D1572713

GEMS and MINERALS of AMERICA

OTHER BOOKS BY JAY ELLIS RANSOM

A Complete Field Guide to American Wildlife, Western Edition
Fossils in America
A Range Guide to Mines and Minerals
The Rock-Hunter's Range Guide
Petrified Forest Trails
Arizona Gem Trails and the Colorado Desert of California
High Tension (A Biography)

Jay Ellis Ransom

GEMS and MINERALS of AMERICA

of AMERICA

A Guide to Rock Collecting

HARPER & ROW, PUBLISHERS
New York, Evanston, San Francisco, London
1817

Portions of this book have appeared in different form in *A Range Guide to Mines and Minerals* and *The Rock-Hunter's Range Guide*, both by Jay Ellis Ransom.

FIRST EDITION

Designed by C. Linda Dingler

Library of Congress Cataloging in Publication Data

Ransom, Jay, Ellis, 1914–
    Gems and minerals of America.

    Bibliography: p.
    1. Precious stones—Collectors and collecting—
United States.   2.   Mineralogy—Collectors and collecting
—United States.   I.   Title.
QE392.5.U5R36   1975   549′.075   72–9147
ISBN 0–06–013512–3
ISBN 0–06–013513–7 (lib. bdg.)

For America's millions of gem and mineral collectors, but especially for Karl Denny, whose thirty years of lapidary production of gem stone jewelry may be found in hundreds of West Coast collections.

Contents

Tables

Acknowledgments

In putting together any large amount of information gleaned from thousands of sources, it is impossible to give a complete accounting of credit where credit is due. I owe a great debt to the geologists, mineralogists, and rock collectors of the past two centuries of exploration of the American continent. In the last half century in particular, many of the three million or so gem and mineral collectors of America have taken the time to offer their detailed knowledge of gems and minerals, fossils, and rocks to others through the pages of the excellent magazines and journals listed in Appendix IV.

Additional credit must certainly go to the authors of hundreds of excellent technical and semitechnical books on geology, gemology, mineralogy, and the lapidary sciences. Many of these fine books, which should be in every rock collector's private library, are also listed in Appendix IV, supplementing in much greater detail the material presented in the body of this volume. These books have served me well as a check against my own inexperience in some of the more technical aspects of the complete rockhound hobby.

Except where specific credit lines are given with photographs, all photography appearing in this book is by the author. The color photographs of gemstones were made possible by Howard and Hazel Michael, of Yreka, California, who opened their home and rock museum to me and provided detailed information for each of hundreds of their exhibits.

While every effort has been made to eliminate errors, I must apologize to the alert reader who, nevertheless, discovers some inconsistency or some outright error. As any author, printer, typographer, and publisher knows full well, an error-free reference work is as rare as feathers on a turtle's back. Thus, in drawing freely from the vast store of geological and mineralogical literature, some typographic errors may have been repeated.

Finally, my special thanks and appreciation to two individuals. The first is my editor, Nahum Waxman, who conceived this book and determined its need in the Harper & Row program of earth science books designed for amateur and professional collectors, geologists, mineralogists, and students. Without a sensitive, understanding editor and a willing publisher, an author is really something of a disembodied spirit working in limbo. The second contributor to this book is my long-suffering wife Wilma, Dutch artist and novelist, who kept me well supplied with coffee, sandwiches, and much needed encouragement during the hours, weeks, and months of writing and typing that went into this book before it reached its publisher.

JAY ELLIS RANSOM

Foreword

Our planet is truly a world of rocks and minerals. All human cultures make important use of hard stones, rocks, sands and ochers, ore minerals, gemmy substances, and crystals. Almost every type of rock in the earth's outer crust has some practical value, not only to the past generations of man but to his modern-day descendants.

Prehuman anthropoids of the late Pliocene period, some 10 million years ago, used wooden tools: clubs for killing, sticks for reaching, vines for tying, and leaves and grasses for making into beds and shelters. Not until humanoids began shaping hard rocks into hand axes, choppers, scrapers, knives, arrow and spear tips, and grinders did the roots of humanity begin swelling into the first fragile trunks of the human species, *Homo neanderthalensis* (men of the Old Stone Age) and *Homo sapiens* (men of the New Stone Age, our direct ancestors, the Cro-Magnon). More than anything else, perhaps, the ability to collect selectively and use the mineral products of the earth brought on the evolution of mankind, as we know ourselves and are a part of it today.

Recently, archaeologists working in the remote Lake Rudolf area of Africa's Kenya found shaped stone implements radiologically dated from 2,160,000 years ago, at the very beginning of the Pleistocene "Ice Ages" period. Those quartzite flakes were evidently fashioned to suit specific purposes, attesting to a mental development that could include planning and execution of a technological problem, with overtones of cultural evolution and the possibility of language.

The Lake Rudolf implements are some 1,800,000 years older than the rounded and shaped hand tools found in the Olduvai Gorge in Tanzania. The older tools, however, seem somewhat more sophisticated and intelligently conceived than were the Olduvai equivalents. The earlier implements, found in what appears to have been a temporary campsite inhabited by a number of cooperating individuals, are thought to have been made for purely domestic use. Although some of the quartzite flakes resemble choppers, they might also have had an aggressive or defensive purpose as well.

Out of such very ancient pre-Stone Age technologies developed the highly sophisticated cultures of both the Old and the New stone ages, beginning in the third interglacial period between the European Riss and Würm glaciations about 100,000 years ago with Neanderthal man and continuing, after around 25,000 B.C., with the Cro-Magnons. Thus, rock collecting with a purpose goes back to the very origins of human society and culture. Indeed, the whole of human history is marked by an increasing knowledge of the use of minerals and the ability to fashion hard stones into implements or decorative objects.

Gems, gemstones, and minerals have always ranked among the most valued substances on earth and, in a multitude of forms, have been prized since the dawn of human existence. In contrast to the hundreds of lovely minerals gathered by modern-day collectors, ancient man (including the American Indians) gathered only thirteen basic rock types. These included amber (most precious of the ancient gems), calcite, fluorspar, jadeite, pyrite, quartz family minerals (agate, carnelian, chalcedony, chert, flint, jasp-agate, jasper, quartzite, rock crystal, amethyst, chrysoprase, opal, etc.), serpentine, and steatite (massive talc), as well as basalt, granite, limestone (and/or sandstone), marble, and the clay minerals for baking into ceramics and pottery or to use as ochers to decorate their bodies.

At a time when Neolithic man was picking up gold and copper nuggets to be hammered into ornaments (20,000–14,000 B.C.), he was already using nephrite (massive jade), sillimanite (prismatic waterworn crystals of aluminum silicate found as clear blue gemmy pebbles), and turquoise. About 2000 B.C. the first true emeralds appear in the graves; by 500 B.C. sapphires and rubies were included in the burial vestments. The very earliest true gem diamond dates only to 480 B.C., although diamond crystals had been used before this time as drilling and cutting tools to work other stones. Even before the onset of the Bronze Age in central Europe, the prehistoric Lake Dwellers were boring holes into garnets and stringing them into necklaces.

The oldest known pieces of wrought jewelry in the world are about 8,000 years old. They were discovered in the most ancient of all Egyptian burials, in the Valley of the Royal Tombs at Abydos west of the ancient city of Thebes. About 1900 Sir Flinders Petrie, an English Egyptologist, discovered the partial remains of a mummy, Queen Zer, who lived about 6000 B.C. and had been buried beside the body of "King" Zer. Only one arm remained of the ancient queen, whose gem-wrapped body had been vandalized some time after burial. But that mummy arm had a story to tell, for it held the jewels which had been left to adorn her in the afterlife: opaque blue turquoise and lapis lazuli, clear red carnelian, purple amethyst, and rock crystal—all mounted in heavy gold settings that were further decorated with blue enamel.

The designs represented birds and flowers, and the ornaments were fastened together with ball-and-loop devices of gold wire; during her life they must have clinked as she walked, and gleamed in the fragile gauze of her robes. One bracelet adorning her arm was formed of turquoise panels alternating with gold plaques, each one surmounted by the royal hawk. Another bracelet had goldwork in the shape of seed pods of a desert plant. A third was of turquoise, amethyst, and hollow gold balls held together with gold wire braided with the hair from an ox tail. The fourth bracelet had brown limestone beads mingled with amethyst and turquoise.

About 3500 B.C. the Egyptians were collecting agates from the desert playas near Jebel Abu Diyeiba, along with rock crystal and amethysts. During the ensuing 2,000 years, agates became a regular trade commodity between Egyptians and Arabians, although archaeologists believe that many trade agates arrived from distant India over the camel caravan routes. Meanwhile, precious opal was introduced about 4000 B.C. from mines in Kenya. This amorphous form of quartz, with its brilliant flickering of rainbow colors, was so highly valued throughout the Mediterranean world that by Roman times a senator, Norius, owned an opal which, though smaller than a hazelnut, was valued at the modern equivalent of nearly $2 million.

The Sumerians, the earliest inhabitants of Mesopotamia, seem to have been the first civilized people who valued agates for their beautiful colors and patterns and who believed that all forms of precious and semiprecious stones had special value as ornaments and, later, as talismans or magical objects. At their cultural peak, around 3000 B.C., the Sumerians were making jeweled ornaments set with precious coral, agate, mother-of-pearl, and lapis lazuli brought from the city of Ur. Certainly, the Sumerians were the first artisans to practice the lapidary arts. The imaginative Mesopotamians cut, carved, and polished an astonishing variety of lovely beads, lavaliers, necklace stones, signet ring settings, and cylinder seals, as well as many kinds of purely ornamental *objets d'art* out of turquoise, malachite, lapis lazuli, rock crystal, onyx, and agate, especially valuing the deep red carnelian variety of chalcedony. Although the Sumerians used almost all the common gemstones available to them, agate is by far the most frequently used in the vast horde of beads found by Marshall Field for the Field Museum of Natural History in Chicago in the excavations made at Kish.

The history of commercial mining is also long, beginning with the Kenya opal mines of 4000 B.C. Mining began with gemstones, instead of metallic ores, and mining for turquoise was enormously extended throughout the Sinai Peninsula by the Egyptians. Indeed, by 1650 B.C., in the time of the Egyptian Pharaoh Sesostris, emeralds were being taken from mines on Mount Zabarah on the west coast of the Red Sea. King Solomon is supposed to have owned emerald mines, and this glistening green gem has often been found in Bronze Age burial jewelry.

A thousand years before Christ, even the wild Gauls of the dark forests of far-off western Europe were collectors of gemmy substances, decorating their helmets with red branches of precious coral traded up from the Mediterranean coasts. The Greeks who first settled the southern coast of France also loved the brilliant red coral. They gathered it and shipped it to India, where coral soon became regarded as a most powerful protection against danger. Among the Romans the precious coral was set with diamonds, and over much of the modern world this organically derived "gemstone" is still highly prized.

The Bible mentions many of the Bronze Age gemstones, generally referring to agate by separate names for its different varieties and including gemstone names of dubious translation. Even in Genesis there are references to onyx and sard. In Exodus 28 an account is given of how the breastplate worn by Moses' brother Aaron was to be made. As the Jewish high priest, Aaron had the right to wear this eight-inch-square ornament, similar to the pectorals made by the Egyptian artisans, hanging from his shoulders by onyx clasps. Made about 1250 B.C., this breastplate was destroyed or stolen in 586 B.C., when the Babylonians desecrated the Israelite temple and took its furnishings to Babylon. In 519 B.C. a second such breastplate was made during the reconstruction of the temple, and this one seems to have existed until the Roman army under Crassus carried away everything of value to Rome in 53 B.C. (When the famous Roman general Pompey, a rival and equal of Crassus, returned from his victorious battles in Asia Minor, he brought back to Rome with him the world's finest collections of gems and gemstones, the beautifully engraved stones of Mithridates, king of Pontus. This collection started a jewel craze among wealthy Romans; even the poor obtained cheaper ornaments of amber, amethyst, and tinted glass.)

Aaron's breastplate had four rows of three gemstones each, representing the twelve tribes of Israel through the twelve sons of Jacob. There is considerable confusion in mineralogically interpreting the names of the stones as listed in the King James or later translations, but here is my interpretation:

First row: sardius (probably red carnelian, assigned to Reuben), topaz (probably citrine or yellow "topaz" quartz, assigned to Simeon), and carbuncle (any bright red stone, probably almandite garnet or possibly red spinel; assigned to Levi, or possibly Manasseh).

Second row: emerald (the only true gem contemporary with the presumed 1250 B.C. date of the exodus, but unknown archaeologically from the time of Jacob; assigned to Judah), sapphire (more probably lapis lazuli, assigned to Dan), and diamond (no doubt rock crystal, i.e., clear quartz, assigned to Naphtali).

Third row: ligure (possibly jacinth, yellow zircon, or hyacinth, e.g., essonite garnet; an undetermined ancient gemstone sometimes labeled also sapphire, although this is unlikely because it was orange red in color; assigned to Gad), agate (perhaps green chalcedony or "chrysoprase";

assigned to Asher), and amethyst (probably a purple sapphire as distinct from Dan's "sapphire" rather than the present purple quartz crystal; assigned to Issachar).

Fourth row: beryl (probably bluish aquamarine or pink morganite; assigned to Zebulon), onyx (assigned to Joseph, or possibly Ephraim), and jasper (most likely the red variety; assigned to Benjamin, Jacob's last son).

Curiously enough, although the best known and most valued of all ancient gemstones was turquoise, well known to the Israelites, this hard, sky-blue mineral was not included on Aaron's breastplate, nor is it mentioned anywhere in the Bible. Because the Egyptians revered turquoise as the "gemstone of the gods," they had been sending great expeditions to prospect and mine for it throughout the Sinai Peninsula since at least 4000 B.C. As float, the migrating Israelites could have picked it up almost anywhere during their wanderings, along with agates, jaspers, and the other gemstones mentioned in the Old Testament. Although its lack of mention in biblical literature casts an interesting sidelight on the thought processes of the Israelites, turquoise seems to have been the first mineral to have been systematically sought for and mined by a civilized people.

About the time that the Israelites were crossing the Red Sea to escape from Egypt, but in another corner of the Mediterranean world of the thirteenth century B.C., the Greek navigator Jason and his companions were sailing from Athens in the ship *Argo* on the heels of a rumor that gold had been discovered on the flanks of the Caucasus Mountains in the land of Colchis (now Soviet Georgia). The picturesque legend of Jason and the Golden Fleece has a great deal of fancy and magic in it, but the simple truth of the matter is that Jason and his hardy adventurers were bona fide prospectors, not unlike the hordes who sailed from Seattle and San Francisco for the Klondike and Alaska thirty-one centuries later.

By 500 B.C. the Greeks and Sicilians were scrabbling for agates among the gravel bars of the river Achates (now called Drillo), which flows through the Val de Noto in Sicily, as well as in the stream gravels of the main Italian peninsula. Grecian tombs have yielded tens of thousands of carved and polished agate ornaments, seals, beads, and signet rings showing that the Greeks considered agate to be one of the most revered and desirable of gemstones. In his book *Stones,* Theophrastus (c. 371–287 B.C.) describes agate as "a colorful stone, usually sold at high prices."

About A.D. 77 the Roman historian Pliny the Elder included in his *Natural History* everything then known about agates, stating that they were first found in Sicily near the river Achates, hence the name "agate." Pliny wrote: "It occurs in large masses and in various colors, hence its numerous names: iaspisachates [agate-jasper, i.e., our "jasp-agate"], cerachates [chalcedony], smaragdachates [green agate], haemachates [red agate, or agate containing red jasper in spots or veins], leucachates [another type of chalcedony], and dendrachates [moss agate]."

That the art of the lapidary was well advanced by the turn of the first century A.D. is attested to by Pliny's further remarks about moss agates imported from India to Rome: ". . . for on them you will find represented rivers, woods, and farm horses; and one can see in them coaches, small chariots, and horse litters and in addition the fittings and trappings of horses." Any modern agate fancier who has ever reveled in the polished moss agates of Montana's famed Yellowstone River gravel bars knows fully whereof Pliny spoke.

Pliny also described how physicians carved mortars and pestles out of agate for grinding their medicaments to a powder. Many modern mortars and pestles used in chemistry laboratories are still carved from agate, as are the fine-edged fulcrums of delicate chemical and postal balances. Indeed, at the time of Pliny's death, the very wealthy considered it a mark of the highest prestige to own and drink from a carved agate or rock crystal goblet. Such cups seemed actually to cool wine.

Perhaps the most extravagant of all Roman rulers was Nero. It is reported that he paid the modern equivalent of $40,000 for a single carved rock crystal goblet, and that during his reign as emperor he made a habit of confiscating for his private collection agate and rock crystal cups, bowls, and goblets wherever he could find them. Indeed, so beloved were such cups that the Roman consul Titus Petronius asked on his deathbed to see once more a large goblet for which he had paid the modern preinflation equivalent of $12,000. In order to prevent Nero from acquiring it, the consul smashed the goblet beyond repair.

Rock collecting as a hobby began in the United States some years after the discovery of Arizona's famed Petrified Forest in 1851 by Lieutenant Lorenzo Sitgreave of the U.S. Army. When specimens of the rainbow-hued, quartz-hard fossil wood reached the Atlantic seaboard, jewelers began buying it up. As transportation opened up the remote fastnesses of the Southwest, visitors toured the area, bringing home beautiful rock souvenirs to be made into bookends and paperweights. At the 1900 World's Fair, Tiffany and Company sparked further interest with its brilliant display of gems, polished slabs, and Arizona petrified wood. So great became the mania for collecting such specimens that in 1906 President Theodore Roosevelt heeded the demands of the Arizona territorial legislature and created the Petrified Forest National Monument to preserve the area from further destruction.

The Great Depression of the 1930's created more rock collectors. Provided with unexpected and unwanted leisure, many outdoors-minded people began to tramp the hills in search of raw materials that could be turned into cash. Lured on by the legends of gold mines stumbled on by the kick of a burro's heel, these latter-day prospectors poked around abandoned gold and silver mines seeking dust or nuggets. Often they found both. More often, however, they found many other mineral forms that could be converted into income—agates, petrified wood, crystals of every kind, jade and jasper, stream tin. From collecting it was a short step to the home workshop, where many an amateur lapidary began turning out creditable jewelry and curios.

Although the glamour of gold has never faded, most of today's non-professional prospectors seek agate, turquoise, jasper, amethyst, carnelian, petrified wood, rock crystal, beryl, tourmaline, topaz, and garnet. Every rock hunter thrills to a find of malachite, chrysocolla, jade, or rhodonite. Today, of course, there are few highly prolific fields. Like the buffalo hunters of the 1870's who believed the herds could never be depleted, early gem and mineral collectors believed that nature's mineral bounty was inexhaustible. Not so. The worst offenders in cleaning out every newly discovered collecting field were rock dealers, with trucks and dynamite, out to make a killing. The second worst offenders, without meaning to deplete their heritage of gems and minerals, have been the rock clubs themselves. A "field trip" used to mean spreading out in long irregular lines to literally sweep over a collecting locality, missing little along the way. Thus, field trips today, except in some areas, are relatively unproductive in gem and mineral finds, although rewarding in friendships and enjoyment of a communal vacation.

Even so, most old gemstone and mineral localities are still good spots, though the rock hunter may find his rewards only through considerable pick-and-shovel work. In seams and pegmatite dikes the liberal application of elbow grease will still open valuable pockets, or vugs, filled with crystals as fine as were ever removed in the good old days. Perseverance should be the watchword of every field collector.

Wherever once famous mines have been commercially worked out and abandoned, one is also sure to find extensive mine dumps sloping steeply down from the shaft or tunnel entrances. On or close to the surface of these piles of weathered gangue material, interesting mineralizations, often secondary forms produced by atmospheric oxidation, can be found. Old mine dumps often reveal a varied assortment of brightly colored ore minerals, raw nuggets of native metal—gold, silver, copper, bismuth, etc.—clumps and crystals of shiny yellow pyrites, and fragile encrustations that make lovely cabinet specimens. Even today it is not unusual for a casual visitor to an old gold rush mine to kick up a solid gold, silver, or native copper nugget simply because the early miners were unbelievably careless in their hasty mining of only the highest-grade ores.

Rock hunters today have a great advantage over the dusty pick-and-pan prospectors of the 1850's. Where the rugged forty-niners tramped over catwalk ridges and camped in the silent canyons of the lands west of the Great Plains, their modern counterparts prospect by pickup truck, camper, jeep, or trailer. Instead of a lonely pursuit, rock hunting—or rockhounding, as it is generally called—is now a true family avocation. An estimated 3 million men, women, and children (often called pebble pups) are registered members of American mineral and gemological societies and subscribe to a vast array of periodicals devoted to the rock hunter's interests. It is for these rockhounds that this book is intended.

This volume updates and replaces two of my previous works. *The Rock-Hunter's Range Guide* (Harper & Row, 1962) dealt primarily with how and where to seek gemstones. *A Range Guide to Mines and Minerals* (Harper & Row, 1964) was concerned with the collecting, preparation, care, and display of colorful ore minerals and offered suggestions on how to convert a small mining prospect into a profitable business. Now, for the first time, both these topics are covered in a complete field guide to every type of gem, gemstone, and ore mineral in the United States.

Part I of this book presents the background for intelligent rock collecting and the proper techniques for preserving and displaying specimens. Part II provides a nationwide compendium of gem and mineral locations that can be reached by the amateur. In the appendixes are listed the characteristics of the most common American gemstones and minerals, a glossary, a list of mineral museums and libraries, and a bibliography. A guide to mineral possibilities can never be entirely up to date, for new fields are found every day; this volume, however, is as current as it is possible to be and is also comprehensive enough to be of value to both the serious collector and the beginner.

In Part I a good deal of basic information is presented, but only in the context of how that information will help each collector to discover new fields for himself or extract quality minerals and gemstones overlooked by his predecessors in old and theoretically worked-out fields. It is always delightful to watch the chagrin of an old-time collector when a knowledgeable newcomer to a supposedly exhausted site comes up with a museum-quality specimen "where nothing has been found for decades."

Only a novice is satisfied with precisely located and known collecting sites that are quickly gleaned of their mineral offerings. Soon it becomes necessary for the advancing collector to learn how to recognize mineral environments, to read topographic and geologic maps, and to translate the ever-fascinating language of geology. All that is required to seek new collecting fields is an imagination that surpasses the limitations of earlier prospectors, mining geologists, and collectors. For this reason Part I includes a section on the techniques of reading a geological map. For a great many areas of the United States, such maps can be bought, at modest prices, from the U.S. Geological Survey or regional land offices; also, they can be examined in major reference libraries. Moreover, U.S. Forest Service topographic maps usually pinpoint every major mine, petrified forest, or other site of significance.

Many localities in the Far West are in remote mountain or desert areas. The beginning collector should always make local inquiry and check his "survival" equipment thoroughly before entering one of these isolated districts, since roads are often not maintained and may be seldom traveled. Too many rockhounds have perished beneath the pitiless southwestern sun to suggest that collecting and prospecting for minerals and gemmy substances is without some occasional danger.

Sooner or later, most gem and mineral collectors begin to consider how to convert some of their best crystals and gemstones into attractive jewelry. Not only is this personally satisfying, but jewelry making constitutes a steady source of collateral income, often producing more than enough outside money to pay the costs of vacation field collecting. Therefore, the concluding chapter of Part I covers the basics of lapidary workmanship, of sawing, cutting, faceting, and polishing—the end products of the dedicated collector's skill and appreciation of form and beauty.

The order of presentation in Part II is based on a simple assumption: that the gem and mineral collector travels widely in his search for new materials and new vacationing possibilities. Collecting localities and their mineral contents are accurately described for every state, alphabetically listed by county and community, range and distance. Whenever the collector crosses a county line, he will find the name of the county he is entering posted alongside the highway. By looking up the state and county, the user of this guide can determine the collecting sites in that county by range and distance from the major cities and towns (also listed in alphabetical order), together with the names of gem and mineral species to be found in or near those locations.

Generalities must sometimes suffice, however, because accurate details were not included in the mineralogical literature. Here the collector must depend on local inquiry. In many regions roads present a confusing complex, and it is not always easy to drive straight to a collecting site or old abandoned mine. Therefore, a field collector must also rely on a good road map—available from oil companies, automobile clubs, and so on—or on a topographic map for details which cannot be included for the thousands of localities listed. Wherever possible, I have given mileages from key points; unfortunately, not all automobile odometers are calibrated precisely. Hence, the traveling field collector must depend on common sense, accurate maps, and extraneous information to reach a specific spot within a particular county.

Many old localities listed here have, literally, been "worked out" as far as surface discoveries of interesting specimens are concerned. Also, expanding urbanization and highway construction may have obliterated many older sites. Nevertheless, the enterprising rock collector is sure to find ways of delving beneath the surface or looking into nearby quarries, road cuts, and bluffs beyond the immediate boundaries of a locality to find worthwhile examples of nature's artistry to carry home with him. A bit of exploration of the surrounding countryside, especially if one has learned to read the contours on a geological map, often turns up unexpected mineral tidbits that can extend one's faith in the old mining camp adage heard in every mineralized area: "There are more minerals remaining under the ground than were ever taken out of the mines." So be patient. Even if you should fail to locate a particular collecting field or old mine, you may stumble on a brand-new outcrop that nobody before you has explored. It happens every day and has for the past two hundred years.

It is wise to plan every rock-hunting vacation trip to take in a number of collecting fields in their order of mileage from your home. Aimless wandering may produce limitless scenic vistas but very little in the way of filling your collecting sacks. In many instances you may have to ask permission to enter private lands, for rock-hunting fields lie on both public and private property. In general, a good rule to follow is never to leave a gate unclosed or a landowner unadvised of your wish to search his property for mineral specimens. Some owners may charge a small fee. Others actually use heavy equipment to open prime collecting strata for your enjoyment. The rules of good etiquette apply as strictly in the most remote territories as they do in a host's home.

Many parts of the West are under military control. Permission to collect on posted land, where it is safe at all, is usually limited to Sundays. In such areas, where dud bombs or shells may lie, it is dangerous to trespass without a permit from the nearest commanding officer, and it is always a courtesy to ask his advice.

The appendixes of this book include in brief form the essential characteristics of most of the more common gemstones and minerals likely to be found in the United States. Of more than 2,000 known mineral species, it is unlikely that more than 10 to 20 percent will appear in any individual mineral collection outside a scientific museum. The others are either rare minerals, subvarieties of the more common species, or laboratory curiosities of interest primarily to the professional mineralogist.

There is always the possibility that you may discover a commercially valuable mineral deposit worth filing on as a mining claim. Indeed, a good seam of agate or asbestos or kaolin fulfills the mining law requirements and can be worth far more per ton than a gold-bearing prospect and be easier to mine commercially. State and federal publications in enormous quantities are to be found in every large reference library, slanted toward helping the commercial-minded prospector contribute toward America's continuing need for strategic minerals.

For every piece of colorful stone brought home, the collector also discovers that, by sawing it in half or into many slices, he doubles or multiplies his material beyond his own inclinations to keep it all for himself. The excess material is therefore available for trading or selling to other collectors.

One well-known southern California rockologist—quite a wag in his own right—was Chuckwalla Slim. For decades he traveled the West with jeep and a monster trailer, attending rock shows and selling gems and minerals wherever he went, always at astonishingly high prices. Speaking before a Los Angeles mineral society, he chided: "All the best rock-hunting localities left in America are in the basements and backyards of rock collectors! I would like to suggest that it would greatly profit the hobby if each collector took all his excess rocks back to the deserts and mountains and scattered them along the roadsides for other collectors to find and pick up again." He had a point there!

For many years my father used field trip expeditions throughout the West as an excuse to fill his automobile trunk to leveled springs with everything he could find. Then whenever he passed a gem and mineral shop in his travels, he sold as much of his rough material as the shop owner would take. He never failed to return from extensive field trips during his retirement years with all expenses accounted for, plenty of the best specimens for himself, and more money in his jeans than he started out with. For him, retirement years spelled adventure. Everywhere he went he found new and interesting friends coursing the backcountry roads on the twisting trails of gemstones and minerals—a great coterie of friendly people: men and women and children—sniffing the breezes of sun-filled days and camping out under the sparkling diamond-dusted skies of night.

Back home in his garage lapidary shop he lapped out slabs and slices, made bookends and paperweights, and neatly sawed out cabochon roughs. By placing small ads in the rockhound magazines, he entertained a modest but definitely profitable worldwide sale of his excess rocks for more than twenty years.

During the course of years of gem and mineral collecting, the amateur rock collector will inevitably build up a considerable personal museum of fine cabinet specimens, slabbed and polished pieces, cabochoned or faceted jewels, and a miscellany of prized examples of nature's handiwork. Most amateurs eventually fill glassed display cabinets with their finest rocks, found on periodic adventurings into the field, purchased from rock dealers and other collectors along the way, or acquired from answering ads in the gem and mineral magazines. Such private collections increase in dollar value year by year; they never decrease in the face of rockhound dealers' needs for salable rocks.

Thus, a well-documented collection of attractive minerals and gemstones becomes "money in the bank," a real legacy for future generations to cash in or to add to. A brief perusal of the ads in any of the rockhound periodicals listed in the bibliography provides a good idea of the commercial value of gem and mineral collecting, measurable more often in the thousands and tens of thousands of dollars than in hundreds. Many philanthropic-minded collectors have also willed their collections to museums.

For many people, rock hunting, mineral collecting, and jewelry making have become a way of life in itself, a phenomenon of the last half of the twentieth century. Not infrequently, the amateur may become professional and earn a part of his retirement income by supplying mineral dealers with quality material. This field guide is, therefore, a high road to a fascinating pastime that began some three million years ago and has no foreseeable end.

part I

The Fundamentals of Rock Collecting

chapter 1

Rocks, Minerals and Gemstones

We can easily recognize rocks on every hand; they are the building blocks of mountains, occurring massively and forming prominent parts of the outer structure of the earth's crust. Rocks, except for a few "rock-minerals," have no uniform chemical nature, being composed of many different mineral substances. The most commonly recognized rocks are basalt and andesite lavas (and their variants known to highway engineers as "traprock"); granites; sandstone and limestone (including dolomite), both of which are also true minerals because they do have a uniform chemical structure; serpentine, which is also a mineral, and a wide variety of mud and clay sediments hardened by time and mineral percolations. These easily split rocks are most readily apparent in mountainous regions as layer piled on layer of sloping and often contorted strata: shale, slate, claystone, and mudstone.

MINERAL CHARACTERISTICS

Except for float transported by rain, wind, and gravity to great distances from its point of origin, most mineral deposits occur within rocky confines. Even though sandstone, limestone, and dolomite are homogenous "rocks" which occur over large areas, the particles which make up their masses are strictly chemical compounds, i.e., minerals: silicon dioxide, SiO_2, for sandstone; calcium carbonate (calcite), $CaCO_3$, for limestone; and magnesium carbonate, $MgCO_3$, for dolomite. Where mineral grains found in other rocks are large enough to be identified, we can name the particular rock form itself. For instance, granite is a speckled light-gray, hard, dense, massively occurring plutonic rock composed primarily of the mineral crystals of quartz, feldspar, and biotite mica; granite is identified primarily by its content of quartz.

Chemists and mineralogists consider that any earthy substance comprising a single chemical compound which can be reduced to a formula, no matter how complex, is a mineral. Halite is the mineralogical name for rock salt (ordinary table salt chemically defined as sodium chloride, NaCl)—a "mineral-rock" that occurs as massive deposits in various parts of the world where ancient salt-water seas evaporated hundreds of millions of years ago, leaving the salt in relatively pure form. Sulfur (chemical symbol S), one of the 92 natural earth elements, is another such mineral-rock which is also an element.

A rock, however, does not satisfy the strict requirements demanded of a mineral: that it have essentially uniform properties and a definite atomic structure which can be written in the symbols of a chemical formula. (Appendix I describes the more common minerals in terms of their properties, and the chemical formulation is given for each one.)

While a rock may loosely be defined as any hard, massive, earthy substance, minerals occur in three general forms: amorphous, that is, completely without form or structure, like powder; massive or crystalline, and actually composed of great quantities of very small crystals packed together; and true crystals. Crystals constitute the raw material of many gems and gemstones used by the lapidary for cutting into cabochons or faceting into the classical jewels.

GEMSTONE CHARACTERISTICS

Not all minerals are gemstones; in fact, the vast majority of mineral species are not. Nor are all gemstones chemically identifiable as minerals. Mineralogists today have described by formula, physical and chemical properties, environments of origin, and locality occurrences nearly 2,000 minerals, a great increase from the 750 minerals recognized at the onset of the twentieth century. Of these minerals, perhaps barely a hundred species provide the lapidary with the potential for cutting and polishing, based on hardness, suitability of pieces of "rough" large enough to handle, and color, translucency, or transparency. Even of this round number, the average rock collector might consider himself among the mineral cognoscenti if he is able to recognize and name one-quarter of the total.

Gemstones not strictly mineral in nature but valued by collectors and lapidaries also include some which are really "rocks." Obsidian in its various colors, striations, and forms is a particular rock form compositionally identical to granite. Marble, which comes in many colors and is found massively in many parts of the world, is another useful rock-mineral derived from limestone by the metamorphic processes of great heat and pressure. Jadeite and nephrite (the latter an amphibole comprising tremolite and actinolite and customarily called jade) occur in or near mountains of serpentine which, in California, lacks the gemstone quality of the same mineral found in Arizona or elsewhere. A considerable variety of colorful granites likewise serve as gemstone substances capable of taking a glossy polish, often used for tombstones and in the construction of building façades.

There are three distinctive types of gemmy substances with two types being chemically identical but quite different in outward appearance. Amorphous gemstones, such as opal (also a "precious" stone) and obsidian, have internal structures without any regular organization: the atoms and molecules occur all jumbled together in varying degrees of concentration. Ordinary glass (technically not a solid at all but a liquid, like frozen syrup) is a good example of amorphous structure. Amorphous materials tend to fracture or break chonchoidally, that is, in curved shell-like surfaces the way thick glass breaks. There are very few varieties of amorphous gemstones.

Most gemmy substances, however, can be seen under high magnification of thin cross sections or by X-ray examination to have a microscopically small crystal structure throughout. The minute crystals are so densely packed together as to give the whole stone the appearance of uniformity. Such dense, compact stones are termed cryptocrystalline or microcrystalline. The physical conditions producing such gemstones did not allow room for the growth of larger crystals. The crystals in jade, for example, are so microscopic as almost to give the mineral an amorphous structure, making jade an extremely tough material.

Crystalline gemmy substances lead to the third type: gemstone crystals. One example well known to all rock collectors is "rock crystal," quartz crystals that often grow to large size but are identical in chemical composition to the cryptocrystalline forms of chalcedony: agate, chert, carnelian, jasper, etc. In gemstone crystals the atoms are arranged in a distinctive lattice structure of great regularity. It is thought that no matter how large a crystal becomes during the process of growth, each one constitutes but a single molecule.

In practice any hard substance, whether synthetic or occurring naturally, which is capable of being cut and polished and has durability, color, and perhaps internal design constitutes a gemstone. The gemstone crystals commonly gathered into rock collections, if free from flaws and large enough, may be cut and faceted into wearable jewels in the forms usually allotted to diamonds, rubies, emeralds, or other precious gems. Indeed, gemstone crystals are often referred to as "semiprecious gems" to distinguish them from the more highly valued classic jewels of antiquity.

Unlike the true gems, many of the gemstone crystals are opaque or semitransparent, or contain interesting inclusions, such as clear quartz crystals shot through with slender needles of rutile (titanium oxide), tourmaline, or asbestos fibers. Such gemstones are often cut cabochon style to bring out the beauty of the inclusions, rather than being faceted to enhance highlights and sparkle.

The term mineral usually gives the layman a picture of a rock form derived from the earth's inorganic chemical processes. However, a pearl found in an oyster or clam shell is also a mineral, chemically identical to calcite and created by organic rather than inorganic processes. The pearl, also a true gem, has been valued highly throughout history.

Other organically derived gemstones from which beautiful jewelry settings are cut and polished may be neither gems nor minerals, nor even stones. Amber, for example, is a form of very ancient, fossilized resin composed of a variety of complicated organic chemical substances, chief of which is succinic acid (hence the occasionally used mineral term succinite). Jet is a compact velvet-black mineral-hard "stone" derived from lignite coal; it is mostly carbon, like diamond and graphite, but contains many impurities characteristic of the coal formation that produced it. The ever-lengthening list of contemporary gemstone substances which can be treated as minerals includes: mother-of-pearl and coral (both are calcite), tortoise shell (the mottled horny carapace of certain species of turtles used for inlaying and making ornamental articles), and ivory (the hard, creamy-white dentine composing the tusks of elephants and walrus). To these natural substances might also be added today's increasing variety of artificial or synthetic gemstones, glass, and hard plastics which lend themselves to the lapidary's art.

THE CRYPTOCRYSTALLINE SILICATES

Perhaps 90 percent of all the minerals and gemstones collected in a person's lifetime or displayed in regional gem and mineral shows belong to the quartz family of minerals, silicon dioxide (silica, SiO_2). Approximately 200 varieties are described in the mineralogical literature. Most of them are subvarieties of chalcedony, of which the endlessly fascinating agates and petrified woods represent the most sought-after and commonly occurring gemstones.

The element silicon, next to oxygen, is the second most abundant element of the earth's crust, making up 26 percent (oxygen makes up approximately 50 percent). Since one atom of silicon readily combines with two atoms of oxygen, the resulting silicon dioxide is the most abundant mineral on earth, both as pure silica itself, e.g., sandstone, and as a "silicate" portion in minerals made up of the other elements. Fortunately for the well-being of Mother Earth, silica is slightly soluble in water, especially in very hot subterranean magmatic waters under tremendous pressure. The eternally changing forces beneath the surface of the earth's crust raise mountains, fracture rock strata, and crumble formations into rubble; silica, dissolved in percolating magmatic or ground waters, fills the cracks and literally heals the wounds. The result is a cross-patterning of veins, stringers, and filled cavities (hollow nodules, geodes, thundereggs, vugs, etc.). To a lesser extent such "healing" is also accomplished by feldspar and calcite. Were it not for the healing capacities of these minerals, the surface of the changing earth would be little more than brecciated rubble.

Rock Quarries. The best place for hunting minerals, crystals, fossil-leaf imprints, and gemmy substances is almost any rock quarry in America.

OPEN PIT MINES. Among the most productive collecting sites are open pits, such as the Sleeping Beauty copper mine at Miami, Arizona, where colorful copper minerals may be picked up.

MINE DUMPS. Huge concentrations of rocks, such as these from the Inspiration open pit mine near Superior, Arizona, may be prospected by the gem and mineral collector for colorful copper minerals, including malachite, azurite, and chrysocolla, while agate, jasper, chalcedony, Apache tears, and many other gemstones occur throughout the surrounding desert.

MILL EXITS. The gangue rocks coming out of this Arizona mill on a conveyor belt may be loaded with crystallizations and colorful minerals which will interest the collector. Throughout America, wherever ore mills are operating, visiting gem and mineral collectors are usually welcomed and given a guided tour through the plant.

Norman's Studio, Globe, Arizona

MINING GHOST TOWNS. Silver City, Idaho, is typical of the mining towns that flourished in the nineteenth century. Fascinating places for rockhounds to visit, their surrounding hillsides and gulches are often prolific in gem crystals and colorful lead and silver minerals, while gold dust and nuggets can be panned from nearly all regional creek sands.

MINING CAMPS. Scattered throughout the Western states are thousands of forgotten ghost mining camps. This gold camp is typical of once populous centers abandoned when rich ore veins played out. Local creek sands may still reveal abundant colors and nuggets of gold, while surrounding hillsides, gulches, and old mine dumps often yield fine gemstones, crystals, and minerals.

COLLECTING FIELDS. This rockhound is shown in California's Mojave Desert examining a piece of seam agate broken from weathered fractures in the adjacent basalt ledge. The surrounding desert is a collector's dream land for agate, chalcedony, jasper in many colors, jasp-agate, quartz crystals, and the ore minerals of copper, lead, silver, and gold.

Jay Ellis Ransom

ABANDONED MINES. Many Western mines were blasted out of solid rock but because of rockfall, it is dangerous to explore the tunnels beyond the range of daylight. Nearly all old mines are abandoned, but their dumps usually produce colorful mineral specimens and gemmy crystals.

Jay Ellis Ransom

A LIMESTONE CREVICE. Limestone formations often show deep crevices and caverns in which the rock collector may find calcite crystals and other gemmy forms of calcium carbonate. The collector is cautioned to be careful and not to hunt alone in areas of subterranean hollows formed from dissolving percolating water.

A PUMICE QUARRY. Commercial pumice occurs at the foot of Glass Mountain in a flow of obsidian on the margin of northeastern California's Medicine Lake Highland. In such mantle-like deposits covering older basalts the rock collector may find gem-quality obsidian in many colors, including rainbow, iridescent, black-and-red banded, snowflake, etc., along with Apache tears weathered out of pumice and pearlite.

A MANGANESE MINE. Where gem and mineral prospecting shows commercial quantities of valuable ore minerals, the rock collector may establish a mine and elect to garner as much wealth as he and perhaps one helper can excavate from veins beneath the surface. In the manganese ore shown here, are fine crystals of calcite and quartz which have a collector's value far above the manganese content of the ore.

A FOSSIL BED. Such areas as this one in Oregon, where rivers have cut deeply into the surrounding terrain, expose for the rockhound fascinating fossils and frequently agates, jaspers, and silicified woods.

Oregon State Highway Commission

AN AGATE BEACH. Low tide gravels, especially following heavy storms at sea, are unusually prolific of fine gem agates, jasper and quartz pebbles, gold-bearing black sand, colorful pieces of petrified wood and moonstones, among others. This Oregon beach is typical of gemstone collecting beaches from Washington's Straits of Juan de Fuca all the way to the northern California coast.

A WESTERN URANIUM MINE. Colorado plateau sandstone formations of the Four-Corners area, where Arizona, Utah, Colorado, and New Mexico come together, were once extensively mined for uranium-bearing carnotite ores. After being worked out commercially, such mines were abandoned and now serve the collector seeking fluorescent mineral specimens.

A TRAVERTINE FOUNTAIN. Natural hot springs calcareous deposits like this gigantic cone at Thermopolis, Wyoming, provide colorful examples of travertine built up through thousands of years of mineral deposition from magmatic waters.

A CONGLOMERATE DEPOSIT. This wave-cut residual thumb of consolidated volcanic breccia conglomerate on Unalaska Island in the central Aleutian Islands of Alaska contains primarily broken andesite rocks, argillite, and pebbles of agate and jasper, many of which are gem quality. Only the most hardy adventurers can ever expect to reach these remote regions, which are dangerous at almost any time of year because of violent storms.

The extremely fine-grained chalcedonies are sometimes termed tectosilicates, from "tectonic," i.e., deriving from deformation of earth strata, particularly through the filling of fault fractures. Many tectosilicates are gemstones, including the many varieties of agate, chert, flint, jasper, tiger's-eye, chrysoprase, and, surprisingly, both the amorphous common and the precious opal.

Silica plays a double role at times. This mineral compound not only crystallizes out of solution to fill cavities and fractures as an earth-healing substance, but by processes not yet understood enters into an oxidation-reduction action that minutely replaces the organic cellular structure of wood. The result is "petrified wood," and where color impurities also occur in the percolating silica-rich solutions, the petrifications become extraordinarily lovely and desirable collectors' material. Petrified wood often has real commercial value, especially the highly colored agatized fossil woods of Arizona and the equally sought-after opalized woods of south-central Washington state. (See Chapter 9 for a discussion of petrified wood.)

PRECIOUS STONES VS. GEMSTONES

There have always been persons, keen of eye and sensitive to natural beauty, who have gathered up shiny, brightly colored, or scintillating crystals glistening in the clear flowing water of gravelly stream beds. No doubt young children were the first gatherers, but their fathers or tribal shamans were the first to conceive of a use for such naturally occurring objects.

Early man's technologic development involved three main techniques: grinding domestic utensils, such as metates, mortars and pestles, oil lamps, and statuary out of dense rocks like granite, basalt, marble, jadeite, and nephrite, among others; chipping and flaking hard crystalline rocks into arrow and spear points, knives, scrapers, and hand axes; and, long later, cutting and polishing gemmy crystals into decorative ornaments and talismanic symbols. Thus, the art of the lapidary was first developed around converting raw crystals of emeralds, rubies, sapphires, aquamarines, chrysoberyl (alexandrite, cat's-eye, etc.), diamond, and garnet, along with lumps of turquoise, into jewels. Though much softer and far more brittle and difficult to work, opal was likewise considered a worthy gem because of its brilliant rainbow colors and strange hidden fires.

Other than precious opal, very few true gems will ever be collected in the field by the amateur rockhound or, for that matter, even by professional gem hunters. In America the principal rough jewels which can be field-collected are sapphire (primarily from the stream gravels of western Montana and Idaho), a few diamonds from privately owned grounds in Arkansas where collecting is permitted for a fee, and precious opal from a rather wide distribution of localities but most importantly from Idaho and Nevada.

The true gems are the most highly valued of all decorative objects because of their great rarity in the rock formations and sediments of Mother Earth. Modern-day imitations or synthetic formulations of classic jewel substances, while every bit as lovely, hard, and durable, lack the intrinsic value which the natural stone engenders. Expert jewelers are readily able to distinguish between nature's product and the chemical equivalent produced in a high-temperature laboratory.

Of all the mineral species on earth, chalcedony, the mother of the quartz family cryptocrystalline minerals, is the most widely distributed and the most varied in its forms. Not only does chalcedony occur in almost every county in America, but no two forms are ever alike.

Agates alone vary tremendously in color (derived from mineral impurities in the otherwise opaque, colorless chalcedony), as well as in internal designs. Agate names, listed in Chapter 9, seem as unscientific and undefinitive as their localities, from which so many names derive, but most agates fall into such basic categories as banded, fortification, saganitic, dendritic, and mossy or plume. In any case, anciently and today, the agate variety of chalcedony allows the imaginative lapidary to bring out an infinitely varied internal patterning and coloration.

All chalcedonies, as well as other members of the quartz family minerals except opal, have the same degree of hardness, 7 on the Mohs scale of hardness (see Table 14), so that they are extremely durable and resistant to even the roughest kind of wear and tear.

When agates first came into written history is well documented, but archaeologists' excavations of Stone Age burials show that agates were gathered and valued enough to be buried with their owners by both the Old Stone Age Neanderthals and the New Stone Age Cro-Magnons.

Unlike all other gemstone species, the agate and jasper varieties of chalcedony occur massively, often in long dikelike veins measuring several feet in thickness—an original deposition of silica colored by impurities in a massive earth fracture. Agate found in such masses lends itself to the carving of fine art objects, such as spheres of all sizes, bowls, goblets, and occasional statuary. The amount of labor which went into such lapidary work anciently not only was tremendous, because it all had to be done by hand, but added greatly to the intrinsic value of each piece. Such museum relics of past civilizations as we have on display today could have been possessed only by the nobility or by extremely wealthy merchants.

Rough gemstone material which can be sliced, cut, and polished into attractive cabochons varies greatly according to the quality of the material, its internal beauty and design, its relative scarcity, the degree of flawing, the colorations, and the size of the rough specimen. A minimum present-day price obtainable for the roughest kind of agate is about 50 cents a pound, but such agate may be found by the ton and produces values much greater than any but the richest gold ore veins. An average price for cabochon material may run from 75 cents to several dollars per pound, field-run and as sold by gem and mineral dealers in the rough.

Because the rockhound hobby is expanding so rapidly and generating such a rising demand for quality materials, dealers seek the world over for supplies; every amateur collector with surplus rocks to sell gets an immediate and attentive ear. For gemmy crystals the rough prices sky-rocket, ranging from less than a dollar per gram (five carats) for flawed material to 15 or 20 dollars a gram for top facet-grade crystals.

COLORFUL ORE MINERALS

Many field collectors look for gemmy substances because these hard-rock minerals so readily lend themselves to lapidary manipulations and have an intrinsic value as decorative pieces. However, the great majority of collectable and colorful minerals are really ores of the metals which provide the base for all cultural activities. Some ore minerals, such as the copper ores of malachite and chrysocolla, also constitute gemstones because of their hardness and capacity for being cut and polished. The primary difference between an ore mineral and a gemmy substance is that ore minerals are usually too soft and fragile for converting into ornamental objects and are generally too unstable chemically to endure.

Nevertheless, of all the earth's mineral substances, those mined for their metallic content or for other commercial reasons often rank among the loveliest and most colorful examples of rock forms. Many ore minerals are widely sought, bought and sold in dealers' shops, and displayed by collectors as cabinet specimens. Most such minerals require special attention in care and handling; many are extremely fragile, so that a breath of air, a drop of moisture, or too dry an atmosphere can alter or destroy them entirely.

Nearly all ore minerals tend to undergo significant changes in coloration, structure, and form when removed from the stable geologic environment in which they were found. Atmospheric gases of a big city corrode or completely change the original mineral compounds; heat and presence or absence of water vapor bring about molecular changes in the minerals, usually to their detriment. In warm dry atmospheres, such as in a collector's home or shop, many delicate minerals, such as gypsum, lose their essential water of crystallization and crumble from beautiful crystal forms to an uninteresting powder. Other minerals, such as halite, absorb moisture out of the air and "deliquesce," or dissolve away in their own solutions.

Despite the fact that beautiful ore minerals require extra care in handling and preservation, sometimes involving immersion in an inert gas like nitrogen, many thousands of rock collectors eagerly include fine specimens in their display cabinets. Certainly, the major mineral museum collections (listed in Appendix III) display as many magnificent examples of minerals taken from the world's historically important metal mines as they do representatives of gems, gemstones, and crystals. Indeed, the prices of museum-quality ore specimens on sale in many rock and mineral shops are higher than for gemstone materials. A perusal of Part II of this book will show that by far the greatest number of collectable minerals listed in the various field sites belong to the classes and categories of commercial ore minerals.

chapter 2

Mineral Environments (I): The Igneous Rocks

North America is a continent of great geological contrasts and immense variety in its mineral environments. Not all parts of the United States, or Canada for that matter, provide equal opportunities for rock collecting, and the variety of rocks one can collect in his own backyard depends very much on where he lives.

Because mineral distributions are discontinuous, it is important that you gain some knowledge of your own regional geology and undertake to learn the significant facts about the mineral environments of whichever more distant region you plan to visit on any gem collecting trip. The geological formations in which collectable minerals were formed or from which they have weathered are quite well defined and easily recognized in the field.

THE AMERICAN SCENE

Two-thirds of the continental United States lies between the 2,000-mile-long Appalachian Mountain system and the equally long Rocky Mountains west of the 100th meridian. The remaining one-third of the country includes a narrow strip of Atlantic seacoast plain and the far western topography of the mountain-studded Great Basin states, the Cascade-Sierra Nevada range, and the Pacific Coast, which includes the much lower Coast Range.

THE EASTERN HIGHLANDS

The eastern quarter of the national geography is dominated by the eroded high peneplains and rounded slopes of the very ancient Appalachian Mountain chain, running southeasterly from northern Maine into northeastern Alabama. These mountains are the uplifted sediments of still older, vanished mountain ranges of the Ordovician, Silurian, and Devonian eras going back half a billion years, compressed and contorted into great arches (anticlines) and downfolds or troughs (synclines). The total amount of compression is equivalent to shortening the circumference of the earth by several hundred miles.

Throughout the Appalachian highlands, deeply buried granite batholiths pushed up domed mountains, fractured the overlying sediments, and intruded into the fractures to produce veins, stringers, pegmatites, and outcroppings of mineral-enriched rocks. The result has been that gem and gemstone collectors are remarkably fortunate in the variety of minerals they can find throughout the region, especially in the pegmatite intrusions (dikes) of New England, New Jersey, Virginia, North Carolina, and Georgia.

PRAIRIES AND PLAINS

Between the Appalachian Plateau and the Rocky Mountains lie some 1,500 miles of nearly sea-level prairies and plains, including the Gulf Coastal Plain, and rising westward from the Mississippi River to the mile-high short-grass plains fronting onto the 100th meridian and the eastern foothills of the Rockies. This great region is one of almost exclusively sedimentary formations, with the roots of extremely ancient mountain ranges buried thousands of feet below the present surface. Only here and there in mid-America do the basal crystalline rocks reach worn and wrinkled knuckles above this vast mantle of sediments, for example, in Minnesota, Arkansas, the Ozarks, and the Black Hills.

For literally hundreds of millions of years, shallow "epicontinental" salt-water seas came and went across the heartland of North America. From the Gulf of Mexico, which once extended a thousand miles farther north, to the Arctic Ocean those shallow seas left in their wakes enormous beds of sandstone, limestone, and chalk. While these sedimentary formations are rich in fossils,* minerals and gemstones are relatively scarce. More often than not, what collectable specimens there are occur sporadically, dropped by the glaciers of the Pleistocene ice ages from Canadian origins. The superheated magmatic waters that accompanied the vast Keweenawan lava flows of nearly one and a half billion years ago probably created as many interesting gems and minerals as did similar volcanic flows in Miocene times in the far western states. Unfortunately, those Keweenawan deposits are buried with the roots of the ancient mountains 3,000 feet beneath the present surface. Where the Mesabi Iron Range reaches low elevations above the northern Minnesota prairies, some of the ancient minerals are exposed to the collector.

THE MOUNTAIN WEST

Between the eastern foothills of the Rocky Mountains and the Pacific Coast lie a thousand miles of extremely interesting, scenic, and min-

---

* See Jay E. Ransom, *Fossils in America* (New York: Harper & Row, 1964).

eralogically productive topography, literally a rock collector's and miner's paradise. This is the "mining West," famed for its enormous production of gold, silver, copper, uranium, and a host of other commercial metallics and nonmetallics since the days of the fur brigades. With the exception of the east–west transverse range of the Uinta Mountains separating Wyoming from Utah and western Colorado, all the mountain systems run north and south, separated by generally arid, brush-covered intermontane valleys and lightly timbered plateaus.

Very new by geologic standards, the entire region is characterized by extinct volcanoes and thick fissure flows of basalt that, everywhere, give startling evidence of how much of the North American continent was created. Rich in silica and other minerals, the associated magmatic waters have left us a heritage of heavily mineralized veins and rich mines, as well as creating a magnificent wonderland of gems and gemstone substances. From the tips of the highest peaks more than 14,000 feet above sea level to the depths of Death Valley, 260 feet below sea level, gemmy substances, crystals, and ore minerals can be found in veins, dikes, stream gravels and benches, outcrops, and as "float" over the widespread lower surfaces with little in the way of vegetation to hide them.

Not the least of the prized gemstones is the great variety of beautiful petrified woods from forests that were destroyed and turned to stone millions of years ago. Some of those forests, with tree trunks several feet in diameter, were wiped out in a matter of moments in the full flower of their growth by volcanic lavas or buried under thousands of feet of volcanic ash and dust, then to be petrified by percolating silica-rich waters while still standing rooted in place. Other petrified forests, especially in the Triassic sandstone formations of Arizona, were not forests in the sense of a mass of standing timber, but rather great accumulations of drift logs from the distant rising Rocky Mountains. Those 230-million-year-old logs were washed down as much as a hundred miles and settled into the muds of lake bottoms. There, beneath the level of oxygen-caused decay, the wood cells were replaced by silica colorfully stained with mineral impurities. Wherever magmatic or percolating ground waters seeped, they left their residues of gems, gemstones, and ore minerals.

THE SOUTHWESTERN PLATEAUS

Volcanism was quite limited throughout the region of the southwestern states, although still geologically important. Instead of the surface of the earth being built up by successive layers of basalts or batholithic instrusions of granite, as in the Rocky Mountains and the Pacific Northwest, earth forces raised up enormous areas of sea-laid sandstone and limy sediments into level plateaus many thousands of feet above sea level. In these Permian, Triassic, and Jurassic sediments the rock collector will find a wealth of petrified wood, quartz family gemstones, uranium ores, jasperized dinosaur bones and gastroliths (dinosaur "gizzard stones")—all magnificent, highly colored specimens and quality cutting material.

NORTH TO ALASKA

The volcanic activity of the Far West, extending from the northern Sierra Nevada Range of California all the way to Alaska, came very late in geologic time, mostly during the Oligocene to Pliocene epochs of the Tertiary period going back less than 40 million years. Nevertheless, these far-flung activities produced some of the most prolific gem and mineral hunting grounds anywhere in North America.

The Cascadian Revolution that produced the Sierra Nevada and the Cascade Mountains of Oregon and Washington, along with the coastal ranges of British Columbia and Alaska, occurred only 12 to 15 million years ago, with volcanic activity continuing right into the present century in many places. Most gemstones found in this region consequently belong to the quartz family, but their variety and loveliness are unparalleled anywhere.

Far to the northwest, in the sprawling state of Alaska, the rock hunter finds himself in virgin territory. Roads are few and far between, and most "mother lode" sources of minerals and gemmy substances are difficult to reach. Most Alaskan gemstones are found as float, rather than in place, distributed by streams, glaciers, and sea action along the rugged coastlines. The collector with the time and initiative to visit the Alaskan terrain will find worthwhile material almost everywhere: on any river bar, in gravel pits, along stream beds, and on the shores of tundra lakes, as well as on the beaches of the North Pacific from the southernmost tip of southeastern Alaska to and including the Aleutian archipelago. From garnets the size of golf balls in the Southeastern Panhandle to the gold and copper minerals of the Interior, tin and platinum of the Kuskokwim, and the jadeite mountains of the far northwestern Eskimo country, Alaska in time may become the country's prime rock collecting region.

THE GEOLOGIC TIMETABLE

Mention has already been made and will be again of some of the names of the time divisions in the earth's crustal history. Geology necessarily deals with yardsticks measured in millions of years, the concrete evidence for which are the layers of rock strata piled one on top of another. The total thickness of such successive rock strata has been estimated at 60,000 feet, encompassing a total time of 4.5 billion years for the earth's existence. With each new edition of a book on paleontology or geology, the time scale is lengthened somewhat, a few more millions of years added here and there to previous calculations, as scientific techniques for determining geologic ages are refined. The figures presented in Table 1 have been updated from those first appearing in *The Rock-Hunter's Range Guide* in 1962.

TABLE 1
GEOLOGIC TIMETABLE

Era	Period or Epoch	Began Yrs. Ago	Characteristics
Quaternary	Recent	10–25,000	Continents high, last glaciers melting, grassy plains; modern man.
Quaternary	Pleistocene (Ice Ages)	2½–3 million	Four great ice advances with warm interglacial periods; Neanderthal man in Old World.
CENOZOIC	An interval of mountain building and volcanism: Alps, Cascades, Sierra Nevada, second Rocky Mountain system, Andes, etc., leading to Ice Ages.		
CENOZOIC — Tertiary Period	Pliocene	13 million	Volcanism and mountain building. Modern type mammals plus extinct forms.
CENOZOIC — Tertiary Period	Miocene	25 million	Five-toed animals and anthropoids, land plants similar to modern; grass.
CENOZOIC — Tertiary Period	Oligocene	40 million	Climax of browsing herbivores. Former mountains worn down to deep sediments.
CENOZOIC — Tertiary Period	Eocene	60 million	3-toed horse; deep sedimentation; Sea of Tethys across Central America.
CENOZOIC — Tertiary Period	Paleocene	70 million	Origins of mammals; chilly, with high mountains eroding away.
	Separating the Cenozoic from the Mesozoic era were vast mountain-building systems (Laramide Revolution) which produced the first Rocky Mountains, Appalachian Reuplift, etc. Vast granite batholithic intrusions along entire west of North America produced enormous mineral concentrations.		
MESOZOIC	Cretaceous	135 million	Age of Reptiles. First small mammals; widespread epicontinental seas produced vast chalk formations.
MESOZOIC	Jurassic	180 million	Climax of ammonites, largest dinosaurs. Lowlands, shallow seas, tropic climate. Ancestral Sierras born.
MESOZOIC	Triassic	230 million	Origins of reptiles and first small dinosaurs; pine forests, ammonites.
	Separating the Mesozoic from the Paleozoic era were major geologic disturbances and building of mountain ranges, i.e., the Appalachian Revolution, the Laurentian (Canadian Shield) Uplift, the Wichita Mountains, etc.		

TABLE 1 (Cont.)

Era	Period or Epoch	Began Yrs. Ago	Characteristics
PALEOZOIC	Permian	280 million	First foraminifera; coral reefs; red sand deserts, potash, salt, gypsum; climate mild to glacial; mountain building.
	Carboniferous — Pennsylvanian	330 million	Coal-forming swamps, widespread seas; amphibians and reptiles increasing in size; mountain building in eastern U.S.
	Carboniferous — Mississippian	355 million	Few land animals; seas over most of N.A.; vast limestone deposits; crinoids at climax. Age of Sharks.
	Devonian	410 million	Widespread seas, forested lowlands; mountains beginning to rise. Age of Fishes; placoderms, lungfish.
	Silurian ·	430 million	Much of N.A. under shallow seas and marine life abundant. "Age of Eurypterids"; pill bugs, scorpions, etc.
	Ordovician	500 million	Graptolites, invertebrates with calcareous shells; first Appalachian Uplift, beginnings of Ozarks, Adirondacks, and Wisconsin highlands.
	Cambrian	620 million	Age of Trilobites. Most of N.A. above sea level; great geosynclines occupied by seas; vast sedimentations.

A vast unconformity separates the Cambrian from the Precambrian crystalline rocks, representing a greater lapse of time than the duration of any one of all the geologic periods following. Separation is also marked by the Killarney (Penokean) Revolution and the 65 distinct Keweenawan lava flows that total 50,000 feet in thickness.

Era	Period or Epoch	Began Yrs. Ago	Characteristics
PRECAMBRIAN		4½–6 billion	Divided variously into Eozoic era (faint fossil trails of marine invertebrates), Proterozoic era (rare worm burrows and calcareous algae), Archeozoic era (faintest traces of algal remains), and Azoic or Formative era (no life forms).

PRELUDE TO UNDERSTANDING MINERAL ENVIRONMENTS

To go on a rock collecting trip without a basic understanding of the earth's surface geology is somewhat like going to a rummage sale and blindly snatching items off the tables; most of what you pick up will be worthless. The basic rule to follow before leaving home was laid down for us nearly four and a half centuries ago by one of the greatest mineralogists and mining engineers of all time—Georgius Agricola.

Christopher Columbus was in the midst of his second great voyage of discovery when this most remarkable man was born Georg Bauer at Glauchau, in Saxony, on March 24, 1494. His name was subsequently Latinized to Georgius Agricola by his teachers in the custom of the Middle Ages. He became first a physician at Joachimsthal, a Bohemian town in the heart of the then most prolific metal-mining district of central Europe, and although he did not enjoy the profession it provided him opportunity to travel extensively throughout the mountainous region ministering to his patients.

Like most rockhounds of today, Agricola grew up with a boy's penchant for collecting pretty rocks and stones: samples of colorful ore minerals from the numerous mines that surrounded his home, gemstones, crystallizations, and fossils. He had a rigorously scientific mind. As his rock collection grew, he arranged his specimens into categories and attempted to classify them according to principles laid down nearly 2,000 years earlier by Aristotle.

While making his rounds as a physician, Agricola spent every spare moment not required for his medical duties in visiting the mines and smelters within a 50-mile radius of Joachimsthal. He questioned the miners and mine managers about gems, gemstones, and minerals; he read everything he could find by ancient Greek and Latin writers on mining and the "natural history" of the earth. Eventually, Agricola mastered everything known in his day about minerals and mining. Not until modern times has his knowledge been superseded.

Agricola's greatest contribution to the sciences of prospecting, mining, mineralogy, and metal extraction was his *De re metallica,** published in 1556, a year after his death. On the first page of Book I Agricola laid out his advice for all prospectors, gem and mineral collectors, and mining geologists who were to follow him, as significant for each of us who takes to the field today as it was for our medieval predecessors:

> For a miner must have the greatest skill in his work, that he may know first of all what mountain or hill, what valley or plain, can be prospected most profitably, or what he should leave alone; moreover, he must understand the veins, stringers and seams in the rocks. Then he must be thoroughly familiar with the many and varied species of earths, juices, gems, stones, marbles, rocks, metals, and compounds. . . .

THE CLASSES OF ROCKS

Agricola undoubtedly recognized the three great and obvious classes of rocks: igneous, sedimentary, and metamorphic. Learning to recognize these rocks is not only relatively easy but a prime necessity for

---

* Translated in 1915 by Herbert Clark Hoover and Lou Henry Hoover from the first Latin edition of 1556 (New York: Dover Publications, Inc., 1950).

understanding mineral environments and knowing what to look for in them. By themselves, rocks are too common for consideration by most collectors, although any well-organized mineral and gemstone collection should contain representative specimens of all rock types.

There was a halcyon time once, a century or so ago, when all you had to do to collect gold nuggets, moss agates by the bucketful, carnelian nodules, gem crystals, or any other mineral tidbit was to get off your horse and start looking around. It didn't matter much where you were, in the Appalachian highlands or the frontier West. Gemmy minerals lay almost everywhere over the earth's surface, but nearly all were simply ignored in the great search for gold.

Surface occurrences of desirable materials have nearly all been garnered into private and museum collections, and those simple days have long gone with the five-cent stogie and the ten-cent beer. Instead, most remaining gem and mineral deposits can be detected only by noting the most modest surface clues, which often require a keenly appraising eye to detect, even when one follows a detailed geologic map (see Chapter 6). In order to interpret these indications that something worth digging for lies nearby, the field rock collector must be able to fit his observations into an orderly pattern of geologic reasoning.

The professional geologist is familiar with a great many differing types of mineralizations, not only surface outcrops but deeply buried concentrations. He is trained to recognize at a glance the large external surface features—mountains, outcrops, intrusions, extrusions, veins, dikes, and all general topographic variations—as well as the more detailed minor signs close at hand. Thus, at Butte, Montana, a huge gossan (decomposed rust-colored rock made up largely of mineralogically worthless oxidized iron pyrites containing only the barest traces of gold and silver) led to the discovery of the "Billion-Dollar Hill"—the richest copper ores in mining history, reaching 4,000 feet deep into the bowels of an otherwise unprepossessing mountain.

FORMATION OF IGNEOUS ROCKS

The view of many astronomers is that the earth and its moon were formed by accretion of cold mineral substances, free ice, and masses of nebular gases somewhere between 4½ and 6 billion years ago as they were being drawn inward toward the growing sun (the solar nucleus) by the forces of gravity. The same gravitational forces acted on the raw earth materials, condensing, compacting, building up internal pressures, and generating enough heat to bring the entire globe to a molten condition. The differing densities of the raw earth materials brought about a condition of magmatic separation, such that the heaviest metals (primarily iron and nickel) settled into a great core 4,314 miles in diameter with a density of 10.93. This core was overlaid successively by layers of less dense materials, with the lightest rocks, granite, forming the continents and "floating" on a layer of slightly denser basalt.

The mantle comprises a layer surrounding the core about 1,782 miles thick, with an average density of 4.93. The continental crust riding on the mantle averages slightly more than 20 miles thick and has a mean density of 2.84, practically that of granite. Taken as a whole, the igneous or "fire-formed" rocks make up approximately 95 percent of the earth's present crust. This external crust long ago cooled to a solid state, but beneath it the mantle rocks are plastic to liquid because of their heat of 1,200 to 1,700 degrees Fahrenheit. The nickel-iron core itself is extremely rigid because of the enormous pressures exerted upon it by the mantle and crust; otherwise it would be fully molten, its temperature estimated at 5,000 to 10,000 degrees F.

Beneath the crust and surging throughout both the core and the mantle, vast convection currents of heat create ever-changing pressures beyond anything that can be reproduced in a laboratory. Under any great pressure all rocks yield and bend, so that we can think of the crust of the earth as a flexible layer of rock overlying a yielding and possibly liquid core. As the convection currents shift about through geologic periods of time, new pressures form against the underside of the crust, buckling the surface along zones of weakness, pushing up mountain ranges here, spewing forth liquid rock (lava, magma) from volcanic vents or fissures there, and allowing pressure-compensating regions to subside or sink elsewhere.

Were it not for the existence of an atmosphere and the hydrosphere of oceans and subsurface waters, the primitive earth might have found a balance between its inner and outer layers, but such was not the case (as is discussed in Chapter 3). That these deeply buried pressures, many of which are triggered off by the surface agencies of weathering, erosion, and transportation of sediments, are still active is dramatically recognizable along any of the earth's great geologic faults. For example, the 700-mile-long San Andreas fault of California, estimated to run 50 miles deep, is a zone of earth movement. The western half of California and all of Baja California are moving steadily northwestward at a rate of one to two inches a year, by the fits and starts that we call earthquakes.

During the ages-long cooling process from the completely molten condition, crustal rocks developed two general types: plutonic rocks, or great bodies of basalts and granites that cooled well beneath the surface, and volcanic lavas that, on being poured forth through vents and fissures, cooled more rapidly on contact with the atmosphere.

MAGMATIC CONCENTRATION

The varying rates at which molten rocks (magma) cooled at different depths and pressures resulted in a process which geologists term magmatic concentration. This means that during the cooling period certain minerals tended to become concentrated in various favorable places within the subsurface melt, enriching such accumulations and leaving the surrounding magmas barren of those minerals. In the latter stages of cooling these concentrated, mineral-rich magmatic liquids, which had a lower melting point than the parent magmas, became squeezed by subterranean pressures into fissures, cracks, and cavities in the overlying crustal rocks to produce veins, stringers, ore bodies, and pegmatite dikes (when later erosion has exposed such filled veins at the surface).

The internal heat may also have vaporized low-temperature minerals. The upward movement of these vapors, particularly where steam and superheated water containing such dissolved gases as fluorine and chlorine assisted, brought penetration into even the most minute fractures in the already solidified overburden. Such fissure fillings may not have been entirely filled, leaving cavities along the way for later filling in with other minerals crystallizing out of solution in percolating ground waters.

Where igneous rocks have cooled on the surface, they often contain bubble holes formed by escaping dissolved gases. These openings are called vesicles. When filled or partially filled by later minerals deposited out of surface water solution, they form geodes or lithophysae. Where cooling has been so rapid that crystallization was impossible, the resulting product is a volcanic glass. The most common type is ordinary obsidian, which, although fairly uniform in appearance, has the varied composition of its mother granite.

CHEMICAL COMPOSITION OF IGNEOUS ROCKS

Almost 99 percent of all the igneous rocks which form the earth's crust are made up of mineral compounds containing no more than eight of the 92 native elements. In their order of abundance these elements are oxygen, silicon, aluminum, iron, calcium, sodium, potassium, and magnesium. Oxygen itself constitutes nearly half the total molecular weight of the primary minerals—basically quartz, feldspar, the pyroxene series, and hornblende. It is easy to see why the silicates (containing oxygen and silicon in various combinations with the metallic elements) make up the bulk of all crustal minerals. Table 2 presents the major igneous rock types with their identifying characteristics and mineral contents, and Tables 3, 4, and 5 provide additional detailed information.

MINERALS FOUND IN IGNEOUS ROCKS

Of the eight most common elements only seven are involved in the major proportion of the gem and mineral species that occur in igneous rocks. Table 2 shows that igneous rocks are predominantly either light-colored or dark-colored. The light-colored rocks contain a high percentage of the white minerals quartz and feldspar. The dark-colored rocks contain minerals made up largely of iron and magnesium (therefore termed ferromagnesian minerals). The ferromagnesian minerals contain large amounts of olivine, the pyroxenes, and hornblende, all dark in color and ranging through various shades of dull green, dark olive, brown, to black. In addition to the primary minerals, both the light and the dark igneous rocks contain readily recognizable accessory minerals in much smaller quantities.

Table 3 presents the secondary minerals of igneous rocks together with their characteristics. Table 4 presents primary and accessory minerals of light- and dark-colored igneous rocks. Table 5 briefly itemizes collector's minerals in the rocks of Table 2.

GRANITE PEGMATITE GEMS AND MINERALS

As a major earth-building rock, granite is the foundation stone of continents. Masses of granite rising from the depths, known as batholiths, make up the gray core of many mountain ranges, such as the Sierra Nevada range of California, the central ranges of the Rocky Mountains in Idaho and British Columbia, and the Great Stone Mountain of Georgia. Granite is easily recognized by its speckled-gray color and the uniformity of its grain and texture. Where weathering is active, as in Yosemite National Park and in the Dakota Black Hills, it leafs off (exfoliates) in slabs that break up into more or less uniform talus debris.

As far as gemstones and ore minerals are concerned, raw granite is almost completely barren and without interest to the collector. However, the coarser the granite and therefore the more easily disintegrated by weathering, the more likely it is to show mineralization through chemical alteration.

PEGMATITE: MOTHER OF GEMS

A pegmatite is a coarsely crystalline igneous granitoid rock. Because of its content of large crystals of feldspar, quartz, mica, and often beryl, it is frequently termed "giant granite." A pegmatite intrusion takes on something of the character of a vein and is often noted for the great variety of unusual primary and secondary gemstone and mineral species. Actually a pegmatite forms during the final stage of cooling of a much larger granite mass, when a highly fluid residue enriched in silica and numerous rare elements separates from the partly congealed magma. Dissolved fluorine, chlorine, and superheated water vapor make the molten residue abnormally fluid, so that the underlying pressures can force it into cracks, crevices, cavities, and fissures where slower cooling allows crystal growth of extraordinary proportions.

It is important for the collector to recognize, when in granite country, that pegmatite dikes represent the final closing stages of rock formation

TABLE 2
PRIMARY IGNEOUS ROCK TYPES

Type*	Name	Color	Gross Features	Texture	Minerals	Identification
Ext	Andesite	Light to dark brown	Thick flows, sheer cliffs, jagged outcrops	Porphyritic	(Cf. basalt)	Feldspar phenocrysts; absence of quartz
Plu	Anorthosite (Cf. gabbro)	Dark	Resistant outcrops	Coarsely granular	Feldspar dominant	Blue feldspar reflections; fine parallel striations
Plu	Diorite	Dark	Weathered outcrops and rounded hills	Uniformly granular, crumbly	Hornblende, olivine, and pyroxenes	Absence of quartz; olivine present
Plu	Dunite	Dark green	Rounded hills; few outcrops	Solid granular mass	Pure olivine	Glassy luster
Plu	Gabbro	Dark	Weathered outcrops and rounded hills	Grainy or granular	Ferromagnesian minerals	Fine parallel striations on feldspar
Plu	Granite and monzonite	Light	Rounded tops, domes and steep sides, right-angle joints	Uniformly granular	Quartz, feldspar, mica	Quartz present; speckled pattern
Plu	Granodiorite	Light	Rounded hills	Grainy	Plagioclase prominent	Diorite with quartz
Plu	Pegmatite	Light	Dikes, rocky ribs; white streaks on mountains	Coarse grains and crystals	Mica, feldspar, schorl	Very large size of crystals
Plu	Peridotite, pyroxenite, and kimberlite	Dark green to black	Rounded hills; few outcrops	Porphyritic and crumbly	Hornblende, olivine, pyroxenes, gemmy pyrope	Glassy lustrous olivine grains

COARSE GRAIN

22

FINE GRAIN

	Rock	Color	Occurrence / Structure	Texture	Minerals	Distinguishing features
Plu	Syenite	Light				
Plu	Trachyte	Light		Subparallel, rough fracture surface	Biotite, amphibole, potash feldspar, pyroxenes	Texture flow around larger phenocrysts; without quartz
Ext	Basalt	Chocolate brown to black	Sheet flows and dikes; columnar structure	Aphanitic, gritty	Olivine, pyroxene, plagioclase	Jointed, vesicular, columnar
Int	Diabase	Brown to black	Columns absent or less perfect than in basalt	Coarser than basalt	(See basalt)	Fissure cavities and lathlike crystals
Ext	Felsites	Rusty to almost white; gray to greenish gray	Flows common; outcrops bouldery to jagged	Compact, solid	Silicic magma; host to sulfide ores	Dull fracture surface, flinty; phenocrysts present
Int	Porphyries	Light	Flows common	Porphyritic	Feldspar, pyroxenes, quartz, olivine, etc.	Phenocrysts in fine-grained matrix
Ext	Rhyolite	Light	Flows common; show weathering	Porphrytic	Granite minerals	Presence of phenocrysts

* Ext = extrusive, Plu = plutonic, Int = intrusive. NOTE: The rocks in this table are related as follows: *granite* (and its surface form *rhyolite*), *syenite* (and *trachyte*), *diorite* (and *andesite*), *gabbro* (and *basalt*). The texture of igneous rocks is determined by the rate of cooling: granitoid (coarse) for slow cooling, felsitic (fine) for more rapid cooling, glassy (for very rapid cooling), and porphyritic (distinct crystals in a fine-grained base or matrix).

TABLE 3
SECONDARY IGNEOUS ROCK TYPES

	Name	Color	Gross Features	Texture	Minerals	Identification
GLASSY	Pitchstone	Dull	Flows common	Silicic glass	(See obsidian)	Pitchy luster
	Obsidian	Gray to black with occasional reddish streaks and iridescence	Flows common	Glassy; flow lines visible	Granite minerals, *q.v.*, Table 2	Conchoidal fracture
	Perlite	Black	Weathered flows	Frothy	(See obsidian)	Lightweight; rounded fresh glossy cores and pebbles ("Apache tears")
	Pumice	White	Old obsidian flows surface-contorted; glasslike forms, cliffs	Glassy; flow lines visible	(See obsidian)	Lightweight; frothy
FRAG-MENTAL	Volcanic breccia	Light	Consolidated angular fragments	Coarse; mixed pieces cemented together	Various extrusive volcanic rock debris	Cemented by volcanic ash or dust
	Volcanic tuff	Light	Consolidated volcanic ash or dust	Fine grains	Basalt or andesite series	Lightweight; may contain fossils

TABLE 4
MINERAL CONTENT OF IGNEOUS ROCKS

LIGHT-COLORED IGNEOUS ROCKS

Primary Minerals	Description
Quartz	White, milky, colorless, often stained brownish; glassy to greasy luster, conchoidal fracture, hardness 7.
Feldspar	Opaque white, often with pinkish to bluish tint; gray; dull porcelain luster when weathered, but glassy when fresh; hardness 6. (Orthoclase and microcline are potassium feldspars; albite, andesine, anorthite, bytownite, labradorite, and oligoclase are "plagioclase" feldspars containing various amounts of calcium and sodium.)
Feldspathoids	Mostly colorless or white minerals close to feldspar in composition, including: cancrinite (yellowish, greasy to glassy luster), leucite and nepheline (mostly colorless to white), and sodalite (blue or pink). Hardness 5.5–6.

Accessory Minerals

Apatite	Colorless, white, brown, green, pink, pale blue, violet, yellow; glassy luster, sometimes transparent; conchoidal fracture. Hardness 5.
Corundum (including ruby and sapphire)	Colorless, brown, black, blue, red, yellow, violet; adamantine luster (bronzy on brown varieties); conchoidal or uneven fracture. Hardness 9.
Fluorite	Colorless, white, brown, black, blue, and many intermediate colors; glassy luster, conchoidal fracture; crystals cubical or octahedral. Hardness 4.
Muscovite mica	White, light green, yellow green, silvery to pale or dark brown; glassy luster, crystals flaky and often in "books"; fracture uneven. Hardness 6–6.5.
Sphene	Brown, yellow, gray, green; adamantine luster, transparent in thin flakes. Usually crystallized in brown "envelope-shaped" crystals. Adamantine luster. Hardness 5–5.5.
Zircon	Brown, colorless, gray, green, reddish, bluish, violet; adamantine luster, conchoidal fracture. Hardness 6.5–7.

DARK-COLORED IGNEOUS ROCKS

Biotite mica	Dark brown to black; crystals tabular or "flaky," transparent to opaque, flexible and elastic; cleavage perfect basal. Hardness 2.5–3.
Hornblende	Dark green (edenite), bluish green (pargasite), to black; dull to glassy luster, subconchoidal fracture. Hardness 5–6.

MINERAL CONTENT OF IGNEOUS ROCKS   (cont.)

DARK-COLORED IGNEOUS ROCKS

Primary Minerals	*Description*
Olivine	Usually dark green, light gray, yellow, olive, brown to black; glassy to greasy luster, conchoidal fracture. Hardness 6.5–7. Alters to serpentine.
Pyroxenes	Dark green to brown and black; glassy luster to silky or submetallic (bronzite), uneven fracture. Hardness 5.5–6. Includes: aegerite, augite, enstatite-hypersthene, diopside-hedenbergite, jadeite, spodumene, and rhodonite.

Accessory Minerals

Ilmenite	Black to brownish black (geikielite), steel gray, or deep red (pyrophanite); metallic to submetallic luster, slightly magnetic, conchoidal fracture. Hardness 5–6.
Magnetite	Dark gray to black; dull to metallic luster, subconchoidal to uneven fracture, brittle. Hardness 6.
Pyrite	Bright brassy yellow ("fool's gold"); metallic luster, conchoidal fracture, brittle. Hardness 6–6.5.
Pyrrhotite	Bronze (less yellow than pyrite); metallic luster, although often coated with a rusty film, subconchoidal fracture, brittle. Hardness 4.

in which all the volatiles and most of the still-uncombined rare elements have become concentrated. During the high-temperature phase, while the congealing granite stock is still largely molten, this residual fluid cleans out nearly all the simpler minerals from the bulk of the granite. The abundant minerals in pegmatites are the same as in the mother granite. Because of a pegmatite's slower, low-temperature-phase cooling, the tiny grains visible in the speckled pattern of granite under a hand lens are able to grow to become the highly prized gems and gemstone crystals most sought after by gem collectors. As Agricola intimated, granite by itself is a rock to leave alone—there is nothing in it—but pegmatite granite demands a collector's closest attention.

(Where quartz and feldspar "join together"—the meaning of the Greek pegma—in a curiously intermingled manner, the resulting solid rock is called graphic granite. This material has some interest to general collectors, for the patterning is unusual and it takes a good polish.)

After a pegmatite has solidified, still beneath the surface of whatever overburden the fluid was squeezed into, later erosion removes part of the overburden to expose the veinlike or dikelike forms as parallel structures, often concentric in overlapping arcs of circles surrounding the dome of granite pushed up from the depths. The gem pegmatites of New England, especially in Maine and New Jersey, and farther south,

TABLE 5
COLLECTOR'S MINERALS IN IGNEOUS ROCKS

Rock	Gemstones, Minerals, Ores
Andesite	A barren lava lacking in significant minerals; sulfur
Anorthosite	Magnetite, ilmenite; gem labradorite (N.Y.)
Basalt	Quartz gemstones, native copper, massive datolite as fillings in small cavities (amygdaloidal)
Diabase	Apophyllite, datolite, prehnite, zeolite minerals (primarily eastern U.S. diabase exposures)
Diorite	Ilmenite, gold ores, copper
Felsites	Primarily a host to sulfide ores of gold, silver, copper, lead, and zinc
Gabbro	Mineralized primarily in New York State and Lake Superior region: iron ores (magnetite, ilmenite), native copper
Granite	Mother of pegmatites and of many commercial ores: tungsten, cassiterite, scheelite, wolframite, molybdenum, black tourmaline (schorl), quartz
Granite pegmatite	Host to many gemstones, gems, etc.; crystals of beryl, quartz, topaz, feldspar, fluorite, zircon, siderite, spinel, etc., and commercial ores of mica, beryllium, lithium, and rare-earth minerals.
Granodiorite-monzonite	Ores of copper, molybdenum, tin, tungsten, gold, silver, lead, zinc, uranium (monzonite, Marysville, Utah)
Peridotite	Pyrope garnet, platinum, chromite; diamond in kimberlite deposits; nickel ores
Porphyries	(See Felsites)
Rhyolite	Opal in cavities; topaz crystals, tourmaline
Syenite	Iron ore (magnetite); gold in quartz veins
Trachyte	Opal; turquoise in altered forms

in North Carolina, as well as those in the Dakota Black Hills and in southern California show this type of formation notably well.

Although the gem collector should certainly learn to recognize pegmatite formations in all granite regions, he should be aware that not all pegmatites contain valuable gems and minerals. Many pegmatites contain only the usual granite components of feldspar, mica, and quartz: in fact, many pegmatites are commercially mined solely for feldspar for use in ceramics, or sheet mica for use in electronic equipment. Such commercial veins are called simple pegmatites, whereas those containing additional and rarer minerals are termed complex pegmatites. The latter pegmatites are the result of several stages of cooling, plus "enrichment" by percolating solutions of water and high temperature and pressure or by mineral-laden gases seeping up from the depths.

Pegmatite Structure

Since original highly fluid granite residues were squeezed into cracks and fissures in the cold overburden, various zones can be seen separating the congealed pegmatite into distinctive parts. Nearest the cold outer rocks, crystallization took place quickly, and therefore the outermost pegmatite crystals are small and compacted. Inside this outer "contact band" which entirely surrounds every pegmatite intrusion is a zone where cooling was slower and crystal growth more distinct. This is especially evident in feldspar and mica, the ore values most often mined, but also in quartz, tourmaline, garnet, and beryl.

Toward the center of the vein or dike, cooling is slowest and most even; crystals have opportunity to grow to immense size. A microcline feldspar crystal grew to be 20 feet across in a Maine pegmatite. Both the New England and the Black Hills pegmatites have produced sparkling blue beryl crystals 18 to 27 feet long, and a spodumene crystal found in the Etta mine near Keystone, South Dakota, was 42 feet long and weighed 90 tons. Such overly large crystals are unusual, to say the least, and within most of them are few areas of gem-quality clarity and purity of color because of flawing and impurities.

In the *core* or heart of a pegmatite, the last to solidify and the narrowest of the zones, the material is most often an uninteresting gray quartz. Here and there may be concentrations of rose or smoky quartz, but little likely to be of gem quality.

Pegmatite Configurations

Pegmatites vary greatly in outward shape. The dikes are long and relatively thin, and project more or less vertically above the erosional surface. Sills are horizontally laid pegmatites that separate older strata of rock. Still other pegmatites may be in the shape of lenses, pipes, or pods. Of whatever configuration, pegmatites may or may not show branching structures radiating outward in all directions as smaller veinlets or extensions. The real shapes of pegmatite intrusions are as endless as the forms of the openings in the overburden into which the fluids penetrated. However, the majority of pegmatites are relatively thin and sheetlike.

The larger pegmatite intrusions generally formed in fractures and fissures surrounding large bodies of rising granite magma, as the crustal rocks were raised, distorted, and broken. Nevertheless, many small pegmatites can be found within masses of raw granite. These special pegmatites should be sought by the rock hunter, because they contain numerous cavities, or pockets, that may be lined with some of the loveliest crystals of all.

When weathering and erosion have revealed a pegmatite dike, the various internal zones are not only quite apparent to the beholder but have great meaning to the gem collector. Of greatest interest, perhaps, is the zonal region adjoining the core. Here, cavities and vugs created by vanished gases may have permitted the finest examples of crystal growth. Not all of each crystal may be of gem quality, but as in the case of a beryl that has grown past the feldspar zone, the tip may have become clearer and less flawed, show smoother and sharper faces, and manifest true gem characteristics.

After gases dissolved in the original molten granite escaped, they frequently left cavities which there was insufficient pegmatite fluid to fill. Within the cooling mass the grains of the mineral constituents pointing into the cavity then had a special chance to grow larger and develop perfect crystal terminations. The end result is a minor, perhaps lenticular, pegmatite without the outer zone of fine-grained crystals. Inside are likely to be found gem-quality crystals of microcline feldspar (amazonite), beryl, topaz, and smoky quartz. Such cavity pegmatites usually measure only a few inches across, although some may reach a diameter of a foot and contain proportionately larger crystals.

The following gems, gemstones, and minerals, described in Appendix I, will be of interest to rock collectors: amblygonite, apatite, aquamarine, arsenopyrite, autunite, beryl, biotite, cassiterite, cat's-eye, chrysoberyl, columbite-tantalite, corundum, cryolite, dufrenite, dumortierite, emerald, epidote, eosphorite, fluorite, gahnite, garnet, gummite, herderite, heterosite-purpurite, hiddenite, ilmenite, kaolin, kunzite, lasulite-scorzalite, lepidolite, magnetite, microcline feldspar (amazonite), microlite, molybdenite, monazite, morganite, muscovite mica, orthoclase, phenakite, phosphuranylite, quartz crystals, ruby, samarskite, sapphire, siderite, spinel, spodumene, topaz, torbernite, tourmaline (including the black variety schorl), triphylite-lithiophilite, uraninite, uranophane, wardite, and zircon.

HYDROTHERMAL MINERAL DEPOSITS

Superheated water under great pressure, especially if containing dissolved gases such as fluorine or chlorine, acts like a highly corrosive acid. It has the capability for dissolving many mineral species and transporting them in solution to suitable areas for redeposition.

Hydrothermal ("water-heat") deposits often contain a wide variety of metallic ore minerals that crystallized out of the solution in stages as the temperature dropped during the final cooling process. Because of the enormous subterranean pressures exerted upon the mineral-laden waters, the solution creeps into and fills every conceivable kind of empty space, from the microscopically narrow threadlike fissures, stringers, and veinlets to major fractures in the overburden. Crystallization takes place from the inside out, eventually filling the cavities in otherwise worthless gangue rock, that is, rock made up of the common mineral species.

It is in such deposits, often enriched by subsequent mineral replacement or surface oxidation, that some of the world's richest mines have been found, especially gold (in quartz veins), silver (in lead veins), gold and silver combined (in copper veins), and lead and zinc combined. Table 6 presents the more common hydrothermal ore minerals (arranged alphabetically in three temperature ranges) and their gangue or associated minerals.

MINERAL REPLACEMENTS

Hydrothermal deposits can be extremely varied. Successive flows of hot water laden with soluble minerals often bring about a replacement process in which some of the original minerals are redissolved, removed, and replaced with new minerals—a metasomatic replacement process. This process occurs throughout all classes of rocks, both those deeply buried under the surface and those on or near the surface.

The petrifaction of wood (see Chapter 9) is one example in which oxidation-reduction occurs simultaneously as any one of some 20 petrifying minerals replaces the wood on a cell-for-cell basis. Where one mineral replaces another mineral's crystal form without changing the original shape of the crystal, the result is a pseudomorph ("false form"). Thus cubic crystals of iron pyrite, FeS_2, may be completely replaced by limonite, $Fe(OH) \cdot nH_2O$, without in any way altering the shape of the original crystal faces. The result is a collector's cabinet specimen mineral known as a pseudomorph after pyrite. Similarly, quartz may replace fluorite and calcite, cassiterite may replace feldspar, and native copper may replace aragonite (an atomic variant form of calcite, $CaCO_3$).

TABLE 6
COMMON HYDROTHERMAL MINERALS

Ore Minerals	Gangue Minerals	Associated Minerals
HIGH-TEMPERATURE DEPOSITS		
Cassiterite	Pegmatite rocks; phosphates	Garnet
Gold	Quartz, granite, rhyolite	Sulfide ores (lead, silver, copper, pyrites)
Magnetite	Chlorite schists	Pyrite, sheet mica, tourmaline
Molybdenite	Igneous rocks, pegmatites	Mica, powellite
Pyrite	Slate, metamorphic rocks	Most metal ores: gold, silver, copper, lead
Scheelite	Limestone, quartz	Garnet, epidote, topaz, fluorite, cassiterite, vesuvianite, apatite, wolframite

Ore Minerals	Gangue Minerals	Associated Minerals
Sphalerite	Quartz, calcite, barite, dolomite, fluorite, siderite	Sphalerite, pyrite, marcasite, chalcopyrite
Wolframite	Quartz, granites, pegmatites (rare)	Ferberite
MEDIUM-TEMPERATURE DEPOSITS		
Arsenopyrite	Phosphate rock, pegmatites	Garnet
Bornite	Igneous intrusives	Other copper ores; rhodochrosite
Chalcopyrite	Barite	Other copper minerals, sulfides, pyrite, galena, sphalerite
Enargite	Igneous intrusives	Copper minerals, sulfides
Galena	Quartz, calcite, barite, fluorite, dolomite, siderite	Sphalerite, pyrite, marcasite, chalcopyrite; gold, silver
Gold	Quartz, granite, rhyolite	Sulfide ores
Pyrite		Most metal ores; gold, silver, lead, copper
Sphalerite	(See galena)	(See galena)
Tetrahedrite	Gangue surrounding copper ores	Copper minerals and associates
Wolframite	Granite, quartz, pegmatites	Ferberite
LOW-TEMPERATURE DEPOSITS		
Aragonite	Calcite, carbonate rocks	Celestite, gypsum, sulfur
Cinnabar	Barite, opalite, quartz	Aragonite, stibnite, realgar, opal, native mercury
Fluorite	A gangue mineral in itself; pegmatite rocks	Various ore minerals
Galena	Quartz, calcite, barite, fluorite, dolomite, siderite	Gold, silver, pyrite, chalcopyrite, sphalerite, marcasite
Marcasite	Calcite, dolomite	Galena, sphalerite
Pyrite	Coal, sedimentary rocks	Most metal ores
Silver, native	Calcite, ground-rock associations with silver ores	Silver ores, native copper
Silver, sulfides	Calcite	Other metal ores; opal, fluorite
Sphalerite	(See galena)	(See galena)
Stibnite	Dolomite	Arsenic minerals, cinnabar
Tetrahedrite	Copper ore gangue minerals	Copper minerals and associates

THE IMPERMANENCE OF IGNEOUS ROCKS

As long as igneous rocks remain beneath the earth's surface, they remain more or less changeless except in the uppermost zone of oxidation, which is only the downward extension of the effects of the earth's outer atmosphere. The earth's moon, lacking even the faintest of atmospheres, has remained a stable body for billions of years. But the earth, clothed in a gaseous envelope of which water vapor constitutes an ever-changing proportion, is subject to constant erosion. Every projection of rock above the mean sea level is subject to wind and rain action, freezing and differential heating, and a continual slow fracturing and chemical disintegration resulting therefrom. Thus, from weathering and erosion stem the two other great classes of rock described in Chapter 3, the sedimentaries and the metamorphics.

Mineral Environments (II): The Sedimentary and Metamorphic Rocks

The primitive earth had an extremely dense atmosphere, perhaps 20 times what it is today. Moreover, the first atmosphere was largely carbon dioxide (as it is today on the planets Venus and Mars), in which the present volume of nitrogen was intermixed with water vapor. There was no oxygen at all, except that locked up in the carbon dioxide molecules.

After the earth's crust had cooled to a solid state, most of the water vapor condensed into the seas and lakes and subsurface hydrosphere— all fresh water in the beginning. Fortunately, carbon dioxide is quite soluble in water, producing carbonic acid. Over the geologic ages all but three-thousandths of one percent of the original carbon dioxide was removed to form the carbonate rocks and the vast coal beds we know today—courtesy of its solubility in the waters of the hydrosphere. When vegetation began appearing on the surface of the land areas of the planet, to produce great coal-forming forests, it served to deposit carbon out of the carbon dioxide and release the gas's content of oxygen to become the 21 percent of today's very much thinner atmosphere. The entire process, ages long, produced profound changes in the igneous rocks of the earth's primal crust.

THE SEDIMENTARY ROCKS

Although 95 percent of the earth's crust is still made up of igneous rocks, most of the surface rocks were formed by the action of weather on the preexisting granites, basalts, andesites, and other igneous intermediates. The process is still actively going on all around us, and it will continue so long as there is an atmosphere to provide the "working fluid" of change.

Weather directly attacks all projections of rock, grinding and abrading by wind-blown sand, washing away by streaming rain and cloudburst waters. Alternate freezing and thawing shatters even the toughest rocks, gradually reducing them to grains of sand. Igneous rocks are further attacked chemically by water solution of carbonic acid, and sulfurous and sulfuric acids around volcanic vents. The resulting new chemical compounds, for example, minerals, are less resistant to weathering than the original igneous rocks, allowing yet further decomposition and formation of still newer mineral compounds. This process has been repeated endlessly throughout the 4½ billion years assigned to the earth's solid crust.

As weathering, differential heating, freezing and thawing, and chemical decomposition inexorably work to reduce mountain ranges of granite and great fissure flows of basalt to minute grains of sand, other forces of gravity and streaming water transport the decayed particles always to lower levels, ending on the beaches of the seven seas. When atmospheric decomposition has broken down the original igneous rocks into sand, clay, muds, and gravels, and wind and water have transported these erosional products to the lowlands, the second great class of rocks is formed—the sedimentaries. Gravels, sands, clays, and muds—taken in descending order of particle size—are true sedimentary deposits, but they are not sedimentary rocks. Only when compaction and solidification produce the rock forms of conglomerate, sandstone, claystone, and mudstone along with various intermediates such as shale, marl, breccia, etc., do we refer to the products of weathering and erosion as sedimentary rocks.

THE COMPOSITION OF SEDIMENTARY ROCKS

About 75 percent of all the earth's land areas is blanketed with a superficial layer of sedimentary rocks immediately beneath the soil (which is not a sediment, but a chemical alteration of the topmost layer of rock). These sedimentary deposits range from a fraction of an inch in thickness to 60,000 feet deep and attest to a great variation in geologic time and climatic conditions.

Approximately 58 percent of continental sediments are shales, that is, hardened muds and clays transported the greatest distance from the igneous mountains that produced them. Sandstone and conglomerates, the latter being gravelly masses hardened into solid rock, constitute 22 percent of all sediments. Nearly 20 percent more are limestones, originally deposited under shallow epicontinental seas in the dim past when the earth's atmosphere was largely carbon dioxide. A modest one percent of all rock debris is made up of such precipitates or evaporites as gypsum, salt, phosphate rock, chert, flint, agate, chalcedony, and the organic sediment coal.

Sedimentary rocks are easy to recognize. Because erosional debris eventually comes to rest on the lowest-lying plains, on lake and sea bottoms, and in canyon depths, brought down by successive floods or winds, it necessarily must lie in parallel bedding planes called strata. The earliest or oldest sediments naturally lie on the bottom, and layer by layer, as the strata pile one upon another, the geologic time scale shortens. Today's dust storm lays down the most recent sediment of all, but tomorrow another wind storm is sure to overlay that deposit with another later one.

Even when later uplift and distortion have changed the horizontal layers into all degrees of tilt to and including the vertical, the parallel bedding planes are clearly visible. Such strata may even be folded or sideslipped by faulting, but the existence of one sedimentary layer laid on another in the original deposition can be remarked because of differences in grain structure, color, and parallel or concentric banding, termed stratification. So clear and distinct does successive sedimentation occur that in Ice Age lake bottoms the *varves* (alternate layers of finer or coarser silt believed to comprise an annual cycle of deposition in still water) may run 30,000 to the inch, revealing 30,000 years of sedimentary deposition which, like the rings of a tree's growth, shows differences between winter and summer climatic conditions.

In addition to outward appearances the stratified sedimentaries contain what no igneous or metamorphic rocks do: animal and plant fossils, some microscopically small; ripple marks from wind or water flow that show even the direction of flow and its force; waterworn pebbles or boulders within the formation that has not yet been ground to sand or mud; and often bits and pieces of petrified wood. A great deal about past geologic periods can be learned from a study of their sediments.

The most common end products of weathering are (1) sand, composed mainly of decomposed quartz grains; (2) clay, from decomposed feldspars and the kaolin minerals; and (3) precipitates, from soluble minerals that include mostly colloidal silica (agate, chert, flint, chalcedony, etc.) and the carbonate and phosphate minerals. Lime, calcite, and the phosphates make up most of the precipitates, forming immense beds spread over wide areas where the earth's surface was anciently covered by shallow seas. Other less important sediments include the clastic (volcanic ash, bombs, lapilli, and cinders), meteoritic (dust and fragments from outer space), and magmatic (hot springs deposits).

FOSSIL CONTENT OF SEDIMENTS

Because all sediments are either chemical precipitates or decompositional products of preexisting rocks, transported and laid down in successive layers, many life forms have been included in those layers since the first Precambrian evolution of life on earth. Fossils include not only plant or animal parts, but traces of life, such as worm burrows and trails, footprints, and gnawings and scratchings. Paleozoic fossils are usually thoroughly petrified, many in true gemstone facsimiles of the original organic forms. Utah provides jasperized dinosaur bones and knuckles in considerable abundance, Triassic and Jurassic in age, which make extraordinarily interesting jewelry and art pieces. By themselves fossils are of major interest mostly to paleontologists, but the gem and mineral collector will find many types worth including in his collection. For example, hardshell clams in purest translucent agate from the western reaches of Washington State tumble magnificently into gemmy conversational pieces guaranteed to excite anybody's interest.

Fossils may be casts of plant parts or cell-for-cell replacements (volume-for-volume substitution) by minerals of life forms that died and became embedded in muds and limy deposits, or were covered by volcanic debris and preserved from the oxidation processes of decay until mineralization could take place from percolating waters. Sediments laid down under the seas contain marine invertebrates principally and, in favored localities, the bones of marine dinosaurs.

Fresh-water sediments are often rich in petrified woods, plant impressions, and casts of leaves or other plant units (trunks, limbs, twigs, nuts, cones, etc.), plus a wide assortment of fossilized animal bones, craniums, and teeth. Petrified wood, often beautifully colored and of gemstone hardness 7, occurs in practically every county in every state. The woods occur in rocks of every geologic age from the Silurian to the Recent. Of these the gem and mineral collector is usually most interested in agatized, opalized, and silicified types, colorfully stained by trace impurities.

CLASSES OF SEDIMENTS

Because of the varied conditions under which sediments were deposited, this class of rock varies more widely in form and texture than do either the igneous or the metamorphic rocks. Each type of sediment has its own typical minerals and/or gemmy substances. Some are the original minerals that were in the decaying igneous rocks; others are secondary mineral depositions brought about by chemical alterations, replacements, enrichments, or accumulations of very hard, very resistant minerals surviving through successive stages of sedimentation, compaction, uplift, renewed weathering, and subsequent redeposition.

Sedimentary rocks occur in the following major categories, nearly all of which contain interesting specimen materials:

ARKOSE: A conglomerate rich in quartz and feldspar grains resulting from the fragmentation of granite by alternate freezing and thawing, plus chemical weathering.

BENTONITE: A very fine-grained, bluish white clay derived from volcanic ash by chemical alteration.

BOG IRON ORE: A precipitated sediment, usually in fresh-water bogs, rich in iron oxide derived from weathering.

BRECCIA: Fragmented, angular rocks cemented together; includes fault and friction breccias, volcanic breccias, tuff, brecciated marble (New England), agglomerates, and others.

CHALK: Fine-grained limestone composed generally of the shells and shell fragments of marine organisms, primarily foraminifera, or resulting from calcium carbonate precipitation in salt water.

COAL: An organic bog or swamp sediment derived from the decomposition of ancient forest vegetation.

CONGLOMERATE: Gravels of water-rounded pebbles firmly cemented together; often called "puddingstone."

COQUINA: Limestone composed of loosely assembled shells and shell fragments, like a shell heap cemented together.

DIATOMACEOUS EARTH: Sediments made up of the fossil siliceous external skeltons of microscopic plants called diatoms; also called diatomite.

DOLOMITE: Massive bedded limestone in which the original calcium (of the carbonate) has been replaced by magnesium. Dolomite is harder than calcareous limestone and less effervescent in acid.

EVAPORITES: A group name for deposits of anhydrite, gypsum, salt, etc., resulting from evaporation of sizable bodies of fresh or salt water.

GYPSUM: Commonly occurring hydrous calcium sulfate deposited in ancient sea beds as rock gypsum, alabaster, gypsite, selenite, or satin spar, left behind by evaporation of sea waters.

LIMESTONE: Marine-deposited calcium carbonate occurring widely and frequently containing marine fossils.

LOESS: Fine-grained, wind-transported dust, sometimes deposited hundreds of feet deep, as in China and Iowa.

MARL: Porous masses of shells and shell fragments in deposits on lake bottoms or around the margins of shallow seas; also a lime mud not containing organic remains.

OOLITE: Resembling cemented fish roe, this rock form may be calcareous, ferruginous, phosphatic, or siliceous. Oolite is built up of concentrically layered small spheres, each one containing a grain of sand or a fragment of shell as a nucleus.

PHOSPHATE ROCK: Derived from apatite-containing minerals, calcium phosphate sediment ($Ca_3(PO_4)_2$) is widely distributed.

SALT: Known mineralogically as halite, deposits of sodium chloride (NaCl) occur very widely, often associated with beds of gypsum; halite derives from the evaporation of bodies of water in which concentrations of salt have built up, as in present-day Great Salt Lake in Utah or the Dead Sea in Palestine.

SANDSTONE: Most interesting, colorful, and varied of the clastic sediments, sandstone is composed of loose sand firmly cemented together, its color depending on the cementing agent. Quartzite is sandstone cemented together by silica to form extremely weather-resistant rock of hardness 7.

SHALE: This is the ultimate end product of weathering and is the finest-grained and usually most thinly bedded sediment, having been transported the farthest by water. A hardened shale produced by consolidation of mud is mudstone.

SILICEOUS SINTER: Hot-water precipitate of silica jelly, dried and hardened; found around geyser basins and as hot-springs deposits.

TILLITE: An unassorted conglomeration of rocks, boulders, pebbles, breccias, clay, and sand particles dropped from glacial ice and later cemented together; found only in Ice Age regions.

TRAVERTINE and TUFA: Light-colored calcareous deposits of earthy, spongy, or porous material from hot mineralized springs; best-known deposits are in Yellowstone National Park and along the Big Horn River adjacent to Thermopolis, Wyoming.

VOLCANIC ASH: Blown by tremendous explosive force from active volcanoes, volcanic ash is simply pulverized andesite or basalt; in the West it occurs in thick beds over widespread areas and is the source of bentonite.

GEMSTONES AND MINERALS FOUND IN SEDIMENTS

Since erosion is a never-ending process, as mountains are pushed up, eroded away, new mountains are pushed up again, and so on cycle after cycle as the geologic ages pass, unusually heavy or resistant minerals like quartz, diamond, tin, platinum, gold, topaz, tourmaline, and zircon may lag behind and become concentrated in "residual" economic deposits. Gemstones like topaz, tourmaline, and zircon, which originally were formed in pegmatite granites, may actually weather through several cycles and gradually be worn down to sand grains, only to be recrystallized from concentrated sands during a period of metamorphism. Such new crystals are often well formed and of high gem quality.

Tables 7, 8, and 9* present the characteristics of sediments when unconsolidated and when consolidated. Table 10 shows the relative distribution of many of the following gems and minerals that occur in various types of sediments: agate, apatite, aragonite, barite, bauxite, borax, calcite, carnotite, celestite, chalcedony, chert, colemanite, concretions, coral, diamond, dolomite crystals, flint, fluorite, fossils, fulgarites, galena, geodes, gypsum, halite, hematite, howlite, jasp-agate, jasper, kaolin, kernite, limonite, magnesite, marcasite, millerite, opal, opalite, platinum, polyhalite pyrite, quartz crystals, septarian nodules, siderite, soda niter, strontianite, sulfur, sylvite, thenardite, ulexite.

---

* These tables are adapted from Frederick H. Lahee, *Field Geology,* 5th edition (New York: McGraw-Hill Book Company, 1952) and Jay E. Ransom, *A Range Guide to Mines and Minerals* (New York: Harper & Row, 1964).

TABLE 7
FRAGMENTED PARTICLES FROM MECHANICAL DISINTEGRATION

Type	Occurrence	Unconsolidated	Consolidated
Rubble (rudite)	Residuals	Gravels	Coarse arkose Arkose conglomerate Arkose breccia
	Transported	Gravel, pebbles Talus, slide Till, volcanic fragments	Conglomerate Talus or slide breccia Tillite, volcanic breccia
Sandy (arenite)	Residuals	Sand	Arkose, from feldspathic rocks Graywacke, from ferro-magnesian rocks
	Transported	Sand (fluviatile, marine) Volcanic ash	Sandstone Tuff
Muds (lutite)	Residuals	Residual clays, laterite, terra rossa, etc.	Residual claystones
	Transported	Clay Mud, loess, adobe	Claystone, argillite Mudstone, shale, slate

TABLE 8
SEDIMENTS OF CHEMICAL ORIGIN, USUALLY COMPACTED

Type	Content
Calcareous	Tufa, travertine, oolitic limestone, dolomite
Siliceous	Siliceous sinter (geyserite), chert, flint, etc.
Iron Ore	Ferrous carbonate (siderite), greensand, hematite, bog iron ore
Phosphatic	Phosphate rock (calcium phosphate derived from apatite-containing minerals and/or fossil bones)
Evaporitic	Evaporite, gypsum, halite, alkali, anhydrite, etc.

TABLE 9
SEDIMENTS RESULTING FROM DIRECT ORGANIC ORIGINS

Group or Series	Unconsolidated	Consolidated
Calcareous	Shells and shell fragments Corals Ooze	Shell limestone Coral limestone Chalk
Carbonaceous	Peat, etc.	Coal series
Siliceous	Diatomaceous earth	Tripolite
Phosphatic	Guano	Phosphate rock

TABLE 10

GEM AND MINERAL CONTENT OF SEDIMENTS

Type Formation	Recognition Features	Mineral Content
Disintegration	Gravel beds	Beryl, cassiterite, chromite, chrysoberyl, corundum (sapphire, ruby), diamond, feldspar, garnet, gold, ilmenite, kyanite, magnetite, mica, platinum, quartz crystals, rutile, staurolite topaz, tourmaline, zircon
Decomposition	Clay (from decomposed feldspar); montmorillonite (from decomposed ferromagnesian minerals and obsidian); illite (from sea bottom muds)	Chlorite, illite, kaolinite, montmorillonite, opal, quartz
Lime precipitate	Limestone (often with clay and quartz impurities)	Aragonite, calcite, dolomite, opal, quartz
Iron and manganese precipitates	Bog iron ore; manganese deposits (black)	Goethite, hematite, pyrite, pyrolusite, psilomelane
Evaporation	Salts of sodium, calcium, potassium, magnesium, etc.; gypsum, anhydrite	Alabaster, anhydrite, boracite, borax, carnallite, celestite, colemanite, dolomite, glauberite, halite, howlite, kernite, langbeinite, mirabilite, nahcolite, polyhalite, satin spar, strontianite, sylvite, thenardite, tincalconite, trona, ulexite

WEATHERED ORE MINERALS

It might fairly be said that for color and beauty few of the classic gems and gemstones can compare with the brightly colored ore minerals found in weathered zones of oxidation in the upper levels of rich mine deposits. Many handsome specimens saved from commercial exploitation at the mine hoist can be seen today preserved in mineral museums everywhere, exciting the admiration and wonder of their beholders. Like unusually large raw nuggets of gold which appear in museum collections, particularly colorful mineral species found in the top zones of copper, lead, silver and zinc mines have an aura all their own. Museum-quality specimens bring top prices on the rockhound market today—worth much more than the intrinsic value of their metal content.

Metallic ore veins are frequently honeycombed with cavities above the water table. Here amazing crystal growths take place, while water and oxygen penetrating to such comparatively shallow depths exert chemical changes that bring out the finest colors imaginable. Unfortunately, such prize specimens as smithsonite in pale green, blue, or yellow; the deep blue of azurite and green of malachite (both copper ores, along with the astonishing royal purple blue of tarnished bornite, known to miners as "peacock" copper ore); the glistening spears of cerussite; and hosts of other minerals are too fragile for use as gemstone materials. Good specimens must be handled very carefully, preserved from further alteration in the new environment and atmosphere of a collection. In the cavities of ore veins such crystallizations reach their peaks of perfection.

SECONDARY MINERALIZATIONS

The exigencies of weathering that include percolating ground waters containing dissolved oxygen along with a miscellany of soluble minerals bring about chemical and physical alterations to underlying massive, drab, and generally uninteresting basic sulfide ores that predominate beneath the zone of oxidation.

The zone of oxidation constitutes only the upper few dozen feet of an ore body, defined usually as that portion of a vein lying above the ground water table. Zones of oxidation run deepest in desert and semi-desert regions, where percolating waters seep deep beneath the arid surface and the regional water table lies at a considerable depth. As the water table drops, percolating surface runoff waters can penetrate more deeply, thereby increasing the opportunity for secondary mineralization of in-depth ores.

Oxidation from dissolved oxygen combines with the dissolving of sulfide minerals to form solutions of corrosive sulfuric acid, which further acts on buried ore minerals. Iron pyrite, found in almost all ore deposits, readily oxidizes into iron sulfate and sets off a chain of chemical reactions and interreactions that form new, or "secondary," mineralizations and produce a broad spectrum of beautifully colored masses, crystals, crusts, and hairlike growths. The whole process carried on over geologic periods of time brings about an "enrichment" in the upper levels of an ore body by removing part of the minerals from the uppermost levels and recombining them with the ore minerals deeper down.

Many of the fabulously rich mines discovered during the nineteenth century were found in veins near the surface of the ground in the zone of oxidation. Collectors are almost sure to find many worthwhile mineral specimens yet remaining around such old mines. More particularly, additional weathering of abandoned mine dumps may not only have consolidated the dump into a rock-hard sediment but may have created yet another generation of secondary minerals. It therefore behooves every rock collector to examine old mine dumps and dig, pry, or blast beneath the surface to search for colorful material and raw native nuggets.

Not all mine dumps will be productive, since sometimes nothing but gangue rock was dumped over the sides. Nor are all parts of a dump equally productive of mineral specimens. Some analysis of how a mine was originally worked is usually necessary to reveal, in the words of Agricola, "where to look and what to leave alone."

A fairly typical experience in the Western mining districts happened to my father while he was hunting mineral crystallizations around an abandoned gold mine dump a few miles out of Wickenburg, Arizona. He kicked over a solid gold nugget a quarter the size of a man's clenched fist. Not being interested in gold, he merely pocketed the lump and went on looking for crystals. When he returned home, he could not recall on which of the many old dumps surrounding Wickenburg he had found the gold. A more commercially minded rockhound would have taken out a lease on the abandoned mine, because if there was one gold nugget mixed in with the gangue, there surely would be more. Early-day miners were unbelievably careless in their hand operations, and many such nuggets of gold or silver or copper escaped their attention.

SOLUTION MINERALS IN SEDIMENTARY STRATA

Sediments are the weathered, eroded, broken or pulverized, and transported materials that made up the primary igneous rocks. Therefore, sediments carry the "fines," that is, the powder, of all the mineral species originally contained in the mountain uplifts disseminated throughout the layers of sedimentation. By comparison with igneous rocks, the sedimentary beds are quite porous, and the particles making up the sediments are much less compacted together. Hence, percolating ground waters and atmospheric moisture readily penetrate sedimentary strata.

The slow movement of ground water serves to dissolve many of the finely disseminated minerals and concentrate them into favorable deposits in cavities, vugs, fracture openings, and loosely compacted areas. Many mineral crystallizations occur in very small size in vesicles, but the crystals are likely to be perfectly formed and useful in micromounts for exhibit under strong magnifying glasses. Wherever sedimentary strata are exposed, as in a road cut or bank, limestone quarry, or building foundation, there the interested rock collector will find minute crystallizations in tiny places: perfect cubes of iron pyrite, tiny dogtooth crystals of calcite, drusy quartz crystals, and fine examples of barite, fluorite, celestite, and gypsum.

Such solution deposits are usually quite spottily scattered throughout sedimentary formations. Silica, however, being quite soluble, may form thin beds of chert in some strata. Indeed, the cryptocrystalline quartz minerals quite commonly occur in the sedimentary formations, filling hollow geodes with lovely clear crystals—usually found in sandstones and shales—and solidly filling hollow volcanic "bombs" to create thundereggs. Similarly, calcite forms septarian nodules in many regions. Where calcite predominates over quartz, such fillings will be characteristic of this softer mineral. Whether quartz or calcite, when sawed and polished, such nodules or thundereggs make interesting items for any rock collection.

SERPENTINES

One of the more common minerals is a soft rock with a greasy feel that can be scratched with a fingernail, usually greenish in color but ranging through white, brownish, yellowish, to black. If such a rock has a hardness of 2 to 3, it is likely to be serpentine, the host to a variety of gemstone minerals and commercially important asbestos. So common is serpentine that entire mountains of it occur, especially in northern California, or it may occur as thick beds between layers of quartzite in Arizona along the Salt River canyon.

Serpentine itself is a secondary mineral, resulting from a hot-water alteration of magnesium silicates in which the silicates take up water from the original volcanic magmas; serpentines are found wherever dark-colored magnesian rocks occur. Moreover, the process of "serpentinization" affects various mineralized areas, altering quite unrelated minerals into forms of serpentine. Its greatest commercial value, however, lies in the several varieties of asbestos which occur as veins cutting through such bodies.

Chrysotile asbestos, mined extensively in Arizona, is considered to be the most prized commercial mineral. Where metamorphism has acted on serpentine to convert it into a marble, the result is a popular verde antique. Gem serpentine is valued for its fine color and ability to be carved into ornamental objects.

Serpentine formations also provide a source of chromite, native platinum, nickel ores, nephrite jade, idocrase (californite), chrysoprase (garnierite-stained chalcedony), and benitoite (a rare gemstone known only from San Benito County, California).

THE METAMORPHIC ROCKS

The "eternal" mountains are anything but eternal. From the moment the first upwelling of a subterranean batholith of granite appears above the surface, weather and gravity begin tearing it down. Mountains rise only because the forces of diastrophism pushing them up are stronger and faster than the forces of erosion acting to tear them down. Eventually, of course, erosion wins out as the subterranean convection currents become dissipated or move elsewhere, and every mountain range sooner or later is worn to sand and clay.

Even the ancient peoples who first coined the myth that mountains lasted forever were aware of the damage to mountainsides done by flooding rains and churning gales. No mountain remains the same from one day to another, or even one hour to the next; all rocks elevated above the mean sea level surface, as well as those beneath, are undergoing a constant and continual change.

From the primary igneous rocks, as we have seen, come the sediments. These clastic and chemically altered products of erosion, exfoliation, and frost action are immediately subject to gravitational attraction and so become removed to lower elevations by falling and by the action of streams, rivulets, and wind. A body of rock being pushed upward by internal earth forces weighs a finite number of tons, which can be calculated by multiplying its measureable or estimated volume by the mean specific gravity. As erosion eats into the original rock and the materials are transported away from it, the weight of the body of rock floating on a basalt substratum diminishes. At the same time, that removed weight, when transported to a distant lowland, is added to the weight of the crustal rocks immediately below the lowland surface. Thus, a continuous state of disequilibrium is set up. The transported sediments bring about a downwarping of the crust, creating a trough.

A good example is the Great Central Valley of California (San Joaquin in the south and Sacramento in the north). For ages the surface of these two valleys which feed into the San Francisco Bay has remained at or near sea level, yet the entire valley contains sediments now measuring approximately 16,000 feet deep. Those sediments were derived from a once towering range of mountains off the present coast of California, known as Cascadia, now entirely vanished except for its worn roots showing in the Santa Barbara Channel Islands. As the weight of those sediments shoved downward, they were almost exactly counterbalanced by an upward push to the east that produced the Sierra Nevada range paralleling the Great Central Valley. Over the length and breadth of North America, similar wearing away and building up of mountain ranges has repeated itself throughout geologic time. In the mid-American heartland the roots of a number of ancient mountain systems are today buried beneath some 3,000 feet of sediments derived from erosion of the first and second Rocky Mountain systems.

When old sediments become so deep that they become compressed by the overburden of yet later sediments, they build up compressional heat. Added to this is new heat developed from the radioactivity of the uranium and thorium minerals contained in all rocks and rock debris. Or the increasing pressures on the underlying mantle force molten masses of basalt to intrude directly into zones of weakness in the sedimentary overburden. Under the steadily increasing build-up of pressure and heat, all rocks which were for a time at least in stable equilibrium become modified. Their internal structures, textures, and even colors readjust to meet the requirements of a new mineralogical equilibrium. This readjustment to new conditions is called metamorphism (Greek meta, change, and morphe, form). Therefore, all transformed or "altered" rocks belong to the third and last great class of rocks, the metamorphics.

When you mold a handful of moist, gray clay into a brick and bake it to the hardness of stone at 3,000° F, you are metamorphosing original sedimentary minerals into something very different in color, texture, and hardness. Rocks most responsive to a new environment are, quite naturally, the fine-grained sedimentaries.

Because igneous rocks were originally formed under great heat and pressure, they are least affected by new applications of either. Also, earlier metamorphics raised anew into mountains are similarly resistant, but in the end erosion converts all uplifts into new sedimentaries; all rocks will eventually change their natures as one geologic age follows another and each cycle is repeated.

Geologic processes are slow but measurable. The pressures building up beneath a trough of sedimentation are necessarily transferred elsewhere through the plastic underlying mantle rocks. Inch for inch, as the downwarping grows deeper, somewhere else, perhaps hundreds of miles distant, a new range of mountains is being pushed up at the same rate.

THE EFFECTS OF METAMORPHISM

Metamorphism affects rocks in two important ways. First, where an intrusion of molten igneous rocks penetrates into an overburden of cold compacted sediments, there is an immediate transfer of great heat into the cold rock along the lines of contact. The effect is termed contact metamorphism. Along such lines, extensive remineralization takes place, and the world's greatest ore bodies, as well as gems and gemstone minerals, are found in such zones of contact. Hot mineral-laden vapors and fluids accompany the intruding magma, redissolving many minerals, transporting and concentrating them, and chemically altering old minerals into new compounds. The process of remineralization is called metasomatism, from the Greek meaning "to exchange at the same time." Contact metamorphism takes place in relatively small, localized areas.

A second and mineralogically less important type of metamorphism takes place over broad regions of a few to several hundred square miles, or more, and is called regional metamorphism. Anyone who has traveled through Oregon or Washington is familiar with the great flows of basalt everywhere in evidence. The Columbia Plateau alone is a sheet of basalt covering nearly 200,000 square miles, many hundreds of feet thick in places. Where thinner layers of the basalt are revealed as sheer cliffs alongside the highways, one can frequently see the cross-sectional line of the original underlying surface—usually earlier sedimentary rocks—and observe how the heat of the congealing basalts changed the texture and color for several feet in depth below the lava. Much of that contact heat has baked the underlying sediments into a bricklike rock. The line separating the older land surface from the later fissure flows of basalt is called an unconformity and represents a geologic age of earlier erosion and sedimentation.

Another type of regional metamorphism occurs when the rocks of the earth's crust are buckled or squeezed by compressional forces acting horizontally, sometimes creating an overthrust of older rocks along the surface of later rocks and extending for many miles. Such compressional forces not only may reverse the seeming normal order of sedimentary rock layering, but they also create sufficient heat to alter the layers in contact with each other. Regional metamorphism involves large areas but introduces no new minerals and makes only minor changes in the chemical structure of old minerals.

METAMORPHIC ROCK TYPES

Most characteristically, perhaps, the metamorphic rocks show a development of foliation, that is, a roughly parallel arrangement of the mineral grains, especially noticeable in schists. There is, therefore, a tendency for metamorphic rocks to split along the parallel graining, most readily seen in slate. Metamorphic rocks include:

GNEISS (pronounced "nice"): Banded, coarsely textured, granitelike rock in which each band is made up of but a single kind of crystalline mineral; gneiss is often called *banded granite*.

GRANITE GNEISS: Derived from moderate metamorphism of granite or rhyolite, or strong metamorphism of impure sandstone or quartzite, and conglomerate. No collectable minerals or gemmy substances.

MARBLE: Very minute calcite crystals, formed from the original unorganized carbonates of limestone or dolomite by relatively low heat and low pressure, giving the broken surface a "sugary" texture. There are no simple cleavage planes. Marbles, perhaps the most interesting metamorphic rock form for collectors, contain a wide variety of lovely and interesting minerals and gemmy substances, especially along contact zones with igneous rocks.

METAMORPHOSED COAL: As the pressure of accumulating sediments on a body of carbonaceous matter increases, it forms a progressive series of organic substances: peat, lignite, bituminous coal, anthracite coal, and finally graphite. Each member of the coal series contains more pure carbon and less water, oils, and gases. The end product, graphite, is pure, elemental carbon and the amorphous sister to diamond.

PHYLLITE: Micaceous, banded, or foliated rock of uniform composition, phyllite is formed from clay minerals under more intensive metamorphism than that which creates slate.

QUARTZITE: Under intense heat and pressure cemented sandstone becomes smooth, glassy (100 percent silica), and dense. Quartzite has the hardness of 7 and can be split, or "cleaved," through the individual sand grains instead of breaking around them as in the original sandstone; often highly colored by mineral impurities, especially iron minerals.

SCHIST: Most representative of metamorphic rocks, the various schists

TABLE 11
METAMORPHIC ROCK TYPES

Constituents	Consolidated Forms	Metamorphic Rocks
PARALLEL GRAIN STRUCTURE CONSPICUOUS		
Gravel	Conglomerate	Conglomerate schist Conglomerate gneiss
Silicates (sand, quartz)	Sandstone	Gneiss, schists (mica, chlorite, horn-blende) Slates, phyllites
Carbonates, calcareous ooze	Limestone Dolomite	Impure marble Impure dolomitic marble Calcareous schist
Iron and quartz	Hematite	Itabirite
Carbonaceous (peat, lignite, etc.)	Coal series	Graphite, anthracite coal
COMMONLY MASSIVE, WITH POORLY DEVELOPED PARALLEL GRAINING		
Silicates (principally quartz)	Sandstone	Quartzite
Clay, mud	Shale	Hornfels
Feldspar	Claystone	Slate, serpentine
Magnesian silicates	Talc	Soapstone
Carbonates	Limestone Dolomite	Marble Dolomitic marble
Iron and quartz	Magnetite	Magnetite rock, lodestone

(mica, hornblende, quartz, limestone, etc.) are composed of definite grainy minerals recognizable by their thin, wavy leaves, or "foliations." Schists are host to almandite garnet crystals, muscovite and biotite micas, quartz, feldspar, chlorite, and other gemmy forms.

SLATE: Dense, usually dark-colored, slate is familiar as the blackboard in a schoolroom; slate easily splits into thin sheets of remarkable uniformity.

Table 11 categorizes the various types of metamorphic rocks.

COLLECTABLE METAMORPHIC GEMSTONES AND MINERALS

The heat and pressure of the metamorphic process varies from weak to moderate to strong, depending on subsurface conditions. Where a single-mineral rock like sandstone is metamorphosed, the result is still the same mineral, quartz in this case but in the form of quartzite—colorful perhaps but certainly not very intriguing to the gemstone collector. Where metamorphism introduces new minerals or chemically alters old compounds, the results can indeed be lovely gems, gemstones, crystals, and enriched metallic ores, as well as other rock-forming minerals. However, in nearly all metamorphic rocks the collector will find examples of collectable pyrite, pyrrhotite, hematite, magnetite, rutile, sphene, and tourmaline. In metamorphosed limestones may be found corundum, garnet (andradite, grossular), graphite, lazurite (lapis lazuli), pyroxenes, spinel, tremolite, and wollastonite. Table 12 presents briefly the principal gemstones and minerals found in the metamorphic rocks according to three degrees of metamorphism.

TABLE 12
MINERALS AND GEMSTONES IN METAMORPHIC ROCKS

Weakly Metamorphic	Moderately Metamorphic	Strongly Metamorphic
Albite feldspar	Actinolite-tremolite	Almandine garnet
Anatase	Almandine garnet	Andalusite-chiastolite
Bixbyite (in Utah with pink beryl, quartz, topaz)	Andalusite	Calcite
	Anthophyllite	Cordierite
Brookite	Axinite	Corundum
Brucite	Calcite	Danburite
Calcite	Chrysolite asbestos	Diopside
Chalcopyrite	Corundum	Dumortierite
Chlorite	Dolomite	Feldspar (plagioclase, potassium)
Dolomite	Epidote	
Epidote	Feldspars (plagioclase, potassium)	Fibrolite
Magnesite		Forsterite
Muscovite mica	Forsterite	Hedenbergite
Pyrophyllite	Hornblende	Hornblende
Serpentine	Idocrase (vesuvianite)	Idocrase (vesuvianite)
Siderite	Ilmenite	Ilmenite
Spessartine garnet	Iolite	Iolite
Talc	Kyanite	Lazulite-scorzalite
	Marialite-meionite	Magnetite
	Mica (muscovite, biotite)	Pyroxenes
	Nephrite jade	Pyrrhotite
	Orthoclase	Rhodochrosite
	Scapolite	Rhodonite
	Serpentine	Rutile
	Spinel	Scapolite
	Staurolite	Scheelite
	Zircon	Sillimanite
		Sphene (titanite)
		Spinel
		Tourmaline
		Wollastonite

VOLCANIC FLOWS

Of all rock formations described in the preceding pages, volcanic fissure flows are perhaps the most spectacular and easily recognized. Basalt sills form vertical cliffs along the Hudson River in New York and New Jersey, in Yellowstone National Park along the sides of the Yellowstone Canyon, and all across the Pacific Northwest from Idaho to the coast.

Most lavas form thin to thick sheets, sometimes separating great sedimentary beds and at other places spreading over tens of thousands of square miles on top of preexisting sedimentaries. Nearly all lavas are much darker in color than the adjoining sediments. Each lava flow represents a separate and distinct convulsion of the earth, as the fluid volcanics oozed out of great fissures and flowed over the landscape to fill in valleys and hollows and inundate low hills.

Most lavas carry little of interest to the gem and mineral collector, yet it is in such volcanic regions where many of the most desirable collecting materials are to be found.

Fissure lava flows did not create the conical mountains we call volcanoes. However, on the sides of volcanic cones that tower above the lower reaches of the Cascade Mountains of western Washington, western Oregon, and northern California are smaller basalt flows attesting to more recent volcanism, within the last few hundred thousand years and extending right up into modern times. Flows around Mount Shasta are estimated to be about 5,000 years old, while to the south Mount Lassen cast down lava in its last eruption in 1917. And, of course, the volcanoes of Hawaii chronically emit long seething flows of basalt. There have been no fissure flows of lava within the last few million years.

Minerals Associated with Volcanics

In a few places gemmy minerals were formed in basalt lavas. On the San Carlos Indian Reservation in Arizona gem-quality olivine occurs in the form of nodules (also at Kilbourne Hole, New Mexico). At Peridot Canyon on the reservation, the basalts of the north wall contain small gemmy peridot crystals.

Nearly all outpourings of subterranean magmas are accompanied by waters rich in dissolved silica. For this reason, all volcanic regions are worthy of detailed examination by the rock collector. Out of the silica-rich solutions come the quartz-family gemstones, usually colorfully stained with metallic mineral impurities that were also dissolved in the water infiltrations.

Veins and stringers of agate fill seams and fractures in lavas; nodules of agate occur repeatedly in beds of volcanic ash. Wherever the siliceous waters seep into the pores of vegetal products, there petrifaction takes place. In the volcanic ash beds of the western states, one may find silicified casts of tree trunks and limbs that were burned out by the flaming magmas, large masses of strongly colored jaspers (usually blood red but also bright yellow), and the solidly filled concretions known as thundereggs.

Not infrequently fissure flows of lava crossed sedimentary formations that were saturated with water at the time of the eruption. As the magma's heat penetrated the water table and converted the water into superheated steam, many new minerals formed and were deposited in cavities and cracks in the congealing lava. Later weathering and erosion may loosen such gemmy substances, so that along the bases of lava cliffs seen to be overlying sedimentary strata is a good place to look for interesting float. Generally speaking, however, the mineral-enriched hot waters tend to rise through the molten magmas. This process tends to concentrate minerals and gemmy substances in the uppermost layers, rather than spreading the existing mineral compounds out through the body of molten rock.

TRAPROCK SILLS: BASALT VS. DIABASE

Volcanic sills occur widely, both as extrusions of basalt and as diabase. Both types are usually termed traprock by the quarrymen who blast them out and highway engineers who use the crushed rock for road ballast. Because such sills may be either entirely barren of collectable minerals, or surprisingly endowed, the collector is advised to learn their distinguishing characteristics.

Where basalt sills show cliffs of a typical columnar structure, few minerals will be evident. But thick basalt flows may be honeycombed with cavities in the upper layers. These cavities are worth investigating because of their possible content of secondary mineral crystallizations.

Diabase sills are often thicker than basalt sills. They tend to be more compact and do not have nearly as many cavities. Whereas basalt has a distinct columnar structure, diabase does not, and the latter breaks more readily into large blocky masses. Where cavities do exist in diabase, they are quite likely to be filled with fine mineral specimens. Diabase cools more slowly than the hotter, more fluid basalt; hence, crystals have more time in which to grow larger. It is a rockhound practice to examine traprock quarries in the eastern states, especially those around Paterson, New Jersey, and in many other road ballast excavations scattered across the nation rock collectors would do well to make periodic examinations following periods of blasting.

VALUES IN AN OUTCROP

Any body of rock that juts out above or to the side of other earth structures is an outcrop, and these features vary considerably in size and appearance. Some outcrops may be residual masses of resistant country rock, even small mountains of quartzite reaching boldly above the regional land surface. Others may be small and obscured by vegetation. Although lacking in prominence, even small outcrops may contain collectable minerals, both primary species and the surface-oxidized secondary minerals. Durable minerals like cassiterite, gold, platinum, scheelite, tourmaline, etc., are likely to remain in the outcrop itself, but softer minerals more subject to weathering may have been eroded away from the exposure. They may also be present in depth.

As a rule of thumb, mountainous and volcanic regions are favorable for metallic ore deposits. In mountainous country one can find many obvious faults and fractures in the naked rocks; these crustal breaks are favorable for the deposition of minerals of many species, thereby producing veins and stringers of ore. Moreover, in rough country you are more likely to encounter outcrops or other rock exposures with indications of values below the ground. Such rock structures are often lacking in flat or rolling country, where sediments provide most of the rock formations.

Agricola observed that the mineral hunter should take note of every physical surface feature of rocks. Odd or unusual colors should especially be investigated, for many metallic minerals take on characteristic colorations during weathering. Color in an outcrop is not a certain criterion of mineral values present, and many minerals show no characteristic hues at all. However, you should be aware of the worth of mineral stains as an aid to prospecting. Many mineral colors are bright and vivid, like the canary yellow of the uranium ore carnotite, the bright blues and blue greens of malachite, the Prussian blue of azurite and bornite, and the shining green translucency of chrysocolla. Other metallic minerals have equally spectacular colors in brilliant reds, oranges, yellows, or in combinations. Nickel and chrome ores are green, cobalt minerals a lovely pink, and the manganese ores rhodonite and rhodochrosite combine a startling gorgeous pink with coal black. A color key to the identification of minerals is provided by D. K. Fritzen in *The Rock-Hunter's Field Manual* (New York: Harper & Row, 1959).

chapter 4

Preparation for
Field Collecting

At least 90 percent of successful gem and mineral hunting is in the preparation. A projected field trip involves acquiring and learning the use of appropriate tools, learning to use and read a topographic or geologic map, and knowing how to survive under possibly difficult environmental conditions. The keys to success, of course, are knowing what to look for, recognizing mineralized environments, and identifying mineral and gemmy substances. Much of your preparation can be done entirely at home, supplemented by visits to the nearest mineral museum and geological library.

Previous chapters have outlined the basic information relating to mineral environments and the three great classes of rocks. Learning to recognize them in the field requires personal visits and rather extensive travel. Preferably, a beginning rock collector should make his first field venturings in the company of people who are familiar with the general subject of gem and mineral hunting. For this reason, it might be desirable to join a local rock and mineral society.

It is a mistake to leave for a vacation with only a vague notion about doing a little rock hunting along the way. The amateur photographer may have little difficulty in aiming his camera at scenery which spreads out in all directions around him, but the amateur as well as the experienced rock collector must be able to pinpoint his sights on specific environments and learn to select the collectable "wheat" from the general run of "chaff" rocks that are certain to surround him on all sides.

FIELD CHECK OF MINERAL OCCURRENCES AND CHARACTERISTICS

The knowledge of how to identify minerals begins at home. In nearly all communities supporting at least a junior college, adult education courses in geology and mineralogy provide numberless examples of minerals with which to practice identification. Lacking access to such inexpensive courses, the beginner will profit from the purchase of a sample

TABLE 13
GENERALIZED OCCURRENCES OF MINERALS

Field Exposures	Mineral Contents
Alluvial deposits and placers	Cassiterite, columbite, diamonds, gold, ilmenite, magnetite, monazite, platinum, zircon, etc.
Fumaroles	Hematite, sal ammoniac, sulfur, sulfates
Igneous intrusives	Dark minerals, feldspar, micas, quartz
Limestone quarries	Calcite, celestite, dolomite, fluorite, galena, gypsum, sphalerite, etc.
Metamorphic rocks	Many valuable ore minerals, metal sulfides, hornfels, high-temperature gemstones, rare-earth minerals
Ore veins or lodes:	Native metals (gold, silver, copper), metallic ore minerals, pyrite, etc.
Contact-metamorphic	Epidote, garnet, scheelite, sulfides, idocrase, etc.
Weathered veins	Copper minerals, anglesite, cerussite, smithsonite, wulfenite, etc.
Pegmatites, miarolitic cavities	Granite minerals (graphic granite, micas, feldspars, hornblende), a host of gemmy crystals and assorted minerals, lithia ore minerals
Volcanic rocks, bombs	Tungsten, molybdenum; contact-metamorphic minerals, olivine, augite; quartz family minerals

rock and mineral kit, available at most mineral dealers and designed to acquaint students with the more important rock forms to be found in the earth's crust. Table 13 summarizes the generalized occurrences of minerals in the environments described in previous chapters.

Although many rock collectors are not accustomed to identifying ordinary rocks, except in the most general terms, the well-informed gem and mineral prospector should be able to recognize the major environmental characteristics which lead to worthwhile investigation.

IDENTIFYING CHARACTERISTICS

While the field exposures listed in Table 13 are fairly obvious and easily recognizable surface indications of gem and mineral environments, the minerals themselves are less readily recognized and identified. The *relative hardness* of minerals is a major identifying characteristic. Table 14 presents the hardness scale developed by German mineralogist Friedrich Mohs in 1822. The scale is not strictly a mathematical relationship, although it approximates a logarithmic scale in that each higher number represents an inconclusive multiple of the hardness of the mineral below it. About all that can be said about it is that hardness 7 (quartz) is considerably harder than 6 (feldspar). Sensitive instruments tell us that if the scale ran from zero to 1,000, a diamond would measure 1,000 (Mohs 10), whereas corundum (Mohs 9) would measure only about 250 and topaz (Mohs 8) about 160.

The softest mineral is talc, and the hardest is diamond, which has no competitor for hardness. In the field rocks can tentatively be identified by the use of a thumbnail, coin, knife blade, or other rocks to determine

TABLE 14
MOHS SCALE OF HARDNESS

Hardness	Mineral	Description
1	Talc	A mineral very easily scratched by the fingernail; it is the base for talcum powder. Minerals of hardness 1 are often slippery in feel.
2	Gypsum	A mineral that can be less easily scratched by a fingernail than talc; used for making plaster. (The fingernail has a hardness of about 2.5 and cannot scratch the next representative.)
3	Calcite	A mineral easily scratched by a coin or knife point, used for making cement; it is often associated with common rock limestone.
4	Fluorite	Used as a flux in blast furnaces, fluorite is scratched by a knife point with some difficulty.
5	Apatite	A mineral very difficult to scratch with a knife point because steel has a hardness of about 5.5. Apatite is an important source of phosphate fertilizer.
6	Feldspar	Feldspar may be orthoclase, microcline, or plagioclase; it cannot be scratched by steel, but can be scratched by the next mineral.
7	Quartz	The hardest of the common minerals, quartz resists weathering and provides a large family of gemstone minerals; quartz easily scratches both glass and steel.
8	Topaz	This gemstone scratches quartz with difficulty, requiring considerable pressure; it cannot be scratched by quartz, but only by the next two representative minerals.
9	Corundum	Known more familiarly as ruby or sapphire, this gem mineral can be scratched only by a diamond. Ordinary corundum makes into grinding powders, exceeded as an abrasive only by diamond bort.
10	Diamond	One diamond can be scratched only by another, and then only with difficulty. Although about four times harder than corundum, this pure, crystallized form of carbon is brittle and burns easily.

"scratchability." If one mineral can scratch another, the one that does the scratching is, naturally, the harder. Two minerals of equal hardness will either scratch each other or, more likely, fail to make any impression either way. In Appendix I, where the hardness factor is given for minerals and gemstones, you will find many in-between hardness ratings given as decimals, e.g., hardness 3.5–4.

Some crystals show a different hardness in different crystal directions. Thus calcite can be scratched along the base by a thumbnail, but the cleavage rhombohedron cannot. Kyanite can be scratched along the prism by a knife point, but not across it. Diamonds are too hard to scratch with another diamond (the only possible tool to use on one diamond is another diamond) parallel to the octahedron face; therefore, they can be cut only across the face.

MISCELLANEOUS PROPERTIES

Table 15 presents the identifying characteristics of the more common rock minerals, based on some of the miscellaneous properties described below.

Color and hardness constitute a quick, field-identifying observation, augmented by noting whether a mineral is opaque, translucent, or transparent. Prospectors of experience also heft a rock specimen in one hand to get the "feel" of its weight in subjective comparison with that of a known object: the heavier it is, the more compact, dense, and likely it is to contain metallic minerals. For example, jade is dense and its heft is heavy; so also are galena and garnet, whereas gypsum and opal feel lightweight. Field identification by heft comes with experience, and it serves primarily to denote the general category or chemical family to which a rock specimen belongs.

Most of the common rocks may also be divided into light-colored vs. dark-colored nonmetallics. These nonmetallics may further be subdivided into hard and soft, those which show cleavage and those which develop only fracture. Cleavage is the property of breaking at any place along one of a series of parallel planes that will reflect light the way a mirror does. Some minerals have no cleavage; some have cleavage in only one direction, others in two or more directions. When there are two or three directions of cleavage, it is important to note whether they are perpendicular or oblique (angle expressed in degrees). Cleavage can be said to be good, fair, poor, or absent. Perfect cleavage occurs in mica books, leafing off sheets like the thin pages of a printed book.

Any break that is not a cleavage is a fracture. The most important fracture for purposes of identification is the conchoidal fracture, a smooth curving break with sharp edges like a break in thick glass. Other fracture types are: rough, splintery, even, uneven, and subconchoidal (not quite conchoidal).

Further identification can be made by noting whether a mineral has

TABLE 15
FIELD CHECK OF COMMON MINERALS

NONMETALLIC, LIGHT-COLORED

Hard, Cleavage

	Hardness	Mineral
Pink to flesh-colored, block cleavage	6	Orthoclase
Grayish, lathlike, smooth (94°)	6	Plagioclase
Green, columnar, prismatic	5–6	Actinolite
Gray to red, greasy, soluble	5.5–6	Nepheline

Hard, Fracture

Green, glassy, granular	6.5–7	Olivine
Glassy, variously colored	7	Quartz
Isometric, garnetlike, dark matrix	5.5–6	Leucite

Soft, Cleavage

Salty taste, cubic crystals	2.5–3	Halite
Colorless, rhombohedron	3	Calcite
	3.5–4	Dolomite
Flexible plates	2	Gypsum
Rectangular cleavage	3.5	Anhydrite
Soapy feel, greasy, micaceous	1	Talc
Elastic, flaky, glistening	2–2.5	Muscovite mica
Fibrous, brittle	3.5–5.5	Zeolite(s)
Fibrous, brittle	2–5	Asbestos
Green, greasy, fibrous, little cleavage	2–5	Serpentine

Soft, Fracture

Yellow, burns blue, suffocating odor	2	Sulfur
Earthy	2–2.5	Kaolinite

NONMETALLIC, DARK-COLORED

Hard, Cleavage

Black, prismatic (87–93°), glossy	5–6	Augite
Green to black, prismatic (56°, 124°)	5–6	Hornblende
Dark green, basal, glossy	6–7	Epidote

Hard, Fracture

Brownish green, uneven, glossy	6–7	Epidote
Dark brown, orthorhombic, glossy	7–7.5	Staurolite
Red, green, yellow, glassy, 12 sides	6–7.5	Garnet
Black, columnar, hexagonal	7–7.5	Tourmaline (schorl)
Pink, green, columnar, hexagonal	7–7.5	Tourmaline
Variously colored, waxy, conchoidal	7	Cryptocrystalline quartz family
Black, mottled, red, green, glassy	5	Obsidian
Dark, crystalline, foliated	5–7	Schist

TABLE 15 (Cont.)

Soft, Cleavage

	Hardness	Mineral
Brown to black, elastic, flaky	2.5–3	Biotite mica
Green to black, micaceous, flexible	2–2.5	Chlorite
Brown rhombohedrons, pearly	3.5–4	Siderite

METALLIC, COLORED

Black

Black streak	6	Magnetite, ilmenite
Black streak	1–3	Coal, graphite
Red streak	1–6.5	Hematite
Yellow streak	1–5.5	Limonite

Red

Metallic, fracture jagged	2.5–3	Copper
Earthy	1–6.5	Hematite

Yellow, Brown

Metallic, black streak	6–6.5	Pyrite
Earthy, yellow streak, brown cubes	1.5–5	Limonite

smell or a slippery feel. Other minerals may be flexible (can be bent only) or elastic (returns to original shape after bending). A few minerals are sectile (can be cut with a knife), malleable (can be hammered into other shapes, like gold, or dented because they are not brittle, i.e., subject to fracturing). A very few minerals are magnetic.

Many minerals are fluorescent (see below) or phosphorescent; some show triboluminescence (giving off small flashes of light when scratched or struck; rock crystal, for example, "sparks" when it is sawed, while agate may glow with buried fires on a grinding wheel). Other minerals, such as fluorite and some calcite, reveal thermoluminescence (a glowing when low heat is applied).

Quartz and tourmaline show pyroelectricity and piezoelectricity during periods of warming or cooling, when temperature or pressure changes cause the minerals to take on an electrical charge and develop positive and negative poles.

Adularescence or labradorescence is a bluish sheen seen in some feldspars, such as moonstone and labradorite, when viewed from certain angles. Pleochroism occurs in some colored transparent or translucent crystals of noncubic structure, revealing different colors when viewed from different directions. So pronounced is this color change in minerals like tourmaline, cordierite, and andalusite that the pleochroism is enough to serve as positive identification.

Star figures characterize certain other minerals. When the micas are struck lightly by a blow from a sharp-pointed needle or knife blade, a percussion figure erupts along the crystal directions in the mineral surface, forming a six-rayed star. Yet other gemmy minerals, when cut cabochon and given a high polish, show the phenomenon of asterism. Thus a point of light appears visible through such crystals as ruby, sapphire, rose quartz, corundum, and even some grayish pegmatite quartz. The appearance is that of a six-rayed star spreading from the point of light caused by reflections from microscopic inclusions parallel to the crystal directions. The star shape may vary somewhat, from four-point to six-point, depending on whether two or three sets of needlelike inclusions are present. The presence of inclusions of a foreign mineral also produces a condition of chatoyancy, or fibrous silklike sheen, which when properly cut makes into cat's-eye gems.

A condition of aventurescence occurs when a crystal gemstone contains tiny platelike inclusions that reflect light strongly, especially quartz and feldspar. The Norwegian aventurine feldspar known as sunstone is a particularly attractive example of aventurescence. Finally, a phenomenon similar to aventurescence results not from inclusions of foreign material but from internal microscopic partings or flat separations along the cleavage planes. The reflection of light rays, known as the schiller effect, is developed most strongly when the gemstone is held in certain positions. A good example of schiller is found in amazonite. Where the internal cleavage-plane separations have been coated with very thin films of iron oxide, as in some chalcedonies, iridescence (reflecting rainbow hues like a film of oil on water) occurs. Such chalcedonies are often termed fire agates.

Metallic, colored minerals are usually distinguished on the basis of color and streak. When a freshly broken mineral specimen is scratched across the surface of a piece of unglazed porcelain or the reverse side of a bathroom tile or pulverized by a hammer against a hard object and the powder examined against a white paper or cloth, the color of the powder —the streak—may be quite different from the overall color of the mineral. The colored mark or powder is a surer method for identifying a mineral in the field than is heft. Not all minerals produce a streak, but those that do leave a clearly recognizable signature.

Appendix I describes the identifying characteristics of the majority of collectable gemstones and minerals that are not included in Table 15.

FLUORESCENT-MINERAL HUNTING

Ultraviolet light, light that has a wavelength beyond the purple end of the visible spectrum, has a strange way of causing many minerals to fluoresce, or glow in the dark with characteristic eerily beautiful colors, which bear little relation to the color of the mineral when viewed by ordinary daylight. Nighttime prospecting with "black light" ultraviolet ray lamps had its heyday during the late 1940's and through most of the 1950's, when commercial-minded rock hunters were looking for government-subsidized scheelite, the commonest ore of strategic tungsten, which was being bought at government-subsidized prices. In the dark of moonless nights tungsten ores lying scattered as nodules over desert surfaces glow with distinctive bright blue, blue white, or pale to bright yellow colors when ultraviolet ray lamps are played over the ground. Many prospectors made small fortunes simply by cruising the desert back roads at night and picking up everything that glowed under their black lights. When the government subsidy ran out, scheelite prospecting ceased commercially, but it has continued as a means of building up rock collectors' black-light cabinet collections.

Many other minerals besides economic species fluoresce delightfully under ultraviolet light. Indeed, many gem and mineral collectors set up special darkroom displays of the fluorescent minerals. By daylight most fluorescent minerals appear unimpressive, like ordinary country rock which one kicks aside while hunting more obvious mineralizations. Actually, the fluorescent minerals occur much more widely than either gemstones or ore minerals, so that the rock collector will find an ultraviolet ray lamp useful wherever he goes. Most rock dealers carry various models at relatively modest prices.

Black light not only reveals fluorescent minerals but also less desirable objects, such as poisonous scorpions beneath creosote bushes on the western deserts. Scorpions fluoresce a beautiful yellowish green, much like some of the uranium minerals, so a collector should beware of simply viewing and grabbing.

Through black light, the gem and mineral hunter is offered an opportunity to extend his collection beyond simple daylight prospecting. A good guide to profitable collecting of fluorescent minerals is the U.S. Government's official list of strategic minerals, obtainable from the Defense Minerals Exploration Administration, Interior Building, Washington, D.C. Favorite hunting grounds include rock quarries, mine dumps, roadside embankments, and exposures of almost every kind of country rock. Table 16 lists many fluorescent minerals worthy of inclusion in gem and mineral collections.

HUNTING FOR RADIOACTIVE MINERALS

Prospecting for uranium minerals with a Geiger or scintillation counter was extensive in the 1950's. Many great uranium deposits were found by amateurs in the far western states, especially throughout the Morrison sandstones surrounding the Four Corners region where Arizona, New Mexico, Utah, and Colorado meet. Many uranium prospectors unwittingly located claims on thorium deposits, too. Both uranium and thorium minerals constitute whole series of radioactive substances, daughter elements of the parent uranium and thorium produced by successive

TABLE 16
COMMON FLUORESCENT MINERALS

Mineral	Daylight Colors	Fluorescent Colors	Remarks
Adamite	Light yellow, greenish, rose, or violet	Yellow green	Often brillanily fluorescent
Alexandrite	Blue green (becoming violet red in artificial light)	Red	A variety of chrysoberyl
Alunite	White, light gray, flesh red	Sometimes orange	Long-wave ultraviolet light
Amber	Yellow, light to dark brown	Yellow, greenish yellow	A fossil resin
Amblygonite	Colorless to white, lilac, light gray green, gray blue	Weakly orange	Long-wave ultraviolet light
Anglesite	Colorless to white or grayish	Yellow orange	
Apatite	Colorless, white, brown, blue, violet, yellow	Yellow to orange	Strong heat required; many specimens do not fluoresce
Aragonite	Colorless, white, light yellow	Yellow, green, red, white	Commonly also phosphorescent
Autunite	Greenish yellow, lemon yellow	Green	One of most brilliantly fluorescent of all minerals
Barite	Colorless to bluish, yellow, brown, reddish	Occasionally yellow orange	Brilliant after roasting; also phosphorescent
Benitoite	Blue to white	Deep blue	Strong glow; a rare mineral
Beryl	White, blue, pink, green, yellow	Weakly yellow	Emerald may fluoresce pink to deep red
Brucite	Pearly white to pale green, yellow, or blue	Blue	Fluorescence is diagnostic
Calcite	Colorless, white, pale tints	Red, pink, yellow, blue, orange, pale green	Phosphoresces orange red (briefly) or persistent blue at Franklin, N.J.

Mineral	Color	Fluorescent color	Remarks
Calomel	White, grayish, yellowish	Red	
Celestite	Colorless to white, red brown, or light blue	Sometimes yellow green	
Cerussite	Colorless, white, gray, light yellow	Yellow	Turns yellow to red brown on heating
Colemanite	White or colorless	White	
Corundum	Colorless, brown, black, yellow, red, blue, violet	Red or orange	Often triboluminescent with orange flashes (See also ruby and sapphire)
Diamond	White, grayish to black	Blue, green, red, orange	Weakly fluorescent; most diamonds do not fluoresce
Diopside-hedenbergite	White, light green, dark green, brown	Blue	Light-colored varieties in dolomitic marble
Fluorite	Colorless, black, white, brown, lavender, purple	Blue, green, yellow	Long-wave ultraviolet light; also thermoluminescent
Glauberite	White, light yellow, mud gray, buff		May phosphoresce
Gypsum	Colorless, white, light tints	Green, pale yellow	Most specimens do not fluoresce; phosphorescent, showing hourglass pattern in crystals
Hemimorphite	White, often stained	Pale orange	Pyroelectric
Herderite	Colorless, white, yellowish, light bluish green	Deep blue	Also thermoluminescent
Hydrozincite	White, light gray, light yellow	Brilliant blue	Almost always brilliantly fluorescent
Leadhillite	White (often tinged with blue, green, light yellow)	Orange	
Marialite-meionite	Colorless, white, violet, pink, yellow, gray	Orange to bright yellow, less often red	Long-wave ultraviolet light best

TABLE 16 (Cont.)

Mineral	Daylight Colors	Fluorescent Colors	Remarks
Natrolite	Colorless or white	Orange	Fluorescence helps identification when it forms embedded masses
Nepheline	Colorless, white, gray, smoky, reddish	Orange red	In portions of crystals only
Opal	Colorless and all light tints and rainbow play; fire	Pale green, yellowish green	Sometimes brightly fluorescent
Pectolite	White to gray	Orange	Long-wave ultraviolet light
Phosgenite	Colorless, white, gray, yellowish brown	Brilliant orange yellow	
Powellite	White, yellowish brown, light blue	Yellow	
Quartz (agate, chalcedony)	Colorless, white, smoky, rose, violet, brown	Greenish, yellowish	Many specimens do not fluoresce
Ruby	Red	Dull to bright red	Some rubies glow brilliantly
Sapphire	Cornflower blue	Orange, red, yellow	
Scheelite	White, brownish, light green	Blue, white, pale yellow	Brilliant; fluorescence is a diagnostic test
Serpentine	Green, white, brown, yellow, red, black	Yellowish varieties fluoresce cream yellow	
Sodalite	Colorless, white, blue, violet, pink	Yellow to orange	Pink variety (hackmanite) brilliant; fades to white in daylight and reverts to pink in ultraviolet light
Sphalerite	Colorless (rare), yellow, red brown, black	Sometimes orange	Also triboluminescent
Spinel	White, lilac, violet, blue, red, orange brown, dark green, black	Red and lilac varieties fluoresce red or yellow green	Red spinels glow

62

Mineral	Color	Fluorescence	Remarks
Spodumene	Buff, white, lavender, greenish; transparent varieties lilac, green, yellow, colorless	Orange	Phosphorescent, thermoluminescent
Thenardite	Colorless, light yellowish, brownish	Weakly yellow green	Also phosphorescent
Thulite (a zoisite)	Pink	Sometimes yellow orange	Long-wave ultraviolet light
Tourmaline	Black, white, blue, green, brown, pink, red, colorless	Yellow	Short-wave ultraviolet light
Uranophane	Yellow, orange yellow	Weak yellow green	Distinguished from yellow iron minerals by its fluorescence
Wernerite	(See marialite-meionite)	Bright yellow	Glows distinctively
Willemite	White, colorless, brown	Green	Brilliant; brown specimens do not fluoresce; also phosphorescent
Witherite	White, gray, light yellowish	Blue	
Zircon	Colorless, gray, green, bluish, brown, violet	Yellow orange	Often with a bright glow

degenerations until radioactively inert lead is produced as the ultimate end product. Thorium is not yet considered a strategic element but may become a primary source for the development of power, and the Atomic Energy Commission is interested in knowing the locations of potential thorium deposits. Present atomic energy plants derive their energy from uranium fission; thorium is about four times more plentiful in the earth's crust than uranium, but techniques for converting its radioactivity into usable power have not yet been economically developed.

Reasonably priced radiation counters are available in many gem and mineral shops, and prospecting for radioactive minerals is easy. The "background count" of cosmic rays striking the counter is first checked. Then, when the instrument is passed over mineralized ground, any increase in the count, registered by flashing light signals or "clicks" or read out directly on a meter, indicates the presence of radioactive minerals.

The uranium ores are quite colorful in canary yellows and chartreuse greens and make excellent cabinet specimens. These specimens are especially interesting if shown in a blacked-out room under ultraviolet light, because most radioactive minerals are also fluorescent. Many pegmatites contain fine gemstone or specimen materials—valuable in themselves as collectors' items—containing radioactive minerals in small quantities but enough to register on a counter. By chipping away at pegmatite quarry walls, one can often discover a pocket of radioactive minerals hiding behind masses of feldspar.

CLOTHING AND CAMP EQUIPMENT

Proper wearing apparel is vital to comfortable field trip adventuring. Since gem and mineral hunting is at its best away from the beaten track, outdoor clothing is mandatory. Even in a city excavation or nearby rock quarry, it pays to wear rough clothes, thick-soled slip-proof shoes or boots, and a hat and glasses to shade the eyes from glare and rain sprinkles. Typical clothing for men and women would be Levi-type pants, a blue denim, khaki, or wool shirt, heavy leather boots with packs, serviceable headgear, and a neckerchief. Carry both canvas and leather-faced gloves and a change of everything.

Western rock fields are often replete with freezing night air (even in midsummer), dehydrating winds (a canteen of water is often worth more here than the finest champagne), blistering dust, and spindrifts of flying gravel. Alkali lies in expanses so glaring under the sun that Polaroid glasses should be used to protect the eyes. Add cloudbursts, thorny and scratchy brush, cactus with needle-sharp hooked spines capable of penetrating automobile tires and the best leather boots, mud, sand, and naked lava rock that can cut boot leather to shreds within an hour, plus a superabundance of overly affectionate biting insects, rattlesnakes, and venom-filled scorpions, and it is easy to see that rock hunting can have its momentary drawbacks.

Fortunately, most gem and mineral collectors thrive on occasional outdoor hardships, but nobody really wants to overdo the survival bit. Therefore, always start out prepared for the worst, and the good things will take care of themselves.

Although it is wise to carry a small snakebite kit in the glove compartment of your car or in the bottom of your carrying sack, the danger from rattlers, scorpions, Gila monsters, or other unpleasant creatures including an occasional tarantula is practically nil. All being cautious animals, they will stay out of your way if you let them. Perhaps the worst field offense is bringing a dog along. Not only do dogs diminish the enjoyment of other hunters, but they have an uncanny way of getting into trouble with cactus, sharp rocks, and poisonous creatures.

The following camping and general prospecting equipment can contribute to your ease and prospecting effectiveness. Of course, any amount of variation can be entertained as long as you know how to use the equipment and have sufficient sense not to overload your car or yourself with little-used or useless supplies.

Camping Equipment	*Prospecting Equipment*
Ax, for cutting wood or stakes	Ultraviolet ray lamp
Bad-weather clothing, hat	Canvas specimen bags, sieve
2-quart canteen for water	Chemical field-test kit, acids
Bucket, for hauling water	Compass, tripod (useful for camera)
Clothes: work, relaxation	Geiger counter or scintillation counter
Coleman stove and lamp	Knapsack or packboard
Cooking, eating utensils	Location notices, stakes
First-aid, snakebite kit	Map portfolio, detailed maps
Folding card table, chairs	Portable map-drawing board
Candles, matches, camera	(Rifle, revolver, ammunition)
Gasoline or water can, filled	Shovel, mattock, pry bar, rake
Reading materials, books	Sledge hammer, wedges
Rope, chain, cable, twine	Snakebite kit, ointments, etc.
Sheath knife (6-inch), hand ax	Simple surveying instruments
Sleeping bag, blankets, tarp	2-quart water canteen
Tent, camp trailer, camperette	Writing instruments, notebooks

Personal cleanliness and a clean, neatly ordered campsite will also contribute enormously to your outdoor enjoyment, besides revealing that you recognize camping amateurishness from professional ability to live comfortably wherever you go.

THE EXPERIENCED CAMPER

If you plan to set up a base camp from which to go farther into the wilderness, as many gem and mineral collectors do by backpacking for one or more days, you will want a packboard or knapsack, some extra socks and underwear, a canteen, and compact army-type cooking and eating utensils, as well as a lightweight water-repellent sleeping bag or blanket roll wrapped up in a pup tent. You may even want to go old-time and use a burro, but the story of how to pack one and keep track of it after camp has been made is best told by an experienced packer while teaching you the ropes.

The art of mineral prospecting is, and probably should forever be, reserved for the professional mining geologist and ore seeker, who is usually employed by a large mining firm which makes all arrangements for efficient field stays and studies. Other professionals usually come from the ranks of ex-miners; they are used to the wild lands and frequently live off the natural game.

The hobby of gem and mineral hunting is, however, more a family or group activity. Because you will meet many other collectors in almost every gem and mineral hunting locality, you may wish to entertain and be entertained somewhat. Therefore, consider what goodies you can stash among your camping equipment for periods of relaxation.

As long as you stick to the paved highways, you will have little use for a canvas water bag. Even in the most desolate, arid reaches of the Great American Desert, you are never more than 5 to 15 miles from a service station. But if you expect to leave the pavement to follow a long-abandoned dirt road toward some hoped-for Potosi, remember the following simple rules necessary for your comfort and ultimate survival: (1) carry one or two 5-gallon cans of water; forget the canvas water bag—heritage of the burro prospector—because its contents evaporate too quickly; (2) carry one or two 5-gallon cans of gasoline and extra quarts of oil; (3) have a 3-ton hydraulic jack and a bumper jack along; (4) take a complete set of tire-repair tools and two spare tires in case of stone bruising or ripped casings; carry one or two mounted spare tires under full pressure and a hand tire pump for emergencies; and (5) carry enough food to last a week in case of breakdown.

Two additional admonitions are extremely important when heading for remote country. Make local inquiry before starting out along any old road in desert or mountain regions, and always leave word of where you are going and when you expect to return. Then check back when you do return, as a courtesy and to preclude an abortive search party being sent after you. In recent years, too many unsuspecting motorists unused to wilderness travel, especially in the blistering summer heat of the Desert Southwest, have perished of thirst and sunstroke because they panicked following a mechanical breakdown and tried to walk out. If you should rupture your oil pan on a jagged rock, and it can easily be done, stay with your car. Help will eventually arrive, rest assured, if you left word of your probable destination and time of return somewhere along your back trail.

One more thing to remember: the West is growing wilder all the time, not more civilized. The old-time mining boom camps are dead and totally abandoned; the roads to them are often washed out and dangerous to travel. Tourists, truckers, and highway patrolmen stick pretty much to the paved highways today, and there are fewer and fewer travelers along the outback tracks that were once the arteries of a mining commerce.

An Irreducible Minimum

You may not be interested in any major prospecting or gem-collecting trip, but only in collecting gemmy materials and colorful cabinet specimens on weekends or holiday trips. Many thousands of collectors belong to this category. Their fine mineral collections attest to the fact that one really needs little more equipment than you can easily carry as you stride along, i.e., a basic knowledge of what you are looking for and how to identify it; a prospector's hammer (or hand pick); a stout sack tucked through your belt or light packsack slung over your shoulders; hand magnifying lens, pocketknife, streak plate (or piece of tile); and a full canteen of water and a lunch bag.

You will never have any real use or reason for carrying lethal weapons. Many sportsmen, however, hunt rock during most of the year but also enjoy game hunting during the seasons. They may wish to combine shooting with gem and mineral hunting.

There are also those who believe that a field trip can be enlivened with target shooting. Too many thoughtless individuals have left their unwarranted marks on highway signposts and in the sagging walls of abandoned mining shacks. Cattlemen are especially disparaging of amateur gunmen shooting up the scenery, injuring stock, smashing electric power line insulators, and generally making nuisances of themselves. The net result has been that many large areas of good rock-hunting ground have been permanently closed and posted against all trespassers, however well intentioned.

A Final Word

A field trip should be comfortable and enjoyable for the whole family. Concerned preparation leads to restful sleeping, adequate food and drink, safety against unforeseen hazards, and the sure knowledge that upon your return to civilization you will have achieved relaxation from the turmoil of the daily grind and are impatient to prepare for the next rock-hunting adventure.

chapter **5**

The Rock Collector's
Working Tools

Gem and mineral hunting is not as easy as it may sound, nor is unearthing and prying out prime specimens quite as simple as nudging an interesting crystal out of an excavation for a new building. Again, proper preliminary preparation is the key to collecting success.

In the past gem and mineral hunters exploring new fields found quantities of fine specimens lying loose on the surface. Today, probably every known collecting area has been gleaned of its surface materials, although collectable fragments may still lie scattered around to attract the eye. Such fragments, or "float," indicate mineralization in the field and suggest to the collector that he seek beneath the surface in favorable-appearing areas. Digging-out tools lubricated with elbow grease are necessary for finding gemstones and mineralizations that lie from a few inches to several feet beneath the soil.

Commercial ore miners who work pegmatites, veins, placers, or other ore-bearing deposits use mass means for excavating their "pay dirt." They are not concerned with preserving fine cabinet specimens and lovely crystallizations, unceremoniously dumping everything together into ore cars for hauling to the hoist and then to waiting trucks. In order for a rock collector to obtain worthwhile cabinet and cutting materials, he must exercise much more refined techniques, similar to those used by archaeologists excavating ancient burials. Broken crystals, fractured crusts, and shattered geodes have about as much value to the rockhound as broken window glass to a home owner.

DIGGING-OUT TOOLS

Most of the tools you will need are simple to use and designed primarily for hand operation. Some tools are as small and delicate as the camel's-hair brush archaeologists use to remove dust from prized vertebrae. The most valuable gems and minerals can be obtained only by delicate and painstaking manipulation.

SHOVELS AND PICKS, HAMMERS AND CHISELS

The prospector's hammer and the cold chisel or gad, chief among the implements useful to the rock collector, are easily transportable during a preliminary sashay across any collecting field. The prospector's hammer (often called the mineralogist's standard hand pick) can be purchased in almost any hardware store. Such hammers are available in several weights, either of all-steel construction or with a steel head and a handle made of wood, plastic, or leather-covered grip. The wooden-handled pick is less tiring to use and has a better balance but usually a shorter working life, since wood splinters from a misdirected blow. The hammer part of the head, used for pounding, is square and made of relatively soft steel; the opposite end may be either pointed, like a small pick, or chisel-shaped for prying and is made of much harder steel. Either type carries nicely when tucked through the belt. The preferred type seems to be the hammer with a pointed end, since it can also be used for prying and has the advantage of being easily inserted into small openings.

For removing or breaking heavier rock masses, a variety of additional small or large sledge hammers can be useful, ranging in weight from 2 to 14 pounds. These hammers are not readily field-portable, but at least one should be carried in the car for shattering country rock surrounding a pocket or cavity containing collectable mineralizations.

The cold chisel vies with the gad for prying rock layers apart. Both come in various lengths and have long or short tapers. Miners often use gads as wedges, since a gad is pointed at the working end and can reach into fractures and crevices not open to the broad-edged chisel. Several gads lined out along a fracture and struck successively with a hammer serve as a most convenient broad wedge to separate one layer of rock from another. A steel wedge has obvious uses in separating fractured rock but is hardly portable for casual rock hunting. (Primitive peoples were quite successful at mining with wedges made out of bone or jade.)

Shovels and pry bars are obvious necessities where considerable soil and rock must be disposed of before getting down to a pocket of gemmy material. The shovel may be a folding army trenching, short-handled variety or any of the longer-handled garden types. A miner's shovel differs from a long-handled dirt shovel in having a shorter shank with a handle grip at the end. Of the garden-type digging shovels, the "ladies' shovel" used by the U.S. Forest Service is the most easily handled and best-balanced digging tool. Prying bars, available in various stock sizes and lengths, have the advantage of enabling great prying leverage to be exerted at the prying tip, while simultaneously permitting very close control over the degree of leverage because of the offset point. A pressure of 100 pounds on the end of the shank may produce several thousand pounds at the prying tip.

SPECIAL CLEANING-OUT TOOLS

Some of the most useful tools available to the rock collector come straight out of a prize flower bed or the kitchen drawer home-repair shop. A garden hand rake or a weeder used for digging dandelions comes in handy for scratching into old mine dumps or as a small prying and chipping tool. An ordinary file with the tip of the steel handle bent into a right angle or a similarly bent screwdriver serves as a small prying bar for separating a crystallization from its underlying matrix.

For the more advanced collector, the ingenious use of a number of discarded dentist's, carpenter's, or stonemason's tools can do wonders in helping to remove delicate gemmy crystals or fibrous crusts from a resistant mine-tunnel wall or quarry side. An ordinary pocketknife, especially if it contains a screwdriver or leather punch, a pencil or horseshoe magnet, and a hand magnifying lens play important roles, too. The magnet helps to distinguish between magnetite and chromite and similar-appearing nonmagnetic ilmenite or rutile. The magnifying glass, preferably one with two or three separate lenses that give magnifications from 5 to 20 times, materially aids in helping you to see very small drusy-type crystallizations that require identifying. A lens also helps to distinguish between flecks of gold "color" and "fool's gold"—iron pyrite or marcasite or bits of mica—a laudable distinction that quickly separates the rank amateur from the semiprofessional.

MISCELLANEOUS TOOLS FOR THE ADVANCED COLLECTOR

Special tools and equipment are often required for specific types of gem collecting and prospecting. For example, hunting for sapphires in the stream gravels of Idaho and Montana requires a box screen to separate the cornflower-blue crystals from worthless gravel. To make a box screen, frame a wooden box 18 by 24 inches and 4 inches deep of half-inch wood fastened together at the corners with steel angle straps. Galvanized iron wire screening of half-inch or other mesh forms the bottom of the box, lapping up the outsides for a half-inch and battened down firmly with thin wooden or metal strips. Two or more such screens, with different sizes of mesh, make for efficient separation of variously sized crystals from the "charge" of gravel.

A shovelful of streamside dirt and gravel is dumped into the coarse screen box and rapidly shaken from side to side. Coarse rocks and gravel are tossed out by hand, and the "fines" passing through the mesh are saved for subsequent screening with the finer-mesh screen or hand sorting. If the material to be screened is damp or wet, shaking the screen beneath the surface of water from side to side, alternating with forward to backward motion, will bring about the desired separation.

Dendritic Agate

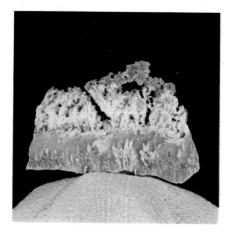

Fire Agate

Fortification Agate

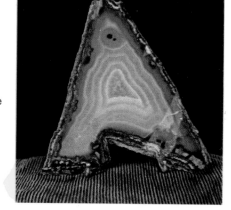

Montana Moss Agate

Amethyst

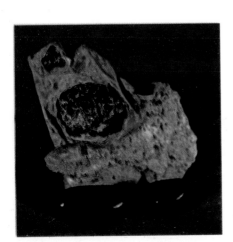

Apache Tears in Perlite

Azurite (L.) and Sodalite (R.)

Bloodstone

Calcite

Calcite "Steeple" Stalagmites

Calcite on Siderite

Carnotite Ore and Wood

Chalcedony Roses

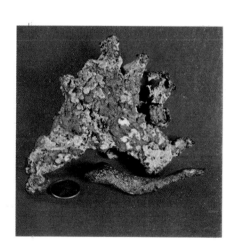

Copper

Eden Valley (Wyo.) Wood

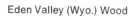
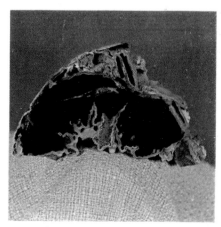

Fluorite on Quartz

Galena (L.), Chalcopyrite on
Dolomite (C.), Cinnabar (R.)

Garnets and Galena in Calcite

Garnets in Diorite

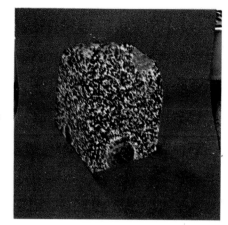

Halite

Iceland Spar

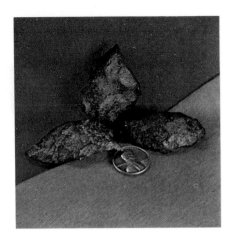

Iron Meteorites

Nephrite Jade

Jasper

THE GOLD PAN

The gold pan is probably the oldest and simplest tool used in prospecting for gold, in cleaning auriferous concentrates, and in hand-working very rich placer ground. The pan is shallow, 15 to 18 inches in diameter at the top and 2 to 2½ inches deep, with the sides sloping at about 30 degrees. A gold pan weighs from two to three pounds and is made of heavy-gauge steel with a rim turned back over a heavy wire for stiffening. Pans are available in almost all hardware stores, especially in mining regions, and may be purchased in many different sizes. The smaller pans are useful for sampling, the largest sizes for production panning.

It takes a bit of practice to learn how to use a gold pan, but a skilled operator can wash from one-half to one cubic yard of detritus in a ten-hour day. The object of panning is to concentrate heavier minerals such as gold, platinum, and various gemmy crystals by washing away the lighter materials. To do this most efficiently, all material in the pan should be of as even a size as possible. The pan is filled about three-quarters full with sand and small gravel, the mass stirred up with the hand, and the larger pebbles thrown out. Then the pan is submerged in water. Panning a bag of material can be done at home in a tub; field panning is usually done in gently flowing stream water near shore. More stirring and tossing out larger pieces and breaking up clay masses with the fingers are done under the surface of the water. Then the operator raises the pan to the surface, gently twirling it back and forth as he does so.

Inclining the pan slightly away from you and giving it a semicircular motion back and forth, combined with a slight upward jerking of the lower lip of the pan, stirs up the mud and dirt. The heavier particles, nuggets, colors, and crystals settle to the bottom while the water washes away the lighter unwanted dross. The panning action is continued until only the heavier minerals, or concentrates, remain, such as gold, black sand, and other minerals having a high specific gravity.

Most mineral hunters save the concentrates in a bottle or tin can until a large quantity accumulates. The larger particles of gold or crystals can be extracted by hand or with a pair of tweezers and saved in a vial or bottle of water for display. Auriferous placer deposits often yield bits of gold which can be mounted in clear plastic for a variety of jewelry making. The smaller particles, or colors, can be amalgamated with mercury, preferably in a copper-bottomed pan. Black sand is often magnetite and can be removed from the fines with a magnet. Table 17 provides a means for calculating the gold values in a cubic yard (one ton) of placer dirt, based on the average weights of the five sizes of gold colors normally found in a gold pan, with nuggets larger than size 5 being weighed or estimated separately.

TABLE 17
GOLD PANNING VALUES

Size	Kind of Colors	Milligrams
1	Very fine	0.05
2	Fine	0.20
3	Small	1.00
4	Medium	2.00
5	Coarse	4.00

The calculation for a yard of pay dirt is based on 181 "struck" pans—that is, 181 pans filled level equal a cubic yard of dirt. Since native gold is not pure, i.e., "1,000 fine," but averages only 80 percent pure (800 fine) to 85 percent (850 fine) and there is about a 25 percent "gravel swell," this number of filled gold pans of standard diameter is taken as the norm. For rapid computation count or appraise the number of each size of colors saved in a representative pan; reduce them to milligrams and add the total weight of all color classes. Of course, any gold found and not sold to the mint carries a much greater value as "specimen gold," and most mineral hunters prefer not to sell to government agencies. One troy ounce equals 7,200 milligrams.

This method of calculating gold values cannot be applied to the extremely fine "flour" gold found in many parts of North America. Capturing flour gold is difficult, because most of it simply floats out of the pan and is lost.

Although not as popular as the gold pan, a batea is often used to perform the same function. The batea is a cone-shaped pan made of either sheet metal or wood; some prospectors say wood is best for concentrating fine gold. Indeed, an ordinary wooden chopping or salad bowl makes an excellent batea. Most such panning instruments measure from 15 to 24 inches in diameter and have angles of slope to the apex of from 150 to 155 degrees.

CARBIDE LAMPS

Many fine crystals have been ruined by carelessly attempting to clean out a pocket of minerals, especially in pegmatites, without benefit of a bright steady light. A light is of course necessary for exploring the workings of old mines—always to be approached cautiously because of the danger of collapsing overhead rock. But even a daylight exposure of a cavity in the wall of a canyon or quarry requires some additional lighting when it comes to delicate hand work.

A flashlight is relatively feeble and has the disadvantage of having to be laid down during operations. The electric headlamp worn by forest service personnel for night tramping in the woods is sometimes useful because the lamp can be angled toward the crystal cavity from its wearing position on the forehead, but its light soon weakens. Moreover, battery cost and replacement are excessive.

The most efficient field light source is the carbide lamp. Operating from a slow dripping of water from an upper chamber onto a small charge of calcium carbide in the lower chamber to produce highly combustible acetylene gas, the ignition is done with an ordinary spark lighter attached to one edge of a polished reflector, similar to lighting a cigarette lighter. Shutting off the water by a lever on top soon stops the production of acetylene, and the light goes out. The illumination from a carbide lamp is bright and steady, and the cost, compared with flashlight batteries, is very minor. In underground workings the intensity of the light is proportional to the amount of oxygen in the air; a feebly burning lamp is an indication that the atmosphere is deficient in oxygen and that it is advisable not to penetrate any farther into the mine.

Carbide lamps can be purchased in many hardware and camping goods stores. The small lamp, measuring about 4 inches tall, can be hung from the belt or from the front of a miner's helmet. The larger size, measuring 6½ inches in height and 3 inches in diameter at the base, can be carried by hand or hung from the wall by its bail-type handle. Both lamps can be purchased with a reflector in a diameter of 2½, 4, or 7 inches. The normal charge of carbide (about two ounces) allows approximately three hours of steady working light with no diminution in intensity.

THE USE OF EXPLOSIVES

It is not the purpose of this book to provide instruction in the use of blasting powder or dynamite. Both are primarily the tools of the experienced miner. However, there are times when a reasonable charge of explosive can be the most effective way to open up a hidden deposit of collectable minerals. Because the use of explosives requires very specialized knowledge, the reader is referred to the *Blaster's Handbook* (Wilmington, Del.: E. I. DuPont de Nemours & Co.), a 516-page compendium for miners, quarrymen, ranchers, and construction men.

At least 99.9 percent of all gem and mineral collectors will have little to no use for explosives in any form. Their indiscriminate use can destroy a gemstone deposit by fracturing everything beneath the surface. A prime collecting site for amethysts in western Arizona was almost completely ruined when a dealer in rocks and minerals set off an excessive charge of dynamite in the expectation of a quick cleanup. Therefore, if a mineral deposit appears to require some dynamiting to remove the enclosing country rock, it is better to call in an expert and pay him to do a proper job.

BRINGING HOME THE BACON

Any field collecting trip has one primary goal besides sniffing the breezes and enjoying long sunny days of outdoor adventuring, and that is to bring home the gems and minerals collected. Whether you go on a one-day trip to a nearby quarry with members of your local mineral society or whether yours is a family vacation safari of several days' duration, you will need to prepare to package delicate specimens against the hazards of transport.

FIELD-TRIMMING A ROCK SPECIMEN

Generally speaking, you will want to bring back gemstone materials without field-trimming them down with a hammer and cold chisel. The reason is that breaking down a large nodule, for example, into smaller pieces may destroy parts of the interior designs or crystals which could be preserved by judicious sawing. But for many minerals and practically all rocks, trimming down to a reasonable size is a necessity.

The best sizes of rock specimens to be taken home for identification or for subsequent rework should always be trimmed from fresh rock, rather than from weathered exposures. Normal sizes are either 4 by 5 by 1 inches or 3 by 4 by 1 inches. These hand specimens are easy to pack away and carry home. While the thickness may vary somewhat, the length and width should approximate the dimensions given.

Trimming is properly done with the flat end of the hammer head, cracking down the larger pieces to the approximate size of the final specimen. Finishing off can be done by striking the rock on its edges so that chips fly off sideways and from both faces at a time. Finally, all hand specimens and any chips that appear to have identification value should be wrapped in newspaper or paper bags to prevent them from scratching, chipping, or bruising one another. Be certain that a label is attached to each specimen (see Chapter 7). A label is extremely important for laboratory analysis, whether you do it yourself or have it done by a mineralogist, since the label information pinpoints the specimen on a reference geologic map.

PACKAGING AND TRANSPORTING

Very seldom can you drive your car directly to a collecting site; sometimes you must tramp for miles, returning loaded down with specimens over rough country, with steep descents down slippery talus slopes and unsure footing at almost every turn. A fall over a boulder can severely damage gems and minerals carried loosely in a cloth or canvas sack at your belt or in a packsack over your shoulders. Therefore, you will find it expedient to carry a supply of soft tissue or cotton for wrapping delicate specimens immediately after picking them up in the field. Old newspapers come in handy for coarser specimens.

It is better to overwrap than not to afford adequate protection. Grass, leaves, and moss sometimes help but usually are too loose; wrapping damp clay around delicate crystals is excellent, when you can get it. Finally, your load must ride easily on your shoulders and not contribute unduly to imbalance that could bring a nasty tumble down a rock slide. (The best knapsack is a standard Boy Scout packboard on a contoured aluminum or wooden frame. With it an experienced outdoorsman can pack 35 to 50 pounds comfortably for long distances.)

Since carrying rocks can be burdensome, it is a good idea not to overload your shoulders but to gather selected specimens all in one place, periodically returning along short lines of investigation to the hub of your radius of hunting. Then, before leaving for camp or your car, you should make a careful selection of the day's harvest, throwing out less attractive rocks, trimming off masses of worthless matrix with your hammer, and reducing the sum total of your day's work to a "high-grader's" minimum quantity of most valuable rocks.

Under good collecting conditions in a new area you may pick up too much good material to carry out in one load; don't overdo it; make as many trips as necessary. Make your first trip out loaded only with the most desirable specimens, the second trip with the second best, and so on. It might well happen that you won't go back a second or third time.

A good supply of old newspapers provides many uses besides folding pieces around prime specimens before placing them in your pack. Around camp, newspapers spread out on the ground and anchored against the breezes with rocks provide a convenient ground cover for spreading out your collection for leisurely examination. Newspapers also make excellent "floor rugs" beside your cot. In the field, newspapers spread several layers thick will protect your knees against small sharp rocks while you carefully clean out a pocket or surface deposit.

The old-time mulepacker knew how to load his mule, or himself if in desperation he had to descend to the ignominy of carrying anything on his own back. Beginning rock collectors, unless thoroughly experienced in Boy Scout distance hiking and backpacking, will find that properly packaging rocks for easy transport is something of a specialized art that improves with time and experience.

Because automobile vibration can severely damage fine mineral specimens, be certain that every rock is well wrapped and secured in place in your car before heading for home. Such unusual mineral specimens as coprolites, the petrified excrement of Triassic and Jurassic dinosaurs occasionally found in ancient sediments, are surprisingly fragile despite their seeming weight and solidity. Small hairlike crystals and delicate mineral encrustations are especially subject to vibration damage. Since you may never return to a particular collecting ground, it pays to exercise great care in packaging and transporting whatever rocks you bring out of the field.

LABELING ROCKS AND MINERALS

Gem and mineral specimens by themselves have only a minimum value. Proper labeling, with the correct species name and field location from which each specimen came, adds a great deal of value to your collection (see Chapter 7 for labeling and cataloging specimens for home or club displays).

It is a good idea always to carry a pocket notebook and a dependable pencil (ballpoint pens have a habit of running dry at the most critical times or refuse to write on paper marked with finger perspiration) in the pocket of your shirt. Field notes are a must for any experienced rock collector or observant visitor to strange wilderness places; you cannot trust your memory for details once your trip is over. Moreover, you may be called upon by your gem and mineral society to give a talk on your experiences; your field notebook assures accuracy in your presentation. A camera also contributes greatly to your record of gem and mineral collecting.

Any field trip will become more interesting in retrospect if you acquire the habit of recording everything you observe in notebooks, each notebook carrying an identifying number and date. One notebook might carry field information pertaining to gemstones and crystals only, another to metallic minerals, a third to nonmetallics, and so on. If you use a camera, you might want a special notebook for recording photographic data—a most useful assist during field reconnaissance and exploration.

A good system for a beginner is to label each specimen immediately when found before packaging it and putting it into his pack, using small squares of adhesive tape pasted on and numbered consecutively for the day's finds. The same numbers should then be jotted down in a pocket notebook, including date, possible identification, common or local name, geologic formation where found, location, and any other pertinent information. At almost any collecting locality, you are likely to find others, perhaps more experienced, who will be pleased to help you identify on-the-spot discoveries as to species, geologic formation, etc.

Back at camp, when you make a final field selection of specimens to transport home, you may wish to renumber your finds. However, keeping a notebook record and field numbers is sufficient until you make the final records and information cards for your home collection. Permanent labels should be applied or attached at home after you have cleaned your specimens and prepared only the finest for display. At that time you substitute a small square of white paint or enamel in place of the adhesive tape and protect the India-ink numbers with a coating of lacquer, plastic, or nail polish.

Older rock collectors, or those less imbued with a knowledge of the scientific method, depend greatly on memory; many exercise an extraordinary recall of every facet of experience connected with every specimen in their collections. This is fine indeed, but eventually the old man with the scythe puts an end to memory. An unlabeled collection becomes like an album of unlabeled photographs two generations old—nothing can be positively identified. Since locality data is even more important than species name—any good mineralogist can subsequently name almost any rock specimen—only the person who found it can supply the information that gives lasting value to his collection.

REPORTS AND MAPS

The three most important and least used tools for successful gem and mineral collecting are mineral reports, geologic maps, and topographic maps (see Chapter 6). Professional ore prospectors use the government-prepared maps to familiarize themselves as much as possible about selected mineralized regions, in other words to provide basic information on where to go, what to look for, and what topographic difficulties may be involved in getting there.

Preliminary research naturally begins in a public library. Research means not only having a well-defined idea of what you would like to find but also knowing what publications to study to find specific answers to technical questions. Numerous government agencies are willing to help you obtain all the background you can absorb on mining and mineralogy, and most universities, colleges, and junior colleges have specialists in the earth sciences. All such sources of direct information are free.

The most readable sources of information are the popular gem and mineral publications listed in Appendix IV. These periodicals are directed to hobbyists and offer interesting personal accounts of other collectors, as well as specific details for reaching new collecting areas. Their advertisements carry a wealth of listings of books and pamphlets on almost every aspect of rock collecting, lapidary work, geology, and mineralogy. Many of these sources are on library shelves.

Your search for mineral and gemstone information necessarily leads you straight to technical mineral, mining, or water resources reports published by state and government agencies. Most of the tens of thousands of pages of fine print contained in the larger libraries are written strictly for scientists and technologists and require a basic knowledge of the vocabulary of all the earth sciences. Nevertheless, most such reports carry readable information about certain areas and their mineral deposits that make their perusal worthwhile.

For a home start, you can write to the U.S. Geological Survey, Washington, D.C. 20242, for the latest supplements and the basic volume of *Publications of the Geological Survey,* free of charge. This paperbound volume and its annual supplements list bulletins, papers, circulars, and monographs by title, author, and date from which you can select publications pertinent to your own interests. The large geological libraries in major university centers and cities usually carry all or most of the publications. Otherwise, you may wish to purchase them from the Superintendent of Documents, Government Printing Office, Washington, D.C. 20402.

Two regional offices of the U.S. Geological Survey handle distribution of the basic volume and supplements for regions west of the Mississippi: U.S. Geological Survey, Distribution Section, Federal Center, Denver, Colorado 80225, and U.S. Geological Survey, 310 First Avenue, Fairbanks, Alaska 99701.

Other important regional offices include one at 345 Middlefield Road, Menlo Park, California. Nearby Palo Alto is noted for Stanford University, whose Branner Geological Library is perhaps the most complete earth science library west of Washington, D.C. This library is open to all free of charge, and the staff is most cooperative in supplying assistance. In Los Angeles there is a center at 1031 Bartlett Building, 215 West 7th Street. In San Francisco there is another distribution center at 232 Appraisers Building.

At any of the regional offices of the Geological Survey is a complete bibliography of publications, available free of charge, organized by state and listing thousands of annual reports, monographs, geologic folios, professional papers, bulletins, water-supply studies (often containing mineralogical data), circulars, geologic quadrangle maps (very important), mineral investigation maps, as well as specialized and general-interest publications. Most of the unclassified papers are for sale at modest prices, and nearly all can be found on open file in larger libraries and centers.

You will find such publications invaluable (if time-consuming to obtain and study) in terms of specific regional information, area maps, diagrams, etc. All will help you to prospect and explore for mineralized deposits in any state and county. To your further advantage, each state bibliography includes a list of all the libraries in the state which maintain a file of these publications, thus affording you opportunity to read up on any particular district free of charge. (See Appendix III for a listing of mineral museums and libraries according to state.)

SKIN-DIVING FOR HEAVY MINERALS

Ever since scuba (self-contained underwater breathing apparatus) was perfected after World War II, skin-diving for gold, platinum, tin, and heavy mineral crystals has been a popular summer pastime for the more athletic generation. This lightweight, flexible diving paraphernalia is not expensive and is commonly used for all sorts of recreational diving, especially in marine waters where divers look for sunken treasure. Underwater prospecting for heavy minerals is only one of scuba's latest uses, and it is rapidly becoming a major weekend hobby in many parts of the country.

Underwater prospecting for gold is probably most popular, simply because there is a fascination for the sun-yellow metal that transcends all other interests in the prospecting mind. Scuba has been instrumental in increasing small-scale placer mining by weekend prospectors, vacationists, and tourists with a yen for excitement—an excitement that becomes a fever once a man has placed his first colors or small nuggets of gold in a vial of water to show to his friends back home. The fever becomes almost deadly when a successful gold hunter discovers he has actually made "vacation wages" during an especially lucky field trip to a mineral-rich area. The fact that most gold hunters never sell their gleanings, but keep them for their displays or for working up into jewelry, is beside the point entirely.

SKIN-DIVING EQUIPMENT

The equipment used in scuba diving may vary considerably. The occasional or beginning underwater prospector may confine himself to a snorkel and gold pan, but as the fever mounts, he is likely to want to invest in an air compressor, a backpack oxygen tank and breathing device, a floating suction dredge, or other more profitable gold recovery equipment. The cost may run from twenty to several thousand dollars.

Because it is usually necessary to clamber up and down steep hillsides, often with no trail to follow, to reach a promising bend in a brawling mountain stream, the most satisfactory equipment is durable, lightweight, and easily transportable by one person and his companion. A minimum complement would include snorkel, face mask, weighted belt, fins, gold pan, and crevicing tool for scraping gold or platinum concentrates out of narrow cracks and crevices under water.

The popular scuba equipment includes mainly a mouthpiece for breathing, an air regulator, and an air supply which may be a gasoline compressor operated from the stream bank or an oxygen tank strapped to one's shoulders and back. The regulator, on the diver's back, automatically feeds air to the diver and releases air only as needed at a pressure identical to that of the surrounding water at whatever depths are necessary to reach pay dirt. The most commonly used source of oxygen is a high-pressure cylinder strapped to the diver's back, allowing him maximum freedom of movement under water.

When a more permanent oxygen supply is desired, an air hose can be connected with a low-pressure air compressor set up on shore. The air compressor and air lines connected to the diver are collectively known as a hookah. Hookahs are used in the majority of larger-scale underwater mining operations. There are many dealers listed in the yellow pages of telephone books in mining regions who provide underwater mining equipment; most of them are willing to provide specialized information and regional prospecting advice.

You may also find that one of the more popular and successful items of equipment is an underwater gold saver known as a jet dredge or sucker, a pipelike device curved at one end. Most models are 6 to 8 feet long and weigh about 20 pounds, with a nozzle from 2 to 12 inches in diameter. A very useful device for prospecting, especially for those who do not own dredge equipment, is a large syringe known as a gold sniffer; it can be homemade from a grease gun, and some of the commercial sniffers are made of transparent plastic. Crevicing tools include large spoons, knives, screwdrivers, crowbars, and many special instruments now on the market. Other useful equipment includes small bags attached to the diver's belt for nuggets, prospector's pick (hammer), hand lens, tweezers, gold scales, and bottles or vials for storing any findings.

GENERAL TECHNIQUES FOR UNDERWATER PROSPECTING

Skin-diving for gold or other heavy minerals is more than just ducking under water and cruising around looking at the sights. Heavy-mineral occurrences have their peculiarities, and a skin diver must learn to recognize the most favorable places along a mountain stream where gold, for example, might be expected to be concentrated by natural forces. A practiced eye can quickly spot a natural feature or a change in the volume of water flow that causes a sudden decrease in stream velocity; such conditions are favorable for examination.

First, naturally, you should examine the stream bank for colors in the sediments between the water level and the high-water mark. In rocky banks any material caught in crevices should be removed with a crevicing tool and carefully panned. Similarly, whatever material may have accumulated on the downstream side of partly buried obstructions should be closely examined. In addition, fine roots, moss, or other vegetable matter near the water's edge may have trapped fine particles of gold during higher water. If you find any colors in the pan, that area of the stream is a good place to follow up with a more determined effort.

Most initial underwater explorations in a stream are undertaken with the snorkel and face mask to determine whether there is enough gold caught in the bottom crevices to make it worthwhile to carry down and set up heavier equipment. Deep, narrow crevices and cracks, especially those that occur in steeply dipping rocks whose strike or trend is perpendicular to the stream flow, are excellent places to prospect. Any natural irregularities at the bottom of a stream act like riffles or pockets to catch gold particles. Sometimes, deep potholes may hold several hundred dollars' worth of heavy minerals, each pocket being a literal strike.

You can expect that metals as heavy as gold, platinum, and stream tin will usually be concentrated near or at the bottom of such natural traps; when they are, such minerals often occur as flat or rounded grains and flakes ranging from microscopically small particles to nuggets several inches across. The coarser gold is usually found at the greater depths.

There will be plenty of other debris, too, in most streams passing through tourist or camping territory: lead shot (suspiciously like platinum!), old nails, pieces of scrap iron, and occasionally corroded coins. One skin diver found a pair of rusty ox shoes which, when cleaned and polished, were the most valuable souvenirs he found in that watershed! When prospecting a crevice underwater, you can partially remove the loose overburden by "fanning" it with cupped hands and removing gold-bearing black sands at the bottom with a crevicing tool. In such a situation, the gold sniffer is a valuable tool.

Once you have selected an area for more intensive mining, you can bring down the heavier equipment and set it up on shore. Ordinarily, the jet dredge is operated by a two-man team. The dredgeman stands in the water and holds the dredge, steadying the long pipe while it sucks up material. In order to be able to stand upright in swift water, the dredgeman will need 40 to 50 pounds of weights on his belt plus heavy weights on his shoepacs.

The second man, known as the "pickup man," lies nearly flat on his stomach and guides the dredge intake along the stream bed. He usually wears about 30 pounds of weights. In addition, he removes rocks too large for the intake and uses the necessary tools to help clean out any crevices. The work should progress upstream so that the discarded tailings will not clog the equipment or obscure the stream bed with mud.

Caution: In many mining districts, especially throughout California, portable dredging of this nature is regulated by law. Only during certain months is dredging permitted, so as not to foul fishing streams with muddy tailings or discharge them where they might spread over good agricultural land. Also, dredge intake sizes may be limited, according to the size of the stream. Local regulations should always be investigated before attempting any type of underwater placer mining, even on a small scale.

It is axiomatic that you should never dive alone; you should also acquire sufficient diving experience in other forms of recreational underwater exploration before taking on the hazards normally encountered in mountain streams.

Your equipment has definite limitations, and you should be thoroughly familiar with them. The hazards include swift and treacherous currents, snags, floating debris, shifting rocks, and chilling water temperatures. For the most part, skin-diving areas are isolated and far from help. It is unfortunate that each season sees some loss of life among mineral hunters, prospectors, and miners because of carelessness, taking too big a gamble, misjudging the power of a mountain torrent, or trying to use equipment inadequate for the job.

OWNERSHIP AND TRANSPORT OF GOLD

At the present time, gold in its natural state may be acquired and transported within the United States without a license. This includes gold nuggets, gold dust, and untreated gold-bearing quartz. But if gold has been amalgamated with mercury, refined, or otherwise treated by heating or by a chemical or electrical process, it must be sold to the United States Mint or to a licensed gold buyer.

There is no limit on how much raw native gold you may keep for specimen material. There is a 200-ounce limit on the possession of retort sponge gold obtained by retorting the gold-mercury amalgam resulting from treating gold fines with quicksilver.

While the easy-to-obtain nuggets of the nineteenth century are almost wholly gone into the world's coffers, enormous subsurface deposits and many placers still remain untouched. Millions of dollars still fill the golden interstices of the Klamath River bench gravels below Happy Camp in northern California, completely untouched since World War II brought a virtual halt to gold mining in that area.

The old-time methods of prospecting for gold still pay off, and the new techniques of underwater mining have a strong appeal to a coterie of enthusiasts that is growing each year.

chapter 6

Maps and How to Use Them

Gems and minerals do not reproduce themselves the way vegetable products do. Therefore, most mineral or gemstone collecting fields become worked out, except for occasional pieces of float, after a period of intensive collecting. Nevertheless, each occurrence of desirable materials can be considered as a particular geologic exposure, and similar outcroppings or exposures can be expected to occur at other, possibly widely spaced locations.

THE GEOLOGIC MAP

A geologic map is really a combination of two maps. Usually both surface and subsurface geologic formations and structures are depicted in a variety of colors relating to the geologic time framework; the maps may also include specific details marked by patterns of bars, stripes, dots, etc., overprinted on an area topographic map. Sometimes only identifying symbols for geologic structures are shown, with their legends given to one side.

Geologic maps are prepared in both broad-scale and small-scale forms. The broad-scale map is a more or less generalized geological picture of a region covering hundreds to thousands of square miles, really more an indication of a large region's underlying structures than a foot-by-foot detailing of outcrops, fault lines, and the like. The small-scale maps provide greater detail and are often prepared to accompany professional reports of geological surveys. A particular mining district or even one notable mine may appear in the geologic literature with a highly detailed map showing every possible geologic feature.

The better-known and certainly the most exploited rockhound fields are those most easily reached by automobile; hence these are early worked out of all surface collectable minerals. Nevertheless, the geologic structures that produced the mineralizations are bound to be much more widely spread and can be expected to outcrop in other areas in the surrounding region. You can discover new collecting fields simply by following the indications shown on a geologic map of the overall area.

Nearly all professional gem and mineral collectors, such as commercial dealers, use this very important technique for extending mineral exploration.

Simply following a hunch is not practical when time is limited; scientific prospecting is not easy, but it is more likely to produce desirable specimens. Since professional mining geologists and prospectors use geologic maps extensively in their explorations for metals, strategic minerals, and fuels, the gem and mineral collector should avail himself of the same means. Geologic maps are just as useful to the amateur as to the professional; each one merely seeks different things.

By skillful interpretation of the lines, colors, and symbols on a geologic map, you learn where to explore for undeveloped sources of gemstones, even though they may be buried beneath the surface. New and promising collecting fields farther off the well-trod path may prove even richer than the original collecting area.

I well remember a noted rock crystal and limonite cube collecting field about nine miles southeast of Quartzite, Arizona. By the early 1950's when I first visited the desert area, the field had been almost worked out by rock collectors on the surface of the ground and in trenches dug into a particular whitish clay formation that outcropped in various spots within the surrounding area. The trip had been to a known and quite exhausted field, and I had not taken the time to study up on the geology of the area. Even at that, enough clear quartz crystals remained on the ground to yield a nice collection of a pound or two.

Once back home, however, a study of a geologic map revealed that the same formations extended many miles eastward into a desolate and arid canyon-ridden land studded with saguaro cactus, creosote bush, and the red-flowered spiny ocotillo. In writing about the field trip for *Desert Magazine,* then perhaps the leading rockhound magazine of the West, I indicated my conclusions gleaned from the map. Subsequently, thousands of other gem collectors penetrated into the farther area by jeep and on foot, discovering great new fields of flawless rock crystal, smoky quartz, and limonite cubes (pseudomorphs after pyrite), thus rejuvenating collecting in the region. I never returned to the quartzite field and so missed a prime opportunity to reap a small fortune in gemmy crystals.

Most of the mining districts described in old reports have been abandoned because the particular ore minerals sought in their heydays became exhausted. However, in nearly all of the long-abandoned mines and on their ore dumps are other minerals and crystallizations which today may have very real value for a collector. Sometimes the old dumps contain commercial minerals now in vogue that make taking out a lease and reworking the dumps a profitable experience. Most old mines were worked for only one or two major metals, such as gold and silver, silver and copper, zinc and lead, and so on, while a host of other minerals worthless in the seventies and eighties were simply ignored and tossed out on the dumps as gangue waste. Thus many old dumps and underground workings were reworked during and after World War II for uranium, tungsten, molybdenum, manganese, quartz crystals for electronic equipment, and many other minerals perfectly collectable today.

Nearly every important old mine of eighty to one hundred years ago was written up in mining reports stacked away in today's libraries. Usually a geologic map of the immediate area was included. A mining geologist hired to make such a map nearly always included mention of all other minerals present (rarely gems and gemstones, unfortunately). But in the newer day of prospecting for noncommercial mineralizations and cutting material, such old maps can be used as a primary guide leading from the known and exhausted mineral deposit to other nearby areas where collectable specimens may still exist.

Early-day prospectors undoubtedly combed the surrounding country for the metallics they hoped to cash in on, but they ignored completely the gems and gemstones and crystals that may have been associated with the ore deposits. Thus the time it takes you to learn to read and understand a geologic map is like adding money to your pocketbook; you can't lose by this sort of investment.

HOW THE GEOLOGIC MAP IS MADE

Every map is a symbolic picture of a portion of the earth showing its physical features projected onto a two-dimensional plane having a definite scale. While most maps depict surface features primarily, maps of an underground mine will also show the subterranean workings and other subsurface geologic features. The title of every map tells you what elements are stressed, such as a road map, topographic map, geologic map, mine map, planimetric map, anomaly map, etc.

While most maps are oriented so that north is at the top of the sheet, others may have been oriented in some other direction because of some peculiarity of surface configuration. Therefore, be sure to check the map for a north arrow. Maps which also show longitude and latitude may not include a north-pointing arrow symbol, since the direction is obvious. Longitude lines run north and south, latitude lines east and west.

A topographic contour map, the base for most modern geologic maps, allows for making satisfactory measurements of altitude, slope, and distance. A little reading practice reveals the astonishing detail with which the natural features of the earth's surface—streams, mountains, valleys, cliffs, and plains—are shown by means of contour lines (which are linear representations of elevation), labels, or symbols. These maps also clearly indicate such man-made features as roads, dams, bridges, towns, canals, individual barns and houses, as well as civil boundaries, property outlines, township and range grid systems, parallels of latitude, and meridians of longitude. It is easy to orient yourself precisely on a topographic map with its pinpointed reference points and lines, if its scale is reasonably large. Once oriented, you can readily identify nearby objects and, from the geologic additions to the underlying topographic map, nearby outcrops and many other features of geologic or mineralogic interest.

The scale to which a map is drawn is important because it indicates the size of the map in relation to the size of the area covered. A scale may be expressed in one of three ways: (1) a written scale, such as 1 inch = 2 miles, or 1 inch = 100 feet; (2) a numerical scale, i.e., 1:500,000, meaning that one inch on the map equals 500,000 inches (8 miles) on the earth's surface; or (3) by a graphic scale, not usual although useful on some types of maps where photographic enlargement or reduction changes the scale proportionately. Any such alteration of the first two indicated map scales involves a recalculation of the scale by the reader.

The map scale also determines the amount of detail which can conveniently be shown on the map. Geographical divisions are usually shown on a small-scale map, e.g., on a 1:1,000,000 scale, whereas a map using a scale smaller than 1 inch = 1 mile (1:63,360) is adequate for indicating prominent features and for general mineral reconnaissance. Underground mine maps may use very large scales, for instance, 1 inch = 50 feet. The majority of U.S. Geological Survey maps are based on the 7½-minute quadrangle with a scale of 1 inch = 2,000 feet (1:24,000), which is large enough to show nearly all man-made surface structures. On such a map, a standard lode claim of 600 by 1,500 feet appears as a rectangle of .3 by .75 inches, large enough to show the mine opening, hoist frame, and buildings.

HOW TO USE A GEOLOGIC MAP

As already mentioned, most geologic maps are made squarely on top of existing topographic maps, simply by adding a variety of lines, symbols, and colors that were adopted and standardized in the eighteenth century. The lines, called contact lines or simply contacts, mark out the line of junction or contact between adjacent bodies of different types of rock. If the contact is clear-cut and can be precisely located, it is drawn with a solid line. If the contact is not clear-cut or is merely inferred (an educated guess), a broken line is used. A dotted line indicates the probable line of contact where it has been buried under later sediments or volcanic flows.

Early mapmaking geologists, beginning with William "Strata" Smith (1769–1839), an English engineer, surveyor, and excavator of canals, soon learned to correlate separated exposures of the same type of rock across considerable reaches of landscape. Where the separate exposures were numerous enough to make a map seem exceedingly complex, they resorted to the use of color to simplify things by painting all the isolated outcrops of a given rock type with the same color. Thus colors on a modern geologic map were arbitrarily selected to identify rock units, or strata, with every map bearing a reference legend for explanation along one side.

MAPPING SYMBOLS

William Smith was the first geological surveyor (he is commonly considered the father of geology) to recognize that sedimentary formations could be dated by the kinds of fossils they contained. The symbols used on geologic maps derive from Smith's original system.

The custom of age-dating sedimentary layers according to their fossil content also provides the symbols used in conjunction with color to show the different varieties of rocks. Thus Quaternary (Q) rocks are usually shown as yellow, Tertiary (T) sediments as orange, and Jurassic (J) deposits as green. Igneous rocks, such as granite, are usually shown in pink or red in order to differentiate them from the sedimentary strata; no fossils occur in the igneous rocks.

The colors used have no relation to the actual appearance of the formations in the field. For instance, most Jurassic sandstones (see Table 1 for approximate ages of the formations named), especially in the southwestern states, are stained reddish with iron oxide. Tertiary sediments may be any color, but browns, grays, and blacks predominate —the colors of ordinary dirt and clay. Table 18 indicates the common map color units and the symbols and names used for the different ages to which time has been loosely attached.

Note that primary age symbols are the capital initial letters, whereas the rock type or, on more detailed maps, the specific rock formation is shown by small letters following the age symbol. Thus "Pc" represents Pliocene continental, i.e., nonmarine rocks of Pliocene age (roughly 13 million years old); "Tm" stands for Tertiary (Monterey formation); and "KJf" is Cretaceous-Jurassic (Franciscan formation). All symbols used on any particular map are summarized with their meanings in the margin. When you locate a formation on a geologic map and can actually see it before you in the field, you will find yourself suddenly understanding and appreciating how vast the scale of geology can be, and how fascinating.

It should be noted here that most geologists couldn't care less about the ages in years assigned to the various formations as listed in Table 1. What is important is that each geologic period given is older than the one above it and younger than the one below. How many millions of years old a formation is has practically no bearing on the subject.

Sometimes a geologic feature is not marked directly on a map but is indicated by simple trigonometric principles, i.e., by symbols for direction and distance from some landmark that also appears on the base map. Direction or bearing is indicated as a horizontal angle between the line from one place to another and a standard north–south line measured by magnetic compass. Thus a description reading ". . . north 30° east" means that when you stand at the designated spot facing north, your line

TABLE 18
COLORS AND SYMBOLS ON A GEOLOGIC MAP

Conventional Map Colors	Symbol	Geologic Period	Characteristic Fossil Types
Yellow	Q	Quaternary	All present life forms and a few extinct mammal species
Orange	T	Tertiary	Mammals, flowering plants, marine snails, clams, oysters
	P	Pliocene	Premankind in Old World
	M	Miocene	Horse (four genera), grass
	O	Oligocene	Titanotheres, flowering plants
	E	Eocene	Creodonts, Eohippus, birds
	Ep	Paleocene	Small five-toed quadrupeds
Yellow green	K	Cretaceous	Reptiles, dinosaurs, ammonites, conifers, sequoia
Green	J	Jurassic	Ammonites, largest dinosaurs
Blue green	Tr	Triassic	Flying reptiles, cycads, pine forests, ammonites, amphibians
Blue	P	Permian	Primitive land plants; corals, tree ferns, clamlike marine animals
	CP	Pennsylvanian	Amphibians, reptiles, coal plants
	CM	Mississippian	Crinoids, sharks
Blue purple	D	Devonian	Fish, crablike trilobites
	S	Silurian	Eurypterids, scorpions, pill bugs
Purple	O	Ordovician	Graptolites, first shellfish
Terra cotta	C	Cambrian	Trilobites
Gray brown	pC	Precambrian	Marine algae, spongelike forms

would run 30 degrees toward your right, or toward the east, with reference to a compass held in one hand.

Distance along the bearing line may be measured in feet, yards, rods, or miles, paced by foot, measured by tape, or obtained from plane trigonometric surveying. Since a compass has 360 degrees, all bearing angles are measured clockwise from the zero point of north. A typical reading may be ". . . mine entrance on the south slope of Bald Mountain 248° and 3,600 yards from bridge over Eagle Creek." By standing on the bridge and using a protractor or compass measured in 360 degrees, you can sight along the line of bearing toward the distant spot. Or you can translate the 248° into 22° south of west (west on a compass is 270° clockwise around the circle from north) by subtracting 248 from 270 and obtain an easier reading of the bearing line.

Plotting the distance on the map itself can be done with a pair of dividers or by extending the marginal "tick marks" onto a crossing at the objective. The map's contour lines will show you how steep and rugged the terrain is between the bridge, for example, and the mine entrance on the mountain.

SURVEY SYMBOLS

Topographic and forest service maps are further broken down into townships, each being a six-mile-square rectangle subdivided into one-mile-square plots of 640 acres each—36 sections to a township. Townships are the larger land units encompassed between ranges and base lines. The range is determined by a north–south principal meridian of which there are 30 spaced from east to west across the United States. A base line is a periodic great circle of latitude. The base lines taken in conjunction with meridianal range lines divide the nation into major blocks of land.

Ranges are numbered in consecutive order east or west of a principal meridian; townships are similarly numbered north or south of the primary base line for the area. Thus T. 18 N., R. 7 W. denominates a 36-square-mile block of land in northwestern Siskiyou County, California, overlapping into Del Norte County (Humboldt and Mount Diablo meridians).

Sections within a township are numbered from 1 to 36, beginning in the upper right-hand corner (the most northeasterly section), proceeding west to number 6, dropping south one level to number 7 and proceeding east this time to number 12, then south one more level to section 13, and west again to number 17, and so on in a back-and-forth manner until the last section, number 36, appears in the lower right corner (most southeasterly position). Each section is further broken down (although not on the maps) into half- and quarter-sections, so that the designation NE¼ designates a 160-acre plot in the northeast corner of a particular section within a township.

Even fractions of quarter-sections are used, so that by symbolic means only very precise localities can be fully determined. County surveyors and water resource departments are more concerned with such minor subdivisions, perhaps, than you will be for rock hunting. Nevertheless, some of the localities cited in Part II of this book are located entirely by these survey symbols, requiring you to use a topographic or geologic map of that particular area.

READING THE GEOLOGIC MAP

Reading a geologic map with comprehension takes a bit of practice. To begin with, it is probably easiest to select a geologic map of an area well known to you, preferably one close to home. The map should be as detailed as possible, with an accurate topographic base and a clearly defined geology. The latter should include symbols to indicate the geologic structures and, perhaps, fossil localities. If a geologic road log (a form of geologic map and description that follows along a given road or highway) is also available for your area, so much the better.

A brief study of the base map features, e.g., roads, streams, towns, prominent landmarks, etc., and their orientation with respect to the indicated geologic features should help you to become scientifically familiar with the area. You should then travel through it and take particular note of the cultural and geologic features shown on the map. An inexpensive hand compass will further help you orient yourself with the map and determine attitudes of any bedded rocks that crop out above the surrounding land surface.

Finally, it would be worthwhile to study the map's geologic features closely. Choose an area within the map where good exposures of flat-lying or only slightly deformed sedimentary rocks are indicated by the appropriate symbols. Examine the actual rocks to familiarize yourself with them and with their map representation by color and symbol. And be sure to look for any of the fossils contained in the rocks by which the geologist who drew the map determined the name and age dating of the strata.

SEDIMENTARY, OR LAYERED, ROCKS

Rock units depicted on a geologic map commonly include the sedimentaries, since by and large these are the most frequently encountered rocks found on continental land surfaces. Although the most extensive geologic formations of sedimentary origin were originally formed flat on an ancient sea bed, features that illustrate many of the basic principles of deposition may be observed along stream channels and around lake shores. In some regions the sedimentary features of ancient stream channels are abundantly exposed in quarries and road cuts—excellent places to prospect for minerals, gemstones, and fossils.

Marine deposits of the past few tens of thousands of years or running back a few million years may be exposed in the cliffs bordering ocean beaches or inland-sea shores. Ancient sea-laid sediments which have been raised high onto dry land, often as great mountain ranges of extraordinary scenery like those in Glacier National Park, are usually tilted one way or another from the center of uplift. The fact that their layers appear superimposed on one another indicates that, indeed, they were once laid down by gradual accumulation of muds, clays, sand, and marls on the level floor of an ancient body of water. The angle of tilt is included on the geologic map as a dip-strike symbol (see below).

As you enter the area covered by a geologic map, you should pay special attention to stream-cut and road-cut exposures of the various geologic units shown on the map. You should also look on the map for contacts between formations and seek out exposures where such contacts may be observed.

If a line of contact is exposed, try to compare its description in the related text with its appearance on the map and how it actually looks as a landscape feature. Is the bedding observable as described? Does the younger (upper) unit lie in normal stratigraphic position over the older (lower) unit? Check the unit's detailed description in the text, or geologic column insert in one margin of the map, with its actual appearance in the outcrop with respect to color, grain size, and textures. Does the measured attitude, i.e., the direction and degree of slope of the bedding planes at this outcrop, agree with that symbolized on the map?

If there seem to be discrepancies in the answers to these questions, you should check to be certain that you have correctly interpreted the bedding plane, allowed for magnetic compass declination, and avoided any nearby pieces of iron or steel that might throw your compass reading off.

It is important to understand the nature of folding and faulting in the area being examined. By projection of the folded bed, you may be able to follow a layer of mineral or gemstone-bearing rock to locate new or unexplored localities farther on for concentrated exploration.

USE OF DIP-STRIKE SYMBOLS

Wherever outcrops of the bedded rocks permit the necessary measurements to be made, their attitude or slope is indicated by the dip-strike symbol⊥.Dip stands for the slope and strike for the angle which the bed makes with a north–south line. Strike directions are readily determined by a simple magnetic compass with an attached level and indicated on the geologic map by straight lines of appropriate direction.

Dip is an angle in a vertical plane and is always measured downward from the horizontal plane, or horizon. Its direction is perpendicular to the strike, which is the direction of the intersection of the surface with any horizontal plane. Taken together, dip and strike determine the position or attitude of a surface with respect to horizontality and to compass directions. Sometimes, the direction of a dip is shown by an arrow with its magnitude by adding a figure in degrees, e.g., 15°.

Since dip and strike are always taken together at an outcrop, they are shown on the map by a combined symbol. The exact location of the outcrop reading is set at the intersection of the two perpendicular lines of the symbol, which on your map may be slanted in any direction to conform with the locality, as: north 45° east, dip 20° southeast. From even a relatively small number of such symbols on a map, it becomes possible to visualize underlying fold structures, even in areas where outcrops are few and far between.

FAULT LINES

Geologic maps show contact zones where rocks have been fractured and one mass of rock has slipped alongside another. Such a fault line may not be easy to see in the field, except in the comparatively rare instances where it is exposed in a road cut or stream bank. In the barren mountains of the West fault lines are quite apparent, and vertical displacements of large bodies of sedimentary strata can be measured in inches or feet. Indeed, along the infamous San Andreas fault, clearly visible from the air, lateral displacements on the earth's surface can actually be measured in miles in some places, where a hill or a mountain was literally sliced in half and the moving western section shoved northwestward for a long distance.

Major fault zones are commonly subdued, poorly exposed features— a result of long weathering and overgrowths of vegetation. A fault may be visible only as a shallow trough or as a number of notches along a hillside. The San Andreas fault, which caused the San Francisco earthquake of 1906, is a noted fault zone which occupies a marked trough, or "topographic depression," visible in many places along its more than 700-mile length.

Questions to ask yourself in the field are: Can any faults be recognized by the offsetting or disruption of bedding planes along a straight line or zone of rubble in any stream bank or road cut? Can the same bed be identified on both sides of the offset? Is this fault shown on the geologic map? Does the map show different rock formations on opposite sides of the fault zone? If so, a closer look at any nearby outcrops might prove quite interesting. Remember that if colorful agates occur in a bed of rock, they should also occur in the same bed no matter how far offset that bed may have become because of shifting movements in the earth's crust.

Note whether the mapped fault zone is marked by foreign rock fragments in the soil, which resemble neither of the adjoining formations in color or texture. If present, these fragments may be fault gouge, that is, ground-up, altered, commonly stained rock fragments, especially fragments of an older, underlying formation which have been dragged to the surface along the plane of fault movement. Such fragments provide concrete indications of minerals which may be buried somewhere below the surface.

A trip over any of the highway passes that cross a mountain range, notably in the great ranges west of the 100th meridian, or along any rugged, mountainous seacoast that is characterized by rocky headlands and deep indentations, should reveal outcrops which will illustrate some or all of the answers to the questions above.

FOLDS

When you have learned to recognize faults in the field, and the various features which indicate rock slippage, you are ready to look at the folded rocks. All rocks are semiplastic and yield under very slow pressures, bending into folds of all kinds, whereas sudden pressure shocks crack or fracture the same rocks into fault slippages. Folds small enough to be visible in their entirety are frequently exposed in stream channels, ocean cliffs, and road cuts, especially in the relatively young, still rising West Coast mountain ranges. Folds too small to show on a standard geologic map may often be recognized in a single road cut.

Larger folds may be recognized by studying the dip of the bedding planes. For example, as you progress through mountainous country, the strata exposed in a road cut may all dip toward the west. As you drive eastward from road cut to road cut, the dip of the beds gradually diminishes in steepness from one exposure to another. Finally, the beds appear to flatten out at the summit and you find yourself at the top of an anticlinal fold (an inverted U). Still farther toward the east, the beds begin to dip slightly, then more steeply, but this time toward the east. In this case, you have just crossed the crest of a north–south trending anticline, or archlike fold. Such anticlines are clearly depicted in road cuts crossing the Pacific Coast Range and through the entire series of the Appalachian mountain ranges. The Appalachians are especially well noted for this type of rock folding. The mountain uplifts are extremely ancient, and their tops, which once held the archlike folds, were completely shaved off ("peneplaned") by erosion. Only the side dips remain today.

Anticlinal crests are well developed in the mountain systems of western America. A simpler, although somewhat rarer structure is a homocline, meaning that the beds all dip in the same direction, a monotonous geologic structure that often ends in sheer cliffs. Homoclines are well exposed along the east front of the California Coast Range west of Red Bluff and Redding in Tehama and Shasta counties and along the seacoast in Santa Barbara County.

GEOLOGIC MAPS AS GUIDES TO NEW FIELDS

Professional dealers in gems and minerals out to ravage as many new collecting fields as possible before amateurs get to them use geologic maps regularly as a means to finding extensions of known fields. As a rule, you have more time to devote to the science of prospecting than most dealers have on weekend trips away from their shops. Therefore, make good use of geologic maps to locate new fields for rock hunting. The colors, lines, and symbols on a map sheet represent the distribution and structural features of widespread formations that may be exposed only here and there above the ground.

If an isolated outcrop shows the presence of tourmaline or topaz or fortification agate, for example, you can be rather sure that these gemstones occur throughout the formation, buried under an overburden of later sediments or volcanics or outcropping many miles away. If collectors before you have cleaned out the specimens from the known outcrop or deposit, naturally your problem is to "discover" similar outcrops or deposits farther on, as shown on your map. Rest assured that commercial ore prospectors have already looked over the more distant scenes, but remember also that they weren't looking for gemstones. Your reward will be many prize specimens, well worth the time it takes you to learn how to "prospect" on paper at home.

After a good deal of practice, the experienced map reader is able to perceive a three-dimensional mental image of the land surfaces portrayed. This ability is most helpful, because topographic variations may also reflect differences in rock types. They may even reflect the attitudes of layered sediments or the relative ages of different rock units.

For example, a gently tilted hillside may be the resistant topside of a hard-rock formation; float may indicate that the hill is made of quartzite. Likewise, the relative age of two mountain peaks may sometimes be inferred from the contours on a topographic map, which show the relative degree of weathering and dissection. The more ridged and dissected, the older the mountain.

You will be able to picture granite intrusions into sediments and note that the green areas on your map mean rocks of Mesozoic age; in these rocks you may find petrified dinosaur bones (almost all fossils in ages preceding the Cenozoic will be petrified). The trained interpreter "sees" tilted, folded, faulted, and sheared rocks instead of merely dip, strike, and shear symbols. In your mind's eye you see rock strata crossing a hill or offset along a stream, rather than a colorful patchwork of lines.

How to Use a Geologic Map in Prospecting

A few simple rules can be set down by which you can follow a geologic map to the discovery of new collecting fields.

Rule 1. Check the index map of the U.S. Geological Survey for topographic quadrangle sheets for an area of interest to you or inquire at the nearest regional land office or forest service district office. Mention was previously made that geologic map overlays have not been made for all areas; in the absence of a true geologic map, you will have to use a topographic base map. Then send for the particular geologic or topographic quadrangle maps that cover known rock-hunting locations you wish to visit.

For any long-distance trip into a remote area, especially if made on foot, on horseback, or by four-wheel-drive vehicle, a topographic map is a necessity. Roads can be quite confusing. Since the heady days of the uranium-boom era of the 1950's, jeep roads have been punched into all sorts of terrain seven ways from the middle, and without a detailed topographic map showing all such roads, as well as other terrain features, you can easily get lost. In many timbered regions, especially throughout the mining districts of northern California, southern Oregon, Idaho, Montana, etc., logging companies have bulldozed out a most disconcerting crosshatching of steep log roads running every which way, making it difficult to find the shortest route to a rich mine of yesteryear. Indeed, in such country it is a good idea to have a compass on deck for picking out conspicuous landmarks and bearings shown on the map or observable from wherever you might stop to look around.

Rule 2. As a starter, visit any well-known rock-collecting field, such as one of those listed in Part II of this volume and covered by a geologic map. Then, map in hand, locate yourself with respect to the map's contour lines. Note all prominent landmarks, such as mountain peaks, stream channels, arroyos, the junctions of watercourses, waterfalls, etc. Streams are especially important, and mapmakers invariably include all watercourses, however minor, on their maps. Because water seeks the easiest way out of an upland region, early-day explorers found it expedient to follow stream beds back into unknown country. This is a good plan for you, whenever you leave the safety and security of a roadway. But be prepared for many difficulties along the way.

Rule 3. Note the type of rock formation from which the known gemstones or minerals originate, by color and symbol. Determine from the map where this mineralized formation trends. Pay close attention to distances, outcrops, canyon breaks, folds. Use a compass bearing to indicate routes of surface travel that cross the formation which has proved by its one known locality to contain the desired materials.

Rule 4. Explore this formation as far as your time permits, checking outcrops, talus slopes, draws, and canyon or stream beds for float. Continue to orient yourself in accordance with the features shown on the geologic map.

Rule 5. Last but not least, be sure to wear the correct clothing for exploratory work, carry a snakebite kit, and be prepared for any emergency. Carry a canteen of water in dry country; you are likely to get very thirsty if the weather is warm. As a good safety rule to follow, never travel into rough country alone; two is companionable and multiplies your chances for getting out of a tight spot safely.

Steps Leading Toward Discovery of New Localities

One of the peculiarities of most human beings is their propensity to follow a known course, like sheep following a bellwether. Of all the gem and mineral collectors in the nation, only a small percentage will ever pioneer a new collecting field. For that reason, it is pretty safe to assume that there are more unexplored gem and mineral localities yet to be collected from than have ever been described in the rockhound magazines or listed in Part II of this book.

Whether you are after gemmy substances or commercially salable ore minerals, if serious about the business of prospecting, you should consider the acquisition of a supply of topographic and geologic maps as only one step in the overall preparation for a satisfying field trip. There are five additional steps to complete your preparations.

Step 1. When entering a new state or county, it is advisable to go to the nearest large public library in order to look up all the available literature and maps relating to that area. County and state road maps are always available from automobile clubs or the various oil companies servicing an area. If you belong to one of the affiliated automobile clubs, you can obtain a complete set of very detailed road maps for all the states in one package simply by asking and showing your membership card. A little additional inquiry will reveal where Forest Service maps, state and federal geologic and topographic maps, and local mining maps can be obtained or examined. Look up or purchase all available copies of pertinent geologic reports put out by federal, state, or private agencies.

Step 2. Nearly every square yard of America has been photographed scientifically from the air. Look up or obtain by purchase any available aerial photographs of the area you would like to explore. These photographs are especially important in regions where mineral literature indicates there may be promising collecting areas. A good technique is to place an acetate overlay sheet on the photograph and mark on it with a grease pencil any notes or symbols that will help you orient yourself in the field. You can then lay the acetate sheet over your map or alongside it for study once you get into the field.

Step 3. Real mineralogical exploration may require several visits to an area; very little can be done in a casual weekend. Make your first, or reconnaissance, trip into the area by whatever means is available. If you have time to travel far off the beaten track, going in by horseback or jeep from a ranch, pack station, or other supply point is the usual practice. En route, you should visit every area of geologic interest, every old gopher prospect hole, abandoned mine, or unusual outcropping, especially if the last feature might appear to be a pegmatite exposure. You should continually reorient yourself with respect to the map and record notes on everything of interest. Keep close track of time and distance and direction if you enter rough country; you may wish to return for another visit at a later date.

Step 4. Trust nothing to memory! Make notes of each investigation, particularly any old mines, and try to relate them to your map. Somewhere back in a major public library, you may find a complete, detailed mining report on that mine, its mineral contents, dollar production, underground geology, and its history. You will probably not have time to investigate all likely prospects thoroughly on any one trip, but the information you jot down for later library research may prove that a follow-up visit will be profitable in terms of collectable materials.

Step 5. When you have a general picture of the region fixed in your mind, select a particular section for more thorough investigation. Note routes into it and which portions are easy to prospect by foot or from horseback or jeep. Make sketches and rough maps in your notebook, and supplement them with photographs if you carry a camera. Add any written observations that seem pertinent to a possible return trip some day. With respect to photographic records, take both area-wide views and detailed close-up shots of promising exposures, using your prospector's hammer or hat as an indicator of size in the picture.

Step 6. Gather plenty of representative mineral and rock samples from the close-up sites. Also note whether float appears and the probable direction of erosion from which it may have originated. Follow up good float showings to higher levels. Label all specimens before putting them into your collecting sack.

Remember that as your experience increases, more and more of what you read in the scientific geology of an area will stick in your mind. The stacks of a geological library will become an open sesame to a lifetime of constructive outdoor recreation. Even though in the beginning stages you may not fully understand everything you find in print, you will certainly absorb a good deal of it by simple mental osmosis. And every little bit added to your knowledge will help you succeed in your next gem and mineral prospecting adventure.

OTHER MAPS USEFUL TO GEM AND MINERAL HUNTERS

Assuming that you will always have an oil company road map to get you into the general area of a collecting site or old mine, the chief and most useful and easily obtained detailed map is the standard topographic quadrangle. The U.S. Geological Survey has mapped every square foot of America, and these maps can be purchased at almost any land office or U.S.G.S. regional and district office or obtained free of charge at the nearest Forest Service ranger station for that station's area of operations.

The average quadrangle is about 25 by 30 inches in size, with various scales from 1:24,000 to 1:125,000. The 7½-minute quadrangles are pretty much confined to Arizona, Utah, and Colorado. Actually, because geologic maps are generally made for specific geological interest, relatively few such maps exist for all topographic coverages.

A planimetric map reveals surface features of general interest, such as place names, drainages, roads, land subdivisions, communities, railroads, and geodetic coordinates. The topographic map is really a modified planimetric or base map to which contour lines have been added to provide a means for visualizing the relief, or variations in elevation of the surface. The usual Forest Service maps are planimetric and lack contour lines connecting points of identical elevation. Contour lines curve with the terrain; the intervals or spaces between them indicate changes in elevation (each line is always marked with its own true elevation); in their place, Forest Service maps show elevations of all prominent peaks. For example, closely spaced contour lines represent a steep declivity or cliff; widely spaced lines reveal areas of slight relief. Isolated concentric ovals, circles, or misshapen closed forms indicate hill or mountain masses rising above a generally lower area.

The anomaly map is valuable chiefly to mineral prospectors who specialize in the radioactive minerals: uranium, thorium, radium, etc. Anomaly maps were originally made by the Atomic Energy Commission after flying airplanes over regions of suspected radioactivity with scintillation counters hung on long cables below the planes to register broad areas of abnormal gamma-ray count. Such a map does not show where a particular radioactive mineral occurs, but only where unusual amounts of radioactivity were perceived by the instrument. Such maps are mainly useful in suggesting wide-scale areas in which detailed ground prospecting via a topographic or geologic map should be done with electronic instruments such as a Geiger counter. You can obtain anomaly maps from the U.S. Atomic Energy Commission, Division of Raw Materials, Washington, D.C. 20025, by requesting "information on airborne radioactivity survey maps."

chapter 7

Care and Preservation
of Minerals

A collection of gems and minerals represents one of the easiest, most practicable, and interesting approaches to the study of the world around us, for the mineral kingdom is everywhere. But collecting gems and minerals is only a beginning; finding an attractive specimen can be easier than maintaining it as a fine example of your skill and acumen. For one thing, almost no field-run rock is ready for display when you find it, and thus proper techniques of care and preparation for display become vitally important.

PREPARING GEMS AND MINERALS FOR DISPLAY

Every gemstone and mineral is stable in the environment surrounding it in nature, when time has permitted all its chemical affinities to be satisfied. Unfortunately, when you remove a mineral substance from its geologic foundation, take it home, and clean and prepare it for cabinet display, you are radically changing the original environmental conditions of atmospheric gases, humidity, temperature, dust, etc.

All minerals are basically chemical compounds, some with molecular structures so complex that they defy analysis. All have a built-in capacity for readjusting to any major change in external conditions as the outer electrons of the atoms which make up the surface molecules become lost or join with electrons from other, more active chemical substances. Thus the appearance of the surface of a mineral—less so for a gem or gemstone—can change surprisingly within a short time after subjecting it to a city or house-interior environment. Most such alterations are detrimental to the appearance and value of specimen materials.

TRIMMING MINERAL SPECIMENS

To achieve a satisfactory display of gems and minerals, many collectors limit the size of their cabinet specimens to maximum diameters of from 2 to 4 inches. Preliminary field trimming done with a prospector's hammer and cold chisel is performed primarily to limit the weight to be packed out of a locality. Much more careful trimming is necessary at home, so that each display specimen may be as pure and typical of its species as possible, with all identifying characteristics clearly visible.

When you have found a crystal surrounded by interesting matrix, like a clear perfectly terminated topaz projecting from a cavity in rhyolite, its value as a display piece or for subsequent sale is enhanced by leaving a small block of the matrix around the crystal to show the rock association and how the crystal actually grew. A cluster of crystals of whatever size makes a more interesting and valuable display if left in its original configuration rather than broken into its separate parts. Even in this case, some external trimming may be necessary to produce a pleasing arrangement. The matrix (country rock) which encases a mineral or gemstone adds to the value of the piece by telling a good deal about its geologic origin.

Cleaning and Evaluating Mineral Specimens

A collection of field-gathered gems and minerals, if left in its natural state, is a pretty drab-looking affair. Many minerals, especially crystals, may be stained with foreign matter that detracts from the appearance of the specimen, though not all stains are undesirable. Where discolorations are characteristic of a mineral, as for example the iron-oxide staining of minerals in the oxidation zone of copper or other metallic ore bodies, it is a natural attribute of the matrix. To attempt to remove such stains might damage the mineral itself.

Nearly all gems and minerals, except the unusually delicate and velvetlike encrustations, can be improved by thorough cleaning. Moreover, as nearly every collector reluctantly admits, there is a continuing gradual dimming of luster and brilliancy in even a tightly enclosed collection through a gradual accumulation of ordinary house dirt, dust, lint, or soot. Periodic cleaning of fine specimens is as necessary as an annual housecleaning and, like rearrangements of furniture, allows for attractive rearrangements of specimens, substitution of newer and more attractive pieces for older ones, and so on.

Primary cleaning requires removal of field accumulations of dirt, impurities, stains, lichens, organic debris, dust, and natural tarnish. The commonest method is to use simple soap and water on raw specimens, sometimes using a toothbrush to get into crevices, wherever such minerals are not soluble in water, e.g., the desert playa sodium and potassium minerals and halite. The water should be lukewarm. Some minerals will expand abruptly and crack under hot applications, while others, like sulfur, may contract and crack in cold water.

No single method of cleaning can be applied to all mineral specimens. Ordinary garden-hose water under low pressure will remove dirt and

clay, assisted by a scrub brush at times. Very fragile hairlike crystallizations or crustal growths cannot be washed at all, for fear of damaging
the tiny protuberances. Good solid specimens, especially those above
hardness 6, can withstand severe scrubbing, even with a wire brush,
while a high-pressure small jet of water can get into tiny crevices and
wash out accumulations of dirt. Geodes or other cavities in matrix rock
can be cleaned by soaking in a bucket of water to loosen the dirt without
unduly disturbing small or loose crystals that may be enclosed.

While water is the most common cleaning fluid, some minerals may
require alcohol or petroleum ether. Iron stains on otherwise water-clear
rock crystal may require treatment with oxalic or other acid. Acetic acid
(the acid in vinegar, available at most photographic supply shops) is an
excellent, harmless acid that gives a brilliant luster to many crystals.
Hydrochloric acid (muriatic acid) is often used, but it is highly corrosive
to fabrics and metal pans, although not dangerous to human flesh; its
fumes are quite unpleasant to the nose when concentrated acid is used.
Household ammonia and dilute acids help to loosen algae and lichens
which often spoil the appearance of field-run gems and minerals.

Where no liquids or scrubbing can be applied because of the delicacy
of the mineral surface, dusting with a syringe blast of air or with a
camel's-hair brush will improve the specimen before it is mounted for
display, especially if it is an intricately grown and fragile needlelike or
fibrous crystallization.

After careful cleaning, gems and minerals may be dried in the air,
spread out on absorbent paper or cloth toweling. At this point should
come your first real appraisal, or evaluation, of your finds. You may find
that the enthusiasm with which you picked up the specimen in the field
degenerates into disappointment. Water or other cleaning solutions en-
liven the natural colors, luster, and sheen of all gems and minerals; when
dry, they may appear much duller and less brilliant. You may wish to set
some aside for more refined cleaning, sawing into them to see whether
anything better is inside or tumbling them (see Chapter 10), or you may
throw away or trade off others which no amount of additional cleaning
can convert into attractive specimens.

REMOVING TARNISH

Natural tarnish affects many mineral species. This is most noticeable
on native copper and silver nuggets, but it also occurs in varying degrees
on many metallic minerals as a result of atmospheric oxidation or sul-
furization. In the southwestern desert region natural tarnish may become
like a solid crust, known as desert varnish—an almost carbon-black
coating of the external surface of everything on the ground, including
nuggets of pure gold. Desert varnish is probably manganese oxide, commonly found in such areas and a mineral mined rather extensively in
some places for manganese. Most tarnishes can be removed by various

chemical processes involving use of alkalis, cyanide, acetic and oxalic acids, and metal polish, i.e., materials normally used by the home owner to remove tarnish or patinas from aluminum, silver, and copper utensils.

The tarnish on silver nuggets is readily removed by immersing the specimens in a warm bath of an ounce each of household baking soda (sodium bicarbonate) and of table salt dissolved in two quarts of water in an aluminum pan. Complete washing with warm water will remove any adhering salt.

Gold, silver, copper, or natural alloys of any combination of these metals can be cleaned with hydrofluoric acid (a weak but very danger-ous acid; a single drop on human flesh requires a minimum of four hours' flushing with cold running water to prevent ulceration), a solution of ammonium bifluoride (which generates the acid), or nitric and hydrochloric acids. As any high school student of chemistry realizes, nitric acid is not only highly corrosive to everything, including human flesh, but its fumes are poisonous.

A safe method for copper that will remove the black copper oxides is to dip the nuggets into a solution of 20 parts by weight of water, three parts by weight of rochelle salts, and one part by weight of common household lye (sodium hydroxide). The same metals may also be cleaned in a dilute solution (about 2 percent) of cyanide, but caution is necessary because all cyanides are quick-acting poisons. Because hydro-fluoric acid dissolves silicates, including glass, it will etch into quartz crystals; its use should be mainly to remove silicate encrustations on other mineral specimens that are not affected by the acid.

MECHANICAL MEANS FOR CLEANING SPECIMENS

Perhaps more so than the home gem and mineral collector, mineral dealers have developed three mechanical means—abrasive techniques, tumbling, and ultrasonic devices—for cleaning rock specimens that are quite effective and can be used on masses of material.

Sandblasting mineral specimens to remove soft matrix surrounding crystals is quite effective, provided that the abrasive used is softer than the crystal itself. Powdery deposits or encrustations adhering to crystal faces can be removed by use of a thin slurry of pumice powder and brisk rubbing with stiff brushes.

Harder gemstones may effectively be cleaned by employing a con-ventional tumbler (described in Chapter 10), adding ordinary sand and water, and allowing the mass to tumble for several hours. Subsequent washing in clear water will allow the collector to examine his specimens for quality and color.

Crystals such as quartz, tourmaline, peridot, topaz, or garnet and lumps of turquoise, jade, or other gemstone can easily be tumbled clean in a small home-type tumbler to remove surface coatings or frosting,

ROCKHOUNDS AT WORK. These mineral hunters are examining rock outcrops for signs that minable ores may be present.

A ROCKHOUND CAMP. This semipermanent desert camp is typical of those established by many serious prospectors seeking minerals and gemstones in a particularly prolific gemstone field. Here in Houserock Valley, Arizona, petrified wood, uranium minerals, gem agate and jasper, and fossils abound in the regional sandstone formations.

MULE TRAIN. Because they often work in inaccessible areas, rockhounds must sometimes use unconventional transport. This mule pack-train is carrying rich carnotite-wood ore valued at several thousand dollars a ton.

Jay Ellis Ransom

HOMEMADE TIRE TUMBLER. Using a truck tire mounted on rollers and plywood and belt gearing to reduce the 1700-rpm one-eighth horsepower electric motor to 3-rpm at the tire, this rockhound tumbles up to a hundred pounds of gemstones at a time. He uses three tires in order of decreasing grit size, with thorough washing of the gemstones between transfers.

CUTTING EQUIPMENT. Machines for such heavy work as converting blocks of Utah wonderstone ("picture" stone, or silicified rhyolite) into attractive scenics can be quite bulky, as this basement installation reveals.

Jay Ellis Ransom

A MOUNTED COLLECTION. This assemblage of mounted Arizona agate cabochons shows typical cut and polished forms. The cabochons are set off by the matched slices of fortification agate in the center. All are brilliantly colored in red, blue, orange, green, and pearl-gray. They were made by Martin Koning of Morristown, Arizona.

GEMSTONE DISPLAY CABINET. This portion of a much broader wall display cabinet along one side of a double garage, utilizing glass shelves and sliding glass doors, was constructed by rockhunter Howard Michael of Yreka, California. Beneath the workbench are drawers filled with gems, gemstones, slices, slabs, and mineral oddities in various stages of being processed on lapidary equipment.

ROADSIDE ROCK SHOP. Typical of rockhound emporiums is this display shop and lapidary service near Tucson, Arizona. At such wayside shops, gem and mineral collectors from all over the United States meet and swap information about collecting fields and, very often, trade prized specimens to one another.

permitting a keener appraisal of their internal color, inclusions, or patterns.

An ultrasonic cleaning device consists of two basic units connected by power cables and housed in a cabinet. When it is plugged into an electrical outlet, household current is converted into ultrasonic waves that pervade a stainless steel tank of water in which the material to be cleaned has been immersed. This method is effective for specimens containing many narrow crevices and recesses which cannot be cleaned with fine tools. Hard gems, crystals, or minerals can be cleaned within a relatively brief time, but softer minerals may require an hour or more of wave generation.

While ordinary water will do the job in the steel tank, adding household ammonia, detergent, or dilute acids that won't attack steel materially assists in the cleaning process. Specimens to be cleaned should not be placed on the bottom, where the vibrating crystals that produce the ultrasonic waves are fastened, but suspended in the tank by a cord.

PRESERVATION OF UNSTABLE MINERALS

The old adage that rocks are eternal is a myth that comes home to roost most inopportunely at times. The collector who has finally found a prize group of botryoidal or stalactitic specimens of chalcanthite ($CuSO_4 \cdot 5H_2O$), for example, brought the mass home safely without damage, and carefully trimmed and cleaned the specimen for display, discovers with horror that in a short time the water of crystallization has evaporated and the mineral has crumbled to pieces. There is no salvaging any of it, although dissolving the whole mass in water and allowing it to recrystallize slowly will produce some interesting "artificial" new crystals—this makes chalcanthite an excellent and colorful salt (it is sky blue) for a student's experimentations in growing crystals.

It is rather amazing how many minerals require special care in order to preserve their form, color, and structure. A few, like pyrite and marcasite, both sulfides of iron, oxidize and rapidly lose their glister; silver specimens tarnish badly from atmospheric sulfur dioxide.

Minerals like chalcanthite and others listed in Table 19 that were collected in damp places retain their water of crystallization only as long as they are kept in a damp atmosphere after removal from their natural habitat. Conversely, many minerals collected from desert-dry habitats suffer from absorption of water vapor when brought into a damper climate and may distintegrate entirely. Halite, ordinary sodium chloride, is a prime example. In the case of marcasite, specimens may develop networks of tiny cracks filled with a white powder that is melanterite as an alteration form in the oxidation of marcasite.

Unstable minerals may be preserved by applying a coating of transparent lacquer after they have been thoroughly cleaned and dried. Other

TABLE 19
INSTABILITY OF SELECTED MINERALS

EFFLORESCENT MINERALS

These minerals lose water of crystallization in dry air and should be kept in sealed containers.

Autunite	Laumontite
Borax	Melanterite
Chalcanthite	Torbernite
Colemanite (also collects dust on pyroelectric areas)	Trona
Halotrichite	Ulexite
Kernite	Zeunerite

DELIQUESCENT MINERALS

These minerals absorb moisture from damp air and may even dissolve into liquid, hence must be kept in dry containers.

Halite (sodium chloride)	Soda niter
Hanksite	Sylvite (potassium chloride)
Melanterite	Thenardite

MINERALS THAT OXIDIZE OR TARNISH

Tarnishing cannot always be prevented, only reduced by keeping specimens in a stable dry atmosphere free of sulfur or acid fumes.

Argentite	Cinnabar	Malachite	Realgar
Arsenic ores	Cobaltite	Marcasite	Silver
Bismuth	Copper	Niccolite	Smaltite
Bismuthinite	Crocoite	Proustite	Sphalerite
Bornite	Cuprite	Pyrargyrite	Stibnite
Chalcocite	Enargite	Pyrite	Sylvanite
Chalcopyrite	Iron	Pyrrhotite	Vivianite
			Zincite

MINERALS AFFECTED BY LIGHT

Apatite (pink variety loses color)	Proustite (alters or turns gray)
Argentite (photochemically alters)	Pyargyrite (grays or alters)
Beryl (brown or orange types may change to pale pink)	Quartz (amethyst, rose, smoky types become paler)
Cerargyrite (changes color or becomes altered)	Realgar (changes to orpiment)
Cinnabar (changes color or alters)	Spodumene (kunzite variety becomes pale or loses color)
Fluorite (green and purple types change color)	Topaz (brown variety loses color)
Orpiment (decomposes)	Tyuyamunite (generally alters)
	Vanadinite (darkens and dulls)
	Vivianite (changes to dull bluish)

delicate minerals may be preserved if kept in an airtight container or in one filled with dry nitrogen. Cleaning with alcohol, drying, and spray-coating with plastic lacquer is a common technique used for preserving many mineral species.

Bright light itself exerts a destructive force on some minerals. Silver minerals may be either bleached or slowly decomposed. Gem crystals of beryl, topaz, and spodumene may have their natural colors altered or completely removed by light, with direct sunlight being the most lethal. Such gem crystals cannot be protected with a plastic coating; they must be kept in the dark and brought out only for showing off.

Table 19 lists a number of minerals which require protection from atmospheric damage or harm resulting from exposure to light.

Since careless handling may destroy delicate crystals and hairlike growths, it is never wise to allow visitors to handle rare or prized specimens. Even the most well-intentioned friend, through ignorance or ineptitude, may so damage a lovely mineral or gemstone that its dollar value is irrevocably lost.

STORING YOUR SPECIMENS

You will need adequate storage space for both cabinet and instructional rock specimens, as well as for the gross materials brought home from the field before they are sorted, cleaned, traded, sold, or broken down into only those pieces worth keeping.

HEAVY ROUGH FIELD MATERIALS

Within an astonishingly few weeks after a beginning gem and mineral collector starts taking to the field on any regular schedule, he makes the discovery that the raw materials of a good rock collection come measured in tons. The average field trip means a car trunk loaded with from 100 to 500 pounds of rock specimens, many of them so large that it is all a man can do to lift one over the bumper guard. Soon the front, back, and side yards are cluttered up with an unsightly miscellany of rocks in all sizes, colors, and degrees of dirtiness. What to do with the inevitable overflow from every collecting trip constitutes a real problem in many homes.

There isn't really much that can be done about large quantities of coarse mineral specimens. Many specimens can be distributed about the flower beds as "garden rock" until such time as they may be sawed up to see what lies inside. Outdoor bins may be built to separate rough rocks by general types, e.g., agates, obsidian, ore minerals with their subbreakdowns according to metallic content, and so on.

One enterprising rock collector periodically held a "field day" in his own backyard. He invited his club members, their friends, and relatives and placed small ads in his local newspaper—"Come one, come all, and start picking." He charged 50 cents a pound and usually managed to get back more than the costs of his field tripping in the bargain, besides reducing the total quantity of rocks to more manageable proportions.

Even at that, when he and his wife decided to move to another state some ten years later, he had to leave more than fifteen tons of good-quality specimens behind—all brought home over the years in the trunk and back seat flooring of his small sedan.

THE FINER SPECIMENS

The finer specimens deserve good storage facilities out of the weather, grouped according to general species for ready accessibility. Such specimens should all be trimmed to a few inches in outside dimensions and thoroughly cleaned—called "dressing a collection." Almost any kind of container will do to hold dressed rocks: cigar, shoe, or cardboard boxes, crates, anything at all that will afford some protection from dust, dirt, excessive light, moisture, and too much handling by visitors.

Egg cartons make ready-made specimen holders for smaller crystals, Apache tears, and gemmy fragments that may eventually be tumbled to a high gloss. Old dresser drawers with cardboard lids can be stacked along the walls of a garage or home workshop. Many collectors build enclosed shelving with drop doors secured by spring latches. However it is done, all good gem and mineral specimens require ordered arrangement and proper labeling for later reference.

Simply dumping specimen material into a drawer or box is not adequate. Every repository requires dividing into separate compartments to prevent specimens from being bumped against one another when the drawer is opened and closed or becoming all mixed together. Rock edges and corners chip rather easily, and crystal corners and points can be knocked off, ruining the specimen. Wooden or pasteboard strips may be used to divide the larger repositories, with or without covers, into smaller compartments.

"Thumbnail" specimens—the term used to describe trimmed rock specimens not more than one inch on a side—fit easily into trays similar to plastic kitchen-drawer silverware containers, further subdivided by cardboard inserts. Thumbnail specimen trays are usually stacked in cabinets which collectors make for themselves. The "miniatures," that is, specimens measuring about 1½ by 1½ by 2 inches, may similarly be stored in slightly larger trays and kept in specially designed cabinets.

The smallest of all categorized specimens, more or less reserved for specialists, are the "micromounts," measuring well under one inch in diameter and consisting mostly of tiny, perfect crystals, bits of colorful matrix, and small fragments or actual microscopically small specimens mounted for display under a microscope or reading-glass type of magnifier. Almost any pharmacy can supply pillboxes by the hundreds, in various sizes, for storing tiny specimens neatly in a larger tray or compartmentalized drawer.

You can buy a wide variety of steel filing cabinets with drawers of varied sizes that slide in and out with a minimum of friction. Old dental tool cabinets are much in demand, since the top drawers are shallow, deepening as one progresses toward the bottom. These cabinets are fairly dustproof and simplify many storage problems. A visit to almost any used furniture store or antique shop will reveal many kinds of old cabinets and cases that may need only a little sprucing up and minor repairs to make handsome and serviceable storage repositories.

YOUR FINEST SPECIMENS

Every gem and mineral collector sooner or later acquires a prized assortment of "bragging stones." These specimens are truly showpieces, either found and prepared for display by the collector himself or purchased elsewhere. Beautiful crystal aggregates and gem crystals in matrix; cut and polished slices, slabs, cubes, and spheres; glittering gold ore specimens and nuggets of gold, silver, platinum, and copper—all these and many more simply cry out for permanent display in glass cabinets. All kinds of china cabinets and bookcases—antique, commercial, modern, homemade—can be used, with shelving covered with black, velvety material and hidden lighting installed. Your finest gems and minerals will comprise only a very small part of your total collection—the *crème de la crème,* as it were—and some provision should certainly be made for showing them off to the best possible advantage.

Such special display cabinets may serve as part of the furnishings of your living quarters or, when time and income permit, be incorporated into the walls of a specially constructed workshop that also contains lapidary equipment along with general storage facilities. Even then, most collectors reserve the finest specimens of all for smaller cabinets on display in their homes where visitors may admire them.

For jewellike crystals or cut and polished gems and gemstones, regular jewelry cases, cuff-link boxes, or ring cases come in handy. Sliding glass door exhibit cabinets purchased commercially are ideal for displays of both larger polished pieces and gems or crystals or fossils, mounted on cotton or velvet in separate "shadow" boxes, like a framed picture, displayed at a slant toward the viewer. Techniques of fine display can be studied by visiting almost any rock and mineral dealer's shop or a jewelry store.

Lighting with separate bulbs or with fluorescent tubes, combined with the skillful use of mirrors to double or magnify elements on display, adds to a collection's interest and brilliance. Often the artistry of some family member helps to create unusual combinations of colorful materials that will bring out the best in each individual specimen.

SPECIAL HOME DISPLAYS

The amount of ingenuity which can be developed for home exhibition of gems and minerals is endless, for both exterior and interior showing.

New home construction permits rough specimens to be worked into façades, cementwork, garden walls, and the outer base structure of fireplaces. Inside, fireplace mantels and sides make ideal settings for highly polished slabs of colorful gemstones.

Collectors with lapidary equipment often create their own lovely bookends or lamp shades from thin translucent slices of such gemstone materials as jade, rhodonite, malachite, chrysocolla, agate, and chalcedony, among many others. By fitting variously sized thin slices together in triangles, squares, parallelograms, or any geometric shape that can be cut from a rough slice, an endless, never-duplicated series of designs can be made that become clearly visible when the light is turned on.

Still others fashion highly polished lampstand and clock bases out of similar stones or large crystal groups. Coffee tables of inlaid polished slabs covered with a sheet of plate glass always make excellent conversation pieces. The popular techniques designed for making leaded stained-glass windows work nicely with thin-sliced and polished gemstone slabs of no particular geometric shape. As you can see, the possibilities for displaying your finer materials are, literally, without end.

An ultraviolet ray display cabinet requires special construction, like a photographic darkroom, which excludes all light and in which ultraviolet ray lamps can be properly installed. A large walk-in closet might serve for a small collection of phosphorescent or fluorescent minerals within a closed glass-fronted cabinet. An automatic timing device which alternately switches from white light to black light may be desirable to show the great differences in appearance between the specimens under daylight or artificial lighting and under long- or short-wave ultraviolet ray light. This is often done in museum displays to save on ultraviolet ray lamps.

LABELING AND RECORDING SPECIMENS

In spite of the spectacular beauty of fine gems and gemstones, they are not as scientifically important to the hobby of rock collecting as the precise recording and labeling of every specimen picked up and brought home, no matter how unspectacular that piece may be.

Here lies the great dividing line between the raw amateur and the truly serious collector. The beginner is always an amateur, but as his interest increases and he begins to understand the ramifications of the rock-collecting hobby, he can enter the high road of professionalism, not necessarily for monetary profit, but in the realm of really understanding what geology, mineralogy, and scientific collecting are all about.

THE MINERAL FIELD LABEL

If you use your field notebook regularly and acquire the habit of recording your observations systematically, you will find that it adds greatly to the interest and value of your rock collection.

The outlined record forms shown can serve as convenient guides to the proper organization of any mineral and gemstone collection. In practice, you should keep the forms as simple as possible, yet include all pertinent information on them. Forms may be dittoed or otherwise inexpensively duplicated; they may vary from the suggested forms according to your particular needs and as your experience dictates. Any printer can make up a batch of record forms at a surprisingly modest cost, and many gem shops sell regular forms in pads.

GEM AND MINERAL RECORD FORMS

MINERAL FIELD LABEL

Specimen No. _____ Local Name _____ Date _____
Species _____ Variety _____ Color _____
Associated Minerals _____
Locality _____
Geologic Occurrence _____
Remarks

Collected By _____ Associates _____

MUSEUM DATA CARD

No. _____ Cabinet No. _____ Species _____ Variety _____ Dana No. _____
Composition _____ Formula _____
Associated Minerals _____
Matrix _____ Geol. Occurrence _____
Geol. Age _____ Collector _____ Date _____
Locality _____
Remarks

Received From _____ Date _____ ☐   ☐
                                                    Trade Purchase

The observations written down in your notebooks or on your mineral field label (carried in a notebook or in pads) will often have to be referenced to individual mineral specimens. The best way to keep a clear record is to use consecutive numbers inked onto a piece of adhesive tape stuck to an inconspicuous spot on each specimen immediately when it is picked up, then noted in your record. (Prolific collecting fields may provide an abundance of specimens, e.g., individual quartz crystals, limonite cubes, etc. Instead of labeling and recording each one separately, it is more convenient to place batches of specimens together in small bags and label each bag with a single sequential number plus the field label information.)

By including as much information as possible gathered on the spot, you will be able to provide each ultimate display specimen with scientifically accurate data.

It is a useful habit to mention whatever else may seem significant to you in the remarks section of your field label, such as a brief description of the terrain (slope, vegetation, etc.); nearby camping facilities, including water and fuel supply; condition of road and trails; and any later references to articles or books dealing with the site.

Few amateurs realize the importance of consistent notekeeping and methodical filing of information. Beginners are often too impatient simply to get out into the fresh air and sunshine of a scenic collecting field to take the time to record their impressions. But the professional knows that by using the techniques of laboratory science, he vastly increases the cash value of his gem and mineral collection. So why not follow demonstrated precedent and, as far as possible, emulate the experts?

MUSEUM DATA CARD OR SPECIMEN LABEL

The museum data card shown is much more important than most gem and mineral collectors realize. Each data card (or museum specimen label) should be prepared with extreme care, reduced in size so as not to obscure the specimen for which it is prepared, and neatly typed, printed, or hand-lettered. This label is designed to be included along with your prize specimens in your display case at home or at a show. The label demonstrates your skill and workmanship, besides providing vital information for all viewers.

For temporary display, a small label measuring about 1¼ by 2 inches is adequate, since it need carry no more information than species name, variety name, and locality. For more permanent display, a larger data card or label is required.

So important is the museum data card that at nearly every gem and mineral show and exposition special credit is assigned to it (for example, 10 to 20 points out of a total of 100 points). This separate assignment of credit points may spell the difference between winning a place award or not winning even an honorable mention. Incidentally, in competitive showings the owner's name is omitted from the labels.

CATALOGING SPECIMENS

Because experienced collectors tend to view any rock specimen displayed without an identifying label as simply another "rock" with little value, in addition to attaching to each cabinet specimen an informative label, you need to develop a cataloging system that includes both the display item and all others in your total collection. The label is primarily important for naming the essentials surrounding a specimen's correct name, locality, and geologic age. Cataloging is something entirely different.

When you apply a piece of adhesive to a flat place on a field specimen, with an inked-on numeral, this is only a temporary solution to the problem of keeping track of your finds by relating the number to its record and pertinent data in your notebook. Not infrequently, some specimens become separated from their labels after a time. To avoid confusion it is expedient back home in the peace and quiet of your workshop or library to reevaluate your finds, throwing out the poor stuff and reorganizing your numbering system for specimens to be retained. This requires a new record book or, preferably, a card file of record forms.

CODED INFORMATION

While there are several methods for applying permanent identification numbers or number-letter combinations to a specimen, perhaps the most common technique is to locate an obscure flat spot on the specimen out of sight of any display position and paint it with a daub of opaque white paint. Then, by using a fine quill-type pen and India ink, the identifying code letters and numerals can be lettered on and the whole label subsequently varnished over with colorless spar varnish. Such labels need not be more than a quarter-inch square. Where a specimen seems to have no flat spots even this small, you can apply a dab of plaster of paris and let it harden or scrape out a smooth place with a hard tool.

While the ink and varnish (or clear plastic lacquer) are drying, you enter the identifying symbols into your record book or onto a file card. In either case, the records should be ordered sequentially according to whatever code system you may devise and tied into the overall organization of your storage or display system. For example, if the specimen belongs to the quartz family, you may wish to file it and all similar family representatives under the initial Q, with a second letter to designate the subspecies, e.g., QA (quartz, agate), QJ (quartz, jasper), QR (quartz, rock crystal), and so on.

Beneath the letter designation should be inked the sequential number of the specimen, that is, the number in order of the specimens found in the field or obtained through trade or purchase. The sequential number relates that particular specimen to its own special description in your field notebook, catalog record book, or catalog card file—the master record which should contain all the details surrounding your acquisition of the specimen.

ACCESSION NUMBERS

When gem and mineral specimens are acquired through trade or purchase, their accession numbers should run consecutively from 1 on, inked onto the specimens as described above. The same numbers should be recorded in a separate catalog book or series of file cards that also include all pertinent data about the item. Some collectors take a dim view of buying specimens, deeming it somewhat unworthy of a dedicated devotee of field collecting; however, outright purchase (accession) has a very real place in a collector's life, filling in gaps in his collection or enabling him to replace an inferior specimen with one of better quality. Nevertheless, for future reference, it is best to keep an accessions catalog file separate from the gem and mineral specimens you find yourself.

The habit of jotting everything down methodically in a field notebook will pay many unsuspected dividends in the long run. True, note taking may at times seem a bit laborious and, in the excitement of harvesting a new mineral field, unnecessarily tedious. But you cannot rely on memory, and so your field notes should be as full and complete as possible, even if the time it takes to jot them down means that you aren't picking up as many specimens as the person galloping ahead of you. The realization that the notes have greater value than the specimens picked up comes slowly to amateur collectors, especially where a field competitive spirit exists among groups all vying with one another to see who finds the biggest and bestest and braggingest rocks. Forget the competition. Write down all your impressions and observations and include accurate distances and directions for reaching each mineralized area.

Professional geologists make a practice of writing on only every other page of their notebooks in order to leave plenty of space for later additions, corrections, sketches, attached photographs, or rough field maps. You will do well to sketch in all significant geologic structures and topographic features, such as ridges, mountain uplifts, watercourses, and man-made objects that will assist you to locate yourself accurately on a topographic map later on.

TAKING PHOTOGRAPHS

Wherever feasible, you might take photographs of field conditions and include them, separately cataloged, along with your enumerated rock and mineral specimens somewhere in your notebook. For each photograph or rough drawing you make, you should record a number, the locality, name, direction or angle of shot, and any remarks as to time of day, light values, length of exposure, diaphragm setting, and focus distance.

A photographic record is one of the most valuable means for illustrating geology. Also, in your display cabinet or at a mineral show, a blown-up scenic view of the area in which prize specimens were found, whether black and white or in color, adds appreciably to viewer interest. Miniature cameras, and the more sophisticated the better, are the most practical, since they are lightweight, easily reloaded, hold many exposures on a roll of film, and cost less for film and processing.

Choose only those views which have a definite bearing on the subject; avoid having another person "mugging" into the camera lens. People in such photographs serve only two possible uses: perspective and size, and action relating to rock examination or digging out specimen material. Although field photographs should answer as many technical questions as can be recorded on film, general photographic principles of artistry, balance, composition, and human interest (i.e., showing a person in the act of hammering, chipping, or picking up a specimen) add greatly to any picture.

Lighting should be carefully considered. Most textured rocks require photography on a cloudy day, as do rock forms of an irregular or rough nature. Too much sunlight causes projecting corners and edges to appear on the finished print as black, uninformative patches. To bring out etched lines, pits, ribbing, or granular texture, it is best to shoot on a bright sunny day with the sun's rays at a low angle to the face of the rock so that minor irregularities will cast shadows and reveal the surface as being three-dimensional.

chapter 8

Your Gem and Mineral Collection

Although there are about 2,000 recognized mineral substances today, including all the gems and gemstone species, you are not likely to include more than 10 to 20 percent of them in your collection. The variety of that small percentage will be surprising, however. Whether you choose to display only your finest materials in glass cabinets or squirrel away the bulk of everything you collect in boxes and drawers, there should be rhyme and reason, order and science, to your collection. All mineral substances can be classified according to specific chemical families.

GENERAL ORGANIZATION

There are any number of ways to organize a mineral collection, but consistency should be the watchword. In the past, before scientific classification was understood, various approaches toward outward mineral relationships were tried, obvious ones being attempts to arrange rocks and minerals simply by their external crystal forms. This did not work very well, because many minerals have much the same crystal structure but are quite apparently not otherwise related. The ultimate and current organization of mineral species accords with the chemical compositions of minerals and has proved to be not only more convenient but the most scientific and authoritative, for it has withstood the test of time.

Mineral specimens in themselves attest only to your ability to collect them and your agility in getting them safely home. Cleaning, trimming, and organization of the collection attest to your awareness of scientific method. As much as anything else in your life, the arrangement of your collection reflects the logic of your mind and the quality of your personality. By whatever means you organize your specimens, it should enable you to find any one representative example in a minimum amount of time and with it a proper label description of its genesis, species name, locality where found, and all other pertinent information attending its original collection.

A Simplified Arrangement

Possibly the simplest means for setting your collection to rights is an alphabetical arrangement according to species name. This system has the advantage of enabling you to locate any specimen or compartment of specimens upon request. Alphabetization is expedient where the complexities of scientific associations are not especially important to you. At least, this method brings a marked, if not scientific, order out of chaos.

Another simple method is to arrange your gems and minerals alphabetically according to the localities where you found them, naming the particular mine dump, quarry, or geographic location taken from a map as so many miles from hither or yon. Many collectors may come to specialize in the gems and minerals from only one or two major collecting fields; they become expert on the minerals and detailed environments surrounding them in these areas.

Such a single field may be a large quarry, like the Crestmore Quarry at Riverside, California, where literally hundreds of different gem and mineral species, some extremely rare elsewhere, occur together in an unusual geologic formation. Another similar quarry is the famed excavation at Franklin, New Jersey, which for rockhound generations has produced some of the finest mineral specimens known anywhere on earth. Then there are the great pegmatite mines of New England, North Carolina, the Black Hills, and around Pala and Rincon in southern California's San Diego County, all famed for their tremendous gem crystals.

Cabinet Display Techniques

Display organization of gems and minerals need not follow the organization you develop for keeping tabs on rough specimens. In general, any display cabinet requires a pleasing arrangement of shapes, colors, crystallizations, or other outstanding characteristics and may cross all boundaries of scientific organization.

There are almost too many possibilities to list in display cabinet arrangements. Your or your family's sense of artistry and imagination will surely devise others than those suggested in Table 20.

The beginning collector will not at first have a very wide selection of gem and mineral specimens to put on display; after a while, he is bound to have entirely too many. It is much too difficult and costly to try to acquire all 2,000 or so mineral species, so many collectors eventually begin to specialize in one or a few types of mineral species: crystals, ore minerals, native metal nuggets, calcite minerals, quartz family gemstones, pegmatite gems, and so on. Specialization permits building up a

TABLE 20
DISPLAY CABINET MINERAL ORGANIZATION

Arrangement	Mineral Contents	Remarks
By size	Any mineral type	Field or hand specimens, micromounts, miniatures, museum types, thumbnails
By locality	Any mineral type	State, county, district, quarry, mine, etc.
Chemical classes (see following entries)	Elements, oxides, sulfides, salts, etc.	The most scientific arrangement, usually found in a museum collection
Mineral groups	Gemmy crystals of garnet, tourmaline, etc., or aggregates	Makes for interesting contrasts and associations
Single species	Varieties of a single mineral, e.g., gold, copper, quartz, calcite, fluorite, etc.	Variations are wide within any mineral species, hence have unique interest
Native metals	Nuggets of gold, silver, copper, platinum	Variety of forms makes for an interesting grouping
Single crystals	Any crystal mineral, small or large	Size may vary from micromounts under a lens to single or double terminations
Multiple crystals	Any crystal type that is a twin, shadow (outline of an interior crystal through the outer crystal), etc.	A wide variety of forms exists in many different mineral species
Crystal inclusions	Rutilated quartz, asbestos, tourmaline, etc.	Crystals may be clear, smoky, or colored; some contain water bubbles
Ore minerals	Metallics, nonmetallics, refractories, etc.	Many are colorful, others dull; all should represent commercial types
Crystal systems	Cubic, hexagonal, orthorhombic, monoclinic, etc.	Refer to any textbook on crystallography
Nodular	Nodules, geodes, thundereggs, agates, jaspers, Apache tears, etc.	Field specimens alone or with cut and polished section to show interiors
Gemstones	Wide variety, hardness of 5.5 and above, both rough and finished	Should be arranged according to species: agates, jaspers, chalcedonies, etc.
Gems	Faceted or cabochon cuts of spinel, tourmaline, amethyst, topaz, garnet, ruby, sapphire, zircon, etc.	Can be combined with rough crystals to show lapidary work

TABLE 20 (Cont.)

Arrangement	Mineral Contents	Remarks
Miscellaneous	Any type of colorful mineral by reason of beauty, shape, or uniqueness	Often reserved for items difficult to classify otherwise
Organic minerals	Amber, jet, coral, pearl	Fossil examples may be included
Petrified wood	Agatized, opalized, silicified, or other	Rough specimens shown with cut and polished slabs for variety
Fossil gemstones	Jasperized dinosaur bone, agatized clams, carnelian shrimp (Colo.), etc.	Rough examples together with tumbled specimens make unusual viewing
Nature's oddities	Fulgarites, pseudomorphs, concretions, mudballs	Any grouping with labels that adds to a viewer's knowledge

truly worthwhile museum-quality collection, but it also involves a great deal of searching for just the right pieces of the finest obtainable quality. A great deal of money can be expended in building such a collection; by the same token, its value invariably increases with time, often faster than the same amount of money salted away in bonds or insurance.

Mineral conventions, rallies, club shows, museums, and other public and private collections should be visited whenever the opportunity presents itself (museums are listed in Appendix III). From them you will gain much of value to assist you in developing a superb organizational and display system for your own materials. Very often, extensive field trips can be combined with visits to regional gem and mineral shows held at county fair grounds or other places; such shows are annually listed with dates and places in the rockhound journals east and west. At these expositions you have a prime opportunity to buy or trade for unusually attractive items for your own collection, thereby increasing its ultimate value.

SPECIALIZED COLLECTIONS

When time and expense have brought about your graduation from generalized collecting to concentrating on the particular type or two of gemstones or minerals that most appeal to you, your next main step is to determine the size range that most nearly meets your space limitations and interest. The basic categories of specimen size are described in Table 21.

With respect to micromount specialization, the minute crystals or crystal groups selected for display are only those that can properly be

TABLE 21
SPECIMEN SIZE CATEGORIES

Category	Title	Size	Remarks
1	Cabinet or museum	Min. 2 inches on one edge	Usually includes larger sizes
2	Miniature	Min. 1 inch to max. 2 inches on an edge	Or in diameter
3	Thumbnail	Less than 1 inch in diameter but containing visible naked-eye crystals or phenocrysts	Very popular with some specialists
4	Micromount	Minute crystals or crystal groupings	Requires mounting under a lens or reading-glass-type magnifier

seen under low-power magnification. Such specimens must be carefully mounted on supports and displayed in a cabinet under a lens positioned above at the focal length to provide the clearest, most instructive viewing. Proper lighting is essential.

Minute crystals, because they are subject to less damage from erosion, often show the greatest perfection and variety of forms. Collectors specializing in micromounts are increasing every year; they frequently consider themselves the aristocrats of all gem and mineral collectors. Specializing in micromounts is one way of assembling a comprehensive and inexpensive collection of the widest possible variety of mineral species and is admirably suited to modern living in relatively limited apartment spaces.

THE FIELD-TRIP SPECIALIST

There is one other major type of mineral collector seldom mentioned in the rockhound literature. That is the person who enjoys field excursions to the utmost and makes of them a literal profession. He is likely to be something of a loner, and he may or may not have a lapidary to saw and trim his finds. In any case, this person is very little concerned with converting gems and minerals for display and seldom indulges in rock shows.

The field trip specialist is a man or woman who goes out to gather rocks in quantity in order to supply rockhound dealers with rough materials taken directly from the field with little more processing than a washing down with a garden hose. The enjoyment of the outdoors is paramount in his psyche; he is relieved of the painstaking chores involved in the finer arts of developing his own individual collection of fine materials.

More power to these rugged individualists; without them gem and mineral shops would soon run out of salable materials which other enthusiasts purchase for their own display collections or to work up into jewelry and art objects. The field-trip specialist frequently is retired and spends the summer months traveling a wide circuit of many rock collecting fields, selling his rocks to gem and mineral dealers in town and city and highway shops encountered along the way. Not infrequently he returns home with only money in his pockets and very little in the way of rocks to clutter up his home. He lacks most of the attributes of the scientific collector, but ask him about any particular specimen, and he will prove to be extraordinarily knowledgeable about every facet of its finding. This collector is not a commercially minded collector or salesman of rocks; invariably, he gathers only a few from here and there, leaving the great bulk of collectable materials *in situ* for others to gather, while he travels on to investigate more fields beyond the blue horizon.

DANA'S SYSTEM OF MINERAL CLASSIFICATION

With the exception of such organic gemstones as amber, jet, ivory, etc., almost all mineral substances can be classed as chemical compounds in which the arrangement of atoms of the contributing elements never varies. In some subfamilies, like the garnets, an interchange of metallic elements produces several varieties, distinguishable mainly by color and degree of transparency but all having the dominant cubic–hexoctahedral crystal shape. Although many minerals do have a relatively simple and easily remembered chemical formula, most have moderate to extremely complicated symbolic representations based not on how the individual contributing atoms are joined but on their percentages of molecular weights.

For all practical purposes, you need use only a simple method of field determination to be able to recognize the more common rocks and minerals. The keys to this recognition are given with each gemstone and mineral listed in Appendix I.

Table 20 indicated that one category for arranging your gem and mineral collection was by chemical class. Whenever you visit a major mineral museum, you are likely to find that the curator has arranged his specimens according to James Dana's classification set down in Volumes I and II of the 7th edition of Dana's *System of Mineralogy* (1944–51) and the 3rd edition of James Strunz's *Mineralogische Tabellen* (1957). In his system Dana classified the minerals according to the order shown in Table 22—a neat, scientific method for organizing any comprehensive collection.

TABLE 22
DANA'S CLASSIFICATION OF MINERALS

Category	Mineral Class	Description
1	Elements	The naturally occurring native elements, or primitive uncombined units of matter are few in number. Of the 92 natural elements, the nonmetallic solids include only carbon (C) in its crystal forms of diamond and graphite and amorphous form soot; and sulfur (S). Among the metallic elements, the collector cannot find more than the liquid mercury (Hg) and the solids copper (Cu), gold (Au), platinum (Pt), silver (Ag), and antimony (Sb). Native silver is rare.
2	Sulfides (including selenides, tellurides) and sulfosalts	This class of minerals represents combinations of metals with sulfur (or selenium or tellurium), such as pyrite (FeS_2), marcasite (identical formula but different appearance and stability), and sphalerite (ZnS). Most minerals of this type look metallic; they are relatively soft, usually brittle, and their crystals when crushed reveal a usually dark to black powder or streak. Thus, pyrite ("fool's gold") can easily be shattered by a hammer blow, whereas true gold, which both pyrite and marcasite closely resemble, merely flattens out because it is malleable.
3	Oxides and hydroxides	Since the gaseous element oxygen is not only the most abundant element on earth but one of the most chemically active, it naturally becomes a major constituent of many minerals. The end product of weathering is the conversion of other mineral classes to their oxides, which represent the most stable natural form. There are many unlike minerals that fall into this class, including ore minerals. Some are hard and resistant, such as corundum (ruby, sapphire) with the simple formula of aluminum oxide (Al_2O_3) and rock crystal (quartz, SiO_2). Many oxygen-containing minerals have more complex formulas and may fall into other categories. The hydroxides (basic minerals) have the chemical negative radical —OH in their formulas.
4	Halides	This class of compounds of metals with any of the four halogens (fluorine, chlorine, bromine, iodine), usually as a fluoride or chloride, includes only one gemstone, fluorite (calcium fluoride, CaF_2) with a hardness

TABLE 22 (Cont.)

Category	Mineral Class	Description
		below that of feldspar. In the field the collector may find only one other commonly crystallized halide, halite (rock salt, NaCl), and only in very dry regions. Most halides are extremely soluble in water, and their crystal forms, usually cubic, are laboratory preparations.
5	Carbonates	Many minor gemstone minerals occur in this category of metals combined with the carbonate negative radical $-CO_3$. Their crystal forms are often translucent to transparent. None is hard enough to resist abrasion; all readily dissolve in acids and produce carbon dioxide gas. Calcite ($CaCO_3$) is often found as water-clear crystals, while rhodochrosite ($MnCO_3$) appears in metamorphic manganese deposits and ore veins as deep rose-pink rhombohedrons.
6	Borates and nitrates	With the exception of a few rare borates occurring in pegmatite granite as remarkably hard minerals, the members of this class are all too soluble to be found in nature. In the dry-lake beds of the western states one will find a few examples of borax minerals, such as howlite, $Ca_2SiB_5O_9(OH)_5$, which can be used as a gemstone material for making bookends, etc.
7	Sulfates	The salts of metals combined with sulfur and oxygen belong here. One group is very soluble and seldom encountered in the field; the second group is insoluble in water. Both types occur deep in the oxidized portions of sulfide ore veins. The collector is most likely to find gypsum or its crystal variety selenite ($CaSO_4 \cdot 2H_2O$) in clay beds and limestone cavities.
8	Selenates, tellurates (including selenites and tellurites)	Relatively sparsely occurring minerals similar to the sulfates except that selenium or tellurium substitutes for the sulfur; not to be confused with the gypsum crystals selenite.
9	Chromates	Chromium salts have the metallic element chromium combined with oxygen in a negative radical. The commonest mineral is chromite ($FeCr_2O_4$ or $FeO \cdot Cr_2O_3$), found mainly in Calif., Ore., and Mont. It is really a ferrous chromic oxide and could be classed with the oxides.

TABLE 22 (Cont.)

Category	Mineral Class	Description
10	Phosphates	Many secondary minerals of metals combined with phosphorous and oxygen belong in this class. A typical primary mineral of gemstone quality is apatite, $Ca_5(Cl,F)(PO_4)_3$, found in pegmatite granites, ore veins, plutonic rocks, and often in sedimentary deposits. Often highly colored.
11	Vanadates, arsenates	Metals combined with oxygen and either vanadium or arsenic belong in this class. They are secondary, usually brightly colored, zone-of-oxidation minerals found around ore bodies which have undergone extensive weathering. These minerals often make attractive cabinet specimens.
12	Tungstates, molybdates, uranates	This mixed group of commercial ore minerals, often highly colored, lends itself mainly to cabinet specimen display. Individual minerals are easily identified; all are soft and heavy.
13	Silicates	Taken altogether, this group contains more than 50 percent of all known minerals and by far the largest number and variety of gemstones. The silicates occur as primary minerals, rather than as products of weathering, as components of rocks, as segregations in rocks, or as crystal druses lining the interiors of rock cavities. The silicates usually have a glassy luster and are variously colored; they make into excellent gemmy items because of their hardness of 7 or greater and their resistance to solution in acids or alkalies.
14	Organic compounds	Organically derived minerals include amber, jet, coral, pearl, and a few other minor substances.

DISPLAY OR STORAGE ORGANIZATION OF MINERALS

You may not at first have enough gem and mineral specimens to fill any single cabinet or display case, but what samples you do have should be arranged in some orderly fashion. If a beginner starts out systematically, learning as he increases the scope of his collection, he will avoid the tedious pitfalls of later on having to reorganize all his specimens into a coherent plan. You may wish to follow Dana's system or develop one of your own.

The following plan of mineral organization describes the museum collection of the California State Division of Mines, one of the largest and most complete in the world. The information has been adapted from "Mineral Exhibit," by George L. Gary and Robert A. Matthews, in *Mineral Information Service* (Vol. 12, No. 9, September 1959).

THE METALLIC MINERALS

The important metallic minerals should be collected together in one display, perhaps subdivided by states or counties, quarries, or mines. Metallic ores include those of chromium, copper, iron, lead, molybdenum, nickel, platinum, silver, tin, tungsten, uranium, vanadium, and zinc, as well as aluminum, antimony, arsenic, bismuth, cadmium, cobalt, gold, manganese, titanium, etc. Iron ores might well be displayed (or stored) as a group to include goethite, hematite, limonite, magnetite, pyrrhotite, and siderite. The lead-zinc minerals form a natural grouping which might include altaite, anglesite, cerussite, galena, linarite, and minium.

The copper minerals are especially colorful and might well be grouped together to include azurite, bornite, brochantite, chalcanthite, chalcocite, chalcopyrite, chrysocolla, covellite, cuprite, dioptase, leadhillite, malachite, and tetrahedrite, with enargite, melaconite, and native copper nuggets adding to the display. The zinc ores, which easily appear in conjunction with copper minerals, can be represented by excellent and sometimes spectacular specimens of calamine (hemimorphite), chalcophanite, franklinite, hydrozincite, smithsonite, sphalerite, willemite, zincite, etc. Nearby would be gathered the nickel minerals, including annabergite, garnierite, genthite, laterite, garnierite and limonite mixed ("chocolate ore"), and nickeliferous pyrrhotite.

The radioactive minerals include the vivid canary-yellow carnotite, as well as autunite, schroeckingerite, torbernite, tyuyamunite, uranophane, and zippeite, which, taken together, make up the lighter-colored uranium minerals. In addition, uraninite and pitchblende represent the darker uranium-radium specimens.

The many fine ore minerals of silver and chromium make a rather spectacular grouping. For example, silver occurs in the form of chlorides, chlorobromides, sulfides, and tellurides with such mineralogical names as argentite, cerargyrite, embolite, freibergite, petzite, and pyrargyrite, along with native silver in the form of raw nuggets or as "wire" silver. The chromium minerals are rather widely distributed and easily collected in some states, especially California; three species will stand out in any collection: one is banded, another is the so-called leopard ore, and the third is massive chromite which is often coated with bright green uvarovite (chrome garnet).

The tin and titanium minerals are often grouped together. The tin minerals include mainly cassiterite, with variations of form according to

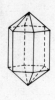

1. APATITE: Hexagonal,
dipyramidal

2. BARITE: Orthorhombic,
dipyramidal

3. BERYL: Hexagonal,
dihexagonal-dipyramidal

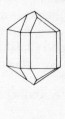

4. CALCITE: Hexagonal,
hexagonal-scalenohedral

5. CASSITERITE: Tetragonal,
ditetragonal- dipyramidal

6. CELESTITE:
Orthorhombic, dipyramidal

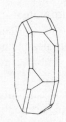

7. CORUNDUM: Hexagonal,
scalenohedral

8. EPIDOTE: Monoclinic,
prismatic

9. FLUORITE: Isometric,
hexoctahedral

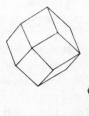

10. GALENA: Isometric,
hexoctahedral

11. GARNET: Isometric,
hexoctahedral

12. GYPSUM: Monoclinic,
prismatic

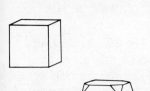

13. HALITE: Isometric, hexoctahedral

14. PYRITE: Isometric, diploidal

15. QUARTZ: Hexagonal; trigonal, trapezohedral

16. RUTILE: Tetragonal, ditetragonal-dipyramidal

17. SCHEELITE: Tetragonal, dipyramidal

18. SPHALERITE: Isometric, hextetrahedral

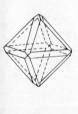

19. SPINEL: Isometric, hexoctahedral

20. STAUROLITE: Orthorhombic

21. TOPAZ: Orthorhombic, dipyramidal

22. TOURMALINE: Hexagonal, ditrigonal-pyramidal

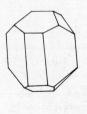

23. WOLFRAMITE: Monoclinic, prismatic

24. ZIRCON: Tetragonal, ditetradonal-dipyramidal

whether the specimens came from a lode, placer, or pegmatite deposit. Titanium ore minerals include ilmenite, rutile, and titaniferous magnetite.

Grouped separately close by might be the various ore minerals of mercury, or quicksilver, as the element is popularly known, with a vial of the silvery liquid representing the elemental form. Mercury minerals include cinnabar, metacinnabar, the mercury oxychloride (eglestonite), and tiemannite (mercury selenide).

In an adjoining miscellaneous group might be placed the ore minerals of aluminum, antimony, arsenic, bismuth, cadmium, and cobalt. The cobalt eye-catcher is the striking pink-purple mineral erythrite, while asbolite and smaltite are other principal cobalt-bearing minerals. Bismuth is usually found native or in the form of bismite and bismuthinite. The cadmium minerals are practically limited to greenockite and a cadmium-bearing smithsonite.

Arsenic and antimony minerals, to be grouped nearby, rank among the more attractive species. Arsenic compounds include arsenopyrite, scorodite, and the highly colored realgar (orange) and orpiment. Antimony often occurs as the native element as well as in the minerals senarmontite and stibnite, while examples of bauxite, diaspore, and laterite pretty well cover the aluminum ores.

Because of the value and comparative rarity of specimens, the gold minerals, either as nuggets, colors, and flower gold or as tellurides (which may also be associated with silver), should be grouped in a separate display case. Minerals containing gold include altaite, hessite, petzite, and sylvanite while, in addition, many common rock types such as quartz, rhyolite, and ordinary country rock found in gold mines carry visible free gold and may make attractive and always interesting specimens.

A special section could be devoted to the manganese minerals, such as the coal-black manganese oxides pyrolusite, psilomelane, manganite, wad (an impure bog manganese oxide), and chalcophanite; the lighter-colored brownish hausmannite; and the intriguing bright pink, black-laced rhodonite and rhodochrosite, specimens of which should also be slabbed and polished and displayed in a glass cabinet with other gemstones.

THE NONMETALLIC MINERALS

The nonmetallics, while often highly valued commercial minerals, are usually less spectacular than those containing the various metallic elements. Asbestos and barite can often be grouped in the same case or storage drawer. Asbestos is represented by four species: chrysotile, tremolite, crocidolite, and anthophyllite, with the long, strong, silky fibers of chrysotile offering excellent interest. Tremolite is a light-colored, weak-fibered variety. Barite is a widely encountered heavy nonmetallic mineral with excellent specimens easily collected in the field. Tabular large barite crystals can also be grouped in another case with other types of crystals.

The industrial minerals, such as pumice, pumicite, and novaculite, go well together, as do the abrasive minerals which include commercial grades of garnet, corundum, sandstone, and emery (fine-grained black disseminations of corundum with magnetite).

Calcite and gypsum are very important mineral commodities, and many collections display as a unit specimens of calcite, Iceland spar (a variety of calcite with double refraction properties), limestone (principally calcium carbonate), dolomite (a magnesian limestone), and the various species of gypsum such as alabaster, satin spar, and selenite. Some of these minerals, although very soft on the Mohs hardness scale, form spectacular crystals and may serve as representative samples in the crystal display cabinet.

Graphite and the feldspars, informative but hardly spectacular minerals of industrial value, make a good grouping along with soapstone (talc, steatite). Graphite may be exhibited (or stored) as examples of vein occurrences, disseminated graphite, or pure graphite. The feldspars would include albite, the green amazonite (a gemmy variety of microcline), labradorite (also a candidate for the gemstone cabinet), microcline, oligoclase, and orthoclase.

THE CRYSTAL MINERALS

Crystals are a highly specialized mineral form crossing many chemical boundaries. Each crystal structure represents the purest form of a mineral, in which the atomic arrangement reaches a height of perfection. Crystals should be grouped separately, subdivided into those with a hardness of 5.5 and above as gem and gemstone materials and those with a hardness below 5.5 as cabinet specimens only.

The nonmetallics fluorite and lepidolite group naturally together. Excellent large crystals of purple, green, blue, and colorless fluorite are rather easily obtainable, either as field specimens or at small cost from a mineral dealer. The distinctive lilac color of lepidolite is representative of the lithium-bearing minerals.

In the same case or drawer, or grouped nearby, should be the mica minerals: muscovite, phlogopite, and sericite—all easily obtained and in themselves exceptionally attractive forms because of their light to colorless transparent leaves—while biotite will add a touch of dark brown to black in the same form. Alongside might then go the magnesium minerals, such as magnesite, brucite, hydromagnesite, and various magnesia products, with a lump of pure magnesium added for good measure.

The borate minerals, mostly found in desert-dry regions and including kernite, ulexite, boracite, borax, colemanite, and inyoite, have an interest all their own. The minerals of sodium and potassium, usually requiring a very dry surrounding atmosphere, offer the viewer some interesting crystal forms, especially thenardite and halite (ordinary rock salt), mirabilite (glauber salt), and natron. The potassium minerals and potash products include sylvite, pirssonite, gaylussite, trona, and hanksite—all important commercially. Strontium and sulfur go hand in glove, and celestite and strontianite from widespread deposits point up the beautiful yellow, coarsely crystalline, and massive specimens of sulfur so easily collected or purchased.

Miscellaneous Mineral Specimens

In many museums special display cases include steatite-grade talc, soapstone, and pyrophyllite, along with typical examples of the silica or quartz family minerals (you may wish to break down the cryptocrystalline gemstones in accordance with any consistent arrangement of subspecies, rough field-run samples, and derived cut and polished halves, single or twinned crystals, and so on).

The quartz family includes massive quartz, quartzite, sand, flint pebbles, chert, agate, tiger's-eye (quartz pseudomorph after crocidolite), chalcedony, rock crystal, jasper, and literally hundreds of subvarieties. Because of color and design the quartz minerals may occupy more than one cabinet or storage case.

In another case might be placed the phosphate minerals, such as apatite and phosphorite (chiefly collophane and phosphatic earths), along with the mineral pigments. The various shades of red, yellow, green, blue, and brown ocher indicate why early American Indians traded extensively for these decorative earths.

The unspectacular clay minerals kaolin, bentonite, fuller's earth, and numerous fire clays should be kept together as representative of earthy substances of great industrial value if not show quality. With these specimens can be placed the siliceous diatomaceous earth and dried aggregates of marine oozes, e.g., radiolarian ooze.

Special Dispensations

Every gem and mineral collection is bound to vary with the interests and personality of its collector, so that individuals may wish to group mineral species into special categories of storage or place them on separate display shelves in cabinets and cases. Whether you specialize in only one or a few mineral and gemstone types, it adds to the value of your whole collection to include mineral forms that exemplify certain peculiar features, as of meteorites, fossils, building stone, garden rock, fluorescence and phosphorescence (in a light-tight cabinet illuminated only by ultraviolet ray lamps); gemstones of many varieties cut, polished, faceted, or rough; as well as a special exhibit of the three major rock types: igneous, metamorphic, and sedimentary. (The basic rock types come in so many varieties of color, texture, graininess, design, and educational value that their collection and organization constitutes a complete geologic approach in itself.)

Igneous rocks might include examples of volcanic rocks, such as obsidian, perlite, dacite, trachyte, andesite, basalt, and others listed in Tables 2 and 3. Under the same category would be representatives of pegmatite granite, aplite, granite, granodiorite, diorite, gabbro, porphyry, diabase, syenite (barkevikite and nepheline), peridotite, saxonite, pyroxenite, dunite, and kimberlite, among others.

The metamorphic rocks would include slate, phyllite, schist (glaucophane, graphite, garnet, hornblende, sericite, chlorite, muscovite, and biotite schists), gneiss, hornfels, marble, serpentines, breccias, silica carbonate rocks, and so on. Contact-metamorphic rocks would include clay shales and stages of metamorphism commonly found in limestone and dolomite.

Among examples of sedimentary rocks you should have little difficulty collecting specimens of are sandstone, conglomerate, mudstone, siltstone, shale, clay, limestone, concretions, stalactites, stalagmites, chert, tufa, gypsum, and coral limestone. There are many others.

A collection showing evidences of earth's diastrophism (resulting from deep-seated movements beneath the earth's surface) could be housed in a special cabinet including examples of anticlinal and synclinal folds (in small scale); slickensides (the polished rock surfaces where one body of rock has slid over another body during faulting); fractures sealed with silica, feldspar, or calcite; and any other technical example described in textbooks of geology.

The Complete Collection

While it is true that the majority of gem and mineral collectors will tend to limit their efforts along some particular line, consideration might well be given to assembling a complete gem, mineral, and rock collection that will embrace all phases of geology. It takes time but very little extra expense to add rock forms to an otherwise specialized collection.

In mountainous regions you can find many interesting rock specimens of the major and altered types that exhibit all geologic features, in addition to those just mentioned: fault gangue, intrusions, columnar jointing (as in basalt), flow lines (as in gneisses and schists), phenocrysts (various small crystals in a fine-grained matrix), and so on. The coarse gravels of mountain stream beds may reveal hundreds of fascinating examples in microcosm, as it were—ready-made specimens of easily manageable size. Such aberrations and modifications in ordinary rock are invariably of real interest to viewers with some background in the earth sciences. Then, of course, your ability to label such exhibits correctly adds to your and their fund of interesting facts.

Collateral with, but somewhat outside, the scope of the average gem and mineral enthusiast is the vast field of fossil collecting. As far as a strictly gem and mineral collection is concerned, there are many fossils with gemstone characteristics, e.g., agatized clams, gem-quality agatized and jasperized dinosaur bones and knuckles, carnelianized gastropod shells of purest translucent gem quality, not to mention the many varieties of petrified woods which appear in practically all gemstone collections and which should be exhibited in a separate cabinet or stored in a separate place. Techniques of the lapidary, described in Chapter 10, can be used to convert gem-quality fossils into jewelry or art objects that provide real satisfaction.

chapter 9

Agates, Opals, and Petrified Wood

A very large percentage of the three million or so gem and mineral collectors in America are interested in three major types of gemstone materials: agates, opals, and petrified wood. Perhaps the interest in agates and petrified wood may be almost 100 percent, despite the fact that agatized and opalized woods occur almost exclusively in the states west of the Mississippi River. The petrified woods of the states east of the Mississippi are plentiful, but the petrifying agents have not always been silica, so they lack color, hardness, or gem interest.

In modern times jewelers have tended to classify only the diamond as a "precious stone," referring to all other gems and gemstones merely as "colored stones." Surely the agates are the most abundant and colorful of this group, and they have a wide appeal. When Theophrastus observed, about 300 B.C., "Agate is a colorful stone, usually sold at high prices," he was stating a fact that holds perfectly true today.

CHARACTERISTICS OF AGATES

As a member of the quartz family of cryptocrystalline minerals, agate has always been the most admired and widely used gemstone. The stones we call agates are really subvarieties of chalcedony (SiO_2), identical in chemical structure to such other varieties as jasper, flint, chert, and their intermediates, as well as much petrified wood, chrysoprase, tiger's-eye, and common and precious opal.

The name chalcedony is given to opaque, concretionary forms of cryptocrystalline quartz with a uniform color, usually white, and no banding or internal design. The distinguishing features which separate agate from its mother chalcedony are internal design and color, for the hardness and chemical composition are the same. Thus the term agate is applied to all forms of chalcedony having translucency, color, patterns resulting from banding, and inclusions of mosslike or dendritic impurities. The quartz hardness of 7 gives to agate its gemstone durability and resistance; the translucency of agate distinguishes it from the opaque though colorful jaspers and the dark opaque flints, cherts, and jaspilite (specularite).

One of the more tangible rewards guaranteed to the modern gemstone collector who specializes in the agates recalls Theophrastus' observation: once you have tumbled or otherwise slabbed, sliced, sawed, cut, cabochoned, and polished the agates you bring home, you will find a ready market for them. The prices of gems have fluctuated markedly over the years, but the prices for agates have remained relatively stable and "usually high."

Table 23 describes the quartz family minerals in alphabetic order, divided according to whether the species are crystalline (quartz) or cryptocrystalline. Table 24 names and describes many agate varieties, but it should be noted that in addition to the listed names there are almost countless regional and privately coined names for local variations. There is nothing scientific about the naming of the quartz family gemstones.

TABLE 23
QUARTZ FAMILY GEMSTONES

Gemstone Name	Description
CRYSTALLINE QUARTZ VARIETIES	
Amethyst	Pale lavender to rich purple transparent crystals; may show color zoning
Apricotine	Yellowish red, apricot-colored quartz pebbles (Cape May, N.J.)
Arkansas candles	Quartz crystals about six times as long as thick, in clusters (Ark.)
Arkansas stone	White porous rock filled with microscopic quartz crystals cemented with chalcedony; see novaculite (Hot Springs, Ark.)
Aventurine	Quartz spangled with mica flecks; variously colored; occasionally termed "crysoquartz"
Binghamite	Crystalline quartz containing goethite replacements (Minn.)
Cairngorm	Scottish name for smoky quartz (q.v.)
Cat's-eye or tiger's-eye	Quartz crystals with a silky luster from fibrous inclusions; somewhat translucent in green, gray, red, or yellow.
Citrine	Transparent pale to rich yellow quartz crystals; frequently showing smoky bands
Crocidolite quartz	Another name for tiger's-eye (q.v.)
Crysoquartz	See aventurine; an uncommon term
Dumortierite	Granular quartz with inclusions of dumortierite; blue, pink, purple, white-speckled

TABLE 23 (Cont.)

Gemstone Name	Description
Falcon's-eye	Another term for hawk's-eye (*q.v.*)
Gold quartz	Milky quartz (*q.v.*) containing gold inclusions; a rich commercial ore of gold
Green quartz	Transparent greenish quartz
Hawk's-eye	Transparent colorless quartz containing fine parallel fibers of blue crocidolite
Herkimer diamond	Unusually pure, clear quartz crystals from Herkimer County, N.Y.
Indian jade	Incorrect term for aventurine (*q.v.*)
Iris quartz	Clear rock crystal containing minute air-filled fractures which produce the effect of iridescence
Lake George diamond	See Herkimer diamond
Little Falls diamond	See Herkimer diamond
Madeira topaz	An amethyst which has been heat-treated
Middleville diamond	See Herkimer diamond
Milky quartz	Translucent to nearly opaque massive quartz; see also gold quartz
Morion	Nearly opaque to deep black smoky quartz (*q.v.*)
Mosquito stone	Quartz containing minute dark inclusions; sometimes called mossy quartz
Novaculite	Trade name for quartz whetstones (Ark.)
Occidental diamond	Little-used term for rock crystal (*q.v.*)
Pincushion quartz	Clustered slender quartz crystals from Collier Creek Mine (Crystal Mountains, Ark.)
Prase	Opaque, dark green quartz colored by inclusions of amphibole
Quartz cat's-eye	Light to dark grayish green crystalline quartz containing fibrous inclusions
Quartz topaz	Incorrect term for citrine (*q.v.*)
Rainbow quartz	See iris quartz
Regalite	A green quartz (*q.v.*) or white quartz with green veins; seldom-used term (Utah)
Rock crystal	Transparent, water-clear quartz crystals with single or double terminations
Rose quartz	Pink or rose translucent quartz
Rutilated quartz	Transparent, sparkling quartz crystals containing needles of rutile
Saganitic quartz	Transparent colorless quartz containing needlelike inclusions of actinolite, goethite, rutile, tourmaline, etc. See rutilated quartz

TABLE 23 (Cont.)

Gemstone Name	Description
Scotch pebble	Pebble chiefly of smoky quartz (q.v.), but in general any variety of quartz pebble
Scotch topaz	Citrine (q.v.) or yellow quartz
Siberian amethyst	Trade name for deep reddish violet or purple amethyst (Twin Peaks, Ariz.)
Silkstone	Crystalline quartz containing fibrous goethite replacements; less pure than binghamite (q.v.)
Sioux Falls jasper	A brown jasperlike fine-grained quartz (Sioux Falls, S.D.)
Smoky quartz	Transparent to opaque smoky brown to black quartz crystal; see also cairngorm and morion
Smoky topaz	Incorrect term for smoky quartz (q.v.)
Soldier's stone	Name, seldom used, for amethyst (q.v.)
Sowbelly quartz	Local Creede, Colo., name for amethystine quartz
Star quartz	Asteriated rose and clear quartz crystal
Thetis hair stone	Quartz crystal containing inclusions of green fibrous hornblende; see also Venus hair stone
Tigerite	Alternative name for tiger's-eye (q.v.)
Tiger's-eye	Yellowish or yellowish brown gem quartz pseudomorphous after crocidolite, cf. cat's-eye; colored by limonite
Topaz quartz	Recommended name for all topaz-colored quartz
Tourmalinated quartz	Transparent quartz crystal containing fine or coarse needles of tourmaline
Trenton diamond	See Herkimer diamond
Venturina	See aventurine
Venus hair stone	Quartz crystal containing inclusions of reddish brown or yellow rutile fibers that appear to be tangled
Water drop quartz	Quartz crystal containing inclusions of water drops or air bubbles

CRYPTOCRYSTALLINE QUARTZ GEMSTONES

Agate	Endlessly varied; see Table 24 for nomenclatures
Algae jasper	Bright-red jasper with cellular pattern (northern Minn.)
Amberine	Yellowish green chalcedony (Death Valley, Calif.)
Banded jasper	Jasper banded with contrasting colors
Basanite	Deep velvet-black amorphous quartz finer-grained than jasper (q.v.); the "touchstone" (q.v.) of the ancients ("Lydian stone"), used by jewelers to test precious metals; not a gemstone
Black chalcedony	Dyed clear chalcedony popular for men's jewelry; sometimes called "black onyx"
Bloodstone	Dark-green jasper spotted with blood-red specks

TABLE 23 (Cont.)

Gemstone Name	Description
Boakite	Brecciated green-and-red jasper; a local name (Nev.)
Brecciated jasper	Jasper of mosaic pattern from resilicified fractured jasper fragments
Bruneau jasper	Local name for jasper found along Idaho's Bruneau River
Cape May diamond	Chalcedony pebbles in various colors (cf. apricotine) from white to smoky found along the Cape May, N.J., seashore
Carnelian	Red to orange chalcedony, often banded; translucent
Carnelian onyx	Any onyx with one or more alternating parallel bands being carnelian color
Cave Creek jasper	Jasper from Cave Creek area of Maricopa County, near Phoenix, Ariz.
Chalcedony	Translucent (rarely transparent), gray, white, bluish, unbanded cryptocrystalline quartz; the mother of agate (q.v.)
Chert	Gray to black unpatterned jasper (q.v.)
Chrysocolla	Bright blue chalcedony stained with copper minerals; see Table 24 for chrysocolla agate. Pure chrysocolla is too soft for lapidary work, and it is not a quartz family mineral
Chrysoprase	Bright yellow-green chalcedony
Creolite	Red-and-white banded jasper (Shasta and San Bernardino counties, Calif.)
Desert rose	Flowerlike, flat, nodular form of chalcedony, pinkish, violet, some with carnelian centers, translucent to opaque, found in desert areas
Dinosaur bone	Agatized and jasperized actual bones and knuckles of Triassic to Jurassic dinosaurs (Utah, Colo.)
Egyptian jasper	Orbicular jasper (q.v.), similar to oregonite (q.v.), found on the beaches of western Strait of Juan de Fuca, Wash.
Emeraldine	Green-dyed chalcedony
False lapis	Chalcedony artificially dyed deep blue to resemble lapis lazuli
Ferruginous jasper	Lake Superior area jasper highly impregnated with iron oxide
Fish-egg jasper	Alternative name for orbicular jasper (q.v.)
Flint	A mixture of quartz and opal, gray, brown to black, opaque; may resemble good-grade jasper
Flower stone	Chalcedony beach pebbles; more properly a "flower" jasper (southern Calif.)
Frost stone	Gray chalcedony (see frost agate, Table 24, but this is not an agate)

TABLE 23 (Cont.)

Gemstone Name	Description
Gastrolith or "gizzard stone"	Any quartz family pebble that served a dinosaur's digestive process (Mountain states)
Green jasper	Jasper colored green by inclusions of iron silicate, chlorite, or chromite; an ornamental stone
Green onyx	Chalcedony dyed dark green; cf. emeraldine
Heliotrope	Dark green chalcedony spotted with red jasper
Iolanthite	Banded reddish jasper from central Oregon's Crooked River
Jasp-agate	A mixture of jasper and chalcedony, with jasper dominant
Jasper	Impure chalcedonic quartz, variously colored and patterned, opaque; varieties are jaspilite, moss, orbicular, banded, striped, ribbon, etc. (*q.v.*)
Jasperine	Uncommon name for banded jasper (*q.v.*) of various colors
Jaspilite	Bright red jasper alternating with black bands of specular hematite
Jasponyx	Opaque onyx in which some or all of the bands are jasper or jasperlike chalcedony; cf. onyx
Kinradite	Trade name for jasper containing spherulites of nearly colorless to clear quartz (Calif., Ore.)
Lavic jasper	Highly colored jasper (red with white markings) from near Barstow, Calif.
Moonstone	Incorrect term for chalcedony which exhibits a sheen; true moonstone is orthoclase feldspar
Morgan Hill jasper	Orbicular jasper (*q.v.*) from Morgan Hill, Calif.
Morrisonite	Local name for banded and colored chert occurring about 22 miles east of Ashwood, Ore.
Moss jasper	An incorrect term for petrified wood streaked with translucent quartz (Ariz., N.M.); see moss agate in Table 24
Myrickite	White to gray chalcedony containing red inclusions of cinnabar; named after "Shady" Myrick (Death Valley, Calif.)
Ochoco jasper	Jasper occurring around Ochoco Lake, east of Prineville, Ore.
Onyx	Chalcedony containing straight, parallel bands of strongly contrasting colors
Orbicular jasper	Jasper containing round spots or "eyes" of contrasting color; may be called kinradite or paradise jasper (*q.v.*)
Oregon jade	Local term for dark green jasper found near Durkee, Ore.
Oregonite	An orbicular jasper, cf. kinradite, occurring north of Holland, Ore.
Oriental chalcedony	Gray or white chalcedony, fine-grained, translucent

TABLE 23 (Cont.)

Gemstone Name	Description
Oriental jasper	An alternative term for bloodstone (*q.v.*)
Paradise jasper	An orbicular jasper (*q.v.*) found near Morgan Hill, Calif.
Pastelite	A waxy jasper with large wavy areas of pastel browns, greens, pinks, and reds (Mojave Desert, Calif.)
Petrified wood, coral, bone (agatized)	Organic fossil remains replaced with chalcedony, agate, jasper
Petrified wood (opalized)	Organic vegetal matter replaced by opal, opalite, etc.
Plasma	Semitranslucent green, nearly opaque chalcedony, occasionally with white or yellowish spots
Point chalcedony	White or gray chalcedony containing tiny flecks of red iron oxide
Poppy jasper	Same as orbicular jasper (*q.v.*)
Poppy stone	See orbicular jasper
Prase	Translucent light or grayish yellow-green chalcedony colored by needle inclusions of actinolite
Puddingstone (jasper)	A conglomerate of brecciated material occurring in the Lake Superior region
Ribbon jasper	Banded jasper with alternating ribbonlike stripes of contrasting colors
Rogueite	Local Oregon term for greenish jasper (Rogue River)
Russian jasper	Jasper flecked with red
Sapphire quartz	Chalcedony of light sapphire blue to pale blue
Sard	Translucent brown to reddish brown chalcedony similar to carnelian (*q.v.*)
Sardoine	Carnelian (*q.v.*) of darker color than sardonyx (*q.v.*)
Sardonyx	An onyxlike chalcedony (or agate) with straight parallel bands of brown to reddish brown, alternating with other colors; an onyx (*q.v.*) containing sard or carnelian in the bandings
Sard stone	Term used for both sard and sardonyx (*q.v.*)
Siliceous malachite	Green chrysocolla (*q.v.*)
Siliceous wood	Any petrified wood in which replacement of cells is with silica
Spherulitic jasper	Jasper containing quartz spherulites of contrasting color; usually an orbicular jasper (*q.v.*)
Stone Canyon jasper	A brecciated jasper (*q.v.*) from Stone Canyon (San Miguel, Calif.)
Striped jasper	Another term for banded jasper (*q.v.*)
Swiss jasper	Jasper dyed blue

TABLE 23 (Cont.)

Gemstone Name	Description
Touchstone	Alternative name for basanite (*q.v.*)
Vabanite	Brown red jasper (Calif.)
White carnelian	White chalcedony with faint reddish tints

Chalcedony and agate have a Mohs scale hardness of 7, the same as quartz. To the gem collector both seem quite dense and solid. They are indeed. Nevertheless, the chalcedonies are really rather porous and absorbent, surprising as that may seem.

When sliced and polished, the chalcedonies can be boiled in a solution of sugar for many hours and then immersed in concentrated sulfuric acid. The sugar solution penetrates the microscopic pores in the various agate bands and is distributed throughout the material along myriads of invisible small channels. The concentrated acid, a thick, syrupy, extremely corrosive liquid, also penetrates the sugar-filled opening, dehydrating the sugar by withdrawing all its hydrogen and oxygen (as molecular water) and leaving behind only the pure black carbon. Thus black chalcedony (cf. Table 23) is a popular material for men's jewelry. The acid treatment can be halted at any stage of the process by thorough soaking and washing in water, so that almost any degree of brown to black coloration may be achieved.

Any variety of colorful dyes can likewise be imposed on the chalcedonies and jaspers, including all the agates, to bring out interesting effects and intensify banding. Successive treatments with different dyes may produce a strangely unnatural variation in hues and shades. The artificial colors thus induced will be only as permanent as the dyes themselves; the sugar and sulfuric acid treatment is permanent.

The bona fide rock collector does not usually tamper with the natural colorations of agates or chalcedony. However, rock shop dealers often display brilliantly colored agates that no natural process would ever have produced: greens, oranges, crimsons, blues, and so on, made by dying natural chalcedonies. While dyed agates may have a dubious place in the jewelry-making profession, they are akin to the paste compounds which double for diamonds; any tampering with nature's own creations destroys the mineralogical value which the natural agates may have had originally.

Even at that, a good percentage of commercial agate used to manufacture novelties, especially the "Uruguay agate" used in making ashtrays, marbles, and other items, is processed agate. Incidentally, the Uruguayan agate found on the market is real agate that comes from the border region between Uruguay and Rio Grande do Sul, Brazil. It occurs in large masses of an uninteresting dull gray, but when treated with heat

TABLE 24
THE VARIOUS NAMES AND FORMS OF AGATE

Common Name	*Description*
Agatized wood	Petrified wood in which cellular matter has been replaced with agate, chalcedony, or jasper
Algae agate	Northern Minn. bright red jasper with cellular patterning; cf. algae jasper, Table 23
Auriferous agate	Uncommon light red stream pebbles of agate
Banded agate	Any agate with colors arranged usually in parallel bands (wavy, concentric, etc.)
Blood agate	Flesh red, pink, or salmon-colored agate (Utah)
Blue agate	Light sky blue to darker blue agate; rare
Botryoidal agate	Spherical "warts" of agate in the form of bunched grapes resting on a matrix of some other material
Bouquet agate	A very fine flower agate (*q.v.*), with flowerlike inclusions resembling arranged bouquets
Brecciated agate	Previously broken agate recemented by silica
Cat's-eye agate	An opalescent agate giving a cat's-eye effect
Chrysocolla agate	Blue green chalcedony; cf. Table 23
Circle agate	Agate with circular bandings
Cloud agate	Light gray, semitransparent chalcedony with larger spots and blotches of darker gray
Concretion agate	Agate found inside concretions; a general term
Coral agate	Agatized coral (Fla.)
Cyclops agate	An eye agate (*q.v.*), showing only one "eye"
Dendritic agate	Agate with inclusion of iron or manganese oxide resembling moss, flowers, ferns, trees, etc.
Dot agate	White chalcedony containing round colored dots
Dryhead agate	Highly colored fortification agate (*q.v.*) from the Dryhead area of northern Wyo. and southern Mont. in the extreme north of the Big Horn Basin
Ellensburg blue agate	Pale blue agate from Ellensburg, Wash., area
Eye agate	Any agate banded concentrically about a dark center
Fairburn agate	Colorful fortification agate (*q.v.*) from an area east of Fairburn, S.D.
Fairhills agate	Similar to Fairburn agate (*q.v.*) but from the Black Hills, S.D.
Fire agate	A chalcedony containing limonite (or goethite), which gives an iridescent firelike sheen
Flower agate	General term for moss agate (*q.v.*); see also bouquet and plume agate
Fluorescent agate	An agate or chalcedony containing uranium-mineral impurities which fluoresce

TABLE 24 (Cont.)

Common Name	Description
Fortification agate	Banded agates in which the bands resemble the angular structure of a fort; bands parallel but show acute cornering
Fossil agate	Any petrifaction (wood, coral, bone) in which cell replacement is with agate
Frost agate	Gray chalcedony containing white patterning resembling snow or frost
Glass agate	Exceptionally transparent agate or chalcedony
Grape agate	Wartlike clusters of small spherical mammillary agate growths attached to a matrix; cf. botryoidal agate
Half-carnelian agate	Yellow agate
Hells Canyon agate	Fortification agate (q.v.), from Hells Canyon, S.D.; similar to Fairburn agate (q.v.)
Horse Canyon agate	A fine moss agate (q.v.) from Horse Canyon (Kern County, Calif.)
Horsetail agate	Dendritic agate (q.v.) in which inclusions resemble a horse's tail (Nipomo, Calif.)
Iris agate	Banded agate exhibiting rainbow hues when thinly sliced and polished
Jasperated agate	A jasper mixed with agate; cf. jasp-agate in Table 23
Keweenaw agate	Agate from Michigan's Keweenaw Peninsula; distinctive
Lake Superior agate	Distinctive agate from the Lake Superior region and from some Iowa deposits of glacial till
Landscape agate	Gray or white chalcedony in which mossy inclusions depict rural landscapes
Macaroni agate	Milky quartz in chalcedony in which streamers have openings suggesting macaroni
Mammillary agate	Small spherulitic inclusions in agate, somewhat similar to grape agate (q.v.)
Mexican agate	Any agate from Mexico; highly colored and popular
Milk agate	Translucent chalcedony with a milky or cloudy effect
Montana (moss) agate	A notably scenic moss agate (q.v.) from southern Mont. in which inclusions make black "scenes" against a usually reddish background; translucent to nearly transparent
Moss agate	Any translucent chalcedony, agate, or other cryptocrystalline quartz containing inclusions that show mosslike, flowerlike, or treelike patterns, and fernlike or leaflike designs
Nipomo agate	A sagenite agate (q.v.) containing marcasite inclusions (San Luis Obispo County, Calif.)

TABLE 24 (Cont.)

Common Name	Description
Ochoco agate	Nodules or agate-filled thundereggs found in eastern Oregon; cf. Ochoco jasper, Table 23
Onyx agate	A banded agate in which the bands of contrasting colors occur in straight parallel layers; commonly black and white, black and red, white and red to brownish red
Oolitic agate	Agate containing grainlike inclusions resembling oolite; cf. grape agate
Pagoda stone	Agate with markings like a Chinese pagoda
Petoskey agate	Not an agate, but a fossil coral found around Petoskey, Mich., and in other Midwest localities
Pigeon blood agate	A carnelian agate found near Cisco, Utah
Pipe agate	Agate containing tubelike or pipelike inclusions
Plume agate	A moss agate (q.v.) with sagenite inclusions resembling plumes (Ore., Tex.)
Point agate	See point chalcedony in Table 23
Polka dot agate	An Oregon agate containing opaque spots in a creamlike background; reddish brown, brownish black, or red spots
Pompom agate	A Texas sagenite agate containing inclusions resembling yellow to orange pompoms or chrysanthemums
Priday Ranch agate	Plume agate (q.v.) from the Priday Ranch near Willowdale, Ore. (Fulton Agate Beds)
Rainbow agate	See iris agate
Redtop moss agate	Montana moss agate (q.v.) that is red at the top (or bottom, however cut) and containing dendritic inclusions
Ribbon agate	Agate containing ribbonlike bands of alternating color; differentiated from ribbon jasper (q.v. in Table 23) by its translucency
Ring agate	Agate with concentric ring banding; less distinctive color contrasts than eye agate (q.v.)
River agate	Miscellaneous agate or jasper pebbles from stream gravels; a general term
Rose agate	Gray or rose banded agate from Brewster County, Tex.
Ruin agate	Agate with fortification patterning resembling ruins; cf. brecciated agate
Sagenite agate	Clear chalcedony containing tiny needles or inclusions of actinolite, goethite, rutile, tourmaline, etc., often densely packed
Sard agate	Sard or sardonyx (q.v. Table 23)
Sardonyx agate	Chalcedony in which straight parallel bands are of reddish brown to brown, alternating with other colors

TABLE 24 (Cont.)

Common Name	Description
Scenic agate	See landscape agate
Seam agate	Agate found in thin veins in sedimentary rocks
Seaweed agate	See sagenite or moss agate; inclusions resemble seaweed palms, fronds, etc.
Shell agate	Agate containing silicified mollusk shells
Star agate	Agate showing star-shaped figures, rather than "asterism"
State Park agate	Fortification agate similar to Fairburn agate (q.v.) from Custer State Park, S.D.
Sweetwater agate	Dark gray chalcedony nodules containing dendritic growths in star patterns; fluorescent; from Wyo.
Tempskya agate	Agatized *Tempskya* tree fern; a petrified wood
Tepee Canyon agate	See Fairburn agate; from Tepee Canyon, S.D.
Texas agate	Any agate from Texas; more specifically a jasp-agate (q.v. Table 23) from Pecos River localities
Thunderegg agate	Agate filling of interiors of thundereggs, especially those occurring in central Ore. and in N.M., usually banded, rarely carnelian
Thundereggs	Volcanic bombs or nodules filled with agate
Topographic agate	Agate containing markings resembling a topographic map; cf. fortification agate
Tube agate	Agate containing tubelike inclusions that may be hollow; rather rare
Turritella agate	Agate containing silicified Turritella shells
Turtleback agate	Clear chalcedony exhibiting a layered effect, resembling a turtle's back, when slabbed and polished
Variegated agate	A moss agate (q.v.), in which the inclusions and colors exhibit no pattern or scenes
Wart agate	See grape agate; wartlike or mammillary protuberances or small spherical growths on colored agate
Wascoite	Part-agate with variegated designs (Wasco County, Ore.)
Wax agate	Yellow or yellowish red chalcedony of waxy luster
White moss agate	Agate with large blotches of white inclusions
Yellowstone agate	See Montana moss agate; from Yellowstone River area
Zigzag agate	Brecciated fortification agate, resilicified

and chemicals, it produces many colorful varieties which can be cut and polished and sold commercially.

OPAL, QUEEN OF THE GEMS

Of all the colorful gems and gemstones which have intrigued man since the Old Stone Age, opal has remained consistently at the top of the collector's list. Precious opal, with its brilliant rainbow play of fiery colors, is worth more than diamonds or emeralds on a carat-for-carat basis. Nodules of Virgin Valley (Nevada) opal only an inch or two in diameter command prices above the million-dollar mark. Yet opal is only a silica gel of the quartz family, an amorphous translucent substance laced with water. Prized precious opal comes primarily from three areas: South Australia, parts of Mexico, and the Virgin Valley in Nevada. In many other places throughout most of America's fifty states less-valued opal and opalite occur to delight the heart of collectors.

CHARACTERISTICS OF OPAL

Opal is formed when silica (SiO_2) is deposited as a gel without any definite crystal structure. Opal is hydrous silica; during its solidification, the mass of the material is penetrated by a maze of microscopic fractures. These minute cracks are later filled with additional silica that differs in water content and, slightly, in density, thereby setting up the internal conditions which give rise to the remarkable play of rainbow colors (opalescence) which characterize the gem.

Nevada precious opal was formed during the petrifaction of an ancient forest, when the bark of trees was replaced by amorphous silica after destruction of the forest by volcanic action. In the same general region there are other deposits of a green fire opal that was not a fossilizing agent, attesting to the fact that in Virgin Valley at least the magmatic waters associated with the regional volcanism were the cause of the opal deposits.

Although composed entirely of silicon dioxide, opal is not as hard as the other quartz family minerals, varying from 5.5 to 6.5, compared with quartz at 7. This seemingly modest difference becomes extremely great when the logarithmic scale of hardness is considered: a faceted quartz crystal is actually hundreds of times harder than precious opal. With due caution against abrasion, an opal cabochon will nevertheless last indefinitely, its flashing internal fires seemingly inexhaustible.

Most varieties of opal contain up to 20 percent water, but precious opal contains less than 10 percent. This water is not in the form of water of crystallization attached to molecules of silicon dioxide, but rather of very finely disseminated true water. Hence some mineralogists, in trying to explain why certain opals gradually lose their fiery colors, assert that there is a tendency for opals to dry out slowly through simple evaporation.

Many techniques of "preserving" opals have been tried, including submersion in water, in a mineral oil (the Smithsonian Institution in Washington, D.C., has done this with exceptionally fine rough opals), and in glycerine. Although these liquids do enhance the display of cabinet-specimen opal, there is no real evidence that they actually preserve the opalescent effect.

Even the finest specimens of precious or semiprecious opal have a tendency to "craze"—to develop myriads of tiny surface cracks—when subjected to lapidary treatment. Crazing is possibly caused by the internal water's expanding from the heat generated by grinding and polishing. The consensus of gem and mineral collectors is that rough field specimens of opal should be retained as cabinet specimens rather than being converted into jewelry. It is so disappointingly easy for the home lapidary to ruin good opal that, with rare exceptions, the processing of precious opal, at least, should be left to experts. As cabinet specimens, rough opal commands the highest prices, and it never fails to intrigue the observer with its play of colors.

SUBVARIETIES OF OPAL

Opalized deposits occur in many parts of North America, wherever water solutions of silica, especially hot water, once permeated the crustal strata. Only when the material exhibits the characteristic flashing play of colors is it termed opal or precious opal. Most of the remaining deposits known from at least fourteen states contain opalite or opalized wood, the latter being ancient wood silicified by opal gel.

Opal itself is semitranslucent, and it appears almost as if you could look right down into the heart of the mineral and see its fires at their source. Opalite and opalized wood are completely opaque, distinguishable from agate primarily by their lustrous sheen and waxy surface. The characteristics of the subvarieties of opal include its gemstone hardness (somewhat harder than precious opal), its amorphous texture, its generally conchoidal fracture like the other quartz family cryptocrystalline gemstones, and its lustrous appearance, like silk under a subdued light.

Both opalite and opalized woods are usually stained various shades of yellow, orange, tan, brown, and red from impurities that permeated the original gel—mostly iron minerals. The commercial value of the subvarieties varies considerably; most opalite comes in large masses or in veins and is commonly used for garden rock in flower beds and rock terraces. Opalized wood, especially that from south-central Washington State, is a true gemstone worth many dollars per pound; it is used for lapping into bookends, paperweights, lamp bases, and other more massive objects.

The varieties and subvarieties of opal are described in Table 25.

TABLE 25
OPAL AND ITS VARIETIES

Common Name	Description
Agate opal	An opal, rather rare, with agatelike banding; some agate may be banded with opal
Agaty potch	Opalized potch in which parallel bands of different-color hues appear like the bands in agate
Amatite	Siliceous sinter; also called pearlite
Amber opal	Opal of golden or amber color
Angel stone	Silicified clay or sandstone often occurring just above a deposit of opal; often contains fractures permeated with precious opal (q.v.)
Azules	Mexican term for blue opal
Black opal	A costly opal in which the background color is dark gray to black, exhibiting subdued to brilliant fires; subject to cracking when sawed
Cachalong	A pale bluish white, opaque to semitranslucent, porcelainlike opal, sometimes banded with chalcedony; used for cutting cameos; cachalong is somewhat porous and readily absorbs moisture
Candlebox opal	General term for low-grade opal
Chloropal	A green opal similar to prase opal (q.v.)
Common opal	Any variety of opal or opalite with no commercial value or real mineralogical interest
Fire opal	Transparent to translucent red to orange opal with or without any play of internal color
Flame opal	A fire opal (q.v.) containing brilliant red color plays in rather irregular streaks
Flash opal	A fire opal (q.v.) in which the play of color is dominant only when viewed in one direction
Gelite	A secondary accessory opal or chalcedony deposited usually in sandstone fractures
Glass opal	Another term for hyalite (q.v.)
Gold opal	Amber or golden opal
Harlequin opal	White opal with patches of close-set mosaics in color, like the clown suit of a harlequin
Honey opal	Honey-colored opal; amber potch
Hungarian opal	Trade name for any white opal
Hyacinth	Reddish brown opal; not to be confused with the biblical essonite garnet (hyacinth)
Hyalite	Colorless common opal; cf. jelly and water opal
Hydrophane	Opal which shows rainbow colors only when immersed in water

TABLE 25 (Cont.)

Common Name	Description
Jasper opal	Opaque common yellow brown opal resembling jasper; really a jasper in which the cementing agent is opal instead of quartz
Jelly opal	Colorless common opal; cf. hyalite
Levin opal	Opal characterized by long, thin flashes of color
Light opal	Opal backgrounded in white, pale cream, or milky hues
Lithoxyl	Opalized wood showing the cellular structure
Mexican opal	Any opal from Mexico, especially the brilliant fire opal (q.v.), of cherry red to orange fires; this is the only opal considered by jewelers to be a true "precious stone"
Milk opal	A pale cream or milky opal
Moss opal	Common opal containing black fernlike dendritic inclusions
Mountain opal	Opal occurring in igneous rocks of mountains; a general term
Noble opal	Same as precious opal (q.v.)
Onyx opal	Common opal with parallel bandings
Opal agate	An opal banded with alternating layers of opal and chalcedony
Opaline	Opal matrix (q.v.)
Opalite	Impure colored varieties of common opal; opaque
Opalized wood	Petrified wood in which the replacing mineral is common or, more rarely, precious opal
Opal matrix	The country rock surrounding an opal inclusion
Perlmutter opal	Common opal with a luster like mother-of-pearl
Pinpoint opal (pinfire opal)	A variety of opal containing pinpoints of fiery flashes; cf. harlequin opal
Pipe opal	A naturally occurring opal cast of long, narrow, cigar-shaped steam vents in sandstone
Pitch opal	Yellowish to brownish common opal with a pitchy luster
Potch	A valueless, colorless opal; an Australian term
Prase opal	Opal colored green from chromium minerals; native to Australia, Brazil, and Hungary
Precious opal	Any opal showing brilliant fiery plays of color; technically restricted to Mexican fire opal (q.v.)
Quincite (quinzite)	Rose-colored common opal
Radio opal	Smoky common opal discolored by radiolaria or organic inclusions in the original gel
Red flash opal	Brilliant red precious opal (q.v.), in which fiery flashes appear and disappear abruptly

TABLE 25 (Cont.)

Common Name	Description
Resin opal	Honey yellow to ocher yellow common opal having a resinous luster
Roebling opal	Proper name given to the largest (2,610 carats) known chunk of precious opal in the world, now in the U.S. National Museum at the Smithsonian Institution. The Roebling opal is a piece of Virgin Valley opalized wood displaying brilliant red and green fire; it is sometimes called the Roebling black opal and is valued at more than $250,000
Rose opal	See quincite
Rough opal	Any unpolished, field-run piece of opal; a general term
Rubolite	Reddish to red common opal
Sobrisky opal	Opal occurring only at Lead Pipe Springs, near Death Valley, Calif.
Sun opal	See fire opal
Volcanic opal	See mountain opal
Water opal	See hyalite; a misnomer for moonstone, which is orthoclase feldspar
Wax opal	Yellow opal with a waxy luster
White opal	Any precious opal with a light-color base
Wood opal	See opalized wood
Yowah nuts	Small ironstone nodules containing precious opal

OCCURRENCE OF OPAL

Although opal is abundant and widespread, only a very small percentage can be classed as precious and somewhat more as semiprecious. Even colorful varieties are scarce, but common opal, like many other quartz family minerals, often replaces wood during the petrifaction process. Common opal occurs in practically all geologic horizons.

Nearly all varieties of precious opal display stronger flashes of color or fire in one direction than in another. For best appraisal it is expedient to immerse suspected precious opals in glycerine or water and view them edge on, whenever possible. Thus viewed, the Virgin Valley opals display the widest range of colors.

Of all the gems and gemstones, only the opal displays a constant shifting of color as the stone is tilted. This play of color gives the mineral its beauty and commercial value. The colors are caused by light rays penetrating the translucent surface and being broken up into rainbow hues as the rays are reflected back as pure prismatic colors. In order to cut an opal to bring out the strongest play of hues, it is first necessary to determine the orientation by which the prismatic colors are most effectively seen.

The beginning collector may sometimes confuse the luster and color play of true opals with color phenomena manifested by some other gemstones, such as adularescence, aventurescence, iridescence, labradorescence, and schiller, described in Chapter 4.

PETRIFIED WOOD

As a mineral phenomenon, petrified or fossil wood has never been well understood. Primitive tribes all over the world developed theories to explain the presence of the substance that looks like wood, including bark, knots, limbs, roots, and trunks, yet is generally as hard and incombustible as quartz.

The Navahos of Arizona and New Mexico considered that the wonderfully colored agatized logs they found scattered all over their lands were the bones of the monster Yeitzo, who was destroyed by the sun, and that the congealed lavas of the same arid lunarlike landscape were the monster's blood.

Petrified wood occurs over nearly the entire earth from the Antarctic continent to Greenland. In America some form of petrified wood can be found in nearly every county and state and somewhere among the gravels of almost every stream. Wherever the geologic conditions were right, woody matter was replaced in a cell-for-cell oxidation-reduction process in which any of some twenty petrifying minerals contributed the necessary preservative.

THE PETRIFACTION OF WOOD

As far as the gemstone fancier is concerned, only three types of fossil wood have lapidary value: agatized, opalized, and calcified. The first two forms can conveniently be lumped under the general term silicified wood. Replacement of woody tissues with calcite is much rare and less colorful, although occurrences of calcified wood tell us a good deal about the ancient plant life of the Paleozoic era. Coal balls found in coal seams everywhere reveal an amazing amount of information about Carboniferous period vegetation. Not of gemstone quality by any stretch of the imagination, the calcified plant remains found in coal balls make excellent cabinet specimens for any complete mineral collection.*

The general term petrifaction applies to all forms of petrified and fossilized wood, most of which is uninteresting to the gem and mineral collector. Petrifying agents most commonly encountered are silica, calcium carbonate, magnesium carbonate, and iron sulfide, the last being either pyrite or marcasite. During the process of petrifaction, woody

* See Jay E. Ransom, *Petrified Forest Trails* (Mentone, Calif.: Gembooks, 1955).

tissues which some cataclysm of nature caused to become deeply buried under sediments beyond the reach of oxygen were permeated with mineralized solutions. The minerals may be chemical compounds of the carbonates, sulfates, phosphates, silicates, and others. The silicates, which are reduced to silicon dioxide, usually bring about petrifaction without combining with any other fossilizing agent. Iron compounds, however, reduce through reaction with hydrogen sulfide (one of the products of decay) to pyrite or marcasite, and these may combine with calcification. One or the other is likely to predominate in the fossil product.

Since two things cannot occupy the same space at the same time, during petrifaction mineral substances deposited in place of the wood cells must drive out the volatile organic materials, such as gases, oils, protoplasm, and water. Not everything is removed, however. When even the hardest silicified wood is dissolved in hydrofluoric acid, some of the ancient original constituents of the wood, including cellulose and lignin, can be shown to have been preserved as organic material.

Petrified wood in the collector's lexicon usually refers to the gemstone agatized and opalized woods; all the other varieties of petrifaction are commonly termed fossil wood. Silicified woods show a multiplicity of colors, enough in certain varieties to delight the heart of the most discriminating gemstone collector. The colors, which result from mineral impurities in the percolating solutions, range from pure white and shades of gray to amber, yellow, brown, red, and jet black with many combinations usually found in the finest gem woods.

Fossil woods are much softer than petrified woods, usually turn white on weathering, and are extremely fragile to powdery. Iron is a frequent impurity and lends rich reds and browns to silicified wood. In the Mountain states the uranium mineral carnotite is highly concentrated in woody tissues, giving them a canary-yellow color but leaving the wood extremely soft and fragile. Brown colors are caused by the retention of humic compounds, and wood that appears to be jet black is often only a light brown when viewed in thin cross sections.

CHEMICAL CHANGES DURING PETRIFACTION

All petrified or fossilized woods reveal that the wood cell walls have undergone a certain amount of original decomposition, perhaps analogous to the chemical changes that occur during the formation of coal. Early decay first disintegrates the softer protoplasmic cell contents, with subsequent breaking down of the cellulose, probably by hydrolysis.

The process may further involve the lignin, leaving a residue of nearly pure carbon, or the disintegration may stop at almost any stage. Petrified wood in which the cell walls have been reduced to microscopic layers of coal is common, especially where the preserving mineral is iron pyrite.

Cellulose itself, along with other compounds that make up woody tissue, is extremely insoluble, and just how silica or other mineral replacement takes place is still something of a mystery.

While many petrified woods examined under the microscope reveal an almost completely mineralized cellular structure, there may have been some decomposition from fungus action or hydrolysis prior to mineral infiltration. Many fossil wood specimens that are grayish or white on the outside are black on the inside. The whitish outer layers intergrade with the darker interior, extending deeper along cracks. This may be the result of weathering accompanied by hydrolysis of the organic matter in the original wood.

AGATIZED AND OPALIZED WOOD

Volcanic ash and hot springs magmatic waters provided the raw silica which converted many great forests in the western states into colorful silicified examples of gem-grade petrified wood. The majority of the forests grew during the Mesozoic and early to middle Cenozoic ages. The great standing petrified forests of Yellowstone National Park and adjoining areas of central Washington, Nevada, and much of the vast Colorado Plateau region were petrified through the action of ash silicates.

Western woods were mainly agatized, opalized, or preserved by carnotite during the long ages of mountain building and volcanism. Such woods are comparatively young by geologic standards. By contrast, the oldest fossil forests in the world seem to have been Devonian treelike seed ferns (*Pteridospermophyta*) which grew to heights of 30 and 40 feet along the brackish shores of an ancient sea that periodically inundated the region around Gilboa, New York. Three such forests, one on top of the other, have been exposed at Manorkill Falls, with remnants of stumps 3 to 4 feet in diameter rooted in shale. The locally well-known Naples Tree (an *Archaeosigillaria*) grew to a height of about 25 feet more than 400 million years ago. A sizable section of its trunk is mounted in the New York State Museum in Albany. These extremely ancient fossil woods were also preserved by silica but lack any of the attractive colors found in the far western, much younger woods.

A relatively modern (Tertiary) petrified forest once grew across the southeastern states and is especially well known from the Lafayette formation in Mississippi, with lesser quantities weathering out of the Wilcox and later Tertiary sediments. Near Flora, about 18 miles northwest of the Mississippi state capital of Jackson, a large petrified forest field once showed logs and tree fragments in varying stages of disintegration lying scattered over a large area. The largest silicified log was 20 feet long and had a diameter of about 6 feet. In the northeastern part of the state whole forests were fossilized by iron oxide, too soft and of an unattractive dark-brown color which did not interest collectors generally. But often the larger chunks of the fossil wood contain cavities and crevices in which water-clear quartz crystals of small size occur—well worth the collector's search.

Silicified woods reveal several forms of silica, but only the crypto-crystalline and amorphous (opal) varieties commonly preserve the original tissues in microscopic detail. Crystal formation destroys cell structure through rupture. However, beautiful quartz and amethyst crystals are often found in cavities in petrified logs, such as in knotholes, hollow stems, or large cracks. Both the Arizona Petrified Forest and the stone forests of Yellowstone National Park are noted for their incidental crystal gems. In fact, Amethyst Mountain in Yellowstone Park received its name from the beautifully colored amethyst crystals found in the silicified logs lying scattered over its slopes. Unfortunately, or perhaps fortunately for posterity, gem collecting is not permitted in any national monument or park.

Agate is one of the commonest petrifying agents which gives to "wood" some of its finest colors and textures. Some of the best-known and loveliest forms of agatized wood are collected regularly from Wyoming's Eden Valley, where fragments of logs weather out of sedimentary formations of Eocene age. In Arizona the petrified forests which weather out of Triassic and Jurassic sandstones contain not only an abundance of richly colored agate but also chalcedony and jasper as petrifying agents. Nevada's petrified wood is extraordinarily rich in fire opal, with cones and small limbs well preserved and marked with the rainbow hues of precious opal.

IDENTIFYING PETRIFIED OR FOSSILIZED WOODS

Unlike nearly all other gem and mineral species, which carry proper names and identifying characteristics, petrified and fossilized woods require that the purist not only be able to distinguish among the petrifying agents but arrve at some identification of what genus or species of plant the original living material was. This is not easy, even for a paleobotanist who specializes in fossil vegetation and ancient plant lfe.

There are several excellent botany textbooks devoted to the technical methods of identifying modern living woods, and in some instances, they may have value in paleobotany. However, the identification of "stonie wood," as Merry Old Englanders called it during the Middle Ages, is something that even the most highly trained experts often argue over. About all that is really necessary is that the perspicacious collector be able to determine to what family or type the fossil wood may belong— oak, elm, pine, redwood, walnut, and so forth. This simple preliminary identification may often be made with an ordinary hand lens on the polished surface of the specimen.

The correct determination of the precise species of wood is a wholly different matter and a complicated problem much beyond the scope of most collectors. Moreover, the identification of fossil woods may be further complicated by the fact that some, indeed most, varieties are entirely extinct, with no surviving modern counterparts for comparison purposes. Owing to the difficulty of identifying most petrified or fossilized woods, it is generally customary to collect and study the fossil leaves, stems, cones, or other fragments that may also be present in the geologic formation from which a particular kind of wood has weathered out.

Another complicating factor is that the original wood structure may be wholly lacking in petrifaction or that it may be present only in a distorted form. It is the exception, rather than the rule, to find petrified wood with perfectly preserved tissue structure. If the structures are wholly gone, it may be impossible to arrive at an exact identification of the specimen.

COMMON PETRIFIED WOODS

Only silica and, rarely, calcite replacements of wood tissues produce petrified wood of a hardness capable of being cut and polished into bookends, paperweights, coffee table inlays, spheres, and other products of the lapidary. Silicified woods are abundant all over North America, although the colorful examples occur primarily west of the Mississippi. Softer, usually less colorful, and often extremely fragile specimens of fossilized wood are produced by replacement with aragonite, azurite, barite, calcite, carnotite, chalcolite, chalcopyrite, chlorite, cinnabar, dolomite, fluorite, galena, gypsum, hematite, limonite, malachite, marcasite, phosphorite, pyrite, sphalerite, sulfur, or talc.

For display purposes, the collector should certainly include on his label the type of petrifying agent that preserved the wood specimen, even if he is unable to denominate the specimen itself as anything other than petrified wood.

Among the fossilized varieties of petrifactions probably carnotite wood ranks highest among the collector's specimens. During the uranium boom of the 1950's, eager prospectors sought the rich canary-yellow, powder-soft fossil wood throughout the vast Four Corners region of Colorado, Utah, Arizona, and New Mexico, as well as in much of Wyoming east of the Continental Divide. Along with the uranium mineral, vanadium and radium minerals also show a propensity for becoming concentrated in woody tissue, and carnotite logs usually contain both vanadium and radium. Each such log represented a literal financial bonanza for its discoverer.

Two carnotite logs found near Calamity Gulch, Colorado, brought their exuberant finders a cool $350,000 from the Atomic Energy Commission. A carnotite log was to a uranium prospector what a pocket, or vug, of solid gold crystals and nuggets was to the gold seeker of the mid-nineteenth century. Uranium is no longer such a desperately sought strategic element as it was after World War II and the development of the atomic bomb, but a carnotite log found today will still bring a very high price at the smelter for its uranium, vanadium, and radium content.

Some types of petrified wood can be identified as to general family at a glance. For instance, conifers and hardwoods will show cross striations even in rough specimens, an easy way to distinguish the woods from similarly hard and colored chert or onyx. The cross or fanlike striations are much finer than the annular ring growths and fan out from the center.

WESTERN VS. EASTERN WOODS

The famed opalized woods of southeastern and central Washington State have turned out under scientific study to be mainly petrified swamp cypress, with lesser amounts of petrified walnut, hickory, and persimmon wood. It is evident that a mixed hardwood forest covered a great region of low-lying rolling plains subsequently covered with volcanic ash from the rising Cascade Mountains to the west 12 to 20 million years ago. In the same general region lies the spectacular Ginkgo Petrified Forest, set aside as a national monument from which collecting is forever prohibited. The ginkgo tree became extinct in North America millions of years ago but persisted in remote parts of China into modern times. Today ginkgo trees are planted in many American parks and estate gardens. A very ancient tree, having originated as a maidenhair tree more than 200 million years ago, the ginkgo is a lone survivor of a very large class of gymnosperms with fan-shaped leaves, sparse branches, and yellow apricotlike fruit.

Most of the colorful Arizona petrified woods seem to be the fossil remains of an ancient pine—the *Araucaria*—with its origins in the Triassic period some 230 million years ago. This pine still survives in the Andes but is extinct in North America. Farther west along the Colorado River boundary between Arizona and California are found great quantities of "petrified palm root" or "wood," really the root stocks of cycadeoids and other primitive palm trees. The material is hard and durable, cuts easily, and takes a high polish but is not very colorful. The original cellular structure is plainly visible. In the same area, weathering out of the sandy benches above the Colorado River, are other, relatively uncolored examples of wood locally called ironwood. This material rings like a bell when struck with a hammer and is so hard that is quickly dulls a diamond saw.

Eastern petrified woods occur in some 30 species in the great geologic formation known as the Catskill delta of northern and eastern Pennsylvania and adjacent ridges of New York State. In addition to the genera named previously, the main constituents include the fern *Archaeopteris,* and the large forest trees of *Aneurophyton* and *Callixylon,* all of

Devonian age. Since they have all been extinct for hundreds of millions of years, there are no common names, only the Latin terms assigned to them by paleobotanists.

Throughout the Mesozoic era and contemporary with the dinosaurs flourished the cycads, a species of ancient plant between a tree fern and a true palm tree, belonging to the Order Cycadeoidales. Petrified remains of this primitive tree are found in many places scattered all over America. The finest of all fossil cycad forests have been set apart as the Fossil Cycad National Monument in the lower Lakota formation of the Rim country just south of the Dakota Black Hills. The ancestors of all modern flowering plants, the cycads reveal true gemstone hardness and beauty in the forms of flowers, foliage, and mature seed cones, along with the downed trunks.

All during the early periods of the Cenozoic, when the Mississippi River was slowly extending its vast delta southward into the ancient Gulf of Mexico, which once reached all the way to present-day Ohio and Illinois, its tributaries brought down huge quantities of driftwood of hundreds of species of plant life from both east and west. This debris was buried under the accumulating sands, muds, marls, and clays also carried by the great river. Specimens now found weathering out of the enormously widespread Wilcox formation, which extends entirely across the southern tier of states, constitute the Wilcox flora, consisting of entire petrified tree trunks, root masses, limbs, seed pods, leaves, twigs, and other plant parts of a basically dense tropical to semitropical forest that covered much of Tertiary America.

Without exception, every state affords a seemingly inexhaustible supply of petrified and fossilized woods in an endless variety of types, colors, and degrees of hardness.

WORM-BORED PETRIFIED WOOD

Ranking high on the collector's list of prize cabinet specimens are pieces of silicified woods that reveal petrified worm borings, found frequently wherever agatized and opalized woods occur. Collectors generally refer to such pieces as teredo wood, although any number of species of cellulose-eating animals may have been responsible for the borings that twisted through the wood and were later filled with silica.

There are two general types of petrified wood showing worm holes: (1) specimens with small holes, presumably made by termites working on dry land or similar water worms or insects working in fresh shallow waters and (2) the marine wood borers, or teredos. The marine worms or mollusks generally completely riddled the original wood, leaving comparatively large holes that can range up to a quarter-inch in diameter.

Gravel pits near Mandan, North Dakota, have yielded many interesting examples of worm-bored petrified wood. In Ransom County specimens clearly show that marine mollusks, similar to present-day teredos, were going about their work of demolishing cellulose more than 100 million years ago. The modern teredo is also known as the ship worm because it attacks wooden boat hulls and pilings. Oregon and Washington teredo-bored woods seem to have been conifer ancestors of the modern redwoods, since the teredos which made the borings were of the redwood type.

Just as in any modern forest downed logs reveal worm borings filled with the animal's excrement, or castings, so also do the petrified woods. The castings are themselves petrified with the same silica that preserved the logs, a remarkable example of nature's fidelity to detail.

COLLECTOR INTEREST IN PETRIFIED WOOD

Although Tiffany & Company, a jewel firm of New York City, demonstrated the beauty of petrified wood at the World's Fair of 1900, interest among gem and mineral collectors has remained primarily a specialization of those living west of the Mississippi River, where the best collecting grounds lie. In the eastern states petrified wood lacks beauty and detailed form; it has value mostly as a cabinet curiosity, although its scientific worth may be much greater. In the west petrified wood is predominantly gem quality.

One of the disadvantages of processing petrified wood is that it requires rather massive equipment; pieces found in the field come in large chunks, whole logs, and limb sections that may dwarf every other kind of mineral and gemstone. Saws for slabbing, lap wheels for polishing, and grinders for rough work must all be rather large and cumbersome, and these take a good deal of workshop space.

Unlike faceted gems, rough opals, or other cabinet display specimens, the finished petrified wood art objects (or slabs, slices, cubes, spheres, etc.) require fairly large-scale display space. Doing justice to the beauty of silicified wood requires that slabs be cut and polished in sizable chunks measuring many inches across and weighing pounds rather than ounces or carats. This requirement rather eliminates collectors whose living and working quarters are confined to apartments.

Nevertheless, petrified wood, whether of gemstone quality or of purely fossil interest, remains one of the major fields of interest to gem and mineral collectors everywhere. What cannot be processed at home can be purchased from any rock dealer. A lovely, highly polished specimen or two of quality agatized or opalized wood adds conversational vitality to any gem collection.

chapter 10

Cutting and Polishing Gems and Gemstones

Sooner or later every gem and mineral collector decides he wants to get the very best out of his most beautiful stones. To do so he must master many of the traditional techniques of cutting, grinding, and polishing. By 1800 a few books of instruction and some lapidary equipment could be purchased in Europe, but it has been largely in the last quarter-century that many new ideas and inventions have made the lapidary arts widely available, and thousands of gemstone collectors have become competent craftsmen in hard, lovely stone.

The lapidaries of the past more or less limited themselves to laboriously carving by hand goblets, bowls, statuary, seals, and signet rings and polishing them to a fine gloss. They also gradually learned to lay out, cut, and polish the rounded oval gemstones we call cabochons. The precise faceting of very hard gem brilliants came much later. Cabochons and faceted gems are still the most popular and widespread among gemstone fanciers for jewelry, since such workmanship requires much less skill or handwork than do carvings.

Actually the modern amateur lapidary is not a true worker in hard stone compared to the traditional artisan. Gem cutting is not nearly as difficult as it was before the era of powered equipment and commercially manufactured sawing, grinding, and polishing machines. Recently a new technique has developed of simply tumbling rough fragments of gemstones in a revolving cylinder, wooden cask, old rubber tire mounted on rollers, or even a cast-iron drum—all using inexpensive abrasives and water. Although the finished stones—called baroque gemstones—possess great beauty and have gemological interest, their processing can hardly be termed lapidary work. It is too automatic, requiring absolutely no skill but simply following directions, buying the proper grits, paying the electric bill, and waiting out the weeks while the tumblers do all the work.

The type of material available for processing dictates how it is to be handled. Clear crystals or fragments of crystals large enough for handling—minimum size about one-eighth inch diameter—are most often used for faceting into cut gems. Faceting means grinding small flat faces, or facets, at precisely dictated angles one with the other all over the surface to bring out the light-breaking or light-reflecting properties of the gem. This causes a crystal to become more brilliant and sparkling than it would be if cut simply cabochon—that is, as an oval, rounded, or flat-faced form. Faceting with the precisely controlled machinery available today is much less of an art than a mechanical skill that increases with experience. The only real requirement from the lapidary himself is a vast amount of patience. Because faceted gems are cut to predetermined norms, very little art and originality are involved.

Not all clear crystals should be faceted. Many kinds contain interesting inclusions—slender needles of rutile, asbestos, tourmaline, or chlorite, among others. Such crystals are best displayed when cut cabochon. The cabochon cut is also best for bringing out the asterism that occurs in some star rubies and sapphires, as well as the cat's-eye effect of chrysoberyl and many lustrous effects of more opaque gemstones. By far the greatest number of gem cutters prefer making cabochons. More artistry is involved. The size and shape of a cabochon can vary greatly to bring out the stone's coloration and patterning, and cabochon cutting lends itself to a much wider variety of materials than does faceting.

Other objects also lend themselves readily to the lapidary's appreciation of form and beauty: carvings by machine and hand, slabbing and polishing for cabinet display, mosaic inlay work for table tops, and a host of other creations dear to the hearts of collectors. A visit to any gem and mineral show will provide a wealth of ideas for the beginning lapidary to consider for his own materials.

Once considered the highly specialized and difficult prerogative of professional jewelers and artisans, fine working in hard gemstones has become a major part of the hobby of gem and mineral collecting. This chapter, of course, cannot offer the detailed techniques of lapidary work but only suggest what can be done. Some excellent, thoroughly detailed, and comprehensive references on gem cutting are included in the bibliography in Appendix IV. Those by Quick, Leiper, and Sinkankas are probably the best for the amateur lapidary.

EQUIPMENT

Lapidary equipment in all sizes, shapes, degrees of complexity, and price ranges can be bought at almost any rock dealer's shop. It is not a good idea to take a dealer's advice on what to buy; the best way to get acquainted with and understand what equipment, including motors, you will need is to visit an experienced rock collector-turned-lapidary. See what equipment experience has taught him to concentrate on. Get him to explain the whys and wherefores behind each item and to let you saw, cut, grind, and polish a specimen while he explains every step.

One of your biggest hurdles may be space. You can get small equipment that produces so little noise that neighbors in the next apartment cannot hear you at work (though motors may interfere with television reception). On the other hand, if you have plenty of workshop or basement space, you can spread out a wide variety of specialized equipment and be little concerned with the noise level.

It is seldom necessary to purchase outright every piece of equipment to start up lapidary operations. Many of today's modern secondary schools have already installed a full complement of saws, grinders, and polishing buffs and welcome outsiders to use them, often establishing evening adult education classes for exactly that purpose. Many beginners and even advanced amateurs willing to trade rocks or donate halves, slabs, or slices from their cuttings to the good cause of friendship are invited to use others' equipment. It is a good idea to join a lapidary or gem and mineral organization, whose perpetual watchword is generosity.

Many amateur lapidaries make all their own equipment from scrap parts. For instance, electric motors taken from old refrigerators or washing machines are commonly used, since the maximum horsepower needed is from one-eighth to one-quarter horsepower. Many lapidary equipment manufacturers make such components as shafts, laps, ball-bearing arbors, diamond-saw parts, and so on, which can be purchased separately as needed at modest prices and incorporated directly into your otherwise home-grown equipment. Outlets for secondhand lapidary machines are listed in the yellow pages of most telephone books.

THE HOME WORKSHOP

Once you have analyzed your space requirements, you are ready to set up your equipment. Placement of the individual components is important, since sawing, grinding, and sanding operations can be messy, requiring a steady small supply of running water and to assist in the operations. Today dry grinding is out and water is in, so a sink with running water should be nearby, for periodically washing specimens for close examination, and for removing the inevitable grit and muck that will get on hands, forearms, and especially beneath the fingernails. If, like most lapidaries, you feed house-supply water to your equipment via small-diameter copper tubing, you will need a catch basin underneath with runoff capabilities. Where ready connection to a house faucet is lacking, an overhead container can be used—a large glass jar or galvanized can—filled from the garden hose, as required. You can recirculate water in a closed system, like an outdoor fish pond fountain, with a small electrically driven pump.

Polishing and buffing equipment should be placed a good distance away so that it will not become clogged with abrasive dust that could scratch a gemstone piece during the final stages of polishing.

Proper lighting is a necessity, especially for the final stages of shaping and polishing. An overhead light casts too many harsh shadows. A lamp with a reflector bulb of at least 150-watt capacity will provide clear illumination at critical times and places. Too high a wattage will, however, tire the eyes. For trimming and slab sawing you will not require more than 60 to 100 watts, so place the lamp about two feet away. Faceting, because of its close tolerances, requires about 100 watts well shaded from the eyes.

An electric motor is bound to set up some vibration, and a table top acts much like an oversize sounding board capable of transmitting noise into the flooring and adjoining walls. To reduce the noise level, insulate table legs from the floor with pads of sponge rubber or felt and the motorized equipment from the table with squares of an insulating board like Celotex or pads of sponge rubber or sponge plastic.

No matter what type of lapidary equipment is used, it should be mounted on as stout and rigid a table or bench as possible; additional bracing may even be required to cut down vibration. Finally, since all stages of lapidary work create dust, grit, grime, and debris, provision must be made for disposal. Periodic washing of tables, benches, shelving, and the floor will also keep the work area in shipshape condition. Cleanliness is not only an important part of producing fine gems; it is the hallmark of professionalism.

OPERATION DIAMOND SAW

Nature provides field-run rock specimens in all sizes and shapes, most of them entirely too large and all of them always too rough. Therefore, the first step in lapidary work is to saw the rocks down to a workable size and thickness or to an approximation of the rough blank. Three general sizes of diamond saw blades charged with minute particles of commercial diamond (bort) are available at any rock shop at relatively modest prices. Large blades are used for slabbing rough stones into blocks or pieces, middle-sized blades for trimming to the rough outlines of the finished product, and small blades for fine sectioning and edging. Each blade is limited to a certain number of square inches of sawing before it has to be recharged with additional abrasive.

Various grades of diamond powder are sold by the carat at lapidary supply houses. Actually, a very little bort, or carbonado as the impure forms of diamond are called, goes a surprisingly long way in terms of the number of square inches of gemstone being sawed. The blade itself does not do any cutting; its notched edge simply holds the diamond powder, which wears through even the hardest rock with remarkable ease.

THE SAW AND ITS MACHINERY

Most amateur lapidaries use a circular saw blade made of soft steel, with variously sized diameters and arbor holes to fit different diameter shafts. An abrasive charge may run from large mesh (50 to 100) to small mesh (120 to 250) grit, mesh referring to the number of holes per inch in the screening through which the grit has been sifted for standardization of size. The notches made around the outer rolled rim of the blade may be either vertical or slanted to the edge. Since sawing tends slowly to wear one edge of the blade somewhat more than the other, reversing the blade on its motor-driven shaft periodically provides greater evenness and accuracy.

Commercial lapidary supply houses sell a variety of assembled saws and operating machinery. However, you can make your own equipment if you are handy. Directions can be found in rockhound magazines, periodicals on popular science and mechanics, and books. Essentially all that is needed is a shaft or arbor of steel (early lapidaries often used the rear axles of Model-T Fords), a pulley and vee-belt arrangement to connect the shaft with a motor, and a solid platform or carriage for holding the material to be sawed.

Beneath the saw should be a tank of cooling liquid—light oil or water—in which the blade spins. The coolant keeps the friction heat down and washes out the rock dust generated by the saw. Also, because the blade throws its coolant upward, the whole setup should be encased and covered with a splash hood which can be hinged down over the saw during its operation.

A diamond saw cuts at the rate of an inch or so every five minutes through relatively soft minerals and more slowly through the harder species. It is not feasible to hold the rough in the hand, since a steady pressure must be exerted upon it to force the rough piece against the whirling edge of the blade. The carriage on which the rough must be securely clamped is moved toward the blade by either an electrically powered feeding mechanism or a weight-feed wire dangling over a pulley at the rear of the saw. Special care is required, however, near the final fraction of an inch of sawing through a rough, for the rock may break along a jagged projection before the saw slices through. At the end of a cut the rough stone usually provides less area to be sawed through; the previous carriage pressure against the blade may be too great. Hence, it is necessary to stop the saw just short of completing the cut and do the final feeding by hand.

Saw blades are rather expensive, and considerable caution must be exercised to prevent bending, kinking, binding, or jamming, any one of which can quickly occur if the clamp holding the rock in place allows any twisting or wobbling during the process.

Bearings and shafts must be equal to the strains imposed on them. Although a half-inch shaft may be adequate for small blades, a five-eighths-inch shaft will give surer service. For larger size slabbing saws, shaft diameters should be three-quarters to an inch.

Since a diamond saw blade is thin and flexible, it requires suitable flanges on each side to ensure true running and reasonable stiffness. Ball bearings holding the ends of the shaft should be used whenever possible to ensure long, accurate, continuous spinning of the shaft; sleeve bearings have a tendency to become worn out of round, resulting in the spinning shaft's wobbling out of control. And, of course, proper lubrication of all moving parts is an absolute necessity.

ROCK-HOLDING DEVICES AND COOLANTS

The saw carriage and clamping arrangement has been pretty well standardized by manufacturers of lapidary equipment. Many carriages have cross-feeds so that a number of slices of any thickness can be sawed from a rough in succession. Strong positive clamps will allow slices to be cut as thin as one-sixteenth inch to as thick as 4 inches. Thicker slices can be achieved by reversing the stone in its clamp.

Several kinds of coolants are commonly used, the most popular being light, almost colorless white or flushing oils which usually have to be specially ordered. Kerosine, another popular albeit odorous coolant, is frequently used with ordinary light automobile lubricating oil added in a ratio of one or two parts oil to ten parts kerosine. Both diesel and transformer oil may also be used, but the odors can be a bit noxious at times.

PROPER SAWING SPEEDS

Saw speeds in terms of feet per minute at the blade rim vary greatly with the diameter of the blade and the revolutions per minute of the motor and the gear ratio provided by the vee-belt and pulley connection between the motor and the shaft. Manufacturers of diamond saws generally recommend that the rim speeds should range from 2,000 to 2,500 surface feet per minute for cryptocrystalline quartz (hardness 7) and 6,000 to 8,000 surface feet per minute for soft minerals like calcite or marble (hardness 3). Because most amateur lapidaries process gemstone minerals of hardness 5.5 or above, the recommended rim speed should be between 2,000 and 3,000 feet per minute.

The wide variety in sizes and ratios that may enter into setting up sawing equipment may require a few relatively simple mathematical calculations to arrive at the desired blade rim speed. There are conversion tables in almost any mechanic's handbook or gem-cutting guide to simplify the calculations.

GRINDING TECHNIQUES

Grinding is simply the abrasive technique necessary to rough out a blank gemstone piece; it refers to the use of ordinary carbide wheels spinning on the same shaft used for the diamond saw and run by the same electric motor. Indeed, the coarsest grinding wheel is usually set close to the sawing hood. Such wheels may be purchased in any size and degree of abrasiveness and are used to preform cabochons and the roughs for faceted gems, for grinding bevels on flats, for rough-shaping carvings, and for many other tasks that do not require refined workmanship.

GRINDING WHEELS

The silicon carbide grinding wheel is preferred by most lapidaries. Grades sold under the trade names of Carborundum, Crystolon, etc., range from 100 grit (coarse) to 1,200 grit (very fine). Common sizes range from a half-inch to 1½ inches in thickness and from 6 to 10 inches in diameter with arbor holes cut out to fit any common shaft. So-called hard wheels soon glaze over as the cutting particles of abrasive wear smooth and are not discharged; soft wheels lose their surface grains quickly, allowing a constant supply of new, fresh grains of abrasive for fast grinding.

The rate of wear on hard and soft wheels depends on the cementing bond holding the abrasive together. For lapidary work with hard gemstone materials, the softer grinding wheels are more efficient. But because very soft wheels have to be replaced rather often, upping the cost of lapidary work, most amateurs prefer to use medium, medium-soft, or medium-hard commercial wheels.

Every home lapidary needs at least two grinding wheels: a coarse wheel of 120 grit and a finer wheel of about 220 grit, placed next to each other on the same shaft and covered with the same housing hood. This propinquity allows for rapid switching from rough to smooth grinding or the reverse when rapid retouching is required. Generally speaking, grinding wheels should spin at a high speed (4,000 to 6,000 surface feet per minute) in order to perform their functions properly. They also require proper flanging according to diameter and ball-bearing supports that will eliminate any tendency to vibrate or wobble.

GRINDING SPLASH HOODS

Any grinding process creates friction heat. Gemstones are subject to fracturing or shattering when sudden heat is applied to the outer surface; therefore, any gemstone mineral must be ground under a thin stream of cooling water. The resulting spray requires a splash hood to protect surrounding equipment and the operator from inundation. Moreover, a hood is a safety device that will protect the lapidary from flying pieces, should the grinding wheel explode under the effects of centrifugal force— not likely, but always a possibility.

Caution: Never allow a grinding wheel to rest in a bath of water. The cementing compound is porous, and soaked-up water seriously unbalances a wheel. Always start the wheel and let it run for a minute or two (to ensure that it isn't going to disintegrate) before turning on the cooling water.

The best method of applying water to the grinding surface of a carborundum or other wheel is with a spray or a series of steady drips across the surface. A spray head is not always available, but spaced water drips can be punched into a copper tube supported above the wheel and angled across the grinding rim.

BUMPINESS IN WHEEL SURFACES

Grinding a gemstone is usually done by hand. Or, if the stone is too small to hold in the hand, it may be attached with sealing wax to a dop stick—a section of dowling 4 to 5 inches long and one-eighth to three-quarters inch in diameter that is squared off at the working end. In either case irregular hand pressure against the grinding surface tends to create pits, bumps, and slopes over the rim of the wheel. The larger the wheel, of course, the slower is the formation of such irregularities.

Bumpiness is a constant annoyance to lapidaries everywhere. When irregularities become intolerable, it is necessary to redress the wheel to return its surface to a condition of smoothness by one of these methods: (1) dressing the surface with a star wheel dresser; (2) smoothing the rim surface with a diamond wheel dresser; or (3) smoothing with a block of another hard abrasive. The third method, using silicon carbide specially pressed into brick form, is slower but produces a more even rim surface on the grinder. Or you can buy a new wheel.

As long as most grinding is done free-hand, it is impossible to avoid developing bumpiness in a grinding wheel. Acquiring skill and steadiness of hand will slow its development. Applying a rough gradually to the wheel and not trying to grind away rough spots too rapidly helps to reduce damage to the grinding surface. And where possible, use the largest grinding wheels you can afford and have space to mount. Do all preliminary grinding on a coarse wheel; use the fine grit for the finishing touches before final polishing.

LAPPING THE FLAT SURFACE

Sawing a rock tends to leave a rough surface showing the characteristic arcs of circles made by the saw. While a grinding wheel can be used to wear down the rough surface, most halves of rough stones are too large even for grinding by hand. Therefore, a lap wheel is commonly used whenever a flat surface is to be smoothed for ultimate polishing. Large agates, slabs of petrified wood, blocks of chrysocolla or malachite, and so on must be lapped to a rather high smoothness before the final polish that will bring out the colors and patterns to the best effect.

THE PRINCIPLE OF LAPPING

Lapping a slab of rock consists simply of rubbing the sawed surface against a revolving horizontal steel plate charged with loose abrasive grit and a little water. Just as in grinding, lapping begins with coarse grits and proceeds through finer grits until the slab surface is ready for its final polishing.

A lap plate can be made of almost any metal, but best results are achieved when it is of mild steel or cast iron. Lap kits are sold commercially, but the amateur can make his own by mounting the lap plate on a vertical shaft so that the top of the plate is flush with the top of the shaft. The shaft is connected to a drive motor with a large pulley geared down to where the plate revolves at a slow speed so as not to throw grit and rock specimens against the side walls of the plate housing. A removable splash pan which can be easily cleaned completes the assembly.

Silicon carbide abrasive, available in one-pound cans, is the least expensive and most popular grinding material for use on a lap plate. The median size used for most work is 220 grit for the first grind, followed by 400 grit, and ending with 1,200 grit.

A first grind done on a medium-sized lap plate may require a full pound or two of the 220 grit. The last grind, working on very fine grit, uses only small quantities of the much more expensive abrasive.

LAPPING TECHNIQUES

Since the lap plate revolves inside a vertical-walled metal tub, the sides of the tub prevent rock specimens from flying off at a tangent. The objective of lapping is simply to flatten and polish the surface of a slab or block in order to remove saw marks, pits, or any other irregularity and produce a smoothness that will take a final high gloss on a buffer.

The grit should be mixed with a little water containing a dash of detergent and brushed onto the rotating plate near its center. Experience soon shows how much water to use—too much and the grit is washed off the plate, too little and the plate runs dry. To make the grit stick more firmly to the plate, some lapidaries add a spoonful of ordinary clay. Others consider the addition unnecessary, since the rock dust ground off the specimen serves the same purpose.

The specimen to be lapped is placed on top of the brushed-on grit slurry, also near the center of the plate. A single specimen may be held on the lap plate by hand or by a fixed arm projecting from one side of the tub, against which the rock rests while the plate revolves slowly beneath it. Unless the specimen is swept more or less continually back and forth over the surface of the plate, the lap will develop a "saddle" as the metal is ground away. One way to prevent this is to place numerous rock blocks or slabs on the plate at the same time; as the lap revolves, the specimens gradually shift places and rotate, thereby covering the grinding surface rather evenly.

From time to time as the lapping proceeds, it is necessary to wash off the specimen at the sink or in a bucket of water to examine the smoothing surface; any "frosted" areas indicate incomplete lapping. Keep checking the specimen, for the ground surface must be perfectly flat and uniform before you go on to the next finer grit.

CHANGING CHARGES OF GRIT

When the surface of the gemstone has been ground smooth and there are no perceptible irregularities or frosted areas, grinding has proceeded as far as that particular grit is concerned. Remove the specimen from the plate and carefully flush off the coarse grit into the splash pan, scrubbing well with slightly soapy water. Save the old grit in a bottle for the next use on rough specimens.

Be absolutely sure that your own fingernails, hands, and forearms are thoroughly scrubbed and washed before attempting to recharge the plate with the next finer grit—for example, 400 size for the second grind. A particle or two of the old, larger grit can seriously scratch the higher polish that is achieved with later grinds.

When you reach the 1,200-grit stage, use very little of the fine abrasive in the brush-on slurry. As grinding proceeds, check regularly to see that the surface is being ground evenly and is not being scratched by particles of coarser grit. Eventually the entire surface should be evenly frosted, almost to the point of a dull gloss; this is as far as the lapping operation goes. The specimen is then ready for the final high-gloss polish.

SANDING DOWN A SPECIMEN

For sanding many lapidaries use one or more wooden wheels (disks) attached to the same drive shaft used for the saw and grinding wheels. Each disk is covered with a stout sanding cloth coated with a layer of silicon carbide, the grit varying from 220 for coarse sanding to 400 or 600 grit for successively finer sanding. Recent developments in sanding cloth allow for either wet or dry sanding; previously, all sanding had to be done dry.

There are several types of sanding disks available, as well as devices of a different nature. Depending on the kind of general equipment you install, you may wish to use a drum sander or a belt sander. And incidentally, either disk or drum sanders fitted with leather yield very fine sanding of gemstones that ordinary abrasive cloth cannot produce.

Whatever type of sander is used, its surface speed should be about the same as for general grinding, neither too fast (the abrasive tends to be thrown off) nor too slow. The fastest speed that can be used without disintegrating the abrasive does the most effective sanding job. Surface speeds from 3,000 to 4,000 feet per minute are recommended: the faster speeds reduce undercutting in gemstones which have differences in hardness across the surface.

Most sanding will normally be done on curved surfaces, also used for flats and slabs, except that curved surfaces are somewhat easier to sand because more pressure can be exerted on any given area. Flats and slabs can best be sanded on drum- or belt-type sanders, maintaining a steady two-hand pressure of the specimen against the sander, keeping it moving constantly, and turning the specimen from time to time to expose new areas to the abrasive.

As with all skills, experience is the best teacher. When coarse sanding is complete, fine sanding should be done at right angles to the microscopic striations produced in the coarse sanding. Again, periodic shifting of the specimen back and forth at various angles helps to smooth out any abrasive markings.

Very hard gemstones, such as ruby, sapphire, and topaz, require the same initial coarse and finer sanding by cloth, followed by sanding on wood or rubber-bonded wheels using various grades of diamond powder. The rubber-bonded wheels have a special application for sanding hard gemstones, including chrysoberyl, and should be operated at the highest feasible speed for improved abrasive action.

THE FINAL HIGH-GLOSS POLISH

Polishing a specimen to a high gloss is the last step in the lapidary process, differing from the preceding grinding and sanding steps in that no abrasive is used. A brilliant glistening surface is produced simply by pressing the stone against a buffing wheel covered with cloth, felt, leather, or porous wood charged with a watery slurry or a polishing agent. Polishing will not take place, however, unless the surface has received as fine a sanding as can be given to it.

POLISHING AGENTS

Several kinds of polishing agent may be used, some for one species of gemstone and some for another (see Table 26). Ordinary boudoir rouge, an iron oxide, was once quite popular but is less so today because it stains everything in and about the polishing wheel, including the operator. Aluminum oxide, otherwise known as alumina, ruby dix, or Linde A (most recommended), is perhaps the most widely used polishing agent. Powdered cerium oxide, zirconium oxide, tin oxide, and chromic oxide (chrome, green chrome; it stains as badly as rouge) also have polishing value.

For very hard stones, tripoli (powdered silicon dioxide) is commonly

Poppy Jasper

Malachite

Marcasite

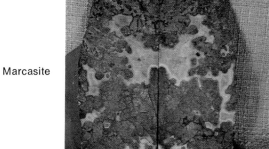

Obsidian with Cristabolite

Onyx

Opal on Petrified Wood

Opalized Wood

Petrified Ironwood

Pyrite Crystals

Quartz Crystals

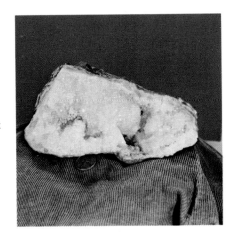

Druzy Quartz

Rutilate Quartz

Smoky Quartz

Quartz Geode

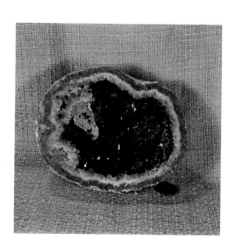

Rhodonite

Rhodonite crested with
Druzy Quartz Crystals

Selenite Crystals

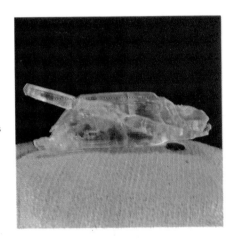

Thunder Eggs

Topaz Crystal in Ryolite

Tourmalines

Turquoise

Wavellite in Ryolite

Wonderstone

Wulfenite

used. For each kind of gemstone, whether hard or soft, a particular combination of polishing agent with a polishing plate of leather, tin, flannel, Lucite, felt, wax, or wood produces the best results.

POLISHERS

Any number of polishers may be used, but two general types prevail: buffs constructed for yielding materials and used primarily for polishing cabochons, flats, spheres, etc., and flat plates for polishing faceted gems and geometrically flat gemstone surfaces. Buffs may be belts, disks, drums, or wheels; the most usual forms are disks and wheels.

Many lapidaries add a felt buff wheel, solidly constructed out of compressed wool, to the general power-driven shaft beyond the fine-sanding disk. Felt buffs come in all sizes and require supporting flanges on each side. In order to keep out unwanted dust and grit, the buff should be covered when not in use.

It is not advisable to change the polishing charge from one kind to another on the same buff; since aluminum oxide polishes the great majority of gemstones effectively, with cerium oxide a second choice, it is best to stick to one kind and use separate buffing wheels for specialized polishing.

TABLE 26
RECOMMENDATIONS FOR USE OF POLISHING AGENTS

Mineral	Mohs	Lap Base	Polisher	Remarks
Actinolite	5–6	Tin	Linde A	Use 1,200 copper lap for cutting facets; material rare
Algodonite	8.4	Leather	Linde A	Somewhat heat-sensitive and difficult to polish; chips and pits
Amber	2–2.5	Wax/wood	Linde A	For large flats
		Felt, flannel, flexible leather	Tripoli or tin oxide	Felt and flannel bases should be impregnated with polisher; use leather damp
Amblygonite	5.5–6	Tin	Linde A	Fast but may groove or furrow
		Wax	Linde A	Recommended, but may round off facet edges
		Tin or wax	Cerium oxide	Will also polish
Analcime (analcite)	5	Tin	Linde A	Faceting crystals rarely over ⅛ inch diameter
		Lucite	Tin or cerium oxide	

TABLE 26 (Cont.)

Mineral	Mohs	Lap Base	Polisher	Remarks
Andalusite	7.5	Tin	Linde A	Finished gem should show reddish hues in green background
Anhydrite	3–3.5	Wax	Linde A	Very difficult to process
Anthophyllite	3	Felt	Cerium oxide	May display schiller effect
		Leather	Linde A	For massive forms
Apatite	5	Tin	Linde A	For prepolish
		Wax	Linde A or cerium or tin oxide	For final polish
Apophyllite	4.5–5	Tin	Linde A	For faceting gems
		Leather	Linde A	To bring out pearly luster
		Felt	Cerium oxide	Also brings out luster
Aragonite	3.5–4	Leather	Tin oxide	For cabochon material
		Wax/wood	Linde A	For faceting crystals
Argillite	Soft	None	None	After sanding, rub with wood shavings and stove polish
Augelite	4.5–5	Wax	Linde A	
Axinite	6.5–7	Lucite	Cerium oxide	Hardness varies according to crystal direction
		Tin	Linde A	Change directions if scratching occurs
Azurite	3.5–4	Wax	Linde A	For transparent crystals
		Leather	Linde A or chromium oxide	For massive azurite
Banded rhyolite	Soft	Leather	Linde A	For cabochon materials
		Wax	Linde A	For flat pieces
		Pitch	Rouge	For flat pieces
Barite	3	Wax	Linde A or tin oxide	Very heat-sensitive
Benitoite	6–6.5	Lucite	Cerium oxide	Recommended
		Tin	Linde A	May cause grooving; fast
Beryl	7.5–8	Tin	Tin oxide	Polishes with difficulty; best for emeralds

TABLE 26 (Cont.)

Mineral	Mohs	Lap Base	Polisher	Remarks
		Lucite	Cerium oxide	Can substitute chromium oxide if gem unfractured
Beryllonite	5.5–6	Lucite	Cerium oxide	Keep lap moist
		Tin	Linde A	May cause scratches
Boracite	7–7.5	Tin	Linde A	Gives fine, quick polish
Bornite	3	Cloth	Rouge	For cabochons
		Leather	Linde A	Thin slurry for cabochons
		Wax	Linde A	Watery slurry for flats
Brazilianite	5.5	Tin	Linde A	Polishes smoothly and fast
Calcite	3	Wax, wood	Any type	Tin oxide or Linde A usual; cannot polish on tin
			Tin oxide	Best for massive calcite; improved by dissolving a few grains of oxalic acid in the tin oxide slurry
Cassiterite	6–7	Tin	Linde A	Make a thick slurry for fast, almost dry lap; facets
		Leather	Linde A	For cabochon material
Celestite	3–3.5	Wax	Linde A	Will not give perfect polish
Cerussite	3–3.5	Wax, wood	Tin oxide	Wax base preferred; neither gives more than fair polish
Chiastolite	4	Leather	Linde A	Tends to undercut
Chlorastrolite	5–6	Felt	Cerium oxide	Soft weathered material will not polish
Chondrodite	6–6.5	Wax, wood	Linde A	
Chrysoberyl	8.5	Hardwood	Diamond dust	For final polish
		Tin, zinc, or copper	Diamond dust (6,400)	For larger facets
		Tin	Linde A	Works for small-facet gems
Cinnabar	2–2.5	Wax	Linde A	Often with tiny grooves
Clinozoisite	6	Tin	Linde A	Requires a little caution to avoid fracturing with either base and polish
		Lucite	Cerium oxide	
Colemanite	4–4.5	Lucite	Tin oxide	Recommended; scratches eliminated by changing directions
		Lucite	Cerium oxide	Rather difficult to polish

TABLE 26 (Cont.)

Mineral	Mohs	Lap Base	Polisher	Remarks
Copper rhyolite	Var.	Leather	Linde A	For massive material
		Wood, or pitch	Linde A	For large flats
Corundum	9	Copper, tin, or bronze	6,400 diamond	Mix grit with oil for pre-polish; finish with tripoli
Covellite	1.5–2	Leather	Linde A	Good polish on both massive and cabochon material
Crocoite	2.5–3	Wax	Linde A	Not entirely perfect polish
Danburite	7	Tin	Linde A	
Datolite	5–5.5	Felt	Cerium oxide	Must be sanded very smooth
		Leather	Linde A	Requires fine presanding
		Lucite	Tin oxide	Change directions on facets
Diopside	5–6	Tin	Linde A or tin oxide	For small facets is suitable
		Wax, wood	Linde A or tin oxide	Recommended
Dioptase	5	Lucite	Cerium oxide	For faceting
		Felt	Cerium oxide	For cabochon material
Domeykite	7.5			See algodonite
Enstatite	5.5	Tin	Linde A	For facets
		Felt	Cerium oxide	For massive bronzite variety
		Leather	Linde A	For bronzite variety
Epidote	6–7	Lucite	Cerium oxide	May require changing direction
		Tin	Linde A	About the same as Lucite
Feldspar	6	Felt	Cerium oxide	For cabochons
		Tin	Linde A	For faceted gem crystals or gemstone varieties (commoner)
Fergusonite	5.5–6.5	Tin	Linde A	Heavy paste on deeply scored tin lap base
Fibrolite (sillimanite)	7.5	Tin	Linde A	Rounded crystals only
Fluorite	4	Wax, wood	Any type	Very heat-sensitive

TABLE 26 (Cont.)

Mineral	Mohs	Lap Base	Polisher	Remarks
Gadolinite	6.5–7	Tin or type-metal	Linde A	Not heat-sensitive
Garnet	6.5–7.5	Leather	Linde A or chrome oxide	Gives fast polish
		Tin	Linde A	For facet material
Glass	4.5–6	Pitch	Cerium oxide	For large flats and lenses
		Pellon	Cerium oxide	Flats, lenses
		Lucite or tin	Cerium oxide	For facets on gems
Goethite	5–5.5	Leather	Linde A	For cabochons
		Wax or well-scored tin	Linde A	For flats
Gypsum	2	Soft buff or leather	Any type	Final polish by hand with felt, wool, or damp leather plus polisher
Hematite	1–6.5	Cloth buff, leather or wood	Cerium oxide	For cabochon material pre-polished on leather with wet silicon carbide 1,200 grit
		Tin, wax	Linde A	For faceting gem material
		Cloth buff	Magnesium oxide	A German technique
Howlite	3.5	Felt	Tin oxide	If material does not undercut
		Leather	Linde A	To prevent undercutting
Hypersthene				See enstatite
Idocrase	6.5	Leather	Chrome oxide or Linde A	For massive material; may undercut
		Wood	Linde A or chrome oxide	For flats; may undercut
Iolite	7–7.5	Lucite	Cerium oxide	For massive material
		Tin	Linde A or tin oxide	For massive material or flats
		Leather	Linde A or chrome oxide	For cabochons
Jadeite	6.5–7	Leather	Linde A	For massive material or cabochons

TABLE 26 (Cont.)

Mineral	Mohs	Lap Base	Polisher	Remarks
		Scored tin	Linde A	High luster for facets using a thick paste
Jet	3–4	Cloth, felt, or leather	Cerium or tin oxide or Linde A	Leather buff most effective
Kyanite	5–7.5	Tin	Linde A	Crystals very brittle
Lapis lazuli	5.5	Leather	Chrome oxide or Linde A	For cabochons or flats
		Tin	Linde A	For faceted gems
Lazulite	5.5–6	Leather or wax	Linde A or chrome oxide	For cabochons
Lepidolite	2.5	Leather	Cerium oxide or Linde A	Subject to undercutting
Leucite	6	Lucite	Cerium oxide	Uncommon clear crystals
Magnesite	3.5–4	Wax	Linde A	Very heat-sensitive
Malachite	3.5–4	Leather	Linde A or chrome oxide	Hand-finish with clean leather dipped in thin slurry containing a little soap
Marcasite				See pyrite
Mesolite	5	Felt	Cerium oxide	Fast polish for cabochons
Microlite	6	Tin	Linde A	Easy smooth polish
Mimetite	3.5–4	Leather	Linde A or tin oxide	For cabochons
		Tin, wax	Linde A	For faceting material
Mordenite				See thomsonite
Muscovite	2–2.5			See lepidolite
Natrolite	5–5.5	Lucite	Cerium oxide	Fast polish
		Tin	Linde A	Slower polish
Nephrite	6–6.5	Leather	Linde A or chrome oxide	For massive material
		Softwood	Tin oxide	For material that won't polish on leather; use almost dry with pressure
		Wood	Chrome oxide	For large flats

TABLE 26 (Cont.)

Mineral	Mohs	Lap Base	Polisher	Remarks
		Tin	Linde A	For facet-grade gems
Obsidian	5	Felt	Cerium oxide	For Apache tears and massive material
		Lucite	Cerium oxide	For faceted gems; keep lap wet, as heat-sensitive
Opal	5.5–6.5	Felt	Cerium oxide	For cabochons; may crack
		Lucite	Cerium oxide	For faceted gems; keep wet to avoid cracking
Pectolite	5	Leather	Linde A	
Peridot	6.5–7	Tin	Linde A	To thick paste add 1 or 2 drops of HCl; keep lap nearly dry
		Wax	Linde A plus HCl	For large facets
Petalite	6–6.5	Lucite	Cerium oxide	For cabochons or facets
		Tin	Linde A	Alternative polish; good
Phenakite	7.5–8	Tin	Linde A	Thick paste, almost dry; slow
		Tin	6,400 diamond	Somewhat faster
Piedmontite	6–7	Leather	Linde A or tin oxide	For cabochons
		Pitch or wood	1,200 grit	For flat surfaces
Pollucite	6.5	Lucite	Cerium oxide	Gives a smooth polish
Prehnite	6–6.5	Leather or tin	Linde A	For cabochons or facets
Proustite	2–2.5	Wax	Linde A	May scratch
Pyrite	6–6.5	Leather	Linde A	For cabochons and massive
		Wax, wood	Linde A	Thick paste, for faceting
		Felt, flannel	Magnesium oxide	German technique
Quartz	7	Felt, leather, wood	Cerium oxide or tripoli	All quartz types
		Leather	Linde A	For types that undercut
		Lucite	Cerium oxide	For faceted gems

TABLE 26 (Cont.)

Mineral	Mohs	Lap Base	Polisher	Remarks
		Tin	Linde A	Also used for faceted gems
Rhodochrosite	3.5–4.5	Leather	Linde A or tin oxide	For cabochons
		Tin	Linde A	To prepolish facet gems
		Wax	Linde A	For final facet polishing
Rhodonite	5.5–6.5	Leather	Linde A	For flats, cabochons, etc.
		Tin	Linde A	For faceted gems
Rutile	6–6.5	Tin	Linde A	Popular, using thick paste; or very thin slurry on very smooth tin lap (say others)
Scapolite	6.5	Felt or Lucite	Cerium oxide	All types
Scheelite	4.5–5	Tin	Linde A	For prepolish
		Wax	Linde A	For final polish
Scorzalite				See lazulite
Serpentine	2.5–4	Leather	Linde A or chrome oxide	Keep leather almost dry
		Tin	Linde A	For faceted clear gems
Shattuckite	3.5–4	Leather or felt	Linde A or tin oxide	May undercut with felt lap
Smithsonite	4–4.5	Felt	Tin oxide	For cabochons
		Tin	Tin oxide (thick)	For facet gems (rare)
Sodalite	5.5–6	Felt or Lucite	Cerium oxide	All types: flats, cabochons, facets
Sphalerite	3.5–4	Tin	Linde A	For prepolishing facets
		Wax	Linde A	For final polish of facets
		Leather	Linde A	For cabochons
Sphene	5–5.5	Tin	Linde A	Tendency to furrow
Spinel	8	Tin	Linde A	
Spodumene	6.5–7	Tin	Linde A	For faceted gems
		Leather	Linde A	For cabochons
Stibiotantalite	5.5	Tin	Linde A	
Tektite	5.5	Felt or Lucite	Cerium oxide	A natural glass originating from outer space
Thaumasite	3.5	Felt	Tin oxide	For cabochons or flats
		Leather	Linde A	Also polishes well
Thomsonite	5–5.5	Felt	Cerium oxide	Makes lovely cabochons

TABLE 26 (Cont.)

Mineral	Mohs	Lap Base	Polisher	Remarks
Topaz	8	Lead	400 grit	For large facets
		Iron	600 grit	For large facets
		Tin	Linde A	For small facets; finish almost dry with thick paste
		Leather	Linde A	For cabochons which have been finish-sanded with 1,200 grit on leather
Tourmaline	7–7.5	Tin	Linde A	For faceted gems
		Leather	Linde A	For cabochons
		Wood	Linde A	For large facets
Tremolite	5–6	Felt	Cerium or tin oxide	For cabochons
		Lucite	Cerium or tin oxide	For facet gems
Turquoise	5–6	Leather	Linde A	
Ulexite	2–2.5	Felt or leather	Linde A or tin oxide	For cross sections use polishers on cloth or leather
Variscite	4.5	Leather	Linde A	Polishes easily, massive
		Felt	Cerium or tin oxide	Massive or cabochons
		Wax, wood, pitch, or Pellon	1,200 grit	For flats or nodule halves and slices
Vivianite	1.5–2	Wax	Linde A	Uncommon faceting material
Willemite	5.5	Tin	Linde A	Polishes easily
		Lucite	Cerium oxide	Will also give a good polish
Witherite	3–4	Tin	Linde A	For prepolish
		Wax	Linde A	For final polish
Wollastonite	4.5–5	Leather	Linde A	Polishes easily
Wulfenite	3	Tin	Linde A	For prepolishing facets
		Wax	Tin oxide	For final facet polishing
Zincite	4–4.5	Tin	Linde A	Change directions periodically
Zircon	7.5	Tin	Linde A	Polishes slowly
Zoisite	6–6.5	Leather	Linde A or tin oxide	

Just as leather is used to hone a straight-edge razor, solid leather buffing wheels have long been used to give gems and gemstones a final high polish. Solid leather wheels are not necessarily required, since good-quality undyed tanned leather can be glued onto a wooden disk and will serve just as well.

The use of leather has its greatest effect in polishing gemmy minerals that have a tendency to undercut during the sanding process—jade, lapis lazuli, rhodonite, serpentine, among others. Almost any polishing agent can be used with leather, but the favorites are aluminum oxide (especially Linde A) and chrome oxide, although the latter may stain any light-colored material that contains tiny fractures or pits. Leather lasts almost indefinitely and produces relatively slow but very fine polishing. Inasmuch as leather will polish almost everything and can be readily cleaned of one polishing agent for use with another, the lapidary who wishes to install only a single buffing wheel should consider using a leather buff or leather-covered disk.

DRILLING HOLES IN GEMSTONES

Sooner or later every lapidary wishes to drill a hole through an agate or other gemstone for a gold chain. Even the most ancient and primitive lapidaries regularly drilled small-diameter bead holes and strung their colorful beads onto necklaces. Of course, they did not have power machinery or diamond bits: they simply used a bow-and-drill arrangement similar to that used in making fire by friction. Ruby sand may have been their grinding agent.

THE DRILLING RIG

Although many types of drilling rigs can be purchased, a large number of amateur lapidaries use an ordinary electric hand drill fitted into a wooden block and strapped in place so that it cannot vibrate. Vertical kits can be purchased or built, or the drill can be operated horizontally against a securely positioned stone. The most important feature is that the drill bit must be able to be moved up and down or in and out of the hole, so that worn-out grit can be replaced with fresh grit as the drilling proceeds.

The Near East Chaldeans used water to cool their hand- or foot-operated drills. Modern Chinese, who still prefer their ancient manually operated drill rigs to modern electric types, also use water along with silicon carbide grit and are expert at drilling holes of any size.

Manufacturers of commercial drills may recommend various oils for use with diamond bort, since the powdered diamond sticks in oil and is less likely to be worked out of the hole. Oil also has the advantage of not splashing as much as water does and, at the same time, acting as an excellent cooling liquid.

Too fast a speed with any type and size of drill leads to splashing of the coolant and consequent loss of abrasive. For large-sized tube drills, a recommended speed is 2,000 rpm or even slower; for small tube-type drills, an rpm of 2,000 to 3,000. For small diamond bits or needle drills, a speed of 4,500 to 5,000 rpm allows relatively speedy drilling with firm control.

TYPES OF DRILLS AND BITS

Commercially available are a variety of tube, core, and diamond-point drilling devices, designed to make holes of various diameters. The techniques vary slightly between tube and core drills and needle-type drill rods. For extremely small holes the diamond-point bit is most efficient and can be made by the lapidary himself. For larger holes, coring tubes in various sizes are used.

A single-point diamond bit is made from a thin drill rod heated red hot and annealed at the drilling tip. After the drilling end is squared off, it is slotted with a jeweler's saw and widened slightly with a riffling file. Into this slot is placed a tiny diamond chip slightly larger than the diameter of the drill rod (the small single chips of diamond bort are quite effective). With a pair of small pliers and as slight a pressure as possible, the lips of the slot are pinched over the holding edges of the bit of diamond. Then, if the tip is dipped into silver solder flux and heated, ordinary silver solder can be applied and the tip heated until the solder fills every remaining crack and crevice. Such a bit is then ready for a careful grinding away of any excess metal on a fine grinding wheel until only diamond extends beyond the circumference of the bit. Finally the drill rod is secured in the powered chuck, and as it spins, a slender neck above the drill tip is filed away.

Most amateur lapidaries are inclined to buy commercial plated diamond bits from a dental supply house, along with any required small disks and grinders, which come in various shapes and sizes.

The finest holes are drilled with an ordinary steel needle mounted accurately at the terminus of a lightweight shaft. Power equipment is rarely used, experienced lapidaries preferring the old-fashioned bow-and-spindle device used by Boy Scouts for making fire by friction. As the bow is drawn back and forth, the drill spins first one direction, then the other, being fed slowly with crushed diamond powder as the actual cutting abrasive. It takes a great deal of practice and experience to develop a truly effective technique with the needle drill.

Powered equipment is ideal for a small-diameter (tube) or large-diameter (core) metal tube made of copper, brass, bronze, aluminum, or steel. The tubes themselves do no cutting, but they guide the abrasive which does. One especially popular small tube is no more than the brass ink container of a used-up ball-point pen. The outer diameter is about one-eighth inch and the tip section about one-sixteenth inch. For most purposes a sixteenth-inch-diameter hole is all that is required.

Regardless of the size of tubing used, it simply cuts a core out of the stone.

ABRASIVES AND DRILLING PROCEDURES

Commercial silicon carbide is the least expensive and most usual abrasive for drilling holes in hard stone. Boron carbide may also be used but is rather slow. The most expensive but certainly the most effective is diamond powder. The cost can be reduced somewhat by mixing diamond powder with boron carbide, which produces somewhat faster drilling.

Usually the stone to be drilled will be a polished slice or ground and polished preform pendant or other small polished stone with flat, polished areas. The piece must be securely attached to a block of wood to prevent shifting during drilling and to prevent chipping out on the back side as the bit grinds through.

With the drill poised precisely over the point to be drilled, a small washer or nut is waxed onto the stone with the hole centered over the drill area to provide a tiny container for holding the abrasive around the spinning needle or tube. Water or oil is added a drop at a time to the abrasive, and the drill tip is lowered as lightly as possible through the grit onto the surface of the stone. The lightest possible initial contact is necessary to keep the drill tip from wandering off and to cut a preliminary pit.

Once the drill tip is set in its preliminary pit, steady power drilling can proceed apace. The drill must be raised every few seconds to allow the abrasive and coolant to penetrate the deepening hole.

Great care must be exercised during the last few seconds, with as gentle a pressure as possible applied to avoid chipping out on the back side. As soon as the drill tip actually breaks through the undersurface, the whole stone should be removed from the wood block, turned over, and rewaxed onto the block. Then final drilling is accomplished through the back side. This not only prevents chipping around the edges of the hole but allows for equalization of the diameter of the hole itself.

A larger tube for drilling a hole big enough, for example, to make an agate ring is done with the same technique. The process takes much longer, naturally, because there is much more stone to be abraded away.

Instead of securing a small washer or nut over the drilling center, it is more efficient to clamp or cement the flat to the center bottom of a small pan and cover the stone with the abrasive slurry so that from a quarter-inch to a half-inch of grit surrounds the drill at all times during the cutting action. The drill must be raised periodically to ensure that the grit and coolant reach the grinding surface.

FACETING EQUIPMENT

It is not the purpose of this chapter to include all the rather complicated details of how to grind facets onto gem crystals. One of the best and most complete manuals for developing faceting techniques is John Sinkankas' *Gem Cutting: A Lapidary's Manual* (listed in Appendix IV), and the reader interested in faceted jewels is referred to it. Faceting equipment can be homemade or purchased from most lapidary supply houses with instructions for its use.

Essentially the process of faceting a gem is simply one of grinding and polishing precisely angled and positioned flat surfaces (facets) onto a crystal so that light reflections from both the surface and the interior reach the viewer's eye as brilliant sparkles of pure prismatic colors or glinting white light. Different gemstones have different refractive indexes, requiring that different crown angles and pavilion angles be used to produce the most satisfactory results. Nor can all gemstones be given specific angle settings. (The part of the gem above the girdle, i.e., the widest part of the gem, is termed the crown; the bottom part of the gem is called the pavilion. The crown consists of many small facets surrounding one large top facet called the table, and it is through this table that most of the light rays pass. The pavilion consists of many small facets drawing toward the point; these facets break up the entering light rays and reflect them back brilliantly through the table, provided that the facets have been cut at the proper angles.) Tables of crown and pavilion angles are given in technical manuals on faceting for each gemstone species.

FACETING HEADS

A faceting head, available in several styles, is a device for holding and rotating a gem fixed to a suitable dop stick so that it remains at a precise angle during the grinding of the facets on a small lap wheel. Except for provision for changing the angle of grind, there are no moving parts; the actual work of grinding is done by the lap plate and its charge of abrasive. As with polishing, different lap plates and abrasives are required for different species of gemstone.

The main parts of a faceting unit are a solid base plate and stand rod, a master lap assembly for operating the cutting and polishing laps, and the facet-head assembly, which securely holds the dop stick. The head includes a quadrant marked in degrees of angle and a pointer. Thus the gem can be set for any angle of cut from zero degrees (horizontal position) to 90 degrees (vertical position).

MASTER LAP ASSEMBLY

Table 26 reveals that with each gemstone a particular lap base is recommended to assist in the final polishing of a gem, cabochon, flat, or other surface. The individual lap "sheets," or bases, are fixed to the master lap assembly as subordinate elements. The master lap assembly itself is the primary lap plate on its rotating shaft. This primary plate is a "dummy" iron or aluminum plate of considerable rigidity used as the support for the interchangeable cutting and polishing laps: tin, copper, Lucite or plexiglass, leather, wood, wax, type metal, or lead. In some instances more than a single final polishing lap is required, one providing a prepolish and another a final polish.

Copper laps are used most often with diamond dust because diamond embeds itself in the copper surface and cannot be discharged. Tin laps, backed by aluminum for additional stiffening, are frequently used for final polishing. Plastic laps are durable and used for a wide assortment of facet-grade gems. Wooden plates may be made from almost any kind of wood and are usually used for polishing gem girdles and the large facets, usually with Linde A or tin oxide polishing powders. Wax laps are simply a coating put onto a stiff metal lap plate with cloth impregnated with beeswax; wax is most effective in polishing very soft gemstone materials and touching up facets on other gemstones that might otherwise be scratched by any other lap base.

TUMBLED GEMSTONES

Ancient lapidaries tried to bring some ordered form to their jewelry-making. Beads had to be round or oval, for example, and some more or less standardized shape lay behind the fashioning of each decorative object. Modern lapidaries still use conventional preforms in making cabochons, lavaliers, pendants, and, of course, all faceted gems.

Tumbled gemstones—irregularly shaped, highly polished pieces of gemmy substance fashioned into fascinating baroque "jewels" are very much newcomers in the long history of the lapidary art, no two of which are alike. Tumbling requires less effort than any other type of lapidary work and produces finished gemstones in the hundreds or thousands simultaneously. The process is nothing more than filling a rotating barrel or other canister part full of broken pieces and fragments of hard rock, adding water and abrasive powder, and turning on the power. Tumbling may proceed unattended for days and weeks on end, requiring only regular recharging of the abrasive to progressively finer grits until the stones are smoothly rounded at all corners and edges and polished to a high reflective gloss.

In tumbling a load of loose stones is carried up one side of a turning canister to the flopover point. At this point the topmost stones begin to slide down across the surface of the rising mass. Since all stones are coated with the abrasive slurry, the constant sliding action (not really tumbling, which would crack and shatter the stones further) provides the grinding and polishing action. An ordinary cement mixer, for example, will make a usable tumbler for large-size gemstones if the baffles are removed. The action is much the same.

TYPES OF TUMBLERS

Since the idea of producing tumbled gems en masse became a major lapidary interest, every imaginable kind of container has been used by amateurs: tin cans, glass jars, oil cans, beer casks, steel drums, and even old truck tires mounted vertically on rollers and held upright by a supporting framework. All must be attached by a belt and pulley connection to a small motor and geared down to where the speed of rotation is no more than just enough to bring the sliding mass of rocks about two-thirds the way up one side and allow them to flop over and start cascading down. As the action repeats itself with an ever-changing rhythm, every rough spot or projection on the stones is rounded off and polished.

Commercial tumblers, available in a wide range of sizes, are often hexagonal in cross section, but round barrels are also available. The deeper barrels allow greater abrasive action and are generally preferred. Many amateurs use modest-sized tumblers in diameters of 6 to 12 inches, so that the quantities of abrasive agents will be kept within reasonable costs and the charge of gemstone fragments will not be so large that it poses the problem of what to do with the finished product.

To prevent undue wear on the sides of the tumbler, a lining must be securely glued or cemented with close-fitting joints. Linings may be of rubber sheeting, Masonite sheeting, or wood. Lining also reduces the noise level considerably. There are other ways of lowering the sound level, and the reader is advised to visit rockhound friends already set up with tumbling equipment for ideas, home-generated techniques, and ample free advice.

It is necessary to halt the action periodically and open the container to allow gas-pressure build-up to escape; some tumblers are equipped with an automatic pressure valve which will allow gas to escape without leaking any of the water charge.

Commercially purchased tumblers come equipped with the proper gearing ratio, since for any given diameter of tumbler, there is a specific recommended speed of rotation. Table 27 presents the rotational speeds in revolutions per minute to use for homemade tumblers during the preliminary grinding process. About half these speeds are used for the final polishing grits.

Most gemstone tumbling is done exclusively with silicon carbide. The preliminary grind requires coarse grits, usually 80 mesh. The second grind takes 400 or 600 grit. Final polishing is rarely done with abrasive powders; instead, ordinary water with detergent may be used or the rock charge leavened with scraps of cork, Masonite, leather, or small cubes of hardwood. Fine-grain polishers, such as nut shells, corncobs, pulverized cork, sawdust, rice hulls, and clay work admirably, in a ratio

TABLE 27
RECOMMENDED TUMBLING SPEEDS

Barrel Diameter in Inches	Revolutions per Minute
6	35 to 55
10	25 to 40
12	15 to 25
16	5 to 15
20-inch truck tire	1 to 3

of a pound of polishing agent (stannic oxide, aluminum oxide, rouge, tripoli, chrome oxide, etc.) with five pounds of the leavening materials to each 20 pounds of gemstones.

The first or coarse grind usually takes from three to four weeks of continuous tumbling to round off the corners and smooth down the surfaces, depending on the shape of the fragmented gemstones and their species properties. The second grind uses about half as much finer abrasive as was used in the coarse grind and will occupy another two or three weeks of continuous tumbling. The final polishing takes only four to seven days; a check should be made every now and then on individual specimens until it is apparent that surface areas are indeed at a high gloss. If specks and spots of frosting show up, it means that additional polishing time is needed.

Charging a tumbler of gemstones means filling the container to half or slightly more of its volume with stones and abrasive, then adding water until the level is at the level of the charge. Even more water can be added, and many experts think that the higher level of the water, the faster the grinding action.

When coarse grinding is completed and finer grit is to be used, the original charge of grit and rocks should be thoroughly washed with water until none of the coarser grit remains. Cleaning and flushing with clear water is always a dirty chore and should be done in a suitable work area. *Do not wash old grits down a drain;* they will eventually clog the lines rather thoroughly.

During the washing operation, examine the semirounded stones. Cull those which have deep holes or pits and those which lack character. Then replace the load in the tumbler (which must also be thoroughly flushed out—sides, lid, everything) and add the finer abrasive, water, and perhaps a little detergent to increase wetting of the stony surfaces, and continue tumbling.

TUMBLED GEMS AS JEWELS

Tumbled gems, which began as raw, rough fragments of gemmy minerals, are usually produced in such quantities, even with a small tumbler, that the lapidary will wonder what to do with them all. Every rock shop has bins full of tumbled stones, with retail prices ranging from 5 cents apiece to rarely more than 15 cents. These highly polished roughs are only the raw materials for baroque jewelry. With any of them the problem has always been how best to fasten the stones securely in their mountings. Because of their varied shapes, drilling holes is neither practical nor desirable.

Many systems have been tried for mounting these irregular polished gemstones for wearing. The most successful is to use small gold-finished metal caps that can be cemented onto a rounded corner with epoxy resins. These bell caps have prongs which can be spread and then squeezed down to fit the contours of the stone; the tiny ring at the top then allows for stringing on a gold or silver chain. Another technique is to slot one end of the stone with a thin diamond jeweler's saw and cement a thin metal ring into the slot.

However you attempt to handle tumbled gems, it is absolutely necessary that scrupulous cleanliness be observed. Even a trace of body oils from the fingers will loosen the epoxy, causing the stone to drop off eventually. To prevent oily contamination, the stones should be thoroughly washed in acetone or any grease-dissolving solvent (except gasoline and cigarette lighter fluid, which are not adequate) and subsequently not touched at all wherever the epoxy is to be applied.

CUTTING CABOCHONS

Whole books have been written on the techniques of cutting gemstones into a multitude of cabochon shapes. Unlike faceted gems, which are cut to bring out sparkle and pure colors, cabochons are made into ovals, squares, rectangles, hearts, or other geometric shapes, usually fairly thin with a rounded top surface and a flat base. A cabochon is often the best form to bring out interior pattern and design or the colors and patterning on the surface of opaque material. The numerous books available on lapidary techniques provide all the necessary instructions for making templates (or buying ready-made plastic templates) and cutting and polishing any shape and style of cabochon and have information beyond the scope of this chapter.

Cabochon cuts are distinctive from the faceting of gems and crystal gemstones. The cabochon cut is a means for displaying color, design, and such phenomena previously described as chatoyancy, aventurescence, adularescence, labradorescence, iridescence, and pattern effects. Opaque gemstones, such as nephrite, jadeite, jasper, jet, etc., make attractive jewels when cut cabochon, as do the crystal gemstones which show asterism. Cat's-eye gems, because of their many hairlike inclusions, are best cut cabochon rather than as faceted gems.

STYLES AND TEMPLATES

Cabochon styles have been pretty well standardized for outline and cross section. The most common style is an oval in a large range of length to width ratios, having a perfectly flat base for easy mounting into a ring or other setting. Various degrees of upper curvature produce "cabs" of low, medium, or high roundness. Nearly all cabochons must be ground and polished by hand.

In selecting cabochon material for processing, the choice should be based on quality and freedom from flawing, cracks, pits, or other irregularities. Many gemstone materials contain soft spots which are likely to undercut during sanding and polishing. Whether opaque, translucent, or transparent, the cabochon rough should be a solid piece that will not break along cleavage planes or shatter or chip during trimming, grinding, sanding, and polishing.

A slab or thin slice of gemstone material is usually the rough material from which a cabochon is cut. Thickness should range from one-eighth to one-quarter inch, with exceptionally large cabochons requiring up to three-eighths-inch thickness. Standard plastic templates cut into various-sized ovals, crosses, rectangles, heart shapes, and pendant shapes can be purchased.

By selecting a particular area of interesting design in the rough slice and positioning one or another template over it, you can use an ordinary lead pencil to outline the shape most appropriate to the design in the stone. Even draftsman's templates can be used. Many shapes in any size can be drawn onto a rough slice of gemstone; careful sawing will separate them into individual cabochon roughs. All that is needed subsequently is the skill to trim them down to the approximate line of the pencil marks and to grind and sand them until the blank is ready for final polishing.

TRIM-SAWING AND GRINDING

The cabochon blanks marked on the rock slice must not only be sawed out but trimmed down to the outline form. The trim-sawing only approximates the curves of the blank, leaving many small corner projections which can be nibbled off with a pair of slip-point pliers. Very tough materials like jade and rhodonite cannot be nibbled, but the quartz family minerals chip off nicely.

Finally, the penciled outline requires grinding right down to the outline itself, a hand-held project that is surprisingly easy. The stone is first held against a coarse grinding wheel and then finished against a fine grinder. By sweeping the blank from side to side to create smooth curves, you can develop astonishing accuracy simply by eye.

Another basic step in preparing a cabochon is beveling the edges to avoid the possibility of chipping. This is done on the same grinding wheels, often simply by hand and eye, although much experience is needed for accurate workmanship. When the rough blank has been preformed to the general shape of the desired cabochon, the final grind and polish must be done with the aid of a dop stick. The cabochon blank is fastened securely to the squared-off end with ordinary sealing wax, stick shellac, or a mixture of the two with beeswax and powdered clay. Some caution has to be exercised if the gemstone is critically heat-sensitive, because the heat of the melted wax may be sufficient to crack or shatter it. Once fastened, the stone is ready for being worked.

Without going into specific details of how to grind bevels, curves, and surfaces onto the gemstone while holding the dop stick in the hand, it is sufficient to state that the dop stick itself serves only as an easily controlled extension of the fingers, allowing fine detailed grinding and polishing at any angle and pressure. All the grinding and polishing techniques so briefly outlined in previous sections apply to finishing off a cabochon.

In Conclusion

There have been great advances in the use of automated and powered lapidary equipment. But no beginner should assume that any equipment has been invented that will take a rough rock specimen and, after a series of buttons have been punched, process it automatically into a finished gem. Hand cutting, grinding, and polishing are still the most expedient means for converting rough stones into beautiful objects, tedious as the process may be.

The art of the lapidary is not a full-fledged science. It remains, as it has for thousands of years, a peculiar skill of mind and eye and hand, augmented and assisted here and there by powered devices. The lapidary arts are entirely separate from the field collecting of gems and minerals, yet closely associated with everything brought home, including the enduring memory of sun and skies and far horizons.

part II

Where to Find Gems and Minerals in America

(Located alphabetically by states, counties, towns, and a progressive order of mileages)

Introduction

With the exception of Hawaii, each of the states in our country has interesting gem and mineral localities. Much of the land in the far-flung western states is government-owned, e.g., 99.7 percent in Alaska, 87 percent in Nevada, and 55 percent in Arizona. All such land is wide open, free of any limitations, to the collector, except where military bombing ranges were established during and after World War II. Even on these restricted and sometimes dangerous lands, collecting is often permitted on weekends, with permission being granted by the cognizant commanding officer.

In most states, especially those lying east of the 100th meridian, almost all gem and mineral collecting fields lie on private lands. Permission is usually given collectors, or entire rock clubs, often involving payment of a small fee. Although some private property has been closed to the public because of past irresponsible acts, such localities have been included here; they may someday be reopened to future collectors.

Wherever possible, every collecting locality has been pinpointed by the nearest community with road map numbers and mileages to the site, prefixed with the average compass direction that can be laid out on a map. Thus: "SOUTHAMPTON, ESE 18 mi. (via U.S. 21 and Rtes. 210 and 346), to Bear Paw Mt., on W side slopes—**garnets**" would be translated as "approximately 18 miles east-southeast from the town of Southampton by following the numbered highways on the map and prospecting the general slopes, draws, and gullies on the west side of Bear Paw Mountain for garnets." Precise road turns and by-passes may or may not be included, but the collector is presumed to have an accurate map along and a reasonably accurate odometer on his car.

Not all collecting sites can be easily reached; many are located in almost inaccessible regions that can be reached only by jeep-type roads or long hikes. The collector must be left to his own devices and accurate topographic maps to find his way thither, if he is so inclined (and a surprising number are willing to tackle such difficult locations, knowing that prime gems are less likely to have been cleaned out).

Abandoned mines and quarries can be dangerous. The collector should exercise the utmost caution to avoid overhanging walls and delicately poised rock masses. Where mines and quarries are still active, permission should be requested from the foreman or superintendent. He will determine the most favorable and safest times and places where collecting can be done without interfering with the commercial operations. Also, he usually has a collection of prime specimens set aside to give away or sell at minuscule prices.

Every state has far more mines and quarries or gravel pits than can possibly be listed in a single volume. For example, the complete list of mines and prospects for San Bernardino County, California, comprises a state-printed book of more than 300 pages! Therefore, for each described locality, the collector is advised to inquire and look around for other, unlisted nearby mines or excavations that may be equally productive of gems and minerals as the one described.

Alphabetization of a state's counties does not, of course, indicate progressive cross-country routing. The collector who plans an extensive collecting trip should use a map and lay out the order of the counties along his preferred route. Unfortunately, so many gem-rich counties lie well off the main transtate highways that special side trips may have to be made in order to reach their gem and mineral fields. Many main highways pass through no mineralized counties at all.

In any state listing, certain counties show a superabundance of localities. In planning a cross-country tour, the collector may wish to develop his own peculiar routing to take in such productive areas.

The county boundaries for each city and town were determined from the collective maps of the American Automobile Association. These maps show all county boundaries, which few of the oil company maps do. Finding a particular productive county by studying a map can be frustrating indeed; therefore, it usually becomes necessary to look up the name of one of the towns alphabetized under the county name in the index provided with each state map and locate it in the number-letter grid system. The name of the county will be shown somewhere nearby. This method will reveal in what section of a state any unfamiliar community and its nearby collecting areas are located.

The following coded information is used: N, ESE, SW, etc., for average common compass directions; "U.S." for main highways and interstate routes; "Rte." or "Hwy." for state highways; and "co. rd." for backcountry roads, often unpaved, with "Farm rd." an alternative.

Where several localities are found near a central starting point, they are numbered in parentheses successively in order of increasing mileages, as (1), (2), etc. Where further breakdowns of localities occur from any one of these numbered subdivisions (as secondary starting points), they are numbered in reasonable order as (a), (b), etc.

The term "AREA" may initiate a county listing to refer to the entire county coverage of old mines, quarries, gravel pits, building excavations, etc., and the collector should refer to a topographic map of the region for detailed information. This term, when used with a particular town starting point, means that all surrounding exposures, such as road cuts, road embankments, stream gravels, farm fields, etc., are likely sources for gems and minerals.

In many cases, some local inquiry may be required to obtain the ultimate road-by-road directions. Such inquiry may further reveal additional collecting localities known only to the local inhabitants that would be worth adding to the listings included here.

ALABAMA

Alabama comprises two major geologic regions. The northeast section is mountainous, constituting the southern end of the Cumberland Plateau and climaxing in 2,407-foot Cheaha Mountain. This crystalline or "mineral region" is composed primarily of metamorphosed Paleozoic rocks which are exposed and commercially mined in Chambers, Clay, Cleburne, Coosa, Randolph, Tallapoosa, and parts of Chilton, Elmore, and Lee counties. In this contorted, structurally complicated region of slates, phyllites, marbles, quartzites, and conglomerates the metamorphic series includes granites, schists (mica, garnet, graphite, quartz), and gneisses, as well as numerous granite pegmatites and ore-bearing veins. Prior to the California gold rush of 1849, this portion of Alabama experienced its own gold rush, largely unprofitable although gold may still be panned in the regional streams.

Most of the rest of the state, i.e., about 60 percent, is the gently rolling to flat Coastal Plain averaging about 500 feet above sea level. From this predominantly farming region the wide-spreading Tuscaloosa formation disgorges chert that has gemmy qualities for cutting and polishing.

For information and locality maps, write: Geological Survey of Alabama, University of Alabama, University.

AUTAUGA CO.

PRATTVILLE, N 6 mi., and just E of the Birmingham to Montgomery hwy., a unique deposit as a vertical vein from 10 to 24 in. wide enclosed in a ferruginous sandstone—**red ocher.** (Such deposits were well known to prehistoric Indians.)

BARBOUR CO.

BAKER HILL, SE 1 mi.: (1) in a deep ravine, as a bed deposit—**yellow ocher;** (2) nearby exposures, deep red to variegated—**ocher.**

BIBB CO.

AREA: (1) county gravel pits along the Cahaba R.—**gemmy minerals, petrified wood;** (2) area limestone quarries—**calcite, celestite, marble;** (3) SIXMILE (hamlet on Sixmile Cr.), area of abandoned mines—**barite** (crystallized, massive, nodular), **fluorite.**

CENTREVILLE: (1) area stream gravels, rd. cuts, banks, etc.—**siliceous gemstones;** (2) N 5 mi. on Rte. 5: (a) chert quarry—**barite crystals, chalcedony, chert, siliceous oolite;** (b) extending another 5 mi. N and E, adjacent to the Cahaba R. and Sixmile Cr., principally in adjacent parts of T. 25 N, R. 10, 11 E—**barite** deposits associated with fairly large crystals of **fluorite, sulfur** (in cavities), **limonite,** some **calcite crystals.**

BLOUNT CO.

BLOUNTSVILLE: (1) W 1 mi., in prospecting pits—**agate, carnelian, chalcedony, chert, sardonyx;** (2) along Hwy. 128, both sides, in gravel pits— **agate, chert.**

BLOUNT-ETOWAH COS.

AREA: (1) West Red Mt., top and NW slopes, and (2) in Murphrees Valley, as a narrow strip of scattered outcrops about 5 mi. long—**manganese minerals.**

CALHOUN CO.

AREA: (1) lead mines—**galena;** (2) sand, gravel pits—**quartz gemstones;** (3) iron mines—**hematite, magnetite, pyrite,** etc.; (4) limestone and dolomite quarries—**barite, calcite.**

ANGEL STATION (NW part of co.), area—**barite crystals.**

CEDAR BLUFF: (1) along shores of the Weiss Reservoir—**rock crystal;** (2) N 3.6 mi. on Rte. 9, on left side of rd.—**fluorite, quartz crystals;** (3) Little R., area—green **calcite.**

CHESTERFIELD, area manganese mines—**manganese minerals.**

JACKSONVILLE, W 5 mi., in Trenton limestone, in old Civil War quarries— **galena.** (Loose pieces of **galena** are found over the entire state, possibly dropped by prehistoric Indians from lead-producing areas of the upper Mississippi Valley. Not a county in Alabama but has a tradition of a "lead mine" worked by Indians.)

PELL CITY, NE 3 mi., area quarries—**black marble.** (The **marble** belt extends through Calhoun, Etowah, and St. Clair counties, with good-quality exposures much restricted.)

CHEROKEE CO.

CENTRE, area Miocene outcrops—**tektites.**

ROCK RUN: (1) area mines and furnaces, intercalated with "brown iron ore"—**limonite, manganite, psilomelane, pyrolusite;** (2) area lenses and pockets (also widely distributed throughout Alabama) along unconformable contacts between Cretaceous and Paleozoic horizons, as large pisolitic samples —**bauxite.**

CHILTON CO.

AREA: (1) east-central region (W and SW of the Coosa R. and E of the Louisville and Nashville RR), area pegmatite outcrops—**muscovite mica;** (2) SE region: (a) B. T. Childers prospect in NW¼ SE¼ Sec. 15, T. 22 N, R. 13 E, on S bank of a creek in the Hillabee schist—**arsenic, arsenopyrite, chalcopyrite, copper, gold, pyrite;** (b) Franklin or Jemison Mine, in NW¼- SW¼ Sec. 8, on tributary of Mulberry Cr., in the Talladega Formation, near remains of a 10-stamp mill—**gold, pyrite.**

CLANTON, W 13 mi. to Sec. 17, the Mulberry Cr. placers (most westerly exposures of the crystalline schists), along a branch of Mulberry Cr. exposing Hillabee schists—**gold.** (Stream gravels of Mulberry Cr. and its tributaries have long been worked for **gold.**)

CLARKE CO.

AREA, vein outcrops along county roads—**chert** (resembles **chalcedony**).

JACKSON: (1) N 1½ mi. and just E of hwy., a bed—**yellow ocher;** (2) NW 1 mi. to Clarke Co. Rd.: (a) 5.7 mi. from Rte. 43 jct. toward Coffeeville via first dirt rd. N, jct. area—**chalcedony;** (b) in road cuts and clay banks and along nearby Fire Tower Rd., and in stream gravels of tributary of the Tombigbee R.—**agate, chalcedony;** (c) 6½ mi. from Rte. 43 jct., in banks and rd. cuts—**septarian nodules;** (3) JACKSON-COFFEEVILLE-GROVE HILL, area deposits in the Tallahatta Formation (worked by prehistoric Indians)—**agate** ("Alabama blue," moss), **silicified wood.**

WALKER SPRINGS, SE 3 mi., near summit of a flat-topped hill, a bed— **dark yellow ocher.**

CLAY CO.

AREA: (1) pegmatite outcrops in the mica schists, as large platy books found in loose, weathered rock—**muscovite mica;** (2) Rte. 9 crossing of Ketchepedrakee Cr., in manganese deposits—**manganese minerals, rhodonite;** (3) Buzzard Cr. and tributaries—gemmy **chlorite, green quartz;** (4) Pyriton District (stretching 17 mi. NE to SW, many mica and gold mines in hills

W. of Rte. 9, reached only by rough roads)—**beryl, feldspar crystals, musco-vite mica, quartz crystals,** etc.

ASHLAND: (1) area: (a) M. & G. Mine—**apatite, garnet, smoky quartz;** (b) Gibson prospect—**garnets;** (c) Shirley prospects—**garnet, kyanite, magnetite, white tourmaline;** (d) along Pleasant Grove Rd., both sides—**quartz crystals;** (e) Coosa and Tallapoosa R. drainage area pegmatite outcrops, numerous old mines—**muscovite mica.** (A line drawn from the Delta Mica Mine in the NE corner of the county with a bearing 45° W will lie at all points about centrally of the observed and developed mica occurrences in Clay Co., as far S as the vicinity of IDAHO, *q.v.*, or immediately N of the Quenelda graphite mines.)

(2) NW 2½ mi., the Southern Graphite Co. quarry—**graphite.** (The known deposits of **graphite** are mostly confined to a zone with a NE–SW trend running from the NE corner of Clay Co. to MILLERVILLE, widening out southward, then, after a gap, showing up near Goodwater (Coosa Co.) and continuing a short way into Chilton Co., a length of about 60 mi. with widths from 2 to 5 mi. Associated with **graphite** are: **feldspar, micas (biotite, muscovite), quartz,** and **sillimanite;** the unweathered ore also carries **apatite, garnet, limonite,** and **pyrite.**

CRAGFORD: (1) area mines (including parts of Randolph Co.), as veins or disseminations in quartz—**arsenopyrite, chalcopyrite, galena, pyrite;** (2) Garrett Pyrite prospect, NE¼NE¼Sec. 17, T. 21 S, R. 6 E, in numerous pits along the creek—**pyrite.** (The pyrite found on the dumps is not solid, but botryoidal aggregates of small crystal pipes or stalactites, with radiating fibrous textures, as in some forms of **limonite.**)

DELTA: (1) the old Delta Mine, on dumps—**beryl, kyanite, tourmaline;** (2) NW 2.6 mi., the Smith No. 1 Mine—gem **beryl, feldspar crystals, garnets** (to 1 in. dia.), **kyanite, black tourmaline.**

ERIN: (1) area RR cuts, as encrustations—**turquoise** (or **wavellite**); (2) S, along W side of Gold Mines Cr. (S of Talladega Cr.): (a) many mica mines and prospects—gem **apatite, beryl** (golden, green), **feldspar (albite, microcline), garnets (rhodolite, almandite), muscovite mica, tourmaline;** (b) E bank of Gold Mines Cr., in boulders—**actinolite, chlorite, olivine** and, upstream, **garnets (pyrope,** massive), **placer gold, sillimanite, talc;** (c) Bob Lee Mine, abundant—**garnets;** (3) Pleasant Grove Church: (a) just S, and (b) N 2½ mi.—**copper minerals, turquoise.**

IDAHO (DISTRICT), in Ashland schists of W part of co. lying SW of the pyrite mines (cf. ASHLAND), in the Hillabee schists: (1) T. 19, 20 S, R. 7 E, several notable old mines—**placer gold;** (2) SW 7 mi.: (a) Harall Gold Mine, Sec. 34, T. 20 S, R. 6 E—**gold;** (b) Prospect Tunnel, SW¼Sec. 23, T. 21 S, R. 7 E—**gold;** (c) Stringfellow prospect, Sec. 19, T. 20 S, R. 7 E—**chalcanthite, chalcopyrite, garnets, graphite, pyrite, turquoise.**

LINEVILLE, E by secondary roads N and S of Rte. 48, starting 1½ mi. E of town: (1) numerous pegmatite outcrops in area bordered by Crooked Cr. (S) and Fox Cr. (N); (2) Barfield, Gibbs, and Griffin mines—**feldspar crystals, garnets, quartz crystals, tourmaline.**

TALLADEGA, S 13 mi. along Rte. 7, in rd. cuts—**alum, azurite, graphite, hematite, kaolin, malachite, pyrite, uranium minerals.**

CLEBURNE CO.

AREA of extreme S border with Randolph Co., no communities shown on map but various mining districts overlap into Randolph Co.: (1) Dyne Cr., outcrops—**kyanite;** (2) Jim Flemming Mine—**beryl, garnet, hornblende crystals, kyanite, quartz crystals, tourmaline;** (3) Morris Mica Mine, near center of NE¼NW¼ Sec. 21, T. 17 S, R. 10 E, in pegmatite—**crystals of garnet, kyanite, quartz** in **hornblende** and **muscovite** schists; (4) extreme S border, area deposits—**barite.**

ARBACOOCHEE (District): (1) Arbacoochee Placer, Sec. 5, 6, T. 17 S, R. 11 E, most extraordinary gold placer in Alabama, covering some 600 acres on the top and sides of Gold Hill, once employing 600 miners—**gold;** (2) Clear Cr. Placer, Sec. 7, long famed for its rich production—**gold;** (3) Anna Howe mines, Sec. 34, T. 16 S, R. 11 E, first gold-bearing quartz discovery in district—**gold;** (4) Valdor property, Sec. 3, T. 17 S, R. 11 E, in bedded vein—**gold;** (5) Hicks-Wise Mine, Sec. 2, deepest gold mine in state —**gold;** (6) Lee Mine, Sec. 2—**gold;**

(7) S of Arbacoochee: (a) Golden Eagle or Prince Mine, Sec. 17, T. 17 S, R. 11 E; (b) Crown Point property, Sec. 25; (c) Eckles property, Sec. 23, T. 17 S, R. 10 E; (d) Mossback property, Sec. 35, T. 17 S, R. 11 E—**gold;** (e) Wood's Copper Mine, Sec. 35, under iron gossan and the first paying copper discovery in Alabama (1874), a rich zone of secondary **chalcocite,** abundant—**azurite, chalcopyrite, copper (native), copper sulfides, cuprite, garnets, gold, malachite, muscovite mica, pyrite** (iron, copper, massive), **pyrrhotite, silver;** (f) Lucky Joe, Sec. 25; (g) Pritchet property, Sec. 36; (h) Ayers prospect, SW¼SW¼ Sec. 33, just E of the Blake cemetery—**gold;** (i) Smith's Copper Mine—**chalcanthite, pyrite, pyrrhotite;** (j) Stone Hill Copper Mine; (k) other nearby mines—**copper sulfides; sphalerite;** (1) Turkey Heaven, area—**kyanite;**

(8) E of Arbacoochee: (a) Middlebrook property, Sec. 3, T. 17 S, R. 12 E; (b) Sutherland property, Sec. 34, T. 16 S, R. 12 E, as low-grade deposits —**gold;** (9) NE of Arbacoochee, Marion White property, Sec. 6, T. 16, S, R. 12 E, once source of rich specimen ore and float—**gold.**

CHULAFINNEE (District): (1) Chulafinnee Placer, Sec. 14, 15, 16, T. 17 S, R. 9 E (mining mostly along Chulafinnee Cr. in gravels which were 5 to 6 ft. under soil surface)—**gold;** (2) Carr Cr. Placer, Sec. 23, 24, some 240 acres in a deposit of gravel and clay, fine—**gold;** (3) Rev. King's property, E½NW¼ Sec. 22 (3 mi. W of CHULAFINNEE), old stamp mill, in decomposed quartz—**gold;** (4) King Mine, Sec. 16, stamp mill, pit covering 2,500 sq. ft.—**gold;** (5) Striplin property, Sec. 22, shallow openings showing stringers of quartz in schist—**gold;** (6) Higginbottom property, adjoining the Striplin on NE, thin quartz veins in decomposed schist, obtainable by panning—**gold.**

MICAVILLE CHURCH (Take Rte. 37 from its jct. with Rte. 9, 2 mi. after crossing the Tallapoosa R. This road branches to the E along the county line.) Along both sides are numerous: (1) old mica mines and prospects— **muscovite mica** and **accessory minerals;** (2) many pegmatite exposures in rd. cuts—**pegmatite gems and minerals.**

COLBERT CO.

ALLSBOROUGH: (1) area outcrops, excellent—**yellow ocher;** (2) NW 4 mi., in Sec. 6, T. 4 S, R. 14 W, in bed and banks of a small stream as a light deposit containing many thin streaks of white clay and overlain by a ledge of ferruginous conglomerate—**yellow ocher.**
MARGERUM, area, highly ferruginous—**bauxite.**

COOSA CO.

AREA: (1) countywide pegmatite outcrops—**muscovite mica** and **accessory minerals;** (2) countywide old gold mines—**gold, rutile, staurolites, zircon;** (a) Flint Hill, Sec. 17, T. 22 N, R. 16 E, in heavy quartz vein as a trace—**gold;** (b) Goldbranch, NE 1 mi., at Stewart or Parsons mines, Sec. 4, T. 23 N, R. 17 E, in 200-ft.-wide auriferous part of the ridge, first worked by open cuts—**gold, bronzy pyrite;** (c) Gold Ridge Mine, Sec. 1, 2, T. 21 N, R. 16 E—**copper minerals, gold, graphite.**
BRADFORD, area pegmatites—**beryl, corundum, feldspar, quartz crystals, sapphires.**
HANOVER, area, as numerous fine crystals—**corundum.**
HATCHETT CREEK: (1) Alum Bluff, near mouth of a creek, Sec. 35, T. 22 N, R. 16 E, on an elevation in an 8-ft. quartz vein—**alum, gold, iron sulfates, pyrite;** (2) old Miller mines (1840)—**gold;** (3) Ivey Mine, NE¼ NW¼ NE¼ Sec. 15, T. 22 N, R. 16 E and 1½ mi. E of the Coosa R. at a point midway between old power plant at Lock 12 and Mitchell Dam—**muscovite mica** and **accessory minerals.**
HISSOP: (1) NE 1 mi., then ¾ mi. SW, area—**golden beryl;** (2) N 1 mi. on rd. toward CREWSVILLE, then secondary rd. left (keep left) to a Y after ¾ mi. (a) Thomas prospect—**aquamarine, gem beryl** (lime green, yellow), **biotite mica,** massive white **quartz;** (b) several mines just N of the Thomas (e.g., Coward, Brown, Hatchet)—**pegmatite crystals.** (The ROCKFORD, q.v., mining district runs about 8 mi. E and 8 mi. W of HISSOP, embracing about 32 sq. mi.)
MARBLE VALLEY, extending in a narrow belt along the border of the metamorphic area through Talladega into Calhoun Co., 35 mi. long and averaging ½ mi. wide, with many regional quarries—**marble** (crystalline, gemmy, takes a fine polish).
ROCKFORD: (1) entire area, as described for HISSOP, old mica and tin mines, abundant—**gems, crystals, minerals;** (2) SE limits of town, excavations—**gold;** (3) N, toward GOODWATER, many pegmatite outcrops—**cassiterite, feldspar crystals, muscovite, quartz;** (4) W 1 mi. on Rte. 22, turn right on trace that dead-ends near the Pond Mine, on dumps—**feldspar, garnets, moonstone, quartz, tourmaline;** (5) NE 1 mi., between Rtes. 11 and 22, on tributary to Jack's Cr., the Millsite Tin Mine—**albite, apatite, cassiterite, epidote, garnets, lepidolite, rock crystal, sillimanite, topaz, black tourmaline;**
(6) W 1½ mi., at Bently tin property in SW¼ Sec. 14, T. 22 N, R. 18 E (only authentic occurrence of tin in Alabama)—**cassiterite.** The crystals

are well-formed octahedral, showing narrow V-faces of the primary prism between the pyramids, to ½-in. dia. Also, some **tantalite** and **tourmaline** are present; (7) W 2 mi.: (a) Pond Mine—**muscovite;** (b) on N side of Rte. 22, the Two Bit Mine—see (5); (8) CREWSVILLE, W 2 mi., the 1400 Tin Mine —see (5); (9) Carroll and Pole Branches, placer sands—**gold;** (10) Gin-House Branch, in stream bed—**gold.**

DE KALB CO.

FORT PAYNE: (1) area iron ore deposits—gemmy **chert, hematite;** (2) NW 4 mi., in Will's Valley, only locality developed to any extent in Alabama— **fuller's earth.**

ELMORE CO.

AREA: (1) gravels of Coosa R. and Tallapoosa R.—**silicified wood** (some palm); (2) along shores of Lake Martin—**silicified wood.**

ETOWAH CO.

AREA, along the S boundary in Greens Creek Valley, deposits—**barite crystals.**

FRANKLIN CO.

WACO, in the Adah Quarry, as large quantities of excellent cabinet specimens—**oolitic limestone.**

GREENE CO.

PLEASANT RIDGE, area deposits of a resinous yellow to brown hydrocarbon —**walchowite.**

JACKSON CO.

PAINT ROCK: (1) area river and tributary gravels—**agate** ("Paint Rock"), gemmy **chert, rock crystal,** brown **sardonyx;** (2) area dry washes, hillsides, coves, banks, cliffs—**agate;** (3) Jacobs Mt.—**agate, chert, jasper.**

JEFFERSON CO.

LEEDS, SW 3½ mi., area deposits—**barite crystals.**

LEE CO.

AREA, sandstone quarries—**itacolumnite** (flexible sandstone).
AUBURN: (1) many nearby localities (check with rock shops in town); (2) 10 mi. distant—gemmy **quartzite** (partly opalized); (3) area abandoned mica prospects—**mica, pegmatite gems, minerals.**
OPELIKA, SE, in springs area fields, rd. cuts, banks, etc., especially behind the Boy Scout camp—**rock crystal.**

MADISON CO.

AREA: (1) stream gravels, as float—**"Paint Rock" agate,** gemmy **chert;** (2) regional barite quarries—**barite crystals.**
GURLEY: SE on Rte. 72, on small mt.—gemmy **chert** (grades into **chalcedony**).

MARENGO CO.

BARTON'S BLUFF, area—**calcite crystals.**

MARION CO.

PEARCE'S HILL (and area outcrops)—**red ocher.**

MARSHALL CO.

GUNTERVILLE, area stream gravels—**rock crystal.**

MONROE CO.

JONES MILL, SW 5 mi., in banks of a small stream—**yellow ocher.**
PERDUE HILL, E 3 mi., in a gully just N of the main hwy to MONROEVILLE, as bright yellow outcrops—**ocher.**

RANDOLPH CO.

AREA: (1) numerous pegmatite exposures throughout co.—**quartz crystals, rutile, tourmaline,** etc.; (2) regional stream sands—**placer gold, rutile crystals;** (3) regional metamorphic or intrusive contact zones—carvable **steatite;** (4) area manganese mines—**ankerite, manganese minerals, siderite.** (There are more than 100 mines, some still active, in this county, with dumps well supplied with minerals, crystals, and gems; most mines are in the belt along the N border with Cleburne Co.; cf. ARBACOOCHEE District.)

MICAVILLE (site of first attempted recovery of mica commercially in the state from what was later known as the Pinetucky Gold Mine)—**muscovite mica.** This district has various mica mines with productive dumps, e.g.: Pinetucky, NW via Rte. 37 (the Micaville Rd.) and numerous side roads, mines near the Cleburne Co. line E of the Tallapoosa R. and W of Pinewood Cr.—**pegmatite minerals;** (2) just N of Pinetucky, group of famous mines: (a) Great Southern Mine, just off Rte. 37, abundant—**apatite, aquamarine, beryl, garnet, black tourmaline;** (b) Liberty Mine—gem **apatite, garnet, pyrite, tourmaline;** (c) Haynes Mine—gem **tourmaline;** (d) Arnott No. 1 prospect—massive **garnet;** (e) Edwards, Crystal Clear, and many nearby mines—**pegmatite minerals;**

(3) Along N border of co.: (a) Gold Ridge property, Sec. 4, T. 17 S, R. 10 E, in highly garnetiferous mica schist—iron-aluminum **garnets** (to 3 in. dia., many much decomposed), **gold** (free-milling, sulfides), **magnetite, manganese minerals;** (b) Pinetucky Gold Mine, Sec. 12, T. 18 S, R. 10 E, a "rich specimen" mine extensively worked in quartz—**auriferous sulfides, garnets, native gold, muscovite;** (4) along W boundary of co. (extending into E section of Clay Co.'s CRAGFORD district, *q.v.*), T. 19, 20 S, R. 9, 10 E, numerous placer mines, e.g., the Manning, Goldberg, Dawkins, Farrar, Bradford Ridge, Pine Hill, Teakle, Morris, Grizzel, etc.—**antimony, arsenic, arsenopyrite, copper, gold.**

MILNER: (1) N, toward Pinetucky, W of connecting rd. and about midway between, the Jones No. 1 Mine—**apatite** (blue, spectacular), **rhodolite garnet, black tourmaline;** (2) W: (a) Vickers prospect, dumps, abundant—**tourmaline;** (b) J. J. New No. 2 Mine—**garnets** (maroon, to 1½ in. dia.); (3) E 2 mi. and just N of Rice Mill—**apatite** (turquoise color), **rhodolite garnet.**

SHELBY CO.

HARPERSVILLE, area deposits—**barite.**

SAGINAW, area of Longview, old pits—**barite.**

SHELBY, NW ½ mi., in abandoned brown iron ore workings—**red ocher** containing pebbles of **hematite.**

VINCENT, in E part of co., including HARPERSVILLE, *q.v.*, and WILSONVILLE districts—**barite.**

ST. CLAIR CO.

AREA: (1) old copper prospects—**azurite, malachite;** (2) Coosa R. banks and gravels —**wavellite;** (3) regional barite pits—**barite;** (4) Beaver Cr. Mts., in limestone exposures—gemmy **chert.**

BROMPTON, E 1¼ mi., at Prescott Siding, once found here—**diamonds.**

SUMPTER CO.

LIVINGSTON, area quarries and gravels of the Tombigbee R. and tributaries, in limestone—**pyrite** (crusts, nodules).

TALLADEGA CO.

AREA: (1) ½ mi. E of Clay Co. line and ½ mi. S of Rte. 48, a metamorphic exposure, the Pitts Mine—gemmy **hornblende gneiss** (pistachio green, veined with white quartz); (2) SE part of co., the Riddle's Mill District (most important gold mining area of the Talladega series), numerous mines in Sec. 16, 20, T. 19 S, R. 6 E, such as Ribble's Mine, Woodford Tract, Storey, Warwick, and Cogburn or Gold Log Mine—**chalcopyrite** (with **bornite** tarnish), **enargite, gold, magnetite, pyrite**.

ALPINE, at a talc mill—carvable **steatite**.

SYLACAUGA, area marble quarries—**ornamental marble** (white and cream color), **snowy marble** (with **pyrite cube** inclusions). This marble deposit is about 32 mi. long, 1½ mi. wide, and 400 ft. thick.

WINTERBORO, area outcrops in Cambrian-Ordovician limestones—**calcite onyx, steatite**.

TALLAPOOSA CO.

AREA: (1) This county contains four major gold-mining districts: Devil's Back Bone, Eagle Creek, Goldville, and Hog Mountain: (a) Goldville District, about 14 mi. long, scene of a major mining boom in the early days; (b) the mines of the Devil's Back Bone and Eagle Creek districts, which occur at varying intervals along a narrow belt of slates, were less important; (2) many active and inactive prospects and quarries—**andalusite, asbestos, bauxite, chromite, ilmenite, monazite, scheelite, spinel**, etc.; (3) Coon Creek, near the Tallapoosa R., a prehistoric Indian quarry, as occasional artifacts and as fine specimens—**soapstone. Soapstone (steatite, talc)** is rather widely distributed in Tallapoosa, Chambers, and Randolph counties as a greenish, schistose rock consisting of a felt or mesh of **actinolite** crystals and **steatite**, frequently studded with **garnets** to an inch or more in dia.; (4) Ham's Cut, on Central of Georgia RR, in igneous dikes—**asbestos, corundum**, etc.

ALEXANDER CITY: (1) W shores of Lake Martin: (a) numerous outcrops —gem **epidote**; (b) Wind Cr. area, large deposit—**actinolite, bronzite, cleavelandite, epidote crystals, feldspar crystals, specular hematite, gemmy quartz**; (c) various unexplored localities along the several hundred miles of lakeshore—**gems, minerals** yet to be found; (2) E shore of Lake Martin: (a) various access areas—**actinolite, feldspar, quartz crystals, unakite**; (b) many unexplored mineral-rich areas around this side of the lake; (3) S, several miles along the river—**corundum. (Corundum—ruby, sapphire**—is often associated with **asbestos** and **steatite**.) (4) NE 13 mi., at Hog Mountain, unique old gold-mining district in that the veins were in granite; this locality was where cyaniding was first introduced into Alabama for the recovery of gold—**arsenic, arsenopyrite, galena, gold, graphite, pyrite, pyrrhotite, sphalerite**, etc.

DADEVILLE: (1) area dikes and veins cutting crystalline schists—**corundum**; (2) area mica mines: (a) Kidd Mine—violet red **garnets, pyrite, quartz crystals, sericite**; (b) Camp Hill, at the Doc Heard prospect—**garnet, graphic** granite, **muscovite, smoky quartz, tourmaline;** (3) NE 11 mi., at Carleton (Buttston) Mine—**muscovite, pegmatite gems.**

DUDLEYVILLE: (1) area mine dumps (N of DADEVILLE and W of DUDLEY-VILLE, on NE–SW angle with N section drained by tributaries of the North Fork of Sandy Cr.)—**margarite, sapphire;** (2) NW 2–3 mi., area—**corundum;** (3) Easton district: (a) area dikes of igneous rocks—**corundum;** (b) E 1¾ mi., at Easterwood Mine—**muscovite;** (c) Mica Hill Mine, on one of the highest peaks (knobs) in SE Alabama; (d) ½ mi. NW of Mica Hill Mine in NW¼SE¼ Sec. 12, T. 22 N, R. 23 E, just S of the Montgomery hwy., at the Berry Mine—**muscovite, garnets.**

ZANA, area igneous outcrops—**lazurite, pyrite, smoky quartz.**

TUSCALOOSA CO.

BROOKWOOD: (1) area stream gravels, iron mines, and pits along the Black Warrior R., W to PETERSON—**agate, chalcedony, fossils, jasper, kyanite, steatite, vivianite;** (2) nearby strip mines reached via local rd. 4 mi. W of town leading N to mines—**nodular hematite, quartz crystals, siderite.**

GOETHITE, Brown Ore Mine, on dumps below washer and tipple—**goethite, limonite.**

TUSCALOOSA, S, in area gravels, abundant and gem quality—**silicified wood.**

ALASKA

America's forty-ninth and largest state has long been facetiously called Seward's Folly or Uncle Sam's Attic, and more truthfully, the Billion-Dollar Land. Hundreds of great mineral strikes made during the first seventy-three years after the fledgling United States purchased Alaska from the Russians for $7 million (about 2 cents an acre) produced a registered total of more than half a billion dollars, to be exact, $579,647,-730 in pre-World War II gold and silver and copper. Even greater wealth in oil is now being developed along the shores of the Arctic Ocean.

From Ketchikan (nearest Alaskan city to Seattle, Washington) to Attu Island fronting onto the Kamchatkan shores of Asia is as far as from New York City to San Francisco—a 3,000-mile span of the far northern longitudes. The main continental bulk of Alaska, reaching to within 1,300 miles of the North Pole, is really the northern terminous of an immense granite batholith that extends along the spine of both South and North America, unbelievably rich in commercial metallic ores and unexplored deposits of gemstones. Owing to its general inaccessibility, Alaska will long remain one of the most mineralized but least explored regions in North America.

Geographically, Alaska is divided into four major regions, rather than counties: Southeastern—rugged coastal mountains, fjords, and timbered islands; Alaska Peninsula and Aleutian Islands—volcanically active peninsula and island archipelago extending across the North Pacific almost to within sight of Kamchatka; Interior—sea-level plains forested with birch and spruce and rolling hills embracing thousands of tundra lakes within the vast drainage systems of the Kuskokwim and Yukon rivers, a region nearly twice the size of Texas; and the Arctic Slope—treeless tundra plains sloping northward from the east-west transverse Brooks Range to the Arctic Ocean. Except for jade in the extreme northwest portion of the state, the ore minerals have completely dominated the gemstones, and today it is oil.

Alaska is 99.7 percent public land. New prospectors, whether for gemmy substances or for commercially valuable minerals, are sure to be welcomed with open-handed prodigality. However, only those rugged individualists who are well financed, are inured to physical hardship and loneliness, and possess an expert's capabilities for prospecting and solving the survival problems to be encountered in any virgin wilderness should try their luck in any area at all off the little-traveled nine state highways.

For more detailed information, write: Department of Mines, University of Alaska, College, Alaska.

ALASKA PENINSULA and BRISTOL BAY

BRISTOL (NUSHAGAK) BAY: (1) area and along the Wood R., many scattered prospects—**cinnabar;** (2) Kujulik Bay, area—**petrified wood;** (3) Mulchatna R., upper reaches, as placers—**gold.**

KATMAI NATIONAL MONUMENT: (1) area outside boundaries: (a) N, Nonvianuk Lake, along shores—**agate, petrified wood;** (b) farther N, Iliamna Lake and Lake Clark, in gravels of inflowing streams, as placer deposits—**gold;** (c) S, Becharof Lake, on N shore and near outlet, as pale red and honey-colored pebbles—**carnelian;** (2) Valley of Ten Thousand Smokes, area fumaroles and volcanic pits—**pumice, sulfur;** (3) far SW peninsular beaches from Chignik Bay to Tuxedni Bay, as seepages—**petroleum.**

ALEUTIAN ISLANDS

This 1,200-mile-long arc of islands begins with Kodiak Island, south of the Kenai Peninsula at the head of the Gulf of Alaska and extends along the south coast of the Alaska Peninsula to Unimak Island, then south and west to Attu across the North Pacific, separating that ocean from the Bering Sea. No transportation exists other than by an occasional ship or by air (usually a chartered "bush pilot" plane). Each summer, however, sees numerous scientific expeditions working in the Aleutian Islands.

(1) ADAK Is., N shore beach gravels—gem **red jasper;** (2) AKUTAN Is., area volcanic deposits—**sulfur;** (3) ATKA Is., area petrified forest remnants, none of gem quality but of great specimen interest—**petrified wood;** (4) ATTU Is., SE beach gravels—gray pebbles of **chalcedony, jasper;** (5) KODIAK

Is., W coast beaches and contributary lodes—**copper, gold, lead, silver, tin, zinc;** (6) POPOF Is., beach placers and area lodes—**gold;**
(7) SEDANKA Is., small area high-grade deposits—**zinc;** (8) SHUMAGIN Is., SAND POINT, area beach gravels—**agate, carnelian, chalcedony, jasper;** (9) TANAGA Is., beach gravels, as pebbles—**agate;** (10) UNALASKA Is.: (a) UNALASKA, DUTCH HARBOR, area beach gravels of Captain's Bay to Priest Rock—**agate** (banded, gray), **chalcedony, green argillite, jasper;** (b) crater of Mt. Makushin—**sulfur;** (11) UNGA Is., Apollo Mine (operating since 1900) —**gold.**

INTERIOR REGION (Yukon River Drainage Basin)

Larger than many midwestern states, this immense territory contains the most important known placer **gold** deposits in Alaska. More than $200 million in gold was recovered from its mines prior to World War II, with the region between Eagle (on the Canadian border) downriver to Tanana being most productive. U.S. Geological Survey Bulletins No. 872 and 907, covering "The Yukon-Tanana Region," are especially detailed in the investigations of the mineral resources of this section of Alaska. In all the gold mining districts listed below, a chief ore mineral associated with gold is **stibnite,** along with **galena** and **pyrite.**

BONNIFIELD DISTRICT (including the Kantishna and Valdez Cr.), long an important mining center: (1) California-Totatlanika Cr. area, as a number of occurrences—**stibnite, lead-antimony sulfides, jamesonite** (fine-grained); (2) Eva Cr., near the Liberty Bell Mine and in float near Caribou Cr.—**ferberite, gold, lead, silver;** (3) Gold King, Marguerite, Moose, Platte, and Portage creeks, many area mines and prospects—**gold, lead, silver, stibnite.**

CACHE CREEK DISTRICT, many placer mines—**gold.**

CHANDALAR DISTRICT (N of Fort Yukon): (1) Big Cr., (2) Dictator Cr., (3) Little Squaw Cr., area placers—**gold.**

CHENA DISTRICT, about 70 mi. E of FAIRBANKS, the Palmer Cr. placers, abundant—**gold, scheelite.**

CHISANA (Shushanna) and NABESNA DISTRICTS: (1) Big Eldorado, Little Eldorado, Bonanza, Beaver Cr., and many other area placer mines—**gold;** (2) between Erickson Gulch and Bonanza Cr., many claims and prospects— **gold;** (3) Nabesna Mine area: (a) area pegmatite outcrops, (b) near MEN-TASTA, books and sheets to 12 in. dia.—**muscovite mica** and accessory minerals.

CHULITNA RIVER, upper reaches, many mines—**gold, lead, silver, zinc.**

CIRCLE DISTRICT: (1) Crazy Mts. area—**stibnite;** (2) Deadwood Cr.— abundant placer **tin, wolframite, cassiterite;** (3) Portage Cr., common— **cassiterite;** (4) S Fork of Birch Cr.—**stibnite.** (Throughout interior Alaska, **placer tin** is found in almost every mining district, except the Kuskokwim region and the Iditarod and Innoko areas. Similarly, **placer scheelite** occurs rather commonly, with **placer wolframite** less abundant, especially in the FAIRBANKS district.)

COLORADO, S 5 mi. along the Alaska RR, on Antimony Cr., lode ore— **stibnite.**

COPPER RIVER DISTRICT (see CORDOVA, SE Alaska): (1) many area wide-

spread mines and deposits—**copper, molybdenite;** (2) Bremmer R. placers—
gold; (3) Canyon Cr.: (a) head of, as lode ore—**nickel minerals;** (b) Mc-
Carthy vicinity in the upper Chitina R. Valley, high-grade deposits—
molybdenite; (4) Kennecott (Nizina) area: (a) part accessible from CHI-
TINA, lode mines—**copper, gold, silver** (the world-famed Kennecott Copper
Corp. mines and railroad access from Cordova were abandoned in 1938);
(b) upper valley area, served by highway from VALDEZ or ANCHORAGE—
copper, gold, silver mines; (c) Chistochina district mines—**copper, gold,
silver;** (d) Nerchina district placers—**gold;** (5) McKinley Lake, area lode
deposits—**gold.**

DONNELLY DISTRICT: (1) Alaska Range, Mt. Hayes: (a) N side, between Mt. Hayes and Ferry, at 5,000 ft., as float—**stibnite;** (b) N, in canyon
on Ptarmigan Cr., rich ore—**molybdenite;** (2) Rapids Roadhouse, S ½ mi.
on Gunnysack Cr. and ½ mi. upstream from rd.—**stibnite** (bearing **gold**).

EAGLE DISTRICT (just W of the Canadian border), placers on Fourth of
July, American, Alder, Barney, Woodchopper, and Crooked creeks, and on
the Seventymile R.—**gold.**

FAIRBANKS DISTRICT (principal gold placer area in Alaska and third most
productive of lode gold): (1) area placer claims covering a broad region—
antimony, gold, tungsten; (2) area creek gravels—lenses of **stibnite, gold,
quartz gemstones, fossils;** (3) FAIRBANKS: (a) N 70° E from Treasure Cr. to
lower Fairbanks Cr., an area 20 mi. long by 1 mi. wide, deposits—**gold,
stibnite, fossils;** (b) Ester Dome area, in a 6-mi.-dia. mineralized zone—
gold, stibnite; (c) NE 15–20 mi., country adjacent to Pedro Dome, placers
—**gold, fossils, petrified wood;** (d) valleys of Cleary, Gilmore, Goldstream,
Engineer, and Pedro creeks, placers—**cassiterite, gold, scheelite.**

FORTYMILE and GOODPASTURE DISTRICTS: (1) between headwaters of
the Middle Fork and the North Fork of the Fortymile R.—**scheelite;** (2)
Chicken, NW 10 mi. in Fortyfive Pup, a tributary of Buckskin Cr., abundant placer deposits—**gold, scheelite;** (3) Ketchumstuk and My creeks:
(a) area deposits of a replacement nature, in limestone—**copper, lead;**
(b) upper Ketchumstuk Cr., large deposit—**stibnite;** (c) E of the last-named,
in the Middle Fork drainage—**stibnite;** (4) Jack Wade, Walker Fork, and
such lesser camps as Stonehouse, Ingle, Lost Chicken, Napoleon, Franklin,
Davis, and Poker Creek, placers—**gold.**

GULKANA, 25 mi. distant, in large pegmatite exposure area—sheet **muscovite mica.**

HOT SPRINGS DISTRICT, S of Hot Springs Dome, in a basalt dike—**cobalt
bloom, nickeliferous pyrrhotite.**

IDITAROD DISTRICT (lower Yukon R. Valley): (1) regional placer and
lode veins, many—**cinnabar, copper, gold, lead, stibnite, tungsten, zinc;**
(2) FLAT, area placers—**gold;** (3) Otter Cr. (2 mi. S of FLAT), rich placers
—**gold.**

INNOKO DISTRICT: (1) Little and Ganes creeks, (2) Yankee Cr., regional
placers—**gold;** (3) OPHIR, S 5 mi. on No. 6 Pup, tributary to Little
Cr., placers—**scheelite.** (In the Innoko, Iditarod, Kantishna, McGrath, and
Sleitmute districts, along with **gold** there is usually **stibnite** associated with
cinnabar.)

KOYUKUK DISTRICT (a region embracing a very large tract of land and
consisting of three rather widely separated mining areas of interest, mostly

placers—**gold**): (1) Gold Cr. gravels, as pebbles—**stibnite;** (2) John R., near Hunts Fork—**stibnite.**

MARSHALL DISTRICT (including practically all of the W part of the Yukon Valley below HOLY CROSS): (1) area near MARSHALL, (2) in the Bonasila or Stuyahok Valley, placer mines—**gold.**

RAMPART DISTRICT: (1) area mines and placers—**gold;** (2) on Little Minook, Slate, and Hoosier creeks, both placer and lode mines, prospects, claims—**gold.** (Between RAMPART and TANANA, along the Yukon R., on N side, a high cliff of **bituminous coal** descends to the water's edge.)

RICHARDSON and FORT GIBBON, area placers—**gold.**

RUBY DISTRICT (an ill-defined region extending from RUBY, on the lower Yukon, for 50–60 mi. to include POORMAN and adjacent camps), mostly placers—**gold, antimony, lead, silver, tin.**

SALCHA DISTRICT, NE of the Splits of the Salcha R., in large area of basic igneous exposures—disseminated **chromite** in **peridotite** and **dunite, nickel minerals, platinum.**

STEVENS VILLAGE (100 mi. NNW of FAIRBANKS): (1) area sands of the Yukon R., by panning—**gold;** (2) S, to mouth of the Dall R., thence upriver in an area about 100 mi. across extending well N of the Arctic Circle, many placer prospects—**gold.**

TANANA, W, in the Gold Hill District on Morelock and Grant creeks, placers—**gold.**

TOK DISTRICT, on Boulder Cr. about 7 mi. above the Dry Tok Cr.—**stibnite.**

TOLAVANA DISTRICT (N and NW from FAIRBANKS): (1) area placers, notably in Lucky Gulch, Amy, Lucile, Ruth, and Olive creeks—**chrome spinels, chromite, cinnabar, gold;** (2) Lillian Cr., N side, cut bank just across highway crossing—**stibnite,** traces of **cinnabar** and **gold, nickel sulfides** and **silicates;** (3) LIVENGOOD, Claim No. 16 above Discovery Claim—**gold, stibnite.**

WADE CREEK, upper part, on property of the Wade Creek Dredging Co.—**gold, lepidolite.**

WISEMAN (200 mi. NW of FAIRBANKS), regional placer and lode mines—**gold.**

WOOD RIVER DISTRICT, near head of Kansas Cr., deposits—**stibnite.**

KOBUK RIVER REGION (accessible by air from Kotzebue)

Prospectors interested in this large region, which includes the drainage systems of the Kobuk, Noatak, and Alatna rivers, should be well financed and thoroughly familiar with technologies of prospecting and survival. Minerals include: **asbestos, coal, copper, iron, jade, lead, quartz crystals, silver,** etc.

CALIFORNIA CREEK (tributary of the Kogoluktuk R. from the E), as float amphibole and cross-fiber—**asbestos.** (The regional streams contain various derivative minerals of **serpentine.**)

DAHL CREEK: (1) area outcrops, as high-grade slip fiber—**chrysotile asbestos;** (2) Asbestos Mt., near top in lenses—**tremolite asbestos, chrysotile asbestos** associated with massive **serpentine, antigorite, magnesite, magnetite,** some **nickel;** (3) Jade Cr., area—**nephrite.**

KOBUK RIVER VALLEY: (1) E section, in vicinity of SHUNGNAK, as placers
—gold; (2) W part, near KIANA in valley of the Squirrel R. and especially
in its Klery Cr. tributary, numerous placers—gold. Both areas are extremely
remote and difficult to reach except by chartered airplane. In all regional
placers are also found platinum nuggets. (3) KOBUK, W 30 mi., Jade Hills
and Jade Mt., and in all regional stream gravels, many outcrops of high-
quality gem nephrite jade.

SHUNGNAK DISTRICT: (1) Shungnak R. area—asbestos, nephrite, serpentine; (2) prehistoric Eskimo village sites between SHUNGNAK and KIANA, in
house pit excavations—asbestos, nephrite (some as carved ornaments); (3)
W 50 mi., in valley of the Ambler R., placers—gold; (4) Squirrel R. District
and Shungnak District are probably the most favorable sections in Alaska
for new discoveries of gemstone and commercial mineral deposits, especially
gold, jade, platinum, etc. These districts lie in a large unmapped and practically unexplored mountainous region between the Kobuk and Noatak
rivers. The deposits on Shungnak R. and Jade Mt. are about 12 mi. W and
35 mi. NW, respectively, of the Dahl Cr. deposits (q.v.) and similarly located with respect to the Kobuk R. Each lies on the S slope of mountains
which sweep up and N from the broad Kobuk lowlands; (5) Cosmos Cr.,
4 mi. E of Shungnak R. and 8 mi. W of Dahl Cr. tremolite deposits, just
above canyon about 11 mi. from the Kobuk R.—asbestos, serpentine (whitish green float, massive); (6) Wesley Cr., 6 mi. W of the Dahl Cr. tremolite
mine, near head of creek—gold and other minerals.

KUSKOKWIM RIVER REGION

This is an enormous, generally sea-level region in southwestern Alaska embracing the drainage systems of the Kuskokwim River and its tributaries, all
south of the lower Yukon River Valley. The richly commerical gold-mining
districts revolve around MCGRATH, TAKOTNA, and MEDFRA in the upper
reaches of the Kuskokwim River in an area roughly 300 miles from NW to
SE by 150 miles wide.

EEK, KANEKTOK, TOGIAK RIVERS, area gravels, placers—gold.

GEORGETOWN DISTRICT: (1) central part of the Kuskokwim Valley (about
45 air mi. S of IDITAROD, Yukon Valley)—gold, platinum-group minerals
(native alloys); (2) GEORGETOWN, TAKOTNA, MCGRATH, NIXON FORKS,
many great placer operations—gold.

GOODNEWS DISTRICT: (1) area placers, especially: (a) on Book Cr. in the
Tolstoi district; (b) Granite Cr. in the Ruby district; (c) Slate Cr. in the
Chistochina district; (d) Cache and Peters creeks in the Talkeetna district;
and (e) from the Kohiltna R. in the Yentna district—gold, platinum and
platinum-group metals; (2) Goodnews Bay (a small indentation on the coast
on the E side of Kuskokwim Bay about 125 air miles S of BETHEL), high-
grade placer mines—platinum group metals, gold.

RUBY CREEK, old Pearson and Strand Mine, lode—gold.

SLEITMUT (SLEETMUTE) DISTRICT: (1) area deposits, widespread—cinnabar; (2) 8 mi. below SLEITMUT on S side of the Kuskokwim R., at the
Red Devil Mine—cinnabar; (3) upper Swift R., tributary to the Holitna R.
(about 75 air mi. from SLEITMUT)—cinnabar.

STONY RIVER, S toward Goodnews Bay across the Hoholitna, Holitna, and upper Aniak rivers, a barely explored mineralized region in need of extensive prospecting—**copper, gold, lead, silver, platinum, tin, zinc.**

TULUKSAK-ANIAK DISTRICT (named from its two rivers), large-scale placer operations—**gold.**

SEWARD PENINSULA (northwestern Alaska)

This westernmost extremity of North America is second only to the Yukon-Tanana region in the production of **placer gold,** mostly from the rich concentrations in the sands of the Bering Sea beaches at Nome. The peninsula mines also produced **copper, bismuth, iron, lead, mercury, silver, platinum, tin,** and **tungsten.** Almost everywhere can be found **cassiterite.**

BENDELEBEN MTS., area pegmatite exposures—**muscovite mica.**

BLUFF: (1) W 7 mi., on California and Coca Cola creeks, placers—**gold;** (2) lower course of Daniels Cr., placers—**gold;** (3) farther N, on Eldorado and Swede creeks—**gold.**

BONANZA DISTRICT (E side of the Seward Peninsula, forming the E border of Norton Sound), area placers—**gold.**

COUNCIL DISTRICT: (1) Aggie Cr. (tributary of Fish R.), (2) Crooked Cr. and on Benson Gulch (tributary of Melsing Cr.), and (3) Ophir Cr., all area placer mines—**gold.**

FAIRHAVEN (including the Candle and Inmachuk districts): (1) Bear Cr., many placer mines—**gold;** (2) Candle Cr.; (3) Inmachuk R.; (4) up the Kiwalik R. (on Quartz Cr. and on Gold Run a few miles below Quartz Cr.), many placer mines—**gold.**

KOUGAROK DISTRICT: (1) on the Kougarok R., near mouth of Henry Cr., many placer mines—**gold;** (2) near head of the Kougarok R., in vicinity of TAYLOR, especially on Macklin Cr. and its tributaries, area placers—**gold;** (3) S part of district: (a) Coffee Dome, area; (b) Iron Cr. and on American Cr. about 8 mi. E of Iron Cr., area placers—**gold.**

KOYUK DISTRICT (includes most of SE Seward Peninsula: (1) Dime Cr., and (2) HAYCOCK vicinity, many placer mines—**gold;** all other area creeks, especially on Monument Cr., numbers of open-cut mines—**gold;** (3) between Little and Dry creeks, extensive dredging operations—**gold.**

PORT CLARENCE DISTRICT (includes W part of peninsula, especially that part adjacent to TELLER and the Imuruk Basin: (1) Coyote Cr., and (2) Gold Run, Offield Cr., American R., area placers—**gold.**

SOLOMON: (1) E 6 mi., placers—**gold;** (2) Big Hurrah, Jerome, Rock, and West creeks, principally open-cut mines—**gold.**

YORK, area placers—**cassiterite, gold.**

SOUTH and SOUTHEASTERN ALASKA

ANCHORAGE (Cook Inlet): (1) Archangel Cr., head of—**gold;** (2) Craigie Cr.: (a) head of, and (b) just N of Willow Cr.—**gold;** (3) Fishhook Cr., head of, most productive area mines—**gold;** (4) NE, Matanuska area, upper part of Willow Creek district at the head of Cook Inlet, second most productive lode-gold area of Alaska—**gold:** (5) Suisitna region, near head of Nugget Cr. in the Yentna district, many substantial veins—**gold.**

CORDOVA, access port to great Kennecott copper deposits along the Copper R. of the Interior (around CHITINA, STRELNA, COPPER CENTER, etc.)— **copper minerals, molybdenite, pyrite,** etc. See: Interior Region, Copper River District.

HAINES, E side of Chilkat Valley, area deposits—**barite, gold, magnetite.**

JUNEAU (Gold Belt): (1) Admiralty Is.: (a) Hawk Inlet and Funter Bay —**gold;** (b) Windham Bay—**gold;** (2) JUNEAU: (a) at edge of city, the famed Alaska Juneau Gold Mine (by far the largest lode-gold mine in Alaska, with a notable "glory hole" behind the mountain, closed for mining but open for tourist visitations), very low-grade granite ores—**gold, silver** (as **electrum**), **lead;** (b) N, in Berners Bay district, at old Kensington and Comet mines—**gold;** (c) Douglas Is. (across Gastineau Channel by bridge), area mines, especially the drowned-out and abandoned great Treadwell Mine— **asbestos, copper, iron, gold, manganese, molybdenum, nickel, stibnite, tremolite;** (d) Indian Reservation, Copper R., area—**star sapphire;** (e) Stevens Passage, between Grand Is. (20 mi. S of Juneau) and Grave Point, 8-sq.-mi. hydraulic operation lying under some 100 fathoms of water, requiring deep-water dredging—**placer gold.**

KENAI PENINSULA (W of SEWARD): (1) Girdwood District, just N of the peninsula and S of ANCHORAGE, extending a few miles N from shores of Turnagain Arm, many mines, especially near head of Crow Cr.—**gold;** (2) MOOSE PASS–HOPE District, an area N of the Moose Pass sta. on the Alaska RR and extending to the old settlements of HOPE and SUNRISE on Turnagain Arm, many mines and prospects—**gold;** (3) Nuka Bay (extreme S part of peninsula), many area lode mines and prospects—**gold.**

KETCHIKAN (District): (1) area, including coastal islands, many mines— **antimony, chromium, copper, gold, iron, lead, limestone, marble, molybdenum, palladium, platinum, silver, zinc,** etc.; (2) Cleveland Peninsula, near Helm Bay, large mining district—**gold;** (3) Kasaan Peninsula, old Mt. Andrews property—**gold;** (4) KETCHIKAN, E, in HYDER District, many old mines—**copper, gold, lead, silver, tungsten;** (5) Porcupine District, area placer mines—**gold;** (6) Prince of Wales Is.: (a) area deposits—**magnetite;** (b) Dolomi area, at old Valparaiso Mine—**gold;** (c) HOLLIS, vicinity, at old Sealevel Mine—**gold;** (d) Sulzer, at the Green Monster Copper Mine— **chalcopyrite, epidote, grossularite garnet, rock crystal.**

LITUYA-YAKUTAGA REGION, area beach placers exposed to ocean wave action—**gold.**

PETERSBURG (Kupreanof Is.): (1) area mines—**barite, chromium, gold, manganese, silver, zinc;** (2) Glacier and Hamilton bays, beach gravels— **agate, jasper, petrified wood.**

SITKA (District): (1) Baranof Is.: (a) Red Bluff Bay, area gravels—**serpentine;** (b) SE of SITKA, at head of Silver Bay—**rhodonite;** (2) Chichagof Is., W part, second most productive mining district in Alaska: (a) Klag Bay (60 mi. NW of SITKA), and (b) a few miles farther NW, near Kimshan Cove —**gold** (more than $20 million in high-grade ore at the old $20-per-ounce price), **copper-nickel ores, gypsum, scheelite.**

SKAGWAY (including the Porcupine placer district), area old mines—**gold.**

VALDEZ (Prince William Sound): (1) many area lode mines—**gold.**

(Most mines in this district can be reached only by boat.) (2) Passage Canal zone, as numerous veins exposed by receding glaciers—**gold**; (3) Knight and Latouche Is., extensive deposits—**copper**; PORT WELLS, area lode mines —**gold**; (4) Tiekel District (35 air mi. N of Valdez), area mines—**copper, gold, lead, silver**; (5) Unakwik Inlet, area vein mines—**copper, gold, lead, silver, zinc.**

WRANGLE (District): (1) area mines—**barite, fluorite, garnets** (to an inch or more in dia.), **gold, graphite, lead, limestone, pyrite, silver**; (2) Woewodsky Is., at old Maid of Mexico Mine—**gold**; (3) Stikine R. mouth, 1¾ mi. SE of Sergief Is., along Garnet Cr.—**almandite garnets**; (4) Zarembo Is.: (a) beach gravels of adjoining Kuiu Is., and (b) gravels of Saginaw Bay— **agate, jasper, petrified wood.**

TOPKNOT OF AMERICA

Well within the Polar Zone lies the Arctic Slope of Alaska, from the Philip Smith and Davidson mountain ranges on the east to Point Hope on the shore of the Chukchi Sea far north of the Seward Peninsula. Reaching about 600 miles east and west and 150 miles south to north, this desolate, treeless, tundra land slopes gently from the foothills of the Brooks Range all the way to the muskeg shores of the Arctic Ocean.

The Arctic Slope, as far east as the lower Colville River, has long been a U.S. Naval petroleum reserve, with major developmental activities centered in Prudhoe Bay, and mineral location is prohibited. Transportation is so difficult and expensive that the exploration for gems and minerals outside the federal oil lands has been minimal. Extensive beds of **coal** are widely distributed throughout this region, and paleontological expeditions from the University of Alaska have mapped numerous fossil areas since World War II. Placer **gold** deposits have been profitably panned in the streams of the eastern sections, principally on the Okpilak River. The north slopes of the Endicott Mountains show mineralized outcrops of **gold** and its usual associates.

ARIZONA

The first white men to visit the "Copper State" were Spanish explorers led by Fray Marcos de Niza, who crossed the Sonoran border at Lochiel, Santa Cruz County, in 1539. They could not have entered Arizona at a more propitious spot, for south-central Arizona is one of America's richest mineral-bearing regions in a state that ranks among the most heavily mineralized terrains on earth.

Southern Arizona, where the Gila River flows across the entire state, is a land of hot desert plains broken by north–south ranges of dry, severely eroded mountains—-an immense, empty land that is still little explored for any minerals other than **gold, silver,** or **copper.** Phoenix not only is the capital city of Arizona but also bears the apt title of the Sun Capital of America.

Northern Arizona is part of the Colorado Plateau, with arid deserts and high, timbered plateaus whose elevations range from 4,000 to 10,000 feet, climaxing in 12,611-foot Humphreys Peak (highest of several peaks in the San Francisco Mountains north of Flagstaff). The Colorado River and the mile-deep Grand Canyon slash across the northwestern corner of the state. The Colorado Plateau itself breaks abruptly in a vast east-west escarpment stretching across central Arizona. Known as the Tonto and Mogollon ("Muggyyone") rims, the sheer cliffs look down to the cactus-studded lowlands of the south.

The dumps of thousands of Arizona mines are fertile hunting grounds for a host of colorful and often valuable ore minerals and a great variety of gemstones, crystals, agatized woods, and specimen materials. Much of the state is also rich in agatized woods and Triassic/Jurassic dinosaur bones, often jasperized. The collector will find no comparable area in the United States so accessible or so prolific in its yield of beautiful gems and fascinating minerals. To avoid climatological problems, collecting in Arizona should be seasonal: the northern half in summer, high and coolish; the southern half in winter, warmly welcoming and gentle.

For additional information, write: Geology Department, University of Arizona, or the Arizona Bureau of Mines, both in Tucson.

APACHE CO.

CEDAR RIDGE, in the Chinle Formation at Echo Cliffs—**agate, jasper, petrified wood.**

CHINLE: (1) area to N—**agate, jasper, petrified wood;** (2) S on Rte. 27 to Beautiful Valley, area—**petrified wood.**

CONCHO to ST. JOHNS: (1) area around CONCHO, and (2) E along both sides of U.S. 180 to just W of ST. JOHNS—**petrified wood, agate** (some dendritic), **chalcedony, gemmy chert.**

GANADO, area SW—**agatized wood.**

MEXICAN WATER: (1) W 5 mi., at Garnet Ridge, in loose sand—**pyrope garnet** ("Arizona rubies"); (2) N 10 mi., Moses Rock field in San Juan Co., Utah—**pyrope garnet.**

NAVAJO, E along both sides of U.S. 66 to Sanders—**agatized wood.**

ROUND ROCK, WSW 12 mi., to Round Rock, area—**agatized wood.**

SANDERS, broad area surrounding town and including Witch Well—**agatized wood.**

ST. JOHNS, area along both sides of U.S. 666, both N and S—**agatized wood.**

TANNER SPRINGS: (1) SW, in Tanner Wash, and (2) N of Pinto Siding (Santa Fe RR)—**silicified wood.**

APACHE, COCONINO, NAVAJO COS.

PAINTED DESERT, region embracing a large geographic area of Triassic Chinle Formation consisting of mauve to variegated clays: (1) as microscopic particles disseminated in the clays—**gold;** (2) on surface of draws, washes, slopes, etc.—**fossils, petrified wood.**

COCHISE CO.

BISBEE (District): (1) area copper mines, dumps, abundant—**azurite, bornite, brochantite, chalcanthite, chalcocite, chalcopyrite, chalcotrichite, chrysocolla, cuprite, malachite, native copper, shattuckite.** (**Chalcocite** is most important in disseminated ore, locally abundant as a secondary mineral in limestone replacement deposits.) (2) Copper Queen Mine (one of the most outstanding U.S. copper localities), as magnificent crystal specimens—**azurite, malachite, native silver.**

CARRIZO MTS., W, in Morrison formation (sandstone)—**carnotite.**

COCHISE (in NW part of Co.), area deposits—**copper, gold, lead, silver, tungsten, zinc.**

DOS CABEZAS (and the Teviston District), placers—**gold.** (Practically all the gulches and dry washes in this area contain **gold**-bearing sands.)

DRAGOON, in Dragoon Canyon (once a refuge of the Apache war chief Cochise), area of 2,260 acres owned by the Dragoon Marble Quarries, Inc., in 7 major veins—**marble.**

GLEASON-COURTLAND DISTRICT: (1) area mines, as important constituents of enriched copper ores—**chalcocite, copper minerals;** (2) turn N from GLEASON just W of old Santa Fe RR to South Courtland (ghost town) and NORTH COURTLAND: (a) just N, old copper mines—**brochantite, copper minerals;** (b) NW ¾ mi., to Turquoise Mt., old Tiffany Turquoise Mine (1880's)—**limonite, gem turquoise;** (3) SE, across abandoned RR to DOUGLAS, turn N to operating copper mine, fine specimen materials—**bornite (peacock copper).**

JOHNSON, nearby in E foothills of the Little Dragoon Mts., as large deposits—**copper minerals, molybdenite.**

PEARCE, Pearce Hills, Commonwealth, and other mines, abundant—**embolite** (major **silver** ore).

TOMBSTONE (District): (1) many area great mines, especially along the Empire-Contention dike, mineral specimens abundant on all dumps—**argentite, aurichalcite, azurite, barite, bornite, bournonite, calamine** (or **hemimorphite**), **cerargyrite, chrysocolla** (widely distributed), **connellite, copper** (native), **covellite, cuprite, galena** (bearing **tellurium**), **gold, hydrozincite, jarosite** (common), **plumbojarosite, pyrite, pyromorphite** (associated with crystals of **wulfenite** in outer layers of oxidized **lead** ores), **rosasite, stromeyerite, sulfur, tenorite, tetrahedrite** (high in **silver**), **thaumasite** (rare), **vanadates (copper, lead, zinc), wulfenite** (common but not abundant);

(2) In addition to these, the following mines carry the further indicated minerals: (a) Empire Mine—**bromyrite, native silver;** (b) Ingersol Mine—**famatinite;** (c) Lucky Cuss Mine—**albandite, hematite** (100 ft. W of the dumps), **hillebrandite;** (d) Silver Thread and Sulphuret Mines—**sphalerite;** (e) State of Maine Mine—**embolite** (as principal **silver** mineral); (f) Tombstone Extension Mine—**galena;** Toughnut Mine—**chalcocite, famatinite, bronchantite, smithsonite;** (g) West Side Mine—**hessite, smithsonite;** (h) West Side Quarry "Roll"—**aurichalcite** (pale blue crystal aggregates).

COCONINO CO.

FLAGSTAFF: (1) area, Brown Onyx Quarry—**onyx;** (2) NE via U.S. 89, Sunset Crater: (a) area of this and nearby cinder cones, and (b) W, in the San Francisco Mts.—**sulfur.**

FREDONIA: (1) W 15 mi. on Rte. 389 into Mohave Co., Pipe Spring National Monument, area—**petrified wood;** (2) W 29 mi., Colorado City, area —**petrified wood, celestite crystals;** (3) E on dirt rd., then N to Paria (ghost Mormon colony), area—**petrified wood;** (4) SW 37 mi., in Hack's Canyon, as extensive **uranium** deposits—**copper minerals, metatorbernite, torbernite;** (5) ESE on U.S. 89 about 3 mi., turn E on dirt road cutting around Kaibab Plateau to House Rock, area gulches and washes of the plateau—**petrified wood.**

GRAND CANYON (S Rim community): (1) area pegmatite exposures (not easy to reach), as octahedral crystals to 1 in. dia.—**magnetite;** (2) scattered regional ore deposits—**bornite, chalcocite, cuprite;** (3) the Inner Gorge (by the trail to the N Rim), ½ mi. downstream from Monument Cr., abundant —**sillimanite.**

JACOB LAKE, region of the Kaibab Plateau in **chert** beds of wide extent, as impregnations—**azurite, malachite.**

LEES FERRY (on the Colorado R. near mouth of the Paria R.)—**petrified wood.**

MARBLE CANYON: (1) SW 2–3 mi. on U.S. 89, in canyon breaks of the Chinle cliffs to the west: (a) scattered over alluvial surfaces—**carnotite wood** (rich in **vanadium** and **radium**), **green agate;** (b) deep within the contributing canyons, weathering out of the sandstone formations—**carnotite logs;** (2) SE on U.S. 89 toward BITTER SPRINGS and THE GAP, area washes and draws—**petrified wood.**

MOENCOPI: (1) NW 9 mi., around Willow Springs, and (2) 10 mi. E of Dunns, in Nokai Cr. Canyon—**siliceous wood.**

GILA CO.

CHRYSOTILE (W of Seneca and U.S. 60) and Cienega, Salt R. Canyon asbestos mines—**chrysotile asbestos, gem serpentine.**

COOLIDGE DAM: (1) park below dam on E side of river, area above roadway—**agate, native copper, rock crystal** (some with **amethyst** tips), **andradite garnet;** (2) SE 12 mi., the Stanley Butte district in Graham Co. (*q.v.*).

GLOBE DISTRICT: (1) Alter Mts. (on Apache Indian Reservation)— **andesine, andesine-sunstone;** (2) area great copper mines: (a) Buffalo and Continental Mines, and (b) Dominion Mine—rich assortment of **copper minerals;** (3) up Pinal Cr. from town, placers—**gold;** (4) SE 6 mi. and E of Sixshooter Cr., at Gap and Catsclaw Flat, placers—**gold;** (5) W 6½ mi., at Keystone and Live Oak Mines—**chrysocolla, chrysocolla**-stained **chalcedony, copper minerals, rock crystal;** (6) WNW: (a) Lost Gulch, and (b) Pinto Cr., area placers—**gold;** (7) N, in the Apache Mts. and W, in small gulches draining into Richmond Basin, placers—**gold;** (8) S 24 mi. on Rte. 77, then W to Dripping Springs, NW of Cowboy Gulch on SW side of Dripping Spring Wash as placers—**gold.**

MAZATZAL MTS., Slate Cr. deposits—**cinnabar.**

MCMILLAN (ghost town)—**silver minerals, native silver.** (This old camp N of Globe on U.S. 60 was originally part of the San Carlos Indian Reservation. The 3-ft.-wide vein of almost pure native silver was so extensive and so rich that political pressure caused the reservation limits to be shifted 12 miles east, thus depriving the Apaches of some $2 million that came from the Stonewall ledge, which extended 10 miles long.)

MIAMI: (1) area great copper mines—**copper minerals, silver minerals, molybdenite,** etc.; (2) broad region N and W—**Apache tears (obsidian);** (3) W 5 mi.: (a) Castle Dome Mine, and (b) NE, the Golden Eagle Mine, in area gulches as placers—**gold.**

PAYSON (District): (1) area copper mines, e.g., the Silver Butte Mine and the Oxbow Mine—**copper minerals, epidote, fluorite, dioptase;** (2) N, toward Tonto and Mogollon rims, area canyons and washes, as float—**gold;** (3) W 4.8 mi. past high school and country club to S-trending dim rd. (parallel to main road, unmarked), then W 1 mi. onto North Peak Trail (on N) with Cypress Thicket due W, both sides of Trail for 1½ mi.—gem **agate, jasper, septarian nodules;** (4) E 14 mi. on Rte. 260 to Diamond Point, turn N 4 mi. toward lookout—**rock crystal;** (5) E about 50 mi. on Rte. 260 to area of USFS guard station, surrounding forest—gem **red jasper;** (6) from (4) go another 8 mi. NW to area about 1 mi. from river, abundant—**agate, jasper, geodes** (crystal-lined), etc.; (7) N on Hwy. 87 14 mi. to W turnoff to Natural Bridge (3 mi. W of Hwy. 87), area—gem **serpentine.**

PERIDOT, area, in volcanic bombs of **olivine** as large crystals—**spinel** (possibly **picotite**).

ROOSEVELT: (1) SE on Hwy. 88 to jct. with Rte. 288, then N 1¼ mi. to windmill, go through gate and up dry creek bed to old blacksmith shop, area, especially upstream—**asbestos, jade,** etc.; (2) 15 mi. NE of E end of Roosevelt Reservoir, area—**agate, jasper.**

SAN CARLOS: (1) SW 2½ mi., at Peridot Mesa—**peridot;** (2) San Carlos Reservoir, S bank of Gila R. below Coolidge Dam, area—**agate, garnets, native copper.**

GILA-PINAL COS.

AREA straddling both sides of the co. line, in outcrops of the Pinal schist near post-Cambrian granitic rocks, locally abundant—**andalusite, sillimanite, tourmaline.**

GRAHAM CO.

ARAVAIPA DISTRICT (W side of Coronado National Forest): (1) Grand Reef system veins—**argentite;** (2) La Clede Mine—**native silver;** (3) Ten Strike Group—**chalcocite** and other **copper minerals.**

BYLAS, N, in many outcrops across the San Carlos Indian Reservation—**black hypersthene, peridots.**

FT. THOMAS, S 18 mi. on U.S. 70, turn onto Black Rock Rd., area both sides—**agate, chalcedony, jasper, silicified wood.**

SAFFORD: (1) N, in Lone Star District, as complex low-grade ores—**copper minerals** and associates; (2) E 10 mi. on U.S. 70 to jct. with U.S. 666, then NE on U.S. 666: (a) all way to GUTHRIE in Greenlee Co., continuous localities along both sides of hwy.—**agate, chalcedony roses, jasper, petrified wood;** (b) 8 mi. NE of jct., rough track turns N, park and walk along it short distance to end, all area—**agate** (red, brown, and green moss rivaling **Montana moss agate** for quality), **chalcedony** (fluorescent green), **chalcedony roses, Apache tears, jasper;** (3) E 14 mi. on U.S. 70, turn N 7 mi. on dirt rd. to Gila R., area chiefly upstream from mouth of Bonita Cr., placers—**gold, ferruginous chert** pebbles, abundant **black sand.**

STANLEY DISTRICT (Crystal Peak, Limestone Mt., Quartzite Mt., ghost town site of Stanley). This area is best reached from COOLIDGE DAM, Gila Co. (*q.v.*), E 10 mi., then S on rough rd.: (1) area along both sides of rd.— **yellow garnets;** (2) 2 mi. S to Stanley town site on N flank of Stanley Butte: (a) widespread area about town site, especially above old post office, and (b) area washes, slopes, draws, etc., on adjoining mts.—**andradite garnet, fluorite** (in **barite** gangue); (c) Cold Spring prospect, contact-metamorphic ores—**stibnite;** (d) Stanley's Deer Cr. Basin and S side of Copper Reef Mt.— **agate, chalcedony** (nodules, roses), **jasper,** etc.; (3) 1½ mi. S of town site, area above an abandoned residence—**garnets, gemmy chert, fossils, quartz crystals.**

WINKLEMAN, 2 mi. up the Gila R., in fissures 6–8 in. wide in exposures of Mississippian limestone along river banks—**nitrocalcite.**

GREENLEE CO.

AREA: Most sections of this county reveal many locations for gemstone hunting, and casual prospecting along the sides of practically all roads is productive—**agate, chalcedony** (nodular, roses), **jaspers,** gemmy **silicified wood,** etc. (1) Ash Spring Mt. and Ash Spring Canyon, slopes, washes, draws, creek beds and banks, etc.—**agate, chalcedony, jasper;** (2) Chase Cr. Canyon, in cliffs of granite porphyry, as bright green encrustations—**gerhardtite;** (3) Peloncillo Mts., area—**agate** (pastel), **chalcedony, jasper.**

CLIFTON: (1) very many gem areas, inquire locally: (2) North Clifton to second bridge above the Phelps Dodge store, cross river 1½ mi. to cattle guard, then E onto right-hand rd. up a canyon, then .2 mi. to trail, park and walk up Limestone Canyon—**gem agate;** (3) E 15 mi.: (a) Mulligan Peak, and (b) Ward Canyon, areas—**red agate;** (4) NW, along the Coronado Trail (U.S. 666), many area mine dumps—**chrysocolla, turquoise;** (5) NE 7 mi., along the San Francisco R., in Limestone Canyon—**purple agate;** (6) S 9 mi. on Rte. 75 and SW on U.S. 666 to Three Way drive-in theater (13.7 mi.), turn through gate on N side of rd., go about 1 mi., all area along both sides of rd.—**fire agate, chalcedony;** (7) SE 14 mi., Mule Cr. Rd., along both sides—**chalcedony geodes;** (8) SE 15 mi., at York, area—**agate** (banded, fire), **carnelian, jasper;** (9) both sides of hwy. S to DUNCAN on Rte. 75— **agatized wood.**

DUNCAN: (1) several area properties—**fluorite;** (2) SE 12 mi. on U.S. 70 from old New Mexico checking station, then 14 mi. on dirt rd., area— **agate, chalcedony, jasper, petrified wood.**

GUTHRIE: (1) both sides of U.S. 666 W toward SAFFORD—**cryptocrystalline quartz gemstones;** (2) SW on U.S. 666 toward SOLOMON: (a) summit of low pass through Peloncillo Mts., area between low rounded knolls, extensive field—**pastel agate, chalcedony, jasper,** etc.; (b) just below summit on W side, area—**nodules (agate, chalcedony), geodes** (crystal-lined, fluorescent apricot); (3) farther W at point where rd. reaches base of mts., turn N 1.6 mi. on rough rd. through low hills, at their top beneath a basalt ledge, abundant—**agate, chalcedony** (nodules, roses), **carnelian nodules.**

MORENCI, area of great mines: (1) Morenci, Detroit, Manganese Blue, etc.—**azurite, chalcotrichite, malachite,** etc. (The mines of the Clifton-Morenci area are rich disseminations of ore minerals in veins, in places as solid seams 2–3 ft. thick—**azurite, chalcocite, malachite,** while in the veins also occur **chalcopyrite, molybdenite, pyrite, sphalerite.**) (2) Copper Mt. and Mammoth Mines, as snow-white mammillary masses—**kaolinite,** with **azurite** and **malachite.**

MARICOPA CO.

AREA: (1) Alama Mt.—**variscite;** (2) Aztec Mt.—**chrysoprase;** (3) Gila Canyon, area gravels and sides—**chrysoprase, garnets.**

AGUILA: (1) Big Horn Mts., area deposits—**pyrolusite** with **manganite** or **psilomelane;** (2) SE, in Vulture Mts., in tuff—**carnotite;** (3) E end of Harcuvar Mts. via dirt rd., area along way—**chalcedony roses** (pink); (4) nearby town, a wash leading toward Harcuvar Mts.—**Apache tears.**

ARLINGTON, turn N at cattle pens to RR to July 4th Butte, all area beyond RR to Saddle Mt., good gem hunting—**agate, chalcedony roses.**

BEARDSLEY, N 12 mi., in White Peak district—**wulfenite.**

BUCKEYE, W 2.7 mi., cross RR onto left fork and turn NW on Salome rd.: (1) NW 5.7 mi. to Wintersburg (ghost camp), area to S on low mesas —**banded Apache tears, smoky topaz;** (2) NW 15.9 mi. to cattle guard, turn S on dirt rd. to base of mt. (or at 17.9 mi. turn S 1 mi. then W 2.9 mi.), park, all surrounding area—**agate, chalcedony roses.** (Best locality around top of north peak.)

CAVE CREEK: (1) area, Red Rover Mine—**chalcocite, argentiferrous tetrahedrite;** (2) CAVE CREEK–NEW RIVER cutoff road: (a) SW 4 mi., both sides of rd.—**agate, gold, orbicular jasper, quartz;** (b) W on cutoff rd. from jct. S of CAVE CREEK 1¼ mi., turn up Cave Cr. ¼ mi., park, hill on far side of creek—**red jasper;** (c) W 2½ mi. to N-trending rd. and on this 1½ mi., area of old Go John Mine—**gold, silver, copper minerals, red jasper, bluestained quartz;** (d) NW 6½ mi., under power line to S-trending private rd. (permission at house), go on it ¼ mi., area—**magnetite;** (e) NW 10½ mi. (2 mi. N of Sears Ranch Rd.), to wide wash, N side of rd. on hillsides— **agate;** (f) in area about 1 mi. NE of a realty venture subdivision (2 mi. E along "Mours Blvd."), in area around a small hill—white **'headcheese"** **agate;** (g) NW 11½ mi., on E side of rd. many diggings and trails up and along a cross wash—**scenic agate;**

(3) Seven Springs–Bloody Basin Rd., all area—**agate, jasper;** (4) from Carpenter's Rock in center of CAVE CREEK, N 8 mi. to poor E-trending rd. to Bartlett and Horseshoe dams: (a) S 2 mi. on poor rd., area—**fluorite;**

(b) W 7 mi. (5 mi. E of jct.) toward Bartlett Dam, turn N 2 mi. to W-trending jeep rd. to quartz outcrop—**radioactive nodules, thundereggs;** (c) 7 mi. N of jeep rd. turnoff to Horseshoe Dam caretaker's house, area to W and N—**agate;** (5) N 13 mi. from Cave Creek, dirt rd. W to Rackensak Mine, farther S to another old mine—**gold;** (6) SEVEN SPRINGS (on co. line), see in Yavapai Co.

GILA BEND: (1) S 15 mi., in sandstone and conglomerate—**celestite, gypsum;** (2) S 23.6 mi. (18.4 mi. N of AJO, Pima Co.), turn E on old rd. across RR, many miles to Hat ("Table Top") Mt.: (a) area draws, washes, slopes, etc.— **agate, chalcedony;** (b) farther E, along ledges—**crystal-lined geodes, chalcedony roses** (many fluorescent).

GLENDALE (inquire locally for rd. to Black Canyon: (1) Arizona Agate Mine, area of surrounding washes, draws, hillsides, etc.—**gem agate** (all varieties); (2) scattered localities along the Cave Cr. rd.—**agate, chalcedony, jasper;** (3) all regional side rds. leading toward the mts.—**gemstones, minerals.**

HASSAYAMPA, NW 22 mi., Saddle Mt.—**fire agate.**

MORRISTOWN, NE 21.9 mi. on gravel rd. toward Castle Hot Springs: (1) then 1.9 mi. N, park at trail entrance to old mine, walk steeply uphill about 1¼ mi., area—**calcite, manganite, pyrolusite, quartz crystals,** etc.; (2) note pegmatite outcrops on roadsides from entrance into mts.—**mica, garnet, hornblende, feldspar, black tourmaline;** (3) area both sides of rd. all way from MORRISTOWN to Castle Hot Springs—**agate, chalcedony, chert, garden rock, jasper, schorl;** (4) Castle Hot Springs (see in Yavapai Co.); (5) road from Castle Hot Springs S along the Agua Fria R., prospect anywhere on both sides of rd.—**quartz family gemstones,** abundant. (This entire region is blanketed with cholla cactus, extremely difficult to penetrate, and the best specimens seem invariably to lie under the largest cacti.)

PHOENIX, N along Black Canyon Hwy. (Rte. 69): (1) N 18 mi. to Skunk Cr. at Mile Post 219 park, walk 1¼ mi. downstream—**pink chalcedony;** (2) NEW RIVER, area stream gravels especially in New R.—**agate, chalcedony, jasper;** (3) N 42 mi. to Mile Post 242, just S of Rock Springs turn E through gate to obvious diggings—**copper-stained minerals** (gem quality); (4) NW of PHOENIX, in area gravels of the Agua Fria R.—**agate, chalcedony, jasper;** (5) NW 45 mi., San Domingo Wash, placers—**gold;** (6) ENE 45 mi. and 9¾ mi. W of Roosevelt Dam, at W base of second peak from S in Four Peaks, elev. 6,500 ft., reached via USFS rd. from dam plus 18-mi. hike, in walls and loose in dirt—**gem amethyst** (among finest in the world).

ROOSEVELT DAM, SW on Apache Trail (Rte. 88) to Port of Phoenix on Canyon Lake Reservoir, then S 1½ mi., area—**chalcedony geodes.**

TONOPAH (NW part of co.): (1) broad surrounding area to W and N toward SALOME in Yuma Co., fine, abundant—**agate, chalcedony roses** (orchid color); (2) W on dirt rd. to Saddle Mt. area of Eagle Tail Mts., area washes and surfaces—**agate** (fire, moss), **carnelian, chalcedony.**

WICKENBURG: (1) Hassayampa R. gravels, sparingly present but notably abundant for several miles below mouth of San Domingo Wash 7 mi. SE of town—**gold;** (2) NE 2 mi., deposits—**bentonite;** (3) SW 14 mi., Vulture Mine (noted in early days for production)—**gold, pyrite;** (4) NE, large mining region, cf. Yavapai Co. (The entire region surrounding Wickenburg shows literally hundreds of old mine dumps and prospects visible from all access roads. Solid **gold nuggets** to several ounces, along with **pyrite, quartz crystals,** etc., are frequently found in the waste gangue. Early miners were unbelievably careless in their mining of only the highest-grade ore.)

MOHAVE CO.

ALAMO CROSSING, of the Bill Williams R. about 40 mi. N of U.S. 60 at WENDEN (Yuma Co.) via typical desert road. The entire region between WENDEN and KINGMAN is one of extreme heat in summer, dangerously rough dirt roads, aridity, and few inhabitants; be prepared to handle all emergencies alone. Be certain to leave word of destination and time expected back. A fascinating region but one of most hostile in the desert Southwest.

(1) Many area old mines, e.g., the Little Kimball Mine 5 mi. back of Alamo Crossing (with its Jim Rogers abandoned mill in Alamo)—**copper minerals, gold, agate, chalcedony, jasper, quartz crystals;** (2) sands and gravels along the bed of the Bill Williams R.—**celestite, gypsum;** (3) N 12.4 mi., bear W on rough dirt rd. 4½ mi. to second jct. (Sally Ann), then .7 mi. to head of Mississippi Wash, park at old homestead, and walk ½ mi. into the wash to huge natural cauldron—Indian petroglyphs, **agate, jasp-agate, jasper, petrified wood** in general area;

(4) N 16 mi., Rawhide. This extraordinarily rich gold "camp" (it never became either a mining camp or a town) straddled the old Owl Hoot outlaw trail and was a stopover where desperadoes could dig out raw gold from Rawhide Butte by the literal bucketful to replenish their finances between crimes. No legitimate prospector, miner, or lawman ever penetrated to Rawhide; hence no town grew up around the rhyolite butte. (a) Area around base of Rawhide Butte (which towers over the campsite), large deposit—**gem jasper, jasp-agate** containing **specular hematite;** (b) area single-jack prospects—**copper, gold, silver;** (c) Rawhide Butte (now a shell of rhyolite) —**gold, copper minerals, copper-silver minerals;** (d) E, SE, and S toward Alamo, area 20 mi. N to S and several miles wide, as nodules and boulders literally covering the surface of the ground, coal-black—**manganese (pyrolusite, psilomelane,** etc.). The main deposit is a 25-mi.-sq. U formation of the richest manganese (and largest) in America, between the Artillery Mts. and the Rawhide Mts. The richest deposits face the NE sides. Mostly on public land, the manganese can be picked up anywhere and trucked to the smelter, but transportation costs about equal the per-ton value. (e) N 5 mi., a U.S. Bureau of Mines operation (trucking out to Congress Jct.)—**manganese minerals.**

BULLHEAD CITY, S along Rte. 95, in gravels of the Colorado R. terrace on both sides of hwy.—**agate, chalcedony** (pebbles roses) **jasper, fossil trilobites, petrified wood** (cycad, ironwood, palm, etc.).

HACKBERRY, S 30 mi., in Aquarius Cliffs, pegmatites—**gadolinite.**

HOOVER DAM: (1) area downstream from mouth of the Grand Canyon, in sands and gravels—fine **placer gold,** with coarser **gold** in more elevated river bars; (2) Lake Meade area, along E side of the Colorado R. near its exit (best locality 3 mi. SSE of Hoover Dam)—**agate, chalcedony;** (3) S 4 mi., in veins—**pyrolusite.**

KINGMAN: (1) area mines and, in N part of co. in sand dunes—**gadolinite;** (2) Emerald Isle Mines, as fine-color material—**chrysocolla, tenorite;** (3) SW 3 mi. and ½ mi. NE of McConnico, at old BiMetal Gold Mine, placers —**gold;** (4) N 5 air mi., at Kingman Feldspar Mine—**allanite, microcline, quartz crystals;** (5) NW 15 mi.: (a) CHLORIDE and MINERAL PARK (*q.v.*) District, notably the Minnesota-Connor, Windy Point, and Queen Bee mines —**arsenopyrite, dufrenoysite;** (b) Distaff and other nearby mines—**silver minerals, native silver;** (c) Golden Gem and Vanderbilt mines—**galena, pyrite, sphalerite, stibnite;** (d) on SW side of the Cerbat Range (extending SE to Mineral Park—**kaolin minerals, turquoise;** (6) S 22½ mi. to within 6 mi. of Goldroad (ghost town), near Sitgreaves or Meadow Cr. Pass, area— **agate** (fire, grape), **chalcedony roses** (to 5 in. dia.), **jasper;** (7) SSE, in the Hualpai Mts., the Boriana Mine—**scheelite crystals;** (8) S 55 mi., in the Aquarius Range: (a) area pegmatite outcrops—**native bismuth, bismuthinite, gadolinite;** (b) W side of Aquarius Range, the Rare Metals Pegmatite Mine—**beryl, bismuth, euxenite, gadolinite, yttrotantalite;** (c) 2 mi. S of the Rare Metals mine, in two small pegmatites mined to shallow depths—**beryl, microline feldspar;** (d) 2 mi. SW of the Rare Metals mine, in pegmatites—**allanite** (blades several inches long), **beryl, columbite, monazite, xenotime** (reddish crystals to 1 in. dia.); (9) SE 60 mi., the Mammoth Claim—**satin spar.**

LAKE MEADE–LAKE MOHAVE, area Colorado R. gravels, E side alluvial terraces and foothills all way S along W border of co.—**agate, chalcedony** (pebbles, roses), **jasper, petrified wood** (cycad, ironwood, palm, etc.)

LITTLEFIELD: (1) area basic dikes—**pentlandite,** with **chalcopyrite** and **pyrrhotite;** (2) Virgin Valley (across extreme NW corner of co.): (a) badlands near Nevada border, deposits—**gypsum, halite;** (b) Quail Canyon and South Mt., as thick beds—**gypsum;** (3) Chin Lee Valley, W 6 mi. and 2 to 4 mi. S of the Utah border, area—**gadolinite, peridot.**

MINERAL PARK (rejuvenated ghost town): (1) E 1 mi., at Ithaca Peak, (2) 1 mi. S of Ithaca Peak, at Aztec Mt.; (3) at end of range of hills ⅓ mi. SSW of MINERAL PARK, (4) on mt. ⅘ mi. SSE of town—**kaolin minerals, turquoise;** (5) old mine dumps in and about town—**copper minerals.** (Such famous mines as the Keystone, Gold Star, Metallic Accident, and Quick Relief are or have been overrun by the Duval Sulphur & Potash Co. in its exploration and exploitation of an enormous deposit of 1 percent **copper** ore containing traces of **molybdenum** and **silver.** Initial discoveries of ore ran $8 per pound of ore in **silver** alone.)

OATMAN: (1) area mines—**gold.** (The discoverer, John Moss, located the Silver Creek Vein in 1863. Legend has it that he extracted $240,000 in **gold** from a pit 10 feet on a side and 10 feet deep. Mining in the Oatman district continued up to World War II.) (2) Black Mts., N part of district, as white to pale green bands or as linings of cavities—**fluorite;** (3) NW 5 mi. and 6 mi. downstream from U.S. 66 in valley of Silver Cr., placers—**gold.**

PIERCE FERRY (accessible from U.S. 93 12 mi. N of the turnoff to CHLORIDE, or 54 mi. SW of BOULDER CITY, Nev.): (1) S 9 mi. from the Colorado R., in T. 28, 29 N, R. 17, 18 W, placer sands—**gold;** (2) S 8 mi. from Colorado R., in T. 29, 30 N, R. 17 W, the King Tut Mine, placers— **gold.**

PIPE SPRINGS NATIONAL MONUMENT. For area, see FREDONIA in Coconino Co., as access point.

TOPOCK: (1) area extending to visible low hills—**gem agate, chalcedony, jasper;** (2) E 2½ mi. toward OATMAN, on E side of rd. in gravels—**quartz gemstones;** (3) N 4½ mi. on rd. to OATMAN, along E side of rd.—**quartz gemstones;** (4) N 5 mi., area of low hills on W extending for 2 mi.—**gem agate;** (5) old Oatman hwy. over Black Mt. via Sitgreaves Pass, areas along both sides of hwy.—**agate, chalcedony roses, jasp-agate, jasper, petrified wood, chert** (containing **fossil corals** and **crinoidal stems**); (6) N 7½ mi., area—**agate, chalcedony, jasper;** (7) SE 18 mi. Gold Wing district (SW part of co. in foothills of the Chemhuevis or Mohave mts., placers—**gold.**

WIKIUP: (1) SE 19 mi. to Burro Cr. crossing by U.S. 93: (a) area under bridge and both sides of hwy., best field in state—**banded agate, chalcedony, opalite, gem chert, jasper;** (b) 2 mi. S of bridge, broad surrounding area— **Apache tears;** (c) 6½ mi. NW of bridge—**agate, amethystine chalcedony, chalcedony roses, chert, jasper, obsidian;** (2) S about 10 mi., turn E on rd. to Bogle Cattle Co., follow 14 mi. (4 mi. beyond ranch turnoff), keeping right, extensive field extending another 2 mi. to old Burro Cr. crossing— **agate** (blue, fluorescent); (3) N 22 mi., Big Sandy R., in gravels—**onyx.**

NAVAJO CO.

AREA: Most of this county, especially southeast of HOLBROOK, is noted for its gem quality **agatized wood** that includes *Araucarioxylon arizonicum, Podozamites arizonica* (cycad type), and *Woodworthia arizonica,* plus some 35 other genera and species of flora, including ferns, fungi, cycads, ginkgo trees, and horsetail rushes. The larger agatized tree trunks often contain cavities filled with **gem amethyst, rock crystal,** etc.

FORT APACHE INDIAN RESERVATION, area outcrops, as large platy crystals —**selenite.**

HOLBROOK, S 22 mi. from U.S. 66, the Petrified Forest National Monument (no collecting permitted), area outside boundaries, abundant—**gem agatized wood.**

MONUMENT VALLEY (N of KAYENTA to MEXICAN HAT, Ut.), regional Shinarump sandstones—**carnotite, fossil wood** (often rich in **uranium, vanadium, radium**). This is part of the Navaho Indian Reservation. During the 1950's many small **uranium** mines were operated by the Navahos. **Carnotite** ore occurs in lenses outcropping wherever the Morrison formation appears.

WINSLOW, area deposits—**gypsum.**

PIMA CO.

AJO: (1) area hills surrounding town—**agate, chalcedony, jasper, silicified ironwood;** (2) area copper mines, including the mammoth open pit in town, one of largest copper deposits in America—**bornite, chalcocite, chalcopyrite, hematite, magnetite, molybdenite, specularite, sphalerite, tennantite;** these minerals occur as grains and veinlets in a gangue of **quartz, orthoclase, albitic plagioclase, sericite,** and **chlorite;** (3) New Cornelia open-pit mine (get permission)—**gem shattuckite,** and in ore body on the S side as a bordering narrow band—**chalcocite.**

ARIVACA, LAS GUIJAS (about 50 mi. SSW of TUCSON): (1) area mines—**azurite, bornite, chalcopyrite, covellite, cuprite, native copper, tetrahedrite,** some **gold;** (2) W, in Cerro Colorado Mts., many regional mines and prospects—**iodyrite (horn silver), stromeyerite, tetrahedrite, native silver.**

CORTARO, SW on Cortaro Rd. to Picture Rock Rd., W to Wade Rd., then N to jct. with Silver Bell Rd., turn W and pass gas line, first rd. S to Little Peak (Safford Peak due W), park, area—**gem agate** (banded, moss, plume).

HELVITIA-ROSEMONT DISTRICT: (1) Leader, Ridely, Pauline mines, as well as many prospects in Madera and Providencia canyons—**molybdenite, gold, copper minerals, tungsten;** (2) Cuprite district, Cuprite Mine—**molybdenite in chalcopyrite** ore; (3) GREATERVILLE district at E foot of Santa Rita Mts. 8½ mi. NW of SONOITA, placers—**gold.**

QUIJOTOA (Pima Indian village about 70 mi. W of TUCSON on Rte. 86), the Quijotoa Mts., area of about 100 sq. mi., placers—**gold.**

REDINGTON, SW, on N slope of Alder Canyon in Santa Catalina Mts., from near the USFS boundary to within a few miles of the San Pedro R., placers—**gold** (coarse, flat, ragged).

ROBLES JCT. (25 mi. W of TUCSON on Rte. 86), SW, in the Baboquivari Mts., the Gold Bullion Mine, in quartz veins—**gold, molybdenite.**

SILVER BELL (District): (1) in old mine workings—**chalcanthite, copper, cuprogoslarite, silver;** (2) El Tiro Mine—**pisanite.**

TUCSON: (1) Tucson Mts., old Yuma Mine, area 1 mi. S on a prospect, as crystals—**willemite;** (2) NW, in the Sierrita Mts.: (a) Mineral Hill district, as efflorescences on walls of old mines—**melanterite,** also **copper minerals, pyrite;** (b) Neptune property, as veins from a few inches to 2 ft. wide—**fluorite;** (3) W, between the Banner Pima mines and the edge of the Papago Indian Reservation, the Mission Mine—**copper minerals;** (4) SW about 30 mi., at PAPAGO or AGUAJITO (S part of co.) in the Papago Mining District, along Ash Cr. on the Sunshine-Sunrise group of claims in Pescola Canyon, placers—**gold;** (5) SW 33 mi. alongside the Banner and Pima mines, the Esperanza Mine (once called the New Year's Eve Mine), rich ores—**copper, molybdenum.** (These are not old mines; ore bodies were discovered entirely by geophysical methods, since no indications of subsurface mineralizations were observable on the surface.)

TWIN BUTTES (SSW of TUCSON and SW of SAHUARITA about 7 mi. by good graded rd. or reached via Mission Rd. to San Xavier, 23 mi. from TUCSON): (1) many area old mine dumps; (2) Glance, Copper King, Copper Queen mines—**azurite, chalcocite, chrysocolla, malachite,** many **fluorescent minerals** (night prospecting of surface), **calcite, covellite, cuprite, pyrite, spar,** etc. The famed Copper King Mine on the E butte is connected at the 700-ft. level underground with the equally famed Copper Queen Mine on the W butte. These two mines and the San Xavier Mine just N produced $25,387,000 in **copper, lead,** and **zinc.** Other collectable minerals include **marcasite** as alteration from **pyrrhotite** and **native copper.** The area mines were all developed in the zone of oxidation veins, with progressive enrichment of ores with increasing depth. Dumps all hold nice specimens.

PINAL CO.

COPPER CREEK DISTRICT (SE corner of co., 8 mi. E of MAMMOTH, *q.v.*, on Rte. 77), then E into Galiuro Mts. in Graham Co.: (1) Blue Bird Mine —**stromeyerite,** with **tennantite** in lower levels; (2) Copper Giant and Old Reliable mines, as coatings on walls of drifts and in fractures—**chalcanthite;** (3) Childs-Aldwinkle Mine, as fine crystallizations—**molybdenite,** with **atacamite, enargite, olivenite.** (**Rhenium** occurs here in the highest known percentages as an associate of **molybdenum.**)

FLORENCE: (1) N side of RR tracks go E through underpass to flag stop of Price (pole 969), turn N for 9 mi., keeping right, to Martinez Silver Bell Mine—**chalcedony roses, copper minerals, galena, geodes;** (2) head of Martinez Canyon to the NE—**agate, jasper;** (3) about 32 mi. SW on U.S. 80, 89 (halfway to TUCSON), area E of hwy. in basalts, as radiating fibrous amygdules—**thomsonite.**

MAMMOTH, the Mammoth Mine, on dumps—**anglesite, caledonite, cerussite** (as magnificent twinned and reticulated crystal aggregates), **crocoite, dioptase, leadhillite, linarite, malachite, phosgenite** (as slender prismatic crystals with **diaboleite** on the 400-ft. level of the Collins vein), **tenorite** (as coal-black nodules surrounded by thin shells of **chrysocolla**), **vanadinite, willemite, wulfenite** (crystals encrusted with bright orange **ecdemite**).

RAY (12 mi. S of SUPERIOR on Rte. 177, then E 3 mi.), old Ray shaft, as sparkling ruby-red aggregates—**cuprite, chalcotrichite.**

SUPERIOR: (1) area perlite mines to SW—**Apache tears;** (2) Belmont and Magma mines—**copper minerals, pyrite, sphalerite;** (3) Silver King and other area silver mines—**silver** (wire, also fine crystallizations), **stromeyerite** (most important ore mineral), **sphalerite.**

PINAL-MARICOPA COS.

APACHE JUNCTION (Pinal Co.), NE into Maricopa Co. 15 mi. along the Apache Trail (Rte. 88) to: (1) first glimpse of Canyon Lake, back up and park at cattle-loading corral, all area along both sides of hwy.—**chalcedony roses,** dark brown **geodes;** (2) Port of Phoenix, see ROOSEVELT DAM, Maricopa Co.; (3) Tortilla Flats, and area side canyons—**chalcedony roses, quartz crystals.**

SANTA CRUZ CO.

DUQUESNE (ENE of NOGALES): (1) very many area mines, both active and inactive, on dumps—**chalcocite, arsenic minerals, chalcopyrite, diopside, epidote, galena, gedrite, hedenbergite pyrite, pyrrhotite, sphalerite, garnets, tourmaline, tremolite, wollastonite;** (2) Westinghouse property—**cerrusite, anglesite, chrysocolla, cuprite, smithsonite, sphalerite** (as magnificent crystal groups).

HARSHAW (10 mi. S of PATAGONIA): (1) Alta Mine, as red gangue—

fluorite, with **embolite** and **pyrargyrite;** (2) between Sonoita Cr. on NW and Alum Canyon on SW, in Quaternary placer gravels—**gold.**

MOWRY DISTRICT, on E slopes of the Patagonia Mts. 15 mi. S of PATA-GONIA and 6 mi. N of Mexico, gravels of Mowry Wash and its tributaries, placers—**gold.**

NOGALES (District): (1) N 6 mi., in Guebabi Canyon—**gold;** (2) E, on W side of Patagonia Mts., the Dura Mine—**stibnite.**

PATAGONIA DISTRICT: many regional rich old mines, e.g.: (1) Double Standard Mine, as reniform masses attached to walls of dolomitic limestone pockets—**arsenic;** (2) Flux Mine—**cerussite, massicot, minium;** (3) Santo Nino and 3 R mines, as striated and twinned crystals or aggregates to 8 in. dia.—**pyrite,** associated with **molybdenite;** (4) Kansas Mine—**galena, garnets, pyrite, sphalerite;** (5) Trench Mine—**albandite, galena, rhodochrosite, sphalerite.**

RUBY (with ARIVACA in Pima Co.) DISTRICT: (1) with nearby ORO BLANCO, a very old mining district, area mine dumps—**copper minerals, gold;** (2) area between RUBY and TWIN BUTTES, both sides of all roads—**fluorescent minerals, pink agate;** (3) Montana Mine—**galena, sphalerite.** (Throughout Santa Cruz Co. and adjoining Pima Co., black-light prospecting at night will reveal **tungsten minerals** scattered everywhere, sometimes in commercial quantities.)

SALERO, SW 2¼ mi. to Tiniall district 1 mi. S of Mt. Allen at SW base of the Grosvenor Hills, on each side of the township line in SW¼ Sec. 35, placers—**gold.**

TUBAC, ENE into national forest, the Compadre Mine—**copper, lead, silver, zinc minerals.**

WASHINGTON DISTRICT: (1) area mines, cf. DUQUESNE; (2) NW 3 mi., the Four Metals Mine; and (3) 2 mi. W of the Four Metals at the Proto Mine—**chalcocite, chalcopyrite, pyrite;** traces of **gold, lead, silver.** In this Patagonia Mts. region some 17 mi. E of U.S. 89 lie more than 40 mineral-rich mines on the dumps of which occur a wide variety of colorful ore minerals and crystals. (4) Red Mt. Mine—cf. Four Metals Mine; (5) Wrightson district: (a) American Boy Mine, as fine crystals—**tennantite (tetrahedrite);** (b) Happy Jack Mine—**uraninite.**

YAVAPAI CO.

ASHFORK: (1) surrounding town are about 50 sandstone quarries within a radius of 25 mi.—colorful **flagstone** (used in buildings, patios, etc.); (2) 8 mi. distant at F. C. Ellington quarry (get directions in town), best quarry for collecting—**flagstone.**

BAGDAD: (1) at crossroads with Hwy. 97, turn N at a tavern for 3 mi. to cattle loader and fence, prospect along fence and in adjoining areas toward E—**gem jasper;** (2) SE, along banks of Santa Maria R. and in sandbars—**agate** (blue, green), **agatized cactus wood;** (3) N to Copper Company open-pit mine (get permission), follow rd. through pit to view of power poles (4 mi. N of town), area around poles in all directions—**gem jasper, crystal "conglomerate," quartz crystals;** (4) area of Eureka District (45 mi. W of PRESCOTT), in pegmatite outcrops—**bismuthinite.**

BLACK CANYON CITY: (1) area mines—**silver** with **proustite;** (2) Howard, several area placers, especially 1 mi. below—**gold.**

BUMBLE BEE (area), Mile Post 252 on Hwy. 79 (52½ mi. N of PHOENIX), Sunset Point Lookout, E on Bloody Basin Rd. to old Piedmont Mine—**copper minerals.**

CAMP VERDE, SW 3 mi., in salt deposits—**halite, glauberite, gypsum, mirabilite, thenardite.**

CASTLE HOT SPRINGS: (1) area around the resort 24 mi. NE of MORRISTOWN (Maricopa Co.)—**agate** (blue, gray, fortification), **agate nodules, chalcedony roses, drusy quartz geodes, dumortierite, jasp-agate, jasper, manganese in quartzite, quartz crystals** (many with inclusions, some rose), **rose quartz, pyrite, pyrolusite, black tourmaline;** (2) Castle Creek mining district, the Swallow Mine—**bismuthinite** altering to **bismite;** (3) 4 mi. N, the Champie Ranch, area—**agate** (blue, gray, fortification), **quartz crystals** (with inclusions), **rhyolite nodules** (**opal** centers), etc.

CHINO VALLEY, area—**agate, chalcedony, jasper.**

CONGRESS JUNCTION: (1) N 2 mi. on U.S. 89, turn SE on dirt rd. for 4½ mi. to big wash, cross and for next ¼ mi. on flats above a steep hill—**fluorite, garnets, pyrite;** (2) E another 1½ mi., old mining camp of Stanton: (a) area—**fluorite, garnets, gold, pyrite;** (b) Rich Hill (flat-topped mt. above Stanton), on or in surface debris—**gold nuggets;** (3) another 2 mi. S, to old camp of Octave—**gold;** (4) N 3 mi., at old Congress Mine (private property)—**gold, pyrite;** (5) NW, to Date Cr., area—**agate, garnet, jasper, limonite cubes, quartz crystals;** (6) E 6–8 air mi. and just NW of Octave, the Weaver and Rich Hill mines, placers—**gold;** (7) S, to Mile Post 261, 200 yds. S of marker, on hillside above a dry wash—**fluorite, garnets, pyrite.**

CONSTELLATION, area mines—**copper minerals, gold, pyrite; amethyst, jasper, quartz crystals.**

CORDES (Jct. 61 mi. N of PHOENIX): (1) NW to MAYER on Hwy. 69, area across Big Bug Cr.—**"Arizona"** or **"paisley shawl" onyx;** (2) Poland Jct., W past power station, take right (upper) rd. in canyon to old mine dumps—**marcasite,** etc.; (3) in stream gravels along the left (lower) rd., placers—**gold.**

DEWEY (83 mi. N of PHOENIX on hwy. to PRESCOTT), just E of PRESCOTT turn S for 8 mi. to ghost town of WALKER, *q.v.,* area—**pyrite.**

HUMBOLDT, POLAND, MAYER (E and S of PRESCOTT on Hwy. 69): (1) area mines of the Big Bug district, e.g., the Mayer, McCabe, and Humboldt placers—**gold;** (2) Boggs Mine, as crystallized material—**bournonite in calcite** masses; (3) Iron Queen Mine, as small coloform masses in partly oxidized ore—**marcasite;** (4) Bradshaw City: (a) area mines—**tetradymite,** associated with **pyrite** in quartz; (b) Minnehaha area and Montgomery Mine, in quartz veins—**gold, pyrite, tetradymite;** (5) Lynx Cr. (central part of co.): (a) Malley Hill Mine, and (b) Tuscambia Mine—**stibnite;** (6) Peck district, the Peck Mine, as main ore mineral—**bromyrite;** (7) Turkey Cr. district—**stibnite.**

JEROME: (1) area mines—**copper minerals;** (2) N 9 mi. toward PERKINSVILLE, many fields along both sides of rd.—**gem agate** (various colors), **jasper.**

KIRKLAND, SSE 9 mi., in Placerita, French, and Cherry gulches, many placer mines—**gold.**

PEEPLES VALLEY, W, along Model Cr., placers—**gold.**

PERKINSVILLE, adjoining areas—**gem chert** (erroneously called **"pink agate"**).

PRESCOTT: (1) area mines—**copper minerals, gold, pyrite;** (2) Columbia district, area black sands—**gold, platinum;** (3) S 4–6 mi., placers—**gold;** (4) S, to headwaters of the Hassayampa R., along entire course of river S from the 7,000-ft. Bradshaw Mts. to the co. line 2 mi. N of WICKENBURG (Maricopa Co.), many productive mines and placers—**gold;** (5) NE 43 mi. via JEROME and Pine Flat on U.S. 89A, to Sycamore Canyon (30 mi. S of WILLIAMS in Coconino Co.), area breaks and side canyons—**agate, chalcedony, jasper, petrified wood.**

ROCK SPRINGS (46 mi. N. of PHOENIX): (1) Mile Post 246, turnoff to Maggie Mine, placers—**gold;** (2) Mile Post 249: (a) turn W to CLEATOR and old Bumble Bee hwy., S ¼ mi. from store to French Lilie Mine, around transformer area—**andalusite crystals;** (b) beyond CLEATOR on old hwy. to MIDDLETOWN, to old Crown King Mine (ghost camp), area—**black tourmaline.**

SEVEN SPRINGS (on Maricopa Co. line N of CAVE CREEK, *q.v.*): (1) N 1 mi. to Camp Cr. campground, area—**red jasper;** (2) N 3 mi., a W-trending rd.: (a) W ½ mi., area—**agate, jasper;** (b) 2 mi. farther W, old onyx mine —**onyx;** (3) N 9 mi. (6 mi. N of onyx mine turnoff), a dim S-trending rd. across a dry wash to old buildings of the Arizona Agate Mine, on N slope of hill in old diggings and all area on both sides of rd.—**gem agate;** (4) N 19 mi., both sides of road—**gem red jasper.**

SKULL VALLEY: (1) E 6.7 mi. on dirt rd. just S of RR into old mining district, many collecting localities: (a) surface workings—**azurite, cuprite, malachite,** etc.; (b) mine dumps—**chalcopyrite, ferrimolybdite, molybdenite, pyrite,** etc.; (2) NE on rd. to PRESCOTT, in Copper Basin District: (a) Copper Basin Wash, N between SKULL VALLEY and the Sierra Prieta, area placers —**gold;** (b) Mercury, Cinnabar Queen, Zero Hour, and Shylock mines—**cinnabar.**

WALKER (7 mi. SE of PRESCOTT): (1) Robinson property—**stibnite;** (2) along creek to its junction with Agua Fria Cr. 13 mi. E of PRESCOTT, placers—**gold.**

YUMA CO.

AREA: Wherever metamorphosed limestones outcrop, look for **idocrase (vesuvianite),** rather abundant.

BLAISDALE, N 16 mi. on U.S. 95 to turnoff to Martinez Lake: (1) NW from jct. about 4 mi., area of petrified forest (shown on most maps)—**petrified cycad, ironwood, palm,** etc.; (2) N 19 mi., turn W at old windmill toward Yuma Test Sta. (bombing range area, permission required for weekend prospecting), all along rd. into the restricted area, especially around a low knoll—**petrified palm, ironwood, cycad,** etc., plus **agate, jasper** (yellow, gemmy), **sand spikes.** (This is about center of a 100-mi.-long collecting region on the terraces and benches above the Colorado R.)

BOUSE: (1) area old mines, in deep-red rhyolite, as free particles—**gold** (specimen value only); (2) E, across RR tracks, at Bouse Butte, some area veining on N and E sides—**seam agate** (green, lavender, moss pink; really a **jasper**); (3) N about 3 mi., area—**variegated agate.**

BRENDA (service sta.), E 1.2 mi., area adjoining S side of hwy. extending in broad arc to the S, abundant—**jasper** (gemmy, red, mossy, some slightly translucent).

CASTLE DOME DISTRICT (38 mi. NE of YUMA via U.S. 95 and dirt rd.): (1) area mines—**barite, fluorite** (greenish, purple, rose-colored, crystals and cleavage masses to several in. dia.), **galena, witherite, wulfenite;** (2) Big Eye Mine—**lead, silver minerals;** (3) E and S of the Big Eye, area placers—**gold;** (4) Castle Dome Mts., area of these "Middle Mts.," scattered localities— **geodes, quartz gemstones, opal, opalite, turquoise;** (5) W of U.S. 95 jct. to the Castle Dome district, 1.9 mi. on dirt rd., take N fork to its end at mile 2½, area—**agate, jasper, geodes** (filled with **fortification agate, banded agate, chalcedony,** or **quartz crystals**).

CIBOLA (due S of BLYTHE, Calif., on E side of Colorado R.), reached 22½ mi. S of QUARTZITE via U.S. 95, jct. with W-trending rd.: (1) W 4.2 mi. to Cibola forks, take S fork .3 mi. to second rd. fork beside steep butte, all area surfaces—high-grade **opalite;** (2) continue W to ghost town of CIBOLA (19 inhabitants in 1920); (a) area draws and washes of the river terrace—**agate, chalcedony, jasp-agate, jasper, chert, petrified wood** (many kinds); (b) area old mine dumps—**gold, pyrite.**

DOME, E, in Muggins Mts., S and central portions of T. 8, 9 S, R. 8, 9, 10 W, especially in Burro Canyon, dry placers—**gold.**

GILA CITY (about 20 mi. E of YUMA at N end of the Gila Mts. and 1½ mi. W of present site of DOME near mouth of Monitor Gulch), area placers —**gold.** The whole area between U.S. 60, 70 and U.S. 80 east of the Colorado R. to the Maricopa Co. line (a region of nearly 5,000 sq. mi.) contains hundreds of old mines and prospects, mostly worked for **gold** but other minerals usually present. The region is one of the hottest, most arid deserts in the Southwest, with prospecting feasible only during the pleasant winter months.

HOPE, W 3 mi. on U.S. 60, 70 to Shell gas station, then S on rd. just W of station for 27 mi., all area to top of hill ½ mi. S (to rock monument), broad locality, especially to E—**gem agate.**

LAGUNA: (1) Laguna Dam, area at E end and about 10 mi. NE of YUMA: (2) Las Flores area; (3) McPhaul area, local placers—**gold;** (4) N of the Gila R. and the Gila Mts., in R. 21, 22 W, embracing the S, SE, and SW portions of the Laguna or San Pablo Mts., area placer sands—**gold.**

QUARTZITE: (1) area nearby mines exposing schists—**kyanite, dumortierite, andalusite;** (2) SE, on top of highest peak visible from town (very long hike), hard-rock mine—**gold;** (3) Plomosa district (including E and W margins of the La Posa Plain and extending in all directions from heart of town, dry placers—**gold:** (a) La Cholla, in area 4–5 mi. long bordering E foot of the Dome Rock Mts. S of Int. 10, placer sands at bedrock level, abundant—**gold;** (b) Middle Camp, just N of the Oro Fino placers, *q.v.*, in rich seams of gravel on bedrock—**gold;** (c) Oro Fino, at E foot of the Dome Rock Mts., in vicinity of Int. 10, dry placers—**gold;** (d) Plomosa (5 mi. SE of QUARTZITE), at E edge of the La Posa Plain and W of the foot of the Plomosa Mts., rather abundant in dry placers—**gold;**

(4) W 9 mi. to ruins of La Paz (S of the Colorado R. Indian Reservation),

along foot of the Dome Rock Mts. and 6 mi. E of the Colorado R., placers —gold; (5) Dome Rock Mts.: (a) area mines—**cinnabar, magnetite, siderite, stibiconite** (as radiating blades of **stibnite** partially altered to **cervantite** and **stibiconite**), **tourmaline;** (b) Colonial property—**cinnabar,** thinly coated with **metacinnabar;** (c) Don Walsh prospect, as crystals to 1 in. dia.—**pyrite;** (6) E 8.3 mi., turn S onto old mine road, campsite about 4 mi. from pavement, area all along way—**agate, chalcedony, jasper,** etc.;

(7) S 9 mi. on U.S. 95: (a) E on poor dirt rd. 7½ mi. to Crystal Peak area, campsite, broad surrounding area to N and NE—**rock crystal, limonite cubes.** (This is a noted location for chatoyant **quartz crystals,** many with inclusions, to large size, but has been pretty well cleaned out.) (b) E 9–15 mi. into mts., all area along the rd., both sides, in whitish clay exposures—**rock crystal, limonite cubes, quartzite;** (8) S 19.2 mi. (4 mi. N of Weaver Pass side rd. to CIBOLA, turn E on dirt rd. 5.4 mi. past turnoffs to Palm Canyon, Kofa Queen, and Kofa Game Refuge, to good campsite: (a) SW ½ mi., as bed—**geodes** (containing white **botryoidal chalcedony** or **quartz crystals,** to 12 in. dia.); (b) area old mines, such as the King of Arizona, Kofa Queen, North Star, etc.—**copper, lead, silver, gold;** (c) all regional draws, washes, hillsides, etc.—**agate, chalcedony** (nodules, roses), **jasper, geodes, petrified wood, quartz crystals,** etc.; (9) SW 22 mi., to Trigo: (a) Dome Rock Mts. in T. 2 N, R. 21 W, area placers—**gold;** (b) Red Cloud Mine—**argentite, argentiferous galena.**

SALOME: (1) S past jail on dirt rd. 10 mi. to ghost camp of Harquahala, noted mining center with a considerable history: (a) area great mines, e.g., Harquahala Bonanza, Extension, Summit Lode, Narrow Gauge, Grand View; (b) to the NE, the Golden Eagle and subsidiary shafts—**gold.** (The free-milling ores were extremely rich; a single nugget sprouting leaves of pure gold out of white quartz brought $10,000 cash at the old price of gold.) (2) SE, along road across desert to TONOPAH (Maricopa Co.): (a) many regional old mine dumps—**copper minerals, lead, gold, silver, pyrite,** etc.; (b) random exploration for surface gemstone fields will reveal many collectable specimens—**quartz family gemstones;** (3) Tank Mt., on pediment near the Puzzles, Golden Harp, Ramey, and Regal prospects at E foot of the mts., placers—**gold.**

VICKSBURG, N 4 mi., in Granite Wash Hills, area—**tellurium.**

WELTON: (1) W 3½ mi. (6.2 mi. E of LIGURTA), dirt rd. S (infamous Spanish Camino del Diablo, i.e., "highway of the devil," traversing the fierce Lechuguilla Desert to Tinajas Altas), at 28.1 mi. turn E on left fork parallel to the Mexican border to mi. 37.6, a large rock circle (mass grave of Mexicans who died en route to the Arizona gold mines), keep right up a black mesa, all area—**agate, chalcedony, jasper, jasp-agate, pyrope garnets, petrified wood, opalite, sard,** etc.; (2) SE, in Cabeza Prieta Mts., area of many unlisted collecting localities—**agate** (banded, red moss), **jasp-agate, jasper, chalcedony, sard, opalite** (two-toned), **petrified wood,** various **geodes** and **nodules;** (3) NW 6 mi. and 6 mi. NE of LIGURTA, Muggins Mts.—**agate** (moss, plume), **jasper, chalcedony roses, petrified wood** (cycad, ironwood, palm); (4) W 8 mi., in Gila Mts., on E side—**kyanite;** (5) W 5 mi., turn N 3 mi. on dirt rd. to abandoned Johnson Ranch, then E 3 mi. to N-trending track for 1½ mi. into foothills (very rugged) to abandoned **bentonite** mine, park and hike 2½ mi. above mine to survey post, collecting area to N, abundant—**gem agate.**

YUMA, N all along the Colorado R. to Ehrenburg, 100 mi. or so, by any access rd. to shores, terraces, and elevated benchlands: (1) in boulders along river banks as fine fibrous material—**dumortierite,** with **kyanite** and **pyrophyllite;** (2) area surfaces—**agate, chalcedony, jasper, opalite, petrified wood** (many kinds), **sard,** etc.

ARKANSAS

Arkansas is almost equally divided geographically between the Early Cretaceous to Quaternary sediments of the Coastal Plain (52 percent) and the crystalline Paleozoic rocks of the Interior Highland (48 percent), with the northwestern counties being mountainous and rather strongly mineralized. The major mountain ranges include the Boston and Ozark systems, really parts of the segmented Ozark Plateau, and the Ouachita Mountains, which are the roots of a very ancient once towering range.

Although some thirty useful minerals are mined or quarried within Arkansas, there are estimated to be another hundred that could be commercially exploited. The Ozark region is notable for its abundance of the ores of **copper, iron, lead, manganese, silver,** and **zinc,** as well as for such nonmetallics as **dolomite, limestone, marble, phosphates,** and **sandstone.** The shales and sandstones of the Arkansas Valley contain coal, commercial clays, natural gas, and some metallic mineral ores.

The mountains of western Arkansas contain great quantities of sparkling quartz crystals. These crystals occur in sizable clusters, always six-sided and perfectly terminated, ranging in size from slender needles to the "Arkansas candles" six times as long as thick.

For maps and information, write: Director of Geology, Arkansas Resources and Development Commission, Little Rock.

BOONE, NEWTON, MARION, SEARCY COS.

AREA: In this far NW part of Arkansas are many regional mines—**aurichalcite, goslarite, hydrozincite, smithsonite, sphalerite, "turkey fat"** (a cadmium yellow variety of **smithsonite**).

CARROLL CO.

EUREKA SPRINGS, area cave deposits in rocks of Ordovician age, translucent and brightly banded—**onyx marble.**

GARLAND CO.

BLAKELY CREEK, area deposits—**galena.**

CHANCE: (1) W 2 mi., area—**quartz crystals** (clear, large); (2) W 9 mi., Miller Mts., area ridges and slopes—**quartz crystals, variscite.**

HOT SPRINGS: (1) ledge near town (inquire at local rock shop), several feet thick—**malachite;** (2) W 2 mi., on S slope of West Mt., area—**pyrite;** (3) Hot Springs National Park, area outside boundaries along all surrounding ridges of the Ouachita Mts.—**rock crystal** (all sizes, perfect, clusters, "Arkansas candles").

JESSIEVILLE, area mt. ridges—**quartz crystals, smoky quartz.**

HOT SPRING CO.

AREA: (1) S of and along the Ouachita R. (co. line with Garland Co.), in pockets or crevices among shales and intrusive rocks—**asbolite;** (2) Novaculite Mts., area—**chalcedony, novaculite** ("Arkansas stone"), **quartz crystals.**

BUTTERFIELD, area deposits of excellent grade—**tripoli** resembling **novaculite.**

GIFFORD, area road and RR cuts—**amber.**

MAGNET COVE. This small area, of great interest to gemologists and mineralogists, has long been known as a locality for many rare and beautiful as well as useful gems and minerals. In granite outcrops are found—**actinolite, aegirite** (with **labradorite** and enclosed in **microcline**), **albite, allophane, ankerite, apatite, arkansite crystals, augite, aventurine, braunite, brookite, cinnamon stone, coccolite, dogtooth spar, fahlunite, garnet (almandite, andradite, aplome, grossularite), geyserite, hornblende, hydrotitanite, hypersthene, idocrase, iolite, magnetite, melanite, mica, octahedrite, oligoclase, opal, ozarkite, pealite** (var. **opal**), **perovskite, pinite, pseudobrookite, rutile, schorlomite, silica, siliceous sinter, smoky quartz, sunstone** (pink, gray), **talc shale, wavellite.**

POINT CEDAR, area—**galena.**

ROCKPORT, extending nearly to Oklahoma, W of DALLAS in Polk Co., forming the Zigzag Mts. about HOT SPRINGS and the Ouachita Mts. S of the Ouachita R.—**novaculite** (a flintlike, compact rock used for making whetstones).

INDEPENDENCE, IZARD COS.

BATESVILLE, regional belt 20 mi. long by 4–8 mi. wide extending through Independence, Sharp, and Izard counties, area mines—**hausmannite, psilomelane, pyrolusite** (associated with **ferruginous manganese** ores, some brown and red **iron oxides).**

MADISON CO.

DELANEY, area mt. ridges and slopes—**quartz crystals.**

MARION CO.

BUFFALO RIVER, at Silver Hollow Bluff, a mine—**zinc.**
YELLVILLE, area lead and zinc mines, especially the Morning Star—
galena, pyrite, smithsonite ("turkey fat"), sphalerite.

MONTGOMERY CO.

AREA: (1) Crystal Mt., surfaces, ridges—**quartz crystals;** (2) Sloan's
Well—**talc** (as incrustations in black shale), **halotrichite.**
BLACK SPRINGS, along rd. to MOUNT IDA, showings in shale—**talc.**
CADDO GAP, NE, in bed of Collier Cr. at Buttermilk Springs—**graphite.**
MOUNT IDA, S, at Fisher Mt., area—**rock crystal, smoky quartz.**
RUBICON (near VIRGINIA CITY), and at the Minnesota, Montezuma, Wal-
nut, and Waterloo mines—**galena.**

PIKE CO.

AREA, Trinity formation exposures of Cretaceous rocks intruded into
Carboniferous formations—**diamond** (mines), **peridotite.**
DELIGHT, area deposits—**tripoli.**
MURFREESBORO: (1) noted area **diamond** mine, small fee—**diamond;** (2)
SSE 2½ mi., at Prairie Cr., area—**amethyst, diopside, epidote, garnet,
hematite, peridote, pyrite, quartz crystals.**

POLK CO.

AREA, Silver World Mine—**stannite (tin pyrites).**
MENA, SE 7 mi., area—**rock crystal.**

PULASKI CO.

LITTLE ROCK: (1) immediate environs; (2) just S of city limits, in
Fourche Mt. district, embracing an area of more than 12 sq. mi.—**bauxite;**
(3) Kellogg District: (a) Kellogg Mine, Sec. 30, T. 3 N, R. 11 W, and
(b) McRae Mine—**lead, silver.**

SALINE CO.

AREA: (1) Rabbit Foot Mine—**bartholomite** (encrustations in crevices
as decomposition of **pyrite**), **melanterite, pyrite;** (2) Wallis' soapstone
quarry, near the old HOT SPRINGS–LITTLE ROCK rd. in NW¼ Sec. 15, T.
1 N, R. 15 W, near Cane Cr.—**massive soapstone.**
BAUXITE (30 mi. SW of LITTLE ROCK), area quarries—gemmy **bauxite
(heliotrope bauxite).**

BENTON: (1) NE 12 mi. and S of the HOT SPRINGS rd. in NE¼ Sec. 15, T. 1 N, R. 15 W, as a good outcrop—**soapstone;** (2) W, near Olsen switch, impregnations in quartz—**native copper.**

BLOCHER, N, in embedded patches in quartz—**serpentine.**

BRYANT (Twp.), 18 mi. SW of LITTLE ROCK in the BAUXITE District, several sq. mi. of outcrops—**bauxite.**

PARON: (1) outcrops in a 6-mi. radius—**quartz crystals** (milky, smoky); (2) broad surrounding area extending into Montgomery Co., i.e., from PARON to a point 5 mi. SW of MOUNT IDA—**calcite, chert, chlorite, feldspar, quartz** (crystals, milky—mostly found along mt. and ridge crests).

SCOTT CO.

BLUE BALL, area exposures—**peridotite, diamond.**

SEARCY CO.

AREA, Sec. 6, T. 16 N, R. 16 W, the Tomahawk Mine—**malachite.** (This mine lies in a district noted for its **zinc minerals.**)

SEVIER CO.

CONBOY, nearby at the Bellah Mine—**galena.**

GILHAM, W, area—**chalcopyrite.** The far N part of this county and adjoining S section of Polk Co., in a rather narrow belt of steeply folded Mississippian shales and sandstones (Stanley Shale), as numerous deposits—**antimony,** associated with small amounts of **copper, iron, bismuth sulfides,** and **zinc.**

WASHINGTON CO.

FARMINGTON, vicinity, as good-grade deposits—**tripoli.**

WHITE CO.

SEARCY, area outcrops—**peridotite, diamond.**

CALIFORNIA

Second largest of the continental United States, California has a diversified topography and complicated geological history. This immense state divides naturally into a number of remarkably diverse geomorphic provinces: Cascade Range, Sierra Nevada, Modoc Plateau, Klamath Moun-

tains, Basin Ranges, Coast Ranges, the Great Central Valley (Sacra-
mento-San Joaquin), the Transverse Ranges, and the Mojave and
Colorado deserts. The southern California deserts further extend by a
series of interlocking intermontane arid valleys all the 900-mile length of
the eastern half of the state to the Oregon line. This desolate region lies
immediately east of the almost impenetrable granite barrier of the Sierra
Nevada Range.

Not only is California noted for its Mother Lode **gold** mines and the
huge deposits of **cinnabar** that enabled early gold miners to extract the
precious yellow metal with quicksilver, first mined by prehistoric Indians
for facial pigment, but the state ranks among the leading gemstone regions of the world. In fact, the Mother Lode counties which later became
the center of gold rush mining were first noted for their gem-quality **gold
quartz,** formerly a prime collector's gemstone.

The gem pegmatites of New England and the Black Hills of South
Dakota are easily matched by the enormously productive gem pegmatites
of southern California's San Diego County. One of the advantages which
California vouchsafes to gem and mineral collectors is its general aridity
and a lack of the covering vegetation which hides so many of the gem and
mineral localities of moister states. In the Golden State mineralized outcrops are everywhere starkly visible. While the vicissitudes of climate and
lack of readily available supplies of water in many mineral regions of
California can make gem and mineral prospecting rather difficult at times,
the great majority of collecting localities can be easily reached by automobile over roads that are paved almost everywhere except in the farther
reaches of the inhospitable desert counties.

For guides and illustrated papers, write: Division of Mines, Department of Natural Resources, Ferry Building, San Francisco.

ALAMEDA CO.

BERKELEY, throughout the Berkeley Hills exposures of andesite containing brilliant crystals—**analcite.**
EAST OAKLAND, at Leona Heights: (1) area pyrite mines—**epsomite** (efflorescence on mine walls and timbers), **pyrite;** (2) Alma Mine—**alunogen**
(as a white powder), **boothite** (with other sulfates of iron and copper),
chalcanthite (massive coatings and crystals) with **melanterite, copiapite,
copper** (as arborescent groups), **salvadorite (kröhnkite).**
LIVERMORE, SE 16 mi., in the Cedar Mt. district, many area mines—
massive **chromite.**
SUNOL, SE, on Apperson Cr.—**talc** pseudomorphs after **actinolite.**

ALPINE CO.

MARKLEEVILLE: (1) S, in the Loope district—**jasper;** (2) Mogus district,
the Morningstar and area mines—**arsenopyrite** (well-formed crystals), **enar-**

gite with massive **pyrite, famatinite;** (3) E 7 mi., the Leviathan sulfur mine, abundant—**chalcanthite;** (4) SSW 10 mi., area exposures of garnetiferous quartzite—bands of **lazulite** with **andalusite** and **rutile, ilmenite.**

MONITOR DISTRICT, on dumps of the Exchequer Mine, as crystals to ½ in. dia.—**arsenolite.**

AMADOR CO.

FIDDLETOWN, Indian Gulch area—**diamond** (occasional), **gold.**

IONE: (1) E 2½ mi., the Mace Mine, as veins in **serpentine**—**chrysotile;** (2) NE 3 mi., the Jackson (Newton) Mine, as chief ore—**chalcopyrite.**

JACKSON: (1) Gwin Mine—crystals of **arsenopyrite** (some including arborescent masses of crystallized **gold**); (2) Mountain Spring House, S 1 mi.—**chromite.**

MARTELL, W 4 mi., quarry on Allen Ranch in vein cutting limestone, as crystals to 1 in. long—**axinite.**

PINE GROVE DISTRICT, the Little Grass Valley Mine, as fibrous sheets—**tremolite.**

PLYMOUTH: (1) Loafer Hill area (near Oleta)—**diamond, gold;** (2) Plymouth Mine, as incrustations on slate—**ankerite.**

VOLCANO: (1) area of Jackass Gulch and Rancheria—**diamond, gold;** (2) area stream gravels—**amethyst, rock crystal, rose quartz;** (3) S 1½ mi., deposits—**psilomelane** mixed with **pyrolusite;** (4) SW 5 mi., the Defender Mine—**marcasite** with **pyrrhotite.**

BUTTE CO.

AREA, T. 21 N, R. 4 E, the Surcease Mine, in **gold** ores—**native antimony, bournonite, gold.**

BIG BEAR LOOKOUT, SE 1½ mi., in andalusite schists—**andalusite.**

BIG BEND, S ½ mi., the Pinkston Mine—**auriferous barite.**

CHEROKEE: (1) area stream gravels, occasional—**diamond;** (2) Cherokee Flat—**diamond, gold.**

FORBESTOWN, Gold Bank Mine, as constituent of schists—**prochlorite.**

OROVILLE: (1) Thompson's Flat, area—**diamond, gold;** (2) N 1 mi., W bank of Feather R., occasional—**diamond.**

PULGA, N side of Feather R. ½ mi. NE of Big Bar Sta.—**californite, grossularite garnet, serpentine.**

YANKEE HILL: (1) area gravels of the Feather R.—**axinite;** (2) area old gold placers—**axinite** (plum-colored, platy, abundant loose clusters and crystals), **diamond, gold.**

CALAVERAS CO.

AREA: (1) Hughes Mine, good—**azurite, malachite;** (2) Morgan Mine—**altaite;** (3) Railroad Flat—**alunite crystals;** (3) Robinson's Ferry, the Frenchwood Mine—**altaite, calaverite, petzite,** and other **tellurides.**

ALTAVILLE, E 5–6 mi., on Janokis Ranch, as good crystals—**diaspore**, with **chlorite** on **chromite**.

ANGELS CAMP: (1) area mines, widespread: (a) Keystone, Lancha Plana, Union mines—**chalcopyrite**; (b) Milton, E 9 mi. and NE 10 mi. at Wright Ranch in Salt Springs Valley; (c) 5 mi. SE of Valley Springs and 4 mi. N of COPPEROPOLIS on rd. to Milton; (d) too many other area occurrences to list—**chromite**; (2) N 7 mi., in quartz exposures as good crystals—**epidote**.

BALD POINT (on the Mokelumne R.), as large crystals—**epidote**.

CAMPO SECO, area—**boothite** (crystals, massive).

CARSON HILL: (1) area mines, abundant—**ankerite, hornblende**; (2) Melones, Morgan, and Stanislaus mines—**calaverite**; (3) T. 2 N, R. 13 E, at Stanislaus mines in large masses—**altaite** (with **calaverite** and **hessite**), **melonite, native tellurium**.

COPPEROPOLIS, area mines—**azurite, bornite, brochantite** (as druses), **chalcopyrite, malachite**.

GARNET HILL, just above confluence of Moore Cr. and the Mokelumne R.—**epidote, andradite garnet, quartz, idocrase**.

MOKELUMNE HILL (District): (1) S of the hill 2½ mi., and (2) Eclipse, the Infernal Mine and other area mines 3 mi. S of the hill—**gold, rock crystal**.

SAN ANDREAS: (1) E ½ mi., the Ford Mine, on the 300-ft. level—**allanite**; (2) N 1 mi., the Golden Gate Mine—**ankerite**.

SHEEP RANCH, SE 2 mi. in NW¼NW¼ Sec. 22, T. 4 N, R. 14 E, on the Hauselt Patent—**cobaltiferous arsenopyrite**.

VALLECITO, just W, on rd. to ANGLES CAMP, large masses—**hornblende**.

COLUSA CO.

AREA, W part of co.: (1) Manzanita Mine in Sec. 29, T. 14 N, R. 5 W—**cinnabar, calcite, chalcopyrite, gold** (leaf, wire), **marcasite, stibnite**; (2) Gray Eagle Mine in Sec. 20, T. 16 N, R. 6 W, in **serpentine—native copper, cuprite, tenorite**.

COOK SPRINGS, NW 1½ mi., area—**chromite**.

LODOGA, S 4 mi., area—green **epidote, hematite**.

STONYFORD: (1) Chrome Wonder Mine—**chromite**; (2) gravels of Stonyford Cr. N of Lodoga—**jasper, nephrite jade, serpentine**.

SULPHUR CREEK: (1) area, massive—**auriferous alunite**; (2) Simmins Spring, W ¼ mi., the Oriental Mine—**cinnabar, free gold**; (3) many area exposures—**onyx**.

WILBUR SPRINGS, about 2 mi. E of the Lake Co. line, in a road quarry—**calcite, datolite, hydromagnesite, prehnite, pectolite, thomsonite, serpentine**.

CONTRA COSTA CO.

BERKELEY (Alameda Co.), E, in Berkeley Hills, rd. cuts along Skyline Blvd. N of Fish Ranch Rd., in Moraga Formation—**chalcedony**.

WALNUT CREEK, E, on Mt. Diablo: (1) E side, in numerous deposits known to prehistoric Indians—**cinnabar;** (2) Mitchell Canyon, at a prospect in a ravine tributary—**bornite** (with **chalcopyrite** and a little **gold**).

SAN PABLO, area schist outcrops—**actinolite, anthophyllite** (fibrous masses), abundant **tremolite.**

DEL NORTE CO.

CRESCENT CITY, area ocean beaches—**agate, chalcedony, jasper, moonstone, petrified wood.**

DIAMOND CREEK (District), area prospects—**native copper.**

GASQUET, S on USFS rd. to Sec. 19, T. 16 N, R. 3 E, the Camp Group of mines—**chromite** coated with **kämmererite, uvarovite.**

ROCKLAND (District), the Keystone Mine—**copper nuggets.**

SHELLY CREEK (and upper Monkey Cr.), area mines, in quartz veins—**arsenopyrite, gold.**

SMITH RIVER, area gravels of the Smith R., occasional—**diamond.**

EL DORADO CO.

AREA: (1) many Mother Lode mines—**arsenopyrite, gold;** (2) regional outcrops of **serpentine** (concentrated around CLARKSVILLE, CUMMINGS, FOLSOM, GEORGETOWN, NEWCASTLE, and VOLCANOVILLE)—**chromite.**

DIAMOND SPRINGS, E 1 mi., the Larkin Mine, as one of the gangue minerals in **gold** quartz veins—**ankerite.**

FAIRPLAY: (1) Alabaster Cave, and (2) old Cosumnes and other area mines in the Foothill **copper** belt, excellent—**azurite;** (3) Boston Mine—**bornite** pseudomorphs after **picrolite;** (4) NE 3 mi., old Cosumnes Mine —**axinite** (small clear crystals with many faces, on **epidote**), massive **bornite** (with **molybdenite** in a coarse pegmatite), **chalcopyrite** with **garnet** (good specimens).

GEORGETOWN, SSE 2½ mi., at Traverse Cr., area—massive **californite, garnet, idocrase.**

GREENWOOD, N 6 mi., at French Hill, as veins—fibrous **chrysotile.**

PLACERVILLE: (1) area gold placers—**gold, phantom quartz crystals, rock crystals** (many with inclusions); (2) W 4½ mi., area **copper** mines—**bornite;** (3) NE 5.6 mi., American R. gravels—**nephrite jade;** (4) Cedar Ravine, Forest Hill, Smith's Flat, Webber Hill, and White Rock Canyon, area gravels—**diamond, gold.**

FRESNO CO.

AREA: (1) Grub Gulch, common—**epidote;** (2) Mt. Diablo Range (W part of co.), many deposits—**chromite;** (3) Picayune Flat, in sands, excellent—**zircon;** (4) Tehipite Dome, opposite at the Uncle Sam Mine on Kings R.—**bornite, magnetite, gold;** (5) Watts Valley, E side and 1½ mi. S of Hawkins schoolhouse and 700 ft. above Watts Cr.—**californite, garnet, serpentine.**

COALINGA: (1) Copper King Mine, abundant—**chalcopyrite**; (2) NW, near head of White Cr. in SE¼ Sec. 4, T. 19 S, R. 13 E, in cavities of a soda-syenite—**albite, aegirite, analcite, barkevikite** (crystals); (3) S 3½ mi., in Jacolito Canyon—**orbicular chert.**

PIEDRA, N side of the N Fork of the Kings R., in rd. cuts as large pseudo-hexagonal plates in veins—**clinochlore,** some **penninite.**

SANGER: (1) E 9 mi., in Clarks Valley, in pegmatite—**apatite** (crystals to 1 in.), large crystals of **andalusite;** (2) N end of Clarks Valley, as crystals to 10 in. long—**epidote.**

SHARPSVILLE, E 1½ mi., in S½ Sec. 20, T. 11 S, R. 22 E, in a narrow pegmatite as radiating masses and prismatic crystals, pink to dark reddish violet color and to 7 in. long—**andalusite.**

TRIMMER, area, as a contact mineral with quartz—**epidote, garnet.**

GLENN CO.

CHROME, a few miles N of Chrome Mt., as float—**native copper.**

FRUTO, 19 mi. distant in T. 19, 20 N, R. 5, 6 W—**chromite.**

GRINDSTONE CREEK, the Mammoth Copper Mine in T. 22 N, R. 9 W—**copper minerals, volborthite.**

ORLAND, W 30 mi., in Sec. 3, T. 22 N, R. 7 W—**chromite.**

HUMBOLDT CO.

AREA, gravels of the Trinity R.—**diamond, platinum nuggets.**

ARCATA, NE 8 mi., at Liscom Hill, in white crystalline veins to 1 ft. wide —**barite.**

BLOCKSBURG, N 12 mi., the Woods Mine—**bementite, neotocite, rhodochrosite.**

CENTERVILLE, S 4 mi., on ocean beach as boulders—**hematite.**

EUREKA: NE 25 mi., on Horse Mt.: (1) area exposures—**chromite;** (2) W side, in schists as large prisms—**epidote** (with **calcite**); (3) N, St. Patricks Point and all beaches—**agate, jasper.**

FORT SEWARD, at the Fort Seward Mine in Sec. 15, T. 3 S, R. 4 E, as primary ore mineral—**braunite.**

ORLEANS, S via USFS rd. to Sec. 29, T. 10 N, R. 6 E, the Red Cap Mine —**bornite, native copper** (as float).

TRINIDAD, N 6 mi., at Patrick's Point, beach boulders—massive **pyrite, chalcopyrite.**

IMPERIAL CO.

COOLIDGE SPRING, area a few mi. S of Fish Springs and W of the old hwy., as concretions—**barite.**

COYOTE WELLS, area to N—**fossils** (clams, oysters).

MIDWAY WELL: (1) E 2 mi. on rd. to True Friend and Silver Mom mines on E flanks of the Chocolate Mts.—**opal, turquoise;** (2) SE 3 mi., the Paymaster district, numerous mines—**argentite** (in **gold quartz** veins), **barite** (as gangue).

NILAND, at Obsidian Butte, in lithophysae in an **obsidian** quarry—**fayalite** (as occasional crystals), **obsidian.**

OGILBY: (1) N 10–12 mi., on either side of Indian Pass, area—**agate, chalcedony, dumortierite, jasper, quartz crystals, petrified palm root;** (2) N, in Cargo Muchacho and Chocolate mts.: (a) area surfaces—see (1); (b) Cargo Muchachago district, area old mines—**arsenopyrite.** (The Chocolate Mts. are mostly locked up in a U.S. military gunnery range with no travel permitted inside the posted boundaries.)

PICACHO (District), the Bluejacket and other area mines—**tetrahedrite.**

WILEY WELL (Region): (1) very many area collecting grounds, with some routes posted by rock clubs—**gemstones;** (2) Hauser geode beds—**agate, jasper, geodes** (fine gem contents), **gem nodules.** (This is a noted collecting locality embracing a considerable area of desert that is extremely hot and hostile in summer.)

INYO CO.

ARGUS RANGE (N of TRONA, in San Bernardino Co.), mines of the Minietta and Modoc districts—**anglesite** (abundant ore) associated with **azurite** and **bindheimite** as oxidation products of **galena.**

BALLARAT: (1) area mine dumps—**cerussite, wulfenite;** (2) American Magnesium Co. mine, as fibrous masses in clay—**alunogen,** with **epsomite;** (3) E 5–10 mi., on W side of the Panamint Range, comprising much of the area schists—**attrelite (chloridtoid)** in dark green oblong plates; (4) NE 10 mi. from Panamint mines, in Surprise Canyon, area—**embolite.**

BIG PINE: (1) SE 9 mi., area—**litharge, massicot;** (2) Owens Valley regional mine dumps—**azurite, chalcopyrite, chrysocolla, cuprite, malachite, tellurides.**

BISHOP: (1) S 4½ mi., area—**cervantite, metastibnite, valentinite;** (2) SW 18 mi.: (a) Bishop Cr. Mine—**arsenopyrite, loellingite, pyrrhotite;** (b) Wilshire **gold** mine, at headwaters of Bishop Cr.—**arsenopyrite, loellingite, pyrrhotite,** other sulfides; (3) W, in the Tungsten Hills, area mines—**bithmuthinite, bismutite.**

CERRO GORDO DISTRICT: (1) area mine dumps—**anglesite** (in masses with crystalline crusts enclosing **galena** cores), **brochantite, caledonite, copper carbonate ores, linarite, smithsonite;** (2) Aries Mine—pseudomorphs of **chrysocolla** after **cerussite;** (3) Belmont Mine—**argentite, tetrahedrite, stephanite** (the **tetrahedrite** contains a large percentage of **silver**); (4) Cerro Gordo Mine—**aurichalcite** (with **hemimorphite** and **hydrozincite**), massive **bournonite, brochantite** (with **caledonite** and **linarite**), **smithsonite,** compact massive **jamesonite** (with **argentiferous galena**), **mimetite, plumbogummite, chrysotile** (long-fibered), **leadhillite** (pale sea green imperfect crystals), **limonite** pseudomorphs after long crystals of **stibnite, liroconite.**

COSO HOT SPRINGS, area **obsidian** outcrops, in spheroidal openings—**fayalite** (small brown crystals) with **cristobalite, tridymite, orthoclase.**

DARWIN: (1) area contact zones, abundant—**epidote;** (2) Fernando Mine —**bismuthinite, barite** and **scheelite** in **bismutite.**

DEATH VALLEY, many area saline lakes and deposits—**borax minerals.**

FISH SPRINGS, S 10–12 mi., the San Carlos Mine—**datolite** (massive white), **idocrase, garnet, lapis lazuli, opal.**

FURNACE CREEK (Death Valley): (1) Furnace Cr. Wash borax mine— **borax, colemanite;** (2) area mines in the Amargosa Range, as immense deposits—**colemanite;** (3) S, in the Greenwater district of the Black Mts.— **azurite, copper minerals** (oxides, silicates, carbonates); (4) Chloride Cliff: (a) area in the Amargosa Range in T. 30 N, R. 1 E, as small, colorless, equant crystals on fracture surfaces of limestone—**adamite;** (b) the Chloride Cliff Mine, in the Funeral Range—**cinnabar, metacinnabar;** (5) Gower Gulch and the Ryan district outside Death Valley—**colemanite.**

KEARSARGE, E 7 mi.: (1) Lucky Boy prospect, in a 15-in. vein—**molybdenite;** (2) Roper iron mine, abundant—**specular hematite.**

KEELER, E 18 mi., at the Lee Mine—**argentite, embolite.**

LAWS: (1) NE 6 mi., in Gunter Canyon, as white veins 2–5 ft. wide, with schists and slates—**barite** (crystals, massive); (2) N 17 mi., area—**pyrophyllite.**

LITTLE LAKE, area—**sanidine.**

LONE PINE: (1) E 1½ mi., in pegmatite, abundant as poorly developed crystals, green—**microcline;** (2) area Owens Valley mine dumps—**azurite, chalcopyrite, chrysocolla, cuprite, malachite,** etc.

LONG LAKE, E, at the Bishop Silver and Cobalt Mining Co., Sec. 14, T. 9 S, R. 31 E— **annabergite, erythrite, smaltite, argentite.**

MANZANAR, E 2 mi., the Reward Mine—**caledonite, linarite, chrysocolla** pseudomorphs after **calcite.**

MOUNT BLANCO (District), area mines—**borax minerals, howlite.**

PANAMINT: (1) NE ½ mi., the Curran Mine—**chalcopyrite, pyrite, pyrrhotite, siderite;** (2) S 4 mi., the Mountain Girl Mine—**siderite;** (3) Sunrise Mine—**argentite;** (3) Panamint Mts., head of Cottonwood Cr., as bottle-green, radial crystals—**brochantite** (in brown **jasper**), **chrysocolla.**

SHOSHONE: (1) W 3 mi., as massive brown deposit—**strontianite;** (2) T. 22 N, R. 7 E, as important deposits in clay-shale—**colemanite, ulexite.**

SWANSEA, the Indiana Mine—**cerargyrite, embolite.**

TECOPA, the Noonday Mine—**scorodite.**

UBEHEBE MINE, as perfect white crystals—**axinite** (with **smithsonite**).

WILD ROSE STATION, in Wild Rose Canyon in light-colored mica schists, abundant—**jarosite, argentite, cerargyrite.**

KERN CO.

AREA: (1) Amalie Mine—**argentite, pyrargyrite, tetrahedrite;** (2) Aldridge Mine (NW¼ Sec. 27, T. 25 S, R. 32 E), abundant crystals—**epidote;** (3) Castle Butte, SE side in foothills N of Hwy. 466—**agate, chalcedony, chert, jasper, petrified wood;** (4) Contact Mine (Sec. 10, T. 10 N, R. 15 W), in vein 6–12 in. wide once mined for **arsenic**—**arsenopyrite;** (5) San Emigdio Canyon, head of, Sec. 10, T. 9 N, R. 21 W—**stibnite.**

BAKERSFIELD, SE, at Walker Cr. in area schists—**chiastolite.**

GORMAN, N 4 mi. (of Quail Lake), at the Meeke (Hogan) tin mine, as nodules and stringers—**cassiterite.**

HAVILAH-KERNVILLE: (1) 4 mi. S of Miracle Hot Springs, at Erskine Cr., nodular masses (to 300 lb.)—**antimony, stibnite;** (2) Little Caliente Spring (S of Piute)—**antimony, stibiconite;** (3) Rayo Mine, Sec. 24, T. 27 S, R. 33 E—**antimony, stibnite;** (4) Sunset, W 12 mi. and 5 mi. NW of Cuddy Valley, at Antimony Peak, area—**antimony.**

HOBO HOT SPRINGS, E ¼ mi., in contact deposit—**actinolite.**

JAWBONE CANYON: (1) Sec. 10, 11, 14, 15, T. 30 S, R. 36 E, as sulfur-yellow fibrous crystals—**ferrimolybdite;** (2) Sec. 5 and 6, area—**antimony.**

ISABELLA DAM: (1) Greenhorn mining district, the Cadillac claims—**epidote, scheelite;** (2) N on Rte. 178 to W-trending gravel rd. through the Greenhorn Mts.: (a) Huckaby and Little Acorn mines—**epidote, quartz crystals, smoky quartz, scheelite;** (b) area scheelite mine dumps—**epidote, scheelite crystals, smoky quartz crystals** (some with **epidote** inclusions); (3) Green Mt., area—**arsenopyrite.**

KRAMER: (1) area 35 mi. SE of MOJAVE and just N of BORON—**howlite;** (2) Pacific Coast and Western Borax Co. mines, and (3) the Suckow Mine—**borax,** with **colemanite, ulexite, probertite (kramerite),** etc.

MOJAVE: (1) Middle Buttes, in stringers of coarsely crystalline materials—**alunite;** (2) N, in Pine Canyon, good crystals—**barite;** (3) Soledad Butte, in several area mines—**argentite;** (4) W 18.6 mi. on U.S. 466 to Cache Cr. rd., along rd. about 7 mi. to Horse Canyon, elev. 5,000 ft. in Tehachapi Mts., noted locality—**"Horse Canyon" agate** (fern, flower, icicle, lace, plume, tube, sagenite, etc.), **fossil horse bones;** (5) see RED ROCK CANYON.

(6) NE 25 mi. via good dirt rds., the El Paso Mts., general region: (a) Dutch Cleanser Pumice Mine, as fine unusual specimens from abandoned workings—**pumice;** (b) all surrounding region as surface float or shallow pockets requiring minor digging—**agate, opal, jasper, gold** (surprisingly abundant), **agatized** and **petrified palm wood** and **twigs.** This excellent collecting area can be entered by any of three routes: from the south via the RANDSBURG road, a spectacular route, from the ruins of Hart's place about 14 mi. N of the RANDSBURG jct. via good dirt rd. heading SE to the Dutch Cleanser Mine; and N from the ruins of Garlock via Mesquite Canyon. Productive old mines and area camps include: Cadahy Camp, Owens Camp, Burro Schmidt's Tunnel, Colorado Camp, Gebracht Camp, plus many old mines unnamed on Kern Co. maps.

RANDSBURG: (1) Yellow Aster and area mines—**arsenopyrite;** (2) S 2 mi., in schist as crystals to 1 in. long—**zoisite.**

RED ROCK CANYON (21 mi. N of MOJAVE on Rte. 14): (1) area lava flows, in cavities—**analcime, calcite, natrolite,** some **opal;** (2) area surfaces —**agate, agatized wood, chalcedony, jasper, precious opal;** (3) Saltdale (on rd. to RANDSBURG), side rd. into Last Chance Canyon—gem **opal, petrified wood.**

ROSAMOND: (1) W to first N-trending rd., then N several mi. to Gem Hill, many prospects: (a) area—**agate, chalcedony, jasper, plasma, uraninite;** (b) N to NW slopes—gem **jasper** (to huge boulders); (2) Portal

Ridge, area—**rhodonite;** (3) Wheeler Springs: (a) area old mines—**gold;** (b) regional surfaces—**agate, jasper, obsidian, arrowheads.**

TEHACHAPI: (1) N, at Tollgate Canyon, large columnar, brittle—**tremolite;** (2) E 7 mi. on Rte. 466 (to 2 mi. E of MONOLITH), to Cache Cr. Canyon, area—**"Horse Canyon" agate, chalcedony, jasper.**

WOODY (district 34 mi. W of Isabella Reservoir), the Greenback Mine—**azurite, copper oxides** and **sulfides.**

LAKE CO.

AREA, SE¼ SE¼ Sec. 20, T. 12 N, R. 7 W, in a gemstone prospect, purple—**cordierite.**

BARTLETT SPRINGS (15 mi. by steep gravel rd. N of Clear Lake), NW 15 mi., on the Eel R., mines—**orpiment, realgar.**

KELSEYVILLE, SE 4 mi., massive green deposit—**fluorite.**

LAKEPORT, S (to S end of Clear Lake), the Sulphur Bank Mine—**sulfur, melanterite** (abundant as stalactites), **aragonite, opal.**

LUCERNE: (1) Clear Lake, and (2) Lower Clear Lake, area, especially along Cole Cr.—**dolomite crystals, obsidian.**

REIFF, area deposits along the KNOXVILLE rd.—**chromite.**

LAKE, NAPA, SONOMA COS.

The Mayacmas–Sulphur Bank districts include hundreds of occurrences of **cinnabar,** with other **mercury minerals** of less importance. Many deposits of ore are in **opalite.**

LASSEN CO.

WESTWOOD, SE 9 mi., in the Meadow Mt. district (Sec. 28, T. 28 N, R. 10 E), copper prospects—**copper minerals, native copper.**

LOS ANGELES CO.

ACTON: (1) S and SW, area hillsides and washes—**agate, chalcedony, jasper, quartz;** (2) W ¼ mi., as sheaves and platy crystals to several inches long—**stilbite;** (3) Free Cuba Mine, in quartz—**copper;** (4) between town and Agua Dulce Canyon, in Escondido Canyon—**agate** (banded, green moss, sagenitic), **amethyst geodes, jasper.**

AZUSA: (1) N, up San Gabriel Canyon, the Felix fluorite mine—**barite** (some), **fluorite** (purple and green masses and cubes); (2) N 8 mi., the Kelsey and O.K. mines—**annabergite, erythrite, native silver, smaltite; argentite, barite,** various **arsenates** (mostly as coatings); (3) site of old Eldoradoville (gold camp of the 1860's), in area canyon detritus—**gold** (colors, nuggets).

CALABASAS, S on Rte. 27 to within 8 mi. of Coast Hwy., area—**agate, jasper, natrolite.**

HOLLYWOOD: (1) area of Cahuenga Pass, W, near Mulholland Dr., in vesicular basalts—**heulandite, natrolite;** (2) Griffith Park, N side along South Riverside Dr., in small dikes, abundant—**barkevikite.**

LANCASTER, Portal Ridge, area deposits, massive, deep pink—**rhodonite.**

LANG, Sterling Borax Mine, extensive deposits—**colemanite, howlite.**

LOMITA, area quarries, crystals—**dolomite, marcasite, pyrite.**

LOS ANGELES: (1) Brush Canyon, in veins and cavity fillings in basalt exposures in the Pacific Electric Quarry No. 3—**analcime, natrolite, prehnite, apophyllite;** (2) San Francisquito Canyon Reservoir area, E edge in quartz veins, abundant—**clinozoisite;** (3) Soledad Pass (New Pass), 7 mi. below summit and 90 ft. above creek bed, as veins and stringers in quartz—**chalcopyrite.**

MALIBU, N, to Malibu Lake, area basalt seams—**analcite.**

MEADOW VALLEY (district), area prospects—**bornite, garnet.**

PALMDALE, W 5 mi., area—**siliceous psilomelane.**

PALOS VERDES ESTATES, area quarries and rd. cuts in the Palos Verdes Hills (extreme SW part of co.)—**barite crystals, fossils** (shells, whale bones).

RAVENNA, N side of hwy. along canyon, area surfaces—**chalcedony, copper**-stained **garden rock, jasper.**

REDONDO BEACH: (1) N along beach to EL SEGUNDO, low-tide gravels (much destroyed now by breakwater construction)—**gem moonstones;** (2) S, in Malaga Cove—**seam agate** (dark brown), **glaucophane** (with **crossite**).

SAN FERNANDO, NE 12 mi. in Pacoima Canyon: (1) area—**annabergite** (with **siderite** and **pyrrhotite**); (2) 12 mi. up from canyon mouth: (a) Denver Mining and Milling property, in veins in schist—**chalcopyrite** (with **galena, pyrrhotite, sphalerite**); (b) Indicator Mine, massive—**sphalerite** (with **galena** and **pyrrhotite**); (3) Sec. 17, T. 3 N, R. 13 W, in pegmatite outcrop—**allanite** (abundant rough tabular crystals to 3 in. long), **apatite, zircon** (abundant clear pinkish crystals).

SAN PEDRO, W at Vicente Point, then ½ mi. N in dikes of limestone and breccia, in vugs—**calcite crystals.**

SANTA CATALINA IS.: (1) area lead mines, abundant—**galena, sphalerite;** (2) Howlands Landing, in a nearby pegmatite outcrop, as good transparent crystals to 1 in. across—**albite;** (3) W tip of island, in **chlorite-lawsonite** schist, as well-developed crystals—**albite.**

SANTA MONICA, W, in the Santa Monica Mts.: (1) area slate exposures along access rds., and (2) jct. of Franklin and Coldwater canyons, in "spotted" (**cordierite**) slates, fair-sized crystals—**chiastolite.**

SAUGUS, NE: (1) Sierra Pelona Valley, N side, in NE¼ Sec. 12, T. 5 N, R. 14 W, in the Pelona schists as a network of pure-white crystals with interstitial **chlorite** and **tourmaline**—**clinozoisite;** (2) Bouquet Reservoir, in Pelona schist on Bouquet Canyon hwy., in SW¼ NE¼ Sec. 28, T. 6 N, R. 14 W, in lenses of greenish gray radiating prisms to 4 in.—**clinozoisite** (in **albite amphibolite**).

SOLEMINT (on U.S. 6 N of SAN FERNANDO), E 6½ mi. to Mint Canyon with dirt rd. to rte. leading into Tick Canyon: (1) up Mint Canyon a short distance to old borax mine, gemmy—**howlite;** (2) in Tick Canyon: (a) area hillsides—**chalcedony** (clear, nodular), **banded agate,** some good **bloodstone;** (b) at old **colemanite** deposit mine—abundant **colemanite** and cauliflower-like masses of **howlite;** (c) head of canyon, in cavities in lava, small crystals —**analcite, natrolite.**

TUJUNGA, N, in Tujunga Canyon, area placer sands—**gold** (colors, nuggets).

MADERA CO.

AREA: (1) Chowchilla R., near Chowchilla crossing on Fort Miller rd., in micaceous schists, crystals—**chiastolite;** (2) Fish Creek, N ½ mi., in the North Fork mining district and about 200 yds. E of the Chiquito trail—**altaite;** (3) Iron Mt., area deposits—**magnetite;** (4) Kaiser Mt. district, 1½ mi. from Huntington Lake rd., abundant crystals—**calcite;** (5) Ritter Range: (a) W side, area exposures—**lazulite;** (b) Shadow Cr. Canyon, S side, in crystalline limestones—**actinolite, rhodonite** (with **epidote** and **garnet**).

COARSE GOLD: (1) N 2 mi., and (2) NE 5 mi., area exposures—**axinite, byssolite** (fibrous **actinolite**), **gold, quartz crystals, sphene.**

DAULTON: (1) W ½ mi., mine dumps—**chiastolite crystals;** (2) SE 1 mi., the Daulton Mine—**cubanite.**

MADERA, area prospects—**chromite** (coated with **zaratite**).

RAYMOND; (1) Mt. Raymond district, the Star Mine, as large cubes—**galena;** (2) N 12 mi., on the I.X.L. claim, in a quartz vein in **andalusite** schist, as crystals and masses to several lbs.—**wolframite.**

MARIN CO.

AREA: (1) Eel R., North Fork, area deposits and float—**nephrite jade;** (2) Point Bonita (foot of Golden Gate Bridge)—**kinradite;** (3) San Francisco Bay shores: (a) Stinson Beach, area exposures of **serpentine,** as impregnations and coatings—**szaibelyite (ascharite, beta-ascharite, camsellite);** (b) Stinson Ranch, area hillsides—**axinite crystals** (with **prehnite**).

FORT BARRY, shale exposures in rd. tunnel, as fibrous tufts—**alunogen** (with **gypsum**).

INVERNESS, NW 1½ mi., on shore of Tomales Bay, crystals in schist layers—**wollastonite** (with **tremolite**).

MT. TAMALPAIS, area exposures, as tabular crystals—**pyrrhotite.**

PETALUMA, SW 5 mi., on E flanks of Massa Hill in Sec. 19, T. 5 N, R. 7 W, in massive **serpentine** as veins and lenses—**nephrite jade, satelite**(fibrous serpentine), **serpentine.**

REED STATION: (1) area **lawsonite** schists, as crystals to ½ in.—**albite;** (2) E ½ mi., in schists—**actinolite** (with **lawsonite**).

SAN FRANCISCO BAY. Around the north shores are numerous outcrops of the Ingleside chert beds (530 ft. thick) and the Sausalito chert beds (900 ft. thick) which yield a high-silica **chert** in bright colors, locally called **kinradite.**

SAUSALITO, on SE corner of Marine Peninsula—**kinradite.**

MARIPOSA CO.

AREA: (1) regional Mother Lode gold mines—**ankerite, arsenopyrite;** (2) Copper Queen Mine in Sec. 19, T. 5 S, R. 19 E—massive **copper, malachite;** (3) Fitch Mine, in Sec. 9, 10, T. 4 S, R. 15 E—**barite, tetrahedrite, sphalerite** (triboluminescent); this **sphalerite** is a mixture of fine-grained **sphalerite, barite, chalcopyrite,** and **kaolinite;** it glows when rubbed; (4) Green Mt. copper group (of mines)—massive **chalcopyrite** (with **pyrite**).

BEAR VALLEY, the Josephine Mine—**cobaltiferous arsenopyrite (danaite),** with **erythrite** and **mariposite.**

COULTERVILLE: (1) Just W, as a belt of coarse white carbonate 300 to 500 ft. wide—**ankerite;** (2) SE, near Pleasant Valley Sta., the Purcell-Griffin Mine—**chromite.**

EL PORTAL: (1) S 2½ mi., the P and L Mine, as fibrous masses on quartzite—**alunogen** (with **graphite**); (2) W 2 mi., as a large deposit—**barite.**

INCLINE, N 1 mi. from Trumbull Peak, in quartzite veins—**celsian** (with **sanbornite** and **gillespite**).

MARIPOSA: (1) SE 6 mi., the Silver Bar Mine—**argentite, pyrargyrite;** (2) S 12 mi., at Moore's Flats in metamorphic rocks and from the Hornitos slates—**chiastolite;** (3) Sec. 23, T. 3 S, R. 17 E, the Surprise Claim—**rhodochrosite, rhodonite, spessartite.**

TRES CERRITOS, SW of Indian Gulch, in quartzite—**alunite.**

MENDOCINO CO.

AREA: (1) Big and Little Red mts., in T. 24 N, R. 16 W, many area mines —**chromite;** (2) Eel R. gravels—**jadeite, nephrite;** (3) Leach Lake Mt.: (a) area sheared serpentines—pale pink **xonotlite, pectolite, nephrite, calcite;** (b) both sides below Leach Lake—**jadeite.**

CLOVERDALE, S, at Ash Cr. and 1 mi. NE of hwy., on or near the Sonoma Co. line—**brewsterite, edingtonite.**

COVELO: (·1) Area rd. cuts along the new Covelo Rd.—**bornite, lawsonite, epidote** (or **clinozoisite,** blades to 24 in., with **lawsonite** and **rutile**); (2) W 6 mi., in boulders of Williams Cr.—**nephrite jade;** (3) in Williams Cr. gravels along rte. to MINA—**jade.**

HEARST, 8 mi. distant at Impassable Rock, Mt. Sanhedrin—**rhodochrosite, inesite** (veins), **bementite, neotocite.**

LONGVALE, E 3 mi., at Syke Rock on the new Covelo rd., as large radiating crystals—**zoisite.**

MINA, on N Fork of the Eel R., as stream-bed boulders—**nephrite jade** (with **crocidolite** and **jadeite**).

NAVARRO, area placers along the Navarro R., in Anderson Valley—**cinnabar, gold, iridium, platinum, zircon.**

PIETA CREEK, NW 3 mi., in rd. cut on the Cloverdale hwy., as large prisms —**actinolite.**

POTTER CREEK, area, large masses, good—**actinolite.**

REDWOOD, NE 6 mi., the Thomas Mine, granular, pale brown—**bementite** (with **neotocite**).

WILLITS, N 12 mi., area—**chromite** (coated with **uvarovite garnet**).

MODOC CO.

FORT BIDWELL: (1) pass between here and Pine Cr., area—**agate, chalcedony, jasper, quartzite;** (2) E flank of Warner Mts., between CEDARVILLE and FORT BIDWELL, area—**agate, jasper.**

GLASS MOUNTAIN (or Buttes, on Siskiyou Co. line)—**obsidian** (banded, black, blue, gold, green, rainbow, red, silver).

GOOSE LAKE, area—**agate, chalcedony, jasper.**

SUGARLOAF MT. (5 mi. E of Davis Cr. Ranger Sta.), area—**obsidian** (all colors).

MONO CO.

AREA: (1) Blind Spring Hill district, the Diana, Comet, Comanche, etc., mines, as principal **copper** mineral and source of most **silver**—massive **tetrahedrite, galena, cerussite;** (2) Epidote Peak, at head of E Fork of Green Cr., massive—**epidote;** (3) Green Lake, W 1 mi., in metamorphic rocks— **andalusite, lazulite,** etc.; (4) Mono Craters, E of U.S. 395, area—**obsidian** (banded, various colors); (5) Mt. Baldwin, SE base, in vugs and fissures in metamorphic rock 200 yds. NW of the S shore of a large lake, as plum-colored crystals to 1 in.—**axinite.**

BENTON DISTRICT, area mines—**argentite, argentiferous galena, gold, silver** (native).

BODIE: (1) S, in lava beds S of the Bodie rd. just N of Mono Lake— **sanidine;** (2) Standard Mine (on SE town slopes), well-defined crystals to 4 in.—**albite** (with **quartz**). (The crystals are often shells studded internally with fine quartz prisms.)

BRIDGEPORT, W 8 mi., in lava cavities as long, slender crystals—**hornblende** (with **tridymite**).

CEDARVILLE, area basalt veins in the Warner Range, optical-quality crystals—**calcite (Iceland spar).**

COLEVILLE, S 7 mi., in quartz veins—some **bismuthinite,** with **brannerite.**

MAMMOTH LAKE, area, as a 4-ft. outcrop—**barite.**

MOCALNO, E 7 mi., on W slope of the White Mts. at the Champion Sillimanite Inc. Mine (large commercial **andalusite** deposit)—**andalusite, corundum, diaspore, alunite** (massive pink and brown), **augelite, lazulite, apatite, pyrophyllite, barite** (fine crystals).

PATTERSON (District), in the Sweetwater Range, area mines—**argentite, cerargyrite** (in **quartz**), **gold, silver.**

TIOGA PASS, the Tioga Mine—**cobaltite, gold.**

WHITE MOUNTAIN (W of DYER, Nev.): (1) W side, area mines— **andalusite, augelite, dumortierite, lapis lazuli, lazulite, quartz, sillimanite;** (2) W slope, between Coldwater and Piute canyons, area mines—**cerussite.**

MONTEREY CO.

BIG SUR, area W side Santa Lucia Range, stream gravels between Point Sur and Salmon Cr. Ranger Sta.—**jade, nephrite, serpentine.**

BRADLEY, NE 18 mi., in Stone Canyon, area—**brecciated jasper.**

CAMBRIA PINES, area ocean beach gravels of Salmon and San Simeon creeks—**jade.**

GORDA, N, on coast: (1) Cape San Martin: (a) area low-tide gravels—**nephrite, serpentine;** (b) Jade Cove (1,250 ft. SE of Plaskett Point and just S of the mouth of Willow Cr. about 1,200 ft. NE of the cape, reached from Rte. 1), gem quality—**nephrite, serpentine;** (2) Plaskett Point, N 8 mi., mouth of Lime Kiln Cr., area beaches—**rhodonite** boulders, **axinite crystals** (in metamorphosed **serpentine** with **epidote** and **quartz**).

JAMESBURG, SE, in SE¼ Sec. 31, T. 18 S, R. 5 E—**cinnabar** in **calcite.**

KING CITY, W in mts., mine—**kämmererite** (with **uvarovite garnet** and **chromite**).

LOS BURROS (District), in quartz veins—**arsenopyrite, gold.**

PARKFIELD, area serpentine belts—**chromite.**

SALINAS, SE 8 mi., the old Alisal **silver** mine—**arsenic.**

NAPA CO.

CALISTOGA, 2 mi. N: (1) Mount St. Helena Mine—**argentite, cerargyrite;** (2) Palisades Mine—**arsenopyrite, argentite, deweylite** (gangue mineral with **gold** and **silver** ores).

KNOXVILLE: (1) 3½ mi. out, the Lone Pine Chromite Mine—**chromite,** common green **opal;** (2) Redington Mine—**aragonite** on **cinnabar, botryogen** (as minute aggregates of small red crystals) with **copiapite, epsomite** (abundant long white fibers in old tunnels), **quartz pseudomorphs** after **barite.**

MIDDLETOWN: (1) E on Rte. 29: (a) T. 10, 11, 12 N, R. 6, 7 W, in decomposed serpentines, and (b) Sec. 36, T. 19 N, R. 10 W, as prospects—**chromite;** (2) NE 2 mi. along hwy. to LOWER LAKE, as fine cleavage fragments—**anorthite;** (3) NW 4 mi., the Copper Prince Mine—**azurite, malachite;** (4) Great Western and Mirabel mercury mines, off Rte. 29—**actinolite, chert, cinnabar, curtisite, dolomite, jamesonite, metacinnabar, millerite, opalite, stibnite, tiemannite;** (5) E 1½ mi. on rd. to Lower Lake, exposures —**pectolite, serpentine;** (6) S 13 mi., high-grade deposit—**chalcopyrite.**

MONTICELLO, W 6 mi., area prospects—**native copper.**

NEVADA CO.

AREA: (1) Buckeye Hill, mines—**chalcocite, native copper, graphite;** (2) Indian Springs, area serpentines, as fine octahedrons—**chromite;** (3) Meadow Lake district, masses—**chalcopyrite** (with **arsenopyrite, galena,** etc.).

FRENCH CORRAL, area stream gravels—**diamond.**

GRASS VALLEY: (1) S 2½ mi., the Allison Ranch Mine—**argentite** (with **pyrargyrite** and **stephanite**); (2) SW 4 mi., at Deadman Flat, the Alcalde Mine—**arsenic** and **gold** in **calcite;** (3) E 5 mi., the Banner Mine—**argentite;** (4) Empire Mine—**altaite.**

NEVADA CITY: (1) area: (a) Blue Tent mining camp, and (b) Sailor Flat—**agate, chalcedony, jasper, opalite, opalized** and **petrified wood;** (2) Providence Mine—**alunogen** (colored blue with **copper**), **altaite** (bunches in the Ural vein intergrown with **native gold** and associated with **pyrite, galena, quartz**); (3) Washington, Red Ledge chrome mines—abundant **rhodochrome, calcite (dogtooth spar), kämmererite.**

ORANGE CO.

AREA: (1) Blue Light Mine (Sec. 11, 14, T. 5 S, R. 7 W), abundant—**sphalerite;** (2) Red Hill, as gangue mineral of a **cinnabar** deposit—**barite** (crystalline); (3) Trabuco Canyon: (a) Santa Ana Tin Mining Co. Tunnel No. 1, yellow crystals, often twinned—**arcanite;** (b) Trabuco Tin Mine—**cassiterite.**

ELSINORE (Riverside Co.) Quadrangle, SW part, N bank of San Juan Cr. about 1½ mi. E of the W quadrangle boundary in vein several ft. wide—**sphalerite** (with **chalcopyrite** and **pyrrhotite**).

PLACER CO.

AREA, gravels of Shady Run—**garnet, rock crystal** (**chlorite** inclusions), **serpentine.**

AUBURN, 12 mi. out, on Wolf Cr. rd., area—**pyrolusite, rhodonite.**

CLIPPER GAP, W 5 mi., at Hotaling, deposit—**magnetite.**

IOWA HILL, E ¼ mi., deposit of white "slip fiber"—**asbestos.**

LINCOLN: (1) E 3 mi., the Kilaga Mine—**alunogen;** (2) N 6 mi., the Valley View Mine (Whiskey Hill)—**chalcanthite, coquimbite, native silver.**

NEWCASTLE, SE 7 mi., in nodular masses—**chromite** (coated with **penninite, kämmererite,** and good crystals of **uvarovite garnet**).

PENRYN, E 1 mi., the Alabama Mine—**argentite** (in **gold quartz,** with **galena** and **tellurides**).

TOWLE, SE 9 mi., in Green Valley, deposits—**chromite,** with **uvarovite garnet** and **clinochlore (kotschubeite).**

PLUMAS CO.

AREA: (1) Gopher Hill, Nelson Point, Sawpit Flat, Upper Spanish Cr., alluvial gravels—**diamond, gold;** (2) Edmonton, Diadem, and Penrose lode mines—**manganite, psilomelane, rhodonite;** (3) Spanish Peak, in **plumasite** —**hornblende** (var. **edenite**). The Walker, Engles, and Superior mines of this co., carrying **bornite-chalcopyrite** ores, have been the leading **copper** producers in California since 1915.

GENESSEE, area gravels and deposits of the Genessee Valley—**rhodonite.**

MEADOW VALLEY, NW, at Rich Bar on Indian Cr.—**tremolite.**

MUMFORDS HILL, area mines—**copper minerals.**

SPRING GARDEN, NE 9 mi., the Walker Mine—**cubanite** (with **chalcopyrite** and **pyrrhotite**).

SUSANVILLE' (Lassen Co.), S 20 mi., in Indian Valley at the Pocahontas Mine—**native copper, cuprite, malachite, native silver, rhodonite.**

TAYLORSVILLE, nearby Peters Mine—**rhodonite.**

THOMPSON PEAK (SW of JANESVILLE), area deposit—white **apatite, black tourmaline (schorl).**

RIVERSIDE CO.

AREA: (1) Box Spring Mt., area mines, crystals to 1½ in.—**fergusonite;** (2) Coahuila Mt., N side, the Fano Mine—**amblygonite, kunzite, lepidolite, tourmaline;** (3) pegmatite outcrops on Lookout Mt.; Red, Little, Coahuila, Thomas mts.; Rouse Hill—**amazonite** (on Thomas Mt.), **idocrase, rose quartz, tourmaline.**

ALBERHILL, area clay pits—**boehmite, gibbsite.**

BLYTHE: (1) Floyd Brown Mine—**fluorite;** (2) Santa Maria Mts., area mines and prospects—**amarantite, magnesian copiapite** (as yellowish brown crystalline masses); (3) SW 20 mi., the McCoy Mt. mining district—**copper minerals.**

CAHUILLA, area pegmatite mines on Cahuilla Mt., especially the Williamson Mine—**aquamarine, beryl, morganite.**

CRESTMORE: (1) The Jensen Quarry—**idocrase, rose quartz, tourmaline,** abundant **brucite** (pseudomorphous after **periclase**). (2) The more than 120 minerals from the famous CRESTMORE quarries grouped about CHINO and Sky Blue Hills, i.e., the Chino, Wet Weather, Lone Star, and Commercial quarries, occur in extensive contact zones in limestone, formed by intrusive plutonic and dike rocks. New, hitherto unidentified minerals are constantly being found. All the great variety of gemstones and minerals are prime collector's items.

DESERT CENTER: (1) S, in Chuckwalla Mts., the Pacific Mining District, at the Red Cloud Mine, abundant—**cuprite;** (2) N, the Eagle Mt. iron deposits—**allanite** (as tiny crystals), **hematite,** etc.

ELSINORE: (1) see Quadrangle, Orange Co.; (2) NE 2 mi., the Chief of the Hills Mine—**cassiterite.**

MIDLAND: (1) area pegmatite outcrops—**spinel;** (2) Midland Mine, in limestone—**tremolite** (small crystals, with **phlogopite**).

NUEVO: (1) wall of Southern Pacific Quarry, as large bladelike plates— **biotite mica;** (2) in area pegmatite, as radial clusters and crystals—**cyrtolite** (with **monazite, xenotime, yttrocrasite**).

PACKARDS WELL, S 2 mi., the Palen Mts., area **copper** mines—massive **epidote.**

RIPLEY, W, in the Mule Mts., area—**agate** (common, fire), **chalcedony** (nodules, roses with **goethite** coating—the so-called **fire agate**).

RIVERSIDE: (1) E 2 mi., Box Springs Mt., area pegmatites—**aquamarine;** (2) S 2 mi., in new city quarry—brown **hematite, allanite** (with **serendibite** and associated minerals); (3) W 4 mi. and just W of the Jensen Quarry, good dark green crystals to 1 in. long—**hornblende;** (4) SW 13 mi., in granodiorite outcrop near the Cajalco Tin Mine—**dumortierite; cassiterite** at the mine; (5) North Hill, in old city quarry, large purple crystals—

axinite; (6) SOUTH RIVERSIDE, SE 5 mi., the Crowell Mine, in bunches—
stibnite.
TEMESCAL (District), Sec. 2, 3, 10, 11, T. 4 S, R. 6 W, area tin deposits—
cassiterite.

SAN BENITO CO.

DALE, E, at Iron Mt. and Iron Age Mine, massive veins—**hematite, magnetite.**
HERNANDEZ: (1) area serpentine belts—**chromite;** (2) in Clear Cr. gravels
along rd. to NEW IDRIA, and (3) area around Santa Rita Peak—**albite, analcite, biotite mica, garnet, jadeite, prehnite, serpentine, sphene, thomsonite.**
HOLLISTER: (1) area stream placers—boulders of **chromite** coated with
zaratite; (2) NE, on Antimony Peak, several claims—**stibnite.**
IDRIA, SW, toward Fresno Co. line, in gravels of headwaters of San Benito
R. (25 mi. N of COALINGA, Fresno Co.)—**actinolite, aragonite, benitoite**
(mine), **joaquinite, natrolite, neptunite.**
NEW IDRIA: (1) area chrome deposit—**artinite** (acicular crystals), red
kämmererite on **chromite** (with **uvarovite garnet**); (2) a nearby quicksilver
mine—**cinnabar, diadochite.** (The NEW ALMADEN mines of Santa Clara Co.
and the NEW IDRIA mines of San Benito Co. are the two most famous cinnabar properties in California.)

SAN BERNARDINO CO.

AREA: (1) Amargosa mines (T. 18 N, R. 7 E, in the Amargosa Sink), as
masses—**arsenolite;** (2) Cottonwood Siding (Santa Fe RR), W 2 mi., the
Gove Mine—**turquoise;** (3) Lead Mt. (T. 10 N, R. 1 W), SW 1 mi., in
barite deposit as greenish yellow crusts on limestone—**alunite, bayldonite;**
(4) Sidewinder Mine, SW 2 mi., area—**brochantite** (small crystals, crusts),
chrysocolla; (5) Wingate Canyon, area—**sagenite agate.**
ADELANTO: (1) N 5 mi. and 1 mi. W of U.S. 95, area **silver** mines of the
Silver Mt. district, masses—**sphalerite** with **silver;** (2) N 30 mi., the Kramer
Hills along U.S. 95, area—**agate, chalcedony, jasper.**
AMBOY: (1) W, at Amboy Crater, area—**jasper, obsidian;** (2) Bristol
Dry Lake, SW margin, extensive deposit, as concretions—**celestite;** (3) Siberia Crater, in volcanic ash—**olivine** (granular, as cores of many volcanic
bombs), **hornblende** (basaltic, crystals).
ATOLIA, area mines, in **scheelite** veins and as part of the gangue rock—
ankerite.
BAKER: (1) W, in Soda Mts., area mines—**brochantite, caledonite, linarite,**
dioptase; (2) W 7 mi., the Blue Bell Mine, abundant—**chrysocolla, malachite;** (3) N 10 mi., area—**agate, jasper.**
BARSTOW: (1) E on U.S. 66 to Milepost 113, area surrounding Lavic RR
siding, abundant, gemmy—**jasper** (called "**Lavic**" jasper); (2) Milepost
115: (a) rd. turnoff to abundant field—gem **jasper;** (b) all surrounding milepost areas—**jasper** (the farther one walks away from the roads, the richer

and more abundant the specimens); (3) NE 6 mi., area fossil beds—**fossil bones** containing tiny crystals of **barite;** (4) NE, on N side of Lead Mt., in old borax mines, cavities lined with slender crystals—**colemanite** on **calcite** crystal crusts;

(5) N 10 mi., in the Mud (Strontium) Hills, Sec. 20, 30, T. 11 N, R. 1, 2 W, large deposits as brown and gray granular masses in limestone—**strontianite;** (6) N 11 mi., in Black Mts., area—**fossils;** (7) N 30 mi., Goldstone Camp, area—**turquoise;** (8) N 40 mi., Eagle Crags: (a) area—**blue agate nodules, bentonite, calcite, chalcedony, chalcedonic quartz, chert, jaspagate, jasper, jasp-opal, opal, opalite, orpiment, siderite, wonderstone;** (b) Leadpipe Springs, NE 1½ mi., on N side of steep hill—**blue agate nodules, chalcedony, jaspers, opal nodules, precious opal, septarian nodules, thundereggs;** (c) 15 mi. NW of Leadpipe Spgs., area—**blue agate nodules, bentonite,** clear **chalcedony** (speckled with **cinnabar**), **milk opal, opalite, quartz crystal geodes;** (9) NW 20 mi., head of Blacks Canyon near Opal Mt., area— **opal;** (10) Solo Mining District, area prospects—**turquoise.**

CALICO (DISTRICT): (1) area borate mines—**colemanite, howlite, ulexite;** (2) area silver mines—**azurite, argentite, cerargyrite, chrysocolla, embolite, strontianite, wulfenite;** (3) Calico Hills: (a) area mines—**copiapite** (with **krausite, coquimbite,** and **alunite**); (b) borate, in **colemanite** ores—**geodes** (lined with **strontianite** and light blue to colorless **celestite** crystals to 1½ in. long); (c) in the "sulfur hole" below the old borax mines, abundant— **alunite,** with **krausite,** etc.; (4) W ½ mi., in the Total Wreck Mine and Langtry Lode, massive—**cerussite** (with **chrysocolla**); (5) Mule Canyon, W side—**petrified palm;** (6) Wall Canyon, area—**barite, cerargyrite, chert, embolite, jasper, orpiment;**

CIMA: (1) E 3 mi., on NW slope of the New York Mts., the Death Valley Mine—**emoblite;** (2) N 14 mi., the Carbonate King Mine—**hydrozincite** (with **cerussite** and **smithsonite**); (3) CIMA-IVANPAH, many regional mines—**argentite,** massive **tetrahedrite.**

COLTON, area limestone quarries—**chondrodite.**

DAGGETT, E 35 mi., at Pisgah Crater (S of U.S. 66), area—**agate, chalcedony** (nodules, roses), **"Lavic" jasper, obsidian.**

DALE, iron ore deposit—**epidote, garnet, hematite, magnetite.**

DANBY, NE 9 mi., area—**cinnabar.**

DEATH VALLEY, area niter beds—**darapskite.**

DEATH VALLEY JCT., W, to W side of Pyramid Peak (E of Rte. 190 and ¼ mi. E of Death Valley boundary)—**onyx.**

EARP, N 5 mi., on S slope of the Whipple Mts., the Blue Cloud Mine— **specular hematite, chrysocolla** (seams, coatings).

GOFFS: (1) Camp Signal, area—**calciovolborthite;** (2) SE 2 mi., in vugs of an outcrop as small crystals—**atacamite;** (3) N 12 mi. and W of rd. to Lanfair, area—**agate, chalcedony, jasper, petrified palm.**

HALLORAN SPRINGS (NE of BAKER on Int. 15), 5½ mi. away at Manvel district in the Turquoise Mts., various small mines, especially the Himalay claims at the head of Riggs Wash 12 mi. ENE of Silver Lake—**turquoise.**

HINKLEY, N 18 mi., off U.S. 91/466 on secondary rd. to N: (1) area— **common opal;** (2) both sides of rd. for 6-mi. stretch—**agate, chalcedony, geodes, jasper.**

HODGE, SE 7 mi.: (1) Globerson Iron Mine—**iron minerals;** (2) 200 yds. W of the mine, in vein—**lazulite** (crystalline and massive), **quartz, muscovite mica, specularite, talc, tremolite.**

IVANPAH, Barnwell area in the New York Mts.—**turquoise.**

JOHANNESBURG, SE 30 mi. and 15 mi. NE of Leadpipe Springs near S end of Death Valley, area mines—**cinnabar** (as inclusions in blue-gray **chalcedony** forming the gemstone called **myrickite**).

LUDLOW: (1) NW 2 mi., the Gallinger-Root mines—**arseniosiderite;** (2) NW 4 mi., in Sec. 29, 30, T. 8 N, R. 7 E, extensive beds—**celestite;** (3) just E, old mine dumps—**agate, chalcedony, chrysocolla, fluorite, jasp-agate, jasper, malachite, psilomelane** (calcite, manganese), **smithsonite.**

MIDWAY (45 mi. E of BARSTOW): (1) all area mesas, gullies, etc.—gem **"Lavic" jasper;** (2) E 3 mi., turn off to Afton Sta., dirt rd. to S to Mojave R. bed, cross, and enter Afton Canyon in the Cady Mts., area—**agate, jasper, chalcedony.** (On the right of the rd. to Afton Canyon along U.S. 91, all areas show abundant **agate** and **jasper** float.)

MORONGO (District), the United Tungsten Copper Mine, as green needles to ¾ in.—**bismutite.**

NEEDLES: (1) W, in S end of the Dead Mts., the Black Mt. Mine—**copper minerals;** (2) N end of the Chemehuevis Mts., Bumper group of claims—**azurite, malachite;** (3) NW 17 mi., area—**epidote, specular hematite;** (4) SW 36 mi. on U.S. 95, to W-trending dirt rd. into Turtle Mts., to Carson Wells and Lost Arch: (a) area mines—**gold, silver minerals;** (b) area dry washes, hillsides, etc.—**agate** (common, moss, sagenitic), **chalcedony** (nodules, roses), **jasper, jasp-agate,** etc. (The barren desert region extending W to the Old Woman Mts. is gemologically unexplored territory and should prove very productive; travel by four-wheel drive only.)

NIPTON (Rte. 68), W to Int. 15 to Mountain Pass 39 mi. NE of BAKER: (1) N 1 mi., at East Clark Mt., the Mountain Pass Antimony Mine—**stibnite;** (2) E 2½ mi., the Desert Antimony Mine—**stibnite;** (3) area **bastnaesite** occurrence, in dolomitic breccias along an extensive zone—**allanite.**

ORO GRANDE, W 5 mi., in the Silver Mt. District: (1) area mines, prominent—**cerussite;** (2) Amazon Mine—**copper oxides;** (3) Black Diamond Mine—**gold, silver, copper minerals;** (4) N 14 mi. and 2½ mi. from the Mohave R., the Scorpion Mine, coarse-fibered—**tremolite.**

RANDSBURG (District), area mines in and out of town—**miargyrite** (most abundant **silver** mineral).

RED MOUNTAIN, the California Rand Mine, as clear, yellow, colorless, or white coatings on vugs in the ore—**cervantite** (with **pyrostilpnite**), **allophane.**

SAN BERNARDINO, N on Int. 15, Cajon Pass area: (1) Blue Cut, area—**actinolite, epidote, slickensides** (not a gemstone or mineral, but a fault-polished rock with geologic interest); (2) Lone Pine Canyon, area—**actinolite;** (3) summit, in alluvial fan dropping to the N—**rhodonite** float.

SARATOGA SPRINGS, 6 mi. away in the Black Mts., the Ibex Mine—**anglesite** (massive, crystalline), **argentiferous galena, cerussite, linarite.**

SEARLES LAKE, area, as colorless tabular crystals—**aphthitalite** (with octahedral **halite** and massive **borax**).

SHOSHONE: (1) W, to S entrance to Death Valley, then SE, in Sperry Wash, area—**petrified wood** (cycad, palm); (2) SW about 30 mi., at Owl's Head

Springs in the Owl's Head Mts., area of Owl's Head Canyon—**sagenite agate.**

TWENTYNINE PALMS, SW 1½ mi., in monzonitic porphyry, as crystals to 7 in. long, abundant, usually as Carlsbad twins—**orthoclase.**

UPLAND, N 12 mi. to Cascade Canyon and 5 mi. by trail up San Antonio Canyon—**diopside, mica, lapis lazuli, quartz crystals.**

VICTORVILLE: (1) E 11 mi., on E side of hill which is W of a limestone quarry—green **diopside, uvarovite garnet, vesuvianite** (crystals, massive); (2) E 17 mi., the Hillis marble quarry—**actinolite, marble;** (3) SE 30 mi., the Wild Rose group of claims—**gold**-bearing **tremolite.**

VIDAL JCT., N, in the Whipple Mts.: (1) Black Metal Mine—**chrysocolla, horn silver;** (2) Braintruster Mine—**azurite, chalcopyrite, malachite.**

YUCCA VALLEY: (1) on rd. to Old Woman Springs, the Pomona Tile Quarry—**allanite, euxenite, ilmenite, monazite;** (2) NW 15 mi. and 1 mi. above Pipes Canyon public camp, area—**onyx.**

SAN DIEGO CO.

ALPINE (on Int. 8 about 35 mi. E of SAN DIEGO), area—**dumortierite, orbicular gabbro.**

BORREGO SPRINGS, N in Anza Borrego Desert State Park, along the Riverside Co. line, area—fine **rhodonite.**

DEHESA, area pegmatite outcrops—**apatite, dumortierite** (violet red), **sillimanite.**

ENCINITAS, E 8 mi., in quartz veins of the Willhite group of claims—abundant **arsenopyrite, chalcopyrite** (masses).

ESCONDIDO, area in Moosa Canyon—**axinite.**

JACUMBA: (1) NNE 8 mi., along RR, Dos Cabezas area—**hessonite garnet;** (2) NW 8½ mi., the Crystal Mine—**beryl.**

JULIAN: (1) area mines—**albandite, arsenopyrite, pyrrhotite, gold;** (2) S 3 mi., a mine, in ores—**copper minerals, cerargyrite;** (3) S 4 mi., the Friday Mine, in **nickel** ores—massive **pyrrhotite,** some **chalcopyrite** (with **pentlandite** and **violarite**), **erythrite** (with **limonite** and **morenosite**).

LAKESIDE, NE 12 mi., the Barona copper claims—**chalcopyrite, copper minerals.**

MESA GRANDE (District): (1) W of Lake Henshaw, near Hwy. 79, many area mine dumps—**aquamarine,** massive **beryl, lepidolite, morganite, quartz crystals, smoky quartz, tourmaline;** (2) Himalaya Mine—**amblygonite, pegmatite gemstones.**

PALA (District): (1) NW 2 mi., on hill about ½ mi. W of the rd., as black masses in quartz veins—**allanite;** (2) N 3 mi., pegmatite on the N. S. Weaver Ranch, as large rough crystals—**allanite;** (3) N and E, in many pegmatite mines on Hiriart Hill, Pala Chief Mt., and Tourmaline Queen Mt., above the San Luis Rey R.—**apatite, aquamarine, beryl, cleavelandite, kunzite, lepidolite, morganite, quartz crystals** (clear, smoky), **rose quartz, spodumene, tourmaline;** (4) Caterina (and other surrounding mines)—massive **amblygonite, rubellite, lepidolite, tourmaline,** etc.; (5) Steward Mine—**bismuth** (long irregular crystals sometimes capping **tourmaline**).

The PALA-RINCON region is in the heart of an extensive pegmatite gem area, extending from the San Jacinto Mts. to the Mexican border. The pegmatites are more or less irregular dikes intruded into igneous rocks of the granodiorite type, or into schists, and rich in **lithium.** The gem-producing mines are as follows: near the summit of the San Jacinto Range (Riverside Co.), Coahuila Mt., Aguanga Mt., PALA, MESA GRANDE, RAMONA, minor occurrences east of JULIAN, and in the Chihuahua Valley, while gem-quality **garnet** occurs in the JACUMBA area. The major gem minerals include: **beryl, kunzite** (similar to transparent lilac **spodumene**), **topaz, tourmaline** (abundant in various colors), **quartz crystals, lepidolite, schorl** (black **tourmaline**), **smoky quartz crystals** (some with inclusions), **morganite, spodumene, aquamarine, cleavelandite,** and various **lithia minerals** (some quite rare).

PALOMAR: (1) E rim of Aguanga Mt., the Ware Mine—**beryl, lepidolite, quartz crystals, schorl, smoky quartz crystals, spodumene, topaz, tourmaline;** (2) Mountain Lily and Pearson mines—**beryl, aquamarine, amblygonite, cassiterite, lepidolite, schorl, smoky quartz crystals, topaz, tourmaline,** etc.

RAMONA (District): (1) ENE 3½ mi., pegmatite outcrops in Hatfield Cr. Valley: (a) W side—**aquamarine, morganite, spessartite garnet, topaz, tourmaline;** (b) many area mines overlooking Hatfield Cr.—**beryl, feldspar, smoky quartz crystals, topaz, tourmaline;** (2) ENE 3¾ mi., the J. W. Ware Emeralite No. 2 Mine—**"emeralite"** (greenish blue **tourmaline**), **tourmaline** (variously colored); (3) SE 7½ mi., the McFall Mine—**epidote, grossularite garnet,** etc.; (4) Little Three Mine—**cleavelandite, schorl, smoky quartz crystals, spessartite garnet:** (a) NE, the Spaulding Mine, and (b) in flats below the Little Three—**diamond, gold.**

RINCON (District): (1) SSE 1½ mi., the Mack Mine—**aquamarine, beryl, morganite, tourmaline;** (2) Victor Mine—**cookeite** (colorless and deep pink coating on **quartz**), **albite, amblygonite** (white cleavable fragments), **bismuth** (as small bright cleavages in **lepidolite**), **kunzite,** pseudomorphs after **kunzite, orthoclase;** (3) E of the Rincon Indian Reservation, in upper part of Pauma Valley, many area mines but especially the Clark (and Victor) mines on SW spur of mts.—**aquamarine, beryl, morganite, tourmaline.**

WARNER SPRINGS: (1) E 3 mi., mine—**asbestos** (fibers to 6 in. long); (2) NE 4 mi., to Hot Springs Mt. on N side of the Chihuahua Valley, many area mines—gem **tourmaline,** etc.

SAN FRANCISCO CO.

CLIFF HOUSE (at Land's End Promontory), NE 1 mi., outcrop—**spherulitic chert.**

COYOTE POINT (S San Francisco Bay and E of the San Mateo Junior College and just N of the yacht harbor)—**chert** (brecciated, orbicular), **jasper.**

FORT POINT, area: (1) altered diabase dike in **serpentine,** as glassy crystals and white veins—**datolite;** (2) basalt fissures, as spherical or massive platy or plumose aggregates replacing the wall rock—**gyrolite;** (3) **serpentine** seams— **apophyllite** (minute colorless crystals), **gyrolite, aragonite, barite, calcite.**

SAN FRANCISCO: (1) Army Street, excavations of Western Pacific RR, in **serpentine** veins—**xonotlite** (with **brucite**); (2) Duboce Street, near Market Street, at site of the U.S. Mint in a **serpentine** ledge, as veins—**chalcedony, curtisite.**

SAN JOAQUIN CO.

CORRAL HOLLOW (Sec. 2, 11, T. 4 S, R. 4 E), the old Ladd Mine—
bementite, hausmannite.

SAN LUIS OBISPO CO.

AREA, Sec. 15, 21, T. 27 S, R. 9 E, the Oceanic Mine—**cinnabar** (as replacements of **fossil shells**).

ARROYO GRANDE, SE 6 mi., on the Fugler Ranch, in a vein 1–2 ft. thick—
barite.

NIPOMO: (1) area fields E of U.S. 101—**agate** (moss, sagenite), **fossil
bone, jasper, petrified wood, stibnite;** (2) W of U.S. 101 toward ocean, on
area farms—**peach agate.** (All the famed sagenite agates lie in the fields,
turned up during plowing, as float from unknown sources back in adjoining
hills.)

PASO ROBLES, area creek gravels—**jadeite.**

POZO, S 5 mi., near Salt Cr. in the Santa Lucia Range 9.7 mi. from Rout-
zahn county park, variously colored—**onyx.**

SAN LUIS OBISPO: (1) along Hwy. 1 all the way to MONTEREY, numerous
accesses to Pacific Ocean beaches, in gravels—**California jade;** (2) N, in the
Coast Range E of and between CAMBRIA and SAN SIMEON, many area prospects, abundant—**cinnabar.**

SAN MIGUEL, E of U.S. 101 in Stone Canyon (private property, so inquire)
—gem **jasper** (brecciated, among finest in America).

SAN SIMEON, area beach sediments above high-tide mark S of turnoff to
the Hearst Castle—**moonstone (feldspar)** to 100-lb. boulders.

SANTA MARGARITA, SW, near summit of Santa Lucia Range, as fine wires
in serpentine—**native copper.**

SANTA MARIA, E, in the Cuyama Valley, N side area dikes of **augite-
teschinite—analcite** (water-clear grains to 6 mm.).

SIMMLER, SE, in the Carizo Plain near dry Soda Lake, large crystals in
dried mud—**bloedite.**

SAN MATEO CO.

PALO ALTO, W 5 mi., in seams and cavities in the siliceous material so
common in the **serpentine** of the cinnabar districts, as minute yellow crystals
—**eglestonite** (with **cinnabar, calomel, dolomite, magnesite, opal, quartz**).

PESCADOR BEACH (45 mi. S of SAN FRANCISCO), area outcrops—**orbicular chert.**

REDWOOD CITY, W 2 mi., in joints and fissures in a siliceous rock replacing **serpentine—montroydite** (long prismatic and bent crystals), with
eglestonite, calomel, native mercury, and **cinnabar.**

SAN MATEO, W, near Crystal Springs Lake on Pacific slope of the redwoods, scattered masses—**chromite.**

SANTA BARBARA CO.

POINT SAL, SW, in hills, a minor mining claim—**chromite.**

SANTA MARIA (straddles San Luis Obispo and Santa Barbara co. line), SE 15 mi., on the Sisquoc, deposit—**barite.**

SANTA YNEZ, N 7 mi., on the J. C. Keyes claim, abundant fibrous crystals which phosphoresce when broken in the dark—**pectolite.**

SANTA CLARA CO.

AREA: (1) regional exposures of **serpentine—chromite;** (2) NE part of co. (NE¼ Sec. 27, T. 6 S, R. 5 E), the Jones Mine—**bementite, rhodochrosite, manganese oxides.**

MADRONE: (1) NE 3 mi., on the Weber Ranch in the Los Animos Hills, and (2) E 4½ mi., on Coyote Cr., deposits—**siderite.**

MILPITAS: (1) SE, Alum Rock Park, in boulders—**albandite** (with **alleghanyite, hausmannite, tephroite,** etc.); (2) NE, at the N end of Calaveras Valley, in **eclogite** and schists—**glaucophane.**

MORGAN HILL, along Llagas Cr. (7 mi. NW of GILROY), a noted gem locality—**poppy (flowering) jasper** known as **Morgan Hill chert.**

NEW ALMADEN (9 mi. SW of SAN JOSE), great mercury mines—**chert, cinnabar, apophyllite, gyrolite.** (Most of these minerals occur as well-developed crystals. The NEW ALMADEN mines were crucial during the Civil War for extraction of Mother Lode **gold** that paid for the war.)

SANTA CRUZ CO.

DAVENPORT, at the Vicente Cr. tunnel—**calcite crystals.**

SANTA CRUZ, W 2 mi., in the Pacific Limestone Products quarry—**frankeite, meneghinite, stannite.**

SHASTA CO.

AREA, the Copper Belt (includes the Bully Hill district, Iron Mt., Afterthought, Balaklala, and other mines), as predominant mineral—**chalcopyrite** (with **barite** as gangue).

COPPER CITY, the Peck Mine, common—**chalcanthite.**

FRENCH GULCH (District), the Greenhorn Mine in Sec. 33, T. 37 N, R. 5 W—**azurite, native copper, copper sulfides.**

GIBSON, W 4 mi., in Sec. 33, T. 37 N, R. 5 W—**ferrimolybdite** (with **ilsemannite** and **molybdenite**).

HEROULT, S 1 mi., on the Pit R—**psilomelane.**

IGO, W 3 mi., the Chicago Mine—**cerussite, galena, pyrite, proustite, pyromorphite, tetrahedrite, quartz.**

LICK SPRINGS, area, as an incrustation—**bechilite** (possibly **ulexite**).

MANZANITA LAKE, area hot springs of Lassen Volcanic National Park, as incrustations—**alunogen, alunite** (as isolated crystals and aggregates).

254 Gems and Minerals of America

REDDING, W 4 mi., the Silver King Mine, as small perfect crystals—**cerargyrite**.

ROUND MOUNTAIN, E 7 mi., in amygdaloidal basalt—**analcime, analcite, chabazite, natrolite, tridymite**.

SHASTA (old ghost town, now a tourist historic site), area mines—**gold**.

SIM'S STATION, E 3 mi., the Stock Asbestos Mine—**anthophyllite asbestos**.

SOUTH FORK (District), the Big Dike Mine in Sec. 17, 18, T. 31 N, R. 6 W—**argentite, native silver, freibergite**, etc.

SIERRA CO.

AREA, Upper Spencer Lake, at the Sierra Iron Mine—**apatite** (crystals to ¾ in.), **chlorite** (crystals, with **magnetite** as replacement of dolomite). Some of the **magnetite** in this large deposit is **lodestone**, i.e., magnetic.

DOWNIEVILLE, E 10 mi., at Four Hills, pure and abundant—**specular hematite**.

FOREST, area talcose slates, as perfect octahedral crystals—**magnetite**.

SISKIYOU CO.

The western half of Siskiyou Co. became the famed "Northern Mines" of gold rush history, its more than 370 gold mines encompassing a highly mineralized gold zone extending in a long belt from north of Yreka (on Int. 5) southwest into adjoining counties. Gold mining has been the county's principal activity (other than contemporary ranching) from 1850 through 1955, with many mines still active seasonally. Raw native **gold**, along with **platinum** and **stream tin**, may still be panned from the regional streams, sometimes in nuggets to fist size. At the same time, in countywide exposures of immense serpentine strata (entire mountains of it in places) are some of the major chromium mines of America, and **chromite** is very common, along with **asbestos** and **iron minerals**. Just as the NEW ALMADEN (Santa Clara Co.) mercury mines enabled the Sierra Mother Lode mines to yield up their gold, so also did the scores of rich **cinnabar** mines along the northwestern border of Siskiyou Co. provide the quicksilver for amalgamating the crushed or placered gold of this extraordinary county.

AREA: (1) E part of co.: (a) Agate Flat, area—**agate, bloodstone, jasper, petrified wood;** (b) Tamarack Flat, W of Garner Mt.—**pumice, obsidian;** (2) Scott Bar Mts., across N end of Scott Valley and due W of YREKA, a heavily mineralized zone extending from Greenhorn summit westward to Scott R., many great gold mines, placers, and hydraulic operations, particularly: (a) N of FORT JONES, around old mining camps of Deadwood, Hooperville, etc., and (b) such tributary creek gulches to Scott R. as French Gulch, Indian Cr., Rattlesnake Cr., etc.—**gold, cinnabar, asbestos, chromite**, and, in the placer tailings, **actinolite, marble, quartz, muscovite mica, jasper,** etc.; (3) Siskiyou Mts., N of the Klamath R. all along the Oregon border and extending N into Oregon to JACKSONVILLE and W to the coast, hundreds of rich mines—**cinnabar, asbestos, chromite, gold,** etc. (All regional access roads are USFS dirt roads; snow blocks many of them until after mid-July.)

(4) W half of co., hundreds of area mines, primarily **gold—chalcopyrite, pyrite, pyrrhotite,** etc.

CALLAHAN: (1) area mines (mainly hidden back in precipitous mts.)— **gold, erythrite** (as coatings on **smaltite**); (2) bed of South Fork of Scott R. from town S toward headwaters—**gold nuggets** (to several ounces); (3) SW, the Martin McKean Mine—**chromite, gold, kämmererite, uvarovite garnet;** (4) SW 3 mi., on Boulder Cr., the Richie Mine—**barite, bornite, galena;** (5) dredger tailings just N of town—**hydrogrossularite (white jade), californite, corylite** (local name for an unusually attractive gemmy material that is mainly clear quartz), green **mariposite** (var. of **muscovite** colored green by **chromium**), **pyrite;** (6) East Fork of Scott R., gravels—**antigorite, gem serpentine, thulite;** (7) Camp Eden: (a) SE, the Blue Jay Mine—**gold, asbestos, scheelite;** (b) Jackson Cr.—**gold, rhodonite;**

(8) E and NE, to Gazelle Mt. summit: (a) area chromium mines—**chromite, serpentine;** (b) area limestone outcrops—**calcite;** (c) Lovers Leap—**galena, copper minerals, calcite;** (d) Grouse Cr., stream placers—**gold, chromite, serpentine;** (9) SE 6 mi. (very steep rd.) to Scott Mt. public camp, area—**chromite, serpentine, asbestos, magnetite.** (During the gold rush years, several thousand Chinese worked in or near CALLAHAN; evidences of their mining lie everywhere.)

DUNSMUIR, S 3 mi., the Brown Mine on Little Castle Cr. (Sec. 2, T. 38 N, R. 4 W), the largest chrome ore body on the Pacific Coast—**chromite, kämmererite** (as coating).

ETNA: (1) S 3 mi. on Sawyers Bar rd., outcrop at sharp turn—**marble** (variegated from pinkish to white, black-streaked, greenish); (2) SW, behind Etna Mt. via jeep rd. and trail, Ruffy Lake area (popular fishing lake) —**rose quartz, snow ("bull") quartz;** (3) S 9 mi. on Rte. 3, Sugar Cr., follow dirt rd. up canyon—**gold, copper minerals;** (4) Scott R. gravels—**actinolite, asbestos, serpentine, marble, muscovite** (in **quartz**), **quartz.**

FORKS OF SALMON: (1) area old mines—**gold, cassiterite;** (2) area stream gravels—**gold, stream tin, platinum;** (3) SE about 10 mi., King Solomon Mine (a famous gold rush mine reached via Matthews Cr. jeep rd.)—**gold, epidote** (crystals in **gold ore**).

FORT JONES: (1) N, area old mines visible on mt. sides—**chromite, serpentine;** (2) W, along Scott R. to its confluence with the Klamath: (a) Indian Cr., stream gravels—**gold, snow quartz;** (b) Jones Beach, area—**olivine crystals** on diabase boulders, **soapstone;** (c) Kelsey Cr. bridge, area—**rhodonite;** (d) Spring Flat, below, in stream gravels—**zircon;** (e) Scott Bar —see under SCOTT BAR.

GAZELLE, the Dewey Mine, plentiful—**arsenopyrite, pyrite.**

GRENADA, E 12 mi., at Canyon Butte (Sec. 13, T. 44 N, R. 4 E), in lithophysae in spherulitic **obsidian—fayalite** (with **cristobolite**).

HAPPY CAMP: (1) area jade mines along Indian Cr. to the N, especially the Chan Jade Mine, the Blue Star and Huey mines—**gold, idocrase, nephrite jade, serpentine.** (The Happy Camp area **jade** has long been sent to China and returned to America as "Chinese jade." Prized specimens are **jade** laced with **native gold.** Individual **jade** boulders, on exhibit in county museums, frequently weigh more than a ton.) (2) N, along Indian Cr. and tributaries, in stream gravels—**williamsite (noble serpentine);** (3) N 9 mi., between East Fork of Indian Cr. and Thompson Cr., on E side of Thompson

Mt.—**gem rhodonite;** (4) NNW 10 mi., South Fork of Indian Cr., gravels—**californite, grossularite garnet, idocrase, serpentine;** (5) N, to Slater Butte Lookout, then N 3 mi., on W side of Thompson Ridge near crest, mine—**rhodonite;** (6) Sec. 33, T. 17 N, R. 8 W, the Preston Peak Mine—**bornite, covellite, chalcopyrite;** (7) Twin Valley Cr., gravels—**jadeite.**

HORNBROOKE, NE, along Jenny Cr.—**agate, carnelian, petrified wood, fossils.**

HORSECREEK: (1) a mercury mine in Sec. 15, 16, T. 46 N, R. 10 W, in seams of **hornblende** schist—**cinnabar;** (2) W, several miles to Honolulu, the Bonanza Mine—**azurite, chalcopyrite, pyrrhotite.**

MOUNT SHASTA, old town of Berryvale, S 6 mi., deposit—**onyx.**

MUGGINSVILLE ("QUARTZ VALLEY"), area old mines—**gold, rhodochrosite.**

OAK BAR, W 4 mi., the Minnehaha Mine on the Klamath R., as semi-transparent crystals—**cinnabar.**

ORO FINO (3 mi. NW of GREENVIEW in Scott Valley), area old mines—**gold, rhodochrosite, rhodonite, jasper.**

QUARTZ VALLEY (about 10 mi. W of FORT JONES and 4 mi. W of GREENVIEW): (1) area gold mines (hidden in surrounding hills)—**gold, quartz, rhodochrosite;** (2) area stream gravels—**gold colors, jasper;** (3) Isingglass Mt., area—**muscovite** (large books and sheets), large **quartz crystals.**

SAWYERS BAR (25 mi. SW of ETNA via very steep dirt rd.): (1) all area stream gravels—**gold, platinum, stream tin;** (2) entire Salmon R. drainage system: (a) area gravels, with very many hydraulic operations evident—**gold, platinum, cassiterite crystals;** (b) East Fork gravels—**gold, platinum;** (c) Little South Fork, on N side of Mt. Caesar at head of watershed, in cliffs above a snowfield area—**azurite, malachite;** (d) North Fork gravels—**gold, platinum, cassiterite;** (e) South Fork gravels, especially near mouth of Black Gulch—**gold, platinum, rhodonite,** massive bladed **actinolite;** (3) E 3 mi., Whites Gulch: (a) numerous old hydraulic operations—**gold;** (b) at head of gulch—**pyrrhotite, rhodonite;** (4) NE, to Idlewild, in gravels of South Russian Cr.—**gold, cassiterite, manganese, rhodonite.** (The extremely rugged mountains to the south constitute the Trinity Alps Wilderness Area and those to the north the Marble Mountain Wilderness Area, with the Salmon Mountains Wilderness Area sandwiched between. Until 1960 only gold rush mule trails crisscrossed the region outside the wilderness boundaries, now somewhat rebuilt as USFS and logging roads, steep, rugged, and often dangerous.)

SCOTT BAR (3 mi. S of confluence of Scott R. and Klamath R., which is about 3 mi. E of HAMBURG), the Scott Bar Mine (operated for more than 100 yrs.)—**hessite** in **gold ore.**

SEIAD: (1) head of Seiad Cr.—**graphite;** (2) Seiad Valley—**epidote** (in area schists), **iddingsite, chromite** (with **uvarovite garnet**); (3) Twp. 46, 47 N, R. 11, 13 W, area mines—**kämmererite,** with **uvarovite garnet.**

SOMES BAR, N 3 mi., in limestone outcrop on Salmon R., as fine divergent specimens—**wollastonite.**

WEED, NE 12 mi., the Yellow Butte Mine—**chalcocite, chalcopyrite, molybdenite.**

YOUNGS VALLEY, area mines—**chromite, kämmererite, uvarovite garnet.**

YREKA: (1) area mines and gravels—**gold.** (Following the torrential flood-waters of Dec., 1964, solid **gold nuggets** to several ounces surfaced in town, especially around the waterworks.) (2) Between YREKA and HORNBROOK via the old U.S. 99, in rd. cut crossing of the Klamath R., as large pale pink crystals in a 2–6-in. vein—**axinite;** (3) N and NW, the Humbug mining district: (a) area mines—**gold, copper minerals, native copper, axinite crystals;** (b) Hungry Cr. gravels, float—**cassiterite crystals, native copper** in slate; (4) SE 14 mi., the Peg Leg Mine—**penninite,** with **uvarovite garnet.**

SOLANO CO.

FAIRFIELD, between town and VACAVILLE, in quarries—**onyx.**

SONOMA CO.

AREA: (1) countywide exposures of underlying Franciscan **serpentines—chromite;** (2) many lava outcrops, as minute prismatic phenocrysts—**enigmatite.**

CALISTOGA, W, area—**opalized wood.** A fabulous petrified forest was discovered here in 1871; the very many prostrate opalized logs surpassed in size and gem quality anything found in Arizona's Petrified Forest (*q.v.*). Individual names were given to giant stone trees, e.g., Queen of the Forest, 80 feet long and 12 feet in diameter. The Monarch had an unbroken length of 126 feet (possibly 300 feet, when fully excavated) and a mean diameter of 10 feet; it was 3,000 years old when the forest was destroyed by volcanic action millions of years ago. These giant stone redwoods are interspersed with the opalized remnants of other trees, principally pines, a Miocene forest which thrived 12 to 20 million years ago until the nearby Mt. St. Helens exploded and blasted the forest into eternity.

CLOVERDALE, at The Geysers, abundant—**alunogen, alunite, boussingaultite** (as crusts and stalactites), with **mascagnite** and **epsomite.**

GLEN ELLEN: (1) E side of Sonoma Valley, in cavities in a **soda-rhyolite**—**aegirite, riebeckite;** (2) along rd. to KENWOOD, in **kaolin** deposit—**precious opal.**

HEALDSBURG, SW 2 mi., exposure—**glaucophane.**

PETALUMA, E 2½ mi. along Adobe Cr., area—**jasper, petrified wood.**

SKAGGS SPRINGS, area mines—**cinnabar, curtisite, metacinnabar, realgar.**

VALLEY FORD, E 2½ mi., area exposure—**glaucophane** (blue crystals), with **clinozoisite.**

STANISLAUS CO.

PATTERSON, W, on Arroyo del Puerto, deposit—**psilomelane.**

VERNALIS, W, at the Buckey Mine in the Diablo Range, mine dumps—**manganese minerals, psilomelane.**

TEHAMA CO.

ELDER CREEK: (1) at the Grau pit, on fracture surfaces of **chromite— aragonite crystals**; (2) North Fork, in Sec. 16, T. 25 N, R. 7 W, large deposit—**chromite.**

TRINITY CO.

AREA: Trinity R. and tributaries, gravels—**chalcedony, gold, jasper, nephrite jade, petrified wood, platinum nuggets, serpentine**; (2) NW¼ Sec. 17, T. 26 N, R. 12 W, the Blue Jay Mine—**barite, copper carbonates, native copper, hausmannite**; (3) Sec. 27, T. 30 N, R. 6 E, the Manganese Queen, Lucky Bill, and Spider mining claims—**bementite, rhodonite, rhodochrosite**; (4) Sec. 17, T. 4 S, R. 6 E, the Shellview Mine—**braunite, rhodochrosite**; (5) Island Mountain copper mine—**bornite, copiapite, pyrrhotite** (as pale brown scaly masses).

CARRVILLE: (1) N 1 mi., at Coffee Cr., area—**anthophyllite** (dark, soda-rich, as cross-fiber **asbestos** veins to 2 in. wide in **serpentine**); (2) NW 2 mi., the Jones Bros. **asbestos** mine—**chrysotile**; (3) Golden Jubilee Mine, large cubes—**limonite** pseudomorphs after **pyrite.**

DEDRICK: (1) area stream beds, as nodules—**rhodonite**; (2) trail from end of rd. into the Trinity Wilderness Area, several-mi. hike to 6-mi.-long ledge—**rhodonite.**

HAY FORK: (1) 15 mi. below the P.O. on the Hay Fork of the Trinity R., area, dark gray—**barite**; (2) Trinity R. gravels—**gold, platinum** (nuggets to 2½ oz.).

TRINITY CENTER (old town now submerged beneath Clair Engle Lake), 3 mi. above, the Enright claim—**gold, platinum** nuggets (**platiniridium,** to several oz.). (This part of Trinity Co. is noted for its immense **gold** placers of the gold rush era, with active mining continuing up to World War II.)

WEAVERVILLE (Quadrangle): (1) Iron Mt. district—**epidote, garnet, sphene, zircon**; (2) W edge of co., as a moderately common mineral in area **gold** ores—**arsenopyrite**; (3) Helena, N along E Fork and especially Indian Cr., gravels—**rhodonite.**

TULARE CO.

AREA: (1) Drum Valley: (a) Consolidated Tungsten Mine—**calcite crystals** (massive), **axinite crystals** (to ¾ in. long), **scheelite**; (b) on a hill between the valley and Slickrock Canyon—massive **epidote, garnet, quartz**; (2) Eber Flat, large divergent-columnar masses—**epidote**; (3) Rocky Hill, SE, along a **serpentine** contact in **quartz-albite** schist, as clusters—**riebeckite** (needles to ¼ in. long); (4) Yokohl Valley, NW¼ Sec. 17, T. 18 S, R. 28 E, exposure—**hornblende** (crystals to 10 in. long).

EXETER: (1) NW, on the D. F. Gassenberger Ranch, in pegmatite— **allanite** (with **rose quartz**); (2) NE¼ Sec. 8, T. 18 S, R. 26 E, the Venice Hill mines—**chrysoprase, opal, serpentine.**

LEMONCOVE, N 3 mi., on N side of a ravine ⅓ mi. NE of Kaweah R. and 1 mi. E of Ward Ranch—**quartzite, rhodonite.**

LINDSAY, ESE 1 mi., pits on N end of a low hill—**chrysoprase, crypto-crystalline quartz gemstones, opal, serpentine.**

MINERAL KING (District), area—**epidote** (common), **arsenopyrite** (old mine dumps).

PORTERVILLE: (1) S 1½ mi. and E of PLANO, area—**chalcedony, chryso-prase, common opal, serpentine;** (2) N 2 mi., at Lewis Hill, in **serpentine** exposure—**nephrite jade** (masses, some of gem quality); (3) E 8 mi. and ½ mi. S of Deer Cr.—**chalcedony, chrysoprase, common opal, serpentine;** (4) S 11 mi., the Deer Creek silver mine—**azurite, silver minerals;** (5) E 30 mi., on Middle Fork of Tule R. in Sec. 30, T. 19 S, R. 31 E, as exposed masses—**copper minerals, native copper.**

THREE RIVERS, area, as crystals to 4 in. long—**epidote.**

VISALIA, E 8 mi., at S end of Venice Hill—**satelite (serpentine).**

WHITE RIVER, E 12 mi., the Green Monster Mine—**scheelite, cupro-tungstite.**

WOODLAKE, Sec. 9, T. 17 S, R. 26 E, in a hornblende-gabbro exposure, as crystals to several in. long—**hornblende.**

TUOLUMNE CO.

AREA: (1) area Mother Lode **gold** mines, widespread as a gangue mineral —**ankerite;** (2) Adelaid Mine—**altaite;** (3) Josephine Mine—**erythrite, arsenopyrite;** (4) Lang Gulch, pegmatite outcrop—**allanite** (crystals to 6 in. long); (5) Ragged Peak, area pegmatite outcrops, in talus blocks— **allanite** (crystals to 17 in. long); (6) Sell Mine—**altaite** (as gray crystals on crystallized **gold**).

COLUMBIA: (1) area—massive **psilomelane** (with **pyrolusite**), **calcite** (showing scarlet triboluminescence); (2) Sawmill Flat, the Barney Pocket Mine—**altaite** (crystals cemented by **gold**).

HORSESHOE BEND, E, on slope of ridge—**bornite** (with **cinnabar**).

JAMESTOWN: (1) S 3 mi., the Mann Copper Mine; (2) Oak Hill and Washington mines at Big Oak Flat—**chalcopyrite.**

SONORA, in the Bonanza and O'Hara mines—**altaite** (in clusters of crystal-lized **gold**).

TUOLUMNE, N 1 mi., pegmatite outcrop—**spessartite garnet** (crystals to 2 in.).

TUTTLETOWN, the Golden Rule Mine—**altaite.**

YOSEMITE VALLEY, NW side at foot of Eagle Peak, in talus blocks from a pegmatite, small amounts—**alunite.**

VENTURA CO.

FILLMORE, E 3 mi., at Sulphur Mt., as deposits—**sulfur.**

FRAZIER MT. (reached from GORMAN, Los Angeles Co., on Int. 5 or via Wheeler Springs on Rte. 33 from Ojai): (1) area deposits—**colemanite;** (2) Lockwood Valley, N, in Russel and area borax mines—**howlite.**

OJAI, NE, at South Mt., as coating in crevices of sandstone outcrops—**boussingaultite.**

TRIUNFO, the Prospect Mine—**azurite.**

VENTURA: (1) N, along U.S. 101, beach gravels of the Rincon from just N of VENTURA to the Santa Barbara Co. line—**"Catalina" marble** (brecciated, patterned), **silicified marine dinosaur bone** (locally termed **"whale bone"**); (2) Ventura Mine (T. 1 N, R. 18 W)—**pyrrhotite** (with **nickel minerals** and **chalcopyrite**).

YUBA CO.

DOBBINS DISTRICT: (1) NW 2 mi., in the Indiana Ranch area, the California M Lode—**arsenopyrite, chalcopyrite, tellurides;** (2) Red Ravine Mine (Sec. 30, T. 18 N, R. 7 E)—**gold, sylvanite.**

MARYSVILLE–YUBA CITY, regional gravels of the Feather R., especially upstream toward the mts.—**axinite, gold.**

COLORADO

Lying within five natural physiographic provinces, each characterized by its own peculiar geology, Colorado ("colored land") is noted for its high mountains in the western half of the state and the Great High Plains of the eastern half. With 51 peaks rising more than 14,000 feet above sea level, the mean elevation of Colorado is 6,800 feet, the highest of any of America's 50 states. As might be expected, most of the state's extensively developed mining districts occur in the mountainous region west of the 100th meridian. In any gem and mineral collecting visit, altitude and rigorous climatic changes, abrupt even in summer, should be taken into account.

Known as the Centennial, or Silver, State, Colorado ranks among the most heavily mineralized regions of the world, although no single mine (other than the Climax Molybdenum Mine at Climax and the Eagle Zinc Mine at Gilman) can really be termed a "large operation." Colorado's highly divergent minerals and gemstones are widely distributed in relatively small concentrations which, fortunately for the collector, lie generally on public land. Like Alaska, Colorado is noted primarily for its metallic mineral wealth (some $3 billion since 1858) because of its enormous production of **copper, gold, lead, molybdenum, radium, silver, uranium, vanadium,** and **zinc.**

While ore minerals built the fortunes of the state, more than 30 varieties of highly prized gems and gemstones (including organic **amber** and **jet**) occur in the region's mines, stream gravels, high-mountain pegmatites, and eastern sedimentaries, and as float. Colorful specimens of an abundance of crystals and minerals occur on the thousands of mine dumps that dot the mining districts, especially **azurite, chalcopyrite, galena, sphalerite,** and others intermixed with the common gangue minerals of **barite, fluorite, quartz,** and **rhodochrosite.**

East of the Rocky Mountain system, occurring almost everywhere as float or as components of the sedimentary Great Plains formations, can be found a wealth of **petrified woods, quartz family gemstones,** crystals of **calcite** and **aragonite,** and interesting pseudomorphs after primary minerals. There are literally thousands more gem and mineral collecting localities than can be listed in this volume, and the collector should be forever on the lookout for other localities known mainly to local specialists and the numerous active rock clubs which hold monthly meetings and periodic shows in all parts of the state.

For information, write: Colorado Geological Survey, 220 Museum Building, Denver.

ADAMS CO.

STRASBURG, area deposits along Clear Cr., placers—**gold.**

ALAMOSA CO.

ALAMOSA, S to ANTONITO, Cumbress Pass hwy., take right bank of river, rd. through MOGOTE to about 20 mi. above ANTONITO (hwy. crosses river and the pass), ¼ mi. beyond river park car and climb a rocky point to a rockslide area—gemmy **lace agate.**

BLANCA (or WEST BLANCA), elev. 10,000–14,000 ft., many area mine dumps—**gold, silver.**

ARAPAHOE CO.

AREA: (1) South Platte R. gravels—**gold. Gold** was discovered in 1858 S of DENVER in bars along this river, as well as in (2) Cherry Cr. and Dry (Cottonwood) Cr., T. 5 S, R. 66, 67 W; (3) all tributary streams, placers—**gold.**

BACA CO.

SPRINGFIELD, SW 45 mi., at Carizzo Cr. (Estelene), in exposures of a white sandstone—**gold, chalcocite** (partly altered to **azurite** and **malachite**).

BOULDER CO.

AREA, coal beds of the Laramie formation—**amber.**

BOULDER: (1) W 4 mi., to Arkansas Mt. (extending W for 9 mi. to vicinity of NEDERLAND, *q.v.*), noted tungsten mining district: (a) Boulder

Canyon—**ferberite** (black, brilliant); (b) Gold Hill—sulfide minerals (**gold, lead, copper, silver, zinc**), massive **fluorite** (fluorescent); (c) Caribou district—**lead-silver minerals, pitchblende;** (2) W 7 mi.: (a) Magnolia (reached via steep grades), numerous high-grade veins—**gold, silver,** some **tungsten;** (b) Sugarloaf, mines—**gold** (with **lead** and **copper** subordinate), **zinc;**

(3) W, on Rte. 119, Grand Island (Cardinal, Eldora), area mines—**copper, gold, lead, silver,** some **zinc;** (4) NW 12 mi., at JAMESTOWN, area mines—**gold** (some as a **telluride**), **copper, lead, silver, zinc, cerite** (radioactive), **fluorite** (massive, fluorescent).

NEDERLAND, N on Rte. 160 toward WARD 3.7 mi., turn E onto Sugarloaf-Sunset rd. to mi. 7, the Oregon Mine—gem **ferberite, biotite mica, fluorite, sulfide minerals.**

WARD (20 mi. NW of BOULDER and 9 mi. N of NEDERLAND), on Rte. 160, area mines—**gold, silver** (predominant, with **lead** and **copper**), low-grade **pyrite.**

CHAFFEE CO.

AREA, Arkansas R. gravels (BUENA VISTA, SALIDA, NATHROP), along river from BUENA VISTA SE 25 mi. to Fremont Co. line and near GRANITE (close to co. line 15 mi. NW of SALIDA), many placers—**gold.**

BUENA VISTA: (1) Chalk Cr. gravels—**sapphire;** (2) S 2 mi. to U.S. 24: (a) E, to Riverside (6 mi. off U.S. 24, last 2 mi. difficult), alt. 12,000–13,000 ft., veins—some **copper, gold, lead, silver;** (b) E 5.9 mi., turn S on Rte. 53 toward BASSAM, left fork to Clora May Mine—**allanite, bismuthinite, bismutite, euxenite, garnet, graphic granite, fluorite;** right fork 1.2 mi. to Crystal No. 8 Mine—**allanite, biotite mica, garnet, gadolinite, fluorite, euxenite, microcline feldspar, monazite, rose quartz, xenotime;** (c) NE 13 mi. and just S of Trout Cr. Pass, mines—**copper, gold, lead, silver, zinc;** (3) W 14 mi., Cottonwood, near head of Cottonwood Cr., small veins—**gold, lead, silver;** (4) SE 5 mi., Free Gold, on Trout Cr.—**gold, silver.**

GARFIELD-MONARCH (District), alt. 10,000–10,500 ft., in T. 49, 50 N, R. 6 E, mine dumps—**copper, gold, lead, silver, zinc.**

GRANITE: (1) S 3 mi.: (a) Clear Cr., area mines, and (b) 4–10 mi. farther SW, placers—**gold;** (2) T. 11, 12 S, R. 79 E (with part of district in Lake Co.), placers and lode mines—**gold, lead, silver;** (3) W 15 mi., La Plata (WINFIELD) on Clear Cr., alt. 9,750–12,000 ft. (mineralized area 1–3 mi. W and SW of WINFIELD, small veins in Tertiary Twin Lakes porphyry—**copper, gold, lead**).

NATHROP: (1) across the Arkansas R. in the Ruby Mt. district via W 1 mi. on U.S. 285 to NW-trending track to the RR bridge: (a) directly across RR, the Dorothy Hill mass; (b) NE from bridge by trail on N side of Arkansas R., Ruby Mt. (directly across river from town), and (c) due N of Dorothy Hill at Sugarloaf Mt.—gemmy colorful—**rhyolite, perlite, Apache tears (marekanite,** locally called "black rubies"), **spessartite garnet, topaz, sanidine, feldspar, quartz crystals;** (2) S 2–3 mi., Browns Cr. (Browns Canyon, near U.S. 285), placers—**gold;** (3) W 16 mi., Chalk Cr. (T. 15 S, R. 80, 81 E), the Mary Murphy Mine—**copper, gold, lead, silver, zinc;**

(4) NNW 9.8 mi. via S on U.S. 285 for 3.8 mi., turn N on Rte. 70 for

1½ mi., bear left and N to John Mohr cabins on Mt. Antero (park, take trail 7+ mi. and climb 5,000 ft. to summit), area pegmatite outcrops: (a) mines and pits—gem **aquamarine, beryl;** (b) summit (14,000 ft.)— **apatite, aquamarine, bertrandite, beryl, bismutite** (or **phenakite**), **brannerite, calcite, cyrtolite, danburite, feldspar (microcline), fluorite, goethite** pseudomorphs after **pyrite, hematite, ilmenorutile** (massive), **limonite, magnetite, mica (biotite, muscovite), molybdenite, molybdite, monazite, pyrite, quartz crystals, sericite, smoky quartz, spessartite garnet, sulfur, topaz, tourmaline;** (c) saddle of Mt. Antero—**aquamarine, common beryl** (crystals to 8 in. long), **bertrandite** (finest in world), **fluorite, phenakite, rock crystal, smoky quartz;** (d) 2 mi. SW of summit at foot of Mt. Baldwin, area pegmatites— gem **beryl;** (e) 5 mi. N of summit, on S slopes of Mt. Princeton—**aquamarine, beryl, quartz crystals;** (f) on adjoining White Mt. (connected to Mt. Antero by a ridge), area pegmatites—**aquamarine, bertrandite, beryl, fluorite, huebnerite, molybdenite, sanadine crystals, smoky quartz, phenakite, topaz, tourmaline;** (g) near head of Browns Cr., dumps of the California Mine—**beryl** (colorless), **aquamarine, ferrimolybdite, fluorite, brannerite, molybdenite, molybdite, jarosite, muscovite mica, quartz crystals, rutile, tourmaline, topaz.**

SALIDA: (1) S 4 mi., Cleora (near U.S. 50), mine—**chalcopyrite;** (2) W, at Monarch Pass: (a) limestone quarry (largest in state)—associative **carbonate minerals;** (b) area mines and dumps—**beryl, copper, corundum, feldspar, fluorspar, gold, graphite, iron, manganese, marble, rare-earth minerals, silver, tungsten, uranium-thorium minerals;** (3) take Rte. 190 toward TURRET: (a) at ½ mi., park and walk to Savilla Queen No. 2 Mine and area prospects—**beryl, garnet, muscovite mica, feldspar, quartz crystals;** (b) at 2.9 mi., TURRET (near ghost town), area mines, particularly the Combination Mine S of rd.—**beryl** (blue, crystals to 12 in. long), **garnet, mica (biotite), feldspar** (red and white), **graphic granite, metallic minerals;**

(4) N 4 mi., in the Trout Cr. Hills via Rte. 291, to the abandoned Sedalia Copper Mine—**actinolite, almandite garnets** (gem crystals to large size, e.g., 15 lbs.), **asbestos, azurite, beryl, cerussite, chalcanthite, chalcocite, chalcopyrite, chrysocolla, chrysoprase, corundum, cuprite, epidote, microcline feldspar, gahnite (spinel), galena, hemimorphite, hornblende, kyanite, limonite, malachite, melanterite, mica (biotite), pyrite, quartz crystals, sphalerite, staurolite, willemite;**

(5) ENE 6 mi., the Rock King prospect, abundant—**graphic granite;** (6) N 7 mi., the Combination prospect—**graphic granite;** (7) W 8 mi., on E side of Arkansas R. valley, at SEDALIA, with ore minerals intimately intergrown with schist minerals—**chalcopyrite,** abundant **sphalerite** (with some **galena** and **silver,** a little **gold**);

(8) NW 10.7 mi. via Rtes. 291, 180, and 190 (in this order from town), to the TURRET mining district, jct. to Calumet Iron Mine: (a) on left side of jct., the Rock King Mine—**beryl, columbite-tantalite, feldspar (albite, microcline), mica (biotite, muscovite), graphic granite, massive quartz;** (b) at mi. 11, the Homestake Mine (a huge quarry)—**albite feldspar, muscovite mica, fluorapatite;** (c) at mi. 11.9, the Calumet Iron Mine—**amphibole, augite, chalcopyrite, corundum, epidote** (crystals to 2 in. long), **grossularite garnet (essonite), magnetite, marble, muscovite mica, pyrite, quartz crystals, sagenite quartz** (crystals to 6 in. long), **sapphire** (gem), **wernerite;**

(9) N 11 mi., on fair roads, at Turret Cr., area mines—**chalcopyrite, gold, silver;** (10) NNE 16 mi., to CALUMET (WHITEHORN, Fremont Co.), alt. 9,500–10,000 ft.: (a) area small mines—**copper, gold, silver;** (b) Calumet Iron Mine, dumps—**actinolite, epidote, magnetite, sapphire** (deep blue), **uralite (amphibole** after **pyroxene).** (While no crystals are visible in the gangue, treatment with HCl will expose some unusual crystal forms, since the specimens are about 25 percent **calcite,** dissolved by the acid.)

TWIN LAKES, Red Mt., from the Continental Divide E to the town P.O., with most mines and prospects above the valley and difficult to reach, alt. 11,000–12,000 ft.—**gold, silver.**

CLEAR CREEK CO.

DAILEY (ATLANTIC), near head of W Fork of Clear Cr. and Butler Gulch, 2 mi. E and SE of Jones Pass, area small mines—**lead,** some **silver, zinc.**

EMPIRE (UPPER UNION), on U.S. 40 and 41 mi. W of DENVER, with main veins 1½ mi. N of EMPIRE on good rds.—**gold.**

GEORGETOWN–SILVER PLUME–QUEENS (GRIFFITH), on U.S. 6 and 40–42 mi. W of DENVER, local steep grades: (1) area mines—complex **sulfides,** varying from **gold-lead-silver** ores to **lead-silver-zinc minerals (gold** subordinate, some **copper);** (2) S 2 mi., the Argentine (West Argentine) District, including mines along Leavenworth Cr. and on SE side of Leavenworth Mt. (also on SE slope of McClellan Mt. at head of Leavenworth Cr. 6 mi. farther SW), mines—**lead-silver minerals, gold,** some **copper** and **zinc.**

IDAHO SPRINGS: (1) mines at Cascade, Coral, Jackson Bar, Paynes Bar, Spanish Bar, Virginia Canyon, via good rds., wide variety of colorful ore types—**gold-silver-lead-copper** ores predominating; (2) NW 2 mi., along Trail Cr., gravels—**amethyst;** (3) NW 2½ mi., at TRAIL (Freeland, Lamartine), on Trail Cr. with the Lamartine Mine 2 mi. SW on divide between Trail Cr. and Ute Cr., good rd. 2–4 mi. from U.S. 40 and 6—**gold, lead, silver, zinc minerals** (in combination); (4) W 6 mi., gravels of Silver Cr.—**amethyst;** (5) NW 10 mi. (2 mi. on U.S. 40 and 8 mi. on Rte. 285), to ALICE (Lincoln, Yankee Hill, alt. 10,000–11,000 ft.), lode mines—**lead, gold, zinc;** (6) Montana (Lawson, Dumont, Downieville), the W extension of the district on U.S. 6 and 40 (38 mi. W of DENVER), area mines—**gold, lead, silver.** (Mineralization here is very similar to the immediate IDAHO SPRINGS area.)

LAWSON-DRUMMOND DISTRICT, Red Elephant Mt., area—**amethyst.**

CONEJOS CO.

MANASSA, E 10 mi. (13 mi. ESE of LA JARA), and 1½ mi. W of the Rio Grande R., the King Mine on Pinon Mt.—**kaolin, quartz** (colorfully stained), **sericite, turquoise.**

PLATORO (W from LA JARA via Rte. 15), the Axel, Gilmore, Lake Fork, Ute, and Stunner districts, many area mines—**gold, silver.**

COSTILLA CO.

SAN LUIS, NE 7 mi. to Plomo (Rito Seco) on Rito Seco Cr.—**gold, pyrite** (in **quartz**).

CUSTER CO.

SILVER CLIFF–WESTCLIFFE, hardscrabble district of relatively small but high-grade veins: (1) area mines—**gold, lead, silver, zinc;** (b) NE, to Oak Cr. (Ilse, Spaulding), on Rte. 143 about 16 mi. SW of FLORENCE (Fremont Co.), area mines—**cerussite,** some **silver;** (3) E 14 mi. on Rte. 96 and 2 mi. on local rd. to Rosita Hills (Rosita, Querida), in veins and pipes—**copper, gold, silver.**

DOLORES CO.

OPHIR, the San Juan Mts. (a triangle between OURAY in Ouray Co., SILVERTON in San Juan Co., and OPHIR, E to the Hinsdale Co. line, a mountainous region of hundreds of old mines, prospects, and abandoned dumps with a varied assortment of minerals—**gold, copper, lead, silver, manganese, tungsten, pyrite,** etc. (Access roads are usually steep and rough; make local inquiry.)
RICO: (1) mines on Rte. 145 and 36 mi. NE of DOLORES and 27 mi. S of TELLURIDE—**argentite, argentiferous tetrahedrite, chalcopyrite, galena, pyrite, quartz crystals, rhodochrosite, sphalerite;** also (2) NW 16 mi. at Lone Cone (Dunton) on W. Dolores R. on Rte. 331.

DOUGLAS CO.

DECKERS, E 7 mi., in Sec. 21, T. 9 S, R. 69 W, the Devils Head prospect—**graphic granite, topaz.**
FRANKTOWN: (1) Cherry Cr. (from town extending several mi. N), and (2) NW 4–5 mi., on Lemon Cr., area placers—**gold;** (3) S 1 mi., Russelville Gulch (tributary of Cherry Cr.), extending along gulch for 3 mi., placers—**gold.**
LARKSPUR, area, as float—**jasper.**
LOUVIERS, along Dry Cr. (tributary of the South Platte R.), in deposits extending NE into Arapaho Co., placers—**gold.**
PALMER LAKE, NW 10 mi., Front Range foothills, area—**alabaster, gypsum, satin spar.**
PARKER: (1) S 1 mi., area float—**petrified wood;** (2) NW 1½ mi. on Rte. 83: (a) Newlin Gulch, and (b) NW of Newlin Cr. in Happy Canyon, as microscopic grains to pinhead nuggets—**placer gold.**
SEDALIA: (1) W 10.2 mi. on Rte. 67 (Jarre Canyon Rd.), turn left on Rampart Range Rd. and keep right to: (a) mi. 20.8 to C. M. S. Topaz

Claim (Devils Head), numerous area prospects—**allanite, amethyst, cassiterite, cyrtolite, gadolinite, feldspar (albite, amazonstone, microcline), fluorite, samarskite, smoky quartz crystals, topaz;** (b) S of summit on top of a ridge below main access rd.—**cassiterite, microcline feldspar, fluorite, hematite, limonite, smoky quartz crystals, topaz;** (c) mi. 21.4, White Quartz Mt., area on both sides of rd. for ½ mi.—**rock crystal, smoky quartz;** (d) regional stream beds and gullies—various **gemstones, crystals;** (e) mi. 26.2, on Bergen Rd., at Long Hollow, area—huge **smoky quartz crystals,** gem **topaz crystals** (to 24 in. long); (2) W 11 mi., Pine Cr., pegmatite outcrops—**amazonite, smoky quartz crystals;** (3) W 13.7 mi. on Rte. 67, to Sprucewood Inn jct., then 2 mi. up mine rd. to mines, tunnel, dumps of the Pine Cr. area—**albite feldspar** (crystal groups), **amazonstone, cassiterite, fluorite** (cubes to 3-in. edges), **rock crystal, smoky quartz crystals.**

EAGLE CO.

EAGLE: (1) W 1 mi. on U.S. 24 and 6–8 mi. up Brush Cr. on rd. to FULFORD, area mines—**cerargyrite, azurite,** and **malachite** (locally staining sandstone), trace of **uranium** and **vanadium;** (2) SSE 20 mi. to FULFORD, head of Brush Cr., area mines—**lead-silver minerals.**

GILMAN, the Eagle Mine (fourth largest **zinc** mine in America)—**copper, lead, silver, zinc.**

McCOY, W along Colorado R., bench gravels—**placer gold.**

MINTURN, SW 10 mi., Holy Cross (Eagle R.), at head of Cross Cr., spotty high-grade ore deposits—**gold, lead** (some), **silver.**

REDCLIFF: (1) Homestake Cr., area mines—**gold, lead, silver, zinc;** (2) Battle Mt., Belden, area mines to GILMAN, *q.v.*—**barite, auriferous sideritic sulfide** bodies (mantos), **chalcopyrite, galena, gold-silver tellurides, marmatite, manganosiderite, pyrite, pyritic gold, pyritic copper-silver** ores, **zinc sulfide** mantos, various complex **sulfides.**

ELBERT CO.

AREA: (1) Bijou and Kiowa Cr. gravels—**petrified wood;** (2) Platte R. gravels, especially SE of ELBERT—**opalized** and **silicified wood.**

AGATE, surrounding region, abundant—**agate, jasper, petrified wood (agatized, jasperized, opalized).**

ELBERT, SE a short distance, abundant logs—**agatized** and **opalized wood.**

ELIZABETH, W and NW 1–1½ mi., Gold Cr. (or Ronk Cr.), on Rte. 86 about 40 mi. SE of DENVER, placers—**gold.**

EL PASO CO.

AREA, regional coal mines in the Laramie formation—**jet.**

CALHAN: (1) all surrounding area—**amazonstone, quartz gemstones (agate, chalcedony, jasper,** etc.), **petrified wood (agatized, jasperized, opalized), rock crystal, selenite;** (2) E 3.4 mi. (U.S. 24 for .4 mi., turn S on paved rd. and at 1 mi. turn E onto Paint Mine Rd.), to Paint Mines: (a) area washes, gullies, surfaces—**agate, amazonstone, jasper, quartz crystals,** selenite; (b) S of the mine dumps—agate, etc. Throughout much of eastern Colorado, in a zone 150 mi. broad, are found petrified woods of gem quality (agatized, jasperized, opalized), and fossils.

COLORADO SPRINGS: (1) NE 4 mi., at Austin Bluffs, area—agate, carnelian, chalcedony, jasper; (2) Eureka Tunnel (NE of rd. summit between city and ROSEMONT, on lower side of rd.)—zircon; (3) NW 6 mi., at Blair Athol in the foothills, placers—gold;

(4) SW 7 mi., the St. Peter's Dome District via Gold Camp Rd. Take Rte. 33 SW toward CRIPPLE CREEK to jct. of Gold Camp Rd. and High Drive: (a) W .3 mi., across canyon, old tunnel and dump—zircon (to 2 in. long); (b) W .6 mi., hillside above rd.—rock crystal, smoky quartz, hematite pseudomorphs after siderite; (c) at 2.4 mi., Fairview RR sta., area both sides of rd.—bastnaesite, fluocerite ("tysonite"), fluorite, quartz crystals; (d) at mi. 2.9 climb low ridge to N to Cook Stove Mt. and another ¼ mi. to Buffalo Cr., area gravels and hillsides—amazonstone, smoky quartz, bastnaesite, fergusonite, fluorcerite, fluorite, genthelvite, lanthanite, phenakite, topaz, zircon;

(e) S of Cook Stove Mt., area—amazonite, smoky quartz crystals, topaz; (f) W 5.8 mi., just before the third tunnel, old dump downslope from a cement building, on USFS access rd.—columbite, cryolite (pink, pale green, translucent), microcline feldspar, milky quartz, pegmatite gems, pachnolite, prosopite, fluorite; (g) on right ⅓ mi., the Eureka Tunnel—see (2); (h) on through the third tunnel to mi. 6.1 to the Eureka Tunnel, q.v.; on left side of stream about 400 ft. below rd.—gem zircon; (i) at mi. 6.6, park and walk on USFS access rd., keeping right at first fork, many area prospect pits—astrophyllite, riebeckite, zircon; (j) at mi. 9.1 (jct. of Rte. 336 and 122) and at mi. 10, the Duffield L.O. at base of St. Peter's Dome, walk ⅓ mi. to Duffield Fluorspar Mine—barite, galena, fluorite, sphalerite.

The prolific St. Peter's Dome District provides not only gemmy minerals (allanite, apatite, feldspar—pink microcline-perthite and oligoclase, magnetite, sphene, and zircon) but also a variety of colorful and interesting gangue minerals, such as fluorite (accompanied by chalcopyrite, galena, sphalerite, pyrite, quartz (some chloritic), chalcedony, some gold and silver, pink barite, specular hematite, and such other rare fluorine minerals as bastnaesite, elpasolite, fluocerite, prosopite, ralstonite, and thomsenolite). Still rarer minerals include astrophyllite, cassiterite, chlorite, columbite, fayalite, fergusonite, genthelvite (danalite), pyrochlore, riebeckite, rutile, and xenotime.

MANITOU SPRINGS, SW 2 mi., at base of Cameron Cone: (1) Crystal Park, and (2) around bases of Mt. Arthur and Mt. Garfield, area pegmatites—amazonstone, columbite, feldspars, fluorite, hematite (in quartz and as pseudomorphs after siderite), hornblende, mica (biotite, muscovite), phenakite, quartz (crystals, smoky), topaz (blue, pinkish, to several inches long), black tourmaline (enclosed in quartz), zircon (rare).

PEYTON: (1) area of E half of co.—gem petrified wood; (2) the Bijou Basin, noted locality—agatized and jasperized wood.

FREMONT CO.

AREA, gravels of the Arkansas R., from Chaffee Co. line downstream to FLORENCE, many placers—gold.

BADGER CREEK (8 mi. SE of SALIDA in Chaffee Co.), with deposits 4 mi. N up cr., placers—**gold** (with some **copper minerals**).

CANON CITY: (1) area, Colorado State Penitentiary (call for permission to dig), section along Skyline Drive—**cone-in-cone calcite, fossils** (*Inoceramus, shark's teeth*); (2) N 4 mi. on U.S. 50; gate to the Cowan Quarries (go 2.3 mi. inside)—gemmy **travertine** (may contain casts of pine needles and cones), **gem marble** ("royal breccia"); (3) NW 4 mi. and ½ mi. S of U.S. 50, in Sec. 14, T. 18 S, R. 71 W, area—**graphic granite, microcline feldspar, quartz;** (4) N 4.4 mi., area of city dump—**barite** (brown crystals), **calcite** (white crystals), **cone-in-cone calcite, septarian nodules;** (5) NW 6 mi. and 1 mi. N of U.S. 50, the School Section Mine (Sec. 16, T. 18 S, R. 71 W)— **graphic granite;** (6) S 7 mi., Curio Hill—finest gem **agate;**

(7) N 6½ mi., Felch Cr., area—**agate nodules, chalcedony, geodes, jasper;** (8) N 7 mi., Garden Park, area—**agate, chalcedony, silicified dinosaur bone;** (9) N 8.2 mi. at S end of Garden Park Dinosaur Monument, area —**agate** (nodules, geodes, seam, banded), **jasperized dinosaur bone** (brown, red, yellow, plainly cellular), **pink calcite, petrified cephalopods;** (10) N 9.8 mi., to Felch Cr., area badlands—gem red **agate, alabaster nodules, geodes** (containing crystals of **barite, calcite, celestite, goethite, quartz**), **gypsum, gem jasper, jasperized dinosaur bone, millerite, satin spar, selenite;** (11) NNE 10 mi., on W side of Eight Mile Cr., at Phantom Canyon **beryl** prospect—**beryl, graphic granite.** (Area is difficult to reach by road; requires 2 mi. by trail that turns off Rte. 67 about 2 mi. S of ADELAIDE.)

(12) NW 12 mi. and 1 mi. S of Twelvemile Park, area—**amethyst, quartz crystals;** (13) W 13 mi. on U.S. 50, Currant Cr. (Parkdale, Micanite), with mineralized area 8 mi. to N on creek, mines—**copper, gold, lead, silver, zinc;** (14) NW 24 mi., the Climax Mica Mine (approx. 3,700 ft. NE of the ghost town of Micanite with mine about 600 ft. S of Park-Fremont Co. line) —**graphic granite, muscovite mica.**

COALDALE, E 1 m., on bank of the Arkansas R. (Sec. 24, T. 48 N, R. 11 E), the McCoy prospects—**graphic granite.**

COTOPAXI: (1) N 4 mi., feldspar prospect (Sec. 8, T. 48 N, R. 12 E)— **feldspar, graphic granite;** (2) N 9 mi. on U.S. 40 to Red Gulch (24 mi. SE of SALIDA in Chaffee Co.), area mines—**chalcocite,** some **silver, coal.**

PENROSE, S 1½ mi. on Rte. 115, area small gulleys and valleys—**calcite crystals** (to 4 in. long).

ROYAL GORGE: (1) area—**aquamarine, beryl, tourmaline;** (2) S 1.3 mi. toward Buckskin Joe, the School Section Mine—**apatite, beryl, beyerite, bismutite, chalcopyrite, columbite, mica (biotite, muscovite), microcline feldspar, garnet, black tourmaline, triplite;** (3) S 2.2 mi., quarry and Van Buskirk Mine—blue **apatite, microcline feldspar, garnet, graphic granite, biotite mica** (to 4 ft. long), **black tourmaline;**

(4) S 2.8 mi.: (a) Meyers Quarry (active)—**andradite garnet, beryl, beyerite, cleavelandite, lepidolite, muscovite mica, tourmaline** (pink, black), **triplite;** (b) Mica Lode Mine (second huge quarry off the main rd.)— **azurite, beryl** (crystals to 6 ft. long), **chalcocite, chrysocolla, garnet (andradite, spessartite, uvarovite), graphic granite, muscovite mica** (greenish blades to 3 ft. long), **rose quartz, tourmaline** (pink, black), **triplite, bismutite;** (5) S of the Mica Lode Mine, on high hill, the Magnuson Mine—**beryl** (greenish, yellow), **pink feldspar, graphic granite;** (6) at entrance to the

Mica Lode Mine, turn right for .3 mi. across uphill field to Border Feldspar No. 2 Mine—**graphic granite, quartz crystals, tourmaline;**
(7) Royal Gorge Park, area of exposed pegmatites on both sides of the gorge: (a) N side, known as Eight Mile Park, and (b) S side, as Webster Park—**andesite, azurite, beryl, beyerite, bismuth** (native), **bismutite, calcite, cerussite** (pseudomorphs after **natromontebasite**), **chalcedony, chalcocite, chlorite, chrysocolla, cleavelandite, columbite-tantalite, covellite, euxenite, feldspar** (**albite, microcline, oligoclase**), **fluorapatite, garnet, hematite, kaolinite, limonite, magnetite, malachite, manganese minerals, mica** (**biotite, lepidolite, muscovite**), **monazite, montebrasite, natromontebrasite, quartz** (crystals, gem **rose**), **silver** (native), **torbernite, tourmaline, tripolite.**
TEXAS CREEK: (1) N 6 mi. on gravel rd.: (a) the Devils Hole Mine—**aquamarine, columbite-tantalite, microcline feldspar, mica, rose quartz.** This pegmatite mine, as well as other area pegmatite outcrops, produces **microcline feldspar** crystals in enormous size, pale pink in color (**albite**) or pale buff. A record crystal measured 75 ft. long by 40 ft. wide; **muscovite mica** books have measured 5 ft. in diameter. (b) ⅓ mi. W of Echo Canyon–East Gulch jct., area—**rose quartz;** (2) N 6½ mi., the Amazon claim in East Gulch—**beryl.**
WELLSVILLE, 3 mi. up Taylor Gulch, huge deposit and quarry—gemmy **travertine, fossils** (pine cones and casts of needles).
WHITEHORN (a district E of and continuous with the Calumet District of Chaffee Co.), area mines—**gold, silver,** etc.

GARFIELD CO.

GLENWOOD SPRINGS, NEWCASTLE, N, on dumps of old mines on Riffle and Elk creeks and on S flank of the White River Plateau (an almost inaccessible area today)—**galena, gold, lead-silver** ores, **sphalerite.**

GILPIN CO.

AREA: (1) northern districts (Perigo, Independence, Pine-Kingston-Apex), covering half a twp. 20–25 mi. SW of BOULDER (Boulder Co.) and 50–60 mi. NW of DENVER, with good access roads, many mines—**gold, silver** predominant, some **lead** and **zinc** minerals; (2) southern districts (Central, Nevada, Gregory, Russel, Quartz Mt.), scattered throughout twp. 40–50 mi. W of DENVER and SW of BOULDER, many mines—**chalcopyrite, bornite, gold, pyrite, silver.**
CENTRAL CITY: (1) East End Mine—**moss agate, labradorite;** (2) SW 2.1 mi. on Rte. 279 past Russel Gulch (ghost camp), area old dumps—**pyrite cubes** (to 1 in. dia.); (3) right, on Rte. 279 (unmarked), then right fork at mi. 3.2, area slopes—**magnetite;** (4) at mi. 3.8, the Gloryhole (enormous open pit with dangerous rim)—**chalcopyrite, native copper, galena, gold, magnetite, pyrite cubes, rock crystal** (doubly terminated), **tennantite;** (5) rd. to ghost town of Apex: (a) at mi. 3, area—**magnetite;** (b) at mi. 6.7, cross Pine Cr., rd. leads to Evergreen Mine dumps—**azurite, bornite, calcite, chalcocite, chalcopyrite, chrysocolla, covellite, cuprite, enargite, galena,**

garnet, specular hematite, malachite, pyrite, sphalerite, sphene, wollastonite, zircon.

GRAND CO.

AREA, Middle Park—**moss agate, chalcedony, chrysoprase.**

GRAND LAKE (Wolverine), E 7 mi. on Rte. 278, mines—**gold-lead-silver** ores.

HOT SULPHUR SPRINGS, NW on Willow Cr., area—**moss agate, chalcedony, fossil wood.**

PARSHALL: (1) jct. of Williams Fork with Colorado R.: (a) area— **jasper** (variously colored); (b) 2 mi. up Williams Fork, area—**moss agate;** (2) S, to head of Williams Fork, the La Plata District extending a few miles SE across the Continental Divide (Jones Pass) into headquarters of the West Fork of Clear Cr. (Clear Creek Co.), in iron-stained veins—**pyrite, lead,** some **gold** locally, **silver, zinc.**

GUNNISON CO.

AREA: (1) Italian Mt., W side, area—**lapis lazuli;** (2) Mt. Beckwith, area—**moonstone.**

ALMONT (on Rte. 306), NE 7 mi., in Spring Cr. Canyon, mines—**lead-silver-gold** ores.

CRESTED BUTTE: (1) NW 10 mi. and a few mi. N of Rte. 135, rich ores —**ruby-silver;** (2) N 22 mi., at Elk Mt., alt. 9,500–11,000 ft. (including ghost town of Gothic), mines—**chalcopyrite** (with **gold** and **silver**), **galena, sphalerite.** (Mineralization is widespread, but veins are small and irregular.)

GUNNISON: (1) N, on W side of North Italian Mt., area metamorphic contact zones—**metamorphic minerals, lapis lazuli;** (2) E 13 mi., at Gold Brick (4–6 mi. N of OHIO, *q.v.,* on fair rd., alt. 9,000–10,000 ft., relatively rich veins—**gold-lead-silver** ores. (The productive veins are concentrated just E of Gold Cr. in an area 4 mi. long by 1 mi. wide.)

MARBLE (40 mi. S on Rte. 133 from GLENWOOD SPRINGS in Garfield Co., on W flank of the Elk Mts. at Rock Cr., with CRYSTAL 6 mi. to the E as central part of the district, alt. 9,000–13,000 ft.): (1) area mines—**barite, calcite, chalcopyrite, fluorite, galena, pyrite, quartz crystals, silver**-bearing **tetrahedrite, specularite,** white **marble** (gemmy, used for finishing and statuary); (2) NW, along highway to CARBONDALE (Garfield Co.), as float—**"Colorado Yule" marble;** (3) town quarry waste, RR road ballast; (4) 2 mi. distant across river, the Yule Quarry; (5) old mill site on W edge of Crystal R. (fantastic ruins); (6) E, at the Strauss Quarry—gem-grade **marble;** this famed marble created the Lincoln Memorial in Washington, D.C., and the first Tomb of the Unknown Soldier in Arlington National Cemetery (from a single 56-ton block), as well as being used for very many state and federal buildings across the nation; (7) head of Yule Cr., as massive beds to 50 ft. thick—**andradite garnet.**

OHIO: (1) W, in the Quartz Cr. area, more than 500 pegmatites—**beryl, columbium-tantalum minerals, graphic granite, lepidolite, mica, monazite,**

tourmaline; (2) SW 1⅞ mi., two rich pegmatite outcrops; (3) SW 2½ mi., at a rd. fork and within a radius of 1,200 ft. to the E, a dozen pegmatites, (4) SW 3.4 mi., a rich pegmatite; (5) SW 3¾ mi., rich pegmatite in hornblende gneiss; (6) many other area pegmatite exposures—cf. (1); this area is one of the most prominent regions in North America for **graphic granite;** (7) the Opportunity No. 1 prospect (open cuts on E side of a N-trending low ridge on E side of Quartz Cr.—**albite, beryl, columbite-tantalite, cleavelandite, graphic granite, microlite, muscovite mica.** (The pits encompass 11 pegmatites with varied, mostly noncommercial, mineral contents.)

PARLIN: (1) the Quartz Cr. district (29 sq. mi.) via Rte. 162, a region of 1,803 pegmatites: (a) area pegmatites contain a total of 27 species—**gemstones, minerals;** (b) the Brown Derby Mine—**pegmatite gems;** (3) S 3–4 mi., at Cochetopa (Green Mt., Gold Basin) and extending from Cochetopa Cr. 2–4 mi. W—free-milling **gold,** some **copper minerals,** possibly **tellurium;** (4) N 8½ mi. on Rte. 162 past the Opportunity and Brown Derby mines, turn onto Fossil Ridge dirt rd. for .2 mi., to the Bucky Mine—**beryl** (blue, green, to 12 in. long), **columbite-tantalite, gahnite, graphic granite, lepidolite, lithiophyllite-triphylite, monazite, muscovite, quartz, topaz.**

PITKIN: (1) NE 1–4 mi. and near rd. to TINCUP, in S end of a mineralized area which includes TINCUP, many mines—**gold, lead-silver, molybdenite** (rare); (2) S 6 mi. and near U.S. 50 about 25 mi. E of GUNNISON, in Box Canyon at old Independence and Camp Bird mines 3–4 mi. N of Waunito Hot Springs Cr. on steep rds., free-milling—**gold;** (3) N 15 mi., TINCUP, at head of Willow Cr. on extreme SE side of Taylor Park and 26 mi. E of GUNNISON via Rte. 162—"blanket deposits" of **gold-lead-silver,** spotty **molybdenite,** some **huebnerite.** (Cumberland Pass, 12,000 ft. alt., separates PITKIN from TINCUP.)

POWDERHORN, in the Cebolla District (Iola, Domingo, Vulcan, White Earth), mines along Cebolla Cr.—**gold, gold-silver, copper-gold-silver, pyrite.**

SARGENTS, N 10 mi., at Tomichi (Whitepine), a ghost town, area—**gold, lead, silver, zinc, bog iron ore, copper.**

HINSDALE CO.

EUREKA (historic ghost town not on most maps), the Sunnyside Mine—pink gem **rhodonite.** (This is a noted locality for **rhodonite;** good material is available at the old mill in town, since the aggregate used in the concrete for the mill foundation was **rhodonite.**)

LAKE CITY: (1) along Henson Cr. above town, mines—**lead-zinc** ores with subordinate **gold** and **chalcopyrite, lead-silver-zinc** ores with considerable **chalcopyrite, gold telluride** (with **silver**); (2) S 5 mi., Lake Fork at N end of Lake San Cristobal, noted for the Golden Fleece Mine—**gold telluride;** (3) SW 12 mi., between Lake Fork and its tributary Henson Cr., in several districts, e.g., Burrows Park (Whitecross), on Rte. 351 near head of Lake Fork of the Gunnison R., alt. 10,500–12,000 ft.—**chalcopyrite, galena-sphalerite, gold-silver,** some **lead** and **zinc.** (This area is a geologic extension of the SILVERTON mining district 14 mi. SW in San Juan Co.) (4) SW 18 mi., Carson, at head of Wagner Gulch, with mineralization extending S across the divide into head of Lost Trail Cr.—**barite** (chief gangue mineral), **lead, silver,** some **copper,** some **gold,** a little **zinc.**

HUERFANO CO.

LA VETA (11 mi. SW of WALSENBURG via U.S. 160 and 5 mi. on Rte. 111), area mines—**silver** (associated with **galena**), **gray copper, chalcopyrite, sphalerite, siderite,** gangue minerals (**barite, calcite, quartz**).

JACKSON CO.

COWDRY, NW 18 mi. on Rte. 125, to Pearl, area mines—**chalcopyrite, gold, silver, sphalerite** (dark).

RAND, SE 9 mi., at Teller, on Jack Cr., alt. 9,000–10,000 ft., an active early-day mining boom camp—**copper, gold, silver.** (Jackson Co. is virtually coextensive with North Park.)

JEFFERSON CO.

AREA: (1) Bear Cr. (between GOLDEN and RALSTON), area deposits—**alabaster;** (2) Drew Hill, area—**chrysoberyl.**

EVERGREEN (12 mi. W of MORRISON on Rte. 74, an important recreational center): (1) ½ mi. above town on Cub Cr., deposit—**chalcocite, quartz-fluorite** (vein), **silver,** yellow **sphalerite;** (2) S 1½ mi. on Rte. 73, the Augusta Mine—**fluorite, galena, azurite, barite, chalcocite, cerussite, lead** and **zinc minerals, sphalerite, limonite, willemite:** (a) SW ¾ mi., on NW side of Cub Cr. along Rte. 334, and (b) ¼ mi. W of Rte. 74, in Augusta Mine-type exposure—**fluorite, gold, silver.**

GOLDEN: (1) along Clear Cr. to E, fine placers—**gold;** (2) North and South Table mts. (basalt mesas near town on sides of Clear Cr.): (a) very many mines and prospects—**apophyllite, aragonite, calcite** (luminescent), **fossils** (vertebrate bones of dinosaurs, crocodiles, etc.), **halloysite, petrified wood** (palm, leaves, etc.), gemmy **zeolite crystals** (many varieties); (b) many area quarries with good access rds.—**dogtooth calcite, heulandite, laumontite, levynite, nordenite, scolecite, stilbite, zeolites (analcime, chabazite, mesolite, natrolite, thomsonite);**

(3) W 8 mi., the Roscoe beryl prospect (Sec. 5, T. 4 S, R. 71 W)—**beryl, graphic granite;** (4) NW 7½ mi. on Rte. 93 toward LEYDEN, the Leyden Coal Mine—**carnotite, coffinite;** (5) NW 9.1 mi. via Rte. 58 to: (a) No Name Pegmatite (in Golden Gate Canyon)—**tourmaline** (crystals to 12 in. long); (b) at mi. 10½, jct. to Robinson Hill, the Robinson Gulch prospect, pegmatite—**feldspar, black tourmaline;** (6) W on U.S. 40, past jct. with Lookout Mt. rd., then .6 mi. to Conoco service sta., area pegmatite exposures in curve in rd.—**allanite, astrophyllite, epidote, grossularite garnet** (to 12 in. dia.), **hyalite opal, hornblende, idocrase, magnetite, scheelite, sphene, vermiculite, wernerite;** (7) W 15 mi., at Centennial Cone, NW flanks, area pegmatites—**aquamarine, beryl, smoky quartz crystals.**

MORRISON, W 3 mi., the Malachite Mine (on divide between Bear Cr. and Mt. Vernon—massive **chalcopyrite** (with dark **sphalerite**), **augite** (altered with **hornblende** as gangue mineral), **copper, labradorite, pyrrhotite.**

KIT CARSON CO.

BURLINGTON, N 20 mi. along S Fork of the Republican R., broad area—
moss opal, petrified wood.

LAKE CO.

AREA, T. 10 S, R. 80 W, at Box Cr., dredger operations—gold.
CLIMAX: (1) SE 1 mi., in valley of the Arkansas R. (10–12 mi. NE of
LEADVILLE), the Alicante Mine—fluorite, quartz crystals, pyrite, rhodo-
chrosite; (2) 4 mi. farther S, the Birdseye Mine on E side of valley—gold,
lead, silver, zinc.
LEADVILLE: (1) area great mines—copper, bismuth, gold, lead, manganese-
iron ores, hematite, pyrite, silver, zinc, siderite, etc.; (2) California, Evans,
Iowa, Empire mines, alt. 10,150 ft., on W slope of the Mosquito Range—
bismuth, copper, gold, iron, lead, manganese-iron, pyrite, silver, zinc, etc.
(The LEADVILLE DISTRICT is one of the leading metal-producing areas in
America, lying in the broad open valley of the Arkansas R. along U.S. 24 at a
two-mile altitude.)
(3) N, the Kokomo mines—pyrite (magnificent crystals); (4) W 4 mi., at
St. Kevin–Sugar Loaf, early metal producers—gold, silver, and on the dumps
considerable amounts of galena, pyrite, quartz, sphalerite (dark brown),
some pink carbonates; (5) NW 6.9 mi. via the Turquoise Lake rd. and
Bear Lake truck rd.: (a) the Turquoise Chief Mine—metatorbernite (disseminations), turquoise; (b) adjacent old Iron Mask Mine—hematite, pyrite,
siderite; (c) W 2,000 ft. from the Turquoise Chief, at the Josie May prospect;
and (d) two mines NE of the Josie May—chrysocolla, malachite, torbernite,
turquoise; (6) SW 22 mi. and 5 mi. W of GRANITE (Chaffee Co.), a district
which includes all of the Lake Cr. drainage W of TWIN LAKES, many area
mines—gold, lead, silver, zinc.

LA PLATA CO.

AREA, Animas R. gravels, placers—gold.
DURANGO, N 25 mi. to the flagstop of Needleton, then E 6 mi. to the
Needle Mts. (Tacoma, Florida R., Vallecito, with Chicago Basin center of
district), alt. 11,000–12,000 ft., many area mines—barite, calcite, chalcopyrite, chalcedonic silica, fluorite, copper, gold, galena, pyrite, rhodochrosite,
silver.
GEM VILLAGE, headquarters town for gem and mineral collectors. Many
local summer field trips to adjoining gem-collecting localities are provided
by residents.
LA PLATA, large surrounding area in the heart of the La Plata Mts., and
area at head of Junction Cr. on E flank of mts., separated from town by
Eagle Pass (alt. 11,700 ft.)—chalcocite veins, chalcopyrite (bearing platinum), gold tellurides, pyritic gold, ruby-silver (veins), silver, etc. (More than
60 mineral species occur in this district.)

LARIMER CO.

BELLVUE (on U.S. 287), SW 3 mi. at Empire (Howes Gulch) and 6 mi. SW of FORT COLLINS, area mines—**chalcopyrite**, some **gold, cupriferous pyrite.**

ESTES PARK, W 31 mi. on U.S. 34 on Trail Ridge rd. to Milner Pass. Just before reaching the Poudre Lakes, take right-hand trail (keeping left) for 1½ mi. to Specimen Mt., numerous localities on W and S slopes—**allophane, calcite** (partly replaced by **chalcedony** and **opal**), **agate, geodes** (agate, green **chalcedony, onyx, opal, nontronite** or **chloropal**), **jasper nodules, rock crystal, topaz, tridymite.**

FORT COLLINS: (1) N 17 mi. to Owl Canyon Trading Post, turn onto side rd. S of the store (keep right) for 1.7 mi. to quarry in a gully—gem **alabaster, onyx marble, satin spar, selenite;** (2) W 15½ mi., the Wisdom Ranch prospect (S½ Sec. 5, T. 7 N, R. 74 W)—**graphic granite;** (3) WNW 33 mi., near line between Sec. 1 and 2, T. 8 N, R. 74 W, the Chaney-Sims beryl prospects——**beryl, graphic granite;** (4) W 45 mi., at Manhattan, then N 3–4 mi. on steep rd. off Rte. 14, placers—**gold.**

RED FEATHER LAKES (District), the Pennoyer Amethyst Mine—**amethyst, quartz crystals.**

LAS ANIMAS CO.

MODEL, NE .7 mi. on U.S. 350, turn E for 8 mi. toward Canyon Sta., exposure of the Van Bremmer dike, in veins and in septarian concretions—**calcite crystals** (some clear as **Iceland spar**), **fossils** (abundant cephalopods and ammonites).

TRINIDAD: (1) SE 34 mi., at Trinchera Mesa in Wet Mt. Valley, in coal seams—**jet;** (2) W 35 mi., at Monument Lake, area rd. cuts and stream gravels—green **jasper ("Stonewall jade").**

MESA CO.

AREA: (1) Black Ridge, fossil beds—**petrified dinosaur bone, gastroliths;** (2) Colorado R. Valley and side canyons W from GRAND JUNCTION to the Utah line—**agate, chalcedony, jasper, opal, opalized** and **jasperized wood, petrified dinosaur bone.**

CORTEZ, area of Goodman's Point—**petrified dinosaur bone.**

DELTA, E 15 mi., area—**alabaster.**

DELTA-WHITEWATER, area called the Indian Hunting Ground—**silicified wood** (black, gemmy).

FRUITA: (1) S 2 mi., area—**gastroliths, petrified dinosaur bone;** (2) S, in regional exposures of the Morrison formation (sandstones)—**petrified dinosaur bone** (especially of allosaurs and brontosaurs); (3) S 3 mi. on Rte. 340, cross the Colorado R., then W on gravel rd. to Opal ("Blue") Hill, on both sides E and W of the ½-mi.-long ridge—**opalized wood;** (4) W 4 mi., at Dinosaur Ridge, exposures of the Morrison formation—**petrified dinosaur**

bone (allosaurs, brontosaurs); (5) SE along Rim Rock Drive (toll, 22 mi. long), area outside the Colorado National Monument—**agate** (banded, moss), **aragonite, amethyst, petrified** and **agatized dinosaur bones, jaspers** (variously colored), **quartz (rock crystal,** milky), **opalized** and **silicified wood, thundereggs.**

GATEWAY: (1) S 3.9 mi. on the URAVAN hwy., cross Dolores R. to log building, in cliff next the rd. an old **barite** mine—**barite, banded alabaster;** (2) at mi. 6.1 S, turn right, a deposit in the Monkopi formation—**alabaster, gypsum** (sugary, banded, white).

GLADE PARK: (1) area, including Pinon Mesa—**opal, opalized wood;** (2) S 3½ mi. to region of Pinon Mesa (extends W into Utah, 40 mi. long by 10 mi. wide, as part of the Fruita division of the Grand Mesa National Forest), lower section—**agate** (banded, mossy, many colors); (3) 8.3 mi. out on main road crossing Pinon Mesa, past Mud Springs campground to area of Windy Point: (a) left "JS" rd. to North East Cr. and Johnson Cr. (on way to S rim of mesa)—**smoky chalcedony, jasper** (various colors), **petrified wood;** (b) right rd. No. 16.55, for 2 mi. toward Fruita Guard Sta., area—**desert rose-quartz** pseudomorphs after **barite.**

GRAND JUNCTION: (1) W 5 mi. on U.S. 6–50, then N toward Book Cliffs, area—**barite crystals, agatized dinosaur bone, uranium minerals;** (2) 13 mi. out on the Serpent's Trail (or 18 mi. from FRUITA via Rimrock Drive), area around Glade Park, *q.v.*—**opalized wood.**

WHITEWATER, SW 15 mi. on Rte. 141, to Unaweep, on East Cr. in Unaweep Canyon, area—**calcite, chalcopyrite,** some **fluorite** (with **pyrite**), **hematite** (conspicuous in places).

MINERAL CO.

CREEDE: (1) mining district on Willow Cr.—**amethyst** (massive crystals), **chalcedony, milky quartz, lead-silver minerals, sphalerite.** (All regional silver mines produce **amethyst** crystals and clusters on their dumps.) (2) N .8 mi., on left fork of West Willow Cr.: (a) bed of creek—**turquoise;** (b) the Commodore Mine—gem **amethyst, lead, "sowbelly" quartz, silver;** (2) W of West Willow Cr.: (a) the Amethyst Lode, numerous area mines—**agate, amethyst, anglesite, barite, cerussite, chalcopyrite, chlorite, galena, wire gold, goslarite, limonite, malachite, pyrite, native silver, sphalerite, thuringite, wad;** (b) gravels between Amethyst and Commodore mines—**turquoise;** (3) Holy Moses Mine—**massicot;** (4) King Solomon, Sunnyside mines (end of Rte. 149, alt. 9,000–11,000 ft.)—**lead-silver** veins, **argentiferous galena, gold, chalcopyrite, pyrite, pyrargyrite, sphalerite** (all in a gangue of **amethystine quartz, chlorite, barite,** and **fluorite**); (5) Ridge Mine—**sphalerite;** (6) Last Chance Mine—**turquoise.**

WAGON WHEEL GAP: (1) E 1.7 mi. via Wagon Wheel Ranch rd. across Rio Grande R. bridge to: (a) Wagon Wheel Gap Mine on E side of Goose Cr.—**barite, calcite, chalcedony, fluorite** (crystals, massive, clusters), **creedite, gearksutite, halloysite, quartz;** (b) ridge E of area hot springs—**barite crystals;** (2) Embargo mining district, area—**agate** (banded, moss), **chalcedony, jasper, quartz.**

WOLF CREEK PASS (SE corner of co., alt. 10,860 ft.): (1) along Wolf

Cr.—**agate, chalcedony, jasper, moonstone, quartz crystals, amethyst geodes, natrolite;** (2) summit of pass: (a) valley to right—**amethyst;** (b) Treasure Falls, in area of a cliff dipping to the left—gem **agate;** (c) gravels below rd.—**agate;** (3) W 6 mi. from summit, area—**agate, chalcedony, jasper, moonstone.**

MOFFAT CO.

AREA: (1) Green and Yampa R. breaks, gravels, etc.—**agate, carnelian, chalcedony, dinosaur bone** (agatized, carnelianized, jasperized), **jasper;** (2) S and E slopes of the Uinta Mts.: (a) hillside gravels along U.S. 40, and (b) N of U.S. 40 between the Utah line and Cross Mt. (15 mi. W of MAYBELL)—**agate, chalcedony, chert, flint, jasperized dinosaur bone, opal, agatized wood.**

CRAIG: (1) area exposures, abundant—**agate, chalcedony, jasper, petrified wood** (agatized, opalized), **dinosaur bone** (agatized, petrified); (2) SW 12 mi., at Round Bottom on N side of the Yampa R., area placer gravels—**gold;** (3) W 19 mi., at LAY on U.S. 40, with the latest operations 6–10 mi. N on Lay Cr., placers—**gold;** (4) N 35 mi., at Fourmile Cr. (and Timberlake Cr.), close to Rte. 13 with BAGGS, Wyo. 5 mi. to N, placer gravels covering the dry, rolling plain along W base of Elk Mts. in an area 30 by 40 mi.—**gold.** The **gold,** which can be winnowed from a dry-placer blower-type machine, is 885–935 fine, with about 600 colors approximating a value of one cent at $35 per troy oz. (5) W 80 mi. and within 5 mi. of U.S. 40, at Skull Cr. (and Blue Mt.), mines—**copper, vanadium.**

GREYSTONE, SW 10 mi., at Douglas Mt., mines—**chalcocite, copper,** some **galena** and **silver.**

MONTEZUMA CO.

AREA, exposures of McElmo Cr. Valley sandstones—**petrified dinosaur bone.**

MANCOS, E 8–14 mi., East Mancos R.: (1) area stream gravels, and (2) the Red Arrow Mine, placer and lode—**gold, silver.**

RICO, SW 15 mi., at Bear Cr.—**placer gold,** some **chalcocite** in ore bodies.

MONTROSE CO.

CIMMARON, E 1 mi., at Goat Hill No. 1 prospect—**graphic granite.**

NATURITA: (1) E 4 mi. on Rte. 145, turn right on Rte. 80 for 17.1 mi. to Basin Store, turn right at mi. 24.2 and proceed to old barn at mi. 26.2, area E of rd. across a cr. and summit of hill—gem **black agate.** The **agate** occurrences extend from PARADOX, *q.v.,* to LONE CONE (San Miguel Co.); (2) T. 46 N, R. 15 W, in sand and gravel bars on benches above the water level along the San Miguel and Uncompahgre rivers, placers—**gold.**

PARADOX (on Rte. 90), 6 mi. out at La Sal Cr. and about 100 mi. S of GRAND JUNCTION and 85 mi. W of MONTROSE, numerous mines—**chalcocite, native copper** and **silver, placer gold** in creeks.

UNCOMPAHGRE, area gravels—**bloodstone.**

URAVAN, SE 3 mi. on Rte. 141 to Tabequatche Cr., then E up cr. for 18 mi. to the Tabequatche Basin, an area noted for its conglomerate boulders on a bench on N side of the basin at a place known as the Copper King prospect, as impregnations in the boulders—**azurite.**

OTERO CO.

LA JUNTA, S, area surfaces on regional ranches—**jasperized dinosaur bone.**

OURAY CO.

MIDDLETON, the Ruby Mine—**huebernite.**

OURAY: (1) area of a radius of 10–15 mi., many old mines—**lead, gold, silver, copper, zinc, pyrite,** etc.; (2) just N, on E side of valley a few miles off U.S. 550 by steep grades to Uncompahgre (Upper Uncompahgre, Ouray), many mines operating in **magnetite-pyrite** ores—**copper, gold, pyrite** (containing **copper** and **gold**), **tellurides (gold, silver),** siliceous and baritic ores containing **lead, silver, zinc;** (3) gravels and banks of the Uncompahgre R.—**bloodstone, quartz geodes;**

(4) S 6 mi., the Treasury Tunnel (Idarado Mining Co.) near U.S. 550—**bismuth**-bearing minerals (e.g., **casolite**), **argentiferous gray copper, enargite, lead-zinc sulfides** (massive bodies), **polybasite, proustite, calcite crystals** (snowy, some fluorescent), **fluorite, quartz crystals** (clear, sugary, to 8 in. long); (5) WSW 8 mi. on Rte. 361, at Sneffels (Imogene Basin): (a) area mines—**argentite, argentiferous tetrahedrite, chalcopyrite, calcite, gold, galena, pyrite, rhodonite, rhodochrosite, sphalerite, silver** (native), **stephanite;** (b) Mt. Sneffels, area—**andradite garnet;** (6) S 12 mi., Red Mt. Pass (alt. 11,018 ft.), the Longfellow Mine—**chalcocite, colusite, enargite, tetrahedrite.**

TELLURIDE, W 7 mi., on Diamond Hill (via jeep rd.), abundant—**rock crystal.**

PARK CO.

AREA, South Park, near Grand R., area—**bloodstone, garnet.**

ALMA: (1) NE ¼ to ½ mi., on E side of the South Platte R., placers, as coarse nuggets to several oz.—**gold;** (2) NW 2–6 mi., in small veins in crystalline rocks—**gold, gold-silver, lead-silver, zinc;** (3) N 5–10 mi., the Consolidated Montgomery Mine, alt. 11,500–13,500 ft.—**gold, lead, silver, zinc,** etc.; (4) Sweethome Mine, in Buckskin Gulch—**rhodochrosite;** (5) area of Mosquito Cr. and its tributaries, alt. 10,500–12,500 ft., mines—**gold, galena, chalcopyrite, lead, pyrite, silver, sphalerite, zinc,** etc.

ANTERO JUNCTION, N .7 mi. on U.S. 285, crest of hill, area—**agate, jasper, travertine.**

BAILEY: (1) area of Beaver Cr., alt. 10,000–10,500 ft., placers in outwash gravels from Wisconsin Ice Age moraines from the South Platte glacier—

gold; (2) W 13–14 mi., area mines—**barite, bismuth, chalcopyrite, copper, gold, lead, silver, tetrahedrite, zinc.**

FAIRPLAY: (1) area SE of town, alt. 10,250–10,500 ft., in gravels of glacial outwash nature—**placer gold;** (2) NE 10 mi., Tarryall Cr. on E slope of Silverheels Mt. W of COMO, important placers extending several mi. SE of COMO—**gold;** (3) W by S 12 mi., Horseshoe, at head of Fourmile Cr., alt. 11,500–12,500 ft., in a glacial cirque—**lead-silver** ores with varying amounts of **copper, gold,** and **zinc;** (4) SW 12 mi. and N of Fourmile Cr., Sacramento, S of Mosquito Cr.—cf. (3); (5) SW, at Weston Pass (alt. 11,900 ft.), at crest of the Mosquito Range on boundary between Lake Co. and Park Co., alt. 11,400–12,500 ft., mines—**lead-silver minerals,** some **zinc.**

GARO, N 1 mi. on Rte. 24, field pits—**agate, chalcedony** (fluorescent), **uranium minerals.**

GRANT, N, at Geneva Cr. (Collier Mt.), head of W Geneva Cr. and continuous with the Montezuma District to NW in Summit Co., alt. 10,250–12,000 ft., area mines—**copper, gold, lead, silver.**

GUFFEY, SW 3 mi., at the Copper King prospect in Sec. 21, T. 15 S, R. 73 W—**graphic granite.**

HARTSEL: (1) area South Platte R. gravels—**agate, jasper;** (2) SE all along Rte. 9 toward GUFFEY, especially over the Agate Plateau—gem **agate, chalcedony, jasper,** etc.; (3) W 1½ mi. on U.S. 24 and Rte. 9, on hill beneath low cliffs—**agate** (various kinds), mammillary **chalcedony,** various **jaspers, petrified wood;** (4) SW 3.2 mi. on U.S. 24, the Hartsel Barite Mine —**barite crystals** (blue, to 5 in. by 2 in., also aggregates); (5) S 20 mi. on Rte. 9, the Meyers Ranch, in pegmatite—gem **rose quartz, beryl** (blue, yellow, to 10 in. across), **bismutite, beyerite, cordierite, columbite, feldspar (albite, microcline crystals** to 6 ft. long), **fluorapatite, garnets, mica (biotite, muscovite** books to 8 in. dia.), **tantalite** (crystals to 6 in. long), **black tourmaline;**

(6) E on U.S. 24 to summit of Wilkerson Pass (alt. 9,525 ft.): (a) area of campground—**galena, garnet, magnetite, scheelite, sphalerite, black tourmaline;** (b) E of pass .6 mi. toward LAKE GEORGE, area pegmatites—**beryl, epidote, feldspar, mica (biotite, muscovite), quartz crystals;** (c) E 2 mi. from pass, the abandoned St. Joe tunnel, and (d) ½ mi. still farther E, an old mine—**azurite, bornite, chalcopyrite, malachite, pyrite.**

LAKE GEORGE: (1) W 2.9 mi. on U.S. 24: (a) area mines—**idocrase, garnets, graphic granite, mica (biotite, muscovite), quartz;** (b) at mi. 6½, ghost town of Gold City, area mine dumps—**idocrase, garnet, hematite, molybdenite;** (2) W 3.1 mi. via U.S. 24 and Rte. 77 (toward TARRYALL): (a) area old prospects—**drusy quartz, quartz crystals** (to 2 in. dia.), **fluorite;** (b) at 3.4 mi., the Kyner Mine (abandoned)—**fluorite, quartz** (crystals, drusy); (c) at 5 mi., the Stevens Ranch (a well-known locality)—**amazonite, goethite, hematite** pseudomorphs after **siderite, smoky quartz;** (3) SW 9.7 mi., at Badger Flats: (a) the Boomer Mine (once the largest beryl producer in America)—**bertrandite, beryl, fluorite, galena, muscovite mica, quartz crystals, siderite, topaz;** (b) on the right, the Blue Jay Mine—**beryl, bertrandite, cassiterite, sericite, topaz, wolframite;**

(4) S 1.1 mi. on U.S. 24 and Eleven Mile Canyon Rd., exposure of the Teller Pegmatite, area pits—**allanite, astrophyllite, biotite mica, gadolinite, monazite, xenotime, yttrofluorite;** (5) W and S 15½ mi. via U.S. 24 and

Eleven Mile Canyon Rd., to Spruce Grove campground, area deposits—
**feldspar, hematite, mica (biotite, muscovite), rock crystal, smoky quartz,
topaz**(to 1 in. long).

PITKIN CO.

ASPEN: (1) area of Roaring Fork, including ASPEN, Richmond Hill,
Lenado, with principal mines located within 1 mi. of town of ASPEN,
e.g., the Mollie Gibson, Smuggler, etc.—**gold** (minor), **lead, silver** (massive, matted-wire), **pyrite** (rare), **zinc.** (ASPEN is noted for its rich **silver**
production, its mines at one time the greatest silver producers in the world,
totaling about $105 million.)
(2) N 10 mi., at Ashcroft, a ghost town on Castle Cr., mines—**lead-silver,**
some **zinc;** (3) SE 15 mi., at Lincoln Gulch, with mineralized area at
head of gulch and 10 mi. from Rte. 82 via poor rd., W side of Ruby Mt.,
vein—**galena, lead-silver, sphalerite** (abundant), occasional **molybdenite,**
iron-stained **pyritized rock.**

PROWERS CO.

LAMAR, S 18 mi., area along both sides of U.S. 287–385—**silicified wood.**

RIO GRANDE CO.

AREA, the Rio Grande R. sands and gravels—**agate, amethyst-**lined
geodes, jasper.
DEL NORTE: (1) W about 8 mi., Embargo Cr., mineralizations along cr.
extending a few mi. on either side of the Rio Grande-Saguache Co. line—
copper, gold, lead, silver; (2) NW 8.8 mi. (into Saguache Co.), park at
foot of Twin Mts., in Old Woman Cr., area at W edge of the San Luis Valley: (a) broad area around parking area—**agate** (banded, dendritic, gem
plume), **bloodstone, chalcedony** (blue, red, white), **chrysoprase, geodes,
jasperized lava,** "Monte Vista eggs" (nodules with green inclusions to 12 in.
dia.), **opal, petrified wood, quartz crystals, thundereggs;** (b) W of parking
area, on S slopes of Twin Mts.—white dendritic **opal.**
MONTE VISTA, SW 30 mi., to JASPER (Decatur), with prospects and mines
½ mi. W on Alamosa Cr.—**galena, gold, enargite, lead, lead-zinc minerals,
pyrite, silver, sphalerite.**
SUMMITVILLE (26 mi. SW of DEL NORTE), at head of Whightman Fork
tributary of Alamosa Cr., alt. 11,000–12,000 ft., mines—**covellite, cupriferous pyrite, enargite, gold.** (The known ore exposures and veins extend
throughout 1½ mi. N–S and about 1 mi. E–W on both sides of South Mt.)

ROUTT CO.

COLUMBINE (22 mi. N of STEAMBOAT SPRINGS), area old mines—**copper,
gold, lead, pyrite, silver,** etc.

HAHNS PEAK (town 4 mi. N of COLUMBINE): (1) area stream beds S of town—**placer gold;** (2) take rd. to Hahns Peak (mt.): (a) area slopes, and (b) summit, via 1½ -mi. trail—**quartz crystals.**

SAGUACHE CO.

AREA, extreme SW part of co., along Embargo Cr., cf. Rio Grande Co., DEL NORTE—**copper, gold, lead, silver.**

LA GARITA: (1) along La Garita Cr. in exposures of volcanic rocks—**agate, chalcedony;** (2) N 1 mi. to turnoff left to Crystal Hill Mine, area dumps and slopes—**quartz crystals (enhydros, rock crystal);** (3) S 2 mi., along edge of mts. to La Garita Cr., follow rd. upstream for 3–4 mi. into hills, all area slopes—**geodes.**

MOFFAT: (1) NE 10 mi. on Cotton Creek, at Blake (Mirage, Cotton Creek), at head of Cotton Cr. on W slopes of the Sangre de Cristo Range, many old mines—**copper, gold, lead, silver, zinc;** (2) E 15 mi., at CRESTONE (Baca Grant), in a band of Precambrian rocks 3–6 mi. wide, scattered occurrences and mines—**copper, gold, lead, silver.**

VILLA GROVE: (1) NW 8 mi., the Hall Mine—**lazulite, turquoise;** (2) W, toward Bonanza along Kerber Cr., in the Cochetopa Hills at NW end of the San Luis Valley, alt. 9,500–10,000 ft., area mines—**bornite, chalcopyrite, enargite, galena, pyrite, sphalerite, stromeyerite, tennantite** (in a gangue of **barite, calcite, quartz,** and **rhodochrosite**), some **bismuth (cosalite), gold, fluorite, tellurides** in some veins in N part of district.

SAN JUAN CO.

AREA: (1) dumps around Chattanooga and along Cement Cr.—**huebnerite;** (2) Engineer Mt., area—**jasper, obsidian** (green).

SILVERTON: (1) S 3 mi., at Molas Divide, area—**pyrolusite;** (2) W 3 mi., mines—**chalcopyrite, tetrahedrite,** etc.; (3) just NE on U.S. 550 (the "million-dollar highway"), at ANIMAS, and covering both sides of the Animas R.—**barite, chalcopyrite** (in **quartz**), **gold**-bearing **pyrite, huebnerite, "rusty" gold, lead, silver.** (The producing mines occur in a belt several mi. wide along the S rim of the SILVERTON caldera.) (4) NE 4 mi., the Senorita Mine—**azurite, malachite,** etc.; (5) N on U.S. 550 to the foot of Red Mt. Pass, area—**galena, pyrite, sphalerite;**

(6) HOWARDSVILLE quadrangle, the Ruby Mine, with turnoff at MIDDLETON —**huebnerite crystals, quartz crystals;** (7) N, at EUREKA (Cement Cr., Mineral Cr., Animas Forks): (a) area—cf. minerals under (3); (b) past EUREKA, the Sunnyside Mine (8.1 mi. NE of SILVERTON)—**albandite, alleghanyite, friedelite, helvite, rhodonite, rhodochrosite, tephroite,** various **sulfide** minerals **(copper, iron, lead, silver, zinc), gold;** (8) N 8 mi., Red Mts., area surfaces—**enargite, pyrite, quartz crystals;** (9) E 19 mi., mostly by trail, and 50 mi. W of CREEDE (Mineral Co.), at Bear Cr. in very rugged terrain —**gold, silver telluride** (possibly **petzite**).

SAN MIGUEL CO.

OPHIR, W, at Mt. Wilson (alt. 14,246 ft.), with the more important mines on the W slope of adjoining Wilson Peak (alt. 14,017 ft.), at head of Big Bear Cr.—**calcite, arsenopyrite, chalcopyrite, galena, molybdenite, sphalerite, stibnite, tetrahedrite, gold**-bearing paystreaks.

TELLURIDE: (1) E, to head of San Miguel R., at Upper San Miguel, alt. 10,000–12,000 ft., many old mines—**argentite, calcite, chalcopyrite, galena, gold, pyrite, rhodonite, rhodochrosite, silver;** (2) SW 9 mi., at Ames, mining area extending E for 6 mi. to Iron Springs—**gold**-bearing **quartz** and **pyrite, galena, molybdenite, sphalerite, tungsten;** (3) NW 14 mi., Lower San Miguel (PLACERVILLE, SAWPIT, NEWMIRE), area placers—**gold.** (The TELLURIDE area, particularly the city which is the county seat, during the nineteenth century was the liveliest **gold**-producing center in Colorado. Some active mining still goes on.)

SUMMIT CO.

AREA, near N co. line along Rte. 9, the Big Four Mine (16 mi. S of KREMMLING in Grand Co.)—**galena, sphalerite,** etc.

BRECKENRIDGE, E and NE in area of about 5 sq. mi., many old mines—**argentite, calcite, chalcopyrite, galena, gold, pyrite, rhodonite, rhodochrosite, silver.**

FRISCO (4 mi. SW of DILLON), area mine dumps—**galena, pyrite, quartz, siderite, sphalerite.**

KOKOMO (Tenmile, Robinson, 19 mi. NE of LEADVILLE in Lake Co.), with many mines along valley of Tenmile Cr. for 2–3 mi. NE and 5 mi. SW to Robinson—**barite, chalcopyrite, galena, marcasite, pyrite, pyrrhotite, sphalerite (marmatite), rhodonite, rhodochrosite.**

MONTEZUMA (Snake River, Peru), with mineralized area extending E 2–5 mi. to the Continental Divide, readily accessible, many old mine dumps —**bismuth sulfides, chalcopyrite, galena, gold, pyrite, silver sulfides, sphalerite, tennantite, tetrahedrite;** gangue minerals include **ankerite, barite, calcite, manganosiderite, quartz, sericite.**

TELLER CO.

CRIPPLE CREEK: (1) area mines—**calaverite, krennerite, gold** and **silver tellurides, turquoise;** (2) N of the co. hospital, on slopes of Mineral Hill— **gem minerals** (wide variety).

FLORISSANT: (1) just N of town, area—**amazonstone, smoky quartz crystals, topaz;** (2) N 2 mi., at (a) Crystal Peak (a 9-sq.-mi. region around the peak, showing hundreds of pegmatite exposures with many great and small mines, as well as adjacent areas of similar exposures in the Pikes Peak granite)—**amazonstone, beryl, cassiterite, columbite, feldspar, fluorite, goethite, hematite** (finest production in America), **limonite, muscovite mica, quartz** crystals, phenakite, pyrite, topaz; (b) ½ mi. NW of Crystal Peak, area—amazonstone, quartz crystals, topaz; (3) S 2.4 mi. via U.S. 24 and Rte. 143 toward CRIPPLE CREEK, entrance to Pike Petrified Forest (largest known petrified tree stumps, collecting inside boundaries prohibited), area outside park boundaries broad and productive, especially in rd. cuts and banks—gem-quality petrified wood.

GOLDFIELD, N, at Pikes Peak (alt. 14,110 ft.), regional granite outcrops covering some 1,000 sq. mi. in several counties are laced with pegmatite dikes containing a great many species of gems, crystals, minerals, e.g.—amazonstone, quartz crystals, topaz, tourmaline, etc.

WELD CO.

RAYMER (9 mi. W of STONEHAM), N 14 mi. on gravel rd. to old community of Kalouse, area—agate, jasper, petrified wood. (The gem-quality agate and jasper are considered the finest in Colorado.)

STONEHAM, E to jct. of Rtes. 14 and 71, take Rte. 14 for 1.1 mi., turn N at crest of hill and go 4.1 mi., turn right on ranch rd. toward "Chalk Bluffs," area of bluffs and badlands—barite crystals (best in America), barite roses, calcite crystals, fluorescent opal coating on some specimens.

YUMA CO.

AREA, SE corner, along the S Fork of the Republican R. (20 mi. N of BURLINGTON in Kit Carson Co.), broad area—agate, chalcedony, jasper, opal (mossy, opaque, white).

CONNECTICUT

This 60-by-95-mile state is about equally divided into three physiographic areas, offering the visitor a surprisingly varied topography. The eastern and western highlands are separated by the fertile Connecticut River Valley, composed mainly of Triassic black shale sediments; along both sides of the valley basalt sills outcrop prominently in vertical cliffs. The surface of the highlands is exceedingly rugged, showing very little level ground. The skyline presents a remarkably straight and nearly level horizon (an ancient eroded peneplain) with a few knolls exceeding 2,000 feet in elevation and culminating in the extreme northwest corner in Mount Bear, at 2,355 feet.

Numerous mines and quarries dot the Connecticut countryside. From them interesting minerals, some fossils, and not a few gemstones can be gathered. Indeed, the basalt sills yield gem-quality prehnite, while the many pegmatite exposures have long been mined for commercial minerals, although stone and clay are the state's chief mineral products.

For more detailed information, write: The Connecticut Geological and Natural History Survey, Trinity College, Hartford.

FAIRFIELD CO.

BRANCHVILLE: (1) area deposits and prospects—**uraninite;** (2) the Old Feldspar Quarry—**aventurine, beryl, columbite, mica** (curved), **spodumene (kunzite).**

BROOKFIELD, area deposits and mines—**calamine** (with **galena**), **cerussite** (on **galena**), **pyromorphite,** some **sphalerite.**

DANBURY, numerous area pegmatite outcrops—**graphite.**

GREENWICH, some area outcrops—**soapstone** (good for carving).

MONROE: (1) some area pegmatite outcrops—**tourmaline;** (2) Lane's Mine —**arsenopyrite, native bismuth, pyrite, sphalerite, wolframite.**

NEWTOWN, area outcrops—**pyrite.**

REDDING, area pegmatite outcrops—**graphite.**

TRUMBULL: (1) area exposures—**chalcopyrite, wolframite;** (2) the Long Hill tungsten mine (1 mi. S of RR station)—**calcite, fluorite** (used as a commercial flux), **pyrite cubes, scheelite,** blue **topaz crystals.**

WILTON, an area lead mine—**arsenopyrite, native bismuth, galena, pyrite, wolframite,** etc., in **quartz.**

HARTFORD CO.

BRISTOL: (1) area granite gneiss exposures—**chalcopyrite;** (2) Bristol Copper Mine—**bornite, chalcocite crystals** (excellent).

EAST GRANBY, at the Roncari Quarry—gem **datolite.**

FARMINGTON: (1) area land surfaces—**agate, prehnite;** (2) area rock exposures—**native copper.**

GLASTONBURY, area feldspar quarries—**columbite, feldspar.**

GRANBY, the Simsbury Mine—**chalcocite, cuprite, malachite.**

MERIDEN, NW 1½ mi., area quarries—**amethyst, quartz crystals.**

ROCKY HILL, area copper deposits and prospects—**azurite, bornite.**

SOUTH GLASTONBURY, in area pegmatite outcrops—**molybdenite.**

WINDSOR, area slate exposures—**pyrite.**

LITCHFIELD CO.

BARKHAMSTED, area outcrops—**actinolite, asbestos, soapstone.**

BRADLEYVILLE, at Prospect Hill—**chalcopyrite, pyrite, pyrrhotite.**

CORNWALL, W section, pegmatite outcrops—**graphite.**

LAKEVILLE, the Davis and Orehill mines—**limonite (bog iron ore).**

LITCHFIELD (and SOUTHBURY), area exposures of mica schists—**corundum, pyrite, staurolite (fairy crosses), talc.**

NEW HARTFORD, area deposits—**actinolite, asbestos.**

NEW MILFORD, N 13° W 5½ mi., the George Roebling or Merryall Mine —**aquamarine, golden beryl, biotite mica, feldspar, garnet, muscovite mica, black tourmaline.**

NEW PRESTON, area iron mines—**magnetite.**

ROXBURY, the Old Iron Mine at Mine Hill—**chalcopyrite, galena, pyrite cubes, pyrrhotite, quartz crystals, opalescent quartz, siderite, sphalerite.**

SALISBURY (and SHARON), large area deposits, mined—**bog iron ore, limonite.**

TORRINGTON (and WOODBURY), area basalt sills—**agate nodules, prehnite.**

WINSTED, area quarry—**bornite.**

WOLCOTT, area deposits—**bornite, chalcocite, malachite.**

MIDDLESEX CO.

CHATHAM, the old Cobalt-Nickel Mine, in small quantities—**arsenopyrite.**

EAST HAMPTON, SE 3½ mi., the Slocum Quarry—**golden beryl.**

HADDAM (TWP.): (1) area gneiss quarries—**molybdenite;** (2) area mines—**bismuthinite** (with some **chrysoberyl**), some **cassiterite crystals;** (3) 5 mi. SSE of MIDDLE HADDAM, the Gillette Quarry on E bank of the Connecticut R.—**aquamarine, beryl, chrysoberyl, garnet, quartz crystals, tourmaline;** (4) HADDAM NECK, area quarries—**cordierite, fluorite.**

MIDDLETOWN: (1) area mines—**galena, chalcopyrite, sphalerite;** (2) various area quarries, especially ½ mi. W of Benvenue at the Riverside Quarry on S bank of Connecticut R.—**aquamarine, beryl;** (3) at an old lead-silver mine—**fluorite, galena, native silver.** (These minerals are found at several localities and were mined for **lead** in Colonial and Revolutionary War times and, for a few years, before the Civil War for **silver.**)

PORTLAND: (1) S 1 mi. from the Portland Reservoir, the Pelton Quarry—**citrine, quartz (rose, smoky, rock crystal);** (2) NE 2½ mi., on W side of Collins Hill, near summit, the Andrews' and Strickland's quarries—**apatite, aquamarine, beryl, citrine, bismuthinite, columbite, morganite, quartz (rose, smoky), rock crystal, tourmaline, uraninite;** (3) the Walden Gem Mine—**pollucite.**

NEW HAVEN CO.

BETHANY, N part, outcrops—**graphite.**

CHESHIRE: (1) area Triassic sandstone exposures, and in small quantities in other formations—**barite;** (2) SE section—**chalcocite.** (The CHESHIRE barite was formerly mined to mix with white-lead paint.)

DERBY, area mines—**arsenopyrite.**

GUILFORD: (1) area around GUILFORD and EAST HAVEN—**agate;** (2) Hungry Horse Hill, outcrops—**iolite (cordierite).**

HAMDEN: (1) area Triassic sandstones or trap—**native copper;** (2) Mt. Carmel, mines—**bornite** (with **diabase**), **chalcocite.**

MADISON, NW, area mines—**magnetite.**

MILFORD, area quarries—**serpentine.**

ORANGE, around Lamberts Mine and in small quantities elsewhere—**chalcopyrite.**

OXFORD, area mines—**arsenopyrite.**

STONY CREEK, area quarries—**apatite, spodumene.**

NEW LONDON CO.

BRANDON, NEW LONDON, ONECO, area quarries—**apatite, spodumene.**
COLCHESTER, area iron mines—**bog iron ore.**
NORWICH, area outcrops—**corundum** (sparingly with **sillimanite**).

TOLLAND CO.

BOLTON, old area quarries in mica schist—**whetstone.**
HEBRON, area mines—**bog iron ore, limonite.**
STAFFORD: (1) area iron mines—**bog iron ore, limonite;** (2) area schist exposures—**quartz (crystals, rose), staurolite.**
TOLLAND, area exposures of schist—**quartz (crystals, rose), staurolite.**
VERNON, area exposures of mica schists—cf. TOLLAND.

WINDHAM CO.

ASHFORD, NW corner, a quarry—**graphite.**
WILLIMANTIC: (1) area iron mines—**bog iron ore, limonite;** (2) area pegmatite outcrops—**topaz.**

DELAWARE

Delaware lies within the province of the Atlantic Coastal Plain to the east of the Appalachian mountain system. The Fall Line, which marks the border between the upland Piedmont region and the Coastal Plain, passes through the northernmost part of the state just south of NEWARK. Along the Fall Line the gneisses and marbles of possibly Precambrian age disappear under the Cretaceous and younger sediments which blanket most of the state.

For more information, write: The Delaware Geological Survey, University of Delaware, Newark.

KENT CO.

EAST DOVER, area mined deposits—**bog iron ore (limonite).**

NEW CASTLE CO.

CHANDLERS HOLLOW, area outcrops, in small quantities—**corundum.**
NEWARK, at Chestnut Hill, a deposit—**limonite.**
WILMINGTON: (1) NE, in feldspar quarries—**asbestos, feldspar, serpentine;** (2) NW 6 mi., area—**serpentine.**

SUSSEX CO.

AREA, various deposits, some mined—**limonite, ocher.**
LAUREL, S 2 mi., at Little Creek—**bog iron ore.**

FLORIDA

Although Florida is a land of comparatively slight relief, its surface features range from the nearly level plain in the coastal region and the Everglades sea-level swamps to the deeply dissected uplands of the northern counties, a region of rolling, pine-clad hills. In this region much of the surface has been trenched by steep-walled valleys. The altitude of the entire subtropical peninsula varies from tidewater to about 200 feet at various points along the ridge which forms the central "backbone" and to about 300 feet near the northern boundaries of Gadsden, Walton, Santa Rosa, and Escambia counties. By contrast, the southern region comprises an area about 150 miles long by 100 miles wide, all with an altitude less than 50 feet above mean tide level.

For added information and an excellent guidebook, write: Florida Geological Survey, Box 631, Tallahassee.

ALACHUA, MARION, SUMTER COS.

AREA: (1) regional limestone quarries—**chert** (boulders, concretions); (2) regional road and RR cuts, building excavations, etc.—gemmy **chert, fossil ivory.**

BRADFORD CO.

LAWTEY, nearby at the Highland Mine—**ilmenite, zircon.**
STARKE, area, E. I. du Pont de Nemours and Co., Trail Ridge Plant—**staurolite.**

CITRUS CO.

AREA, the limonite quarries, road and RR cuts, excavations, etc.—**chert** (nodules, crystal-filled vugs), **fossil ivory.**
CRYSTAL RIVER, area limestone quarry seams and vugs—**calcite crystals** (clear, pale yellow), **drusy quartz, chert, fossils** (replacement by **calcite**).

DUVAL CO.

SOUTH JACKSONVILLE, the Skinner Mine—**ilmenite, rutile, zircon.**

GADSDEN CO.

AREA, along the Georgia line, many old fuller's-earth mines, in sandy strata—**silicified wood, fossils** (invertebrate shells, vertebrate bones).

JAMIESON, area NW, N, and NE, in fuller's-earth pits—**silicified wood, fossils.**

QUINCY-HAVANA, area fuller's-earth mines and pits: (1) 8 mi. N of QUINCY, and NE of the Willacoochee R. on E side of Rte. 65; (2) at the Georgia state line, Rte. 159 turns E toward JAMIESON, two mines; (3) at HAVANA, a N turn onto U.S. 27 leads to a fuller's-earth mine and plant—**silicified wood, fossils.**

HAMILTON CO.

JASPER, area phosphate pits—gem **coral** (fossil).

WHITE SPRINGS: (1) area phosphate pits—gem **fossil coral;** (2) Stephen Foster Memorial: (a) area—**silicified coral heads** (to 4 ft. dia.); (b) banks of the Suwannee R., beginning at the memorial and extending for some 12 mi. upstream—**coral heads** (agatized); (c) all tributary creeks of the Suwannee R. from the right side (fossiliferous formation is more than a mile wide)—**coral heads.**

HERNANDO CO.

BROOKSVILLE, area dragline operations, cuts, quarries, excavations, etc.—**calcite** (crystals, tiny stalactites and stalagmites), **echinoid geodes (crystal** interiors), **silicified coral** heads (golden **calcite** as petrifying agent).

HILLSBOROUGH CO.

TAMPA: (1) Ballast Point (and Davis Is.) area, in the City Park—gem **agatized corals (chalcedony** pseudomorphs as bottle-shaped, fans, finger, and branching coral types), carnelian-red **geodes** (also coral); these chalcedony replacements are variously colored, often contain sparkling **quartz crystals** or **opal,** etc.; (2) regional shores at low tide—**agatized coral:** (a) access via Bayshore Blvd., and (b) access via Interbay Blvd.—**coral, chalcedony enhydros, fossil shells** replaced by **chalcedony (carnelian, sardonyx, agate);** (3) N, along the Hillsborough R., banks and breaks—**brain coral, finger coral, agate.**

INDIAN RIVER CO.

AREA, the Florida Minerals Co. and Rutile Mining Co. (Jacksonville Mine)—**ilmenite, rutile, zircon.**

VERO BEACH, the Winter Beach Mine, Sec. 4, T. 32 S, R. 39 E, the Florida Minerals Co.—**zircon.**

JACKSON CO.

AREA: (1) many inactive quarries—**crystals, fossiliferous limestone;** (2) area streams and rivers, banks—**fossils, chertlike limestone;** (3) Crystal River Formation, area exposures—**chertlike limestone, crystal-lined vugs.**

COTTONDALE: (1) area streams and creeks, banks—red **fossiliferous chert;** (2) N 1 mi., a limestone quarry—polishable **limestone** (patterned with marine fossils).

MARIANNA, area limestone quarry—**crystals, gemmy limestone** (patterned with marine fossils).

LEE CO.

FT. MEYERS BEACH, area deposits around Estero Bay, used as mineral paint—**ochers.**

LEVY, LAFAYETTE, GILCHRIST, SUWANNEE COS.

AREA: (1) stream gravels, pits, quarries, excavations—gemmy **chert, agatized corals** (some as **geodes**), **silicified wood;** (2) exposures along the Suwannee R.—gemmy **silicified corals;** (3) Cross State Barge Canal, banks—**fossils, silicified coral.**

MANATEE-MARION COS.

AREA, old fuller's-earth pits—**silicified wood,** polishable **fossils.**

MANATEE-SARASOTA COS.

AREA, all along the Gulf beaches: (1) especially from TARPON SPRINGS to FORT MEYERS—**corals, shark teeth, fossils, sponges, manatee bone,** etc.; (2) Englewood Beach, one of the most productive areas—same materials.

PASCO CO.

AREA, banks of rivers and streams from Bailey's Bluff E to the Withlacoochee R. near DADE CITY—**silicified corals** (to 100 lbs.).

BAILEY'S BLUFF, area quarries, excavations, etc.—**silicified coral, chalcedony.**

NEW PORT RICHEY: (1) dredger tailings of the Flor-a-Mar, and (2) area quarries and excavations, abundant—**agatized corals** (rather cherty but polishable, in amber, blue, bone white, charcoal, gray, honey, peach colors), **chalcedony** pseudomorphs after **calcite** and **selenite, crystal-**lined **shell pseudomorphs, crystal-**lined **"sea-worm" tunnels.**

PINELLAS CO.

CLEARWATER, on several offshore islands—**silicified coral.**
DUNEDIN: (1) banks of the Caladesi Causeway—**chalcedony roses** (deep blue black); (2) W end, tidal exposures—**coral geodes.**

PINELLAS-HILLSBOROUGH COS. (N to Georgia line)

AREA: (1) all beaches, and (2) all regional excavations or dredging operations—**agate, carnelian, chalcedony, chert, fossil corals, chalcedony** replacements of **coral, chalcedonized marine invertebrates,** etc.

POLK CO.

AREA, phosphate quarries and pits, dredging operations, etc.—**gemmy fossils (mastodon ivory, silicified bones, shark teeth), gypsum, petrified wood, uranium minerals, vivianite.**
BARTOW: (1) SW corner of city limits, a phosphate mine; and (2) S, between Rte. 35 and the Peace R. and N of Ft. Meade, a phosphate mine—**gypsum, uranium minerals, vivianite.**
BRADLEY JCT., E and SE along rd. encircling Lake Hookers Prairie, phosphate mines—cf. AREA.
FORT MEADE, E 1½ mi. on N side of Rte. 630, a phosphate mine—cf. AREA.
LAKELAND: (1) E 2 mi., at Saddle Cr.: (a) a phosphate mine, and (b) 1 mi. S of the mine rd.—**gypsum, vivianite** (crystals, crusts), **uranium minerals;** (2) 2 mi. NE of Lake Parker between Rte. 33 and U.S. 92, a phosphate mine—see above; (3) NE 7 mi., area—**chalcedony, silicified coral.**
MULBERRY: (1) area phosphate mines—**gypsum, uranium minerals, vivianite** (crystals, crusts); (2) N side of Rte. 60 toward BARTOW, phosphate mines—cf. AREA.
PLANT CITY, S 1 mi. on Rte. 39, then 2 mi. E on a mine rd., a phosphate mine—**gypsum, uranium minerals, vivianite.**

ST. JOHNS CO.

AREA: (1) beaches—**"coquina rock"** (coquina shells and pieces cemented by **calcite**). (The first quarry in America was opened here by the Spanish to build Castillo de San Marcos in ST. AUGUSTINE, the oldest fort in the United States.) (2) In exposures from above ST. AUGUSTINE to below COCOA: (a) along the beaches, and (b) regional quarries—**"coquina rock."**

SUWANNEE CO.

DOWLING PARK, SE 5 mi., mine—**malachite.**

VOLUSIA CO.

SEVILLE, E 12 mi., and at several points on the Florida East Coast RR, in cuts—**limonite.**

WASHINGTON CO.

AREA, stream banks, rd. cuts, abandoned quarries—**chert, flint.**
CHIPLEY: (1) area fossiliferous limestone exposures, polishable—**chert-like limestone;** (2) sinkhole and rd. cuts—**calcite, chalk, chert;** (3) SW from Falling Water 1½ mi., on both sides of the rd.—**chert** (light blue, in seams and pockets); (4) S of the airport, in a RR cut—**calcite** (ivory color, fossiliferous).

GEORGIA

Georgia's nearly 59,000 square miles makes it the largest of the Atlantic seaboard states. It is situated at the southern end of the Appalachian chain of mountains. These ranges extend into the northeast corner where Brasstown Bald, a part of the Nantahala Mountains, achieves the highest elevation in the state of 4,784 feet.

Beginning in the northwest, where the Lookout and Sand mountains loom over rich agricultural valleys, Georgia easily divides into five major physiographic provinces, each one formed during different geologic ages and under varied conditions: the Cumberland Plateau, the Appalachian Valley, the Appalachian Mountains, the Piedmont Plain (occupying about 30 percent of the state), and the Atlantic Coastal Plain. Thus rocks of every geologic age are exposed somewhere over the state's varied surfaces. The upland northern counties are heavily forested with hardwoods, merging into other forests of stately pines on the Piedmont. Beneath the highland forests lie some of the oldest crystalline rocks in the East, both igneous and metamorphic, strongly mineralized and dotted with once-rich abandoned and some still-active mines.

Dividing the stratigraphically complicated Piedmont Plain from the coastal lowlands is the Atlantic Coast Fall Line, so named from the falls or rapids in rivers at places where they pass from the Piedmont crystalline rocks to the softer and less resistant formations of the Coastal Plain. This Fall Line extends southwesterly across the state roughly on a line connecting Augusta, Milledgeville, Macon, and Columbus.

The first real gold rush in America occurred in Georgia following two simultaneous discoveries of **gold** by Negro slaves in 1828, one on the Lovelady place near Loudsville in White County and the other on Bear

Creek near Dahlonega in adjoining Lumpkin County. Not only was placer and lode gold found in abundance here and elsewhere, but the early miners and prospectors panning the regional stream gravels discovered **diamonds,** the largest a pale yellow crystal of 4½ carats picked up near Morrow Station in Clayton County in 1887. Since then, many fine diamonds have been found and are still being occasionally washed out of gold pans. Many other gem crystal species occur in pegmatite exposures, such as **aquamarine, beryl,** some ruby-red **corundum, spodumene,** and **topaz.**

Georgia has been actively prospected for gold since colonial times, and the modern gold panner should concentrate his efforts in the known gold-bearing areas. Lode deposits usually consist of quartz veins in solid rock, while placer deposits occur in a great many regional streams. Much of the colors are "flour gold," too fine to be retained in any commercial operation. The two most important gold belts include (1) the Dahlonega Belt that extends from near Tallapoosa northeastward through Dahlonega County to Rabun County, and (2) the McDuffie County Belt, extending through portions of McDuffie, Warren, Wilcox, and Lincoln counties. In many places, but most notable in the lode gold districts, numerous other colorful minerals occur in association with **gold,** such as **chalcopyrite, galena, pyrite, pyrrhotite,** and some **sphalerite.**

For more detailed information, write: Department of Mines, Mining and Geology, 425 State Capitol Building, Atlanta.

BANKS CO.

MAYSVILLE, area gravels along adjoining co. line—**rock crystal.**

BARROW CO.

WINDER, along rd. to JEFFERSON and 1½ mi. inside the co. line in a hornblende-gneiss exposure—**beryl, black tourmaline.**

BARTOW CO.

AREA, Saltpeter Cave, as float—**jasper.**
CARTERSVILLE: (1) area **barite** pits—**barite, geodes, goethite, hematite, limonite, iron minerals;** (2) area mines, as important producers—**barite, manganese, ocher. Manganese** deposits have a wide geographic distribution in NW Georgia, but most important occurrences are in the vicinity of CARTERSVILLE and CAVE SPRINGS (NW Polk Co. and SW Floyd Co.). (3) E 1 mi., extending in a N–S trending belt about 8 mi. long and less than 2 mi. wide, with its S end W of EMERSON and about 2 mi. S of the Etowah R., many mines, prospects, and excavations—**ochers** (light to bright yellow, dark yellow).

EMERSON: (1) extensive area deposits (mined)—**barite, graphite;** (2) U.S. 41 bridge over the Etowah R., area **barite** pits—**barite, geodes** (crystallined).

KINGSTON, S, in area fields, streams, rd. cuts, etc.—**agate** (banded, various colors), **jasper.**

BURKE CO.

GIRARD, along the Ga. side of the S.C. border—**"Savannah River" agate, chalcedony, quartz gemstones, silicified oolite.**

CARROLL CO.

CARROLLTON: (1) E 1.3 mi., in gravels of the Tallapoosa R.—**rubies;** (2) E 1.3 mi. and just off Rte. 166, vein exposures—**asbestos, garnets, olivine crystals.**

VILLA RICA: (1) area, and (2) at Reid's Mt., extensive deposits—**pyrite.**

CATOOSA CO.

GRAYSVILLE, SE 1½ mi., in Knox dolomite exposed in an abandoned quarry—**barite, calcite, fluorite** (purple cubes), **galena.**

CHATTAHOOCHEE CO.

AREA: (1) stream gravels—gemmy **chert, quartz pebbles** (pastel colors), **petrified wood, pyrite;** (2) rd. cuts, banks, cliffs—**selenite crystals.**

COLUMBUS, SE section along Rte. 103 toward BUENA VISTA in Marion Co., area of Randall Cr. near FT. BENNING, as float over a broad area—**silicified wood.**

CUSSETA, NW 2 mi. on U.S. 27, a rd. cut—**selenite crystals,** decorative **fossil shark teeth.**

CHATTOOGA CO.

GORE, N 6 mi., along lower slopes of Taylor Ridge—**halloysite.**

SUMMERVILLE: (1) S 2½ mi. on U.S. 27: (a) along both sides of hwy.—**agate;** (b) quarry on W side of hwy.—**agate, chalcedony,** gemmy **chert, common opal;** (2) area of state fish hatchery on Cloudland Rd.—**agate** (cloudy, vivid red-banded); (3) W 3 mi. and 2 mi. N: (a) at the Marble Springs Quarry—gemmy **marble** (red and green); (b) E, in Taylor Ridge area—**agate;** (4) SE 3 mi., on left side of U.S. 27N, on the Roland Handcock farm, a pit—gemmy **chert.**

CHEROKEE CO.

BALL GROUND: (1) area: (a) local deposits—**talc;** (b) S and W of town, area fields, etc.—**staurolites;** (c) numerous area mines—**kyanite;** (d) the Bennett, Chapman, and Hendrix mica mines—**aquamarine, beryl, amethyst, garnet, smoky quartz crystals, black tourmaline,** etc. (the accessory minerals of all area mica mines include **almandite garnet, feldspar, black tourmaline,** etc.); (e) the Alexander and Cooley mines—opaque **beryl;** (f) between town and CANTON, area—**almandite garnet;** (g) Harmony Church, area pegmatite outcrops—**beryl;** (h) Hickory Flat, 2 mi. NE on rd. to ORANGE—**corundum;**
(2) 1 mi. W of Fairview Church, on E side of Sharp Mt., area—**staurolite;** (3) NE 2½ mi.: (a) the Cochran Mica Mine (1 mi. from the Cherry Grove School)—**agate, aquamarine, beryl** (yellow green), **rutilated quartz crystals;** (b) 1 mi. W of the school, exposed pegmatites—**rutilated quartz crystals;** (4) SW 3½ mi., near Four Mile Church and Shiloh Church, mines —**kyanite;** (5) W 4½ mi., on N side of Bluff Cr., along Rte. 1—**staurolite;** (6) SE 7 mi., on the Etowah R., at the Creighton-Franklin Mine—**gold.** (This mine was at one time the most extensive gold producer in Georgia.)

CHEROKEE-PICKENS COS.

NELSON (Pickens Co.), a 300-sq.-mi. region surrounding this town contains many pegmatite dike mines—**mica minerals, quartz crystals, aquamarine, beryl, black tourmaline,** etc. The most productive mining districts surround the communities of HOLLY SPRINGS, TOONIGH, WOODSTOCK, CUMMING, ARNOLD, ORANGE, CANTON, NELSON, BALL GROUND, CENTERVILLE, JASPER, TATE, BETHANY CHURCH, DUG GAP, FEDERAL SCHOOL, MARBLE HILL, DAWSONVILLE, and HOLCOMB P.O.

CLARKE CO.

AREA, many old mines and prospects—gemmy **blue quartz.**
ATHENS, along Alps Rd. across from the airport, in a field—gem lime-green **beryl, quartz crystals.**

CLAYTON CO.

MORROW (13 mi. S of ATLANTA, co. seat of Fulton Co.): (1) creek beds—**diamond;** (2) the Laurel Creek Mine—**aquamarine, beryl, corundum** (red).

COBB CO.

BELMONT HILLS, on SMYRNA-BELMONT HILLS rd. ½ mi. out of BELMONT, turn E for ½ mi. on dirt rd., in quartz exposures—**quartz** (translucent-rose, milky).

MARIETTA, area near the National Cemetery—**banded agate, mossy chalcedony, kyanite, jasper.**
POWDER SPRINGS, S 2 mi., outcrop—**corundum.**

CRISP CO.

CORDELE, area fields, cut banks, etc.—**moss agate, jasp-agate, jasper.**

DADE CO.

RISING FAWN, S 1 mi., on E slope of hill—**halloysite.**

DE KALB CO.

ATLANTA, Emory University, area pegmatite outcrops—**quartz crystals** (clear, smoky).
BARNESVILLE, THOMASTON, area mica mines—many **gemmy minerals.**
BERMUDA, Rockbridge Rd. to Macedonia Church (near Stone Mt.), area —**quartz crystals.**
LITHONIA: (1) area quarries—**calcite, epidote, fluorite, garnet, thulite, tourmaline, zoisite;** (2) Rock Chapel Quarry—cf. area quarries; (3) N side of Arabia Mt.—**quartz crystals, tourmaline,** etc.; (4) Flat Rock Quarry— **hyalite opal;** (5) Lithonia High School, N 60° W 1 mi. and 1 mi. NW of the COVINGTON hwy. on the Philips rd., a pegmatite—green **muscovite** (containing small **garnets), feldspar, quartz.**
STONE MOUNTAIN: (1) two area granite quarries—**beryl, feldspar, hyalite opal;** (2) area granite outcrops, in joints—**uranophane** (thinly coated with **hyalite opal**).

DODGE CO.

DUBOIS, EMPIRE, JAY BIRD SPRINGS, PLAINFIELD, Miocene exposures in all regional fields—**tektites** (translucent, bottle green).

ELBERT CO.

AREA: (1) Rock Branch Church, old **mica** mine—**beryl;** (2) Harmony Church, area—**aquamarine;** (3) Broad River pegmatite exposures—**sillimanite.**
DEWEY ROSE, at Antioch Hill, exposures—**aquamarine, rock crystal, amethysts.**
ELBERTON: (1) area **sillimanite** mines—**muscovite mica, sillimanite.** Mica-bearing pegmatites occur in Carolina gneiss between ELBERTON and HARTWELL in Hart Co. The known **mica** district includes some 250 sq. mi., with most mining revolving around the old Chapman Mine in Elbert Co. Similar mines occur also in Madison Co. (2) N 10 mi., on N side of Cold Water Cr.:

(a) the Chapman Mica Mine—**aquamarine, garnet, quartz crystals, tourmaline;** (b) the nearby Alexander Mine—**beryl.**

OGLESBY, 3 mi. distant on N side of the Little Broad R., the Yellow Mine —**amethyst, beryl,** etc.

FANNIN CO.

AREA: (1) stream beds, loose soil of fields, schist exposures, rd. cuts and banks, etc.—**staurolites;** (2) extreme N part of co., a short distance from the famed DUCKTOWN copper mining district of Tennessee (Polk Co.), *q.v.,* area—**copper minerals.**

BLUE RIDGE: (1) take COPPERHILL Rd. 1.6 mi. to a sawmill, turn left for 1 mi. on a dirt rd. to Hackney farm—**staurolites;** (2) SW 4 mi., at the Bailey farm, area exposures—**kyanite;** (3) W of Cole's Crossing—**staurolite.**

MINERAL BLUFF: (1) cross RR on Murphy Rd. to COPPERHILL, along sides of rd. and adjoining forest—**staurolite;** (2) NW, at Windy Bluff, area— **staurolite;** (3) ½ mi. SE of UNION, from where a schist outcrop crosses Mill Cr.—**staurolite;** (4) 1½ mi. NW of Hogback Mt., on the Thomas farm— **kyanite crystals, quartz crystals;** (5) S ½ mi., exposure—**talc.**

FAYETTE CO.

FAYETTEVILLE, on the Homer Kellin farm (make local inquiry), loose in field soil—**gem amethysts** (some rutilated), **rutilated quartz.**

FLOYD CO.

HERMITAGE, E of Hermitage Jct. on Rte. 53 6 mi. (NE toward CALHOUN in Gordon Co.), turn E at jct., many area mines—**bauxite, chert, jasper, lignite, marcasite.** (This is the locality where **bauxite** was first discovered in America, in 1887.)

ROME: (1) W on Rte. 20 to the Rice Springs Farms, area—**botryoidal chalcedony, geodes** (lined with **quartz crystals** or **botryoidal chalcedony**), **rose quartz,** etc.; (2) at the Ledbetter Quarry—**calcite crystals** (**pyrite** inclusions).

FORSYTH CO.

CUMMING: (1) area stream beds—**ruby;** (2) E 2 mi., a small placer ground—**gold.**

OSCARVILLE: (1) area rd. cuts, pegmatite outcrops—**beryl,** etc.; (2) N side of SILVER SHOALS–OSCARVILLE rd. and E of jct. with rd. to Four Mile Church—**beryl, pegmatite gemstones.**

SHELTONVILLE, area pegmatite outcrops—**amethyst, beryl, quartz** (clear, smoky).

SUGAR HILL, the Simmons Mine—**gold.**

FRANKLIN CO.

LAVONIA, area prospects and narrow lensy **mica** pegmatites crossing the LAVONIA-ROYSTON rd. between LAVONIA and BOWERSVILLE—**muscovite mica** (dark green), **galena, quartz.**

FULTON CO.

BIRMINGHAM, area of N part of co. (old Milton Co.), many narrow pegmatite exposures—**muscovite mica.** (Many beginners in geology from ATLANTA have had their first field experiences in this district, even though no actual mining was ever done.)

GORDON CO.

AREA, the Piedmont Mine, abundant sources—**argentiferous galena.**

RANGER, the Black Marble Quarry on U.S. 411—**calcite,** green **fluorite, pyrite, serpentine, talc.**

HABERSHAM (and RABUN) COS.

AREA: (1) Alec Mt., mines in decomposed schists—**corundum, garnet;** (2) Piedmont Orchard—**margarite, ruby** (brilliantly fluorescent).

CLARKSVILLE: (1) area mines—**xenotime;** (2) S of the North Georgia Vocational School, in fields and woodlands leading to the Soque R.—**kyanite;** (3) E ½ mi., stream gravels and banks, veins—**kyanite;** (4) NE of the school on E side of the Soque R., in **biotite-quartzite** pegmatite—**kyanite crystals;** (5) W 2 mi., area—**banded agate, chalcedony, jasper;** (6) N, in U-shaped belt about 30 mi. long and from 100 ft. to ¼ mi. wide, most important area in Georgia for mining purposes—**kyanite.** (Veins and lenses of coarsely bladed **kyanite** occur in **mica** schists, locally associated with **quartz** lenses and boulders of **kyanite.**)

DEEP CREEK, STONEPILE CHURCH, TURNERVILLE, WOODLANDS, many regional vein pegmatite exposures and mines—**kyanite.**

HALL CO.

GAINESVILLE: (1) area: (a) exposures along the Chattahoochee Ridge—**itacolumite** (flexible sandstone); (b) Glade Cr., gravels—**diamond;** (2) regional creeks emptying into the Chattahoochee R., many prospects and placers—**gold;** (3) W 1 mi., in stream bed—**corundum;** (4) NW 1½ mi. via Grape St., the Old Hope or Merck Mine, as good specimens—**muscovite mica, feldspar, smoky quartz.**

LULA, E 4½ mi. into Banks Co., on the Thurmond Standridge farm, a deposit—**kyanite crystals, sericite, vermiculite.**

HANCOCK CO.

Sparta: (1) area fields, rd. banks, etc., as float—**carnelian, chalcedony, jasper;** (2) W, along shores of the Sinclair Reservoir—**quartz gemstones.**

HARALSON CO.

Draketown, NW 4 mi., at the Waldrop Copper Mine near the Polk Co. line—**copper minerals, pyrite.** (This **copper** district also includes the counties of Lincoln, Lumpkin, and Fulton.)

HART CO.

Area, the old Water Hole Mine at Cross Roads—gem **beryl.**
Bowersville, area schist outcrops—**sillimanite.**
Hartwell: (1) area **mica** mines—associative **gems, minerals;** (2) a quarry near the Hartwell Dam—gem **beryl, garnet, microcline** (gemmy), **moonstone spar;** (3) SW 6 mi., at headwaters of Coldwater Cr., as crystals in **biotite gneiss—sillimanite.**

HENRY CO.

McDonough, N 6 mi. (5 mi. S 25° E of Stockbridge), just N of the Stockbridge-Millers Mill rd. and 1 mi. W of Millers Mill, a pegmatite mine —**muscovite mica, pegmatite gems, minerals,** etc.

IRWIN CO.

Area, regional farm field exposures of Miocene rocks, especially around Osierfield—gemmy **tektites.**

JACKSON CO.

Commerce: (1) area: (a) hard-rock exposures—green **epidote;** (b) Double Top Mt.; and (c) Sugar Loaf Mt., area—**rhodolite garnet;** (2) on the J. T. Cheatham farm—gem **beryl;** (3) NE on Rte. 59 and 5 mi. E of co. line—gem **beryl.**
Jefferson, E 5 mi. on the Brockton rd., pegmatites: (1) near the Harris School—gem **beryl, smoky quartz;** (2) the Venable farm across rd. from the school; (3) N of the school, at the Potts farm; (4) E of the school, the Webb farm—gem **beryl, mica, quartz crystals,** etc.
Nicholson: (1) several area pegmatite exposures—gem **beryl;** (2) W side of U.S. 441 toward Commerce, in pegmatite exposure—gem **aquamarine.**

JASPER CO.

AREA, all plowed fields throughout co.—**beryl, quartz** (blue, smoky).

HILLSBORO: (1) area rd. cut (well known to gem collectors)—**amethyst, quartz crystals** (blue, asteriated, rose, smoky, clear), **mica, vermiculite;** (2) E 3 mi. on unpaved rd., the Barron Fullerton Hospital, area—**amethyst, quartz crystals** (all kinds).

KELLY, NE 1½ mi., in kaolinized pegmatite, in **mica** schist—**"rum" mica.** (**Mica** pegmatites are rather common in this co., where they frequently intrude **hornblende gneiss** and other basic rocks. Considerable **vermiculite** is produced locally, with some pegmatites containing this mineral in sheets.)

MONTICELLO: (1) S along Rte. 83, area plowed fields—**gem crystals;** (2) fields along rd. to HILLSBORO—**beryl, quartz crystals** (blue, smoky); (3) in dumps of 13 area mines—**amazonite, garnet, mica, graphic granite.**

JONES CO.

ROUND OAK, area—**agate, jasper, petrified wood.**

LAMAR CO.

AREA, old mines and prospects (many)—**mica** ("rum," scrap), **feldspar crystals, white quartz** (containing impressions of **mica** books).

BARNESVILLE: (1) an old **mica** mine—blue **beryl crystals, mica;** (2) SE 5 mi., in area soils—**apatite, garnet, mica, quartz;** (3) E 7 mi. and .8 mi. N of the FORSYTH (Monroe Co.) hwy., an old mine shaft in a pegmatite— **"rum" mica;** (4) S 80° E 7 mi. and 1½ mi. due S of the FORSYTH hwy. at the point where it crosses the co. line—scrap **mica, white quartz** (containing impressions of **mica** books), some **feldspar crystals.**

MILNER: (1) 1 mi. W of the BARNESVILLE-GRIFFIN (Spalding Co.) hwy., and (2) ¾ mi. SW of the Lighthouse, pegmatites—**mica** books, **quartz** (milky, smoky).

RAMAH CHURCH, W ½ mi., near the Early-Vaughn Mine, pegmatite outcrop—**aquamarine, golden beryl, mica, quartz, spar.**

LINCOLN CO.

LINCOLNTON, W 6 mi. on Rte. 378 to Graves Mt.: (1) on N side, a mine of the Aluminum Silicates Corp., fee—**lazulite crystals,** gem **rutile** (deep red), **pyrophyllite crystals;** (2) Paschal and Phelps mines, abundant specimens—**galena;** (3) base of mt. at picnic ground 1 mi. E of Washington Co. line, take footpath to saddle and top of mt., area—**gem crystals.**

LUMPKIN CO.

AREA, stream gravels, from placers—**gold.** (Total yield of **gold** has exceeded $40 million.)

AURARIA: (1) S 2 mi., stream gravels of Baggs Branch, placers—**gold;** (2) W, at: (a) Battle Branch Mine—**galena, native gold;** (b) McKlusky Cr., the Topabri Mine close to the Etowah R.—**gold, pyrite.**

DAHLONEGA (gold mining center): (1) many area mines—**gold;** (2) area placer claims (fee to collectors)—**gold, gem crystals;** (3) E, the Lockhart Mine on Yahoola Cr.—**garnet, gold;** (4) S 3 mi., Turkey Hill (original **gold** discovery site), many area mines and prospects—**garnet, gold, ruby, staurolite, tourmaline, zircon;** (5) SE, at jct. of Long Branch with the Chestatee R., the Long Branch Mine—**gold;** (6) SE, in bottom of the Barlow Cut, the Barlow Mine (largest of the old saprolite workings in the district—**gold sulfides.** (The term *saprolite* means "weathered rock in place"; such deposits characterize the Piedmont region of the southern Appalachians and should be distinguished from lode deposits. Saprolitic rock is part of the zone of oxidation, exposed to hydration, and passes in depths into unaltered hard rock, sometimes not until depths of 100 ft. The difficulty in saprolite mining is the recovery of the very fine **gold** disseminated throughout the weathered clay. Lumpkin Co. has produced many millions of dollars in saprolitic gold, and deep open cuts scar the hillsides in many areas.)

(7) NE several mi., the McDonald Mine—**gold, pyrite;** (8) NE 9½ mi., the Williams Mica Mine (2½ mi. SW of Ward Gap)—colorless **topaz.**

PORTER SPRINGS, SE 1 mi., exposure—**corundum.**

LUMPKIN, UNION, FANNIN, TOWNS COS.

Many **mica** mines occur in these counties, primarily along the Blue Ridge crest near the Lumpkin-Union co. line. The mining section extends into the N part of Union Co. and the S and E portions of Fannin Co. A total area of about 400 sq. mi. is involved, and nearly all mines (which are locatable on topographic maps) can easily be reached by automobile.

MADISON CO.

AREA, see ELBERTON in Elbert Co. Numerous scattered mines containing the gems and minerals described.

McDUFFIE CO.

THOMSON: (1) area old mines, such as the Columbia, Park, Hamilton, Seminole or McGruber, and others; and (2) NW 12 mi., adjacent to the Little R., a **quartz** mine—**gold.**

MERIWETHER CO.

FEDERAL SCHOOL, SW ¾ mi., the Bozeman Mica Mine—**beryl crystals, mica.**

GREENVILLE, N 40° W 6 mi. (12 mi. SE of HOGANSVILLE in Troup Co.), mines—**muscovite mica.**

MASSINGALE, ½ mi. distant at the Stozier farm, in pegmatite—**aquamarine, common beryl.**

WARM SPRINGS, 1 mi. out of town along RR, area—**agate, chert, jaspagate, common opal.**

WOODBURY, W 5 mi. and 3–4 mi. due W of Cane Cr. Church—**muscovite mica.**

MONROE CO.

CULLODEN: (1) area mines and prospects, numerous—**mica;** (2) N 4 air mi. and 1 mi. S of Monroe-Lamar Co. line, pegmatite site of extensive **mica** mining in large open cut, with many other area cuts and old pits— **mica (muscovite, biotite), feldspar, quartz;** (3) N 4½ air mi., near co. line, pegmatite—**feldspar, mica, quartz** (milky, smoky).

FORSYTH: (1) area mines and prospects, and (2) S 47° W 7¼ air mi. (9 mi. by rd.) and 3 mi. SW of BRENT, the Peters Mine—**biotite** and **muscovite mica** (both minerals as large books), **feldspar, rose quartz.**

JULIETTE, many area pegmatite mines and prospects—**feldspar, mica (biotite, muscovite), quartz** (milky, smoky).

MORGAN CO.

APALACHEE, W, near Adair Plantation, outcrop—**aquamarine.**

BETHANY (CHURCH), SE 1 mi., the Denson Mica Mines near Rock Cr.— gem **beryl, muscovite mica.**

BUCKHEAD: (1) area farm of Benny Ray, in cavities in massive **quartz** vein—**amethyst;** (2) E 2 mi., area exposure—**amethyst, quartz crystal.**

MADISON: (1) NE 1½ mi., mine—**mica;** (2) area toward RUTLEDGE: (a) Hard Labor Cr., in drainage area and tributary creeks—**corundum, rutile, pink sapphire, spinel;** (b) 1.6 mi. SW of Talking Rock, in **mica** prospect—**beryl;** (c) gravels of confluence of Little R. and Shoal Cr.— **corundum.**

MURRAY CO.

AREA, stream beds and banks, fields, rd. cuts, etc.—**quartz gemstones.**

CHATSWORTH, 3 mi. distant at Fort and Cahutta Mts., deposits—**talc.**

ETON, area mines—**barite, talc.**

HOOKER SCHOOL, N on dirt rd. to Fincher Bluff—**silicified oolite.**

SPRING PLACE, area rd. cuts along Rte. 225 to the S—**agate, chalcedony, silicified oolite.**

MUSCOGEE CO.

AREA, gravels along the Chattahoochee R. and its tributaries—**chalcedony** (variously colored), **chert, flint, jasper, common opal, opalized wood** (in brilliant colors) etc.

COLUMBUS, E 10 mi. via Rte. 103 to Randall Cr., turn right on dirt rd. to a sandpit—**quartz gemstones** (as for AREA).

PAULDING CO.

AREA, 5.2 mi. E of the New Georgia Church, several granite pegmatite outcrops—pink **feldspar, scrap mica** books.

DALLAS: (1) from W of Rte. 92 just NE of town, an area of many **corundum** mines extending S to BROWNSVILLE—**corundum** (blue, gray, lavender, deep red); (2) SE 6 mi., loose in soil—**almandite garnets;** (3) SW to within 2½ mi. of the Carroll Co. line and 3½ mi. SE of Rose's Store (old Embry), near headwaters of Turkey Cr., area of active mining around 1914, many old mines—**corundum, "rum" mica** (containing **biotite** specks); (4) N on Rte. 61 (halfway to CARTERSVILLE in Bartow Co.), at Burt Hickory Ridge, placers —**gold.**

HIRAM: (1) the Little Bob Copper Mine—**almandite garnet, azurite, garnet** pseudomorphs, **limonite, malachite, pyrite;** (2) at nearby Garnet Hill, area—**gem garnets.**

PICKENS CO.

AREA, Sharptop Mt., exposures—**kyanite.**

JASPER, S 2½ mi. to Harmony School and halfway to Refuge Church— **kyanite.**

TATE: (1) area quarries in the TATE-Marble Hill district—**almandite garnet, kyanite,** gemmy **marble** (with **pyrite** inclusions), **mica, staurolites;** (2) immediately S, at jct. of Rtes. 5 and 143, a nearby outcrop—**beryl, feldspar, rutile, smoky quartz;** (3) SW 1 mi., the Holly Springs Quarry, in area forest—**apatite, magnetite,** green **talc, verde antique;** (4) E 2 mi., as boulders or massively in **mica** schist—**kyanite;** (5) E 2½ mi., residual boulders—**kyanite;** (6) W 4 mi.: (a) the Cook Farm, outcrop—**beryl;** (b) the Denson Mica Mine—**aquamarine, mica;** (7) SE 2 mi., as buttonlike lenses—**kyanite.**

POLK CO.

AREA, including much of Date, Walker, Chattooga, and Catoosa counties for a distance of approximately 175 mi., as unusually rich deposits and outcrops, especially in the Red Mt. formation series—**limonite, fossil iron ore.**

CEDARTOWN, area iron mines—**rhodochrosite.**

RABUN CO.

AREA: (1) many regional old mines—**gold, quartz crystals, beryl,** etc.; (2) extreme NE part of co., the Laurel Creek Mine—**corundum.** (This mine has been the chief source of **corundum** in Ga. for many years, although the mineral is found in many of the northern counties.)

CLAYTON: (1) many area old mines—**mica, beryl, quartz;** (2) SE 4 mi., area of Germany Mt.—**amethyst** (gem quality); (3) E 7 mi. and S of War Woman Dell, the Becky Beryl Mine—**beryl** (as large flawed crystals in pegmatite, with clear portions suitable for cutting); (4) SW 7½ mi., old **mica** mine on Dicks Cr. rd.—**beryl, mica.**

RABUN GAP: (1) the Kell Mica Mine—asteriated **quartz crystals;** (2) N 1 mi., along Black Cr.—gem **amethysts.**

TALLULA FALLS, area creeks—**quartz crystals (citrine,** clear, smoky).

ROCKDALE CO.

MAGNET, NW 2 mi. and 1 mi. N of the South Ocmulgee R., in a pegmatite —weathered **sulfides, muscovite mica, feldspar, milky quartz.**

SPALDING CO.

GRIFFIN, SW 2½ mi., rock outcrops—gem **beryl, quartz crystals, tourmaline.**

VAUGHN, N 2 mi. and slightly W: (1) in fields of the J. T. Allen farm— gem **beryl, rose quartz, black tourmaline;** (2) along both sides of the rd.— same minerals.

TOWNS CO.

AREA: (1) extending into Clay Co., N.C., a region of **mica** schist exposures reaching from (a) Winchester Cr. valley, along rd. as loose crystals— **sillimanite,** blue-bladed **kyanite;** (b) across Hunter Knob, NE side, a 100-ft. zone—**graphite, muscovite mica, quartz crystals, sillimanite;** (c) through the Brasstown Church section (church yard and area rd. cuts to NE, numerous zones)—**sillimanite,** locally associated with **kyanite, biotite,** and **muscovite mica;** (d) along Brasstown Cr., extending to Brasstown Bald—**corundum, sillimanite** (in pegmatite outcrops); (e) along an abandoned hwy. to SW of Brasstown Cr., zone of schist 30–35 ft. thick—**sillimanite, sericite** (as alteration mineral). (This mineralized zone extends to TUSQUITEE, Clay Co., N.C.) (2) Regional stream beds, banks, adjoining fields and hillsides—gem **amethyst;** (3) many regional old mines and prospects along the Appalachian Trail—**corundum, sillimanite.**

HIAWASSEE: (1) at Charlie's Cr., in banks and gravels—gem **amethyst;** (2) area of Hog Cr., disseminated in minute crystals—**chromite** in **chrysolite;** (3) SW 2 mi., the Hog Creek Mine—gem **rubies;** (4) W for several mi., as linings in rock cavities of exposures—**rhodochrosite;** (5) Lake Chatuge (reached via Hwy. 76 or side rds. E from Rte. 69): (a) beach gravels— **corundum, garnet, kyanite, quartz crystals, rutile;** (b) Elf, area around Mt. Pleasant Baptist Church—**corundum.**

TROUP CO.

LA GRANGE: (1) area: (a) pegmatite outcrops near La Grange Airport— **aquamarine, beryl** (blue, opaque), **quartz** (milky, rose), **black tourmaline;**

(b) along the Young's Mill rd., a pegmatite exposure—**beryl, quartz crystals;**
(c) N along U.S. 27 a short distance, on both sides of rd.—**gem beryl;**
(2) N 1 mi. from town square, prospects in pegmatite—green **muscovite mica** books (containing numerous **garnets**), **smoky quartz** (crystals, nodules);
(3) S on Rte. 219 to Cleveland Crossroads, the famed Big Beryl Mine (formerly the Hog Mine)—**amethyst, aquamarine, beryl** (crystals to more than 60 lbs.), **garnet, mica, quartz** (rose, rutilated), **black tourmaline,** etc.;
(4) S 8 mi. to Smith's Store: (a) S 100 yds. on W side of Rte. 219, the Stevens place reveals a pegmatite outcrop—**gem beryl;** (b) W .6 mi., on N side of dirt rd. to Grady Hill School, a peculiar pegmatite outcrop— **feldspar, mica (biotite, muscovite), quartz** (rose, smoky), **tourmaline;** (c) S 1 mi. from Smith's Store and Hardins Crossroads, on W side of Rte. 219 in a pegmatite—**aquamarine, beryl,** green **muscovite mica, quartz** (smoky, rose), **black tourmaline;** (5) SW 10 mi. on the GABBETVILLE rd., pit on the Hugh Allen place—**gem beryl, quartz** (milky, rose).

LOUISE, just N of the Calloway Airport, the Chromite prospect—**beryl, chromite.**

UNION CO.

AREA: (1) Gumlog Mt., area schist exposures—**corundum, kyanite** (crystals, clusters), **black tourmaline;** (2) 2 mi. S of Hightower Bald, between Jacks Branch and Shoal Branch—**amethyst, quartz crystals.**
BLAIRSVILLE: (1) S 4–5 mi., area—**gold, sillimanite;** (2) NW 5 mi., in Teece Cr. valley, 1 mi. below hwy. crossing—**gold, kyanite** (crystals to 2 in. long).

UPSON CO.

CREST: (1) area, gravels of Hurricane Cr.—**beryl, kyanite, quartz crystals;** (2) N 1 mi., on W side of Town Mt.—**garnet, feldspar, kyanite, quartz;** (3) SW 2 mi., pegmatite prospects—**mica** books to 3 in. dia.; (4) Mica Hill—**biotite** and **muscovite mica.**
THOMASTON: (1) area: A broad region of rich mines extends from SW of THOMASTON S of the THOMASTON-YATESVILLE airline to E and N of YATESVILLE almost as far N as Topeka Jct., more than 50 mines—**kyanite, mica,** and associated **gem minerals;** (a) area **mica** mines—**citrine, corundum, garnet;** (b) Goat Rock, rd. cuts along Rte. 19—**gem crystals;** (2) SW 3½ mi., on the Dolly Cherry place—**gem kyanite, staurolites** (finest twinned crystals in Ga.); (3) E 4 mi. and about 1 mi. off the THOMASTON-BUTLER hwy., the Mauldin Mine (well known locally)—**albite,** glassy **microcline, apatite, mica (biotite** books common, **muscovite), smoky quartz;**
(4) NE 6 mi., near jct. of THOMASTON-YATESVILLE hwy., in banks and cliffs of Wilmot's Ravine—**gem agate, jasper;** (5) S 20° W 3½ mi. airline (4½ mi. by rd.) and ½ mi. due E of Bell Cr., the old Bell Mine in a pegmatite—**potash feldspar, muscovite mica, quartz** (milky, smoky); (6) S 5 mi. and 1 mi. W of THOMASTON-BUTLER hwy., on the Parker Ferry rd., pegmatite—cleavable **feldspar, mica (biotite, muscovite), smoky quartz** nodules;

(7) S 50° W 5½ mi. and 1 mi. N 35° W of jct. of Potato and Womble creeks and between the two, a pegmatite mine—**mica** (books to 4 in. dia.). (Many **mica** mines have been developed in the pegmatites found within a radius of 8–10 mi. of THOMASTON.) (8) SE 7½ mi., the Mitchell Creek Mine—**apatite, muscovite.**

YATESVILLE: (1) Just outside of town, the Herron Mine—**apatite, beryl** (crystals to 7 in. long), **mica, quartz;** (2) N 3 mi. by unimproved rd. that lies .8 mi. E of paved rd. to BARNESVILLE, the Adams Mine—gem **beryl;** (3) S 46° W 3.8 mi., the Charlie Nims Mine, pegmatite—**mica** books to several in. dia. on dumps. (Many pegmatite mines occur in this area, with all dumps containing collectable gems and minerals.)

WALTON CO.

BLASINGAME, 6 mi. out on dirt rd. to the Malcom farm, a pegmatite exposure in a field—gem **aquamarine, beryl** (common, star), **mica, quartz, tourmaline.**

WASHINGTON CO.

SANDERSVILLE, S 4 mi. on Rte. 15 and 2 mi. from Buddy's Service Sta., at the Hugh Taubutton farm—**cryptocrystalline quartz** gemstones.

WHITE CO.

AREA, widespread stream gravels, placers—**gold.** The first gold discoveries in Georgia in 1828 were followed by so many placer prospects that in 1831 the legislature held a lottery for 35,000 plots of 40 acres each with drawings being made by some 130,000 prospectors. The first gold coins were struck at DAHLONEGA in 1838, with eventually more than $7,500,000 coined from Georgia gold. Gold mining continued here up to World War II. In the gold placers are also found **diamonds, topaz, rubies,** and **aquamarines.**

CLEVELAND: (1) numerous **gold**-mining areas (including HELEN)—**gold, gem crystals;** (2) N 4 mi., at the Dunbar Mine, placers—**gold.** (Several extensive mines exist in this area.)

NACOOCHEE: (1) area mines—**asbestos;** (2) placer gravels of Bean Cr.—**gold;** (3) 3 mi. and just W of the CLEVELAND-HELEN hwy., placers—**gold** (sizable nuggets have been found here); (4) the Horshaw Mine—**gold, diamond.**

WHITFIELD CO.

DALTON, cut banks and gravels along Tarr Cr.—red **oolitic jasper,** black **siliceous oolite.**

WILKES CO.

ADASBURG, area outcrops—**rock crystal.**
WASHINGTON: (1) SE 7 mi., on the Wingfield plantation on the WRIGHT-BORO rd., extensive outcrop of quartzite—**kyanite crystals;** (2) E on U.S. 378 to co. line, turn onto first right-fork rd., then take a left fork to crest of a hill, the Magruder Mica Mine—**azurite, barite, bornite, chalcopyrite, galena, gold, malachite, pyrite, garnet,** gem **spinel.**

WILKINSON CO.

GORDON, gravels along nearby lake shore—**opalite, quartz gemstones.**
MCINTYRE, area mines—**bauxite.**

HAWAII

Of the twelve Hawaiian islands which lie approximately 2,000 miles west of San Francisco (usually spoken of as composing the main group of volcanic islands), four are mere barren rocks, and four are large, extremely mountainous islands culminating in Mauna Kea (13,900 ft.) and Mauna Loa (13,700 ft.). Four other islands are of lesser extent, but all are composed of basalt.

Almost the only minerals present on any of the islands are **sands,** some **gravel,** and **limestone,** including deposits of **calcareous algae** and the skeletons of stony **corals.** In the craters of the still-active volcanic cones one can find **sulfur.**

For information, write: Geology Department, University of Hawaii, Honolulu.

IDAHO

With an oddly configured "panhandle" shape, Idaho reveals a varied topography. The central and northern portions are extremely rugged, encompassing the massive Sawtooth and Salmon River mountain systems, with many lakes, and snow-laden peaks that rise more than 12,000 feet high. The mountains have been extensively prospected and mined for **copper, gold, lead, silver,** and **zinc.** As a **gold**-producing state, Idaho ranks ninth in America, and it is credited with producing 8,323,000 ounces from 1863 through 1965. Many abandoned mining ghost towns dot the mineralized areas.

The promisingly mountainous nature of Idaho led early prospectors from Virginia City, Nevada, and Bannock and Virginia City, Montana, into its labyrinthine watersheds in search of **gold** and **silver.** Idaho's mountain systems are the result of enormous batholithic intrusions that took place during the Laramide revolution some 70 million years ago. Known to geologists as the "Idaho batholith," this granite mass covers from 16,000 to 20,000 square miles and is probably the largest and best-known such geologic phenomenon in America.

The earliest known **gold** discovery in Idaho was an auriferous sandbar along the Pend Oreille River in 1852. Then in 1860 Captain E. D. Pierce found **gold** near what became the town of Pierce in Clearwater Co., with other rich placers soon being mined at Elk City, Orofino, Boise Basin, Florence, and Warren. Although many of the richer placers were exhausted by 1870, the following half-century led to intensive exploration for lode-**gold** deposits. Most of the state's **gold** came from lode mines after 1900.

In addition to the basic and noble metals, produced in astonishing abundance, Idaho provided large amounts of strategic minerals of inestimable value to the emergencies of World Wars I and II. Potentially, at least, the Panhandle State ranks above all others in America in the importance of its mineral resources. Aside from the commercially valuable minerals, the state provides an unusual abundance and variety of **gemstones, gem crystals, silicified woods,** and other mineral items valued highly by the collector—occurring throughout the state in far more localities than can be enumerated here.

For more information, write: Idaho Bureau of Mines, Moscow.

ADA CO.

AREA: (1) very many localities along co. roads, prospect almost anywhere—**agate, chalcedony, jasper, petrified** and **opalized wood;** (2) gravels of Musselshell Cr. tributary of the Snake R.—**zircon.**

ADAMS CO.

AREA: (1) very many regional old mines and dumps—**azurite, native copper, gold, malachite,** etc.; (2) Sturgill Cr., area deposits, prospect pits, and mines—**manganese** (in numerous parts of this co. are interesting old mines and dumps profitable for the mineral collector); (3) Rock Flat gravels—**diamond, garnet, ruby, sapphire, topaz.**

COUNCIL, SE 10 mi., the Mica Queen Mine in Sec. 8, T. 15 N, R. 2 E—**muscovite mica.**

MESA, in all area deposits of volcanic ash—**opalized wood.**

NEW MEADOWS, E 5 mi. along Little Goose Cr. Canyon, in gravels—**diamond.**

BANNOCK CO.

LAVA HOT SPRINGS, numerous area mines—**manganese minerals.**
POCATELLO, the Moonlight Mine (inquire directions)—**bornite, chalcocite.**

BEAR LAKE CO.

CLEVELAND, SE 1 mi., on E side of Bear R.—nodules of mixed **psilomelane** and **pyrolusite, wad.**
MONTPELIER: (1) E 3 mi., in limestone fissures—**gypsum;** (2) area of Paris Canyon, the Hummingbird Mine—**quartz** (impregnated with **cuprite** and **malachite**).

BENEWAH CO.

FERNWOOD: (1) SE 5 mi., Emerald Cr. and its East Fork—**almandite garnet;** (2) S 2 mi., gravels of Ruby Gulch—**almandite garnet.**

BLAINE CO.

AREA, basalt exposures throughout co., especially in the Pole Cr. area—**chalcedony geodes** (with **amethyst** linings), **quartz crystal geodes.**
BELLEVUE: (1) SW corner of co., in the Wood River District: (a) Wood R. and tributaries in T. 1 S, R. 17, 18 E, placers—**gold;** (b) area mines—**galena, dufrenoysite, magnetite, malachite, marcasite;** (c) Camas, Croesus, and Tip Top mines—**pyrrhotite.**
CAREY, gravels of the Little Wood R.—**agate, chalcedony, jasper.**
HAILEY: (1) SW, in T. 1 N, R. 17 E and S of Croy Cr.—**galena, gold, monzonite, sphalerite, uraninite;** (2) W, in T. 2 N, R. 17 E, the Deer Cr. deposits—**barite** (the Blaine Co. **barite** deposits were noted during the development of the area **lead-silver** lodes in the early 1900's); (3) area mines and dumps—**galena, silver, sphalerite.**
KETCHUM: (1) area **lead** mines in T. 4 N, R. 17, 18, 19 E—**argentiferous tetrahedrite, arsenopyrite, galena, siderite, sphalerite;** (2) the Sawtooth District, area mines—**proustite** with **pyrargyrite**).

BOISE CO.

AREA: (1) the Banner **silver** veins—**gold, pyrargyrite, silver;** (2) Deadwood Gulch—**garnets, gold;** (3) Willow Creek District, at (a) Checkmate, (b) Gold Hill, and (c) many other regional mines—**gold, pyrite, silver.** This co. has many old mines; the dumps yield **quartz crystals,** brilliant **pyrite,** etc., in addition to other minerals.
BANKS, SE 11 mi., the Vaught prospect in Sec. 19, T. 8 N, R. 5 E—**columbite, mica.**
CENTERVILLE: (1) N to Garden Valley, pegmatite outcrops—**aqua-**

marine; (2) along Grimes Cr. on way toward PLACERVILLE; and (c) along the Boise R. near Twin Springs, area placers—**gold.**

IDAHO CITY: (1) both sides of Moore Cr.—**precious opal;** (2) area: (a) vicinity of town, (b) along Mine Cr., and (c) near Horseshoe Bend of the Payette R., placers—**gold.**

PIONEERVILLE: (1) the Quartzburg area, and (2) around Grimes Pass, lode deposits—**gold.**

BONNER CO.

CLARK FORK (District): (1) area old mines—**copper minerals;** (2) mines in T. 55, 56 N, R. 2 E—**lead-silver minerals.**

BOUNDARY CO.

CARRIETOWN: (1) along Little Smoky Cr., in T. 2, 3 N, R. 14, 15 E, placers—**gold;** (2) mines in T. 4, 5 N, R. 13, 14 E, lode—**gold.**

PORTHILL, SW 26 mi., in T. 64 N, R. 4 W—**gold, lead, silver.**

BUTTE CO.

ARCO, W 20 mi., in the Lava Cr. district—**manganese minerals, tourmaline.**

CANYON CO.

MARSING, from rd. toward HOMEDALE turn left at abandoned "Y" Inn to Graveyard Point, then left on canal rd. over bridge and 2 mi., crossing canal bridge and backtracking ¾ mi.—gem **opal.**

CARIBOU CO.

SODA SPRINGS, S a few miles: (1) Sec. 2, 11, 13, 14, T. 9 S, R. 42 E, and (2) Sec. 14, T. 10 S, R. 43 E, regional deposits—**gypsum, sulfur.**

CASSIA CO.

BURLEY, mines along the Snake R.: (1) T. 9, 10 S, R. 24, 25 E, placers—**gold;** (2) T. 15, 16 S, R. 21 E, mines and dumps—**copper, gold, lead-silver.**

MOULTON, NW 5 mi. and just W of ALMO—**topaz.**

CLEARWATER CO.

AREA: (1) Kelly and Morse creeks in T. 39 N, R. 10, 11 E, placers—**gold;** (2) North Fork (of Clearwater R.) and its tributaries, T. 37, 38, 39 N, R. 1, 2, 3, 4 E, placers—**gold;** (3) Rhodes Cr., gravels—**zircon.**

PIERCE: (1) area placer mines, and (2) along Orofino Cr. between ORO-

FINO and PIERCE, T. 36, 37 N, R. 2, 3, 4 E, placers—**gold;** (3) N 11 mi., near HEADQUARTERS, area—asteriated **almandite garnet.**

CUSTER CO.

AREA: (1) Alto district, near Wild Horse Cr., mines—**scheelite;** (2) Bayhorse, T. 12, 13 N, R. 18 E, area mines—**lead minerals;** (3) Bonanza and Custer mines on Yankee Fork, T. 12, 13 N, R. 14, 15 E, lodes—**gold;** (4) Nicholia district, rich early-day strikes—**lead-silver minerals;** (5) toward head of Big Lost R., as well as all other Tertiary basalts outcropping over a broad region—**chalcedony geodes (amethyst** linings).

CHALLIS, a 7½-mi.-long belt extending from the Pacific Mine near Bayhorse on the S to Mill Cr. on the N, most deposits being in T. 13 N, R. 18 E—**fluorite.**

CLAYTON: (1) area of Squaw and Thompson creeks in T. 11, 12 N, R. 16 E, mines—**scheelite,** lode **gold;** (2) mines in T. 11, 12 N, R. 17 E—**lead minerals.**

MACKAY, area **copper** mines and dumps—**azurite, chalcopyrite, chrysocolla, malachite, pyrite, pyrrhotite.**

STANLEY: (1) area stream gravels of the Stanley Basin—**corundum, gold, sapphire;** (2) placer mines in T. 10, 1 N, R. 12, 13 E; and (3) along the Salmon R., particularly between Robinson Bar and CLAYTON in T. 11 N, R. 15, 16, 17 E—**gold;** (4) the Willis placers along Stanley Cr.—**cinnabar, gold.**

ELMORE CO.

AREA: (1) along the Boise R.: (a) Middle Fork, in T. 6 N, R. 10 E; (b) South Fork, in T. 2 N, R. 10 E; (c) at Twin Springs, in T. 3, 4, 5 N, R. 5, 6, 7 E, placers—**gold;** (2) the Neal district, area mines—**stibnite.**

MOUNTAIN HOME, NE 25–50 mi.: (1) PINE (mining district), as stringers in granite—**cinnabar, gold;** (2) FEATHERVILLE and ROCKY BAR, regional old mines—**gold;** (3) ATLANTA, famous old **gold** camp: (a) T. 5 N, R. 11, 12 E, mines—**gold;** (b) W 20 mi., on East Fork of Sevenholm Cr., in Sec. 13, T. 6 N, R. 9 E, the Hermada deposit, high grade—**stibnite.** (The original old mining camp of PINE now lies under the waters of the Anderson Ranch Reservoir.)

FREMONT CO.

ST. ANTHONY, N 18 mi. and 8 mi. SE of IVAN, at Crystal Butte, area—**andesine.**

GEM CO.

EMMETT: (1) take rd. toward Horseshoe Bend and up Black Canyon about 1 mi. to old diggings in rock walls—**precious opal** (containing red and green fire); (2) 5 mi. E of Squaw Butte—**agate.**

PEARL, extending NE to co. line and including parts of T. 6, 7 N, R. 1 E, many old mines—**gold.**

GOODING CO.

GOODING, area along both sides of Clover Cr. extending E into Lincoln Co. and embracing a considerable region—**opalized wood.**

IDAHO CO.

AREA: (1) Bear Valley, a deposit in T. 12, 13 N, R. 9 E—**monazite, uranium minerals;** (2) Lolo, Musselshell, and Eldorado creeks, many once-rich placer mines—**gold;** (3) Resort area placers—**corundum, gold, zircon;** (4) Salmon R. sands and gravels, both sides and all tributaries—**agate, chalcedony, jasper, petrified wood,** etc.; (5) Slate and McKinsey creeks—**agate, jasper,** etc.; (6) T 33 N, R. 5 E, six or more ledges within a few square miles—**amphibole asbestos.** (The western and southern halves of this large county are extensively mineralized and contain very many old abandoned mines, ghost mining camps, and deposits of collectable minerals and gemstones.)

BURGDORF-WARREN (the entire region S of the Salmon R.), many area placers, especially in T. 22 N, R. 4, 5, 6 E—**gold, monazite, topaz.**

DIXIE, N side of the Salmon R. along Sheep and Crooked creeks—**gold.**

ELK CITY, region along the American R. and the South Fork of the Clearwater R., many old mines and placers—**gold.**

KOOSKIA: (1) S, along the South Fork of the Clearwater R., including areas around STITES and HARPSTER, placers—**gold;** (2) E, along the Middle Fork of the Clearwater R., and on Maggie Cr., placers—**gold.**

LUCILLE-RIGGINS, regional placers along the Salmon R.—**gold.**

OROGRANDE, SW, the Buffalo Hump mining district, many mine dumps—**copper minerals.**

ROOSEVELT, E 10 mi., the Pringle-Smith Mine at Sugar Cr.—**cinnabar.**

WHITE BIRD, area gravels of the Wind and Salmon rivers, to 6 mi. N of town—**gold.**

IDAHO-LEWIS COS.

AREA, the Lolo District, many mines—**copper minerals.**

KOOTENAI CO.

BAYVIEW, S and SW sides of Lake Pend Oreille, many mines and prospects —**argentiferous galena.**

COEUR D'ALENE (District), many area mines—**gold, lead, silver.** Gold was first discovered here in 1860 in minor amounts, but the real mining boom began in 1882 with the discovery of some of the world's richest **lead-silver** mines, such as the Bunker Hill and Sullivan mines at KELLOGG and WALLACE in adjoining Shoshone Co., *q.v.* These are still active mines.

HAYDEN LAKE, area: (1) T. 51, 52 N, R. 1, 2 W; and (2) T. 48, 49 N, R. 2 W, many mines—**lead-silver minerals.**

SETTERS, area land surfaces—**common opal** (yellow to brown).

LATAH CO.

AREA: (1) NW part of co., along Emerald and Ruby creeks—**garnet;** (2) the Hoodoo District, area mines—**copper minerals.**

AVON: (1) N 6 mi., on flanks and crest of Mica Mt. in Sec. 15, 22, 23, 27, T. 41 N, R. 2 W, in pegmatite outcrops with numerous mines—**beryl, mica (biotite, muscovite);** (2) the Fitzgerald property and adjoining exposures in Sec. 27—**graphic granite.** The pegmatites found in a belt about 1 mi. wide extend for about 24 mi. in a NE-SW direction; there are many prospects and old workings along the outcrops.

MOSCOW, W, toward WHELAN and squarely on the boundary between Idaho and Washington, in decomposed basalt exposures—**precious opal.**

LEMHI CO.

AREA: (1) Blue Wing district, on W slope of the Lemhi Range in Sec. 23, T. 14 N, R. 23 E, the Ima Mine—**tungsten (huebnerite)** with **tetrahedrite, chalcopyrite, galena, scheelite, sphalerite;** (2) Parker Mt. district, area—**agate, chalcedony.**

COBALT, the Panther Cr. valley 6 mi. below headwaters in porphyry dike extending 1½ mi. along cr.—**opal** (common, precious, nodular).

GIBBONSVILLE: (1) T. 25 N, R. 21 E; (2) T. 26 N, R. 21 E, regional mines—**autunite, galena, hematite, gold, pyrite, torbernite;** (3) along the Salmon R. and area creeks, as placer sands—**gold;** (4) back of the Salmon R., as lode mines—**gold.**

GILMORE, T. 13 N, R. 26 E, lode mines—**gold.**

LEADORE, T. 13 N, R. 27 E, area mines—**lead minerals.**

LEESBURG, area placers—**gold, petrified wood.**

MAY, nearby exposure—massive **opal, opalite.**

MEYERS COVE, near Camas Cr. in T. 18 N, R. 17 E, 2–3 mi. NW, as vein fillings in composite lode-type veins in Challis volcanics and Miocene porphyries—**barite, fluorite, quartz.**

SALMON, SW 45 mi.: (1) Blackbird District, on Blackbird and Meadow creeks in T. 20, 21 N, R. 18 E, numerous mines and prospects—**cobaltite, chalcopyrite, pyrite, pyrrhotite,** minor **lead-silver-zinc** ores; (2) T. 20, 21 N, R. 21, 22, 23 E, many regional mines of considerable richness—**azurite, bornite, chalcopyrite, cuprite, malachite.**

SHOUP, the Salmon R. and its tributaries in N part of co. (near GIBBONSVILLE, *q.v.*), as placers and lode deposits in same region but extending farther S near LEESBURG and SALMON—**gold.**

LEWIS CO.

KAMIAH, SE 14 mi., exposures—**amphibole asbestos.**

LEWIS, NEZ PERCE, IDAHO, ADAMS, WASHINGTON COS.

The Seven Devils mining district, extending along the Snake R. for about 120 mi., known as the Snake River Copper Belt, very many mines and prospects—**azurite, bornite, chalcocite, chalcopyrite, covellite, malachite,** etc.

LINCOLN CO.

SHOSHONE, large surrounding area, especially W into Gooding Co.'s Clover Cr. region—**opalized wood.**

NEZ PERCE CO.

AGATHA, area E and N—**opal, opalized wood.**

LEWISTON: (1) gravel bars all along the Clearwater R. between town and DENT—**agate, jasper** (with **sillimanite** inclusions), cherty **"Clearwater picture stone"** (gray, with black stripes); (2) Clearwater R. gravels upstream from town for about 100 mi., but especially between LEWISTON and MYRTLE —**fibrolite** (gem **sillimanite**); (3) all regional streams—**agate, aquamarine, garnet, gold, quartz crystals;** (4) 8 mi. down the Snake R. on N side, on weathered basaltic hillsides—**fire opal** (in black matrix); (5) 11 mi. downstream to gravel pits at Silcott, take steep hill trail to caves near top in basalt—fine gem **fire opal.**

OWYHEE CO.

BRUNEAU: (1) entire region of the Bruneau Desert, along almost any access rd.—**agate, chalcedony, jasper;** (2) SE, in the Bruneau Canyon area (advisable to hire a local rockhound guide)—**"Bruneau Canyon" jasper.**

CLIFFS (40 mi. S of JORDAN VALLEY, Ore.), the Brace Brothers ranch—**precious opal.**

ENTERPRISE, W 3 mi. and 2 mi. SW of Sommer Camp, in open cuts and pits in perlitic rhyolite—**opal.**

GRAND VIEW, along the Snake R., area placers—**gold.**

HOMEDALE, S 2 mi. on U.S. 95 to Graveyard Point marker, then 4 mi. W and 1 im. S to area of Idaho–Oregon boundary. A very rich gem **agate** collecting area which, since it lies mainly on the Oregon side, cf. in Malheur Co. at Nyssa (4).

NAMPA: (1) area of Graveyard Point, SE—**plume agate;** (2) SW 8 mi., at Squaw Cr. Canyon, just below jct. of Squaw and Little Squaw creeks and 3 mi. back of the Snake R., in basalt gas cavities—**chalcedony** (banded, common), **chalcedonic opal, precious opal, onyx;** (3) W, along Sucker Cr.— **plume agate.**

OREANA: (1) area old mines—**lead-silver minerals;** (2) SE 6 mi., along Castle Cr.—**precious opal.**

SILVER CITY: (1) Black Jack and Trade Dollar mines in town—**chalcopyrite, gold, lead, silver;** (2) War Eagle and Florida Mt. veins in T. 4, 5 S, R. 3, 4 W, all fissure-type deposits with mineralizations occurring as ore shoots—**argentite, cerargyrite, electrum, jamesonite, pyrargyrite, stibnite, silver-**bearing **tetrahedrite,** etc.; (3) scores more regional mines, all abandoned, with occasional summer prospecting and placering—**gold, lead, silver,** and on dumps associated with **agate, calcite, chalcedony, geodes, jasper, marcasite, pyrite, quartz crystals,** etc.;

(4) NW a short distance to ghost camp of DE LAMAR, lode deposits and huge mines—**gold, lead, silver.** The DE LAMAR–SILVER CITY mines, although the longest and richest producers in Idaho, are now virtually abandoned. My mother, as a teacher, witnessed the demise of SILVER CITY as a mining camp in 1909, when the stampmills ceased operation one January night. As the county seat of Owyhee Co., SILVER CITY survived until 1935, when the courthouse was dismantled block by block and reassembled in the new county seat of MURPHY. In "The Death of Silver City" (*Westways,* Vol. 52, No. 1, Jan., 1960), she wrote: "In the middle of a night late in January [1909] I awoke as if shocked out of a horrible dream. For dazed moments my eyes followed the dim lights and shadows flickering on the wall opposite my bedroom window as a dull apprehension gripped me. Finally, in a sort of horror, I realized that the months of roaring and pounding of the stamps had ceased, leaving such a crashingly deafening silence over the midnight city that every soul alive had awakened, as I had done. As a mining camp, Silver City had died at last."

SHOSHONE CO.

AREA: (1) region of the Coeur d'Alene mining district (as extension from Kootenai Co., *q.v.*): (1) the Idaho Giant and other mines, as center of one of the world's richest **lead-silver** zones—**argentiferous tetrahedrite, barite, galena, pyrite, pyromorphite, siderite, sphalerite,** etc.; (2) the "Silver Belt," in T. 48 N, R. 3, 4 E, an area in which the chief product is **silver** extending about 6½ mi. E–W and 2½ mi. N–S, very many famous mines—**argentiferous tetrahedrite, galena, sphalerite,** etc.

AVERY: (1) the area to S, and (2) around Bathtub Mt.—**staurolite.**

CALDER, W, in the ST. JOE (Benewah Co.) mining district: (1) many area mines in Shoshone Co.—**copper minerals;** (2) along the St. Joe R., in T. 45 N, R. 3, 4, 9 E, lode mines—**gold.** (Most **gold** from Shoshone Co. comes from ores mined primarily for **copper, lead, sliver,** and **zinc.**)

KELLOGG, the Bunker Hill and Sullivan mines (now combined as one of the world's largest lead producers)—**lead-silver minerals.** (Labor troubles in 1899 led to the blowing up of the huge Kellogg Mill, an incident in a long-drawn Idaho labor war.)

KINGSTON, area of the Pine Cr. district in T. 48 N, R. 1, 2 E, numerous old mines—**arsenopyrite, gold, pyrite, stibnite.**

MURRAY (principal **gold-**mining part of co.), lode mines—**gold.**

PRICHARD, area creek placers—**gold.**

WALLACE (distributing center for E portion of the Coeur d'Alene mining district): (1) many area mines, some world famous, such as the Sunshine Mine—**gold, lead, silver;** (2) T. 47, 48 N, R. 4, 5 E, placers—**gold.**

TWIN FALLS CO.

AREA, along Hwy. 93 and 3–4 mi. N of the Nevada state line—**chalcedony geodes.**

CASTLEFORD, W, across Salmon Falls Cr. to Balanced Rock, take dirt rd. W and SW to Bruneau R. Canyon (Owyhee Co., cf. BRUNEAU), area—**"Bruneau Canyon" jasper.**

VALLEY CO.

BIG CREEK: (1) area streams in T. 20, 21 N, R. 9, 10 E, placers—**gold;** (2) NW, to the Ramey Ridge district (extending into S part of Idaho Co.), many mines—**copper minerals;** (3) E, to Long Valley, near confluence of Big Cr. with the Salmon R., one of richest **thorium** placers in Idaho—**ilmenite, garnet, monazite, zircon.**

EDWARDSBURG, T. 20 N, R. 9 E, lode mines—**gold.**

STIBNITE, area old mines—**arsenopyrite, gold, pyrite, stibnite.**

YELLOW PINE: (1) T. 18 N, R. 8 E, placers—**gold;** (2) general region, in volcanic exposures—**opal** (white, spotted with **cinnabar**); (3) T. 19 N, R. 8, 9 E, area mines—**arsenopyrite, gold, pyrite, stibnite;** (4) T. 19 N, R. 9, 10 E, as deposits distributed over an area of about 4 sq. mi.—**cinnabar;** (5) T. 18, 19 N, R. 11 E, Monumental Cr., near Thunder Mt., lode veins—**gold;** (6) SSW about 40 mi. to Warm Lake, T. 15 N, R. 6, 7 E—**placer gold.**

WASHINGTON CO.

EATON, E 5 mi., along Grouse and Hog creeks—**agate** (banded, iris), **chalcedony.**

SEVEN DEVILS mining district, the Peacock claim—**bornite, garnet, melaconite, powellite, specularite.**

WEISER: (1) Nutmeg Mt., at the Idaho-Almaden deposit in T. 10, 11 N, R. 3 W—**opal, chalcedony, cinnabar, opalite, pyrite;** (2) N 30 mi., on the Snake R. in Sec. 7, 8, 17, 18, 20, T. 13 N, R. 7 W, many deposits as banded lenses—**gypsum;** (3) NW 16 mi., in Fourth of July Canyon at jct. of July and Mann's creeks, in volcanic ash 500 ft. above creek beds, high quality—**opalized wood.**

ILLINOIS

Known as the Prairie State, Illinois exhibits a length of 378 miles and a width of 210 miles, with its 56,000 square miles sloping slightly to the southwest. Containing more than 275 rivers, the state is bounded along three-fourths of its circumference by navigable waters, primarily the Ohio and Mississippi rivers. The highest elevations are the "mounds" along the northern borders, rising only to altitudes of 900 to 1,000 feet above sea level.

Though well endowed with fossils, Illinois has little to offer gem and mineral collectors, even though the state produces more **sandstone, silica sand,** and **fluorspar** than any other state in America. Most specimen collecting is done in the **lead-zinc** mining districts of northwestern Illinois, the glacial drift of the Late Pleistocene Wisconsin glaciation, the bluffs and detritus of the Ohio and Mississippi rivers, and the **fluorspar** region of the south.

Fossil hunters are well acquainted with the famed "Coal Measures" so often mentioned in Illinois geology. These measures constitute the Upper Carboniferous system of repeated alternations of sandstone, shale, bituminous slates, thin bands of limestone, and seams of coal usually underlaid with clay. In these coal seams the collector may often find **marcasite** and **pyrite.** The measures are 1,200 to 1,400 feet thick in the south, grading to 600 to 800 feet thick in the north.

For information, write: Illinois State Geological Survey, Urbana.

ALEXANDER CO.

FAYVILLE, area stream gravels—**agate, jasper,** rare alluvial **diamond.**

THEBES: (1) area gravel deposits, pits, bars of the Mississippi R.—**agate, jasper;** (2) RR siding of Clay—**agate.**

CALHOUN CO.

AREA, shores of the Mississippi R., in the Warsaw formation that surrounds WARSAW, HAMILTON, and NAUVOO in western Illinois—**geodes** (lined with **botryoidal chalcedony,** occasionally with pale **amethysts,** or **quartz crystals**).

CRAWFORD CO.

PALESTINE, area deposits—**siderite.**

EDWARDS CO.

AREA, T. 1 S, R. 10 E, regional deposits—**siderite.**

FULTON CO.

FARMINGTON, W 6 mi. on Rte. 116 to the Rapatee No. 5 strip mine—**pyritized gastropods** (Pennsylvanian age).

GRUNDY CO.

AREA: (1) regional road and RR cuts and banks of Mason Cr.—excellent fossils; (2) Coal City, on area mine dumps from sedimentary overburden—oval concretions (containing "Mason Creek" fossils).

EAST BROOKLYN (SE of GARDNER), area coal mine dumps—marcasite, pyrite.

HANCOCK CO.

HAMILTON: (1) area gravels and glacial drift deposits—agate, jasper, geodes (containing gemmy blue gray chalcedony; (2) S of the Keokuk bridge, in stream banks and gravels—geodes (lined with crystals).

NAUVOO, area stream and creek tributaries and Mississippi R. gravels, in cuts, pits, banks, etc.—geodes.

NIOTA: (1) area excavations, pits, stream banks and gravels—fossils, geodes; (2) S 2 mi., at Tyson Cr.—crystal-lined geodes (filled with thick oil; no oil deposits are known in the area).

WARSAW, area rd. cuts, pits, quarries, gravels, banks along regional creeks and streams—geodes.

HARDIN CO.

CAVE-IN-ROCK: (1) area fluorspar mines, and (2) NW 4½ mi., mines—cerussite, chalcopyrite, fluorspar, galena (as a by-product), pyrite, silver, smithsonite, witherite.

ROSICLARE: (1) area mines—calcite crystals, fluorite; (2) the Empire and Fairview mines—fluorite, galena, pyrite; (3) E, numerous mines—cf. CAVE-IN-ROCK; (4) N .8 mi. on Rte. 1 from Rte. 146 jct., then W on gravel rd. 2 mi. to the Mahoning Mine No. 3, on dumps—fluorite crystals; (5) Fairview Landing, area mines—cf. CAVE-IN-ROCK. (This fluorspar region extends W into Pope Co.)

HENDERSON CO.

TERRE HAUTE, area gravels, pits, mine dumps—"Mason Creek" fossils (type).

HENRY CO.

CORDOVA, Mississippi R. banks N through Whiteside, Carroll, and Jo Daviess counties to EAST DUBUQUE (actually on both sides of the river to include Iowa)—agate.

GALVA, N, at Bishop Hill, area—agate, jasper.

JEFFERSON CO.

Mᴛ. Vᴇʀɴᴏɴ, W 9½ mi. on U.S. 460 from jct. with Int. 57, area cr. gravels (about 3½ mi. E of Aꜱʜʟᴇʏ, Washington Co.), occasional—**diamond.**

JO DAVIESS CO.

Gᴀʟᴇɴᴀ: (1) area mine dumps—**cerussite, galena** (cubes, coated with **marcasite**), **"plume" marcasite** (plumes are of **pyrite;** the local name is **radiant pyrite**), **pyrite, sphalerite;** (2) NE 20 mi., many regional mine dumps—**calcite crystals, cockscomb marcasite, lead-zinc minerals.**

McDONOUGH CO.

Mᴀᴄᴏᴍʙ, area stream and cr. gravels, occasional—**diamond.**

POPE CO.

Aʀᴇᴀ, mines, including the Pittsburgh, McClellan, etc.—**cerussite, chalcopyrite, fluorite, fluorspar, galena, pyrite, silver, smithsonite, witherite.** (The mining district extends E into Hardin Co.)

RANDOLPH CO.

Sᴘᴀʀᴛᴀ: (1) area mine dumps, pits, etc.—**pyrite disks** (radiating); (2) W, on dumps of numerous mines—**fossil blastoids,** etc.

UNION CO.

Aɴɴ, Jᴏɴᴇꜱʙᴏʀᴏ, Wᴇꜱᴛʟᴀᴋᴇ, regional deposits with large production and refineries at Jᴏɴᴇꜱʙᴏʀᴏ and near Wᴇꜱᴛʟᴀᴋᴇ, lesser occurrences elsewhere in area—**tripoli.**

VERMILION CO.

Dᴀɴᴠɪʟʟᴇ, area quarries in dark shale—**marcasite** replacements of marine **fossils.**

WILL CO.

Lᴇᴍᴏɴᴛ, area quarries—glistening **quartz replacements of fossils.**
Wɪʟᴍɪɴɢᴛᴏɴ, regional mines in the coal formations, on dumps—**fossils** (wide variety), **marcasite, pyrite.**

INDIANA

The geologic formations of the Hoosier State are predominantly sedimentaries of Ordovician to Pennsylvanian age, that is, from 500 million to 330 million years ago, with many Silurian exposures (430 million years old) outcropping east and west across the state in the latitude of Newton and Adams counties. The oldest formations occur in the eastern counties, with the youngest rocks appearing in the southwest. The most important formation is the Mississinewa shale, lowest of the Niagaran series, and loaded with fossils. There are no igneous or metamorphic rock outcrops in Indiana.

The four great ice advances of the Pleistocene period successively smoothed off any irregularities that may originally have existed in the northern counties. The debris pushed ahead by the ice was dropped throughout the central agricultural area, blanketing nearly five-sixths of the state to considerable depths in places. This morainal detritus contains what few gems and minerals there are in Indiana, mainly **agate, jasper, fossilized corals,** and **petrified wood. Copper** nuggets have been found scattered over eighteen counties between the eastern and western boundaries and as far south as Vanderburgh Co., brought down by the ice from the Lake Superior **copper** regions. Similarly, cubes of **galena** transported by the ice have given rise to many false reports and legends of **lead** mines in Indiana.

The moraines of thrice-glaciated Morgan Co. yield **quartz gemstone** pebbles, some **topaz,** and now and then bits of **corundum.** This and adjoining Brown Co. have also produced an astonishing 30 **diamonds** over the last century. These glacial-drift gems were found during **gold-**panning operations in the regional streams that produced small quantities of the yellow metal. However, from the collector's viewpoint, Indiana is disappointingly barren.

In the central and southern counties are many **coal** mines containing the usual associative minerals of **goethite, marcasite, pyrite, selenite,** and **sphalerite.** Regional limestone quarries produce some gemmy **apatite, calcite, glauconite, marcasite, pyrite,** and **quartz,** with now and then occurrences of **barite, celestite, dolomite,** and **siderite.**

For information, write: Department of Geology, Indiana University, Bloomington.

ALLEN CO.

FORT WAYNE: (1) area farms (inquire permission), as glacial float—**agate, jasper;** (2) gravels of the Maumee R.—**agate, jasp-agate, jasper, fossil coral, petrified wood.**

BARTHOLOMEW CO.

ELIZABETHTOWN, NE 2 mi., at the Meshberger Stone Co. quarry—**calcite, fluorite** (several colors), **marcasite.**

BROWN CO.

AREA: (1) glacial drift gravels throughout co.—**corundum, quartz** pebbles, **topaz,** occasional **diamond;** (2) stream sands, especially of Greenhorn Cr., placers—**gold;** (3) rd. and RR cuts throughout co., stream beds, banks, cliffs, washes, pits, quarries, etc.—**"geodized fossils,"** which is local terminology for **crystal geodes** which have the shapes of fossil brachiopods, pelecypods, crinoid heads, corals, etc., but do not contain any actual fossil material.

BEANBLOSSOM (5 mi. N of NASHVILLE), along Beanblossom Cr.—**geodes.**

NASHVILLE, SW 2 mi., in rd. cut on Rte. 46, 100 ft. N of entrance to Brown Co. State Park—**geodes** containing crystallized **goethite (limonite),** prismatic crystals of **marcasite,** or **aragonite crystals** on **quartz crystals.** (In some geodes, **pyrite** has been altered to nearly perfect spheres of **goethite.**)

TREVLAC: (1) area stream beds, particularly Bear Cr.—**geodes** (quartz-lined); (2) gravels of Lick Cr. (about 15 mi. SE of MARTINSVILLE in Johnson Co.—**diamond;** (3) N, to Yellowwood State Forest, along the Yellowwood Trail—**geodes.**

CASS CO.

LOGANSPORT, E 2½ mi., the France Stone Co. quarry—**apatite** (associated with **collophane**), **calcite** (crystals with **marcasite** along cleavage planes), **pyrite, quartz.**

CRAWFORD CO.

AREA, caves and caverns (some commercial) in limestone formations of the hilly Ohio R. country—**aragonite, calcite, travertine.**

MARENGO, NE edge, roof of Marengo Cave—**aragonite, hydromagnesite.**

WYANDOTTE, just NW, in Wyandotte Cave—**calcite, alabaster, flint, epsomite** (beautifully crystallized).

DEARBORN CO.

WEISBURG, area RR and rd. cuts, of Ordovician age—**trilobites** (well preserved).

DECATUR CO.

NEW POINT, N 1 mi., a stone quarry—**chalcopyrite** (as tiny crystals encrusting blackish **dolomite**).

FOUNTAIN CO.

ATTICA, S 2½ mi., in a coal mine—**sphalerite,** associated with "notable quantities of cobalt" (1862). (The "cobalt" turned out to be **remingtonite,** a supposed hydrous cobalt carbonate now discredited as a mineral species.)

KINGMAN, NE, at the Morgan Company coal mine—**marcasite, pyrite.**

HARRISON CO.

CROYDEN, area quarries—**calcite, fluorite,** pink **dolomite crystals, quartz.**

HUNTINGTON CO.

HUNTINGTON, E edge, in Erie Stone Co. quarry—**calcite, marcasite** (crystals), **pyrite** (fine-grained), **quartz geodes** (small), **sphalerite.**

KNOX CO.

BICKNELL, area coal mines—**marcasite, pyrite.** (An area of coal mines extends S into Pike Co.)

LAWRENCE CO.

AREA: (1) all regional stream beds and banks, road and RR cuts, pits, excavations, etc., especially around towns of CLEARSPRING, ERIE, GUTHRIE, HELTONVILLE, PINHOOK, and ZELMA—**"Indiana" geodes;** these geodes contain inclusions of **quartz crystals, calcite crystals, siderite, sphalerite, goethite, dolomite, limonite, kaolin, celestite, fluorite, chalcedony;** (2) Garner Mine Ridge, Sec. 21, T. 4 N, R. 2 W—**allophane, allophane-evansite, crandallite, halloysite;** (3) Sec. 28, T. 5 N, R. 2 W, as a deposit—**hematite;** (4) entire co. exposures—**fossils.**

BEDFORD: (1) N, at community of OOLITIC, in exposures of limestone—**oolitic limestone;** (2) E, in area cuts, pits, banks, etc.—**geodes** (containing traces of **petroleum**); (3) E 6 mi., in cr. banks—**geodes.**

BUDDHA, SE 2 mi., abandoned quarry and cut along the Baltimore and Ohio RR—**barite, calcite, celestite, gypsum, strontianite.**

GEORGIA, W ½ mi., the Nally Quarry—**barite** (crystals), **dolomite, strontianite.**

GUTHRIE, area excavations, stream gravels, pits, rd. cuts, banks, etc.—**geodes.**

HELTONVILLE: (1) cf. GUTHRIE; (2) Salt Cr. gravels—**quartz geodes.**

MEDORA, E 4 mi., in cr. banks and gravels—**geodes.**

MITCHELL, NE 2 mi., the Lehigh Portland Cement quarry—**anhydrite** (weak to moderate pink fluorescence), **gypsum.**

SPRINGVILLE: (1) SW 2 mi., the Ralph Rogers Co. quarry—**allophane;** (2) SW 3½ mi., the Webster Quarry—**barite crystals.**

MARION CO.

INDIANAPOLIS (practically coterminous with co.): (1) all area cr. beds—
moonstone (feldspar); (2) Williams Cr.—**amethyst, quartz crystals.**

MARTIN CO.

SHOALS, S, near Coal Hollow—**siderite.**

MIAMI CO.

ERIE, area stream banks, rd. and RR cuts, excavations, etc.—**geodes.**
PERU, area morainal deposits—**diamond.**

MONROE CO.

BLOOMINGTON: (1) area quarries, wide variety of minerals—**fluorite,** a
new species **smytheite** (dark acicular crystals included on peach-colored
dolomite, often as pockets in a greenish matrix); (2) N ½ mi., the Bloomington Crushed Stone Co. quarry, 15 recorded species of collectable minerals, including—**aragonite,** mammillary **calcite, barite, strontianite** (as fuzzy
white hemispheres encrusting crystals of **calcite**). (Some **strontianite** contains
inclusions of minute cubes of **pyrite;** other **strontianite** occurs on **drusy
quartz crystals.**) (3) N 2 mi., in rd. cut on Rte. 37—**quartz geodes** (containing velvety-brown micaceous plates of **goethite**), with **aragonite, calcite,
pyrrhotite, siderite.**
HARRODSBURG: (1) area rd. and RR cuts—**calcite, dolomite;** (2) N on
Rte. 37, rd. cuts—**aragonite.**
STANFORD, S 2.8 mi., the Quimby and Stephen Quarry—**marcasite, pyrite.**
UNIONVILLE, E ½ mi. on Rte. 45, a quarry—**barite, dolomite, glauconite,
goethite, pyrite.**

MORGAN CO.

AREA: (1) all regional stream and cr. gravels and glacial moraines—
quartz pebbles, corundum, rare **diamonds, topaz;** (2) Highland Cr. gravels
(7 mi. NNW of MARTINSVILLE in Johnson Co.)—**hematite, magnetite, placer
gold, pyrite, ilmenite, corundum, garnet, diamond, zircon.** (Diamonds from
Indiana's stream gravels, found while panning for **gold** in placer sands,
have come principally from this county.) (3) Gold Cr., gravels—**ruby, massive sapphire, corundum, gold, diamond, zircon.**
WILBUR: (1) co. area glacial moraines—cf. AREA; (2) area glacial gravel
bars—**quartz, corundum, diamond, topaz;** (3) surrounding cr. sands, especially Greenhorn Cr., placers—**gold;** (4) along Highland Cr., numerous
glacial gravel bars—cf. AREA.

OWEN CO.

FREEDOM, SW 3 mi., the Hahn Bros. Quarry—**collophane, hematite.**
SPENCER: (1) area limestone quarries, cr. banks, rd. and RR cuts—**barite, celestite, siderite;** (2) NE 3½ mi. in Dunn Limestone Quarry (4 mi. E of jct. of Rte. 46 and a secondary rd. leading toward GOSPORT)—**barite, celestite, siderite.**

PARKE CO.

COXVILLE, area coal mines and dumps—**pyrite.**

PARKE CO.

AREA, coal mines, dumps, seams, banks, cuts, excavations, etc.—**goethite, marcasite, pyrite, selenite, sphalerite.** (The mines, rd. cuts, banks, etc., of most of central and southern Indiana produce an abundance of these minerals.)
SPURGEON, NW 2 mi., the Enos Coal Mine—**concretions (marcasite, pyrite).** (The coal and shale beds of SW Indiana contain the state's largest **marcasite** and **pyrite concretions.**)

SHELBY CO.

MORRISTOWN, W ½ mi., the Cave Stone Co. quarry—**calcite** (lamellar), **fluorite, marcasite.**

SPENCER CO.

MAXVILLE, W 2½ mi., rd. cut on Rte. 70 about .2 mi. W of jct. with Rte. 66, encrusting shale above Coal Measure III as euhedral crystals to 1 mm. dia.—**copiapite,** with other sulfates (perhaps **melanterite, coquimbite, siderotil**).

WARREN CO.

RAINSVILLE, W 1½ mi., in bluff along Mud Pine Cr.—**sphalerite** (in fossil wood preserved by **limonite**), **barite,** nodules of **siderite, marcasite,** or **pyrite.**

WASHINGTON CO.

PEKIN, W 1¼ mi., an abandoned quarry—**barite, calcite, selenite, sphalerite** (in vugs, as twinned crystals).

WAYNE CO.

RICHMOND, SE 3 mi., the Debolt Quarry—**calcite, dolomite, marcasite, pyrite, apatite, barite** (fluorescent), **goethite** (red coatings or as pseudomorphs after **pyrite**).

WELLS CO.

BLUFFTON, N 1½ mi., the Erie Stone Co. quarry—**dolomite, marcasite, pyrite.**

IOWA

Iowa is primarily a prairie state of moderate relief, with low hills in the unglaciated northeastern section and rich, rolling tablelands interrupted by many streams elsewhere. The highest point in the state is a knoll rising 1,675 feet above sea level west of Sibley in the northwestern corner of Osceolo Co. The present surface features are a result chiefly of the uneven mantling of preexisting indurated rocks by glacial drift, since all of Iowa was included within the region of the Pleistocene ice fields.

For much of the Mesozoic era, and especially during the whole of the Cretaceous period, Iowa lay under a broad, shallow, epicontinental sea; therefore, the subsurface formations are dominated by sedimentary deposits. Throughout the state almost any road or railroad cut, erosional gulley, cut bank, stream break, quarry, or other excavation, however shallow, is a promising place in which to look for **quartz family gemstones, crystallizations,** or **fossils.** Indeed, beautifully colored **silicified colony corals** and **stromatoporoids** are commonly encountered, capable of being cut and polished into unusual gemstone art objects. These gemmy fossils occur principally in Devonian limestone exposures which outcrop over much of Iowa, being most typical and best-known around Iowa City.

For information, write: Iowa Geological Survey, Iowa City.

ALLAMAKEE CO.

HARPERS FERRY, area Mississippi R. mud beds, in mussel shells—gem **pearls.**

LANSING, an abandoned nearby mine (make inquiry)—**cerussite.**

NEW GALENA, area mines and dumps—**galena.**

APPANOOSE CO.

CENTERVILLE: (1) area quarries—**gypsum;** (2) on all regional coal mine dumps (very many scattered from ALBIA in Monroe Co. to COAL CITY on Missouri border SE of CENTERVILLE)—**pyrite, selenite.**

BLACK HAWK, BREMER, BENTON COS.

AREA, any limestone quarry, rd. or RR cut, stream bank, gravel bar, or pit—**"Coldwater"** agate (nodular, fortification type, gem quality; filled with blue, gray, pink, amethystine centers, or crystals).

BUCHANAN CO.

BRANDON, in cr. bed both inside and outside of town—**geodes, fossils.**

CLAYTON CO.

AREA, many mines and dumps in the **lead** and **zinc** region—**lead minerals** (mainly **galena**), **limonite, pyrite, sphalerite.**
GUTTENBERG: (1) area mines—**galena, smithsonite;** (2) both N and S of town, in washes, cut banks, etc.—**agate** (gray, banded vein type), **cave onyx,** (3) S of town, in washes, etc.—also **jasper** (black and various colors).

CLINTON CO.

BUENA VISTA, area mines—**galena, smithsonite.**

DE MOINES CO.

BURLINGTON: (1) all area Mississippi R. gravels and commercial dredging operations (get permission)—**Lake Superior agates.** (These gem **agates** are found in all Mississippi R. gravels along the entire east boundary of Iowa.) (2) Geode State Park (no collecting, but a most interesting display of gemstones and geodes); (3) all regional cr. beds—**Lake Superior agates, quartz crystals, crystal geodes.**

DUBUQUE CO.

DUBUQUE: (1) all regional **lead** and **zinc** mines of co.—**galena, cerussite, limonite, sphalerite;** (2) all Mississippi R. gravels and commercial dredging operations (get permission)—**Lake Superior agates, moss agates, moonstone spar, jasper, petrified wood, fossils, diamond** (rare), occasional **oolitic agate.**

FAYETTE CO.

AREA, all regional stream and cr. gravels—**Lake Superior agates.**

FRANKLIN CO.

CHAPIN, in area limestone quarry—**geodes** (crystal-lined, to baseball size).

FREMONT CO.

AREA, all Devonian limestone outcrops, gemstone quality—**fossil corals and stromatoporoids.**

HAMILTON CO.

STANHOPE, N to second crossrd., turn W and then N to a bridge, cross and park, area of Bells Mill, in veins and beds of sedimentary rocks—**cone-in-cone calcite** (coal-black, to 12 in. high).

HARDIN CO.

ELDORA: (1) area limestone quarries—**crystal geodes;** (2) area stream gravels—**geodes.**
HUBBARD, S 5 mi. on Hwy. 65, then W 4 mi. on paved rd., turn S to next intersection and go 6 mi. W, then S to a quarry just N of the next intersection, in brown limestone formation—**geodes** (crystal-lined).
UNION: (1) all area quarries—**crystal-lined geodes;** (2) regional stream beds—**geodes.**

HENRY CO.

AREA, the Skunk R. gravel bars from ROME SE to LOWELL—**"Keokuk" geodes, petrified corals ("Petoskey stones"),** area deposits of brown **limonite.**
MT. PLEASANT, S edge in exposures of Mississippian limestones—gemmy banded colored **chert, quartz crystal geodes.**
NEW LONDON, regional stream beds, banks, cuts, etc.—**agate, jasper.**

JACKSON CO.

AREA, gravel pits—**agate, carnelian.**
BELLEVUE, Mississippi R. gravels and commercial dredging operations (get permission)—**Lake Superior agates, jasper, moonstone spar, moss agate, petrified corals,** etc.

IRON HILLS, area deposits—**limonite (brown iron ore), hematite** (principal **iron** ore).

JASPER CO.

MONROE, area mines, used in the manufacture of metallic paints—**hematite.**

JOHNSON CO.

CORALVILLE (suburb of IOWA CITY): (1) area farms (inquire)—**silicified corals** (similar to Michigan's "**Petoskey stones**"); (2) area quarries (including IOWA CITY)—**silicified** or **calcified corals.**

LEE CO.

FARMINGTON, area gravel pits—"**Keokuk**" **geodes, "Petoskey stones**" (silicified or calcified *Hexagonaria* corals).

KEOKUK: (1) in all tributaries of the Des Moines R. NW to OTTUMWA in Wapello Co.; (2) along the Des Moines R. in gravel bars, banks, bluffs, etc.; (3) all regional quarries, gravel pits, rd. and RR cuts, excavations between the Mississippi R. at KEOKUK and OTTUMWA—"**Keokuk**" **geodes, "Petoskey stones.**" The famed Keokuk Geode Beds outcrop in a broad area around the junction of the Des Moines and Mississippi rivers, where the states of Illinois, Iowa, and Missouri come together. The **geodes** occur in the Warsaw formation and may contain any or any combination of the following: **amethyst, ankerite, aragonite, calcite** (pink variety highly prized), **chalcedony, dolomite, goethite, kaolin, limonite, marcasite, millerite** (as dark green, hairlike inclusions in **calcite**), **pyrite** (glittering), **sphalerite.** The extraordinarily abundant **geodes** vary in size from golf ball, baseball, soft ball, to beach ball, the commonest **geodes** being 4 to 6 inches in diameter.

LINN CO.

CEDAR RAPIDS, entire co. area stream gravels—**silicified** or **calcified corals.**

MAHASKA CO.

OSKALOOSA, area limestone quarries—**concretions** (coated with white **calcite crystals**), **concretions** containing **dolomite crystals** (bronze to black, iridescent).

MAHASKA, WAPELLO, JEFFERSON, HENRY COS.

AREA, extending SE from OSKALOOSA to its jct. with the Skunk R., the bed, banks, and gravels of Cedar Cr.—**silicified** and **calcified corals.**

MARION CO.

KNOXVILLE: (1) regional coal mine dumps—**concretions** (containing crystals of **barite, calcite,** and **dolomite; siderite**); (2) SE 8 mi. on Hwy. 60, turn E ¾ mi. to the Pershing Mine—**calcite crystals** (very long), **pyrite crystals** (rare type).

MONROE CO.

ALBIA, entire region S through Monroe and Appanoose counties to COAL CITY, innumerable coal mine dumps—**pyrite, selenite crystals.**
LOVILIA, all area mine dumps—**calcite crystals** (honey-colored or with dark hairlike **goethite** needle inclusions), **fossils.**

MONTGOMERY CO.

RED OAK, W on Hwy. 34 1 mi., turn N at motel onto country rd. to an area a short distance N of some large structures on the E, continue to large limestone quarry W of rd. (get permission)—gemmy **chert,** locally termed **"protozoa"** (or **"rice"**) **agate.**

MUSCATINE CO.

MUSCATINE: (1) center of Mississippi R. **pearl**-dredging operations (extending along entire Iowa border) with a second center at MCGREGOR in Clayton Co. far to the N, in mussel shells—gem **pearls** (pink, gold, pigeon blood; gems, slugs, baroques, **mother-of-pearl**); (2) S of town, gravel pits in a large alluvial flat—**agate** (Lake Superior, moss, sagenitic), **chalcedony, quartz crystals;** (3) S on U.S. 61 through town past a pearl button factory and mill, turn E on Oregon St. to Steward St. gravel operations (thence on to other rock piles), get permission from commercial dredge operators—**Lake Superior agates, silicified** and **calcified corals, moss agate, jasper, petrified wood, moonstone spar.**

PALO ALTO CO.

EMMETSBURG, regional stream gravels—**agate, jasper, petrified wood.**
GRAETTINGER: cf. EMMETSBURG.

STORY CO.

AMES, area stream gravels, quarries, excavations—**chalcedony, fossils.**

VAN BUREN CO.

FARMINGTON, area stream beds, banks, excavations, etc.—**quartz crystal geodes.**

WEBSTER CO.

FORT DODGE, regional quarries—**gypsum.**

KANSAS

As a mineral-producing state, Kansas is seldom appreciated, even by its own residents. Economically, the mineral industry is second only to agriculture, and the state outranks most others except California in its mineral production. However, the mineral wealth derives primarily from **coal, zinc, lead, gypsum,** and **volcanic ash,** in this order, now being superseded by great new reserves of **petroleum** and **natural gas.** As a source for collectors' gems and gemstones, Kansas is likely to be bypassed by the traveling rock hunter, although in-state collectors find many interesting specimens worthy of being added to their home collections.

Western Kansas comprises the rather rugged, semiarid Great High Plains. The land surface is thinly covered by Pleistocene and Recent gravels, with extensive Pliocene lavas capping the buttes and mesas. Few gemstones but an enormous variety of fossil vertebrate bones weather from the cut banks and washes.

About 1,750,000 years ago northern Kansas was invaded by the Kansan glacier, second of the four Pleistocene ice advances, as far south as the Kaw Valley and the Little Blue River. In this region's gravel pits, quarries, and morainal deposits can be found a variety of glacial drift gemstones. By contrast, southeastern Kansas constitutes an extension of the Ozark Plateau into what is termed the "Tri-State District," where Kansas, Missouri, and Oklahoma join boundaries. This district is interesting to the mineral collector because of its many highly productive **zinc** and **lead** mines. Dumps rising 100 feet high are known as "chat mountains" (chat being a mispronunciation of **chert**) and produce an abundance of desirable mineral specimens of **barite, calcite, chalcopyrite, cerussite, dolomite crystals, galena, pyrite,** and **sphalerite.**

To be noted on geologic maps is the widespread Ogallala formation (Tertiary), embracing the counties of Clark, Ellis, Logan, Ness, Rawlins, and Wallace. In this formation are found **dendritic opal,** white translucent **opal** as irregular masses or nodules, **opalized bones,** and much **petrified wood.** From the western Cretaceous chalk beds exposed in the counties of Cherokee, Logan, Norton, and Phillips, one can gather color-ful gemmy **chert** (some dendritic with **manganese**) and **jasper.** Anderson, Brown, Chase, and Franklin counties yield fine crystals of **barite.** In general, the surfaces of draws, washes, and sandhills of all the western half of Kansas produce **agate, chalcedony, chert, jasper,** and **petrified wood,** although very little is quality gemstone material, especially along the Smoky Hill River in Gove, Logan, Trego, and Wallace counties. Regional outcrops of shale disgorge good **selenite crystals.**

For information, write: State Geological Survey, University of Kansas, Lawrence.

ANDERSON CO.

GARNETT, N 3 mi. on U.S. 59, a RR quarry—**crystals, fossils.**

BARBER CO.

AETNA: (1) area draws, washes, etc.—**agate, agatized wood;** (2) along the Medicine Lodge R. and on adjoining buttes and terraces—**agate, jasper, agatized wood.** (Gemstone collecting is good over all the regional surface all the way to KIOWA in the SE corner of the co. and also includes **chert, chalcedony,** and **petrified wood.**)

SUN CITY, area **gypsum** quarries, especially in S hills—**calcite crystals, gypsum.**

BARBER-COMANCHE COS.

AREA, all regional **gypsum** quarries and mines, widespread—**gypsum, calcite crystals,** etc.

BOURBON CO.

FORT SCOTT, on Marais des Cygnes, in Pennsylvanian "Coal Measures" as interstratifications—**siderite.** (Beds of **coal** interstratified with **siderite** outcrop along regional tributaries of the Neosho R. for several counties to the west.)

BUTLER CO.

DAVID CITY, in breaks and cut banks along the Walnut R. in S section of the Flint Hills (inquire locally)—**crystal-lined geodes.**

CHASE CO.

STRONG CITY, area gravel pits—**chalcopyrite, geodes** (lined with **quartz crystals**).

CHEROKEE CO.

AREA of the Tri-State District, e.g., the BADGER, PEACOCK, GALENA, and LAWTON districts, very many huge **lead-zinc** mines with towering dumps (chat mountains)—**galena** (as most abundant **lead** ore), **sphalerite** (**zinc** ore), **barite, calcite, cerussite, marcasite, pyrite, smithsonite.**

BAXTER SPRINGS, area mines with ore bodies occurring in Mississippian limestone which outcrops predominantly in the very corner of Kansas— **"chat"** (local term for **chert** which is mixed throughout the **lead-zinc** ores), **galena, pyrite, sphalerite.** (This extensive mining region embraces SW Missouri, SE Kansas, and NE Oklahoma.)

COLUMBUS, all area **coal** mines (including entire co.)—fine crystals of **pyrite, calcite, dolomite, marcasite, sphalerite.**

GALENA, many area mines and huge dumps—**calamine** (secondary mineral in **zinc** ores), **galena, hydrozincite, marcasite, pyrite, smithsonite, sphalerite.**

WEST MINERAL, many area mines—typical **lead** and **zinc minerals,** with **marcasite** and **pyrite** occurring in **coal** veins.

CLARK CO.

ASHLAND, N, in steep hills of Bluff Cr. and near Mt. Casino—**moss agate, moss opal, jasper.**

CLOUD CO.

CONCORDIA: (1) N, in area called the Old River Bed—**agate** (clear, banded, mossy), **jasper, petrified wood;** (2) all cut banks, tributaries, and gravels of the Republican R. (and extending outside co. boundaries)— **agate, jasper, petrified wood.**

COMANCHE CO.

AREA, N part of co., extending E to 12 mi. N of SUN CITY in Barber Co., *q.v.,* all along the valley of Salt Fork Cr., as beds—**gypsum.**

WILMORE, beds extending from 1 mi. N of town to 5 mi. S, commercially exploited—**volcanic ash.**

COWLEY CO.

ROCK, area draws, gulleys, cut banks, and regional cr. and stream beds— **crystal-lined geodes.**

DICKINSON CO.

AREA, gravels of the Smoky Hill R.—gem **agatized wood.**
HOPE, area quarries—**gypsum, associated minerals.**
SOLOMON, area quarries—**gypsum, calcite,** etc.

ELLIS CO.

HAYES, W, in valley of the Smoky Hill R., as massive outcropping beds—Niobrara **chalk.**
YOCEMENTO, local cement plant quarry—**rock wool.**

ELLSWORTH CO.

CARNEIRO: (1) area known locally as the Mushroom Rocks—**pyrite concretions;** (2) S 5 mi., in Cretaceous outcrops (banks) of the Smoky Hill R., in lignite beds—**amber.** The old collecting area is under the waters of the Kanopolis Reservoir, but hunting may successfully be done in lignite beds outcropping back from the impounded waters. Also collectable are **barite roses ("walnuts").**
ELLSWORTH, area quarries or mines—**halite.**
KANOPOLIS, area quarries or mines, especially to the E and SE, and as local deposits—**halite, volcanic ash.**
MORRILL, NW 2 mi., in banks of Pony Cr. in veins in Permian shales—**celestite crystals.**

FORD CO.

DODGE CITY, NE 7 mi., a quarry—**rock wool.**

FRANKLIN CO.

OTTAWA: (1) area Rose Quarry (inquire directions)—**crystals, fossil plants;** (2) S 4 mi. on U.S. 59 to the Buildex Quarry—**crystals, fossil plants.**

GEARY CO.

JUNCTION CITY: (1) countywide area sand and gravel pits—gem **agatized wood;** (2) regional rd. and RR cuts—**geodes** (**quartz** and **calcite**); (3) gravels of the Republican R.—**agate, jasper.**

GOVE CO.

QUINTER: (1) area surrounding town—**concretions** (cemented by **calcite**); (2) SW 10 mi., on E side of a S-flowing tributary of Hackberry Cr., as deposit—**volcanic ash.**

HARPER CO.

ANTHONY, area mines—**halite.**
HARPER, N, along the Chikaskia R. in gravel bars—**agate, jasper, petrified wood.**

JEFFERSON CO.

McLouth, area glacial moraines and gravel drift—**Lake Superior agate, chalcedony, jasper, petrified wood.** (Good collecting of gemmy substances can be found over much of the county's rocky hillsides, stream beds, gravel pits, etc.)

JEWELL CO.

Burr Oak, area deposits—**volcanic ash.**

KINGMAN CO.

Kingman, area mines—**halite.**

KIOWA CO.

Greensburg, E on U.S. 54 to the Kimberley Ranch (noted area for thousands of pounds of specimens)—**meteorites** of the stony-iron type called **"pallasites."**

LOGAN CO.

Elkader, up and downstream of the Smoky Hill R., weathering out of chalk bluffs—**moss opal.**

McPHERSON CO.

Freemount (just S of Rte. 4), area—**septarian nodules.**
Roxbury, just outside of town at Roxbury Hill—**septarian nodules.**

MARION CO.

Florence, area gravel pits—**crystal-lined geodes.**

MARSHALL CO.

Blue Rapids: (1) gravel beds of the Big Blue R., extending beyond co. boundaries, all its tributaries, and on all surrounding hillsides and in washes —**agate, chalcedony, chert, jasper;** (2) S, area mines—**gypsum.**

MEADE CO.

Fowler, W 7½ mi., largest producing area in Kansas—**volcanic ash.**

MITCHELL CO.

BELOIT, area of the Blue Hills in W section of co.—**septarian nodules.**
GREAT SPIRIT SPRING, surrounding area—**banded travertine, tufa.**

MONTGOMERY CO.

INDEPENDENCE, local cement plant quarry—**rock wool.**

NEOSHO CO.

CHANUTE, local cement plant quarry—**rock wool.**

NORTON CO.

DELLVALE, area deposits, mines—**volcanic ash.**
NORTON, E, to vicinity of CALVERT: (1) area deposits—**volcanic ash;**
(2) area land surfaces, washes, draws, etc.—**concretions** (cemented by **calcite**).

OSBORNE CO.

HOBBIE LAKE, S 1 mi., area—gemmy **septarian nodules** (filled with yellow **calcite** veining).
OSBORNE, S 2 mi., area—**septarian nodules** (with yellow **calcite** veining).

OTTAWA CO.

ADA, area to N and NW—**petrified wood.**
MINNEAPOLIS: (1) SW 2½ mi., area, largest in state—giant **concretions** (far too large to collect, but a tourist attraction in the Smoky Hills region); (2) Smoky Hills (W section called the Blue Hills), area outcrops of clay, sandstone, and limestone—**"fence post" limestone** (not gemmy material; the fresh-quarried limestone is cut into large fence posts for use as such through much of the region where wood is extremely scarce.)

RENO CO.

ARLINGTON, area of central part of co., large salt-producing companies, mines—**halite.**

RICE CO.

LYONS, area mines—**halite.**
STERLING, area mines—**halite.**

RILEY CO.

BALA, area volcanic plug—**magnetite.**
STOCKDALE, area igneous rock exposures, as granules—**pyrope garnet.**

SALINE CO.

SALINA, W about 7 mi., in old Saline Quarry (2 mi. W of BAVARIA)—**barite roses ("walnuts"), sand concretions.**

TREGO, WALLACE COS.

AREA, valley sand and gravel beds, pits, etc.—**geodes (chalcedony, calcite, quartz).**

WALLACE CO.

WALLACE, S 5 mi., in rd. cut—**moss opal** (milky, with **manganese** dendrites; scenic).

WASHINGTON CO.

WASHINGTON, NE, along Mill Cr., in Permian outcrops—**celestite crystals.**

WILSON CO.

BUFFALO, along the Verdigris R.—**agate, jasper, chalcedony, petrified wood.**

WOODSON CO.

YATES CENTER, S 8 mi., area—**amethysts, quartz crystals.**

WYANDOTTE CO.

BONNER SPRINGS, in the Lone Star Quarry—**quartz-crystal geodes.**

KENTUCKY

The Blue Grass State is relatively little explored from the gemstone collector's viewpoint, and very few rock clubs have been organized within its boundaries. The minerals which contribute most to Kentucky's economic prosperity, about $400 million annually, are the staples of **coal, limestone, fluorspar, rock asphalt, stone, gravel,** and **sand**—all products of sedimentation. The state is part of a very old land surface, lying within the eastern uplifted Appalachian Plateau and the westerly Interior Low Plateaus. During most of the Paleozoic and Mesozoic eras, Kentucky lay beneath the sea, and thus its rock formations are predominantly sedimentary shales, sandstone, limestone, etc., with almost no igneous or metamorphic intrusions.

The rugged hardwood-timbered Cumberland Plateau that comprises part of eastern Kentucky rises to 4,100 feet in Big Black Mountain, highest of numerous peaks that straddle the Virginia border in the range of the same name along the boundaries of Bell and Harlan counties. This plateau breaks toward the "bluegrass" heartland in the Pottsville Escarpment, marked by a belt of rounded shale hills known as the "Knobs." To the west in the low Mississippian Plateau, a region of rocky hillsides denotes an extensive area of underground streams which have carved such great caverns as the famed Mammoth Caves in the limestone substrata.

The region lying east of the Tennessee River emerged from the Paleozoic seas toward the close of the Mississippian period some 340 million years ago. Outcropping rocks in this region range from the Middle Ordovician to the Pennsylvanian, containing few collectable minerals and gemstones but great quantities of fossils. Nevertheless, wherever the Fort Payne and Warsaw formations of the Mississippian Period crop out, gemmy **geodes** appear abundantly. These interesting nodules are found in many sizes from walnut to beach ball. Some contain beautifully banded **chalcedony,** while others have interiors lined or filled with lovely crystals of **calcite, celestite, fluorite, goethite, pyrite,** and **quartz.** The most productive area for collecting **geodes** surrounds the Bluegrass, southward into Tennessee. Throughout this considerable region, investigation of creek and stream beds and banks, runs (local term for a small stream or rill), road and railroad cut banks, excavations, etc., almost always reveals an abundant supply of **geodes.**

The lands lying west of the Tennessee River, known as the Purchase Region, did not emerge from the sea until Tertiary times only 40 to 50 million years ago. This region remained for long ages as the head of a great embayment extending north from the ancient Gulf of Mexico, thus receiving largely estuarine deposits. Cretaceous and Tertiary formations are developed principally in the Jackson Purchase area, while Pleistocene alluvium occurs plentifully in the valleys of western Kentucky and along the Ohio and its tributaries.

For information, write: Kentucky Geological Survey, Lexington.

ADAIR CO.

AREA, countywide creeks, rivers, beds and banks, rd. cuts exposing the Warsaw formation—**quartz** and other **geodes.**
COLUMBIA, the Shamrock Stone Co. limestone quarry—**geodes.**

ALLEN CO.

SCOTTSVILLE, area quarries in the Warsaw formation—**quartz geodes.**

BALLARD CO.

WICKCLIFFE, E, in a ravine as a deposit—**yellow ocher.**

BARREN CO.

CAVE CITY, area commercial quarries, as pink and yellow gemmy varieties —**marble.**

BATH CO.

OWINGSVILLE, area **iron** mines—**hematite.**

BOURBON CO.

MILLERSBURG, area mines—**barite, galena.**
PARIS, area mines (make inquiry or check a topographic map)—**barite, galena.**

BOYD, CARTER, GREENUP COS.

ASHLAND (Boyd Co.): these counties in the extreme NE corner of Kentucky comprise a considerable mining district for **iron** ores, mines and dumps producing as the original mineral—**siderite.**

BOYLE CO.

DANVILLE, many area mines and dumps—**barite.**

CALDWELL CO.

AREA, many mines throughout W part of co.—**barite, calcite, fluorite,** etc.
CRIDER, N, in fault exposures—**fluorite,** etc.

FREDONIA, area mines—**barite.**
PRINCETON, area quarries (numerous)—**calcite, fluorite.**

CALDWELL-CRITTENDEN COS.

AREA, many well-known old mines, such as the Ashbridge, Glendale, Tabor, and other regional mines back of the Ohio R.—**galena, fluorite.**

CARLISLE CO.

LAKETON, in bluffs of a nearby cr., a deposit—**yellow ocher.**

CRITTENDEN CO.

AREA along the Ohio R. (Ky. side of similarly famed **fluorite** region of Ill., *q.v.*), many **fluorite** mines, such as the Old Jim, Brown, Hodge, Columbia, etc.—**barite, calcite, dolomite crystals, fluorite** (crystals to 5 in. on an edge; blue, green, canary yellow, hyacinth, rose, violet; etched, striated, color-zoned), **galena, marcasite, pyrite, silver** (some recovered from **lead** concentrates from **fluorspar**), **smithsonite, sphalerite.** (The mines were opened in the 1870's in massive fault-replacement veins in Mississippian limestone.)

MARION: (1) N 3 mi. from jct. of U.S. 60 and Rte. 1668, on E side of rd., the Crittenden Springs fault—cf. AREA minerals; (2) NW, off Rte. 387 at Hickory Cane Mine dump (W of rd. and up Caney Cr. from the Glendale Baptist Church on Glendale Church Rd.)—**mica, fluorite, peridotite;** (3) from jct. of U.S. 60 and Rt. 855, go 1 mi. left to the old Kirk Mine— cf. AREA minerals; (4) SW 5 mi., as scattered deposits—**ocher.**

MEXICO, SW on U.S. 70, turn left at the Crider Fluorspar Co. sign .8 mi. from town, then left at .3 mi. (1.1 mi. from town) across RR to the Pigmy Fluorspar Mine (an open pit)—cf. AREA minerals.

SHERIDAN, the Big Four Fault, NE to SW of Rte. 297 (the La Rue, Cartwright, Macer, etc., **lead** mines)—**anglesite, cerussite, fluorite, galena, pyromorphite, smithsonite, smoky quartz crystals.**

ELLIOTT CO.

AREA, igneous outcrops in the Little Sandy R. area—**apatite, almandite garnets, chromite, diopside, enstatite, feldspar, quartz.**

ISONVILLE, in **peridotite** outcrops along the banks of Ison Cr., especially just W of confluence with Johnson Cr. and across from the Ison Johnson school—**enstatite, ilmenite, magnetite, mica, olivine, peridotite, pyrope garnet, serpentine.**

FAYETTE CO.

LEXINGTON: (1) area mines (check a topographic map)—**barite;** (2) vicinity of Morton's Mill, mines—**fluorite;** (3) area of Elk Lick Falls ("Petrified Falls"), a large deposit—**cave onyx** (banded in browns and yellows).

FRANKLIN CO.

FRANKFORT, area of KISSINGER (not on AAA map), as gangue mineral in the Clerk vein—**barite,** with **galena** as main ore.

GARRARD CO.

LANCASTER: (1) N on Rte. 52 on Boone Cr., in **barite** prospect—crystals of **barite, calcite, fluorite, sphalerite;** (2) W 4 mi., a deposit—**barite.**

GRAVES CO.

FARMINGTON, HICKORY, SEDALIA, VIOLA, regional gravel and clay pits, as pebbles—**agate, chalcedony, chert, jasper, petrified wood.**
HARD MONEY, S 2½ mi., small quantities in gravel beds—**hematite.**
MAYFIELD, SW 5 mi. on U.S. 45 (and just N of PRYORSBURG), area clay pits, as pebbles—**agate, chalcedony, chert, jasper, quartz, silicified wood.**

HARDIN CO.

ELIZABETHTOWN, area quarries in the Warsaw formation—**quartz geodes,** etc.
VINE GROVE, area excavations, pits, quarries, cut banks exposing the Warsaw formation—**quartz geodes.**

HARRISON CO.

CYNTHIANA, SE 3 mi., in Ordovician limestone as a deposit—**barite.**
LAIR, area mines and pits—**barite, galena.**

HART CO.

ROWLETTS, area rd. cuts, banks, stream gravels—banded **calcite onyx, petrified wood.**

JEFFERSON CO.

LOUISVILLE: (1) area beds and banks of the Ohio R.—**fossil corals** (cutting material), **petrified wood;** (2) N end of LOUISVILLE-JEFFERSONVILLE bridge—**petrified wood, silicified corals;** (3) E via U.S. 60: (a) By-pass 60 to Grinstead Ave., turn right to quarries N of the by-pass near jct.; (b) first left turn off Grinstead Ave., a quarry; (c) across the by-pass at E end of park—**silicified fossils** (corals, crinoids), **oolite;**
  (4): (a) rd. cuts along U.S. 42; (b) the County Quarry (reached from

Grinstead Ave. N from By-pass 60 to STILZ, then left to Frankfort St., and Hillcrest to U.S. 42), quarry is 2½ mi. from the jct.—**silicified fossils** (corals, wood, crinoids); (c) rd. cuts N of the quarry—**silicified fossils;** (5) Coral Ridge, S 1½ mi. to Buttermold Knob and ½ mi. E of the Old National Turnpike, an exposure—**silicified corals.**

VALLEY STATION, S to Muldraugh's Hill (on or near co. line; reached also from WEST POINT in Bullitt Co.), numerous roadside exposures of the Warsaw formation—**quartz geodes.**

LINCOLN CO.

AREA, countywide exposures of the Fort Payne and Warsaw formations (Mississippian age)—**geodes** (containing crystals of **calcite, celestite, goethite, fluorite, quartz, pyrite;** some lined with botryoidal and banded **chalcedony**), clear **quartz crystals.**

ROWLAND, N, on rural roads to just S of Rte. 52, on Boone Cr. near confluence of Hanging Rock Cr. and Dix R., numerous pits and prospects—**barite, calcite, fluorite, sphalerite.**

STANFORD: (1) S 6 mi. via Rte. 78 to near Hall's Gap, bed and banks of the Green R.; (2) along the S and E banks and in the Green R. bed from Green River Church SW to New Bethel Church—**geodes** (crystal-lined). (These fascinating **geodes,** most prized of which contain pink **calcite crystals** along with sharply terminated, brilliantly clear **quartz crystals,** occur abundantly through Lincoln Co. and adjacent counties. Some stream beds are literally choked with the **geodes.**)

LIVINGSTON CO.

BIRDSVILLE, nearby on Rte. 137, two abandoned quarries—**calcite, dolomite crystals, fluorite, quartz.**

BURNA, area sandstone quarries—**calcite, fluorite, quartz crystals.**

CARRSVILLE: (1) area **fluorspar** mines—**barite, calcite, dolomite crystals, fluorite** (crystals to several in. on an edge; variously colored, color-zoned, striated), **galena, marcasite, pyrite, smithsonite, sphalerite,** some **lead-silver** minerals in **fluorspar;** (2) E 1 mi. and S of Rte. 387, the Ellis Mine—**calcite, fluorite, quartz crystals,** etc.; (3) E, on N side of Rte. 3872, a fault near the Ohio R. exposing brecciated sandstone—**fluorite cubes.**

JOY, area **fluorspar** mines—**calcite, fluorite, galena, quartz.**

SMITHLAND, N, at Dyer Hill **fluorspar** mine, in cavities in a massive **fluorspar** vein in the Dyer Hill fault—**calcite, fluorite, galena, quartz crystals, sphalerite.**

LYON CO.

AREA: (1) along the E shoreline of Kentucky Lake, and (2) all area rd. cuts and quarries—**calcite geodes, jasper, quartz.**

EDDYVILLE, area gravel pits, rd. cuts, excavations—**agate, chalcedony, jasper.**

KENTUCKY DAM, 6 mi. above at Milepost 30 on the Tennessee R., in the State Quarry revealing an unusual exposure of the Warsaw formation—**calcite, jasper, quartz geodes.**

KENTUCKY STATE PARK, rd. cuts at entrance show Warsaw formation exposures—**"Fort Payne" chert.**

MADISON CO.

BEREA, SE on U.S. 25, area rd. cuts and banks—**oolitic limestone, quartz geodes.**

McCRACKEN CO.

PADUCAH, E 3 mi., mines and pits—**ocher.**

MARSHALL CO.

CALVERT CITY, area of Highland Landing on the Tennessee R., a deposit on the banks—**ocher.**

MERCER CO.

AREA: (1) area of the Kentucky R. bend (NE of HARRODSBURG), and (2) the Two Chimneys and Fantail mines—**barite, calcite, fluorspar.**

HARRODSBURG, area mines—**barite, calcite, fluorite, galena, sphalerite.**

MONROE CO.

TOMPKINSVILLE, regional quarries, excavations, and other exposures of the Warsaw formation—Warsaw-type **geodes.**

OWEN CO.

GRATZ, N, on N bank of the Kentucky R. immediately W of Rte. 355, dumps of the Gratz Mine—**barite, calcite, fluorite, galena, sphalerite.**

ROCKCASTLE CO.

BOONE: (1) area rd. cuts; (2) S toward MOUNT VERNON in all rd. cuts and banks—**chert, jasper, geodes, oolite;** (3) in area limestone quarry—**calcite, oolitic limestone, quartz.**

MOUNT VERNON: (1) N on U.S. 25 1 mi. from city limits, in a rd. cut—**chert** (black, gemmy), **jasper** (several colors), **"topographic" limestone** (brecciated, with maplike patterning); (2) W, in a limestone quarry—**chert, jasper, geodes.**

ROWAN CO.

ELLIOTTVILLE, FARMER, HAYS, MOREHEAD, SUMMIT, all regional quarries and excavations, cut banks, stream beds, etc.—**crystals, fossils, minerals.**
SALT LICK, W 5 mi. and 3 mi. N of Rte. 60, the old Rose River strip **iron** mines—**hematite** (nodules), **jasper** (red, mixed with **hematite**).

SCOTT CO.

GEORGETOWN, area of Duval Sta., 1½ mi. distant at the Johnson vein—**barite** (gangue mineral), **galena.**

WHITLEY CO.

CUMBERLAND FALLS, area quarries and stream banks, rd. cuts, etc.—**"Rockcastle" conglomerate** (a sandstone matrix filled with well-cemented pebbles of **flint, jasper, quartz,** etc.; makes excellent attractive cutting material). This unusual conglomerate caps the entire Pottsville Escarpment that separates the Cumberland Plateau from the lower Mississippian Plateau and the Bluegrass, crossing many counties.

WOODFORD CO.

TROY, SW 2 mi. on Mundy's Landing rd., dead-ending at mines and prospect pits—crystals of **barite, calcite, fluorite, galena, sphalerite.** (There are many regional mines within this co., as at Shyrock Ferry and Spring Sta., Faircloths Ferry, etc.—**barite, galena, sphalerite.**)

LOUISIANA

Louisiana lies in the lower Mississippi River Valley, only in recent times elevated above the surface of the ancient Gulf of Mexico. The land has a maximum elevation above sea level of 500 feet, sloping gently southward from the Arkansas line with an average elevation of 400 feet. A very low dividing ridge runs almost centrally through northern Louisiana, separating the Ouachita and Red river drainage systems east and west. Along these two rivers the flood plains and second bottoms, or "hammocks" as they are locally called, form a very minor topographic feature in the generally monotonous landscape.

The state lacks gemstones and minerals generally. Brown **hematite** and **limonite** occur in Tertiary sands in numerous deposits in the northwestern parishes (counties) of Bienville, Bossier, Caddo, Claiborne, Lincoln, and Union. The northern counties also reveal various exposures of hard **limestone, gypsum, salt,** and **marl** in separated exposures of Cretaceous strata. Tertiary formations (Eocene and Oligocene) outcrop in nearly every parish to yield **petrified wood** (mostly hickory, oak, poplar, and palm). Large silicified logs have been found in De Sota Parish. The whole history of the Tertiary laminated sands and lignitic shales is that of a gradually receding sea, too recent to allow formation of the type of minerals and gemstones most sought after by collectors.

For information, write: Louisiana State Geological Survey, State University, Baton Rouge.

LIVINGSTON, TANGIPAHOA PARISHES

Regional stream gravels, occasional—**carnelian.**

OUACHITA PARISH

WEST MONROE, S 12 mi., in gravels of the Ouachita R.—**banded agate, petrified** and **opalized wood.**

RAPIDES, VERNON PARISHES

Regional stream gravels—**silicified palm** (*Palmoxylon*).

MAINE

The topography of Maine was sculptured by Pleistocene glaciers two miles thick in places, eroding the original Tertiary land surfaces right down to bedrock. Thus, the state rests on its ancient foundation of limestone, sandstone, and shale. The generally mountainous, heavily forested western region slopes northward to the St. John River basin and eastward toward the Penobscot River. Receding glaciers dammed the valleys with long drift ridges to form some 2,200 lakes. In the more than 5,000 rivers and streams, gravel beds yield up many interesting gem and mineral specimens.

Where deep-seated earth forces caused molten granite to intrude the basal sedimentaries and recrystallize them, many valuable mineral and gemstone deposits were formed. Indeed, the mineral wealth of Maine is notable, especially for the wide variety of gemstone minerals which occur in the state's extraordinary pegmatites. These dikes are essentially coarse-grained concentrations of **feldspar** and **quartz,** developed during the closing stages of widespread granitic intrusions through the foundation rocks.

The great glaciers exposed most of the dikes, easily traceable as pod-shaped or sheetlike bodies ranging from a few inches to more than 4,000 feet in length.

The Maine pegmatites have been mined for more than a century for **potash feldspar**, along with occasional production of **quartz, sheet mica, beryl, spodumene,** and other industrial minerals. Substantial quantities of semiprecious gem crystals have made the Maine pegmatites world famous, because of the high gem quality of their **aquamarine, beryl, garnet, rose quartz, spodumene, topaz, tourmaline,** and many other gemstones. Perhaps nowhere in the world is there an area of comparable size productive of such an array of quality gems as Oxford County. Here, in particular, the Newry mines near Rumford and the mica mines near Paris are a collector's mecca.

For information, write: State Geologist, Geological Survey, Orono.

ANDROSCOGGIN CO.

AUBURN: (1) Kennedy Mine—**aquamarine, beryl, topaz;** (2) W 4 mi. (1¼ mi. ENE of MINOT, *q.v.*), many area mines such as the Androscoggin Tourmaline, Fisher, Hatch Farm, Greenslaw, Keith (Towne), Maine Feldspar, Pulsifer, etc.—**amblygonite, apatite** (purple), **beryl, feldspar, garnet, lepidolite, spodumene, tourmaline, morganite.**

LEWISTON, area of Mt. Robinson, pegmatite outcrops—**vesuvianite (idocrase).**

MINOT: (1) Bell (Giddings) prospect—**feldspar, muscovite mica, black tourmaline;** (2) La Flamme Mine—**feldspar, muscovite, pollucite, black tourmaline;** (3) Phillips Mine—**autunite, feldspar, amethyst, black tourmaline;** (4) Pitts Mine—**feldspar, muscovite mica, quartz;** (5) Pitts-Tenney Mine—**beryl, diopside, feldspar, grossularite garnet;** (6) Sturtevant Mine—**feldspar, black tourmaline;** (7) ENE 1¼ mi., mine on Mt. Apatite—**tourmaline;** (8) E 1½ mi., mine on Mt. Apatite—**apatite, beryl, morganite, tourmaline.**

POLAND, the Berry Quarry (1¼ mi. SE of MINOT)—**apatite, beryl, cassiterite, microcline feldspar, lepidolite, muscovite mica, tourmaline.**

AROOSTOOK CO.

AREA: (1) Castle Hill, at the Dudley Mine—**bementite, braunite, collophane (manganese, iron), manganiferous carbonate;** (2) Hammond Place, the Carpenter Mine—**ferrorhodochrosite;** (3) Hovey Mt. (with Maple Mt. continuous), area mines—**bementite, braunite, hematite, manganian talc, neotocite, penninite, pyrophanite, rhodochrosite, rhodonite, spessartite garnet, stilpnomelane.**

LINNEUS, the Adams Mt. Mine, in shale—**manganese minerals.**

LITTLETON, area molybdenite mine—**molybdenite.**

NEW LIMERICK, the Drew Hill Sulfide Mine—**marcasite, pyrite, pyrrhotite.**

CUMBERLAND CO.

AREA, the Piscataqua Mine—**copper, gold, nickel.**
BALDWIN, the Kelley prospect—**biotite mica, feldspar, muscovite mica, quartz.**
BRUNSWICK: (1) Garland Mine—**beryl, feldspar, muscovite mica, quartz;** (2) Grant Quarry—**feldspar, muscovite mica, quartz;** (3) LaChance Mine—**beryl, biotite mica, columbite, feldspar, muscovite, quartz, black tourmaline;** (4) Larrabee quarries (Helie Mine)—**beryl, biotite mica, feldspar, quartz;** (5) Morse Quarry—**feldspar.**
CASCO, the Chute prospect—**feldspar.**
FALMOUTH, the Falmouth Copper Mine—**copper pyrites, nickel arsenate.**
POWNAL, the Tyon Mt. quarries—**feldspar, mica (biotite, muscovite).**
WINDHAM, area exposures of micaceous slates—**staurolites.**

FRANKLIN CO.

AREA: (1) Township D, the Mountain Brook prospect—**scheelite;** (2) Township E, the Harden-Keith-Small prospect—**columbite, microcline feldspar, muscovite mica, quartz, spodumene, tourmaline.**
BYRON, the east branch of the Swift R., area near Tumbledown Mt. via Rte. 17, in low-water gravel bars, abundant placers—**gold.** (Local residents have been panning or sluicing **gold** from all area stream gravels for generations. The source of the gold is unknown, and there has never been a gold mine, as such, in Maine. Gravel caught in natural potholes and between up-ended ledges of rock makes for productive panning.)
FARMINGTON, area mines—**scheelite.**
RANGELEY, the Wing Mine—**calcite, pyrite, pyrrhotite.**

HANCOCK CO.

BLUE HILL: (1) Atlantic Mine—**pyrites (copper, gold, silver);** (2) Blue Hill Manganese Mine—**manganese minerals, rhodonite;** (3) Blue Hill Mine—**chalcopyrite, pyrite;** (4) Douglas Mine—**arsenopyrite, chalcopyrite, copper** (native), **cuprite, galena, magnetite, molybdenite, pyrite, pyrrhotite, sphalerite, stibnite, tennantite, tetrahedrite;** (5) Granger Mine—**bornite, chalcopyrite, pyrite, native silver;** (6) Mammoth Mine—**chalcopyrite, galena, pyrite, pyrrhotite, specularite, sphalerite;** (7) Owen Lead Mine—**chalcopyrite, galena, magnetite, pyrite, pyrrhotite;**
(8) Owen Mine—**chalcopyrite,** native **copper, magnetite, pyrite, pyrrhotite;** (9) Stewart Mine—**chalcopyrite, magnetite, pyrite, pyrrhotite;** (10) Stover Hill Mine—**chalcopyrite, pyrite;** (11) Twin Lead Mine—**bornite, chalcopyrite, magnetite, pyrite, pyrrhotite.**
BROOKLIN, the Brooklin Mine—**gold, silver.**
BROOKSVILLE: (1) Abner Gray Mine—**carbonate minerals, copper sulfurets;** (2) Cape Rosier Mine (Rosier Consolidated)—**chalcopyrite, galena, pyrite, pyrrhotite, sphalerite;** (3) Dodge Mine—**argentiferous galena, copper**

sulfuret, zincblende; (4) Jones & Dodge Mine, and (5) Tapley Mine—chalcopyrite, galena, pyrite, pyrrhotite, sphalerite.

CASTINE: (1) Castine (Castine Head) Mine—copper, gold, lead, silver; (2) Emerson Mine—galena, magnetite, pyrite, pyrrhotite, sphalerite; (3) North Castine Mine—chalcopyrite, galena, pyrite.

DEER ISLE: (1) Belle of Deer Isle Mine—galena; (2) Deer Isle Mine—chalcopyrite, galena, magnetite, pyrite, native silver, sphalerite, tetrahedrite.

ELLSWORTH: (1) Boston Silver Mine—argentiferous galena; (2) Brimmer Mine—silver.

FRANKLIN: (1) Franklin Extension Mine—gray copper, galena, ruby silver, native silver; (2) Frenchman's Bay Mine—galena.

GOULDSBORO: (1) Globe Mine—galena; (2) Gouldsboro Mine—galena, sulfurets.

HANCOCK: (1) Custer Mine (Copperopolis)—chalcopyrite, pyrite, rhodochrosite; (2) McFarland Mine—argentiferous galena, chalcopyrite.

LAMOINE, the Little Sue prospect—galena.

LITTLE DEER ISLE, area exposures, gem quality—serpentine.

MOUNT DESERT (Somesville), area outcrop—amazonite.

PENOBSCOT: (1) Annear Mine—copper minerals; (2) Hercules (Dunbar) Mine—arsenopyrite, chalcopyrite, gray copper, copper silicates, native copper, galena, pyrite, pyrrhotite, native silver, specularite, sphalerite.

SEDGEWICK, the Eggemoggin Mine—arsenopyrite, chalcopyrite, galena, pyrite, sphalerite, native silver.

SORRENTO, the Boss o' the Bay Mine—native copper, copper minerals.

SULLIVAN: (1) Beacon Hill Mine—galena (with lead, copper, silver, zinc), pyrite; (2) Milton Mine—chalcopyrite, pyrite, native silver; (3) Salem and Sullivan mines—argentiferous galena, chalcopyrite, pyrite, silver (ruby, native), stephanite; (4) Sullivan Falls Mine—argentiferous galena.

SURRY: (1) Blue Hill Bay Mine—copper, silver; (2) Sunburst Mine—bornite, chalcopyrite, galena, malachite, pyrite, red copper oxide.

KENNEBEC CO.

GARDINER: (1) the Iron Hill Mine—nickel pyrrhotite; (2) W 5½ mi. into LITCHFIELD Twp., an outcrop 2,000 ft. SW—sodalite.

LITCHFIELD: (1) area pegmatites—zircon; (2) 1,000 ft. N of Spears Corner—sodalite.

VIENNA: (1) Nurse Farm prospect—feldspar, muscovite mica; (2) Vienna Mt. prospect—feldspar.

WINSLOW, the Winslow Tin Mine—beryl, cassiterite, galena, fluorite, margarite, lepidolite, quartz, tourmaline.

KNOX CO.

APPLETON, the Appleton Mine—chalcopyrite, garnet, pyrrhotite, tourmaline.

CUSHING, the State Prison Farm prospect—albite feldspar, quartz, spodumene.

ISLE AU HAUT, mine of the same name—**copper, silver.**
ROCKLAND, the Rockland City Mine—**argentiferous galena.**
ROCKPORT: (1) Porterfield Mine—**copper, gold, nickel, silver;** (2) River-side Mine—**arsenopyrite.**
SOUTH THOMASTON, the Owl's Head Mine—**gold, silver.**
UNION, the Union Pyrrhotite Mine—**pentlandite, pyrrhotite, chalcopyrite, magnetite, sphalerite, labradorite.**
VINALHAVEN, the Island City Mine—**galena.**
WARREN: (1) Starrett Mine, and (2) Starrett prospect—**microcline feldspar, muscovite mica, quartz, spodumene.**

LINCOLN CO.

EDGECOMB: (1) the Poole prospect—**feldspar, muscovite mica, quartz;** (2) Williams Mine—**feldspar, muscovite mica, quartz.**
WALDOBORO, the Benner prospect—cf. EDGECOMB.
WICASSET, the LaPoutre prospect—cf. EDGECOMB.

OXFORD CO.

ALBANY (Twp.): (1) area: (a) Frenchman Mt., along the crest—**aquamarine, rose quartz;** (b) Rattlesnake Mt., area pegmatite outcrops—**gem beryl;** (2) regional mines and prospects, e.g.: (a) the Donahue prospect—**beryl, feldspar, muscovite mica, quartz, black tourmaline;** (b) General Electric Glass Quartz prospect—**beryl, columbite, feldspar, garnet, quartz;** (c) Holt prospect—**muscovite mica;** (d) Guy Johnson Mine—**beryl, feldspar, muscovite mica, quartz, black tourmaline;** (e) Pingree prospect—**beryl, columbite, feldspar;** (f) Sterns prospect (Hornet Mine)—**beryl, feldspar, muscovite mica, quartz, black tourmaline;** (g) Wardwell Mine—**beryl, mica (biotite, muscovite), feldspar, rose quartz;** (h) Wentworth Mine—**apatite, beryl, feldspar, muscovite mica, quartz, pyrite.**
ANDOVER: (1) W, in area of Baldpate Mt., pegmatite outcrops and float—**aquamarine;** (2) Leach Beryl prospect, as small crystals—**gem beryl;** (3) Spruce Mt., area pegmatites (inquire locally)—**massive beryl;** (4) West Surplus, Frye Brook–West Branch (inquire locally)—**gem beryl.**
BATCHELDER'S GRANT, the Peabody Mt. Quarry—**apatite, feldspar, muscovite mica, quartz, tourmaline.**
BETHEL, SSE 6.4 mi. and 1.2 mi. SW of Town House, the Bumpus Quarry—**beryl, plagioclase feldspar, muscovite mica, rose quartz.**
BUCKFIELD: (1) SW 2 mi., the Lewis Mine, and (2) the adjoining J. H. Fletcher Mine—**cesium beryl, tourmaline;** (3) SW 2½ mi., the Robinson Dudley Mine—**aquamarine, cesium beryl, pollucite** (rare); (4) SW 2½ mi. and ¼ mi. S of Rte. 117, exposure (mine)—**amblygonite, arsenopyrite, beryl, cassiterite, feldspar, loellingite, mica, pollucite, tourmaline;** (5) W 3 mi. and ½ mi. N of the Bennett farmhouse, the Bennett Quarry—**amblygonite, apatite, aquamarine, arsenopyrite, beryl, cassiterite, columbite, feldspar, garnet, lepidolite, morganite, muscovite mica, pollucite, quartz, rhodochrosite, spodumene, tantalite, topaz, tourmaline;**

(6) Regional mines, e.g.: (a) Bessey Mine—**arsenopyrite, beryl, feldspar, muscovite mica, smoky quartz** (with liquid inclusions), **sphalerite**; (b) Cummings Mine—**quartz;** (c) Dudley prospect (Neville-Owl's Head)—**amblygonite, beryl, pollucite;** (d) Fletcher Mine—**beryl;** (e) General Electric Co. mine (Dudley Mine)—**pollucite;** (f) Irish (Westinghouse) Mine—**beryl, pollucite, tourmaline** (black, green); (g) Orchard Mine—gem **apatite, beryl, cassiterite, columbite, feldspar, rose quartz, spodumene, topaz,** gem **tourmaline.**

BYRON, an area mine—**diopside, pyrite, quartz, scheelite.**

CANTON, N 47° W 2¼ mi. (from bridge in center of town), the Clark Mine —**chrysoberyl, muscovite mica.**

DENMARK: (1) the Lord prospect—**feldspar, mica (biotite, muscovite), quartz;** (2) Warren Quarry (Howe Mine)—**amethyst.**

GILEAD: (1) Peaked Hill Mine—**feldspar, garnet, mica (biotite, muscovite), quartz;** (2) Peaked Hill prospect—gem **beryl;** (3) Wheeler Mine(s)—**beryl, feldspar (cleavelandite), muscovite mica.**

GREENWOOD (Twp.): (1) Diamond Ledge (Yale or Yates Quarry)—**quartz crystals;** (2) Emmons Quarry (Uncle Tom Mine)—**amblygonite, beryl, lepidolite, pollucite, spodumene,** gem **tourmaline;** (3) Nobles Corner, NW 2 mi. and ½ mi. E of Mud Pond, a pegmatite—**tourmaline;** (4) Tamminen Quarry (at base of Noyes Mt.)—**albite feldspar, apatite, beryl, morganite, petalite, pollucite, quartz, spodumene, topaz, uraninite;** (5) Tamminen-Waisanen Mine—**apatite, bertrandite, feldspar, herderite, spodumene;** (6) Tiger Bill Mine—**autunite, bertrandite, feldspar, herderite, spodumene;** (7) Waisanen Mine (the Nubble)—**beryl, feldspar, muscovite mica.** Other mines in the GREENWOOD mining district include: Heath Quarry, Harvard Quarry (Noyes Mt. Quarry), Hayes Ledge, Heikken Quarry, Mustonen Ledge, and Ohtonen's Quarry, at which some or all of the following minerals and gemstones occur—**apatite, beryl, or feldspar (cleavelandite, microcline), garnet, lepidolite, mica (biotite, muscovite), quartz crystals, spinel, pyrite, tourmaline** (black, green).

HARTFORD (Twp.): (1) Dickvale, SE 2 mi. on S slope of Hedgehog Hill, pegmatite—**aquamarine, golden beryl;** (2) 2 mi. S of S end of Worthley Pond in area of Ragged Jack Mt., exposure—**chrysoberyl.**

HEBRON (Twp.): (1) area of Mt. Rubellite: (a) 1½ mi. NE of HEBRON at N end of Greenwood Hill, and (b) 2½ mi. N of HEBRON, in pegmatite outcrops and prospects—**rubellite** (pink **tourmaline**), gemmy green **tourmaline;** (2) regional mines: (a) Conant Mine—**feldspar;** (b) Hibbs Quarries—**beryl, feldspar, garnet, mica (biotite, muscovite), quartz, black tourmaline;** (c) Hill No. 4 Quarry—**cassiterite, feldspar,** gem **tourmaline;** (d) Rubellite (Cushman) Mine—**beryl, pollucite, rubellite,** green **tourmaline;** (e) Streaked Mt. prospect—**feldspar;** (f) Sturtevant (Sanitarium) Mine, inquire locally—gem **beryl.**

HIRAM, Cutler Mt. area, the Frenchman's Gold Mine—**feldspar, muscovite mica, quartz.**

LOVELL, the Forks Farm—**beryl, feldspar, muscovite mica.**

MASON, the Anderson Mine—**muscovite mica.**

MEXICO, the Gogan prospect—**feldspar, muscovite mica.**

NEWRY (Twp.): (1) area mines: (a) Dunton Mine (Newry Gem Mine), and (b) the Newry Mines (False Mine, Lower Mine, Nevel Quarry)—**am-**

blygonite, apatite, autunite, beryl, beryllonite, cassiterite, chalcedony, columbite, cookeite, eosphorite, fairfieldite, feldspar, francolite, galena, garnet,
hatchettolite, herderite, lepidolite, microlite, montebrasite, muscovite, opal,
pollucite, purpurite, pyrite, quartz, reddingite, siderite, sphalerite, spodumene,
tantalite, torbernite, tourmaline (gem, black), triphylite, uraninite, vivianite,
zircon; (c) the Scotty Mine—beryl, feldspar, muscovite mica, quartz, spodumene;

(2) Plumbago Mt.: (a) area pegmatites and prospects—beryl, spodumene;
(b) E knoll, area mines—albite, amblygonite, beryllonite, eosphorite, herderite, tourmaline; (c) E spur 3.9 mi. N 40° W of RUMFORD POINT—aquamarine; (d) summit of E spur, the Dunton Tourmaline Mine—aquamarine,
tourmaline (gem); (e) NE side, the Lower Nevel Quarry—spodumene; (3)
Puzzle Mt. area (inquire locally), in pegmatite exposures, prospects, mines
—gem beryl.

NORTH WATERFORD, the Scribner Ledge Quarry (1 mi. N of the pump-
ing sta.)—rose quartz.

NORWAY: (1) BB No. 1 Quarry—garnet, muscovite mica, pollucite, spodumene; (2) the Dunn Mine—beryl, feldspar, muscovite mica, quartz; (3)
Tubbs Ledge—cassiterite, lepidolite, rose quartz, tourmaline (green).

OXFORD, the Jordan prospect—feldspar, muscovite mica, quartz.

PARIS: (1) area: (a) E 1½ mi., mines on Mt. Mica—amazonite, beryl
(gem, lithia), cassiterite, cesium, cookeite, feldspar (cleavelandite, microcline), garnet, lepidolite, montmorillonite, morganite, muscovite mica, pollucite, quartz crystals (citrine, rose, smoky), sagenite, tourmaline (black,
blue, green, pink); (b) Little Singepole Group (of mines), such as the
Foster Mine, Haveringen Mine, and Mills Quarry—apatite, beryl, columbite,
feldspar, garnet, muscovite mica, pollucite, quartz, tourmaline;

(2) Regional mines, such as: (a) Bowker Mine—rose quartz; (b) Hoopers
Ledge (Twitchell Mine)—beryl, chrysoberyl, feldspar, rose quartz; (c) Immonen Ledge No. 1—beryl, feldspar, garnet, muscovite mica, rose quartz;
(d) Immonen Ledge No. 2—fibrolite; (e) Mt. Marie Mine—apatite, beryl,
columbite, feldspar, garnet, muscovite mica, pollucite, quartz, tourmaline;
(f) Perham Mine—apatite, aquamarine, feldspar, garnet, mica (biotite, muscovite), pyrite, quartz, tourmaline; (g) Ryerson Hill Mine—beryl, columbite,
feldspar; (h) Scott Colby Mine—feldspar, rose quartz; (i) Slattery Mine—
bertrandite, beryl, feldspar, rose quartz; (j) Stearns Farm Mine—rose quartz
(fused for optical use); (k) Stony Brook Mine—feldspar, lepidolite, muscovite mica, quartz, tourmaline (damourite); (l) Whispering Pines Mine—
feldspar, rose quartz.

PERU (Twp.): (1) Hedgehog Hill, S side, the Hedgehog Hill Mine—gem
beryl (golden, pink), biotite mica, chrysoberyl, garnet, muscovite mica; (2)
Lobikis Mine—beryl, muscovite mica, pyrrhotite, quartz, triphylite, vivianite;
(3) Perry prospect—autunite, spodumene, triphylite.

ROXBURY: (1) Binford prospect—muscovite mica; (2) Partridge Peak
Mine—scheelite.

RUMFORD (Twp.): (1) area: (a) Black Mt., area quarries—apatite,
beryl, cassiterite, columbite, feldspar, garnet, hornblende, lepidolite, magnetite, muscovite mica, purpurite, quartz crystals, sphene, spodumene, tantalite,
tourmaline, uraninite; (b) Whitecap Mt., area mines and prospects—apatite,
feldspar, garnet, muscovite mica, quartz crystals, tourmaline;

(2) Regional mines and prospects: (a) Beliveau prospect—**feldspar, muscovite mica, quartz crystals;** (b) Black Mt. Mica Mine—**spodumene;** (c) Brown-Thurston prospect—**beryl, muscovite mica, plagioclase feldspar, rose quartz;** (d) Carver prospect—**beryl, feldspar, purpurite;** (e) Elliot Mine —**apatite, beryl, feldspar, garnet, muscovite mica, quartz crystals, black tourmaline;** (f) Leach quartz prospect—**quartz crystals;** (g) Red Hill Mine— **beryl, feldspar, triphylite;** (h) Roy mines (Goddard Ledge)—**beryl, corundum, feldspar, pyrrhotite, sphalerite;** (i) Whitehall prospect—**beryl.**

STONEHAM (Twp.): (1) area of Butters Mt., mines and prospects—**golden beryl, garnet;** (2) area mines and prospects: (a) Aldrich prospect—**beryl, feldspar, muscovite mica, pyrite, serpentine;** (b) Andrews Ledge—**beryl, muscovite mica;** (c) Foster Hill prospect—**feldspar, muscovite mica;** (d) Lord's Hill Mine (on Lord's Hill ½ mi. SE of Harndon Hill)—**autunite, beryl, beryllium minerals, chalcopyrite, columbite, feldspar, fluorite, phenakite, quartz crystals, topaz, tourmaline;** (e) Melrose prospect—**bertrandite, aquamarine, beryllonite;** (f) Styles Mt. prospect—**beryl;** (g) Willis Warren Quarry—**apatite, beryl, feldspar, garnet, muscovite mica, tourmaline;** (3) WSW in area of NORTH LOVELL: (a) Chapman Hill, 3 mi. N, mine— **gem blue beryl;** (b) Durgin Mt. (inquire locally), 4 mi. N 30° W, on E side, mines—**gem beryl** (various colors); (c) WNW 2¾ mi., at base of McKean Mts., mines—**apatite, beryl, beryllonite, cassiterite, feldspar, muscovite mica, quartz crystals** (smoky), **triplite;** (d) N 5 mi., mine on Speckled Mt.—**golden beryl;** (e) Sugar Hill, area prospects—**aquamarine, beryl, beryllonite.**

STOW (Twp.): (1) Colton Hill prospect—**feldspar, quartz;** (2) Deer Hill area (Big Deer Hill, 4½ mi. N of Stow or 1¾ mi. ESE of NORTH CHATHAM, N.H.), mine—**amethysts, feldspar, garnet, muscovite mica, pyrite, quartz crystals.**

WATERFORD: (1) Beech Hill (Waterford Mica) Mine—**microcline feldspar, garnet, mica (biotite, muscovite), quartz crystals;** (2) Knight (Coye or Foye) Mine—**beryl, columbite, muscovite mica;** (3) Saunders Mine— **chalcopyrite, feldspar, garnet, magnetite, muscovite mica, pyrrhotite, quartz crystals, black tourmaline;** (4) South Waterford prospect (Bear Mt.)— **muscovite mica;** (5) Stearns Hill Mine—**feldspar.**

WEST PARIS, S 70° W 8.8 mi. and ½ mi. NE of Flints Mt., the Scribner Mine—**apatite, golden beryl, feldspar, garnet, mica (biotite, muscovite), rose quartz, black tourmaline.**

WOODSTOCK, area mine—**copper, lead, gold, silver.**

PENOBSCOT CO.

CARMEL, the Carmel Antimony Mine—**stibnite.**
CORINNA, the Dearborn Mine—**argentiferous galena.**
EXETER, area mine—**galena, some gold.**
GARLAND, area mine—**chalcopyrite, galena.**
GREENFIELD, the Cemetery Hill Mine—**iron, manganese.**
HAMPDEN: (1) the Hampden Consolidated Mine—**lead, copper, silver;** (2) Latrence Mine—**galena;** (3) Silver Drift Mine—**auriferous iron pyrite, galena;** (4) Queen City Mine (near BANGOR)—**gold, lead, silver.**
LAKEVILLE, the Getchell Mt. prospect—**feldspar, magnetite, biotite mica,**

rose quartz.

LOWELL: (1) the Shorey Mine—**sulfurets (antimony, gold, silver);** (2) Vinegar Hill Mine—**arsenopyrite, chalcopyrite, pyrite.**

PISCATAQUIS CO.

BLANCHARD, many area quarries—**slate.**
BROWNVILLE, area quarries—**slate.**
DOVER-FOXCROFT, the Foss Farm Mine—**chalcopyrite.**
GUILFORD, area mine—**argentiferous galena, chalcopyrite.**
KATAHDIN IRON WORKS, reached by private rd. from N of BROWNVILLE JCT.—**chalcopyrite, ilmenite, limonite, linnaeite, magnetite, marcasite, pyrrhotite.**
MONSON, many area quarries—**slate.**

SAGADAHOC CO.

BOWDOIN: (1) the Combs Quarry—**beryl, feldspar, garnet, mica (biotite, muscovite), pyrite, quartz crystals, black tourmaline;** (2) the Ordway mines —cf. Combs Quarry; (3) Trufant prospect (inquire locally at the U.S. Gypsum Co. in LISBON FALLS)—**beryl, feldspar, garnet, mica (biotite, muscovite), quartz crystals.**

BOWDOINHAM: (1) the Booker prospect—**feldspar;** (2) Consolidated Quarries—**feldspar, mica (biotite, muscovite), quartz;** (3) Dunn prospect—**feldspar;** (4) Harriman Mine—**feldspar, quartz;** (5) Lang Mine—**feldspar;** (6) McFee Mine—**feldspar.**

GEORGETOWN: (1) Consolidated Quarry—**autunite, beryl, feldspar, gummite, lepidolite, muscovite mica, quartz, tourmaline;** (2) Cunningham Mine—**feldspar;** (3) Moffatt mines—**feldspar, tourmaline;** (4) Thorne prospect—**feldspar, bertrandite, mica (biotite, muscovite), herderite, spodumene;** (5) Todd Mine—**beryl, feldspar.**

PHIPPSBURG (Twp.): (1) McKay Farm prospect—**beryl, feldspar, garnet, mica (biotite, muscovite), quartz crystals, black tourmaline;** (2) Parker Head: (a) numerous area mines and prospects (inquire locally)—**beryl, feldspar, ilmenite, magnetite, muscovite mica;** (b) 1.3 mi. S 17° W of tide mill, the Thoman Feldspar Quarry—**aquamarine, golden beryl;** (3) Perry Mine—**feldspar;** (4) Robbins Mine—**beryl, feldspar, magnetite;** (5) Rogers Mine—gem **beryl, feldspar, black tourmaline;** (6) Thomas Quarry—**apatite, beryl, feldspar, muscovite mica, tourmaline.**

TOPSHAM (Twp.): (1) N, overlooking the Cathance R., **feldspar** quarries at BRUNSWICK—**aquamarine, smoky quartz crystals, topaz, tourmaline;** (2) 2 mi. NW of Cathance Sta., the Willes Feldspar Quarry—**beryl, tourmaline;** (3) N 2½ mi., a pegmatite dike outcrops on a low hill just N of the Cathance River and Fisher Quarry—**apatite, beryl, cassiterite, columbite, feldspar (albite, cleavelandite), gahnite, herderite, lepidolite, muscovite mica, topaz, torbernite, tourmaline;** (4) area mines: (a) Chapman, Given, Graves, Mallett, Trenton—**feldspar, muscovite mica, quartz;** (b) Direnzo (Cormier Farm) prospect—**feldspar, muscovite mica, quartz;**

(5) Numerous area quarries: (a) Great Divide (Undivided), Ingalls, Purington, Standpipe Hill, Alice Staples, William Staples, Rumrill, William Willes, some or all of the following—**beryl, cassiterite, columbite, albite feldspar, gahnite, garnet, herderite, lepidolite, mica (biotite, muscovite), quartz crystals, topaz, torbernite, tourmaline;** (6) Consolidated Quarries (several)—**beryl** (some), **feldspar, garnet, magnetite, mica (biotite, muscovite), quartz crystals, tourmaline;** (7) Fisher Quarry—**beryl, columbite, feldspar, muscovite mica, quartz crystals, topaz, tourmaline.**

WEST BATH, the Davis Mine—**apatite, beryl, microcline feldspar, garnet, muscovite mica, quartz crystals, tourmaline.**

WOOLWICH: (1) Trott Cove Mine—green **apatite, beryl, feldspar, garnet, muscovite mica, quartz crystals, black tourmaline;** (2) Woolwich Mine—**azurite, bornite, malachite.**

SOMERSET CO.

CONCORD, the Robinson Mine—**arsenopyrite, bornite, chalcopyrite, galena, pyrite, pyrrhotite.**

ST. ALBANS: (1) the Gould prospect—**copper, lead, silver;** (2) Indian Lead Mine—**galena;** (3) St. Albans Mine—**galena,** trace of **gold.**

WALDO CO.

KNOX, the Stone Mine—**gold, silver.**

PROSPECT, the Fort Knox Mine—**copper, lead, gold, silver.**

WASHINGTON CO.

CHERRYFIELD: (1) the Britton Mine—**galena;** (2) Cherryfield Mine—**chalcopyrite, galena, gold quartz, pyrrhotite, silver sulfurets, sphalerite.**

COOPER, Cooper (American Molybdenum) Mine—**native bismuth, iron molybdate, molybdenite.**

CUTLER, the Johnson Mine—**copper, silver.**

JONESPORT, area mines—**argentiferous galena.**

MARSHFIELD, the Crocker prospect—**lead, silver.**

PEMBROKE: (1) The Big Hill Mine—**chalcopyrite, galena, pyrite, pyrrhotite sphalerite;** (2) Pembroke Mine—**azurite, bornite, chalcopyrite, galena, malachite, pyrite, sphalerite;** (3) Young's Point Mine—**argentiferous galena.**

TRESCOTT-LUBEC, the Trescott Mine—**galena.**

WESLEY: (1) the Bacon & Snow Mine—**chalcopyrite, pyrite, sphalerite;** (2) Rollins Mine—**bornite, cuprite, galena, pyrite, pyrrhotite, sphalerite.**

YORK CO.

ACTON: (1) the Acton Mine—**arsenopyrite, chalcopyrite, galena, pyrite, pyrrhotite, sphalerite;** (2) Acton Consolidated Mine—cf. Acton Mine; (3) Acton-Lebanon Mine—**galena, pyrite, native silver.**

CORNISH, the Berry Mine—**calcite, diopside, grossularite, garnet, idocrase, pectolite, scapolite, scheelite.**

LIMERICK, 4 mi. distant at Straw Hill, in seams and boulders—**sodalite.**

LYMAN, the Brock prospect—**beryl, feldspar, muscovite mica.**

NEWFIELD (Twp.): (1) Bergendahl Mine—**chalcopyrite, molybdenite, pentlandite, pyrite, pyrrhotite, sphalerite;** (2) Davis Mine—**arsenopyrite, pyrite, scheelite;** (3) Pease Mt. Mine—**diopside, grossularite garnet, idocrase, scheelite;** (4) Piper Hill Mine—**grossularite garnet, scheelite;** (5) Tin (Newfield) Mine—**cassiterite.**

SANFORD, the South Sanford Mine—**molybdenite, molybdite, powellite, scheelite, vesuvianite.**

WATERBORO, the Caton prospect—**feldspar, quartz.**

MARYLAND

Divided by the drowned canyon of Chesapeake Bay, Maryland is characterized by three strikingly different geological provinces. The Coastal Plain extends westward from the present margin of the continental shelf to the Fall Line, passing through the cities of Baltimore and Washington, D.C.—a flat, almost featureless sea-level plain underlain by unconsolidated clays, sands, and gravels of Mesozoic and Cenozoic age dipping at a low angle toward the southeast.

The Piedmont Plateau forms the central part of Maryland, extending westward from the plains, or Fall Line, to the east side of South Mountain. This region is an undulating upland with a maximum elevation of 1,000 feet, formed of ancient, intricately folded and greatly faulted strata thoroughly metamorphosed by intense crushing and extensive igneous intrusions. In the west and north the Piedmont rises to the Blue Ridge and the hills of Pennsylvania.

The Appalachian Province spans the region between South Mountain and the West Virginia border, divided into three main districts: the Blue Ridge, the Greater Appalachian Valley, and the Allegheny Plateau. Here, in the extreme southwestern corner of Garrett County almost on the West Virginia line, rises the highest point in Maryland, Backbone Mountain, 3,360 feet above sea level. This province provides the gem and mineral collector with some excellent lapidary materials, derived from a series of metamorphosed volcanic flows and tuffs. Replacement mineralizations yield some relatively rare mineral species, while vugs and cavities often contain interesting secondary minerals.

From the gem collector's viewpoint, the most rewarding gemstones occur in the **serpentine** and **chromite** deposits that are widely distributed through five northern counties (Cecil, Harford, Baltimore, Carroll, Frederick) in a region locally known as the "Barrens" because of the stunted nature of its vegetation. Here a gemmy **serpentine** called **"greenstone"** has long been quarried for building stone and for railroad ballast. The associated **verde antique,** laced with twisting white veinlets (the "serpents" that originally gave **serpentine** its name), is greatly valued for its decorative nature. Another metamorphic type, locally called **baltimorite,** is valued by collectors as cutting material because of its pale blue green color and compact fibrous texture.

Associated in these deposits are **picrolite,** a rare form of foliated blue green **serpentine** closely resembling **asbestos,** and **brucite,** a silvery mineral with green and red inclusions in a fibrous matrix. Here, also, occurs a gemmy, jadelike **serpentine** called **williamsite,** much valued by collectors. Indeed, because of its apple-green color and translucency, **williamsite** ranks among the most sought-after gemstones in Maryland. All these gemstones occur in the famed State Line Pits that straddle both sides of the Maryland-Pennsylvania boundary, especially in Cecil Co., Maryland, from the Susquehanna River eastward to the Delaware line. Other associated gemstones and minerals include clear and smoky **quartz crystals, jasper, olivine crystals, enstatite, tourmaline, rutile** (in the form of red, lustrous, prismatic crystals), **vesuvianite,** light-green massive **talc** useful for carving, pink to purple **kämmererite, magnesite, hydromagnesite,** and **deweylite** (a hydrous magnesian silicate), with apple-green **genthite** representing a **nickel** replacement of **magnesium.**

Following the Civil War, Maryland was extensively prospected for **gold. Gold quartz** ores were found in the Piedmont, and although mining did not prove profitable, one can still pan for colors in the regional stream gravels. For years Maryland was a leading producer of **copper, lead, iron, manganese, molybdenum, titanium,** and **zinc,** while pegmatites outcropping in the eastern Piedmont have been abundantly mined for **mica** and **feldspar.** Much **asbestos** has also contributed to the mineral economy of the state.

Visiting gem collectors to the State Line Pits must necessarily include both the Maryland and Pennsylvania mines. At least a hundred mines and prospects surround the crossroads towns of Cecil County, Maryland, west to east from the Susquehanna River, of Pilot, Oakwood, Rock Springs, Goat Hill, Sylmar, and Calvert, while almost as many other workings on the Pennsylvania side of the boundary surround the communities of Pleasant Grove, Wakefield, Lyles, Wrightsdale, Nottingham, Chrome, and White Barrens. Since all collecting areas are privately owned, permission to collect must be given primary importance.

For information, write: Department of Geology, Mines, and Water Resources, Johns Hopkins University, Baltimore.

ALLEGANY CO.

CUMBERLAND: (1) area deposits, prospects, etc.—**fluorite;** (2) old mining town of ROBERTS and on the W side of Wills Mt., area of abandoned strip mines—**hematite.**

FROSTBURG, area **coal** mine dumps (park car at Dan's Mt. State Park)—
barite crystals, siderite.

ANNE ARUNDEL CO.

AREA, the Fort Dorsey and Loper Hall **iron** mines—**jet.**
RIVIERA BEACH (S of BALTIMORE and NW of ANNAPOLIS): (1) Magothy
R.: (a) area exposures of the Magothy Formation—**pyrite.** (Deposits of this
pyrite were mined and the mineral roasted for the manufacture of sulfuric
acid.) (b) Area of North Ferry Point, in river bank lignite seams—**amber,
fossils;** (2) lignite seams along the Severn R., especially at Sullivans Cove—
amber.

ANNE ARUNDEL and PRINCE GEORGES COS.

AREA, regional exposures of the Patapsco and Arundel formations, as
deposits—**ocher.**

BALTIMORE CO.

ALBERTON, area quarries or mines in pegmatites—**copper minerals,** massive
quartz, garnet, tourmaline.
BALTIMORE: (1) area: (a) in metropolitan district, the Bare Hills
(1-mi.-sq. mining district since 1839)—**actinolite, copper minerals** (such as
malachite), **epidote, feldspar, garnet, marble, moss agate, pyrite, quartz,
serpentine, tremolite, zoisite;** (b) the Dyer Quarry—**serpentine;** (2) SE of
city, in gravels, and (3) NE, in Germantown gravel exposures—**silicified
cycad wood;** (4) quarries along the Gunpowder R., especially the Arundel
Gneiss Quarry—**aquamarine, beryl.**
BUTLER, area mines, prospects—**serpentine, williamsite.**
CATONSVILLE, area old prospects, in **quartz** veins—**gold.**
COCKEYSVILLE, area quarries—fine-grained white **marble.**
DELIGHT, old **chrome** mines in Soldier's Delight area—**feldspar, metamor-
phic minerals, quartz, chromite, magnesite,** etc.
GRANITE, area pegmatite quarries—**copper minerals, garnet,** massive
quartz, tourmaline.
GREAT FALLS (on Liberty Lake), area mines—**copper minerals.**
HOLLOFIELD: (1) area pegmatite quarries—**copper minerals, quartz** (mas-
sive), **garnet, tourmaline;** (2) S ½ mi. on old FREDERICK rd., quarry—
serpentine.
JONES FALLS, area quarries, as traces—**galena.**
MARRIOTTSVILLE, area quarries—**quartz crystals.**
REISTERSTOWN: (1) area quarries—**serpentine;** (2) area **chrome** mines—
chromite, feldspar, metamorphic minerals, quartz.
TEXAS: (1) area quarries—fine-grain white **marble;** (2) the Campbell
Quarry—**tourmaline.**
WHITE HALL, SE 1 mi. and 2½ mi. NE, area mines—**magnetite.**
WHITE MARSH, area exposures of pegmatite—**amethyst.**

BALTIMORE, CARROLL, FREDERICK, HOWARD COS.

AREA, the Blue Ridge district, regional exposures of crystalline rocks, as veinlets, stringers, discolorations, etc.—**malachite**.

BALTIMORE, HARFORD COS.

AREA, quarries in inferior deposits of fibrous **serpentine—chrysotile asbestos**.

CALVERT CO.

PRINCE FREDERICK, both N and S along the shores of Chesapeake Bay: (1) Breezy Point to Cove Point, in cliffs and strata and weathered out onto beaches, great variety of gemstone-hard, colorful, and lapidary quality—**fossils**. (Many species names are listed in J. E. Ransom, *Fossils in America*, Harper, 1964.) (2) Calvert Cliffs State Park (no collecting inside boundaries), area beaches outside park—**gemstone fossils, shark teeth**, etc.

CARROLL CO.

AREA, W part of co. and E part of Frederick Co., in limestone exposures —**galena**.

ELDERSBURG, N 1½ mi.: (1) at the Monroe prospect dumps—**azurite, malachite**; (2) 1 mi. E of the Monroe prospect, on both sides of Rte. 32, the Beasman prospect, abundant—**pyrite**.

FINKSBURG: (1) E 1 mi., on both sides of U.S. 140 and Rte. 526: (a) the Patapsco Mines—**cobalt** and **nickel minerals**; (b) 200 yds. S of Rte. 526, the Wildesen Mine—**cobalt** and **nickel minerals**; (c) between U.S. 140 and Rte. 526, the Orchard Mine—**cobalt, nickel**; (2) Union Bridge, a quarry—**marble** (pink and green, swirling cloudlike patterns); (3) SW 7 mi., at Mineral Hill, area mines—**bornite, chalcocite, gold, specularite**.

MIDDLEBURG, between town and Big Pipe Cr., sparingly in outcrops of a red sandstone—**chrysocolla**.

NEW WINDSOR, area mines, prospects—**azurite, bornite, calamine, malachite, smithsonite, sphalerite**.

SYKESVILLE: (1) area, as the center of a once important mining district, many old mine dumps and pits—**actinolite**, some **native copper** and **gold**, **epidote, garnet, malachite** (some), **lead-zinc minerals, marble** (gemmy), **quartz, soapstone, specular hematite** (on dumps of **iron** mines), **tremolite, zoisite**; (2) NW ½ mi.: (a) the Springfield Mine—**copper** and **iron minerals**; (b) across Piney Run to the NE, the Carroll Mine—some **copper, epidote, garnet, iron minerals, specularite**.

CECIL CO.

AREA: see introductory paragraphs to Maryland for State Line Pits and regional crossroads villages. The hundred or so mines, prospects, and pits are dangerous, often water-filled, and require great caution to investigate. Recommended collecting methods are to avoid the old pits and dig around in general brushy areas between or adjacent to the excavations, particularly in areas where the **chrome** miners dumped their gangue rock—**kämmererite, gemmy serpentine, soapstone, williamsite,** etc., **chromite, zaratite, brucite, magnesite.**

BALD FRIAR, CONOWINGO CREEK, FLINTVILLE, PILOT, area mines and **feldspar** quarries—**feldspar crystals, garnets, mica, quartz crystals,** massive crystalline **quartz** (locally termed **"flint"**).

CONOWINGO: (1) N on U.S. 222 to within ½ mi. of the Pa. line, then E on dimly marked Connelly Rd. to State Line Pits (long abandoned **chrome** mines here), on dumps and brush-covered surfaces—some **kämmererite, soapstone, serpentine, williamsite;** (2) other area mines (some periodically operating), e.g., the Red Pit, Wood Chrome, Wet Pit, Hillside, North Rock Springs (Jenkins Mine), Cedar Hill (a noted operating mine, i.e., the Stolfus Quarry), and Newbold—gemmy **serpentine, williamsite.**

ROCK SPRINGS CROSSROADS, N ¾ mi., area pits—**brucite,** purple **kämmererite, magnesite, serpentine, williamsite.**

WEST NOTTINGHAM, area quarry, forming wall rock—**serpentine.**

FREDERICK CO.

CATOCTIN FURNACE : (1) area **iron slag** dumps—gemmy **slag** (fluorescent, brightly colored, can be cut and polished); (2) SW, mine on hill—**magnetite, silver.**

FREDERICK, in area crushed stone quarry—pink **fluorite.**

JOHNSVILLE: (1) area mines, e.g., the Liberty, Bare Hill, etc.—**bornite, chalcocite, malachite;** (2) SE 1 mi. and ½ mi. N of the Coppermine Rd., at the Repp Mine—**copper minerals** (abundant on N dumps), **brecciated marble** (pink and purple), **milky quartz;** (3) SE 1½ mi., on E side of Beaverdam Cr.—**barite crystals, marble;** (4) NE 1¾ mi., near an old stone church, the Cox Mine dumps (brush-covered)—**copper-lead-zinc minerals.**

LANTZ, Catoctin Mt., area outcrops, as specimen material only—**native copper.**

LIBERTYTOWN: (1) area mine dumps—**copper, gold, silver, zinc minerals.** (This is the heart of the old Linganore mining district. The mine dumps carry also **azurite, chrysocolla, covellite, malachite, tenorite, cerussite, anglesite, smithsonite.**) (2) E ¾ mi. and ¼ mi. S of Rte. 26, on both sides of Dollyhyde Cr., the Dolly Hyde Mine—**copper minerals,** some **marble;** (3) SW ¾ mi., on dumps of the Hammond prospects—**bornite,** pink **calcite, covellite, malachite, rock crystal;** (4) N 2 mi., the Liberty Mine, and (5) ¾ mi. W of Rte. 75 on S side of Coppermine Rd., many open cuts and pits—**bornite, calcite, chalcocite, galena, hematite, malachite, pyrite, quartz, sphalerite;** (6) regional land surfaces, especially hillsides around town—**barite crystals,** gemmy **conglomerate (jasper, rhyolite).**

MIDDLETOWN, valley occurrences, mines, pits, etc.—**stibnite.**

NEW LONDON, in SW corner of town, the New London Mine—**barite, marble** (bearing **copper**).

POINT OF ROCKS: (1) on area state highway land, gemmy—**puddingstone** (a colorful conglomerate); (2) an area deposit—**pyrolusite;** (3) a quarry between town and Washington Jct.—**calcite, jasper, marble, quartz.** (The **marble** is locally named "Calico" or "Potomac" **marble,** a breccia of **calcite** and not true **marble.**)

UNIONVILLE, NW ¾ mi. at the Young place on S side of an old mine rd., a producing mine—**lead-zinc minerals, pyrite, quartz.**

HARFORD CO.

CAMBRIA, BROAD CREEK, area quarries—**serpentine.**

CARDIFF, area quarries—**garnet, pyrite, serpentine (verde antique,** i.e., **"green marble"), staurolites.**

CASTLETON, N 1 mi., extending W along the Susquehanna R.—**quartz crystals, tourmaline.**

CHERRY HILL: (1) SE, and just E of Chrome Hill, mine pits—**chromite, serpentine;** (2) E ½ mi., area surfaces—**smoky quartz crystals** (singles, groups); (3) Chrome Hill, mine dumps—**actinolite, bronzite, garnet.**

COOPSTOWN, NW 2 mi., the Wilkens Mine (and the Reed Mine)—**chromite, gem serpentine, soapstone,** etc.

DEER CREEK, area quarries—**serpentine.**

DUBLIN, area mines—**serpentine, soapstone.**

FLINTVILLE, area hills, draws, etc.—**moss agate, jasper.**

MINEFIELD, SE 1 mi., a small mine—**magnetite.**

PYLESVILLE, W 2½ mi., in **serpentine** mine—**magnetite, rutile.**

WHITEFORD (on Rte. 136 just S of the Penn. line), E to foot of a hill, the Green Marble Quarry and mill —gemmy **verde antique, chrysotile asbestos** (can be ground, not cut, and polished into art objects).

HOWARD CO.

CLARKSVILLE, area quarries—**marble.**

DAVIS: (1) S 1 mi., the Frost Feldspar Quarry—**garnet, smoky quartz crystals, sphene, vesuvianite;** (2) SE ½ mi., quarry—**marble.**

HIGHLAND: (1) S, at Browns Bridge Rd. near Lime Kiln Rd. 1 mi. NE of ALPHA, a quarry—**marble;** (2) Browns Bridge N .3 mi. a schist outcrop—**garnets, staurolites;** (3) below Snell Bridge and .7 mi. S of HENRYTOWN on the Tunnel Rd.—**garnets, staurolites;** (4) Bear Island (in the Potomac R.), exposures—**apatite, epidote, amphibolite, sphene, zircon.**

ILCHESTER, area and regional **feldspar** quarries, especially the Day Mine operating in pegmatite—**pegmatite minerals, gems.**

MARRIOTTSVILLE (cf. Baltimore Co.): (1) W 1 mi., at Carroll's Mill, and (2) N 2 mi., at Nicols, quarries—**marble.**

SCAGGSVILLE: (1) SW 1 mi., the Ben Murphy Mica Mine—gem **beryl** (green, yellow), **autunite, gahnite, mica;** (2) NW, the old Maryland Mica Mine—**amethyst, black tourmaline,** various **minerals.**

SIMPSONVILLE, the Maryland Mine (once the richest **gold** mine in the state)—**beryl, galena, gold** (in quartz veins and dikes), **pyrite, silver.** Cf. also GREAT FALLS in Montgomery Co.

WOODBINE, some old area mines (make local inquiry)—**gold.**

MONTGOMERY CO.

ASHTON: (1) E 2 mi., (2) Woodfield, and (3) Cedar Lane, area quarries —**serpentine, steatite.**

BROOKEVILLE, area abandoned mines—**pyrolusite.**

BURNT MILLS, the Kensington Mica Mine—**golden beryl, mica.**

ETCHISON, area mines—**chrome tourmaline.**

GAITHERSBURG, N, along the 6 mi. to Seneca Cr., as float—**serpentine, steatite.**

GREAT FALLS, the Great Falls Mine—**gold, tetradymite.**

ROCKVILLE (a suburb of WASHINGTON, D.C.), NW on U.S. 70: (1) W a short distance on Rte. 28, a large quarry—**diopside;** (2) NW, in a concrete aggregate quarry near Hunting Hill—**calcite, chlorite, diopside, grossularite garnet** (massive), **idocrase, opal, serpentine;** (3) Hunting Hill (massive **serpentine** body over 4 mi. long), area quarries—**calcite, gem diopside, garnet, common opal, serpentine;** (4) 6 mi. out along the Darnestown rd.— **talc.**

PRINCE GEORGES CO.

AREA, exposures of the Potomac formation—**petrified wood.**

BELTSVILLE, old area mine dumps—**hyalite opal, quartz crystals, silicified wood.**

OXON HILL, area old mines—**pyrite** (originally mined for **gold**).

WASHINGTON CO.

CAVETOWN, area quarries—**calcite, onyx.**

HANCOCK, area quarries—**fossils, quartz crystals.**

HARPERS FERRY (Jefferson Co.), N 3 mi., mine on N shore of the Potomac R.—**pyrolusite.**

MASSACHUSETTS

The Connecticut River Valley divides Massachusetts, with its mean elevation of 500 feet above sea level, into an eastern coastal plain, marked by short, swift rivers, and a western region of minor uplands that rise toward the Berkshire Hills in north-central Berkshire County. These hills, which climax in Mt. Greylock at 3,491 feet, are but the glaciated remnants of an Ordovician mountain-building "overthrust" of such magnitude that the whole of New England was narrowed by several hundred miles. The crumpling of Cambrian and Ordovician sedimentary strata raised up the Taconic Mountain range, which borders the western part of the state.

The Connecticut River Valley is characterized by sill-type exposures of vast basalt flows. Gas cavities in the basalts often contain such collectable items as **agate, chalcedony,** and **geodes** which are sometimes lined with excellent **amethysts.** Although extensive **limonite iron** ore beds of considerable economic value occur in the West Stockbridge area of Berkshire County, and **coal** is found in Norfolk County, the mineral industry of Massachusetts is definitely secondary in importance to industrialization.

For information, write: Department of Geology, University of Massachusetts, Amherst, or Massachusetts Institute of Technology, Cambridge.

BERKSHIRE CO.

DALTON, area mines, quarries—**asbestos, talc.**
HOOSAC TUNNEL, area mines—**talc.**
WILLIAMSTOWN, area deposits, once mined—**ocher, sienna.**
WINDSOR, area quarries—**soapstone.**

DUKES CO. (Martha's Vineyard Island)

AREA, various exposures and deposits scattered over the island—**alum.**
GAY HEAD, in area exposures of lignitic clays—**alum, amber.**

ESSEX CO.

NEWBURYPORT: (1) area **lead** mines (make inquiry)—**chalcopyrite, galena, pyrite, sphalerite, siderite, tetrahedrite;** (2) S, in area quarries—**noble serpentine, verde antique.**
ROCKPORT, area pegmatite exposures—**amazonstone.**
ROWLEY, area fields, cuts, excavations—**jasper.**

FRANKLIN CO.

BERNARDSTON, area mines—**hematite.**
CONWAY: (1) area gravel pits—**agate;** (2) area exposures of quartz veins (once mined)—**psilomelane, pyrolusite;** (3) area quarries—**fluorite.**
DEERFIELD: (1) area basalt sills—**agate nodules;** (2) area quarries—**fluorite;** (3) gravel beds of the Deerfield R.—**agate, chalcedony.**
EAST DEERFIELD, the Cheapside Quarry—**amethyst, chalcedony geodes, prehnite.**

GREENFIELD, area mines—**chalcopyrite.**

LEVERETT, area mines—**chalcopyrite.**

MONTAGUE, area mines—**chalcopyrite, hematite.**

NORTHFIELD: (1) area quarries—**fluorite;** (2) area pegmatite exposures (mines, prospects, pits)—**garnet, golden beryl;** (3) Northfield Mt., area deposits, material suitable for cutting—**garnet.**

ROWE: (1) area mines or mills—**talc;** (2) the Davis Mine—**chalcopyrite, cupriferous pyrite.**

WARWICK, area mines—**hematite.**

ZOAR, area mines and mills—**talc.**

HAMPDEN CO.

BLANDFORD, area pegmatites and quarries—**beryl, feldspar.**

CHESTER: (1) area deposits—**garnets** (fine crystals); (2) area old **emery** mines—**diaspore, emery** (impure **corundum**), **jasper, pyrrhotite;** (3) three area outcrops of **serpentine—chromite.**

MONTGOMERY, area mines—**galena.**

NORWICH, area pegmatite outcrops (quarries, prospects)—gem **beryl.**

RUSSELL, area deposits—**garnets** (as fine crystals).

SPRINGFIELD, W on U.S. 20, between town and Westfield, the Lane Quarry —**datolite, prehnite.**

HAMPSHIRE CO.

AMHERST, area gravel pits—**agates.**

CHESTERFIELD, area deposits, pegmatites—gem **beryl, kyanite, staurolites.**

CUMMINGTON: (1) area mine in Silurian schist exposure, as fine gem-stone material long mined for ornaments—**rhodonite;** (2) Forge Hill, S 6 mi., area—**ankerite, garnet, quartz crystals, rhodochrosite, rhodonite.**

GOSHEN: (1) area pegmatite outcrops—gem **beryl;** (2) N 80° W 1½ mi., a pegmatite dike 300 yds. N of the N end of Lily Pond—**emerald, goshenite** (colorless to amber **beryl**), **smoky quartz crystals, tourmaline.**

LITHIA, the Barrus Farm, pegmatite outcrop—**spodumene.**

LOUDVILLE, area mines—**chalcopyrite, wulfenite.**

MIDDLEFIELD, N section, fine bed associated with exposure of **serpentine— soapstone.**

NORTHAMPTON, area mines—**fluorite, galena, wulfenite,** some **chalcopyrite.**

NORWICH BRIDGE, area pegmatites—gem **beryl.**

PELHAM, area mines—**asbestos, apatite, emery.**

SOUTHAMPTON, area mines—cf. NORTHAMPTON.

WEST SPRINGFIELD, area mines—cf. NORTHAMPTON.

MIDDLESEX CO.

FRAMINGHAM, area deposits of minor extent—**jade** (possibly only **williamsite**).

MALDEN, area beds of argillaceous slates—**novaculite.**

SOMERVILLE, area quarries—**prehnite.**

WESTFORD, exposures of metamorphic rocks—**chiastolite crystals**. (Exposures are argillaceous slates.)

WORCESTER CO.

BOLTON, E 2 mi., a limestone quarry—**scapolite** (crystals, massive, pink).
HUBBARDSTON, area mines (for **copperas**)—**pyrite**.
ROYALSTON, N 68° E 2½ mi., at Beryl Hill, the Reynolds Mine (most productive locality in state for blue and yellow gem-quality material)—**beryl, smoky quartz crystals, muscovite mica**.
STERLING, area exposures of micaceous slates—**chalcopyrite, siderite**.
STURBRIDGE, area mines in gneiss—**graphite**.

MICHIGAN

Michigan is separated into two distinct parts by the Ice Age waters of Lake Michigan. In the far northwest the Upper Peninsula extends from the Wisconsin boundary to front onto southwestern Lake Superior, where a long arm, the Keweenaw Peninsula, curves into that great body of fresh water. This remote region is the northern woods country, known facetiously as a land with "ten months winter and two months poor sledding." Here, enormous **copper** deposits were early ruthlessly stripped of great masses of the native metal, as well as unbelievably rich ores, with active mining continuing right up to the present.

Mined primitively by prehistoric Indians for useful nuggets of **native copper** that could be hammered into ornaments, the deposits also produced many such huge unworkable masses as one single "nugget" that weighed more than 420 tons, when eventually broken up and excavated by white miners. The most productive mines and gem-rich dumps occur in the Copper Range, about 25 miles long, extending from Painesdale in Houghton County to Mohawk in Keweenaw County. However, virtually every community shown on maps of the Upper Peninsula is a mining center and consequently of interest to the rock collector.

Also occurring in the Upper Peninsula are almost equally important and extensive bodies of high-grade **iron** ore. Where the **copper** mine dumps yield up very many gemstone materials and colorful ore minerals, the **iron** mine dumps are more gemologically noted for a rather extraordinarily attractive gemstone known as the **Kona dolomite**. This impure dolomite is really a breccia of silicified algae of Huronian age, 2½ to 3 billion years old. The fossil algae grade into **chert** and **quartzite** in various shades of pink, orange, brown, and red intricately laced with steel-black **hematite**.

The gem and mineral collector will find that there are two different types of collecting to be considered in Michigan: hunting along the state's lake beaches for gemstones, especially Lake Superior-type **agates,** and working over the almost countless **iron** and **copper** mine dumps. The Keweenaw Peninsula, especially in Houghton and Keweenaw counties, contains the richest **copper** mines. At the same time, the Lake Superior beaches surrounding the peninsula are rich in **agates,** with **thomsonite** and **chlorastrolite** occasionally encountered.

The **agates** are generally small but richly banded and quite colorful. An occasional large nodule may be found, as witness the 17-pound prize reported from Keweenaw Point. They represent a subvariety of the Lake Superior type, differing in that their primary color is brown, with generally tone-on-tone bands and a tendency toward greater opaqueness. The associated **thomsonite** is a pastel pink and green cutting material (perhaps a pink **prehnite**) occurring in radiating sunburst patterns. The **chlorastrolite,** locally termed "**greenstone,**" is a rare **zeolite** gemstone. Along with these sought-after materials the collector is likely to find waterworn specimens of **chalcedony, jasper,** gemmy **chert,** and **adularia** (a colorless **orthoclase feldspar** that doubles for **moonstone**).

The **copper** district mine dumps are especially interesting to the perspicacious collector. The dumps contain abundantly the usual assortment of blue-green-purple ore minerals plus frequent nuggets of **native copper, native silver,** and a naturally occurring native combination locally termed "**half-breeds.**" In addition occur such other gemmy materials as **ankerite, calcite crystals** (many with raw **copper** inclusions), **domeykite, epidote, laumontite, prehnite,** and **tenorite** (with **chrysocolla**). Indeed, the Keweenaw Peninsula mines and beaches, including Isle Royale, afford at least 60 desirable gemstones and minerals to delight the heart of any collector.

The Lower Peninsula, constituting most of Michigan, also contains a considerable mineral wealth, but mainly in such less spectacular earth products as **gypsum, sandstone, limestone, salt** (**halite**), and a little **petroleum.** One exception to the general paucity of gemmy materials is locally abundant occurrences of the famed calcified *Hexagonaria* (or other) corals known as **Petoskey stones** or **Petoskey agates.** These gemmy fossils are most abundant along the beaches of Travers Bay from Petoskey, Emmet County, to Charlevoix, in the county of the same name, a stretch of about 14 miles, as well as in the regional gravel pits and quarries back from the beaches. Elsewhere in lower Michigan, quarries and gravel pits yield up crystals of **calcite, celestite, dolomite, pyrite, sphalerite,** and various kinds of quartz family gemstones.

For information, write: Geological Survey Division, Department of Conservation, Lansing.

ALPENA CO.

ALPENA: (1) area quarries and gravel pits—**fossils, Petoskey stones;** (2) N 9 mi. on U.S. 23, then E 1½ mi. to the Rockport Quarry—**fossils** (bryozoans, cup and horn corals, favosites or honeycomb coral, shells), **Petoskey stones, pyrite.**

BARAGA CO.

L'ANSE, area pits, quarries—**graphite.**

CHARLEVOIX CO.

NORWOOD: (1) area exposures of the Traverse limestone (also statewide outcrops)—gemmy **chert** (colorful); (2) N, along Lake Michigan beaches—**Petoskey stones;** (3) all regional quarries, gravel pits, etc.—**fossils, Petoskey stones.**

CHEBOYGAN CO.

AFTON, area quarries—**fossils, Petoskey stones.**
BURT LAKE, area beach gravels—**fossils, Petoskey stones.**

CHIPPEWA CO.

RABER, area quarries—**silicified coral** (gemmy).
TROUT LAKE, E, in Scott's Quarry—**agatized coral, chert, flint.**

DICKINSON CO.

FELCH, at Rian's Quarry—**actinolite, asbestos, dolomite crystals, biotite mica, wollastonite.**
IRON MOUNTAIN, LORETTO, NORWAY, QUINNESEC, RANDVILLE, VULCAN, WAUCEDAH, all regional **iron** mines, richest **iron** ore in Michigan—**hematite.**
RANDVILLE: (1) area quarries—**beryl, quartz crystals, tourmaline;** (2) the Metro-Nite Quarry—**fluorite, phlogopite, pyrite, pyroxene,** various **ore minerals.**

EATON CO.

BELLEVUE, the Cheney Quarry—**calcite,** brilliant **marcasite, pyrite.**
GRAND LEDGE, W 1 mi., a quarry—**calcite, sphalerite.**

EMMET CO.

AREA, widespread exposures and outcrops of the Traverse limestone—**Petoskey stones (calcite** replacements of *Hexagonaria percarinata* corals).
PETOSKEY: (1) W, to CHARLEVOIX in Charlevoix Co., in lake beach grav-

els, abundant—**Petoskey stones;** (2) all regional quarries (extending E clear across Mich.—**Petoskey stones.**

GOGEBIC CO.

BESSEMER, IRONWOOD, WAKEFIELD, all regional **iron** mine dumps—**hematite, specularite.**

HOUGHTON CO.

CALUMET, W about 6 mi. to the F. J. McClain State Park (on the beach), beach gravels all the way to Five Mile Point—**adularia, chalcedony, chert, jasper, Keweenaw agates, thomsonite.**

HANCOCK, area dumps of the Arcadian and Quincy mines—cf. minerals of the KEWEENAW PENINSULA. (The Quincy Mine is noted for its high-quality gem **datolite.**)

HOUGHTON: (1) area mine dumps of the Clark, Delaware, Iroquois mines; (2) Quincy Mine (across Portage Lake)—**datolite, prehnite;** (3) Old Huron Mine—**quartz crystals;** (4) Sheldon-Columbia Mine (on Portage Lake)—**algodonite, domeykite.**

KEARSARGE, dumps of the Wolverine Mine—**Keweenaw agate, chrysocolla, epidote.**

LAKE LINDEN, S, in beach gravels around shores of Torch Lake—**fossils, Petoskey stones.**

SOUTH RANGE, the Baltic Shaft No. 2—**bornite, chalcite, chalcopyrite.**

HOUGHTON and KEWEENAW COS.

AREA, the Copper Range (extending 25 mi. from PAINSDALE in Houghton Co. to MOHAWK in Keweenaw Co.), many mines and prospects—**copper minerals, native copper.** Famous mines include, in order from SW to NE: Champion, Trimountain, Baltic, Atlantic, Superior, Houghton, Isle Royale, Hancock, Quincy, Franklin, Osceola, LaSalle, Calumet and Hecla, Tamarack, Centennial, South Kearsarge, Wolverine, North Kearsarge, Allouez, Ahmeek, Mohawk, and Objibway. **Copper minerals** occur abundantly on all mine dumps, along with **datolite, algodonite, chalcedony, chrysocolla, domeykite, prehnite, quartz crystals,** etc.

HURON CO.

BAY PORT, area limestone quarries—gemmy **chert nodules.**

POINTE AUX BARQUES, in shale exposures around the lighthouse, abundant —**marcasite.**

SEBEWAING, area **coal** mines—**marcasite.**

IOSCO CO.

ALABASTER, area quarries—**alabaster, gypsum.**
NATIONAL CITY, area quarries—**alabaster.**
TAWAS CITY, N, in gravel pits, finest in state—**quartz crystals.**

IRON CO.

AMASA, CRYSTAL FALLS, IRON RIVER, MANSFIELD, STAMBAUGH, all regional **iron** mines and dumps—**hematite, specularite.**

ISLE ROYALE (off tip of the Keweenaw Peninsula)

AREA (a National Park with collecting prohibited, but scuba diving off-shore is prolific)—massive **chlorastrolite, specular thomsonite:** (1) Black Creek Beach, where creek enters Lake Superior—**onyx** (black and white); (2) old workings at the Epidote Mining Claim and at Thomsonite Beach—**chlorastrolite ("greenstone"), datolite nodules, thomsonite;** (3) Seven Mile Point Beach—**agate** (purple-banded); (4) head of Siskowit Bay and on N shore of Tobin Harbor, toward Blake Point, and on adjoining island beaches as well as inland on prehistoric lake beaches from McCargo Cove (as well as on most Isle Royale beaches)—**agate nodules, carnelian, quartz crystals;** (5) S shore of Siskowit Lake, in gravels—**chlorastrolite.**

KENT CO.

GRAND RAPIDS, extreme W suburb of GRANDVILLE, area **gypsum** quarries —**alabaster, gypsum.**

KEWEENAW CO.

AHMEEK: (1) area beaches, quarries, gravel pits—**Keweenaw agate, thomsonite;** (2) area **copper** mines—**azurite, algodonite, bornite, chryso-colla, domeykite, native copper, malachite.**
ALLOUEZ, dumps of the Allouez Mine—**chalcedony, chrysocolla, native copper.**
CENTRAL, CLARK, CLIFF, DELAWARE, MANDAN, PHOENIX, all regional mines (most named after these communities)—cf. minerals described for the KEWEENAW PENINSULA.
COPPER FALLS: (1) Copper Falls Mine dumps—**zeolite crystals,** plus minerals described under KEWEENAW PENINSULA; (2) N, area—**amethysts.**
EAGLE HARBOR: (1) local beach gravels, quarries, pits—**Keweenaw agate, thomsonite;** (2) S, to area of AHMEEK, beach gravels—**agates, adularia, chalcedony, chert, jasper, thomsonite** (variety of pink **prehnite**).

KEWEENAW POINT, area beach gravels—**Keweenaw agate, adularia, chalcedony, chert, jasper, thomsonite.**
MOHAWK, area **copper** mines—cf. AHMEEK minerals, plus **chlorastrolite.**

KEWEENAW PENINSULA (Ontonagon, Houghton, Keweenaw Cos.)

AREA, all regional **copper** mine dumps (very many)—**ankerite, calcite** (crystals which may have inclusions of **native copper**), **chlorastrolite, native copper, native silver, native copper-silver** (locally called "half-breeds"), **datolite** (massive, nodular, often with **native copper** inclusions), **domeykite, epidote, laumontite, prehnite, quartz crystals, tenorite** (with **chrysocolla**).

MACKINAC CO.

ST. IGNACE, NW 10 mi., at Pointe Aux Chenes, area quarries—**gypsum, satin spar.**

MANITOU ISLAND (off E tip of Keweenaw Peninsula)

AREA: (1) all beaches surrounding island, (2) N shore of bays especially productive—**Lake Superior agates.**

MARQUETTE CO.

AREA, all communities shown on maps surround great mines of the same name, e.g., Champion, Gwinn, Humboldt, Palmer, Princeton, Republic, etc., mines, plus many other regional mines with productive dumps—**hematite, specularite, jasper, jaspilite,** etc.
CHAMPION, the Champion Mine (in pegmatite)—**hematite, sapphire, sericite, specularite.**
GWINN, the Archibald Mine—**gypsum** (crystals on **hematite**), **hematite** (specular), **magnetite.**
ISHPEMING: (1) area prospects in T. 48 N, R. 27 W—**gold;** (2) near town, the Ropes Mine—free **gold, auriferous pyrite, chalcopyrite;** (3) all regional occurrences of glacial drift gravels, by panning—**gold colors;** (4) Lindberg Quarry (get permission)—gemmy **Kona dolomite** (brown, orange, pink, red); (5) Jasper Hill—**jasper, jaspilite;**
(6) All area iron mine dumps—**iron minerals:** (a) the Lake Shaft—**hematite, greenstone, jasper, quartz;** (b) Section Sixteen Mine—**hematite, limonite** (massive, kidney, grape, needle, specular, stalactitic), **jasper, calcite** (concretions on **hematite**), **quartz crystals, pyrite crystals** (on **limonite**), **talc;** (c) the Holmes Mine—**hematite, hematite** with **jasper, limonite, calcite** (filling cavities in **hematite**), **mica** (with **ferruginous quartz**), **magnetite crystals, specular hematite;** (d) the Cliffs Shaft Mine—**chert** (iron-stained), **jasper, pyrite, specular hematite** (hard, compact); (e) the Morris-Lloyd Mine—**hematite** (with blue jasper), **iron minerals.**

MICHIGAMME: (1) area outcrops, prospects, etc.—**jaspilite;** (2) Mt. Shasta, outcrops—**garnets;** (3) Michigamme Mine—**chalcedony, hematite, jaspilite.**

NEGAUNEE: (1) the Cambria Mine—**kidney ore,** massive **hematite, specular hematite** (schist), **talc;** (2) Lucy Mine—**barite;** (3) the Baltic Mine dump, massive—**rhodochrosite.**

REPUBLIC: (1) area outcrops, abundant—**jaspilite;** (2) area pegmatite outcrops, prospects, pits—**beryl, quartz crystals, tourmaline;** (3) the Republic Mine—**hematite, specularite, jasper, jaspilite.**

MONROE CO.

MONROE, the France Stone Quarry, as crystals—golden **calcite, dolomite.**

OCEANA CO.

HART, S about 3½ mi., Crystal Lake beach gravels—**fossils, Petoskey stones.**

ONTONAGON CO.

AREA, S and SW part of co. adjoining Houghton Co., *q.v.,* as a southward extending mineral belt, such mines as the Lake, Mass, Adventure, Michigan, and Victoria—**copper minerals, native copper, native silver:** (1) Lake and Algomah mines—**copper minerals, chrysocolla;** (2) Indiana Mine and adjoining properties—**chrysocolla, malachite, native copper** (in masses of **felsite**), **native silver.**

MASS: (1) area mine dumps (many)—cf. minerals of KEWEENAH PENINSULA; (2) the Mass Mine (on Hwy. 26)—**chrysocolla, datolite, malachite,** etc.

ONTONAGON, area Lake Superior beach gravels—**adularia, Keweenaw agates, chalcedony, chert, jasper, thomsonite** (pink and green).

ROCKLAND, area mine dumps—cf. KEWEENAW PENINSULA minerals.

SILVER CITY: (1) area around Gull Point in beach gravels—**Keweenaw agates;** (2) W about 8 mi., area of the Porcupine Mts. (outside the state park): (a) area mines—**hematite, chalcedony, jasper, jaspilite, specularite;** (b) area exposures of abundant gemmy masses—**jaspilite** (a **jasper** laced attractively with steely **specularite**).

PRESQUE ISLE CO.

ONAWAY, area quarries, gravel pits, etc.—**fossils, Petoskey stones.**

PRESQUE ISLE, area beach gravels of Lake Huron—**agate, chalcedony geodes,** gemmy brown **sandstone** (veined with **calcite**).

SCHOOLCRAFT CO.

WHITEDALE, area quarries, pits—**silicified corals.**

WAYNE CO.

DETROIT, S to ROCKWOOD, the Sylvania Quarry—**geodes** (containing yellow **calcite** or **celestite**).

MINNESOTA

This nearly level and most northerly of the continental United States is a broad glaciated plain with an elevation of 1,000 to 1,500 feet above sea level. More than 11,000 Pleistocene ice-scoured basins are filled with sparkling lake waters, remnants of the great Pleistocene Lake Agassiz, 700 miles long by 250 miles wide, that covered much of northwestern Minnesota some 10,000 years ago, and lesser lakes elsewhere that impounded the glacial melt waters as the ice retreated northward. Only the extreme southeastern corner of the state, in the eastern parts of Winona and Houston counties, escaped the Ice Age glaciers. Thus immense deposits of glacial drift, consisting of till, gravels, and stratified sands and clays, dominate the state's surface topography.

The only section that might be termed at all mountainous lies in the northeastern triangle. Here the Lake Superior hill ranges (Sawteeth, Mesabi, Cuyuna, Gunflint, Giant's Range, Vermilion) rear a few worn and rounded "peaks" to elevations near 2,000 feet above sea level, or 500 feet above the surrounding countryside. Even these ranges from which much of the world's richest **iron** ores have come are heavily drift-covered.

By far the most widely distributed and popular gemstone, for which Minnesota is especially noted, is **Lake Superior agate,** distinguished by its translucency, rich glowing colors, and fine parallel banding. Usually found in sizes from one-half to two inches in diameter, an occasional nodule weighing several pounds is picked up, high-grade gem quality throughout. Three forms are recognized: **eye agates,** an onyxlike **banded agate,** and **fortification agate** that resembles the famed **Fairburn agates** of South Dakota. Practically every glacial moraine or drift deposit, every gravel bank and stream bar, every lake beach, quarry, excavation, and gravel pit in the entire state yields up a surprising abundance of these eagerly sought-after gemstones.

For information, write: Minnesota Geological Survey, University of Minnesota, Minneapolis.

BLUE EARTH CO.

MANKATO, all regional quarries, gravel pits, stream gravels, etc.—**Lake Superior agates.**

CARLTON CO.

CARLTON, all area mine dumps—**Lake Superior agate, garnets, greenalite, magnetite, marcasite, minnesotaite, pyrite.**
CLOQUET: (1) area gravel pits, stream gravels, excavations—**Lake Superior agates;** (2) area mine dumps—cf. CARLTON.

CHIPPEWA CO.

MONTEVIDEO, area gravel pits, excavations, stream gravels—**Lake Superior agates.**

CHISAGO CO.

TAYLOR FALLS, area mine dumps—**argentiferous chalcocite.**

COOK CO.

GRAND MARAIS: (1) both E and W, all along the N shore of Lake Superior from U.S. 61 (wherever one can get through private property), all regional beach gravels—**lintonite** (var. **thomsonite** lacking fibrous structure and olive green translucency throughout), **thomsonite;** (2) SW 5½ mi., Thomsonite Beach (a 1-sq.-mi. area of basalt outcrops extending a mile inland and 1 mi. from Terrace Point)—**chlorastrolite, lintonite, thomsonite nodules** (pink, red, green sunbursts and eyes in a creamy background); (3) E 14 mi., basalt outcrops along Lake Superior shoreline—**Lake Superior agates.**
GRAND PORTAGE, E to Pigeon Point, area mines—**argentiferous chalcocite, chalcopyrite, pyrite.**

CROW WING CO.

BRAINARD, area and regional gravel pits, excavations, stream beds, lake shores—**Lake Superior agates.**
CROSBY, IRONTON: (1) area **iron** mine dumps of the Cuyuna Range; (2) the Arco and Portsmouth mines (get permission)—**agate, chalcedony, jasper,** gem **binghamite** ("silkstone," a crystalline quartz replacement of fibrous **goethite** stained red with **hematite** or yellow with **limonite**), **iron** and **manganese minerals.**

FARIBAULT CO.

BLUE EARTH, area and regional quarries, gravel pits, stream beds, etc.—**Lake Superior agates.**

FILLMORE CO.

SPRING VALLEY, area glacial drift deposits, by panning—**gold.**

GOODHUE CO.

RED WING, area and regional quarries, gravel pits, stream gravels, etc.—
Lake Superior agates.

HENNEPIN CO.

OSSEO (NW suburb of MINNEAPOLIS), S ¼ mi. on Rte. 110, then W on
rd. dead-ending in a series of gravel pits (get permission at first three pits)—
Lake Superior agates, chalcedony, jasper.

HOUSTON CO.

CALEDONIA, area sand quarry—**calcite crystals.**

LAKE CO.

BEAVER BAY, E and W, area Lake Superior beach gravels—**Lake Superior
agates, thomsonite**, etc.

LAKE OF THE WOODS CO.

AREA, Sec. 6, T. 167 N, R. 33 W, a mine—**feldspar.**

LE SUEUR CO.

KASOTA (just S of ST. PETER via Rte. 22 and W of this rte.), area quarries
along the Minnesota R.—gemmy **fossil corals.**

MORRISON CO.

LITTLE FALLS: (1) area gravel pits, stream gravels, excavations, etc.—
Lake Superior agates; (2) in sands of Elk Cr.—**garnets, staurolites;** (3)
Blanchard Dam area (S of town via U.S. 10 for 6.3 mi. from St. Gabriel
Hospital, turn W 1.2 mi. on township rd., then N 1.6 mi. to a dirt rd. and
½ mi. to the dam parking area)—**garnets, staurolites;** (4) Charles Lindbergh
State Park, in area stream sands—**staurolites.**

ROYALTON, W 3 mi., along both sides of the Mississippi R. (W side
reached from BOWLUS and ROYALTON)—**staurolites.**

OLMSTED CO.

AREA, all co. stream gravels, by panning—**gold colors.**
ROCHESTER: (1) area and regional rd. cuts, banks, etc.—**Lake Superior agates, chalcedony, fossils;** (2) E 5 mi., a quarry—**agates, fossils.**

PINE CO.

PINE CITY, area deposits or showings along banks of the Snake R.—**chalcocite.**

PIPESTONE CO.

PIPESTONE, N 1 mi., Pipestone National Monument Indian Reservation (no collecting)—**catlinite (pipestone).** This 1-sq-mi. monument preserves the only area of pre-White Plains environment and ecology in Minnesota, heritage of the Sioux tribes of the mid-nineteenth century. Here were the original prehistoric Indian diggings from which **pipestone** came and which made this area of ancient quarries a universal no-man's-land of eternal peace for all tribes, now open to the public with guided tours along prehistoric trails. Here, also, are the sheer cliffs of **quartzite** which Longfellow called the "mountains of the prairies" in *The Song of Hiawatha.* The beautiful red gemstone **catlinite** is available for purchase in town.

REDWOOD CO.

REDWOOD FALLS, area deposits and pits, as kaolinized gneiss and granite—**mineral paint (ocher).**

ST. LOUIS CO.

BIWABIK: (1) W 1 mi., the Mary Ellen Mine; (2) W 2 mi., the Corsica Mine; and (3) all in-between stream gravels, rd. cuts and cut banks, and all abandoned mine waste dumps—**Lake Superior agate, iron minerals, "Mary Ellen" jasper** (silicified algae with colorful swirling designs), other **jaspers.** (These minerals are found in all regional outcrops of the Mesabi Range Sudan formation.)
ELY, SW, Vermilion Range regional creeks, washes, breaks, etc.—**gem jasper** (many varieties), **quartz crystals, chalcedony.**
EVELETH, entire region WSW for 50 mi. to GRAND RAPIDS in Itasca Co., mainly along U.S. 169 but including side rds., all mine dumps—**iron minerals, Lake Superior agates, jasper.**
FLOODWOOD, area mine dumps—**Lake Superior agates, garnets, greenalite, magnetite, marcasite, minnesotaite, pyrite.**
HIBBING: (1) area gravel pits, excavations, stream beds—**Lake Superior**

agates; (2) regional mine dumps—**iron minerals, agate, jasper, marcasite, pyrite,** etc. The original town site was moved 1 mi. south to make way for the world's largest open-pit **iron** mine. (3) CHISHOLM area dumps—**gem goethite** (botryoidal, stalactitic).

WINTON, area gravel deposits, glacial drift, etc.—**Lake Superior agate, "evergreen" jasper.**

ST. LOUIS, LAKE, COOK COS.

DULUTH, starting at Lake Ave. and U.S. 61, follow hwy. NE along shore of Lake Superior: (1) mi. 12.2, French R. beach gravels—**Lake Superior agates;** (2) mi. 18, Knife R. beaches—**agates;** (3) telephone pole No. 1385, beach—**agates;** (4) mi. 28.2; beach—**agates;** (5) mi. 34.6, beach and stream gravels—**agates;** (6) pole No. 1915, beach gravels—**agates;** (7) pole No. 2120, Gull Rock (get permission), beach gravels—**agates;** (8) mi. 62.5, beach gravels—**thomsonite;** (9) mi. 64.5, mouth of Little Marais R.—**thomsonite, zeolites;** (10) mi. 103.2, Thomsonite Beach—cf. GRAND MARAIS in Cook Co.

SCOTT CO.

JORDAN, area glacial drift deposits, panned from gravels—**gold colors.**

SWIFT CO.

APPLETON, area gravel pits, stream gravels, excavations—**Lake Superior agates.**

WABASHA CO.

WABASHA, N side of RR station, an adjoining gravel pit—**Lake Superior agates.**

WASHINGTON CO.

STILLWATER, area between bluffs of Browns Cr., a deposit—**tripoli.**

WINONA CO.

WINONA: (1) area quarries, gravel pits, stream gravels, etc.—**Lake Superior agates;** (2) beach gravels around shores of Lake Winona—**Lake Superior agates;** (3) Goodview (suburb of WINONA), in gravel pit beside U.S. 61—**agates;** (4) all along right of way of U.S. 61, especially in roadway gravel beds—**agates;** (5) gravelly shores of a boat harbor (on Mississippi R.) just behind the Northwestern shops—**agates.**

MISSISSIPPI

Although its surface is everywhere characterized by Cretaceous to Tertiary sediments less than 100 million years old, Mississippi lends its name to a 25-million-year-long depositional epoch in American geology that began some 355 million years ago during the Lower Carboniferous period. Like other adjoining states that also anciently lay beneath the extended Gulf of Mexico, all of the state's formations were laid down under salt water as the gulf slowly receded southward from its northernmost Paleozoic reaches below the present Ohio River Valley. Such sedimentation is still actively going on, wherever rivers discharge their burdens of mud, silt, and sand into the modern Gulf of Mexico.

The sixteen counties that embrace most of north-central Mississippi are part of a very low North Central Plateau, underlaid by Eocene formations of 60 million years ago. In the two most northeastern counties of Alcorn and Tishomingo, the Tennessee River Hills achieve maximum elevations of 700 feet, while the general statewide surface is at or near sea level.

Few gemstone localities exist in Mississippi. However, the state yields a great abundance of fossils of many geologic ages. Petrifactions occur in the northeastern and central counties, where the preservative is primarily unattractive **iron oxide.** In some areas the state's fossil trees contain lovely, small, water-clear **quartz crystals,** as well as **drusy quartz** linings of cracks and fissures. Considerable quantities of this fossil wood weather out of exposures of the widespread Lafayette formation, with smaller quantities occurring in the Wilcox and other Tertiary sediments. A considerable petrified forest area, once noted for its abundance of fossil logs that reached six feet in diameter, occurs in Madison County near Flora, 18 miles northwest of the state capital of Jackson.

For information, write: State Geologist, Mississippi Geological Survey, University of Mississippi, Oxford.

BENTON, LAFAYETTE, MARSHALL, TIPPAH COS.

AREA, these northeastern counties contain many notable deposits, many mined—**siderite.**

COPIAH CO.

WESSON, E 4 mi., in a gravel pit—**agates** (banded), **chalcedony, petrified wood.**

HARRISON CO.

GULFPORT, NW 18 mi., gravel beds of Bell Cr.—**agates.**

TALLAHATCHIE CO.

CHARLESTON, area exposures—**amber,** in Tuscaloosa formation.

TISHOMINGO CO.

IUKA, extensive area deposits, formerly mined—**ochers** (red, yellow).
PADEN, area exposures of the Tuscaloosa formation—**amber.**

WAYNE CO.

WAYNESBORO, NW 7 mi., area excavations, cut banks, etc.—**fossils, petrified palm.**

MISSOURI

Missouri lies in the greater Mississippi Basin and provides excellent exposures of a wide range of Paleozoic formations from the Cambrian period through the Permian. Cretaceous marshes and swamp forests left many **coal** deposits throughout the state, while epicontinental seas laid down thick beds of sand and limestone. The youngest of the stratified rocks are the Cretaceous Coal Measures which comprise the northwestern two-fifths of the state, while the south-central one-third is occupied by the oldest rocks, those of the great Magnesian Limestone series. However, from the north extending as far south as the Missouri River, approximately, a thick mantle of Pleistocene detritus derived from the glaciations of more northern regions overlies the more ancient structures.

The state's chief topographical feature is the Ozark Uplift, a broad plateau with gentle slopes rising to 1,500 feet above sea level extending entirely across the southern part of Missouri, bordered on all sides by deep grooves and narrow gorges. This Ozark region, containing rock formations of several different geological ages, is one of the most heavily mineralized areas in the world. Many great mines and pits enrich the state's economy with their production of **barite, clay, hematite, lead,** and **zinc,** with **silver** as a by-product.

Missouri's mineral wealth is found in three main regions: **coal** in the west and north-central counties, **lead** in the southeast, and **zinc** in the

southwest around Joplin that includes the Tri-State District surrounding
the junction of Missouri with Kansas and Oklahoma, as described in the
introduction to Kansas.

A considerable variety of gemstones also occurs in Missouri. Typical
Lake Superior agates are abundant in the glacial drift deposits of Gentry,
Daviess, Grundy, and Livingston counties, along with **agatized coral** and
bone, chalcedony, jasper, and **petrified wood.** All along the Mississippi
River, which is the eastern boundary of the state, gravel operations yield
an endless supply of fine, high-quality **agates** and other quartz family
gemstones. In Clark Co., around Kahoka, exposures of the Warsaw
formation disgorge great quantities of **geodes** which differ from the Iowa
type in that more of them are hollow and lined with brilliant crystals of
pink **calcite, fluorite, goethite, millerite,** and **pyrite.** The regional stream
beds contain many such geodes, which are constantly being weathered
out of surrounding ledges. Elsewhere, an interesting and colorful gemmy
chert, locally called **mozarkite,** makes rock hunting productive in such
central Missouri counties as Benton and Hickory, while another variety
of cutting-quality **chert** is well known from McDonald Co.

Gemmy crystals of **"crested" barite** are much sought after in St. Francois and Washington counties in eastern Missouri, while directly across
the state in Jasper Co., gorgeous crystals of **lead** and **zinc minerals** make
dramatic cabinet specimens. These crystals occur abundantly deep in the
Joplin and Tri-State area mines: brilliant cubes of **galena,** a distinctive
bronzy cockscomb **marcasite,** delicately curved flesh-pink crystals of
dolomite, honey-colored **calcite,** and the ever-popular deep ruby-red
massed crystals of **sphalerite.** Because of their high mineral value, such
crystallizations, including iridescent **chalcopyrite,** are not thrown out on
the many extensive mine dumps but must be purchased locally as cabinet
specimens.

For information, write: State Geologist, Division of Geological Survey
and Water Resources, Rolla.

BENTON CO.

LINCOLN, area quarries, rd. cuts, gravel pits, etc.—**chalcedony,** gemmy
chert (compact, colorfully pink, blue, or lavender; locally called **mozarkite**),
jasper.

WARSAW: (1) all area of low hills along the W edge of the Ozark Uplift,
and (2) throughout the SE ("Bootheel") part of co.—**agate,** gemmy **chert.**

BENTON, HICKORY, POLK, DADE COS.

AREA, all rd. cuts, banks, breaks, excavations, etc., along the W slopes of
the Ozark Mts., gemmy, colorful—**chert.**

BOLLINGER CO.

LUTESVILLE, all co. gravel pits, rd. cuts, excavations, etc., extending E through Cape Girardeau Co. to the Mississippi R.—**agates, petrified wood.**

CAPE GIRARDEAU CO.

CAPE GIRARDEAU, all co. area excavations, rd. cuts, gravel operations, etc. —**agates, petrified wood.**

CHARITON CO.

DALTON, extensive area quarries—**tripoli.**

CLARK CO.

ALEXANDRIA, WAYLAND, FOX CITY, regional cr. and river banks—**"St. Francisville" geodes.**
KAHOKA: (1) area shale outcrops along the Fox R., abundant—**geodes;** (2) in banks of all area tributary streams—**geodes.**
ST. FRANCISVILLE: (1) base of all area bluffs along the Fox R.—**gemmy chert, quartz crystal geodes;** (2) in banks of Weaver's Branch, abundant—**geodes** (containing inclusions of pink **calcite crystals, fluorite, geothite, millerite, pyrite**).

COLE CO.

EUGENE, HENLEY, HICKORY HILL, regional mines—**barite.**

CRAWFORD CO.

STEELVILLE: (1) area mines, and (2) E, along Hwy. 8, on mine dumps—**amethysts, hematite, quartz crystals, pyrite.**

DADE CO.

GREENFIELD, all co. area excavations, quarries, cut banks, gravel pits—**agate, chert, petrified wood.**

DAVIESS CO.

GALLATIN, all regional gravels along the Grand R.—**fossils, agate, chalcedony, jasper, petrified wood,** etc.

FRANKLIN CO.

LESLIE, area mines—**marcasite, pyrite.**
MORRELTON, ST. CLAIR, area mines—**barite.**
STANTON, the Ruepple Mine—**amethysts, quartz crystals.**
SULLIVAN, area mines—**azurite, chalcocite, chalcopyrite, pyrite.**

GASCONADE CO.

OWENSVILLE, W and N 8 mi., scattered over area hillsides and in an abandoned clay pit—blue-gray **quartzite** boulders (containing **brachiopod casts**).

GENTRY, DAVIESS, GRUNDY, LIVINGSTON COS.

AREA, all regional glacial drift gravels, excavations, pits, etc.—**Lake Superior agates, jasper, fossils, petrified wood.**

HICKORY CO.

HERMITAGE, area rd. cuts, banks, excavations—**chalcedony,** gemmy **chert.**

IRON CO.

IRONTON, regional mines—**hematite** and other **iron minerals.** A visit to the Elephant Rocks State Park near GRANITVILLE NW of IRONTON will intrigue all rock collectors because of massive boulders which have weathered from enormous granite extrusions (no gemstone contents)—which characterize much of the St. Francois Mts.

JASPER CO. (cf. also Ottawa Co., Okla.)

JOPLIN DISTRICT (Tri-State District Missouri mining towns of ALBA, CARTERVILLE, CARTHAGE, DUENWEG, JOPLIN, NECK, REEDS, SARCOXIE, THOMS STATION, WEBB CITY), all great regional mines—**smithsonite, sphalerite** (principal ore) in underground workings, and as fine tabular crystals in the ores and on mine dumps—**anglesite, calamine, calcite** (museum-type crystals), **cerussite, greenockite, marcasite, pyrite.** (Many of the regional mine dumps also yield good specimens of **barite, chalcopyrite, dolomite crystals, galena,** etc. This enormously rich mineral district extends westward into northeast Oklahoma and southeast Kansas.)

JEFFERSON CO.

VALLES MINES, area **zinc** mines, as principal ore—**smithsonite.**

LAWRENCE CO.

Aurora, area deposits and mines—**calamine.**

LEWIS CO.

La Grange, N and S, in all regional gravel deposits along the Mississippi R. (a favorite collecting area) and local gravel pits—gem **agate, chalcedony, jasper.**

MADISON CO.

Fredericktown: (1) area mines—**chalcopyrite;** (2) S of Rte. 72, on dumps of the Einstein Silver Mine—**arsenopyrite, fluorite, pyrite, quartz crystals, sphalerite.**

Mine La Motte, area lead mines (numerous)—**chalcopyrite, galena, pyrite, sphalerite.**

Zion, all regional cut banks, excavations, etc., in the hill country extending E into Bollinger Co. and on surfaces—**jasper.**

McDONALD CO.

Powell, area of Bee Bluff along the Elk R.—gemmy blue **chert** (containing pockets and vugs of **drusy quartz crystals**).

MILLER CO.

Bagnell, Etterville, regional mines—**barite.**

MONITEAU CO.

California, countywide gravel pits—**barite crystals.**

MORGAN CO.

Versailles, countywide gravel pits—**barite crystals.**

NEWTON CO.

Granby (8 mi. NE of Neosho), area mines—**calcite, cerussite, chert, dolomite crystals, calamine, galena, marcasite, pyrite, quartz crystals, sphalerite.**

Racine, Seneca, extensive area quarries—**tripoli.**

Wentworth, area mine dumps—**lead-zinc minerals, pyrite, sphalerite.**

OZARK CO.

GAINESVILLE, N on Rte. 5 to Timbered Knob, area—gemmy **chert** (white and yellow bands).

RALLS CO.

NEW LONDON, N on U.S. 61, in rd. cut near the Salt R. bridge—**silicified conodonts** (fossil microscopic toothlike structures composed of calcium phosphate).

RIPLEY CO.

DONIPHAN: (1) E along U.S. 160 toward the Butler Co. line, area farms, hillsides, etc.—gemmy **flint** (many colors); (2) along banks and in gravels of the Current R., sometimes to giant size, gemmy—**chert nodules.**

SHANNON CO.

EMINENCE, the nearby Slater, Tyrell, and Jerktail mines—**chalcocite, malachite.**

ST. FRANCOIS CO.

AREA, many large deposits and pits throughout co.—**"crested" barite.**
IRON MOUNTAIN, area mines and pits—**hematite, quartz crystals.**

STE. GENEVIEVE CO.

CORNWALL, area mines—**chalcocite, cuprite, malachite.**
STE. GENEVIEVE, area mines—**chalcopyrite.**

STODDARD, DUNKLIN COS.

DEXTER, S, along both sides of Rte. 25 to MALDEN in Dunklin Co., and in all regional gravel pits and stream beds—**chert, fortification agate** (blue, gray, pink, white).

WASHINGTON CO.

OLD MINES (village 7 mi. N of POTOSI on Rte. 21), area mine dumps—**barite, gemmy chert, drusy quartz crystals.**
POTOSI, area deposits, pits, mines—**barite crystals.** (There are numerous

barite mines around such unmapped centers as Barytes, Cadet, Fertile, etc., in this county.)

MONTANA

Montana was named from its mountains. Dominated by the complex Rocky Mountain system that originated with the Laramide revolution to close the Mesozoic era and initiate the Cenozoic, western and southwestern Montana carries the Continental Divide on the rugged granite shoulders of the Bitterroot Range that is the state's western boundary. Every few years, earthquakes smashing across the mountain regions remind us that the mountain-building forces are still dramatically at work.

Early prospectors, who followed trails pioneered by Lewis and Clark in 1805 and the fur *voyageurs* of subsequent decades, came as losers from the California gold fields. They discovered enormous new sources of mineral wealth in **gold, silver, lead, copper, manganese,** and **zinc,** causing Montana to become known primarily as a mining state. Long later, a different kind of mineral wealth in **Montana moss agates** and **sapphires** contributed to the state's high placement in every gem and mineral collector's roster of places to visit on a rock-hunting vacation.

Montana is seventh in the list of America's gold-producing states, having yielded a total of 17,752,000 ounces between 1863 and 1965. Gold was first discovered in 1852 in placers in Powell Co., but not until a decade later did a truly great influx of prospectors arrive, and then in the Bannack district of Beaverhead Co. Many other rich placers were subsequently found in rapid succession, best known of which was in Alder Gulch, where Virginia City (1864) now slumbers as the county seat of Madison Co. Such placers, which produced nearly half the state's total gold, were most active prior to 1870 but continued pouring out the yellow metal until halted by World War II. Today, panning for **gold** is a major summer hobby.

Inauspicious showings of "colors" in an **iron** gossan covering a minor butte in Silver Bow Co. in 1864 created a modest **gold** and **silver** camp known as Butte. But when the underlying **copper** ores were penetrated in 1880, Butte erupted into the greatest **copper** center on earth, adding more than $2 billion to America's coffers—one of the few metal-mining districts in the world ever to produce such enormous raw new wealth. The **copper** brought the railroads into Montana and greatly facilitated settlement of the state.

Although for nearly a century Montana made exciting economic and political news with its great metal mines, later comers began making Montana world famous for **Montana moss agate.** The gray **chalcedony** nodules shaped like Idaho potatoes occur in the gravel bars and adjoining benches along the Yellowstone River for some 250 miles eastward from the river's exit from Yellowstone National Park all the way to North Dakota. The most prolific area extends some 140 miles eastward from Billings to Miles City, with numerous side streams out of Wyoming contributing a minor supply. This extraordinary gemstone consists of unusually translucent **chalcedony** laced with **manganese dioxide** against a background often of brilliant red **carnelian.** When sliced, the nodules reveal delicate landscape scenes of mountains, forests, trees, bushes, ferns, lakes, clouds, and human and animal figures. Slice for slice, **Montana moss agate** brings the highest prices in the world's agate markets. A single potato-sized nodule, when slabbed into thin slices, can be worth well in excess of $100.

Two other highly desired gems, purple **amethysts** and cornflower-blue **sapphires,** are notable from Montana. The gold mines of Jefferson Co., east of Butte, produce high-quality **amethysts** as a by-product, along with lovely water-clear **quartz crystals.** The **sapphires** come mostly from the stream gravels of Lewis and Clark Co., out of Helena, although other western counties also produce the blue gem **corundum.**

For information, write: Montana State Bureau of Mines and Geology, Montana School of Mines, Butte.

BEAVERHEAD CO.

Argenta: (1) area mines—**lead-silver minerals.** (Here was the first discovery, early in the 1860's, of **lead-silver** ore in Mont.) (2) NE ½ mi., mine—**pyrophyllite.**

Armstead, SW, the Anderson deposit—**chrysotile asbestos.**

Bannack, area placer mines—**gold.** (The first significant **gold** was discovered here. Bannack became the first territorial capital, now marked by a state monument, a ghost town with well-preserved buildings dating back to 1862. Here originated the famous vigilante activities which filled Boothill with desperadoes; each grave is now marked with an appropriate signpost.)

Dillon: (1) area NW: (a) Frying Pan Basin, and (b) Camp Cr., regional gravels, surfaces, etc.—**corundum, opalized** and **silicified wood;** (2) NW 27 mi., the Rothschild Mine—**vanadinite;** (3) SE 11 mi., on Axes Cr., an exceptionally pure deposit—**talc:** (a) 2 mi. S of Axes Cr., the Timber Gulch Deposit, and (b) 8 mi. NE of Axes Cr., the Keystone Mine—**talc;** (4) E 14 mi., in Sec. 3, 4, T. 7 S, R. 6 W, area outcrops—**dumortierite.**

Glen, NW 6 mi., at Brown's Lake, abundant mine ores—**scheelite.**

Hecla (Bryant), area placers and lode deposits—**gold, lead, silver.**

Polaris, S toward Bannack, in gravels of Grasshopper Cr., rare—**diamond.**

BIG HORN CO.

Hardin, SW about 50 mi. via dirt rds. to Dryhead (cattle ranch above the Big Horn Canyon on steep E slopes of the Pryor Mts.), a considerable area of exposures of the Jurassic Chugwater Red Beds (sandstone): (1) many regional prospects—**uranium minerals;** (2) all area surfaces, especially along the canyon rim—**agate** (Dryhead fortification, with brilliant alternating red and white bands, opaque), **chalcedony, jasper, sandstone concretions** (resembling petrified tortoises), **silicified coral,** Jurassic invertebrate **fossils.** This remote, rugged area is best reached via four-wheel-drive vehicle, either from HARDIN or from BILLINGS (Yellowstone Co.). From the latter take Int. 90 W to jct. with U.S. 212, turn S to EDGAR on Rte. 789 (U.S. 310), then E on dirt rd. for about 35 mi. via PRYOR. The colorful **Dryhead agate,** which I originally discovered and named on the TX Ranch in 1955, is widely distributed, mostly on ridge tops, over this section of southern Montana and adjacent northern Wyoming. The collecting areas are on the Crow Indian Reservation or on privately owned ranches, and permission to enter must be obtained.

BROADWATER CO.

AREA (old ghost mining camps): (1) Confederate Gulch, placer and lode mines—**gold;** (2) Park (Hassel, Indian Creek), area mines—**gold;** (3) White Creek, area mines—**copper minerals.**

RADERSBURG: (1) area mines—**gold** (veins in andesite flows), **silver** (in sediments); (2) the Keating Mine—**gold, silver, tetradymite.**

WINSTON (Beaver Creek), area mines—**lead, silver, zinc.**

CARBON CO.

FROMBERG, W 1 mi., coal mine—**coal, pyrite.**

RED LODGE, two area mined deposits, podiform—**chromite.**

WARREN, N and E in the Pryor Mts. toward the Big Horn Canyon, very many scattered prospects, claims, and mines—**uranium minerals.** (All the regional surfaces yield fossils, quartz family gemstones, etc. See Dryhead minerals under HARDIN, Big Horn Co.)

CARTER CO.

ALZADA, area of the Black Hills, 9 good deposits—**bentonite.**

CASCADE CO.

AREA, Narrow Gauge Gulch, a mine—**pyromorphite.**

MONARCH, area pegmatite outcrops—**beryl.**

NEIHART: (1) area district mines—**galena, polybasite, native silver, sphalerite;** (2) Big Bend deposit—**molybdenite;** (3) the Hartley Mine, gemmy—**sphalerite;** (4) area S in Little Belt Mts., placers and lode veins in gneiss and diorite—**gold, silver.**

VAUGHN, area surfaces—black **silicified wood, teredo wood** (filled with **chalcedony**).

CHOUTEAU CO.

WARRICK, area of the Bearpaw Mts., the Black Diamond prospect—
apatite, augite, magnetite.

DAWSON CO.

GLENDIVE, all regional surfaces, draws, washes, etc.—**agate, jasper, moss
opal.** (Most of eastern Mont. is covered by Tertiary sediments washed down
from the rising Rocky Mts. far to the west, and **quartz family minerals** can
be found as float almost everywhere.)

DEER LODGE CO.

ANACONDA, area: (1) French Cr., placers—**gold;** (2) Rable Mine—**argentite, arsenopyrite, azurite, bornite, chalcocite, chalcopyrite** (with **gold**),
chrysocolla, hematite, marcasite, pyrrhotite.
CHAMPION, E 5 mi., in gravels—**gold, sapphires.**
GEORGETOWN: (1) area placers—**gold;** (2) Cable Mine—**gold, chrysocolla;** (3) Southern Cross Mine—**gold.**

FERGUS CO.

GILT EDGE, MAIDEN: (1) area placer mines—**gold;** (2) area lode mines,
veins as replacements in limestone—**gold;** (3) in the Judith Mts., the Spotted
Horse Mine—**gold telluride.**
NORTH MOCCASIN (Kendall), area mines, ore mostly in bituminous and
argillaceous sediments near top of Madison limestone—**gold.**

GALLATIN CO.

BOZEMAN, area: (1) Salesville, and headwaters of Elk Cr.—**emery, corundum;** (2) Horseshoe Hills, area—**dendritic shale, trilobites;** (3) S, on summit
of Mt. Blackmore, elev. 10,196 ft.—**agate, chalcedony, hyalite opal, gem
opal, petrified wood.**
MANHATTAN, NW 5 mi.—**onyx.**

GLACIER CO.

BLACKFOOT, Nelson Hill area, rare—**diamond.**

GRANITE CO.

PHILLIPSBURG: (1) SW 2½ mi., the Granite Mine, as important ore mineral—**cerargyrite** (this important mining district contains numerous mines,

on the dumps of which are found **chrysocolla** and **rhodochrosite** in addition to various metallic ore minerals); (2) First Chance (Garnet) Mine, veins in granodiorite—**pyritic gold-copper minerals;** (3) Granite-Bimetallic Mine— **argentite, arsenopyrite, azurite, bornite, chrysocolla, malachite, tennantite;** (4) Boulder Cr., area mines, veins in granite, especially the Royal Mine as chief producer—**gold, silver;** (5) Flint Cr., area mines, replacements in limestone—**gold, manganese, silver;** (6) Henderson Cr., lode mines—**gold, scheelite;** (7) W several mi., Rock Cr., area gravels, particularly in Anaconda and Sapphire gulches and along all tributary draws—**quartz crystals, sapphires.**

HILL CO.

ROCKY BOY, Bearpaw Mts., in exposures of carbonate rocks—**columbite.**

JEFFERSON CO.

BASIN, the Boulder Basin District: (1) regional placer and lode mines along: (a) Basin, Cataract, and Lowland creeks, and (b) the upper Boulder R.—**silver, gold** (as by-product); (2) N 7 mi., on Jack Cr. in Sec. 7, T. 7 N, R. 6 W—**dumortierite;** (3) Mill Canyon, pegmatite outcrops—**tourmaline.**

CORBIN, area mines—**arsenopyrite, cerussite.**

ELKHORN (District): (1) area contact metamorphic deposits—**auriferous silver-lead** replacements, **gold sulfides, arsenopyrite, cerussite;** (2) Elkhorn Peak, area mines—**hematite, magnetite.**

PIPESTONE: (1) N to Int. 90 then W 7 mi. (to milepost 19 out of BUTTE), turn N for 5 mi. to (a) Homestake mining district, area mine dumps— **amethysts, rock crystal;** (b) W side of Rider Cr.— **amethysts, rock crystal;** (2) the Pohndorf Amethyst Mine (2 mi. NE of Toll Mt. picnic grounds and 2 mi. N of U.S. 10)—**amethysts, feldspar crystals, mica, smoky quartz crystals, black tourmaline.**

WHITEHALL (Cardwell), area mines in **quartz** veins—**galena, gold, pyrite, sphalerite.**

WICKES, CLANCY, COLORADO (includes Warm Springs and Clancy creeks and Lump Gulch), area placers and mines—**arsenopyrite, cerussite, gold.**

JUDITH BASIN CO.

UTICA, SW 15 mi., in Yogo Gulch, occurring in area igneous dikes intruded into limestone outcroppings on hills above the gulch—**gold, ruby, sapphire.**

LEWIS AND CLARK CO.

GARDINER, area mines—**arsenopyrite** (with **gold**).

HELENA (Last Chance Mining District): (1) area mines along the N contact of the Boulder batholith—**gold;** (2) Golden Messenger Mine (on W side of Big Belt Mts.), operated until 1942—**gold;** (3) McClellan Cr., area placers—**gold**; (4) Missouri R.–York (Trout Cr.) District, area **quartz** mines, in replacements—**gold**; (5) Sevenmile-Scratchgravel District, early placers with some renewed activity in the 1930's, panning for colors a seasonable hobby—**gold**; (6) Stemple (Gould)–Virginia Cr. District, area mines with veins in sediments—**gold**; (7) American Bar (long a noted occurrence of gem **sapphires**)—**cassiterite (stream tin), chalcedony, garnet, gold, kyanite, limonite** (pseudomorphs after **pyrite**), **sapphire, topaz**; (8) N and SE, all gravel bars along the Missouri R.—cf. American Bar; (9) Prickly Pear Cr. in lower end of Magpie Gulch: (a) Emerald Bar—cf. American Bar; (b) Metropolitan Bar, and (c) Spokane Bar—**gold, sapphires**; (10) NE 12 mi., the Eldorado Bar: (a) area gravels—cf. American Bar; (b) SE 6 mi., at French Bar—cf. American Bar; (11) very many other gravel bars, benchlands, and tributary draws and streams (make local inquiry at any rock shop in town)—**gold, sapphire, garnet, chalcedony, cassiterite, topaz,** etc.

LINCOLN, area placers and some lode mines—**gold.**

MARYSVILLE (Ottowa)–Silver Cr. (includes Bald Butte S of the main part of the district, the Drumlummon Mine as main producer—**gold, silver.** (This rich mine operated for nearly a century, closing in 1956.)

RIMINI-TENMILE District, area mines—**lead, silver, zinc.**

LINCOLN CO.

LIBBY (Snowshoe): (1) SW 4 mi., the Rainy Cr. District, mines in **quartz** veins associated with **iron** and **copper sulfides—aegirite** (containing **vanadium**), **tremolite asbestos, vermiculite**; (2) S 20 mi., a small area containing mines and prospects in veins—**gold**; (3) SE 35 mi., mines in massive vein cutting Belt **argillites—barite.** (All mines and prospects around LIBBY yield also **gold, lead,** and **silver.**)

SYLVANITE-YAAK, area mines and prospects along the Yaak R. and surrounding tributaries—**gold, pyrite,** etc.

MADISON CO.

AREA: (1) Cow Camp, Elk Mt., Finnegan Ridge, regional surfaces, draws, etc.—gemmy **chert, jasper**; (2) Greenhorn Gulch, area gravels—rare **diamond, quartz crystals**; (3) N part of co., in the Sappington pegmatites (see geologic quadrangle map for distribution)—**fergusonite, muscovite mica,** etc.; (4) Pole Cr., area gravels—**garnet, gold, quartz crystals, rubies, sapphires**; (5) South Boulder Cr., area gravels—**quartz crystals**; (6) South Meadows, between there and Moore Cr., pegmatite outcrops—**spinel,** etc.

ALDER: (1) Alder Gulch, many great mines—**gold**: this was one of the richest **gold**-producing areas in Montana after 1863; along with nearby VIRGINIA CITY, *q.v.*, it yielded approximately $30,000,000 (old price of gold) in three years; (2) Bismark Mine—**molybdenite, pyrite, chalcopyrite**; (3) California Gulch, head of, in placers—**fergusonite, gold**; (4) S, upstream along the Ruby R.: (a) area gravels, (b) gravel beds near Ruby Dam, and (c) all regional tributary cr. beds—**almandite garnets.**

ENNIS: (1) SW 13 mi., area pegmatite outcrops—**andalusite, kyanite,**

sillimanite; (2) S 15 mi., deposit in pegmatites—**muscovite mica;** (3) S 20 mi., in Johnny Gulch, deposit—**talc.**

HUTCHINS RANCH (community on U.S. 287 about 38 mi. S of ENNIS), S to Cliff Lake (extreme SE part of co.), area deposits—**chrysotile asbestos, serpentine.**

SILVER STAR (Rochester District): (1) gravels of the Jefferson R., and (2) surfaces of all area hills—**agate, chalcedony, jasper, petrified wood;** (3) near S end of the Boulder batholith, mines in **quartz** veins—**gold.**

TWIN BRIDGES (Tidal Wave): (1) W, at Crystal Butte, area—**rock crystal;** (2) mines in contact veins on W side of the Tobacco Root batholith —**gold.**

VIRGINIA CITY, area great mines—**gold, garnets.** Founded in 1863 with discovery of rich placers in Alder Gulch, *q.v.*, this present county seat mushroomed with miners, gamblers, road agents, dance hall women, etc., to become the first town incorporated (1864) in Montana Territory, with the first newspaper published in the territory the same year. The city became successor to BANNACK, *q.v.*, in Beaverhead Co., as territorial capital, later losing that distinction to HELENA, present state capital. VIRGINIA CITY carries on Madison Co. legal business and survives principally on tourism.

MINERAL CO.

SUPERIOR: (1) Cedar and Trout creeks, area placers—**gold;** (2) Snowbird property (in SW part of co.)—**fluorite, calcite, quartz.**

MISSOULA CO.

GREENOUGH: (1) placers and lode mines (**quartz-pyrite** veins) on Elk Cr. in the Elk Cr.–Coloma District—**gold;** (2) 2 mi. S of Elk Cr., deposits— **barite.**

LOLO, area surfaces in the Lolo Cr. District—**quartz crystals** (clear, smoky).

MINERAL POINT, area mines—**arsenopyrite** (containing **silver**).

NINEMILE CREEK, placers in glacial moraines—**gold.**

PARK CO.

CARBELLA, area draws, cr. beds, hillsides, etc.—**agate, jasper, petrified wood, quartz crystals.**

CLYDE PARK, area rock exposures—**calcite (Iceland spar).**

COOKE CITY (New World), negligible area placers (panning for colors good) and numerous contact–metamorphic vein mines—**gold, gold sulfides.** This tourist town is the present gateway to the northeast corner of Yellowstone National Park via U.S. 212 from RED LODGE in Carbon Co. Dubbed the "Million-Dollar Highway" because it cost that much per mile to construct during the Depression years, this route into the park ranks among the most scenic in the world. COOKE CITY was a noted **gold**-mining camp in the early days, with many mines inside and immediately outside its environs.

EMIGRANT, small-scale placers along Emigrant Cr., some lode veins—**gold.**
GARDINER, area land surfaces, gravels, stream beds, etc.—**agatized wood, travertine.**
JARDINE (Sheepeater), small placers and replacement vein mines—**arsenic, gold, tungsten.**
LIVINGSTON: (1) area hillsides, ranchlands, etc.—**agatized wood;** (2) all regional gravels of the Yellowstone R.: (a) S toward Yellowstone National Park, (b) E toward SPRINGDALE, and (c) all regional tributary stream gravels—**agate** (some **Montana moss**), **natrolite, silicified wood.**
MINER, area land surfaces—**agate, chalcedony, jasper, petrified wood.**

PHILLIPS CO.

LANDUSKY, area old mines—**gold, malachite, pyrolusite.**
ZORTMAN, some placers, some veins in porphyritic laccolith—**gold.** These two old near-ghost camps lie on opposite sides of the Little Rock Mts. ("Little Rockies") and were the stomping grounds of such outlaws as Butch Cassidy, Kid Curry, and the notorious Wild Bunch. Full-scale placering was under way by 1890; in 1893 Pike Landusky discovered and developed the noted August Mine, a lode operation in Alder Gulch, followed by the opening of such other mines as the Goldbug, Pole Gulch, Independent, Mint, Alabama, Fergus, Ella C, and Hawkeye. The mines were closed during World War II. A recent real estate boom has revived both towns as centers for recreation in the Little Rockies.

POWELL CO.

AVON (Ophir), area placers, veins in Paleozoic limestone—**gold.**
FINN DISTRICT (includes Washington, Jefferson, and Buffalo gulches), numerous placer and lode mines—**gold.**
GOLDCREEK, area placers—**gold.**
PIONEER, area placers where the first actual **gold** was discovered in Montana Territory (1852), veins in granite—**calcite, chalcopyrite, gold, quartz crystals, pyrite.**
ZOSELL (Emery), area placers and **quartz-sulfide** veins in volcanics—**gold.**

PRAIRIE CO.

FALLON, to E and N of the Yellowstone R., in side tributaries of Crackerbox, Hatchet, Sand, and Whoop-up creeks, finest gem grade—**Montana moss agates, chalcedony, chert, jasper.**
TERRY: (1) area land surfaces, draws, washes, etc.—**petrified wood, chalcedony, jasper,** etc.; (2) area gravel bars of the Yellowstone R. across entire co.—**Montana moss agate.**

RAVALLI CO.

AREA: (1) Crystal Mt., mine that is Montana's largest producer—**fluorite;** crystals range from white or pale green to deep purple; (2) Eightmile Cr., near the White Cloud Mine, pegmatite outcrop—**"parasite" beryl;** (3) Hughes Cr., area placers small and sporadic, but panning for colors good—**gold.**

CONNER, on Sheep Cr. (tributary of the West Fork of the Bitterroot R.), a large, mined deposit—**allanite, ancylite, fergusonite** (with **euxenite** and **fersmite**), **monazite.**

HAMILTON, W, in pegmatite outcrops of the Bitterroot Mts.—**fergusonite.**

SULA: (1) area pegmatite outcrops, and (2) N 2 mi., pegmatites—**beryl** (green, prisms to 3 in. long).

SILVER BOW CO.

AREA: (1) Brown's Gulch, alluvial gravels—**sapphires;** (2) Highland District (ghost town of early-day placers, veins, chimneys, and contact deposits)—**gold.**

BUTTE: (1) dumps and underground workings that are open to visitors of the Alice, Allie Brown, Lexington, Rainbow, and other city mines—**bornite (peacock copper), pisanite, rhodochrosite, rhodonite** (gemmy gangue mineral). The city mines, many reaching to depths of 4,000 feet, are interlaced with more than 3,000 miles of tunnels on 100+ levels so that visitors and miners may travel from one part of the city to another entirely underground, entering or emerging via scores of shafts. The "richest hill on earth" produces **copper** primarily, with by-products of **lead, gold, silver,** and **zinc.** Visitors are escorted (dressed in rubber suiting because of the ubiquitous water) at timed intervals through the largest workings; temperature rises rapidly with depth to near boiling point in the lowest workings. Collection of lower-grade ore specimens may be allowed, and specimens of the flamboyantly gorgeous, Prussian-blue **peacock copper** can be purchased. Visitors to BUTTE should also visit nearby ANACONDA in Deer Lodge Co. to view one of the largest smelters in the world, with a brick chimney more than 500 ft. tall.

(2) The Emma Mine, massive—**rhodochrosite;** (3) E, along the foothills of East Ridge, numerous mines—**chrysocolla** and other **copper minerals;** (4) S, in the Gravelly Range, deposits—**silicified rhyolite ("onyx");** (5) Summit Valley, area placers and complex veins in **quartz monzonite—gold.**

MELROSE-GREGSON, extreme SW corner of co., area mines—**bentonite.**

WALKERVILLE, upper 4 mi. of Dry Cottonwood Cr. starting 12 mi. NW of BUTTE, area stream gravels—**gold, sapphires.**

STILLWATER CO.

COLUMBUS, SW 42 mi., the Mouat Mine—**lead, silver.**

YELLOWSTONE CO.

BILLINGS to CUSTER, all gravel bars of the Yellowstone R. (including to W boundary of co. W of LAUREL)—**Montana moss agate, chalcedony, jasper.**

NEBRASKA

This rectangular Great Plains state rises 4,460 feet east to west, from 840 to 5,300 feet, yet so imperceptibly that the traveler is impressed with its seeming completely level topography. The highest elevation, 5,424 feet, almost straddles the extreme southwestern corner of Kimball Co. where it overlooks both Colorado and Wyoming. The subsurface rock strata of the entire state are all undisturbed sedimentaries: sandstone, limestone, shale, and clay, with the oldest formations lying in the southeastern corner where Pennsylvanian rocks crop out. These formations resulted from Tertiary erosional debris spreading out from the Rocky Mountains as they rose during the Larimide revolution of 100 million years ago that closed the Mesozoic era. Thus, as one travels westward across Nebraska he finds successively younger formations appearing in cut banks, in draws and breaks along the regional rivers, and outcropping through the Quaternary gravels of the surface.

Greatly eroded sandhills fan out across the west and northwest counties, while the farthest west reaches rise to the high, arid sagebrush plains of eastern Wyoming, disclosing spectacular bedrock formations. Northwestern Nebraska contains most of the gem fields in the state, inasmuch as both the Black Hills of South Dakota and the scenic Badlands thrust long spurs into this part of the state. In this rough, uncurried region are found the famed **Fairburn agates,** brilliantly fluorescent **chalcedonies,** and **jaspers** that rival the colors of the rainbow.

The western Nebraska-South Dakota borderland from Sheridan Co. to the Wyoming line is good rock-hunting country, especially along the southern slopes and ridges of the Pine Ridge Escarpment and along Whiteclay Creek near the Sioux Indian community of the same name in Sheridan Co. The extreme northwestern counties of Sioux and Dawes have many localities for fascinating things to hunt for: **concretions, barite and celestite crystals, chalcedony rosettes, agates, jaspers,** and **fossil** plant and vertebrate remains. The breaks of the White River north of Crawford in Dawes Co. and the rather extensive rock beds east of the Orella railroad station rank among the finest collecting grounds in the Midwest for gemstone materials.

An extensive collecting region for **agatized** and **opalized wood** of high gem quality is the Sandhills country around Valentine in Cherry Co., extending along the Niobrara River eastward into Brown Co. The Sandhills Museum in town is well worth the rock hunter's visit. Draws, cuts, and breaks in the hills along the Minnechaduza Creek and the Niobrara, as well as all tributary canyons, creeks, and washes, reveal an abundance of gem-quality **petrified wood,** often occurring as huge stone logs lying on the surface of the ground. A great deal of **agatized** and

opalized mastodon ivory in pastel colors weathers from the same regional formations.

Eastern Nebraska has few gemstone localities, but quarries, gravel pits, and other excavations throughout the more settled counties will pay investigation for **geodes, chert nodules, fossils, calcite crystals, marcasite, and pyrite cubes.** The area around the confluence of the Loup River with the Platte River in Platte Co. is well known for its **agate, chalcedony, jasper,** and gem **petrified wood.**

For information, write: State Geologist, Conservation and Survey Division, University of Nebraska, Lincoln.

BUFFALO CO.

KEARNEY, area gravel bars and pits along the Platte R., especially to the W of town—**agate, chalcedony, jasper, petrified wood.**

CASS CO.

WEEPING WATER, SE, on rd. to NEHAWKA, in the Snyderville Quarry—**chalcedony, jasper, fossils** (crinoids, brachiopods, horn corals).

CHERRY CO.

VALENTINE, in the Sandhills country along the Niobrara R. and Minnechaduza Cr.: (1) regional cuts, draws, hillside surfaces—**agatized** and **opalized wood, agate, jasper;** (2) in draws and washes and gravel beds of Spring Cr. and the Keya Paha R.—**agatized** and **opalized wood, silicified mastodon tusks, arrowheads, flaked points** (of gem **agatized wood**).

CHEYENNE, DEUEL, GARDEN, KEITH COS.

AREA, between North and South Platte rivers and in all tributary branches and creeks: (1) especially along Lodgepole Cr., (2) region S of SIDNEY to OGALLA, (3) along banks of the South Platte R., (4) south banks of the North Platte R., in regional sand pits, breaks, rd. cuts, etc., gem quality—**agatized** and **opalized wood.**

DAWES CO.

CRAWFORD: (1) N, in breaks of the White R. reached by numerous ranch rds. (get permission to enter), choice—**Fairburn agates;** (2) all regional federal grazing lands (leased by area ranchers or get USFS permission)—**Fairburn agates, jaspers, petrified wood,** etc.; (3) NW on Rte. 2 to the Orella RR sta.: (a) N 1 mi., turn E on ranch rd. and NW 2 mi. to a lone butte, one of best collecting areas in the midwestern states—**Fairburn agates, jasper, agatized** and **opalized wood, silicified** *Tempskaya superba, Tempskaya* **ferns, agatized bog, agatized palm, teredo wood, cycads,** etc., **chalcedony nodules** (pseudomorphic, filled with **agate, carnelian, opal,** with much of the **chalcedony** brilliantly fluorescent); (b) S from Orella ½ mi., turn W across RR tracks on ranch rd. for 3 mi. into steep breaks—**Fairburn** (and other) **agates, fossils, jasper, agatized** and **opalized wood,** etc. (Gemstone materials and fossils lie scattered or in local concentrations over a broad region surrounding the Orella RR sta., eroding out of gullies and ravines or scattered throughout the prairie grass that makes this entire region a cattle grazing province. Judicious chipping of specimens is required, since agate exteriors give little to no indication of interior beauty.) (4) N 20 mi., all area of the Little Bad Lands—**fossil** remains of alligators, oredonts, rhinos, saber-toothed tigers, etc.; (5) Pine Ridge, area—**quartz concretions, agates, petrified wood, fossils,** etc.

DAWES, SIOUX COS.

AREA, the entire region embraced by these two adjoining NW cos., in gravels, cut banks, breaks, draws and washes, gullies, hill slopes, etc.—**chalcedony roses, celestite crystals, fossils** (plant and animal), **concretions** (containing **calcite-**coated pillars), **agatized** and **opalized wood,** etc.

DEUEL CO.

CHAPPELL, all regional surrounding surfaces, breaks, etc.—**agate (Fairburn** and other), **jasper, chalcedony, petrified wood.**

DOUGLAS CO.

AREA, Platte R. gravels and all regional gravel pits—**agate** (banded, moss), **chalcedony, chert, flint, moss opal, agatized** and **opalized wood.**

OMAHA, W to the Platte R., then S and E to PLATTSMOUTH in Cass Co., both sides of the Platte R. for about 75 mi. (reached by many side rds.), very many localities with abundant specimens in gravel pits and bars along the river—**agates** (banded, moss), gemmy **chert** pebbles, **jasper, petrified wood.**

GAGE CO.

WYMORE (and BLUE SPRINGS): (1) all regional gravel pits and quarries —**calcite, quartz crystals;** (2) SE 3 mi., quarry on E bank of the Blue R.—**geodes** (lined with **quartz crystals** or rare blue **celestite**); (3) SW of HOLMESVILLE, quarry on the Blue R.—**geodes, flint, fossils.**

JEFFERSON CO.

FAIRBURY, regional gravel pits and stream gravels—**agate, chalcedony, jasper, petrified wood.**
STEELE CITY, area gravel pits, quarries, stream gravels—cf. FAIRBURY.

MORRILL CO.

ANGORA, 2 mi. E of Angora Hill on ranch rd., abandoned mine dumps— fluorescent **moss opal nodules** (in limestone, coated with white **calcite**), **opal arrowheads.**
BAYARD, area gravel pits, sandhills, stream gravels, etc.—**agate, chalcedony, chert, flint, fossils.**

NEMAHA CO.

AUBURN, gravel beds of the Little Nemaha R.—**agate** (common, moss), **chalcedony, jasper, petrified wood** (cycads).

PLATTE CO.

PLATTE CENTER, in gravels and pits surrounding the confluence of the Loup and Platte rivers—**agate, chalcedony, jasper, silicified wood.**

SCOTTS BLUFF CO.

SCOTTSBLUFF: (1) N 8 mi., in rd. cut on Hwy. 87, gemmy—**petrified wood** (**opal** replacement with black dendrites, fluorescent); (2) S, in Scottsbluff Badlands—**concretions, fossils.**

SHERIDAN CO.

HAY SPRINGS, area gravels, cut banks, breaks, etc.—**chalcedony, agate, jasper, petrified wood.**
WHITECLAY: (1) area gravel bars along Whiteclay Cr.—**Fairburn agates, petrified wood;** (2) entire region W to the Wyo. line (on both sides of the Nebr.–S.D. border), all breaks, badlands, cut banks, eroded topography, etc.—**agates** (**Fairburn** and other types), **chalcedony, jasper, agatized** and **opalized wood, fossils.** (This is mainly ranching country, with many access roads; permission must be obtained from area ranchers to collect on private property, including federally owned lands leased to the ranchers.)

SIOUX CO.

AREA, NE corner of co., take W-trending rd. 3 mi. S of ARDMORE, S.D., turn S and W for 9 mi. to area of Montrose on Hat Cr., area gravel beds, cut banks, etc.—**fossils, agate, jasper,** etc.

AGATE (20 mi. S of HARRISON, *q.v.*, the Agate Fossil Beds National Monument (no collecting inside), area outside—**agates, fossils, agatized** and **opalized wood,** etc.

HARRISON, E about 18 mi. toward CRAWFORD on U.S. 20 (about halfway to the Dawes Co. town), in extensive sandy rd. cut—**sand spikes.**

NEVADA

This large semitriangular state, lying entirely within the Great Basin of interior drainage, is cut off from the moisture of the Pacific Coast by California's Sierra Nevada Range. Nevada's watercourses are few and dust-dry, and the state itself is extremely arid, characterized by scores of short, high, greatly eroded Paleozoic mountain ranges that mostly trend north and south. Precambrian and Cambrian crystalline rocks dominate the state's formations and contain extraordinary concentrations of most of the commercially valuable metallic and nonmetallic ore minerals.

The mining of ore minerals and gemstones in Nevada began during pre-American times, when primitive Uto-Aztecan Indians first dug for **turquoise,** later followed by Mexican Indians and early Spaniards seeking **gold.** Ever since the first California-bound pioneers struggled across the state's barren wastes and threaded their ways through arid valleys, alkali sinks, and around the ragged ranges, Nevada has been dominated by its ores: **antimony, arsenic, copper, gold, iron, lead, magnesium, mercury, molybdenum, silver, tungsten,** and many others. Nevada's fame was guaranteed by such great strikes as Virginia City's "Big Bonanza" that enriched the silver kings: J. W. Mackay, J. G. Fair, W. S. O'Brien, and J. C. Flood; the 1900 discovery of the rich **silver** veins at Tonopah; the lucky find of gold at Goldfield in 1902 that made the city the "richest gold camp on earth"; and the enormous open-pit concentrations of **copper** excavated from Ely and Ruby, in White Pine Co., after 1868.

The enormously rich **silver** mines of Virginia City and, later, Aurora in present-day Mineral Co. (originally part of Esmeralda Co.) not only added hundreds of millions of dollars in raw new wealth to the American economy of the nineteenth century but paid for much of the Union's expenses for the Civil War, as well as resurrecting San Francisco after the earthquake and fire of 1906. Goldfield's tremendous outpouring of **gold** between 1902 and 1912 caused the world's financiers to fear for the

gold standard, because the yellow metal was seemingly to become as common as iron.

Although Nevada's focus is still basically on commercial ore minerals, there are almost numberless tapped and untapped sources for gems and gemstones: **quartz family minerals, pegmatite gem crystals, turquoise, agatized** and **opalized woods** (whole forests of logs), and some of the world's most highly valued **opal.** In the following list of gem and mineral localities, commercial ore minerals are not generally named, only the metal constituents. Few unusual, rare, or exotic ores are found; the collector who is at all familiar with metallic ores, especially of the base metals, will have little difficulty in recognizing the individual mineral species on old mine dumps from the names of their principal metals. Thus, when **copper** is listed, the collector will expect to find such mineral species as **azurite, bornite, chrysocolla, malachite,** and so on, along with interesting gangue minerals, **marcasite, pyrite, quartz crystals,** and the usual assortment of associative materials.

For information, write: Nevada Bureau of Mines, University of Nevada, Reno.

CHURCHILL CO.

AREA: (1) far E part of co.: (a) Dry Lake area, on slopes of the Clan Alpine Mts., old camp of Alpine (Clan Alpine, approx. 79 mi. E of FALLON), veins and shear zones in Tertiary volcanics—**gold, molybdenum, silver;** (b) old camp of Bernice, veins in sedimentaries—**gold, silver;** (2) extreme N-central part of co., at Mineral Basin (approx. 25 mi. SE of LOVELOCK in Pershing Co.), area mines—**iron, mercury;** (3) far NW part of co., reached N from FERNLEY in Lyon Co.; (a) NE 15 mi., old camp of Leete, veins in rhyolite, dacite, and andesite—**gold, lead, silver;** (b) NE 23 mi., old camp of Fireball —**gold.**

DIXIE VALLEY (approx. 37 air mi. NE of FALLON reached via dirt rds. from FRENCHMAN on U.S. 50): (1) NW to old camp of Buena Vista, mines in Triassic sedimentaries cut by granite intrusives—**iron minerals;** (2) old camp of White Cloud (Coppereid), replacement and contact metamorphic veins in Triassic sediments cut by granite and diorite—**copper, iron, silver, zinc.**

EASTGATE (on Rte. 2, 5 mi. E of U.S. 50 and about 60 mi. E of FALLON): (1) area mines with veins in broken **quartz** and **talc**—**gold, lead, silver;** (2) NE, in Desatoya Mts., old camp of I.X.L. (Silver Hill), veins in granite and slate—**copper, gold, lead, silver;** (3) SSW 18 mi. (via Rte. 23), the Gold Basin district, area mines with veins in Tertiary volcanics (**quartz-latite** predominating)—**gold.**

FALLON: (1) quarry 14 mi. out (make local inquiry)—**wonderstone;** (2) E about 25 mi., on W slope of the Stillwater Range in Grimes Canyon, old camp of Copper Kettle with veins in diorite overlain by altered porphyry —**copper minerals;** (3) E 30 mi., Mountain Wells (La Plata), area mines— **silver;** (4) N 26 mi. on U.S. 95, turn E on dirt rd. for 23 mi., then N to area of Pershing Co. line, mining district E of Humboldt Lake on W flank of

Humboldt Lake Range (extending into Pershing Co.), lodes in Jurassic shales—**antimony, lead, silver.**

FRENCHMAN (on U.S. 50 about 34 mi. SE of FALLON; a very considerable mining region 20–30 mi. S via Rte. 31 in adjoining Mineral Co. and SE via Rte. 23 in Mineral and Nye counties. See RAWHIDE and HOT SPRING in Mineral Co. and GABBS in Nye Co.): (1) E 11 mi. and S on Rte. 23: (a) old camp of Fairview, veins in Mesozoic sediments—**copper, gold, lead, silver;** (b) 7 mi. S of Fairview to old camp of South Fairview, veins in Tertiary volcanics—**gold, silver;** (c) 1 mi. E of Fairview, approx., Bell Mt., area mines with veins in Tertiary volcanics—**gold, silver;**

(2) E, to Chalk Mt., area mines with vein replacements in Triassic limestones—**lead, silver;** (3) E 6 mi. to N-trending dirt rd. (to DIXIE VALLEY): (a) NE 3 mi. to 5-way crossrds., take NE-trending dirt rd. 11 mi. to old camp of WONDER (Hercules), veins in Tertiary volcanics and lake sediments—**copper, gold, silver, zinc;** (b) NE 3 mi. to crossrds., then N on improved dirt rd. for 12–20 mi., area of old mining camps around Table Mt. (Boyer, Cottonwood Canyon, Bolivia), veins in Triassic sediments cut by diorite—**antimony, cobalt, copper, gold, lead, silver;** (4) S about 20 mi. on Rte. 31 to Shad Run, veins in **quartzite—gold, lead, silver.**

JESSUP (on U.S. 95 Alt., 10 mi. NW of Huxley RR Sta. [White Plains] and about 35 mi. SW of LOVELOCK in Pershing Co.), area mines—**gold.**

LAHONTAN: (1) W end of Lahontan Dam, and (2) along NE shore of the Lahontan Reservoir, area surfaces—**agate, chalcedony, jasper, petrified wood.**

SALT WELLS (15 mi. SE of FALLON), area deposits—**halite.**

SAND SPRINGS (23 mi. SE of Fallon on U.S. 50), area mines in Tertiary volcanics intruding Triassic and Jurassic sediments—**gold, silver.**

TOY (Browns), 2 mi. S of RR section house, mine with veins in contact metamorphic zone of sediments cut by granite—**tungsten.**

WHITE PLAINS (Huxley Sta.), SW 8 mi., Desert (White Plains) Mine, rich ore—**gold** (in **hematite** gangue).

CLARK CO.

AREA (old mining camps not shown on contemporary maps, but on co. topographic maps, *q.v.*): (1) Bullion district, area mines—**azurite, chrysocolla, malachite;** (2) Dike, N 1 mi., veins in Paleozoic limestones—**lead;** (3) Sutor, W 2 mi., mines with veins in sandstones underlying Permian limestone and on fractures and joints as patches—**carnotite, radium oxide** (cf. also SLOAN and JEAN for similar minerals); (4) White Basin, area deposit, fibrous—**ulexite.**

ALUNITE (Railroad Pass, Vincent; about 19 mi. SE of LAS VEGAS via U.S. 93): (1) area mines with veins and stringers in igneous rocks—**gold;** (2) SW, to Black Mt., area mines—**iron, manganese.**

BUNKERVILLE (5 mi. SW of MESQUITE on side rd. S of U.S. 91): the Copper King District (Bunkerville, Great Eastern, Key West mines), veins in Precambrian gneiss intruded by basic dikes—**cobalt, copper, gold, nickel, platinum, silver, tungsten;** (2) S about 15 mi., mining district of St. Thomas, area mines—**copper, silver;** (3) S about 30 mi. on dirt rds., Gold Butte, area mines with replacement veins in Precambrian complex—**copper, gold, silver, zinc.**

HENDERSON, S 1¾ mi. then 4½ mi. W to range of low hills, area surfaces —**chalcedony, jasper, onyx.**

JEAN: (1) NW 8 mi. on Rte. 53, the Yellow Pine District (GOODSPRINGS, Potosi), area mines with veins as replacements in Paleozoic sediments cut by dikes—**antimony, cobalt, copper, gold, lead, nickel, palladium, platinum, radium, silver, zinc;** (2) SE 15 mi. to Sunset (Lyons), veins in granite— **gold.**

LAS VEGAS: (1) area gravels in Las Vegas Wash—**amethysts;** (2) SE 16 mi. via U.S. 93 to the Las Vegas Mining District (cf. also ALUNITE), area mines with replacement veins in Tertiary volcanics—**manganese;** (2) NW 35 mi., old mining camp of CHARLESTON, area mines—**lead, silver, zinc.**

NELSON (approx. 20 mi. NNE of SEARCHLIGHT or 22 mi. S of BOULDER CITY via U.S. 95 and Rte. 60): (1) E 7 mi. on Rte. 60 to Eldorado Canyon Camp, area gravel beds of the Black Canyon of the Colorado R.—**almandite garnet;** (2) the Eldorado and Colorado mines (in the Opal Hills), veins in Precambrian granite and gneiss cut by acidic intrusives—**copper, gold, lead, silver.**

NORTH LAS VEGAS, N 18 mi. to Gass Peak (elev. 6,943 ft.), area mines with veins in Paleozoic limestones—**gold, silver, zinc.**

SEARCHLIGHT: (1) area mines, with veins in Precambrian complex cut by quartz monazite—**copper, gold, lead, silver;** (2) W about 10 mi. on Rte. 68 to Crescent (about 6 mi. E of NIPTON, Calif.), then 3 mi. ESE and just S of Crescent Peak, mines and prospects—**copper, gold, lead, molybdenum, silver, turquoise, vanadium.**

SLOAN (17 mi. S of LAS VEGAS and 2 mi. W of Int. 15), S 2 mi., a Tertiary rhyolite flow, coating on walls of joints—**radium oxides.**

DOUGLAS CO.

AREA: (1) extreme E side of co.: (a) Buckskin (adjoins the W side of the YERINGTON mining district of Lyon Co. and extends SW across the Pine Nut Mts. to the Mt. Siegel mining district, best reached N from WELLINGTON in Lyon Co.), area mines with contact metamorphic veins and placers (Triassic sediments cut by granite)—**copper, gold, iron, palladium;** (b) toward S end of the Pine Nut Mts., area pegmatite outcrops—**thulite** (pink **zoisite**), **topaz;** (2) extreme SE corner of co.: (a) old camp of Silver Glance (W side of the WELLINGTON, Lyon Co., mining district), veins in quartz monzonite of probable Cretaceous age—**copper, gold, silver;** (b) Topaz Lake area of S end of Pine Nut Mts., practically on the Calif. boundary, old camp of Mountain House (Holbrook, Pine Nut), area mines—**gold, silver.** (A rough dirt rd. runs along the entire E boundary of the county along the east side of the Pine Nut Mts. Best access is from WELLINGTON in Lyon Co.)

GARDNERVILLE: (1) Eagle mining district, area mines with veins in diorite, Tertiary volcanics, and lake sediments—**gold, copper, silver;** (2) SE 4 mi., in Red Canyon (Silver Lake camp), contact metamorphic veins in Triassic sediments cut by quartz monzonite—**gold, lead, silver;** (3) ESE about 18 mi., Mt. Siegel (elev. 9,450 ft.), area placers—**gold, platinum.**

GENOA, W, on E slope of Sierra Nevada Range, veins, replacements, placers in Triassic sediments intruded by Cretaceous granite—**copper, gold, silver, platinum.** (This community is also known by its pioneer name of Mormon Station, the western terminus of the transcontinental Pony Express trail and the eastern terminus of its extension over the Sierras to Sacramento, Calif.)

ELKO CO.

CARLIN: (1) area pegmatite outcrops in surrounding hills—**rose quartz;** (2) nearby, at the Carlin Mine—**gold.** Opened in 1965 as a result of geophysical prospecting (no surface evidence of mineralization), the Carlin Mine is considered to be the largest **gold** discovery in America since 1910. The deposit is thought to contain some $120 million dollars in **gold** at the $35 per oz. price, based on geological study and interpretations published by the U.S. Geological Survey.

CATLIN STATION, veins and replacements in Paleozoic sediments cut and capped by Tertiary volcanics—**gold, silver.**

CHARLESTON (95 mi. NNE of ELKO via dirt rds., reached from NORTH FORK on Rte. 51), the Copper Mt. and Cornwall mines, contact metamorphic replacement veins, placers in Paleozoic sediments cut by granite—**gold, copper, lead, antimony, platinum, silver.**

COBRE (NE corner of co. 4 mi. SW of LORAY, off Rte. 30), E, veins in quartzites and limestones (not a mining district)—**copper, lead, iron.**

CONTACT (NE part of co. on U.S. 93 S of Idaho line), area mines, e.g., Kit Carson, Porter, Salmon River, contact metamorphic replacement veins in Paleozoic sediments cut by granite—**azurite, malachite,** etc., **gold, silver.**

CURRIE (SE part of co. on U.S. 95): (1) SE 8 mi., old camp of Kinsley, contact metamorphic veins—**copper, lead, silver;** (2) NE 25 mi., old camps of Delker and Dolly Varden (Mizpah, Granite mines), contact metamorphic veins—**copper, gold, lead, silver;** (3) WSW 40 mi., Mud (Medicine) Springs, replacement veins in Permian limestones, shales, and quartzites—**barite, lead, silver, zinc.**

DEEP CREEK (68 mi. NNW of ELKO on Rte. 11): (1) old camp of Cornucopia, veins in Tertiary volcanics—**gold, silver;** (2) area of Bull Run and Centennial mts., old camp of Aura (Bull Run, Columbia mines), veins and placers in Paleozoic sediments cut by granodiorite—**gold, lead, platinum, silver, zinc;** (3) area of Lime Mt. (80 mi. N of Elko), contact metamorphic veins—**copper, gold, silver.**

DELANO MINES (Delano, Delno), in extreme NE corner of co. reached via dirt rds. N 34 mi. from MONTELLO: (1) area mines—**copper, lead, silver;** (2) Elk Mt. (approx. 90 mi. SSE of TWIN FALLS, Ida.), area contact metamorphic veins—**antimony, copper, silver, gold, lead.**

ELKO: (1) NW 5 mi., old camp of Good Hope: (a) area veins in Tertiary volcanics—**gold, silver;** (b) W 10 mi., old camp of Burner in the Burner Hills, veins in andesite—**lead, silver;** (2) SSW 27 mi. (12 mi. SE of PALISADE) via rough dirt rd., replacement contact metamorphic veins in Ordovician limestone—**copper, gold, lead, silver, zinc;** (3) SE 28 mi., old camp of LEE (on the Te-Moak Indian Res.), area mines—**copper;** (4) NW

28 mi. via poor dirt rds., old camp of Merrimac (Lone Mt.)—**copper, gold, lead, silver.**

FERGUSON (far E part of co. 20 mi. SSW of EASTLINE on U.S. 50 Alt.); (1) SW to old camp of White Horse on SW flank of Mt. Pisgah, veins in quartz monzonite—**copper, lead;** (2) W to Ferguson Spgs. (Alleghany) on W side of the Toana Range, replacement veins in Paleozoic limestones—**copper, lead;** (3) S about 20 mi. to old camp of Ferber (40 mi. S. of WEND-OVER, Ut., and in extreme SE corner of co.), contact metamorphic veins—**copper, gold, lead, silver.**

HALLECK (20 mi. NE of ELKO on Int. 80 and just S of hwy. on Rte. 11), SE 25 mi. to Warm Creek on SE side of Warm Creek Ridge, replacement veins in fossiliferous limestone and shale—**lead, zinc.**

JARBRIDGE (well-known ghost town on dirt rd. halfway between MOUNTAIN CITY and CONTACT, *q.v.*, and about 95 mi. S of TWIN FALLS, Ida.), area mines—**gold, silver.**

JENKINS (on rough rd. about 38 mi. SW of TUSCARORA, *q.v.*), area Rock Cr. mines—**lead, silver.**

LORAY (13 mi. SW of MONTELLO on Rte. 30), veins in crystalline limestone—**copper, iron, lead, silver.**

MIDAS (W side of co. on Rte. 18): (1) 10 mi. distant at the Rand Mine—**common opal;** (2) SW, the Gold Circle and Summit mines, replacement veins in Tertiary volcanics—**gold, mercury, silver;** (3) SE about 30 mi. by rough rds., old camp of Ivanhoe, veins in rhyolite flow breccia—**mercury.**

MOUNTAIN CITY (N-central part of co. on Rte. 51 and just S of the Idaho line), area mines—**azurite, malachite;** (2) Cope and Van Duzer mines, veins and placers in Paleozoic sediments—**copper, gold, lead, silver, zinc;** (3) Edgemont (Centennial) mines, veins in Paleozoic sediments—**gold, lead, silver;** (4) SE, to Island Mt.: (a) Gold Creek Mine, veins and placers—**gold, platinum, silver;** (b) 8 mi. N of Gold Cr., in the Alder district, area mines—**gold.**

ROWLAND (Gold Basin district about 20 air mi. NE of MOUNTAIN CITY and 12 air mi. NW of JARBRIDGE, *q.v.*, on dirt rd. 6 mi. S of Idaho line), area mines—**copper, gold.**

RUBY VALLEY (on rough dirt rd. about 55 air mi. SW of WELLS on W side of Franklin Lake), the Smith Cr. mines with lenses in Paleozoic limestones—**lead, silver, zinc.**

TECOMA: (1) S, at old camp of Lucin, replacement veins in Carboniferous sediments—**copper, lead, silver;** (2) NNE 10 mi., mines with replacement veins in limestone—**copper, gold, lead, silver.**

TUSCARORA (W-central part of co. on Rte. 18 about 42 mi. E of MIDAS, *q.v.*): (1) area mines with veins and placers in Tertiary volcanics—**gold, lead, platinum, silver;** (2) area gravels, surfaces, and outcrops—**citrine, rose quartz, wonderstone** (banded **rhyolite**); (3) NW 8 mi., to divide at head of Dry Cr., area mines and prospects—**gold, silver.**

WELLS: (1) S and SW to Valley View (not a mining district), contact metamorphic replacements—**copper, gold, lead, silver, tungsten, zinc;** (2) SSE 15 mi. on poor dirt rd. to old camp of TOBAR, N 4 mi., old camp of Lafayette—**lead, silver;** (3) SSE about 40 mi. to Spruce Mt. (camp of SPRUCEMONT on S side about 25 mi. S of TOBAR), area mines with replacement veins in Paleozoic sediments—**copper, gold, lead, manganese, silver.**

ESMERALDA CO.

ALKALI SPRINGS (11 mi. NW of GOLDFIELD), area thermal deposits as surface salts—**calcium** and **magnesium carbonates, halite,** etc. (A truly desolate area with graded dirt rd. rounding Silver Peak Marsh en route to mining center of SILVER PEAK, all land surfaces below bajadas rising to arid mts. coated with snow-white salts.)

BLAIR JUNCTION: (1) SW 4–8 mi. on dirt rd., Emigrant Peak (Emigrant Pass elev. 6,145 ft.), area surfaces, draws, washes, etc.—**silicified wood;** (2) N 8 mi., Castle Rock mines—**gold, mercury, silver;** (3) NE 9–11 mi., on E flanks of the Monte Cristo Range, area mines and regional float—**variscite;** (4) E via rough dirt rds, to Lone Mt. (old camp of West Divide): (a) area replacement veins in Cambrian sediments—**copper, gold, lead, silver, zinc;** (b) old camp of Alpine, replacement veins in Paleozoic limestones—**gold;** (c) S 13 mi. from U.S. 95 by rough rd. to S flank of the Lone Mts., WEEPAH (short-lived Model-T Ford boom camp of the early 1930's)—**gold, silver;** (5) SW 25 mi., Windypah (Fesler), via dirt rd., area mines—**gold, platinum, silver.**

COALDALE: (1) NE 3–6 mi., in the Monte Cristo Range: (a) area mines—**variscite;** (b) area draws, washes, surfaces—**agate, chert, jasper, turquoise;** (2) SSW 10 mi., on W side of Fish Lake, area land surfaces—**Apache tears;** (3) SW 13 mi. and 1 mi. E of Rte. 3A, the "Sump Hole," area—**opalized wood;** (4) Rock Hill Siding (along the abandoned right of way of the Tonopah and Goldfield RR (torn up during World War II), area mines—**variscite.**

COLUMBUS, NW 1½ mi., area prospects and mines—**variscite.**

DYER (23 mi. S of COALDALE on Rte. 3A): (1) area lode mines—**gold, lead, silver;** (2) S and E about 15 mi. to old camp of Good Hope (7 mi. S of Piper Peak on W flank of the Silver Peak Range), veins in Ordovician slates—**silver;** (3) E, in Fish Lake Valley, and (4) along flanks of the White Mts. near the Calif. line, regional mines and prospects—**cinnabar, opalite.**

GOLDFIELD (see also under Nye Co. for access to the Ralston Desert region; co. line lies about 2 mi. E of town): (1) city mine dumps (very many, huge; extensive open-pit workings), replacement veins in Tertiary volcanics underlain by Cambrian sediments—**alum, copper, gold, lead, manganese, pyrite, silver, zinc, quartz crystals.** GOLDFIELD was the scene of the gold rush of 1903 (one of the largest such rushes in the world, with great numbers of prospectors and miners coming from the Canadian Yukon (DAWSON) and Alaskan gold fields). From its discovery in 1902 on the flanks of inconspicuous Columbia Mountain until its virtual destruction by fire in 1923 (repeated exactly twenty years later in 1943, when I was teaching in the Goldfield High School), GOLDFIELD was ranked among the greatest gold camps on earth. The city achieved a maximum population of 40,000 (estimated). It is still the county seat of Esmeralda Co. (pop. about 100), and the history-minded visitor will find much of interest. The county courthouse retains century-old newspaper files from AURORA (now in Mineral Co. but in the 1870's county seat of a vastly extended Esmeralda Co.).

(2) W 3 mi., past the city dump, an outcrop, massive—**opalite** (good for garden rock); (3) W and SW 7 mi. by various jeep mine rds. crossing the "Malapai," large region surrounding and embracing Montezuma Mt.: (a)

very many old mines and prospects with replacement veins in Cambrian sediments—**copper, gold, lead, silver;** (b) all regional surfaces—**chalcedony, chert, jasper, quartz crystals, obsidian, opalized wood;**
(4) E on various rough dirt rds. (mainly used by local stockmen) into the Ralston Desert of Nye Co., area land surfaces—**chert** (the W boundary of the Nellis Air Force bombing range with travel restricted on all roads begins about 8 mi. due E of GOLDFIELD and the Nye Co. line about 2 mi. E of town);
(5) S 14 mi., old vanished camp of Cuprite, replacement veins in Cambrian sediments—**copper, gold, lead, mercury, silver;** (6) SW 25 mi. (via a dirt rd. that turns W from U.S. 95 just S of the Goldfield Summit 6 mi. S of town): (a) old camp of Hornsilver (Lime Point), veins in Cambrian limestone and shales—**copper, gold, lead, silver, zinc;** (b) Railroad Springs, lode mines— **copper, gold, silver.**

GOLD POINT (14 mi. by dirt rd. SW of STONEWALL and U.S. 95), area mines—**copper, gold, silver.**

LIDA (19 mi. W of U.S. 95 from STONEWALL via Rte. 3), veins and impregnations, placers in Cambrian sediments—**copper, gold, lead, platinum, silver.**

MILLERS (15 mi. W of Tonopah in Nye Co. and 1 mi. S of U.S. 695), NW 11 mi. to Crow Springs: (1) area mines with veins in Tertiary volcanics —**copper, gold, lead, silver;** (2) W another 2 mi. to old camp of Gilbert (Desert), lode mines—**copper, gold, lead, silver.**

NIVLOC (8 mi. SW of SILVER PEAK, *q.v.*), the Nivloc (Red Mt.) Mine— **gold, lead, silver.**

PALMETTO (11.7 mi. W of LIDA, *q.v.*, on Rte. 3, or 13.2 mi. E of jct. of Calif. Rte. 168 with Nev. Rte. 3 at OASIS, Calif.); (1) Palmetto Canyon, area surfaces—**citrine, quartz crystals, agate, chert, jasper;** (2) N 5 mi., the Palmetto Mine, veins in Paleozoic sediments intruded by granite producing contact metamorphic replacement deposits—**gold, lead, silver.** This is one of the oldest mining camps in the co., and the mine was the first big producer, with total production exceeding $6.5 million. Nonmineral souvenirs include old bottles, square hand-hammered nails, purple "desert" glass shards, and other oddments of a once active mining district. (3) Regional placers in Paleozoic sediments—**gold, lead, platinum, silver;** (4) S on rough rd. to Sylvania (Green Mt.) in the Sylvania Mts. (12 mi. E of OASIS, Calif.) and near the state line, veins in limestone—**lead, silver.**

SILVER PEAK (Mineral Ridge, Red Mt.; 20 mi. S of BLAIR JUNCTION, *q.v.*): (1) major area mines active until the 1950's—**gold, lead, silver;** (2) area rock outcrops—**rose quartz.** This mining district was located in 1863, with primary **silver** ores found on Red Mt. The Silver Peak Marsh to the NE is a large sink encrusted with **sodium-magnesium salts;** hot saline springs bubble up on the NE fringes (cf. ALKALI SPRINGS).

TOKOP (old Gold Mt., Oriental Wash; 15 mi. W of BONNIE CLAIR in Nye Co., *q.v.*): (1) area mines and placers—**copper, gold, lead, platinum, silver;** (2) area slopes of Gold Mt. (elev. 8,139 ft.)—**citrine, quartz crystals.**

TONOPAH (county seat of Nye Co., as center from which to reach adjacent Esmeralda Co. mineral localities): (1) S 7 mi., Divide (Gold Mt.), veins in Tertiary volcanics—**gold, lead, silver;** (2) SW 12 mi., the Dolly Mine, veins in Tertiary volcanics—**gold, lead, silver;** (3) S 14 mi., Klondyke and South

Klondyke (about halfway to GOLDFIELD and W of U.S. 95), lode veins, placers—**copper, gold, platinum, silver.**
WEEPAH (see above, BLAIR JUNCTION).

EUREKA CO.

AREA: (1) old abandoned mining camps not on maps (make inquiry in EUREKA): (a) Alpha, E 5 mi., sheeted zones and replacements in Devonian limestone—**lead, silver;** (b) Mineral, SE 5 mi., Mineral Hill, replacement veins in Paleozoic sediments—**copper, lead, silver, zinc;** (c) Mt. Hope Station, W 2 mi., area mines—**lead, silver, zinc;**
(2) Extreme N part of co. (reached via dirt rds. from CARLIN in Elko Co.): (a) NW 9–15 mi., the Maggie Creek District (Schroeder), area mines, especially the Copper King Mine, replacement veins—**antimony, copper, gold, faustite, lead, montmorillonite clays, silver, turquoise;** (b) NW 20 mi., veins and placers in the Tuscarora Mts.—**gold, platinum.**
BEOWAWE (W side of co. on Rte. 21 about 6 mi. S of Int. 80), area mines and prospects—**cinnabar.**
EUREKA: (1) area, including Pinto, Prospect, Ruby Hill, Secret Canyon, Silverado, and Spring Valley; replacement veins in Paleozoic sediments, granite, porphyry, rhyolite, and basalt (according to the particular district and mine)—**arsenic, copper, gold, lead, silver, zinc;** (2) Ruby Hill District, area mines—**azurite, malachite,** etc.; (3) NNE about 25 mi. via dirt Rte. 46, old camp of Diamond, veins in limestone—**lead, silver;** (4) N 27 mi. on Rte. 51, then SW on dirt rd. to old camp of Roberts, veins in syenite and limestone —**lead, silver, zinc;** (5) SW about 25 air mi. to extreme SW corner of co., old camp of Antelope—**copper, lead, silver.**
In the 1870's and '80's EUREKA was known as the greatest lead-silver mining camp on earth. Between the 1864 discovery date until the mines were flooded out in the late '80s, the mines produced $122 million in **lead, silver, zinc,** and **gold.** So much lead was produced that several operators had up to 4,000 tons each stockpiled in town, seriously affecting the world price of lead. Flood waters closed the Ruby Hill Mine on the edge of town, leaving an estimated $100 million in lead remaining beneath the flood zone. The coming of cheap electric power in 1972 will enable the Ruby Hill and other famous mines to be pumped out to initiate a new era in the mining of strategic metals.
PALISADE (9 mi. SW of CARLIN in Elko Co.): (1) W 6 mi., old camp of Safford (Barth, Palisade), veins in Tertiary volcanics—**copper, gold, lead, silver;** (2) SSW 35 mi., Buckhorn (Mill Canyon), area mines—**gold, lead, silver.**

HUMBOLDT CO.

The whole western two-thirds of this county is virtually uninhabited desert, requiring safety precautions for visitors and their vehicles. Roads are generally rough dirt, and few are on standard maps. Nearly all roads end in a mining area or connect old abandoned mining camps in a crosshatch of ancient wagon freight tracks difficult for modern automobiles to traverse. Here the finest **opals** in the world are found, as well as most of the county's supply of other gemstones.

AREA, the Virgin Valley, approx. 37 air mi. SW of DENIO, *q.v.*, at the end of a rd. that turns S from Rte. 8A a few miles E of the Summit Lake Indian Res. (also reached W via dirt rds. from QUINN RIVER CROSSING 26 mi. S of DENIO on Rte. 140, or E 60–70 mi. from CEDARVILLE, Calif.). This remote, waterless, arid region provides no supplies, sources of help, or accommodations. Collecting requires several days' minimum time, and the collector must be prepared for extremely hot weather in summer, the only months in which travel or camping is feasible.

(1) W side of valley; with the exception of the Green Fire Mine, cf. below, all **opal** localities are on the W side of the Virgin Valley: (a) many area prospects, pits, etc., and (b) the Rainbow Ridge Mine—**opal** (precious, black fire, common), **opalized wood, rhodonite.** The mine has yielded the world's most spectacular and valuable **precious opal** specimens, some to 7 lbs. in wt.; the mine is open to collectors on a fee basis in summer. An abundant supply of **common opal** occurs in blue, green, orange, purple, or red colors.

(2) E side of valley: (a) regional land surfaces—**agate, chalcedony, chert, flint, jasper, opal** (common, float), **silicified lignite** (black), **opalized** and **petrified wood** (many pine and spruce cones); (b) the Green Fire Mine, as irregular seams and masses—gem **opal** (black, fire), **common opal** in various colors.

DENIO, W approx. 25 air mi., the Warm Springs District (Vicksburg, Ashdown, Pueblo mines), ores in a **quartz** gangue—**copper, gold, lead, silver.**

GOLCONDA: (1) ESE 3 mi., mines with bedded lenses in Tertiary sediments and volcanics—**copper, gold, iron, lead, manganese, tungsten, zinc;** (2) E 5 mi., the Preble (Potosi) Mine—**gold, silver;** (3) S 15 mi., the Gold Run (Adelaide) Mine, replacement veins, contact metamorphic deposits, placers in Triassic sediments—**copper, gold, lead, platinum, silver;** (4) S 22 mi., the Black Diablo Mine (just over Pershing Co. line)—**copper, gold, lead, silver;** (5) NE 20 mi. on Rte. 18: (a) turn S 6 mi. on dirt rd., the Red House Mine—**gold, silver,** etc.; (b) turn N 10 mi. on dirt rd., the Getchell Mine—**copper, gold, silver,** etc.

MCDERMITT (approx. 73 mi. N of WINNEMUCCA on U.S. 95 and just S of the Ida. line): (1) general area; inquire locally: (a) old camp of National, veins in Tertiary volcanics—**antimony, gold, silver;** (b) W, old Jackson Creek District, contact metamorphic veins—**copper, lead, silver;** (c) W, old camp of Disaster, veins and placers—**gold, platinum;** (2) SW 11 mi., the Cordero Mine—**copper, lead, gold, silver.**

OROVADA (on U.S. 95 about 43 mi. N of WINNEMUCCA): (1) N 11 mi., the Rebel Creek District (New Goldfields, Willow Creek), veins and placers—**gold, platinum, silver;** (2) WNW approx. 30 mi. and W of the Kings R. Valley by rough dirt rds., Agate Point, area surfaces—**agate, chalcedony, chert, flint, jasper,** etc.

PARADISE VALLEY (44 mi. NNE of WINNEMUCCA via U.S. 95 and Rte. 8B), the Mt. Rose and Spring City mines, veins, placers in Mesozoic metamorphic slates—**gold, platinum, silver.**

SULPHUR (60 mi. W of WINNEMUCCA on Rte. 49), N, in the Black Rock Desert, area surfaces—**opalized** and **petrified wood;** (2) NW a short distance, the Red Butte Mine—**antimony, copper, mercury;** (3) the Black Rock Mine—**gold, lead, silver;** (4) S into Pershing Co. 12 mi., the Rabbithole Mine, veins in Tertiary rhyolite and water-laid tuffs—**mercury, silver;** (5) numerous other Pershing Co. area mines via rough dirt rds., e.g., Rosebud, Scossa, Placeritas (10–15 mi. SW of SULPHUR) and the Poker Brown Mine 25 mi. SE of Rabbithole—**gold, lead, silver, mercury.**

WINNEMUCCA: (1) SE 5 mi., the Sonoma Mt. (Harmony) Mine—**copper, gold, silver, zinc;** (2) WNW 5 mi., the Winnemucca (Barrett Spgs.) Mine, veins, placers in metamorphosed slates, diorite—**copper, gold, lead, platinum, silver;** (3) NW 10 mi., the Ten Mile Mine—**gold, silver;** (4) W on Rte. 49; (a) 17 mi. to Pronto, area mines; and (b) another 17 mi. to Jungo, area mines—**gold, lead, silver,** etc.; (5) NNE 20 mi., the Willow Point Mine—**copper, silver;** (6) N 23 mi., the Sherman Mine—**gold;** (7) W 25 mi., the New Central Mine—**gold, lead, silver;** (8) S 26 mi. (into Pershing Co.), old camp of Grandpap—**gold, silver;** (9) N 28 mi., the Shone Mine, veins in granite—**gold, silver;** (10) NW 30 mi., old camp of Amos (Awakening, Slumbering Hills mines), veins, placers—**gold, platinum, silver.**

LANDER CO.

AREA, general prospecting along any co. rd. in washes, draws, and regional land surfaces is productive of some type of gemstone—**chalcedony, jasper, opal** (common), **opalite,** etc. Make local inquiry in regional rock shops along main highways.

AUSTIN (cf. also under Nye Co. for access to localities in that adjacent co.): (1) NW 9 mi., the Skookum Mine, contact metamorphic veins—**gold, silver;** (2) W 16 mi. on U.S. 50, then NW 11 mi. by dirt rd., the New Pass District, veins in limestone—**gold;** (3) NNW 20 mi. (7 mi. W of the Silver Cr. Siding on the N.C. RR), the Ravenswood (Shoshone) Mine, veins in Cambrian shales—**copper, gold, lead, silver;** (4) NE on Rte. 21, old camp of Spencer, veins in Paleozoic sediments—**antimony, gold, silver;** (5) S 10 mi., Big Creek mines, veins in sedimentaries—**copper, gold, molybdenum, silver;** (6) S 24 mi. (via 2 mi. W on U.S. 50, 8 mi. SW on Rte. 2, 5 mi. on dirt Rte. 21, turn S on rough rd.), the Kingston District (Bunker Hill, Santa Fe, Summit, Victorine mines), veins in limestone—**gold, silver;** (7) SW 36 mi. via Rte. 2 to the Campbell Cr. Ranch, the Gold Basin District (cf. under EASTGATE in Churchill Co.), old camp of Carroll on the co. line, area mines —**gold, silver,** with traces of **copper** and **lead.**

BATTLE MOUNTAIN: (1) area, SW, the Reese R. District (Amador, Austin, Yankee Blade mines), veins in Paleozoic sediments—**arsenic, copper, gold, lead, silver, zinc;** (2) W, in the Galena Range near the Humboldt Co. line, the Buffalo Valley mines (17 mi. S of VALMY in Humboldt Co.), replacement veins in limestone—**gold** (this adjoins the Copper Basin area, *q.v.*); (3) SW 8–20 mi., the Copper Basin District: (a) Bannock, Copper Basin, Copper Canyon, Cottonwood Creek, Rocky Canyon, Galena mines; replacement veins and contact metamorphic—**antimony, arsenic, copper, gold, lead, platinum, silver, zinc;** (b) the Blue Turquoise Mine—**turquoise;**

(4) SE 14 mi., the Lewis District (Dean, Mud Springs, Pittsburg mines), veins in Paleozoic sediments—**gold, silver;** (5) SE 18 mi., the Hilltop District (Kimberly, Mayesville mines), veins—**copper, gold, lead, silver;** (6) SE 20–50 mi. (best reached from BEOWAWE in Eureka Co. via Rte. 21), the Bullion District: (a) the Campbell, Lander, Cortez, Mt. Tenabo mines, replacement veins and placers in Paleozoic sediments—**arsenic, copper, gold, lead, platinum, silver, zinc;** (b) the Pedro Claim and (c) the Fox Turquoise Mine—**turquoise.**

(7) SSW 30 mi., the McCoy and Horse Canyon mines, veins in diorite and limestone—**gold;** (8) S 35 mi., the Hot Springs District, area mines and prospects—**turquoise;** (9) SSE 40 mi., GOLD ACRES (best reached via paved Rte. 21 SW 29 mi. from BEOWAWE in Eureka Co.), area mines—**copper, gold, silver;** (10) NE 30 mi., the Lynn District, area mines and prospects —**turquoise;** (11) NE 45 mi., the Ivanhoe District (over line in Elko Co., q.v. under MIDAS)—**opalite** and other minerals.

LINCOLN CO.

AREA: (1) Sugar Loaf Peak, area surfaces surrounding base and numerous prospecting pits—**turquoise;** (2) W edge of co., old camp of Tem Piute in the Timpahute Mts., lode veins—**copper, gold, silver, zinc.**

CALIENTE: (1) W 16 mi. on U.S. 93, turn onto SW-trending dirt rd. for 6 mi., then branch left for 6 mi. to old camp of Delmar—**gold, silver;** (2) S 43 mi. on dirt rd., old camp of CARP: (a) SE ¼ mi., the Viola Mine in the Mormon Mts.—**copper, lead, silver, zinc;** (b) S 21 mi. by rough dirt rd., old camp of Rox or Vigo, then 24 mi. E into the Mormon Mts., a mine—**manganese;** (3) NNW 8 mi. in the Chief Range, the Chief (Caliente) Mine, veins in Paleozoic sediments—**copper, gold, lead, silver;** (4) WNW 30 mi., the Ferguson (Delmar) Mine, replacement veins in Paleozoic quartzite—**gold, silver.**

HIKO: (1) the Pahranagat Mine, veins in Paleozoic sediments—**copper, lead, silver;** (2) SW 18 mi. on Rte. 25, turn SW 24 mi. on rough dirt rd. to old camp of Groom, veins in limestones and shales—**lead, silver.**

PANACA, E 8 mi. on paved Rte. 25: (1) SW 10 mi. on dirt rd., old camp of Crestline; and (2) 13 mi. farther S, old Acoma District, area mines— **copper, gold, lead, silver;** prospecting the general surrounding land surfaces —**chalcedony, chert, flint,** etc.

PIOCHE: (1) area mines, replacement veins in Paleozoic sediments—**copper, gold, lead, manganese, silver, tungsten, zinc;** (2) NW 3 mi. on U.S. 93, turn W on dirt rds.: (a) 4 mi. to old camp of Mendha, and (b) 11 mi. to Comet (Mill), area mines in replacement veins—**copper, gold, lead, silver, tungsten, zinc;** (3) WNW 7 mi., the Highland Mine, replacement veins— **copper, gold, lead, silver;** (4) NW 12 mi. on U.S. 95, turn W on dirt rd. 10 mi.: (a) the Bristol (Jack Rabbit) Silver Mine, replacement veins—**copper (azurite, malachite, chrysocolla), gold, lead, manganese, silver;** (b) the Silverhorn Mine, replacement veins in limestone—**nickel, silver;**

(5) E 15 mi., old camp of Ursine: (a) area mines—**gold, lead, silver;** (b) S 2 mi. on dirt rd., the Eagle Valley District (Fay, State Line mines), veins in Tertiary volcanics—**gold, lead, silver;** (6) W 16 mi., the Lone

Mountain Mine, replacement veins—**lead, silver;** (7) N 28 mi. on U.S. 93, then NE 21 mi. on dirt rd., the Atlanta District: (a) area land surfaces—**chalcedony, chert, flint;** (b) area mines (Silver Park, Silver Springs), veins in quartzites and limestones—**copper, gold, lead, radium, silver;** (8) N 52 mi. on U.S. 93, turn W 11 mi. over Patterson Pass (elev. 7,400 ft.), the Patterson District (Cave Valley, Geyser mines) at S end of the Shell Cr. Mts., replacement veins—**gold, lead;** (9) W 75 mi., the Worthington (Freiberg) Mine, best reached via dirt rds. from Rte. 25 near the Nye Co. line, veins in rhyolite—**gold, silver.**

LYON CO.

DAYTON: (1) S 10 mi., old camp of Como (Palmyra, Indian Spgs.)—**gold, silver;** (2) NE 17 mi. (into Storey Co.), Red Mt. area mines, contact metamorphic veins—**iron.**

FERNLEY: (1) S 5½ mi., area on W flank of hills—**agate, chert, jasper;** (2) S 14 mi., the Talapoosa Mine, veins in Tertiary volcanics—**copper, gold, silver.**

FORT CHURCHILL (old adobe-ruins military post, now a state historical monument), N a few mi., in basin on SE slope of Churchill Butte, a mine—**tungsten.**

SILVER CITY (5 mi. S of VIRGINIA CITY in Storey Co.), the Chinatown, Dayton, Devils Gate, Gold Canyon mines; veins, placers, in Tertiary volcanics—**gold, iron, platinum, silver.**

SILVER SPRINGS (16 mi. S of FERNLEY), NW a few mi., old camp of Ramsey, veins—**native gold, silver.**

WELLINGTON, N along the Pine Nut Mts. (straddling the co. line, not a mining district), lode mines, placers—**copper, gold, iron, lead, platinum, silver.**

YERINGTON: (1) area, W, in the Singatse Mts., mines—**chalcanthite ("bluestone");** (2) NNW 1½ mi., area mines and prospects—**turquoise;** (3) W 2 mi., the Mason and Ludwig mines, contact metamorphic, placers—**copper, gold, lead, platinum, silver;** (4) the Ludwig Mine—**thulite;** (5) WNW 8 mi., mines and prospects—**turquoise;** (6) S 11 mi. on Rte. 3, turn SSE on dirt rd. for 14 mi.: (a) W 5 mi. on rough rd., the Pine Grove Mine; and (b) S 5 mi., the Rockland Mine—**gold, platinum, silver;** (7) S 15.6 mi., Wilson Canyon (noted collecting area)—**agate, chalcedony, chert, jasper, silicified wood, turquoise;** (8) S 30 mi., old camp of Washington—**copper, gold, silver.**

MINERAL CO.

AREA: (1) extreme NE wedge of co. immediately S of the Churchill Co. line and 16 mi. S of U.S. 50 via Rte. 23, BROKEN HILLS (with the Quartz Mt. mining district to S just over the Nye Co. line), area old mines—**gold, lead, silver,** etc.; old camp of Acme (Fitting), replacement veins in Tertiary volcanics and placers in Triassic sediments—**copper, gold, lead, silver.**

BABBITT: (1) NE 5 mi. to THORNE: (a) area mines—**gold, lead, silver;** (b) SE 5 mi., Ryan Canyon, area mines—**gold, lead, silver, thulite;** (2)

N on U.S. 95: (a) along the shores of Walker Lake, and (b) area land surfaces back of the lake—**agate, chalcedony, fossils, petrified wood, turquoise.**

BASALT (extreme SE corner of co. on U.S. 95): (1) SW 5 mi., summit of Montgomery Pass (elev. 7,167 ft.), area of Queen Mt.—**obsidian;** (2) SW 10 mi., the Buena Vista District (Basalt, Mt. Montgomery, Oneota mines), veins in Tertiary volcanics—**copper, gold, lead, silver, zinc;** (3) N 17 mi. on Rte. 10 and E 8 mi. on rough rd., old camp of Candelaria (Belleville, Columbus), replacement veins: (a) area mines—**copper, gold, lead, nickel, silver;** (b) S 1 mi., in E foothills of the Candelaria Mts. and 1 mi. W of the Mt. Diablo Silver Mine, claims, pits, prospects, etc.—**variscite;** (c) the Mt. Diablo Silver Mine—**lead, silver;** (d) the Reik Mine—**turquoise.**

HAWTHORNE: (1) make local inquiry for the Lucky Boy, Palmico mines, veins in Cambrian sediments—**copper, gold, lead, silver, tungsten;** (2) NW 10–15 mi.: (a) the Walker Lake District (Buckley, Cat Creek mines), W of Walker Lake on the E slope of the Wassuk (Walker River) Range, veins in granodiorite—**copper, gold, silver;** (b) the West Walker District, on W slope of the Wassuk Range, area mines—**gold, silver;** (3) SE 16 mi., the Whiskey Flat Mine, veins in granite-limestone contact—**copper, gold, silver;** (4) SE 18 mi., the Sulphide Mine—**gold, tungsten;** (5) SW 30 mi. via rough rds., old and famed ghost town of AURORA (Cambridge, Esmeralda), usually reached 8 mi. E from BODIE (historic mining camp state monument), Calif.: (a) area draws, washes, steep hillsides in town—**jasper, quartz crystals;** (b) many area mines, inside and outside of town, veins in Tertiary volcanics—**gold, silver.**

AURORA was a somewhat later sister camp to VIRGINIA CITY, 1869–99, and so lawless that the state's first vigilante organization was formed here. Mark Twain dared stay only one night and departed hastily for VIRGINIA CITY the next morning. The mines produced tens of millions of dollars, and at its peak the city boasted 10,000 residents, two newspapers, a "whore town," and a two-story stone county courthouse that served both Nevada and California, for both states claimed the city and collected taxes from the citizenry. Eventually state boundary line surveyors laid out the line between AURORA and the still later booming mining camp of BODIE, California, 8 miles to the west, barely in time to avert an interstate civil war over courthouse jurisdiction and tax collections. Originally the county seat of Esmeralda Co., AURORA in its decline was relegated to a remote corner of Mineral Co. that was split off after discovery of the great GOLDFIELD bonanza in present-day Esmeralda Co. AURORA is now totally abandoned, its once fine brick buildings demolished to their foundations to save on county assessments. The ruins of a military fort still stand squarely on the county line with Mono Co., California, attesting to the warlike intentions of AURORA's Nevada residents not to be included in California. Millions of dollars in taxes collected by California (paid into the Mono Co. seat of BRIDGEPORT) were never returned to Nevada after the boundary line was firmly established. But, by that time, AURORA had become a dying mining camp, although for many years Mineral Co. tried unsuccessfully to reclaim the taxes paid into California's coffers. The city's newspaper files are retained in the GOLDFIELD, Esmeralda Co., courthouse.

LUNING: (1) area mines—**gold, silver, axinite** (plum color); (2) E, the Santa Fe District (Luning, Kincaid mines), contact metamorphic veins—

antimony, copper, gold, lead, silver. (During World War II, this district was noted for its emergency production of **magnesium.**) (3) S 13 mi. on U.S. 95, then SE to SODAVILLE and E 18 mi. to the Pilot Mt. mines, contact metamorphic veins and placers—**gold, lead, mercury, platinum, silver, tungsten.**

MINA (10 mi. S of LUNING on U.S. 95): (1) area contiguous mines, including Gold Range—**copper, gold, lead, magnesium, silver, tungsten;** (2) SW 8 mi. in E end of the Excelsior Mts., area—**banded rhyolite (wonderstone), turquoise, variscite;** (3) SW 26 mi. by rough rds., the Marietta and Black Mt. mines, contact metamorphic veins—**copper, gold, lead, magnesium, silver, tungsten;** (4) NW 15 mi., the Garfield Mine, veins in limestone—**copper, gold, lead, silver;** (5) NW 20 mi., old camp of Mable, area mines—**gold, lead, silver;** (6) NE 23 mi. by rough rds., the Cedar Mountain District (Simon, Bell, Omco mines), veins in Triassic limestones—**gold, lead, silver, zinc;** (7) NE 30 mi. (over the Nye Co. line; cf. under GABBS for the Golddyke and Warrior mines area), the Athena Mine, veins in Tertiary eruptives and lake beds—**gold, silver.**

RAWHIDE (24 mi. S of FRENCHMAN in Churchill Co. via Rte. 31 and 5 mi. on dirt rd. S and W from Nevada Scheelite Mill): (1) area, the Regent Mine—**copper, gold, lead, platinum, silver, tungsten;** (2) N 6 mi. and 2 mi. W on dirt rd., area close to Churchill Co. line—**opalized wood;** (3) SE 11 mi. on rough rd., Hot Spring, on E side of Alkali Flat (can also be reached via rough rd. 34 mi. N of LUNING, or 23 mi. W from GABBS in Nye Co.), area mines in volcanic tuffs—**barite, gold, silver;** (4) SE, the King Mine, veins in Tertiary volcanics—**gold, lead, silver;** (5) S 18 mi., the Rand Mine—**turquoise;** (6) SE 14 mi. on rough rd., Hot Spring (Sunnyside Mine), veins in **quartz** and diorite—**gold, silver.**

SCHURZ: (1) W 8 mi., the Granite Mt. District (Mountain View, Reservation mines), veins in granite—**copper, gold, lead, silver;** (2) N 9 mi., the Benway Mine, veins in granite—**gold, silver;** (3) NE 12 mi., old camp of Holy Cross (Fallon, Terrell mines), veins and replacements in Tertiary volcanics—**gold, manganese, silver;** (4) E 28 mi., the Bovard District (Copper Mountain; Rand, *q.v.* under RAWHIDE, mines), replacement veins in Tertiary volcanics—**copper, gold, lead, manganese, silver.**

NYE CO.

AREA: (1) NW corner of co.: (a) 28 mi. SSW of AUSTIN in Lander Co., old camp of Washington, veins in Paleozoic sediments—**lead, silver;** (b) old Westgate district (42–54 mi. ESE of FALLON in Churchill Co.), veins in Jurassic limestone—**gold, lead, silver;** (c) 45 mi. S of LANDER, old district of Millett (North Twin River), pockets in limestone and slate—**copper, gold, lead, silver;** (d) 50 mi. S of LANDER, the Twin River district, veins in slate—**silver;** (2) see also under GABBS for other access dirt roads into the general mineralized region.

BEATTY: (1) area mine dumps in or around town—**cinnabar, opalite;** (2) NW 4 mi., ghost town of RHYOLITE (noted for its "bottle house" and never-used railroad station converted into a casino; tracks were never laid on the RR right of way S from GOLDFIELD in Esmeralda Co.): (a) area mines—**copper, gold, silver;** (b) nearby old site of Pioneer, veins in Tertiary vol-

canics—**copper, gold, lead, mercury, silver;** (c) W 8 mi., old site of Bullfrog, area mines in Tertiary volcanics—**azurite, amethyst, gold, malachite;**
(3) E 6 mi., old site of Fluorine (Bare Mt., Telluride mines)—**gold, mercury, silver;** (4) S 8 mi. on U.S. 95, site of ghost town of CARRARA, area old mines—**gold;** (5) NE approx. 15–18 mi., Yucca Mts., area surfaces—**geodes, gemmy nodules;** (6) NE, old camp of Johnnie (25 mi. NE of Death Valley and 14 mi. SSE of Amargosa in the NW end of the Spring Mts.), lodes, placers—**gold, lead, platinum, silver;** (7) WNW 22 mi., old camp of Grapevine, veins in rhyolite—**gold;** (8) E 30 mi., old Wahmonie Mine—**gold, silver.**

BONNIE CLAIR (old camp and mill on Rte. 72 into N end of Death Valley, 6 mi. W of Scotty's Jct. on U.S. 95), area mines—**copper, gold, silver.**

CLARK STATION (33 mi. E of TONOPAH, *q.v.*, on U.S. 6): (1) the Clifford Mine, veins in Tertiary volcanics—**gold, silver;** (2) the old Blakes Camp (32 mi. ENE of TONOPAH), the Golden Arrow Mine, contact metamorphic veins—**gold, silver;** (3) N 48 mi. on dirt rd. to Crockers Ranch (or old stop of Morey), then W in the Hot Creek Range, area mines with veins in granite—**gold, lead, silver.**

CURRANT (NE part of co. at jct. of U.S. 6 with Rte. 20): (1) E, in the Grant Range, area mines with veins in limestone—**copper, gold, lead;** (2) S 30 mi., Troy Peak (elev. 10,280 ft.), old camp of Troy at base (Irwin Canyon, Nyala mines; NYALA lies 39 mi. SSW of CURRANT), veins in sedimentaries—**gold, lead, silver.**

GABBS: (1) E 3 mi., the Stokes Iron Mine—**iron minerals;** (2) E 16 mi. to dirt crossrds.: (a) E 4 mi., old camp of GRANTSVILLE, area mines—**copper, gold, silver.** (A short distance NE lies the Ichthyosaur Paleontologic State Monument, where the fossil bones of Mesozoic dinosaurs are exposed.) (b) N 4 mi., turn E on old rd. to ghost camp of BERLIN (Union Mine), and (c) N 7 mi. to old camp of IONE, veins in Tertiary volcanics and placers in Carboniferous sediments—**copper, gold, lead, mercury, silver;** (d) old camp of Bruner near IONE, the Phonolite Mine, veins in andesite and rhyolite—**gold, silver;** (3) N 3 mi., turn NE on dirt rd. from Rte. 23 to old camp of Downieville, area mines—**copper, gold, silver;**
(4) N 12 mi. on Rte. 23, turn right on dirt rd. to old camp of Quartz Mountain: (a) area mines—**gold, lead, silver;** (b) nearby old camp of Westgate (possibly over line in Mineral Co.)—same; (c) NW 3–4 mi., old mining district of Broken Hills (in Mineral Co. and straddling co. line)—**gold, lead, silver;** (d) old camp of Lodi (Ellsworth, Mammoth, Marble mines), veins in granite and limestone—**copper, gold, lead, silver, tungsten;** (5) SSE 10 mi., old camp of GOLDDYKE, and (6) 8 mi. farther S, the Warrior Mine—**gold, lead, silver;** (7) SSE 14 mi., the Fairplay and Atwood mines (at or near GOLDDYKE), veins in granite—**copper, gold, lead, silver, tungsten.**

GOLDFIELD (Esmeralda Co., *q.v.*), access to Ralston Desert to E in Nye Co. (Nearly all the region for 70–80 mi. E of U.S. 95 and extending 70–80 air mi. S of TONOPAH constitutes the highly restricted area of the Nellis Air Force bombing range and the Atomic Energy Commission nuclear testing site. No travel is currently allowed on the region's rough dirt access roads, except by regional cattle ranchers.) (1) NE approx. 12 mi., Cactus Peak area prospects and pits—**turquoise;** (2) E 24 mi., in NW end of the Cactus Range, old camp of Cactus Springs, replacement veins in Tertiary volcanics—**gold, silver;** (3) SE 27 mi., Gold Crater Mine—**gold, silver;**

(4) E 35 mi., Swab Mt., on S side of the Cactus Range, area surfaces—**jasper, petrified wood;** (5) ESE 30 mi., the Antelope Mine—**gold, silver;** (6) ESE 38 mi., old camp of Wilson, veins in Tertiary volcanics—**gold, silver;** (7) ESE 40 mi., the Trappmans Mine, veins in granite—**gold, silver;** (8) SE 46 mi., the Silverbow Mine—**gold, silver;** (9) E 54 mi., the Kawich (Gold Reed) district, veins in monzonite porphyry, rhyolite—**gold, mercury.**

LATHROP WELLS, E 26 mi. on U.S. 95 and N on side rd., MERCURY, area mines—**cinnabar, opalite.**

POTTS (44 mi. SE of AUSTIN in Lander Co. and just S of the Nye Co. line): (1) area, old camp of Jackson (Gold Park), overlapping into Lander Co., veins in Paleozoic sediments, granite porphyry, and Tertiary volcanics —**copper, gold, lead, silver;** (2) SE on rough rd. into the Monitor Range, old camp of Danville, veins in limestone—**gold, silver.**

SCOTTY'S JUNCTION (35 mi. S of GOLDFIELD on U.S. 95 and entrance into N end of Death Valley): (1) S 6 mi. and ½ mi. E of U.S. 95, area—**arrowheads** and **cores** of **obsidian, obsidian float;** (2) ESE about 10 mi., old camp of Tolicha (20 mi. E of BONNIE CLAIR) and Monte Cristo Mine, veins in Tertiary rhyolite—**gold, silver.**

STONEWALL (16 mi. S of GOLDFIELD on U.S. 95 and 1 mi. E of jct. with Rte. 3): (1) area mines, veins in Paleozoic sediments—**gold, mercury** (some), **silver;** (2) E 20 mi., old camp of Wellington (O'Briens), veins in Tertiary volcanics—**gold, silver.**

SUNNYSIDE (extreme E edge of co. on Rte. 28, on E side of the Egan Range), area mines—**azurite, malachite.**

TONOPAH: (1) area mines in town and on adjoining hills, replacement veins in Tertiary volcanics—**copper, gold, lead, silver, tungsten.** (Here was the scene of a truly great **silver** rush in 1902, the same year **gold** was first discovered in GOLDFIELD 28 mi. to the S in Esmeralda Co.) (2) E a few mi., old camp of Ellendale, veins and stringers in Tertiary volcanics—**copper, gold, silver;** (3) E 10–12 mi., area—**petrified algae** and **bogwood, jade;** (4) E 20 mi., the Hannapah district (Silverzone, Volcano mines), veins in Tertiary volcanics—**gold, mercury, silver;** (5) N 10–15 mi. in the San Antonio Mts., area—**jade, petrified wood, wonderstone (banded rhyolite);** (6) NW 20–25 mi., in the San Antonio Mts., old San Antone district (San Antonio, Royston Mines), veins in Tertiary volcanics—**copper, gold, lead, silver;**

(7) N 42 mi. via Rtes. 8A and 82, turn SW on MANHATTAN-BELMONT dirt rd.: (a) old camp of Spanish Belt (Barcelona Mine), veins in granite and shale—**mercury, silver;** (b) nearby old camp of Arrowhead, replacement veins—**gold, silver;** (8) NW 42 mi. via Rte. 89: (a) Cloverdale district (Republic, Golden mines), lodes and placers—**copper, gold, lead, platinum, silver;** (b) N 12–15 mi. from Cloverdale on rough rd., old camp of Jett, mines in limestone and slate—**lead, silver, zinc;** (9) N 40 mi. on Rte. 8A, turn E 7 mi. on Rte. 92, old semighost town of MANHATTAN, replacement veins and placers in Paleozoic sediments—**arsenic, gold, platinum, silver;**

(10) NNE 46 mi. via Rtes. 8A and 82, old ghost town of BELMONT: (a) the Philadelphia, Silver Bend mines, veins in Paleozoic sediments—**copper, gold, lead, mercury, silver;** (b) N 18 mi. then W, old Jefferson Can-

yon district (Concordia, Green Isle mines)—**gold, silver;** (11) N 52 mi. on Rte. 8A, turn E 3 mi. to ghost town of ROUND MOUNTAIN, veins and placers —**gold, lead, platinum, tungsten;** (12) N approx. 57 mi. on Rte. 8A, the Jackson (Gold Park) district, about 44 mi. S of AUSTIN in Lander Co., area mines—**gold;** (13) N 66 mi. via Rtes. 8A and 82 to area of turnoff W to the Northumberland Caves (recreation area), old camp of Northumberland in the Toquima Range, veins in granite porphyry—**silver.**

WARM SPRINGS (49 mi. E. of TONOPAH on U.S. 6): (1) the Bellehelen Mine—**gold, silver;** (2) E about 6 mi., the Eden (Gold Belt) mines, veins in Tertiary volcanics—**gold, silver;** (3) E about 20 mi., old camp of Beveille—**copper, lead, silver;** (4) NE 8 mi. on U.S. 6, turn NW 4 mi. on dirt rd. to crossrds.: (a) W 4 mi., old camp of Tybo, replacement veins in Paleozoic sediments, and (b) N 12 mi., old camp of Hot Creek—**antimony, copper, gold, lead, manganese, silver;** (5) SE 40 mi. on Rte. 25, the Willow Creek district at S end of Railroad Valley, replacement veins in Paleozoic sediments and Tertiary eruptives—**copper, gold, silver.**

ORMSBY CO.

CARSON CITY (Nevada state capital and county seat): (1) W, in foothills of the Sierra Nevada, the Voltaire district (Washoe, Eagle Valley mines), veins in Triassic schists—**gold, silver, platinum, arsenic, copper;** (2) E 9 mi., Carson R., area mines—**arsenic, copper, gold, mercury, silver.**

DELAWARE, the Sullivan Mine in Brunswick Canyon in E part of co., veins in andesite—**copper, gold, lead, silver.**

PERSHING CO.

AREA (far E part of co.): (1) the Iron Hat Mine (20 mi. SW by rough rd. from VALMY on U.S. 40 in Lander Co.), veins in limestone—**copper, lead, silver;** (2) the Jersey Mine (43 mi. SW of BATTLE MOUNTAIN in Lander Co. by rough rd. via Alkali Flat, on E flank of the Augusta Mts.), veins in **quartzite** and porphyry—**lead, mercury, silver;** (3) the Kennedy Mine (55 mi. S of WINNEMUCCA in Humboldt Co. via dirt rd., on E side of Granite Mt.), veins in Triassic sediments—**gold, lead, silver.**

BLACK DIABLO MINE (22 mi. S of GOLCONDA in Humboldt Co.)—**copper, gold, lead, silver.**

GOLDBANKS (36 mi. S of Winnemucca in Humboldt Co. via dirt rd.), replacement veins in quartz porphyry—**gold, mercury, silver, copper, lead.**

IMLAY (4 mi. W of MILL CITY, *q.v.*, on Int. 80): (1) S 6 mi. and 4 mi. E of the Humboldt R., the Prince Royal, Humboldt, and Eldorado mines, replacement veins in Jurassic sediments—**copper, gold, lead, mercury, silver;** (2) W 23 mi. on dirt rd. to crossrds., then N 6 mi. on rough rd., the Haystack Mine (7 mi. S of JUNGO in Humboldt Co.), veins in granite and **quartzite**—**gold;** (3) W 29 mi. via dirt rds.: (a) the Rosebud Mine, and (b) another 4 mi., the Rabbithole Mine, with (c) other area mines such as the Scossa and Placeritas to the S and E—cf. all under SULPHUR in Humboldt Co.

LOVELOCK: (1) S a few mi., the Wild Horse Mine on E side of the Humboldt Range—**antimony, arsenic, copper, lead, silver;** (2) S 7 mi. on Rte. 59, turn E on dirt rd., then S to lake—cf. FALLON locality (4) in Churchill Co.; (3) SE a few mi., the Sacramento Mine on W flank of the Humboldt Range, placers, veins in Triassic sediments—**gold, silver, platinum;** (4) SE 25 mi., the Mineral Basin (on the Churchill Co. line), area mines—**iron, mercury;** (5) ESE 9 mi., the Muttleberry Mine—**copper, lead, silver;** (6) NE 10 mi., the Loring district (Lovelock, Willard Mines) in the Humboldt Range, contact metamorphic veins—**gold, iron, mercury, silver, tungsten;** (7) E 22 mi., Antelope Springs (Relief Mine), veins in Triassic limestones— **antimony, gold, mercury, silver;**

(8) NE 28 mi., the Spring Valley district (American Canyon, Fitting mines) on E flank of the Humboldt Range, veins and placers—**copper, gold, lead, mercury, platinum, silver;** (9) W 10 mi., the Velvet Mine, veins in Tertiary eruptives—**gold;** (10) NW 12 mi., then 8 mi. W on improved rd., the EAGLE PITCHER MINE—**copper, gold, silver, tungsten;** (11) SW 20 mi., then NW 20 mi. (from HUXLEY in Churchill Co.), contact metamorphic veins in the Juniper Range—**copper, gold, silver, tungsten;** (12) NW 24 mi.: (a) the Vernon Mine, and (b) 2 mi. farther N, the SEVEN TROUGHS MINE, veins in Tertiary volcanics—**copper, gold, lead, silver;** (13) N 36 mi. via Rte. 48 and dirt rd. that turns N to PLACERITAS and large mining district, cf. under SULPHUR in Humboldt Co.—**antimony, copper, gold, lead, mercury, silver, petrified** and **opalized woods;** (14) NW 45 mi. (and 10–15 mi. E of GERLACH in Washoe Co.), the Farrell (Stone House) Mine, veins and lenses in Tertiary rhyolite—**gold.**

MILL CITY: (1) N 7 mi., on SE slope of the Eugene Mts.: (a) TUNGSTEN (largest **tungsten** mill in America), contact metamorphic veins—**copper, silver, tungsten;** (b) 5 mi. farther N, the Keystone Mine—**lead, silver;** (2) S 10 mi. on Rte. 50, the Star Creek Ranch district: (a) the Santa Clara Mine, veins, lenses—**antimony, silver;** (b) SW to Star Peak (elev. 9,835 ft.), area of E side—gemmy **geodes** and **nodules;** (c) S 6 mi., then 4 mi. W, the UNIONVILLE district (Buena Vista Mine) on E slope of the Humboldt Range, replacement veins in Triassic sediments—**antimony, copper, gold, iron, lead, silver;** (d) S 16–20 mi. to N end of the Humboldt Range at Black Knob, area mines with veins in Jurassic calcareous shale—**antimony;** (e) S 30–35 mi., the Indian Mine in Indian Canyon on E flank of the Humboldt Range, veins, placers—**gold, silver;** (3) SE 10 mi., the Sierra district (Sunshine, Oro Fino mines), veins in limestone, placers—**copper, gold, lead, platinum, silver;** (4) E via various rough dirt rds.: (a) 8 mi. NE, the Dun Glen Mine; (b) 11 mi. E, the Straub Mine; and (c) 15 mi. SE, the Rockhill Mine—**copper, gold, lead, silver;** (5) W 20 mi., the Antelope (Cedar) Mine in the Antelope Range, veins—**antimony, arsenic, copper, gold, lead, mercury, silver, zinc.**

NIGHTINGALE (extreme SW corner of co., approx. 40 mi. WSW of LOVELOCK), on E flank of the Nightingale Range; (1) contact metamorphic veins —**copper, gold, silver, tungsten;** (2) area—**garnets.**

OREANA (14 mi. NE of LOVELOCK on Int. 80): (1) W 5 mi., the Trinity district (Arabia, Oreana mines), veins in altered granodiorite—**antimony, copper, gold, lead, mercury, silver, tungsten;** (2) N 6 mi., Gypsy Queen Canyon, area—**dumortierite quartz;** (3) NE 5–6 mi., mines in Wrights Canyon, contact metamorphic veins—**tungsten;** (4) E 9 mi., the ROCHESTER-LOWER ROCHESTER district: (a) Nenzel Mine, veins, placers—**antimony, copper, gold, lead, platinum;** (b) W side of Lincoln Hill, area—**dumortierite;** (c) Echo (Ryepatch Mine), contact metamorphic veins—**copper, gold, lead, silver, tungsten.**

RYE PATCH DAM, W 5 mi.: (1) the Poker Brown Mine, and (2) W another 4 mi., the San Jacinto Mine, veins in slate and granite—**arsenic, lead, silver.**

TOULON SIDING (on the Southern Pacific RR), W 10 mi., the Copper Valley (Ragged Top) Mine, contact metamorphic veins in limestone—**copper, tungsten.**

STOREY CO.

VIRGINIA CITY: (1) area, including Comstock, Gold Hill, Silver Star, Flowery, etc., main veins in diorite and Tertiary volcanics—**copper, gold, lead, mercury, silver.** (This fabulous mining district virtually paid for both the Union side of the Civil War and the rebuilding of San Francisco after the 1906 earthquake and fire. One of the greatest and richest mining districts in the world, VIRGINIA CITY has been preserved as a monument—still inhabited by some 1,000 residents, although in its heyday it was by far the largest mining camp of the bonanza era—and is an exciting tourist attraction. An estimated $700 million in **silver** bullion came from the Comstock lode alone.) (2) N 01 mi., the Castle Peak (Red Mountain) Mine—**mercury.**

WASHOE CO.

AREA: (1) W side of Mt. Davidson, the West Comstock (Jumbo) Mine (reached from VIRGINIA CITY in Storey Co.), veins in diorite—**gold, silver;** (2) Renard, W 15 mi., the Sheephead Mine—**gold;** (3) Sano, E, the Cottonwood (Round Hole) Mine, veins in sedimentary rocks—**gold, lead, silver;** (4) Steamboat Springs, impregnations in Tertiary volcanics, mines and prospects—**mercury;** (5) far NE part of co., High Rock Canyon (best reached from CEDARVILLE, Calif., 38 air mi. to the W by rough rds., via VYA, *q.v.*: (a) around headwaters of Little High Rock Cr., area, and (b) surrounding the canyon crossing of the Lost Creek Canyon rd.—**obsidian nodules.**

GERLACH: (1) SW in the Smoke Creek Desert, area of Deep Hole, placers—**gold;** (2) N 38 mi. on Rte. 34, old ghost town of Leadville: (a) area mines, veins in Tertiary volcanics—**gold, lead, silver, zinc;** (b) N 1 mi., the Donnelly (Gerlach) Mine, veins in sedimentary rocks—**gold, silver;** (c) N 8 mi., area both sides of Rte. 34—**agate, silicified wood.**

RENO: (1) NE 4 mi., the Wedekind Mine, replacement veins—**gold, lead, silver, zinc;** (2) NW 10 mi., the Peavine district (Reno, Crystal Peak mines), replacement veins, placers—**copper, gold, lead, platinum, silver, tungsten;** (3) N 34 mi. via Rte. 33 and dirt rd. on W side of Pyramid Lake, PYRAMID (Mine), veins in Tertiary volcanics—**copper, gold, lead, silver.**

SPARKS, area draws, washes, fields, land surfaces—**agate, garnet, idocrase, obsidian.**

VYA (extreme NW part of co., best reached 22 mi. E from CEDARVILLE,

Calif.), S 30 mi. on Rte. 34, area on W side of rd.—**opal** (common). (May also be reached on Rte. 34 50 mi. N from GERLACH, *q.v.*, but rd. is generally rough.)

WADSWORTH, W 9 mi., the White Horse (Olinghouse) Mine, contact veins, placers—**gold, platinum, silver.**

WASHOE CITY (17 mi. S of RENO on U.S. 395), N 1 mi., the Galena Mine, veins in granite—**arsenic, copper, gold, lead, silver, zinc.**

WHITE PINE CO.

AREA, far W part of co., Bald Mt. (about 75 mi. S of ELKO in Elko Co. and N of Pancake Summit on U.S. 50), lode mines, placers—**copper, mercury, platinum, silver, tungsten.** (This is a mineral-rich co., and there are very many old mines and districts shown on topographic maps that are not listed here.)

BAKER (4 mi. W of the Utah line and 5 mi. S of U.S. 6/50): (1) area mines—**copper, gold, lead, silver.** (This is the entrance point for the Lehman Caves National Monument.) (2) SE, on E flank of the Snake Range, practically on the Utah border, the Snake (Bonita) Mine, veins in granite—**silver, tungsten;** (3) the Eagle district (Kern, Pleasant Valley, Regan, Tungstonia mines), veins in sedimentary rocks—**copper, gold, lead, silver, tungsten.**

CHERRY CREEK (45 mi. N of ELY on U.S. 93, turn W 9 mi. on Rte. 35): (1) area mines, veins and secondary enrichments—**copper, gold, lead, manganese, silver, tungsten;** (2) the Eagle Canyon Mine in the Egan Range—cf. area; (3) W 5 mi., the Gold Canyon Mine—cf. area; (4) SE 18–36 mi. (area also reached NW from McGILL, *q.v.*) and 10 mi. E of old camp of Melvin, many old mines such as the Aurum (Muncy Creek), Queen Springs, Ruby Hill, Schellbourne, Schell Creek, Siegel, Silver Canyon, Silver Mountain, contact metamorphic veins—**copper, gold, lead, manganese, silver.**

ELY: (1) area mines, contact metamorphic veins—**copper, gold, lead, manganese, silver;** (2) SE 10 mi., replacement veins in limestone—**manganese, silver;** (3) S 19 mi., the Ward (Taylor) Mine on S side of Ward Peak (elev. 10,936 ft.), contact metamorphic veins—**copper, gold, lead, silver.** (This is the site of the Ward Charcoal Ovens Historic State Monument.) (4) SE 35 mi. on U.S. 50, turn E 4 mi. on dirt rd.: (a) old camp of Osceola, veins and placers—**gold, lead, platinum, silver, tungsten;** (b) the nearby Sacramento (Sacramento Pass) Mine on W flank of the Snake Range, veins in limestone and slate—**gold, silver, tungsten;**

(5) SE 45 mi., on SW flank of the Snake Range and S of the Lehman Caves National Monument, the old Tungsten district (Hub, Lincoln mines), veins in **quartzites** and **argillite—silver, tungsten;** (6) ESE 49 mi., the Black Horse Mine—**gold, silver;** (7) W 36 mi. on U.S. 50 to Little Antelope Summit (elev. 7,433 ft.), area surfaces—**wonderstone (banded rhyolite).**

HAMILTON (approx. 35 air mi. W of ELY and 10 mi. S from turnoff 9 mi. E of Little Antelope Summit), replacement veins in Paleozoic sediments—**copper, gold, lead, silver, zinc.** (This was a noted **silver** camp of the late nineteenth century, now a ghost town.)

KIMBERLY (5 mi. NW of ELY on U.S. 50 and 4 mi. W on Rte. 44), NW 1 mi., Robinson Canyon, area surfaces to the S—**garnets.**

McGILL: (1) NW 3 mi., the Duck Creek (Success) Mine, replacement veins in limestone and shale—**copper, gold, lead, silver, zinc;** (2) S 3 mi. on U.S. 93 to W-trending dirt rd.: (a) NW 21 mi., old camp of Steptoe (Granite Mine), replacement veins in Paleozoic sediments—**gold, lead, silver,** and SW a short distance, old camp of Hunter, replacement veins in dolomitic limestone—**copper, lead, silver;** (b) NW 28 mi., turn SE toward Magnusons Ranch, the Warm Springs Mine, quartz veins—**gold, silver.** (This road leads N to the CHERRY CREEK district, *q.v.*)

RUTH (8 mi. W of ELY), open pit operations—**copper.** (Enormous development of the **copper** ores in the Egan Range has resulted in an awesome "glory hole," one of the largest man-made holes on earth.)

SHOSHONE (48 mi. SE of ELY via 28 mi. on U.S. 6/50, 3 mi. on U.S. 93, and paved local rds. to the E and S), the Minerva and Lexington mines, veins in limestone—**silver, tungsten.**

STRAWBERRY (29 mi. NE of EUREKA in Eureka Co. via Newark Pass), on E slope of the Diamond Mts., the Newark Mine, veins in limestone—**copper, gold, lead, silver.**

NEW HAMPSHIRE

New Hampshire, in the heart of New England, bears two appropriate names: the Granite State, because of its extensive bedrock exposures, and the Land of Peace and Beauty. During the Pleistocene epoch, the entire state was buried beneath a succession of glaciers estimated to have been more than two miles thick. In their original advances from the north, the great sheets of ice scraped the mountains, peneplained the upland regions, and rerouted watercourses. In receding after 100,000 years or so, the last, or Wisconsin, glaciation left precipitous streams, innumerable lakes, and the barren Precambrian granite over which only a relatively thin layer of soil has formed in the last 8,000 to 10,000 years.

The residual White Mountains of the northern Appalachian chain stretch across the southern part of Coos Co. Many peaks rise more than 4,000 and 5,000 feet above sea level, culminating in Mt. Washington. At 6,288 feet this peak is the highest mountain in the New England states. Immediately to the north the Presidential Range lifts five other rugged peaks to near 6,000-foot heights, and cutting through the New Hampshire mountains are many sharp "notches" familiar to all travelers through the northern counties. South of the mountain and lake region, the generally level uplands are noted for isolated minor peaks of resistant rock, called "monadnocks."

Commercial mining for **copper, gold, lead, silver,** and **zinc,** as well as **feldspar, fluorspar,** and **serpentine,** at various times and places has contributed minor amounts to the state's economic wealth. However, New Hampshire primarily interests the gem collector because of its pegmatite mines, quarries, and exposures which yield top-quality gem crystals. These include **amethyst, apatite, aquamarine, beryl, garnet, rock crystal** (clear, rutilated, rose), **staurolite, topaz,** and **tourmaline,** among others. Panning for **gold** is a regular summer hobby activity in the northern streams, especially around the headwaters of Indian River in the extreme northern part of Coos Co. Gold occurrences in northern New Hampshire from unknown sources seem to reflect similar occurrences in the Chaudière River watershed of southern Quebec, just across the international boundary between Canada and southwestern Maine, said to be the most important placer **gold** field east of the Rocky Mountains.

For information, write: Department of Geology, University of New Hampshire, Durham; or Dartmouth College, Hanover.

BELKNAP CO.

ALTON, area mines—**arsenopyrite, pyrite.**
GILMANTON, area fields, rd. cuts, etc.—**jasper**.

CARROLL CO.

CONWAY, NW 2½ mi., the Lovejoy Gravel Pits—**microcline feldspar, smoky quartz crystals, topaz.**
JACKSON, area mines—**arsenopyrite, bornite, cassiterite, wolframite.**
MADISON, area mines—**galena, silver, sphalerite.**
NORTH CHATHAM (extreme NE corner of co., on Rte. 113), W 3½ mi., on South Baldface Mt., area pegmatites—**mica (biotite, muscovite), microcline feldspar, phenakite, smoky quartz crystals.**
OSSIPEE (co. seat and site of the Ossipee Summer Fish Hatchery), area mines—**chalcopyrite, lead-silver minerals.**
REDSTONE (Conway Twp.), the Redstone Red Quarry—**amethyst, apatite, quartz crystals** (clear, smoky), **topaz.**

CHESHIRE CO.

CHESTERFIELD, N 2–4 mi. on Rte. 63, on W side of Spofford Lake and just W of the hwy., area mines—**fluorite.**
GILSUM: (1) NNW 2¼ mi. on a connecting rd., the Island Mice Mine—**beryl,** etc.; (2) NNW 3½ mi., the Britton Mine, pegmatite—**beryl,** etc.; (3) N 5½ mi., the Wenham Mine, in pegmatite—**rose quartz.**
HINSDALE, area pegmatites—**tourmaline,** etc.
KEENE: (1) E 4½ mi., on S side of Horse Hill, pegmatite outcrops—**aquamarine, beryl,** etc.; (2) ENE 5 mi., Bassett Hill, area pegmatite outcrops, pits, etc.—**beryl.**
WALPOLE, area pegmatites—**tourmaline.**

WESTMORELAND: (1) area mines—**fluorite;** (2) S 3–5 mi.—cf. CHESTER-FIELD.

WINCHESTER, area pegmatite exposures, pits, etc.—**tourmaline.**

COOS CO.

AREA: (1) in the topsoil of the regional mountain ridges surrounding the communities of BERLIN, DUMMER, LANCASTER, MILAN, NORTHUMBERLAND, and STRATFORD—**amethysts, quartz crystals;** (2) Indian Stream (extreme NW part of both co. and state), headwater branches, numerous regional placers—**gold** (colors, nuggets).

GORHAM, area mines—**chalcopyrite.**

MILAN: (1) all area pegmatite exposures—**albite, amethyst, beryl, chlorite, feldspar, fluorite, knebelite, limonite, molybdenite, muscovite mica, pyrite, quartz crystals** (smoky), **sericite, topaz;** (2) area mines—**bornite, chalcocite** (with **gold** and **silver**), **chalcopyrite, galena, pyrite, sphalerite;** (3) Greens Ledge, area pegmatite exposures—cf. item (1).

PERCY, NNW 1¾ mi., Victors Head area pegmatites—cf. MILAN item (1).

SHELBOURNE: (1) area **copper** and **zinc** mines—**bornite,** some **sphalerite;** (2) area **lead-silver** mines—appropriate minerals, **pyrite.**

STARK: (1) all regional pegmatite exposures—cf. MILAN; (2) N 5–6 mi., Percy Peak, pegmatites exposed on Diamond Ledge—cf. MILAN; (1) Hutchins Mt., area pegmatites—cf. MILAN.

WEST MILAN, the Milan Mine—**pyrite, silver minerals.**

GRAFTON CO.

AREA, in soils and gravels around shores of Mink Pond—**staurolites.**

BATH, area mines—**chalcopyrite, gold, lead, silver.**

FRANCONIA: (1) area mines—**malachite, essonite;** (2) regional stream gravels, fields, hill surfaces—**andradite garnet.**

GRAFTON CENTER, NW 1½ mi., the Ruggles Mine (a noted producer)—**copper, lead, silver.**

HANOVER: (1) area gravels, pits, surfaces—**jasper, rutilated quartz crystals;** (2) area mines—**malachite.**

HAVERHILL: (1) area mines—**arsenopyrite;** (2) a nearby large deposit, mined—**soapstone.**

LEBANON, area mines—**arsenopyrite.**

LISBON: (1) area mines—**copper, gold, lead, pyrite, silver;** (2) area ridges, hillsides, fields, in topsoils—**staurolites.**

LITTLETON: (1) area mines—**chalcopyrite, gold, lead, silver;** (2) the White Mountain Mine—**bornite, chalcopyrite, malachite.** A mineralized belt containing many mines and prospects extends SW along Rte. 10 for 12–15 mi., including LYMAN, LISBON, and BATH, and yields ore specimens named in item (1).

LYMAN: (1) area mines—**arsenopyrite, chalcopyrite, gold, lead, silver;** (2) the Dodge Mine—**native gold.** From the Dodge Mine some $70,000 in **gold** was taken between 1865, the year of discovery, and 1875. A quartz mill was constructed in LISBON to process the ore. The veins pinched out into unproductive slate at a depth of about 100 ft.

MONROE, area mines—**copper minerals**.

NORTH GROTON: (1) WSW ¾ mi., the Charles Davis Mine—**aquamarine, beryl, brazilianite, lazulite;** (2) SW 2 mi., the Palermo Mine and quarry—**brazilianite, lazulite** (massive).

ORFORD, area mines—**copper minerals, pyrite**.

SUGAR HILL: (1) S 1½ mi., on S side of Ore Hill, area surfaces, in topsoil—**amethyst, rock crystal;** (2) summit of Ore Hill, in topsoil—**staurolites**.

TINKERVALE, NW, on Gardner's Mt. (elev. 2,330 ft.), area mines—**chalcopyrite, gold, lead, pyrite, silver**.

WARREN, area mines, especially the Warren Mine—**chalcopyrite, essonite**.

WOODSTOCK, area mines—**sphalerite**.

HILLSBOROUGH CO.

FRANCESTOWN, general area land surfaces, gravel pits, etc.—**jasper**.

MERRIMACK CO.

DANBURY, NW, on co. line area about 3¼ mi. SE of GRAFTON in Grafton Co., on Severance Hill, area pegmatites—**beryl**, etc.

PITTSFIELD, the Silverdale Mine—**chalcopyrite, pyrite, galena**.

WILMOT, N, a mine long worked for abrasive—**garnet**.

ROCKINGHAM CO.

RAYMOND, the Chandler Feldspar Mine—**feldspar, spodumene**.

SULLIVAN CO.

CLAREMONT, area outcrops of micaceous slates—**staurolites**.

CROYDON, area mines—**chalcopyrite, cupriferous pyrite**.

GRANTHAM, area micaceous slate outcrops—**staurolites**.

NEWPORT, the Smith Mica Mine at Chandler's Mill—**augelite, lazulite**.

SPRINGFIELD, NE to ROBINSON CORNER (straddles co. line 2¾ mi. SSW of GRAFTON in Grafton Co. and best reached from there), near summit of Pillsbury Ridge, the Columbia and Reynolds mines—**aquamarine, beryl**, etc.

UNITY: (1) area mines—**chalcopyrite, cupriferous pyrite;** (2) S 6–7 mi., various localities around ACWORTH and Beryl Mt., pegmatite exposures, prospects, etc.—**beryl, garnet, quartz crystals**.

NEW JERSEY

Known as the Garden State, New Jersey ranks among the world's three most noted gem- and mineral-producing regions. More than 200 mineral species have been named and described from a single locality and a great variety from hundreds of other places. Of these minerals, at least 40 were first identified in this state, and many of these have thus far never been found elsewhere.

In this 160-by-60-mile state sandwiched between the Hudson and Delaware rivers, the geology of New England merges with the geology of the Appalachian Highlands. The northern one-third of the state lies within the mountain provinces, culminating in 1,803-foot High Point on Kittatinny Ridge in High Point State Park of northwest Sussex Co. The rock formations of this region are mainly folded and faulted limestones, sandstones, and shales of middle Paleozoic age, although the Highlands reveal many Precambrian metamorphic outcrops. Another three-fifths of New Jersey constitutes the Atlantic Coastal Plain, separated from the Highlands by the Triassic-age Piedmont.

New Jersey has always ranked high in its production of such industrial earth products as **limestone, sandstone, serpentine,** and commercial **clays. Iron** mining began around 1710 and continues to this day from **limonite, magnetite,** and **bog iron ores.** The initial production of **zinc** first opened the astonishing gemstone quarries at Franklin in Sussex Co. Although **zinc** is no longer mined, the production of gems and gemstones through collector activity continues at a great rate. Here, most of the 200 mineral species are concentrated in a geographically very small area, unmatched anywhere else on earth.

While the Franklin deposit may be considered a gem mecca for mineral collectors, the state's traprock quarries are of almost equal interest. Not only do the New Jersey quarries lead the world in the production of road ballast, but the gemstones found in cavities in the basalt or diabase lavas are a never-ending source of excitement to discriminating collectors. The most gem-abundant quarries occur in the Palisades of the Hudson River in Bergen Co., the Watchung Mountain basalts of Somerset Co., and the diabase intrusions exposed between the Delaware and Raritan rivers across the center of the state.

Quarries are not the only excavations that uncover traprock. Railroad tunnels, road cuts, and building excavations of every description also produce high-quality gems. Perhaps the most famous collecting area is Bergen Hill in Hudson Co., part of the Palisades basalt sill that extends from Bergen Point to Edgewater. Another high, narrow crescent of gem-rich diabase parallels the Hudson River from above Haverstraw, New York, to below Jersey City, New Jersey. Cavities in these lavas contain abundant **banded agate** and **opal** (common, fire), **amethysts,** clear and smoky **quartz crystals,** and clear, pastel lime-green crystals of **datolite.** Such cavities may also contain gem **apatite** and **malachite,** needlelike **natrolite** crystals, and such **zeolite**-associated gemstones as **analcime, apophyllite, chabazite, gmelinite, heulandite, laumontite, mesolite, pectolite,** and **scolecite.** The railroad tunnels and cuts in Bergen Hill may be reached from the cities of Edgewater, Guttenberg, Weehawken, Union City, Hoboken, Jersey City, and Bayonne.

Nearby is Snake (Laurel) Hill, just east of the Hackensack River off the New Jersey Turnpike two miles west of Jersey City. Excavations in both Bergen and Snake Hills have produced some of the most spectacular minerals ever found, when **zeolite** species occur in a contrasting matrix of **calcite, dolomite, quartz,** or other base mineral. These two hills continue to yield magnificent specimens of **albite, epidote, galena, siderite** (both rhombohedral crystals and **spherosiderite**), and fine **talc** pseudomorphs after **pectolite.**

Of all the localities to be found in America, New Jersey produces the most and finest **amber,** mainly from counties where exposures of Cretaceous marl sands occur. The best collecting localities are in marl, clay, sand, and gravel pits scattered over the state. In addition, the **copper** deposits of the Watchung Mountains yield excellent gem **turquoise.** In several counties gem **amethysts, agate,** and jadelike **serpentine** occur along with a wide variety of gemstones rare in most of the rest of America and the world. For instance, **prehnite,** one of the most beautiful and valued of lapidary gemstones, is practically a New Jersey "state stone."

For information, write: Bureau of Geology and Topography, 520 East State Street, Trenton.

BERGEN CO.

AREA, every basalt and diabase outcrop exposed in rd. cuts, railroad tunnels, building excavations, or other across the entire state, including adjoining Passaic, Hudson, Morris, Somerset, Union, Essex, Hunterdon, and Mercer counties to the Delaware R. and north of TRENTON—**agate, amethyst** (druses, geodes, crystals), **carnelian, chalcedony, datolite, natrolite, opal** (common, fire), etc.

BURLINGTON CO.

AREA, extreme NW corner of co., at Crosswicks Cr. (4 mi. S of TRENTON in Mercer Co.), area marl and sand pits—**amber.**

BURLINGTON, HAINSEPORT, RIVERSIDE, RIVERTON, regional sand and gravel pits—**amber.** (Amber occurs in the sands and gravels all the way SW through Salem Co. adjoining upper Delaware Bay, in greater quantity and quality than anywhere else in America.)

VINCENTOWN, area sand and gravel pits—**amber.**

BURLINGTON, CAMDEN COS.

AREA, all the W part of New Jersey along the Delaware R., especially between TRENTON in SW Mercer Co. (30 mi. N of PHILADELPHIA, Pa.) to

420 Gems and Minerals of America

PENNS GROVE (20 mi. S of PHILADELPHIA), in any sand or gravel pit in or near any community—**jasper,** striped clear **agate, amber.**

CAPE MAY CO.

CAPE MAY, area ocean beach sands and gravels—**"Cape May diamonds"** (water-polished clear and opaque **quartz crystals**), **chalcedony** (pebbles in all colors from colorless to smoky, including **apricotine**).

ESSEX CO.

BELLEVILLE, BLOOMFIELD, area old mines—**malachite.**

GLOUCESTER CO.

AUSTINVILLE, BRIDGEPORT, GIBBSTOWN, regional sand pits—**amber.**
HARRISONVILLE (E of Rte. 45 and N of U.S. 40), at Oldmans Cr., a marl pit—**amber** (to large-size chunks).
MULLICA HILL, area marl and sand pits—**amber, fossils.**
SEWELL: (1) sands and gravels of nearby tributary of Mantua Cr.—**amber;** (2) the Inversand Co. greensand marl pit—**amber.**

HUDSON CO.

AREA: (1) the Arlington Mine—**chalcopyrite;** (2) Bergen Hill (reached from EDGEWATER, GUTTENBERG, WEEHAWKEN, UNION CITY, HOBOKEN, JERSEY CITY, BAYONNE), all area RR cuts, tunnels, etc., between EDGEWATER and Bergen Point along the Hudson R., including regional quarries in the diabase substratum—**agate** (banded), **albite, amethyst, analcime, apatite, apophyllite, calcite crystals, chabazite, datolite** (lime green, gem), **dolomite crystals, epidote, galena, gmelinite, heulandite, laumontite, malachite, mesolite, natrolite crystals, opal** (common, fire), **pectolite, quartz crystals** (clear, smoky), **scolecite, siderite, spherosiderite, sphalerite, sphene, talc** (pseudomorphs after **pectolite**); (3) Snake Hill (Laurel Hill), just off the New Jersey Turnpike E of the Hackensack R. 2 mi. E of JERSEY CITY—cf. Bergen Hill.
EAST BELLEVILLE, old mine—**malachite.**
EDGEWATER, GUTTENBERG, BAYONNE, area RR and rd. cuts—cf. Bergen Hill.
HOBOKEN: (1) area basalt exposures, in cavities—**agate, amethyst, opal** (common, fire), etc.; (2) area **serpentine** outcrops—**magnesite, serpentine;** (3) Castle Point, area quarries in **serpentine**—**brucite, dolomite crystals, magnesite, hydromagnesite.**
JERSEY CITY: (1) W 2 mi. at Snake (Laurel) Hill—cf. Bergen Hill; (2) NW, the Schuyler Mine—cf. Bergen Hill, plus **allanite** (black prismatic crystals), **chalcocite.**

MONTVILLE, area scattered deposits in limestones—**serpentine.**

PALISADES (not a town but basalt cliffs fronting the Hudson R. for more than 70 mi.), in cavities and talus debris—cf. Bergen Hill.

STEVENS POINT, as projections into the Hudson R., formerly quarried—**serpentine.**

WEEHAWKEN, in cavities in area basalt exposures—**allophane** and other Bergen Hill minerals.

HUNTERDON CO.

BRYAN, area quarries—**spinel.**

CLINTON, area old mines—**braunite.**

FLEMINGTON, the Flemington Mine—**chalcopyrite.**

LAMBERTVILLE (on the Delaware R. near the state boundary): (1) area quarries—**axinite crystals** (in regional traprock cavities), **tourmaline;** (2) S 1 mi., Goat Hill, in area veins—**pectolite, stilpnomelane;** (3) Barber and Irelands Quarry—**byssolite** (locally called **"mountain leather"**); (4) the Kingston Quarry—**actinolite crystals;** (5) the Lambertville Quarry—**prehnite** (as tiny micromount, perfect crystals); (6) W, in quarries along the Delaware R.; (7) N 2½ mi., on Mt. Gilboa; (8) S 2½ mi., on Belle Mt., at Moore's Sta., all regional quarries—**gem minerals** typical of the region.

MERCER CO.

HOPEWELL: (1) area quarries near the Hunterdon Co. line, and (2) at the NE end of Pennington Mt.—**gem minerals.**

MOORE: (1) the Mercer Co. Workhouse Quarry (a few mi. S of the Hunterdon Co. line), and (2) a quarry on Rte. 29 between MOORE and LAMBERTVILLE in Hunterdon Co.—**analcime, aurichalcite** (in **calcite** veins as pale blue rosettes), **calcite crystals, chalcopyrite, epidote, heulandite, natrolite** (delicate needles), **scolecite, stilbite;** (3) a quarry on Pennington Mt. just E of Rte. 69, in diabase—cf. above.

PRINCETON: (1) area quarries, and (2) N 4 mi., the Rocky Hill Quarry—**albite, chalcocite, chrysocolla, galena, goethite, malachite, prehnite, quartz gemstones** (various), **stilpnomelane, tourmaline.**

MIDDLESEX CO.

GRIGGSTOWN, area mines—**chalcopyrite.**

MILLTOWN, MATAWAN, PERTH AMBOY, WOODBRIDGE, area gravel pits—varied assortment of **gem minerals.**

NEW BRUNSWICK: (1) area mines—**chalcocite, chalcopyrite;** (2) East Brunswick, area gravel pits—**gems, minerals.**

SAYREVILLE: (1) area sand and gravel pits—**marcasite** (balls, rosettes), **pyrite crystals, petrified wood;** (2) pits between town and MIDDLETOWN—**marcasite** (nodules), **pyrite.**

MONMOUTH CO.

LONG BRANCH, area ocean beach gravels—**quartz crystals.**

MANASQUAN, S, along the ocean beaches through Ocean, Atlantic, and Cape May counties (approx. 100 mi.), in beach gravels and cliff talus debris —**"Cape May diamonds"** (*q.v.* under Cape May Co.), **fossils, petrified wood.**

MORRIS CO.

DOVER: (1) area, as vein fillings in **magnetite—isopyre opal;** (2) nearby: (a) at Ferromonte, large deposit—**apatite** (mixed with **magnetite**); (b) Golden Corner Mine, as large crystals—**apatite** (in **pyrite**); (3) the Dell and Fichtor mines—**menaccanite (ilmenite);** (4) on Mine Hill, the Alan Wood Iron Mine (near summit)—aventurescent **feldspar (sunstone;** bright, spangled); (5) W 2 mi., the Scrub Oaks Iron Mine (in the Dover **magnetite** district and the last active **iron** mine in N.J.): (a) on the dumps—**bornite, calcite** (fluorescent), **chalcopyrite, chlorite, garnet, hematite, magnetite, pyrite** (abundant crystals), **quartz crystals** (smoky, bluish rutilated), **spinel, sunstone** (with copper-colored inclusions), rare-earth (**thorium, uranium**) minerals, **tremolite;** (b) pegmatite exposures at the mine—**allanite, apatite, calcite, chevkinite, doverite, hornblende, monozite, muscovite mica, pumpellyite, rutile, sphene, xenotime, zircon.**

HIBERNIA, area mines—**apatite, pyrite, pyrrhotite.**

HOPATCONG, area gravels and surfaces at Nolands Point, around Lake Hopatcong, and Ironia—**garnets.**

HURDTOWN, old regional mines, e.g., Old Copperas, Hibernia, Hurdtown —**apatite** (as yellow crystals in **pyrrhotite,** especially in the Hurdtown Mine).

JEFFERSON and Mt. Olive twps., area quarries—**gem crystals.**

KENVILLE, PEQUANNOCK, RIVERDALE, STANHOPE, WHIPPANY, all regional quarries and pits—**prehnite,** etc.

LAKE VALHALLA, W, on Turkey Mt., old quarries—**diopside, marble, serpentine.**

MILLINGTON, area quarries near the Passaic R. off Rte. 512—**prehnite,** etc.

MONTVILLE: (1) N, on W shore of Lake Valhalla, *q.v.,* an abandoned quarry—gem **serpentine;** (2) other area quarries and pits—various **gems** and **minerals.**

MT. FREEDOM, area pits—**allanite, amphibole** (green and gray crystals), **augite, chalcopyrite, chondrodite, coccolite** (pyroxene, as blue, green, and white crystals).

MT. HOPE, area quarries—**apatite, pyrite, pyrrhotite,** etc.

MT. PLEASANT, area quarries—**apatite, pyrite, pyrrhotite.**

STIRLING, in gravels of Stirling Brook—gem **carnelian.** (The nodules are best found by digging 2 ft. under the silt layer overlying bedrock gravels.)

TAYLORVILLE, the Rockaway Valley area mines—**magnetite.**

WARREN (Twp.), bedrock gravels of Carnelian Brook—**agate** (banded, moss), **chalcedony** (red, green, red orange, botryoidal), **jasper, petrified wood, quartz crystals (amethyst, cat's-eye citrine,** clear, smoky), **sard, sardonyx.**

OCEAN, ATLANTIC COS.

AREA, entire stretch of the Atlantic Ocean beaches from the NE co. border to Cape May Co., in beach gravels, and weathering out of the cliffs—"Cape May diamonds" (*q.v.* under Cape May Co.).

PASSAIC CO.

CLIFTON: (1) W 3 mi. on U.S. 46, the Great Notch Quarry, and (2) the Frascinco Bros. Quarry—**agate, albite, amethyst, apophyllite, calcite** (snowy crystals sprinkled with dark green **babingtonite**), **chrysocolla** (some, not gemmy), **datolite, epidote, natrolite, opal** (cachalong), **pectolite, prehnite** (green crystals and globular crusts in various quarries), **rock crystal, scolecite, selenite, thaumasite, thomsonite;** (3) the two quarries of Houdaille Industries adjoining the Great Notch RR sta., and (4) a quarry immediately SW of the sta.—cf. above.

HALEDON, NORTH HALEDON, area quarries—cf. HAWTHORNE.

HAWTHORNE, the Braen's Quarry—**agate** (a prime locality for this gemstone), **datolite crystals, dendritic pyrolusite, goethite.**

LITTLE FALLS, the Great Notch Corp. quarry—cf. CLIFTON.

MONTCLAIR, the Upper Montclair Quarry (on the co. line), on Edgecliff Rd.—**agate** (banded), **amethyst, analcime, babingtonite, chabazite, chalcedony, chrysocolla, datolite, goethite, laumontite, opal, prehnite, scolecite, selenite, stilbite.**

PATERSON: (1) area quarries, especially the gem-renowned Prospect Park Quarry (at the end of Planten Ave.)—**agate** (banded), **amethyst, apophyllite, barite, babingtonite, byssolite, calcite, chalcedony, covellite, cuprite, datolite, dolomite crystals, galena, goethite, greenockite, hematite, mesolite** (on **calcite**), **opal** (cachalong), **prehnite, quartz** (pseudomorphs after **glauberite,** crystals to 3 in. long; other quartz family gemstones), **silver** (native wire), **stevensite, thaumasite** (tabular crystals); (2) W 9 mi. on U.S. 202, quarry at Pompton Lakes—cf. area; (3) SE, to Bergen Hill extension from Hudson Co., in all RR tunnels and cuts as fine, brilliant crystals—**analcite** (with **datolite, natrolite, stilbite**).

RINGWOOD: (1) gravel quarries on Rte. 511 near the Ringwood State Park —many **gemstones;** (2) the Ringwood Iron Mine—**calcite, chalcopyrite, crocidolite, corundum, epidote, garnet, hornblende, limonite, orthoclase feldspar, pyrite, serpentine, zircon;** (3) the Hope Mine—**garnet, magnetite.**

WAYNE, area gravel quarries along the Pompton R. (on the Morris Co. line)—wide variety of **gemstones.**

WEST PATERSON, in the New Street quarries: (1) area quarries on both sides of New Street, (2) the New Street Quarry itself, (3) the Upper New Street Quarry, (4) Burger's Quarry—very many gems and minerals, including **prehnite** (gorgeous green), **thomsonite,** etc.; cf. PATERSON.

SALEM CO.

AREA, all co. gravel and sand pits and stream sands—**amber.**

HARRISONVILLE, regional sand pits and river sands—**amber.**

SOMERSET CO.

BARNARDSVILLE, the Somerset Crushed Stone Co. Quarry—**agate, quartz geodes,** etc.

BELLE MEAD, the 3M Quarry—**quartz family minerals.**

BOUND BROOK, area quarries—**agate, prehnite, quartz gemstones.**

CHIMNEY ROCK, area quarries—**bornite, chalcocite, native copper** and **silver, cuprite, malachite, tourmaline.**

KINGSTON, the Kingston Trap Rock Co. Quarry—cf. BOUND BROOK.

MARTINSVILLE, the Dock Watch Quarry Co. quarry—**gemstones** characteristic of the county.

PYSON STATION, area pits and quarries—**quartz geodes.**

SOMERVILLE: (1) area quarries—**agate, albite feldspar, datolite, native copper** and **silver, quartz crystals, serpentine;** (2) N 3 mi., old **copper** mine on First Watchung Mt.—gem **turquoise, copper minerals;** (3) the American Copper Mine—**chalcocite, chalcopyrite, malachite, native copper.**

WATCHUNG, area quarries—**carnelian, citrine, jasper, sardonyx.**

SUSSEX CO.

ANDOVER: (1) area quarries—**amphibole asbestos** (blue), **aragonite (flos ferri);** (2) the Old Iron Mine—**garnet, hematite, limonite, magnetite.**

EDISON, the Ogden Group mines—**bustamite, calcite, cleiophane** (colorless **sphalerite**), **cyprine, franklinite, friedelite** (translucent, dark carnelian color, resembles **chalcedony,** found as stringers in **calcite**), **hodgekinsonite, magnetite, molybdenite, rhodonite (zinc), willemite, zincite.**

FRANKLIN: (1) area mines—**azurite, gahnite, bementite, beryl, corundum, ruby, fowlerite (rhodonite)** as splendid crystals, **smithsonite, sphalerite;** (2) turn off Rte. 23 at corner of Franklin Ave. to the Buckwheat Mine dumps on the Wallkill R., fee—approx. 200 gems and minerals (some 30 fluorescent), including **friedelite, cleiophane, hodgkinsonite, willemite** (rarest of the fine area gems as transparent orange and yellow crystals), **zincite,** etc.; (3) The Taylor Mine dumps, as purple octahedrons and crystal masses in limestone—**fluorite;** (4) N, the old Parker Mine dumps (now built over, but investigation of area openings, excavations, etc., is in order), many fluorescent—**axinite, apatite, azurite, calcium larsenite, cerussite, corundum, franklinite, galena, hardystonite, hydrozincite, malachite, margarosanite, pectolite, smithsonite, wollastonite;** (5) numerous mine dumps along Cork Hill and Taylor rds., and (6) the Noble and Passaic pits (mammoth size, opened in the 1870's)—**apatite, azurite, cerussite, corundum, franklinite, galena, fluorescent minerals;**

(7) Such regional mines as: (a) the Ogden Mine, as rose-colored crystals—**fluorite;** (b) the Franklin and Williams Mine—**apatite;** (c) Stanhope and Ahles mines—**magnetite, molybdenite;** (d) the Trotter shaft—**amazonite, garnet (almandite, spessartite, melanite);** (e) the Williams Mine, abundant—**zircon** (in **magnetite**); (8) S on Rte. 517 to OGDENSBURG: (a) all regional limestone exposures, in contact zone with the enclosing country rock, facet quality—**corundum;** (b) various mines and dumps of the New Jersey Zinc

Co.—cf. EDISON. The FRANKLIN-OGDENSBURG-STERLING HILL district produces both gem-quality minerals and materials not useful to the lapidary. Especially sought after in many other localities are gemmy crystals of **corundum** (pale blues and reds), **cleiophane, epidote** (green, polishable), **jaspers** (various colors and combinations), **friedelite, hodgkinsonite, quartz crystals,** and carvable **serpentine.** Many specimens, especially if associated with **calcite,** fluoresce beautifully.

FRANKLIN FURNACE, area **zinc** mines—**fluorite, franklinite** (most abundant ore mineral), **magnetite, tephroite, willemite, zincite.**

McAFEE, SIMPSON, CEDAR HILL, area mines—**hematite.**

MINE HILL, area quarries, mines—**axinite.**

NEWTON: (1) area limestone quarries—**corundum** (blue, pink), **ruby;** (2) S 4 mi., the Andover Group mines—**magnetite.**

OGDENSBURG, across the Wallkill River Valley at STERLING HILL—cf. FRANKLIN item (2) respecting the 200 or so species of minerals and gems, including fine crystals of **amphibole, apatite, augite (pyroxene), calamine (hemimorphite), chalcophanite, chalcopyrite, fowlerite (rhodonite), franklinite** (crystals to 8 in. on a side and the principal ore mineral), **gahnite, tephroite, willemite, zincite** (abundant). (The Sterling Hill Mine is still active.)

ROSEVILLE, area mine—blue **amphibole asbestos.**

SPARTA: (1) area quarries (in limestone)—**corundum** (blue, pink), **ruby;** (2) SE 3½ mi., the Ford Mine—**magnetite.**

SPARTA JUNCTION, area limestone quarry—**actinolite, barite, biotite mica, fluorite, pyrite, quartz crystals, rhodonite, rutile, sphene, spinel, tourmaline.**

UNION CO.

MOUNTAINSIDE, area quarries in the Watchung Mt. traprock that underlies the region E and NE of the First and Second Watchung mts.—**agate** (banded, neutral, pastel), **albite feldspar, apophyllite** (green crystals), **bornite, chalcedony** (varicolored), **chrysocolla** (not gemmy, but specimen material), **datolite, galena, hematite, opal** (common, fire), **orthoclase feldspar** (pink crystals), **pumpylite** (dark green crusts).

PLAINFIELD: (1) area quarries—cf. MOUNTAINSIDE; (2) the Wilson's Quarry—**albite feldspar** (pink), **datolite, malachite, native silver, zeolites (analcime, gmelinite, natrolite).**

SCOTCH PLAINS, area quarries—cf. MOUNTAINSIDE.

SUMMIT, area traprock quarries—cf. MOUNTAINSIDE, plus **pectolite.**

WARREN CO.

AREA: (1) the Cummings Iron Mine—**garnet, hematite, magnetite;** (2) the Taylor Mine—**algerite** (altered **scapolite**).

HARMONY: (1) the Franklin and Marble Hill Quarry—**actinolite;** (2) the Marble Mt. Mine—**hematite.**

OXFORD, the Oxford Furnace Mine—**magnetite.**

PHILLIPSBURG, area quarries—**serpentine** (quarried for decorative use), **soapstone (talc).**

NEW MEXICO

Often called the Land of Enchantment, New Mexico straddles the Continental Divide and has a mean elevation of 5,700 feet above sea level. The state, which is roughly bisected by the Rio Grande, exposes an array of Paleozoic rock formations in its usually isolated and remote semiarid mountains and plateaus. Topographically, New Mexico is noted for its spacious grasslands, wide sweeping deserts, broken mesas, volcanic necks, and densely pine-forested mountains marked by high, barren peaks.

Not only does New Mexico contain a very considerable wealth in **copper, gold, iron, lead, manganese, molybdenum** (one of the largest **molybdenum** mines in America is here), and **zinc,** but the empty reaches are especially enchanting to the gem and mineral collector because vast areas are public domain and therefore open to collecting. Much of the grazing land is leased to ranchers and farmers, and there are many mining claims. Courtesy requires permission to collect, almost always hospitably given.

The U.S. Geological Survey reports that from 1848 through 1965 New Mexico produced 2,267,000 ounces of **gold.** Although small-scale lodes were worked as early as 1833 by Spanish miners, major prospecting and mining did not take place until the 1860's and 1870's, when rich lode and placer **gold** mines were developed. Also, many rich **silver** and **lead-silver** discoveries were made in rapid succession. By 1900, the zone-of-oxidation ores were mostly depleted, and mining interest turned to developing the primary base-metal ores from which additional **gold** is produced as a by-product. The major **gold** districts are Elizabethtown-Baldy, Mogollon (pronounced Muggyyone), and Lordsburg.

Both **native silver** and **turquoise** were mined rather extensively by prehistoric aborigines for personal adornment, and many **turquoise** deposits are active today. **Potash** is mined from one of the world's largest deposits, but the enormous **coal** beds remain almost untouched because of the long hauling distance to any substantial manufacturing center requiring fuel. Generally speaking, the gem and gemstone minerals of New Mexico have received little attention, and vast areas have never been prospected for them. Few roads penetrate the backcountry, and those that do are mostly rough dirt roads used by stock ranchers, miners, and Indians. Therefore, caution is urged for all adventurous rock collectors bent on exploring the hinterlands; they are blisteringly hot in summer and bitterly cold in winter and always deficient in supplies of water. Accommodations exist only along the major highways or at guest ranches in the "outback."

For information, write: New Mexico Bureau of Mines and Mineral Resources, Campus State, Socorro.

BERNALILLO CO.

AREA, W side of co. but E of the Continental Divide, the Rio Puerco Valley, all area gravels, surfaces, draws, washes, etc.—**agate, chalcedony, jasper, opalized** and **petrified wood.**

ALBUQUERQUE: (1) WNW, on N side of the new freeway, in area sand dunes—**agatized wood;** (2) W 11 mi. on U.S. 66 to Tepee Service Sta., turn S ½ mi. on dirt rd. (making only rt. turns for ¼ mi.): (a) in banks of arroyos leading toward the river and on all adjacent ridges—**agatized wood, agate, jasper;** (b) along E side of range of low hills all the way to the Isleta Indian Res., in sandy arroyos and erosional breaks in the grazing lands—**agatized algae** and **wood.**

ISLETA PUEBLO (on E side of the Rio Grande across from ISLETA), E, into the Isleta Indian Res., all area surfaces, draws, washes, etc.—**opal** (milk white), **opalized** and **petrified wood.**

TIJERAS, the Tijeras Canyon in the Sandia Mts., area mines—**fluorite.**

CATRON CO.

AREA, SE corner of co., the Taylor Cr. District (extending into Sierra Co.), area mines and deposits—**fluorite,** colorless **topaz.**

APACHE CREEK, NW 5 mi. on Rte. 32 to national forest boundary, park on N side. On left, across Apache Cr., are N to S the Lee Russell and Kerr canyons. Hike 4 mi. up Lee Russell Canyon (take drinking water): (1) along way, area surfaces—**agate** (many varieties); (2) into Turkey Flat and Elk Horn Park—gem **agate** (many colors and patterns).

HORSE SPRINGS, S, in the widespread Plains of San Augustine, in exposures of volcanic tuffs—**moss agate, jasper.**

LUNA: (1) W 2 mi. on U.S. 180, surface of ridge N of hwy.—**amethyst crystal geodes;** (2) W 4.3 mi. on U.S. 180 to the San Francisco R. bridge, area N side of hwy.—gem **banded agate;** (3) S on U.S. 180 to W-trending logging rd. into the San Francisco Mts., area along both sides of rd.—**agate** (clear, translucent); (4) SE 10 mi. on U.S. 180, on N side of hwy.—**agate** (blue, banded), **amethysts, quartz crystals** (clustered); (5) many other regional localities—**agate, chalcedony, jasper, quartz crystals,** etc.

MOGOLLON (District), area mines and surfaces—**agate, chalcedony, jasper, fluorite.**

QUEMADO: (1) area (inquire in town for specific directions to numerous gemstone localities)—**agate, chalcedony, jasper, agatized wood;** (2) N about 12 mi. on Rte. 117 to E-trending dirt side rd., then E on this rd. ¼ mi., broad area of diggings—**agatized wood, Indian artifacts;** (3) N to end of pavement, turn NE on old rd. to Horse Camp, area draws, washes, surfaces, etc.—**agatized wood, artifacts.**

CHAVES CO.

LAKE ARTHUR, E 16 mi., along Eddy Co. line, area—**aragonite crystals.**

ROSWELL, E to the Pecos R., entire area on both sides of the river: (1)

80 mi. N to Fort Sumner in De Baca Co., and (2) S 70 mi. to Carlsbad in Eddy Co., in river-bed gravels and regional benchland gravels—**quartz crystals** (clear black, clear white, clear red, red and white, etc.).

COLFAX CO.

AREA, Moreno and Ute creeks—**chalcopyrite, gold, pyrite, pyrrhotite.**

CIMARRONCITO, ELIZABETHTOWN, area mines but in small quantities—**gold, chalcopyrite, pyrite, pyrrhotite,** etc. (The once rich **gold** mines have been abandoned since around 1900, and the towns are ghostly.)

RATON, the Sugarite Mine in the area **coal** fields—**amber.**

DE BACA CO.

FORT SUMNER: (1) S, along both sides of the Pecos R. all the way to CARLSBAD in Eddy Co. (about 150 mi.), in river gravels and benchland surfaces—**"Pecos diamonds"** (**quartz crystals:** clear, rose, red, smoky); (2) W about 28 mi. along U.S. 60 (about halfway to VAUGHN in Guadalupe Co.), in bench, terrace, and gravel beds of all tributaries to the Pecos R.—**"Pecos diamonds."**

DOÑA ANA CO.

AREA: (1) many co. deposits and **fluorspar** mines (cf. area topographic maps)—**fluorite;** (2) Black Mt., placer sands of Texas Cr.—**gold.**

HATCH, NE on dirt rd. into the Caballo Mts.: (1) regional mt. breaks, draws, washes, etc., especially along the Sierra Co. line—**agate, chalcedony, jasp-agate, jasper, quartz crystals;** (2) many area old mines (dumps good collecting localities)—**goethite, fluorite, quartz crystals;** (3) S of cattle pens (passed en route to mining area), area washes, loose in soil—**rock crystal.** (Area topographic maps locate many **fluorspar** and other mines, all with dumps worth prospecting.)

KILBOURNE HOLE (extinct volcano), best reached W on Rte. 273 out of EL PASO, Tex., WNW on turnoff from Rte. 273 (1 mi. N of jct. with Rte. 260), cross RR after 5 mi. to STRAUSS, then NW 5 mi. to VEVAY, turn W about 13 mi. to N–S crossrd., then N to Hunts Hole and the volcano (about 5 mi., all very sandy desert, so be prepared): (1) in sands around rim of volcano, and (2) in crater bottom, weathering out of basalts—**augite, peridot crystals** (gemmy, to 1 in. dia.). (Best to inquire of local EL PASO rock shops or rock club members.)

LAS CRUCES: (1) S, along both sides of U.S. 80, and (2) W 5 mi. on side rd. to MESILLA, all area—**obsidian.**

ORGAN (District): (1) area mines—**brochantite, cerargyrite, cerussite, chalcopyrite, molybdenite;** (2) the Quicksilver Mine, on dumps—**chrysocolla, onyx, rock crystal** (with **chlorite** inclusions).

EDDY CO.

ARTESIA, E on U.S. 82, cross Pecos R., then E ½ mi., turn S on ranch rd. to range of low hills near the river, all area draws, washes, surfaces, etc. —**"Pecos diamonds."**

WHITES CITY (entrance to Carlsbad Caverns National Park), area limestones (but no collecting inside park boundaries)—**onyx.**

GRANT CO.

AREA: (1) Bullards Peak district, area mines—**pyrargyrite;** (2) many regional mines, e.g., the Black Hawk, Chloride Flat, Kimball, Lone Mt., Steeplerock, Pyramid, etc.—**argentite.**

CENTRAL (District): (1) Burro Mt.: (a) area mines—**azurite, chalcocite, chalcopyrite, cerargyrite, chrysocolla, fluorite, galena, malachite, pyrite, onyx;** (b) Cap Rock Mt., and (c) Mimbres Mt., W slopes—**agate, chalcedony, chert, chrysocolla, jasp-agate, jasper, fluorite, rock crystal;** (2) Sylvanite District, the Wood Mine—**pyrolusite** (with **hematite** and **limonite**) coatings on **quartz.**

CLIFF, the Gila R., both sides in Sec. 19, 20, 29, 30, T. 13 S, R. 13 W, in area mines, outcrops, etc.—**alunogen, halotrichite.**

FIERRO-HANOVER, JUNIPER, MEERSCHAUM districts, area surfaces—**chert** (various colors, gemmy).

FORT BAYARD, area surfaces—**opal** (common, fire).

GEORGETOWN, the Commercial Mine—**argentite, descloizite.**

GRANITE GAP, the Hanover Mines—**argentite, cerussite, cuprite, sphalerite,** etc.

HACHITA (District): (1) area mines—**cerussite, silver, stilbite, wolframite;** (2) the American Mine—cf. area mines; (3) W 2 blocks, then S on ranch rd. 1.6 mi., passing cemetery to an E-trending dirt rd. (dim, very rough), then S about 4½ mi. to the old Apache Mine, dump No. 2—**calcite** (stained green), **chrysocolla, malachite, turquoise.** (Area arroyos contain Indian artifacts.) (4) SW on Rte. 81 into Hidalgo Co., the Little Hachita Mts., many area mines and dumps—**moonstones.**

MULE CREEK (far NW corner of co.): (1) area surfaces along the Arizona state boundary fence, high gem quality—**Apache tears;** (2) S, in the old Carlisle mining district—**amethysts.**

PINOS ALTOS, E, into the Black Mts.: (1) the Great Republic Mine, and (2) all W side slopes, draws, etc.—**albite, amethyst, biotite mica, sanidine, sphene;** (3) N 28 mi. on Rte. 15: (a) Sapillo Cr., area gravels, and (b) Alum Peak, area surfaces—**banded-agate geodes, carnelian.**

REDROCK, NE 6 mi., in Ricolite Gulch, area—**ricolite** (gemmy banded **serpentine**).

SANTA RITA (District), area mine dumps—**copper minerals, cuprite, molybdenite.**

SILVER CITY: (1) Gold Hill, large mine dumps—**argentite, pyrargyrite, native silver, sphalerite;** (2) SW 10 mi. (1½ mi. N of TYRONE): (a) the

Azure Mine (especially the "Elizabeth Pocket"); (b) in all regional prehistoric Indian excavations; (c) SE ½ mi., the Parker Mine; and (d) many
other area mine dumps—**halloysite, quartz crystals, turquoise;** (3) W 12 mi.,
and 24 mi. N, area pits and prospects—**meerschaum;** (4) N 15 mi., on both
sides of the Gila R., large deposit—**alum.**

SYLVANIA (District), the Golden Eagle and Handcar mines—**tetradymite**
(containing **gold**).

GUADALUPE CO.

SANTA ROSA, area coal mines, on dumps—**jet.**

HIDALGO CO.

AREA, NE corner of co. (best reached from HACHITA in Grant Co., *q.v.*):
(1) Playas Dry Lake, and (2) Hatchet Mt., area surfaces—**agate** (fortification, moss, plume), **moss opal.**
LORDSBURG: (1) area mines (Pinos Altos, Santa Rita, Steeple Rock, Sylvanite, etc.)—**bornite, cerussite, chalcopyrite, gold.** (The **gold** mines were
extremely productive between 1870 and 1900.) (2) S 2 mi. to rd. fork: (a)
W fork to ghost town of Shakespear (the town "too mean to live"); (b) SE,
around cemetery about 1 mi., turn W to base of chain of low mts., many area
pits and dumps—**azurite, bornite, galena, linerite,** etc.; (c) S through Pyramid Mts., some 85 old mines, e.g., the Atwood, Manner, Silver & Gold, etc.
—**copper, gold, silver,** etc.; (3) Pyramid and Peloncillo mts. (SW corner of
co.), area—**agate, chalcedony** (common, roses), **jasp-agate, jasper;** (4) N on
U.S. 70 to jct. with Rte. 464, then N on Rte. 464 for 21 mi. to REDROCK,
q.v., in Grant Co., E from post office to first rd. N, cross the Gila R. 3.3 mi.
(keep rt. at all forks) to Ricolite Canyon—**ricolite** (gemmy green-banded
serpentine, abundant in all sizes and grades).

LINCOLN CO.

ANCHO, area draws, washes, land surfaces—**jasper.**
HIDALGO (District), area mines and prospects—**fluorite.**
JICARILLA, NOGAL, WHITE OAKS: (1) area mines—**gold, huebnerite;** (2)
area deposits—**onyx.**

LUNA CO.

COLUMBUS: (1) W 4 mi., area—**onyx;** (2) NW 12 mi., the Tres Hermanas
Mts., area mines—**dumortierite, hydrozincite, pyrolusite, quartz crystals,
smithsonite, willemite.**
DEMING: (1) area: (a) all draws, washes, surfaces for miles around—
agate, chalcedony, chert, jasper, etc.; (b) regional **fluorspar** mines—**fluorite**
(this region is one of the major producers of **fluorspar** in America); (2) NE
5.1 mi. on Rte. 26 to N-trending ranch rd., then 5–6 mi. on the dirt rd.

toward Masacre Peak (elev. 5,600 ft.), center of rich rock-hunting area about 15 by 25 mi., scattered over entire area but excluding some hills— **carnelian** (deep red, translucent), deep red **jasper;**

(3) S 8 mi. on Rte. 11, then W and S by turns for 16 mi. to famed "Big Diggins," i.e., the Westmorland claims (open to gemstone collectors on a fee basis, as deposits are bulldozed out commercially): (a) the "Big Diggins" —**agate** (high grade, vein type, bordered with **sagenite,** clear with red and black banding, to 50-lb. chunks; (b) several other nearby claims. (When in DEMING, stop in local rock shops for complete description of localities.)

(4) E 7 mi. on Int. 10, then S 5 mi. to noted Spanish Stirrup Guest Ranch: (a) all surrounding ranch lands—**agate, geodes** (crystal-lined); (b) low saddle of the Little Florida Mts.—**agate** (sagenitic), blue **chalcedony, jasper.** (The nearby Rockhound State Park is equipped with picnic and camping facilities geared to the gem and mineral collector.)

(5) SW 27 mi., area ranch lands open for a fee—**agate** (all sizes; banded, plume, sagenite); (6) SW 38 mi. toward HERMANAS (20 mi. S from "Big Diggins"), then W via fence gate and crooked rough rd., several well-known area nodule beds (inquire at Deming rock shops)—**agate nodules** (crystal-lined, banded, **opal** centers, **amethyst** interiors); (7) SW 46 mi., 19 mi. S of item (5) fee ranch, broad collecting area—**agate nodules** (brilliantly colored fortification), **agate geodes** (containing brown to clear **quartz crystals**), **amethysts, opal** (poor quality, but some containing fire).

FREMONT, area mines—**azurite, bismuth, chalcopyrite, galena, malachite.**

NUTT, SW to Cooks Peak (elev. 8,408 ft.): (1) area mines—**anglesite, cerussite, galena, plumbojarosite;** (2) area on and surrounding the peak embracing approx. 20 sq. mi., mostly flats and low hills covered with gemstone float—**agate, carnelian, chalcedony, jasp-agate, jasper, fluorite,** etc.

VICTORIA (District), area mines—cf. NUTT item (1).

McKINLEY CO.

AREA, E slopes of Furry Mt.—**garnets.**

MCGAFFEY, E, in the Zuni Mts. (extending SE into Valencia Co.), area surfaces—**agate, chalcedony, jasper, petrified wood.**

SAN MATEO, NE, at Willow Spgs., area—**agate, jasper, petrified wood.**

THOREAU, SE 12 mi.: (1) area coal mines—**amber (wheelerite);** (2) in coal seams S of Devil's Pass and regional outcrops—**amber.**

OTERO CO.

OROGRANDE, N ½ mi. on U.S. 54, turn W on ranch rd. around the Jarila Mts.: (1) low range of hills immediately W of the turnoff from U.S. 54 (SW of the Jarila Mts.), area—**andradite garnets;** (2) N to the Jarila mining district, park car at old mine dumps and prospect to W and S: (a) area mines—**chalcocite, chalcopyrite, chrysocolla, galena, gypsum, jarosite, kaolin, limonite, malachite, turquoise;** (b) contact zones between exposed area beds of limestone and quartz monzonite—**orthoclase feldspar crystals** (often rose color, to 2 in. long, various types of twinning).

TULAROSA, S 1½ mi. to Bent, area—**"Mexican" onyx.**

RIO ARRIBA CO.

ABIQUIU (District): (1) area mines—**copper minerals;** (2) area basalt outcrops—**labradorite;** (3) E on U.S. 84 to jct. with Rte. 96, turn N 3.8 mi. to Carson National Forest marker, turn W opposite the marker to gate in fence with arroyo on S and steep climb to ancient pueblo ruins on mesa top, many mines in the arroyo—**fluorite.**

BROMIDE, area mines—**amazonite, chalcopyrite, copper minerals, fluorite, gold, molybdenite.**

COYOTE, area mines—**azurite, malachite.**

DIXON, E 6½ mi. (into Taos Co.): (1) N to old Calcite Mine—**calcite;** (2) S .6 mi. to rd. jct., then W and S to the Harding Mine—blue **apatite,** purple **lepidolite,** rose **muscovite mica, quartz crystals,** green **tourmaline.**

GHOST RANCH MUSEUM (and recreation park, on U.S. 84 on N side of a lake): (1) area—**agate;** (2) W 2.1 mi. on Rte. 96 (S side of lake), area of a low saddle in the hills, abundant—**agate;** (3) W 6 mi. from U.S. 84 toward YOUNGSVILLE on Rte. 96, to schoolhouse ruins, then S about 3 mi., all area benchlands to Pedernal Peak—**agate, chalcedony, chert, jasper.**

HERMOSA, area prospects—**chalcocite.**

HOPEWELL, area mines—**chalcopyrite** (minor ore), **gold.**

LA MADERA, E 1½ mi. (across a bridge) on Rte. 519 to an abandoned mine between survey posts 7500 and 7600: (1) on mine dumps—**book mica;** (2) area hillsides above mine—**calcite crystals** (pseudomorphs after **ilmenite**), **limonite crystals** on **calcite, crystal-lined geodes;** (3) N another .9 mi., canyon area—**geodes** (lined with **rock crystal**); (4) N another 10 mi. to Cervilleta sign, area E of rd.—**rhyolite nodules** (coated with **agate**); (5) N another 3 mi., turn E toward a dry wash, area on both sides—**calcite crystals, pseudomorphs** after **ilmenite, crystal-lined geodes.**

LAS TABLAS, SW 1½ mi. and ¾ mi. SE of Persimmon Peak, the Canary Bird Mine—**tourmaline.**

PETACA (13 mi. N of OJO CALIENTE on Rte. 519): (1) area prospects—**amazonite, fluorite, mica;** (2) 3½ mi. SW of SOUTH PETACA, above Alamos Canyon, the Sunnyside Mine (W of the Globe rd.), in pegmatite—**aquamarine, beryl;** (3) W on mt. rd. toward VALLECITOS: (a) W 1 mi., on S side of rough rd., a mine dump—pink **feldspar, book mica,** pink **mica** in **quartz;** (b) W another 3 mi., all area along route—pink **feldspar, mica** (books to 2 in. dia.); (c) all area mine dumps (easily reached)—**feldspar, mica,** black **columbite,** green **beryl,** green **amazonstone, pitchblende;** (4) from Cerro Pedernal to W side of San Pedro Mt., especially ½ mi. SE of LA MADERA—**dumortierite, specularite, "Pedernal" chert** (gem quality).

YOUNGSVILLE, area around store, abundant—gem **agate.** See also GHOST RANCH MUSEUM item (3), as the schoolhouse ruins are 4 mi. E.

SANDOVAL CO.

AREA: (1) SE part of co., the Jemez Mts. (from Rte. 44 on W to U.S. 85 on E, 60 mi. across), along Rte. 22 SW of LOS ALAMOS (beginning with SAN YSIDRO on Rte. 4 NE, around mts. to SANTO DOMINGO PUEBLO): (a) very many collecting localities, so prospect anywhere—**agate nodules, Apache tears, jasper, obsidian;** (b) La Jara Canyon, in first small tributary canyon to left of entrance, area surfaces—gem **jasper** (banded, brown, red, yellow); (2) Nacimiento Mts., regional draws, washes, etc.—**agate, azurite, chalcedony, chrysocolla, malachite.**

CABEZON, the regional Rio Puerco **coal** fields, area mine dumps—**wheelerite** (fossil resin).

COCHITI: (1) area mines—**gold;** (2) area of Upper Percha Cr.—**common opal.**

COOPER, MINERAL HILL, TECOLOTE, area mines—**copper minerals.**

CUBA: (1) area mines—**copper minerals;** (2) SE about 10 mi. to cattle guard (logging area), turn N ½ mi. into old mining district (Blue Bird, Eureka, etc., mines), on all old dumps—**copper minerals** (and associates), gemmy **chrysocolla conglomerate.**

JEMEZ (District): (1) area lava outcrops, in cavities—**moonstones;** (2) area small-scale mines—**sulfur;** (3) the Sulfur District, at Battleship Rock, area surfaces—**obsidian, opalized wood** (in volcanic tuffs); (4) the Rio Puerco Valley, area both sides—**agate, chalcedony, jasper, quartzite, silicified wood.**

NACIMIENTO (District), area mines—**chalcocite** (principal ore of the red beds), **chrysocolla.**

PLACITAS (District): (1) area mines—**copper minerals;** (2) area limestone outcrops, in caves—**cave onyx.**

SAN JUAN CO.

AREA: (1) regional **coal** mines (DURANGO, Colo., to GALLUP in McKinley Co.), on dumps—**jet;** (2) W part of co., region bounded by the San Juan R. and its Chaco R. tributary, numerous exposures of the Ojo Alamo Formation (as shown on area geologic map)—**chert, garnet, jasper, quartzite** (colorful), **petrified wood.**

BLANCO TRADING POST (on Rte. 44, 28 mi. S of BLOOMFIELD), S on Rte. 57 to the Chaco Canyon National Monument, along both sides of rd. entire distance—**chalcedony.**

FARMINGTON, S 27 mi. to the Bisti Trading Post, broad area of strange geological formations—**agatized dinosaur bone,** gemmy **carbonized wood, silicified mudballs** (banded brown and red).

SAN JUAN-McKINLEY COS.

NAVAJO INDIAN RESERVATION, numerous locations (inquire at trading posts)—**pyrope garnet ("Arizona rubies").**

SAN MIGUEL CO.

LAS VEGAS, N, general area—**petrified wood.**

PECOS, N along the Pecos R. canyon on old rd. 14 mi. to the Terrero Store, turn E around store (1 mi. uphill), long mine dump extending to

Willow Cr. (campground)—**actinolite, garnets, lepidolite, mica, peacock copper (bornite), pyrite, tourmaline.**

Rociada, Tecolote, area mines—**chalcocite, copper minerals, molybdenite.**

SANTA FE CO.

Area, regional **copper** mines (locations on topographic map)—**bornite, chalcopyrite, galena, malachite, pyrite,** etc.

Cerrillos: (1) area prospects—some **chalcopyrite** (containing **gold** and **silver**); (2) park car E of Tongue Wash and power lines: (a) N, a sandy mt., area—**carbonized fossil wood;** (b) big wash on S, all contributing arroyos—**red jasper;** (c) numerous adjoining localities in general vicinity—**agate, chalcedony, chert, jasper,** etc.; (3) NNE 6 mi. on Rte. 14 (30 mi. SSW of Santa Fe): (a) Turquoise Hill (3 mi. from Mt. Chalchihuitl in the Cerrillos Hills), and (b) area slopes and draws on Mt. Chalchihuitl—**agate, chalcedony, petrified wood, turquoise.**

Golden, SE, the San Pedro Mts.: (1) area placer mines—**gold;** (2) area hard-rock mines—**chalcopyrite** (principal ore), some **chalcocite.**

SIERRA CO.

Area: (1) Mud Spgs. Mt., NE flanks—**agate, opalized** and **silicified wood, petrified palm;** (2) extreme NW corner of co., on W side of the Continental Divide, the Taylor Cr. District (cf. Catron Co. Area)—**fluorite.**

Caballo, E, in the Caballo Mts., area mines—**azurite, chalcocite, chalcopyrite, fluorite, malachite.**

Chloride, the Apache and Phillipsburg mines—**chalcopyrite, cerussite, bornite** (containing **silver**), etc.

Cutter, area opposite the Aleman Ranch—**gem jasper.**

Derry, area washes, draws, etc.—**chert** (colorful, gemmy).

Engle: (1) area—**agate, chert;** (2) along both sides of rd. to Elephant Butte—**agate, chert, chalcedony, jasper;** (3) E to the San Andreas Mts., W side of Mockingbird Gap, area—**dendritic jasper.**

Hillsboro (Fremont): (1) area mines and prospects—**cerussite** (rich in **silver**), **gold;** (2) W, toward Kingston, a high cliff just before reaching an iron bridge across Percha Cr., in talus—**"flowering" rhyolite** (gemmy, pink, gray).

Kingston (District): (1) area mines—**proustite** (in **silver** ore), **pyrargyrite;** (2) the Comstock Mine—massive **rhodonite;** (3) on W side of town turn N on old mine rd., cross cr. and on for about 1 mi. to a gate, park car, small mt. on the E, area—**quartz crystals** (unusual, clusters, double-terminated, scepter-shaped, resembling a halo or a crowned hollow tooth); (4) E 9 mi. on Rte. 20, cross Percha Cr. on iron bridge, in cliff talus—**"flowering" rhyolite** (cf. Hillsboro).

Lake Valley (District): (1) area washes, draws, etc.—**chert** (colorful, gemmy); (2) area mines and dumps—**dolomite** (massive, pinkish), **magnetite, psilomelane, pyrolusite crystals;** (3) the Apache, Bella, Grande mines—

iodyrite (with **vanadinite**), **manganite, cerussite** (rich in **silver**), **native silver, embolite, enlichite;** (4) both sides of loop rd. NW of the old town—**agate, calcite crystals, jasper.** (This is a ghost town dating from 1878.)

TIERRA BLANCA (District), area mines—**bromyrite, gold, silver.**

TRUTH OR CONSEQUENCES: (1) N, on W side of the Fra Cristobal Mts., area—**agate, jasper;** (2) E 13 mi., Hot Spgs. (in the Jornada Valley), area—**agate, chalcedony, "elixirite" (silicified wonderstone,** i.e., **banded rhyolite), jasper, petrified wood;** (3) NE 38 mi. to abandoned Ft. Craig, take canal rd. S 11½ mi. to mile post 1370, park car; cross old river bed to hills on E, in all sandy outcrops, excellent, black—**opalized wood;** (4) E on Rte. 52 to ENGLE, *q.v.*, then S on ranch rd. paralleling the RR for 13 mi. to a ranch, turn W through ranch, cross RR tracks into low hills (a spur of the Caballo Mts.) for 2 mi., all along both sides of rd.—**carnelian agate.**

SOCORRO CO.

AREA: (1) SE corner of co.: (a) the Sierra Oscura Mts., regional prospects and mines—abundant **chrysocolla,** some **chalcocite;** (b) the Joita Hills, and (c) around the Socorro Peaks S to Mockingbird Gap (cf. ENGLE in Sierra Co.), regional washes, draws, surfaces, etc.—**agate, chalcedony, jasper** (common, dendritic), **quartz crystals, quartzite** (colorful, gemmy), **petrified wood;** (2) the Mogollon Mts., area mines—**bornite, chalcocite, chalcopyrite, native silver.**

BINGHAM, E ½ mi. on U.S. 380, then S several mi. to the famed Blanchard Mine (claims) in the Sierra Oscura Mts. (pay collecting fee at the Blanchard cabin)—**atacamite, azurite, barite, brochantite, celestite, cerussite, cyanatrichite, dolomite crystals, fluorite, galena, limonite, linarite, malachite, murdochite, plattnerite, quartz crystals, spangolite.**

COONEY (Mogollon; district includes Mill Canyon, Silver Mt., and Rosedale), area mines—**bornite, chalcocite, chalcopyrite, gold.**

HANSONBURG (San Andreas, San Lorenzo): (1) area mines—**copper minerals;** (2) Grandview Canyon, area mines—**fluorite.**

LAVA (straddles Sierra-Socorro co. line at end of rd. N from ENGLE in Sierra Co., *q.v.*): (1) the Fra Cristobal Range, N end and NE side of Elephant Butte Reservoir; and (2) S of the E end of Bernado Bridge over the Rio Grande, area—**opalized wood** (logs, limbs, stem sections). (This field extends S into Sierra Co. along the mts. and E into the Jornada Valley to the E of TRUTH OR CONSEQUENCES, *q.v.*, in Sierra Co.)

MAGDALENA: (1) area mines—**anglesite, cerussite, chalcophanite, cuprite, galena, hydrozincite, smithsonite, sphalerite;** (2) SE 3 mi. to ghost town of KELLY, on all old mine dumps—gem-quality **smithsonite** (blue green), **zinc minerals** in **quartz, fossils** (crinoids, mollusk shells). (Once this was a boom town of 3,000 people; the Kelly Mine, and others, produced millions of dollars in zinc from 1904 to 1931.) (3) W, at Silver Hill, on WSW side—**garnets;** (4) N 16 mi. on gravel rd. to jct. (Riley, 4 mi.), turn W on dim ranch rd. for 5 mi., area surfaces—**agatized "picture wood"** (large pieces), **petrified cycad and palm.**

SOCORRO: (1) NW 4 mi., and (2) on E side of Strawberry Peak, area—**satin spar.**

TAOS CO.

GLENWOODY, area gravels—**staurolites.**

MOLYBDENUM, area mines—**molybdenum minerals.**

PICURIS: (1) area mines—**chalcocite, chrysocolla, cuprite;** (2) area gravels, slopes, washes, etc.—**staurolites.**

PILAR: (1) area mine dumps between mts. and U.S. 64—gem-quality **lepidolite** and **sericite;** (2) both sides of rd. to VELARDE—**garnets, staurolites.**

RED RIVER, area mines—**fluorite, gold.** (Wheeler Peak, elev. 13,161 ft.; to the south is the highest peak in N.M.)

TRES PIEDRAS, W on Rte. 519. See LA MADERA in Rio Arriba Co. and reverse order of localities.

TWINING, area mines—**copper minerals.**

TORRANCE CO.

ESTANCIA, the area surrounding the Estancia Lakes—**epsomite, glauberite.**

MANZANO, TORREON, TAJIQUE (adjoining towns on Rte. 14 N of MOUNTAINAIR, W, in the Monzano Mts., area schistose outcrops—**staurolites**).

UNION CO.

AREA, extreme NE corner of co.; (1) the Tri-State Marker (N. Mex., Colo., Okla.): (a) area, extending into Okla. to KENTON, Cimarron Co.—**petrified algae** and **cycad wood;** (b) a hill near the marker, area surfaces—rose-colored **agate;** (2) Ute Cr., deposit—**alum.**

VALENCIA CO.

AREA: (1) regional coal mine dumps and seam exposures—**jet;** (2) NW part of co., in the Zuni Mts.: (a) area mines of the Copper Hiss District in the "Red Beds"—**azurite, chalcocite, malachite;** (b) regional slopes, draws, washes, etc.—**agate, chalcedony, jasper, petrified wood.**

BELEN, N to LOS LUNAS, *q.v.*, area surfaces, draws; washes, etc.—gem **agate.**

GRANTS, the "Grants Uranium District," very many mines and exposures of radioactive rocks—**andersonite, autunite, boyleyite, carnotite, ilsemannite, liebigite, meta-autunite, metatyuyamunite, montroscite, pascoite, thenardite, thermonatrite, todorakite, tyuyamunite, uranopilite, zellerite, zippeite.** Associated with these radioactive minerals (many fluorescent) are often **barite, calcite, coffinite, jordisite, marcasite, pyrite, gray selenium,** and **gypsum.**

This large area of radioactivity extends from GALLUP in McKinley Co. on the west to the western edge of the Rio Grande trough on the east, approximately 110 mi. long by 20 mi. wide. The principal mining areas revolve around (1) GALLUP, (2) CHURCH ROCK, (3) SMITH LAKE, (4) AMBROSIA

LAKE, (5) GRANTS, (6) PAGUOTE or JACKPILE. These areas are grouped into three major mining districts: GALLUP, GRANTS, and LAGUNA. It was the presence of poisonous **selenium** in the abundant "locoweed" (sp. *Astragalus*) that led a Navajo sheepherder, Paddy Martinez, to the first discovery of **tyuyamunite** in a Todilto Limestone outcrop in Sec. 19, T. 13 N, R. 10 W at the base of Haystack Butte in 1950. **Uranium** was subsequently found in the Dakota Sandstone and in the Brushy Basin Shale, as well as in the West-water Canyon members of the Morrison formation.

LAGUNA, area surfaces—**agate, jasper.**

LOS LUNAS, W 6 mi. on Rte. 6, then S on dirt rd. to Dalies (water tank and cattle pens) on the RR, continue S into low hills (taking right forks en route), area of arroyos and breaks leading to the Rio Puerco, abundant— agate (red, red-banded), **Apache tears, agatized palm wood, obsidian.**

NEW YORK

Called the Empire State, New York is irregularly shaped, not only from a geographical standpoint but in its multivaried rock formations. The eastern part of the state is dominated by the great valley of the Hudson River and Lake Champlain, while the rolling hills of northern ("upstate") New York rise from the Mohawk River to the rugged Adirondack Mountains. Here, in 1892, the state legislature established a wilderness preserve, the Adirondack Park, larger than any other national or state park in America. Its 5,693,000 acres, or 8,895 square miles, makes it greater in area than the state of Massachusetts. Western New York is a rolling, hilly region extending to Lakes Erie and Ontario, cupping many sapphire-blue lakes in the folds and wrinkles of a thoroughly glaciated terrain. Most of the southern counties belong to the Allegheny Plateau that culminates in the Catskill Mountains.

Pleistocene glaciers covered all parts of New York State. Geologists think that at least 1,000 feet of ice once lay over what is now New York City and Long Island and that 2,500 feet of ice buried the Catskills. The outer (Ronkonkoma) and inner (Harbor Hill) moraines on Long Island are notable examples of glacial termination, while Central Park in New York City exposes many glaciated boulders still clearly showing the scratch marks (striations) made on them thousands of years ago by the moving ice sheets.

More noted for their fossil content than for commercial minerals, gems, and gemstones, the state's rock formations represent almost every class of deep-seated igneous rocks and nearly all the important sedimentary groups from the earliest Cambrian to the most recent periods. The state depends primarily on the importation of raw materials to supply its great industries, but does have some mineral resources, such as **iron, lead, oil, natural gas, salt, gypsum, cement,** and **limestone.**

For information, write: State Geologist, New York State Science Service, Albany.

CAYUGA CO.

AUBURN, sparingly in area (inquire locally), old pits—**fluorite**.

CLINTON CO.

AREA, the Palmer Hiss Mine and Finch ore bed, abundant—**fluorite**.
ARNOLD HILL (just NW of CLINTONVILLE), area mines and workable ore bodies—**magnetite**.
LYON MOUNTAIN, area mines—**molybdenite**.

COLUMBIA CO.

ANCRAM, area mines—**barite, galena, sphalerite**.

DUTCHESS CO.

AREA, NE corner of co., various old mines—**galena**.

ERIE CO.

BUFFALO: (1) E 2½ mi., the Fogelsanger Quarry—**calcite, favosites** (petrified honeycomb coral), **petrified corals** (other types); (2) Eighteen Mile Cr., area deposits—**pyrite**.

ESSEX CO.

AREA, the Opalescent R., gravel beds, bars—**labradorite**.
BURTON HILL, area mines—**fluorite, magnetite**.
CASCADE (Lakes), area gravels, outcrops—**labradorite**.
CROWN POINT: (1) area outcrops and gravels—**sunstone**; (2) SW 7½ mi., old mine—**feldspar, graphite, mica**.
INDIAN LAKE, SE on Rte. 28 to within 5 mi. of NORTH RIVER in Warren Co., the Crehore Mine—**garnet** (crystals to 8 in. dia.), **hornblende**.
IRONVILLE, area mines—**hematite, magnetite**.
KEESEVILLE: (1) area quarries—**labradorite**; (2) area mines on Mt. Bigelow—**garnet** (commercial abrasive).
LEAD HILL, area mines—**graphite**.
LEWIS, area mines—**arsenopyrite, rhodonite**.
MINEVILLE, area high-grade **iron** mines, abundant minerals—**apatite, fluorite, hematite, magnetite, pyrite**. (It is claimed that this mining district supplied the iron for the Civil War Union ship *Monitor*.)

NEWCOMB, E 1 mi., Lake Harris, area pegmatite outcrops—**albite feld-spar, amphiboles** (various), **apatite, graphite, muscovite mica, pyrite, pyroxene, quartz crystals** (smoky), **scapolite, tourmaline, tremolite.**

NORTH CREEK, S 4 mi., on Oven Mt., old mines—**garnet.**

OLMSTEDVILLE, W 1 mi. on rte. to MINERVA, area—**idocrase, gem microcline feldspar crystals, scapolite.**

TAHAWUS, area **iron** mines—**hematite, magnetite, titanium.** (In addition to production of **iron,** the Tahawus Mine is the chief source of **titanium** in America.)

TICONDEROGA, Bear Pond area mines—**graphite, pyrite.**

FRANKLIN CO.

DUANE, large area bed, mined—**pyrite.**

HERKIMER CO.

FAIRFIELD, area quarries—**barite.**

MIDDLEVILLE, area sandstone exposures—**"Herkimer diamonds"** (unusually water-clear quartz crystals, perfectly terminated), found principally: (1) on N side of rd. to NEWPORT along a NW belt; (2) E 1 mi. toward the N side of the FAIRFIELD hwy. (Rte. 29); and (3) from town 3 mi. S, most prolifically on top of a hill between town and HERKIMER. All collecting localities are on private land; make local inquiry and obtain permission.

JEFFERSON CO.

ALEXANDRIA BAY, area mines—**galena.**

PHILADELPHIA, area **serpentine** outcrops—**hematite, pyrite, siderite.**

PILLAR POINT, area quarries—**barite crystals.**

THERESA, Muscalonge Lake: (1) area quarries—**fluorite;** (2) NE shore of lake, mines—**fluorite.**

LEWIS CO.

LOWVILLE, area mines—**fluorite.**

MARTINSBURG, area **lead** mines—**galena.**

NATURAL BRIDGE, NE 3 mi., a quarry—**serpentine, talc.**

MONROE CO.

ROCHESTER, regional quarries—**fluorite.**

NIAGARA CO.

LOCKPORT, area limestone quarries—**fluorite.**

ONONDAGA CO.

FAYETTEVILLE, area quarries—**fluorite.**
MANLIUS, area quarries—**fluorite.**
SYRACUSE, area peridotite outcrops—**peridotite.**

ORANGE CO.

AMITY, area limestone outcrops—**corundum** (blue, white), **fluorite.**
BLOOMING GROVE, along the Hudson R., area—**bloodstone, jasper.**
EDENVILLE: (1) area mines, and (2) between town and Mt. Adam, mines
—**arsenopyrite, leucopyrite, scorodite.**
MONROE, near Lake Mombasha, pegmatite outcrop—**phlogopite mica**
(greenish).
OTISVILLE, the Phoenix Mine—**galena, sphalerite.**

OTSEGO CO.

TODDSVILLE, area gravel pits, stream beds—**sapphire.**

PUTNAM CO.

BREWSTER, NW 6 mi., the Tilly Foster Iron Mine—**apatite, chondrodite,**
fluorite, garnet (grossularite, uvarovite), hematite, magnetite, sphene.
COLD SPRING, just E, a mine—**chrysotile asbestos.**
KENT CLIFFS, in the Highlands near Pine Pond, a mine—**arsenopyrite,**
asbestos, leucopyrite (iron diarsenide), pyrite.
WEST POINT, S 3½ mi., on bank of the Hudson R., quarry—**chrysotile as-**
bestos.

RICHMOND CO. (Borough of New York City)

TOMPKINSVILLE, area quarries—**asbestos.**
TOTENVILLE, SW tip of Staten Island, the Androvette Clay Pits (near
KREISCHERVILLE on the shore of Arthur Kill)—**serpentine.**

SARATOGA CO.

BATCHELLERVILLE: (1) area quarries, in pegmatites—**feldspar, muscovite**
mica; (2) N 12½ mi., at Overlook, area—**rose quartz.**
SARATOGA SPRINGS, intersection of Rte. 9 with the twp rd., W ½ mi., a
pegmatite outcrop—**chrysoberyl.**

SCHOHARIE CO.

AREA, numerous exposures of sedimentary rocks—**silicified coral.**

SCHOHARIE: (1) area exposures of the Brayman shales and the Roundout Waterline (cf. on geologic map)—**barite crystals, celestite** (as nodular aggregates of delicate crystals); (2) town courthouse, vicinity exposures of water limestone—**barite crystals** (associated with **strontianite**); (3) N 2 mi., on face of Terrace Hill (within sight of rd. to Schoharie Jct.), an old mine—**strontianite.**

ST. LAWRENCE CO.

BRASHER IRON WORKS, area mines—**iron minerals.**

CANTON, the High Falls Mine—**pyrrhotite.**

DEKALB, area quarries—**barite, fluorite.**

EDWARDS: (1) area mines, and (2) area quarries—**barite, galena, sphalerite, fluorite.**

FOWLER, (1) area quarries—**barite, fluorite;** (2) area sedimentary exposures, stream beds and banks—**geodes** (containing **barite** and **hematite**); (3) NW on Rte. 58, the Loomis Talc Mine—**talc, tremolite.**

FULLERVILLE IRONWORKS, area mines—**iron minerals, pyrite.**

GOUVERNEUR: (1) area quarries—**barite, fluorite;** (2) area mines—**garnet** (abrasive); (3) N 3 mi., as a body of rock—**garnets** (crystals to ¼ in. dia.); (4) various outcrops along the Oswegatchie R.—**serpentine.**

HAILSBORO, area limestone quarries—**apatite.**

HAMMOND, area quarries—**barite, fluorite.**

HERMON, area mines—**pyrite.**

MACOMB, area mines—**barite** (gangue), **fluorite, galena.**

OSWEGATCHIE, area pegmatite mines, pits—**muscovite mica.**

PIERREPONT, area pegmatite exposures—**tourmaline.**

PYRITES, area mines—**pyrite.**

RICHVILLE: (1) area of the Reese Farm, in pegmatites—**pyroxene, tourmaline** (white dravite), **tremolite;** (2) N 5 mi. and 3 mi. NE, various area outcrops of pegmatites—**achroite, diopside, white tourmaline (dravite).**

ROSSIE, area mines—**barite** (gangue), **galena.**

SOMERVILLE, N 2 mi., as good crystals—**phlogopite mica.**

STAR LAKE, area open-pit **iron** mine (one of the world's largest)—**magnetite.** More than 200 **iron** mines have been worked in the Adirondacks in St. Lawrence, Franklin, and Essex counties. In addition to **iron** and **titanium,** the mines also produced abrasive **garnet, granite, marble, talc, graphite,** and **zinc.**

TALCVILLE, area quarries—**talc.**

SULLIVAN CO.

SUMMITVILLE, area mines—**sphalerite.**

SULLIVAN, ULSTER COS.

AREA, the Shawangunk Mts., many regional mines—**sphalerite.**

ULSTER CO.

ELLENVILLE, area mines—**sphalerite.**
NAPANOCH, area mines—**siderite.**

WARREN CO.

BRANT LAKE (HORICON), NE to Brant Lake: (1) S shore, in rd. cut through pegmatite—**apatite, calcite, diopside, graphite, muscovite mica, pyrite, rutile, tourmaline;** (2) N shore, a deposit—**asbestos.**
GRAPHITE, area mines—**graphite.**
NORTH CREEK: (1) WSW 4 mi., mines around Gore Mt.; (2) W, mines on Ruby Mt.; (3) S, mines on Oven Mt.—**garnet.**
NORTH RIVER, W, into extreme NW corner of co., the Thirteenth Lake, SW 6½ mi. from S end of lake, at Humphrey Mt., area mines—**garnet.**
WEVERTOWN, area quarry—**garnet.**

WASHINGTON CO.

DRESDEN STATION, area South Bay mines—**graphite.**

WESTCHESTER CO.

BEDFORD (Twp.): (1) area quarries—**cyrtolite, feldspar;** (2) SE ¾ mi., the Kinkel Quarry: (a) this quarry; (b) ½ mi. W, the Baylis Quarry; (c) 1½ mi. SE, along the Mianus R. in North Castle, the Hobby Quarry— **golden beryl, citrine, quartz crystals** (rose with asterism, smoky).
PEEKSKILL: (1) area—**sunstone;** (2) SE, an area of igneous rocks known as the Cortlandt series (7 mi. E–W by 5 mi. N–S), regional deposits and mines—**emery, spinel, thomsonite.**
PLEASANTVILLE, area mines—**muscovite mica.**
RYE, area **serpentine** bosses (constituting about 15 sq. mi.)—**asbestos (amphibole, chrysotile).**

NORTH CAROLINA

With more than 300 species of gems, gemstones, and minerals, this remarkable state is geared for rock collecting as few other states are. Blessed with extraordinary scenic beauty, North Carolina has a gem history equaled nowhere else in North America and innumerable tales of discoveries of **amethyst, aquamarine, bronzite, diamonds** (first found abundantly in the **gold** placers in the middle 1850's), **golden beryl, rubies, sapphires,** and **topaz.** Moreover, North Carolina has the only true **emerald** mines in America, discovered about 1875. To these gems can be added the clear emerald-green **spodumene** crystals called **hiddenite** after William Hidden, supervisor of one of the larger **emerald** mines. This new gem was discovered and identified late in the nineteenth century, along with a second new gem, **rhodolite,** a rose pink gem-hard crystal found in Cowee Creek near Franklin, Macon Co., about the same time.

Mining history really began in North Carolina in 1799, when a twelve-year-old boy unearthed a 17-pound **gold** nugget on his father's plantation in Cabarrus Co. Young Reed sold his nugget to a local jeweler for the unheard-of price of $3.50. Eventually, millions of dollars in nuggets were produced by the plantation, and millions of other dollars in **gold** began coming from other parts of the state as intensive prospecting for **gold** and **silver** got under way. It was in the placer gravels that incidental discoveries of many species of gem crystals, especially **diamonds,** were made.

(**Gold** was subsequently found throughout a multistate region east of the Appalachian Mountains, about 700 miles long by 150 miles wide. North Carolina became the principal producer, inasmuch as the noble metal was found to occur almost universally wherever the rocks were not covered by drift, both free and in association with **chalcopyrite, iron,** and **pyrite.** In order of decreasing production, the other states in this region are South Carolina, Georgia, Virginia, and Alabama. In North Carolina, certainly, the seasonal **gold** panner will find literally hundreds of profitable stream gravel bars in which to wield pick, shovel, and pan.)

The sharply defined provinces of North Carolina constitute part of the Atlantic seaboard between the Atlantic Ocean and the Appalachian Mountains. From the tidewater swamps of the coast the land rises to an elevation of 500 feet along the western edge of the upper Coastal Plain before beginning the rolling hill country of the Piedmont, with its many swift, gem-rich Fall Line streams descending eastward. On the west the land juts abruptly into the Blue Ridge, 3,000 to 4,000 feet high, then dips sharply to the broad Carolina Highlands backed up against the Great Smoky Mountains. Here, in Yancey County, Mt. Mitchell, at 6,684 feet, is the highest peak in America east of the South Dakota Black Hills.

The Mountain and Piedmont regions expose rocks from Precambrian to Carboniferous ages, enormously folded, faulted, broken, and crushed by diastrophic forces. The older rocks were repeatedly intruded by granites and diorites, and the entire region is blanketed with metamorphic schists, gneisses, quartzites, and slates. The igneous rocks produce a great abundance of commercial minerals, and this state leads the nation in its production of **feldspar, kaolin, mica,** and **pyrophyllite** and stands high in **asbestos, crushed** and **dimension stone, granite, marble, olivine,** and **vermiculite.** The mining of **copper** and **tungsten** is also a major contributor to the state's economy. At least 50 species of minerals are mined today, not counting the scores of gem crystals most sought after by rock collectors, while another 20 or so have economic potential.

Gems and gemstones occur in almost every county, but most abundantly in Alexander, Mitchell, Yancey, Macon, and Cleveland counties. Easy access to the main gem-producing districts is from the 470-mile-long Blue Ridge Parkway that follows the spectacular crest of the Appalachian Mountains. Not only do many old mines allow gem collecting on a fee basis, but throughout the Mountain and Piedmont regions sparkling streams yield up a never-ending supply of alluvial **gold, diamonds, rubies,** and **sapphires.** The state's pegmatites, mined mainly for **feldspar, mica,** and **quartz,** are rich in the usually associated gems: **amethysts, aquamarine, golden beryl, corundum, garnet, moonstone, rock crystal, spodumene,** and **topaz.** Granite outcrops provide an abundance of the "state stone," **unakite,** named after the Unaka Mountains, as well as the unusual **leopardite.** **Petrified wood** is found in the alluvial gravels of many counties, particularly Anson, Cumberland, Moore, Montgomery, and Wayne. Public and private campgrounds, many with trailer hookups, abound throughout the gem-producing regions; indeed, many fee gem mines offer free camping facilities.

For information, write: North Carolina Division of Mineral Resources, Raleigh.

ALAMANCE CO.

AREA: (1) general countywide surfaces, as float—**serpentine;** (2) area mines: (a) Dixon's Mine (on both sides of the Haw R.), placers; (b) the Holt Mine; (c) the Anthony Mine; (d) Newlin's Mine—**gold;** (3) Buck Hill, area, massive and opaque—**quartz.**

BURLINGTON: (1) area fields, streams, cuts, etc.—**quartz crystals,** red gemmy **quartzite, serpentine;** (2) the Superior Stone Quarry—**copper** and **iron minerals;** (3) on a farm ½ mi. from the quarry, loose in soil—**limonite** (pseudomorphs after **siderite**), **quartz crystals.**

ALEXANDER CO.

AREA, Poplar Spgs., area—**rutile crystals** (geniculated, acicular in **limonite** and **quartz**), **spodumene.**

ELLENDALE, All Healing Spgs. (W part of co. N of Rte. 90): (1) near Lambert Cr., pegmatite—**beryl** (golden, green, yellow); (2) near Little R. Church, pegmatite—**beryl** (pale green, yellow).

HIDDENITE: (1) area: (a) in loose soils surrounding town—**emeralds;** (b) in the Mertie Pegmatite—**quartz crystals** (champagne color, clear, smoky amber); (c) many area old mines and dumps—**aquamarine, beryl, quartz** and **rutile crystals;** (d) the old Ellis Mine (½ mi. N of the old Hiddenite

School, near a creek)—**emeralds,** blue **beryl, rose quartz, rutile;** (e) just S of town, in rd. cuts, massive—**smoky quartz.**

(2) E ¼ mi., old mine—**aquamarine, calcite, chalcopyrite, dolomite crystals, emeralds, hiddenite, monazite, muscovite mica, quartz** and **rutile crystals, black tourmaline;** (3) E 1½ mi., on ridge between Davis Cr. and the Little Yadkin R., pegmatite exposures—**aquamarine, beryl, quartz** and **rutile crystals;** (4) W ½ mi., mine—cf. item (2); (5) SW 1 mi., old **beryl** prospect on the Charles Payne farm—**beryl, mica,** etc.; (6) SW 2 mi., the Gwaltney prospects—**garnet, feldspar, quartz crystals** (with inclusions), **beryl, tourmaline;**

(7) SW 3½ mi., the Dagenhart Mine—**beryl, feldspar, garnet, quartz crystals** (with inclusions), massive **smoky quartz, tourmaline;** (8) S 6 mi., the Hammer prospects—**rutilated quartz crystals;** (9) N 1 mi.: (a) the Warren Farm (near Salem Church and 300 yds. from Rte. 90)—**albite, amphibole, ankerite, apatite, aquamarine, arsenopyrite, beryl, calcite, chlorite, emerald, feldspar (orthoclase), hiddenite, muscovite mica, pyrite, quartz** and **rutile crystals, black tourmaline, siderite, spodumene;** (b) NW 1,000 ft., the Osborne-Lackey farm—same, plus **aragonite crystals;**

(9) NE 1.2 mi., the old Revis Farm—**quartz** (rose, rutilated); (10) NE 2 mi. on rd. to Smith's Store, as area float, and at the Lackey farm on the same rd.—**rutilated quartz crystals;** (11) N 3.2 mi., pegmatite dikes along the South Yadkin R.—**quartz crystals** (smoky, rutilated).

STONY POINT: (1) area—**chlorite, goethite, monazite** (fine crystals), **quartz crystals** (rutilated and with **byssolite** inclusions), **spodumene** (fine transparent green crystals); (2) the Hiddenite Mine: (a) mine dumps—**emeralds, smoky quartz crystals, rutile crystals, black tourmaline;** (b) just S of the mine, pegmatite outcrop—**rutilated quartz crystals** (with inclusions of **goethite, diorite, tourmaline, byssolite;** also, some enhydros).

TAYLORSVILLE: (1) area: (a) mine dumps—**beryl, columbite, quartz crystals** (rose, smoky), **rutile crystals, scorodite, tourmaline;** (b) N several mi., in the Brushy Mts. (on the Wilkes Co. line), area mines—**asbestos, chalcopyrite, graphite,** tabular **quartz crystals;** (2) SE, at headwaters of the South Yadkin R. (¾ mi. SE of HIDDENITE), the O. F. Patterson Mica Mine—gem **beryl, muscovite mica;** (3) SE 2 mi., near Paynes Store on the Kever farm (exposures of pegmatites extend ½ mi. NE to the Payne place), several types—**quartz crystals;** (4) SW 5 mi., the Blakenship prospect—**muscovite mica, quartz** (asteriated), **moonstone feldspar.**

WHITE PLAINS: (1) area mines—cf. TAYLORSVILLE area mine dumps; (2) Liberty Church, near Millholland's Mill—**rutile crystals.**

ALLEGHANY CO.

AREA, Bullhead Mt., area mines—**garnet,** gem **kyanite, magnetite.**

DOUGHTON PARK, N 2½ mi., area of Air Bellows Gap in sandstone schists —fine **iron garnets.**

GLADE VALLEY, the Monroe Holloway farm—showy **magnetite crystals, talc** (foliated).

ENNICE, several outcrops along the New R., showy—**magnetite crystals.**

ROARING GAP, area mine—**auriferous chalcopyrite, bornite.**

SPARTA, NE 3 mi. on Rte. 18, turn W 1 mi. on unmarked rd., the Crouse Manganese Mine (S of Bald Knob)—**alleghanyite, galaxite, garnet** (massive **spessartite**), **rhodonite, tephroite.**

STRATFORD, W, near Elk Cr., the Peach Bottom Mine dumps—**chalcopyrite, cuprite, galena, malachite, molybdenite, pyrite, native silver, sphalerite** (red).

TWIN OAKS; NE, and 1½ mi. S of the state line (7 mi. SE of INDEPENDENCE, Va.), below Bald Knob, mine—**spessartite garnet, pyrolusite, rhodonite.**

ANSON CO.

WADESBORO: (1) the Jesse Cox Mine—**gold;** (2) SE 2 mi., the Hamilton (Bailey) Mine, in **quartz** veins—**gold;** (3) S 2 mi., a vein—**gold;** (4) SW 2 mi., in small patch of crystalline rocks on S side of the Triassic sandstone belt—**gold.**

ANSON-UNION COS.

AREA, stream gravels—**placer gold.**

ANSONVILLE, FAIRVIEW, regional stream gravels and mines—**calcite, garnet, galena, gold, pyrite, siderite, rutile, sphalerite.**

PEE DEE, in gravels of the Pee Dee R. and its tributaries, as float—**agatized** and **petrified wood, chalcedony, jasper,** etc.

ASHE CO.

AREA: (1) Helton Cr., near mouth—**magnetite;** (2) Horse Cr., area— **epidote, manganese garnet, magnetite;** (3) S part of co.: (a) near headwaters of the New R., the Copper Knob (Gap Creek) Mine—**bornite, chalcocite, chalcopyrite, chrysocolla, gold, epidote, hematite, malachite, native silver;** (b) S Fork, near mouth—**chalcopyrite, chrysolite, magnetite.**

BEAVER CREEK: (1) SW 1½ mi., the South Hardin Mica Mine—**aquamarine, golden beryl** (crystals to 8 in. long), **muscovite mica.**

CHESTNUT HILL (Twp.): (1) area—**rock crystal;** (2) area farms on Chestnut Mt. along Long Shoal Cr., weathering out of decomposed granite outcrops —**rock crystal** (to extraordinary size, the largest found to date weighing 300 lbs.).

CRUMPLER, E ½ mi., on N Fork of the New R., in outcrops of **biotite-muscovite** gneiss—**staurolites.**

ELK (Crossroads), NW 2 mi., the Walnut Knob Mine (¾ mi. S of Black Mt.)—**aquamarine.**

JEFFERSON: (1) S, at Blue Ridge, pegmatites—**muscovite mica, black tourmaline;** (2) E 3 mi., at Mulatto Mts., area mines—**chalcopyrite;** (3) 2–6 mi. distant, mines—**chalcopyrite, pyrite.**

ORE KNOB, N on Rte. 88, the Ore Knob Mine—**apophyllite, arsenopyrite, calcite, chalcocite, chalcopyrite, native copper, cuprite, epidote, malachite, pyrite, stilbite, thomsonite.**

PINEY CREEK: (1) area granite exposures, fields, cuts, etc.—**rock crystal** (some with inclusions of **chlorite, manganese,** or **rutile**); (2) N Fork, area stream gravels—**rock crystal.**

WEST JEFFERSON: (1) area old **mica** mines—**aquamarine, beryl;** (2) SW 1.2 m., the Duncan Mica Mine—**beryl, muscovite mica.**

AVERY CO.

CRANBERRY: (1) area RR cut banks, and (2) SW 1 mi., on dumps of the Cranberry Iron Mine—gem **epidote, garnets, hematite,** gem **kyanite, unakite.**

ELK PARK, ½ mi. up Roaring Cr. from hwy., the Bill Burleson farm, fee —gem **moonstone.**

PLUMTREE: (1) area pits, rd. cuts, gravels—gem **feldspar crystals, melanite garnets, moonstone,** gem **oligoclase crystals;** (2) NE .8 mi., the Plumtree Mine—**moonstone, oligoclase crystals;** (3) NE 1 mi. and about ½ mi. off U.S. 19E, the Meadows Mine—**moonstone, soda feldspar crystals;** (4) N, on Lick Log Cr., the old Elk Mine—**garnets;** (5) SE 2 mi., the Johnson Mine— **garnets.**

SPEAR, W 2½ mi. and just off U.S. 19E, the Birch Mine—**epidote, soda feldspar crystals.**

BUNCOMBE CO.

AREA: (1) Cane Cr., in gravels—**calcite, gold, hematite, limonite;** (2) Ivy R., area—**chrysolite, genthite, hornstone, talc, tremolite asbestos;** (3) Reams Cr., as large crystals—**garnets;** (4) Pisgah Mt. (10 mi. N of ASHEVILLE), area—**meteoritic iron;** (5) Tremont Mt., area—**chrysoprase.**

ASHEVILLE, E and S along the Blue Ridge Parkway: (1) Potato Gap; (2) NE of the Craggy Gardens picnic area—**almandite garnets;** (3) Balsam Gap, ½ mi. N of the Parkway, the Balsam Gap Mine—**albite, allanite, green beryl, columbite, corundum, black garnet, margarodite, mica (biotite, muscovite), sapphires** (opaque, muted).

BLACK MOUNTAIN: (1) Black Mt. Sta., mine near the Blue Ridge Parkway—**aquamarine,** gem **kyanite;** (2) just N (and 1.4 mi. SE of Balsam Gap), (3) Lookout Mt., area—**kyanite crystals;** (4) NE 2 mi., the J. C. Dude Ranch—**corundum, sapphires.**

DEMOCRAT (N-central part of co.): (1) area mines—**nickel minerals;** (2) W on Rte. 197 for ½ mi., turn N .2 mi. on secondary rd., the Goldsmith Mine—**chalcedony, feldspar crystals,** gem **garnets, moonstone, olivine crystals, vermiculite.**

SWANNANOA GAP: (1) area pegmatite outcrops—**corundum** (in **kyanite**), **damourite;** (2) S, at Ridgecrest—gem **corundum;** (3) SW 2 mi., old mine— **limonite.**

BURKE CO.

AREA: (1) in the **gold** placers of the co. (many) also occur—**anatase, brookite, chromite, corundum, epidote, fibrolite, hematite, limonite, mag-**

netite, **menaccanite, monazite, palladium, pyrope garnet, rutile crystals, tourmaline** (black, green), **wolframite, xenotime, zircon;** (2) SW corner of co., near Bee Bridge: (a) Brindleton Cr., numerous area mines and prospects —**corundum, diamonds, pyrope garnet, rutile crystals, tourmaline;** (b) gravels of Hall and Silver creeks—cf. Brindleton Cr.

(3) Brown Mt., mines—**albite, fluorite, gold,** some **platinum;** (4) Linville Mt., mines—**hematite, itacolumite, graphite, menaccanite, pyrophyllite** (radiated); (5) High Peak, N .3 mi., area—**garnets;** (6) Scott's Hill, area mines —**cerargyrite, gold, psilomelane, pyrite, native silver, zircon;** (7) South Mt., area mines—**garnet, graphite, quartz crystals** (clear, enhydros); (8) Sugar Mt., area mines—**asbestos, beryl, gold, magnetite, quartz crystals** (doubly terminated), **rutile;** (9) Tremont Mt., area mines—**chrysoprase.**

BRIDGEWATER, area mines—**garnet, gold, manganese minerals.**

BRINDLE TOWN, area mines—**actinolite, anatase, asbestos, beryl, brookite, chromite, columbite, corundum, epidote, fergusonite, fibrolite, gold, graphite, hematite, kyanite, limonite, magnetite, menaccanite, monazite, montanite, pyrope garnet, rutile, samarskite, smoky quartz crystals, talc, tellurium, tetradymite, tourmaline, tremolite asbestos, xenotime, zircon.**

BURKE CHAPEL (SE part of co.): (1) S ½ mi. on gravel rd., turn rt. on dirt rd. for ½ mi., area S of rd. extending N about .3 mi. to N side of rd.— **quartz crystals** (clear, smoky, rutilated); (2) go 4 mi. on unnumbered rd. to Rte. 18, then rt. for 4 mi.: (a) area on N side of rd.—**quartz crystals;** (b) N .3 mi., in **mica** schist outcrop—**garnets.**

GLEN ALPINE, W, in pegmatite dike exposure—**pegmatite gems.**

MORGANTON: (1) area: (a) Burkmont Mt., area pegmatites—gem **beryl;** (b) Buzzard Roost Knob, and (c) Walker's Knob—gem **beryl;** (d) South Mts. (cf. Blue Ridge region described under Burke, McDowell, Rutherford counties), area pegmatites and **mica** mines—**aquamarine, beryl, feldspar** and **quartz crystals;** (2) E 4 mi., and 1 mi. S of U.S. 70, the Grill prospect— **quartz crystals;** (3) S 4–6 mi., area mines—**actinolite, chlorite, chrysolite, breunnerite, garnet, hematite, magnetite, serpentine, tremolite asbestos;** (4) S 8 mi., and ½ mi. E of Walker, the Walker prospect—**aquamarine, beryl** (golden, green);

(5) SE 8 mi., area gravels along Laurel Cr.—**pyrope garnets;** (6) SW 9 mi., pegmatite outcrops—**aquamarine, beryl;** (7) N 4 mi., an old mine—**corundum** (altered into **damourite**), **galena, quartz crystals;** (8) N 13 mi., on Kingy Branch (tributary of Upper Cr.), the Brown Mt. Mine, in quartz veins —**gold.**

MORGANTON SPRINGS, area mines—**titanite.**

RAMSEY, NE 1.6 mi., at Shoup's Ford, many old area mines and prospects —**corundum, beryl, diamonds, garnet, gem kyanite, sillimanite, tourmaline.**

BURKE, McDOWELL, RUTHERFORD COS.

AREA. The Blue Ridge region in which the South Mountain Belt, comprising the South Mountain Range, forms one of the most prominent eastern outliers of the Appalachian Mountain system, constitutes the most important **gold**-bearing belt in North Carolina. The auriferous region embraces from

250 to 300 square miles, and panning for **gold** can be successfully done in practically all streams.

CABARRUS CO.

AREA (with overlap into S Rowan Co., *q.v.*): (1) very many old mines, going back to pre–Civil War times (cf. on regional topographic maps)— **azurite, gold, malachite, quartz crystals, scheelite, sphalerite**, etc.; (2) specifically: (a) Cosby's Mine—**cuproscheelite, siderite, scheelite, stilpnomelane, wolframite**; (b) Cullin's Mine—**azurite, cuprite** (cubes), **malachite, pseudomalachite, scheelite, tetradymite**; (c) Flowe's Mine—**barite, scheelite, tungstate of lime** (rhombic crystals), **wolframite**; (d) McMakin's Mine—**argentite, barite, galena, goslarite, magnesite, proustite, pyromorphite, pyrolusite, rhodochrosite, native silver, sphalerite, tetrahedrite** (var. **freibergite**); (e) Union Copper Mine—**copper minerals, native copper** (as arborescent or crystalline plates).

CONCORD: (1) area: (a) mines—**agate, bornite, chalcopyrite, gold, hyalite opal, goethite** (acicular crystals in **quartz**), **malachite, magnetite, quartz crystals** (rose, rutilated), **tourmaline**; (b) regional fields and stream gravels between town and HARRISBURG—**agate, carnelian, chalcedony, common opal**; (2) SE, the Firness Mine—**barite, epidote, malachite, scheelite**; (3) SE 7 mi.: (a) the Phoenix Mine—**gold**; (b) S 1 mi., the Tucker (California) Mine, and (c) nearby other mines and prospects—**gold**;

(4) SE 10 mi., the Rocky River Mine—**chalcopyrite, galena, gold, pyrite, sphalerite**; (5) SE 11 mi., the Allen Furr Mine (23 mi. E of CHARLOTTE)— **gold, pyrite, sphalerite**; (6) S 13 mi., the Pioneer Mills group of mines (not worked since Civil War days)—**barnhardite, chalcocite, chalcopyrite**, some **gold, molybdenite, molybdite**; (7) SE 12 mi., the Nugget (Biggers) Mine— coarse **gold, galena**.

FAGGART: (1) E 1½ mi., the Barnhardt Mine—**gold**; (2) NE 3 mi., the Faggart Mine—**gold**.

GEORGEVILLE: (1) NE 1 mi., the Buffalo Mine—**auriferous pyrite**; (2) SE 1½ mi., the Reed Mine—**gold**. This is the site of the first discovery of **gold** in North Carolina. More than 150 lbs. of **gold,** in huge solid nuggets, were taken from the Reed property, some nuggets weighing between 15 and 28 lbs. each. Between 1804 and 1846, an estimated $1 million in **gold** nuggets was obtained. The last nugget of any size was discovered on April 11, 1896, weighing 10.072 lbs. (3) N 2½ mi., the Crayton Mine—**gold** (minute grains in **quartz**), **pyrite**.

MOUNT PLEASANT: (1) SW 5 mi., the Harkey Mine, veins in diorite— **chalcopyrite, gold, marcasite, pyrite**; (2) SW 8 mi., the Snyder Mine—**gold**.

TUCKER, N 3 mi., the Quaker City Mine—**gold**.

CALDWELL CO.

AREA: (1) S part of co., a broad band of **mica** schist runs NE to SW, in all regional outcrops—**sillimanite** (best in nodular form); (2) Davis Mt.,

W slope near the river, the Baker Mine—**anglesite, chrysotile asbestos, cerussite, galena, marmolite, pyromorphite, serpentine;** (3) Grandmother's Mt., area placers—**gold, pyrite, quartz.**

COLLETTSVILLE: (1) N 1.7 mi., in rd. cuts near Rte. 90—massive **epidote, pyrite** cubes; (2) S, the Hercules Mine (12 mi. N of MORGANTON in Burke Co.)—**gold.**

DUDLEY SHOALS: (1) SW ½ mi., the Teague Farm (via Cedar Valley rd. W 1 mi., turn S for ½ mi. on country rd.)—**sillimanite** nodules; (2) N 3 mi., the Travis prospect—**quartz crystals.**

HARTLAND, NW 1½ mi., adjoining mines (Miller, Scott Hill)—**gold.**

HARTWELL, pegmatite exposures inside town limits—**beryl, garnets.**

LENOIR: (1) SE 3 mi., on Hibreton Mt. (4½ mi. W of U.S. 321), area—gemmy **feldspar;** (2) NW 4 mi., on NE slope of Bee Mt., the Bee Mt. Mine, in **garnetiferous mica** gneiss with pegmatite intrusions—**gold;** (3) E 7½ mi., on low ridge 1.3 mi. N of Rte. 90 in the Oak Hill district: (a) area old **mica** mines—**garnets, sillimanite,** massive **quartz;** (b) 2 mi. E of Oak Hill Sta. on Rte. 90, the Land farm—**quartz crystals;** (4) E 9 mi. (2 mi. N of Rte. 90), the Reid prospect—**feldspar** and **quartz crystals,** etc.

YADKIN VALLEY, area 2 mi. NW of Rte. 268 and 5 mi. E of U.S. 321, the Broyhill **mica** deposit—**beryl, garnets.**

CASWELL CO.

AREA, the Carolina Igneous Belt (comprising Caswell Co. and parts of PERSON, ALAMANCE, GUILFORD, RANDOLPH, DAVIDSON, DAVIE, ROWAN, CABARRUS, MECKLENBURG counties, and the E fringes of LINCOLN and GASTON counties), the second most important **gold-**bearing section of N.C., varying from 15 to 30 mi. wide, very many old mines—**gold.** (The gold deposits are confined largely to GUILFORD, DAVIDSON, ROWAN, and MECKLENBURG counties.)

BLANCH, area old **mica** mines—**allanite, mica.**

LEASBURG, W 3 mi., area prospects—**chlorite, epidote, tourmaline** (fibrous).

MILTON: (1) area old **mica** mines—**allanite, mica;** (2) SW 3¾ mi., the Slaughter prospect—**allanite.**

SEMORA, area old **mica** mines—**allanite, mica.**

YARBORO, area mine dumps—**albite, garnets, quartz crystals.**

CATAWBA CO.

AREA: (1) extreme SW corner of co.: (a) E of Rte. 18 and about 1 mi. E of the Burke Co. line, between two tributaries of Jacob Cr., the Bessie Hudson Mine—**almandite garnets,** gem **beryl;** (b) the Tallent prospect (5 mi. NE of TOLUCA in Lincoln Co.)—**quartz crystals, sillimanite;** (2) Hooper's Quarry—**calcite, gold, graphite, pyrite.**

CATAWBA, 4½ mi. slightly S of E, the Shuford Mine (and quarry) on the

Southern RR, in numerous auriferous **quartz** seams—**gold,** with **calcite, magnetite, rose quartz.**

CONOVER: (1) area N and W, old **mica** mines: (a) 1 mi. from town, the Bowman Mine (extending 7 mi. to the Hefner Mine)—**apatite, beryl, feldspar crystals, garnets, mica, staurolites;** (b) 2½ mi. N of Wray's Gin on Rte. 10 and 2.6 mi. NE of co. line, the Abernathy Water Mine—**quartz crystals** (with inclusions); (2) NW 4½ mi., the Drum Mine—**apatite,** yellow **beryl, garnets, mica;** (3) N 7 mi. on Rte. 16, turn E on dirt rd. for .9 mi., area on E side—**corundum.**

DRUMS CROSSROADS, SE 2.3 mi., exposures—**steatite.**

HICKORY: (1) area mines—**amethysts, chalcopyrite, garnets, graphite, hematite, limonite, magnetite, muscovite mica, pyrite, pyrrhotite, pyrolusite, quartz crystals;** (2) NE 5 mi., near the Catawba R. dam, the Sigmon Mine—**apatite** (green crystals).

MAIDEN: (1) many area mines and prospects—**gold;** (2) E 6 air mi. (on Rte. 16 E for 7 mi., then S for ¾ mi. on co. rd.), pegmatite dike—**pegmatite minerals.**

NEWTON: (1) many area mines and prospects—**gold;** (2) E 2 mi. (and N of Rte. 10), at McLin Cr., deposit—**steatite.**

SOUTH CREEK, area 1 mi. NE of Rte. 16—**steatite.**

CHATHAM CO.

AREA, Battle's Dam, area mines—**garnets, hematite, manganese minerals** (such as **psilomelane**), **rose quartz.**

BENNETT: (1) area old **copper** mines and prospects—**chalcedony, jasper, rose quartz** along with **copper minerals;** (2) SE 4½ mi.: (a) the Phillips prospect (via Rte. 22 for 2.6 mi. SE, turn E 2 mi. to crossrds., prospect on the N); and (b) the adjoining Bear Creek prospect—**azurite, malachite, pyrite, quartz crystals,** etc.; (3) the Clegg Mine—**azurite, bornite, calcite, chalcopyrite, cerussite, chrysocolla, cuprite, galena, pseudomalachite, malachite, pyrite.**

PITTSBORO, N 1½ mi. on Rte. 87, in area rd. cuts—**limonite** (pseudomorphs after **pyrite**).

SILK HOPE, NW to co. line area (3.3 mi. SE of SNOW CAMP in Alamance Co.), an old **pyrophyllite** mine—gemmy **chert, quartz crystals** (with **pyrite** inclusions).

CHEROKEE CO.

AREA: (1) Hanging Dog Cr., area gravels—**staurolites, tourmaline;** (2) in stream gravels where Peachtree Rd. crosses Valley R.—**chloritoid** (dark green **mica**), **ottrelite, metamorphic minerals;** (3) Little Snowbird Mts.: (a) area at headwaters of Vengeance Cr.—**calcite, garnet, marble, quartz crystals, staurolites;** (b) area from Vengeance Cr. to VALLEYTOWN, a distance of 12–15 mi. along the lower slopes of the mts., many "diggings" in the drift —**gold, staurolites;** (4) very many countywide exposures of schists in the mt. regions—**metamorphic gems** and **minerals, chloritoid, ottrelite.**

ANDREWS, MARBLE, area 2 mi. from Palmer Museum, on the Bettis Bros. farm—**staurolites.**

MARBLE: (1) area cr. beds, dike exposures, gravel pits—**sillimanite** (cat's-eye), **staurolites;** (2) SE 1 mi.: (a) Valley R. gravels—**placer gold;** (b) between Parson's and Burnt branches—**almandite garnets;** (3) N 1.3 mi., in Hyatt Cr., Fishermare Branch, and Allmon Cr.—**almandite garnets, staurolites;** (4) NW, in the Snowbird Mts., the Parker Mine—**garnets, gold, staurolites.**

MURPHY: (1) area mines—**cerussite, dravite** (brown **tourmaline**), **galena, gold, lead, pyrolusite, sillimanite, silver, talc, tremolite asbestos;** (2) the No. 6 Mine—**calcite, argentiferous galena, gold, tremolite asbestos;** (3) N 1½ mi., the Hitchcock Mine—**dravite, marble, sillimanite, steatite, tremolite;** (4) SW ½ mi., area along U.S. 64—**limonite** cubes; (5) SW 4.2 mi., the Metals and Minerals Mine—cf. item (3).

UNAKA: (1) area gravels, pits, etc.—**staurolites;** (2) E ½ mi. on rd. toward MURPHY, gravels of Beaverdam Cr.—**agate, epidote,** pink **feldspar,** placer **gold, jasper, petrified wood, smoky quartz crystals, staurolites.**

CLAY CO.

AREA: (1) E-central part of co. N of U.S. 64, Buck Cr.: (a) area mines in peridotite-dunite—pink **corundum, smaragdite** (green **amphibolite**), **anorthite feldspar, olivine crystals, spinel, zoisite;** (b) the Cullakanee Mine (6 mi. N of the Ga. state line and 20 mi. SW of FRANKLIN, Macon Co., via U.S. 64)—**bronzite, corundum, opal, peridot;** (c) the Maney Cut—pink **corundum, smaragdite;** (d) S side of U.S. 64, area boulders—**unakite;** (e) the Buck Creek Dude Ranch, SW .3 mi., the Herbert Mine (on Little Buck Cr.)—**corundum;** (f) the Buck Creek Campground, area—**serpentine;** (2) The Cat Eye Cut (600 ft. W of Chestnut Knob)—**"cat eye" corundum** (asteriated); (3) Chestnut Knob, area—**corundum** (white, star); (4) Park Gap (near Chunky Gal Mt.): (a) area—**garnets;** (b) on NE slope of the mt., area—**staurolites;** (5) Red Corundum Knob, area—**actinolite,** pink **corundum, gem kyanite, olivine crystals, ruby, serpentine.**

BRASSTOWN: (1) area prospects and mines—**gold;** (2) W ½ mi., on N side of U.S. 64, area—**garnets;** (3) E 1 mi., on Tusquitee Cr., near HAYESVILLE, *q.v.,* area—**staurolites;** (4) in rd. cuts along Greasy Cr.—**staurolites;** (5) Greasy Cr. gravels—**almandite garnets, staurolites.**

HAYESVILLE: (1) Corundum Knob (½ mi. W of the Bureau of Mines Sta.), area—**corundum** (two-toned); (2) E, on Penland Bald, area—**garnets;** (3) E 12 mi., near U.S. 64, area **amphibole** exposure—**rubies, sapphires, smaragdite.**

SHOOTING CREEK: (1) area exposures and gravels—**hyalite opal geodes;** (2) N 1.8 mi. on U.S. 64, near Muskrat Rd., in outcrop of **mica** schist—pink **corundum;** (3) W, near Spring Hollow, area—**rutile crystals;** (4) W, at Elf: (a) area—**corundum** (red, in nodules found in green **amphibolite**), **opal, quartz crystals, smaragdite;** (b) as float around Lake Chatuge—**corundum** (deep to gray blue, pink), **smaragdite;** (c) area near Myers Chapel—**corundum.**

CLEVELAND CO.

CASAR: (1) area, NE via Rte. 10 into NE corner of co.: (a) Carpenter's Knob, .3 mi. NE of rd. following E side of the hill, on W bank of a farm rd. trending NW, area—corundum (black, blue, gray) enclosed in sillimanite; (b) 1.6 mi. W of TOLUCA, Lincoln Co., on SE-flowing tributary of Knob Cr., the A. F. Hoyle Mine—apatite, autunite, garnet, zeolite minerals; (c) area around St. Peters Church, numerous old mines—gem crystals; (d) mining area centered at Carpenter Grove Church—gem crystals; (2) S, on farms reached after crossing Ward's Cr. W of town and along W fork of the Broad R.—quartz crystals (rutilated); (3) N, on N side of Old Sheep Knob (just N of a dirt rd.), area mines—corundum; (4) W 2 mi., area—agate, quartz crystals (rutilated); (5) SW 2½ mi., the Cooke Mine—beryl; (6) SW 3½ mi., the Elliott Mine—beryl.

FALLSTON: (1) E 1 mi. and N 3.8 mi.: (a) the Norman Mine—garnets, tourmaline; (b) ¼ mi. NW of this mine, the Gantt Mine (½ mi. W of the rd.)—graphic granite; (2) E 1.3 mi., on S side of the main rd., the Fallston prospect—smoky quartz crystals; (3) SE 3 mi., the Mauney Carpenter Mine—quartz crystals (clear, smoky).

GROVER, N 2½ mi. on U.S. 29E, then N on co. rd., pegmatite—aquamarine.

HOLLYBUSH, W side of Broad R., pegmatite—yellow beryl.

KINGS MOUNTAIN (major mineral district): (1) area gravels—diamonds; (2) the Foote Mineral Co. Mine, more than 30 gems and minerals, including —apatite, beryl, bikitaite, calcite, cassiterite, childrenite, fairfieldite (hydrous phosphate of calcium and manganese, as exceptional crystals), moonstone feldspar, purpurite, rhodochrosite, roscherite, spodumene, black tourmaline, vivianite; (3) 1 mi. NW of jct. of U.S. 74 and U.S. 29, the Bun Patterson Mine—beryl; (4) the Mountain Mine—alunogen, arsenopyrite, galena, garnet, gold, graphite, muscovite mica, melanterite, pyrite (abundant crystals), rock crystal, tourmaline.

LATTIMORE: (1) S ½ mi., the Jones Mine—milky quartz crystals; (2) SE 1 mi., the Hunt Mine, abundant—quartz crystals; (3) W 1½ mi., the Joe Humphries Mine—beryl, feldspar crystals (penetrating massive quartz), tourmaline; (4) the L. Yates Brooks Farm, area—anatase (blue crystals), muscovite mica; (5) 1 mi. from the Yates farm (inquire way), area—anatase crystals, muscovite mica.

POLKVILLE: (1) NE .9 mi., the Gettys No. 1 Mine—mica, marcasite, quartz crystals, spar, sillimanite; (2) NW 3¾ mi. and just W of Duncan's Cr., dumps of the Lattimore Mine, abundant—beryl, quartz crystals, black tourmaline.

SHELBY: (1) area mines (very many), all highly mineralized: (a) N to Union Church and Double Shoals; (b) W to MOORESBORO and LATTIMORE —anatase crystals, actinolite, beryl, emerald, magnetite, moonstone feldspar, muscovite mica (large books), quartz crystals, tourmaline, etc.; (c) S along Rte. 18 all way to BLACKSBURG, Cherokee Co., S.C., in regional fields, streams, cut banks, etc.—gem crystals;

(2) S on Rtes. 18 and 150 at the forks, then W 1.8 mi. to a secondary rd., turn S ½ mi.: (a) area along the Broad R., in fields on both sides of rd.,

several localities—**quartz crystals;** (b) Charon Church crossrd., S 1 mi., area —**quartz crystals;** (c) ¼ mi. due N of the Stice Dam, area—**corundum** (bronze, gray), **quartz crystals;** (d) 1.3 mi. due E of EARL, on tributary of Buffalo Cr., area—**aquamarine, garnets;** (e) 1½ mi. E of the Stice Dam, the Turner Mine—**aquamarine;** (f) 1 mi. NE of the dam, the Old Plantation Mine—**gem beryl;**

(3) N, along Little Harris Cr. near rd. to DOUBLE SHOALS, numerous **mica** mines: (a) 1 to 1¾ mi. SW of Union Church, mines (especially the Spangler Mine)—**garnets, rock crystal** (with green **mica** inclusions); (b) 1.1 mi. S of the church, the Weathers Mine—abundant **garnets;** (c) 2½ mi. SE of Union Church, area—**garnets, mica;** (d) on N side of cr. by DOUBLE SHOALS, the Bowen Mine—**garnets, mica;** (e) ½ mi. from the Bowen Mine, at edge of woods S of Little Harris Cr., the Harris Mine—**feldspar crystals, garnets, smoky quartz crystals;** (f) 1½ mi. SW of DOUBLE SHOALS on S side of dirt rd., the Mary Gold Mine—**sillimanite** (gem);

(4) NW 2.7 mi., the Niagara Mine—crystals of **feldspar, pyrite, quartz;** (5) NW 3.3 mi., the McGinnis Mine—crystals of **feldspar, pyrite, quartz;** (6) NW 4¾ mi., the Martin Mine—crystals of **feldspar, pyrite, quartz;** (7) S 30° W 4¾ mi., near E bank of First Broad R. and ½ mi. NE of the dam, area—**aquamarine, beryl, emeralds, mica (biotite, muscovite), smoky quartz crystals, tourmaline;** (8) SW 4¾ mi., the Allen property, area 6-ft.-thick dike —**aquamarine, emeralds, moonstone, rutilated quartz crystals;** (9) W 6.2 mi., near creek ¼ mi. S of U.S. 74, the McSwain Mine—**garnets, sillimanite;** (10) SW 6.2 mi., the Mill Race Mine, in **mica** schist—**garnets.**

CUMBERLAND CO.

AREA: (1) Countywide stream gravels and alluvial deposits, gravel pits, excavations, rd. cuts, etc.—**agate, chalcedony, chert, jasper, common opal, agatized wood;** (2) Cape Fear R. and tributaries, gravel beds—cf. (1).

DAVIDSON CO.

AREA, very many regional mines—**chalcopyrite, gold, arsenical pyrite, tetradymite.**

CID: (1) area mines—cf. AREA; (2) W, the Emmons (Davidson) Mine (12 mi. SE of LEXINGTON)—**calcite, chlorite, gold, siderite, silver.**

LEXINGTON: (1) area S and E, noted old **gold-silver** belt, many abandoned mines—**gold, silver, marcasite, pyrite,** etc.; (2) E 6 mi., the Conrad Hill Mine—**chalcopyrite, limonite, malachite, silver, specular hematite.**

LINWOOD, NW 5 mi. and 1 mi. S of TYRO, area—**amethysts.**

SILVER HILL (5 mi. SE of LEXINGTON, an old mining town): (1) area mines—**anglesite, argentite, calamine, calcite, cerussite** (fine crystals, massive, pseudomorphic after **pyrite**), **chalcanthite, chalcocite, chalcopyrite, cuprite, argentiferous galena, goslarite, malachite, melaconite, pyromorphite, silver, sphalerite, stolzite, wavellite** (green, brown, black, colorless, yellow), **zoisite**(?).

(2) N ¼ mi., old mine—**argentite, feldspar crystals, malachite, pyromorphite, scheelite, wavellite;** (3) S 1 mi., on W side of Flat Swamp Cr. Valley,

NW of the Silver Valley crossrds., the Silver Valley Mine—**chalcopyrite, galena, gold, pyrite, silver, sphalerite;** (4) W 5 mi., David Beck's Mine—**chalcopyrite, gold, arsenical pyrite, tetradymite.**

THOMASVILLE: (1) SE 1½ mi., the Loftin Mine—**gold;** (2) SE 2 mi., the Lalor (Allen) Mine: (a) on old dumps—**copper pyrites, gold, limonite, hematite;** (b) ½ mi. W of the Lalor Mine, the Eureka Mine—**gold.**

DAVIE CO.

AREA mines, including Butler, County Line, Isaac, Allen, and several old mines on Callahan Mt.—**gold.**

FARMINGTON, E 2 mi. to Rte. 801, turn N for 1½ mi., area pegmatite exposures—**autunite, columbite.**

OAKS FERRY, W 1 mi., near the Yadkin R. on the Hairston farm—gemmy **orbicular gabbro-diorite** (a mixture of whitish **feldspar** with **hornblende** "eyes").

DURHAM CO.

BETHESDA, W of U.S. 70, area fields, cuts, gravels, etc., as float—**silicified wood.**

DURHAM: (1) W, near jct. of U.S. 75 and Rte. 98, area float—**petrified wood;** (2) inquire in town rock shops for directions to a major quarry about 15 mi. distant—**calcite, biotite mica, kobellite** (steel-gray var. of **jamesonite**), **siderite** (gemmy olive green crystals).

WEAVER, gravels of the Eno R.—**agatized wood.**

FORSYTH CO.

KERNERSVILLE, area fields, rd. cuts, gravels, etc.—**chrysolite, enstatite** (var. **bronzite**), **tourmaline.**

WINSTON-SALEM: (1) area quarries, pits, deposits, etc.; and (2) S 4 mi., mines—**halloysite, hematite, magnetite, manganese garnet.**

FRANKLIN CO.

AREA: (1) N part of co., many pegmatite outcrops—**beryl, mica;** (2) the Portis Mine—**diamonds, gold.**

CENTERVILLE: (1) area: (a) the Taylor place on Rte. 561 W of the crossrds., outcrop—**amethysts** (royal purple); (b) old mine dumps near Rte. 58 on rd. to Inez—**gold;** (c) near Sandy Cr., on S side of first rd. out of town leading NW from Rte. 561, the Van Alston prospect—**gold;** (2) NW several mi., near Rte. 58, many pegmatites—**beryl, feldspar** and **quartz crystals, tourmaline,** etc.

FRANKLINTON, W 4 mi., several pegmatite outcrops, some mined—**gems, minerals.**

LOUISBURG: (1) area gravels, fields, etc.—**amethysts;** (2) E 18 mi., old placers—**gold, diamonds.**

YOUNGSVILLE: (1) NW 4 mi., the Mitchell Mine, and (2) NW 5 mi., near rd. to POKOMOKE, the Gully Mine, both in pegmatites—**gems, minerals.**

GASTON CO.

ALEXIS: (1) E 2.4 mi., in area fields as float—gem **kyanite-lazulite, rutile crystals;** (2) Clubb's District (variously called): (a) many area mines—blue **corundum, dumortierite,** gem **lazulite,** gem **kyanite, lithiophyllite;** (b) Clubb's Mt., area—**corundum** (red, blue), **damourite, gold, manganese garnet, hematite, magnetite, margarite,** gem-blue **kyanite crystals** (translucent), gem-blue **lazulite, leopardite, muscovite mica, pyrophyllite, quartz crystals, rutile crystals, talc, tourmaline;** (c) Crowder's Mt.—cf. Clubb's Mt. plus **barite, chalcopyrite, emery, argentiferous galena, limonite, menaccanite, monazite, pyrite, sphalerite, topaz.**

BESSEMER CITY: (1) S, in the Devil's Workshop area—**goethite;** (2) E 2.3 mi., near Long Creek Church, a pegmatite dike exposure—**apatite, beryl, spodumene.**

CHERRYVILLE, N of Rte. 277 and E along Little Beaverdam and Beaverdam creeks: (1) at confluence, pegmatite exposure—**cassiterite;** (2) SE 3½ mi., the Big Bess Mine—gem **apatite, beryl, garnet, feldspar** (chatoyant), **marcasite, pyrite, quartz** (blue), **rutile crystals, sillimanite, tourmaline, zircon;** (3) SE 4.3 mi., the Self Mine—**feldspar crystals, smoky quartz, zircon;** (4) SE 5 mi. on Rte. 274, the Huskins Mine—**beryl, garnet, tourmaline.**

CRAMERTON, S, in extreme corner of co.: (1) the Oliver Mine (12 mi. SW of CHARLOTTE, Mecklenburg Co.) on W side of the Catawba R.—**galena,** abundant **gold, pyrite** (this mine is possibly the earliest operated mine in North Carolina, with work traditionally started before the Revolutionary War); (2) the McLean or Rumfeldt Mine (15–16 mi. SW of CHARLOTTE); (3) the Duffie Mine (16 mi. SW of the same town); and (4) the Rhodes Mine (18 mi. SW)—**gold.**

CROWDERS, the King's Mt. area, numerous old mines—**altaite, bismite, calcite, chalcopyrite, galena, gold, magnetite, nagyagite, pyrrhotite, sphalerite, tetrahedrite.**

DALLAS, NW 6 mi., the Long Creek Mine (3 veins)—**gold.**

KING'S MT. STATION: (1) S 1½ mi., the Catawba (King's Mt.) Mine, in limestone—**gold;** (2) E side of King's Mt. and 4 mi. E of the Catawba Mine, the Crowder's Mt. (Caledonia) Mine—**gold.**

GRANVILLE CO.

AREA: (1) N half (with overlap into Person Co. on W), very many regional **copper** and **gold** mines, including: Royster (Blue Wing), Holloway, Mastodon, Buckeye, Pool, Gillis, Copper World, and Yancy—**bornite, chalcocite, native copper, gold, pyrite;** (2) area stream gravels—**topaz;** (3) area mine dumps, rock exposures, etc.—**andalusite, carnelian, malachite;** (4) Reed's Cr. gravels—**agate, jasper, jasp-agate, quartz crystals;** (5) Oak Hill, S, on Mountain Cr.—**agate, jasper;** (6) Long Mt., area—**agate, jasper.**

BULLOCK: (1) E and SE, area exposures, abundant—**pyrite;** (2) NE 1½ mi.: (a) outcrop of metabasalt porphyry—**clinozoisite, epidote, labradorite,** titanite; (b) ½ mi. farther N—**epidote, hornblende, quartz crystals;** (3) NW 6 mi. and ¾ mi. from state line, area—**limonite, hematite, quartz crystals.**

BUTNER, area—**agate, amethyst, jasper.**

CREEDMORE-GRANVILLE-OXFORD, a 15-mi.-long stretch along U.S. 15 and Int. 85, area both sides of highways—**cryptocrystalline quartz gemstones.**

POCOMOKE, N 2 mi., area—**lepidolite** (with **rubellite**).

STEM, 2 mi. distant on Bowling Mt., deposit—**pyrophyllite.**

VIRGILINA: (1) area tó S, many old **copper** mines—**copper minerals, native copper** and **silver, epidote, hematite, malachite,** pink **feldspar, pyrite, quartz;** (2) S 2 mi. and 1 mi. W, the Holloway Mine—cf. AREA item (1); (3) the Blue Wing Church: (a) N, the Blue Wing Mine—**azurite, calcite, argentite, chlorite,** etc.; (b) across rd. from the church, prospect pits—**malachite, specular hematite.**

WILTON, E 2 mi., a granite quarry—**calcite, epidote, feldspar, molybdenite, quartz.**

GUILFORD CO.

BIGSONVILLE, area—**quartz crystals** (green, with **actinolite** and **asbestos** inclusions).

FRIENDSHIP: (1) N, the Tuscarora Iron Mine—**limonite, hematite, magnetite, corundum;** (2) NE, the mine on the McCarvisten farm—**iron minerals.**

GREENSBORO: (1) SW 5 mi., the Fisher Hill Mine—**chalcopyrite, gold, hematite, magnetite, menaccanite, pseudomalachite, pyrite, siderite;** (2) SE 6 mi., the Hodges Hill Mine—**gold, malachite, chalcopyrite, limonite, siderite;** (3) SSW 6 mi., the Mills Hill Mine—cf. Fisher Hill Mine; (4) SW 6 mi., the Twin Mine—**gold;** (5) SW 8 mi., the Gardner Mine—**chrysocolla, gold, malachite;** (6) S 9 mi., the North Carolina (Fentress) Mine, old, with **gold** vein traced for 3 mi. along the outcrop—**copper minerals, gold.**

JAMESTOWN: (1) NE 2–3 mi., the Gardner Hill Mine—cf. item (5) under GREENSBORO; (2) S 2¼ mi., on N side of Rte. 29, the North State (McCullough) Mine—**chalcotrichite, native copper, copper pyrites** (fine crystals), **cuprite, malachite, gold, siderite.**

HALIFAX CO.

AREA, all exposures of Quaternary gravels throughout co.—**petrified wood.**

BRINKLEYVILLE, S, on property of the Boy Scouts of America, area—**chalcopyrite, molybdenite, pyrite, sericite.**

GLENVIEW, W 1.7 mi., old mine—**gold.**

ROANOKE RAPIDS, the Gaston Ore Banks—**limonite, hematite** (iridescent, specular), **magnetite.**

HAYWOOD CO.

AREA: (1) several pegmatite mines in co. are open on a fee basis; make inquiry at any rock shop—**tourmaline** and other gems, etc.; (2) Hall's Mine—**chlorite, chrysolite, corundum, talc, tremolite.**

CANTON, NW 4 mi., the Presley Mine—**albite, amphibolite, corundum** (blue, gray, altered into **damourite** and **albite**), **damourite** (large crystals and scales), **sapphire** (clear, color-zoned, opaque, star).

HAZELWOOD, S 21° E 3.9 air mi., on SW slope of Roberson Ridge between two unnamed branches of Deep Gap Cr., the Big Ridge Mine—**ankerite, apatite, garnets, hedenbergite, margarodite, menaccanite, mica (biotite, muscovite), pyrrhotite, quartz crystals, tourmaline.**

WAYNESVILLE: (1) area, Newfound Gap, pegmatite—**rubies;** (2) N 2 mi., old mine—**talc, tremolite asbestos;** (3) S 2 mi., on Richland Cr., old mine—**damourite, garnet, limonite, psilomelane;** (4) SE 6 mi., on the Pigeon R., the J. H. Edmondson property at Retreat—**almandite garnet, corundum,** gem **kyanite.**

HENDERSON CO.

BAT CAVE: N on Rte. 9: (1) 1 mi., in gneissic outcrops—**moss epidote;** (2) ½ mi. farther, in rd. cut—**unakite.**

ETOWAH, on SE slope of Forge Mt., the Boylston Creek Mine (12 mi. W of HENDERSONVILLE)—**gold.**

MILLS RIVER, W, along the Green R. on the S side of the Blue Ridge, area—granular **calcite, xanthitane, zircon.**

TUXEDO: (1) area pegmatite mines, in a zone running NE to SW for several mi. semiparallel with the Green R.: (a) ½ mi. E of town, the Freeman Mine; (b) 1.8 mi. SW of town, the Pace Mine; (c) ½ mi. E, the Jones Mine; and (d) 3 mi. SW of the Freeman Mine—**apatite, epidote, garnet, octahedrite, sphene,** abundant **zircon;** (2) W shore of Lake Summit, at W end—**agate.**

IREDELL CO.

AREA, countywide scattered outcrops of **quartz**—**quartz crystals, specular hematite.**

HARMONY-TURNERSBURG, along the South Yadkin R., area—**beryl, corundum, tourmaline,** etc.

MOORESVILLE, WNW 4½ mi., area—**agate, amethyst, quartz crystals.**

NEW HOPE: (1) area old **mica** mines—**beryl, garnet, mica, quartz crystals, tourmaline,** etc.; (2) ½ mi. S of the post office, the McClelland prospect—**beryl, quartz crystals;** (3) SW 2 mi., the Campbell prospect—**beryl, rock crystal** (various colors).

STATESVILLE: (1) area: (a) the Statesville Quarry—**oligoclase sunstone;** (b) the Cook farm, ½ mi. W, area, and 1½ mi. S, area—**agate, amethysts, quartz crystals;** (2) area fields just N of town—**amethysts;** (3) N on U.S. 21 and 1.6 mi. N of the Prison Camp—**corundum** (pale blue); (4) W, at the Acme (Collins) Mine—**sapphires** (in stream gravels behind a drive-in theater; old mine dumps have been built over);

(5) S 3 mi., area—**agate, amethysts, quartz crystals;** (6) W 5 mi., near old city airport, area—**zircon;** (7) S 12½ mi., area—**agate, amethyst, quartz crystals;** (8) SW 14 mi., at Snow Creek: (a) N, on the Campbell property;

cf. also item (3) under NEW HOPE—beryl (golden, green), white quartz, black tourmaline; (b) Fox Mt., area—rutile crystals; (9) NW 14 mi.: (a) on farms along Rte. 115; (b) S of Rhyne's store—citrine, quartz crystals (smoky, clear, some with inclusions of colored clay); (c) ½ mi. N of Rhyne's store, a massive outcrop—rose quartz.

JACKSON CO.

AREA: (1) countywide cr. gravels, particularly along the S slopes of the Blue Ridge, e.g., near HOGBACK, Chimney Top Mts., and CASHIERS, q.v., placers—gold; (2) regional pegmatite outcrops—golden beryl; (3) confluence of Johns Cr. with Caney Fork, a ridge 1¼ mi. SSE, outcrop—golden beryl; (4) E-central border, near Pinhook Gap, the McCall Mine—feldspar, garnet, mica, quartz crystals, tourmaline, uranium minerals; (5) Halls Sta., area—almandite garnets; (6) the Wolf Creek Mine—chalcocite, chalcopyrite, chrysocolla, native copper, malachite; (7) 1¾ mi. E of summit of Whiteside Mt. and ½ mi. NE of Whiteside Cove, the Grimshawe Mine—golden beryl; (8) SW of Toxaway Mt. and ¼ mi. NW of U.S. 64, pegmatite outcrop—beryl, aquamarine, garnets, black tourmaline, etc.; (9) S of U.S. 64 on Transylvania Co. line: (a) area mines, especially the Rice Mine—aquamarine, sapphire; (b) along S shore of Sapphire Lake, the Sapphire Mining Co. Mine—sapphires.

BALSAM, S 57° E 2 air mi., the Big Flint (Grassy Ridge) Mine—biotite mica, garnets.

CASHIERS: (1) E 4¼ mi., between Fairfield Lake and a tributary of Horsepasture R., in peridotite exposure spanned by U.S. 64 and extending to Little Hogback Mt. on the N—corundum; (2) Sheepcliff Mt., the Sheepcliff Mine —aquamarine, golden beryl, feldspar, garnets (various colors), mica, quartz crystals, radioactive minerals; (3) Whiteside Mt., area old mines—pegmatite gems; (4) cf. also item (7) under AREA.

CULLOWHEE: (1) the Cullowhee Copper Mine—chalcocite, chalcopyrite, malachite, melaconite; (2) S 41° W 3½ air mi. and 2,000 ft. NW of Presley Cr., on a steep E-facing slope (elev. 3,000 ft.), the Bowers Mine—rum mica.

DILLSBORO, S 23° W 7½ air mi., the Engle Cope Mine (above Savannah Cr. and U.S. 23, about ½ mi. W of the Cowee sawmill)—mica (biotite, muscovite), garnets, pyrite, pyrrhotite.

HOGBACK, the Hogback Mine—chromite, chrysolite, corundum, damourite, dudleyite, margarite, quartz crystals (drusy), rutile in corundum (rare), tourmaline.

MONTVALE: (1) area stream gravels—ruby, sapphire; (2) the Grimshawe Mine—aquamarine, gem corundum.

SAPPHIRE: (1) area stream gravels along border of Transylvania Co. line—golden beryl, corundum; (2) SSW 2 mi., the Beryl Mines (½ mi. N of summit of Sassafras Mt.)—golden beryl, corundum; (3) the Sapphire and Whitewater mines—golden beryl, corundum.

WEBSTER: (1) near town, an outcrop—gem olivine; (2) area dunite outcrops—bronzite (altered enstatite), websterite (bronzite-diopside); (3) area mines—actinolite, chalcedony, chromite, chrysolite, corundum, deweylite, enstatite, genthite, magnesite (crystalline, earthy), marmolite, penninite,

pyrolusite, drusy quartz crystals, serpentine, talc, tremolite, wad; (4) SE, via Rtes. 107 and 116, area deposits—**actinolite, bronzite, chromite, diopside, garnierite, genthite, goethite** (botryoidal), **drusy quartz crystals, serpentine, steatite, websterite** (mixture of **bronzite** and **diopside**); (5) large pegmatite dike exposed in W-central part of co.—**gems, pegmatite minerals.**

WILLETS: (1) area not far E of town and SYLVIA—**rhodolite garnets;** (2) SE 1 mi., on Sugarloaf Mt., via U.S. 19A and old rd., a mine—**garnets.**

LINCOLN CO.

AREA: (1) an extensive **tin-spodumene** mining belt shared with adjoining co.: (a) regional old mines, and (b) regional stream gravels, as float— **cassiterite nodules** (pegmatites are most exposed SE of LABORATORY and E of U.S. 321); (2) Pumpkin Center, SE 1 mi., old mines dating back to the Civil and Revolutionary wars—**goethite, hematite, tin minerals.**

COTTAGE HOME, area gravels—**diamond.**

DENVER: (1) S 1.3 mi., at the Forney farm—**amethysts, rock crystal;** (2) SW 1¼ mi. and 2 mi. NE of IRON STATION, *q.v.*, a farm—**amethysts.**

FALLSTON: (1) NE 2½ mi. and extending for some distance, series of pegmatite outcrops (some mined)—**gem crystals** and **minerals;** (2) NE 3 mi., the Biggerstaff place (¼ mi. N of residence), the Deadman Mine—**feldspar crystals, garnets, hornblende, quartz crystals, tourmaline;** (3) NE 4 mi. (on way to FLAY, *q.v.*): (a) the Brown and Carbine mines, and (b) the Foster Mines—**beryl, garnets,** blue **quartz,** green **feldspar.**

FLAY (near FALLSTON, *q.v.*): (1) area mines—**apatite, corundum, mica, sillimanite** (schist), **black tourmaline;** (2) S, at the Baxter Mine (off Rte. 274, almost on the Gaston Co. line)—**quartz crystals** (smoky); (3) S 2 mi. and ½ mi. W of Rte. 274, the Eaker Mine—**gem garnets.**

IRON STATION: (1) area all way to DENVER, *q.v.*, in NE part of co., scattered localities—gem **amethysts;** (2) NE 1.7 mi., on the Lynch farm— **amethysts;** (3) NE 2 mi., at the Randleman (Goodsen) farm, fee—museum-quality **amethysts;** (4) NE 4 mi., the Graham Mine—**chalcopyrite, gold.**

LINCOLNTON, near, the Hope Mine—**gold.**

MACPELAM CHURCH, E 2 mi., old mine—**manganese garnets, chalcopyrite, pyrite.**

MACON CO.

BURNINGTOWN (3 mi. N of FRANKLIN), off Rte. 28 via co. rd., in gravels of Burningtown Cr.—**sapphires** (orchid, pink).

ELLIJAY (3 mi. SE of FRANKLIN), the Mincey Mine—**corundum** (various kinds, chatoyant, bronzy, etc.), **ruby, sapphire** (bronze, star).

FRANKLIN ("Gem Capital of the World"): (1) area mines, prospects, and "diggings"—**amethyst, bronzite, epidote, fibrolite, rhodolite garnet, jasper, kyanite, menaccanite, quartz crystals** (dendritic), **rhodochrosite, rubies, rutile crystals, sapphires, sphalerite, staurolites, wad;** (2) E 1½ mi. at Corundum

Hill, in dunite and **serpentine**—industrial **corundum, rubies, sapphires** (blue, green, orchid, pink, yellow; to large size), **bronzite, chromite, olivine crystals;** (3) ESE 4½ mi., on S slope of Higdon Mt. ½ mi. N of U.S. 64, W of Crows Branch Cr. jct. with the Cullasaja R. (part of Corundum Hill), area outcrops (dunite) and mines—**actinolite, anthophyllite, cerolite, chalcedony, chromite, chrysolite, corundum, culsageeite, deweylite, diaspore** (rare), **enstatite, genthite, kerrite, maconite, margarite, magnetite, hyalite opal, penninite, prochlorite, drusy quartz crystals, rock crystal, ruby, rutile** (rare), **sapphire, serpentine, spinel** (crystals, granular), **tourmaline, talc, tremolite, willcoxite;**

(4) E 6½ mi., the Mincey Mine—cf. under ELLIJAY; (5) S, along the Tennessee R., area—**columbite, damourite, garnets, kyanite, staurolites;** (6) NW 1¼ mi. (from center of town), the Allman Cove group of mines—**feldspar, mica (biotite, muscovite), quartz;** (7) N 6 mi., the Cowee Valley (take Rte. 23–141 N 3 mi. from FRANKLIN, turn NW on Rte. 28 about 4 mi. into signposted mining district and up Cowee Cr. past the Cowee Baptist Church): (a) many area mines, fee—**garnets, rubies, sapphires,** etc.; (b) confluence of Calor Fork and Cowee Cr., area gravels—**corundum** (pink, orange, violet, white), **corundum nodules** (in **saprolite**); (c) turn E to the famed Cowee Creek Ruby Tract (of mines) along the Calor Fork of Cowee Cr., e.g., Dale, Demko, Carter, Cowee Valley, Gibson (in creek flume diggings), Holebrook, Rockhound Haven Gem, Shuler, etc., fees charged at all mines—**corundum, garnets, rubies, sapphires.** The regional mine dumps also contain **beryl, bronzite, chromite, fibrolite, gahnite (zinc spinel), gold, hornblende, ilmenite, iolite** (colorless), **kyanite, monazite, pleonaste** (black **spinel), pyrite, quartz crystals, rutile crystals, staurolite** (transparent), **tremolite,** and **zircon.**

HIGHLANDS: (1) in city limits, a pegmatite outcrop just N on U.S. 64—**beryl;** (2) SW on U.S. 64 (NW of town) and W 2 mi. to Dry Falls, then take co. rd. southerly along Turtle Pond Cr.: (a) in area gravels—**corundum, almandite garnets, quartz crystals,** etc.; (b) an old mine in area—**beryl** (common, golden), **feldspar, muscovite mica, quartz crystals, black tourmaline;** (3) 3 mi. out on U.S. 64 turn onto gravel rd. ¾ mi. to Whiteside Mt., area—**almandite garnets;** (4) SE 4½ mi., N of rd. just W of the Jackson Co. line, the Ammon Mine—**amethysts;** (5) SW 5½ mi. on Rte. 106, to Little Scaly Mt.: (a) in area rock exposures, and (b) area mines—**asbestos,** gem **corundum, rutile crystals, serpentine, vermiculite;** (6) 6 mi. out on Rte. 106, the Waggoner Mine (on Abe's Cr.)—**amethysts.**

OTTO (9 mi. S of FRANKLIN): (1) E ⅗ mi.: (a) a mine on Tessentee Cr. —**amethysts** (in **kaolinite** weathered from pegmatite); (b) area stream gravels—**amethysts, garnets;** (c) near headwaters of Tessentee Cr., old mine —**amethysts, beryl, corundum;** (2) mouth of Tessentee Cr.: (a) NE 2 mi., the Connally Mine; and (b) E 4 mi., area gravels—**amethysts, quartz crystals.**

WESTS MILL (6 mi. N of FRANKLIN via Rte. 28), S 1.6 mi. from the Wests Mill bridge to slopes of Mason Mt.: (1) area stream gravels—**corundum** pieces, **garnets, hornblende** and **quartz crystals;** (2) the Rhodolite Mine—**rhodolite garnets** (abundant), **gedrite, hypersthene, biotite mica;** (3) ½ mi. S of crest of Mason Mt., a quarry—**rhodolite garnets, gedrite, hypersthene, kyanite, biotite mica, quartz crystals.**

MADISON CO.

AREA: (1) many rock exposures along co. rds. and hwys.—**unakite;** (2) N parts of co., many localities—**essonite garnet, vesuvianite;** (3) W parts of co., in mined deposits—**limonite, hematite, magnetite, psilomelane, pyrolusite;** (4) Bear Cr., 2 mi. above mouth, area—**calcite, chlorite,** green **coccolite, epidote, garnet** (large crystals), gem **kyanite, magnetite, staurolite, talc;** (5) gravels of Reed's Cr.—**jasper;** (6) Lemon Gap, S ½ mi. on East Fork Cr., area—**allanite.**

BLUFF: (1) area outcrops—**unakite, jasper;** (2) NE 1 mi., old mine—**barite crystals;** (3) SW 2 mi., Roaring Fork Cr.: (a) ½ mi. W of confluence with Meadow Fork, outcrop—**unakite** (green **epidote** with red **feldspar** and white **quartz**); (b) 1 mi. N of confluence with Spring Cr. (which empties into French Broad R.)—**unakite.**

DEMOCRAT, N 1.7 mi. to first E-trending rd. after passing the Pleasant Gap Methodist Church, then ½ mi. to the Carter Mine (at head of Holcombe Branch)—**beryl, chromite, chrysolite, corundum** (pink, white), **culsageeite, hornstone, hyalite opal** (aqua color), **menaccanite, olivine crystals, prochlorite, drusy quartz crystals,** gem **serpentine, spinel, tremolite.**

HOT SPRINGS: (1) area, a new discovery—orange fluorescent **barite crystals;** (2) area gravels, float in fields, rd. cuts, etc.: (a) along the French Broad R., (b) around Knapp's store, and (c) near Reed's Cr.—gem **jasper;** (3) just S and extending to JOE and E to Big Laurel and Walnut creeks, the Max Patch Mts., type locality, with many outcrops in a broad area along the Tennessee border—**unakite, jasper** (as red float in regional stream gravels).

MARSHALL: (1) area—**bornite, calcite, chalcopyrite, epidote, fluorite, galena;** (2) gravel beds of Little Pine Cr.—**rhodolite garnet.**

REDMON: (1) just N, above RR tracks—gem **almandite garnet;** (2) SW 2 mi., on Little Pine Cr., the Little Pine Garnet Mine—**almandite garnets;** (3) SW, near headwaters of Paw Paw Cr., old mine—**barite.**

WALNUT: (1) area exposures, occasional—**staurolites** (many twinned crystals); (2) Walnut Cr., near the French Broad R., area—green **coccolite** in **calcite, phlogopite.**

MACON CO.

AREA: (1) Hanging Dog Cr., gravel beds; and (2) Persimmon Cr.—**staurolites.**

McDOWELL CO.

AREA: (1) stream gravels of co.—**pyrope garnets, placer gold;** (2) area **mica** mines (many)—**garnets, mica,** etc.; (3) Glade Cr., North Muddy Cr., and South Muddy Cr.—**gold, platinum,** etc.; (4) Hunt's Mt., area—**gold, platinum;** (5) Second Broad R., between Vein Mt. and Huntsville Mt., the Vein Mountain Mine—**chalcopyrite, gold, pyrite;** (6) the old toll rd. to Mt.

Mitchell, near Greybeard Mt. (almost on the Buncombe Co. line), pegmatite outcrop—**almandite garnet, autunite, beryl, columbite, smoky quartz crystals, samarskite;** (7) many other pegmatite exposures in area—same.

BRACKETTOWN, in the valley of the headwaters of South Muddy Cr., the Marion Bullion Co. Mine—**chalcopyrite, diamonds, galena, gold, platinum, pyrite, sphalerite.**

DYSARTSVILLE: (1) numerous area old Civil War era **gold** mines, placers—**gold;** (2) South Muddy Cr. crossing of Rte. 26: (a) in creek gravels—**diamonds, gold;** (b) nearby placer mines—**corundum, gold, zircons;** (c) a tributary 1.2 mi. SE of town, the Mills farm—**corundum;** (3) SW 2 mi., on N side of paved rd. to U.S. 221, as float in stream gravels—**corundum.**

GRAPHITEVILLE, area exposures, extending into Buncombe Co.—**graphite, gem kyanite, quartz crystals.**

MARION: (1) S, in pegmatite dike exposures—**gem crystals;** (2) Lincolnville Mt.: (a) area—**rock crystal;** (b) ½ mi. S of North Cove School, on the Gregg and Lonon farms—**psilomelane, pyrolusite;** (c) near the North Cove along Honeycutt Cr. and Tom Cr. N of U.S. 221, in **mica** prospects on the Swofford property—**mica, uranium minerals;** (3) headwaters of North Fork of the Catawba R.—**pyrite, sphalerite;** (4) SW 6 mi., the Sugar Hill area, on the Charles Laney farm—**amethysts.**

NEBO: (1) RR and rd. cuts along Rte. 105—**quartz crystals;** (2) outcrops of **mica** schist in the banks of Lake James, abundant—**garnets.**

OLD FORT: (1) W, in the Brevard Belt, area mines—**graphite;** (2) W 4½ mi., along Mills Cr., area **mica** prospects—**beryl, mica.**

WOODLAWN: (1) quarry near U.S. 221—**calcite** (dogtooth crystals); (2) a few hundred yds. N, area—phantom **quartz crystals.**

MECKLENBURG CO.

AREA, Clear Creek Twp., on a high plateau from which flow McAlpine's Cr. to the SW, Reedy Cr. to NE, and Clear Cr. to SE: (1) the Surface Hill Mine (famed for its yield of large **gold** nuggets)—**chalcopyrite, gold;** (2) old mine on Clear Cr.—**diamonds, gold.**

CALDWELL, area float—**agate, carnelian, chalcedony.**

CHARLOTTE: (1) building excavations in city—**jasper, leopardite;** (2) S ½ mi. from town center, the St. Catherine (Charlotte) Mine, and (3) S 1 mi., the Rudisil Mine—**copper pyrites, gold, iron,** massive **pyrite, silver** (trace); (4) W 2½ mi., the Clark Mine—**gold;** (5) NW 5½ mi., the Capps Mine (between Rossel's Ferry and Beattie's Ford rds.)—**copper minerals, gold** (this mine was long noted for the amount and quality of its ore, from four well-known **quartz** veins); (6) W 9 mi., the Stephen Wilson Mine—**gold;** (7) NW 11 mi., the Hopewell (Kerns) Mine, and other nearby mines and prospects—**copper minerals, gold, pyrite,** etc.

MITCHELL CO.

AREA: This is a generally rugged, mountainous county with so many gem mines that detailed topographic quadrangle maps, or such rockhound maps as are put out by the Baker's Motel and Tainter's New Service in SPRUCE

PINE, *q.v.*, are required for pinpoint accuracy in locating any of the prolific collecting localities. Nearly all such localities are old or active mines, privately owned, and require either permission to enter or payment of a modest fee. Almost all the mines listed here are in the SPRUCE PINE surroundings, although many are presented from local post office centers reached by various roads out of SPRUCE PINE.

(1) Countywide stream gravels and gravel pits—**agate;** (2) Grassy Cr.: (a) area gravels—**aquamarine, golden beryl;** (b) the prehistoric Indian "Sink Hole Mine"—blue **beryl;** (c) the Meadows Mine—blue **beryl;** (3) the Buchanan Mine—**albite, allanite, asbestos, beryl, gummite, manganese garnet (andradite,** black), **graphite, muscovite mica, kyanite, phosphuranylite, yttrogummite** (?).

BAKERSVILLE: (1) nearby Clarence Wilson farm, exposure of a **feldspar** matrix—gem **epidote crystals;** (2) the Kona area, exposures—**epidote;** (3) Medlock Mt., area—**feldspar crystals** (inclusions of glittering **hematite** or **goethite**); (4) SE 1 mi. on White Oak rd., the Pannell Mine (reached by turning left out of town on Rte. 226)—**bronzite, corundum, mica, vermiculite;** (5) SE 1.2 mi., the Pannell farm, exposures—**ruby, sapphire;** (6) S 2½ mi., a mine—**actinolite, chromite, chrysolite, deweylite, enstatite, magnesite, penninite, quartz crystals, rutile** (in **corundum**), **saponite, serpentine, talc, tremolite;**

(7) E 3 mi., area—**albite, epidote;** (8) N 1 mi., at base of Meadows Mt., area—**moonstone, oligoclase crystals** (transparent); (9) NE 1½ mi., Clarence E. Wilson property—**epidote** (doubly terminated crystals); (10) N, on McKinney Cove rd., at Lick Ridge, area—chatoyant **moonstone, epidote** (dark crystals), **sphene;** (11) N on the Roan Mt. rd. (Rte. 261) to area of scenic Roan Mt. (elev. 6,267 ft.): (a) turn W .3 mi. S of CARVERS GAP, *q.v.*, opposite sign "Pete's Crest Farm," a mine—**uranium minerals;** (b) area outcrops on Roan Mt.—**unakite;** (12) NE 7 mi., on the Dillinger farm—gem **kyanite** (bladed green crystals).

BANDANA: (1) the Sink Hole Mine—**albite, beryl, apatite, garnet, kyanite, thulite;** (2) N 9 mi., the Abernathy Mine—**apatite, biotite mica,** various **fluorescent minerals.**

CARVERS GAP: (1) W 1½ mi., on N bank of the Roan Peak rd.—**unakite,** massive green **epidote;** (2) S 3 mi., granite outcrops—**unakite.**

CROSSNORE, N, at the Hanshaw Mine—**garnets.**

FLAT ROCK: (1) area—**chrysoberyl;** (2) from 4 mi. NW of SPRUCE PINE turn N at Lawson Jct. to Rag Branch, pegmatite mine—**hyalite opal** (fluorescent), **thulite, uranium minerals;** (2) the major area mine—**albite, autunite, epidote, garnet, gummite, menaccanite, muscovite mica** (pink, white), **phosphuranylite, uraninite, uranotil, zircon, zoisite** (var. **thulite**).

GILLESPIE GAP (on the Blue Ridge Parkway S of SPRUCE PINE), N 4 mi., turn E on co. rd. 1117 (Carter Ridge rd.) for 1.2 mi., on N side of rd., the Wiseman Aquamarine Mine (no collecting on Sunday)—**aquamarine.**

GLEN AYRE (NE of Spruce Pine): (1) the Biddix place—**moonstone;** (2) NE 2.4 mi. (½ mi. E of Rte. 261), mine owned by Benton McKinney—**orthoclase feldspar** (crystals with **sunstone** sheen).

HAWK (4½ mi. ENE of SPRUCE PINE on co. rd. 1211, about halfway between Rte. 226 and U.S. 19E): (1) N 1 mi., the Hawk Mine—**allanite, apa-**

tite, epidote, oligoclase feldspar (water-clear crystals), pyrite, thulite, black tourmaline; (2) E 1 mi., the Stagger Weed Mine—coral feldspar, milky quartz; (3) the Sugar Tree Mine—garnets (huge clear crystals); (4) S, at the Clarissa Mine—gem garnets; (5) E 2.6 mi.: (a) old mine dumps—corundum, kyanite, ruby, sapphire, tremolite; (b) the Dillinger farm—ruby, sapphire.

INGALLS, W on co. rd. 1143 (area starting 3 mi. E of SPRUCE PINE leading from main hwy.), area fields, cuts, etc.—actinolite crystals (in boulders), foliated talc, steatite.

KINGS MOUNTAIN, the Foote Mineral Co. Mine—cassiterite, spodumene.

LINVILLE FALLS, E 4 mi., at Wiseman View, area—dendritic sandstone (polishable), quartz crystals.

LITTLE SWITZERLAND (on the Blue Ridge Parkway), NW via co. rd. 1100 and 1104 to the Big Crabtree Emerald Mine—emeralds, emerald matrix (for cabochons).

MOUNT PLEASANT, NW 2½ mi. on rd. to HUGHES, turn left on dirt rd. at HUGHES, the Lieback Mica Mine—fine large red garnets.

PENLAND: (1) E .2 mi., in horseshoe bend of the North Toe R., the Deer Park Mine—autunite, feldspar crystals, garnet, hyalite opal, mica, monazite crystals, thulite, torbernite, uraninite; (2) Penland Jct.: (a) in rd. cut on Rte. 226—gem epidote; (b) N 1½ mi., Bear Cr. Gap (on Bear Cr. rd. N of Rte. 226), area—gem kyanite.

SPEAR, many area mines and dumps—beryl, garnets, epidote crystals, mica. (Most mine roads require four-wheel drive.)

SPRUCE PINE. This community of about 2,500 population is located on U.S. 19E about 4 mi. N of the Museum of North Carolina Minerals at Gillespie Gap on the Blue Ridge Parkway, a center for a large feldspar and kaolin mining industry. Within a radius of 20 mi. are far too many gem and mineral mines to list here, other than a few of greatest interest to the collector. Many of the commercial mines are open to collectors on weekends only, or weekdays if no blasting is scheduled. Because of the rugged terrain, it is advisable to hire a local guide and use his truck, usually a four-wheel-drive vehicle, to reach the most prolific gem mines with the least waste of time. Information about localities, mines, maps, and available guides is provided by the Mitchell County Chamber of Commerce in SPRUCE PINE, as well as at a dozen or so rock shops in the area. Mine owners usually charge a modest fee and will assist the collector in every way possible.

(1) Area mica and feldspar mines (very many)—actinolite, amazonite, autunite, garnet, hyalite opal, gem kyanite, foliated talc, thulite, tourmaline, etc.; (2) E on U.S. 19E to English Knob (.4 mi. W of the Avery Co. line), mine on E side of hwy.—autunite, columbite, cyrtolite, gummite, monazite, pitchblende, samarskite, torbernite; (3) E on U.S. 19E to jct. with co. rd. 1143 (second rd. branching N), then: (a) N 1 mi., a mine—actinolite, talc; (b) N 1.3 mi., turn right on unmarked rd. (leading to city dump) .2 mi. to the Wiseman Uranium Mine (closed on weekends) and .9 mi. to the Pink Mine (3 mi. from town; closed on weekends)—apatite, garnets, uranium minerals; (c) N 5 mi., the Spread Eagle Mine—feldspar, garnets, gummite, rare uranium minerals. Five mi. out on co. rd. 1143 is a 3-way fork (the right fork leading to INGALLS, q.v.). The center fork has two mines on a

trail to the right—**smoky quartz crystals, radioactive minerals;** the left fork leads to three mines (the most distant being 6 mi. from town)—**garnets, hyalite opal, pegmatite minerals.**

(4) S on Rte. 226 leading toward the Blue Ridge Parkway, three major mines: (a) 1½ mi. from town, the Henry Mine—**steatite, foliated talc;** (b) ½ mi. ESE of Chalk Mt., the McHone Mine—**amazonite, aquamarine, golden beryl,** gem **spodumene;** (c) 2½ mi. from town, the Wiseman Mine—**aquamarine** (sea blue), **golden beryl, mica, spar;** (5) SE 2½ mi. (air) and SE of Brush Cr. (follow Rte. 226 to LITTLE SWITZERLAND 5 mi. S of SPRUCE PINE, turn right on co. rd. 1100 to a church, take co. rd. 1104 to the Crabtree Emerald Mine (elev. 5,000 ft.), fee—**emeralds, garnets, beryl** (pale colors, yellow), **black tourmaline;**

(6) W to jct. with Crabtree Rd. (co. rd. 1002): (a) S on Crabtree rd. to the McKinney Mine (famed locality)—**amazonite, autunite** (staining **feldspar**), **beryl** (massive opaque green or blue), **bornite, chalcopyrite, columbite, covellite,** chatoyant **feldspar, gummite, hyalite opal** (blue, translucent, brilliantly fluorescent), **malachite, muscovite mica** (with brilliant **garnet** inclusions), **samarskite, sphalerite, sunstone, torbernite, uraninite;** (b) W to next S-trending rd., S to a fork, turn W to the Old No. 20 Mine (5 mi. SW of SPRUCE PINE on W fork of Crabtree Cr.)—**beryl, crystolite, cryolite** (amber), **feldspar,** gem red **garnets, gummite** (orange), **hyalite opal, muscovite mica** (greenish), **thulite, torbernite, uraninite;** (c) nearby Ray Olivine Mine—**asbestos, chlorite, chromite, olivine, serpentine, talc;**

(7) W 2 mi. on U.S. 19E, then SW 1 mi. on a mine rd., the Chalk Mt. Mine (a working mine with a 200-ft. sheer face)—**autunite, feldspar, hyalite opal, muscovite mica, quartz crystals, thulite, torbernite;** (8) NW 1 mi. on Rte. 226 (toward BAKERSVILLE): (a) area rd. cuts—**byssolite,** gem **epidote crystals, stilbite, zeolites;** (b) 1½ mi. up Sullins Branch rd., the Sullins Mine —**autunite, hyalite opal, torbernite;** (9) NW 1.7 mi. on Rte. 226 to dirt rd. leading ½ mi. N, the Southers Branch Mine—**garnets, hyalite opal** (stalactitic forms longer than 2 in.), pink **orthoclase crystals, unakite** (as blue stalactites);

(10) NNE 1.8 mi., the Wiseman Tract (¼ mi. SW of English Knob)—**aquamarine, golden beryl;** (11) NW 2 mi. on Rte. 226 and 1½ mi. NE of MINPRO on a private rd., the Pine Mt. Mine—**autunite, hyalite opal, torbernite;** (12) N on Rte. 226 about 4 mi., turn NE onto first unmarked mine rd., park car, hike 2½ mi. uphill to the Chestnut Flats Mine—**garnets, uranium minerals;** (13) NW 5 mi., the Putnam Mine (and on dumps of adjoining Deer Flat and Pine Mt. mines)—pink **thulite;** (14) NW 8 mi. on Rte. 226 and 2 mi. on the Slagle gravel rd., in the Snow Cr. section, the R. B. Phillips Mine—**garnet, mica.**

MONTGOMERY CO.

AREA: (1) regional abandoned silica quarries—**quartz crystals** (clear, smoky, some with **rutile** inclusions); (2) Beaver Dam Cr. jct. with the Yadkin R., NE 2 mi., the Beaver Dam Mine—**gold, pyrite;** (3) regional mines, especially in the extreme NW corner of co.—**gold.** (Such mines as the Bright,

Ophir, Dry Hollow, Island Creek, Deep Flat, Spanish Oak Gap, Pear Tree Hill, Tom's Creek, Harbin's, Bunnell Mt., Dutchman's Creek, Worth, etc., have played a prominent part in the state's mining history.) (4) Extreme N part of co. along the Randolph Co. line, the Uwharrie Mts., numerous mined deposits—**anatase crystals** (clear blue, bicolor, to 5 mm. size, encased in **quartz**), **limonite.**

CANDOR: (1) W 2½ mi., the Montgomery Mine—**gold;** (2) W 3 mi., the Iola Mine—**gold, siliceous pyrite.**

ELDORADO: (1) area old mines—**azurite, calcite, gold, hydrozincite** (strongly fluorescent), **malachite, pyrite, silver, smithsonite, sphalerite;** (2) SE 2 mi., on E side of the Uwharrie R., a mine—**gold;** (3) E 3 mi., the Riggon Hill Mine—**gold;** (4) S 8 mi., the Moratock Mine—**copper minerals, gold, pyrite;** (5) N 1½ mi.: (a) the Coggins (Appalachian) Mine, in argillaceous slates and schists—**gold;** (b) E, at the Eldorado Mine—**gold, silver, pyrite,** etc.; (6) N 3 mi., near the Randolph Co. line, the Russell Mine in silicified slate—**calcite, gold.**

STAR, W 3 mi., the Carter Mine (one of the oldest mines in the state)—**gold.**

TROY: (1) area stream gravels—**petrified wood;** (2) a nearby old mine—**leopardite;** (3) NE 14 mi., the Black Ankle Mine—**gold.**

WADEVILLE: (1) W, to within 3 mi. of the jct. of Rtes. 24 and 27, the Sam Christian Mine—**gold** nuggets (this mine was remarkable for its large, fine nuggets); (2) area abandoned **silica** quarries—**quartz crystals** (smoky, rutilated).

MOORE CO.

AREA: (1) mines such as the Bat Roost, Grampusville, and Schields—**gold;** (2) gravels of Deep Cr.—**petrified wood;** (3) gravels of Shut-In Cr.—**jasper** (gemmy, showy).

CARTHAGE: (1) NW 8 mi., the Bell Mine—**gold;** (2) NW 11 mi.; the Burns (Alfred) Mine—**gold:** (a) ¾ mi. N, the Cagle Mine, and (b) ¼ mi. W of the Cagle, at the Clegg Mine—**gold.**

GLENDON: (1) area **pyrophyllite** mine—**fluorite, hematite, lazulite, pyrite;** (2) NE 1.6 mi. (go 1 mi. E from town, turn E 1.3 mi. on old logging rd. and take rt. fork to an old copper mine on the Haw Branch rd.)—**azurite, calcite, malachite.**

ROBBINS, SW, at confluence of Cabin and Dry creeks, on the Moore farm —**amethysts, rock crystal.**

NASH CO.

AREA: (1) regional mines such as Conyer's, Nick Arrington, Thomas, Kerney, Taylor, Mann, Davis, etc.—**gold;** (2) Portis Mine: (a) on dumps—**gold, iron, manganese minerals;** (b) SE 1 mi., the Arrington Mine—**gold.**

ARGO (NW corner of co. and 5 mi. SE of Ransom's bridge), the Mann-Arrington Mine, in chloritic and porphyritic schist—**gold.**

NASH, FRANKLIN COS.

AREA, the N portions of these two counties plus the S sections of WARREN and HALLIFAX counties, known as the Eastern Carolina Belt, comprises some 300 sq. mi. containing very many old mines—**gold.**

ORANGE CO.

CHAPEL HILL: (1) area woods, fields, creek gravels—**moss agate, petrified wood;** (2) area mines—**chalcopyrite, epidote, hematite, hematite** pseudomorphs after **pyrite, limonite, magnetite, pyrite, serpentine;** (3) NW 12 mi., the Robeson Mine in **quartz** (a main producer, now abandoned)—**gold.**

HILLSBORO: (1) area fields, stream gravels, rd. cuts, etc.—**moss agate, sagenitic quartz crystals** (**chlorite** inclusions); (2) area mines—**barite, chlorite, epidote, pyrite cubes, pyrophyllite;** (3) S, in abandoned **barite** pit—**barite, calcite, celestite;** (4) NE 5 mi. and just S of city, near RR crossing on Rte. 86, area—**andalusite crystals, pyrophyllite** rosettes.

PERSON CO.

REGION, extending SW, covering part or all of the counties of DURHAM, ORANGE, ALAMANCE, CHATHAM, RANDOLPH, MOORE, MONTGOMERY, DAVIDSON, STANLEY, CABARRUS, ANSON, and UNION. Known as the Carolina Slate Belt, this region contains many once rich **gold** mines in a zone from 15 to 50 mi. wide. The chief gangue minerals in the mines are: **bornite, calcite, chalcopyrite, quartz, rhodochrosite, siderite.**

ALLENSVILLE, NE ¼ mi., then N on secondary rd. 1 mi. to the old Durgy Copper Mine—**malachite.**

LONGHURST, NW 2 mi. to Hager's Mt., **quartz** vein exposed between rd. and Marlowe Cr. to the W—gem **kyanite** (with **pyrophyllite**).

SURL: (1) N 2.3 mi. on paved rd. to Mt. Tirzah (S part of co.), on W side of rd. across from a church, area fields, rd. cuts—**actinolite, hematite, limonite, manganese minerals, rock crystal** (with **chlorite** inclusions); (2) 1 mi. E of Mt. Tirzah along rd. to MORIA, area fields and cuts—**pyrite crystals, limonite** pseudomorphs after **pyrite** (most cubes found ¼ mi. W of Mt. Tirzah).

POLK CO.

AREA: (1) the many regional **gold** mines are in extensions of the South Mountain region and include such noted old mines as the Double Branch, Red Spring, Splawn, and Smith—some **chalcopyrite, gold, pyrite;** (2) regional stream gravels—**garnets, placer gold, rutile crystals, staurolites, zircons.**

PEA RIDGE: (1) area old mines, and (2) S ½ mi., the North Star Mine—gem **feldspar** and blue **quartz, garnets, tourmaline.**

SALUDA, SE 5 mi., an old mine—**calcite, epidote,** brecciated **jasper, feldspar crystals, pyrite, quartz crystals.**

RANDOLPH CO.

ASHEBORO: (1) area granite outcrops—**unakite;** (2) W 6 mi. and N of U.S. 64, abandoned road dept. quarry via secondary rds.—**epidote, feldspar;** (3) W to near co. line, the Jones (Keystone) Mine (18 mi. E of S from LEXINGTON, Davidson Co.)—**gold, limonite, pyrite;** (4) NE 10 mi., the Alred Mine, open cuts—**limonite** pseudomorphs after **pyrite, gold.**

FARMER: (1) on S side of rd. between town and DENTON, Davidson Co., at Copper Hill—**quartz crystals** (with rare mossy-green inclusions of **actinolite**); (2) the Hoover Hill Mine (17 mi. E of S from HIGH POINT, Guilford Co.) in **quartz** veins—**gold.**

STALEY, W 4½ mi., the Bernhardt **pyrophyllite** mines—**andalusite crystals, barite crystals,** pearly **diaspore, lazulite** (crystals, massive), **pyrophyllite** (radiating green crystals), foliated green **ottrelite, pyrite.**

RICHMOND CO.

ELLBERLE, area creek gravels—**petrified wood.**

ROCKINGHAM CO.

PRICE: (1) very many regional mine dumps—**gems, minerals;** (2) W 1 mi., on state line, the Clifton Mine—**garnets,** variegated **quartz;** (3) SW 3¼ mi., on S side of the PRICE-Sandy Ridge rd., the Short Top Smith Mine, reached via Va. Rte. 692 left of U.S. 220, Rte. 691 (left of Rte. 692) to third graded co. rd. (mine rd.), turn left ½ mi.—**allanite, autunite, tourmaline, uranophane, uraninite;** (4) W and S, a broad region of rural rds. (requires topographic quadrangle map): (a) SW 5 mi. (leave town on U.S. 220, turn immediately left to reach Va. Rte. 692, cross Va. state line and immediately turn left on Va. Rte. 691 to first ungraded rd., turn left 1 mi.), the Long Tom Smith Mine—**garnet, rock crystal, smoky quartz;** (b) 1 mi. farther along same rd., the Rosa Evans Mine, on steep slope—**spessartite garnet, smoky quartz crystals.**

ROWAN CO.

GOLD HILL: (1) area mines, numerous—**magnetite, manganese garnet;** (2) a nearby quarry—**amethysts, sunstone** (the most notable of the county's gemstones is **amethyst,** and the county has by no means been thoroughly prospected for them); (3) SW 1 ½ mi., the Mauney Mine—**gold;** (4) E 3 mi., the New Discovery Mine—**gold;** (5) E 3½ mi., the Dun's Mt. Mine—**gold, pyrite;** (6) E 6 mi.: (a) the Reimer Mine, on the Yadkin R.—**gold;** (b) 1½ mi. E of the Reimer, the Bullion Mine (little worked), in outcrops as traces—**gold;** (7) SE 9 mi., the Gold Knob Mine—**gold;** (8) SE 10 mi., the Dutch Creek Mine—**gold, pyrite.**

GRANITE QUARRY, area outcrops and exposures of granite—**smoky quartz crystals.**

MT. ULLA, area fields, gravels, pits, etc.—**amethysts, quartz crystals.**

SALISBURY: (1) area fields, gravels, rd. cuts—**amethysts;** (2) regional pegmatite outcrops—**tourmaline** (color-zoned pink and green, crystals small); (3) E 3½ mi. the Dun's Mt. Mine—**gold.**

WOODLEAF, area quarry—pale green **prehnite crystals.**

RUTHERFORD CO.

AREA: (1) many old **gold** mines, in **quartz** mostly—**gold,** some **platinum;** (2) Sandy Level Church, area mine dumps—**gold, platinum, diamonds** (rare); (3) the J. D. Twitty placer mine—**gold, diamonds.**

ELLENBORO: (1) on outskirts of town, the Maurice Mine—**tourmaline;** (2) NE 3.2 mi., on W banks of Sandy Cr.: (a) the Dycus Mica Mine—**beryl, perthite, rose quartz;** (b) farms of Martin and Toney, pegmatite outcrops—**beryl;** (3) NE 5 mi., the D. G. McKinney Mica prospect—**beryl.**

GILKEY, E, on W side of Blacksmith Shop rd. 1.4 mi. S of the Green Hill School, pegmatite outcrop—**corundum, fuchsite mica.**

HOLLIS, N, in area of Huckleberry Mt. and Lisenberry Mt., many old mines—**mica, quartz crystals.**

RUTHERFORDTON: (1) area mines, such as the Ellwood and Leeds—**gold;** (2) NW .6 mi., in gravels of Hollands Cr.—**diamonds, platinum** nuggets, **quartz crystals** (blue, banded, distorted, enhydros); (3) N on country rd. between Rtes. 221 and 64, a short distance S of the Oak Springs Baptist Church, a deposit—**corundum, fuchsite, sericite;** (4) N 3½ mi. on U.S. 221, near Isinglass Hill, outcrop—**unakite;** (5) NE 4 mi., the Marville Mica prospects—**mica;** (6) N 5 mi., on divide between Cathey's Cr. and the Broad R., the Alta (Monarch, Idler) Mine, showing 13 parallel **quartz** veins—**gold;** (7) W 3½ mi., the Wilkins Mine—**mica;** (8) W 15 mi. on U.S. 74, pegmatite outcrops—various **gems** and **minerals.**

SUNSHINE: (1) W, on Duncan's Cr. rd., the McFarland farm (2 mi. E of rd. to SUNSHINE), a **mica** prospect—**golden beryl, quartz crystals** (blue, star).

THERMAL CITY: (1) area gravels of Stony Cr.—**garnets;** (2) N 1 mi., the McDaniel Mine—**garnets;** (3) W 2½ mi., the Flack Mine; and (4) W 7 mi., the Kay Mine—**garnets;** (5) the Whitehouse area, on E side of Shingle Hollow rd. 1 mi. NW of the Welcome Home Church, an old prospect—**bornite, chalcopyrite, galena, marcasite, pyrite.**

WESTMINSTER: (1) N 4 mi., granite gneiss outcrops on Marlin's Knob E of U.S. 64—**garnets, unakite;** (2) outcrops and gravels along Puzzle Cr. all the way to ELLENBORO, *q.v.*—**garnets.**

STANLY CO.

ALBEMARLE: (1) NW 2½ mi., the Haithcock and Hern mines, in **quartz** —**gold;** (2) E 4 mi., the Crawford (Ingram) Mine, placer—**gold;** (3) NW 7 mi., the Parker Mine, **quartz** veins in greenstone—**gold** (this locality was long a source for many sizable nuggets).

MISENHEIMER, the Barringer Mine (4 mi. SE of GOLD HILL, *q.v.,* Rowan Co.)—**gold.**

NEW LONDON: (1) W, in area stream gravels of Mountain Cr. (in Cabarrus Co.)—**golden beryl, diamonds, placer gold;** (2) E 1 mi., the Crowell Mine, in silicified, sericitic, and chloritic schist—**gold, pyrite.**

STOKES CO.

DANBURY: (1) area stream gravels—**agate, carnelian, chalcedony, jasper, hyalite opal, hematite, amethysts, sardonyx;** (2) SW 3 mi., a deposit—**itacolumite.**

DAN RIVER, area quartz outcrop—**rose quartz** (cat's-eye, star).

FRANCISCO, SE 4 mi., on N bank of Big Cr. near confluence with the Dan R. (take dirt rd. left from Rte. 89 midway to DANBURY), the Hole Mine —**garnets, moonstone, quartz crystals** (milky, smoky).

GAP, Coffee Gap on Rte. 66 near Hanging Rock State Park, center of a gem and gemstone region: (1) area in the Sauratown Mts., a well-known **quartz** outcrop—**lazulite** (dark blue gem crystals, massive in **quartz** excellent for cabochons), **quartz crystals;** (2) 2 mi. SW of GAP, an extensive deposit—**itacolumite.**

SANDY RIDGE: (1) W 1 mi. on Rte. 770, turn SW on co. rd. 1½ mi. to dumps of the Hawkins Mine—**garnet, perthite crystals, pyrite, quartz crystals;** (2) SW 4½ mi. (turn left off Rte. 704 1 mi. W of Oak Ridge onto unmarked rd. for 1½ mi.), the Moorefield Mine—**rock crystal, tourmaline** (dark).

SURRY CO.

BURCH STATION, E 1½ mi. from Rte. 268 to the Clarence Greenwood farm —**jasper, quartz crystals.**

DOBSON, N 10 mi., area mines—**actinolite, breunnerite, chlorite, hausmannite, magnesite, magnetite, manganese garnet, pyrolusite, serpentine, steatite, talc** (green crystals), **wad.**

ELKIN, MT. AIRY: (1) area outcrops—**rock crystal** (some with inclusions of **iron, chlorite, actinolite**); (2) Mt. Airy: (a) a nearby **feldspar** quarry— **oligoclase crystals** (clear); (b) NE, in large granite quarry—**jasper, quartz;** (3) gravels of the Mitchell R.—yellow **chalcedony,** gemmy **hornblende crystals, steatite;** (4) W, on Pleasant Hill (Wilkes Co.), near Rte. 268—**quartz gemstones.**

PILOT MOUNTAIN: (1) area—**rutilated quartz crystals;** (2) NE 1.3 mi., on the Phillips and Cos farms—**rutilated quartz crystals.**

SWAIN CO.

BRYSON CITY: (1) area: (a) region extending from town to the Deep Cr. Church, (b) extending to the Franklin Grove Church, area—**allanite, garnet, magnetite, moonstone, quartz crystals, pyrite;** (c) a few hundred yds. from the Deep Cr. Church—same minerals plus **graphic granite, feldspar crystals,** mica; (2) N 1½ mi. and just N of the Deep Cr. Campground, in **graphite** vein exposures—**kyanite, staurolites;** (3) 2½ mi. N of Proctor on Gold Mine Cr., mine—**copper minerals;** (4) just N of Toot Hollow Branch, the Cox No. 1 Mine—**almandite garnets, feldspar** (chatoyant crystals), **biotite mica, pyrite.**

TRANSYLVANIA CO.

AREA at the end of the Blue Ridge Parkway: (1) SE of the Parkway at Looking Glass Rock, just E of U.S. 276: (a) above the Pink Beds Recreation Area—**smoky quartz crystals;** (b) vein extends about 1 mi. up the mt. along old rd.—**smoky quartz crystals;** (2) E of the mt., area of Looking Glass Falls—**garnets;** (3) in rd. cuts along U.S. 276 about 23 mi. S of the falls, in a pine grove N of the hwy., area—**almandite garnets.**

CEDAR MOUNTAIN, on unnumbered rd. leading E from U.S. 276, along the Carolina Power & Light Co. line between Cedar Mt. and Blue Ridge—**almandite garnets, pyrite crystals.**

FAIRFIELD VALLEY, along Georgetown Cr., as placers—**gold.**

MONTVALE, area mines—**sapphires.**

OAKLAND, N, on E side of Great Hogback Mt., area old mines in **peridotite—bronzite,** gem **corundum.**

ROSMAN: (1) E, on the Tinsley farm N of the Girl Scout Camp, area—dogtooth **calcite;** (2) N off U.S. 64: (a) 1 mi. toward BALSAM GROVE, then W on secondary rd. crossing North Fork, on S side of rd. W of the river, area—**quartz crystals;** (b) 2.2 mi. SW of BALSAM GROVE, in pasture of the Hogsed farm (reached via rd. W from the main rd. 2 mi. S of Balsam Gap), as float—**quartz crystals.**

WAYNESVILLE, SE, on U.S. 276 to Bethel (first crossrd. stop, up side rd. to recently opened cr. bed mine, fee), abundant—**sapphires.**

UNION CO.

MONROE, W (including much of the W side of co.): (1) area mines, such as: Lemmonds (Marion), New South, Crump, Fox Hill, Phifer, Black, Smart, Secrest, Moore Hill (group) 2 mi. S of Indian Trail—**calcite, gold, pyrite,** etc.; (2) N 14 mi., in extreme NW corner of co., the Crowell Mine: (a) on dumps—**gold;** (b) ¾ mi. SW, the Long Mine, and (c) 3 mi. SE of the Long Mine at the Moore Mine—**calcite, chalcopyrite, galena, gold, pyrite, siderite, sphalerite.**

POTTER'S STATION, N 1½ mi., the Bonnie Belle (Washington) Mine—**chalcopyrite, gold, pyrite.**

WAXHAW, E 3 mi. (22 mi. S of CHARLOTTE, Mecklenburg Co.), the Howie Mine—**gold, pyrite.**

VANCE CO.

BULLOCKSVILLE: (1) area along Nutbush Cr., pegmatite outcrops—**gems, minerals;** (2) SW 1.7 mi., area—**quartz crystals** (with inclusions of **sillimanite**).

GRASSY CREEK: (1) W 2 mi., the Yancey farm on Jonathan Cr., area—abundant **pyrite;** (2) NW 2 mi., area outcrops—**quartz minerals;** (3) SW 3 mi., area—**pyrite;** (4) the Graystone quarry—**hornblende crystals,** gemmy pink **pegmatite.**

HENDERSON: (1) NE, near the Kerr Reservoir on the state line, in **phyllite** gneiss exposures—**quartz** and **rutile crystals, sillimanite;** (2) NW 13 mi. (9 mi. E of CLARKSVILLE, Va.), center of a mining region with major deposits S of the Kerr Reservoir in drainage of Island Cr. (tributary of the Roanoke R.): (a) area surfaces, gravels, etc.—**agate, chalcedony, rock crystal, tourmaline;** (b) area mines—**specular hematite, pyrite, quartz crystals;** (3) N 18 mi., in the Hamme Tungsten District (NE part of co., extending into Va.), between Big Island and Little Island creeks, many area mine dumps—**apatite, chalcopyrite, fluorite, galena, hyalite opal, huebnerite, quartz crystals, rhodochrosite, scheelite, sphalerite, tetrahedrite.**

KITTRELL, N, along U.S. By-pass 1, in granite outcrops—**hyalite opal** (highly fluorescent).

TOWNSVILLE: (1) W, area as float—**rock crystal;** (2) E of Marrow Chapel, as float—**rock crystal;** (3) around Townsville Lake—**quartz crystals;** (4) SW 2 mi., at the Devil's Backbone, area—**quartz gemstones.**

WILLIAMSBORO, NW, as area float—**rock crystal.**

WAKE CO.

AREA: (1) NW corner of co., many regional deposits, mined—**asbestos, actinolite, kyanite, serpentine, steatite;** (2) Barton's Cr., area mines—**chlorite, hematite** pseudomorphs after **pyrite, margarodite, pyrite** (large crystals), **tourmaline.**

PURNELL: (1) area: (a) the Powell farm, between Newlight Cr. and Water Fork, area—**corundum;** (b) BAYLEAF, area contact zone exposures (take rd. W from the village leading to Rte. 50, 2 mi. to Barton's Cr. crossing; or via the Neuse R. NE of village, or go to the jct. of Buckhorn and Newlight creeks)—carvable **steatite, actinolite;** (2) S 2 mi., near Horse Cr., a pegmatite outcrop on the Thompson farm—**allanite** (black), **beryl** (green and yellow, opaque).

RALEIGH: (1) E, in area of Wilder's Grove: (a) E ½ mi. on U.S. 64, turn N on dirt rd. 1 mi., area near the Neuse R. to the E—**amethysts** (large, color-zoned); (b) W 2½ mi., near U.S. 64, area—**amethysts;** (c) N 1 mi. on paved rd. to jct. with a secondary rd., then E .7 mi. to entrance to a dim trail S of the rd., area—**amethysts;** (2) N, turn off U.S. 70 on N side of Crabtree Cr. bridge onto paved rd. 3½ mi. to Mine Cr., area exposures—**gem kyanite;** (3) S 5 mi.: (a) area **mica** mines in pegmatite—**feldspar crystals, garnets;** (b) ½ mi. E of U.S. 15A, on the Coburn farm—**feldspar, garnet, mica,** snowy **quartz;** (4) NE 5 mi., area—**amethysts, quartz crystals.**

WAKE FOREST, W 3 mi. and 2 mi. S of Rte. 264, the Wakefield Mica Mine—**mica,** massive **quartz** (gray, pale blue).

WARREN CO.

CENTERVILLE, NW 3 mi. and near Rte. 58, between Isinglass and Shocco creeks, the Alston Mine—**graphic granite, perthite, quartz.**

INEZ: (1) S 2 mi. to the Franklin Co. line, many area pegmatite exposures—**gems, minerals**; (2) S 2½ mi., on E side of Rte. 58, pegmatite on the Fowler farm—**amethysts, beryl, lepidolite, smoky quartz crystals, staurolites**; (3) just E of the Fowler farm, on both sides of Rte. 58, the Harris deposits—**mica, quartz crystals**.

WATAUGA CO.

AREA, Rich Mt.: (1) head of Cove Cr., area—**actinolite, chromite, chrysolite, epidote, quartz crystals, penninite, tremolite**; (2) mouth of Squirrel Cr., area—**chrysotile asbestos**.

BLOWING ROCK, area stream gravels, placers—**gold**.

BOONE: (1) area stream gravels, especially Hardings Cr., placers—**gold**; (2) N 8 mi., at Elk Knob, area old mines—**azurite, garnets, epidote, limonite, malachite, calcite, cuprite, pyrite, pyrrhotite**, etc. (mainly primary **copper minerals**).

WILKES CO.

AREA: (1) E part of co., on Zeb Souther farm—**smoky quartz crystals**; (2) Bending Rock Mt., area exposures—**itacolumite**; (3) headwaters of Honey Cr., area gravels—**amethysts, rock crystal, smoky quartz crystals**.

CHAMPION, area old **mica** mines—**beryl, garnet, mica**.

DEEP GAP, E 6 mi.: (1) the Flint Knob Mine—**galena**, some **gold, pyrite, silver**; (2) the Laurel Spur of Flint Knob, area—**calcite, galena**.

NORTH WILKESBORO, area old **asbestos** mine—gem **serpentine**.

TRAP HILL: (1) area fields, cuts, gravels, etc.—**agate** (silvery, mossy), brecciated **jasper, chalcedony** (brown, yellow, reddish); (2) the Trap Hill Mine—**auriferous chalcopyrite, garnet, galena, magnetite, pyrrhotite, pyrite, rutile crystals, tourmaline**; (3) E side of Bryan's Knob, in **quartz** veins—**chalcopyrite, pyrite, pyrrhotite**; (4) Bryan's Gap on E face of the Blue Ridge, a bold outcrop of **quartz** (has been traced for nearly 3 mi.)—**gold, pyrite**.

WILKESBORO, N 2 mi., area—**garnet, serpentine, talc**.

YADKIN CO.

AREA: (1) area pegmatite outcrops, many—**beryl, garnet**; (2) area stream gravels—**carnelian** (reddish, dendritic or mossy, locally called **"tree carnelian"**).

YADKINVILLE: (1) E 6 mi., on SW side of a creek, at the Hauser Mine—**feldspar crystals, perthite crystals, smoky quartz crystals**; (2) SE 8 mi., the Dixon Mine—**gold**.

YANCEY CO.

AREA: (1) on Blue Rock Rd., the Spider Mine—**thulite**; (2) the Guggenheim Mine—**albite, apatite, autunite, halite, manganese garnet, margarodite,** muscovite mica, tourmaline; (3) the Hampton's Mining Creek Mine—**actinolite, bronzite, chromite, chrysolite, deweylite, epidote** (fine green crystals), **enstatite, magnesite, penninite, serpentine, talc, tremolite;** (4) the Young's Mine—**asbestos, bronzite, chlorite, chromite, chrysolite, enstatite, manganese garnet, muscovite mica, pyrite, serpentine, talc, tourmaline;** (5) the North Toe R., area gravels—**dithene** (gem **kyanite** crystals); (6) Yellow Mt., area outcrops—**dithene.**

BOWDITCH, E 1.9 mi., the Gibbs Mine on W bank of the Smith Toe R.—**oligoclase crystals** (transparent, greenish).

BURNSVILLE: (1) many area mines—**garnets, mica, platinum,** etc.; (2) E ½ mi. to trail leading S of U.S. 19 E ½ mi. to the Doe Hill Mine—**feldspar, garnets, mica (biotite, muscovite), pyrite;** (3) SE 2½ mi., on Hurricane Mt.: (a) the Ray Mica Mine—**eschynite, albite, amazonstone, apatite, aquamarine, autunite,** gem **beryl, columbite** (?), **emeralds, fluorite, fluorite** pseudomorphs after **apatite, garnet,** gem **kyanite crystals, monazite** (rare), **muscovite mica,** gem **oligoclase crystals, rutile crystals, smoky quartz crystals, sunstone, tourmaline** (black, also greenish yellow), **yttrocerite** (?), **zircon;** (b) along the right fork of the rd. to the Shanty Mine—**apatite, garnets, hyalite opal;**

(4) Parrot's Ford (3 mi. distant from town), area—**tantalite, tourmaline;** (5) SW 5 mi. on Rte. 197, the Ray Olivine Mine—**apatite, asbestos, beryl, chlorite, chromite, columbite, garnets, olivine crystals, serpentine;** (6) W 6 mi. on rd. to Red Hill, on E side of rd. at Green Mt., area outcrops visible from rd.—**chromite, olivine crystals;** (7) N 6 mi., area—**labradorite, platinum** (?); (8) NW 10 mi., on W side of Sampson Mt. via U.S. 19 to LEWISBURG, turn SW along Bald Mt. Cr. (with Sampson Mt. visible 5 mi. to the S): (a) the Hayes Mine—**corundum** (blue, gray, beige, white, cat's-eye, chatoyant) and (b) head of Bald Mt. Cr., the Cattail Branch Mine—**gem beryl, garnets.**

CELO: (1) area: (a) Celo Ridge, area mine dumps—**sapphires;** (b) Toe R. gravels—**corundum, sapphires;** (c) mine dumps about town—**feldspar, garnet,** gem **kyanite, mica;** (2) NE 1½ mi., the Little Gibbs Mine, on the South Toe R.—gem clear **oligoclase crystals** (dewdrop).

MICAVILLE: (1) N 2 mi., the Presnell Mine—**apatite, almandite garnets, columbite, mica;** (2) SE 2.7 mi.: (a) the Fanny Gorge Mine—**apatite, columbite, autunite, garnets, pitchblende, thulite;** (b) on S side at the Spec Mine—**aquamarine, almandite garnets;** (3) SE 3½ mi., the old Charles Mine—blue **apatite crystals,** pink **thulite.**

NORTH DAKOTA

This fertile state, geographic center of North America, is everywhere surfaced by Quaternary soils and sediments overlying rock formations of greatly varied ages. The eastern half, known as the Lowlands, once lay beneath the vanished waters of the great Pleistocene Lake Agassiz. Deeply buried beneath the lake sediments are rock formations of Mississippian, Jurassic, and Cretaceous ages. The western counties expose here and there much older formations, of Devonian age. West of the Red River Valley, abrupt escarpments rise 300 feet to the glacial drift prairies of scattered lakes, occasional moraines, and extensive, rolling, grass-covered hills. Along the Little Missouri River lie the strongly eroded, scenic, and almost inaccessible spires and minarets of the famed Badlands, extraordinarily rich in fossils that reach back to the era of the dinosaurs.

The state's mineral resources are limited almost exclusively to organic fuels and inorganic clays. Vast **lignite** beds, so close to the surface as to permit strip mining, cross the western counties, and North Dakota leads the nation in the production of this fuel. In close proximity to the lignite beds are large deposits of **commercial clays** in several varieties. Last, but not least, the discovery of oil in the Williston Basin some years ago has made **petroleum** production a prominent contributor to the state's mineral economy.

From the standpoint of the gem and mineral collector, it can truthfully be said that North Dakota really needs intensive prospecting. From east to west and north to south, the alluvial gravels underlying the topsoil are rich in **quartz family gemstones.** But the sparse population has afforded only one or two rock shops in the entire state, and the number of local hobbyists is minimal. Therefore, prospecting alluvial gravels, quarries, excavations, and stream beds everywhere should be productive of much more **agate, chalcedony, jasper, silicified wood,** and **quartz crystals** than would appear in the small list of known localities mentioned here. The eastern counties reveal Lake Superior–type **agates,** while the western counties yield types reminiscent of Fairburn and Montana **moss agates.** All gemstone occurrences are, of course, products of erosion from long-gone ranges of mountains and water distribution over the state character-istic of Tertiary epochs.

For information, write: North Dakota Geological Survey, Grand Forks.

ADAMS CO.

HETTINGER, N 10–12 mi., NE, and E, along both sides of the entire course of the Cedar R.—**agatized wood.**

BILLINGS CO.

MEDORA, area buttes and badlands formations—**agate, chalcedony, silicified wood, concretions** (filled with yellow **calcite crystals, aragonite,** or **siderite**).

BURLEIGH CO.

BISMARK, area gravel pits and alluvial beds along the Missouri R.—**agates, chalcedony, petrified wood, jasper.**

GOLDEN VALLEY CO.

SENTINEL BUTTE, area **uranium** mines and prospects, especially in T. 137 N, R. 100 W (Lutheran Church) and T. 139 N, R. 104 W (Sentinel Butte)— **uranium minerals.**

GRANT CO.

CARSON, area breaks along the entire course of the Cannonball R.—**agate, chalcedony, jasper, silicified wood.** Much of the gem-quality wood is *Sequoia dakotensis,* with wood, stems, limb sections, and walnut-sized cones beautifully preserved. Other species found are *Tempskaya* fern, *Osmundites,* and the silicified pods of the katsura tree.

HETTINGER CO.

MOTT, N 11 mi., along steep hillsides on both sides of the Cannonball R.— **agate, chalcedony, jasper, silicified wood** (including pine cones), **selenite crystals.**

HETTINGER-STARK COS.

AREA: (1) from MOTT to RICHARDTON, a broad area along both sides of Rte. 8—**agate, chalcedony, jasper, jasp-agate, agatized wood;** (2) from NW of MOTT 150 mi. to WILLISTON (Williams Co.), area breaks, rd. cuts, etc.— **selenite crystals.**

KIDDER CO.

TAPPEN, E, in regional gravel pits—**agate, chalcedony, jasper,** etc., **fossils.**

McHENRY CO.

DENBIGH, regional gravels of the Mouse R. SW to VELVA—**quartz gemstones, fossils.**

McKENZIE CO.

AREA, gravels of the Yellowstone, Missouri, and Little Missouri rivers— **Montana moss agate, jasper, agatized wood,** etc.

EAST FAIRVIEW, in gravel bars near confluence of the Missouri and Yellowstone rivers—**Montana moss agate, jasper, silicified wood,** especially around CARTRIGHT just to the E on Rte. 23/200.

GRASSY BUTTE, W and N, gravels of the Little Missouri R.—**Montana moss agate, agatized wood, jasper, plasma.**

SEARING, broad general surrounding region—**petrified wood.**

MERCER CO.

GOLDENVALLEY, S, the Crowley Flint Quarry (a historical site)—**gem flint.**

HAZEN, area mines—**uranium minerals.**

MORTON CO.

MANDAN: (1) area hills, draws, washes, etc.—**agate, chalcedony, chert, silicified teredo wood;** (2) area gravel pits—worm-bored **"teredo" wood** (borings filled with **calcite** or **chalcedony**).

MOUNTRAIL CO.

STANLEY, N and W around several highly saline lakes (White Lake, Cottonwood Lake), area mine dumps, as crystals—**glauberite, halite, thenardite.**

PEMBINA CO.

CONCRETE (on the Tongue R.): (1) area blue-gray limestone exposure—**crystals, fossils;** (2) regional limestone quarries—**calcite, fossils;** (3) deltas of the Pembina, Elk, and Sheyenne rivers—**fossils, quartz gemstones, petrified wood.**

RAMSEY CO.

DEVILS LAKE: (1) area gravel pits (in bed of the prehistoric Lake Agassiz) —gem **agate, jasper,** etc.; (2) gravel bars of all regional (countywide) streams, especially the James and Sheyenne rivers—**quartz gemstones, petrified wood,** etc.

RANSOM CO.

LISBON, in gravel bars along the lower Sheyenne R.—**quartz gemstones, teredo wood.**

ROLETTE CO.

DUNSIETH, on edge of the Turtle Mts.: (1) a large gravel pit—**quartz gemstones;** (2) area slopes and draws of the mts.—**manganese minerals.**

STARK CO.

DICKINSON: (1) area land surfaces—**agate, chalcedony;** (2) N 6 mi. on Rte. 22, a large gravel pit—**agate, jasper, petrified wood.**

WARD CO.

MINOT, S, in numerous area gravel pits, great variety—**quartz gemstones, fossils.**

WILLIAMS CO.

AREA, regional stream gravels—**Montana moss agate.**

OHIO

Only Paleozoic rock formations underlie Ohio's Pleistocene surface debris and Quaternary soils. For long ages Ohio lay beneath a shallow sea which received successively enormous quantities of Ordovician, Silurian, Devonian, Mississippian, and Pennsylvanian sediments—the erosional products of some 200 million years. Few, if any, Mesozoic rocks appear within the state, but every one of Ohio's 88 counties is surfaced with Pleistocene debris. The state was buried completely four times by the Ice Age glaciers, leaving the land surface nearly level but with some fairly rugged low hills in the southeastern corner. There are few localities containing worthwhile gems or minerals, although excavations in the underlying black, Upper Devonian (New Albany) shales occasionally produce pieces of **silicified wood,** mostly *Callixylon oweni* and *Callixylon newberryi.*

Ohio ranks first in the nation in the production of **limestone** and **dolomite,** and second in the production of **clays.** Lesser production of **iron, petroleum, natural gas,** and **coal** from thick beds contributes to the mineral economy. But as far as the gem collector is concerned, Ohio is unique in but a single gemstone, an exceptionally high-quality, colorful **flint** that is mostly a mixture of **chert,** translucent **chalcedony, jasp-agate,** and **common opal,** rivaling in beauty when cut and polished Arizona's **agatized wood.** This gem **flint** occurs in the 8-mile-long Flint Ridge, between Newark, Licking Co., and Zanesville, Muskingum Co., a region of delightful, rolling, wooded hills. Here, prehistoric Indians quarried the toolmaking material for arrowheads, knives, scrapers, drills, etc., centuries before the coming of the white man.

While occurrences are widespread throughout Ohio, the chief deposits of true **flint** (characterized by ease of working) include the highly colored "Vanport" flint of the Flint Ridge and the Upper Mercer flint exposed in Hocking, Perry, and Coshocton counties. Early American settlers also quarried a rough, porous **flintstone** from outcrops, especially around McArthur, Vinton Co., for making the burstones they needed for grinding grain in their water mills.

Other collectable minerals are rare, although quarries in the western counties, especially the Clay Center quarry 12 miles southeast of Toledo but in Ottawa Co. between routes 51 and 579, yield good specimens of **celestite, dolomite crystals, fluorite, galena, marcasite, pyrite, selenite,** and **sphalerite.** A few alluvial **diamonds** have been found.

For information, write: Ohio Geological Survey, Columbus.

ASHTABULA CO.

CONNEAUT, area pits, quarries, rd. cuts, etc.—**cone-in-cone calcite.**

CLERMONT CO.

MILFORD, area creek gravels and alluvial deposits, rare—**diamonds.**

CLINTON CO.

WILMINGTON, area of Todd's Ford, a mined deposit—**hematite.**

COSHOCTON CO.

AREA, townships of WASHINGTON, VIRGINIA, BEDFORD, JACKSON, JEFFERSON, BETHLEHEM, MONROE, and CLARK; on regional knobs and ridges and just above areas of drainage in townships of FRANKLIN, KEENE, MILL CREEK, and TUSCARAWAS, as hard dark gray to black nodules—**flint.** (This region was worked by prehistoric Indians, especially in Jefferson Twp.)

CUYAHOGA CO.

CHAGRIN FALLS (on Geauga Co. line), area quarries—**oilstone.**

DELAWARE CO.

DELAWARE, area co. exposures of blue clay, as clusters and nodules—**pyrite** (crystals sharply cubical).

FRANKLIN CO.

COLUMBUS, area countywide exposures of blue clay in rd. cuts, pits, quarries, excavations—**pyrite** (clustered cubical crystals) .

HIGHLAND CO.

SINKING SPRING, area ore deposit (most important in Ohio)—**hematite.**

HOCKING CO.

AREA exposures throughout co. of the Upper Mercer horizon, commonly represented by black **flint** of excellent quality: (1) Benton Twp. map, Sec. 24, along high ridges and knobs, as nodules—**flint;** (2) Green Twp., 2½ mi. SW of KACHELMACHER and 1 mi. W of Freeland School—**flint** (high quality, once quarried by prehistoric Indians); (3) Sec. 23, east-center, in a hollow as scattered nodules—**flint;** (4) Washington Twp., SW part of Sec. 31 in a gully on the knob—**flint.**

HOLMES CO.

AREA, townships of BERLIN, HARDY, KILLBUCK, MECHANIC, PAINT, and SALT CREEK (with occurrences in shale or sandstone), and conspicuous deposits in townships of CLARK (limestone occurrences), PRAIRIE, and WALNUT CREEK—**flint.**

JACKSON CO.

AREA, townships of BLOOMFIELD, COAL, HAMILTON, JEFFERSON, FRANKLIN, LICK, MADISON, and MILTON, as nodules in the Vanport member—**flint.**

LAWRENCE CO.

AREA, townships of DECATUR, ELIZABETH, PERRY, SYMMES, UPPER, and WASHINGTON, as nodules in limestone exposure—**flint.**

LICKING-MUSKINGUM COS.

AREA, from 3 mi. SE of NEWARK, Licking Co., to 12 mi. NW of ZANESVILLE, Muskingum Co., 8 mi. long by ¼ mi. wide: (1) Flint Ridge—**agate, amethyst, carnelian, chalcedony, chert** (various colors), **jasperlike flint, jaspagate, jasper, quartz crystals** (smoky), **rock crystal.** From BROWNSVILLE, Licking Co., take U.S. 40 E 3 mi., turn N to Flint Ridge State Park, and area of 10-mi. radius of private lands (make inquiry)—gem **flint**. This is a noted prehistoric Indian **flint** industry locality, and occasional arrowheads are found in the debris of aboriginal pits. (2) Regional rd. cuts, banks, stream banks and beds—gem **flint, arrowheads,** and **flakes**. This famed **flint** is extremely varied in pattern, from dendritic scenes in translucent **chalcedony,** banded swirls, to clear fortification; numerous cavities are lined with **drusy crystal quartz.**

LUCAS CO.

SYLVANIA, SW, at jct. of Brint St. and Centennial Rd., the Medusa Quarry (SW of 4 quarries), very many specimens—fine **fossils** (some replaced by **marcasite,** hollow shells lined with **calcite crystals** or **marcasite;** "doublets" of one **fossil** on another).

WHITEHOUSE, area quarries—**celestite, gypsum.**

MUSKINGUM CO.

AREA, cf. Licking-Muskingum counties.

ZANESVILLE, area mined deposits—**hematite.**

OTTAWA CO.

CLAY CENTER, area limestone quarry, famed—**calcite, celestite, dolomite crystals, fluorite, pyrite, fossils** (corals, gastropods).

GENOA, SE, in area quarries—crystals of **calcite, celestite, dolomite** and **fluorite; marcasite, pyrite,** various **fossils.**

GREEN (or STRONTIAN) ISLAND, Put-in-Bay, Lake Erie, as fine crystals and in large masses filling fissures in the waterlime rock—**celestite.**

PERRY CO.

AREA: (1) countywide deposits worked by aborigines, as nodules—**flint;** (2) townships of MONDAY CREEK, SALT LICK, PIKE, and CLAYTON, area—**flint.**

ROSS CO.

CHILLICOTHE, W several mi. (inquire at local farms), in regional exposures of blue clay, as large masses—**pyrite** crystal clusters.

SANDUSKY CO.

WOODVILLE, area quarries—**calcite, celestite, dolomite, fluorite, marcasite, pyrite,** various **fossils.**

SCIOTO CO.

PORTSMOUTH, countywide regional quarries—**catlinite.**

SENECA CO.

MAPLE GROVE (N of Tiffin to Fort Seneca on Rte. 53 and W 2 mi. on section line rd., then N ½ mi. to the Maple Grove Quarry)—**calcite, celestite, dolomite, marcasite, pyrite, fossils,** etc.

TUSCARAWAS CO.

CANAL DOVEL, MIDVALE, NEW PHILADELPHIA, ROSWELL, WAINWRIGHT, regional mines—**pyrite.**

TUSCARAWAS, STARK, SUMMIT, PORTAGE COS.

AREA, from the NW part of Tuscarawas Co., in numerous townships along the valley of the Tuscarawas R. from BOLIVAR to ZOAR STATION, as nodules in limestone outcrops—**flint.**

VINTON CO.

AREA: (1) Swan Twp., on Upper Mercer horizon exposed along an old rd. in SE part of Sec. 9—**flint;** (2) townships of RICHLAND (Sec. 1, central part along an abandoned rd.), WILKESVILLE, VINTON, CLINTON, and ELK, in Vanport limestone exposures as nodules—**flint.**

WAYNE CO.

AREA, Paint Twp., Sec. 24, near center, as black nodules—**flint.**

WOOD CO.

BOWLING GREEN, W and S, at the Pugh Quarry—crystals of **barite, calcite, celestite, fluorite, pyrite** (all in cavities and veins).

OKLAHOMA

The Sooner State occupies approximately 70,000 square miles of nearly level land in the southern part of the Great Plains. The western

Oklahoma Panhandle is part of the arid, short-grass Great High Plains, broken by the Black Mesa in the northwest corner of Cimarron Co. and the Wichita Mountains in the southwest. Black Mesa, at 4,978 feet elevation, is the highest point in the state. From the Panhandle the land slopes gently east and south to a minimum elevation of less than 350 feet in the extreme southeastern corner of the state. There are elevated regions, ranging from 200 to 1,200 feet higher than the surrounding plains, in the Wichita, Kiamichi, Ouachita, and Arbuckle mountains and in the westward extensions of the Missouri Ozarks.

Parts of Oklahoma are mineralogically important. Extensive **coal** beds occur around McAlester, Pittsburg Co., and the great mines of the extreme northeastern corner, known as the Tri-State Area, are famed for their production of **lead** and **zinc** along with similar production from adjacent mines in southeastern Kansas and southwestern Missouri. While western Oklahoma produces a good deal of **gypsum,** it is the immense **petroleum** deposits which have given the state much of its fame and wealth.

Barite occurs at many localities in maroon sediments of Lower Permian age, with the greatest concentrations south and east of the Wichita Mountains and in the central counties of Comanche, Kiowa, Stephens, and Tillman, with locally abundant exposures in McClain and Garvin counties. In the **barite** districts, the mineral occurs as veins, nodules, and **barite-clay-carbonate** concretions in shale or as **sand-barite** concretions in sandstone. The "state stone" of Oklahoma, if it can be called that, is a peculiarly roselike crystal aggregate of **barite-in-sandstone.** Prized by mineral collectors everywhere, these rose-shaped crystal aggregates occur abundantly in the central counties and are variously termed **barite roses, barite rosettes, petrified roses, rose rocks, petrified walnuts, sand barites, sand crystals, sand rosettes,** or **sand barite crystals.**

Southwestern Oklahoma, especially in Beckham and Tillman counties, produces **alabaster, agatized** and **petrified wood,** and other **quartz family gemstones** from regional gravel pits and stream beds. Along the Cimarron and North Canadian rivers, gravel bars carry **agate, jasp-agate, jasper,** and **petrified wood,** along with **fossil bones** and **teeth** of Pleistocene mammals.

For information, write: Oklahoma Geological Survey, Norman.

ALFALFA CO.

Jet, W 6 mi. on U.S. 64, then N 3 mi. on dirt rd. to crossroads, then E 1¼ mi. to gate; collecting areas on the Salt Plains National Wildlife Refuge are posted—**selenite crystals.** Collecting on the refuge is permitted from 8 A.M. to 5 P.M. only on Saturdays, Sundays, and holidays between April 1 and October 15; per person limits are 10 lb. plus one crystal or cluster per day. Natural salt (**halite**) coating the plains, 7 mi. long by 3 mi. wide, was used by prehistoric Indians.

ATOKA CO.

AREA, Impson Valley, W side, on branch of Tenmile Cr. in fissure veins in Stanley shale—**grahamite.**
ATOKA, area quarries—**novaculite.**

BECKHAM CO. (with Blaine, Greer, Harper, Jackson, and Major)

AREA, **gypsum** quarries—**alabaster, selenite, petrified wood.**
ELK CITY, area quarries—**alabaster, selenite.**

BLAINE CO.

AREA (extending SW into Custer Co.), regional quarries—**borate minerals** (e.g., **priceite, probertite, ulexite**).
SOUTHARD, area quarries—**borate minerals.**
WATONGA, NE 6 mi., quarry—**borate minerals.**
WINNVIEW, area, scattered through clay shale exposures, as raw nuggets—**native copper.**

CADDO CO.

APACHE, SW 4 mi., quarry—**calcite rhombs** (fluorescent).

CANADIAN CO.

EL RENO (W end of the OKLAHOMA CITY complex), in gravel bars along the North Canadian R.—**agate, jasper, petrified wood.**

CIMARRON CO.

KENTON: (1) E 2 mi. on Rte. 18 to turnoff to Roberts Ranch and 2.3 mi. to ranch house, fee, collecting area—**agatized algae, agatized cycad wood, Indian artifacts;** (2) N to Tri-State Marker (Okla., Colo., N.M.), on hill—rose **agate;** (3) E ½ mi., turn N across Cimarron R. 11.2 mi. into Colo., turn E 2.3 mi. to the Layton Ranch, fee; collecting area in bed and sides of Carrizozo Cr. S from Colo. into Okla.—rose **agate, agatized algae** and **cycad wood,** some **coprolites.**

COAL CO.

LEHIGH, HUNTON, area mines—**manganese minerals.**

COTTON CO.

RANDLETT: (1) E 3 mi., and (2) E 6 mi., as small fissures in red shale—**malachite.**

DEWEY CO.

SEILING, TALOGA, area—**agate, jadeite, jasp-agate, jasper, petrified wood,** etc.

GARFIELD CO.

ENID, T. 24 N, R. 8 W (NE¼ SE¼ Sec. 24), area—**native copper.**

GARVIN CO.

PAULS VALLEY, area of Sec. 18, T. 4 N, R. 1 E, in red sandstone—**malachite.**

GREER CO.

AREA, the Wichita Mts., regional mines—**amphibole, zircon.**
MANGUM: (1) area quarries—**alabaster;** (2) N of town, general area—**agatized wood.**

HARPER CO.

BUFFALO, area—**agate, chalcedony, chert, jasper.**

HUGHES CO.

WETUMKA, area of Sec. 30, T. 8 N, R. 9 E, as clear, transparent, coarsely crystalline masses—**barite.**

JACKSON CO.

ALTUS, area draws, washes, cut banks, gravels—**smoky quartz crystals.**

JOHNSTON CO.

MILL CREEK: (1) area mines—**manganese minerals;** (2) NE 6 mi., on old Thompson Ranch near W line of NW¼ Sec. 15, T. 1 S, R. 5 E—**barite, iron oxides.**

LINCOLN CO.

AGRA, area of N part of co.—red **"medicine rock."**

LOGAN, OKLAHOMA, CLEVELAND, GARVIN COS.

REGION, a north-south line just E of center (to west-central part of Garvin Co.), very many localities—**barite.**

MAJOR CO.

FAIRVIEW, area gravels, cut banks, surfaces, etc.—**agate, jadeite, jasper.**

McCLAIN CO.

BYARS: (1) SW¼ Sec. 33, T. 5 N, R. 2 E, in Permian sandstone—**malachite;** (2) W 5 mi., surface workings—**malachite, silver, barite concretions** (radiating needles common).

McCURTAIN CO.

AREA, SE corner of co., the Ouachita Mts., regional stream gravels, cuts, washes, etc.—**rutilated quartz crystals, zircon.**
GLOVER CREEK, area gravels—**quartz crystals.**
WATSON: (1) SW 2 mi., in SE¼ NW¼ Sec. 33, T. 1 S, R. 26 E, the Eades Mine—**barite, galena, sphalerite;** (2) S 3½ mi., near center of Sec. 10, T. 2 S, R. 26 E, old pit—**barite, galena, sphalerite.**

MURRAY CO.

AREA, the Arbuckle Mts., numerous mines—**sphalerite.**
DAVIS, area mines—**smithsonite.**
SULPHUR, S, at a prospect pit in Sec. 3, T. 2 S, R. 3 E—**barite.**
WHITE MOUND, Sec. 20, T. 2 S, R. 3 E, in Sylvan shale exposures as thin, flat, circular crystal aggregates known as "dollars"—**barite.**

OKFUSKEE CO.

OKEMAH, area of SW part of co. in SE¼ SW¼ Sec. 31, T. 12 N, R. 7 E, a fault zone with mine veinlets—**azurite, malachite, chrysocolla, chalcocite, native copper, hematite, calcite, dolomite, limonite, pyrite** (coated with **melanterite**), **tenorite.** (Considered an unusual "Red Bed" **copper** deposit. Drill holes to depths of 50 ft. encountered **galena, pyrite,** and **sphalerite.**)

OTTAWA CO.

MIAMI-PICHER, regional **lead-zinc** district mines as important contributors to the Tri-State District (including SE Kans. and SW Mo.) mineral production (cf. also in introduction to Kans. and under Jasper Co., Mo.)—**anglesite, aragonite, barite, calamine, calcite, chalcopyrite, chert, dolomite, galena, greenockite, gypsum, marcasite, melanterite, quartz crystals, pyrite, smithsonite, sphalerite.**

The major producing mines occur within an area of 25 to 30 miles revolving around the mining towns of PICHER, CARDIN, CENTURY, and QUAPAW. This is the most important district in a much larger mining region extending N into Kansas and NE into Missouri, referred to by the U.S. Geological Survey as the Joplin Region, for that part outside Oklahoma, and the Miami District, Quapaw District, or Miami-Quapaw District for the Oklahoma portion.

PEORIA, QUAPAW, area mines—**calamine, cerussite, galena.**

SENECA, area mines—**tripoli.**

PUSHMATAHA CO.

ANTLERS: (1) area draws, washes, gravels—green **quartz crystals;** (2) the Impson Valley, McGee Creek, and Moulton mines—**impsonite** (bitumen).

WOODS CO.

ALVA: (1) countywide regional fields, washes, stream beds, cut banks, etc., especially (2) S of ALVA—**agate** (banded, mossy), **chalcedony, chert, jasper.**

OREGON

The geologic character of Oregon was formed during Tertiary times when millions of years of volcanic activity during the Oligocene and Miocene epochs raised the Cascade Mountains and layered nearly the whole surface of the state with thick beds of volcanic ash and flows of basalt. The Cascade Range, with its numerous snow-covered volcanic cones, divides the 100-mile-wide strip of rain-wet western Oregon from the high, arid plateau country of the eastern two-thirds of the state. Northeastern Oregon is part of the 225,000-square-mile basalt Columbia Plateau, one of the largest raw-lava regions of the world.

Central and eastern Oregon embraces many thousand square miles of some of the most prolific gemstone collecting land in America; here almost every type of **quartz family mineral** can be found, along with such oddities of the mineral kingdom as **geodes, nodules, fossils,** and a great array of **silicified woods.** The fertile western region is also heavily endowed with gemstones, and nearly every creek and river gravel bar, regional gravel pit or other excavation, and road cut reveals attractive minerals, gemstones, **fossils,** and **petrified wood.**

The rock-collecting hobby did not really begin in Oregon until about 1940, but today it is a major recreational activity throughout the state, aided and abetted by state, federal, and local chamber of commerce promotionalists. A federal law passed in 1962 limits collecting rocks from public lands to not more than "25 pounds plus one piece per person per day, not to exceed 250 pounds per year," and **petrified wood** may not be sold or bartered to commercial collectors. Full details respecting mining claims, permission to collect on private land, and penalties for violating federal laws are obtainable from the U.S. Forest Service, Portland, or the Bureau of Land Management office in Prineville. A particularly informative and colorful "Central Oregon Rockhound Guide" is available free of charge, published by the Forest Service in cooperation with the Bureau of Land Management, and the Prineville-Crook County Chamber of Commerce.

The "state rock" of Oregon was officially designated on March 5, 1965, as the **thunдеregg,** one of the most distinctive and sought-after mineral oddities in the world. These spherical masses of **agate** core in a volcanic matrix range in size from less than an inch to several feet in diameter, with most specimens being slightly larger than baseballs. The exterior surface is an uninteresting, drab rind of chocolate brown rhyolite or silicified volcanic tuff, nearly always knobby in appearance. This rind encloses a solid core of a peculiarly geometric, multisided mass of translucent **chalcedony** which may be **banded agate** in contrasting colors, deep red **carnelian, jasp-agate,** or **chalcedony** containing a small unfilled cavity lined with **quartz crystals.** No two **thundereggs** are ever alike, and no matter how one is sawed or sliced, the interior presents a star shape in lovely contrasting colors against the dark brown, buff, or tan rind matrix. The most prized specimens contain **carnelian** (rather rare) or reveal exquisite and colorful designs ranging from five-pointed stars to miniature landscapes. Not a few **thundereggs** are actual doubles enclosed in an elongated rind. Such nodular gemstones are invariably associated with highly siliceous volcanic rocks and are found abundantly in rhyolite flows and welded volcanic tuffs in a broad zone north and west of U.S. Highway 26. The geology exposed in this area is mainly the Clarno formation of Eocene age (60 million years old) and includes basic flows and andesite intrusives. The genesis of **thundereggs** is almost completely unknown.

Some of Oregon's coastal beaches are considered by rock collectors as the finest collecting areas in the world for **agates** (clear, ribbon), **jaspers, agatized wood, coral, bloodstones,** and **fossils.** Agate Beach near Newport in Lincoln Co. was well named. Other beaches well known to collectors are Otter Rock, Bob Creek, Ten Mile, Heceta Head, and beaches both north and south of Yaquina Bay. The best hunting is right after winter storms and after extreme high tides have churned up the sands.

Oregon also ranks tenth in the **gold**-producing states of America, having yielded up 5,797,000 ounces of **gold** between 1852 and 1965. The major rush to Oregon occurred about 1861, following a rich placer discovery at Griffin Gulch, Baker Co. Mining the yellow metal declined after the early 1900's but became greatly rejuvenated in 1934 when the price of **gold** rose from $20 to $35 an ounce; mining continued at a fairly lively pace until World War II diverted attention to more strategic minerals. The **gold**-panning hobbyist may still reap small seasonal fortunes in nuggets and colors from the streams of northeastern Oregon's Blue Mountains and those descending the Siskiyou Mountains of far southwestern Oregon.

For information, write: Oregon State Department of Geology and Mineral Industries, 1069 State Office Bldg., Portland.

BAKER CO.

BAKER: (1) area land surfaces, draws, washes, etc., many varieties—**quartz family gemstones;** (2) area mining districts, including Baker, Buck Gulch, Virtue, etc., regional mines (lode and placer)—**gold, pyrite, pyrrhotite** (bearing **gold**), **tetrahedrite;** (3) N 2 mi., a quarry—**gypsum, satin spar;** (4) Shirttail Cr., area—**agate, chalcedony, jasper, "Oregon jade"** (green **plasma agate**), **agatized wood;** (5) E, in volcanic rocks and in Powder R. gravels along the Richland Valley—**chalcedony geodes** (lined with **drusy quartz crystals**).

COPPERFIELD (NE part of co.), the Copper Butte District (including the Lower Snake R.), regional mines, especially the Copper Queen—**chalcocite, malachite, pyrite.**

CORNUCOPIA (ghost town), the Bryan Mine and others—**gold, pyrite, sylvanite.**

DURKEE, area washes, draws, slopes—**quartz family gemstones.**

GEISER, the Bonanza District regional mines—**gold, pyrite.**

HOMESTEAD (extreme NE corner of co.), the Iron Dike District mines, as predominant metal—**silver** (minerals).

HUNTINGTON, area around U.S. 30 milepost 393—**quartz crystal geodes** (to large size, lined with brilliant **rock crystal**).

PLEASANT VALLEY, area draws, washes, hillsides—**garnets** (resembling **rhodolite**), **opalized wood** (banded black and white).

RICHLAND, area surfaces, draws, etc.—**quartz family gemstones.**

RYE VALLEY, area mines—cf. SUMPTER.

SPARTA (14 mi. NW of RICHLAND), area mines—**arsenopyrite, galena.**

SUMPTER: (1) area mining districts of Cable Cove, Elkhorn, and Burnt River Divide (Sumpter), regional mines—**argentite, arsenopyrite, cinnabar, galena, pyrite, pyrolusite, specularite** (in **argillite**), **sphalerite, tetrahedrite;** (2) Cracker Creek District; and (3) N, in the Bourne District, area mines (several deep)—**gold, pyrite.**

WHITNEY (11 mi. SW of SUMPTER): (1) Greenhorn District: (a) area gravels, surfaces—**gold, agate, silicified** *Tempskaya* **wood;** (b) Greenhorn Mts., area NW of the Owyhee Reservoir—**agate.**

BENTON, LANE, LINN, CLACKAMAS, MULTNOMAH COS.

Area, all low-water gravel bars of the Willamette R. and its tributaries—**agate** (among finest in world), **jasper, bloodstone, petrified wood,** etc.

CLATSOP CO.

Astoria, Pacific Ocean beaches in gravels as waterworn pebbles—**bloodstone, jasper,** some **agate.** (The ocean beach gravels of the entire 400-mi.-length of the Oregon coast produce gem **agate,** with best collecting after severe winter storms.)

Pittsburg, Mist, Jewel, Elsie, Nehalem (taken E to W along the Nehalem R. from Columbia Co. NE of Vernonia), low-water stream gravels all way to ocean—**agate, carnelian, jasper.**

COLUMBIA CO.

Gable, Columbia R. shores, in gravels—**thomsonite.**

Vernonia: (1) SW, in gravels of Clear Cr.—**plume agate, carnelian, jasper;** (2) in gravel bars of Clear Cr. and town—**agate, carnelian, chalcedony, jasper;** (3) cf. Pittsburg and Mist under Clatsop Co.; (4) area logging RR cuts—**zeolite minerals, fossils.**

COOS CO.

Area, ocean beach gravels entire length of co.—**agate.**

Bandon, just N, at Bullards Beach State Park, in beach sands—**platinum.**

Coos Bay, W to ocean beaches, both N and S of the bay entrance along entire coast of co.—**agates,** fine **petrified wood.**

Myrtle Point, including the Eden and Randolph districts, regional stream placers—**gold.**

CROOK CO.

Area: (1) W side of co., especially in broad triangle between U.S. 26 on the N and U.S. 20 on the S, all land surfaces, draws, washes, etc.—**agate, chalcedony, chert, jasper, petrified wood, quartzite** (gemmy, colorful); (2) Howard area black-sand placers—**cinnabar, gold;** (3) McAllister Butte (near Ochoco Cr.), area—gem **moss agate.**

Paulina, SW 5½ air mi., in T. 17 S, R. 22 E: (1) Sec. 14, 15, Congleton Hollow, area—**agatized limb casts;** (2) Sec. 8, 29, the South Fork, area—**agatized limb casts.**

POWELL BUTTE, area draws, washes, breaks, slopes, etc.—**plume agate** (high quality).

PRINEVILLE. Most of the following localities have been abstracted from "Central Oregon Rockhound Guide," published in Dec. 1971 by the U.S. Forest Service in cooperation with the Bureau of Land Management and the Prineville–Crook County Chamber of Commerce. Visitors should obtain a free copy in PRINEVILLE, since all localities, roads, etc., are clearly depicted on a standard-type topographic map laid out by section, township, and range. This broad region ranks among the finest gemstone collecting areas in America for **moss agate** (all sizes of boulders in red, green, blue, yellow), **quartz crystal geodes** (all sizes), massive **botryoidal agate,** and **thundereggs.** Many of the listed localities comprise free collecting claims owned by the PRINEVILLE chamber of commerce; many others are on private land and permission to collect must be obtained and an occasional fee paid.

(1) Area, Viewpoint (make local inquiry), several excellent localities on private lands, fee charged—**thundereggs;** (2) E 5 mi. on U.S. 26, Ochoco Lake shores above the dam, area—**"Ochoco" jasper;** (3) E 6 mi. on U.S. 26, on NW side of the Ochoco Reservoir in Sec. 14, T. S, R. 16 E, area— **"Ochoco" jasper;** (4) E approx. 19½ air mi., in T. 14 S, R. 18 E, Sheep Cr. (NW¼ Sec. 25), area—green **moss agate;** (5) E, into the Clarno Basin, all regional land breaks, washes, erosional slopes—**fossils** (mammal bones), **"Clarno nuts"** (fossil cones);

(6) ENE on U.S. 26 to dirt rd. turnoff NE along Ochoco Cr., then NE approx. 12 mi. (into Wheeler Co.): (a) turn W, back into Crook Co. to Coyle Spring (Sec. 34, T. 12 S, R. 19 E), area—green **jasper;** (b) Sec. 35, Ahalt Cr., area—**vistaite;**

(7) NE approx. 12 air mi. (6.2 air mi. due N of the E end of the Ochoco Reservoir), in T. 13 S, R. 17 E, Dry Cr.: (a) line between Sec. 7 and 8, SW¼ Sec. 8, area—**jasper;** (b) due N ½ mi. or so, area—**thundereggs;** (8) NE approx. 16 air mi. (11 mi. NNE of E end of the Ochoco Res.), in T. 12 S, R. 17 E: (a) S part of Sec. 22, Harvey Cr., area—**thundereggs;** (b) NW¼ Sec. 22, Harvey Gap—**thundereggs;** (c) nearby, in Sec. 30, T. 12 S, R. 18 E, at Forked Horn Butte, area—**thundereggs;**

(9) NE approx. 16 air mi.: (a) T. 13 S, R. 18 E, White Fir Spring (Sec. 7), area—**thundereggs;** (b) Sec. 5, White Rock (immediately SE of Wildcat Mt.), area—**thundereggs;** (10) NE approx. 19 air mi., at Wildcat Mt., the famed Ochoco Nodule Beds, area—**plume agate, chalcedony, opal, thundereggs** (agate centers); (11) NE approx. 25 air mi., in Sec. 26, T. 11 S, R. 18 E (area reached via USFS rd. 1223), area—green **moss agate;** (12) NE approx. 26 air mi. via U.S. 26 to the Ochoco Divide, turn W on dirt rd. to Whistler Spring in T. 12 S, R. 18 E: (a) Sec. 11, area about the springs—**thundereggs;** (b) Sec. 16, Desolation Canyon, area—**thundereggs;**

(13) S about 15 mi. on the Crooked R. rd. to the Prineville Reservoir dam, then continue S and E about 6 mi. to rd. fork at Bear Cr.: (a) turn N to mouth of Bear Cr. in Sec. 4, T. 17 S, R. 16 E, area—**agate;** (b) from fork turn S and E about 12 mi. (past Little Bear Cr. turnoff, then up Bear Cr. from its confluence with Sage Hollow Cr.), then fork N on crooked dirt rd. about 3 mi. to Sec. 15, T. 18 S, R. 17 E, Fischer Canyon (on the Crook Co. side of the Deschutes Co. line), area—**petrified wood;** (14) S approx. 19 mi. on

Rte. 27 and 2 mi. S of confluence of Bear Cr. with the Prineville Res., on E side of Taylor Butte (Sec. 9, T. 17 S, R. 16 E): (a) area—**moss agate, chalcedony, drusy quartz** in agate; (b) gravel bars of the whole length of Bear Cr.—**moss agate, chalcedony, drusy quartz** (filling cavities in **agate**);

(15) SSE about 12 mi. on the Juniper Canyon rd. to Antelope Cr.: (a) area E toward the Carey Ranch in Sec. 11, T. 16 S, R. 16 E, the famed Carey Agate Beds—**"Carey" plume agate** (flame-color plumes), **chalcedony, jasper;** (b) SW about 3 mi. to end of rd. in Sec. 21 (a short distance W of the Prineville Res.), area of Reservoir Heights—black **moss agate;**

(16) SE approx. 12½ air mi. to Eagle Rock in Sec. 29, T. 15 S, R. 17 E, area N of the Prineville Res. and Crooked R.—dendritic **agate;** (17) SE approx. 30 air mi. into Ochoco National Forest, in Sec. 1, 2, T. 17 S, R. 19 E, at Shotgun Cr., area—varied **moss agate;** (18) SE approx. 40 air mi.: (a) 4½ mi. S of Logan Butte, in SE¼ SE¼ Sec. 12, T. 19 S, R. 19 E, Smokey Mt., area—**agatized limb casts;** (b) approx. 4 mi. SE of Logan Butte at Owens Water-South Pole Cr. in Sec. 3, 9, T. 19 S, R. 20 E, area—green **agatized wood.**

CURRY CO.

AREA: (1) ocean beaches along entire co., but especially N and S of the mouths of the Chetco and Rogue rivers—**agate, californite (idocrase), jasper;** (2) Rogue R. gravel bars from MARIAL in the NE corner of co. to its mouth at WEDDERBURN—**agate, garnets, gold, jasper, petrified wood.**

AGNESS: (1) area Rogue R. gravels—**agate, carnelian, chalcedony, grossularite garnet, gold, jasper, quartz crystals;** (2) old mines and prospects along the lower Illinois R.—**copper minerals, native copper.**

BROOKINGS, area ocean beach gravels—**agate, jasper, nephrite jade.**

CHETCO, CORBIN, ECKLEY, MARIAL, OPHIR, PORT ORFORD, SELMA, many regional streams with placer sands, formerly mined and yielding colors and nuggets to the casual seasonal panner—**gold.**

PORT ORFORD, area ocean beach sands—**platinum.**

SIXES, E on rural rd. into Coast Range approx. 15 mi. to Sugarloaf Mt., area talus slopes and stream gravels—**nephrite, serpentine.**

WEDDERBURN (at mouth of the Rogue R.), area river gravels—**grossularite garnet.**

DESCHUTES CO.

LAPINE (30 mi. S of BEND on U.S. 97), N 5 mi., turn E for approx. 13 mi., area between Paulina and East lakes—**obsidian.**

DOUGLAS CO.

AREA, Cedar Springs Mt., the Ball Mine—**azurite, chalcocite.**

GLENDALE, area old hydraulic placers and lode mines—**gold.**

OAKLAND, SE, area old mines—**cinnabar.**

REEDSPORT, W, all ocean beach gravels N and S of Winchester Bay—**agate.**

RIDDLE, NW, at Nickel Mt., area mines—**chrysoprase, nickel minerals.**

ROSEBURG: (1) SE 9 mi., area quarries—**marble;** (2) E 12 mi., in gravels of Davis Cr.—**orbicular jasper;** (3) area gravels of the Umpqua R.—**"Oregon jade"** (massive **grossularite garnet**); (a) N, in gravel bars of the North Umpqua R., and (b) especially 22 mi. E in same river gravels, and (c) S, in gravel bars of the South Umpqua R.—**agate, chalcedony, carnelian, jasper, petrified** and **silicified wood** (some of it teredo, or worm-bored, with borings filled with **calcite** or **silica**).

GRANT CO.

AREA, many old mining districts in NE part of co., including Alamo, Crane Creek, etc.—**gold.**

CANYON CITY (just S of JOHN DAY on U.S. 395), several area old placer mines—**gold.**

GRANITE (far NE part of co. and 14 mi. NW of SUMPTER, q.v., in Baker Co.), many dredger tailings and area mines—**arsenopyrite, galena, gold,** etc.

JOHN DAY, NE, in very broad area extending to AUSTIN (30 mi., the Poker Flat mining district, hydraulic placers—**gold**) and GRANITE (38 air mi., q.v.), all regional draws, washes, land surfaces—gem **jasper.**

PRAIRIE CITY: (1) the Quartzburg District mines—**cobaltite, chalcopyrite, gold;** (2) the Copperopolis claims—**malachite;** (3) Saw Mill Gulch, hydraulic placers—**gold.**

SUSANVILLE (District), many area old mines—**cinnabar, chalcopyrite, gold, sphalerite,** etc.

HARNEY CO.

AREA, the Steens Mts. in SE corner of co. (follow any desert rd. into the general surrounding region of these abrupt, high, isolated mts.): (1) rds. S from PRINCETON 40 mi. SE of BURNS via Rte. 78 lead to W side of the Steens, and (2) rds. SW from Folly Farm 30 mi. SE of PRINCETON leading to the Alvord Ranch, Andrews, and Fields give access to the E side of the range, all regional land surfaces, draws, washes, etc.—**moss agate, jasper, thundereggs, geodes, quartz crystals,** etc.

BURNS: (1) W, broad general area, and (2) E to BUCHANAN, area of the Harney Valley—**agate, chalcedony, jasper, geodes, quartz crystals,** etc. (3) N 18 mi. on U.S. 395, then 7 mi. W, Silvies Canyon in Myrtle Park—**wood opal;** (4) E 40 mi., the Warm Springs Reservoir: (a) area surfaces—**agate, chalcedony, jasper, petrified wood;** (b) at milepost 171 on U.S. 20 turn S on dirt rd. 14.2 mi. to the reservoir, on E side of rd. along the lake and on surfaces of surrounding hills—**agate** (black dendritic and white plume).

DENIO, the Pueblo Mts. (S of the Steen Mts.), mines, as large masses—**uraniferous silica.**

HARNEY CITY, area placers—**gold.**

JACKSON CO.

AREA. This co. and including adjoining Josephine Co. to the W are located in a mountainous region of SW Ore. (the N watersheds of the Siskiyou Mts. of the northern Calif. boundary) containing one major and several minor valleys. To the S, over the Calif. line, is the rugged Klamath Mountains system which, like the Siskiyous, is an E–W transverse system of sharp forested peaks and alpine meadows. Both range systems are notably famed in the **gold** rush history of the region for the extraordinarily rich "Northern Mines" containing more than 700 lode and hydraulic mines along a mineralized belt to the N, NW, W, SW, and S of YREKA, Siskiyou Co., Calif. The **gold**-producing mines of SW Ore. belong to the same mineralized belt. Each summer sees many hobby **gold** panners, scuba divers, prospectors, and hardrock miners camped along the regional streams.

APPLEGATE (District): (1) area diggings and hydraulic placers along the Applegate R. (originally mainly worked by Chinese in the early days)—**jade** (botryoidal, or Monterey type), **soapstone,** placer **gold;** (2) Upper Applegate District (i.e., area drained by the Applegate R.): (a) area mines, (b) the Queen Anne Mine, and (c) the Sterling Mine—**arsenopyrite, calcite, gold, pyrite.**

ASHLAND: (1) Big Butte, area—**agate;** (2) SE, on Green Springs Mt. (elev. 4,551 ft.), area, slopes, draws, etc.—**agate nodules, carnelian, chalcedony, jasper;** (3) mining district, including Mt. Ashland (noted winter recreational ski area) or Siskiyou Peak, Pilot Knob, and Grizzly Peak plus the intervening Bear Cr. Valley, with several tributaries leading N as far as PHOENIX (8 mi.): (a) ASHLAND area mines—**gold, pyrite, pyrrhotite, quartz crystals, sericite;** (b) Columbine mines—**chalcopyrite, gold, marcasite, pyrite, pyrolusite;** (c) Crackerjack mines—**bornite, chalcopyrite, calcite, gold, pyrite;** (d) Mattern mines—**calcite, gold, pyrite;** (e) Palmer Cr., small prospect —**cinnabar;** (f) Reeder, area mines—**calcite, chlorite, gold, pyrite;** (g) Shorty Hope, mines—**calcite, chalcopyrite, galena, gold, pyrite, pyrrhotite.**

BUTTE FALLS, area stream gravels—**bloodstone.**

CENTRAL POINT, area from 4 mi. E of town to 6 mi. NE at EAGLE POINT, *q.v.:* (1) Rogue R. gravel bars, and (2) gravels of Antelope and Butte creeks and their tributary draws—**moss agate.**

EAGLE POINT, area stream gravels—**moss agate, bloodstone.**

GOLD HILL (District), includes the Rogue R. Valley from CENTRAL POINT and Table Rock W to Josephine Co., a great many important regional old mines scattered in the backcountry, most of which have similar minerals on their dumps—**arsenopyrite, bornite, calcite, chalcopyrite, galena, gold, pyrite, pyrolusite, pyrrhotite, sphalerite.**

JACKSON (Medford District), historic community oriented toward tourism. The district adjoins the ASHLAND District on the NW and includes all of the Bear Cr. Valley between PHOENIX and CENTRAL POINT; to the SW it extends to the divide between Bear Cr. and the Little Applegate R.; to the NE it is limited by Antelope Cr.: (1) the Norling Mine—**gold, pyrite;** (2) the Opp Mine—**calcite, chlorite, gold, pyrite, telluride (petzite?);** (3) the Town Mine —**gold, pyrite, quartz;** (4) the Yellow King Mine—**gold, pyrite.**

MEDFORD: (1) on hills above McCloud on Rte. 62 to Crater Lake; (a) area basalt outcrops—**natrolite;** (b) draws, washes, slopes, etc.—**quartz crystals** (acicular, radiating, individual crystals to 8 in. long); (2) Big Butte, area—**medfordite** (green and white **jasper**); (3) Big Falls, area—**bloodstone;** (4) NE 10 mi. on Rte. 62, broad area—**carnelian moss agate;** (5) N 12 mi., Table Rock (prominent landmark), area—**agate, petrified wood.**

JEFFERSON CO.

AREA, N and E parts of co., tributaries of the John Day R., in regional gravels, draws, washes, etc.—**fossil ferns** (*Osmundites oregonensis*).

ASHWOOD: (1) area—**agate, chalcedony, geodes, jasper, thundereggs;** (2) E 22 mi., the Horse Heaven Mine—**morrisonite (chert).**

MADRAS: (1) general region—**agate, chalcedony, geodes, jasper, thundereggs;** (2) NE 17 mi. and 4 mi. SE of WILLOWDALE, *q.v.,* the Fulton Agate Beds (formerly known as the Priday Ranch), one of the best-known gemstone collecting areas in Oregon—**agate** (lace, plume, polka dot), **chalcedony, jasper, precious opal, thundereggs** (with centers of **agate, chalcedony, carnelian,** cavities lined with perfect small **drusy quartz crystals**). (The "Priday Ranch" **thundereggs** are found in all sizes from tiny to huge; sliced and polished, they appear in almost every museum collection in America. The ranch owners, who charge a modest fee per lb., keep the best collecting grounds opened up with bulldozers.)

WILLOWDALE, general area surfaces, draws, washes, etc.—**agate, chalcedony, jasper, geodes, thundereggs.**

JOSEPHINE CO.

AREA, Josephine Cr., placer gravels—**gold, josephinite** (a nickel mineral), **platinum nuggets.** (All streams show **platinum.**)

CAVE CREEK JUNCTION: (1) area gravels and placer mines along Cave Cr. —**gold, rhodonite;** (2) E 18 mi. to famed Oregon Caves, all area surrounding the caverns—**agate, chalcedony, gold nuggets** (in area alluvial gravels of watercourses), **jasper, petrified wood, rhodonite.**

GALICE (District), occupies the Rogue R. Valley NW of the mouth of Jump-Off-Joe Cr. to the W boundary of co., many area old mines—**arsenopyrite, azurite, bornite, calcite, chalcopyrite, chrysocolla, galena, gold, malachite, pyrite, pyrolusite, pyrrhotite, sphalerite.**

GRANTS PASS (District), occupies the Rogue R. Valley SE of the mouth of Jump-Off-Joe Cr. (except the Applegate Valley), many old mines—cf. GALICE.

HOLLAND, S 1½ mi. along Althouse Cr., area—**agate, garnet, gold nuggets, jasper, quartz crystals, serpentine.**

KERBY, W 10 mi., mine—**chrysotile asbestos.**

WALDO (District), occupies the SW corner of co., an area drained chiefly by Althouse and Sucker creeks and the East Fork of the Illinois R.: (1) a few placer and lode mines—**azurite, bornite, chromite, chrysocolla, galena, gold, malachite, quartz crystals, silver;** (2) near headwaters of the Illinois R., at Sailor's Diggings, placer—**gold.** (This is an area of large **gold nuggets;** a record single nugget weighed 15 lbs., and was valued at $3,100 at the old $20 per troy oz. price.)

KLAMATH CO.

AREA: (1) Crater Lake National Park (no collecting inside boundaries): (a) all area surrounding park—**agate, petrified wood,** etc.; (b) immediately S of park, area—**"Crater Lake flower" jasper;** (2) Klamath R. gravel bars— **agate, chalcedony, jasper,** etc.

LAKE CO.

AREA, far NE corner of co. (reached 12 mi. SE of HAMPTON, Deschutes Co. via U.S. 20), on SE side of hwy., Glass Butte (elev. 6,393 ft.), center of a vast volcanic area (**obsidian** flow) denominated as the Glass Butte Recreational Rockhound Area in Sec. 3, 10, 14, T. 23 S, R. 22 E (the Glass Butte– Black Butte area)—**obsidian** (banded, black, brecciated, green, irridescent [rainbow], red, snowflake).

LAKEVIEW: (1) all surrounding desert area—**agate, jasper, geodes, nodules, sanidine, sanidine-sunstone;** (2) S 8 mi., in Crane Canyon, area—**agate, jasper, thundereggs;** (3) N 6 mi. on U.S. 395, turn E on Rte. 140 to Warner Canyon, general area with long N–S dirt rd. giving access from Crane Mt. on the S to Crook Peak on the N—**quartz family gemstones, petrified wood.**

PLUSH, NE to Hart Mt.: (1) W flank and draws—**agate, chalcedony, geodes, jasper, opal** (common, precious), **thundereggs;** (2) summit, cavities in Tertiary basalts—**chalcedony, opal** (common, precious).

QUARTZ MT. (E side of Quartz Pass on Rte. 140 about 66 mi. E of Klamath Falls, Klamath Co.), area of the pass—**agate, chalcedony, jasper,** etc.

LANE CO.

BOHEMIA (S part of co. 15 mi. SE of DISSTON), a mining district comprising placer claims on Sharps, Martin, and Steamboat creeks and tributaries—**gold, barite, cerussite, chalcopyrite, pyrite.**

GOSHEN, E 3 mi., Mt. Pisgah, area—**agate, calcite, heulandite, jasper, malachite, mesolite, quartz crystals.**

HAMPTON, LANDAX (on Rte. 58 about 30 mi. SE of EUGENE), W, at June Mt., a ledge—**saltpeter.**

LINCOLN CO.

AGATE BEACH (famed Ore. coast collecting locality, especially after every winter storm), in beach gravels, prized gemstone—**agates, moonstones, jasper, chalcedony,** etc.

NEWPORT: (1) area beaches, especially at Agate Beach to the N—**agate,** chalcedony, jasper, petrified teredo wood, quartz crystals (waterworn); (2) Yakina Bay to TOLEDO, area black sands—placer gold.

YACHATS: (1) area beaches—sagenite agate, chalcedony, orbicular jasper, moonstones, silicified coral enhydros (water-filled chalcedony geodes); (2) beaches S to FLORENCE, Douglas Co.—agate (sagenite and others), jasper, petrified wood, coral enhydros, moonstones; (3) beach gravels 2 mi. N of the mouth of China Cr. to Commings Cr. beach 3 mi. S of town—cf. above; (4) gravels of Big Cr.—garnets.

LINN CO.

SWEET HOME, HOLLEY, area: (1) the Sweet Home Petrified Forest (embracing some 20 sq. mi.), especially along Ames Cr. and the shores of the Calapooya R., area—banded agate, crystal geodes, gem silicified wood (beautifully colored and patterned). This fossil forest has been a prime collecting area for half a century. The most abundant specimens have so far been found on farms between the two communities, which are about 4 mi. apart, with many "diggings" extending E and S. The wood occurs in the Eocene Tyee sandstones but appears to be of Oligocene age; (2) Chandlar Mt. SW of HOLLEY, area—agate (purple or Calapooya blue), carnelians (to large size).

QUARTZVILLE, in placer sands of Quartzville Cr.—gold. This is a summer hobby panning area, and colors are abundant.

MALHEUR CO.

BROGAN, all surrounding area—agate, chalcedony, chert, jasper, petrified wood.

IRONSIDE: (1) all surrounding area—agate, chalcedony, chert, jasper, petrified wood; (2) NE, to the Willow Cr. Reservoir, all surrounding area—same.

JORDAN VALLEY: (1) all area draws, washes, surfaces—chert, jasper; (2) gravels of Jordan Cr.—agate, chert, jasper, petrified wood. (A dirt rd. runs E, rough and very steep in places, to the highly mineralized region of DE LAMAR and SILVER CITY, Owyhee Co., Ida., a "back door" entrance passable for stout cars and pickup trucks; many great silver mines, ghost towns, and long-abandoned ranches.)

MALHEUR, area extending NE to RYE VALLEY, Baker Co., q.v., many regional mines (some very deep lodes)—gold.

NYSSA: (1) area immediately surrounding town—agate, geodes, nodules, jasper, petrified wood, thundereggs; (2) basalt rimrocks along regional cr. valleys—moss agate, jasper, chalcedony, thundereggs; (3) SW 8 mi. to OWYHEE, then W and S on co. rd. to the Owyhee Reservoir Dam: (a) NW 10 mi., near Nigger Rock, area—agate, chalcedony, jasper, gemmy quartzite, petrified wood; (b) the Morrison Ranch near S end of the reservoir, area—morrisonite (a beautiful gemmy jasp-agate); (4) S 35 mi., broad area extending over the Ida. state line, best reached S from HOMEDALE, Ida., on U.S. 95, then S 2 mi. to large sign: "Graveyard Point, 4 mi. W and 1 mi. S."

(The brass plaque monument was erected in 1954 by the Northwest and California Federations of Mineralogical Societies to mark a small cemetery at the base of a prominent landmark on the Ida. side of the Ore. state line, now a famed collecting area in both states.) From the monument head S along a ditch bank to a bridge, cross W, and take main dirt rd. on right of an emergency airstrip, up a hill, through a gentle gap, and across a cattle guard back into Ore.:

(a) all area surrounding both sides of the state line, high-quality gem—**agate;** (b) W 2 mi. from the cattle guard to a rd. fork, take rt. fork, all area hills along both sides of rd. showing pits, trenches, and sizable excavations—**agate, arrowheads.** (This fine **agate** comes in all sizes, to over 100-lb. chunks. It is an unusual, beautiful moss type and occurs in seams and fissures underlying the surface in a square-mile area.)

ROCKVILLE (at S end of the Sucker Cr. Canyon about 43 mi. S of NYSSA), upstream along Sucker Cr. for entire length—**agate, chalcedony, chert, jasper,** colorful gemmy **quartzite, opalized wood.**

MARION CO.

DETROIT, the Santiam District, area placers—**gold.**

MORROW CO.

HEPPNER, SE, to area of buttes—**opal**-filled **nodules.**
PARKERS MILL, S, at Opal Butte, area—**hyalite opal.**

POLK CO.

DALLAS, area land surfaces—**jasper.**

SHERMAN CO.

BIGGS, S 5 mi. along U.S. 97, and 5 mi. S of RUFUS, area—**agate, jasper** (**wascoite** type).

TILLAMOOK CO.

AREA, ocean beach gravels of entire co. S to OCEANLAKE, Lincoln Co.—**agates, jasper, bloodstone, moonstone.**

UNION CO.

STARKEY, the Orofino Mine: (1) area—**agate, jasper;** (2) mine dumps—**gold.**

WALLOWA CO.

JOSEPH, along the Lower Inmaha R., area—**agate, prase.**

WASCO CO.

ANTELOPE: (1) general area—**agate** (iris, moss), **chalcedony** (roses, geodes), **jade, jasp-agate, jasper;** (2) E 1¼ mi., a quarry—red **jasper;** (3) E 10½ mi., area—**jasper;** (4) S 6.8 mi. on rd. to ASHWOOD, Jefferson Co., *q.v.,* area—green **moss agate;** (5) SE 15 mi., area—fossil ferns (*Osmundites oregonensis*).

MOSIER, area stream gravels—**petrified wood, silicified pine cones.**

PINE GROVE, W, and SE of Bear Springs Forest Camp, at Sunflower Flats (popular rockhound area on the Wapinitia Cutoff), all hillsides and creek gravels—**jasper, thundereggs.**

SIMNASHO, the Warm Springs Indian Reservation: (1) general area—brecciated **jasper;** (2) S flanks of the Mutton Mts., area—**agate, chalcedony geodes, geodes** (containing black **agate**).

THE DALLES: (1) W, gravels of upper Chenowith Cr. (E side of mts. from MOSIER, *q.v.*), area—white **opalized wood;** (2) S 13½ mi. on the Mill Cr. rd., area—**opalized** and **silicified wood.**

WAPINITIA, N, in mts., area—**agate, chalcedony, jasper.**

WHEELER CO.

ANTONE, in gravels of Spanish Gulch, placers—**gold.**

DAYVILLE: (1) NW 7 mi., and (2) E 13 mi., area—**fossil bone, petrified wood;** (3) gravels of the John Day R. (through entire co.)—**fossils, petrified wood.**

FOSSIL, S and W 16 mi., the famed Clarno Fossil Beds, area—**agate, jasper, fossils, petrified wood.**

PENNSYLVANIA

Known as the Keystone State, Pennsylvania manifests an extraordinary geologic history. Except for the coastal plains southeast of Philadelphia and around Lake Erie, the state is mostly hills and steep, high mountain ridges slashed by narrow valleys. Central Pennsylvania is a 2,500-foot plateau with a generally Arctic character, marked by the sprawling parallel Blue and Allegheny mountain systems. Through these mountains drainage rivers, older than the mountains themselves, cut spectacularly scenic "water gaps" that enabled colonial pioneers to penetrate the rich interior limestone valleys.

During the Ordovician and Silurian periods, Pennsylvania was part of a great western syncline lying beneath shallow epeiric seas and being steadily filled by the wasting away of the western slopes of Precambrian Appalachia. This ancient continental land mass, now entirely gone and with its granite roots sunk beneath the Atlantic Ocean off the shores of New England, was the "source land" for the basic rock strata of the state—the coarse, deltaic Pottsville conglomerate. The sedimentary deposits reached thicknesses of 4,000 and 5,000 feet, and the widely extended beds of Pennsylvanian marine limestones were formed while much of America lay under the epicontinental seas.

During the 50-million-year period of the Upper Carboniferous epoch, undoubtedly the greatest coal-forming era in the world, vast, luxuriant, tropical forests of *Sigillaria, Lepidendron,* and *Calimites* were extracting carbon dioxide from a steaming atmosphere to convert into the enormous **coal** beds for which the state is famed. This Pennsylvanian epoch, which began some 330 million years ago, derives its name from "Penn's Woods," the name given to the colony by the original Dutch who first began settling the land in 1681.

Although most of the gemstone and mineral localities of Pennsylvania are found in the southeastern counties, with a few in the south-central and southwestern portions of the state, a few minerals played an important role in the state's economic development. The **iron** which was important in the Revolutionary War came largely from the Great Cornwall Ore Banks of Lebanon Co., opened about 1735 on South Mountain at Cornwall, the greatest concentration of iron east of the Mississippi River. While coal constitutes the greatest of Pennsylvania's natural resources, it was the associated **petroleum** which really began the world's oil industry after Colonel Drake drilled his first famous wagon-wheel well near Titusville, Crawford Co., in 1859, striking an oil gusher at 69½ feet.

Nickel and **copper** were mined in Lancaster Co. before the Revolutionary War, and the Wood Chromite Mine provided most of the **chromite** used in America before the Civil War. Very little gold and silver have been found, and what **gold** was produced came as a by-product of the Cornwall Iron Mine. Most of the minerals mined in the state, other than a little **lead** and **zinc**, are in the nature of **marble, limestone, sandstone, building stone, clay, sand,** and **gravel.** From 1839 to 1892 a good deal of **corundum** came from several mines in Chester and Delaware counties, and gem **corundum crystals** are still gathered from pegmatite exposures in these counties. Mountain stream gravels produce collectors' items in **epidote, calcite, quartz crystals,** and **silicified woods** and **corals.** Many quarries and gravel pits prominent along most of the state's great rivers yield a never-ending supply of cryptocrystalline and crystalline **quartz gems.** Hundreds of **coal** mines produce high-quality **pyrite cubes** and carving-quality **anthracite coal.** Limestone quarries yield the usually familiar crystals of **calcite, dolomite,** and **pyrite.**

For information, write: Topographical and Geological Survey, Department of Internal Affairs, Harrisburg.

ADAMS CO.

AREA, S part of co. along the Md. state line, many regional **copper** mines—**azurite, cuprite, malachite**, etc.

CASHTOWN: (1) 2 mi. N of Newman School at head of the Buchanan Valley, in large **quartz** vein—**specular hematite;** (2) W 1 mi. (W of VIRGINIA MILLS and N of MARSHALL), area outcrops—**specular hematite, piedmontite** (a red **epidote**); (3) Charmain, outcrop along RR—**piedmontite;** (4) E, at Fox Fills, area—**garnets;** (5) N, on W side of Piney Mt., area—**piedmontite;** (6) Caledonia State Park, area—**agate, jasper.**

FAIRFIELD, N 1½ mi., at foot of Sugarloaf Mt., area—**garnets.**

GETTYSBURG: (1) Culp's Hill, Bushman's Quarry on S slope—decorative **granite, native copper;** (2) E 2 mi. to Rocky Grove School (2½ mi. SE from the Baltimore Turnpike), many area quarries along the rte.—**granite, copper;** (3) SE 2½ mi. on U.S. 140, on W bank of Rock Cr. (just before the Powers Hill Jct.), the Teeter Stone Quarry—**chabazite** (peach-colored crystals), **epidote, malachite** (as outside coatings), **pectolite,** massive **quartz;** (4) NE 4 mi., Granite Hill, area quarries—**feldspar, magnetite, olivine, quartz,** etc.

MARIA FURNACE: (1) SW 2 mi., on N banks of Tom's Cr., the Reed Hill Mine; (2) Pine Mt., on rd. from town: (a) NE ½ mi., on W side of rd., the Bingham Mine; (b) W ¾ mi., the Virgin Mine—**azurite, native copper, cuprite, epidote** (on Pine Mt.), **malachite, quartz, orbicular rhyolite.**

YORK SPRINGS, NW, area—pink **marble, quartz** pebbles (white, smoky).

ALLEGHENY CO.

ETNA, N 2 mi., at Wittmen and RR cut near Rte. 8—**barite, calcite, pyrite, sphalerite, wurtzite.**

GLASSMERE, area quarry—**barite, calcite, pyrite, sphalerite, wurtzite.**

TRAFFORD CITY, S ⅓ mi., a limestone quarry—**crystals, minerals,** abundant **fossils.**

ARMSTRONG CO.

APOLLO, GIRTY, KITTANNING, MCWILLIAMS, many regional limestone quarries and mines extending for many miles along a major outcrop: (1) mine dumps—**specular hematite, magnetite,** etc.; (2) area quarries—**calcite, chert, pyrite,** etc.

EDDYVILLE, S, in large old quarry—**gem crystals, minerals.**

KAYLOR, on Sugar Cr. between town and Snyder's Run, a large quarry—**calcite, iron minerals, fossils, pyrite.**

MANORVILLE, area quarries—**pyrite cubes.**

NORTH VANDERGRIFT, in stream bed of Gravel Bar Hollow, old **lead/zinc** pits—**galena, calcite,** massive **barite, geodes, sphalerite,** etc.

SOUTH BETHLEHEM, all along Redbank Cr. (N boundary of co.), area both upstream and downstream—**jasper, petrified wood.**

BEDFORD CO.

BARD, BUFFALO MILLS, HYNDMAN, MANNS CHOICE, NAPIER, all regional quarries (many)—**crystals, fossil corals.**
EVERETT, NE 6 mi. and 4 mi. S of HOPEWELL, between Ray's Hill and Broad Top Mt., the Sherman Valley: (1) 2 mi. N of HOPEWELL, mine dumps and in cuts and exposures along the Sherman Valley rd.—**calcite, chlorite, cryptomelane** (gemmy, botryoidal), **orthoclase feldspar, limonite, quartz crystals, tourmaline, zircon;** (2) ½ mi. E of Cypher Sta., near gap on Ray's Hill; (3) 1½ mi. E of the Sherman Valley open-cut mine—cf. item (1).
ST. CLAIRSVILLE, take the Pennsylvania Turnpike at the Bedford Interchange, go 6 mi. on Rte. 220, take rt. turn E over Brumbaugh Mt. to Morrison Cove, an area of 10 sq. mi.—**Herkimer diamonds** (doubly terminated **rock crystal,** to 2 lb.), **amethysts, calcite crystals.**
WATERSIDE: (1) area fields all way to NEW ENTERPRISE—**amethysts, rock crystal;** (2) S 1 mi., at Morrison Cove; and (3) N 1 mi., on W side of Yellow Cr., area—**calcite, chalcedony, chert, marble.**

BERKS CO.

BIRDSBORO, S 1 mi., in quarry—**zeolite crystals.**
BLANDON, HANCOCK, TOPTON, READING, area deposits—**ochers.**
BOYERSTOWN, W ½ mi., on Ironstone Cr. (first **iron** furnace erected in Pa.)—**magnetite.**
EARLVILLE, 2 mi. W of Hill Church, the Dotterer Mine—**specular hematite.**
FURNACE HILL, ROCKLAND, area **iron** mines—**specular hematite.**
JACKSONWALD, S 1.3 mi. on the LORANE rd., in rd. cut at base of hill—**calcite** (orange), **chabazite** (peach color), **prehnite** (green), **epidesmine** (rare var. of **stilbite,** as white translucent crystals and rosettes).
MORGANTOWN: (1) E 1¼ mi. on Rte. 122, the Grace Mine—**actinolite, apophyllite, byssolite, calcite, epidote** (massive, pale moss green), **garnets, natrolite, quartz** (massive white and smoky), **selenite, stilbite, tremolite;** (2) the Jones Mine—**malachite.**
READING: (1) area: (a) Alsace Twp., area mines—**pyrrhotite;** (b) gravels of the Schuylkill R.—**jasper;** (c) the Fritz Island Mine—**azurite, malachite, magnetite, chalcopyrite;** (2) E 1 mi., old mine—**sienna.**
SINKING SPRING, S 2 mi. on the FRITZTOWN rd., turn E ½ mi. on Chapel Rd., then N on Wheatfield Rd. for 1 mi. to the Wheatfield Magnetite Mine—**calcite crystals, fluorite** (amber crystals), **magnetite, melanite garnets.**

BLAIR CO.

ALTOONA: (1) NE, in village of CULP (on W and N borders); and (2) W of the Birmingham Sta., all area **lead/zinc** mine dumps (very many)—**anglesite, barite, calcite, cerussite, dolomite, galena, hemimorphite, pyrite,**

smithsonite, sphalerite; (3) Bald Eagle and Dunning mts., area mine dumps —cf. above.

CANOE CREEK (and Sinking Valley), many regional mines—**calamine, galena, smithsonite, sphalerite, calcite, cerussite, anglesite, dolomite, hemimorphite, pyrite.**

CLAYSBURG, SPROUL, regional quarries—gemmy **chert, quartz crystals.**

DUNCANSVILLE, HOLLIDAYSBURG, ROARING SPRING, ROYER, TYRONE, many regional limestone quarries—**crystals, gems, minerals.**

BRADFORD CO.

NEW ALBANY, the Carpenter Mine—**azurite, chalcopyrite, cerussite, malachite, melaconite.**

BUCKS CO.

AREA, countywide cr. beds and banks—**petrified wood.**

BUCKINGHAM, EUREKA, NEW HOPE, RUSHLAND, TREVOSE, regional limestone quarries—**gem crystals, minerals.**

BUCKMANVILLE, area mines—**copper minerals, native copper.**

COOPERSTOWN, E 2 mi., area—**"black granite"** (gemmy diabase).

DURHAM (Twp.), at Mine Hill, area—**feldspar, hematite, magnetite, quartz.**

FEASTERVILLE: (1) area outcrops—**sunstone;** (2) Triassic rock outcrops: (a) S and SE of Holland Sta., (b) NE of Leonard's Sta., (c) ¼ mi. SE of Roelof's Sta., (d) 1½ mi. N of Woodburne Sta., (e) numerous other outcrops (cf. on a geologic map of area)—**agate, chalcedony, chert, silicified wood.**

MORRISVILLE: (1) gravels of the Delaware R. opposite TRENTON, N.J.—**jasper** pebbles; (2) all regional gravel pits between town and 20 mi. S of PHILADELPHIA, Philadelphia Co. (distance of about 50 mi.)—**jasper.**

NESHAMINY, N 2 mi. and ¾ mi. W of Neshaminy Cr., the Vanartsdalen Quarry—**"chesterlite"** (blue **orthoclase moonstone**).

NEW BRITAIN, area mines—**galena, sphalerite.**

NEW GALENA, area mines—**galena, sphalerite.**

NEWTOWN, W, and ¼ mi. SE of Roelof's Sta., in Neshaminy Cr.—**jasper, petrified wood.**

PERKASIE, N 2 mi., at Rock Hill (largest quarry in co.)—**gem crystals** (in pockets and vugs).

QUAKERTOWN, area traprock quarries, in pockets—**gem crystals.**

RIEGELSVILLE, area stream gravels and gravel pits—gem **quartz minerals.**

VAN SCIVER, gravel operation (largest in state)—**gem crystals, minerals.**

CARBON CO.

BOWMANSTOWN, S, at Lehigh Gap (on Pennsylvania Turnpike on the Lehigh Co. line), area mines—**siderite.**

CHRISTMANS (in the LEIGHTON quadrangle), S 2,000 ft., on both E and W sides of the Lehigh R. gorge—**uranium minerals.**

JIM THORPE: (1) area fields, stream gravels, etc.—**jasper;** (2) .4 mi. S of the courthouse and ¾ mi. E of RR bridge over the Lehigh R. (1 mi. S of town), area—**uranium minerals;** (3) E, on N side of nose of Mt. Pisgah, area—**allanite, andersonite, autunite, carnotite, chlorite, metatorbernite, mica, pyrite, quartz, schroeckingerite, tyuyamunite, uranophane, uraninite.**

MAUNCH CHUNK: (1) N ¾ mi., on Mt. Pisgah in exposure of conglomerate—**carnotite;** (2) SE 7 mi., extending in a SW direction for 20 mi., many regional mines, especially at HAZARD and MILLPORT—**ocher.**

CHESTER CO.

AREA, many regional **corundum** mines in co.—**corundum, feldspar, diaspore** (clear crystals), **kyanite, margarite** (pearly plates), **sillimanite, spinel, tourmaline.**

AVONDALE (London Grove Twp.): (1) the Leiper Quarry—**garnets (almandite, essonite);** (2) N ¼ mi., area—**apatite;** (3) E ¼ mi., area—**quartz crystals** (clear, smoky), **rutile crystals.**

CHATHAM, SW 1 mi., area—**apatite.**

CHESTER, NORTHROP, area pegmatite outcrops—gem **beryl, garnets.**

COATESVILLE, NW 1½ mi., pegmatite outcrop on Rte. 30 by-pass, on S side of hwy. (park on side rds., walk), area—**amethyst, epidote, garnets, graphic granite, smoky quartz crystals.**

DOWNINGTON, N on Rte. 282 through LYNDELL, turn NE to crossrds. of CORNOG, to the Keystone Trap Rock Co. quarry on N side of hwy.—**byssolite, epidote, feldspar, garnet, prehnite, quartz crystals** (smoky, clear, with silky inclusions, blue), **sphene, tourmaline.**

EAST BRADFORD TWP., S and SW of SCONNELTOWN, between Brandywine Cr. and Plum Run, area—**rock crystal.**

EAST NOTTINGHAM TWP., 1½ mi. NE of CHROME, area pegmatites—**corundum.**

FAIRVILLE, area quarries—**labradorite, oligoclase sunstone.**

FREMONT (West Nottingham Twp.), SW 2 mi., area—**corundum, albite crystals.**

GOAT HILL, area bounded by co. line and the Md. border, numerous old pits and prospects—**albite, magnesite, sepiolite (meerschaum).**

HAUTO, area—**quartz crystals.**

KENNETT SQUARE: (1) SE ½ mi., at Pierce's Paper Mill (on E branch of Red Clay Cr.); and (2) SE 2 mi., on Cloud's farm (on a brook that enters the E branch)—**labradorite, oligoclase sunstone.**

KNAUERTOWN, ⅛ mi. N of village of ST. PETERS, at French Cr. **magnetite** mine and dumps—**apatite, apophyllite crystals, azurite, calcite** (green crystals with inclusions of **byssolite** or **malachite** on **chalcopyrite**), **chrysocolla, erythrite (cobalt bloom), malachite, pyrite crystals, quartz crystals, rhodochrosite, stilbite, wernerite.**

LYNDEL, the Cornog Quarry—blue **quartz** (gemmy).

NOTTINGHAM: (1) general area, exposures—**sunstone;** (2) SW 2 mi., on S bank of Black Run, numerous quarries (largest is the Brandywine)—gem **serpentine, garnets, feldspar** (various kinds), **tourmaline;** (3) Nottingham Park: (a) across cr. bordering park and S of the main office, trails lead through woods to many old mines, on dumps—**albite moonstone, chrome minerals;** (b) SW 1¼ mi., the Keystone Quarry; and (c) W, at the Sparvetta Quarry—**fibrous actinolite, apatite, asbestos, moonstone,** massive **quartz, tourmaline, williamsite;** (4) Cooper School, N, in fields—**colerainite** (in rosettes with **feldspar), goethite.**

OXFORD, S, on the Md. state line (cf. state line pits in introduction to Md., and Cecil Co., Md.), very many old **chromite** mines of the Scott, Pine Groves, and White Barrens—gem **serpentine, williamsite.**

PARKESBURG, area pegmatite outcrops—**rutile crystals.**

PHOENIXVILLE: (1) area **lead/zinc** mines, e.g., the Jug Hollow Mine in Schuylkill Twp.—**barite, cerussite, chalcopyrite, galena, malachite, melaconite, gold-**bearing **pyrite;** (2) S, to the Wheatley Lead Mine and the Chester County Mine (.2 mi. S of rd. between PICKERING and WILLIAMS CORNER)— **azurite, barite** (clear crystals), **chalcopyrite, cuprite, fluorite, galena, hydrozincite** (fluorescent), **linarite, malachite, mimetite, pyromorphite** (green and yellow), **quartz crystals, silver minerals, native wire silver, sphalerite** (rare), **sulfur, wulfenite.**

POMEROY, area—**rutile crystals.**

UNIONVILLE (Newlin Twp.): (1) area farms, small mines and prospects— **corundum;** (2) NE ½ mi., at Corundum Hill, in pegmatite exposures—gem **beryl, corundum, diaspore,** yellow **quartz crystals;** (3) 1 mi. N of Corundum Hill, area—**corundum, serpentine.**

WAKEFIELD, S on U.S. 222 to near the Md. border, turn E on rural rd. to Cedar Hill Quarry—**verde antique, williamsite.**

WARWICK (Twp.), French Cr., area **iron** and **copper** mines—**chalcopyrite, native copper, specular hematite, limonite, magnetite.**

WEST CHESTER: (1) N, area—gem **serpentine;** (2) ¼ mi. E of Pocopson Sta. (in Birmingham Twp.), many outcrops in area—**rutilated amethyst, quartz crystals** (clear, smoky); (3) S 1.4 mi. to Darlington Corners, the Brinton Quarry (on Radley Run on N side of Rte. 926, W of Rte. 322, just SW of center of Darlington Corners)—**actinolite,** gem **beryl, bronzite, clinochlore, feldspar crystals, garnets, quartz crystals, tourmaline, williamsite** (translucent green gems), **zircon;** (4) S 2½ mi., on W side of Osborn Hill, area—**corundum, quartz crystals** (clear, smoky).

WEST PIKELAND TWP., Opperman's Corner, on Rte. 113, NE ½ mi., at old Ben Franklin Mine (reached via exit 23 from the Pennsylvania Turnpike onto Rte. 111, S for ½ mi. to Rte. 113), quarries on the N—**garnets, graphite, limonite, quartz** (gemmy, blue), **pyrite crystals, zircon.**

WESTOWN TWP., many area outcrops—**quartz crystals** (clear, smoky).

WILLOWDALE (East Marlboro Twp.), SW 1 mi., on W branch of Red Clay Cr., area—**rock crystal.**

COLUMBIA CO.

ESPY, area mines—**calamine.**

CUMBERLAND CO.

BOILING SPRINGS: (1) SE 2 mi., (2) SE 3 mi., (3) White Rock, 1 mi. E of Reading Bank, area—**cryptomelane** (gemmy, blue black), **goethite, quartz**

crystals, tourmaline, zircon; (4) N, in traprock dike crossing the co.—**marble, calcite, fluorite, quartz crystals.**

CARLISLE: (1) area farm fields—banded **agate, quartz crystals;** (2) E 1 mi. from the Carlisle Interchange on the Pennsylvania Turnpike, area on S side of Rte. 11—banded **agate;** (3) NW 1½ mi., area—**agate, jasper, amethystine quartz, quartz crystals** (clear, smoky).

CLEVERSBURG–PINE GROVE FURNACE, South Mt., area mines—**copper minerals, native copper.**

MT. HOLLY SPRINGS: (1) W, general area of fields, ditches, cut banks, etc.—**agate nodules** (not gem quality); (2) SW 1 mi., area mine dumps—cf. BOILING SPRINGS; (3) S on Rte. 34 through Holly Springs, turn W at main intersection for ½ mi., take rt. fork rd. to a farm 1.2 mi. from Rte. 34 on N side of rd., area fields S of farm, ditches, banks, along fences, etc., prolific—**agate, chalcedony, jasper;** (4) SW 3 mi., on N flank of South Mt., the Wharton Mine—gem **cryptomelane;** (5) W 3½ mi. on Huntsdale rd., turn S opposite cannery by RR to South Mt. phosphate mine dumps—**apatite, braunite, cacoxenite,** banded **chalcedony, quartz crystals, strengite, wavellite** (crystals, rosettes, sunbursts, often banded with **pyrolusite**); (6) W 4 mi., in vicinity of Moores Mill, area mines—**wavellite.**

PINE GROVE FURNACE, N 1 mi. along Little Rocky Ridge, in area **quartz** outcrops—**specular hematite, quartz** (milky, smoky, yellow).

DELAWARE CO.

AVONDALE (Springfield Twp.): (1) area quarries, in small amounts—**chalcopyrite;** (2) Leiper's Quarry (on E side of Crum Cr.)—**aquamarine, golden beryl.**

BARKER: (1) area quarries—**amethysts, smoky quartz crystals;** (2) area rd. cuts, excavations, etc.—**amethysts, quartz crystals.**

BOOTHWYN (Upper Chichester Twp.): (1) SW ⅜ mi., and W of the E branch of Naaman's Cr., on N side of the B&O RR sta.—**sphene;** (2) N ½ mi., on the Armstrong farm E of the CHELSEA rd.—**amethysts** (clear purple, rutilated); (3) N 2 mi. and E of the CHELSEA-BOOTHWYN rd., area—**amethysts** (clear purple, some rutilated).

CHADD'S FORD: (1) SW 1 mi., area—transparent **oligoclase crystals;** (2) S 1½ mi., in gravels and banks of the Brandywine R.—**amethysts.**

CHELSEA: (1) SW 1 mi., mined as an abrasive—**garnet;** (2) W 2 mi., a pegmatite mine—**garnet.**

CHESTER (Twp.): (1) area gravels of Chester Cr.—**amethysts, smoky quartz crystals;** (2) area quarries—gem **beryl, feldspar, rock crystal;** (3) E ¼ mi., the Shaw & Earey Quarry (N of the B&O RR)—**amethysts, smoky quartz crystals;** (4) Bridgewater Sta. on the Pennsylvania RR, opposite, at John Mullen's Quarries (on E side of Chester Cr.)—**mica, quartz crystals** (various colors), **sphene.**

CHESTER HEIGHTS (Aston Twp.), S 1 mi., in gravels of Green's Cr.—**almandite garnets.**

CROZIERVILLE: (1) area fields, rd. cuts, etc.—**amethysts;** (2) W ½ mi., on S side of Chester Cr. opposite LENNI, area—**amethysts.**

CRUM LYNNE, Ward's Quarry on Crum Cr.—gem **beryl, feldspar, quartz crystals.**

DARBY (Upper Providence Twp): (1) Sycamore Mills, E along Ridley Cr., pegmatite dike exposures—**amazonite,** transparent **oligoclase crystals, orthoclase sunstone;** (2) 3½ mi. below, at the Shaw & Ezrey Quarry (near CHESTER and WHITE HORSE)—**aquamarine, beryl.**

ELWYN STA., area farm fields—**corundum.**

GLENDALE (SW corner of Lansdowne quadrangle in Haverford Twp.), take rd. N of Darby Cr., 1 mi. S of jct. of cr. with Rte. 3, a pegmatite mine—gem **beryl** (to 4 in. long), **garnets, feldspar, quartz** (several varieties), **tourmaline** (black).

GLEN MILLS (Thornbury Twp.), area—**amethysts, albite moonstone, rutilated quartz crystals.**

LEIPERVILLE (Ridley Twp.): (1) W ½ mi., at Deshong's Quarry on E side of Ridley Cr.—**aquamarine, golden beryl;** (2) E ¾ mi., in fields of Sherz's and Hibbard's farms—**corundum;** (3) cf. CRUM LYNNE (RR sta.), S ½ mi., at Ward's Quarry on E side of Crum Cr.—**amazonite,** gem **beryl, feldspar, quartz crystals.**

MARPLE TWP.: (1) general area—**amethysts, quartz crystals** (clear, rutilated); (2) Palmer's Mill, area mines—**chromite.**

MEDIA (Middletown Twp.): (1) the Media Quarry—gem **beryl, feldspar, rock crystal;** (2) W: (a) in area pegmatite outcrops—**corundum;** (b) on the Schofield and Hibbard farms—**corundum;** (3) W 1 mi., at Mineral Hill: (a) area farm fields, rd. cuts, etc.—**albite moonstone, amazonite, corundum, orthoclase sunstone;** (b) the Mineral Hill Quarry (W of Ridley Cr. and N of Blackhorse) **albite** (opalescent), **amazonite, aventurine, aquamarine, gem feldspar, garnets, moonstone, sunstone;** (4) N, at the Phillips Chromite Mines—gem **serpentine;**

(5) Black Horse: (a) S ¼ mi. along rd. to ELWYN, area—**corundum;** (b) SE ½ mi., pits in pegmatites—**corundum** (crystals to 6 in. long; in area farm fields as gray, blue, white, and brown crystals), **amazonite, beryl, feldspar, kyanite, moonstone, sillimanite, sunstone** (many of these gem crystals are noted for asterism); (c) NE ¾ mi. (1 mi. W of MEDIA), area—**albite moonstone, amazonite, sunstone (oligoclase, orthoclase);** (d) SW, to Chrome Run, area of widespread pegmatite outcrops—**albite moonstone,** transparent **oligoclase crystals, orthoclase sunstone;**

(6) NW 2½ mi., Blue Hill, area—**amazonite, beryl, feldspar, oligoclase crystals** (clear), **orthoclase sunstone;** (7) NW 2½ mi.: (a) ¾ mi. NE of Sycamore Mills, at Blue Hill Crossroads—**quartz crystals** (blue, green); (b) 1 mi. E of Rose Tree dam on Crum Cr., area—**amethysts** (deep purple); (8) Lenni Sta.: (a) E, in RR cut—**albite moonstone, amazonite, oligoclase sunstone;** (b) N 1 mi., on Dismal Run, area—transparent **oligoclase crystals.**

MORGAN STATION: (1) S ¼ mi., area—**corundum;** (2) W, area fields, cuts, etc.—**amethysts;** (3) Dutton's Mill rd., a pegmatite dike outcrop—**amethysts;** (4) Village Green, area—**corundum,** yellow **quartz crystals.**

MORTON, NW, in area quarries—**garnet, feldspar crystals, rock crystal.**

NEWTON SQUARE (Newton Twp.): (1) W 1 mi., in pegmatite outcrops and rd. cuts—**oligoclase moonstone;** (2) a mine near Ox Run, in **serpentine—chromite.**

SWARTHMORE, S, on Crum Cr., in Leiper's Quarry—gem **beryl** (golden yellow to pale yellow green), **amethysts, garnets, quartz crystals.**

SYCAMORE MILLS, E, in fields of Reece's farm on Ridley Cr.—**corundum.**

TRAINER STA. (Lower Chichester Twp.), N 1½ mi., on a knoll near the Linwood Mill dam—**quartz crystals** (clear, smoky).

UPLAND: (1) area quarries on Chester Cr.—**feldspar, garnets, quartz crystals;** (2) E: (a) area around Henvi's Quarry N of Chester Cr.—**amethyst geodes;** (b) area around Waterville rd.—**amethyst geodes.**

UPPER DARBY (P.O.), W ½ mi., area—**quartz crystals** (large, clear, smoky).

WAYNE, E, area quarries and stream gravels—**garnet,** blue **quartz crystals.**

FRANKLIN CO.

AREA: (1) South Mt., in gemmy rhyolite porphyries, breccias, and conglomerates; and (2) Pigeon Hills, area—gem red **jasper.**

CALEDONIA PARK: (1) area around the Caledonia State Park—**agate, jasper;** (2) N slope of Huckleberry Hill—**garnets.**

CHAMBERSBURG, area mines—**barite.**

LANCASTER STA., area quarries—**fluorite.**

WAYNESBORO, area mines—**barite.**

FRANKLIN, ADAMS COS.

AREA, the Blue Ridge Summit (E of WAYNESBORO), E on Rtes. 16 and 116 (toward FAIRFIELD), with GREENSTONE being a center for a large area of many old mines and mills: (1) on mine dumps—**copper minerals, native copper, quartz;** (2) the Ruberoid Quarry—**copper minerals, epidote** (in rhyolite, some with **native copper** inclusions); (3) the Bingham Mine—**cuprite;** (4) Mt. Hope area quarries and mine dumps—**talc, native copper** (at the Bechtel Copper Mine); (5) the Snively Copper Mine (a popular rock club field trip locality)—**cuprite.**

FULTON CO.

FORT LITTLETON, N 1 mi., pits and trenches along Aughwick Cr.—**barite, calcite, chalcopyrite, pyrite, quartz crystals.**

NEEDMORE: (1) Beaverdam Pond, area—**manganese minerals;** (2) Duvall Cove, along Oregon Cr.—**manganese minerals;** (3) McConnell's Cove, area limestone quarries—**gems, minerals;** (4) W 4 mi., on Sideling Hill at Whips Cove—**cryptomelane, psilomelane, pyrolusite.**

GREENE CO.

CARMICHAELS, DURBIN, MT. MORRIS, WHITELEY, regional quarries in sandstone—**quartz crystals.**

JEFFERSON, along Tenmile Cr. to Laurel Run, area quarries—**quartz crystals.**

MORRIS TWP., SE section, along Browns Run, area—**iron minerals** and **nodules.**

OAK FOREST, 2 mi. above, at Pursley Run—**iron minerals** and **nodules.**

TRUMBULL, on S bank of Tenmile Cr., a quarry—**calcite, pyrite.**

WAYNESBURG, S 1½ mi., in a sandstone quarry—**quartz crystals.**

HUNTINGTON CO.

MAPLETON, area quarries—**quartz crystals.**

MCCONNELLSTOWN, ORBISONIA, UNION FURNACE, area limestone quarries —**calcite crystals, fluorite,** etc.

MT. UNION, THREE SPRINGS, in area sandstone quarries—**quartz crystals.**

WARRIORSBURG, S 3 mi., on S slope of Dry Hollow Ridge, numerous **iron** mines—gemmy **cryptomelane, jasper, quartz crystals** (with inclusions).

LANCASTER CO.

BAINBRIDGE (Paradise Twp.): (1) N 1 mi., area fields—**petrified wood;** (2) Kinzer, area—**rutilated quartz crystals;** (3) 2 mi. NW of Churchtown, and (4) 3 mi. NE of Churchtown, area—**petrified wood.**

BLUE BALL: (1) many area quarries—**gems, minerals;** (2) N on Rte. 23 to the Showalter Quarry on N side of rd.—**dogtooth calcite, fluorite, specular hematite, quartz crystals, rutile.**

BROWNSTOWN, a nearby quarry on Conestoga Cr.—crystals of **calcite** and **quartz.**

CENTREVILLE, an abandoned quarry on Chickies Cr.—crystals of **calcite** and **quartz.**

COLUMBIA: (1) E, a quarry—crystals of **calcite, dolomite,** and **quartz;** (2) N 1 mi. from jct. of Rte. 30 with the St. Joseph's Academy rd., then N toward Chestnut Hill, park car on summit, area fields to E and W—**limonite** (geodes, pseudomorphs after **pyrite**); (3) 1 mi. farther NE, to Grubb Lake and Mud Lake, area—**limonite** (geodes, massive).

EAST PETERSBURG, SILVER SPRINGS, TALMAGE, very many area quarries— crystals of **calcite, quartz,** etc.

EPHRATA, SW 1 mi., a quarry—**dolomite** (tinted pink and green, porcelain-like).

GAP: (1) SW 4 mi., the Gap Nickel Mine—**chalcopyrite, millerite, pyrite, pyrrhotite;** (2) many area quarries—**gems, crystals, minerals.**

JENKINS CORNER, W ⅓ mi., at Rock Springs Run (Fulton Twp.) and 1¼ mi. NNE of Rock Springs, Md., area—**moss agate.**

LANCASTER: (1) area quarries along Conestoga Cr.; (2) quarries along Little Conestoga Cr.—crystals of **calcite, dolomite,** and **quartz;** (3) NE, in the Stoner Quarry, abundant—**pyrite crystals;** (4) the Blue Ball Quarry— **calcite, dolomite, fluorite, hematite, pyrite, quartz crystals, rutile;** (5) area **zinc** mines—**calamine, cerussite, smithsonite;** (6) N 1 mi., near Fruitville Pike, on E side on the property of a nursery—**limonite cubes.**

LITITZ, N, in a quarry—pink **calcite crystals.**
MILLERSVILLE, W 1 mi., a quarry—**calcite crystals, pyrite.**
MT. PLEASANT (Bart Twp.), NW 1 mi., area—**amethysts.**
PEQUEA, the Pequea Mine—**galena, sphalerite, wulfenite.**
QUARRYVILLE, SE on Rte. 472 to UNION, turn W onto left-trending rd. before reaching edge of village, go ½ mi. to the Stillwell Quarry—**brucite, chlorite, chrysotile, magnetite, williamsite.**
TEXAS, area outcrops—**serpentine.**
WAKEFIELD, S, the famed State Line District: (1) the Cedar Hill Quarry (Just N of the Pa.-Md. state line, reached from U.S. 222 via an E-trending rd.—**agate, aragonite, bloodstone, brucite, calcite, chalcedony, chromite, deweylite** (fluorescent), **dolomite crystals, hydromagnesite, magnesite, common opal, prase, williamsite,** many other minerals; (2) the Octoraro Cr. district, in **serpentine** exposures—**chromite.**
WINGDALE, SE 3 mi. on rd. to Lee's Bridge (9 mi. SW of OXFORD), the old Wood Chromite Mine shafts, dumps and adjoining pits—**brucite, cacoxenite, banded chalcedony, chromite, uvarovite garnet, millerite, serpentine, steatite, vesuvianite, williamsite.**

LEBANON CO.

ALMA, AVON, CLEONA, MILLARDSVILLE, MYERSTOWN, PALMYRA, very many regional quarries, wide assortment—**gems, crystals, minerals.**
CORNWALL: (1) many area quarries—**gems, minerals;** (2) area mines—**azurite, chalcopyrite, magnetite, malachite, pyrite;** (3) S, and just NW of a rd. at Big Hill (on old Rte. 322), extensive mine dumps—**actinolite, calcite crystals, chlorite, diopside, epidote, fluorite, garnet (grossularite, andradite), gold** (traces), **labradorite, magnetite, moonstone spar, prehnite, pyrite crystals,** gemmy **quartz** (massive, and clear, white, and smoky crystals), **sphalerite, sphene, talc, tremolite, wurtzite** (crystal form), **zeolites.**
JONESTOWN: (1) S 1 mi., in Bunker Hills, in white sandstone—**quartz crystals;** (2) S 2 mi., a traprock quarry—**gem crystals.**

LEHIGH CO.

ALBURTIS, BREINIGSVILLE, area deposits—**ocher.**
ALLENTOWN: (1) area hills, washes, fields—gemmy **jasper;** (2) area granite quarries—gemmy red **granite;** (3) S 7 mi., near the Pennsylvania Turnpike, area fields, washes, rd. cuts—colored **chert.**
BETHLEHEM, S 4 mi. on Rte. 12, at FRIEDENSVILLE: (1) area **zinc** mines—**aragonite, calamine, greenockite, jasper, quartz crystals, prase, pyrite, smithsonite, sphalerite;** (2) ½ mi. W of main town intersection, the New Jersey Zinc Mine—**aragonite crystals** (fluorescent), **nicholsonite** (fluorescent, phosphorescent), **pyrite crystals, quartz crystals, smithsonite** (banded), **sphalerite crystals, spinel.**
MACUNGLE, SE 2 mi. (½ mi. N of SHIMERVILLE), area—blue **corundum (sapphires;** large crystals, asteriated).
SHIMERVILLE, N ¾ mi., area—**sapphires** (large, asteriated).

VERA CRUZ (13 mi. S of the Lehigh Interchange of the Pennsylvania Turn-pike), in regional hills—**jasper** (red, brown, yellow), **sapphires.**

LUZERNE CO.

HAZELTON, WEST PITTSTON, area anthracite **coal** mine dumps—gem-hard **anthracite** (takes good polish, can be carved), compact gemmy **pyrite.**

WHITE HAVEN: (1) area quarries—gemmy red **quartzite;** (2) N 5 mi., the Moosehead mines—**ocher.**

WILKES-BARRE, area **coal** mines: (1) W, at NATICOKE, (2) S, at ASHLEY (4 mi. S of Ashley Jct., near village of Mountaintop)—gemmy **anthracite, pyrite.**

LYCOMING CO.

BEAVER LAKE: (1) W .7 mi., on the Leon Myers farm (just S of Straw-bridge), in a sandstone outcrop—**radioactive minerals;** (2) E side of Beaver Lake, ½ mi. N of outlet, a sandstone outcrop and an old **copper** mine—**copper minerals** (radioactive); (3) S ½ mi. from the Beaver Lake Hotel, on W side of Beaver Run 250 ft. from hwy. crossing of creek, an old **copper** mine—**copper minerals** (radioactive); (4) SW of the S end of Beaver Lake 1 mi., on hill facing S between two branches of Beaver Run, old **copper** mine—**azurite, chalcocite, chalcopyrite, malachite, fossils** (plant).

TIVOLI, N edge of town, on N side of Big Run 200 ft. NW of U.S. 220, area—**copper minerals** (radioactive), **fossils** (plant, invertebrate).

MONROE CO.

AREA: (1) SE part of co., all regional limestone quarries—**calcite, pyrite,** etc.; (2) Delaware Gap, area quarries—**fluorite.**

KUNKLETOWN: (1) area stream beds and banks—**quartz crystals** (some coated with tiny crystals of **azurite**); (2) S, in sand and clay pits—**quartz crystals.**

STROUDSBURG, area close to the N.J. line—**agatized corals, quartz** (crystals, other gemstones).

MONTGOMERY CO.

AREA: (1) Alsace Twp.: (a) Spies Church, NNW 1½ mi., and (b) 1½ mi. S of Jacksonwald, at Kensey Hill, area—**chalcedony, jasper, jasp-agate;** (2) Edge Hill (and near Spring Hill), area mines—**pyrolusite;** (3) Lower Providence Twp., the Eaton Mine—**cerussite, copper minerals, iron minerals.**

BOWERS STA.: (1) S 1 mi., on Flint Hill (on Rte. 320 on the Schuyl-kill R.), and (2) Olney Furnace, NE 1¾ mi., at Green Hill, area—**amethyst, chalcedony, silicified wood.**

BRIDGEPORT, SE ½ mi. on Rte. 202, the Bridgeport Dolomite Quarry (alongside the RR)—calcite, chalcedony, dolomite, goethite, jasper, malachite, rock crystal, sphalerite.

CONSHOHOCKEN, GLENSIDE, MONTGOMERYVILLE, NORRISTOWN, PLYMOUTH, all regional quarries—gem serpentine, steatite.

DURHAM (Twp.), general area outcrops of Cambrian quartzites—chalcedony, jasp-agate, jasper.

JARRETTOWN (on Rte. 152 N of DRESHER on the Pennsylvania Turnpike), area—quartz gemstones, petrified wood.

JENKINTOWN, W 2 mi. at Hill Crest, quarry—gem serpentine, talc.

LAFAYETTE STA. (Lower Merion Twp.): (1) SE, in quarries on both sides of the Schuylkill R.—serpentine, steatite; (2) NE bank of river, at Prince's Quarry, variety—gemmy minerals; (3) the Lafayette Soapstone Quarry (on the Schuylkill R.)—serpentine, steatite; (4) Lafayette Hill, a quarry—chalcopyrite, soapstone.

MONT CLARE (across the Schuylkill R. from PHOENIXVILLE, Chester Co., q.v., near confluence of river with Perkiomen Cr. and trail to Audubon's Home, a wildlife shrine): (1) many area old copper mines; (2) the Perkiomen Mine—azurite, chalcopyrite, barite, malachite; (3) N of bridge over small cr., mine—goethite, linarite, malachite, mimetite, pseudomorphs after glauberite (copper and quartz).

MORGANVILLE STA.: (1) E ¼ mi., and (2) Maple Glen, area gravel pits—petrified wood.

PERKIOMENVILLE, E ½ mi. on Rte. 29 and about 8 mi. SW of the Quakertown exit of the NE extension of the Pennsylvania Turnpike, in a quarry—actinolite, calcite (fluorescent), chlorite, epidesmine (crystals, with pyrite and calcite), epidote, fluorite (purple, translucent), garnet, heulandite, limonite pseudomorphs after pyrite, natrolite, pyrite crystals, rock crystal (in groups), stilbite, zeolites.

PHILADELPHIA (Philadelphia Co.), N and W, in cr. beds and rural country fields, cut banks, etc.—agate, chalcedony, chert, jasper, quartz crystals, petrified wood.

ROSE GLEN, NW ¾ mi., at the Gladwyne quarries, many kinds—quartz gemstones.

SUMNEYTOWN: (1) nearby mine in Upper Salford Twp.—azurite; (2) S 1 mi., on the Kobers farm, an old copper prospect—azurite, tenorite, zeolites.

WEST MANAYUNK, along Rock Hill rd., many quarries—gem serpentine, steatite.

NORTHAMPTON CO.

BETHLEHEM: (1) many area quarries—chert, oolitic flint, crystals, fossils; (2) NE 3½ mi., the Camels Hump Mine—ocher; (3) E 5 mi. and S of REDINGTON (Lower Saucon Twp.), on South Mt., area—cat's-eye, chalcedony, chert (many colors), prase, quartz crystals.

EASTON: (1) area: (a) mines—ocher; (b) limestone quarries below town —oolitic chert, dark flint; (c) quarries along Bushkill Cr.—chert, flint; (2) N, on the Williams farm—marble; (3) N side of Rte. 611 and 1.3 mi. N of jct. with Rte. 22, at Chestnut Hill (Forks Twp.), area quarries—apatite, asbestos, bronzite, diopside, epidote, pyrite, quartz crystals, radioactive min-

erals (rare), **noble serpentine, sphene, talc, tremolite, vesuvianite, williamsite.**
FREEMANSBURG, HANOVERVILLE, HELLERTON, ISLAND PARK, many regional limestone quarries—**chert, oolitic flint, crystals, fossils.**

PHILADELPHIA CO.

FRANKFORD: (1) area gneissic outcrops—**chalcopyrite;** (2) Falls of Schuylkill, area—**fluorite;** (3) Wissahickon Cr., area gneiss outcrops—**chalcopyrite.**

SCHUYLKILL CO.

AREA, numerous anthracite **coal** mines—**pyrite crystals.**
MAHONEY CITY, area anthracite mines, gemmy—**pyrite crystals.**
POTTSVILLE: (1) the Mammoth Coal Bed—gem **pyrite crystals;** (2) the Diamond Bed—**pyrite crystals.**

SULLIVAN CO.

LAIRDSVILLE, NE 1 mi., turn N from Rte. 115 for ½ mi., turn right 1 mi. to second rd. fork, bear left 2.7 mi. (from Rte. 115) to an abandoned house, behind it an old prospect pit—**galena, chrysocolla** (turquoise color), **copper** and **uranium minerals (malachite** coatings, **azurite** stains), **marcasite, metatorbernite** (flakes), **uranophane,** plant **fossils.**
STRONESTOWN, S ½ mi. on Rte. 220, Eagles Mere, S on rd. opposite jct. ¼ mi., a hillside exposure—**copper** and **uranium minerals.** Cf. also BEAVER LAKE, Lycoming Co.

WESTMORELAND CO.

ALEXANDER, area farm fields, cut banks, ditches, etc.—**chalcedony, jasper,** variously colored **quartz.**
DERRY, area exposures, gravels, quarries—**rock crystal.**
GREENSBURG: (1) area limestone quarries—**marcasite, pyrite;** (2) area clay beds—**petrified wood;** (3) E 7 mi., a quarry—**quartz crystals.**
HUFF, IRWIN, JEANETTE, PENN, area shale exposures in pits, rd. cuts, quarries—**marcasite, pyrite.**
HUNKERS, SE, in a sandstone quarry—**sandstone** (banded, can be cut and polished), **quartzite** (pink, yellow, etc.).
KINGSTON: (1) area fields—**jasper;** (2) ½ mi. above the waterworks, in Loyalhanna Gap, area—**calcite, marcasite, pyrite, fossils;** (3) gravels of the Conemaugh R.—**petrified wood.**
LIGONIER, W 3 mi. on U.S. 30 to a large quarry (½ mi. long)—**quartz crystals, limestone fossils.**

McChance, W 1 mi., at Long Bridge, an extensive quarry—**quartz crystals, fossils.**

YORK CO.

Delta, Peach Blossom, a quarry on the York Co.–Md. boundary—**verde antique** (called **"Cardiff green marble"**).

Dillsburg: (1) S ½ mi. on U.S. 15, a diabase exposure—**analcime, apophyllite, calcite, laumontite, leonhardite, natrolite, pyrite, quartz crystals, sphalerite;** (2) N 2½ mi., a limestone quarry, many varieties—**gem crystals, minerals;** (3) the James Iron Mine—**magnetite, pyrite.**

Harrisburg, S on Int. 83 to Reesers Haven via Lemoyne and New Cumberland interchanges, 1 mi. beyond an overpass, area—**agate, amethysts, chalcedony, andradite garnets, opal, quartz crystals, silicified wood.**

Lisburn, N, in gravels of Yellow Breeches Cr., a conglomerate decorative stone—**"Potomac" marble.**

March Run, on W bank of the Susquehanna R., area, gemmy, brecciated —**marble conglomerate.**

Mount Hope: (1) the Bechtel Mine (in town); (2) S 1 mi., mine; (3) NE 1 mi., on E side of mt., the Snively Mine—**azurite, bornite, chalcocite, native copper, malachite, cuprite.**

Thomasville: (1) area quarries—**fluorite, pyrite, quartz crystals;** (2) S on U.S. 30 (5½ mi. SW of West York, q.v.), quarries along both sides of rd. N of the RR intersection—**calcite crystals** (some fluorescent), **fluorite, hematite, marcasite, pyrite, quartz crystals.**

West York, W 1 mi. on Rte. 234, in cement quarries—**azurite, calcite crystals, chalcopyrite, galena, malachite, quartz crystals.**

York Haven, S and SW 2 mi., area fields—**petrified wood.**

RHODE ISLAND

Smallest and most densely populated of the fifty states, Rhode Island was named from the principal island in Narragansett Bay. With a western boundary only 42 miles long and a maximum width across the south of 35 miles, the surface of this state is rolling and hilly, cut by short, swift streams that pour over many waterfalls. Sandwiched between Connecticut and Massachusetts, Rhode Island's geology partakes of both. Sedimentary deposits, other than Pleistocene to Recent, are extremely rare, since the whole state was scoured to bedrock by Ice Age glaciers.

The state's geology was extensively studied in the nineteenth century, with some areas being prospected and mined for **iron, graphite, manganese,** and **talc.** There are few gemstone occurrences of any consequence.

For information, write: Rhode Island Development Council, State House, Providence.

BRISTOL CO.

BRISTOL, area gravel pits and deposits, as pebbles—**jasper.**

KENT CO.

WARWICK, in gravels along the shores of Narragansett Bay—**carnelian** pebbles.

NEWPORT CO.

TIVERTON, S 4 mi., a mine—**graphite.**

PROVIDENCE CO.

AREA: (1) Calumet Hill, area quarries—**agate, chalcedony, jasper, sagenite quartz crystals;** (2) Fenner Ledge, a large mine—**graphite;** (3) Mt. Hope Bay, area beach gravels—**agate, amethyst, carnelian** and **jasper** pebbles.

BRIDGETON, PAWTUCKET, VALLEY FALL, area mines—**graphite.**

CRANSTON, area deposits—**graphite, hematite.**

CUMBERLAND HILL: (1) area quarries—**agate, chalcedony, jasper, quartz crystals;** (2) near Sneech Pond, area extensively prospected during the second decade of the nineteenth century, mines and prospect pits—**chalcopyrite, magnetite** (especially in beach sands on the S side of the pond), **manganese ore** (resembling **knebelite,** in a bed 40 ft. thick), **molybdenite, rhodonite, wad.**

DIAMOND HILL: (1) area quarries—**agate, chalcedony, jasper, quartz crystals;** (2) area mines—**hematite;** (3) area limestone exposures, in pockets—**agate, chalcedony, amethysts, quartz crystals** (clear, smoky).

MANVILLE, area quarries—**talc.**

PAWTUXET, area beach gravels—**agate, amethyst, carnelian** and **jasper** pebbles.

PROVIDENCE, 5 mi. N of North Providence, at DEXTER: (1) an area lime quarry—**bowenite (jadelike serpentine);** (2) the nearby Conklin and Harris quarries—**bowenite.**

SMITHFIELD, area quarries in **mica slate** and from outcrops of **quartz-mica schist—whetstone.**

WOONSOCKET, E 2½ mi., the Iron Mine Hill (and as a prominent constituent of the regional gabbroid rock)—**magnetite.**

WASHINGTON CO.

KINGSTON, Tower Hill, area mines—**galena.**

SAUNDERSTOWN, area mines—**graphite.**

SOUTH CAROLINA

This subtropical state divides roughly into three main geologic regions: the broad sea level Coastal Plain, separated from the rolling Piedmont down the middle of the state by the Fall Line, and the small Inner Piedmont in the extreme northwestern corner as part of the Blue Ridge of the southern Appalachian Mountain system. The "upcountry," as the Inner Piedmont is known, covers approximately 500 square miles of mountainous territory that culminates near the North Carolina boundary in Pickens County at Sassafras Mountain, 3,560 feet high.

The underlying rock formations of the Inner Piedmont are primarily gneissic schists and granites of Precambrian to early Paleozoic age, cut by granite intrusives and smaller bodies of dunite and peridotite. Regional pegmatite exposures provide sources for **amethysts, beryl, corundum, garnets,** smoky and clear **quartz crystals, tourmaline, topaz,** and **zircon.** These more showy gem crystals were discovered early, but not commercialized, during the initial geologic surveys of the nineteenth century, when considerable prospecting was undertaken for metallic deposits. Although mining of **copper, lead,** and **zinc** remained minor, some placer **gold** was worked. The pegmatite gems were found in the stream gravels, along with an occasional alluvial **diamond.**

In the northern Kings Mountain Belt the regional metamorphism that accompanied intensive folding and faulting produced widespread conglomerates, marble, quartzites, and schists in which **vermiculite** became the major minable mineral. The many **vermiculite** mines scattered throughout the Inner Piedmont also yield collectable gemmy specimens of **asbestos, barite, copper minerals, feldspar, garnets, kyanite, marble,** and **mica.**

With the exception of the Piedmont and the Blue Ridge section, South Carolina's surface is largely Upper Cretaceous (Tuscaloosa formation) laden with **fossils,** Tertiary, and Recent sediments. Primarily **kaolin clays, cement, granite, monumental stone, gravel,** and **limestone** contribute to the mineral economy.

For information, write: South Carolina Geological Survey, University of South Carolina, Columbia.

ABBEVILLE CO.

AREA: (1) countywide stream gravels, rock exposures, cut banks, fields, etc.—**beryl, corundum, epidote,** blue **jasper;** (2) regional mines (in long belt extending NE across several counties)—**gold.**

ABBEVILLE: (1) area mines—**gold;** (2) S 9 mi. and ½ mi. E of Beula Cross Roads, a mine—**gold.**

CALHOUN FALLS, area mines—**chalcopyrite, graphite, ilmenite.**

DONALDS, SE 4 mi., on the J. T. Algary farm—**amethysts.**

DUE WEST, at the nearby Ellis-Jones Amethyst Mine—**amethysts** (largest gem crystal weighed 45 lbs.).

LOWNDESVILLE: (1) N 1.8 mi., and (2) just S of town on the McCalla farm—gem **amethysts;** (3) S 46° W 3 mi., a mine—**gold.**

MCCORMICK STATION, the Dorn Mine—gold.

AIKEN CO.

AREA, Silbur Bluff on the Savannah R., at base of alluvial deposit, mined— **manganese minerals** (bearing **cobalt**).

AIKEN, area of Herse Cr. Valley, 1 mi. off old U.S. 1 near CLEARWATER, as area float and in gravel pits—**amethysts, chalcedony, ilmenite, monazite, quartz crystals** (clear, smoky, rutilated), **rutile crystals, zircon.**

ALLENDALE, S on U.S. 301 across the Savannah R. bridge, turn N on co. rd. 8 mi. to a sharp left turn, take dirt trail along track—**"Savannah River" agates** (really a **chert** laced with impure **chalcedony,** some with cavities filled with **drusy quartz crystals**).

ANDERSON CO.

AREA: (1) Savannah R. boundary of co., on NE bank of river ¼ mi. from mouth of Big Generostee Cr.: (a) the old Gaillard Mica Mine, and (b) the Fretwell prospect—**aquamarine, golden beryl;** (2) numerous exposures along a belt extending from near ANDERSON past IVA on to Lake Secession to DUE WEST, Abbeville Co.—**amethysts.**

ANDERSON: (1) W 2 mi., area, as occasional clear crystals—**beryl;** (2) E 3 mi., several pegmatite exposures: (a) area—**beryl, almandite garnet, limonite cubes, mica, quartz crystals** (clear, smoky), **black tourmaline;** (b) ¼ mi. NNE, area—**aquamarine;** (3) SW 8 mi., in narrow veins—**asbestos;** (4) N 9 mi., near dam on Twenty-six Mile Cr., the Burgess Mine—red **feldspar, garnets, mica, quartz crystals.**

IVA: (1) NW 1¾ mi. along Wilson's Cr. on Rte. 413, on the Frank Pruitt farm—**golden beryl;** (2) S, area of the Sherard farm near MOFFETTSVILLE, in exposure of **mica slates**—**amethysts** (single crystals and clusters); (3) SW 3 mi., the J. B. Anderson farm—**golden beryl;** (4) N 5.7 mi. on U.S. 187, the Martin-Blackwell-Ferguson Mine—gem **beryl;** (5) SE 11 mi., on the Thompson and Jackson farms—gem **corundum, garnets,** white **quartz, zircons** (orange brown).

PELZER, on co. line, pegmatite outcrop (extends 1½ mi. SW of PIEDMONT to 1 mi. S of PELZER)—**aquamarine, indocolite tourmaline.**

CHEROKEE CO.

AREA: (1) E part of co., in prospect pits, mines, rd. cuts, stream gravels and banks—**barite, hematite,** gem **kyanite, sillimanite,** etc.; (2) the Bowen R. region, in exposures of Archean gneiss—**corundum ("ornamental emerald"), gem sapphire.**

BLACKSBURG: (1) NW, the Bowen R. drainage basin, extending to Buffalo Church: (a) area **slate** exposures—**corundum, garnets;** (b) regional stream gravels—**corundum;** (c) tributaries of the Bowen R., in gravel beds—**corundum, garnets;** (2) NW 2½ mi. on Rte. 83 (the "Buffalo Church" rd.) and on the Andrew Moore farm—**emeralds, sapphires;** (3) Porter's Hill, area stream gravels—**corundum, garnets, quartz crystals, topaz, zircon,** etc.; (4) Earles Sta. (10 mi. S of SHELBY), area pegmatites—**emeralds,** etc.

BUFFALO CHURCH: (1) area stream gravels—**amethysts, rutile crystals;** (2) W, on the W. T. Gibbons farm—**amethysts, corundum,** etc.

COWPENS, NE 3 mi., several area mines—**corundum** (particles), **gold, monazite, pyrite, tourmaline.**

GAFFNEY: (1) area, pegmatite dike outcrops—**cassiterite;** (2) NE 1¼ mi., the Ross Mine, and other nearby mines—**cassiterite, feldspar crystals, fibrolite** (banded **kyanite**), **quartz crystals, pyrrhotite;** (3) SE 2.8 mi., on Limestone Cr. (tributary of the Broad R.), the Cameron Mine—**argentiferous galena, pyrite, pyromorphite, siderite;** (4) SW 8 mi., at Love Springs, the Troy Blanton Mine—**garnets, mica, tourmaline;** (5) SE 11 mi. (and 1 mi. W of Smith's Ford on the Broad R.), the old Darwin Mine—**gold;** (6) SE 12 mi., near the 12-mi. post, Flint Hill, area mines—**gold.**

KINGS CREEK: (1) area mines—**barite;** (2) SW 2 mi., the Barkat Mines—**gold;** (3) Canaan Church, W, mines (e.g., Bolin, Wyatt)—**gold;** (4) E from Rte. 97 (and S of Rte. 5), mines (e.g., Dixon, Eutis, Southern Gold, Wallace)—**gold, chalcopyrite, copper minerals, galena, hematite, kyanite, quartz crystals, pyrite, sillimanite, steatite.**

WALHALLA, N 15 mi., area mines—**galena.**

CHESTERFIELD CO.

AREA, numerous old mines—**gold, pyrite.**

JEFFERSON: (1) area N of Rte. 265, along the Lynches R., numerous old mines—**topaz;** (2) W 3 mi. to Brewer Knob on the Lynches R. (co. line), the old Brewer Mine—**cassiterite, covellite, enargite, gold, kyanite, pyrite, quartz crystals, rutile crystals, staurolites, topaz** (massive, champagne, golden). (From the Civil War until 1930 an estimated 1,000 tons of **topaz** were mined for ceramics and porcelain manufacture.)

DARLINGTON CO.

DARLINGTON, E to the Pee Dee R. crossing of Int. 95, on W side of river near bridge, abundant—**petrified wood** (gemmy, honey to golden color).

HARTSVILLE, along Bellyache Cr.—**petrified wood.**

DARLINGTON, FLORENCE COS.

REGION, all fields, stream beds, cut banks, rd. cuts, etc.—**gem petrified wood.**

EDGEFIELD CO.

EDGEFIELD, N 6° W 12 mi. (2½ mi. N of Meeting St.), E side of Sleepy Cr., a large area of old mines—**gold.**

FAIRFIELD CO.

AREA: (1) countywide sand and gravel pits—**petrified wood;** (2) Lake Murray Dam, in rock exposures along river banks—**garnets, kyanite crystals.**
LITTLE MOUNTAIN, E, to the W side of the Broad R., an old mine—gem **kyanite.**

GREENVILLE CO.

GREENVILLE: (1) N 5 mi., near E end of Paris Mt. State Park, pegmatite exposure at jct. of two streams, the Boling prospect—**beryl, garnet, quartz crystals** (clear, smoky), **sillimanite, black tourmaline;** (2) SW 7 mi., just W of Rte. 20 across RR near Saluda R., the Cleveland Mica prospect—gem **beryl, mica;** (3) SE 9 mi., the Willimon Mine—gem **kyanite;** (4) numerous old area **vermiculite** mines, on dumps—**amazonite** (pale aqua color), **feldspar** (chatoyant, peach color), **rutile crystals, sunstone, xenotime** (resembling **zircon**).
GREER: (1) area mines, and (2) NW 8 mi.: (a) the McBee Mine, and (b) 1 mi. above, on opposite side of Middle Tyger R., mines—**gold, pyrite.**
MARIETTA, 4 mi. distant, area mines—**polycrase.**
PRINCETON, NW 3 mi., the Desota Mine—**gold.**
TIGERVILLE, E 1 mi. on Rte. 414, near Baptist church, a **vermiculite** mine —gem **crystals, minerals.**

GREENWOOD CO.

AREA, NE part of co., from 4 mi. SE of SHOALS JCT. to 1 mi. SW, across co. line E of DUE WEST, Abbeville Co., numerous exposures, outcrops, fields, etc.—**amethysts, quartz crystals,** etc.
BREEZEWOOD, W 2 mi., mine—**psilomelane.**
GREENWOOD: (1) NW to jct. of U.S. 25 and U.S. 178, then N 4.3 mi., in rd. cut—**limonite cubes** (to 2 in. dia.); (2) S 5 mi., area mines—**psilomelane.**
SHOALS JUNCTION: (1) SE 1½ mi., and (2) SW 1 mi. (3 mi. SE of DON-ALDS, Abbeville Co.), area fields, cut banks, etc.—**amethysts, quartz crystals;** (3) as float near Lake Greenwood—**amethysts.**

HORRY CO.

MYRTLE BEACH, area beach gravels—**agate, chalcedony, quartz, fossil shark teeth.**

KERSHAW CO.

CAMDEN, NW 9 mi. (1 mi. NW of Getty's Bridge over Sawney's Cr.), the Lamar Gold Mine—**gold.**

LANCASTER CO.

KERSHAW: (1) area mines, (2) N 51° E 3.8 mi., the Haile Gold Mine (large scale)—**gold, pyrite, drusy quartz crystals,** etc. (The Haile Mine is the largest **gold** producer in all the southeastern states and was closed in 1942 because of World War II.) (3) N 5° E 8 mi., on Flat Cr. tributary of the Lynches R., the Blackmon Gold Mine—**gold, pyrite, sericite;** (4) the Maile Mine—**molybdenite.**

LIBERTY HILL, a deposit near the Wateree Reservoir on a tributary of the Catawba R.—gem **smoky quartz crystals** (to 6 in. long and 2½ in. dia.), **zircons.**

LAURENS CO.

CROSS HILL, S on Rte. 39 to jct. (marked by white house on the right), turn right on dirt rd. to next right turn, in farm field (get permission)—**amethysts.**

McCORMICK CO.

McCORMICK: (1) area creek sands, placers—**gold;** (2) S 2½ mi., old mine—**gold;** (3) W 2 mi. on Rte. 378, turn left on Plum Branch rd. 2 mi. to cr. bridge, area on right just before bridge—excellent **limonite cubes.**

NEWBERRY CO.

PROSPERITY, area, as crystal masses—**rutile.**

OCONEE CO.

AREA, gravel beds of the Toxaway and White Water rivers, old placer mines of the 1850's—**gold.**

ADAMS CROSSING, SW 3 mi., a mine—**gold.**

CHERRY, SW 1½ mi., a mine—**gold.**

PULASKI, N 4 mi. (10 mi. N 40° W of FT. MADISON), a mine—**gold, graphite.**

SENECA: (1) area mines—**asbestos;** (2) N 2 mi., on the Leroy farm—gem cat's-eye **sillimanite crystals;** (3) S 5½ mi., old mine—**gold.**

WALHALLA: (1) N 11½ mi., old mine—**gold, pyrite;** (2) W 14 mi. (1 mi.

W of Rogues Ford and 2 mi. below Cannon's Stone), on E scarp of the Chatooga R., the Henckel Mine—**gold;** (3) N 15 mi., on the Middle Fork of Cheohee Cr., old mine—**gold, peridotite, pyrite.**

PICKENS CO.

CALHOUN, N 1 mi., mine—**gold, mica.**
CLEMSON: (1) area of **mica** mines around Clemson College; (2) N 4½ mi. and .7 mi. NW of Twelve Mile Cr., the Head prospect; and (3) NW 7 mi. (SW of creek 1 mi. E of the Seneca R.), the Davis prospect—**garnets, quartz crystals.**
EASLEY, area schist outcrops—carvable **steatite** (with **chlorite**).

SALUDA CO.

SALUDA, NE 6 mi. (12 mi. S of NEWBERRY), in fork of Big Cr. and the Little Saluda R., the Culbreath Mine—**amphibolite, chalcopyrite, chlorite, gold,** green **hornblende crystals, magnetite, niccolite, pyrite.**

SPARTANBURG CO.

AREA, countywide stream gravels—placer **gold,** rare **diamonds.**
COWPENS, N 2 mi., old **mica** mine—**garnets, muscovite mica, quartz crystals, tourmaline.**
CROSS ANCHOR, area old **mica** mines—**mica, black tourmaline.**
ENOREE: (1) area of jct. of Enoree Rd. and Dutchman's Cr.—gemmy red **quartzite;** (2) E 5 mi. on Rte. 92, then 1 mi. on Rte. 30 and 3 mi. E on co. rd. to **vermiculite** prospects (in Cross Anchor Twp.)—massive **quartz, pegmatite gems** and **minerals.**
GLENN SPRINGS, S 8 mi., area mines—**psilomelane.**
SPARTANBURG: (1) area mines—**asbestos;** (2) area stream gravels, placers —**gold, zircons;** (3) E, in a granite quarry—**crystals, minerals.**

UNION CO.

AREA, numerous old mines scattered through co.—**gold.**
WEST SPRINGS, on Fair Forest Cr., the Nott Mine—**gold, native copper, pyrite.**

YORK CO.

AREA, numerous well-known old **gold** mines in co. (check on regional topographic maps)—**gold.**
BETHANY, N 3 mi., on W side of Rte. 161, the Patterson Mine—**gold, pyrite, quartz crystals.**

BLACKSBURG, E, to Kings Mt. Battleground: (1) S 1.3 mi., area pits—**barite**; (2) E 2 mi., the Ferguson Mine—**gold, pyrite, quartz crystals.**

CATAWBA JUNCTION, SE 4 mi., extensive exposure—**wad** (bog **manganese** ore).

CLOVER: (1) NW 3 mi. on Rte. 508, in rock exposures on Henry Knob—**andalusite, gem kyanite, lazulite, staurolites, tourmaline**; (2) SW 5.7 mi., old mine on Bullock's Cr. of the Broad R.—**gold, magnetite, monzonite, pyrite, sericite, slate.**

HICKORY GROVE: (1) N 1 mi., the Wylie Mine—**gold**; (2) SE 2 mi., alongside Rte. 211, the Thunderhead Mine—**gold, pyrite**; (3) W 2.2 mi., on Smith's Ford rd., at head of a branch of Guin Moore's Cr. on S side of rd., the Magnolia Mine—**gold, malachite, biotite mica, quartz crystals**; (4) SW 3.2 mi., old mine—**gold**; (5) SW 4 mi., and (6) ½ mi. NW of Rte. 211, area —**andalusite, kyanite, lazulite, staurolites, tourmaline.**

HICKORY GROVE–SMYRNA, area of **quartz** vein outcrops extending NE between both towns, some 50 **gold** mines and prospects along both sides of Rtes. 5, 97, and 211—**calcite, galena, gold** nuggets, **sphalerite, tourmaline.** (A total of 28 gemstones and minerals have been reported from the old mine dumps.)

KINGS CREEK, SW 3 mi., the Carroll & Ross Mine (on Wolf Cr. tributary of the Broad R.)—**gold, pyrite.**

PIEDMONT SPRINGS, N 1 mi. and just N of Rte. 55, numerous pits (mainly W and N from Zoar Church on Rte. 731)—**barite.**

ROCK HILL, W 5 mi. and .2 mi. S of jct. of co. rd. 46–102 with co. rd. 46, as area float—**sillimanite.**

SMYRNA: (1) NE 1 mi., the Horn Mine; (2) E 2 mi., the Castles and Scoggins mines—**gold, pyrite, quartz crystals**; (3) W 1 mi., the Martin Mine —**gold** (nuggets, some of record size); (4) SW 3 mi., area rock outcrops—**andalusite, kyanite, lazulite, staurolites, tourmaline**; (5) W 3½ mi., the Hull Mine—**calcite, galena, gold, black tourmaline** (sunbursts), etc.; (6) SW 4.4 mi.: (a) the Dorothy Mine, and (b) an old prospect ½ mi. E of the mine—**gold, malachite**, etc.

YORK: (1) area mines, such as (a) the Big Wilson Mine, and (b) E 4 mi., the Mary Mine—**chalcopyrite**; (2) NE, an old **copper** mine—**malachite, cuprite, native copper**; (3) Five Points crossrds. on Nanny Mt.: (a) ¼ mi. W of jct. of Rtes. 49 and 56, on right side of rd. leading to CLOVER, along the N.C. boundary, area fields, cuts, breaks, etc.—**black corundum**; (b) area mines 11 mi. NE of YORK on Nanny Mt.—**pyrrhotite.**

SOUTH DAKOTA

This northwestern Great Plains state varies from nearly level farmland to hill ridges, increasing steadily in elevation from 1,000 feet on the eastern border with Minnesota and Iowa to 3,500 feet along the western boundary with Wyoming. In the far western counties of Lawrence, Meade, Custer, and Pennington the land rises abruptly into the 6,000-square-mile Black Hills region enclosed by the Belle Fourche and

Cheyenne rivers. These pine-covered mountains, higher than the Alleghenies, culminate in Harney Peak in southern Pennington Co. At 7,242 feet this peak is the highest point in America east of the Rocky Mountains.

Cambrian rocks are exposed as thick bands around the entire mountain system. The rising granite mass intruded the famed Cretaceous Dakota sandstone, which underlies most of the Great Plains, and bent the broken edges sharply upward into steep hogbacks unusual in outward appearance. These hogbacks catch the regional precipitation and channel it into the underlying porous sandstone. Laid down in Early Cretaceous times, as the continental seas were advancing from the south, the Dakota sandstone represents "topset" beds, wave-reworked, and spread as a vast deltaic accumulation of water-absorbing sands covering tens of thousands of square miles with extraordinary homogeneity. Throughout the Great Plains, wells drilled deep into this formation provide an inexhaustible supply of cold, artesian, Rocky Mountain snow-melt water.

Harney Peak is the crest of the geologically notable granite "dome uplift" which also produced a most remarkable series of pegmatite dikes ranking with those in Maine and Southern California for their production of gems and minerals. The pegmatites are offshoots of the otherwise barren granite. From them have come some of the world's most spectacular crystals of **beryl** and **spodumene.** For instance, a single **spodumene** crystal from the Etta Mine near Keystone on the east side of the Mount Rushmore National Memorial in Pennington Co. measured 42 feet long and weighed 90 tons. Also, monstrous crystals of sparkling blue **beryl** from the Black Hills pegmatites have measured from 18 to 27 feet in length, weighing many tons apiece. Such giant crystals are exceptions, of course. They are usually flawed and rather impure, but nevertheless each such crystal contained many areas of gem-quality material. In addition, gem **garnets, quartz crystals, topaz,** and **tourmaline** add to the bounty from these fascinating pegmatites.

In 1874 when General George A. Custer's expedition was reconnoitering the Black Hills, two miners attached to the expedition discovered **gold** in gravel bars along French Creek near present-day Custer in the county of the same name. From that date through 1965 more than 31,208,000 ounces of **gold** were taken from placer operations (worked out by 1880) and lode veins, placing South Dakota third in the nation's roster of **gold**-producing states. Most of the yellow metal actually came from a single great lode mine, the Homestake at Lead in Lawrence Co., discovered in 1875. This mine not only became the largest **gold** producer ever developed in America, but it is still in active operation.

The commercial production of minerals, principally **gold, silver, copper, iron, lead, manganese,** and **zinc,** along with lesser amounts of **beryllium, cesium, lithium, tantalum, tin, tungsten,** and **uranium,** has come only from the core of the Black Hills region. Two divisions are recognized: a "northern section," centered in Lead and Deadwood in

Lawrence Co., and a "southern section" covering a somewhat larger area around Harney Peak. The northern section is characterized by vein deposits, while the Southern Hills District includes both veins and the extensive pegmatite dike exposures and mines.

For information, write: South Dakota State Geological Survey, Vermillion.

BON HOMME, CHARLES MIX COS.

SCOTLAND to WAGNER, regional rd. cuts, breaks, river banks, stream beds, excavations, etc.—**selenite roses.**

CAMPBELL CO.

MOUND CITY, W to the Missouri R., regional hillsides, ridges, cut banks, tributary gravels, etc.—**petrified wood, wood opal.**

CORSON CO.

LITTLE EAGLE: (1) area ridges, slopes, stream beds, etc.—**petrified** and **opalized wood;** (2) along the Grand R. through entire co., regional banks, breaks, gravels, etc.—**petrified wood, wood opal.**

CUSTER CO.

BUFFALO GAP, entire region W 37 mi. to the Wyo. line, in stream gravels, cut banks, breaks, hillsides, etc.—**"Fairhill" agates.**

CUSTER: (1) N, near Laughing Water Cr., many area mines—**columbite, gold, silver,** etc.; (2) E 6 mi., on French Cr., the Scott Rose Quartz Quarry —**aquamarine, quartz** (milky, rose), **spodumene;** (3) W 7 mi., the Tin Mountain area, to Deer Camp rd., turn in ¼ mi.: (a) in rocky uplift alongside the rd., and (b) adjoining stream gravels—gem **almandite garnets, quartz crystals, mica;** (4) W 14 mi. on U.S. 16 to Tepee Canyon, diggings on N of hwy. extending up canyon—**agate** ("Hells Canyon," "Park," etc.), **beryl, almandite garnets, lepidolite, staurolites, tourmaline,** etc.; (5) E on U.S. Alt. 16 for 15–17 mi. (near Rte. 79), pegmatite outcrops—**rose quartz;** (6) S along U.S. 385 for 32 mi. to HOT SPRINGS in Fall River Co., all regional side rds., look for limestone outcrops and ridges—**"Fairhill" agates.**

FAIRBURN: (1) NW about 10 mi. and just S of the Game Farm (zoo) on U.S. Alt. 16, area—**Fairburn agates;** (2) W on unmarked dirt rd. and S several mi. into hilly area to old windmill, park car; in dry bed of Lame Johnny Cr., as large waterworn boulders, gemmy—**jasper conglomerate** (variously colored **jasper** pebbles cemented in **quartzite**); (3) E 15 mi. on co. rd. to S-trending side rd. (just E of the McDermond ranch) leading to picnic ground, continue on N toward bandlands buttes to end of rd., all area from picnic grounds to road's end—gem **Fairburn agates, agatized wood,** yellow **jasper;** (4) E 15 mi.: (a) general area, and (b) S to the Cheyenne R., along both sides and on adjoining slopes—**Fairburn agates.**

FOURMILE, W 14 mi. to Jewel Cave National Monument, then N up Hell Canyon from U.S. 16, area—banded **agate, jade, jasper, fossils** (bone, coral, cycads, palm), **geodes.**

PRINGLE: (1) area to MINNEKAHTA in Fall River Co. (best locality)— **"Fairhill" agates;** (2) W on Rte. 89 to Rte. 316, then W to Carter Ranch and S along Pleasant Valley Cr. in Red Canyon, area—cf. FOURMILE; (3) E on U.S. 385 about 10 mi. (halfway to Cave Park boundary), on N side of rd. a few yds., outcrop—**rose quartz.**

DOUGLAS CO.

CORSICA, S on U.S. 281 to ARMOUR, area rd. cuts, stream banks and gravel beds, excavations, etc., occurring mainly in black gumbo—**selenite** (crystals, roses).

FALL RIVER CO.

ARDMORE, E 7 mi. on dirt rd. to ranch (inquire), then S and E several mi. into badland breaks, area—**Fairburn agates, agatized wood, jasper** (green, lavender, red, yellow), **chalcedony** (clear, patterned with black), **quartz nodules** (rose, white).

BURDOCK, E, in S part of the Elk Mts., many mines and prospect pits— **carnotite.**

HOT SPRINGS: (1) area quarries—**gypsum;** (2) E on U.S. 18 for about 3 mi. to first bridge, in banks of the Fall R.—**tufa, travertine;** (3) S about 7 mi. on rd. to ghost town of Cascade, area gravels of Cascade Cr.—**tufa** (a hot springs calcification resembling petrified moss, reeds, watercress, or twigs and variously so called by local collectors); (4) W 12 mi. on U.S. 18 to RR siding of MINNEKAHTA, then S on USFS rd. (to top of Parker Peak), take left fork to dam and through 3rd gate beyond to a large open flat, all general area—gem **agatized cycads, petrified palm wood;** (5) W all way 12 mi. to Parker Peak, all regional breaks, cut banks, washes, land surfaces— **silicified cycad wood.**

MINNEKAHTA (RR siding), all around Parker Peak (1½ mi. E of U.S. 18, 2 mi. S of siding) and all area outside the Cycad National Monument— **silicified cycad stumps.**

OELRICHS, E from hwy. intersection in town: (1) 1 mi., take S-trending side rd. toward nearby buttes, park at fence, area to S—gem **Fairburn agates;** (2) 1½ mi., on buttes to S—**agate, jasper;** (3) 7.4 mi. to new hwy. cuts in badlands area, land surfaces to N—gem **agates;** (4) E 9 mi., at stock dam, area breaks, etc.—**agates;** (5) E 18.4 mi., on N side of U.S. 18, area—**agates;** (6) S from town on U.S. 385, turn E on first dirt rd. for 1 mi., then S for 2 mi. (past large ranch), then E along winding track for 4 mi. to a dim N-trending track and follow 1½ mi. NW to huge alluvial gravel area, abundant—**agate, chalcedony** (banded, water type, etc.), **jasper, jasp-agate, cone-in-cone calcite** (some fluorescent), **agatized wood, concretions,** etc.

HARDING CO.

CAMP CROOK, regional gravel bars of the Little Missouri R. and all tributary creeks—**moss agate, chalcedony nodules** (dendritic).

LAWRENCE CO.

This county and Pennington, western Meade, and Custer counties comprise the core of the Black Hills region in which **gold** and **silver** deposits occur as **quartz** veins scattered throughout most of the Precambrian and Cambrian crystalline rocks in shear zones. Several famous mining districts are locally recognized, and many hundreds of mines, prospects, and mineralized outcrops afford the gem and mineral collector fine specimens.

DEADWOOD, on W edge of town on U.S. 14A, the Broken Butte Gold Mine—**arsenopyrite, galena, gold, pyrite, sphalerite.** This city of 3,045 pop. has only one main street in the bottom of a deep, narrow canyon, the residential areas straggling up the canyon sides. Here is where Wild Bill Hickok was murdered. Visitors tour the mine from May through September each year for a modest charge.

LEAD: (1) S side of town on U.S. 14A and U.S. 85: (a) the Homestake Gold Mine, and (b) other area mines—**arsenopyrite, galena, gold, pyrite, sphalerite.** The Homestake Mine, the largest **gold** mine in the Western Hemisphere, has been operating continuously since 1878, except during part of World War II. Visitor tours are available June through August daily except Sundays and holidays. (2) W about 3 mi. to TROJAN (on W slope of Bald Mt.): (a) the Carbonate and area mines—**atacamite, cerargyrite, cerussite, fluorite, galena, lead carbonate, matlockite, plattnerite, pyromorphite, wulfenite, vanadinite** (large deposit): (b) the Ulster Mine—**fluorite.**

PIEDMONT: (1) E ¾ mi., area—**selenite crystals;** (2) SE 3 mi. on U.S. 14, area—**fossil belemnites.**

SAVOY, the Ragged Top Mountain District (5 mi. long, lying immediately W of Spearfish Cr. in the large bend of Spearfish Canyon, center of a productive mining district with the first mines opened ½ mi. N of Ragged Top Mt. 2 mi. NE of town, at DACY)—**gold, fluorite** (abundant, purple crystals), **silver, tellurium.**

SPEARFISH: (1) area quarries—**gypsum;** (2) S, in gravels of adjoining Spearfish Canyon—**amethysts, amethyst-**lined **geodes, chalcedony, chalcedony geodes, silicified cycad** and **palm wood.**

TINTON, area pegmatite mines—**cassiterite, columbite, scheelite.**

WHITEWOOD (6½ air mi. NE of DEADWOOD), gravel bars and banks of Whitewood Cr.—**amethysts, geodes** (amethyst-lined, **chalcedony**), **silicified cycad** and **palm wood, pyrite** (a large deposit).

MEADE CO.

MAURINE, ESE 5 mi., on top of Fox Ridge, area—**moss agate.**

SCENIC: (1) the Badlands region, all breaks, washes, etc.—blue **chalced-**

ony; (2) W on co. rd. about 2 mi., to buttes on N side of rd., area ravines—black gemmy **agate;** (3) SE to IMLAY along Rte. 40, both sides of hwy., extensive collecting field all the way—gem **chalcedony** (some with **carnelian** spots). This **chalcedony** occurs as nodules, masses, and huge sheets. The type varies from one hill to another over many square miles in all directions; many kinds of **geodes** occur, some transparent, some with pinkish crystal linings or polka dot interiors, other interiors containing **dolomite crystals** or botryoidal **chalcedony,** etc. Also find **aquamarine, beryl, carnelian, garnets, jasper** (plain and orbicular).

MINNEHAHA CO.

SIOUX FALLS, all regional stream gravels, cut banks, gravel pits, excavations, etc.—**agate, catlinite, jasper.** About 30 air mi. NE are the great prehistoric **catlinite (pipestone)** quarries a mile N of PIPESTONE, Minn., *q.v.,* under Pipestone Co.

PENNINGTON CO.

AREA, gravels of Bear Butte Cr., Box Elder Cr., and Warrens Gulch—**amethysts.**

HILL CITY, area mines (in a belt extending from 6 mi. SW of town to 5 mi. NE), deposits in **quartz** veins, fissure veins, and mineralized shear zones—**cassiterite, columbite, graphite, wolframite.**

KEYSTONE: (1) area mine dumps (in a belt about 5 mi. long extending from 3 mi. W of town to 1½ mi. SE): (a) on dumps—**tourmaline** (blue, green, red); (b) the Etta Mine dumps—**lepidolite,** gem **kunzite, spodumene;** (c) the Bob Ingersoll Mine—**autunite, golden beryl, garnets, gummite, quartz crystals, spodumene, tourmaline, uraninite;** (2) regional pegmatite outcrops (over a broad area)—**apatite, aquamarine, beryl** (golden, green); (3) S 1 mi., the Peerless Mine and nearby claims—**amblygonite;** (4) S 4 mi., on co. line, area mines (with **iron** mines on Iron Mt.)—**hematite, ocher;**

(5) S 4 mi. and 2 mi. E, in the Spokane district, area mines—**arsenopyrite, galena** (bearing **gold** and **silver**), **gold, pyrite, silver, sphalerite;** (6) tunnel on U.S. 16A (between U.S. 16 and town), park car and take trail around tunnel, in rock piles on both sides, abundant—**pegmatite minerals;** (7) take shortcut rd. W from town toward HILL CITY: (a) on first mine dump—**scheelite;** (b) on dumps of other area **tin** mines—**cassiterite, scheelite;** (c) area stream gravels—**cassiterite, columbite, scheelite, tantalite, tungsten minerals;**

(8) W to Mt. Rushmore area: (a) regional pegmatite outcrops (very many)—green **beryl;** (b) along rd. behind Mt. Rushmore (connecting U.S. 16A with Rte. 89), on both sides for whole length—**apatite, epidote, garnets, rose quartz, staurolites, black tourmaline;** (c) all regional canyon breaks—**chert, jasper, smoky quartz** (black "morion" type). (The **chert** and **jasper** nodules are locally called **Black Hills thundereggs.**)

MOON, at Nigger Hill in the Hills District (almost on the Wyo. line), in gravels of Bear Gulch and other area creeks—**cassiterite, columbite, scheelite, zircons.**

OREVILLE, E 1½ mi., the Tin Queen claim—**amblygonite, cassiterite, scheelite,** etc.

PACTOLA, area mines and prospects—**cinnabar.**

RAPID CITY, E along Int. 90 to WALL in Meade Co., in all regional rd. cuts, breaks, washes, and on hillsides, as huge concretions—gem golden **barite crystals, fossil shells** (encrusted with **barite** and **calcite crystals**).

ROCHFORD District (includes mines in a belt 9 mi. long, extending from 4 mi. SW of town at MYERSVILLE to 5 mi. N 30° W at NAHANT in Lawrence Co.): (1) regional mines and prospects—**cinnabar;** (2) many mines in the "hornblende belt" and the "iron quartz–tremolite belt"—**arsenopyrite, galena, gold, pyrite, silver, sphalerite.**

SILVER CITY, N 2 mi., area mines on Rapid Cr.—**arsenopyrite, chalcopyrite, gold, jamesonite, mica, sericite, silver, sphalerite.**

WASTA, N on gravel rd. to Elk Cr. (second cr. crossing), turn W through farm (get permission), park car by a dry cr. bed, all surrounding territory—concretions of gemmy **golden barite, calcite crystals** (clusters, some fluorescent), **quartz crystals.**

SHANNON CO.

OGLALA, in breaks along the rd. to SMITHWICK in Fall River Co. in the badlands region—**agate, chalcedony, jasper,** etc.

RED SHIRT, area, especially in breaks along the Cheyenne R.—**agate, chalcedony** (some blue), **jasper.**

ROCKYFORD, W, in regional breaks and washes—blue **chalcedony.**

TODD CO.

MISSION, W 12 mi. on U.S. 18: (1) in banks of the Little White R., and (2) in gravels of the South Fork—gemmy coal-black **opalized wood,** brown **agatized wood.** (All regional stream banks, gravel pits, excavations, etc., throughout co. are noted for **vertebrate fossils,** but collecting is prohibited without a federal permit.)

WALWORTH CO.

MOBRIDGE, N and S along the Missouri R., in cut banks, breaks, tributary gravels—**petrified wood, wood opal.**

WASHABAUGH CO.

CEDAR PASS: (1) area to NW, on S side of U.S. 16—**agatized wood, agate, chalcedony, jasper, jasp-agate,** etc.; (2) in regional gravel beds, banks, and tributary draws of the White R.—**agate, chalcedony, petrified wood, fossils.**

INTERIOR, general region to N and E, abundant everywhere—**"eye" agates** (really a **jasper**), **chalcedony** (black and white), **"fish egg" agates, jasper.**

(Throughout the entire badlands area outside the Badlands National Monument are extensive gem fields in all directions and at all distances.)

YANKTON CO.

YANKTON, W 4 mi., on Gavin's Point rd., on S side in an abandoned brick-yard's clay pits—**selenite** (crystals, roses).

ZIEBACH CO.

DUPREE, SW, at famed geological formation of Rattlesnake Butte, on top and slopes of the south butte—**sand calcite crystals** (often perfectly terminated, to 8 in. long and over 2 in. dia.).

TENNESSEE

This narrow, 450-mile-long scenic state extends across much of the south-central United States and can roughly be divided into three main physiographic regions: the Cumberland Plateau and the associated Unaka and Great Smoky mountains, the rich gently rolling grasslands of central Tennessee, and the alluvial river bottomlands of western Tennessee. The craggy, heavily forested mountains of the eastern part of the state constitute a vast geologic "thrust mass" which developed along the Appalachian fault belt, so that very ancient Precambrian and Cambrian granites, gneisses, schists, quartzites, conglomerates, sandstones, slates, and shales, all intensely folded and faulted, overlie much younger sedimentary rocks, a reversal of the normal order of rock deposition.

Although these three main topographic regions roughly describe Tennessee, they subdivide irregularly into eight distinct and well-defined geologic provinces: the Valley of Eastern Tennessee, the Cumberland Plateau, the Unaka Mountains of Unicoi Co., the Highland Rim (and its enclosed Central Basin), the Plateau Slope of Western Tennessee, the Western Valley, and the Mississippian Alluvial Plain. The Cumberland Plateau crosses Tennessee as a vast tableland averaging 2,000 feet above sea level extending northeast–southwest through southern West Virginia, extreme southwest Virginia, eastern Kentucky, and eastern Tennessee into northern Alabama; it is relatively rich in minerals, especially **coal.** Most of the plateau is underlain with Pennsylvanian age sandstones and conglomerates interbedded with shales and coal seams. The plateau escarpment drops off on the west in sharp breaks, exposing even older Mississippian formations.

Extending from the Cumberland Plateau to the Western Valley is the province of the Highland Rim, which also encloses an oval-shaped area

80 miles long by 50 miles wide known as the Central or Nashville Basin. The Mississippian limestones which underlie the basin dip away in all directions from the central rise of the Nashville Dome, exposing Ordovician, Silurian, and Devonian limestones and shales wherever stream erosion has deeply dissected the formations. Far western parts of the Highland Rim are capped by Cretaceous gravels.

About 35 miles southeast of Knoxville, in southeastern Tennessee, a series of craggy peaks of the Great Smoky Mountains culminate in 6,642-foot Clingmans Dome in southern Sevier Co. on the North Carolina boundary. The 1,900 square miles of the Great Smoky Mountains National Park, stretching 54 miles across southern Blount, Sevier, and Cocke counties and 35 miles wide with overlap into western North Carolina, embraces some of the oldest rock formations in America, well exposed throughout the park. Trails outside the park boundaries, especially the Appalachian Trail which follows the ridge crests, lead to countless gem and gemstone localities, not yet well prospected, all along the mountains northeast to Virginia.

West and north of the mountains, extending for 135 air miles northeasterly across the state from Chattanooga in southern Hamilton Co. on the Georgia line to the Cumberland Gap in northern Claiborne Co. on the Kentucky line, is the broad Valley and Ridge Province. As its name implies, the region is characterized by a succession of northeast–southwest ridges averaging 2,000 feet high and separated by narrow fertile valleys a thousand feet lower. The underlying formations are mainly Cambrian and Ordovician limestones, dolomites, sandstones, and shales dipping toward the southeast.

Farther west lie the long narrow Valley of the Tennessee River, the West Tennessee Uplands, and the West Tennessee Plain sloping gently toward the Mississippi River. Many of the western counties yield **agates, jasper, petrified wood, travertine,** and **fossils** from gravel pits, stream beds, and excavations. Counties in central Tennessee offer **calcite crystals** and **quartz** pebbles (not really gemmy material) to collectors who prospect the regional gravels and quarries. But, as far as gems and gemstones are concerned, Tennessee has been little prospected, and mainly the mountainous regions offer opportunities for the collector to investigate practically virgin territory.

The eastern mountain counties have produced most of the state's commercial minerals, principally **barite, coal, limestone, marble, clay,** the plebian **gravel** and **building stone,** and the nation's top production of **pyrite** and **zinc.** Tennessee also ranks in the top four states for the production of **sandstone, phosphate rock,** and **marble.** The first **marble** quarry was opened near Rogersville in Hawkins Co. in 1838, and this district remains today the most important source for **marble** in America. Many **iron** mines were operated for decades in various counties, with the Bumpass Cove Forge near Erwin in Unicoi Co. dating back to the Revolutionary War period. Another major metal mined for more than a century is **copper,** principally from the single district of Ducktown in southeastern Polk Co. From these mines has come most of the **gold,** a by-product of **copper** refining, produced in Tennessee. The yellow metal was actually discovered as early as 1827, mostly in placer sands along a 50-mile strip in Monroe and Polk counties along the North Carolina boundary, where a few rare alluvial **diamonds** turned up in the early operations.

For information, write: Department of Conservation, Division of Geology, State Office Building, Nashville.

BEDFORD CO.

SHELBYVILLE: (1) ENE via any of several rtes. (Fairfield Pike, Rte. 64, Railroad Ave., Horse Mt. rd.) to the famed Horse Mountain gem fields, area, wide variety, sizes, and colors, high quality—**"Horse Mountain" agate** (nodules, some with crystal-lined cavities; iris, etc.), **agatized corals** or **casts:** (a) Pannell Ridge on the Horse Mt. rd. (about halfway between SHELBY-VILLE and WARTRACE, area plowed fields, ditches, cr. beds; (b) area around Philippi Church; (c) all regional side rds. and stream gravels, cut banks, etc., along the Nashville, Chattanooga and St. Louis RR; (d) all hwy. dept. limestone quarries in region—**agatized corals** and **casts;**

(2) W, in rd. cuts, fields, stream beds; and (3) SW, along Rte. 64, at Sugar Cr., area—**agatized corals;** (4) widespread exposures throughout region of the Hermitage formation—**"Horse Mountain" agate, agatized corals** (*Stromatocerium*).

WARTRACE: (1) the Velmer Cutlow farm on mail rte. 2, pay fee; and (2) the W. E. Dye farm on same mail run, fee—**"Horse Mountain" agate, agatized corals.**

BLOUNT CO.

FRIENDSVILLE: (1) area quarries—**marble** (a gemmy **marble** exposure extends 125 mi. long by 20 mi. wide over the Valley and Ridge Province to the NE, in places 400 ft. thick); (2) NE 2½ mi., a quarry—**"French Pink" marble;** (3) S, a quarry—**marble** (black, cedar color, white).

MARYVILLE, area of Montvale Springs: (1) regional stream gravels, placers—**gold;** (2) placer sands E of the Chilhowee Mts.—**gold.** The principal **gold** deposits in Tenn. occur in a narrow strip of placer gravels about 50 mi. long in southern Blount, Monroe, and Polk counties along the N.C. boundary.

BRADLEY CO.

CLEVELAND: (1) area mines—**sphalerite;** (2) S 6 mi., at Blue Springs, area mines—**galena.**

MINERAL PARK, S a few mi., mine (20 mi. E of CHATTANOOGA in Hamilton Co.)—**galena.**

CAMPBELL CO.

JELLICO, regional rd. cuts along U.S. 25W to LA FOLLETTE—**agate, chalcedony, jasper,** etc.

CANNON CO.

AREA, countywide creek gravels, cliffs and bluffs, rd. cuts, plowed fields, quarries, etc.—**calcite, fluorite, crystal geodes** (of fossil origin, to 12 in. dia.), **goethite, limonite, pyrite, celestite.**

WOODBURY, E 5 mi. on U.S. 70S, area rd. cuts, plowed fields, stream and cr. gravels—**crystal geodes.**

CARTER CO.

ELIZABETHTON, area mines—**bauxite.**

ROAN MOUNTAIN: (1) along U.S. 19E from ELK PARK to BLEVINS; (2) along Rte. 143 to S, all area rd. cuts, stream beds and banks, excavations, etc. —gem **unakite;** (3) in exposures on both sides of Roan Mt.—**unakite.**

SADIE (12 mi. NE of ELIZABETHTON): (1) area mine dumps—**pyrite;** (2) Stony Cr., a mine in black shale—**pyrite, pyrolusite.**

CLAIBORNE CO.

NEW TAZEWELL, SW 5 mi., the Straight Creek district, area mines—**galena, sphalerite.**

COCKE CO.

AREA, Rag Mt. and Bluffton, regional stream gravels—**unakite.**

DEL RIO: (1) area stream gravels, gemmy—**unakite;** (2) area mines—**barite, calcite, celestite,** etc.; (3) the Mine Ridge prospects—**copper, iron, lead, zinc minerals.**

HARTFORD: (1) area gravels and banks of tributaries of Big Cr., weathering out of igneous exposures as pebbles—various **gemstones, quartz** (gemmy, light green); (2) S of Cogdill Chapel, on the Coggins farm, prospects—**copper, lead, zinc minerals;** (3) SE 1.3 mi., on Raven Branch in **quartz** vein, various—**crystals, minerals;** (4) E 2½ mi. along the Gulf Fork of Big Cr., area mines—**chalcopyrite, galena, pyrite, sphalerite.**

NEWPORT, the Yellow Springs Mine and other area dumps—**psilomelane.**

CUMBERLAND CO.

CROSSVILLE, E 4 mi., numerous quarries—**"Crab Orchard stone"** (polishable varicolored sandstone).

DAVIDSON CO.

HAYSBOROUGH, area **lead** mine—**barite, galena.**

FENTRESS CO.

BOATLAND, N side of Boles Cr. and 1 mi. from the church—**calcite, celestite, dolomite crystals, geodes** (containing crystals of **calcite, celestite,** or **quartz;** locally called "cannon balls"), **marcasite, pyrite,** etc.
JAMESTOWN: (1) NW 2½ mi., at Carpenter Hollow; and (2) SW 3½ mi., in the Buffalo Cove section, all area quarries—cf. BOATLAND.

FENTRESS, OVERTON, WARREN COS.

AREA, these counties constitute the state's primary **celestite** region, in Mississippian age limestone exposures, quarries, etc.—cf. BOATLAND in Fentress Co.

GREENE CO.

AREA: (1) scattered co. hwy. dept. quarries (Cove Cr., Dog Walk, Midway, Radcliffe, etc.)—gemmy **chert, crystals, fossils;** (2) Davy Crockett Lake, area mines—**mica,** etc.
GREENEVILLE: (1) area mines—**sphalerite;** (2) 12 mi. distant, veins in dolomite outcrop—**barite crystals.**
MOSHEIM: (1) jct. of U.S. 11E and rd. into town, N 2.7 mi. to exposure of the Mosheim anticline (a highly mineralized belt)—**dolomite** and **quartz crystals, quartz geodes** (to large size). The anticline is 8 mi. long and nearly 2 mi. wide, with many regional rds. leading to mines, prospects, and quarries, all good collecting localities. (2) N 3 mi. to ½ mi. N of the MOSHEIM-ALBANY crossrds., then W on gravel rd. to Gethsemane School, N ½ mi. on dirt rd. to the Brown-Tipton Mine—**calcite, cerussite,** gem **chert, dolomite, galena, pyrite, smithsonite, sphalerite.**

GREENE, HAWKINS, SULLIVAN, WASHINGTON COS.

AREA: (1) all regional limestone quarries, rd. cuts, excavations, etc.—**calcite crystals, celestite, dolomite crystals, fluorite,** golden **jasper, pyrite, quartz crystals;** (2) region bounded by GREENEVILLE (Greene Co.), ROGERSVILLE (Hawkins Co.), KINGSPORT (Sullivan Co.), and JOHNSON CITY (Washington Co.): (a) all regional quarries, rd. cuts, banks, stream beds, excavations, etc.—**quartz crystals** (clear, smoky, doubly terminated); (b) all regional old **barite** mines—**barite, jasper, rock crystal;** (c) regional **iron** mines —**jasper, iron minerals, rock crystal;** (d) all regional building excavations, gravel pits, prospect holes—**agate, jasper, quartz crystals,** etc.

HAMBLEN CO.

RUSSELLVILLE, area gravels, pits, rd. cuts, etc.—**quartz geodes.**

HAMILTON CO.

CHATTANOOGA, area mines at nearby Missionary Ridge—**bauxite.**

HARDIN CO.

AREA, countywide river and stream gravels (Tennessee, Elk, Cumberland, Clinch, and Wagauga rivers; Snake, Owl, Indian, and Holland creeks), buried in muds and sands, fresh-water mussels—**pearls.**

MILLEDGEVILLE, area of Coffee Landing (at Coffee Bluff on banks of the Tennessee R.), in sands—**amber.**

HICKMAN CO.

CENTERVILLE, area mines—**cobalt** in **wad, nickel minerals.**

JEFFERSON CO.

MOSSY CREEK, area exposures of the Knox Dolomite are mined—**calamine, smithsonite** (locally called **"dry bone"**), **sphalerite.**

NEW MARKET, extensive area mines—**smithsonite.**

KNOX CO.

MASCOT, extensive area mines—**sphalerite.**

LAWRENCE CO.

LAWRENCEBURG, area rd. cuts, excavations, cut banks, etc.—**chalcedony, chert, geodes (calcite, quartz).**

MARION CO.

AREA: (1) Iron Ridge, mines—**jasper, hematite;** (2) regional pits, quarries, stream gravels—**barite, fluorite, galena, pyrite, selenite.**

JASPER, the Chattanooga Shale Quarry—fine gem **crystals.**

MONTEAGLE, just S, in a rd. cut, as masses—**calcite onyx** (peach, pink, some crystal clear).

MONROE CO.

AREA: (1) in reddish clay banks along the Little Tennessee R.—**rock crystal;** (2) SE part of co., Coker Cr., much early activity and many old mines—**gold;** (3) Coco Cr. at mouth on Hiwassee R., the Buck Miller Mine —**argentiferous tetrahedrite;** (4) Whippoorwill Branch of the Tellico R., gravels and area lode mines—**gold.**

SWEETWATER (District): (1) area mines and quarries—**barite;** (2) E 5 mi., near village of ROCKY, on rd. to VONORE, the Bullard Barite Mine— **barite, fluorite,** yellow **sphalerite.**

TOQUA, in clay banks of the Little Tennessee R.—**rock crystal.**

OVERTON CO.

LIVINGSTON, NW 4 mi., near ALLONS and W of Rte. 52, a quarry— **calcite, celestite, dolomite crystals, geodes** (containing crystals of **calcite, celestite,** or **quartz**), **marcasite, pyrite,** etc.

MONROE, SE ¾ mi., on NE side of Pilot Knob, area mines—cf. LIVINGSTON.

POLK CO.

COPPERHILL: (1) area streams, rd. cuts, etc.; and (2) the many regional **copper** mines of the Ducktown–Copperhill District (producers since the early 1800's), dumps scattered over many square mi.—**azurite, chalcopyrite, garnets, gold, pyrite, pyrrhotite, malachite, quartz crystals** (many aventurescent), **staurolites** (some with inclusions of **garnet**), **chalcanthite, chalcocite, cuprite, galena, graphite, melaconite.**

DUCKTOWN: (1) area mines—cf. COPPERHILL; (2) the Cherokee Mine— same as area mines but **pyrite cubes** to very large size.

PUTNAM CO.

MONTEREY, N 2 mi. on U.S. 70N, mine dumps, **calcite, celestite,** pink **dolomite crystals, fluorite, quartz crystals.**

ROBERTSON CO.

SPRINGFIELD, area rd. cuts, stream gravels, etc.—**quartz gemstones.**

SEVIER CO.

GATLINBURG: (1) all area stream banks and gravels—**gemstones, minerals;** (2) Pigeon R. and tributaries along numerous improved side rds.—**black chert, quartz** (blue, smoky), **moonstones, unakite;** (3) the Webb, English, and Chilhowee mts.: (a) regional surfaces and outcrops, and (b) regional stream gravels, varied—gemmy **minerals;** (4) the Unaka Mts., in outcrops of the Max Patch granite—**epidote, quartz** (gemmy, variously colored), **unakite.**

SEVIERVILLE, E 8 mi., in Nun's Cove district, numerous old mines—**calcite,** bluish **chert, barite, sphalerite** (pale yellow crystals).

SHELBY CO.

MEMPHIS, at Richardson's Landing, area dredging operations, stream gravels and banks, etc.—**agate** (Lake Superior type), **agatized fossils** (corals, sponges, wood).

SMITH CO.

CARTHAGE, W 8 mi., the Foley Mine—**fluorite.**
TROUSDALE: (1) area mines—**calcite, fluorite, sphalerite;** (2) mines on the Ferry-Lebanon rd. (into Wilson Co.)—**barite.**

SULLIVAN CO.

KINGSPORT: (1) area quarries—**limestone minerals;** (2) cuts in hillsides just outside town, massive—**barite;** (3) the Rockway and Lambert limestone quarries—**calcite, celestite, dolomite crystals,** etc.; (4) rd. cuts along Int. 81 —**limestone minerals;** (5) cf. also combined counties beginning with Greene.

UNICOI CO.

AREA: (1) N section of co., in regional limestone quarries—**calcite, celestite, dolomite crystals;** (2) Unaka Mts., area—**unakite.**
ERWIN: (1) area pits and quarries of the Brooks Sand & Gravel Co. and the Unicoi hwy. dept.—**chalcedony, gem jasper;** (2) 4 mi. out at Bumpass Cove (a noted mineral district with many mines and dumps reached from EMBREEVILLE on co. rd. 107 and an unmarked rd. paralleling Bumpass Cr. and an old RR grade): (a) drive SW around the "Horseshoe" of the Nolichucky R., mines along both sides of rd.—brown **jasper** (patterned with **pyrolusite,** to 25-lb. pieces, attractive gemstone for all lapidary arts); (b) mines and dumps of the Bumpass Cove district—**anglesite, chalcopyrite, cerussite, hematite, hemimorphite, galena, psilomelane, sphalerite.**
FLAG POND (village): (1) area outcrops of **epidotized granite** (laced with **quartz** veins)—red **feldspar;** (2) halfway to ERWIN and ½ mi. from U.S. 23: (a) granite exposures N of hwy., and (b) granite extending as main body to S—**unakite;** (3) NW 2¾ mi., the Chandler Mine—**barite, quartz, unakite;** (4) W, at the Higgins property, as well as the nearby Willis, Lloyd, and Stockton farms, and the Del Rio Stackhouse exposures—**gem unakite** (with Max Patch granite, i.e., red and gray, coarse-grained, showing **biotite, epidote,** and pink **feldspar**). U.S. 23 crosses a massive body of Max Patch

granite just E of the village of FLAG POND, the larger portion extending S to the Walnut Mts. of N.C. Highway cuts reveal the gemmy variety of the Beech granite which is usually associated with the Archean Cranberry granite.

ROCK CREEK, area quarries and mine dumps—**barite, hematite.**

UNION CO.

NEW PROSPECT, area mines and at Stiner's Zinc Mine—**calamine, smithsonite, sphalerite.**
POWELL RIVER, area mines—**calamine, smithsonite.**

WARREN CO.

MCMINNVILLE, S 5 mi., on W side of Ben Lomond Mt. between Bennett Hollow and McCorkle Hollow—**calcite, celestite, dolomite crystals, geodes** (containing crystals of **calcite, celestite,** or **quartz**), **marcasite, pyrite,** etc.

WAYNE CO.

WAYNESBORO, all countywide area limestone exposures (most extensive outcrop in Tenn.)—gemmy **chert, agatized fossils, flint, quartz crystals,** etc.

WILLIAMSON CO.

NOLANSVILLE, area mines—**galena.**

TEXAS

This huge spade-shaped state, second in size only to Alaska, reveals a varied topography and geologic structure. Its rock formations run the gamut from Upper Cambrian of the Llano Estacado, or Staked Plain, to Pleistocene alluvials along the Gulf Coast from Harding to Hidalgo counties. The eastern portion, between Sabine, in Jefferson Co. on the Louisiana boundary, and the Trinity River running through Liberty and Chambers counties, is a region of cypress swamps and pine-covered knolls. Central and northern Texas comprise rolling blackland prairies, among the most fertile farmlands in the world, underlain by Cretaceous formations. Especially notable is the Comanche series of the Lower to Middle Cretaceous, outcropping in a line south from the Oklahoma border all the way into central Mexico and forming a broad east-west belt from the Arkansas line to the westernmost county of El Paso.

These Cretaceous rocks are not only enormously rich in **fossils** but are productive of such characteristic sedimentary formation minerals as **alum, barite, celestite, gypsum, fluorite,** and **limestone.**

The Texas Panhandle and all of west Texas is high arid land rising westward by sweeping plains and eroded uplands. In far northwest Culberson Co., the Guadalupe Mountains achieve the highest point in Texas in 8,751-foot Guadalupe Peak. The mountain range itself is actually a great uplifted sea reef of corals and calcareous algae more than 280 million years old. The flat-topped escarpment is protected from erosion by a cap rock of massive Permian limestone.

A north–south geologic divider occurs along the Balcones Escarpment, a long curving fault line through central Texas marked by rough, tree-covered hills and many waterfalls. West of the escarpment lie the Edwards Plateau and that portion of the Great Plains known as the "north-central short-grass plains." The Cap Rock separates the short-grass plains from the high, wind-swept, canyon-cut Llano Estacado, famed for its bitter winter blizzards and searing hot summers.

Commercial mining plays very little part in the Texas economy, which, as everyone knows, is primarily based in **petroleum.** So vast are the subterranean oil deposits that in places, such as at Kilgore in the east Texas county of Gregg, the oil wells actually crowd the buildings. The equally productive oil fields of west Texas were discovered in the 1940's.

Generally speaking, the gemstone fields of Texas can be grouped into several broad areas in each of which specific collecting localities are far too numerous to list. The gravel beds of the Rio Grande delta area from north of Laredo in Webb Co. to 20 miles south of the Falcon Reservoir Dam in Starr Co. yield great quantities of **agate** of every description, **chalcedony, carnelian, flower jasper, quartz** (amethystine, **geodes, rock crystal**), and a host of subvarieties of cryptocrystalline **quartz gemstones.** The Big Bend region, including Needle Peak and Bouquet, from 17 miles south of Marfa in Presidio Co. to Loma Linda on the Mexican side of the east end of Big Bend National Park in Brewster Co., is productive of all types of **agates, jaspers, fire opal, spinel,** etc., although especially noted for its **"pompom"** or **"bouquet" agate.**

The Catahoula group of counties, which stretches 350 miles in a south-west-to-northeast direction and includes a region some 100 miles broad from the lower Rio Grande to the Louisiana border, produces **agate, petrified ferns** and **palm wood,** silicified tropical **woods,** and **opalized** golden pine **wood.** Taken in southwest–northeast order, collecting centers are at Freer, Duval Co.; George West, Live Oak Co.; Gonzales, Gonzales Co.; Kennedy, Karnes Co.; Giddings, Lee Co.; Bryan, Brazos Co.; and Nacogdoches, Nacogdoches Co.

For information, write: Bureau of Economic Geology, University of Texas, Box B, Austin.

ARMSTRONG CO.

WAYSIDE, N and E by ranch rds., in banks and bed of Prairie Dog Town Fork of the Red R.—**agatized wood.**

BASTROP CO.

SMITHVILLE: (1) wide surrounding region, in breaks, cuts, surfaces—**agate, petrified wood;** (2) N 7.2 mi. on Rte. 71 to cr. crossing (7.8 mi. SE of BASTROP), at abandoned hwy. bridge on the E, 100 yds. up cr. in bank walls on S side in red shale—**selenite crystals** (to 12 in. long, water-clear; crosses, diamonds, phantoms).

BAYLOR CO.

SEYMOUR, take rd. to RENDHAM, then E and NE along the escarpment (capped by Beaverburk limestone), as small cleavable masses in red shale—**barite.**

BREWSTER CO.

ALPINE: (1) N 10 mi., in gravels of Musquiz Cr.—small **moonstones;** (2) E about 15 mi., on W side of the Glass Mts., area—**agate** (moss, plume), **chalcedony, jasper, quartz crystals;** (3) SW 6 mi. on U.S. 90 to RR water tank, beyond tank in valley, area—fine **agates, geodes;** (4) S 16 mi. on Rte. 118, area lava flow—**agate nodules** (moss, plume), **chalcedony, jasper, quartz crystals;** (5) S 16–17 mi. on Rte. 118 to the Woodward Ranch (free camping, collecting fee charged or can purchase roughs)—**"Texas plume"** agate (among most beautiful **agates** in world), **pompom agate, jasper.** (Make inquiry about ranch leases on N side of the Big Bend National Park—**plume** and **pompom agates, jasper,** etc.) (6) S 58 mi. on Rte. 118 to W-trending side rd. (locked gate), then WSW 10 mi. to the Agua Fria Ranch (32,000 acres), area draws, flats, slopes, etc.—**agate, agatized wood, Indian artifacts;** note Indian petroglyphs on high cliff face.

ALTUDA, area mines—**argentiferous galena.**

MARATHON, S on U.S. 395: (1) 37 mi., the Love Ranch, fee, then 2 mi. to collecting area—**agate;** (2) 39 mi. to SE-trending side rd. (just N of Big Bend National Park), then 6.2 mi. to the Stillwell Ranch and Trailer Park, collecting fee, area—**agate;** (3) 50 mi., on E side of Maravillas Cr. and E, SE, or NE of Dog Canyon in the Santiago Mts., area deposits—**barite.**

SOLITARIO (District), area mines, excellent specimens on dumps—**galena.**

STUDY BUTTE: (1) SE, in NW portion of the Chisos Mts., area mines—native **alum;** (2) SW, to Needle Peak (inquire way at store), a broad area—**agate** (pompom and "thistle").

TERLINGUA (ghost town): (1) area mines in Cretaceous limestones and shales—**cinnabar, eglestonite, fluorite, native mercury, montroydite, terlinguaite,** and on dumps also **pompom agate** pseudomorphs after **aragonite**

crystals (to 6 in. long and in clusters). (This old mining district primarily produced **mercury,** with millions of dollars' worth coming from the rich mines. A single cavity in one mine yielded 150 lbs. of pure **native quicksilver.**) (2) Bed and banks of Terlingua Cr. all along W side of co.— **amber, agate, chalcedony, jasper,** etc.

BROWN CO.

BLANKET, W and SW, in the Cretaceous Glen Rose Formation, as replacement deposits—**barite.**

ZEPHYR, area of E part of co., extending into portions of both Comanche and Mills counties, numerous mined deposits—**celestite.**

BURLESON CO.

CALDWELL to SOMERVILLE, and W to GIDDINGS in Lee Co., a broad region (take any side rd. and prospect all regional cr. beds, breaks, hill slopes, etc.) —**petrified** and **agatized wood.**

BURNET CO.

BURNET, the Silver Creek area, mines and prospects in calcareous sandstones—**galena.**

CHILDRESS CO.

CHILDRESS, N on U.S. 83 across the Red R., deposits in area between the Red R. and U.S. 62 in NE part of co.—**alabaster.**

COMAL CO.

NEW BROUNFELS, area stream beds and banks, plowed fields, rd. cuts, excavations—**petrified wood.**

CORYELL CO.

GATESVILLE, S 1 mi. to Rte. 107, then SE 11 mi., rd. cuts 2 mi. W of RR tracks show limestone—**turritella agate.**

OGLESBY, S 3 mi. to Rte. 107, then W 2 mi., area rd. cuts cutting Turritella Limestone—**turritella agate.**

CULBERSON CO.

KENT, N, to Seven Hearts Gap (between the Apache and Delaware mts.), area about 1 mi. long by ¼ mi. wide, replacement deposit in limestone— **barite.**

VAN HORN: (1) W on U.S. 80, rd. cut on S lane of freeway—**talc;** (2) 1 mi. N of the Texas & Pacific RR, area on NE side of the Carrizozo Mts., prospects—**limonite cubes, turquoise;** (3) W 5 mi., area prospects—**turquoise;** (4) N 32 mi., area mines and prospects—**wolframite.**

DONLEY CO.

CLARENDON, N 5 mi. on Rte. 70, just across the Salt Fork of the Red R. bridge, in rd. cuts, gemmy pink—**dolomite.**

DUVAL CO.

FREER: (1) areas to SW—**agate, silicified** and **teredo wood;** (2) W 15–18 mi., along co. rd. 44, area—**petrified palm wood.**

ELLIS CO.

MIDLOTHIAN: (1) area immediately NW, along both sides of U.S. 287 —**fossil shark teeth;** (2) SE 5.2 mi. on U.S. 287, along both sides of creek N and S of hwy.: (a) both sides, area—**pyrite roses** (often encased in limestone); (b) S side of hwy. in shale formation near cr. bank—**fossils** (leaf prints).

EL PASO CO.

AREA, the Quitman Mts.: (1) E side, the Bonanza Mine—**chalcopyrite, galena, sphalerite;** (2) W side, the Sierra Diablo and other mines—**chalcopyrite, galena;** (3) the Old Hazel Mine—**lead, silver.**

DAHLBERG, N, as a mined deposit—**muscovite mica.**

EAGLE FLAT, area mines—**smithsonite.**

EL PASO: (1) N, along Rte. 375 (connecting Int. 10 with U.S. 54), all rd. cuts in the Franklin Mts.—**garnets, mica, serpentine** (pink banded); (2) N 12–15 mi., mines—**cassiterite, wolframite;** (3) N 14–16 mi., area mines in the Franklin Mts.—**cassiterite.**

FAYETTE CO.

LEDBETTER, S on Rte. 957, across Rabs Cr. to the Nechanitz and Matejowsky store: (1) along Rabs Cr.—**petrified palm, opalized wood;** (2) all surrounding farmlands—same.

WARDA, S 1 mi. on U.S. 77, turn E on co. rd. mail rte. for about 6 mi., all area farms and rd. banks to the Matejowsky store—cf. LEDBETTER.

FISHER CO.

ROBY, E of Buffalo Cr., in the HOBBS community, regional mines—**celestite.** From N to S in Fisher, Nolan, and upper Coke counties, the Nolan

Mining District constitutes a narrow belt of deposits about 45 mi. long, with major mining centers described under Nolan Co., *q.v.*—**celestite** (commonly in white, somewhat massive, crystalline aggregates).

GILLESPIE CO.

FREDERICKSBURG: (1) S 8–9 mi. on U.S. 87, rd. cut on E side of hwy.— **fossils;** (2) N 24 mi. on Rte. 16 (30 mi. via rd. from ROUND MOUNTAIN, Blanco Co.), area about 9 mi. NNW of WILLOW CITY, quarries and exposures—**barite** (some), **serpentine, soapstone.**

WILLOW CITY, NE 9.6 mi., a mined lenticular deposit—**barite.**

GILLESPIE, LLANO, BLANCO COS.

AREA, the Coal Cr. and Comanche Cr. districts, many mines and quarries —abundant **magnetite, asbestos, nickel (zaratite), serpentine** (prospected for **chromite), soapstone.**

GONZALES CO.

GONZALES: (1) all general area farms, and (2) bed and banks of Peach Cr.—**agate, petrified wood.**

GRIMES CO.

BEDIAS, broad surrounding area—**"bediasites"** (**tektites,** walnut size common). The town is center of a famed location for "moon rocks," locally called **"black diamonds"** or **"fire pearls."** These extraterrestrial gemmy minerals, presumably knocked off the moon by an in-plunging asteroid, appear black but become dark green when faceted.

LAMB SPRINGS, SW 2 mi. to 2 mi. NE of KIETH: (1) area, and (2) in gravels of Alum, Dinner, Jarvis, and Lake creeks, and around the head of Gibbons Cr.—**tektites (bediasite).**

HIDALGO CO.

SULLIVAN CITY, E to Rte. 886, then S about 2 mi., cross RR and turn W on old military rd. to gravel pits next the Rio Grande: (1) all along the rd., and (2) in the many pits—**"Rio Grande" agates, chert, jasper, agatized wood,** etc. (All gravel exposures along the Rio Grande show an abundance of these gemstones, usually coated with a white patina.)

HOUSTON CO.

CROCKETT, broad triangular area (including GROVETON and TRINITY in Trinity Co.), all regional stream beds, draws, washes, side rds., rd. cuts, bar pits, etc.—**agatized wood, jasper,** etc. (The region is mostly pine timber country, open to collecting; dirt rds. are passable only in dry weather.)

HUDSPETH CO.

ALLAMOOR, broad general region: (1) area, and (2) along S edge of the Quitman Mts. (cf. VAN HORN in Culberson Co.)—**agate, amethysts, carnelian, chalcedony, jasper, petrified wood, etc.;** (3) S, the Van Horn Mts., general area—**agate, chalcedony, jasper,** etc.

INDIAN HOT SPRINGS, E, in the Eagle Mts., area mines—**barite.**

SIERRA BLANCA, NW 8 mi., in the Sierra Blanca, area mines and prospects —**turquoise.**

JASPER CO.

JASPER: (1) area of McGee Bend Dam—**agatized wood;** (2) N 11½ mi. on U.S. 96, make inquiry at the Browndell store, area—**agatized wood** (including palm).

JEFF DAVIS CO.

CHISPA STA. (on the S.P. RR), W 5 mi. and S, area mines—**barite, manganese.**

FORT DAVIS, broad general area—**chalcedony, jasper,** etc. Of special interest are the nearby Davis Mts. State Park and the ruins of the old frontier fort.

KARNES CO.

FALLS CITY: (1) NE 1.1 mi. on co. rd. to GILLETT, crossing a creek, to the Erdman farm (Maymes Rock Haven), small fee, directions, and guide service, area—**petrified palm wood, opalized wood,** other **plant fossils** (horsetail reed, fern buds, etc.); (2) SW 9.3 mi. on Rte. 791 to jct. with Rte. 1344, then NW 1¾ mi. to the Tessman farm (fee, directions), area—golden **agatized palm wood, Indian artifacts.**

LAMPASAS CO.

LAMPASAS: (1) N 5 mi., exposure of the Glen Rose limestone, as large crystals filling pockets—**celestite;** (2) N 6 mi., bed and banks of Little Lucy Cr.—**celestite.**

LA SALLE, McMULLEN, LIVE OAK COS.

COTULLA (La Salle Co.), E along Rte. 97 across McMullen Co. to THREE RIVERS in Live Oak Co., entire area of the Catahoula formation, regional rd. cuts, farm fields, excavations, etc.—**petrified palm wood, agatized fern buds.**

LAVACA CO.

MOULTON, area gravel pits, stream gravels, farm fields, etc.—agate, petrified wood.

LEE CO.

DIME BOX, NE, at Nails Cr. State Park on S side of Somerville Lake (no collecting inside park), all outside draws, washes, adjoining farms (usually pay a small fee)—"East Texas moon rocks" (tektites).

GIDDINGS, S 20 mi. to LA GRANGE (center of a large collecting area), inquire at any service station—petrified wood.

LIVE OAK CO.

THREE RIVERS: (1) W on Rte. 72: (a) at 2.8 mi. turn S on Rte. 1545 for 6.3 mi., to gate to the H. D. House Ranch, fee (inquire first at Antlers Restaurant and Motel in town), area—agatized fern buds and palm, chalcedony, jaspers; (b) continue W approx. 70 mi. (including Rte. 97) across McMullen Co. to COTULLA in La Salle Co., all area rd. cuts, banks, farm fields, excavations en route, exposing the Catahoula formation—Catahoula gemstones (listed above); (2) NE via any rtes. or side rds.: (a) approx. 90 air mi. across Karnes Co. to GONZALES in Gonzales Co., and (b) beyond, another 47 air mi. NE to LA GRANGE in Fayette Co., then (c) E approx. 190 air mi. to the La. border, all regional exposures along all regional rds. of the Catahoula formation—Catahoula gemstones.

LLANO CO.

AREA, all countywide pegmatite exposures (many)—topaz, zircon, etc.

BABYHEAD: (1) SSE 1¾ mi., a series of llanite dikes reaching to summit of Miller Mt.—llanite (a gemmy granite containing pink feldspar spots and blue-agate spherules), opal-quartz; (2) S side of Babyhead Mt. (between LLANO and Wilbern's Glen and E to Wilbern's Gap), area outcrops—llanite, opal-quartz.

BARRINGER HILL, area mines—allanite (some specimens containing occluded hydrogen), cyrtolite, fergusonite, fluorite, gadolinite, ilmenite, mackintoshite, nivenite, rowlandite, tengerite, thorogummite.

FIELD CREEK, E and about 2 mi. S of the San Saba-Llano co. line, the Pecan-Wolf Cr. area, as thin exposed veins—barite.

KINGSLAND, area mines—allanite, etc.

LLANO: (1) N 9.4 mi. on Rte. 16, rd. cuts on both sides of hwy. and along all regional ranch rds.—llanite (camping available at a roadside park just N of the collecting area in low granite mts.); (2) S 15 mi. on Rte. 16, to Rte. 965, then W 8 mi. to Enchanted Rock (about 5 mi. SW of OXFORD), area of the Charles Moss ranch, in crevices in granite—epidote (large clusters, green crystals), pink **feldspar crystals, quartz crystals** (clear, smoky). (Pay small fee at ranch, camping permitted; very scenic area.)

OXFORD: (1) area mines—**magnetite, serpentine, soapstone, vermiculite;** (2) S 5 mi., to Rte. 965, then W to Enchanted Rock—cf. LLANO item (2).

LLANO-GILLESPIE COS.

AREA, the Llano Uplift formation: (1) ranches along Rte. 16 (get permission)—**calcite** (fluorescent), **fluorite,** phantom **quartz crystals, wollastonite,** gemmy **fossils,** etc.; (2) ranches along Sandy Cr. (24 mi. SW of LLANO and along co. rd. 2323), fees charged—same gemstones.

MADISON CO.

MADISONVILLE, farm rd. 978 to NORMANGEE, to Rte. 39, between hwy. and RR south to CROSS and all surrounding region, banks, cuts, fields, draws, washes, etc.—**petrified wood.**

MASON CO.

AREA, countywide granite outcrops of the Llano Uplift formation— **amazonite, feldspar crystals, smoky quartz crystals, topaz** (blue, colorless), **black tourmaline.**

GRIT, area pegmatite outcrops—**topaz, zircon,** etc.

KATEMCY (12 mi. N of MASON)—cf. AREA.

MASON: (1) area along E side of U.S. 87—cf. AREA; (2) SW on co. rd. 1871 to the Llano R., camp and picnic area, walk short distance upstream from low-water bridge, area, weathering out of gray to black limestone— gemmy **crinoid stem sections** (some with star centers); (3) NW on U.S. 87 and Rte. 377 for 5 mi. to jct. with Rte. 29, roadside park camping and picnicking: (a) W on Rte. 377 .6 mi. to locked gate of N-trending rd. to the Seaquist Ranch (get gate key at Hill Top Diner in MASON), park car at end of rd., hike up cr. to collecting locality (cr. bed and hillsides)—**topaz** (gem, large crystals); (b) W 3.3 mi. to S-trending rd., then S 1.2 mi. to locked ranch gate (get key at ranch, fee charged), area in hills N of ranch reached via another locked gate—large **topaz** and **quartz crystals.**

STREETER (8 mi. W of MASON)—cf. AREA.

MAVERICK CO.

EAGLE PASS: (1) area—**agate, amber, chalcedony, jasper;** (2) N 10 mi. on U.S. 277 to W-trending rd.: (a) first house on left (Helms Ranch, pay fee), area—**"Rio Grande" agate** (banded, moss, plume, etc., hidden under white coating), **chalcedony, jasper, petrified wood;** (b) 1½ mi. W of the Helms Ranch to a power plant, all surrounding area, abundant—**"Rio Grande" agate, jasper;** (c) 1½ mi. W of the Helms Ranch to canal, then 2 mi. to

entrance to the Cunningham Ranch, small fee, camping—gem **"Rio Grande"**
agate.
QUEMADO, NW 2.7 mi. on Rte. 1908, to entrance of the Villarreal Ranch
(fee at ranch house ½ mi. inside gate), area, abundant—**"Rio Grande"**
agate, jasper, etc.

McMULLEN CO.

TILDEN: (1) W 5½ mi. on Rte. 72, gravel pit on S side of rd.—**agatized**
wood; (2) cf. also COTULLA in La Salle Co.

MONTAGUE CO.

SAINT JO, area quarries—**sphalerite crystals** (in **calcite**).

MONTGOMERY CO.

NEW CANEY, E, in area cr. beds and banks—**jasper, petrified palm wood.**

MOORE CO.

DUMAS, S 12 mi. on U.S. 87/287 to E-trending co. rd., then E to NW tip
of Lake Meredith, along Plum Cr. near the public campground, in prehistoric
Indian quarries and all regional breaks—**"Alibates" flint** (multicolored).

NACOGDOCHES CO.

DOUGLASS, E 4 mi. on Rte. 21 to Loco Cr., W of bridge, in rd. cut on N
side of rd.—**pyrite, selenite.**

NOLAN CO.

BLACKWELL (extreme S part of co., with deposits extending S into upper
Coke Co.), from the valley of Brushy Cr. N to the W-trending co. rd. to
MARYNEAL, with central part of district near the Antelope School (4 mi. W
of BLACKWELL and 1.2 mi. N of the Nolan-Coke co. line), area mines—
celestite.
SWEETWATER, S and W about 5 mi.: (1) area mines and pits, and (2)
Boothe district, ½ mi. N of the Ada School, on top of a low bluff on E side
of Sweetwater Cr., open-pit mine—**celestite.**

PARKER CO.

WHITE SETTLEMENT, the Stover Peak area, outcrops—**prase.**

POLK CO.

CAMDEN, E along U.S. 287 or co. rd. 1745, to CHESTER in Tyler Co., large region, inquire at any U.S. Forest Service station—**petrified palm wood** (often coated with white lime).

PRESIDIO CO.

, MARFA: (1) S 7 mi. on U.S. 67, turn SE 18 mi. on Rte. 169 to the Bishop Ranch, pay fee at ranch house, area—**agate** (black, bouquet, plume). (The **Texas bouquet agate** ranks among the most beautiful **agates** in the world, containing as many as five colors in the flowerlike plumes.) (2) U.S. 67 all way to Presidio (59 mi.), both sides of hwy.—**Texas bouquet agate;** (3) the area between MARFA and VAN HORN in SW Culbertson Co. via U.S. 90 (NW about 71 mi.) is the Lobo Valley, oldest **agate** collecting region in Texas (permission mandatory from all area ranchers)—**Texas plume agate;**
(4) SW about 30 mi., all along rd. to the Chinati Mts., regional draws, washes, surfaces, etc.—**agate** (common, bouquet, plume), **chalcedony, jasper;** (5) S 80 mi., mines in Fresno Canyon—**alum;** (6) NE, along Rte. 17, to FORT DAVIS in Jeff Davis Co., *q.v.,* all regional side rds., cuts, breaks, ranchlands, etc.—**agate, chalcedony, jasper,** etc.
RUIDOSA, E, in the Chinati Mts., SW side and in San Antonio Canyon, area mines with good specimens on dumps—**galena.**
SAN CARLOS, area coal mines, on dumps—**jet.**
SHAFTER, W 2 mi., area mines—**smithsonite.**

RANDALL CO.

CANYON, E 20 mi. on Rte. 217, into Palo Duro Canyon State Park (extending into Armstrong Co.), area of canyon outside park boundaries—**agatized wood.**

REAL CO.

LEAKY, N on U.S. 83 to jct. with Rte. 39, the Horsecollar Roadside Park: (1) S ½ mi. down hill to steep bank on W—**calcite crystal geodes** weathering out of white limestone (large, containing clear dogtooth crystals); (2) 1½ mi. S of the **geode** field via U.S. 83, and S of bridge on W side of rd.—**fossils** (ox-heart type).

REEVES CO.

BALMORHEA: (1) area quarries—**onyx;** (2) Balmorhea State Park: (a) on mt. sides and in washes of flats, and (b) around N and E sides of Lake Balmorhea, area—**"Balmorhea blue"** agates (nodular, to very large size, blue-banded, some laced with black plumes); (3) E 17 mi., all area along Barilla Draw—**agate.**

PECOS, W 18 mi. on U.S. 80, any ranch rd. in area, on either side—**agate, petrified wood.**

TOYAH, all area ranch rds. running out of town, W, NW, NE, S (most popular is S toward BALMORHEA), entire area and the farther off the main traveled rds. the better—**plume agate** (to 10-lb. chunks), **agatized wood.**

TOYAHVALE, E, on rd. around Lake Balmorhea on N side, in area washes, draws, slopes, etc., of a low range of volcanic mts. from N of the lake around to the SE side (extensive collecting area)—**"Balmorhea blue"** agate, black-plume agate (gem quality, to large size). (Excellent camping, fishing, swimming.)

SAN PATRICIO CO.

MATHIS, area rd. cuts, breaks, banks, gravels, etc.—**moss agate.**

SAN SABA CO.

BARTON, NE, in gravels and banks of Hinton Cr.—**chalcedony, chert.**

SAN SABA, W on U.S. 190 for 2.2 mi., turn S on co. rd. 1030 for 6.9 mi. to a red barn and E-trending rd., then 2 mi. on the side rd. to the Lambert Ranch (inquire directions, pay small fee)—**fossils** (gemmy pink, black, gray crinoid stem sections and heads, embedded in limestone). (The **limestone** is gemmy enough for cutting and polishing. The ranch is the site of a prehistoric Indian camp, and the owners permit camping.)

STARR CO.

RIO GRANDE CITY, all gravels of the Rio Grande both E and W to co. boundaries—**Rio Grande agates, chalcedony, jasper,** etc.

TARRANT CO.

FORT WORTH, in bluff at NE corner of jct. of West Freeway and Rte. 183 (in town, across hwy. from the Carswell runway)—**fossils.**

TAYLOR CO.

BUFFALO GAP, area exposures of red shales (22 mi. SW of ABILENE), as thin veins running vertically—**barite.**

TRAVIS CO.

AUSTIN: (1) W 5 mi., on Mt. Bonnell (near Colorado R.), area mines—**celestite, strontianite;** (2) E a few mi., large area, in cuts, draws, washes, fields, etc.—**agatized wood, petrified palm,** etc.

TRINITY CO.

CARLISLE, large surrounding area N of Lake Livingston—**petrified palm wood** (often coated with white lime).

GROVETON, TRINITY, all surrounding areas in cut banks, draws, washes, slopes, etc.—**agate, chalcedony, jasper, petrified wood,** etc. (See CROCKETT in Houston Co.)

TYLER CO.

CHESTER, W along U.S. 287 into Polk Co. (and along Polk co. rd. 1745) to CAMDEN in Polk Co., broad region along both sides of rds., inquire at any U.S. Forest Service station—**petrified palm wood** (usually coated with white lime).

VAL VERDE CO.

AREA, valley of the Pecos R., numerous mined deposits—**manganese minerals.**

COMSTOCK, W on U.S. 90 to the Pecos R., under E end of bridge, in limestone outcrop—**turritella fossils** (polish nicely).

LANGTRY, NW 26 mi. on U.S. 90 to CEDAR STA. (Terrell Co.), inquire and pay small fee to enter the Kothman Ranch, area—**agate, petrified wood.**

PANDALE, W 1¼ mi., on W slope of a divide separating Howard Draw from the Pecos R., mine—**barite.**

WEBB CO.

LAREDO: (1) within city limits: (a) the Laredo Gravel Pit (on the Rio Grande bank off Santa Maria St.)—**Rio Grande agate, chalcedony, jasper, agatized wood;** (b) river bars at low water and in gravels of islands—**agates, agatized wood, jasper,** etc.; (2) all stream beds and bars of the Rio Grande and tributaries—**agates, chalcedony, jasper, petrified wood;** (3) N on U.S. 81 to jct. with Rte. 1472, then NW 7½ mi. to the Pico Ranch, turn in for 2.2 mi. to ranch house (fee, directions to high-quality fields, camping)—**agate** (moss, many colors), **agatized wood, jasper.**

WEBB, ZAPATA, STARR COS.

AREA, all regional gravels of the Rio Grande and its tributaries SE from EAGLE PASS in Maverick Co., *q.v.,* to RIO GRANDE CITY in Starr Co. (more than 150 mi. along the Rio Grande)—**Rio Grande agates, chalcedony, jasper, petrified wood.**

WILSON CO.

POTH, SW 7 mi. on Rte. 541 to jct. with Rte. 1344, then 6¼ mi. SE to entrance to the Tessman farm (fee and directions)—golden **agatized palm wood, Indian artifacts.**

WISE CO.

ALVOND, SE 1.8 mi. to old iron bridge crossing a cr. bed, in gravel bars and banks—**carbonized wood, pyrite cubes.**
BRIDGEPORT, on NE side of Lake Bridgeport 2.6 mi. N of Rte. 24 (on Rte. 1658), area—gemmy **fossil crinoids, trilobites.**

ZAPATA CO.

LOPENO, W of U.S. 83, area surfaces, draws, etc., of low hills, many varieties—**agates, agatized palm wood, chalcedony, jasper,** etc.
ZAPATA: (1) the Ramirez Ranch (get key and directions at the Falcon Rock Shop in town), via N on U.S. 83 past a roadside park to gate on W side of hwy., area abounds in material—**agate, agatized wood, jasper,** etc.; (2) S 12 mi. on U.S. 83 to Rte. 2687, turn W 8 mi. on rd. to Falcon Lake to Bob's Nob (center of the famed Falcon Reservoir **agate** field), area—gem **agate, jasper, petrified wood.**

UTAH

Visitors to Utah cannot help but be impressed by the state's great contrasts. Although Utah has an overall average altitude of one mile above sea level, the topography is dramatically halved into a relatively low-lying (4,000 feet) western desert region and an extremely rugged mountain and plateau eastern half, spectacularly bounded on the north by the Uinta Mountains along Wyoming's southern border. The Uinta Range, capped by snowy 13,498-foot Kings Peak, is the only major east–west mountain system in North America south of the transverse Brooks Range in northern Alaska. These wild boundary mountains descend sharply southward to uninhabitable pine-graced plateaus that break sheer in enormous exposures of red and white sandstone cliffs. The Jurassic-age formations were formed primarily by the consolidation of sand dunes of truly Herculean magnitude, clearly revealed in the wind-rippled and cross-bedded layers of Zion National Park in Washington Co.

The southeastern one-third of Utah comprises the major portions of the sandstone plateau-and-canyon region, nearly waterless and almost roadless. Here **agate** occurs in many varieties, with literally thousands of unmarked localities far from what few roads penetrate the region. There is also an abundance of gem **jasper** and **septarian nodules,** colorful **fossil wood** petrified by **uranium** and **vanadium minerals,** especially the canary-yellow **carnotite,** and **radium** derivative minerals. Moreover, the almost ubiquitous **jasperized dinosaur bone,** blood red and revealing every microscopic detail of bone cellular structure, might truly be denominated the "Utah state stone."

The two-mile-high wall of the Wasatch Range bisects the state from the Idaho boundary south, marking an abrupt transition between the mountain-and-plateau region to the east and the arid desert playas and saline lakes of the western half. The level, gravelly deserts are bottom-lands of the awesome Pleistocene Lake Bonneville. Wave-cut fossil beach lines mark the regional mountain sides as if the white calcareous residues had been deposited only yesterday, showing that at its maximum size some 64,000 years ago, Lake Bonneville's waters were not only 1,500 feet deeper than present-day Great Salt Lake, its much reduced remnant, but that the lake extended all the way westward to the California Sierra Nevada. The barren peaks and higher rises above the present bare desert floor, then, were literally thousands of "islands" lapped by the Ice Age waters. As one drives through any of the Great Basin states, he can see a number of the fossil beach lines and their absolute parallel levelness. The beach lines were repeated in descending order as the lake waters drained or evaporated away, level by level down the mountain sides, following the retreat of the continental glaciers far to the north and east.

The rock strata exposed everywhere throughout this essentially barren state range from Cambrian crystallines to Pleistocene debris. Thick layers of Mississippian and Pennsylvanian age limestones characterize the rugged Wasatch Mountains and the lesser Oquirrh Range southwest of Salt Lake City. Utah's great concentrations of mineral wealth lie in this central zone of transitional mountains, with **copper** from the Oquirrh Range being the chief metal mined and smelted. Bingham Canyon, within sight of Salt Lake City, contains the world's largest open-pit **copper** mine.

The proximity of high-grade **iron** ores, **coal,** and **limestone** early brought huge steel plants to Provo, Utah Co. In the Wasatch Mountains immediately to the east of the state capital city many rich mines also produced spectacular amounts of **gold, lead,** and **silver.** Between 1863, when the first **gold** was discovered in **lead** ores in Bingham Canyon, and 1965 the state produced 17,765,000 ounces of gold, thereby ranking Utah sixth in the nation's **gold-**producing states. Placer grounds were also found nearby in 1864. At the ghost camp of Mercur in the southwest corner of the Oquirrh Range, **gold** mining and processing history was made when the cyanide process, brought from Australia, was first used in North America and developed here to its highest efficiency.

Discoveries of very rich **lead-silver** ores were made in the Cottonwood,

Park City, and Tintic districts in the late 1860's and early 1870's, but it wasn't until the early 1900's that large-scale mining of low-grade copper ores of the Bingham district began, with **gold** an important by-product. By 1965, the Bingham district, in addition to being one of the major **copper** producers in the world, was the second-largest **gold** producer in America, exceeded only by the Homestake Gold Mine at Lead, South Dakota. Following the impetus of World War II, immense quantities of **uranium** were found as **carnotite,** along with **vanadium** minerals, in the sandstones of the Chinle and Morrison formations in the southeastern counties. Also, it was from the **carnotite** ores first mined near Thompson, Grand Co., that the great French chemist Marie Curie first isolated and identified **radium.** In the Topaz Mountains 90 miles south and southwest of Salt Lake City, in Juab Co., unusually rich **beryllium** deposits comprise the largest known source of this strategic metal used in the manufacture of missile and space vehicle nose and reentry cones.

Of major interest to gem and mineral collectors, the state of Utah is almost 70 percent public domain, mostly unexplored and roadless but abounding in gem and gemstone species. Although in recent years Utah officials have begun to enforce strictly an ill-defined ordinance against hunting **fossils,** involving heavy fines and based on a loose interpretation of the Federal Antiquities Act, such regulations do not apply to hunting either gems or the much sought-after **jasperized dinosaur bone.**

For information, write: Utah Geological and Mineralogical Survey, University of Utah, Salt Lake City.

BEAVER CO.

AREA, numerous mines in co. (see on a topographic map)—**plumbo-jarosite, copper minerals,** etc.

BEAVER: (1) area mines—**bismuthinite;** (2) S, in Blue Valley, area washes, draws, surfaces, etc.—black **agate.**

MILFORD: (1), in the Mineral Mts., area mines—**azurite, malachite, opal, smoky quartz crystals, scheelite crystals;** (2) W approx. 13 mi. on Rte. 21: (a) old ghost mining town of Frisco, area mines, especially the Horn Silver Mine—**beaverite, casolite;** (b) regional draws, washes, surfaces, etc.—**garnets;** (c) Copper Gulch, area—**garnets.**

MINERSVILLE (and Minersville State Park), area mines—**copper minerals,** etc.

SULPHURDALE (1 mi. E of Int. 15 immediately S of the Millard Co. line), area mines—**sulfur.**

BOX ELDER CO.

AREA, the Copper Mt. Mine—**copper minerals, chrysocolla.**

LUCIN, NW 5 mi., on N side of Utahlite Hill—**variscite** (a notable locality).

PARK VALLEY (District), area lode mines—**gold.**
PROMONTORY POINT, area surfaces, draws, etc.,—**obsidian.**

CACHE CO.

NETWON, area lode mines—**gold.**

DAVIS CO.

KAYSVILLE, area co. mines (see on topographic map)—**azurite, malachite,** etc.

EMERY CO.

AREA: (1) Castle Valley, area mines—**azurite, malachite,** etc.; (2) Wild Horse Canyon, many area mines and prospects—**carnotite, vanadium minerals.**

CASTLE DALE: (1) SE, along the San Rafael R., area mines—**sulfur;** (2) E, all region to the Green R. (few rds.), draws, washes, etc.—**agate, agatized dinosaur bone** (locally called **"dinny" bone**), **petrified wood.**

EMERY, SW 15 mi. on Rte. 10 to near co. line, huge fossil reef along N side of hwy.—gem **agate, jasperized dinosaur bone ("dinny" bone).** (The dinosaur bone makes into beautiful blood-red slabs 8 in. in dia., as well as most attractive cabochons.)

GREEN RIVER: (1) W 18 mi., on E flank of the San Rafael Swell, many regional mines and prospects reached via jeep rds.—**carnotite;** (2) SW 30 mi. along Rte. 24, in the San Rafael Valley: (a) regional mines and prospects—**carnotite, petrified (carnotite) wood;** (b) regional surfaces, draws, washes, etc.—**agate, chalcedony, chert, petrified dinosaur bones** and **knuckles, gastroliths, jasper, petrified wood** (carnotized, silicified).

SUMMERVILLE, area mines—**azurite, malachite,** etc.

WOODSIDE: (1) S 4½ mi., in Morrison formation exposures—**agate, carnotite** (stained sandstone, wood, some mined or prospected lens deposits), **chalcedony, chert, petrified dinosaur bone, gastroliths, jasper** (various colors), **silicified wood;** (2) SW 10 air mi., Point of Cedar Mt., area mines—**sulfur.**

GARFIELD CO.

AREA: (1) E part of co.: (a) Circle Cliffs (reached via dirt rd. S from CAINEVILLE in Wayne Co.), area—**agate, chalcedony, jasper, petrified wood;** (b) Henry Mts. (reached via improved rd. S from HANKSVILLE in Wayne Co. plus regional jeep rds.; numerous peaks over 11,000 ft. high), many regional mines and prospects, particularly along Crescent and Trachyte creeks—**carnotite, bentonite** (upper part of Crescent Cr.); (2) Coyote Cr. Valley, mines and prospects in shale—**antimony oxides, orpiment, stibnite;** (3) White Canyon District, area placer mines—**gold.**

BOULDER, E on dirt rd. 12 mi. to crossrd., follow sign 9 mi. to Horse Canyon, area—**petrified wood** (gem quality).

ESCALANTE, area draws, washes, sandstone outcrops, etc.—**gastroliths, petrified dinosaur bone.**
HATCH, S 1½ mi. along Mammoth Cr., area quarries—**onyx.**

GRAND CO.

AREA, Wilson Mesa, regional lode and placer claims—**gold.**
AGATE SWITCH—cf. MOAB item (1).
CASTLETON, in the La Sal Mts., especially on Pack Cr., many regional mines—**uranium minerals.**
CISCO: (1) in hills along the Colorado R., draws, washes—**agatized clams** (to 5 in. dia.), **agatized** and **jasperized dinosaur bone, jasper;** (2) NE, in the Grand R. Valley, regional deposits—black **gypsum;** (3) S 20 mi. and, in general, all exposures throughout eastern Utah of the Morrison and Dakota sandstones, very many regional mines and prospects—minerals of **uranium, vanadium,** and **radium.**
MOAB: (1) gravel bars of the Colorado R. across entire SE corner of co., along with adjoining tributary canyons, slopes, washes, etc.—**agate, chalcedony, chert, jasper, opal, opalized wood, quartz crystals;** (2) N 5 mi., in outcrops of the Cutler formation—**agate, chalcedony, chert, silicified dinosaur bone,** gemmy **silicified shale, petrified wood.**
THOMPSON: (1) entire area, especially to S all way to the Arches National Monument, in draws, washes, breaks (all exposures of the widespread Morrison and Dakota sandstones)—**agate, agatized clams, carnotite** (regional mines usually in lens deposits), **carnotite wood** (rich in **vanadium** and **radium**), **gastroliths, jasper, jasperized dinosaur bone** and **knuckles** (blood-red, revealing microscopic details of bone cell structure), **lizard tails** (sandstone casts of tail segments of dinosaurs), **petrified wood.** (N boundary of general region is U.S. 6/50, W boundary is U.S. 160, and E boundary is Rte. 128, a completely barren landscape exposing almost continuously the sandstones of the Morrison and Dakota formations.)
(2) S 9–12 mi. on dirt rds., the Cactus Rat and Yellow Cat mines, and many other regional prospects and mines—cf. area. (In 1910 Marie Curie received a shipment of **carnotite** and **pitchblende** ore from the Yellow Cat Mine and from it first isolated the then unknown radioactive element **radium.**) (3) SE 22 mi., many regional mines—**calcium vanadate, carnotite,** other **uranium-vanadium minerals, petrified dinosaur bone, jasper, petrified wood,** etc.

IRON CO.

AREA: (1) Gold Springs and Stateline, area lode mines—**gold;** (2) Sand Springs, area placer mines—**gold.**
CEDAR CITY, E, along Rte. 14 to Cedar Breaks National Monument, all regional draws, washes, breaks, etc. outside monument boundaries—**agate** (common, moss), **chalcedony, jasper, petrified wood.**
NEWCASTLE: (1) all regional washes, draws, flats, hillsides—**chalcedony geodes** (to 24 in. dia.); (2) ESE on Rte. 56, old Iron Town, extensive mineralized district reaching S into Washington Co.—regional mines—**magnetite.**

JUAB CO.

FISH SPRINGS, area mines—**gold, lead, silver.**

JERICO: (1) area draws, washes, surfaces—**plume agate;** (2) W approx. 40 air mi., to the Thomas Mts.: (a) N end of mts. at Topaz Cove (just N of Thomas Pass on Rte. 148), area—**beryl, bixbyite, calcite, fluorite, garnet, hematite, pseudobrookite, quartz crystals, topaz;** (b) NE part of range and 3–4 mi. S of Dugway Rd.—same minerals.

LEVAN: (1) area mined deposits—**gypsum, celestite;** (2) S 13 mi., in hillside seams of area—**fortification agate, chalcedony.**

TINTIC District, a great many regional mines—**anglesite, argentite, azurite, barite, bismuth, chalcopyrite, chrysocolla, cuprite, enargite, galena, malachite, manganiferous silver ores, pyrite** (original mineral mined for).

WEST TINTIC, area mines—**gold, lead, silver** (cf. TINTIC).

KANE CO.

GLEN CANYON, area sandstone exposures in regional draws and washes, etc.—**uranium minerals, petrified wood,** some **agate.**

KANAB: (1) area deposits—**gypsum;** (2) E 10–20 mi. on dirt rd. to ghost town of Paria, area of the Vermilion Cliffs, all exposures of the Chinle formation in draws, washes, canyons, etc.—**uranium-vanadium minerals, fossil wood** (containing radioactive minerals); (3) NE on dirt rd. to Paria, area mines (small)—**gold, silver.** This long-abandoned Mormon farming community on a canyon tributary of the Colorado R. (the Paria R.) was once the scene of an abortive mining boom, mostly an exercise in stock selling; an assay building still stands. (4) E 28 mi. on U.S. 89, due S about 6 mi. in roadless territory, an area of a petrified forest—**petrified wood.**

MT. CARMEL–ORDERVILLE, regional washes, draws, hillsides—**septarian nodules** (to 12 in. dia., beautifully laced inside with **calcite**).

PAHREAH, S 9 mi., area mines of the **uranium** boom of the early 1950's—**autunite, uranospinite.**

MILLARD CO.

AREA, the White Mts., vast deposits—**gypsum.**

BLACK ROCK (on Rte. 257 about 30 mi. N of MILFORD in Beaver Co.), area draws, washes, surfaces—**snowflake obsidian** (red, black, combined colors).

CLEAR LAKE (RR Sta.), NE ½ mi., in lava upthrust in center of an alkali flat—**labradorite.**

SUGARVILLE, NW 20 mi. to the Topaz Mts., area outcrops—**topaz,** etc.

PIUTE CO.

AREA: (1) the Annie Laurie Mine—**argentite;** (2) Kimberley and Ohio mines—lode **gold.**

MARYSVALE: (1) area, large deposits—**alunite, tiemannite;** (2) SE 5 mi., area mines—**onofrite, cinnabar, native mercury, tiemannite.**

SALT LAKE CO.

ALTA (District), area old mines—**barite, galena, gold, silver, wulfenite.** (This old mining district SE of SALT LAKE CITY lies at an altitude of 10,000 ft., now a noted ski resort.)

BINGHAM (in Bingham Canyon in the Oquirrh Range SW of SALT LAKE CITY): (1) area great mines (including the largest open-pit **copper** mine on earth)—**barite, bornite, chalcocite, chalcopyrite, covellite, galena, tenorite, tetrahedrite;** (2) placer sands of Bingham Canyon—**gold;** (3) the old Jordan Mine, on dumps—**opal;** (4) Bingham Jct., from smelter bullion—**bismuth.**

BRIGHTON, area old mines—**copper minerals, gold silver.** (Today mainly a ski resort.)

COPPERTON, area mines—**copper minerals, chrysocolla, gold.**

MAGNA, area smelter tailings—**slag** (some capable of being cut and polished).

MURRAY, area quarries—**onyx.**

SALT LAKE CITY: (1) E, in Big Cottonwood Canyon, area mines—**azurite, malachite;** (2) E, in Little Cottonwood Canyon: (a) area mines—**azurite, malachite;** (b) mine on S side—**molybdenite;** (3) due E, on mt. side a short distance above the Pioneer Monument, a large cement slab closes entrance to a tunnel into the mt. Rumor has it that here is an undeveloped, extremely rich **gold** mine owned by the Church of Jesus Christ of Latter-day Saints (Mormons), as a "reserve" source of wealth should the church ever need it.

SAN JUAN CO.

AREA: (1) SE corner of co., reached from MEXICAN WATER, Ariz., on U.S. 164 halfway between KAYENTA and TEEC NOS POS (both in the heart of the Navajo Indian Reservation): (a) N 10 mi. into Utah, at Moses Rock, all area sandstones (and wind-produced erosional debris); and (b) 2 mi. N of the Moses Rock field, area along the W edge of Comb Ridge, in wind-blown sand deposits—**pyrope garnets** ("Arizona rubies"). Cf. also under MEXICAN WATER, Apache Co., Ariz. (2) the Blue Mts., area mines—**gold.**

BLUFF, area stream sands—**gold.**

HITE (S of HANKSVILLE, *q.v.* in Wayne Co.): (1) broad area of mines and prospects—**uranium minerals;** (2) SE 8 mi., in White Canyon: (a) area mines and prospects, and (b) mines and prospects outside the canyon itself —**uranium minerals.**

LA SAL (mining district), area mines—**azurite, malachite.**

MEXICAN HAT, broad surrounding region of mines and prospects—**uranium minerals.** (During the 1950's this was an important **uranium** mining region, crisscrossed by very many jeep and truck rds.)

MONTICELLO, N, in Dry, Big Indian, and Lisburne valleys, many regional mines and prospects—**uranium minerals.** This country in the extreme SE corner of Utah fronts visually into Colo., very rugged, dissected with deep canyons separated by high mesas. Sandstone exposures everywhere show radioactivity. Automobile travel throughout the region requires great caution, and all travelers must carry ample supplies of water and provisions.

SANPETE CO.

GUNNISON, area deposits, some mined—**gypsum.**

SEVIER CO.

AREA, the Ball Mine—**azurite, malachite,** etc.

SALINA, on Rte. 4 toward EMERY in Emery Co., to N is a large fossil reef, area draws, washes, etc., and on ridges—gem **agatized dinosaur bone** (to 8 in. dia., blood-red).

SUMMIT CO.

PARK CITY (a considerable mountainous area at the end of Rte. 248 off U.S. 40, laced together by numerous very steep jeep rds.), many great mines and dumps—**anglesite, galena, sphalerite, tetrahedrite.** (An interesting old town to visit, now devoted entirely to skiing and the tourist trade.)

TOOELE CO.

AREA: (1) the Drum Mts., N side, regional draws, washes, surfaces— **agate, amethysts, jasper, quartz crystals;** (2) SW part of co., the Dugway Range (rough dirt rds. and entry barred to the nearby Dugway Proving Grounds between the Dugway Range and the Cedar Mts. farther N), Dugway Pass, area surfaces, draws, etc.—**amethysts, quartz crystals.**

CLIFTON (old mining district in SW corner of co. no longer shown on most maps): (1) area mines—**azurite, malachite, pyrope garnets;** (2) Deep Creek District, area mines—**bismuthinite, copper minerals, gold, galena, huebnerite, silver, scheelite.**

GOLD HILL (far SW corner of co.), the Gold Hill Mine—**scorodite, gold.**

IBAPAH (extreme SW corner of co. about 35 mi. WSW of SIMPSON SPRINGS), on Ibapah Mt., area pegmatite outcrops—**aquamarine, beryl.**

MERCUR (no longer shown on maps, but reached from Rte. 36 S of TOOELE a short distance S of the Rte. 73 turnoff E to OPHIR, a rather rough access rd.), area mines—**cinnabar, orpiment** (good crystals), **gold.** This mining camp, totally destroyed years ago by fire, once held some 12,000 people (1902), then one of the great **gold** camps of the world, surpassed in its day in the West only by GOLDFIELD, Esmeralda Co., Nev., and Utah's only such mining camp. Here, the cyanide process was first developed in North America (the enormous settling basins still stand), and the first long-distance power transmission line (from PROVO) ever developed to that time was put into use. Adjoining MERCUR are: (1) Sunshine (4 mi. S, in Sunshine Canyon) and (2) West Dip (on the W extremity of the Oquirrh Range), their mines—**galena, gold, pyrite,** etc.

OPHIR (adjoining the MERCUR, or Camp Floyd District, on the N), area mines (still operating)—**galena, gold, pyrite, silver, sphalerite.** This is an active mine in a rather scenic steep canyon facing W across the Great Salt Lake Desert; the dumps are unusually prolific in excellent **pyrite crystals** and **quartz crystals.**

RUSH VALLEY, WILLOW SPRINGS, regional mines—**galena, gold, pyrite, silver.**

SIMPSON SPRINGS (on W side of the Camel Back Range in the far S-central part of co.), area draws, washes, etc.—**geodes,** gemmy **nodules, morganite.**

STOCKTON (7 mi. S of TOOELE), W 9 mi. (or 10 mi. S 65° W of TOOELE), the Amatrice Mine—**quartzite, variscite, copper, gold.**

WENDOVER, E 10 mi. on U.S. 40/50A, the Crystalline Salt Beds—**salt crystals** (various minerals, hydroscopic).

UINTAH CO.

AREA, the Dyer Mine—**azurite, malachite,** etc.

BONANZA: (1) area prospects and claims—**gilsonite (uintaite);** (2) S and W, via Rte. 45 and Rte. 207, into Sweet Water Canyon, regional flats, draws, washes—**agate, chalcedony, jasper, petrified wood.**

BROWNS PARK, area mines—**carnotite, copper minerals.**

CARBONATE, area lode mines—**gold.**

DRAGON, area deposits—**gilsonite (uintaite).**

FORT DUQUESNE: (1) the Uinta Basin, many areas; and (2) the Cowboy claims—**gilsonite.**

JENSEN-OURAY, gravels and sands of the Green R., placers—**gold.**

RED WASH (SW of jct. of U.S. 40 with Rte. 45), in exposures of Precambrian quartzites, as small occurrences—**carnotite.**

UTAH CO.

AMERICAN FORK, area mines—**gold, lead, silver.**

COLTON, area mines—**ozokerite** (mineral wax).

FAIRFIELD: (1) area draws, washes, surfaces—**chalcedony, chert, limonite, pyrite-in-variscite,** white **quartz;** (2) W 1½ mi., in Clay Canyon, area—**variscite;** (3) W 5½ mi.: (a) the Utahlite Mine—**calcite, crandallite, dehrnite, deltaite, dennisonite, lewistonite, variscite,** and such additional rare phosphate minerals as **englishite, gordonite** (colorless), **millisite, montgomeryite, overite, and sterretite;** (b) a nearby low pass with dirt rd. running N past a series of open-cut mines and prospects—cf. the Utahlite Mine. The regional exposures of soft rock disgorge **variscite** as rounded nodules to 12 in. dia., the cores varying from dark green to pale green and framed with rims of other phosphate minerals. The side rd. through the low pass should be a must for all who head for MERCUR, Tooele Co., via this rte. All the regional foothill gulches contain many species of Mississippian age fossils weathering out of the limestones clearly exposed across the S end of the Oquirrh Range.

LEHI, Pelican Point, area—**onyx.**

PROVO, SE 2 mi., a quarry—**slate.**

SANTAQUIN, SILVER LAKE districts, regional mines—**gold, galena, silver.**

SOLDIER SUMMIT, area deposits—**nigrite, ozokerite** (mineral wax).

WASATCH CO.

HEBER CITY: (1) county area: (a) North Fork and (b) Snake Cr., area mines—**gold;** (2) Grey Head Mt., NE (an area of about 100 sq. mi., lying about 50 mi. W of DUCHESNE in Duchesne Co. via U.S. 40): (a) Indian Lake, (b) Avintequin, and (c) Sams Canyons, many mines and prospects—lode **gold.**

WASHINGTON CO.

AREA, the Lucern claims—**garnets.**

CASTLE CLIFF, NW, in Beaver Dam Wash, area—**agate, jasper, "picture stone"** (banded **rhyolite**).

CENTRAL (24 mi. N of ST. GEORGE on Rte. 18), area basalt exposures, as blue-banded nodules to 60 lbs.—**chalcedony geodes.**

HURRICANE, on far side of river from Rte. 15 through town, area—**scenic sandstone** (slabs cut nicely and will take some polishing; often used in fireplace or wall construction).

LEEDS, W 1 mi., old ghost town of Silver Reef, area mines—**lead** and **silver minerals.**

ST. GEORGE, the Dixie Apex Mine—**azurite, malachite,** etc.

WAYNE CO.

HANKSVILLE: (1) broad surrounding area—**agate, jasper, petrified wood;** (2) W 3 mi., scattered over broad area—**agates, jasper, petrified wood;** (3) S 10 mi., Coaly Basin (in Coaly Wash 5 mi. W of the Fairview Ranch), area **coal** mine dumps—**jet;** (4) SW, in N end of the Henry Mts. (main range in Garfield Co.), many area mines and prospects—**carnotite.**

TORREY, regional draws, washes, breaks, surfaces—**agate, jasp-agate, jasper, dinosaur bone** (jasperized, petrified).

WEBER CO.

OGDEN: (1) numerous mines in co.—**azurite, malachite,** etc.; (2) Strongs Canyon, area—**garnets.**

VERMONT

Although not blessed with many gem and mineral localities, the Green Mountain State appeals to visitors because of its majestic mountain ranges, deep river valleys, quiet lakes, and rushing mountain streams. All 9,564 square miles (including lake waters) are readily accessible via an excellent highway system that includes well-maintained backcountry byways. Probably far more gemstone localities exist than have been recorded, since the basal formation of Vermont is granite, but the rock-collecting pastime has so far not been particularly notable within the state.

While several mountain systems characterize Vermont, it is the Green Mountains—really a collection of several mountain systems—that more or less divide the state into two halves. Toward the north end in the far east side of Chittenden Co., Mount Mansfield rises to the highest point in the state at 4,393 feet. Four other peaks spaced along the Long Trail, a wilderness hiking trail that follows the crests of the Green Mountains, rise above 4,000 feet. East of the Green Mountains system lie the Granite Hills, well named because of the excellent **monument granite** and **building stone** that are quarried in many places. The granite industry is centered at Barre in Washington Co., while Rutland at the south end of the Green Mountains in Rutland Co. is famed for its production of fine **marble.**

In the southwestern corner of Vermont the geologically famed Taconic Mountains stretch from northwest of Rutland, west of the Green Mountains, for 150 miles along the New York State boundary into Massachusetts to include the Berkshire Hills. The mountains lend their name to a very ancient mountain-building period—the Taconic Orogony—and afford a good illustration of metamorphism during which widespread limestone sediments were converted into high-quality **marble.** The rocks are least crystalline in the northern and western sections of the Taconic region. Additionally, Cambrian rock exposures occur most notably in the extreme northwest corner of the state, especially around Highgate Springs in northwestern Franklin Co.

Other than fine marble, there are few gems or minerals to be found in Vermont. However, the Rochester Valley in Windsor Co., the Warren Valley in Washington Co., and the Windham Valley in Windham Co. have numerous deposits and quarries which yield highly prized **verde antique serpentine,** another product of metamorphism. Other commercial mineral products are **asbestos, lime, slate,** and **talc.**

For information, write: Vermont Geological Survey, East Hall, University of Vermont, Burlington.

BENNINGTON CO.

BENNINGTON, area deposits—**ocher.**
NORTH DORSET, some area deposits—**ocher.**
READSBORO, area mines (lode)—**gold.**

CHITTENDEN CO.

BURLINGTON, N 9 mi. on U.S. 2, fields and outcrops, etc. on the Parrott farm—**agate, chert, jasp-agate, jasper.**
WEST MILTON, near Lake Champlain, area mines—**hematite, manganese minerals.**

LAMOILLE CO.

EDEN, area mines or quarries—**asbestos.**
MORRISTOWN, area talcose slate exposures—**galena.**

ORANGE CO.

AREA, some scattered **copper** mines in co.—**copper minerals.**
COPPERFIELD, the Ely Mine—**chalcopyrite, pyrrhotite.**
CORINTH (P.O., or COOKVILLE), area mines—**chalcopyrite.**
SOUTH STRAFFORD, the Elizabeth Mine—**chalcopyrite, pyrrhotite.**
STRAFFORD, the Copperas Hill area mines—**chalcopyrite, pyrite** (a large mineralized deposit).
THETFORD CENTER, quartz vein in talcose slate—**galena.**

ORLEANS CO.

LOWELL (and CHRYSOTILE), area mines or quarries—**asbestos.**
TROY, as ore mined in small beds—**titaniferous magnetite.**

RUTLAND CO.

BRANDON, area mines—**psilomelane, pyrolusite.**
CHITTENDEN, area mines—**galena.**
RUTLAND (Sta.), SE 3¾ mi., on N side of Round Hill (on W flank of the Green Mts.), area—green **aventurine.**
SHERBURNE, area pegmatite exposures—**muscovite mica.**
SOUTH WALLINGFORD, area mines—**psilomelane, pyrolusite.**

WINDSOR CO.

BRIDGEWATER, area old prospects—**gold, galena.**
CHESTER, area pegmatite outcrops—**muscovite mica.**

PLYMOUTH, area prospects and talcose slate exposures—**galena, magnetite, pyrite, siderite.**
TALCVILLE, area mines and quarries—**talc.**

VIRGINIA

Like other eastern states tied into the mineral-rich Appalachian Mountain granites, Virginia manifests an abundance of gemstone and mineral localities. The state divides topographically into three main regions: the Tidewater, or Eastern Section, more noted for fossiliferous formations than mineralized rocks; the rolling Piedmont Plateau west of the coastal flats; and the Blue Ridge Mountains and Appalachian Plateau in the west. The far western counties show evidence of being part of the vast thrust mass along the Appalachian fault which, as mentioned for Tennessee, inverted the stratigraphic order. It is in the plateau and mountain counties where the gem and mineral collector can best prospect for lapidary and cabinet specimen materials, especially for **apatite, epidote, garnet, graphic granite,** clear and smoky **quartz crystals, tourmaline, unakite,** and many typical pegmatite gems.

Western Virginia comprises a good portion of the Valley and Ridge Province that crosses into West Virginia, covers all of central Tennessee, and reaches into northeastern Alabama. The far southwestern corner of the state is part of the Appalachian Plateau, marked by steep-sided ridges, scenic gorges, and swift sparkling streams. Carboniferous age **coal** seams are extensively mined throughout this area. Adjoining the province are the Blue Ridge Mountains, climaxed by 5,929-foot Mount Rogers in western Grayson and Smyth counties just above the North Carolina boundary. Following the crést of the Blue Ridge is the spectacularly scenic Blue Ridge Parkway, affectionately called the Skyline Drive by Virginians, which provides access to many gem localities on both sides.

The granitoid nature of Virginia's Precambrian and Cambrian structures, especially throughout the Piedmont and Plateau regions, has produced numberless pegmatite formations; approximately 150 gem and mineral species appear in the exposures or erosional debris. The Piedmont region was strongly folded, faulted, and metamorphosed, and the rock exposures include **biotite-hornblende gneiss, marble, quartzite, greenstone** (a **chlorite schist** that has been quarried since the 1930's), and a long belt of **phyllite** (a **mica**-rich slate with a dull micaceous luster). The **phyllite** belt, known as the "Martic line," crosses the state diagonally and parallel to the mountains on the west.

Early nineteenth-century **gold**-prospecting literally started the search for commercially valuable minerals. Today, the annual $250 million mineral contribution to the Virginia economy comes mainly from **coal,** followed by **sand, gravel, limestone, tin,** and **zinc,** with smaller amounts of **feldspar, gypsum, iron, kyanite, petroleum, rutile,** and **salt.** The gems and gemstones for which Virginia is becoming increasingly well known were originally found as by-products of the early prospecting and mining of commercial minerals and, except for **diamonds,** almost entirely by-passed by their finders. The first faceting **feldspar crystals** were reportedly gathered in 1887, with high-grade gem **amethysts** appearing around 1902. **Rose quartz** and **rock crystal** were found, and by-passed, during the **gold**-prospecting era. **Tourmaline** was not particularly remarked until it appeared in the **lead** and **zinc** mines that were opened before World War I, with **malachite** and **chrysocolla** showing up in **copper** deposits. Later discoveries brought other gem materials to the forefront, and many of the old commercial mines are now being reworked for such sought-after gemstones as **apatite, epidote, moonstone feldspar,** apple-green **prehnite,** clear and smoky **quartz crystals, rhodonite,** the comparatively rare **turquoise crystals,** and many others.

Extensive **iron** ore deposits have long been mined in the western counties. Of interest to specialists are deposits of **titanium** minerals that occur near the northwest margin of the Piedmont Plateau in a zone that trends northeasterly across Amherst and Nelson counties. The latter county lends its name to dikelike ore bodies of **nelsonite,** outcropping particularly around Piney River in Nelson Co. These dikes may be relatable to a large **anorthosite**-type intrusion approximately 19 miles long and 2 to 6 miles wide. The **nelsonite** is peculiar in that it is characterized by the presence of **apatite** with **rutile,** or by **apatite** with **ilmenite,** or both.

For information, write: Department of Conservation, Geological Survey Division, University Station, Charlottesville.

ALBEMARLE CO.

AREA, the Green Mts., paralleling the Blue Ridge SW into Campbell, Bedford, and Franklin counties, a belt of micaceous schists—**soapstone.**

CHARLOTTESVILLE: (1) area: (a) Buck Mt. Creek—gray **agate;** (b) Sugar Hollow Cr.—red **jasper;** (c) N and W, in gravels of the Moorman R., as float—**epidote, jasper;** (d) NE, on W foothills of Southwest Mt., a vein cutting micaceous schists once worked for iron—**chalcopyrite;** (2) S of city along Rte. 795, in cuts and rd. banks—**amethysts** (color-zoned, some with **goethite** inclusions); (3) SW 3½ mi., area boulders—**epidote, microcline feldspar, unakite;** (4) SW 6 mi. on U.S. 29, the Red Hill Quarry—green **epidote crystals,** pink **microcline feldspar, unakite.**

COVESVILLE: (1) area quarries—**serpentine, soapstone;** (2) a quarry at Boyd Tavern—**quartz crystals;** (3) S 1 mi. on U.S. 291, area cut banks, etc.—**amethysts** (color-zoned, some with **goethite** inclusions).

CROZET: (1) N, in gravels of the Moorman R.—**amethyst, epidote;** (2) Stockton Ford, S, in river gravels—**amethysts.**

FABER: (1) 2 mi. slightly N, in E part of the Blue Ridge foothills, the

Faber Mine—**azurite, cerussite, chalcopyrite, fluorite, galena, smithsonite, sphalerite, stibnite;** (2) NE 3 mi., old Civil War **lead-zinc** mine—**fluorspar** (gangue mineral), **galena, quartz crystals, silver** (some), **smithsonite, stibnite.**

NORTH GARDEN, area abandoned Revolutionary War **iron** mine—**iron minerals, quartz crystals** (clear, smoky).

SHADWELL: (1) area cuts, banks, stream gravels—gemmy green **quartzite** (spangled with **chlorite**), **unakite** with **epidote** (in massive exposure of the Catoctin Greenstone).

STONY POINT, area old **copper** mine, productive dumps—**copper minerals.**

AMELIA CO.

AREA, many regional **mica** mines—**fluorite (chlorophane).** (This mineral fluoresces from the heat of the hand, thus affording a fluorescent gemstone which, however, is not hard enough to resist wear.)

AMELIA COURT HOUSE: (1) area: (a) various exposures—**soapstone;** (b) the James Anderson **mica** prospect—**aquamarine;** (2) S, on Rte. 627 from U.S. 360, cross Smacks Cr., then uphill to right, the Winfree prospect (pay fee)—massive **quartz, quartz crystals** (clear, rose, smoky); (3) N of jct. of Rtes. 651 and 616 for 1½ mi., the Ligon Mine—**beryl, garnets, quartz crystals** (asteriated, smoky opalescent), **tourmaline;** (4) N 1¼ mi., the Rutherford Mine—**albite, amazonite, amethyst, circrolite, cleavelandite, feldspar (microcline, moonstone), microlite, muscovite mica, quartz crystals,** blue **topaz;**

(5) N 35° E 1¼ mi., the Richeson Mica Mine—**amazonite, muscovite mica;** (6) N 2 mi., at the Truehart place on Nibbs Cr.—**beryl, quartz crystals, black tourmaline;** (6) N 60° E 4 mi. (S of CHULA), as a belt of exposures—**soapstone;** (7) ENE 4 mi., off Rte. 628, the Morefield Mine—**amazonite, aquamarine, amethysts,** green **beryl, cleavelandite, feldspar** (massive, **moonstone**), **spessartite garnets** (brilliant), **microlite, quartz crystals** (clear, smoky), **phenakite,** blue **topaz crystals, zircons;** (8) NW, off Rte. 632, the Champion Mine—**quartz crystals** (blue, some with **chlorite** inclusions).

JETERSVILLE: (1) many important area **mica** mines in pegmatite dikes—**allanite, apatite, beryl, columbite, feldspar, fluorite, spessartite garnets, helvite, microlite, monazite, muscovite mica, quartz crystals, tourmaline, zircon.** This district is famed for such big mines as the Jefferson, Berry, Winston, Pinchback, and Schlegal. Much **soapstone** also occurs throughout the belt. (2) N 4½ mi., area mines—**soapstone.**

AMHERST CO.

AMHERST: (1) E about 3 mi. to the Schaar farm (inquire way; drive to abandoned buildings of an old service sta., take farm rd. 659, then E to next crossrd. and follow signs to the farm, where permission is granted), in cr. bed about ¼ mi. from house—gem **amethysts;** (2) E several mi. to marked fee site—**amethysts;** (3) E 7 mi. from center of town via farm rds. 604 and 624, to the Earley farm, then .9 mi. beyond a red house on the left; park at first two woods rds. and walk down second rd. a few hundred yds. to the abandoned Folley Mine—**malachite** (gemmy); (4) NNW 7 mi.: (a) ⅓ mi. N of old Sandiges post office, in diggings; and (b) at scattered spots in soils of the Fancy Hill ridge—**amethysts, quartz crystals;** (c) in area out-crops of granite, gneiss, and granodiorite—**apatite, epidote.**

PINEY RIVER, E 2 mi., area mine dumps—**ilmenite, rutile.**

SWEET BRIAR, E 2 mi., area prospects—**chrysocolla.**

APPOMATTOX CO.

AREA, 2 mi. upstream from mouth of Wreck Island Cr., old mine—**chrysocolla.**

BECKHAM: (1) area **manganese** mines, and (2) SW 8 mi., on Bent Cr. (just beyond jct. with Rte. 623), mines of the Enterprise Mining Co.—**cryptomelane ("black malachite"), manganite** (crystals, nodules), gemmy **quartzite** (some containing brilliant **drusy quartz crystals**).

BENT CREEK, 8 mi. out at the old Enterprise Mine—**psilomelane, cryptomelane.**

CONCORD, vicinity SE of Mt. Athos, deposits—**manganese.**

ARLINGTON CO.

ARLINGTON, along Kirkwood Rd., in banks of Spout Run—**jasper.**

AUGUSTA CO.

CRIMORA, SW 2½ mi., the Crimora Mine (most important producer in Va.) and other area mines—**psilomelane, pyrolusite, wad.**

SPOTTSWOOD, area gravels—**quartz crystals.**

WAYNESBORO: (1) NW 2½ mi., deposit—**ocher;** (2) the South River Mine (on Rte. 702 toward VESUVIUS in Rockbridge Co.)—**chert, goethite, hematite, psilomelane, quartz crystals;** (3) the Cold Springs Clay Mine (on Rte. 608)—gem **chert,** impure **chalcedony;** (4) S 27 mi. on the Blue Ridge Park-way to Tye River Gap (on W side just inside co. line and near the Rock-bridge Co. sites, q.v.), NE ½ mi., area outcrops—**epidote,** decorative **unakite.**

BATH CO.

MILBORO SPRINGS, N on Rte. 629 to Rte. 640, turn E to the third farm (fee, get directions), noted locality on Chestnut Ridge—**rock crystal.**

BEDFORD CO.

BEDFORD: (1) area of Otter Hill (cf. BELLS), in nearby Craighead Mine (feldspar-mica deposit)—**beryl, columbite,** red **garnets, moonstone, quartz crystals, tantalite, tourmaline;** (2) N on Rte. 43 to first side rd. to E and the

Rosa Arrington store: (a) take rd. uphill to W, an old mine—**feldspar;** (b) at church, turn left onto bad rd. into mts. to old **quartz** mine, on dumps—gem **quartz crystals** (red and green); (c) at store, turn N on good rd. about 1 mi. to W-trending rd. to old mine (a huge excavation)—**feldspar;**
(3) NW 5 mi., the Peaksville Mine—**quartz crystals** (some phantom, some with green **fluorite** inclusions); (4) N about 11 mi., the Peaks of Otter region (a state park), many area old mines and prospects, in **feldspar** and **quartz** veins—gem **feldspar, amethysts, quartz crystals,** etc.; (5) SE 6½ mi. on Rte. 54, the Mitchell Mine—**albite feldspar** (some chatoyant), bluish **apatite;** (6) SE 6½ mi. on co. rd. 714, area—**moonstone;** (7) E 7 mi. (and 300 yds. SW of the Little Otter R., the Hottinger Mine)—**amazonite, garnets, smoky quartz crystals.**

BELLS: (1) S 1 mi. (and E of the Otter R.), the Bells Mines—**amazonite, garnets, smoky quartz crystals;** (2) halfway between town and Otter Hill, on NE side of small NE-flowing stream, the Otter Hill Mine—**feldspar crystals, spessartite garnets, smoky quartz crystals.**

FOREST: (1) area pegmatites—**rutile;** (2) 2½ mi. out, the Everett prospect (on NE side of small stream), abundant—**spessartite garnets.**

MONETA: (1) SE 1 mi., the Moneta Mine—**amazonite, spessartite garnets, graphic granite, plagioclase feldspar, smoky quartz crystals, vesuvianite;** (2) S, on S slope of a hill, the Yong Mine—**amazonite, perthite crystals** (white, flesh color), **spessartite garnets, pyrite, quartz crystals, rutile;** (3) area from town to the Big Otter R. (30 mi. long and 2–5 mi. wide), very many pegmatite exposures, mines, prospects—**garnets, pyrite, quartz crystals, rutile, perthite, tantalite, tourmaline, zoisite,** etc.

THAXTON: (1) area prospects—**sphalerite crystals;** (2) NW 3 mi. (between BEDFORD and ROANOKE), an interesting deposit—**barite, galenite,** some **sphalerite.**

BLAND CO.

POINT PLEASANT , N side of Walkers Mt., area—**quartz crystals.**

BOTETOURT CO.

HOUSTON, 1 mi. out at the Houston Mine—**manganese minerals.** (During the 1880's, this mine was the main producer of **manganiferous iron** ores in Va.)

BUCKINGHAM CO.

AREA: (1) Spiers Mt., and (2) Willis Mt., area mines and prospects—gem **kyanite, manganese minerals.**

ARVONIA, GOLD HILL, JOHNSTON, NEW CANTON, many regional old mines—**copper minerals, gold.** (These district mines were originally operated for **gold.**)

DILLWYN: (1) S side of town at the historical marker, area hillsides, mines—**gold;** (2) SW 4 mi., the Booker Mine (extensively worked prior to the Civil War)—**gold.**

SPROUSE'S CORNER, area mines—gem **kyanite.**

CAMPBELL CO.

AREA: (1) central part of co., and (2) NE part of co., Mt. Athos (cf. also CONCORD in Appomattox Co.), regional mines—**manganese minerals.**

BROOKNEAL: (1) NE, on the Rush farm; and (2) NE 10 mi., on the Clay farm—**amethysts.**

EVINGTON, E and SE a few mi., several mines, such as the Hewitt, Saunders, Anthony, etc.—**barite.**

LYNCH (STATION): (1) area **copper** mines and prospects—**copper minerals, turquoise;** (2) SW of confluence of Old Woman Cr. with the Staunton R., in exposures of **kyanite** and **quartz** veins—**paragonite** (pseudomorphs after **andalusite**); (3) the Bishop Mine (park at the Rock Service Sta., pay small fee)—**chalcosiderite, turquoise crystals** (only generally known locality on earth).

LYNCHBURG: (1) area quarries—**"Virginia greenstone"** (gemmy **actinolite-chlorite** and **chlorite-tremolite** schist), **ankerite, calcite, kyanite, pyrite, magnetite, rutile, steatite;** (2) SW 1 mi., and at the Leesville dam, area excavations, quarries—**epidote;** (3) E and S, large mined deposit—**manganese minerals;** (4) S 6 mi., the old Bell Mine—gem **epidote crystals;** (5) SE 6 mi.: (a) area quarries—gem **epidote crystals;** (b) on the Graves farm, in pegmatite mass—**amazonite;** (6) S 7 mi., area quarries—**epidote;** (7) S 9 mi., area quarries—**epidote crystals.**

RED HOUSE, W 3 mi., area—**amethysts.**

CAROLINE CO.

LADYSMITH, SW 6 mi. (via 4½ mi. on Rte. 229, 1 mi. on Rte. 603, and 1 mi. on dirt rd.), the Last Chance Mine—**beryl** (green, to 5-in.-dia. crystals), **feldspar crystals,** massive **quartz, black tourmaline.**

CARROLL CO.

GALAX (straddles boundary with Grayson Co.; see also localities under GALAX in that co.): (1) area mines—**lead, zinc,** and **silver minerals, marcasite, pyrite;** (2) E, at Pipers Gap, on W side of Rte. 97, area—**hornblende, serpentine, talc;** (3) N 3 mi., on W side of co. rd. 607, area old mine dumps —**apatite** (gemmy green crystals), **chalcopyrite, pyrite** (iridescent), **rutile crystals** (singles and twins, to 1+ in. dia.), **selenite crystals, siderite** (in radial clusters, nearly transparent), **vivianite** (dark blue, bladed crystals).

HILLSVILLE: (1) area mine dumps (an **iron**-mining region stretching from 6½ mi. N for more than 20 mi. to the SW of OLDTOWN in Grayson Co.); (2) the Iron Ridge Mine (near GOSSAN); (3) the Betty Baker Mine (northernmost mine), on all dumps—**arsenopyrite, azurite, barite, chalcocite,** chalcopyrite, chrysocolla coquimbite, cuprite, galena, halotrichite, pyrite, pyrrhotite, siderite, sphalerite, etc.

LAUREL FORK (cf. also Patrick Co. for areas reached from this center): (1) NW 1 mi.: (a) on the Marshall farm—gem **quartz crystals;** (b) the Hall farm just NE—**quartz crystals** (to 3 lbs.); (2) SW 1 mi.: (a) on the Jackson farm—**quartz crystals** (clear, milky, opaque, smoky; to 6 lbs.); (b) ¼ mi. SE, at the Bowman farm—giant gem **quartz crystals** (to 15 in. long).

CHARLOTTE CO.

CHARLOTTE COURTHOUSE: (1) many regional old mines (belt extends 10 mi. from CULLEN, q.v., to jct. of Ward's Fork with Roanoke Cr.), on dumps —**corundum, spessartite garnet, muscovite mica, rutile, spinel, tourmaline;** (2) W 1.2 mi. (and ½ mi. N of Rte. 645), at the Vasser farm, pits, excavations—gem **beryl;** (3) near Rte. 647 and .6 mi. S of its jct. with Rte. 40, at the Moore prospect in pegmatite—gem **beryl, perthite crystals, quartz crystals** (blue, pale gray); (4) W about 2½ mi. on Rte. 40, to abandoned dirt rd. (crossing both sides of Rte. 40), park on S side, walk over bridge remnants and up trail about 200 yds.: (a) well short of an abandoned brick house, in area diggings—gem **amethysts** (some phantom, some clustered), **quartz crystals** (clear, many with phantoms); (b) area of the old brick mansion, buried in soil (to depths of 6–8 ft.)—gem **amethysts;**

(5) WNW 2¼ mi., area fields—**amethysts;** (6) NW 2½ mi., the Donald Plantation, area mines and prospects (mined in 1912)—gem **amethysts, smoky quartz crystals;** (7) W 4 mi., in 200-ft.-long quartz vein—**smoky quartz crystals;** (8) S several mi., area mine dumps—gem **amethysts.**

CULLEN, N 1 mi., the Crews No. 1 Mine—**beryl (aquamarine,** green, yellow).

PHENIX, W on Rte. 40 to area of Campbell Co. line: (1) ⅓ mi. NNE of BROOKNEAL in Campbell Co., and (2) NE 10 mi. from BROOKNEAL, area diggings—gem **amethysts.**

CHESTERFIELD CO.

BERMUDA HUNDRED, nearby, deposit on the Appomattox R.—yellow **ocher.**

ITTERDALE, area fields, gravels, excavations—**petrified** and **opalized wood.** SKINQUARTER, area fields, gravels, etc.—**petrified** and **opalized wood.**

CULPEPER CO.

DRAKESVILLE, area mines—**azurite, malachite,** etc. WILDERNESS, W 3 mi., the Culpeper Mine—**gold.**

DINWIDDIE CO.

DINWIDDIE, area hills, pastures, cr. beds and banks, etc.—**Indian artifacts** (many of gemstone nature).

FAIRFAX CO.

AREA, N part of co., along the Potomac R., a **quartz** outcrop near Difficult Run—**apatite, specularite, tourmaline.**

ANNANDALE, E 2 mi., largest deposit in co., quarry—**soapstone.**

CENTREVILLE: (1) area rd. cuts, banks, etc.—some **amethysts;** (2) the Fairfax courthouse, area cuts—**agate;** (3) stream gravels of Doctor's Run and Four Mile Run, S of the Columbia Turnpike—**quartz** (pebbles, blue, chatoyant); (4) Camp Washington, area exposures—**hyalite opal;** (5) W, at the Centreville (Bull Run) Quarry (on S side of U.S. 29/211)—**apophyllite, moss agate, byssolite, prehnite, thaumasite;** (6) the nearby Chantilly Quarry—gem **prehnite;** (7) E 4 mi. on U.S. 29/211, the Fairfax Quarry—**apophyllite crystals, epidote, pyrite crystals, quartz crystals, thaumasite, sphene,** gem **prehnite** (some with **byssolite** inclusions).

FALLS CHURCH, E, a deposit—**soapstone.**

TENLEY, E 1 mi., second largest deposit in co.—**soapstone.**

FAUQUIER CO.

MORRISVILLE, several area mines—**gold.**

FLOYD CO.

AREA: (1) Blue Ridge, general regional soils, draws, cr. beds, etc.—**staurolites;** (2) SE headwaters of the South Fork of the Roanoke R., near confluence of Lick Fork and Flat Run, area mines—some **arsenopyrite, chalcopyrite, pyrite, pyrrhotite.**

BURKES FORK: (1) area of the Carroll Co. line: (a) ¼ mi. E, and (b) 1½ mi. E of line, on hillsides, in draws, etc.—**garnets;** (2) S, at the Vaughn farm (6¾ mi. N and 1 mi. E of LAUREL FORK in Carroll Co.), in loose soil—**quartz crystals** (clear, smoky, to several in. long); (3) 5½ mi. E of LAUREL FORK—**quartz crystals** (to 100 lbs.).

FLOYD: (1) E 2 mi., on old mine dumps—**amphibolite, prehnite;** (2) NW 2 mi., area exposures—**quartz crystals** (reticulated, some rutilated), massive **quartz** (silky, pale blue, will cut star stones).

INDIAN VALLEY, W, the Toncrae Mine (about 5½ mi. NW of the SW corner of the jct. of Floyd and Carroll co. line)—**almandite garnets, biotite mica.**

REWALD P.O. (about 17 mi. S of CHRISTIANSBURG in Montgomery Co. on Rte. 8, near summit of the Blue Ridge at 3,200 ft. elev.), area mines and prospects—**arsenopyrite.**

WILLIS: (1) SE 2.2 mi., exposure—giant **quartz crystals;** (2) ESE 2.2 mi., area soils, cuts, etc.—**rock crystal;** (3) SW 6 mi. and 1 mi. E of the Buffalo Mt. Church, on the Moles farm—**rock crystal.**

FLOYD, CARROLL, GRAYSON COS.

REGION, the SW Virginia "Great Gossan Lead" area, very many mines—**chalcopyrite, pyrite, pyrrhotite,** etc.

FLOYD, MONTGOMERAY COS.

REGION, W side of the Blue Ridge, at SE base of Pilot Mt., area placer deposits along Brush and Laurel creeks—**gold.**

FLUVANNA CO.

AREA. A **gold** belt traverses the boundary between Fluvanna and Goochland counties, crossing the James R. at Bremo Bluffs into Buckingham Co. This belt was extensively worked between 1830 and 1860, old mines including the Tellurium (cf. under COLUMBIA), Bowles, Payne, Page, Hughes, Moss, Fisher, Busby, Taugus, Gilmore, and many others—**gold.**

CENTRALPLAINS: (1) area quarries, carving quality—**serpentine;** (2) W 6 mi. to Kid's Store, turn N from Rte. 620 to ½ mi. NW of the store, old **manganese** mine (get permission to collect at rock shop in DIXIE, *q.v.*)—gem **rhodonite;** (3) W on Rte. 6 to extreme SW corner of co. (with SCOTTS-VILLE just W of line in Albemarle Co.), area quarries, gravel pits, etc.—cuttable **quartz.**

COLUMBIA, 6 mi. out, the Tellurium Mine (discovered in 1832 and active until 1886)—**gold.**

DIXIE: (1) at crossrds. of Rte. 6 and U.S. 15, a rock shop (get permission and directions to an abandoned **manganese** mine), can be purchased—gem **rhodonite;** (2) for way to mine, drive toward SCOTTSVILLE on Rte. 6, then N on bad dirt rd. into brushy country to end of rd., park car and hike 1 mi. down steep hill, crossing a creek, and up steeply to old mine dumps—high-quality gem **rhodonite.**

FORT UNION, W on Rte. 6 to nearly ghost town of ESMONT (not on most maps), site of old slate industry—fine **pyrite crystals.**

NAHOR, area quarry—cuttable **quartz.**

FRANKLIN CO.

AREA: (1) regional **mica** mines—**apatite, garnet, mica, staurolites, tourmaline;** (2) SE part of co.: (a) between Chestnut and Snow creeks, on Chestnut Mt. (via Rte. 619 and dirt rds.), numerous **mica** mines and prospects—**beryl, garnets, tourmaline;** (b) top of Chestnut Mt., 1 mi. on dirt rd. from Rte. 619, the Chitwood Mine—**garnets, biotite mica, quartz crystals, tourmaline;** (c) on SE side of Chestnut Mt., 1½ mi. by rd. SW of Rte. 619, the Plant Mine—**feldspar crystals, garnets, quartz crystals, tourmaline;** (d) ½ mi. SW of Rte. 619 and 3.4 mi. NW of Rte. 108, the Chimney Mine

—**feldspar** and **quartz crystals, garnets, tourmaline;** (3) extreme W side of co., about ½ mi. from Huff's Store (near the ROCKY MOUNT–FLOYD courthouse rd.), a mine—**chalcopyrite, pyrrhotite;** (4) cf. also Henry Co.

FERRUM, NW 5 mi., the Howell prospect, on dumps—**calcite, pyrite, quartz crystals, sphalerite.**

PENHOOK, S on Rte. 890 to S corner of co. (21 mi. N of MARTINSVILLE in Henry Co.), the Center Ridge Mine (best reached from Henry Co. via U.S. 108, Rte. 619, and 3 mi. on a dirt rd.)—**beryl,** abundant **tourmaline.**

ROCKY MOUNT, jct. of Rte. 619 and Rte. 632: (1) W 1.8 mi., the Klondike Mine—**beryl** (gem crystals, massive blue); (2) W 1.9 mi., the Simms Mine —pale blue gem **beryl** (silky, opaque).

GILES CO.

NEWPORT, WSW 3½ mi., area gravels of Spruce Run—**quartz crystals** (distorted).

GOOCHLAND CO.

AREA. A mineralized belt extends from the central part of co. into E Powhaton Co., 30 mi. long by 15 mi. wide, very many old pegmatite mines (some operating through World War II)—**beryl, columbite, feldspar crystals, garnets, mica, quartz crystals, rutile, sillimanite, tantalite, tourmaline,** etc.

GOOCHLAND: (1) NW 2 mi., on SW side of Rte. 6, the Irwin Mine— **perthite** (flesh color), **smoky quartz crystals;** (2) gravels of Byrd Cr.— placer **gold,** chatoyant **quartz phenocrysts;** (3) NW from the courthouse via U.S. 522 and co. rd. 632, to a Texaco service sta., inquire way to old mine about 3 mi. out along area creek—**beryl** (in **smoky quartz crystals**); (4) NE 3 mi., and ½ mi. W of Rte. 49, on W slope of a hill, the Salter prospect—**garnets, sillimanite,** etc.; (5) NE 3.9 mi. via farm rds. 612 and 634 (and less than 1 mi. from U.S. 250), the Amber Queen Mine—**spessartite garnet,** crystals of **quartz** and **feldspar** (some chatoyant).

OLIVER, the O. W. Harris Mica Mine Farm (7.7 mi. W of Rte. 1 along Rte. 738), in area creek gravels—**garnets,** gem **kyanite, moonstone, rutile crystals.**

PERKINSVILLE, S ½ mi., the Wiltshire prospect—**garnets.**

GRAYSON CO.

AREA, various small hamlets not shown on many maps: (1) Cox's Mill, Edmonds (N 1 mi.), Eona, Baywood (½ mi. S, at Five Forks), Hanks Knob, etc., in area cut banks, gravels, quarries around each community— **garnets, pyrite, pyrrhotite, quartz crystals, rutile,** etc.; (2) Adkins Church (2 mi. N of Rte. 95)—**ilmenite** (massive), **quartz crystals, rutile crystals,** etc.

ELK CREEK, on slope of Iron Mt. 1¼ mi. E of U.S. 21 (and ¾ mi. S of the Wythe Co. line), area—**chalcedony.**

GALAX: (1) on W edge of town, at the J. C. Pierce prospect—gem **kyanite** (broad-bladed crystals), violet **garnets, perthite, quartz crystals** (clear, gray), **rutile crystals;** (2) SW 1.2 mi., on the Nichols farm—gem **kyanite** (bladed, blue, to 18 in. long), **garnets;** (3) a gneiss exposure belt extending from 2 mi. NE into Carroll Co., *q.v.,* to 6 mi. SW of town, area exposures—**spessartite garnet** (massive), **staurolites;** (4) SW 6 mi., in gneiss exposure—**spessartite garnet;** (5) SW 7 mi., area exposures—massive **spessartite garnet.** (Since GALAX straddles the co. line, see also in Carroll Co.)

GRANT: (1) SW ½ mi., in vein exposure—**marble, sphene;** (2) S, at Mink Ridge, a good-quality deposit, mined—**soapstone.**

HAMPTON FORD, on N side of the New R., the Hampton Mine—**garnets,** gem **kyanite, staurolites** (clear, yellow), **tourmaline.**

INDEPENDENCE: (1) just SW of Chestnut Yard, the Iron Ridge Mine, and (2) SE 1½ mi., area exposures—**epidote, hornblende, spessartite garnet;** (3) S 3 mi., near the old Greek Post Office, area—**staurolites;** (4) E 5 mi., near the Appalachian Power Co. dam, veins in gneiss—gemmy green **chlorite;** (5) NE 5 mi. (and ¼ mi. E of the New R.), the Poole prospect—**barite, fluorite, gypsum,** etc.

NEW RIVER, N side of village and ¾ mi. from mouth of the Little R.: (1) the Hampton Mine—**garnets, quartz crystals,** clear **staurolites;** (2) the Wingate Mines (E of Peach Bottom Cr.) on the Hendricks farm—massive **epidote.**

OLDTOWN, N .6 mi. along Rte. 634, area—**rutile crystals.**

TROUTDALE, SE 2½ mi. on Rte. 16, several outcrops along rd. and area side rds.—**epidote,** red **jasper,** pink **feldspar,** gemmy **unakite.**

GREENE CO.

BACON HOLLOW (a hamlet on the E side of the Roach R. Valley): (1) in a dikelike outcrop in area—gem **unakite** (as veins); (2) in area stream gravels, as pebbles and boulders, gemmy—**unakite.**

ELKTON, E 7 mi., area mines—**copper minerals.**

STANDARDSVILLE, N 5 mi., area mines— **copper minerals.**

HALIFAX CO.

VIRGILINA (District): (1) area of many old mines and dumps—**azurite, bornite, chalcocite, native copper, cuprite, gold, malachite,** etc.; (2) N 6 mi., two mines—**gold.** (This district extends about 18 mi. N–S, into N.C., very productive and with most mines located on a low, flat-topped ridge.)

HANOVER CO.

AREA, many pegmatite exposures in co.—**ilmenite, rutile,** etc.

ASHLAND, area fields, gravels, etc.—**staurolites.**

GUM TREE, W 7½ mi. on Rte. 738, the Mica Mine Farm (fee), ¼ mi. to a creek: (1) area of many old mines, on dumps and in creek gravels—**mica,** gem **quartz, orthoclase moonstone;** (2) in area pastures—**amazonstone,** also **feldspar** and **quartz crystals,** gem **kyanite, rutile.**

HEWLETT: (1) area outcrops—**garnets;** (2) SE 3½ mi. (9 mi. NW of ASHLAND), the four Saunders Mines: (a) on dumps—**garnets, graphic gran-**

ite, gem **quartz, mica;** (b) ½ mi. W, the Poteat Mine—**garnets, moonstones, quartz crystals.**

MONTPELIER, COATSVILLE, VERDON, area quarries in granite—**gem minerals, crystals.**

NEGRO FOOT, E 1.3 mi., near Rte. 671, the Rose Hill prospect on the Langford farm—**epidote,** gem blue **quartz, unakite.**

OLIVER (a hamlet): (1) area stream gravels, cuts, ditches, banks, excavations, old mine dumps, etc.—**moonstone;** (2) take Rte. 738 from U.S. 1 for 7.7 mi. to the Harris Mica Mine Farm—cf. under GUM TREE.

HENRICO CO.

AREA, stream gravels and pits of co.—**unakite,** etc.

RICHMOND, downtown building excavations—**vivianite crystals** (among finest and most perfect on record).

HENRY CO.

AREA: (1) countywide distribution of **mica** mines (cf. under RIDGEWAY for mineral species) also shown occasional—**epidote, ilmenite, magnetite, rutile, sphene,** and **zircon** as accessory minerals; (2) gravels of countywide streams, especially Leatherwood Cr. and the Smith R.; and (3) regional fields, rd. cuts, excavations, pits, etc.—gem blue **quartz.**

AXTON, area soils, gravels, etc.—**garnets.**

BASSETT: (1) W, around boundaries of Fairy Stone State Park (no collecting inside)—**staurolites;** (2) W about 1 mi. to the Clark's service sta. (brochure, permission to collect), in soils behind sta.—**staurolites.**

MARTINSVILLE: (1) SW 5.4 mi., in old placer grounds on SW side of Rte. 687—**corundum, garnets, quartz crystals, zircon;** (2) SE 7.8 mi., in rd. cut in S bank of the Smith R.—gem **kyanite, staurolites.**

RIDGEWAY: (1) area gravels, soils, etc.—**garnets;** (2) N ¼ mi. from RR sta., on W side of U.S. 220 in rock exposures, the Ridgeway Mines— **feldspar crystals, garnets, quartz** (smoky, white); (3) S 1.9 mi., and 1.3 mi. E of U.S. 220, the Eanes No. 2 Mine (and adjoining Garrett Mines), in pegmatites along both sides of a dirt rd. leading from Rte. 658—lavender **garnets, black tourmaline** (crystals in **quartz**); (4) SW 2½ mi. on U.S. 220 and Rte. 689, the DeShazo Mine —**feldspar crystals, garnets, graphic granite,** green **hornblende crystals, quartz crystals;** (5) SW 6 mi. on U.S. 220 and Rtes. 692 and 691, the Coleman Mines (in a steep valley) and on ridge above mines—**garnets, graphic granite, feldspar** and **quartz crystals, tourmaline.**

LOUDOUN CO.

AREA, many traprock quarries in co.—**calcite, datolite, heulandite, epidote, laumontite, natrolite, stilbite,** etc.

ARCOLA: (1) area traprock quarries—cf. AREA; (2) a quarry in SE corner of co.—gem brown **sphene.**

ASHBURN, from jct. of Rtes. 7 and 659, S 1 mi. on Rte. 659 to the Arlington Trap Rock Quarry (on Goose Cr.)—gemmy **hornblende, prehnite.**

HILLSBORO, area quarries—cf. AREA.

LEESBURG: (1) the Arlington Quarry—**quartz crystals;** (2) N 1 mi. (belt of exposures extends 3 mi. N), numerous deposits—**ocher;** (3) all regional quarries—**flourite, prehnite, sphalerite;** (4) SE 4 mi., the Belmont Quarry— some **fluorite** (as gangue mineral), **prehnite, sphalerite.**

MOUNTVILLE: (1) area **lime** and **marble** quarry—**garnets (andradite, grossularite), chlorite, calcite;** (2) the Virginia Lime and Stone Quarry—**andradite garnet, serpentine** (waxy).

LOUISA CO.

LOUISA, an area quarry—gemmy green **granite.**

MINERAL: (1) RR sta. on the Cheapeake and Ohio, three major mines within 3½ mi., the Arminius, Smith, and Sulphur—**calcite, chalcopyrite, galena, limonite, pyrite, sphalerite;** (2) N 5 mi., upstream on Contrary Cr., large mining area: (a) on dumps—**garnets** (in shale, to walnut size), **sulfur;** (b) outlying mines—**copper minerals, gold, mica;** (3) N, to near co. line: (a) area around Contrary Cr.—**actinolite, garnets, pyrite, serpentine, tremolite;** (b) the Valcooper Mine—**chalcopyrite, galena, pyrite cubes, quartz crystals, smithsonite, sphalerite,** etc.

PENDLETON, S 1 mi., follow dirt rd. beginning just N of a farm pond to W, to dead end on the McPherson farm, take trail about 1 mi. into woods to old mine—**gold** (obtained by crushing ore detritus and panning).

TREVILIANS, SW 4 mi., in area gravels, pits, trenches, cuts, soils, etc.— **amethysts, quartz crystals.**

MADISON CO.

AREA, 1 mi. SE of Milam's Gap, in Dark Hollow at head of the Robinson R., area mines—**copper minerals.**

CRIGLERSVILLE: (1) cross bridge and turn W on Rte. 670: (a) stream gravels of the Rose R., abundant—**unakite;** (b) a rock mill at edge of town— **quartz** (massive, star, clear); (2) SW on Rte. 670 to Rte. 642 and the Blakey Ridge fire rd., up ridge to fire tower, collecting area on the S—gem **quartz** (blue, light to deep color, semitransparent, chatoyant).

SYRIA: (1) W, near town, area cut banks and stream gravels along Rtes. 670 and 648—gem **epidote, jasper, quartz crystals** (blue, asteriated); (2) in gravels of Rose Run—**jasper;** (3) 8 mi. out on unpaved Rose R. rd. to picnic grounds: (a) in river gravels—**black chert,** massive **epidote, quartz** (pebbles, clear and smoky); (b) also in gravels of all regional streams; (4) take Rte. 600 N of Old Rag Mt., area—**gemstones, minerals,** etc.

MECKLENBURG CO.

FINCHLEY, area extension of the Halifax Co. VIRGILINA, *q.v.,* mining district, the Pontiac Mine—**azurite, bornite, calcite, malachite,** etc.

MONTGOMERY CO.

AREA, exposures of the Luster's Gate dolomites—**quartz crystals.**
SHAWSVILLE, SW, at Bonys Run, area prospects—**smithsonite.**

NELSON CO.

ARRINGTON: (1) NW 7 mi., area mines—**ilmenite, rutile;** (2) NW 8½ mi., the old American Gem and Pearl Co. Mine—**amethysts** (high quality, lavender).
JAMES RIVER, N 2 mi., in SE part of co.: (a) area, and (b) around Warminster and Midway Mills, ore deposits—**manganese minerals.**
LOWESVILLE, nearby, on the Saunders farm, pegmatite outcrop, high quality, lavender— **amethysts.**
MONTEBELLO: (1) SW: (a) area quarries and mines—**moonstone, cassiterite;** (b) gravels of Irish Cr.—blue **moonstone, cassiterite;** (2) just E of jct. of Rte. 56 with the Skyline Drive (not far from Tye River Gap), in outcrop, high quality—**unakite.**
ROSELAND: (1) area mines—**ilmenite, rutile;** (2) area stream gravels—**quartz** (brilliant blue pebbles and crystals), **ilmenite, rutile crystals.**
SCHUYLER: (1) area mines and quarries—carvable **steatite;** (2) a nearby **soapstone** quarry—some **chrysotile, talc** (abundant, good carving material).
WILLKIE, E, in pegmatite outcrop—gem **unakite.**

ORANGE CO.

ORANGE, N, the Rapidan R. area, several old mines—**copper minerals, gold.**
SOMERSET, large area schist exposures—**graphite, pyrite.**

PAGE CO.

IDA: (1) area mines—**copper minerals;** (2) NW about 1 mi.: (a) gravels of East Hawkbill Cr., and (b) mine dumps over 60 acres near Hoak Hill—**azurite, chrysolite, cuprite, epidote, jasper** (orbicular, red, scarlet, maroon, yellow, vermilion, banded), **malachite, hematite.**
MARKSVILLE, S 3 mi., near W base of the Blue Ridge where the Shenandoah Valley RR crosses Stony Run, area mines—**ocher.**
MAUCK, mines near Fisher's Gap—**azurite,** etc., and **unakite.**
STANLEY, S, near Jollett just off Skyline Dr., several exposures—gem **unakite, apatite, chlorite, iron minerals, zircon.** (In the immediate area are 8 distinct **unakite** outcrops.)

PATRICK CO.

AREA: (1) NW part of co., Hurricane Knob (1 mi. from tri-county corner of Patrick-Carroll-Floyd counties, area)—gem **kyanite;** (2) Fairy

Stone State Park (NE corner of co.), area outside boundaries—**staurolites.** (See also BASSETT in Henry Co.)

MEADOWS OF DAN, W: (1) the Barnard farm (3¾ mi. E and 1 mi. S of LAUREL FORK in Floyd Co.)—**quartz crystals** (clear, to 100 lbs.); (2) ½ mi. NW of Barnard's, on the Robinson farm—giant clear **quartz crystals.**

STUART (center of a broad **staurolite** belt): (1) area stream beds, rd. cuts, **mica** schists (from some mi. SW to about 20 mi NE of town)—**almandite garnets, staurolites;** (2) area exposures similar to those in Fairy Stone State Park in NE part of co.—**staurolites;** (3) S 2 mi., at Bull Mt., exposures—**corundum,** gem **kyanite, margarite.**

WOOLWINE, S, in a lime quarry—**almandite garnets, sphene, tourmaline.**

PITTSYLVANIA CO.

AXTON: (1) area pegmatite outcrops—**feldspar, garnet,** gem **kyanite, mica, quartz crystals, tourmaline;** (2) NW, at the Holland Mine—**beryl** (green, yellow), **black tourmaline;** (3) N 3 mi.: (a) the L. P. Willis Mine—**garnets;** and (b) just E on a hilltop, the Turner Mine—**smoky quartz crystals;** (4) NE 5½ mi., the Will Rogers Mine—pegmatite **gems** and **minerals.** (Most regional mines can be reached from U.S. 58 via dirt rds.) (5) E 7½ mi., the Tyler Mine— pegmatite **gems** and **minerals.**

CHATHAM, SW 5 mi., the George Easley Mine, abundant—**gem garnets.**

DANVILLE, area **chlorite** schist exposures—**chlorite,** some **platinum.**

GRETNA: (1) area fields, rd. cuts, stream gravels E of U.S. 29—translucent blue **quartz;** (2) Skyline Estates: (a) area stream gravels and banks, and (b) in **quartz** vein at crest of hill— **mica,** gemmy blue **quartz.**

HURT: (1) area fields, rd. cuts, stream gravels and banks E of U.S. 29—translucent blue **quartz;** (2) from NE corner (near ALTAVISTA in Campbell Co.), a 10-by-12 mi. **mica** mining district lies S of the Roanoke R., many pegmatite exposures (mostly in rugged backcountry)—**feldspar crystals, garnets, pyrite, quartz crystals, tourmaline;** (3) from TOSHES a mining belt extends N to LYNCHBURG in Campbell Co., many old **barite** mine dumps—**barite, epidote, marble,** blue **quartz, tourmaline.**

MOTLEY, S ½ mi., the Motley prospect—pink **perthite,** white **quartz, tourmaline.**

SYCAMORE: (1) E ¾ mi., dumps of the Sycamore Mine—**marble** (in thin area veins), **quartz** (blue, milky, gray); (2) W 4 mi., the Bloomfield prospects—**perthite, quartz.**

WHITTLES, area quarries, excavations, etc.—some **corundum.**

POWHATAN CO.

FLAT ROCK: (1) NE, at the White Peak Mica Mine—**mica,** asteriated **quartz crystals, smoky quartz;** (2) NE 3.6 mi. on Rte. 613, the Hebbe No. 2 Mine—**beryl** (to 5-in.-dia. crystals), **amazonite, cleavelandite, columbite-tantalite, garnets, quartz crystals.**

MOSELEY, area fields, excavations, gravels—**petrified** and **opalized wood.**

PRINCE EDWARD CO.

AREA, extreme W part of co. (5½ mi. S of PAMPLIN in Appomattox Co. on Rte. 47, cross RR, turn sharp E on co. rd. 681 for 2½ mi., turn N on co. rd. 681), the Baker Mt. Kyanite Mine (get permission)—gem **kyanite crystals, garnet, fuschite, pyrite, turgite,** etc.

PROSPECT, SE 1 mi., old **kyanite** mine—**garnets,** gem **kyanite, rutile crystals, staurolites, topaz.**

RICE: (1) many area mines and prospects, especially: (a) the Briery Mine, and (b) at Leigh Mt.—**garnets, kyanite, rutile, staurolites, topaz;** (2) N 1 mi., an old mine—cf. area; (3) N 3 mi. on Rte. 619, wide area of pegmatite outcrops around the Smith farm—**amethysts** (color-zoned, to 6 in. long); (4) on both sides of Sayler's Cr., area surfaces, outcrops, etc.—**amethysts, feldspar, graphic granite, quartz crystals** (clear, milky, smoky).

PRINCE WILLIAM CO.

CATLETT, area mine—**barite.**

DUMFRIES, NW 1½ mi., the Cabin Branch Mine—**chalcopyrite, garnets** (occasional on dumps), **gold, galena, pyrrhotite, sphalerite.**

MINNIEVILLE, W, area—**amethysts, quartz crystals.**

PRINCESS ANNE CO.

VIRGINIA BEACH, 1 mi. NE of jct. of Int. 64 and Rte. 58 (Virginia Beach Blvd.), just N of the Hollywood subdivision, in area pits—**"clam geodes"** (fossil clam shells packed with ivory and clear **dogtooth calcite crystals**).

RAPPAHANNOCK CO.

AREA, extreme N corner of co., about 6½ mi. S from FRONT ROYAL in Warren Co., area mines and prospects—**copper minerals.**

ROANOKE CO.

AIR POINT, on edge of BENT MT.: (1) a rd. cut, as a fine-grained deposit —**unakite;** (2) nearby exposures—**apatite, rutile.**

ROANOKE: (1) S 9 mi. on U.S. 220 and Rte. 921 to the Shepherd farm, in **epidote** exposure—**anatase** (yellow pseudomorphs after **sphene**), black **zircon;** (2) Mason Cove (via Rte. 311), in black shale exposure on W side of river—**rock crystal.**

SALEM: (1) in a rd. cut behind the Dixie Caverns—smoky **agate;** (2) N, at foot of Catawba Mt., in black shale exposure—**barite crystals** (clear, tabular).

ROCKBRIDGE CO.

BUENA VISTA, N on U.S. 60 to CORNWALL (inquire directions): (1) Irish Cr., and (2) tributary Panther Cr., area **tin** mines—**amethyst, apatite, beryl, cassiterite crystals** (to ½ in. long, translucent), **fluorite, moonstone, tourmaline, zircon.**

FAIRFIELD, ½ mi. out, large mined deposit—**ocher.**

GLASGOW, the Lone Jack Quarry in town—**calcite, fluorite, quartz crystals** (clear, smoky).

VESUVIUS: (1) S, in Big Mary's Cr., *in situ* and in gravels of area—gem **unakite**; (2) S on Rte. 56 a short distance: (a) rock quarry—gem **unakite**; (b) on E across the Blue Ridge Parkway, then S by twisting dirt rd. and W back under the parkway to the Irish Creek Tin Mine (on left of trail a few hundred ft. above a forest service bldg.)—**beryl**, some **cassiterite crystals, quartz crystals, scheelite;** (3) SE 1½ mi., exposed lenses—gem **unakite** (with brilliant red **microcline feldspar** crystals to several in. long); (4) ½ mi. farther S on same rd., exposed dikes—green **unakite** (with **quartz** and red **orothoclase feldspar**); (5) several mi. farther (to about ½ mi. W of the Blue Ridge Parkway), an exposure—**unakite** (with green **quartz monazite** and pink **orthoclase feldspar**); (6) W 2 mi., an old quarry—**unakite** (with red orange splotches in yellow green base color); (7) E, at Tye River Gap: (a) area gravels of Irish Cr.—**beryl, quartz crystals;** (b) mines along Irish Cr.—**arsenopyrite, cassiterite, pyrite, wolframite;** (c) on W side of the parkway just inside co. line and near Rockbridge Co. sites, *q.v.*—decorative **unakite.**

ROCKINGHAM CO.

ELKTON: (1) W 1 mi., area—**quartz crystals;** (2) SE, at High Knob, area outcrops and mines—**azurite,** etc.; (3) N, toward SHENANDOAH STA. (on Norfolk and Western RR. in Page Co.), about 5 mi. SW of sta., area mines along Naked Cr.—**ocher.**

HARRISONBURG, nearby quarry—gemmy dark-colored **marble.**

TIMBERVILLE, nearby **lead-zinc** mine—**calcite crystals** (cream color), **galena, sphalerite,** etc.

RUSSELL CO.

CASTLEWOOD, N 10 mi., area mines—**smithsonite.**

LEBANON, a 30-mi.-long region of many mined deposits, the S slope of Kent Ridge along the Clinch R. extending NE to NORTH TAZEWELL in Tazewell Co.—**ocher.**

SMYTH CO.

CHATHAM HILL, immediately S on Rte. 16: (1) area mines—**smithsonite, sphalerite;** (2) just SW of this site, another mine—**hemimorphite.**

MARION: (1) E, and just off Int. 81, the Henderlite Quarry—**barite, calcite, iron minerals, limonite** (pseudomorphs after **chalcopyrite**), **malachite, pyrite;** (2) a 3-mi. radius about town: (a) SW 2 mi., along a prominent ridge; (b) NW 2 mi.; (c) along the Middle Fork of the Holston R.; and (d) NE of Mc-MILLAN in the Wassum Valley—**barite, calcite, iron minerals, limonite** (pseudomorphs after **chalcopyrite**), **malachite, pyrite,** etc.; (3) S 6 mi., near SUGAR GROVE, *q.v.,* along Comers Cr. (in the Glade Mt. **manganese** district), area mines—**cryptomelane, psilomelane,** etc.

SALTVILLE, flats area—well-preserved **fossils** (cavities filled with sparkling crystals of **apatite** and **calcite**).

SUGAR GROVE: (1) area mines—**rhodonite;** (2) the Sugar Grove Mine (200 yds. N of the South Fork of the Holston R. and ½ mi. NW of the Holston Grove School)—**calcite, dolomite crystals, fluorite.**

SPOTSYLVANIA CO.

CHANCELLORSVILLE: (1) N 2 mi., area mines—gem **kyanite;** (2) WNW, into extreme NW corner of co., near the Rappahannock R., oldest **gold** mines in co.—**gold.**

POST OAK, SW on Rte. 208 to co. line along the Anna R., the Edeton Mica Mine (reached also by 5½ mi. on U.S. 522 and 5 mi. on Rte. 208 out of MINERAL, *q.v.,* in Louisa Co.), on dumps—**feldspar crystals, quartz** (clear crystals, milky, star).

STAFFORD CO.

AREA, countywide excavations, pits, gravels, etc., occasionally found—gem **vivianite.**

HARTWOOD: (1) in area, the Eagle Mine (12 mi. NW of FREDERICKSBURG in Spotsylvania Co.), extensively worked until 1894—**gold;** (2) 2 mi. farther NW, the Rappahannock Mine, operated before and after the Civil War—**gold.**

MORRISVILLE, GOLDVEIN (on U.S. 17 NW of FREDERICKSBURG in Spotsylvania Co.), many area very old mines (make local inquiry)—**gold.**

QUANTICO, area banks and gravels of the Potomac R. and area pits and excavations—**petrified** and **opalized wood.**

TAZEWELL CO.

NORTH TAZEWELL, a 30-mi.-long area extending SW along the Clinch R. to region of LEBANON in Russell Co., *q.v.,* deposits on S slope of Kent Ridge, many mines—**ocher.**

WARREN CO.

BENTONVILLE, just S, numerous old mines and prospects (oldest **copper** exploration district in Va.)—**copper minerals.**

BROWNTOWN (village SW of FRONT ROYAL on the Skyline Drive), huge outcrop (mineral-rich, but collecting not allowed from the parkway)— **biotite mica, quartz crystals** (white, smoky), gem **unakite.**

FRONT ROYAL: (1) area stream gravels (which drain the main outcrop area)—**biotite mica, quartz crystals,** gem **unakite;** (2) E and S, many regional prospects and mines—**copper minerals.**

RIVERTON, area outcrops—**calcite** and **quartz crystals.**

WASHINGTON CO.

BRISTOL: (1) on rd. through gap between White Top and Mt. Rogers, in rhyolite outcrop in vugs and pockets—**calcite, fluorite, selenite, siderite;** (2) Hayters Gap area: (a) just N, in shale exposure—**pyritized fossils;** (b) 2 mi. distant, on N bank of the North Fork of the Holston R., as crystals— **calcite, celestite;** (3) a rd. cut near jct. of Int. 81 and Rte. 381, large-size crystals—**calcite.**

GLADE SPRING, NW 4½ mi., on N side of and about ½ mi. from the Saltville branch of the Norfolk and Western RR, a mine—**barite.**

HOLSTON, area extending NE from PLASTERCO to within 3 mi. of CHATHAM HILL, *q.v.,* in Smyth Co., many regional mines, quarries, pits—**gypsum, halite.**

WYTHE CO.

AUSTINVILLE: (1) area, S part of co., many active and inactive **lead-zinc** mines over a broad region—**aragonite, asbestos** (on one dump only), **calcite, fluorite, hemimorphite,** massive **bornite, marcasite, smithsonite, sphalerite;** (2) the huge New Jersey Zinc Co. mines, on dumps—**dolomite crystals, marcasite** (makes into lovely cabochons), gem **pyrite** (massive), minerals of **lead, silver,** and **zinc** (most of the metallic minerals are sulfides); (3) E 10 mi., the Bertha Mine (famed for its limestone "chimneys")—**barite, calamine, calcite, cerussite, fluorite, galenite, smithsonite.**

IVANHOE, area mines (both active and inactive)—massive **bornite, aragonite, calcite, fluorite, hemimorphite, marcasite, smithsonite, sphalerite.**

WYTHEVILLE, area sandstone quarry—**anatase.**

WASHINGTON

The Evergreen State in the far northwestern corner of continental America has a remarkably varied, bold, and geologically interesting structure and topography. It resembles its neighbor Oregon to the south, but the general terrain is rougher and the climate moister, although the Coast Range is lower. As in Oregon, the Cascade Mountains divide the state into a timbered, wet, sea-girt western part and an eastern two-thirds that is arid, basaltic, and cut by the great gorges of the Columbia River and its tributaries.

Puget Sound, with its more than 300 forested islands, bisects the northern half of the western portion with its salt waters to create the Olympic Peninsula on the west. Here, in the Olympic National Park, one of the most rugged and inaccessible wilderness regions in America, Mt. Olympus rises 7,954 feet; it is sheathed in the lower regions with the densest rain forest in North America. To the south Grays and Willapa harbors reach far inland, surrounded by heavily timbered hills. Throughout the western portion, the gem and mineral collector will find road cuts and banks, stream beds, and farmers' fields productive of highly prized **agatized clams** and **oysters,** along with other types of Miocene fossils, as well as gem localities too numerous to be listed in their entirety for **agate, carnelian** (some of the deepest translucent red in the world), **chalcedony,** and **jasper.**

The Cascade Range stretches 230 miles from the Canadian boundary to the Columbia Gorge that forms the Oregon state line. East of Tacoma, Mt. Rainier rises to 14,408 feet, the highest point in Washington. Other glaciered volcanic cones crest the Cascade skyline, rising from sea level into the sky: Mt. Baker on the north, 10,750 feet, and on the south, Mt. Adams, 12,307 feet, and Mt. St. Helens, 9,671 feet. These peaks are snow-covered all year round. During the 30 million years of the Oligocene, Miocene, and Pliocene epochs when the Cascades were rising, extremely fluid basic lavas poured from the volcanoes and from great fissures again and again to fill all preexisting valleys, lakes, and swamps and bury residual granite knobs to depths of 500 to 3,700 feet under successive layers of basalt. The lavas covered much of the western part of the state and virtually all of eastern Washington, with overlap into Canada, Idaho, and Oregon. The flows of basalt and the widespread holocausts of pulverized volcanic ash came in many series, often separated by long geologic intervals of time during which soils formed and great forests grew. Subsequently, the forests were buried under thick blankets of volcanic ash, rich in silica, or were destroyed by the fiery basalts. Eastern Washington is part of the 225,000-square-mile Columbia Plateau, one of the greatest expanses of raw lava in the world. Today's gem collectors find in the debris of the ash-buried forests some of the loveliest gem-quality **opalized** and **silicified woods** in the world.

Throughout Oligocene and Miocene times, as the volcanoes poured out their own basalts along with suffocating clouds of ash, the Columbia River maintained its original westward course. The river carved the Columbia Gorge transversely through the rising formations of the Cascade Range, now many thousands of feet deep, while its principal tributary, the Wyoming-spawned Snake River, cut its own mighty chasm through the southwest corner of the state. Thus the sands and gravel bars of the Columbia River carry great quantities of gemstones, as well as prehistoric Indian artifacts. Tens of thousands of the finest arrowheads in America, chipped out of gem **agate, carnelian, jasper,** and **obsidian,** have been screened from the river sands.

There are so many mines scattered over the state that it is possible here to list only the more important ones. Therefore, reference is made to the "Inventory of Washington Minerals," Parts I and II, by Marshall T. Hunting, State Division of Mines and Geology, Bulletin 37, *Geology,* Olympia, Washington, 1956. Each part consists of two volumes, one for text and one for detailed maps, and every metallic and nonmetallic mine in the state is accurately described and specifically located.

According to the U.S. Geological Survey, Washington is one of the few states in which **gold** production has increased in recent years, principally from the Knob Hill Mine near Republic in Ferry Co. and the Gold King Mine near Wenatchee in Chelan Co. Between 1860 and 1965, **gold** production reached 3,671,026 ounces, placing Washington eleventh in the roster of **gold**-producing states. The yellow metal was first discovered in 1853 in stream sands of the Yakima River Valley in Yakima and Benton counties. Rich placers were worked along many of the major streams of the state through the 1880's, with most sources depleted by the early 1900's. Lode deposits were found in the 1870's, and these eventually supplanted placers as the chief source of **gold.**

For information, write: Division of Mines & Geology, 404 Transportation Building, Olympia.

ASOTIN CO.

CLARKSTON: (1) area sand and gravel exposures, and (2) sand bars of the Snake R.—placer **gold.**

BENTON CO.

COLD CREEK, NW 1 mi., area draws, washes, etc.—**opalized wood.**
PROSSER, all regional draws, washes, etc. of Horse Heaven Hills area— **opalized wood.** (Cf. under ALDERDALE, Klickitat Co.)

CHELAN CO.

AREA: (1) Horseshoe Basin and Railroad Creek districts, many mines— **chalcopyrite** (bearing **gold** and **silver), galena;** (2) mining districts of Bridge Creek, Lakeside, Pehastin, very many lode mines—**gold;** (3) Negro Cr., N side, the Davenport property—**geodes, nodules.**
ENTIAT, LEAVENWORTH, many area mines—**gold.**
PEHASTIN (District), the Ivanhoe and Pole Pick mines—**gold, silver.**
WENATCHEE: (1) regional lode mines—**gold;** (2) in Number One Canyon, area—**onyx.**

CLALLAM CO.

ARCH-A-WAT (W of Neah Bay on the coast), S along ocean beach to Shishi Beach (2 mi. NW of Point of Arches), placer sands—**gold, iridosmine, platinum.**
DUNGENESS, gravels of the Dungeness R.—**agate, orbicular jasper.**
FAIRHOLM, 1 mi. NW of W end of Lake Crescent, area—**jasper.**
JOYCE, N: (1) Agate Beach, and (2) Crescent Beach, in beach gravels—**agate, chert, jasper.**
LA PUSH: (1) area ocean beach gravels—**agate, jasper;** (2) gravels of the Soleduck R. (extending NE to SAPPHO, *q.v.*)—**agate, orbicular jasper.**
OZETTE, gravels of the Ozette R. and Yellow Bank, placers—**gold.**
SAPPHO, gravels of the upper Soleduck R.—**agate, orbicular jasper.**

CLARK CO.

AREA, the Bell Mt. Mine—**plasma agate, rock crystal.**
BRUSH PRAIRIE, area placer sands—**gold.**
CAMAS, sandbars of the Columbia R.—**placer gold.**
WASHOUGAL: (1) area, and (2) especially NE 2½ mi., area—**moss agate, amethysts.**

COWLITZ CO.

CLOVERDALE, E 4 mi., area—**fortification agate, carnelian, chalcedony, geodes (amethyst-**lined).
KALAMA, hills to E—cf. CLOVERDALE.
KELSO, S, at base of cliffs along Int. 5—**agate** (containing water bubbles).
ST. HELENS, area mines—**copper minerals, galena, pyrite.**

DOUGLAS CO.

AREA, Columbia R. sands, placers—**gold.**
BRIDGEPORT, area exposures—**jadeite.**
WATERVILLE, area gravels, pits, excavations, etc.—**common opal.**

FERRY CO.

AREA, the Belcher, Lone Star, and Sanpoil districts, area mines—**copper minerals.**
AENEAS, Lyman Lake, the Crown Point Mine to W—**gold, quartz crystals.**
COVADA (Enterprise district), the Longstree, and other mines and prospects, on dumps—**stibnite.**
DANVILLE, area mines—**gold.**
KELLER: (1) area mines—**cobalt minerals;** (2) the Congress Mine—**nickel minerals.**

NESPELEM, Columbia R. placer sands (between mouths of Nespelem and Kettle rivers) to S and E via COULEE DAM—**gold.**

REPUBLIC: (1) area mines, such as the Tom Thumb, Quilp, Lone Pine, Surprise, etc.—**gold, silver;** (2) Granite Cr., area placer gravels—**gold.**

WEST FORK, placer mines along Strawberry Cr. (tributary of the Sanpoil R.)—**gold.**

FRANKLIN CO.

RINGOLD, area gravels of the Columbia R. benches—**agate.**

GRANT CO.

GRAND COULEE, regional lava outcrops, in debris—**opalized wood** (logs).

MOSES LAKE, area of Moses Coulee, in regional lava outcrops—**opalized wood.**

QUINCY: (1) area diatomaceous earth deposits (mined), as nodules—**common opal;** (2) W 6 mi. on Rte. 10, area—**silicified wood.**

SCHAWANA, S, in the Saddle Mts., all washes, draws, surfaces—**opalized wood** (among the finest gem quality in the world). The Saddle Mts. are a center of a belt some 150 mi. E–W and 50 mi. N–S, extending well into Kittitas Co. and the NE portion of Yakima Co., containing this finest of **opalized wood.** The wood weathers out of volcanic ash exposures, often as huge perfectly silicified logs.

TRINIDAD, area outcrops of lava—**opalized wood.**

GRAYS HARBOR CO.

MOCLIPS, N, along ocean beaches and in regional stream gravels—**agate, jasper.**

OAKVILLE, N 10 mi., regional rd. cuts and stream banks—**agatized** and **chalcedonized clams** and **oysters.** The fossils, which are really **agate** or **translucent chalcedony** casts of Miocene bivalves (no traces of any original organic or shell matter remains), tumble beautifully into unusual gem-fossil specimens.

JEFFERSON CO.

AREA: (1) W-central part of the Olympic National Park, at Mt. Anderson, elev. 7,326 ft. (reached only by trail from rd. ends): (a) outcrops on mt. —**rock crystal;** (b) gravels of Rustler Cr.—**rock crystal;** (2) central part of the park, near summit of Mt. Olympus, elev. 7,965 ft. (reached only by many miles of rugged trail)—**rock crystal.** Entry into the Olympic National Park, with few exceptions around the perimeters, is by foot or horse trail. This is a true primeval wilderness, but the Park Service maintains trails and camping areas, and provides food and lodging.

KALALOCH, area beach gravels—**agate, jasper.**
QUEETS, area ocean beach gravels—**agate, chert, jasper.**

KING CO.

AREA: (1) Bear Basin, Devil's Canyon, and W side of Denny Mt. (above Denny Cr.)—**rock crystal;** (2) the Great Republic Mine—**stibnite.**
BARING, SW, the Climax claims—**bornite** (with **silver**), **chalcopyrite** (bearing **gold** and **silver**).
BERLIN, 6 mi. distant at Money Cr., area lode mines—**gold.**

KITTITAS CO.

CLE ELUM: (1) area: (a) Fish Lake mining district, area lode mines—**gold;** (b) NE, in basalt flows—blue **chalcedony nodules;** (2) E 8 mi. to U.S. 97, then N toward LIBERTY: (a) 2 mi. N to old logging rd., park car, walk 1¾ mi. up RR track to old skid rd., area—**agate** (blue, in large masses); (b) in canyons N of RR, sides and bottoms—blue **agate;** (c) Mineral Spgs. Camp, W on dirt rd. 5 mi. to Crystal Mt., area—blue **chalcedony geodes** (must be dug out); (d) N to Medicine Cr. rd., then W to end, park car, climb to summit of Red Top Mt. (elev. 5,300 ft.), along summit of Teanaway Ridge—gem blue **agate, geodes** (occur along entire route on both sides of rd. and including the parking area); (e) gravels of the Middle Fork of the Teanaway R.—**agate, chalcedony geodes;** (f) N to RYEPATCH, all surrounding area—**agate;** (3) N 20 mi. and a little W, deposit—**hematite.**
ELLENSBURG, N, in lava flows, weathering out—blue **chalcedony nodules.**
LIBERTY: (1) old placer mining operations along Liberty Cr., abundant—**gold;** (2) N, along Williams, Boulder, and Swauk creeks, placer and lode mines—**gold;** (3) NE 2 mi., a 2-sq.-mi. area of stream beds, washes, and talus slopes—**agate, chalcedony nodules.**
VANTAGE: (1) area: (a) almost entire E part of co., (b) all region outside boundaries of the Petrified Forest State Park, (c) Columbia R. gravels and sands W and S of town for many mi.—**opalized** and **silicified wood** (finest in the world); (2) S, in the Saddle Mts. (extending into Yakima Co.): (a) all regional exposures of volcanic ash in canyon sides, summits, draws, washes, etc.; and (b) Crab Canyon, area—gem **opalized wood** (entire logs weighing many tons are common). The State Park and its fine museum have polished specimens of ginkgo wood and other species (all beautifully opalized) on display.

KLICKITAT CO.

ALDERDALE, N and E into the Horse Heaven Hills (extending E into Benton Co.), all regional cuts, canyons, hillsides, draws, washes, etc.—gem **opalized wood.** This range of hills of the Eocene Latah formation reveals exposures of whitish volcanic ash along some 120 mi., extending from GLENWOOD in the NW corner of the co. E across entire co. and into Benton

Co. with overlap into adjoining Yakima Co. on the N. The top-quality **opalized** and **silicified wood** occurs abundantly, weathering out of volcanic ash exposures, in the following order of abundance: redwood (*Sequoia*), oak (many varieties), swamp cypress (*Taxodium*), elm, maple, willow, cedar, poplar, chestnut, alder, birch, persimmon, and laurel.

BICKLETON, CLEVELAND, all regional canyons, draws, slopes of the Horse Heaven Hills—**opalized** and **silicified wood.**

GLENWOOD (E end of the Horse Heaven Hills which, here, extend N into Yakima Co.)—cf. ALDERDALE.

GOLDENDALE, NE 20 mi. (and 2 mi. W), at WARWICK, area—**agate, carnelian, jasper, opalized wood.**

LYLE: (1) E 2 mi., on area hillsides—**petrified wood;** (2) 6 mi. distant along the Klickitat R., area—**petrified wood.**

ROOSEVELT: (1) N, on steep hillsides of the Horse Heaven Hills—cf. ALDERDALE; (2) take co. rd. to Wood Gulch, area—cf. ALDERDALE. The co. rds. leading N from Rte. 14 (following the N bank of the Columbia R.) from ALDERDALE on the E to ROOSEVELT on the W are the principal access rds. into the Horse Heaven Hills from the S side.

LEWIS CO.

ADNA, W, along Rte. 6 to Lucas Cr. (tributary of the Newaukum R.), area rd. cuts, banks, etc.—**agate, carnelian, chalcedony, geodes, jasper, petrified wood.**

CENTRALIA, regional stream gravels, cut banks, etc.—cf. ADNA.

DOTY: (1) area lava outcrops—**peridot;** (2) gravels of the North Fork of the Chehalis R.—cf. ADNA.

FOREST, gravels of the Newaukum R. and its tributaries—**geodes, nodules.**

MARYS CORNER: (1) area farm fields, stream gravels, etc.—cf. ADNA; (2) Salmon and White rivers and all tributaries: (a) in gravels and banks, and (b) loose in soil of all farm fields in the drainage region—**agate, "Salmon River" carnelian, geodes.** This **carnelian,** found in clear and translucent deep red (almost ruby red) nodules from 1 to 6 in. dia., ranks among the finest in the world.

MINERAL, area mines—**realgar.**

MORTON, area **mercury** mines—clear **chalcedony** (spotted with **cinnabar**), **cinnabar.**

PE ELL, regional stream banks and gravels—cf. ADNA.

TOLEDO, regional stream banks and gravels—**geodes, nodules.**

LINCOLN CO.

DAVENPORT: (1) Hell Gate Bar (a few mi. above SANPOIL), and (2) Peach Bar, area placer mines—**gold;** (3) N 15 mi., area mines of the Crystal District, as prominent metal—**silver.**

MONDOVI: (1) N ½ mi., (2) NW 1 mi., area lava outcrops—**precious opal;** (3) NW 3–4 mi., lava outcrops—**fire opal.**

OKANOGAN CO.

AREA, very many mining districts in co., located mostly on regional topographic maps, both placer and lode mines—**gold.**

LOOMIS, NW and W about 35 mi., near Cathedral Peak, area mines—**wolframite.**

METHOW: (1) area mines—**stibnite;** (2) Upper Methow Cr., area mines—**chalcopyrite** (bearing **gold** and **silver**).

NESPELEM: (1) N, gravels of the Nespelem R.—**agate, chalcedony;** (2) the Moses mining district: (a) the Apache Mine, and (b) the Little Chief Mine—**argentite, pyrargyrite;** (3) N 12 mi., the Stepstone prospect—**nickel minerals.**

NIGHTHAWK: (1) area lode mines—**gold;** (2) S, the Palmer Mt. mining district: (a) area lode mines—**gold;** (b) the Golden Zone Mine, and (c) the Gold Hill Mine—**chalcopyrite** (bearing **gold** and **silver**).

OROVILLE, N, Osoyoos Lake, area mines S of the Canadian boundary—**copper minerals, pyrite.**

RIVERSIDE, NE 7 mi.: (1) just above mouth of Tunk Cr. (a tributary of the Okanogan R.), area—**quartz crystals;** (2) gravels of Tunk Cr.—**corundum** (blue, pink), **quartz crystals, thulite** (pink **zoisite**).

TWISP: (1) area lode mines—**gold;** (2) W, mines along the Twisp R.—**chalcopyrite** (bearing **gold** and **silver**); (3) Myers Cr. district: (a) many area placers, (b) Mary Ann Cr. (tributary of Myers Cr.), placers—**gold;** (c) the Monterey and Yakima mines—**galena** (bearing **gold** and **silver**); (4) the Squaw Cr. district, many area mines—**chalcopyrite** (bearing **gold** and **silver**).

WAUCONDA, numerous area lode mines—**gold.**

PACIFIC CO.

BROOKLYN, area cr. banks, gravels, and rd. cuts of the Willapa Hills—**agatized fossil shells** (casts of clams, oysters, etc.).

LEBAM, area gravels of the Willapa R.—**agatized fossil shells, chalcedony casts** of ammonites, gastropods (snail shells), etc.

LONG BEACH, area beach gravels, as pebbles—**agate, chalcedony, jasper, quartz.**

OCEAN PARK, cf. LONG BEACH.

RAYMOND: (1) E along Rte. 6 to PE ELL, q.v., in Lewis Co., in every stream bed and bank along hwy. for some 40 mi.—**agate, carnelian, chalcedony, jasper,** etc.; (2) S, at Greens Cr. (on Rte. 6 above MENLO), in stream bed and banks—cf. item (1).

PEND OREILLE CO.

METALINE FALLS, the Josephine Mine—**smithsonite.**

NEWPORT: (1) area stream gravels, pits, etc.—**amethysts;** (2) S, at Sacheen Lake, area around lake shores—**garnets.**

PIERCE CO.

FAIRFAX (NW corner entrance to Mt. Rainier National Park), the Carbon R. mines—**copper minerals, pyrite.**

SKAGIT CO.

DIABLO, SE, the Thunder Creek District (along Thunder Cr.), numerous area mines—**silver.**

HAMILTON: (1) along S bank of the Skagit R., deposits, mines—**hematite;** (2) Skagit R. gravel bars along entire length—placer **gold.**

LYMON, S 10 mi., numerous mines on Bald Mt.—**copper minerals.**

MARBLEMOUNT, 7 mi. above town, former mine—**talc.**

SKAMANIA CO.

AREA, Gifford Pinchot National Forest at Table Mt., region W and NW and N of a line drawn between Mt. St. Helens and Mt. Adams (best reached from COUGAR in Cowlitz Co. via Forest Service rds.)—**agate, carnelian, chalcedony, jasper, quartz crystals.**

SNOHOMISH CO.

DARRINGTON: (1) area stream gravels—**placer gold;** (2) area lode mines— **gold.**

GOLD BAR, placer sands along the Skykomish R.—**gold.**

GRANITE FALLS: (1) gravel bars of regional streams—**gold;** (2) area lode mines—**gold.**

INDEX, regional mines and prospects—**bornite, chalcocite, chalcopyrite** (bearing **gold** and **silver;** primarily mined for **gold** content).

MONTE CRISTO (District), area mines—**native arsenic, arsenopyrite, azurite, chalcopyrite, malachite, melaconite, pyrite** (gold-bearing), **pyrrhotite, realgar, scorodite.**

SILVERTON, area placer sands—**gold.**

STARTUP, area mines—**gold.**

STILAGUAMISH (District): (1) area mines, and (2) especially the Forty-Five Mine—**arsenopyrite, chalcopyrite, gold, pyrite, silver, tetrahedrite.**

SULTAN: (1) area placer mines along the Sultan R.—**gold;** (2) mines on the NE rim of the Sultan Basin—**azurite, malachite, garnets.**

SPOKANE CO.

CHATTAROY (N of SPOKANE on U.S. 2), gravels of the Little Spokane R. for entire length N and S—**garnets, quartz crystals.**

SPOKANE, SE 12 mi., at Silver Hill, area prospects—**cassiterite.**

STEVENS CO.

COLEVILLE: (1) area mines, as chief **silver**-bearing ore—**galena;** (2) the Copper King Mine—**chalcopyrite** (bearing **gold**).

LOON LAKE: (1) area **copper** mines—**azurite, argentiferous cosalite, huebnerite, malachite, pyrite;** (2) NE 5 mi., scattered through exposures of **quartz** veins—**pyrite.**

MARCUS: (1) area placers—**gold;** (2) Wilmot Bar, placers—**gold.**

MYERS FALLS, ORIENT (districts), regional lode mines—**gold.**

NORTHPORT, SE, near Deep Lake, area mines—**hematite.**

SPIRIT, E in Cedar Canyon (best reached from METALINE FALLS in Pend Oreille Co.): (1) area mines—**argentiferous cosalite, wolframite;** (2) in the adjoining Deer Trail District, the Silver Queen and Orchid mines—**argentite, cerargyrite.**

WHATCOM CO.

AREA, E side of co. and E of the S end of Ross Lake in the Pasayten Wilderness (a very rugged region open only 4–5 months per year; ref. USFS map for Okanogan and Mt. Baker National Forests, 1972), numerous lode mines of the Slate Cr. District, e.g., the New Lite Mine, the Allen Basin Mines, etc., in the Slate Cr. and Barron Cr. watersheds (best reached NW from MAZAMA in Okanogan Co. via dirt rds.)—**gold** (some **placer gold** in regional cr. gravels), **pyrite,** etc.

WHITMAN CO.

AREA: (1) gravel and sandbars of the Snake R., placers—**gold;** (2) Bald Butte, S side, area draws, washes, etc.—**smoky quartz crystals.**

PULLMAN, NE 5–6 mi. (near the Ida. line), area lava outcrops—**fire opal.**

YAKIMA CO.

AREA: (1) American R., (2) Morse Cr., (3) Summit District, (4) Surveyors Cr., regional placer operations—**gold.**

MABTON: (1) all regional draws, washes, hillsides, breaks, etc.—**opalized** and **petrified wood;** (2) regional stream gravels, placers—**gold.**

SUNNYSIDE: (1) NE 11 mi. on Rte. 241, area of S side of the Rattlesnake Hills—**opalized** and **petrified wood;** (2) NE 12–15 mi. (a few mi. S of jct. of Rte. 241 with Rte. 24), in the Rattlesnake Hills, all regional washes, draws, canyons, hillsides, in exposures of whitish volcanic ash—**opalized** and **petrified wood.**

YAKIMA: (1) E via jeep rds. to area of hills and flats, all regional draws, washes, etc.—**petrified wood;** (2) ENE, to the Yakima Ridge (restricted area of the Yakima Firing Center), E end of ridge at Cairn Hope Peak, area of S side (best reached from COLD CREEK in Benton Co.)—**opalized** and **petrified wood;** (3) ESE, in the Rattlesnake Hills (extending E into Benton

Co.), all regional draws, washes, canyons, hillsides, in volcanic ash exposures—**opalized** and **petrified wood** (often as entire logs). (The hills are part of the Yakima Ridge formations.)

WEST VIRGINIA

West Virginia is an irregularly bounded state of many contrasts and spectacular scenery, much of which remains almost in the same primeval wilderness first encountered by its pioneer settlers. With an average elevation above sea level of 1,500 feet, the state ranks as the highest geographic entity east of the Mississippi River. It has a low point of 247 feet at historic Harpers Ferry on the Potomac River in Jefferson Co. and a high point of 4,860 feet at Spruce Knob in Pendleton Co. near the Virginia boundary. About one-sixth of West Virginia lies in the Valley and Ridge Province east of the Allegheny Escarpment, where 15 counties expose fossiliferous Devonian strata. The rest of the state is covered by the Allegheny Plateau. The main range of the Allegheny Mountains runs in a series of rounded parallel ridges through the state from northeast to southwest, exposing igneous rocks most abundantly in Pendleton Co. and metamorphic rocks in Jefferson and Pocahontas counties.

More than half the state's 55 counties are occupied principally with **coal** mining or the production of **petroleum** and **natural gas. Clay, sand, gravel, sandstone, limestone,** and **slate** help place West Virginia fifth in the nation in basic mineral production. The 1943 discovery of some 2,400 square miles of **salt** bodes well for development of major chemical industries requiring sodium chloride as a basic ingredient.

Unlike other states in the general Appalachian belt, West Virginia lacks metallic minerals in minable quantities. **Gold** was saltatorially found in the 1920's on a few farms in Tucker Co. Only one important alluvial **diamond** has been found—a truly magnificent pale green crystal valued at $25,000. It was found by one "Punch" Jones while playing horseshoes and was loaned to the Smithsonian Institution. While **fossils** are found abundantly throughout exposures of Silurian, Devonian, and Mississippian formations, few gems or gemstones have ever been found, perhaps because the state has never been much prospected for them.

For information, write: West Virginia Geological and Economic Survey, Box 879, Morgantown.

BERKELEY CO.

AREA: (1) countywide limestone quarries (many flooded), in exposed levels and adjoining surroundings—**calcite, dolomite crystals, quartz crystals;** (2) 13 mi. W of the Blue Ridge, in the Slate District, regional pegmatites—**muscovite mica, pyrite.**

MARTINSBURG: (1) S 2 mi., limestone quarries, as gemmy crystals—**calcite, dolomite, quartz;** (2) NE 3 mi., poor-quality occurrence—**slate;** (3) N 3½ mi., on E side of U.S. 11, active limestone quarries—crystals of **calcite, dolomite,** and **fluorite; travertine** (banded, yellow).

BRAXTON CO.

STRANGE CREEK, deposit at mouth of cr. of same name—**siderite.**

CABELL CO.

BARBOURSVILLE, regional deposits along the Guyandot R.—**ocher.**

CLAY CO.

AREA, Standing Rock Run, some mines—**siderite.**
CLAY, some mines along Little Sycamore Cr. (tributary of the Elk R.)—**siderite.**

GRANT CO.

AREA, SE part of co., at South Fork Mt., area prospects—**hematite.**
MAYSVILLE: (1) quarry on Rte. 42, in Tuscarora sandstone—**rock crystal;** (2) Gosmer Gap, area deposit—**hematite;** (3) Kline Gap, E, mined deposit—**hematite.**
PETERSBURG: (1) E 2 mi., an abandoned quarry—**calcite, chert, dolomite** and **quartz crystals;** (2) 6 mi. out on Rte. 28, in North Fork Gap, a limestone quarry—**calcite, celestite, dolomite crystals, travertine.**

GREENBRIER CO.

AREA, around the Eckle School in fields, ditches, banks, etc., and excavations—**calcite, pyrite, rock crystal, sphalerite.**
ALVON, area **manganese** mines—botryoidal **psilomelane** and other **manganese minerals.**
FORT STRING, in the Acme Limestone Co. Quarry—**calcite, celestite, dolomite** and **quartz crystals, oolitic limestone.**
GLENMORE, area Oriskany formation **iron** ores—**hematite, fossil iron ore, manganese minerals.**
LEWISBURG, area at confluence of a small cr. (running parallel to Rte. 60) with the Greenbrier R.—**quartz crystals** (smoky brown, perfectly terminated).
RENICK (Sta.), E 1 mi., abandoned quarry on hillside above RR along river—**calcite, fluorite.**
RONCEVERTE, W 4 mi., area—**rock crystal.**
WILLIAMSBURG, area excavations, stream gravels, etc.—red **silicified coral, quartz crystals** (with inclusions).

HAMPSHIRE CO.

AREA, several exposures of the Keefer sandstone in co. (cf. on a geologic map)—**jasper.**

HANGING ROCK, S 1 mi., in outcrops of the Helderberg limestone—**rock crystal.**

MECHANICSBURG, E 2 mi. on U.S. 50, a quarry—**calcite** and **fluorite crystals.**

ROMNEY: (1) S 3 mi., in gap in Mill Cr. Mt. on U.S. 220, the Tonoloway Limestone Quarry—**calcite** and **dolomite crystals, chert, celestite, rock crystal;** (2) N 4 mi. on Rte. 26 (where Poland Rd. turns E), a quarry—**barite concretions, calcite, pyrite.**

HARDY CO.

AREA, numerous **iron** mines in co., on dumps—**iron minerals, jasper, pyrite.**

BAKER, NW 5 mi., on E slope of Branch Mt., area—**rock crystal** (clear, slightly smoky), **hematite.**

MOOREFIELD: (1) S 4 mi. on U.S. 220, rd. cut—**septarian nodules** (veined with **barite** and **dolomite crystals**); (2) 2 mi. from Asbury Church to slopes of South Branch Mt., area—**quartz crystals** (clear, milky, with **micaceous hematite** inclusions).

PERRY, area mines—**hematite.**

WARDENSVILLE: (1) area mines—**hematite;** (2) SW 9 mi. on Rte. 55, quarry on hillside N of Lost R. near the Baker Lime Plant—white **calcite,** crystals of **calcite** and **dolomite, travertine** (banded, yellow); (3) S 5 mi. on the Waites Run rd., old mine dumps—**hematite,** etc.

JEFFERSON CO.

AREA, SE part of co., turn N from Rte. 7 at Snickers Gap for 2 mi. on narrow rd., area rd. cuts, fields, banks, etc.—**amphiboles** (blue, green, fibrous), **quartz** (with **epidote**).

CHARLES TOWN: (1) E, at (a) the Moler Quarry (just W of the village of MILLVILLE), and (b) 1 mi. N of village at the Martin Marietta Co. Quarry—**dolomite** and **quartz crystals, pyrite;** (2) SE 7 mi., on E bank of the Shenandoah R., the Howell Zinc prospect in limestone—**dolomite crystals, galena, sphalerite.**

HARPERS FERRY, deposits along the Lost R.—**ocher.**

RIPPON, S, near state line on U.S. 340, a rd. cut through pegmatite—**tourmaline, zircon.**

SHEPHERDSTOWN: (1) area mines or excavations—**fluorite, ocher;** (2) a nearby quarry—**calcite, fluorite.**

KANAWHA CO.

CHARLESTON: (1) across South Side Bridge, then left onto Loudon Heights Rd. to Connell Rd., then 1½ mi. on to Woodvale Dr. and ¾ mi. to a sharp turn, area woodlands—**silicified wood;** (2) W 4 mi. on Rte. 14 to Davis Cr. bridge, then along the Davis Cr. rd. leading to the Berry Hills Country Club: (a) area stream banks and gravels—**petrified wood;** (b) soils and breaks in the timbered hills N of creek—**petrified wood.** (Some of the **petrified wood** has cavities lined with **drusy quartz crystals.**)

MERCER CO.

BLUEFIELD, a quarry on U.S. 21 By-pass—nodules of **chert** (jet black).
WILLOWTOWN, area quarries—**calcite onyx** (green-banded, semitranslucent).

MINERAL CO.

BURLINGTON, NW 1.9 mi., on Dry Run (off Mill Cr.), in outcrop of white **quartz—galena.**
KEYSER: (1) SE 1 mi., area mines—**hematite;** (2) 1.6 mi. W of SHORT GAP, the Aurora Stone Co. Quarry (just E of crest of Knobly Mt.)—**calcite** and **dolomite crystals, fluorite cubes, sulfur** (in **calcite**); (3) E along Rte. 46, on E face of Knobly Mt., a quarry—**chalcedony** (small **geodes,** massive variety containing prints of marine **fossils**), **rock crystal, sphalerite;** (4) E, at foot of a mt., two quarries—**calcite, chert, dolomite, celestite, fluorite,** gemmy black **limestone, banded travertine, native sulfur.**
NEW CREEK: (1) area, in angle between U.S. 50 and U.S. 220, a quarry—**calcite, chert;** (2) E 1 mi., prospects—**hematite,** red **quartzite.**
RIDGELEY: (1) S, at Cedar Cliff (on W face of Knobly Mt.), in limestone outcrop—blue **celestite crystals;** (2) S another mi., in RR cut on W base of Knobly Mt.—blue **calcite crystals.**

MONONGALIA CO.

BARKER, area coal mines, especially the Connellsville Coal Co. No. 1 Mine—**calcite, marcasite, pyrite, petrified wood.**
CASSVILLE, W, at heart of Scott Run—**opal stalactites.**
COOPERS ROCK, N 2½ mi., exposure—**hematite nodules, opal.**
MORGANTOWN: (1) NW 3 mi., at mouth of Scott Run—**pyrite** (concretions); (2) S of Booths Cr., rd. cut on hillside—**coal seam, pyrite** (with green **melanterite**); (3) S 4 mi., at UFFINGTON (on Rte. 73), in exposure of Brush Creek shale—**siderite** (nodules); (4) SE 8 mi., at GREER, area quarries—pink **calcite crystals.**
WESTOVER, S from rd. to EVERETTVILLE, at Grant Chapel turn right down steep hill to Lock 13 (on the Monongahela R.), walk ¼ mi. to sandstone cliffs above RR, area—**barite, melanterite, selenite, siderite nodules, sphalerite, travertine.**

MONROE CO.

ALDERSON: (1) halfway along rd. to Blue Sulphur Springs, exposures along rd.—**rock crystal** (brilliant, doubly terminated); (2) soils and cuts in Frankford and Neff's orchard—**agate.**

SWEET SPRINGS, area of Moss Mt.: (1) on summit, and (2) on SE flanks, diggings—**chert nodules, iron minerals, manganese minerals, psilomelane** (irregular nodules), **quartz crystals** (clear, smoky).

UNION: (1) area exposures and gravels along Turkey Cr.—**quartz crystals** (with clay inclusions); (2) the Fullen Bros. farm, loose in soils—**rock crystal;** (3) slopes of a hill between town and KNOBS, in rd. cuts—**rock crystal.**

MORGAN CO.

BERKELEY SPRINGS, NE, along Warm Springs Ridge (beginning 1 mi. NE of resort office and extending 4 mi. along U.S. 522), in area glass sand quarries—**calcite,** some **jasper, pyrite cubes, quartz** (crystals, milky), **selenite.**

ROCK GAP, 2 mi. N of entrance to Capapon Mt. State Park, on side rd. off U.S. 522, in a limestone quarry—crystals of **calcite, dolomite,** and **quartz.**

PENDLETON CO.

AREA, many igneous dike exposures in heavily forested region (little explored mineralogically)—igneous rock **crystals** and **minerals.**

FRANKLIN: (1) W 4 mi. on U.S. 33, near Friends Run in exposure of Oriskany sandstone—**chert, quartz crystals** (clear, smoky); (2) 7 mi. E of U.S. 220 jct. with U.S. 33, a quarry at Hively Gap on S side of rd.—**calcite crystals** (clear, white), **celestite, selenite** blades, **sulfur.**

JUDY GAP, limestone quarry between U.S. 33 and Rte. 28—**calcite crystals** (enclosed in **dolomite crystals**), **quartz crystals** (sparkling, silvery smoky), **travertine.**

RIVERTON: (1) E 3 mi. on U.S. 33 to quarry near Seneca Caverns—**barite,** banded **travertine;** (2) N 4 mi. on Rte. 28, turn onto Mill Cr. rd. for 1.6 mi., the Germany Valley Limestone Quarry—**fluorite cubes, lithographic limestone.**

SMOKE HOLE, area limestone cliffs—**fossils, geodes, gypsum, pyrite.**

POCAHONTAS CO.

EDRAY, E, off U.S. 219 on the Clover Lick rd. to State Road Commission quarry—**calcite, celestite** (light blue), **dolomite crystals, fluorite, gypsum** (chatoyant, nodules), **anhydrite.**

HILLSBORO: (1) just N of Mill Point, on N side of jct. of U.S. 219 with

Rte. 39, area—red **silicified corals;** (2) S 2 mi., off U.S. 219 along Locust Cr., gravels and banks—blue **silicified corals** (many varieties).

HUNTERSVILLE, the Possom Hollow mine dumps (1½ mi. SE of Browns Cr. and 1 mi. back of Rte. 89), as gemmy nodules—**chert.**

MINNEHAHA SPRINGS, S 9 mi., on **iron** mine dumps on SE slope of Beaver Lick Mt.—**iron minerals, psilomelane.**

RANDOLPH CO.

ELKINS: (1) off U.S. 219 on the Simmons farm, area—**pyrite cubes;** (2) the Paulina Limestone Quarry on U.S. 33—**calcite crystals** (pink, white).

HARMAN: (1) area exposures of the Greenbrier limestone—**calcite, dolomite crystals, quartz crystals;** (2) a local quarry—**travertine.**

HUTTONSVILLE, E 7 mi. on U.S. 250, a quarry—**calcite, rock crystal, pyrite.**

VALLEY BEND, S 2½ mi. on U.S. 219, in outcrop of gray sandstone—abundant **pyrite,** carbonized **fossils.**

TUCKER CO.

PARSONS: (1) outcrops of **quartz** in Sissaboo Hollow—**pyrite.** (This is an area of an abortive **gold** rush in 1927; assays show small amounts of **gold** in the outcrop.) (2) 8 mi. out at the Riley Moore farm on Clover Lick Run, in **quartz** outcrops—**pyrite.**

WETZEL CO.

NEW MARTINSVILLE, SW 3 mi., in sandstone exposures along the Ohio R. —**muscovite mica.**

WISCONSIN

Bordered by rivers and lakes, the Badger State is laid on a foundation of Precambrian gneisses, granites, syenites, and crystalline rocks of a hornblendic, micaceous, and chloritic nature. The oldest rocks are Eozoic in age, outcropping immediately south of Lake Superior, while a broad exposure of Upper Cambrian crystallines occurs throughout the west-central counties. Ordovician formations form a crescent-shaped belt extending from Green Bay in Brown Co. to the Illinois boundary and thence north to St. Croix Co. Silurian exposures extend all along the eastern part of the state, fronting onto Lake Michigan, while a very narrow strip of Devonian rocks outcrops between Sheboygan and Milwaukee in counties of the same names.

The highest point in Wisconsin is Rib Mountain in Marathon Co. with an elevation of 1,941 feet above sea level. Low, rounded hills of the Keweenaw and Gogebic ranges—Ordovician dome uplifts of Precambrian rocks—stretch across the northern counties, rich in **iron** ore. Topographically, Wisconsin was fashioned by the advance and retreat of all four great ice sheets of the Pleistocene epoch. The state lends its name to the last great advance of ice, which reached its maximum about 20,000 years ago and is still retreating from the Northern Hemisphere. Nevertheless, with some overlap into bordering states, nearly 10,000 square miles of the southwestern corner escaped the ice. This Driftless Area was protected by the Keweenaw and Gogebic ranges, which effectively deflected the slow-moving ice. Today, the Driftless Area presents many interesting examples of how the pre-Pleistocene land surfaces must have appeared throughout the northern states before the glaciers scraped and scoured it to bedrock.

The earlier Paleozoic formations which outcrop in numerous places reveal some carbonaceous beds, limestones, and **iron**-ore deposits. Thus **iron** mining has contributed a substantial share to an otherwise statewide farm and dairy economy.

Gems and gemstones are quite commonly found in Wisconsin; perhaps the most abundant and intrinsically interesting species is **Lake Superior agate,** which occurs in every county in almost every gravel deposit or pit, stream bed, excavation, mine, or quarry. Wherever the **agate** is found, there too are usually fine **quartz crystals.** Other gemstones frequently encountered are a brownish red to orange **aventurine,** a gemmy **albite peristerite** known locally as **Wisconsin moonstone** or **labradorite.** Along with these occur **epidote, rhodonite,** and **unakite,** while the **catlinite (pipestone)** so valued by prehistoric Indians is found in Barron Co. Metallic minerals often found, especially in the mining districts, include fine crystals of **calcite, galena, marcasite, pyrite,** and **sphalerite,** most of which are remarkably brilliant and sparkling.

Among the candidates for "Wisconsin state stone" must surely be the **pearl.** Practically every unpolluted stream or creek in the state, especially in the southern counties along the Mississippi River, is noted for **pearl**-growing fresh-water mussels. One of the English crown jewels is a Wisconsin **pearl,** originally valued at more than $20,000, that was found in a Mississippi River mussel bed at Prairie du Chien in Crawford Co. Another true gem that is found all over the state in glacial moraines, and most abundantly from the counties around Milwaukee, is **diamond.** These alluvial crystals were brought into Wisconsin by the Pleistocene glaciers from completely unknown sources. The first **diamond** found in Wisconsin was discovered in Waukesha Co., and the largest find, a 21-carat crystal, was made in adjoining Washington Co.

For information, write: State Geologist, Wisconsin Geological and Natural History Survey, 115 Science Hall, University of Wisconsin, Madison.

ASHLAND CO.

AREA, regional stream gravels—**agate, jasper.**
MELLEN, N, area of Copper Falls State Park, some—**native copper.**

BARRON CO.

RICE LAKE, E 5 mi., area quarries—**catlinite,** gemmy **quartzite** (banded red and white).

BAYFIELD CO.

AREA, stream gravels, pits, excavations—**agate, jasper.**
GRANDVIEW, area **marble** quarries—gemmy **marble.**

CHIPPEWA CO.

AREA, Penokee Gap (along the Chippewa R.), mixed ores in area mines—**hematite, magnetite.**
CHIPPEWA FALLS, area quarries and gravel pits—**Lake Superior agates, quartz crystals.**

CLARK CO.

NEILLSVILLE, regional stream gravels of co., particularly in the Black R. and its tributaries—**agate, jasper.**
OWEN, area gravels of pits, streams, etc.—**jasper.**

CRAWFORD CO.

PRAIRIE DU CHIEN: (1) area quarries, stream gravels, excavations, etc.—**agates;** (2) Mississippi R. beds, fresh-water mussels (commercially dredged) —gem **pearls.**

DANE CO.

OREGON, SW 2½ mi., gravels of the Kettle Moraine—**diamond.**

DODGE CO.

IRON RIDGE, MAYVILLE, regional mines—**hematite ("Clinton" or "fossil" iron ore).**

DOUGLAS CO.

AREA, sandstone exposures along the Annicon, Brule, and Black rivers—
native copper.
GORDON, on banks of Ounce Cr., an abandoned **copper** mine—**diopside,
epidote, copper minerals, native copper.**

DUNN CO.

COLFAX, area quarries—**fossils.**
MENOMONIE, area gravel pits and quarries—**Lake Superior agates.**

FLORENCE CO.

COMMONWEALTH, FLORENCE, mines in the W extension of the Menominee
Range, especially in T. 40 N, R. 18 E, in beds of great thickness—**hematite**
(hard red **iron** ore), **limonite.**
HOMESTEAD, S, in area schist exposures—**chalcopyrite.**

GRANT CO.

BOSCOBEL, Wisconsin R. bed, mussels—gem **pearls.**
CASSVILLE, regional gravel deposits, quarries, stream beds—**agates, quartz
crystals.**
CUBA CITY, area mines—**barite, calcite, galena, marcasite, pyrite, smith-
sonite, sphalerite,** etc.
HAZEL GREEN, regional mine dumps—cf. CUBA CITY.
MUSCODA, area quarries, stream gravels, pits, etc.—**agates.**
PLATTEVILLE, area mine dumps—cf. CUBA CITY.
POTOSI, in beds in the Grant R., mussels—gem **pearls.**
TENNYSON, area mine dumps—cf. CUBA CITY.
WERLEY, area mine dumps—**barite, dogtooth calcite crystals, galena,
marcasite, pyrite, smithsonite, sphalerite,** etc.

GRANT, IOWA, LAFAYETTE COS.

REGION. The **lead** and **zinc** mines of these three counties constitute what
is known as the "zinc region," with very many active and inactive mines and
sizable dumps—**azurite, barite** (deleterious gangue mineral), **chalcocite,
chalcopyrite, cerussite** (a secondary mineral), **flint nodules** (abundant,
gemmy), **galena, marcasite, pyrite, smithsonite, sphalerite,** etc.

GREEN CO.

MONROE, area mines—**galena,** etc.

GREEN LAKE CO.

BERLIN, UTLEY, regional quarries—gemmy **rhyolite.**

IOWA CO.

COBB: (1) W ½ mi., in NW¼NW¼Sec. 2, T. 6 N, R. 1 E; (2) SW 4–5 mi., at Centerville; and (3) N 5 mi., the Eberle Mine (on Rte. 80), on all dumps—**aurichalite, azurite, chalcocite, chalcopyrite, cuprite, malachite, smithsonite, sphalerite,** etc.; (4) W 5 mi., co. line mines around MONTFORD (in Grant Co.)—**galena, pyrite, smithsonite, sphalerite,** etc.

DODGEVILLE, mines in E part of town—**barite, calcite, galena, marcasite, nickel minerals, pyrite, smithsonite, sphalerite.**

HIGHLAND, LIVINGSTON, MIFFLIN, all regional mines—cf. DODGEVILLE.

LINDEN, area mines near Rte. 39—**barite, calcite, galena, marcasite, nickel minerals, pyrite, smithsonite, sphalerite,** etc.

MINERAL POINT, area mine dumps—**azurite, barite, chalcocite, chalcopyrite, calcite, native copper, galena, pyrite, marcasite, smithsonite, sphalerite, wad,** etc.

IRON CO.

AREA: (1) regional sandstones and epidotized traprock, especially along the Montreal R.—**native copper;** (2) regional stream gravels, gravel pits, excavations, etc.—**agate, jasper;** (3) E side of co., in the Penokee-Gogebic Range, as large ore deposit of soft red or brownish red consistency—**hematite, specular hematite** (hard, steely).

HURLEY: (1) the Montreal Mine (deepest **iron** mine in the world, with shafts 4,000 ft. deep), on dumps—crystals of **bladed barite, bladed selenite, calcite, manganese, rhodochrosite, goethite** (radiating, stalactitelike), **vanadinite** (first discovered here in state); (2) E 1 mi., the Cary Mine—cf. item (1).

POWELL, area mine dumps—**garnets,** gem **kyanite.**

LA CROSSE CO.

LA CROSSE: (1) area quarries, gravel pits, stream gravels—**Lake Superior agates;** (2) bluffs of the Mississippi R. (along entire W boundary of state)—**Lake Superior agates, jasper,** occasional **diamond, fossils.**

LAFAYETTE CO.

BENTON, SHULLSBURG, all regional mine dumps—**barite, calcite, galena, marcasite, pyrite, smithsonite, sphalerite,** etc.

MARATHON CO.

HALDER, W to jct. of Rte. 153 with Rd. H, then N 1 mi., area outcrops—**epidote, unakite.**

WAUSAU: (1) SW side of town, at Rib Mt. (highest elevation in state at 1,941 ft.), along rd. leading to summit—massive **rhodochrosite, quartz crystals;** (2) N, to intersection called Little Yellow Schoolhouse, area pegmatite dikes—gemmy bright red **granite,** abundant **albite peristerite ("Wisconsin moonstone" or "labradorite").**

OCONTO CO.

MOUNTAIN, S, in granite quarry—**arsenopyrite, chalcopyrite.**

TOWNSEND, N 3.3 mi. on Rte. 32, park by entrance to old trail, walk 500 yds. to a **quartz** outcrop—gemmy **quartz crystals, specular hematite.** A giant **quartz** outcrop known locally as McCauslin Mountain extends for 20 mi. along the boundaries of Oconto, Forest, and Marinette counties, 4 mi. wide, bounded on the W by Rte. 32, on the N by Rd. C, and on the S by Rd. F.

OUTAGAMIE CO.

GREEN BAY, ONEIDA, SEYMOUR, regional stream gravels and gravel pits—gem **rubies** and **sapphires.**

OZAUKEE CO.

SAUKVILLE, area glacial moraine gravels, occasional—**diamonds.**

PEPIN CO.

DURAND, area quarries and gravel pits—**Lake Superior agates.**

PIERCE CO.

DIAMOND BLUFF, in the area moraine gravels, occasional—**diamond.**

ROCK ELM (Twp.), gravels of Plum Cr.—placer **gold, diamonds.**

PORTAGE CO.

STEVENS POINT, area mines—**actinolite asbestos.**

RACINE CO.

BURLINGTON, area moraine gravels (in pits, excavations, etc.)—**diamonds.** In regional quarries along Rte. 83 all way to WAUKESHA in Waukesha Co. are found **fossil crinoids** and **tribolites** (to several in. long, fully extended).

RACINE: (1) area quarries, excellent specimens—gem **crystals, fossil crinoids;** (2) the Ives Quarry—gemmy **calcite crystals,** large bladed **marcasite crystals.**

SAUK CO.

AREA, the Baraboo Range, regional deposits and mines—**hematite.**

BARABOO, S, at Devil's Lake (State Park), extensive **quartz** deposit extending E toward Columbia Co., many regional quarries—**Lake Superior agates.**

ROCK SPRINGS, N, at Ableman Narrows, in rd. cuts exposing **quartzite,** as fine pinkish crystals to 1 in. long—**quartz crystals** (matted over **quartzite** matrix).

SAWYER CO.

OJIBWA, regional stream gravels of co., especially along the Chippewa R.—**agate, jasper.**

SHAWANO CO.

TIGERTON, in gravels of the South Branch of the Embarrass R.—gem **beryl crystals.**

WAUKESHA CO.

EAGLE, in gravels, pits, excavations in the Kettle Moraine—**diamonds.** This large glacial moraine deposit extends N and NE for approx. 15 mi. and has been the source of many fine gems.

MILWAUKEE: (1) Estabrook Park (along the Milwaukee R.)—**millerite crystals** (in **calcite**); (2) outside park boundaries, on W side of river—**geodes;** (3) Franklin Quarry—**calcite crystals, trilobites;** (4) the Hartung Quarry—**fossil trilobites.**

WAUKESHA, WASHINGTON, RACINE, OZAUKEE, DANE COS.

REGION, all stream gravels and gravel pits in these southeastern counties, among the most abundant sources for alluvial crystals in America—**diamonds.**

WAUPACA CO.

CLINTONVILLE, area deposits—**ocher** (red, yellow).

WINNEBAGO CO.

OSHKOSH, the Lutz Quarry—**calcite, galena, marcasite, pyrite, sphalerite, fossils** (sometimes lined with **drusy quartz crystals**).

WOOD CO.

AREA: (1) central part of co., in stream gravels; and (2) on regional mine dumps of co.—**agate, aventurine, quartzite** (gemmy).

MARSHFIELD to WISCONSIN RAPIDS, a large and varied **quartz** occurrence, in numerous sandstone quarries in contact zones of pre-Keweenawan igneous rocks and Upper Cambrian sandstone—gemmy colored **quartz,** gem **aventurine.**

WYOMING

A state of many contrasts, from barren sagebrush-covered deserts to high plateaus and perennially snow-crested mountain ranges, Wyoming literally marks the western end of the Great Plains. From the South Dakota border, the Black Hills break westward into eroded badlands and sagebrush plains that sweep outward to the Powder River ("a mile wide and an inch deep"). Near the middle of this nearly square state the Great Plains end abruptly in the steep slants of the Big Horn Mountains. Stretching 150 air miles south from the Montana line and 50 air miles broad, this mammoth fault-block range divides the northern half of the state and crests in Cloud Peak, 13,165 feet high, on the eastern edge of Big Horn County. The generally high tablelands of southeastern Wyoming are interrupted by the snowy Laramie and Medicine Bow ranges, while western Wyoming is mostly high, rugged, practically impenetrable mountains that support the erratic Continental Divide. To the south the giant transverse range of the Uinta Mountains looms along the skyline of Utah.

The character of western Wyoming was formed predominantly by extremely violent volcanic activity which followed the Laramide revolution of 100 million years ago, separating the Mesozoic and Cenozoic eras. Yellowstone National Park, where much of the later volcanism is prominently displayed, dominates the northwestern corner of the state. This geologically important park is guarded on its approaches by such great ranges as the Miocene volcanic-conglomerate Absarokas on the east, the Gros Ventre and Wind River ranges on the southeast, and the Precambrian Tetons to the south.

In the central part of the state southwest of the Big Horn Mountains, the strongly eroded, barren Owl Creek Mountains along the south-western boundary of Hot Springs Co. reveal the entire geologic history of North America. Clearly defined exposures along the 20-mile Wind River Canyon rise from the most ancient Precambrian schists, stratum by stratum, right up to the last Quaternary gravels in streams still flowing at full spring runoff—a time span exceeding 4 billion years. State highway markers along U.S. 20 between Shoshoni in Fremont Co. and Thermop-olis in Washakie Co. label the succession of formations, as layer by layer in the steeply dipping uplift the road cuts sliced through them. This is quite possibly the only easily reached spot in the entire continent where all the major pages of geologic history are readable in unbroken suc-cession.

South of the glaciated Wind River Range that begins at the south-eastern corner of Teton National Park lies the Great South Pass, made famous by the Old Oregon Trail between 1828 and 1869. Here, at either Atlantic City or South Pass City—both ghost mining camps immediately east of the Continental Divide—the gem and mineral collector finds him-self in the heart of a fabulous, historic **gold**-mining, **gemstone,** and **petrified wood** country 8,000 feet above sea level. To the east and south lies the vast Red Desert, with the heart of the famed Wyoming **jade** fields at Lander in Fremont Co. Farther west on the sunset side of the Con-tinental Divide lie entire mountains of **fossil fish** and widespread **opalized** and **silicified forests** containing uncounted stone stumps and tree trunks two to six feet in diameter. These petrified logs contain cavi-ties lined with lovely **amethyst** and **quartz crystals** of exceptional bril-liance and color.

Nearly every county affords the collector with a wide variety of in-teresting gems, gemstones, colorful minerals, and fossils. The plains and mountains have been prospected for minerals since 1842, and there are many ghost mining camps hidden in the farther reaches. Probably the first mineral actually mined was **hematite ocher,** used by prehistoric In-dians in war paint through a hundred centuries of man's occupancy of the Great Basin states. Modern commercial minerals which contribute to a basic stock-raising economy include an enormous wealth in **petroleum** and **natural gas,** great untouched reserves of **coal, gypsum, bentonite, ceramic clays, glass sands,** and **uranium.** Wyoming is also a minor **gold**-producing state with a total output through 1965 of about 82,000 ounces, primarily from Douglas Creek and the Atlantic City-South Pass City mines in Fremont Co.

For information, write: Geological Survey, University of Wyoming, Laramie.

ALBANY CO.

AREA: (1) extreme NE corner of co., 8 mi. NW of Laramie Peak (10 mi. SW of ESTERBROOK in Converse Co.), in SE corner of T. 28 N, R. 73 W, the

Hoosier Group (of mines)—**chalcocite, chalcopyrite;** (2) Sportsman Lake, E 1 mi., a prospect—**gypsum.**

COMO BLUFF: (1) in N½ Sec. 35, T. 23 N, R. 77 W, extensive deposit—**gypsum;** (2) N side of U.S. 30/287 and near adjoining Carbon Co. line, area —**petrified dinosaur bones.** Here is the site of the world-renowned "dinosaur graveyard" discovered in 1877 and considered the most prolific fossil bed ever discovered for reptilian remains.

CUMMINS CITY, SW ½ mi., the Copper Queen Mine—**chalcocite, native copper, cuprite, tenorite,** etc.

HOLMES: (1) the Rambler Mine—**barite, lorandite** (deep red crystals), **orpiment, realgar;** (2) Grand Encampment District, area mines and prospects —**azurite, malachite.**

JELM (BOSWELL): (1) S end of Jelm Mt., in Sec. 24, T. 13 N, R. 77 W, area mines—**bismutite, native bismuth;** (2) W, in pegmatite in SE¼ Sec. 32, T. 13 N, R. 78 W, the Many Values prospect—**muscovite mica** (books speckled with **magnetite** and ruled), **fergusonite** (?), **garnets** (pink euhedral, orange subhedral), **tantalite.**

LARAMIE: (1) numerous outcrops within city limits, abundant—**gypsite;** (2) NE 5 mi., outcrops, pure—**gypsum.**

MARSHALL: (1) area draws, washes, surfaces, etc.—**agate, opalized** and **silicified wood;** (2) E and SE, on E slopes of the Laramie Mts.: (a) all regional draws, canyons, washes, etc.—**agate, chalcedony, jasper,** etc.; (b) in regional metamorphic rock exposures throughout the mts.—**iolite (cordierite).**

RED BUTTES, area 1 mi. S of the Red Buttes, a deposit—**gypsum.**

RED MOUNTAIN, regional outcrops—**gypsum.**

WOODS LANDING, just S of bridge in weathered brown **mica** schists, large numbers of low-grade but interesting crystals—**garnets.**

BIG HORN CO.

AREA: (1) Big Horn Mts., Willet Cr., SE, two dikes—**galena, pyrite;** (2) SE corner of co., the Zeismann Ranch, in SE¼ Sec. 34, T. 49 N, R. 89 W, a number of area outcropping beds—**gypsum.**

BASIN, E, at Stucco in T. 53 N, R. 94 W, area mines—**gypsum.**

CLOVERLY, E, in Red Gulch, interbedded deposits in 125-ft.-thick stratum of red shales—**gypsum.**

COWLEY, N 5 mi., in Dry Gulch near its head, a deposit—**bentonite.**

FRANNIE: (1) E 8 mi., a deposit in the Thermopolis Formation—**bentonite;** (2) the Silver Tip Coal Mine in Sec. 29, T. 58 N, R. 100 W—**bentonite, coal.**

GREYBULL: (1) N, the Wyo-Ben Mine—**bentonite;** (2) NE, the Magnet Cove Mine—**bentonite;** (3) N 3 mi., on N side of Shell Cr., in a 47-ft.-thick bed—**gypsum.** (The red sandstone beds that encircle Sheep Mt. to the N and extend E to the base of the Big Horn Mts. contain many nearly pure deposits of **gypsum,** usually at the base of the Chugwater Formation.) (4) E: (a) 10 mi., at the Reeves Ranch, in SE¼ Sec. 11, T. 52 N, R. 92 W (3 mi. SE of Shell Cr.), in the Morrison formation—**uranium minerals** (often found in **petrified dinosaur bones**); (b) all the badlands region stretching E of the Big Horn R. to the Big Horn Mts., regional draws, canyons, washes, outcrops, etc.— **gastroliths, petrified dinosaur bones, marine fossils** (Jurassic age); (5) N 18 mi., in T. 54 N, R. 95 W, an outcrop 1 mi. long—**bentonite.**

HYATTVILLE, numerous outcrops and beds in surrounding region—**gypsum, dinosaur bones, gastroliths, marine fossils.**

KANE, S at RR section stop of SPENCE, S ¼–½ mi., in bluffs above W side of RR tracks—**calcite crystals.**

LOVELL: (1) S 3 mi., various ranges of low barren hills, scattered deposits and mines—**calcite, gypsum;** (2) SE 3–10 mi., on W hogbacks and low buttes surrounding Sheep Mt.—**gypsum, marine fossils** (Jurassic age); (3) E and SE, extensive badlands region extending to base of Big Horn Mts., regional draws, washes, canyons, bluffs, etc.—**fossil ammonites, cephalopods, dinosaur bones, gastroliths;** (4) E 30 mi., to summit of Big Horn Mts. (most usual approach), area of Bald Mt. City and the Medicine Wheel—see in Sheridan Co.; (5) N 40 mi., the TX Ranch (straddling the Mont. line at E end of the Pryor Mts.): (a) area surfaces along the crest of Black Canyon of the Big Horn R.— **concretions** (resembling petrified turtles, to 2 ft. dia.), **"Dry Head" agate** (fortification, in briliant red-and-white patterning), **Indian artifacts.** (Through this ranch in the **agate** area the prehistoric Old Sioux Trail crosses from the Montana Yellowstone R. country into the Wyoming Big Horn Basin, a seasonal migration route worn 4 ft. deep in places, probably of Uto-Aztecan origins many thousands of years prior to Sioux or Crow Indian entry into the region.) (b) The Little Mt. area in T. 58 N, R. 94 W (a long anticlinal ridge trending NW–SE between East Pryor Mt. in Mont. and the main mass of the Big Horn Mts. in Wyo., many area prospects and mines—**metatyuyamunite, tyuyamunite** (both **uranium minerals** associated with **calcite**).

PAINTROCK, area along Paintrock Cr., in Upper Chugwater beds as deposits —**gypsum.**

SHELL: (1) W on U.S. 14 to N-trending dirt rd., then N several mi. to famed dinosaur beds—**petrified dinosaur bones, gastroliths,** etc.; (2) mouth of Shell Cr. Canyon, 12-ft.-thick bed—**gypsum.**

CARBON CO.

AREA, large geographic triangle cornered by RAWLINS on the W, MEDICINE BOW on the E, and LEA-KORTEZ DAM on the N, all regional washes, draws, cut banks, etc.—**jade.**

BAGGS: (1) surrounding region, and (2) Poison Basin area, many radioactive mines and prospects—**coffinite, ilsemannite, meta-autunite, pyrite, schroeckingerite** (erratically distributed), **uranophane, uraninite.**

ELK MOUNTAIN: (1) area, extensive beds covered with Tertiary debris— **gypsum;** (2) N and NE, and to S of Sheephead Mt., the Rattlesnake Creek Syncline, numerous beds—**bentonite.**

ENCAMPMENT (District): (1) SW 1½ mi., deposit—**amphibole asbestos;** (2) W, to 2 mi. NW of Bridger Peak (elev. 11,007 ft.) and about ¼ mi. E of rd. between RUDEFEHA and SARATOGA, the Creede Mine—**cobaltite, erythrite, linnaeite, pyrrhotite;** (3) S 6 mi., a mine—**bismuth minerals, native bismuth;** (4) W, in the Sierra Madre: (a) many regional mines and prospects— **copper minerals;** (b) head of Jack Cr., near the Continental Divide, the Leighton-Gentry prospect—**cobalt minerals.**

MEDICINE BOW: (1) E and SE, numerous exposures—**bentonite;** (2) W 1–3 mi., at base of the Mesaverde formation, a mine—**bentonite;** (3) N, the Flattop Anticline (extending several mi. along the Little Medicine Bow R.), many regional outcrops—**gypsum;** (4) N 35 mi. (on Rte. 487 to jct., then NE on dirt rd.), petrified forest area in Shirley Basin (shown on maps)—**opalized wood.**

SARATOGA: (1) N, along both sides of Rte. 130 all way to WALCOTT, regional draws, washes, surfaces, etc.—**opalized wood** (fluoresces green); (2) in the Saratoga Mts., at E end (about 6 mi. from the Buzzard Ranch), on N side of the Ferris Mts. near Sand Pass, a mine—**arsenopyrite;** (3) SW 19 mi., the Meta Mine—**barite.**

SEMINOE, S of Freezeout Mt., in Chugwater beds in Sec. 11, 14, T. 24 N, R. 79 W, deposits—**gypsum.**

CONVERSE CO.

BILL, the Powder R. Basin, S area: (1) in the monument Hill district of the Dry Fork of the Cheyenne R., and (2) S, in the Box Cr. district, many regional mines and prospects—**uranium minerals.**

COLD SPRING, NE, in N end of the Laramie Mts., many mines and prospects—**copper minerals.**

DOUGLAS: (1) SW 12 mi., Moss Agate Hill (on maps), area slopes, washes, etc.—**moss agate, chalcedony, jasper,** etc.; (2) SW 30 mi., the Copper King Mine (on Crazy Horse Cr.)—**chalcopyrite,** etc.

GLENROCK: (1) E, in Boxelder Cr. Canyon, S of its jct. with the N Platte R., area surfaces, draws, etc.—**chalcedony geodes, quartz crystals;** (2) NE, in Sec. 20, T. 32 N, R. 75 W, the Stardust claim—**chrysolite, vermiculite;** (3) SW 15 mi., the Deer Creek Mine (in Sec. 11, T. 31 N, R. 77 W, along the steep-walled valley of Deer Cr. Canyon)—**chromite, kammererite, wolchonskoite.**

CROOK CO.

AREA, Warrens Peak, regional mines—**azurite, malachite.**

SUNDANCE: (1) E, in the Black Hills, N section, many exposures—**bentonite.** (In the beds which encircle the Black Hills are very many exposures of **bentonite.**) (2) NW approx. 8 mi., the Copper Prince Mine—**chrysocolla,** some **gold, malachite;** (3) N 10 mi., in the Bear Lodge District in the Black Hills National Forest, numerous mines—**fluorite, gold.**

FREMONT CO.

AREA: (1) far S part of co.: (a) in gravels of the Sweetwater R.—**agates;** (b) Long Cr., N to its jct. with the Sweetwater R.—**agates, nephrite jade;** (2) all SE part of co. N of the Sweetwater R., regional washes, draws, cr. beds, etc.—**agate, chalcedony, jasper,** etc.; (3) N of the Sweetwater R. in Twps. 30, 31 N, Ranges 89, 90, 91 W, all regional surfaces, draws, washes, etc.—**"Sweetwater" agates;** (4) Copper Mt., 14 sq. mi. between mt. and Cedar

Ridge, numerous mines and prospects—**uranium minerals;** (5) NW of the Granite Mts., area—**chalcedony;** (6) NW part of co., the Bridger District, the Yankee Jack Mine, as fine specimens—**argentite, native bismuth.**

ATLANTIC CITY (ghost town 24 mi. S of LANDER and just E of the Continental Divide off Rte. 28—4 mi. E of SOUTH PASS CITY, *q.v.*—in the foothill plateau at the SE end of the Wind River Mts., alt. about 7,800 ft.): (1) many area placer and lode mines—**arsenopyrite, copper minerals, gold, orpiment, realgar:** (2) N 4 mi., the Fire King deposit in Sec. 15, T. 31 N, R. 97 W—**asbestos.**

ATLANTIC CITY-SOUTH PASS CITY, regional stream gravels, draws, washes, gulleys, hillsides, etc.—**agate, chalcedony, gold, nephrite jade, jasper, muscovite mica, quartz crystals, agatized** and **opalized wood, searlesite, shortite crystals,** massive **tourmaline.**

BURRIS, W, on slopes and in draws, washes, etc., of the NE flank of the Wind River Mts., many exposures—**bentonite.**

FT. WASHAKIE, NW 10 mi., in broad area along both sides of U.S. 287—**moss agate, chalcedony, jasper,** etc.

JEFFREY CITY: (1) S, in Green Mts.: (a) area washes, draws, etc., and (b) N side of Beaver Divide, area—**agate** (banded, moss), **aventurine, garnets, sapphires;** (2) E on U.S. 287 to co. line and corner where Fremont, Natrona, and Carbon counties meet, all regional draws, washes, gravels, etc. —**"Sweetwater" agates, nephrite jade.**

LANDER: (1) region, including COTTONWOOD, HAYPRESS, and WARM SPRINGS, heart of the famous **jade** region. The collecting region runs approximately 140 mi. E–W and 60 mi. N–S, including parts of Carbon, Natrona, Sublette, and Sweetwater counties. It takes in FARSON (W of the Great South Pass), the Red Desert (S and SE of South Pass in Sweetwater Co.), and SEMINOE DAM and ALCOVA in Carbon Co.—**agate, jasper, nephrite ("Wyoming" jade).** (2) SE 40 mi. on U.S. 287 to the Sweetwater R., entire area on both sides of river for many mi.—**"Sweetwater" agates** (gray, bluish, dendritic, speckled).

MARION, area gravels—**rhodonite, rubies.**

RIVERTON, gravel beds of the Wind R. and its tributaries—**agates, chalcedony, jasper,** etc.

SHOSHONI: (1) NE 15 mi. (20 mi. SE of THERMOPOLIS in Hot Springs Co.) and E of the Wind River Canyon, pegmatite outcrops—**aquamarine, beryl, feldspar crystals, muscovite mica;** (2) NW many mi. via dirt rds., to W end of the Owl Creek Mts.: (a) the Abernathy deposit in Sec. 5, T. 7 N, R. 5 W (Wind River Meridian), and (b) Sec. 7, T. 42 N, R. 104 W (standard meridian), area mines—**amphibole asbestos.**

SOUTH PASS CITY (4 mi. W of ATLANTIC CITY, *q.v.*): (1) area mines—**gold.** This historic ghost town was noted for its early-day mining, especially the Carissa Mine high on the hillside above town, which still operates occasionally. Site of the inception of woman suffrage in America, the town is a center for mineral collectors and historians. (2) Burnt Ranch in the headwaters of the Sweetwater R., 10 mi. upstream, at point where the old Camp Stanbaugh rd. crossed the stream, abundant in stream gravels—**garnets;** (3) SW, the Beaver Cr. deposit (5 mi. S of Beaver Hill in Sec. 19, T. 30 N, R. 100 W)—**chrysotile asbestos.**

WARM SPRINGS, regional foothills and draws of the Wind R. Range—**agate, chalcedony, jasper, nephrite jade, quartz crystals, silicified wood.**

GOSHEN CO.

FT. LARAMIE, NW: (1) in NE¼ Sec. 26, T. 28 N, R. 65 W, the Vaughn or Vulcan claims, as nodules—**arsenopyrite;** (2) in N-central part of Sec. 35, the Savage claim, in pegmatite—**beryl** (crystals to 4 ft. long have been found).

JAY ELM, regional land surfaces, draws, washes, gravels, etc.—**agate, malachite, onyx.**

HOT SPRINGS CO.

AREA: (1) regional quarries in co.—**alabaster;** (2) far W end of co., along headwaters of Owl Cr., SE of the Washakie Needles, rich placer sands—**gold.**

THERMOPOLIS: (1) within city limits are numerous high, conical natural fountains flowing water sheets down sides, brightly colored—**geyserite;** (2) area along the Big Horn R. as colorfully formed high mineral bluffs and at short intervals between the river and Owl Cr.—**selenite crystals, travertine;** (3) W 2½ mi., a deposit of **gypsum;** (4) SW 18 mi., area mines—**copper stains, limonite.** THERMOPOLIS is the site of Hot Spring State Park, a prehistoric Indian "peace spa" donated in perpetuity to the white man to be "forever free to all races of men." The enormous hot springs rank among the largest in the world, and indoor and outdoor plunges, as well as baths, attract visitors from all continents.

JOHNSON CO.

BUFFALO: (1) NE 12 mi., along both sides of U.S. 16—**agate, chalcedony, gastroliths, jasp-agate, jasper, petrified wood, quartz crystals;** (2) E about 20 mi. on Int. 90, to region of Crazy Woman Cr. and the Crazy Woman Petrified Forest, general region—**opalized** and **silicified wood;** (3) SW, at head of Kelley Cr., placers—**gold;** (4) W about 40 mi. on U.S. 16, to summit of Powder R. Pass in the Big Horn Mts. (elev. 9,666 ft.), on a ridge just N of hwy. in SE¼ Sec. 4, T. 48 N, R. 85 W, mines—**azurite, malachite, pyrite.**

KAYCEE, area mines—**bentonite.**

LARAMIE CO.

AREA: (1) the Adams Copper King Mine—**barite, copper minerals;** (2) the Silver Crown District, area mines—**copper minerals, gold, silver;** (3) NW corner of co., in gravels of Chugwater Cr. (extending NE to CHUGWATER in Goshen Co.)—**bloodstone (heliotrope).**

GRANITE CANYON, 4 mi. away in Sec. 25, 26, T. 15 N, R. 70 W, area mines—**copper minerals, gold, silver.**

IRON MOUNTAIN, area mines and prospects—**iron minerals.**

LINCOLN CO.

AREA, all regional outcrops of the Green R. formation in this and adjoining counties—**agate, turritella agate** (brown **agate** filled with silicified shells of *Goniobasis*), **chalcedony, chert, jasp-agate, quartz crystals, petrified** and **silicified wood.**

BORDER, area deposits, claims, and mines within 3 mi.—**orpiment.**

KEMMERER: (1) badlands region along the Green R., (2) especially along Hams Fork, and (3) all surrounding area breaks, washes, etc.—cf. AREA. (4) W 12 mi., a mountain of **fossil fish.**

NATRONA CO.

AREA: (1) gravels of Sage Hen Cr.—**agate, chalcedony, jasper,** etc.; (2) extreme SW corner of co., in gravels of the Sweetwater R., especially in area 8 mi. E of Split Rock—**"Sweetwater" agates.**

CASPER: (1) area quarries—**agate, alabaster, amazonite;** (2) 8 mi. out, at the Casper Mt. **asbestos** deposit in Sec. 16, 17, T. 39 N, R. 79 W—**chrysotile asbestos;** (3) S about 9 mi., the Haystack Range District (covering about 2 sq. mi.), many pegmatite outcrops—**beryl, muscovite mica, black tourmaline;** (4) W 40 mi.: (a) gravels of Poison Spider Cr., and (b) washes, draws, breaks, and gravels of a broad surrounding region—**agate, chalcedony, jasp-agate, jasper,** etc.

PARK CO.

AREA, the Brown Bear deposit in Sec. 19, 20, T. 47 N, R. 116 W—**asbestos (amphibole, chrysotile).**

CODY: (1) SW, a quarry—**gypsum;** (2) W 3 mi.: (a) along U.S. 14/20, in Sec. 3, 10, T. 52 N, R. 102 W, a mine on S side of the Shoshone R.—**sulfur;** (b) along E side of Cedar Mt., from the Shoshone R. south for about 2 mi., as a terrace formed from mineral hot springs—**travertine;** (c) on N side of the Shoshone R. at foot of Rattlesnake Mt. in T. 53 N, R. 102 W, a deposit containing an estimated 25 million tons—**anhydrite;** (3) NW 4 mi., a mine—**bentonite.** (On the W side of the Big Horn Basin, **bentonite** is common throughout a stratigraphic range of 1,500 ft.) (4) NW approx. 50 air mi., the Sunlight Basin District (in the Absaroka Mts. and 35 mi. SE of COOKE CITY, Mont.): (a) area mines—**copper, lead;** (b) regional draws, canyons, soils, etc.—**agate, chalcedony, placer gold, jasper, petrified** and **opalized wood;** (c) Sulphur Lake, near Sunlight Cr., in a NW–SE series of deposits—**sulfur.** (The Sunlight Basin region is exceptionally rugged, and roads require much caution.)

MEETEETSEE: (1) area gravels of the Greybull R.—**agate, jasper;** (2) S 38 mi., near headwaters of the North Fork of the Wood R., the Kirwin Mine (in T. 45 N, R. 104 W)—**azurite, barite, chalcopyrite, cuprite, galena, gold, limonite, malachite, molybdenite, pyrite, quartz crystals, siderite, specularite, sphalerite, stephanite, tetrahedrite.**

PLATTE CO.

HARTVILLE: (1) W, in regional draws, washes, flats, etc.—**agate** (seam, moss-seam), **chalcedony;** (2) region of the Hartville Uplift, ½ mi. W of the highest peak of the Rawhide Buttes, the Copper Belt mines, e.g., the Omaha, Gold Hill, and Emma claims—**azurite, bornite, chalcocite, chrysocolla, malachite,** etc.

SUNRISE: (1) the N½ Sec. 7, T. 27 N, R. 65 W, a mine—**barite, copper minerals;** (2) the Green Hope Mine in NW¼ Sec. 26, T. 29 N, R. 65 W— **arsenopyrite.**

WHEATLAND, area of the Cooney Hills, a large deposit—**garnet.**

SHERIDAN CO.

SHERIDAN, W about 60 mi. on U.S. 14 and 14A: (1) dirt rd. turnoff to old mining camp of Bald Mt. City: (a) headwaters of the Little Big Horn R. (elev. 9,000 ft.), mines in T. 56 N, R. 91 W, low-grade, free-milling ores— **gold.** This short-lived mining camp of original log cabins (now entirely removed) was established in 1882 following discovery of gold by Ed Sealey, a hog buyer for Swift & Co. The flour **gold** was in black dirt and hard **quartzite,** and a log stamp mill was built about 1 mi. W of town. (b) Take USFS rd. to summit of Medicine Rim (walk last ¼ mi. from parking space), W and N on the narrow limestone plateau, in limestone crevices—**petrified corals.** On the crest of Medicine Rim (most usually reached from LOVELL, *q.v.,* in Big Horn Co.) lies the Medicine Wheel, a prehistoric Indian monument probably constructed by Uto-Aztecans two millennia ago as a primitive calendar system that may have been the forerunner of the Aztec calendar stone in Mexico City. (2) Area of Pass Cr. (near the Wyo.-Mont. line), S to Little Goose Cr., a continuous outcrop—**gypsum.**

SOAP CREEK, N of the North Platte R. in Sec. 24, T. 33 N, R. 81 W, bedded deposits—**bentonite.**

SWEETWATER CO.

AREA, all regional exposures of the Green River formation—**agate, chalcedony, chert, jasp-agate, jasper, petrified** and **silicified wood, quartz crystals, turritella agate** (silicified *Goniobasis* shells in brown **agate** matrix; takes a high polish, with every microscopic detail of the shells visible).

EDEN, the Eden Valley (famed petrified forest area), loose in surface gravels of draws, washes, flats, etc.—**"Eden Valley" wood** (coal black, silicified, takes a high polish; found as pieces of logs, limbs, twigs, stumps).

FARSON: (1) gravels of the Big Sandy R. and all tributary gulches and draws (river is a dry watercourse); (2) E and NE, widespread region of foothills, canyons, draws, flats, etc., of the distant Wind R. Range (no motorized travel within boundaries of the wilderness preserve)—**agate, chalcedony, chert, jasp-agate, jasper, quartz crystals, "Eden Valley" wood**, etc.

GRANGER, in talus debris of buttes along U.S. 30 to BLACK FORK—**turritella agate**.

GREEN RIVER, W, along both sides of U.S. 30 as far as FT. BRIDGER in Uinta Co., broad region of draws, flats, washes—**agate, chalcedony, chert, jasper, silicified wood**.

RINER, W, along both sides of Int. 80 (including all side rds.) to ROCK SPRINGS: (1) region of the Red Desert, and (2) the vast expanses of the Great Divide Basin (both sides of the Continental Divide, which here is literally as "flat as a pancake" with a completely imperceptible rise, elev. around 7,000 ft. above sea level)—cf. FARSON. (Cf. SUPERIOR, on N side rd. from THAYER JCT.)

ROCK SPRINGS, E, along Int. 80—cf. RINER, in reverse direction.

SUPERIOR, N 15 mi., slopes and draws of Steamboat Mt. (in the Leucite Hills)—**agate, chalcedony, jasper, petrified wood**.

WAMSUTTER: (1) SW 3½ mi., along Bitter Cr., extending for 3 mi. as a ledge of lignite and shale in which occurs—**alum (stschemigite)**; (2) S 8 mi., then W to the famed **turritella agate** beds, high quality—**turritella agate**; (3) SW 15 mi., regional flats, draws, canyons, etc. of the Delaney Rim—**turritella agate**.

TETON CO.

AREA, NE corner of co.: (1) region of the SW side of the rugged Absaroka Range, in draws, flats, canyon gravels—**opalized wood**; (2) the Thorofare Wilderness, area stream gravels—**agate, jasper, opalized** and **silicified wood**.

MORAN JCT.: (1) N, on co. or USFS rds. to the Buffalo Fork of the Snake R. (about 35 mi. SE of SNAKE RIVER on S boundary of Yellowstone National Park), area mines—**copper minerals**; (2) N on U.S. 89/287 to within 6 mi. of the south entrance to Yellowstone National Park, headwaters of Berry Cr. and 2 mi. E of the Teton Range watershed, a deposit—**asbestos (amphibole, chrysotile)**; (3) E on U.S. 26/287 to summit of Togwotee Pass (elev. 9,658 ft.): (a) SW 3 mi., the Black Rock Meadows (in T. 44 N, R. 110 W), a deposit—**bentonite**; (b) S 10 mi., in Teton Canyon, area—**bentonite**.

UINTA CO.

AREA, NE corner of co.: (1) along Black Fork Cr. (cf. GRANGER in Sweetwater Co.)—**silicified algae, turritella agate**; (2) regional outcrops of the Green River formation—**agate** (common, turritella), **chalcedony, chert, jasp-agate, jasper, quartz crystals, petrified** and **silicified wood**.

EVANSTON, S 6 mi., and just W of Meyers Bridge in Sec. 30, T. 14 N, R. 119 W—**bentonite**.

FORT BRIDGER, regional gravels (streams, flats, washes, etc.)—**agate** (common, turritella), **jasper, silicified algae**.

WASHAKIE CO.

TENSLEEP: (1) NW 2 mi., along W side of No Wood Cr. and the N side of U.S. 16, as well as in many other regional exposures—**gypsum;** (2) SE 12 mi., at the head of Bud Kimball Draw, a deposit—**bentonite.**

WORLAND, broad regional bench gravels and sides and bottoms of regional draws, washes, etc.—**agate, chalcedony, jasper** (red, yellow), **quartzite.**

WESTON CO.

NEWCASTLE: (1) SE, E, and NE, along Stockade Beaver Cr., an extensive deposit—**gypsum;** (2) N 10 mi., in the valley 2 mi. SE of Mt. Pisgah, deposits—**gypsum.**

YELLOWSTONE NATIONAL PARK

While no collecting is permitted within park boundaries, an enormous amount of gemstone minerals which can be listed for the park itself also can be found in the regional streams, talus slopes, and erosional debris outside its boundaries; unfortunately, there are no access roads, only trails requiring wilderness survival techniques—**agate, amethyst, chalcedony, chert, jasp-agate, jasper, geodes, fossils, nodules, obsidian** (notably whole mountains and giant cliffs along the main hwy.), **opal, opalized** and **silicified woods, quartz crystals, thundereggs, travertine** (including **geyserite**), etc.

Appendixes

Gemstone and Mineral Essentials

The gemstones and minerals which are to be found in the collecting sites identified in Part II are listed here in alphabetical order together with their essential characteristics. Those with a Mohs scale hardness of 6 or above may be termed *gemstones* as well as *minerals,* the generic term for all rock species. Abbreviations used are: H, hardness; G, specific gravity.

achroite Colorless **tourmaline,** *q.v.*

acmite (aegirite) A soda **pyroxene,** *q.v.*, $NaFeSi_2O_6$; monoclinic-prismatic; luster glassy; color black, brown, or green in thin sections; H, 6–6.5; G, 3.4–3.5; fracture uneven; cleavage easy prismatic; brittle; translucent on thin edges.

actinolite (tremolite) Calcium magnesium (iron) silicate: **actinolite,** $Ca_2(Mg,Fe)_5Si_8O_{22}(OH)_2$; **tremolite,** $Ca_2Mg_5Si_8O_{22}(OH)_2$. Monoclinic–prismatic; luster glassy; color white, light green, dark green, violet; H, 5–6; G, 3–3.3; fracture subconchoidal to uneven; cleavage perfect prismatic; transparent to translucent.

adamantine spar Bronzy brown chatoyant **corundum,** *q.v.*

adamite Basic zinc arsenate, $Zn_2(OH)AsO_4$; orthorhombic–rhombic bipyramidal; H, 3.5; G, 4.3–4.4; fracture uneven; cleavage domal; brittle; transparent to translucent; often fluorescent yellow green.

adularia Variety of orthoclase **feldspar,** *q.v.* Named from Adular, Switzerland. This mineral forms colorless to white prismatic crystals, glassy, sometimes quite large.

aegirite Cf. **acmite.**

agalmatolite Cf. **muscovite.**

agate Colorfully banded **chalcedony,** *q.v.*

alabaster Cf. **gypsum;** a calcium sulfate occurring massively in hydrous form, most often found as sedimentary beds from the alteration of **anhydrite,** *q.v.*

albandite Manganee sulfide, MnS; isometric, usually granular massive; perfect cubic cleavage; submetallic; iron black to dark brown; streak green; H, 3.5–4; G, 3.95–4.04.

albite Cf. **feldspar.** Sodium aluminum silicate, $NaAlSi_3O_8$; triclinic–pinacoidal; luster glassy, color white; H, 6; G, 2.63; fracture conchoidal; cleavage good at 94°, poor prismatic; internal flashes.

albite moonstone Variety of **albite,** *q.v.,* with bluish reflections.

algodonite (domeykite) Associated minerals of Keeweenaw Peninsula, Mich., copper mines. **Algodonite:** bright steel gray, luster metallic (tarnishes dull); H, 4; G, 8.4; **domeykite:** silvery, luster metallic (tarnishes yellowish to dark brown); H, 3–3.5; G, 7.5; occurs as masses or veinlets in white quartz.

allanite Rare-earth silicate $(Ca,Ce,La,Na)_2(Al,Fe,Be,Mn,Mg)_3(SiO_4)_3$-(OH); monoclinic-prismatic; luster resinous; color black to dark brown; H, 5.5–6; G, 2.7–4.2; fracture subconchoidal to uneven; cleavage poor; translucent on edges; radioactive.

allanite-orthite Cf. **allanite;** a basic calcium-iron-aluminum-cerium silicate.

alleghanyite Basic manganese fluosilicate, $Mn_5(SiO_4)_2(OH,F)_2$; orthorhombic, in irregular grains; H, 5.5; G, 4; color bright to grayish pink. May be identical to **tephroite,** *q.v.*

allophane Hydrous aluminum silicate, $Al_2SiO_5 \cdot nH_2O$; amorphous, incrustations; very brittle; luster vitreous; colorless, pale sky blue, green, brown; streak colorless; H, 3; G, 1.85–1.89.

almandine garnet Cf. **garnet.** Iron aluminum silicate, $Fe_3Al_2S_3O_{12}$; cubic –hexoctahedral; luster glassy; color deep violet red; H, 6–7.5; G, 4.3; fracture conchoidal to uneven; cleavage none; transparent to translucent.

alstonite Cf. **bromlite** and **witherite.**

altaite Lead telluride, PbTe; isometric, small octahedrons and massive; luster metallic; sectile; color tin-white to dark gray, with a yellowish tinge tarnishing to bronze-yellow; H, 3; G, 8.16. The yellow coating of lead and the violet solution for tellurium help to identify this mineral.

alunite Hydrous aluminum potassium sulfate, $KAl_3(SO_4)_2(OH)_6$; hexagonal–ditrigonal pyramidal; luster vitreous to pearly; color white, grayish, flesh red; H, 3.5–4; G, 2.6–2.9; fracture flat conchoidal to uneven; cleavage fair basal, poor rhombohedral; brittle; translucent to transparent; may fluoresce orange.

alunogen Hydrous aluminum sulfate, $Al_2(SO_4)_3 \cdot 16H_2O$; monoclinic, fibrous masses; luster vitreous to silky; color white; H, 1.5; G, 1.6–1.8.

amalgam Cf. **gold amalgam.**

amarantite Hydrous iron sulfate, $Fe_2O_3 \cdot 2SO_3 \cdot 7H_2O$; triclinic, crystals slender prismatic; usually columnar or bladed aggregates, sometimes radiated; clevage perfect pinacoidal; brittle; H, 2.5; G, 2.11.

amargosite Cf. **montmorillonite.**

amazonite Variety of microcline **feldspar,** *q.v.;* color bright green.

amber Fossil resin; luster oily; color yellowish to reddish brown or yellowish brown; H, 2–2.5; G, 1.05–1.10; fracture conchoidal; cleavage none; transparent.

amblygonite Lithium aluminum fluophosphate, $LiAl(PO_4)(F,OH)$; triclinic–pinacoidal; luster glassy; colorless to white, light greenish gray; H, 5.5–6; G, 3–3.1; fracture uneven; cleavage perfect basal; brittle; transparent to translucent; often fluorescent weakly orange.

amethyst Variety of crystal **quartz,** *q.v.;* color violet to purple.

ammonia alum Cf. **tschermigite.**

amphibole In this group are a series of complex silicates of magnesium, iron, calcium, and aluminum, or varying combinations of these elements. Amphiboles, which include **anthophyllite, actinolite-tremolite,** and **hornblende,** *q.v.,* are common rock-forming minerals, found in both igneous and metamorphic rocks.

amphibolite Metamorphic rock composed of **amphibole** or **hornblende,** *q.v.* (Massive hornblende is amphibole.)

analcime (analcite) Hydrous sodium aluminum silicate, $NaAlSi_2O_6 \cdot H_2O$; cubic–hexoctahedral; luster glassy; colorless, white, greenish, reddish; H, 5–5.5; G, 2.3; fracture subconchoidal; cleavage slightly cubic; transparent to translucent.

anapite Hydrous calcium and iron phosphate $(Ca,Fe)_3(PO_4)_2 \cdot 4H_2O$; triclinic, usually in tabular crystals; two cleavages; luster vitreous; color pale green; H, 3.5; G, 2.8. Becomes magnetic on heating and yields water in a closed tube.

anatase Titanium oxide, TiO_2; tetragonal–ditetragonal bipyramidal; luster adamantine to submetallic; color blue, brown, light yellow; H, 5.5–6; G, 3.8–3.9; fracture subconchoidal; cleavage perfect basal and pyramidal; streak white; brittle; translucent to transparent.

anauxite Hydrous aluminum silicate, $Al_8(Si_4O_{10})_3(OH)_{12} \cdot 3H_2O$; monoclinic, in crystal plates with hexagonal outline; perfect basal cleavage; luster pearly; color white to pale brown; H, 2.5; G, 2.5.

ancylite Hydrous basic carbonate of strontium and cerium, $Sr_3Ce_4(CO_3)_7(OH) \cdot 3H_2O$.

andalusite Aluminum silicate, Al_2SiO_5; orthorhombic–rhombic bipyramidal; luster glassy; color brown, gray, pink, white; H, 7.5; G, 3.1–3.2; fracture conchoidal; cleavage fair prismatic; transparent to translucent.

andersonite Secondary hydrous sodium calcium uranium carbonate, $Na_2Ca(UO_2)(CO_3)_3 \cdot 6H_2O$; common in western U.S. uranium mines.

andesine Variety of **plagioclase,** *q.v.;* H, 6; G, 2.68. Derived from fine-grained **andesite** lavas.

andesite Basic volcanic lava composed mainly of **plagioclase feldspar,** *q.v.*

andradite garnet Cf. **garnet.** Calcium iron silicate, $Ca_3Fe_2Si_3O_{12}$; cubic–hexoctahedral; luster glassy; color pale brown to black; H, 6–7.5; G, 3.8; fracture conchoidal to uneven; no cleavage; transparent to translucent.

anglesite Lead sulfate, $PbSO_4$; orthorhombic, prismatic and tabular crystals; massive, granular to compact; brittle; luster adamantine; color white, yellow, gray, green; streak colorless; H, 2.5–3; G, 6.3–6.9.

anhydrite Calcium sulfate, $CaSO_4$; orthorhombic–rhombic bipyramidal; luster glassy to pearly; colorless, gray, lilac, white; H, 3–3.5; G, 3; fracture uneven to splintery; cleavage good pinacoidal; transparent to translucent.

ankerite Carbonate of calcium, magnesium, iron, and manganese, $CaCO_3 \cdot (Mg,Fe,Mn)CO_3$; hexagonal–rhombohedral; in rhombohedral crystals, but also crystalline massive, granular; cleavage like **calcite,** *q.v.;* luster vitreous to pearly; color white to brown; H, 3.5–4; G, 2.95–3.1.

annabergite Hydrous nickel cobalt arsenate $(Ni,Co)_3(AsO_4)_2 \cdot 8H_2O$; apple green masses or capillary crystals, isomorphous with **erythrite,** *q.v.*

anorthite Cf. **feldspar.**

anorthoclase Cf. **feldspar.**

anthophyllite   Basic silicate of magnesium and iron $(Mg,Fe)_7Si_8O_{22}(OH)_2$; orthorhombic, prismatic, commonly lamellar or fibrous massive; cleavage perfect prismatic; luster vitreous; color brownish gray, brownish green; streak colorless or grayish; H, 5.5–6; G, 2.85–3.2. (Cf. also **amphibole**.)

antimonite   Antimony sulfide, Sb_2S_3; orthorhombic–bipyramidal; luster metallic; color steel gray; H, 2; G, 4.5–4.6; fracture subconchoidal; cleavage perfect side pinacoid; sectile. (Cf. **stibnite**.)

antimony   Native element, Sb; hexagonal–rhombohedral, generally massive, lamellar; perfect basal cleavage; brittle; luster metallic; color and streak tin-white; H, 3.5; G, 6.7.

Apache tears   Variety of **obsidian,** *q.v.,* as small nodules.

apatite   Calcium fluo- (or chloro-) phosphate, $Ca_5(Cl,F)(PO_4)_3$; luster glassy; colorless, blue, brown, green, violet, white, yellow; H, 5; G. 3.1–3.2; fracture conchoidal; cleavage slightly basal; brittle; transparent to translucent; may fluoresce yellow orange.

aphthitalite (glaserite)   Sulfate of potassium and sodium $(K,Na)_2SO_4$; hexagonal–rhombohedral, tabular crystals; massive and in crusts; cleavage prismatic; brittle; luster vitreous; color white; H, 3; G, 2.7.

aplite   A fine-grained, whitish granite consisting almost entirely of quartz and feldspar; found generally in dikes.

aplome   Dark brown or green **andradite garnet,** *q.v.,* containing manganese.

apophyllite   Hydrous calcium potassium fluosilicate, $KCa_4FSi_4O_{10}\cdot8H_2O$; tetragonal–ditetragonal bipyramidal; luster glassy; colorless, greenish, pale pink, white; H, 4.5–5; G, 2.3–2.4; fracture uneven; cleavage perfect basal; transparent to translucent.

aquamarine   Blue and blue green varieties of **beryl,** *q.v.*

aragonite   Calcium carbonate, $CaCO_3$; orthorhombic–rhombic bipyramidal; luster vitreous; colorless, light yellow, white; H, 3.5–4; G, 2.9–3; fracture subconchoidal; cleavage poor; brittle; transparent to translucent; fluorescent and phosphorescent. (Cf. **calcite**.)

aragotite   Cf. **idrialite.**

arcantite   Potassium sulfate, K_2SO_4; orthorhombic, thin plates; luster vitreous; colorless to yellowish; H, 2; G, 2.66.

argentian gold (electrum)   A pale yellow natural alloy of gold and silver.

argentite   Silver sulfide, Ag_2S; cubic–hexoctahedral; luster metallic; color dark lead gray; H, 2–2.5; G, 7.3; fracture subconchoidal; cleavage poor cubic; sectile.

argillite   A soft gray metamorphosed clay with no slaty cleavage, used for carving by Haida and Thlingit Indians of the Pacific Northwest; takes a fine polish and is easily carved by ordinary steel tools.

Arizona ruby   **Pyrope garnet,** *q.v.*

arsenic   Native element, As; hexagonal–rhombohedral, generally granular massive; sometimes reticulated, reniform, or stalactitic; cleavage perfect basal; brittle; luster metallic; color and streak tin-white, tarnishing to dark gray; H, 3.5; G, 5.7.

arseniosiderite   Basic calcium iron arsenate, $Ca_3Fe(AsO_4)\cdot3Fe(OH)_3$; tetragonal or orthorhombic; in fibrous concretions; cleavage basal; luster silky; color yellowish brown; H, 1.5; G, 3.5–3.9.

arsenolite (white arsenic)   Arsenic oxide, As_2O_3; isometric, commonly in fibrous crusts and earthy; cleavage octahedral; luster silky or vitreous; colorless or white; H, 1.5; G, 3.7.

arsenopyrite   Iron sulfarsenide, FeAsS; monoclinic–prismatic; luster metallic; color silver white; H, 5.5–6; G, 5.9–6.2; fracture uneven; cleavage prismatic; brittle.

artinite   Hydrous basic magnesium carbonate, $Mg_2(CO_3)(OH)_2 \cdot 3H_2O$; monoclinic, as crusts of acicular crystals; botryoidal masses of silky fibers, as spherical aggregates of radiating fibers and as cross-fiber veinlets; cleavage pinacoidal (100) perfect, basal pinacoidal (001) good; brittle; luster of fibrous aggregates silky, of individual crystals vitreous; color and streak white; transparent; H, 2.5; G, 2.02. Soluble in cold acids with effervescence.

asbestos   Fibrous or asbestiform **serpentine,** *q.v.,* as an alteration product of basic igneous rocks rich in magnesian silicates. (Cf. **chrysotile.**)

asbolite   Cf. **psilomelane.**

ascharite   Cf. **szaibelyite.**

atacamite   Hydrous copper oxychloride, $Cu_2Cl(OH)_3$; orthorhombic, slender needles and fibrous reticulated masses; cleavage one perfect; brittle; luster adamantine to vitreous; color bright green to black green; streak apple green; H, 3–3.5; G, 3.7. Soluble easily in acids.

augelite   Basic aluminum phosphate, $Al_2(PO_4)(OH)_3$; monoclinic–prismatic; luster glassy; colorless, rose, yellowish, white; H, 4.5–5; G, 2.7; fracture conchoidal; cleavage good (two); brittle; transparent to translucent.

augite   Cf. **pyroxene.** A mixed silicate mineral of calcium, magnesium, iron, and aluminum $Ca(Mg,Fe,Al)(Si,Al)_2O_6$; monoclinic–prismatic; luster glassy; color dark green to black; H, 5–6; G, 3.2–3.4; fracture uneven; cleavage perfect prismatic. (A constituent of basic lavas.)

aurichalcite   Basic carbonate of zinc and copper, $2(Zn,Cu)CO_3 \cdot 3(Zn,Cu)(OH)_2$; monoclinic; plumose, tabular, laminated; in drusy incrustations; luster pearly; color and streak pale green to sky blue; H, 2; G, 3.54–3.64. Easily soluble in acids with effervescence.

autunite   Hydrous calcium uranium phosphate, $Ca(UO_2)_2(PO_4)_2 \cdot 11H_2O$; tetragonal–ditetragonal bipyramidal; luster glassy to pearly; color lemon to greenish yellow; H, 2–2.5; G, 3.1; cleavage perfect basal and prismatic; brittle; translucent; fluorescent brilliant green.

aventurine   Name given to various minerals, such as the **feldspars,** because of contained waferlike inclusions that reflect light like tiny mirrors, an effect known as aventurescence.

awaruite (terrestrial nickel-iron)   A native alloy of **nickel** and **iron,** approximately $FeNi_2$; isometric, grains and nuggets; color tin-white to steelgray; H, 5; G, 8.1; magnetic.

axinite   Hydrous borosilicate of calcium, manganese, iron, and aluminum, $H(Ca,Mn,Fe)_3Al_2B(SiO_4)_4$; triclinic–pinacoidal; luster glassy; color gray, violet brown, yellow orange; H, 6.5–7; G, 3.3–3.4; fracture conchoidal; cleavage one good; transparent to translucent.

azurite   Basic copper carbonate, $Cu_3(OH)_2(CO_3)_2$; monoclinic–prismatic; luster glassy; color light blue, dark blue, to black; H, 3.5–4; G, 3.8; fracture conchoidal; cleavage one good, two poor; brittle; transparent in thin slivers.

azurmalachite   A double mineral containing **azurite,** *q.v.,* and **malachite,** *q.v.,* in alternating bands.

babingtonite   Hydrous calcium iron silicate, $Ca_2Fe''Fe'''Si_5O_{14}(OH)$; triclinic–pinacoidal; luster glassy; color black; H, 5.5–6; G, 3.4; fracture conchoidal; cleavage two pinacoidal; translucent on edges.

bakerite   Hydrous calcium silicoborate, $Ca_4B_4(BO_4)(SiO_4)_3·H_2O$; amorphous, massive; color white to faint green; H, 4.5; G, 2.7–2.9.

banded rhyolite (wonderstone)   Porous **rhyolite** in which mineral-laden infiltrations of water have left bands; color cream, pale brown, red, yellow; H, 2.5–3.5; G, 4.3–4.6.

barite   Barium sulfate. $BaSO_4$; orthorhombic–rhombic bipyramidal; luster glassy; colorless to bluish, brown, reddish, yellow; H, 3–3.5; G, 4.3–4.6; fracture uneven; cleavage perfect basal and prismatic; brittle; transparent to translucent. Very heat-sensitive.

barkevikite   A soda-**amphibole**, *q.v.*, i.e., a **hornblende** rich in ferrous iron and alkalis.

barytocelestite   Cf. **celestite.**

bassanite   Hydrous calcium sulfate, $2CaSO_4·H_2O$; monoclinic, pseudohexagonal; fibrous; color snow white; H, undetermined; G, 2.7.

bastite   An altered **enstatite**, *q.v.*, having the approximate composition of **serpentine**, *q.v.*, with a bronzy iridescent luster (a schiller effect) on its chief cleavage face; occurs as green or brown foliated masses in igneous rocks.

bastnaesite   Rare-earth fluocarbonate, approximately $(CeLa)(CO_3)F$; hexagonal, usually massive, occasionally tabular crystals; cleavage indistinct; luster vitreous to greasy; color wax-yellow to reddish brown; transparent to translucent; H, 4–4.5; G, 4.9–5.2.

bauxite   A mixture of aluminum oxides, $Al(OH)_3 + Al$ and H_2O; amorphous; luster dull; color white to red brown; H, 1–3; G, 2–2.5; fracture earthy.

bavenite   Hydrous beryllium aluminum and calcium silicate, $Ca_4BeAl_2Si_9O_{25}(OH)_2$; monoclinic, in fibrous-radiated groups of prismatic crystals; one cleavage; colorless to white; H, 5.5; G, 2.7.

bayldonite   Basic arsenate of copper and lead $(Cu,Pb)_2(AsO_4)(OH)(?)$; possibly monoclinic; minute mammillary concretions with fibrous structure and drusy surface, also massive and as crusts; luster resinous; color light green to apple green and yellow green; subtransparent to transparent; H, 4.5; G, 5.5. (Primarily from Tsumeb, South West Africa.)

beaverite   Hydrous copper lead iron sulfate, $Pb(Cu,Fe,Al)_3(SO_4)_2(OH)_6$; microscopic canary yellow plates.

beckite (beekite)   Silicified **coral**, *q.v.*

beidellite   Hydrous aluminum silicate, $Al_8(Si_4O_{10})_3(OH)_{12}·12H_2O$; orthorhombic(?), in thin crystal plates; one cleavage; luster waxy to vitreous; color white, reddish, or brownish gray; H, 1.5; G, 2.6; becomes plastic in water.

bementite   Hydrous manganese silicate, $Mn_5Si_4O_{10}(OH)_6$; orthorhombic, fine fibrous masses and granular; luster vitreous to pearly; color pale grayish yellow to light brown; H, 4–6; G, 2.98.

benitoite   Barium titanium silicate, $BaTiSi_3O_9$; hexagonal-ditrigonal bipyramidal; luster glassy; color blue to white; H, 6–6.5; G, 3.6; fracture conchoidal; cleavage poor pyramidal. (Most specimens badly flawed.)

bentonite   Chemically altered volcanic ash; cf. **montmorillonite.**

berthierite   Iron-antimony sulfide, $FeSb_2S_4$; orthorhombic, long prismatic, usually fibrous massive; luster metallic; color dark steel gray; streak grayish black; H, 2–3; G, 4–4.3; becomes magnetic when roasted.

bertrandite Hydrous beryllium silicate, $Be_4Si_2O_7(OH)_2$; orthorhombic–hemimorphic, small tabular or prismatic crystals; cleavage perfect prismatic; colorless to pale yellow; H, 6–7; G, 2.6. A rare pegmatite mineral associated with **beryl.**

beryl Beryllium aluminum silicate, $Be_3Al_2Si_6O_{18}$; hexagonal-dihexagonal bipyramidal; luster glassy; color blue (**aquamarine**), yellow brown (**golden beryl**), yellow green (**green beryl**), green (**emerald**), pink or purplish pink (**morganite**), white (**goshenite**); also pale orange, pale reddish orange; H, 8; G, 2.6–2.8; fracture conchoidal; cleavage poor basal; transparent to translucent. Most common gem beryl is greenish aquamarine; emerald usually flawed.

beta-ascharite Cf. **szaibelyite.**

beyerite Carbonate of bismuth and calcium, $Ca(BiO)_2(CO_3)_2$; tetragonal, thin rectangular plates flattened parallel to the basal pinacoid; compact earthy masses; luster vitreous in crystals; color bright yellow to lemon yellow, but yellowish white to grayish green and gray in massive material; fracture conchoidal in crystals; H, 2–3; G, 6.56 (less in massive, porous material).

bieberite Hydrous cobalt sulfate, $CoSO_4 \cdot 7H_2O$; monoclinic, stalactites and crusts; luster vitreous; color flesh and rose red; H, 2; G, 2; has an astringent taste.

bindheimite Pyroantimonate of lead, $Pb_2Sb_2O_6(O,OH)$; isometric, as cryptocrystalline masses, dense to earthy; incrustations; nodular and reniform masses with concentric layering, sometimes opaline; pseudomorphous; fracture earthy to conchoidal; luster resinous to dull or earthy; color yellow, brown, reddish brown, gray, white, greenish; streak white to yellow; opaque to translucent; H, 4–4.5; G, 4.6–5.6; widely distributed in oxidized ores.

biotite Hydrous silicate of potassium, magnesium, iron, aluminum, $K(Mg,Fe)_3AlSi_3O_{10}(OH)_2$ monoclinic–domatic; luster glassy; color dark brown to black; H, 2.5–3; G, 2.8–3.4; flexible-elastic (a mica); cleavage perfect basal; opaque to translucent.

bismite Bismuth ocher, Bi_2O_3; monoclinic, massive, compact granular to earthy and pulverulent; luster subadamantine to dull; color grayish green, greenish yellow to bright yellow; streak grayish to yellow; H, 4.5 (less in earthy material); G, 8.64–9.22.

bismuth-gold (maldonite) An elemental compound, Au_2Bi; isometric, massive, granular and in thin coatings; malleable and sectile; luster metallic; color pinkish silver white on fresh fracture, tarnishing copper red to black; H, 1.5; G, 15.46. Soluble only in aqua regia.

bismuthinite Bismuth sulfide, Bi_2S_3; orthorhombic, usually fibrous massive; luster metallic; color and streak lead-gray; H, 2; G, 6.4–6.5.

bismuth ocher Cf. **bismutite.**

bismutite Bismuth carbonate, $(BiO)_2CO_3$; incrusting fibrous, or earthy and pulverent; luster vitreous to dull; color white, green, yellow, gray; streak greenish gray; H, 4; G, 7; effervescent in acid. Derived chiefly from alteration of bismuthinite and native bismuth. Also called **bismutosphaerite.**

black jack Cf. **sphalerite.**

black lead Cf. **graphite.**

bloedite Hydrous magnesium and sodium sulfate, $MgSO_4 \cdot Na_2SO_4 \cdot 4H_2O$; monoclinic, prismatic crystals, granular massive; luster vitreous; colorless to greenish, yellowish, red; H, 3; G, 2.23. Soluble in water.

bloodstone   Dark green **agate,** *q.v.*, spotted with blood-red dots; a variety of moss agate with iron oxide inclusions.

blue vitrol (bluestone)   Hydrous copper sulfate; cf. **chalcanthite.**

boehmite   Basic oxide of aluminum, $AlO(OH)$; microscopic orthorhombic plates; cleavage good in one direction.

boothite   Hydrous cupric sulfate, $CuSO_4 \cdot 7H_2O$; monoclinic, fibrous massive; luster vitreous; color greenish blue; H, 2–2.5; G, 1.94. Differs from **chalcanthite** (blue vitrol) in having two additional molecules of water of crystallization.

boracite   Magnesium borate with chlorine, $Mg_6Cl_2B_{14}O_{26}$; isometric–tetrahedral, crystals cubic and tetrahedral, massive; color greenish, white, inclining to gray; H, 7; G, 2.9–3.0; no cleavage.

borax   Hydrous sodium borate, $Na_2B_4O_7 \cdot 10H_2O$; monoclinic–prismatic; luster glassy; colorless, bluish, grayish, yellowish; H, 2–2.5; G, 1.7; fracture conchoidal; cleavage three, one good; brittle; transparent to translucent; efflorescent.

bornite   Copper iron sulfide, Cu_5FeS_4; cubic–hexoctahedral; luster bronzy metallic, tarnishing to purple; H, 3; G, 4.9–5.4; fracture uneven; cleavage poor octahedral; brittle.

botryogen   Hydrous iron and magnesium sulfate, $Fe_2O_3 \cdot 2MgO \cdot 4SO_3 \cdot 15H_2O$; monoclinic, very small crystals; reniform and botryoidal; cleavage one perfect; luster vitreous; color brick red, hyacinth red, ocher yellow; H, 2–2.5; G, 2.04–2.14.

bournonite   Lead copper sulfantimonide, $PbCuSbS_3$; orthorhombic–bipyramidal; luster metallic-adamantine; color grayish black to black; H, 2.5–3; G, 5.8–5.9; fracture subconchoidal to uneven; cleavage one good, two less at right angles; brittle.

boussingaultite   Hydrous ammonium magnesium sulfate $(NH_4)_2SO_4 \cdot MgSO_4 \cdot 6H_2O$; monoclinic, fibers, crusts, veriform aggregates and stalactites; luster silky; color pure white; H, 2; G, 1.68–1.72; cleavage one perfect, another distinct; astringent taste. Often found around hot springs from escaping hot gases.

boydite   Cf. **probertite.**

brannerite   A rare-earth oxide $(U,Ca,Fe,Y,Th)_3Ti_5O_{16}$ (?); possibly orthorhombic, slender prisms; color black, with dark greenish brown streak; H, 4.5; G, 4.5–5.45; radioactive; decomposes in hot sulfuric acid.

braunite   Compound manganese silicate, $3Mn_2O_3,MnSiO_3$; tetragonal, small pyramids and massive; luster submetallic; color and streak brownish black; cleavage perfect pyramidal; H, 6–6.5; G, 4.75. Infusible; soluble in HCl.

brazilianite   Basic sodium aluminum phosphate, $NaAl_3(PO_4)_2(OH)_4$; monoclinic; luster glassy; color chartreuse yellow; H, 5.5; G, 2.98; fracture conchoidal; cleavage one perfect; crystals wedge-shaped transparent.

breunnerite   Magnesium iron manganese carbonate (ferruginous **dolomite** or **magnetite,** *q.v.*), $(Mg,Fe,Mn)CO_3$; an isomorphous system.

brewsterite   A zeolite containing barium and strontium $(Sr,Ba,Ca)O \cdot Al_2O_3 \cdot 6SiO_2 \cdot 5H_2O$; monoclinic, prismatic crystals; cleavage one perfect; luster submetallic; color white; H, 5; G, 2.45; fusible.

brittle mica   Cf. **margarite.**

brittle silver ore   Cf. **stephanite.**

brochantite Basic copper sulfate, $Co_4(SO_4)(COH)_6$; monoclinic–prismatic; luster glassy; color bright to dark green; H, 3.5–4; G, 4; fracture conchoidal; cleavage perfect side pinacoidal, splintery or flaky; transparent to translucent.

bromlite (alstonite) Carbonate of barium and calcium $(Ba,Ca)CO_3$; orthorhombic, in pseudohexagonal pyramids. **Bromlite** stands midway between **witherite** and **strontianite**, *q.v.*

bromyrite Silver bromide, AgBr; isometric; color bright yellow to amber yellow, slightly greenish; H, 1–1.5; G, 5.5; fracture conchoidal; no cleavage; very sectile; luster adamantine. (One of a series with **cerargyrite**. *q.v.*)

bronzite Variety of **enstatite**, *q.v.*, showing strong submetallic brownish luster; a silicate of magnesium and iron.

brookite Titanium oxide, TiO_2; orthorhombic-rhombic bipyramidal; luster adamantine to submetallic; color black, reddish brown; H, 5.5–6; G, 3.9–4.1; fracture subconchoidal to uneven; cleavage poor prismatic and basal; streak white to gray or yellowish; brittle; translucent to opaque.

brown hematite Another name for **limonite**, *q.v.*

brucite Magnesium hydroxide, $Mg(OH)_2$; hexagonal–scalenohedral; luster waxy or pearly; color greenish, blue, yellow, pearly white; H, 2.5; G, 2.4; cleavage micaceous; flexible, nonelastic plates; sectile; transparent; fluorescent blue.

bultfonteinite Basic calcium fluosilicate, $2Ca(OH,F)_2 \cdot SiO_2$; triclinic; crystals colorless to pink; H, 4.5; G, 2.73; cleavage basal and side pinacoidal fairly good. Occurs in radiating spherulites and groups of small radiating acicular crystals.

burkeite Carbonate-sulfate of sodium, $2Na_2SO_4 \cdot Na_2CO_3$; orthorhombic, crystals tabular, twinned; no cleavage; brittle; luster vitreous; colorless; H, 3.5; G, 2.57.

bustamite Calcium manganese **pyroxene**, *q.v.*; $CaMnSi_2O_6$.

bytownite Variety of plagioclase **feldspar**, *q.v.*, a sodium calcium silicate; triclinic; H, 6; G, 2.73; crystals often twinned; color white to colorless; transparent.

cacoxenite Hydrous iron phosphate, $Fe_4(PO_4)_3(OH)_3 \cdot 12H_2O$; yellow or brownish radiated tufts.

calamine Cf. **hemimorphite**.

calaverite Gold telluride, $AuTe_2$; monoclinic, crystals with striated faces, also massive granular; brittle; luster metallic; color pale bronze yellow to yellowish silver gray; streak yellowish gray; H, 2.5; G, 8.2; fracture uneven, no cleavage. See also **sylvanite**.

calciovolborthite Basic calcium copper vanadate, $CuCa(VO_4)(OH)$.

calcite Calcium carbonate, $CaCO_3$; hexagonal–hexagonal scalenohedral; luster glassy; colorless, pale tints, white, yellow; H, 3; G, 2.7; fracture conchoidal; cleavage rhombohedral, perfect in three directions; brittle; transparent to translucent; phosphorescent. Cf. also **aragonite**. Massive forms include stalactites and stalagmites in limestone caverns.

calcite onyx Cf. **onyx**. Used in lamp and inkstand bases.

caldeonite Basic sulfate of copper and lead $(Pb,Cu)SO_4 \cdot (Pb,Cu)(OH)_2$; orthorhombic, small prismatic crystals; cleavage perfect basal; luster vitreous to resinous; color bluish green, dark emerald-green; H, 2.5–3; G, 6.4. Easily fusible.

California iris Cf. **spodumene**.

California jade   Another name for **vesuvianite (idocrase),** *q.v.,* under **californite.**

californite   Massive green variety of **vesuvianite,** *q.v.,* in which **grossularite garnet,** *q.v.,* is intimately mixed with the mineral.

calomel   Mercurous chloride, HgCl; tetragonal, small crystals; sectile; luster adamantine; color gray, white, brown; streak pale yellowish white; H, 1.2; G, 6.48. Easily reduced to liquid mercury by fusion with soda.

campylite   Cf. **mimetite.** Orange yellow, rounded (melon-shaped crystals).

camsellite   Cf. **szaibelyite.**

carnelian   Red to yellowish red variety of **chalcedony,** *q.v.*

carnellite   Hydrous potassium magnesium chloride, $KMgCl_3 \cdot 6H_2O$; occurring commonly as white or reddish deliquescent masses; a good source for potassium.

carnotite   Hydrous potassium uranium vanadate, $K_2(UO_2)_2(VO_4)_2 \cdot 3H_2O$; orthorhombic (?); luster earthy; color bright canary yellow; soft; G, 4.1; crumbly, powdery; sectile; opaque; uranium fluorescent.

cassiterite   Tin oxide, SnO_2; tetragonal–ditetragonal bipyramidal; luster adamantine to greasy; color black, red brown, yellowish; H, 6–7; G, 6.8–7.1; streak white; fracture subconchoidal to uneven; cleavage poor prismatic; brittle; transparent to translucent.

castanite   Cf. **hohmannite.**

catlinite (pipestone)   Very fine-grained metamorphosed clay; luster glossy; color red; texture smooth; compact; sectile (easily carved). Minnesota catlinite is **sericite,** cf. **muscovite,** partly replaced by **pyrophyllite,** *q.v.,* and stained with **hematite,** *q.v.*

cat's-eye   A silky chatoyancy found in such gemstones as corundum, tourmaline, hypersthene, nephrite, quartz, apatite, etc., due to presence of inclusions, tubes, or starlike radiations; not to be confused with true asterism, as in star sapphire or star ruby.

celadonite   Hydrous iron magnesium and potassium silicate, close to glauconite, *q.v.;* earthy or in minute scales; color olive green to apple green; greasy feel; H, 1; G, 2.7. Fusible; soluble in HCl.

celestite   Strontium sulfate, $SrSO_4$; orthorhombic–rhombic bipyramidal; luster glassy; colorless to bluish, red brown, white; H, 3–3.5; G, 3.9–4; fracture uneven; cleavage perfect basal and prismatic; brittle; transparent to translucent.

celsian   Cf. **feldspar.**

centrallsite   Hydrous calcium silicate, $Ca_4Si_6O_{15}(OH)_2 \cdot 5H_2O$; platy, lamellar to compact; color white; H, 2.5; G, 2.51. Associated with **prehnite** and **datolite** at Crestmore, Calif.

cerargyrite   Silver chloride, AgCl; cubic–hexoctahedral; luster adamantine; colorless to greenish gray or gray; H, 1–1.5; G, 5.5; fracture conchoidal; no cleavage; sectile. Cf. also **bromyrite.**

cerussite   Lead carbonate, $PbCO_3$; orthorhombic–rhombic bipyramidal; luster adamantine; colorless, yellowish, gray, white; H, 3–3.5; G, 6.5–6.6; fracture conchoidal; cleavage good prismatic; brittle; transparent to translucent; fluorescent.

cervantite   Antimony oxide, $Sb_2O_4(?)$; orthorhombic, acicular crystals; usually a crust or powder, sometimes massive; color yellow to white; H, 4.5; G, 4; an alteration product of **stibnite,** *q.v.,* or native **antimony.**

chabazite Hydrous silicate of calcium, sodium, aluminum, and potassium $(Ca,Na,K)_7Al_{12}(Al,Si)_2Si_{26}O_{80}\cdot40H_2O$; hexagonal–hexagonal scalenohedral; luster glassy; colorless, pink, white; H, 4–5; G, 2.1–2.2; fracture uneven; cleavage good rhombohedral; transparent to translucent.

chalcanthite Hydrous copper sulfate, $CuSO_4\cdot5H_2O$; triclinic–pinacoidal; luster vitreous; color sky blue; H, 2.5; G, 2.3; fracture conchoidal; cleavage three poor; transparent to translucent.

chalcedony Microcrystalline variety of **quartz,** *q.v.,* usually colorless to white. Banded chalcedony is agate; H, 6.5–7; G, 2.6; luster glassy; fracture conchoidal; translucent.

chalcedony roses Flowerlike growths of **chalcedony,** *q.v.;* luster glassy; color pink, violet, sometimes **carnelian** (red) centers.

chalcocite Cuprous sulfide, Cu_2S; orthorhombic–bipyramidal; luster metallic; color lead-gray; H, 2.5–3; G, 7.2–7.4; fracture conchoidal; cleavage poor prismatic; slightly sectile.

chalcodite Cf. **stilpnomelane.**

chalcolite Cf. **torbernite,** a uranium mineral.

chalcophanite Black hydrous manganese and zinc oxide (Zn,Mn,Fe)-$Mn_2O_5\cdot nH_2O$; luster metallic, changes under heating to a copper color.

chalcopyrite Copper iron sulfide, $CuFeS_2$; tetragonal–scalenohedral; luster metallic; color golden; H, 3.5–4; G, 4.1–4.3; fracture uneven; cleavage one poor; brittle.

chalcosiderite Hydrated basic copper iron phosphate as end product of a **turquoise** series, *q.v.,* in which all aluminum is replaced by iron, $CuFe_6$-$(PO_4)_4(OH)_8\cdot4H_2O$; rare green crystals.

chalcotrichite Cf. **cuprite.**

chert Microcrystalline **quartz,** *q.v.,* without banding; luster glassy; color dull gray to black; H, 7; G, 2.6; fracture conchoidal; opaque.

chesterlite Variety of orthoclase **moonstone,** *q.v.* under **feldspar,** gray to black, found in Chester Co., Pa.

chevkinite Silicotitanate of iron, calcium, and rare-earth elements; approximately $(Fe,Ca)(Ce,La)_2(Si,Ti)_2O_8$.

chiastolite Earthy variety of **andalusite,** *q.v.*

childrenite Hydrous basic iron aluminum phosphate $(Fe,Mn)Al(PO_4)$-$(OH)_2\cdot2H_2O$; crystals orthorhombic, translucent, pale yellowish to dark brown; H, 4.5–5; G, 3.18–3.24.

chili saltpeter Cf. **soda niter.**

chlorastrolite Possible variety of **prehnite,** *q.v.,* or related to the **zeolites.** Called **greenstone** around Lake Superior, or "green star"; H, 5–6; G, 3.2. Also called **pumpellyite.** Color pale gray green to green black.

chlorites A group of soft, micaceous aluminosilicates of iron and magnesium grading one into the other by continuous variations in composition. **Chlorites** are common constituents of metamorphic rocks, and it is often impossible to distinguish variety or species without extensive chemical and optical examination. General formula $(Mg,Fe,Al)_6(Si,AlO_4)O_{10}(OH)_8$; monoclinic–prismatic; luster glassy to pearly; color black, brown, green, rose, yellow, white; H, 2–2.5; G, 2.6–3; flexible leaves; cleavage perfect micaceous; opaque to transparent. See also **clinochlore, penninite,** and **prochlorite.**

chloritoid Hydrous iron magnesium manganese aluminum silicate $(Fe,Mg,Mn)_2Al_4Si_2O_{10}(OH)_4$; monoclinic or triclinic; foliated, massive, scales;

luster pearly to vitreous; color dark gray, black, grass green; streak uncolored to grayish; H, 6.5; G, 3.52–3.57; cleavage perfect basal, plates flexible but inelastic. A synonym **ottrelite** is used for varieties rich in manganese.

chloromagnesite   Magnesium chloride, $MgCl_2$; color white; soft, soluble in water, easily fusible, usually occurs as an efflorescence around waters of some springs and lakes.

chloropal   Hydrous ferric silicate, $Fe_4Si_4(OH)_8·5H_2O$; compact, massive, opallike; luster dull; color pistachio green, greenish yellow; H, 2.5–4.5; G, 1.72–2.49. Becomes magnetic on intense heating; gelatinizes with HCl. Varietal name **nontronite.**

chlorophane   A thermoluminescent (greenish glow) **fluorite,** *q.v.*

chondrodite   Magnesium fluosilicate, $2Mg_2SiO_4·Mg(OH,F)_2$; member of the **humite** group, *q.v.;* orthorhombic, monoclinic; luster glassy; color yellow to reddish brown; H, 6–6.5; G, 3.1–3.2; fracture subconchoidal; cleavage basal; transparent to translucent. (Deep brownish red crystals resemble garnet.)

chromite   Common oxide of iron and chromium, $FeCr_2O_4$; cubic–hexagonal; luster submetallic; color black, streak brown; H, 5.5; G, 4.1–4.9; fracture uneven; no cleavage; brittle. **Magnesium-chromite** is a common variant in which magnesium in part replaces chromium; **trautwinite** is an impure variety. Often found as lenses in serpentine.

chromrulite   Possibly chromium **rutile** mixed with a silicate; tetragonal, crystals prismatic or equant; color brilliant black.

chrysoberyl   Beryllium aluminum oxide, $BeAl_2O_4$; orthorhombic–rhombic bipyramidal; luster glassy; color blue green, gray, greenish yellow, yellow, brown (**alexandrite** variety turns violet purple in artificial light); H, 8.5; G, 3.5–3.8; fracture conchoidal to uneven; cleavage three fair; brittle; transparent.

chrysocolla   Hydrous copper silicate, $CuSiO_3·2H_2O$; orthorhombic (?); luster glassy; color green, greenish blue, sky blue; H, 2–4; G, 2–2.4; fracture conchoidal; brittle to sectile.

chrysolite   Golden yellow variety of **olivine,** *q.v.*

chrysopal   Common **opal,** *q.v.*, stained by nickel minerals.

chrysoprase   **Chalcedony,** *q.v.*, colored a warm green by infusion of nickel silicates.

chrysotile   Fibrous and silky variety of 'serpentine, *q.v.;* a hydrous magnesium silicate of formula $Mg_3Si_2O_5(OH)_4$. The commercially most valuable form of **asbestos,** *q.v.*

cinnabar   Mercuric sulfide, MgS; hexagonal–trigonal trapezohedral; luster adamantine; color bright to brick red; H, 2.5; G, 8.1; fracture subconchoidal; cleavage perfect prismatic; transparent to translucent.

cinnamon-stone   Self-explanatory term for **grossularite garnet,** *q.v.*

citrine   Iron-stained crystal **quartz,** *q.v.;* amber to yellow color.

claudetite   Arsenic oxide, As_2O_3; monoclinic, platy crystals; luster pearly to vitreous; colorless to white; H, 2.5; G, 3.85–4.15; cleavage one perfect.

cleavelandite   Bladed variety of **albite,** *q.v.*

clinochlore   Hydrous magnesium aluminum silicate, a **chlorite,** *q.v.*, $H_8Mg_5Al_2Si_3O_{18}$; monoclinic; plates, scales, earthy, compact; luster pearly; color deep grass green, olive green, rose red; streak uncolored to greenish white; H, 2–2.5; G, 2.65–2.78; cleavage perfect basal, plates flexible but inelastic, thus distinguished from mica. Common in schists and an alteration product of magnesium-iron minerals.

clinoferrosilite   Cf. **pyroxene.**

clinohumite   Basic fluosilicate of magnesium, $Mg_{10}(SiO_4)(OH,F)_2$; monoclinic, crystals or crystalline grains common; luster vitreous to resinous; color white, light yellow, honey yellow, to chestnut brown; H, 6–6.5; G, 3.1–3.2.

clinozoisite   Basic calcium aluminum silicate, $Ca_2Al_3(SiO_4)_3(OH)$; monoclinic, crystals slender prisms, usually striated; colorless, light yellow, green, pink; H, 6; G, 3.25–3.5; cleavage one perfect. A member of the **epidote** group, *q.v.*, but nearly iron-free.

cobalt bloom   Cf. **erythrite.**

cobaltite   Sulfarsenide of cobalt (Co,Fe)AsS; isometric, commonly in cubes and pyritohedrons, also massive; luster metallic; color tin-white; streak grayish black; H, 5.5; G, 6–6.3; cleavage perfect cubic. Residue after roasting becomes magnetic.

coccinite   Iodide of mercury, HgI_2; isometric; color scarlet.

coccolite   Variously colored granular variety of **pyroxene,** *q.v.*

colemanite   Hydrous calcium borate, $Ca_2B_6O_{11}\cdot5H_2O$; monoclinic–prismatic; luster glassy; colorless to white; H, 4–4.5; G, 2.42; fracture subconchoidal to uneven; cleavage perfect side pinacoid; brittle; transparent, often with minute inclusions.

collophane   Cf. **apatite.**

coloradoite   Mercuric telluride, HgTe; isometric; massive, granular; luster metallic; color iron-black; H, 2.5; G, 8.07; cleavage octahedral.

columbite   Columbate of iron and manganese $(Fe,Mn)(Cb,Ta)_2O_6$; orthorhombic–rhombic bipyramidal; luster submetallic to resinous; colorless to black and reddish brown; H, 6; G, 5–8; streak brown to black; fracture uneven; cleavage front and side pinacoid; opaque to transparent. See also **tantalite.**

colusite   Sulfide of copper and arsenic, tin, vanadium, iron, and tellurium; $Cu_3(As,Sn,V,Fe,Te)S_4$; as tetrahedral crystals, color bronze.

concretion   Nodular sandstone ball cemented about a nucleus, which may consist of a fossil, agate, or other hard substance. Takes various forms; some resemble fossil turtles.

connelite   Hydrous copper sulfate chloride, $Cu_{19}(SO_4)Cl_4(OH)_{32}\cdot3H_2O$?; commonly as slender prisms.

cookeite   Hydrous lithium aluminum silicate $(Li,Al)_4(SiAl)_4O_{10}(OH)_4\cdot2H_2O$; monoclinic, in pseudohexagonal plates or rounded aggregates; color white, yellowish, pale pink, deep pink; H, 2.5; G, 2.67; cleavage micaceous.

copiapite   Basic ferric sulfate $(Fe,Mg)Fe_4(SO_4)_6(OH)_2\cdot10H_2O$; triclinic–pinacoidal; luster pearly; color ocher to sulfurous; H, 2.5–3; G, 2.1; cleavage micaceous; translucent.

copper   Element, Cu; cubic–hexoctahedral; luster metallic; color copper; H, 2.5–3; G, 8.9; ductile and malleable.

copper glance   Cf. **chalcocite.**

copper pyrites   Cf. **chalcopyrite.**

copper rhyolite   A term preferred by some to **cuprite,** *q.v.*

coquimbite   Hydrous ferric sulfate, $Fe_2(SO_4)_3\cdot9H_2O$; as white or slightly colored masses.

coral   Organic calcareous form of branching structure, often found in limestone regions fossilized or silicified; calcium carbonate, $CaCO_3$, handled like massive calcite.

cordierite (iolite)   Magnesium aluminum silicate with iron (cf. **dichroite**) $(Mg,Fe)_2Mg_2Al_4Si_5O_{18}$; orthorhombic–rhombic bipyramidal; luster glassy; color gray and blue; H, 7–7.5; G, 2.6–2.7; fracture subconchoidal; cleavage poor pinacoidal transparent to translucent.

coronadite   Oxide of lead and manganese, $MnPbMn_6O_{14}$; tetragonal or pseudotetragonal; massive, in botryoidal crusts, fibrous; luster dull to sub-metallic; color dark gray to black; streak brownish black; H, 4.5–5; G, 5.44.

corundophyllite   Cf. **chlorite.**

corundum   Aluminum oxide, Al_2O_3; hexagonal–scalenohedral; luster ada-mantine; colorless (**corundum**), red (**ruby**), blue (**sapphire**), green, brown with schiller (**adamantine spar**); also yellow, violet, black; H, 9; G, 3.9–4.1; frac-ture conchoidal to uneven; no cleavage; brittle but tough; transparent to trans-lucent; fluorescent orange, yellow, or red; triboluminescent.

cosalite   Lead bismuth sulfide, $Pb_2Bi_2S_5$; lead gray or steel gray; H, 6.39–6.75.

covellite   Cupric sulfide, CuS; hexagonal–dihexagonal bipyramidal; luster metallic; color blue, tarnishing purple to black; H, 1.5–2; G, 4.6; flexible plates; cleavage basal; sectile; translucent in thin plates; blue green.

crandallite   Hydrous calcium aluminum phosphate, $CaAl_3(PO_4)_2(OH)_5 \cdot H_2O$; white to grayish fine fibrous masses.

crednerite   Oxide of copper and manganese, $CuMn_2O_4$; monoclinic (?); foliated masses; luster metallic; color iron-black to steel-gray; H, 4.5; G, 4.95–5.5; cleavage perfect one direction.

creedite   Hydrous basic calcium aluminum sulfate, $Ca_3Al_2F_4(OH,F)_6$-$SO_4 \cdot 2H_2O$; monoclinic, in grains, prismatic crystals and radiating masses; usually colorless, rarely purple; H, 4; G, 2.7; cleavage one perfect.

cristobalite   Silicon dioxide, SiO_2; tetragonal–trapezohedral; luster glassy; color white; H, 5–7; G, 2.3; translucent; often confused with **quartz** or **tridymite,** *q.v.*

crocidolite   A soda-amphibole; cf. **amphibole.**

crocoite   Lead chromate, $PbCrO_4$; monoclinic; long prismatic crystals, granular; luster adamantine to vitreous; color bright red; streak orange yel-low; H, 2.5–3; G, 5.9–6.1; cleavage prismatic; sectile; transparent.

crossite   A soda-amphibole, intermediate between **glaucophane** and **riebec-kite,** *q.v.*

cryolite   Sodium aluminum fluoride, Na_3AlF_8; monoclinic–prismatic; luster glassy; color white or colorless; H, 2.5; G, 2.9–3; fracture uneven, no cleavage; brittle; translucent.

cryptomelane   Oxide of manganese and potassium, probably $KMn_8O_{16} \cdot H_2O$; constituent of manganese ores.

cubanite   Copper-iron sulfide, $CuFe_2S_3$; orthorhombic, generally massive; luster metallic; color bronze yellow; streak black; H, 3.5; G, 4.7.

culsageeite   Cf. **vermiculite.**

cummingtonite   Basic silicate of magnesium and iron $(Mg,Fe)_7Si_8O_{22}$-$(OH)_2$; an **amphibole,** *q.v.*, which occurs in brown fibrous or lamellar masses similar to **anthophyllite,** *q.v.*

cuprite   Cuprous oxide, Cu_2O; cubic–gyroidal; luster adamantine; color red; H, 3.5–4; G, 5.8–6.1; fracture conchoidal; cleavage poor octahedral; brittle; translucent.

cuprodescloizite   Cf. **descloizite.**

cuprogoslarite   A copper-containing **goslarite,** *q.v.*

cuproplumbite   Cf. **galena.**

cuproscheelite   Cf. **scheelite.**

cuprotungstite   Hydrous copper tungstate, $WO_3 \cdot 2CuO \cdot H_2O$; cryptocrystalline, fibrous; color green; H, 4.5.

curite   Cf. **gummite.**

curtisite   A hydrocarbon, $C_{24}H_{18}$; probably orthorhombic, granular; luster vitreous to adamantine; color yellow to pistachio green; H, less than 2; G, 1.2+; fracture conchoidal; cleavage perfect basal; inflammable. Occurs often in serpentine.

custerite   Basic silicate of calcium with fluorine, $Ca_4Si_2O_7(OH,F)_2$; monoclinic, fine granular masses; H, 5; G, 2.91; three cleavages (basal and prismatic); color greenish gray.

cyanite   See **kyanite.**

cyanosite   Cf. **chalcanthite.**

cycad wood   Silicified wood of the genus *Cycadeoidaceae;* members of family have ovoid or short-columnar trunks covered by long persistent leaf bases and multicellular hairs.

cyprine   Massive blue **idocrase,** *q.v.*

cyrtolite   A zirconium silicate, cf. **zircon,** but containing uranium, yttrium, and other rare-earth elements. Occurs in pegmatites.

dahllite   Cf. **apatite.**

damourite   Cf. **muscovite.**

danalite   Silicate and sulfide of iron and beryllium, usually containing zinc and manganese; $(Fe,Zn,Mn)_8Be_8Si_6O_{24}S_2$; isomorphous with **helvite** and **genthelvite,** *q.v.*

danburite   Calcium borosilicate, $CaB_2Si_2O_8$; orthorhombic-rhombic bipyramidal; luster glassy; colorless, gray, white, brownish, light yellow; H, 7; G, 3; fracture uneven to conchoidal; cleavage poor basal; transparent to translucent.

danite   Cf. **arsenopyrite.**

darapskite   Hydrous sodium nitrate and sulfate, $NaNO_3 \cdot Na_2SO_4 \cdot H_2O$; monoclinic, square tabular crystals; colorless; H, 2.3; G, 2.2; cleavages two perfect. (**Nitroglauberite** may be a mixture of **darapskite** and **soda niter,** *q.v.*)

dark ruby silver   Cf. **pyrargyrite.**

datolite   Basic calcium boron silicate, $Ca_2B_2(SiO_4)_2(OH)$; monoclinic–prismatic; luster glassy to porcelaneous; colorless, yellow green, reddish, white; H, 5–5.5; G, 2.8–3; fracture conchoidal to uneven, no cleavage; transparent to translucent.

dehrnite   Basic phosphate of calcium, sodium, and potassium; $(Ca,Na,K)_5(PO_4)_3(OH)$.

deltaite   Basic hydrous phosphate of calcium and aluminum, $Ca_2Al_2(PO_4)_2(OH)_4 \cdot H_2O$; crossection of crystals triangular.

descloizite   Basic lead copper zinc vanadate $(Zn,Cu)Pb(VO_4)(OH)$; orthorhombic–rhombic bipyramidal; luster greasy; color brown, black, green, cherry red, yellow brown; H, 3.5; G, 6.2; streak brownish red to yellow orange; fracture small conchoidal areas, no cleavage, brittle; transparent to translucent. See **mottramite.**

deweylite   Hydrous magnesium silicate, $4MgO \cdot 3SiO_2 \cdot 6H_2O$; amorphous, massive, gumlike; luster greasy; color whitish, yellowish, reddish; H, 2–3.5; G, 2–2.2.

diaboleite   Basic lead copper chloride, $Pb_2CuCl_2(OH)_4$.

diadochite   Basic hydrous ferric phosphate and sulfate, $Fe_2(PO_4)(SO_4)$-$(OH) \cdot 5H_2O$; brown or yellowish.

diamond   Elemental C; cubic–hextetrahedral; luster adamantine; color white to gray-black tints; H, 10; G, 3.52; fracture conchoidal; cleavage perfect octahedral, brittle; combustible.

diaspore   Hydrous aluminum oxide, $HAlO_2$; orthorhombic, crystals prismatic or in foliated masses; luster brilliant; colorless, purple, white, gray, green, brown; H, 6.5–7; G, 3.3–3.5; cleavage good, very brittle.

diatomaceous earth   Massive deposits of opaline silica formed from the tests of diatoms, i.e., the siliceous shells of microscopic single-celled algal plants which once flourished in fresh or brackish waters.

dichroite   Blue and yellow variety of **cordierite,** *q.v.*

dinosaur bone   Calcareous skeletal remains of Mesozoic dinosaurs preserved by silica infusions: agatized, jasperized, silicified; often highly colored, especially red (**jasper**); luster glassy; H, 7; fracture conchoidal.

diopside   Calcium magnesium silicate, $CaMgSi_2O_6$; monoclinic–prismatic; luster glassy; color green, brown, white; H, 5–6; G, 3.27–3.31; fracture conchoidal; cleavage perfect prismatic; transparent to translucent. See also **hedenbergite.**

diopside-jadeite   An intermediate between **jadeite,** *q.v.*, and **diopside.** A silicate of sodium, calcium, and aluminum.

dioptase   Hydrous copper silicate, H_2CuSiO_4; hexagonal–rhombohedral; luster glassy; color emerald-green; H, 5; G, 3.3–3.4; fracture conchoidal to uneven; cleavage perfect rhombohedral; transparent to translucent.

disthene   Cf. **kyanite.**

dolomite   Calcium magnesium carbonate, $CaMg(CO_3)_2$; hexagonal–rhombohedral; luster glassy to pearly; colorless, pinkish, white; H, 3.5–4; G, 2.8; fracture conchoidal; cleavage rhombohedral; brittle; transparent to translucent.

domeykite   Cf. **algodonite.** Silvery masses occurring in veinlets of white quartz; tarnishes to yellowish, then to dark brown.

dreikanter   Three-cornered stones shaped by wind blasting in desert areas; luster smooth polished; color varied but usually dark; H, 5–7; a mineralogical curio.

dudleyite   A variety of **vermiculite,** *q.v.*

dufrenite   Basic iron phosphate, $Fe_5(PO_4)_5 \cdot 2H_2O$; monoclinic; generally as dull green powdery films, sometimes as rounded nodules or crusts with fibrous radiating structure; dull olive green; luster earthy to silky; H, 3.5–4.5; G, 3.2–3.4; streak yellow green, cleavage side and front pinacoid, brittle, translucent.

dufrenoysite   Lead arsensic sulfide, $Pb_2As_2S_5$; monoclinic, generally massive; luster metallic; color dark lead gray; streak reddish brown; H, 3; G, 5.55–5.57; cleavage perfect one direction, brittle.

dumortierite   Hydrous aluminum borosilicate, $Al_8BSi_3O_{19}(OH)$; orthorhombic–rhombic bipyramidal; luster glassy to pearly; color blue, violet pink, violet; H, 7; G, 3.3–3.4; fracture conchoidal; cleavage poor pinacoidal; translucent.

eakleite   Cf. **xonotlite.**

ecdemite   Lead arsenate and chloride (uncertain composition), as yellow or green crystals, masses, or crusts; sometimes orange.

eclogite   A metamorphic rock in which soda-rich **pyroxine** and magnesia-rich **garnet** are essential minerals.

edenite   An **amphibole,** *q.v.*

edingtonite   A zeolite, hydrous aluminum barium silicate, possibly $BaAl_2Si_3O_{10}{\cdot}3H_2O$; orthorhombic, pyramidal crystals; H, 4.4; G, 2.69.

eglestonite   Mercury oxychloride, Hg_4Cl_2O; isometric, minute crystals; luster resinous to adamantine; color yellowish brown changing to black; H, 2.3; G, 8.327.

elbaite   Pink **tourmaline,** *q.v.*

electrum   Cf. **gold,** var. **argentian.**

elixirite   Local New Mexico name for a **banded rhyolite,** *q.v.* A colorful silica gemstone similar to **wonderstone** as an alteration of sandstone; color brown, orange yellow, purplish brown, yellow brown; H, 6.5; G, 2.8.

embolite   Silver chlorobromide, $Ag(Br,Cl)$; isometric, generally massive; luster resinous; color grayish green, yellow; H, 1–1.5; G, 5.31–5.43; sectile. Often found in small amounts with **cerargyrite,** *q.v.*

emerald   Green **beryl,** *q.v.*

emery   Dark gray to black massive **corundum,** *q.v.*

enargite   Copper arsenic sulfide, $Cu_3(As,Sb)S_4$; orthorhombic, crystals and massive; luster metallic; color and streak grayish black; H, 3; G, 4.4; cleavage perfect prismatic; contains up to 6 percent antimony.

enigmatite   Essentially a sodium, iron, titanium silicate; formula uncertain; formerly classed as an **amphibole.** Occurs as black triclinic crystals; G, 3.74–3.80.

enstatite   Magnesium iron silicate, $Mg_2Si_2O_6$; orthorhombic–rhombic bipyramidal; luster glassy to silky; color bronzy, greenish, grayish, yellowish; H, 5.5–6; G, 3.2–3.9; fracture uneven; cleavage perfect prismatic; translucent to transparent on edges; occasionally clear crystals. **Bronzite** is massive **enstatite** displaying metallic reflections.

eosphorite   Hydrous basic manganese aluminum phosphate $(Mn,Fe)Al$-$(PO_4)(OH)_2{\cdot}H_2O$; monoclinic–prismatic; luster glassy; color brown; H, 5; G, 3.1; fracture uneven; cleavage perfect front pinacoid; brittle; transparent to translucent.

epidesmine   Cf. **stilbite.**

epidote   Hydrous calcium iron silicate, $Ca_2(Al,Fe)_3(SiO_4)_3(OH)$; monoclinic–prismatic; luster glassy; color greens, brown; H, 6–7; G, 3.25–3.5; fracture uneven; cleavage perfect basal; transparent to translucent. Also called **pistacite** because of characteristic pistachio-green color. Pleiochroistic.

epistilbite   A zeolite, aluminosilicate of calcium, $Ca_5NaAl_{11}Si_{29}O_{80}{\cdot}25H_2O$; monoclinic, habit prismatic; radiated spherical aggregates, granular; H, 4; G, 2.25; cleavage one perfect. Easily fusible.

epsomite   Epsom salt, hydrous magnesium sulfate, $MgSO_4{\cdot}7H_2O$; orthorhombic, disphenoidal, usually in bunches of long slender fibers and fibrous crusts; luster vitreous to earthy; color and streak white; H, 2–2.5; G, 1.75; cleavage one perfect; bitter taste; soluble in water.

erubescite Cf. **bornite.**

erythrite (cobalt bloom) Hydrous cobalt arsenate, $Co_3As_2O_8\cdot8H_2O$; monoclinic, crystals prismatic, incrustations earthy; luster pearly to adamantine; color and streak crimson to gray; H, 1.5; G, 2.95; cleavage one perfect; sectile. (Coatings and incrustations of erythrite are common on primary cobalt minerals, serving to locate and identify cobalt.)

eschynite (aeschynite) Rare oxide of titanum, columbium, cerium, etc.; $(Ce,Ca,Fe,Th)(Ti,Cb)_2O_6$; as nearly black prismatic crystals.

essonite (hessonite) Brownish or brownish red **grossularite garnet,** *q.v.,* of facet grade.

eucairite (gray copper) Selenide of copper and silver; CuAgSe; massive and granular; color between silver-white and lead-gray; streak shining; H, 2.5; G, 7.6–7.8; somewhat sectile.

euclase Silicate of beryllium and aluminum, $HBeAlSiO_5$; prismatic crystals; luster glassy; color blue, green, yellow; H, 7.5; G, 3.05–3.1; one cleavage perfect; brittle; transparent.

euxenite Oxide of rare-earth metals, including yttrium, cerium, uranium, and thorium, with calcium $(Y,Ca,Ce,U,Th)(Cb,Ta,Ti)_2O_6$; orthorhombic, stout prismatic crystals, commonly in parallel and subparallel semiradical aggregates, also massive; twinning common; luster brilliant, submetallic, to greasy and vitreous; color black, with greenish or brownish tint; streak yellowish, grayish, or reddish brown; H, 5.5–6.6; G, 5; fracture subconchoidal; transparent in thin splinters; radioactive.

evansite Basic aluminum phosphate, $Al_3PO_4(OH)_6\cdot6H_2O$; massive.

fahlunite An altered form of **cordierite,** *q.v.*

fairfieldite Hydrous calcium manganese phosphate, $Ca_2Mn(PO_4)_2\cdot2H_2O$; white or pale yellow, fibrous or foliated; G, 3.07–3.15.

fairy crosses Cf. **staurolite.**

famatinite The antimony equivalent of **energite,** *q.v.;* Cu_3SbS_4; cubic structure; reddish-gray copper antimony sulfide.

faustite A **turquoise,** *q.v.,* in which zinc replaces copper; formula $ZnAl_6(PO_4)_4(OH)_8\cdot5H_2O$.

fayalite Iron silicate, Fe_2SiO_4; orthorhombic, mostly in small crystals; luster vitreous; color yellow, brown, black; H, 6.5; G, 4.1; cleavage distinct. Soluble in HCl, yielding a gelatinous silica on evaporation.

feldspar The feldspars are a group of the most abundant and important rock-forming silicates of aluminum and sodium, calcium, potassium, or barium similar in hardness, cleavage, specific gravity, and twinning. Gem varieties include **amazonite, labradorite, moonstone, peristerite,** and **sunstone.** The **albite-anorthite** feldspars are commonly termed the "plagioclase" feldspars, containing varying percentages of the albite molecule, $NaAlSi_3O_8$, and the anorthite molecule, $CaAl_2Si_2O_8$. The feldspars include **albite, andesine, celsian, labradorite, microcline, oligoclase, orthoclase (adularia, moonstone, sanadine, valencianite, perthite).** H, 6; G, 2.54–2.67; mostly massive, rarely in crystals; luster glassy; color white, whitish gray, whitish pink, colorless, bluish, pale yellow; most varieties show distinct cleavage; transparent to translucent. (As rock-forming minerals, the feldspars are too widely distributed to be listed by localities.)

ferberite Cf. **wolframite.**

fergusonite Oxide of titanium and the rare earths $(Y,Er)_8(Cb,Ta,Ti)_8O_{32}$; tetragonal, crystals prismatic to pyramidal; luster externally dull, on fracture brilliantly vitreous and submetallic; external color gray, yellow, brown, but on fracture surfaces brownish black, velvety black; streak brown; H, 5.5–6.5; G, 5.6–5.8; radioactive.

ferrimolybdite (molybdite) Hydrous iron molybdate, $Fe_2O_3 \cdot 3MoO_3 \cdot 8H_2O$; orthorhombic, fibrous crystals in radiating tufts, earthy; color sulfur-yellow; H, 1.5; G, 4.5; cleavage one distinct. (Dissolving the powdered mineral in concentrated sulfuric acid with a pinhead-size bit of paper produces a deep-blue solution which soon turns brown.)

fersmite Oxide and chloride of calcium and columbium with cerium and titanium $(Ca,Ce)(Cb,Ti)_2(O,F)_6$.

fibroferrite Hydrous iron sulfate, $Fe_2O_3(SO_3)_2 \cdot 10H_2O$; orthorhombic, fine fibrous aggregates; luster silky; color pale yellow to white; H, 2–2.5; G, 1.9; becomes magnetic on heating; soluble in water.

fibrolite Cf. **sillimanite.** Usually massive with fibrous appearance; rarely as transparent pale blue crystals.

fireblende Cf. **pyrostilpnite.**

flint Fine-grained quartz mineral similar to **chert,** *q.v.*

flos ferri Cf. **aragonite.**

fluocerite Fluoride of cerium and related elements $(Ce,La,Nd)F_3$; reddish yellow.

fluorite Calcium fluoride, CaF_2; cubic–hexoctahedral; luster glassy; colorless, brown, black, white, all pastel intermediates; H, 4; G, 3–3.3; fracture conchoidal, brittle; cleavage perfect octahedral; transparent, fluorescent, thermoluminescent. (Predominant colors are purple, blue, green, and yellow; seldom free of inclusions or bubbles.)

forsterite Magnesium silicate, Mg_2SiO_4; orthorhombic, small equidimensional or tabular crystals or grains; color white, greenish, yellow; H, 6–7; G, 3.2–3.3.

fortification agate Any **agate,** *q.v.,* in which bands take sharp abrupt corner turns.

frankeite Sulfide of lead, tin, and antimony, $Pb_5Sn_3Sb_2S_{14}$; orthorhombic, crystals in thin tabular form, elongated; luster metallic; color and streak black; H, 2.5–3; G, 5.9; cleavage one perfect, plates flexible but inelastic. Soluble in nitric acid.

freiburgite Cf. **tetrahedrite.**

friedelite Basic manganese silicate with chlorine, $Mn_8Si_6O_{18}(OH,Cl)_4 \cdot 3H_2O$; rose red; H, 4–5; G, 3.07.

fuchsite Cf. **muscovite.**

fulgarite Silicic tube of sandstone glass formed by lightning in sand, sometimes forked; luster glassy; brittle. Literally "fossil" lightning. See also **lechatelierite.**

fuller's earth Naturally occurring earthy material resembling potter's clay, consisting chiefly of **montmorillonite,** *q.v.*

gabbro-diorite Compart white orbicular **feldspar,** *q.v.,* with inclusions of circular spherules of dark green **hornblende,** peculiar to Davie Co., N.C.

gadolinite   Silicate of iron, beryllium, and various rare-earth minerals, thus a source of rare earths; luster vitreous; color black, brown, brownish black; H, 6.5–7; G, 4–4.5; brittle. Faceted as a curio gem.

gahnite   Dark green **spinel,** *q.v.*

galaxite   Black grains of **spinel,** *q.v.,* found near Galax, N.J.

galena   Lead sulfide, PbS; cubic–hexoctahedral; luster metallic; color lead-gray; H, 2.5–2.7; G, 7.4–7.6; fracture even; cleavage perfect cubic; brittle.

garnet   A series of silicates of aluminum with magnesium, iron, and manganese; with a second series of calcium silicates with aluminum, chromium, and iron; luster glassy; H, 6–7.5; G, 3.5–4.3; fracture conchoidal to uneven, no cleavage; translucent to transparent. (For color and formula, see under individual names: **almandine, andradite, grossularite, pyrope, rhodolite, spessartite,** and **uvarovite.**)

garnierite   Hydrous nickel magnesium silicate, probably $(Mg,Ni)_3Si_2O_5(OH)_4$; apple green to pale green, earthy luster and texture; G, 2.3–2.8. An important ore of nickel.

gaylussite   Hydrous carbonate of calcium and sodium; $CaCO_3 \cdot Na_2CO_3 \cdot 5H_2O$; monoclinic, crystals often elongated or flattened wedge shape; luster vitreous; color whtie, yellowish white; streak colorless to grayish; H, 2–3; G, 1.94; fracture conchoidal, very brittle; cleavage perfect prismatic. Easily effervesces in acids.

gedrite   An aluminous variety of **anthophyllite,** *q.v.*

gehlenite   Calcium aluminum silicate, $Ca_2Al_2SiO_7$; tetragonal, in short square prisms, massive granular; luster vitreous to resinous; color gray to brown; streak white; H, 5.5–6; G, 2.9–3.07; brittle. Almost infusible, gelatinizes with HCl.

geikielite   Black to brownish **ilmenite,** *q.v.*

genthelvite   Silicate and sulfide of zinc and beryllium, $(Zn,Fe,Mn)_8Be_6Si_6O_{24}S_2$; isomorphous with **danalite** and **helvite,** *q.v.*

gerhardtite   Basic copper nitrate, $Cu_2(NO_3)(OH)_3$; emerald green.

geyserite   Hot-springs opal deposited around geysers, forming terraces, basins, and cones. Basically $SiO_2 \cdot nH_2O$.

gibbsite   Aluminum hydroxide, $Al(OH)_3$; crystals monoclinic, light colored, translucent; also in stalactitic and spheroidal forms.

gillespite   Micaceous silicate of barium and iron, $BaFeSi_4O_{10}$.

gilsonite   A variety of asphalt; lustrous and brilliant; streak rich brown; color black; H, 2–2.5; G, 1.065–1.070; burns with a brilliant flame.

ginkgo wood   Agatized, opalized, or silicified wood of the order *Ginkgoales;* the maidenhair tree, *Ginkgo biloba,* is the sole surviving member of this Mesozoic species. Occurs primarily in eastern Washington.

glaserite   Cf. **aphthitalite.**

glauberite   Sulfate of sodium and calcium, $Na_2SO_4 \cdot CaSO_4$; monoclinic, crystals tabular; luster vitreous; color yellowish white, gray; streak white; H, 2.5–3; G, 2.7–2.85; brittle; cleavage perfect basal. Partly soluble in water; completely soluble in dilute acid.

glauber salt   Cf. **mirabilite.**

glauconite   Essentially a hydrous iron aluminum potassium silicate, $K_2(Mg,Fe)_2Al_6(Si_4O_{10})_2(OH)_{12}$; monoclinic, cryptocrystalline or granular; luster dull or glistening; color olive green, blackish green, yellowish green, grayish green; H, 2; G, 2.2–2.4; cleavage one perfect. Found abundantly in ocean sediments near continents.

glaucophane   A **soda-amphibole,** $Na_4Mg_6Al_4Si_{16}O_{44}(OH,F)_4$; widespread constituent in schists of Californian coast ranges.

gmelinite   A zeolite isomorphous with **chabazite,** *q.v.,* $(Na_2,Ca)Al_2Si_4O_{12}\cdot$-$6H_2O$; colorless or light colored; H, 4.5; G, 2–2.2.

goethite   Hydrous iron oxide, $HFeO_2$; orthorhombic–rhombic bipyramidal; luster adamantine-metallic to silky; color black to brownish black; H, 5–5.5; G, 3.3–4.3; streak yellow to brownish yellow; fracture uneven; cleavage side pinacoid; brittle; thinly translucent.

gold, var. **argentian** (electrum)   A natural alloy of gold and silver.

gold amalgam   A native alloy of gold and mercury, rare.

gold element   Au; cubic–hexoctahedral; luster metallic; color bright to silvery yellow; H, 2.5–3; G, 19.3; malleable, ductile.

golden beryl (heliodor)   **Beryl,** *q.v.,* of a golden yellow color.

goshenite   Colorless **beryl,** *q.v.,* found at Goshen, Mass.

goslarite   Hydrous zinc sulfate, $ZnSO_4\cdot7H_2O$; white, usually massive. Formed by oxidation of **sphalerite,** *q.v.*

grahamite   Complex bituminous asphalt; black, lustrous.

graphic tellurium   Cf. **sylvanite.**

graphite   Elemental C; hexagonal–dihexagonal bipyramidal; luster submetallic; color black; H, 1–2; G, 2.3; streak black; plates flexible, greasy feel; cleavage perfect basal; opaque.

gray copper ore   Cf. **tetrahedrite.**

greenalite   Hydrous ferrous silicate, as granules of earthy green color in chert associated with iron ores of Minnesota's Mesabi Range.

greenockite   Native cadmium sulfide, CdS; as yellow translucent crystals or as an earthy encrustation.

greenstone   Cf. **chlorastrolite.**

grossularite garnet   Cf. **garnet;** $Ca_3Al_2Si_3O_{12}$; member of the second or calcium garnet series; color various pale tints but never red; G, 3.5.

gummite   Uranium oxides with water; luster greasy to waxy; color grayish yellow to orange red; H, 2.5–5; G, 3.9–6.4; brittle, no fracture or cleavage; translucent; radioactive.

gypsite   Cf. **gypsum.**

gypsum   Hydrous calcium sulfate, $CaSO_4\cdot2H_2O$; monoclinic–prismatic; luster glassy, pearly, silky; colorless, light tints, white; H, 2; G, 2.3; fracture fibrous or conchoidal; cleavage two, one perfect micaceous; sectile; fluorescent. (**Alabaster** is a granular translucent variety in pale colors; **satin spar** is a fibrous, brilliantly chatoyant form in white to pale pink or orange.)

gyrolite   Hydrous calcium silicate, $Ca_2Si_3O_7(OH)_2\cdot H_2O$; as white concretions.

halite   Sodium chloride (table salt), NaCl; cubic–hexoctahedral; luster glassy; colorless, white; H, 2.5; G, 2.1–2.6; fracture conchoidal, brittle; cleavage perfect cubic; transparent; soluble in water.

halotrichite (iron alum)   Hydrous aluminum iron sulfate, $FeSO_4\cdot Al_2(SO_4)\cdot$-$22H_2O$; monoclinic, fibrous; luster silky; color yellowish white; H, 2; G, 1.9; soluble in water, with "ink" taste.

hanksite   Sodium potassium sulfate-carbonate-chloride, $9Na_2SO_4\cdot2Na_2$-

CO_3·KCl; hexagonal, prismatic, tabular; luster vitreous; color white; H, 3–3.5; G, 2.562; strongly luminescent. Taste salty, easily soluble in water.

hardystonite   Zinc calcium silicate, $Ca_2ZnSi_2O_7$.

hatchettolite   A uranium-bearing **pyrochlore,** *q.v.*

hausmannite   Manganese tetroxide, Mn_3O_4; an opaque mineral.

hawk's-eye   Crystals of **quartz,** *q.v.*, in which hairlike inclusions are arranged in parallel streaks, exhibiting a silky luster and strong chatoyancy; also called **tiger's-eye** or **falcon's-eye.**

heavy spar   Cf. **barite.**

hebronite   Cf. **amblygonite;** named after Hebron, Maine.

hectorite   Cf. **montmorillonite.**

hedenbergite   Cf. **diopside;** calcium iron silicate, $CaFeSi_2O_6$.

heliodore   Cf. **golden beryl.**

heliotrope bauxite   Cf. **bauxite;** a spotted red and green variety locally named in Saline Co., Ark.

helvite   Sulfide of manganese and beryllium, usually also containing iron and zinc; $(Mn,Fe,Zn)_8Be_6O_{24}S_2$; isomorphous with **danalite** and **genthelvite,** *q.v.*

hematite   Ferric oxide, Fe_2O_3; hexagonal–scalenohedral; luster earthy or metallic; color red, black; H, 1–6.5; G, 4.9–5.3; streak red; fracture conchoidal to uneven, no cleavage; brittle. Faceted gems sometimes called "Alaska diamonds."

hemimorphite   Hydrous zinc silicate, $Zn_4Si_2O_7(OH)_2$·H_2O; luster glassy; color white, often stained; H, 4.5–5; G, 3.4–3.5; fracture uneven, poor conchoidal; cleavage prismatic; transparent to translucent.

herderite   Calcium beryllium fluophosphate, $CaBe(PO_4)(OH,F)$; monoclinic–prismatic; luster greasy to glassy; colorless, bluish green, yellowish, white; H, 5–5.5; G, 2.9–3; fracture subconchoidal; cleavage usually prismatic or partially; brittle; transparent to translucent; may fluoresce deep blue.

hessite   Silver telluride, Ag_2Te; isometric, generally in distorted octahedrons, sometimes massive; luster metallic; color lead-gray.

heterosite   Cf. **purpurite.**

heulandite   Hydrous silicate of sodium, calcium, potassium, and aluminum $(Ca,Na,K)_6Al_{10}(Al,Si)Si_{29}O_{80}$·$25H_2O$; monoclinic–prismatic; luster glassy; color reddish, yellowish, white; H, 3.5–4; G, 2.2; streak white; fracture subconchoidal to uneven; cleavage perfect side pinacoid; transparent to translucent.

hexagonite   Lilac variety of **tremolite,** *q.v.*

hiddenite   Green gemmy **spodumene,** *q.v.*

hillebrandite   Hydrous calcium silicate, $Ca_2SiO_3(OH)_2$; as amorphous white masses.

hohmannite   Hydrated iron sulfate, Fe_2O_3·$2SO_3$·$8H_2O$; triclinic, crystalline aggregates, clusters or prismatic crystals; luster vitreous; color orange to dark brown; H, 3; G, 2.2; cleavage one perfect, two less perfect. Decomposed by hot water, easily soluble in HCl. Alternative name **castanite.**

hornblende   A series of aluminous amphiboles lumped together, $CaNa(Mg,Fe)_4(Al,Ti,Fe)_3Si_6O_{22}(O,OH)_2$; monoclinic–prismatic; luster glassy; color green (**edenite,** *q.v.*), bluish green (**paragasite**), black; H, 5–6; G, 2–3.4; fracture subconchoidal to uneven; cleavage prismatic; edges translucent to transparent.

horn silver   Cerargyrite-bromyrite, *q.v.,* so named because of its waxy or hornlike luster.

hornstone   A variety of **quartz,** much like **flint,** *q.v.,* but much more brittle.

howlite   Calcium silicoborate, $Ca_2SiB_5O_9(OH)_5$; monoclinic, "cauliflower" heads in borate deposits; luster dull to subvitreous; color white with black markings; H, 3.5; G, 2.5–2.6; fracture even, no cleavage; translucent to opaque. Carved by steel tools.

huebnerite   Cf. **wolframite.**

humite   A group of magnesium fluosilicates that includes **chondrodite, clinohumite, humite,** and **norbergite,** *q.v.* Humite formula is $3Mg_2SiO_4\cdot Mg(OH,F)_2$; orthorhombic and monoclinic; luster glassy; color reddish brown to yellow; H, 6–6.5; G, 3.1–3.2; fracture subconchoidal; cleavage basal; transparent to translucent.

hureaulite   Hydrous manganese phosphate, $H_2Mn_5(PO_4)\cdot 4H_2O$; monoclinic, crystals in groups or short prisms; massive, compact; H, 5; G, 3.18; color orange red, rose, nearly colorless; cleavage one distinct.

hyacinth   Orange to reddish brown **grossularite garnet,** *q.v.*

hyalite   Clear, colorless **opal,** *q.v.;* also called "water opal."

hydromagnesite   Basic magnesium carbonate, $Mg_4(OH)_2(CO_3)_3\cdot 3H_2O$; as small white crystals or chalky crusts.

hydrophane   Chalky, white, opaque **opal (cachalong** type) which is water-absorbent, becoming clear after soaking, when some may show typical opal color play.

hydrothorite   Cf. **thorogummite.**

hydrozincite   Basic zinc carbonate, $Zn_5(OH)_6(CO_3)_2$; monoclinic; luster dull; color light gray, yellowish, white; H, 2–2.5; G, 3.6–3.8; fracture irregular, no cleavage, earthy; translucent, fluorescent blue.

hypersthene   Magnesium iron silicate $(Mg,Fe)_2Si_2O_6$; orthorhombic-rhombic bipyramidal; metalloidal sheen similar to **bronzite** in massive form, occasionally clear crystals; cf. **enstatite.**

Iceland spar   Double-refracting form of **calcite,** *q.v.*

iddingsite   Hydrous magnesium iron silicate, $MgO\cdot Fe_2O_3\cdot 3SiO_2\cdot 4H_2O$; luster bronze; color chestnut brown to yellowish green; H, 2.5–3; G, 2.84; orthorhombic, lamellar crystals; cleavage one perfect. Becomes magnetic when heated; decomposed by HCl.

idocrase (vesuvianite)   Hydrous calcium iron magnesium silicate, $Ca_{10}Al_4(Mg,Fe)_2Si_9O_{34}(OH)_4$; tetragonal–ditetragonal bipyramidal; luster glassy; color blue (**cyprine**), brown, green, yellow; H, 6.5; G, 3.4–3.5; fracture conchoidal to uneven; cleavage poor prismatic; transparent to translucent. Abundantly massive, rare crystals. Cf. **californite,** for cabochons and art objects.

idrialite (aragotite)   A hydrocarbon; bright scales, color honey yellow; streak white; H, 1; G, 1.1; transparent, volatile.

ilmenite   Iron titanium oxide, $FeTiO_3$; hexagonal–rhombohedral; luster metallic to submetallic; color brownish black to black; streak brownish red to ocher yellow or black; H, 5–6; G, 4.1–4.8; fracture conchoidal to subconchoidal, no cleavage, brittle, weakly magnetic.

ilsemannite   Hydrous oxide (possibly sulfate) of molybdenum, $Mo_3O_8\cdot nH_2O$; as blue, blue black, or black earthy masses.

indicolite   Blue **tourmaline,** *q.v.*

inesite   Hydrous manganese calcium silicate $(Mn,Ca)_3Si_3O_8(OH)_2$; triclinic, prismatic crystals, sometimes fibrous radiating or spherulitic; luster vitreous; color rose red; H, 6; G, 3.03; cleavage one perfect; decomposed by HCl. Commonly associated with **psilomelane,** *q.v.*

infusorial earth   An earthy **opal,** *q.v.*

inyoite   Hydrous calcium borate, $Ca_2B_6O_{11} \cdot 13H_2O$; monoclinic, in large crystals; luster glassy; colorless; H, 2; G, 1.875; cleavage basal, brittle; transparent. Easily soluble in acids.

iodyrite   Native silver iodide, AgI; yellowish or greenish hexagonal crystals usually occurring in thin plates; a halide closely related to **horn silver,** *q.v.*

iolite   Cf. **cordierite.**

iridium   Native element, Ir (probably **iridosmine**), occasionally found with platinum and gold, often with some rare rhodium and ruthenium.

iridosmine (siserskite)   Native alloy of iridium and osmium (Ir,Os); hexagonal–rhombohedral, generally in grains; luster metallic; color tin-white to light steel-gray; H, 6.7; G, 19.3–21.12; cleavage perfect basal. **Iridosmine** is iridium-rich; **siserskite** osmium-rich.

iron   Native element, Fe, rare except in meteorites; cubic–hexoctahedral; luster metallic; color steel-gray; H, 4–5; G, 7.3–7.8; fracture hackly; cleavage cubic; magnetic.

iron alum   Cf. **halotrichite.**

iron pyrites   Cf. **pyrite.**

iron roses   Thin flat scaly growths of **hematite,** *q.v.*

isopyre   Impure **common opal,** *q.v.,* found in Morris Co., N.J.

itabirite   A **quartzite,** *q.v.,* containing micaceous **hematite,** *q.v.*

jade   Cf. **jadeite** and **nephrite.** The term "jade" is collectively applied to both minerals, which are chemically distinct. **Jadeite** is a **pyroxene,** *q.v.,* while **nephrite** belongs to the amphibole group close to **actinolite,** *q.v.*

jadeite   Sodium aluminum silicate, $NaAlSi_2O_6$; monoclinic–prismatic; luster glassy to silky; color green (light, malachite, emerald), lilac, reddish-brown, yellow brown, violet, white; H, 6.5–7; G, 3.3–3.5; fracture difficult, as toughness is characteristic, hence splintery; cleavage prismatic; translucent to opaque. A deep green to black variety is called **chloromelanite.**

jamesonite   Lead antimony iron sulfide, $Pb_4FeSb_6S_{14}$; monoclinic–prismatic, usually as finely fibrous or loosely matted hairs and in solid "feathered" masses; H, 2.5; G, 5.5–6; luster metallic, color dark gray; cleavage across elongation; brittle. An associate of other "feather" ores difficult to distinguish, including **plumosite, meneghinite, boulangerite,** and **zinkenite,** all of which lack the iron (Fe).

jarosite   Basic hydrous iron potassium sulfate, $KFe_3(SO_4)_2(OH)_6$; hexagonal–ditetragonal pyramidal; luster vitreous to subadamantine; color clove brown to ocher yellow; H, 2.5–3.5; G, 2.9–3.3; fracture uneven, cleavage perfect basal, brittle or sectile; translucent.

jasp-agate   Intermediate between **agate** and **jasper,** *q.v.;* luster glassy, fracture conchoidal; H, 7; G, 2.7; translucent to opaque. An opaque moss or plume agate.

jasper   Silicified material ranging from pure **chalcedony,** *q.v.,* to consolidations of miscellaneous material into hard (7), compact, colorful masses; an impure **chalcedony** of slight translucency and no banding, related to **chert** and **flint**, *q.v.*

jaspilite   Cf. **specularite.**

jelinite   Brownish to yellowish dark-colored **amber**, *q.v.*, found in Ellsworth Co., Kans.; luster resinous to waxy; fracture conchoidal; cloudy to translucent.

jet   Variety of **lignite**, *q.v.;* color black, streak brown; H, 3–4; G, 1.3; tough, easily carved with steel tools; combustible; takes a high polish.

joaquinite   A silicate of sodium, iron, and titanium; found on San Joaquin Ridge, San Benito Co., Calif., as honey yellow orthorhombic crystals.

josephinite   A nickel-iron alloy found as nuggets in gold placers.

kalinite   Cf. **potash alum.**

kaolin   Hydrous aluminum silicate, $Al_2Si_2O_5(OH)_4$; monoclinic–prismatic; luster dull; color white or stained black, brown, or red; H, 2–2.5; G, indeterminable but usually taken as 2.6; earthy, cleavage micaceous; opaque.

kaolinite   Principal clay mineral, basically aluminum silicate as an alteration product of **microcline** or **orthoclase**, *q.v.;* color gray, brown, red, yellow, white. Strong clay odor when damp.

kernite   Hydrous sodium borate, $Na_2B_4O_7 \cdot 4H_2O$; monoclinic; luster vitreous to pearly; colorless to white; H, 3; G, 1.953; cleavages two perfect, one distinct; slowly soluble in cold water. Principal ore mineral of Kern Co., Calif., borate deposits.

kimberlite   Variety of **peridotite**, *q.v.*, in which diamond occurs.

kinradite   San Francisco Bay regional chert in which colorful spherules are found, Marin Co.

knebelite   Iron manganese silicate $(Fe,Mn)_2SiO_4$; variously colored.

kramerite   Cf. **probertite.**

krausite   Hydrous iron potassium sulfate, $K_2SO_4 \cdot Fe(SO_4)_2 \cdot 2H_2O$; monoclinic; rough crystals, often prismatic; luster brilliant; color lemon yellow to yellowish green; H, 2.5; G, 2.84; cleavage one perfect, one good; soluble in acid.

krennerite   Gold telluride, $AuTe_2$.

krohnkite (salvadorite)   Hydrous copper sodium sulfate, $Na_2Cu(SO_4)_2 \cdot 2H_2O$; massive, azure blue.

kunzite   Gemmy lilac crystals of **spodumene**, *q.v.;* color pinkish to pale purple.

kyanite   Aluminum silicate, Al_2SiO_5; triclinic–pinacoidal; luster glassy; colorless to bluish or greenish in splotches; H, 5 lengthwise, 7 across prism; G, 3.6–3.7; fracture splintery across crystals; cleavage perfect pinacoidal; transparent to translucent.

labradorite   Member of **plagioclase** series, *q.v.;* coarsely crystalline; color blue (butterfly's wing); H, 6; G, 2.71; displays "labradorescence."

langbeinite   Potassium magnesium double sulfate, $K_2Mg_2(SO_4)_3$; crystals colorless, isometric; much used in fertilizer industry.

lanthanite   Hydrous lanthanum carbonate $(La,Ce)_2CO_3$; earthy, or as white crystals.

larsenite   Lead zinc silicate, $PbZnSiO4$; colorless orthorhombic prisms.

laumontite   Hydrous calcium aluminum silicate, $CaAl_2Si_4O_{12}\cdot 3H_2O$; crystals white, monoclinic; luster vitreous. On exposure to air it loses water, crumbles, and becomes opaque.

lawsonite   Calcium aluminum silicate, $CaAl_2Si_2O_7(OH)_2\cdot H_2O$; orthorhombic, prismatic and tabular crystals; luster vitreous; color pale blue to white; H, 7–8; G, 3.09; cleavages two perfect. Widespread in West Coast schists and metamorphic rocks.

lazulite   A high-magnesium phosphate $(Mg,Fe)Al_2(PO_4)_2(OH)_2$; monoclinic–prismatic; luster glassy; color blue; H, 5.5–6; G, 3.1–3.4; fracture uneven, cleavage poor prismatic, brittle; transparent to translucent. Cf. **scorzalite.**

lazurite (lapis lazuli)   Sodium aluminum silicate plus sulfur, $Na_{4-5}Al_3Si_3$-$O_{12}S$; cubic–hexoctahedral; luster glassy; color blue, greenish blue, violet blue; H, 5–5.5; G, 2.4–2.5; fracture uneven, cleavage poor dodecahedral; translucent.

lead   Native element, Pb; isometric; crystals rare, usually in thin plates and pellets; luster metallic; color lead-gray; H, 1.5; G, 11.4; malleable.

leadhillite   Hydrous carbonate-sulfate of lead, $4PbO\cdot SO_3\cdot 2CO_2\cdot H_2O$; monoclinic, tabular crystals; luster vitreous to pearly; color white, yellowish, greenish; streak uncolored; H, 2.5; G, 6.26–6.44; cleavage perfect basal.

lechatelierite   Fused **quartz,** q.v., found in lightning-created **fulgarites** in sand, q.v.

leopardite   A black-spotted **quartz porphry** found at Belmont Springs, Mecklenburg Co., N.C.

lepidocrocite   Basic iron oxide, $FeO(OH)$; orthorhombic, usually isolated flakes or groups of scalelike crystals; massive, bladed, to fibrous; luster submetallic; color ruby red to reddish brown; streak dull orange; H, 5; G, 4.09; cleavage one perfect, one good; brittle. Often associated with **goethite,** q.v.

lepidolite   Hydrous fluosilicate of lithium, potassium, and aluminum, $K_2Li_3Al_4Si_7O_{21}(OH,F)_3$; monoclinic domatic; luster pearly to vitreous; color gray green, lilac, light yellow, pink, to purplish; H, 2.5; G, 2.8–3.3; elastic plates, cleavage perfect basal or micaceous; transparent to translucent.

lepidomelane   A dark form of **mica,** q.v., near **biotite** in composition but characterized by a large amount of ferric iron; color brown, black; H, 3; G, 3.1; cleavage perfect basal.

leucite   Potassium aluminum silicate, $KAlSi_2O_6$; tetragonal–trapezohedral; luster glassy; colorless to gray and white; H, 5.5–6; S. G, 2.4–2.5; fracture conchoidal, cleavage imperfect dodecahedral; transparent to translucent. Faceted gems show peculiar color flashes.

levynite   Hydrous calcium aluminum silicate, $NaCa_3Al_7Si_{11}O_{36}\cdot 15H_2O$; white or light colored rhombohedral crystals.

lewistonite   Basic phosphate of calcium, potassium, and sodium; $(Ca,K,Na)_5(PO_4)_3(OH)$.

lignite   A low-grade coal in which woody structure is distinct.

lime-dravite   White **tourmaline,** q.v., $CaMg_3B_3(Al_3Si_6O_{27})(O,OH)_4$.

limonite   Various hydrous ferric oxides, $FeO(OH)\cdot nH_2O$; amorphous; luster dull to glassy; color brownish black to yellow; streak brown to yellow; H, 2–5.5; G, 2.7–4.3; fracture conchoidal; earthy, no cleavage, brittle. **Limonite cubes** are pseudomorphs after **pyrite.**

linarite   Basic sulfate of lead and copper $(Pb,Cu)SO_4\cdot(Pb,Cu)(OH)_2$; monoclinic, crystals small, divergent columnar and platy; luster vitreous to adamantine; color deep azure blue; streak pale blue; H, 2.5; G, 5.3–5.45; cleavage one perfect. Often associated with **caledonite,** *q.v.*

linnaeite (linneite)   Cobalt sulfide, Co_3S_4; isometric crystals or massive; pale steel gray, luster metallic.

lintonite   Variety of **thomsonite,** *q.v.;* extremely compact, olive green, translucent.

liroconite   Basic hydrous aluminum copper arsenate, $Cu_2Al(AsO_4)(OH)_4$·- $4H_2O$; sky blue or verdigris green monoclinic crystals; H, 2–2.5; G, 2.88– 2.99.

litchfieldite   A soda-rich **syenite** found at Litchfield, Kennebec Co., Maine.

litharge   Lead oxide, PbO; orthorhombic–rhombic bipyramidal; forms red edge on scales of **massicot,** *q.v.*

lithia tourmaline   Red, green, to blue **tourmaline,** *q.v.*, with basic formula $Na(Al,Fe,Li,Mg)_3B_3Al_3(Al_3Si_6O_{27})(O,OH,F)_4$.

lithiophilite   Lithium manganese phosphate, $LiMnPO_4$; orthorhombic, commonly massive; luster vitreous; color pale pink to yellow and brown; H, 4.5–5; G, 3.42–3.56; cleavage perfect basal; acid-soluble.

lithomarge   Cf. **kaolinite.**

llanite   An igneous rock in Llano Co., Tex.; a reddish porphyry containing reddish **microcline, albite, orthoclase, quartz,** and flakes of **biotite mica.**

lodestone   Cf. **magnetite.**

loellingite (leucopyrite)   Iron arsenide, $FeAs_2$; isomorphous with **arsenopyrite,** *q.v.;* tin white, usually massive.

loranite   Thallium sulfarsenide, $TlAsS_2$; monoclinic crystals, deep cochineal) red.

mackintoshite   Cf. **thorogummite.**

magnesia alum   Cf. **pickeringite.**

magnesiocopiapite   Possibly a variety of **copiapite,** *q.v.* Hydrous basic sulfate of ferrous and ferric iron with variable amounts of chromium, aluminum, nickel, and magnesium; luster vitreous; color greenish yellow; H, 2.5–3; G, 2.08–2.17; triclinic, tabular crystals; cleavage perfect pinacoidal.

magnesioferrite   Iron magnesium oxide, $MgFe_2O_4$, and member of the **magnetite** series, *q.v.;* crystals cubic, octahedron, and dodecahedron; luster metallic-adamantine; color and streak black; H, 5.5–6.5; G, 4.6; nearly opaque; magnetic.

magnesite   Magnesium carbonate, $MgCO_3$; hexagonal–hexagonal scalenohedral; luster dull to glassy; colorless, light tints, white; H, 3.5–5; G, 3–3.2; fracture conchoidal to smooth; cleavage rhombohedral; brittle; transparent to translucent.

magnetic pyrites   Cf. **pyrrhotite.**

magnetite   Ferrous and ferric iron oxide, Fe_3O_4; cubic–hexoctahedral; luster metallic; color and streak black; H, 6; G, 5.2; fracture subconchoidal to uneven; cleavage none, brittle, magnetic. Also called **lodestone.**

maitlandite   Cf. **thorogummite.**

malachite   Basic copper carbonate, $Cu_2CO_3(OH)_2$; monoclinic; luster silky to vitreous; color dark green; H, 3.5–4; G, 3.9–4; fracture splintery, cleavage basal, brittle; translucent.

malacolite   White fluorescent crystals of **diopside,** *q.v.*

maldonite   Cf. **bismuth-gold.**

manganapatite   Variety of **apatite,** *q.v.,* in which crystals resemble green **tourmaline** but are softer; H, 5.

manganite   Manganic hydroxide, MnO(OH) or $Mn_2O_3 \cdot H_2O$; monoclinic, pseudoorthorhombic; occurs in prismatic crystals; color dark steel-gray to iron-black, streak chocolate brown; H, 4; G, 4.3. Commonly altered to **pyrolusite,** *q.v.* An important ore of manganese, often mixed with **psilomelane,** *q.v.*

manganocalcite   Cf. **calcite.**

manganosiderite   An intermediate member of the **siderite-rhodochrosite** isomorphous series.

manganotantalite   Cf. **columbite.**

marcasite   Iron sulfide, FeS_2; orthorhombic–bipyramidal; luster metallic; color brass-yellow; H, 6–6.5; G, 4.9; fracture uneven, cleavage poor prismatic, brittle.

marekanite   Mahogany **obsidian,** *q.v.,* in which both black and reddish brown streaks and swirls occur.

margarite   Hydrous calcium aluminum silicate, $CaAl_4Si_2O_{10}(OH)_2$; monoclinic–prismatic; luster pearly; color gray, pink, violet, white; usually in aggregated laminae, sometimes massive, scaly; H, 3.5 (cleavage face), 5 (prism face); G, 3–3.1; no fracture, cleavage perfect micaceous, brittle; transparent to translucent. Prominent in **glaucophane** rocks.

margarodite (damourite)   Cf. **muscovite.**

margarosanite   Lead calcium silicate, $PbCa_2(SiO_3)_3$; as colorless lamellar masses.

marialite   Cf. **scapolite.**

mariposite   Essentially a **muscovite,** *q.v.,* colored green by chromium (may be identical to **fuchsite**); luster vitreous; color apple green, white; monoclinic, in hexagonal plates and scales, foliated, micaceous; H, 2.5–3; G, 2.78–2.81; cleavage perfect basal. Abundant in Sierra Nevada gold belt, Calif.

marmatite   Ferruginous **sphalerite,** *q.v.;* dark brown to black.

marmolite   Micaceous **serpentine,** *q.v.*

mascagnite   Ammonium sulfate $(NH_4)_2SO_4$; usually in crusts and stalactitic forms; luster vitreous to dull; colorless, yellowish, greenish; H, 2; G, 1.76; cleavage one distinct. Occurs around geysers. See also **geyserite.**

massicot   Lead monoxide, PbO; orthorhombic, usually in scales or scaly masses; color brownish orange, red, yellow; soft; G, 9.29. Easily reduced to lead on charcoal.

matlockite   Lead chloride and fluoride, PbFCl.

meerschaum   Hydrous magnesium silicate, $Mg_3Si_4O_{10}(OH)_2 \cdot 4H_2O$; a fine white soft clay, extremely lightweight; used to make tobacco pipes.

meionite   Cf. **scapolite.**

melaconite   Cf. **tenorite.**

melanterite (copperas)   Hydrous ferrous sulfate, $FeSO_4 \cdot 7H_2O$; monoclinic; fibrous, stalactitic, concretionary, also massive; luster vitreous; color green to white, streak colorless; H, 2; G, 1.89–1.9; cleavage basal, brittle; astringent taste. A common alteration product in mines containing **marcasite** or **pyrite,** *q.v.*

melonite   Nickel telluride, $NiTe_2$; hexagonal, commonly granular and foliated; luster metallic; color reddish white, streak dark gray; H, 1; G, 7.3; cleavage perfect basal.

menaccanite   Cf. **ilmenite.**

meneghinite   Lead antimony sulfide, $Pb_{13}Sb_7S_{23}$; orthorhombic; crystals slender prismatic, also massive, fibrous to compact; H, 2.5; G, 6.36; luster metallic; color blackish lead-gray, streak black; cleavage one perfect, brittle.

mercury   Element, Hg; hexagonal–rhombohedral (frozen at $-40°$ C); luster metallic; color silver-white; liquid at normal temperatures; G, 13.6. Obtained by direct heating of **cinnabar**, *q.v.* Also called **quicksilver.**

mesolite   Member of the **zeolites**, *q.v.*, often confused with **natrolite**, *q.v.* Sodium calcium aluminum silicate $(Na,Ca)_2Al_2S_3O_{10}\cdot 3H_2O$; monoclinic; luster glassy; colorless, cream, green, yellow, white; H, 5; G, 2.2; cleavage prismatic. Compact masses cut into cabochons.

metacinnabar   Mercuric sulfide, HgS; isometric, usually massive; luster metallic; color grayish black, streak black; H, 3; brittle but sectile when massive. Distinguishable from **cinnabar**, *q.v.*, by its black color. Also termed **metacinnabarite.**

metastibnite   Antimony trisulfide, $Sb_2S_3(?)$; luster submetallic, color purplish gray, streak red; H, 2–3.

metastrengite   Iron phosphate, $2(FePO_4)\cdot 3½H_2O$; orthorhombic; crystals prismatic, often in minute spherules; H, 3–4; G, 2.76; cleavage one perfect. (**Strengite** is the iron-rich end member of the **variscite-strengite** series.)

meteorite   Stony or iron-nickel masses from outer space, usually iron with nickel or chromium, and magnetic. Etching of a polished surface with acid shows a crystal pattern known as Widmanstaetten lines. Cannot be cut with a diamond saw, which will clog and glaze.

miargyrite   Silver antimony sulfide, $AgSbS_2$; monoclinic, in complex crystals or massive; luster metallic-adamantine; color iron-black to steel-gray, streak cherry red. (In thin splinters color is deep blood red.) H, 2–2.5; G, 5.1–5.3. Abundant in some silver mines.

mica   Cf. **biotite, muscovite, lepidolite, phlogopite.** A rock-forming mineral.

microcline   A **feldspar**, *q.v.* Potassium aluminum silicate, $KAlSi_3O_8$; triclinic–pinacoidal; luster glassy; color flesh, green, red brown, white; H, 6; G, 2.5–2.6; fracture conchoidal; cleavage two good at near $90°$, poor prismatic; translucent.

microlite   Complex tantalum oxide with calcium, sodium, oxygen, and hydroxyl $(Na,Ca)_2Ta_2O_6(O,OH,F)$; cubic–hexoctahedral; luster resinous; color greenish yellow, yellow, yellow brown, red brown; H, 5–5.5; G, 4.2–6.4; fracture subconchoidal to uneven; no cleavage, brittle; transparent to translucent.

milky quartz   Crystal **quartz**, *q.v.*, of milky coloration.

millerite   Nickel sulfide, NiS; hexagonal–dihexagonal bipyramidal; luster metallic; color brass-yellow; H, 3–3.5; G, 5.3–5.6; fracture uneven, cleavage two rhombohedral, brittle.

mimetite   Lead chloroarsenate $(Pb,Cl)Pb_4(AsO_4)_3$; hexagonal, prismatic crystals rounded to globular forms; luster resinous; color pale yellow, light brown, colorless; streak white; H, 3.5; G, 7–7.25; brittle; soluble in nitric acid. (Yellow orange rounded masses can be cut cabochon with brilliant luster and unusual color.)

minervite   Cf. **taranakite.**

minium (red lead)   Lead oxide, Pb_3O_4; powder; luster dull; color bright red mixed with yellow, streak orange yellow; H, 2.3; G, 4.6. An oxidation product of **galena** and other lead minerals.

minnesotaite   Hydrous iron silicate, $Fe_3Si_4O_{10}(OH)_2$; may be isomorphous with **talc**, *q.v.*

mirabilite (glauber salt)   Hydrous sodium sulfate, $Na_2SO_4 \cdot 10H_2O$; monoclinic, generally as crusts and efflorescences; luster vitreous; color white; H, 1.5; G, 1.48; cleavage one perfect. Taste salty and bitter. Occurs on walls of mines where sulfide ores are decomposing; also as crusts about dry alkali lakes.

mojavite (mohavite)   Cf. **tincalconite.**

molybdenite   Molybdenum disulfide, MoS_2; hexagonal–dihexagonal bipyramidal; luster metallic; color lead-gray, streak gray; H, 1–1.5; G, 4.7–4.8; flexible leaves, cleavage perfect micaceous, brittle, sectile.

molybdite   Cf. **ferrimolybdite.**

monazite   Cerium lanthanum phosphate $(Ce,La,Y,Th)(PO_4)$; monoclinic–prismatic; luster subadamantine to resinous, color reddish brown to yellow, streak yellow brown; H, 5–5.5; G, 4.9–5.3; fracture conchoidal to uneven, cleavage one good, brittle; transparent to translucent.

montanite   Basic bismuth tellurate, $Bi_2(OH)_4TeO_4$.

montebrasite   Basic phosphate of aluminum and lithium, $LiAlPO_4(OH)$; isomorphous with **amblygonite** and **natromontebrasite**, *q.v.*

montmorillonite (saponite, hectorite)   Hydrous magnesium calcium aluminum silicate $(Al,Mg)_8(Si_4O_{10})_3(OH)_{10} \cdot 12H_2O$; massive, claylike; luster feeble; color white to rose red; very soft; G, 2; cleavage perfect basal. (The clay **bentonite**, *q.v.*, derives from the alteration of volcanic ash or tuff and is usually composed of montmorillonite.)

montroydite   Mercuric oxide, HgO; orthorhombic, prismatic crystals; luster brilliant, color and streak deep red; H, 1.5–2; cleavage one perfect; volatile.

moonstone   Adularescent **orthoclase feldspar**, *q.v.*, color silvery blue.

mordenite   A **zeolite**, *q.v.*, closely related to **heulandite**, *q.v.*; color white to cream; found as nodules.

morenosite   Hydrous nickel sulfate, $NiSO_4 \cdot 7H_2O$; orthorhombic; in acicular crystals, fibrous, as an efflorescence; luster vitreous; color apple green to greenish white; H, 2–2.5; G, 2; metallic taste.

morganite   Pink **beryl**, *q.v.*

morrisonite   Colorful banded **chert**, *q.v.*, found near Ashwood, Ore.

mottramite   Basic lead copper zinc vanadate $(Cu,Zn)Pb(VO_4)(OH)$; cf. **descloizite.**

mountain cork (mountain leather)   An amphibole; cf. **tremolite.**

muscovite (potash mica)   Hydrous potassium aluminum silicate (K,Na)-$(Al,Mg)(Si,Al)_4O_{10}(OH)_2$; monoclinic; hexagonal plates, plumose aggregates, scales, compact massive; luster vitreous; colorless, gray, brown, pale green, yellow, pink; streak colorless; H, 2–2.5; G, 2.76–3; cleavage perfect basal. **Sericite-margardorite-damourite** is a fine-grained, greasy-feeling muscovite forming sericitic schists. **Fuchsite** is an emerald-green chrome-muscovite; **agalmatolite** is in part a grayish compact or altered muscovite and in part a compact **pyrophyllite.** Muscovite mica is a common constituent of granites, pegmatites, gneisses, and schists, also called **mica** or **isinglass,** and is of economic importance when occurring in a large transparent "book" of sheets. Widespread and often mistaken for gold colors when panning.

nagyagite Sulfide of lead, gold, tellurium, and antimony; $Pb_5Au(Te,Sb)_4S_{5-8}$.

nahcolite Sodium bicarbonate, $NaHCO_3$; a naturally occurring baking soda.

napalite Hydrocarbon occasionally found with **cinnabar,** C_3H_4; luster resinous, color reddish brown; H, 2; G, 1.02; brittle.

natrolite Hydrous sodium aluminum slicate, $Na_2Al_2Si_3O_{10}\cdot10H_2O$; orthorhombic–rhombic pyramidal; coarse, prismatic crystals; luster glassy, colorless to white; H, 5–5.5; G, 2.2; fracture uneven, cleavage good prismatic; transparent to translucent; fluorescent orange.

natromontebrasite Basic phosphate of sodium, lithium, and aluminum (cf. **montebrasite**); $(Na,Li)Al(PO_4)(OH,F)$.

natron Hydrous sodium carbonate, $Na_2CO_3\cdot10H_2O$; occurs as a solid only in very dry regions, usually with other salts.

neotocite Hydrous manganese silicate, $MnO\cdot SiO_2\cdot nH_2O$; amorphous; luster dull, color black to dark brown; H, 3–4; G, 2.8; a manganiferous **opal.** (Sometimes the manganese may be removed by solution, leaving a spongy framework of **opal.**)

nepheline (nephelite) Sodium potassium aluminum silicate.$(Na,K)AlSiO_4$; hexagonal; rough prisms or massive, grains in syenitic rock; luster vitreous to greasy (which distinguishes this mineral from **feldspar,** *q.v.*); colorless, white, gray; H, 5.5–6; G, 2.5–2.6; cleavage none to poor. An essential constituent of some rocks.

nephrite Intermediate "jade" mineral between **actinolite** and **tremolite,** *q.v.,* and member of amphibole group; a calcium magnesium silicate with some iron; luster glassy, color greenish to dark green to black; H, 5–6; G, 2.9–3; fracture splintery, as material is fibrous and extremely tough.

neptunite Sodium potassium iron manganese titanosilicate $(Na,K)(Fe,Mn,Ti)Si_2O_6$; monoclinic–prismatic; luster glassy; color black, reddish; H, 5–6; G, 3.2; fracture splintery, cleavage perfect prismatic; translucent on edges.

nickel bloom Cf. **annabergite.**

nicolayite Cf. **thorogummite.**

nitrocalcite Native calcium nitrate, $Ca(NO_3)_2\cdot4H_2O$; as an efflorescence (often on old walls and in limestone caves).

nitroglauberite Cf. **darapskite.**

nivenite The mineral **uraninite,** *q.v.,* with cerium and yttrium; velvet black color.

nontronite Cf. **chloropal.**

norbergite Member of **humite** group, *q.v.,* $Mg_2SiO_4\cdot Mg(OH,F)_2$.

novaculite Pure white porous **quartz** cemented with **chalcedony,** known as "Arkansas stone," often colorfully stained and dendritic; occurs brecciated in shades of black, brown, green, gray, orange, red, and yellow.

obsidian Extrusive, glassy igneous rock, mostly silica and alumina with small quantities of iron oxide, potassium and sodium oxides, lime, and magnesia; color black (primarily), red- to brown-streaked, snowflake or "flowering," rainbow, black with gold or silvery inclusions, etc.; no crystal structure, hence considered a rock rather than a mineral; H, 5; G, 2.3–2.4; fracture conchoidal, brittle; nodular (**Apache tears,** *q.v.*), or massive as in Yellowstone National Park, northeast Calif., etc.

oligoclase   A plagioclase series **feldspar,** *q.v.;* sodium aluminum silicate, $NaAlSi_3O_8$; triclinic–pinacoidal; luster glassy; color bluish to clear, or reddish gold (**sunstone**); H, 6; G, 2.65; fracture conchoidal; cleavage two good at 94°, two poor prismatic; transparent to translucent.

olivenite   Basic arsenate of copper, $Cu_2(AsO_4)(OH)$; olive green, dull brown, or yellowish.

olivine   Name applied to a series of magnesium iron silicates $(Mg,Fe)_2$-SiO_4; luster glassy; color brown, green, light gray; H, 6.5–7; G, 3.3–3.4; fracture conchoidal; cleavage one fair, one poor; transparent to translucent. (Gem **periodt** is the **chrysolite** variety of olivine, while **dunite** is a pure olivine.)

onyx   Variety of **calcite,** *q.v.,* or a type of **chalcedony** showing strongly contrasting straight color bands, usually black and white. **Calcite onyx** is soft (3), like marble, whereas siliceous (agate) onyx, i.e., "true onyx," has a hardness of 6–7. **Cave onyx** is **travertine,** *q.v.,* color brown, deposited from cold water.

onyx marble   Cf. **aragonite.**

oolite   Silicified **limestone** containing small spherical concretions; color red or black. The name refers to its appearance like fish roe, and "oolitic" may be applied to jaspers, cherts, and flints.

opal   Silicon dioxide, $SiO_2 \cdot nH_2O$; amorphous; luster glassy to resinous; colorless and all light tints, rainbow, fire, black; H, 5–6; G, 1.9–2.2; fracture conchoidal; transparent to translucent; fluorescent yellow green.

opalite (myrickite)   Impure, usually massive form of opal; often colored red by inclusions of **cinnabar.**

opal wood   Petrified wood in which **opal,** often colorfully stained, has replaced the cell structure.

orbicular jasper   Cf. **jasper,** closely related to orbicular **chert,** *q.v.* Any of a variety of jaspers containing spherules of earthy matter as nuclei for radial growth of chalcedony-type quartz crystallizations; also called **"fish-egg" jasper, "flower" jasper,** or **"poppy" jasper.**

orbicular rhyolite   A **copper rhyolite,** cf. **cuprite,** consisting of small oval amygdules of clear **quartz, epidote,** and **copper ores** in a colorful pattern; color patchy green, orange, and red.

orpiment   Arsenic trisulfide, As_2S_3; monoclinic–prismatic; luster resinous to pearly; color yellow to orange yellow; H, 1.5–2; G, 3.4–3.5; flexible leaves, cleavage perfect micaceous, sectile; transparent to translucent.

orthoclase   A **feldspar,** *q.v.* Potassium aluminum silicate, $KAlSi_3O_8$; monoclinic–prismatic; luster glassy; colorless, brown, flesh, yellow, white; H, 6; G, 2.6; fracture conchoidal; cleavage two good at 90°, fair prismatic; transparent to translucent.

ottrelite   A variety of **chloritoid,** *q.v.;* as gray to black small scales in some schists.

ozokerite   A waxy hydrocarbon mineral mixture, colorless or white when pure, but often greenish, yellowish, to brown; may have unpleasant odor. Used to make ceresin, candles, impressions.

pachnolite   Hydrous fluoride of sodium, calcium, aluminum; $NaCaAlF_6 \cdot H_2O$; crystals monoclinic, colorless to white; H, 3; G, 3.

paragonite   Basic sodium aluminum silicate (a **mica** corresponding to **muscovite**, *q.v.*, but with sodium in place of potassium), $NaAl_3Si_3O_{10}(OH)_2$.

pargasite   Bluish green **hornblende**, *q.v.*

peacock copper   Cf. **bornite.**

pectolite   Hydrous calcium sodium silicate, $Ca_2NaSi_3O_8(OH)$; triclinic–pinacoidal; luster silky; color gray to white; H, 5; G, 2.7–2.8; fracture splintery, fibrous, translucent. Takes a fine polish.

penninite   A **chlorite,** *q.v.* Hydrous magnesium iron aluminum silicate, $H_8(Mg,Fe)_6Si_4O_{18}$ to $H_8(Mg,Fe)_5Al_2Si_3O_{18}$; monoclinic; plates, scales, scaly massive; luster vitreous to pearly; color emerald green, grass green, violet, rose red; H, 1.5–2; G, 2.6–1.85; similar to **clinochlore,** but with more iron. (A peach-blossom red variety, **kämmererite,** is associated with **chromite;** another similar mineral is **rhodochrome.**)

pentlandite   Nickel iron sulfide $(Fe,Ni)_9S_8$; isometric; massive, granular; luster metallic; color light bronze yellow, streak light bronze brown; H, 3.5–4; G, 5; octahedral parting, brittle; easily fusible, yielding a magnetic globule; soluble in HNO_3.

peridot   **Chrysolite** variety of **olivine,** *q.v.*, often found as gemmy crystals, color bright yellow green; H, 6.5–7; G, 3.3–3.5; transparent, often filled with inclusions of black spinel (?).

peridotite (pyroxenite)   Dark rock composed principally of **olivine,** *q.v.*, and **pyroxene,** *q.v.;* a matrix for diamonds.

peristerite   Variety of **albite,** *q.v.*, resembling moonstone; shows internal reflections of blue, green, or yellow.

perlite   Porous, puffy, lightweight **obsidian,** *q.v.*, as an alteration material due to weathering and entrapment of air; often contains **Apache tears,** *q.v.*, and larger masses of **obsidian.**

perovskite   Calcium titanate (may contain cerium and other rare-earth metals), $CaTiO_3$; cubic crystals or reniform masses; brown, grayish black, yellow; H, 5.5; G, 4.02–4.04.

perthite   A variety of feldspar in which several species, e.g., **albite** and **microcline,** *q.v.*, are interbraided and crisscrossed; cf. **amazonite.** Colors green, flesh red, green and white.

petalite   Lithium aluminum silicate, $LiAl(Si_2O_5)_2$ or $(Li,Na)AlSi_4O_{10}$; monoclinic; crystals rare, usually massive; luster vitreous to pearly, color white; H, 6–6.5; G, 2.39–2.46; brittle and shatters, cleavage one good; transparent to pearly. May be called **castorite;** sometimes confused with **spodumene,** *q.v.*

petzite   Silver gold telluride, Ag_3AuTe_2; isometric (?), massive; luster metallic; color steel-gray to black, streak black; H, 2.5–3; G, 8.7–9. Both **petzite** and **hessite,** *q.v.*, may grade into each other; usually associated together with **sylvanite** and **calaverite,** *q.v.*

phenakite   Beryllium silicate, Be_2SiO_4; hexagonal–rhombohedral; luster glassy; colorless, white; H, 7.5–8; G, 3; fracture conchoidal, cleavage poor prismatic, transparent to translucent. Resembles **quartz,** *q.v.;* prismatic crystals are main distinguishing characteristic.

phlogopite   Hydrous potassium magnesium aluminum silicate, $KMg_3AlSi_3O_{10}(OH)_2$; monoclinic–prismatic; luster pearly to metallic, color brown; H, 2.5–3; G, 2.7; flexible elastic leaves, cleavage perfect basal, translucent.

phosgenite   Chlorocarbonate of lead $(PbCl)_2CO_3$; tetragonal, prismatic crystals; luster adamantine, color white to yellow, streak white; H, 2.5–3; G, 6–6.3; cleavage prismatic and basal distinct. Effervesces in dilute nitric acid.

phosphoferrite Manganese ferrous hydrous phosphate $(Fe,Mn)_3(PO_4)_2 \cdot 3H_2O$; as white or greenish crystalline masses; H, 4–5; G, 3.2.

phosphosiderite Cf. **metastrengite.**

phosphuranylite Hydrous calcium uranium phosphate of indeterminate composition, $Ca_2(UO_2)_2(PO_4) \cdot xH_2O$; orthorhombic; luster glassy, color light yellow; soft, cleavage basal, brittle, transparent. Usually occurs as a crust; nonfluorescent.

pickeringite (magnesia alum) Hydrous aluminum magnesium sulfate, $MgSO_4 \cdot Al_2(SO_4)_3 \cdot 22H_2O$; monoclinic, fine acicular crystals and as an efflorescence; luster silky; colorless, white, yellowish, pink; H, 1; G, 1.85; taste bitter, astringent; soluble in water.

picotite Cf. **spinel.**

picrolite Columnar **serpentine,** *q.v.*

piedmontite Calcium aluminum manganese silicate, $Ca_2(Al,Mn)_3(SiO_4)_3 (OH)$; a reddish variety of **epidote,** *q.v.* Luster glassy to greasy; H, 6–7; G, 3.2–3.5; fracture conchoidal, cleavage one perfect; monoclinic crystals, transparent to translucent.

pinite Greenish **mica** pseudomorphs after **spodumene.**

pirssonite Hydrous calcium sodium carbonate, $Na_2Ca(CO_3)_2 \cdot 2H_2O$; crystals white to colorless, orthorhombic; H, 3; G, 2.35.

pisanite Hydrous copper iron sulfate $(Fe,Cu)SO_4 \cdot 7H_2O$; monoclinic; long slender prisms, stalactitic; luster vitreous, color greenish blue; H, 2–3; G, 2.15; cleavage one easy.

pisolite A limestone composed of rounded concretions about the size of a pea, giving rise to the adjective "pisolitic."

pistacite Distinctively pistachio-green **epidote,** *q.v.*

pitchblende Impure **uraninite,** *q.v.,* in black pitchlike masses.

plagioclase A continuous series of sodium calcium aluminum silicates from **albite** $(NaAlSi_3O_8)$, through **oligoclase, andesine, labradorite, bytownite,** to **anorthite** $(CaAl_2Si_2O_8)$; triclinic–pinacoidal; luster glassy; color black, reddish gray, yellow, white; H, 6; G, 2.6–2.8; fracture conchoidal; cleavage two good at 94°, two poor prismatic; transparent to translucent.

platiniridium Native elemental alloy of platinum and iridium (Pt,Ir); isometric, generally in grains and nuggets; luster metallic, color silver-white; H, 6–7; G, 22.65–22.84. (Much of the so-called platinum found in gold placers is really this alloy, widespread in Calif., and often mistaken for **lead.**)

platinum Element, Pt; cubic–hexoctahedral; luster metallic, color grayish white; H, 4–4.5; G, 14–19; fracture hackly, no cleavage, malleable, ductile; usually found impure.

plattnerite Native lead dioxide, PbO_2; usually occurs as iron black masses, luster submetallic.

pleonaste Cf. **spinel.**

plumbago Old name for **graphite,** *q.v.,* meaning "black lead."

plumbojarosite Iron lead sulfate, $PbFe_6(OH)_{12}(SO_4)_4$; rhombohedral, in minute tabular crystals; G, 3.67; color dark brown, cleavage rhombohedral.

pollucite Hydrous cesium aluminum silicate, $2Cs_2O \cdot 2Al_2O_3 \cdot 9SiO_2 \cdot H_2O$; isometric; in cubic crystals, also massive; colorless; H, 6.5; G, 2.9–2.94; quite brittle; crystals may be gray, yellowish, or pinkish and contain numerous small inclusions.

polybasite   Silver antimony sulfide, Ag_9SbS_6; monoclinic; tabular crystals and massive; luster metallic, color iron-black, streak black; H, 2–3; G, 6–6.2; resembles **stephanite,** *q.v.,* often mixed and seldom differentiated; can be distinguished in crystal form.

polycrase   Columbate and titanate of yttrium group metals, isomorphous with **euxenite,** *q.v.;* $(Y,Ca,Ce,U,Th)(Ti,Cb,Ta)_2O_6$; H, 5–6; G, 5.

polyhalite   Hydrous potassium calcium magnesium sulfate, $K_2Ca_2Mg(SO_4)_4 \cdot 2H_2O$; triclinic–pinacoidal; luster resinous, colorless to white; H, 3.5; G, 2.8; splintery, cleavage one good.

potash alum (kalinite)   Hydrous aluminum potassium sulfate, $K_2SO_4 \cdot Al_2(SO_4)_3 \cdot 24H_2O$; isometric, mealy crusts and fine fibers; luster vitreous, colorless or white; H, 2; G, 1.76; water-soluble.

prase   Quartz, *q.v.,* containing very numerous dark grayish green inclusions of **actinolite,** *q.v.*

prehnite   Hydrous calcium aluminum silicate, $Ca_2Al_2Si_3O_{10}(OH)_2$; orthorhombic–rhombic pyramidal; luster glassy; color greens, white; H, 6–6.5; G, 2.8–2.9; fracture uneven, cleavage basal; transparent to translucent. Splits easily along fibers but tough in thick sections.

priceite   Calcium borate, $Ca_4B_{10}O_{19} \cdot 7H_2O$; snow white, occurs massively.

probertite (kramerite)   Hydrous sodium calcium borate, $NaCaB_5O_9 \cdot 5H_2O$; monoclinic, in radial glassy aggregates; luster vitreous; colorless; H, 2.5–3.5; G, 2.14; cleavage perfect prismatic, brittle. Locally termed **boydite** in Inyo Co., Calif.

prochlorite   Hydrous iron magnesium aluminum silicate, a **chlorite,** *q.v.,* $H_8(Mg,Fe)_5Al_2Si_3O_{18}$; monoclinic or triclinic, forming large flaky masses in schists; luster pearly to vitreous; color green, blackish green, brown; streak uncolored or greenish; H, 1–2; G, 2.78–2.96 cleavage perfect basal. Iron-rich varieties become magnetic on heating.

prosopite   Basic fluoride of calcium and aluminum, $CaAl_2(F,OH)_8$; occurs pseudomorphically.

proustite   Silver arsenic sulfide, Ag_3AsS_3 hexagonal–ditrigonal pyramidal; luster adamantine, color reds; H, 2–2.5; G, 5.6–5.7; fracture conchoidal, cleavage rhombohedral, brittle; transparent to translucent. A very soft silver ore of which crystals may be cut into unusually beautiful rich-red faceted gems with a semimetallic luster.

pseudobrookite   Iron titanium oxide, Fe_2TiO_5; crystals small, orthorhombic, brown or black; G, 4.4–4.98.

pseudomalachite   Basic hydrous copper phosphate, $Cu_{10}(PO_4)_4(OH)_8 \cdot 2H_2O$; monoclinic, usually prismatic crystal aggregates forming drusy or botryoidal surfaces; luster vitreous; color dark emerald-green (crystals), lighter green (massive); streak pale green; cleavage one distinct, translucent to subtranslucent. A secondary mineral associated with **malachite,** *q.v.,* in the oxidized zone of copper deposits.

psilomelane   Basic barium oxide with manganese, $BaMnMn_8O_{16}(OH)_4$; orthorhombic; luster dull to submetallic, color black to steel-gray, streak brownish black to black; H, 5–6; G, 3.3–4.7; fracture conchoidal to smooth, no cleavage, brittle.

pumice, pumicite Lightweight volcanic glass (cf. **obsidian**); brownish, yellowish, gray, white, rarely red; hardened volcanic froth with many cavities. Powdered form used as an abrasive; **pumicite** is the naturally occurring volcanic dust.

purpurite Hydrous iron manganese phosphate $(Fe,Mn)_2O_3 \cdot P_2O_5 \cdot H_2O$; orthorhombic, in small irregular masses; luster satin, color deep red or purple; H, 4–4.5; G, 3.4; cleavage one. Similar to **vivianite**, *q.v.*, in its chemical reactions.

pyrargyrite (dark ruby-silver) Silver antimony sulfide, Ag_3SbS_3; hexagonal–rhombohedral; prismatic crystals, also massive; luster metallic, color grayish black or dark red, streak purplish red; H, 2.5; G, 5.85; cleavage distinct, brittle. Found in silver ore veins with **argentite, polybasite, stephanite, tetrahedrite,** and other silver minerals; often embedded in quartz, and good crystals may occur in cavities in quartz.

pyrite Iron sulfide, FeS_2; cubic–diploidal; luster metallic, color bright yellow; H, 6–6.5; G, 5; fracture conchoidal, no cleavage, very brittle (distinguishes itself as "fool's gold" from gold). Very abundant in ore deposits, coal veins, sediments; gem-quality cubes rare; usually flawed, impure, or likely to fall apart; makes beautiful, shining cabinet specimens; readily replaced by **limonite**, *q.v.*, to form "pseudomorphs after pyrite."

pyrochlore Oxide and fluoride of sodium, calcium, and columbium; $NaCaCb_2O_6F$, isomorphous with **microlite**, *q.v.;* brown or dark red.

pyrochroite Manganese hydroxide, $Mn(OH)_2$; hexagonal–rhombohedral, in hexagonal plates; luster pearly; color white, altering to brown and black; H, 2.5; G, 3.26; cleavage perfect basal.

pyrolusite Manganese dioxide, MnO_2; tetragonal–ditetragonal bipyramidal; luster metallic, color steel-gray to black, streak black; H, 6–6.5; G, 4.4–5; fracture uneven, cleavage prismatic, brittle to soft.

pyromorphite Lead chlorophosphate, $Pb_5(PO_4,AsO_4)_3Cl$; hexagonal–hexagonal bipyramidal; luster resinous; color greens, gray, brown; H, 3.5–4; G, 6.5–7.1; fracture subconchoidal to uneven, cleavage prismatic, brittle; translucent.

pyrope garnet Cf. **garnet.** Magnesium aluminum silicate, $Mg_3Al_2Si_3O_{12}$; H, 6–7.5; G, 3.5. Called "Arizona ruby," of deep yellow red color, transparent; used for gem faceting and in manufacture of garnet paper.

pyrophanite Deep red **ilmenite**, *q.v.*

pyrophyllite Hydrous aluminum silicate, $Al_2Si_4O_{10}(OH)_2$; monoclinic–prismatic; luster pearly to greasy; color greenish, silvery, white (often stained brown to black); H, 1–2; G, 2.8–2.9; flexible flakes, cleavage perfect micaceous, opaque to translucent.

pyrostilpnite (fireblende) Silver antimony sulfide, Ag_3SbS_3; monoclinic (?), crystals lathlike or tabular, slightly flexible in thin plates; luster adamantine, color hyacinth red, streak orange yellow; H, 2; G, 5.94; cleavage one perfect.

pyroxene Group name for a series of complex silicates of magnesium, iron, calcium, and aluminum, or varying combinations of these elements. The pyroxenes are common rock-forming minerals, found in both igneous and metamorphic rocks. The series includes: **augite,** commonest of all the pyroxenes, dark green to black; **enstatite,** magnesium silicate, $MgSiO_3$, also termed **bronzite; hypersthene,** iron magnesium silicate $(Fe,Mg)SiO_3$, sometimes termed **clinoferrosilite,** $FeSiO_3$; **diallage,** near **diopside** in composition, but usually with more or less aluminum; **diopside,** $CaMg(SiO_3)_2$, also known by the varietal names of **omphacite** and **diallage; hedenbergite,** $CaFeSi_2O_6$, a principal skarn mineral found with scheelite, magnetite, and garnet; **acmite-aegirite,** sodium iron silicate, essentially $NaFe(SiO_3)_2$; and **jadeite,** sodium aluminum silicate, $NaAl(SiO_3)_2$. **Augite** is an essential constituent of diorites, gabbros, diabases, andesites, pyroxenites, and other basic eruptives. **Clinofer-rosilite,** the pure-iron member, is characteristic of lithophysae in obsidians. **Enstatite** is a rock-forming mineral characteristic of gabbros and gabbro derivatives, e.g., serpentinized rocks. **Hypersthene** is a constituent of basic eruptive rocks, especially gabbros and andesites. **Diallage** is the common pyroxene of gabbro; **diopside,** grass green to purple, is characteristic of crystalline limestones, metamorphosed eruptives, and some schists. The soda-pyroxene **acmite-aegirite** is a rock-forming mineral prominent in some syenites.

pyrrhotite (magnetic pyrite) Ferrous sulfide, $Fe_{1-x}S$; hexagonal; crystals rare, commonly massive, either granular or compact; luster metallic, color bronze-brown, streak grayish black; H, 3.5–4.5; G, 4.58–4.64; brittle; usually magnetic, becoming more strongly so on heating. Often associated with **pyrite, chalcopyrite,** and **arsenopyrite,** and sometimes found in large lenticular masses. Common in gold and copper districts; occasionally it is accompanied by nickel minerals.

quartz Silicon dioxide, SiO_2; hexagonal–trigonal trapezohedral; luster glassy; colorless, clear, amethyst, rose, brown, smoky, green, black, white, almost any tint owing to impurities; H, 7; G, 2.6; fracture conchoidal, cleavage rhombohedral, transparency dependent on impurities and color. Four types of quartz include: **crystalline:** amethyst, asteriated, aventurine, cat's-(tiger's-) eye, citrine, cristobalite, dumortierite, ferruginous, green, prase, rock crystal, rutilated, sagenite, smoky, tridymite; **cryptocrystalline;** agate, bloodstone (heliotrope), carnelian, chalcedony, chrysoprase, gastroliths, jasper, onyx, petrified organic remains, plasma, sardonyx; **intermediate forms:** chert, diatomite, flint, novaculite, siliceous sinter, tripolite; **massive quartz:** milky quartz, quartzite, rose quartz, sandstone.

quartzite Metamorphosed sandstone cemented by silica so that breakage is through, not around, the individual grains; often highly colored by impurities. For characteristics, cf. **quartz.**

quartz porphyry Cf. **leopardite.**

quicksilver Cf. **mercury.**

rainbow obsidian Iridescent **obsidian,** *q.v.*

rasorite Cf. **kernite.**

realgar Arsenic sulfide, AsS; monoclinic–prismatic; luster resinous, color orange red; H, 1.5–2; G, 3.5; fracture subconchoidal; cleavage perfect side, fair basal; sectile, transparent to translucent.

red copper ore Cf. **cuprite.**

reddingite Hydrous manganese phosphate, $Mn_3(PO_4)_2 \cdot 3H_2O$; crystals orthorhombic, pinkish or yellowish white; isomorphous with **phosphofer-rite,** *q.v.*

red lead Cf. **minium.**

red ocher Cf. **hematite.**

rhodochrosite Manganese carbonate, $MnCO_3$; hexagonal–hexagonal scalenohedral; luster vitreous to pearly; color brown, gray, pinks; H, 3.5–4; G, 3.4–3.6; fracture conchoidal, cleavage perfect rhombohedral, brittle; translucent to transparent.

rhodolite   Pale red to rose **garnet,** *q.v.*

rhodonite   Manganese silicate, $MnSiO_3$; triclinic-pinacoidal; luster glassy, color gray to pink; massive, rarely as crystals; H, 5.5–6; G, 3.4–3.7; fracture splintery, cleavage prismatic, brittle; transparent to translucent. Often attractively veined with black and brown.

rhyolite   Light-colored felsitic extrusive igneous rock, often characterized by flow lines.

ricolite   Fine-grained, curiously banded **serpentine,** *q.v.,* found near Rico, N.M.

riebeckite   Basic sodium ferrous and ferric iron silicate—a **soda amphibole** in which **crocidolite** is the finely fibrous form ("blue asbestos")—$Na_6Fe''_6$-$Fe'''_4Si_{16}O_{46}(OH)_2$.

rock crystal   Transparent, colorless **quartz,** *q.v.*

rock salt   Cf. **halite.**

rosasite   Basic carbonate of copper and zinc (a zinky **malachite,** *q.v.*) $(Cu,Zn)_2(OH)_2(CO_3)$.

roscherite   Hydrous basic phosphate of aluminum, manganese, calcium, and iron; $(Ca,Mn,Fe)_2Al(PO_4)_2(OH)\cdot2H_2O$; as dark brown monoclinic crystals.

roscoelite (vanadium mica)   Hydrous potassium aluminum vanadium silicate, $K_2(Mg,Fe,V,Al)_4(Si,Al)_8O_{20}(OH)_4$; monoclinic; in minute scales, often in stellate groups; luster pearly; color clove brown, greenish brown, dark green; H, 2.5; G, 2.97; cleavage perfect basal.

rosolite   Rose pink **grossularite garnet,** *q.v.*

rowlandite   Yttrium silicate with iron and fluorine; massive, grayish green.

rubellite   Red **tourmaline,** *q.v.*

ruby   Red **corundum,** *q.v.*

ruby silver   Cf. **pyrargyrite, proustite.**

ruby zinc   Bright red **sphalerite,** *q.v.*

rutilated quartz   Cf. **rock crystal (quartz);** contains needlelike inclusions of **rutile,** *q.v.*

rutile   Titanium oxide, TiO_2; tetragonal–ditetragonal bipyramidal; luster metallic-adamantine; color black, golden to brownish red; streak brownish; H, 6–6.5; G, 4.2–4.3; fracture subconchoidal to uneven, cleavage basal and prismatic; thinly translucent to transparent. Natural rutile suitable for faceting only in dark red crystals.

sagenite   Any **quartz,** *q.v.,* containing needlelike inclusions is collectively known by this term. Usually, however, it relates to sagenitic **agate** or **chalcedony,** in which slender needles of foreign mineral materials penetrate and crisscross in translucent **chalcedony.**

sal ammoniac   Ammonium chloride, NH_4Cl; isometric; crystals, crusts, efflorescences; luster vitreous; color white, yellowish, grayish; H, 1.5–2; G, 1.528; rather brittle; soluble in water, volatilizes.

samarskite   Complex mixture of rare-earth elements with columbium and tantalum oxide; luster vitreous to resinous, color velvety black (on fresh surface), streak reddish brown to black; H, 5–6; G, 4.1–6.2; fracture conchoidal, cleavage one poor, brittle; thin edges translucent. Often found in pegmatites, may be faceted.

sanbornite   Triclinic barium silicate, $BaSi_2O_5$; rare.

sanidine   Variety of **orthoclase feldspar,** *q.v.,* peculiar to volcanic rocks as flat tabular crystals, bluish. Cf. **moonstone.**

saponite   Cf. **montmorillonite.**

sapphire   Cornflower blue **corundum,** *q.v.*

sard   Pale brown **chalcedony,** *q.v.*

sardonyx   **Sard** or **carnelian,** *q.v.,* showing alternating white bands.

satelite   Fibrous **serpentine,** *q.v.;* silky, grayish green, opaque, chatoyant.

satin spar   Fibrous variety of **calcite,** *q.v.;* term also applied to a silky variety of **gypsum,** *q.v.*

scapolite   Group name for a series of aluminum silicates with sodium and calcium (**meionite, missonite, marialite, wernerite**); tetragonal; luster dull to greasy; color gray, milky, blue, pink, violet, yellow, white; H, 5.5–6; G, 2.7; fracture subconchoidal, cleavage poor prismatic, transparent to translucent; may fluoresce orange to yellow, and red.

scheelite   Calcium tungstate, $CaWO_4$; tetragonal–tetragonal bipyramidal; luster adamantine; color brownish, greenish, white; H, 4.5–5; G, 5.9–6.1; fracture uneven, cleavage three, transparent to translucent; fluorescent blue to yellow.

schorl   Black **tourmaline,** *q.v.*

schorlomite   Iron calcium titanate and silicate, $Ca_3(Fe,Ti)_2[(Si,Ti)O_4]_3$; black masses, luster vitreous, related to **garnet**; H, 7–7.5; G, 3.81–3.88.

schroeckingerite   Hydrous carbonate, sulfate, and fluoride of calcium, sodium, and uranyl; $NaCa_3(UO_2)(CO_3)_3F\cdot10H_2O$.

scolecite   Hydrous calcium aluminum silicate, $CaAl_2Si_3O_{10}\cdot3H_2O$; monoclinic; crystals slender prismatic, also massive, fibrous; luster vitreous, silky when fibrous; color white; H, 5–5.5; G, 2.16–2.4; cleavage nearly perfect prismatic. A **zeolite,** *q.v.,* formed as a secondary mineral in cavities of igneous rocks and sometimes as veins.

scorodite   Hydrous ferric arsenate, $Fe(AsO_4)\cdot2H_2O$; orthorhombic–rhombic bipyramidal; luster glassy to subadamantine, color brownish green to green; H, 3.5–4; G, 3.1–3.3; fracture uneven, cleavage poor, brittle; transparent to translucent.

scorzalite   High-iron magnesium aluminum phosphate; cf. **lazulite;** $(Fe,Mg)Al_2(PO_4)_2(OH)_2$.

searlesite   Hydrous sodium borosilicate, $NaB(SiO_3)_2\cdot H_2O$; monoclinic; prismatic, in radiate-fibrous spherulites; very soft, G, about 2.45; color white, cleavage one perfect. Named from its occurrence as crusts of white spherulites at Searles Lake, Calif.

selenite   Variety of **gypsum,** *q.v.,* occurring as transparent crystals to considerable size; monoclinic; H, 2; glassy.

senarmontite   Native antimony trioxide, Sb_2O_3; as octahedral crystals or in masses.

sericite   Cf. **muscovite.**

serpentine   Hydrous magnesium silicate, $Mg_3Si_2O_5(OH)_4$; monoclinic–prismatic; luster greasy, silky, waxy; color brown, black, red, yellow, green, white; H, 2–5; G, 2.2–2.6; fibrous, cleavage none, greasy feel; opaque to translucent, sometimes fluorescent; includes **antigorite** (platy), **chrysotile asbestos, marmolite** (micaceous), **ophiolite, picrolite, retinalite, williamsite.** The popular **verde antique** ("ancient green") type is used in building decoration. **Precious serpentines** are those of light color, compact, and translucent; **bowenite** varieties are pale green; **williamsite** rich bluish green, highly translucent; **satelite** is fibrous and makes into "cat's-eyes."

shale   Solidified clay, always sedimentary.

shattuckite   Hydrous copper silicate, $2CuSiO_3 \cdot H_2O$; massive, fibrous, blue; G, 3.8.

shortite   Sodium calcium carbonate, $Na_2Ca_2(CO_3)_3$.

siderite   Iron carbonate, $FeCO_3$; hexagonal–hexagonal scalenohedral; luster vitreous to pearly; color brown, gray, white; H, 3.5–4; G, 3.8–3.9; fracture conchoidal, cleavage rhombohedral, brittle; transparent to translucent.

siderotil   Hydrous ferrous sulfate, $FeSO_4 \cdot 5H_2O$.

sienna   Brownish yellow earth (iron oxide) used as a pigment in oils; turns orange red to reddish brown when burned.

siliceous oolite   Limestone in which many spherical concretions are replaced by silica; color black, red.

silicified coral   Fossil **coral** replaced by **chalcedony,** *q.v.*

sillimanite   Aluminum silicate, Al_2SiO_5; orthorhombic–rhombic bipyramidal; luster satiny; color brownish, greenish, white; H, 6–7; G, 3.2–3.3; fracture splintery, cleavage perfect pinacoid; transparent to translucent.

silver   Element, Ag; cubic–hexoctahedral; luster metallic; color bright white, usually tarnished to black; H, 2.5–3; G, 10–11; malleable, ductile.

siserskite   Cf. **iridosmine.**

slate   Metamorphosed clay, resembling shale; characterized by small mica flakes; splits easily into thin sheets.

smaltite   Cobalt arsenide $(Co,Ni)As_{.5-1}$; isometric, generally massive; luster metallic, color tin-white, streak grayish black; H, 5.5–6; G, 6.1–6.8; brittle. Becomes magnetic when roasted.

smaragdite   Green foliated **amphibole,** *q.v.*

smithsonite   Zinc carbonate, $ZnCO_3$; hexagonal–hexagonal scalenohedral; luster subadamantine; color bluish, greenish, yellow, white; H, 5; G, 4.3–4.4; fracture conchoidal, cleavage rhombohedral, brittle, translucent.

smoky quartz   **Rock crystal,** cf. **quartz,** colored blackish or smoky.

snowflake obsidian   A variety of **obsidian,** *q.v.*, in which light gray to bluish gray spots occur, looking like snowflakes in the glossy black obsidian.

soapstone   Cf. **talc.**

soda-dravite   Brown **tourmaline,** *q.v.*, $NaMg_3B_3Al_3(Al_3Si_6O_{12})(OH)_4$.

sodalite   Sodium aluminum silicate with chlorine, $Na_4Al_3Si_3O_{12}Cl$; cubic hexoctahedral; luster glassy; colorless, blue, pink, violet, white; H, 5.5–6; G, 2.2–2.3; fracture conchoidal to uneven, cleavage poor dodecahedral; transparent to translucent, often fluorescent yellow orange.

soda niter (chili saltpeter)   Sodium nitrate, $NaNO_3$; hexagonal–rhombohedral; crystals, incrustations, massive; luster vitreous; color white, reddish, grayish, yellowish; H, 1.5–2; G, 2.24–2.29; cleavage perfect rhombohedral; cool taste. Occurs as white incrustations formed by evaporation in very arid regions.

spangolite   Hydrous basic sulfate and chloride of aluminum and copper, $Cu_6Al(SO_4)(OH)_{12}Cl \cdot 3H_2O$; dark green hexagonal crystals.

specularite Jaspery material laced with bands of dark steel-gray **hematite**.

spessartite garnet Cf. **garnet**. Manganese aluminum silicate, $Mn_3Al_2Si_3$-O_{12}; color dark brown to pinkish, reddish, black; G, 4.2.

sphalerite Zinc sulfide, ZnS; cubic-hextetrahedral; luster adamantine; colorless through black, reddish brown, yellow; H, 3.5–4; G, 3.9–4.1; fracture conchoidal, cleavage perfect dodecahedral, brittle; opaque to transparent.

sphene Calcium titanium silicate, $CaTiSiO_5$; monoclinic–prismatic; luster adamantine; color gray, green, brown, yellow; H, 5–5.5; G, 3.4–3.5; fracture conchoidal, cleavage fair prismatic; transparent to translucent. Cf. also **titanite**.

spinel Magnesium aluminum oxide, $MgAl_2O_4$; cubic–hexoctahedral; luster glassy; color blue, green, black, violet, orange brown, white (in fact all colors but rarely pure or clear); H, 7.5–8; G, 3.5–4.1; fracture conchoidal, cleavage none, brittle; opaque to transparent.

spodumene Lithium aluminum silicate, $LiAlSi_2O_6$; monoclinic–prismatic; luster glassy; color buff, greenish, lavender, opaque, white, i.e.: **hiddenite**, bluish green; **kunzite**, lilac, pink, violet; H, 6.5–7; G, 3.1–3.2; fracture uneven, cleavage perfect prismatic; transparent to translucent; thermoluminescent, often fluorescent and/or phosphorescent orange.

stannite Copper iron tin sulfide, Cu_2FeSnS_4; tetragonal; crystals rare, massive granular; luster metallic, color steel-gray to iron-black, streak blackish; H, 4; G, 4.3–4.5; cleavage poor. Decomposed by nitric acid.

staurolite Iron aluminum silicate, $FeAl_4Si_2O_{10}(OH)_2$; orthorhombic–rhombic bipyramidal; luster glassy, color brown; H, 7–7.5; G, 3.6–3.7; fracture subconchoidal, cleavage fair pinacoidal; transparent to translucent. Also termed **fairy crosses** because the crystal form is a perfect cross.

steatite Cf. **talc**.

stellerite Cf. **stilbite**.

stephanite Silver antimony sulfide, Ag_5SbS_3; orthorhombic–pyramidal; luster metallic, color iron-black; H, 2–2.5; G, 6.2–6.3; fracture subconchoidal to uneven, cleavage two poor, brittle; darkens to black on standing.

stibnite Antimony sulfide, Sb_2S_3; orthorhombic–bipyramidal; luster metallic, color steel-gray; H, 2; G, 4.5–4.6; fracture subconchoidal, cleavage perfect side pinacoid, sectile.

stilbite Hydrous calcium sodium aluminum silicate $(CaNa)_3Al_5(Al,Si)Si_{14}$-$O_{40}\cdot15H_2O$; monoclinic–prismatic; luster glassy; color brown, reddish, yellow, white; H, 3.5–4; G, 2.1–2.2; fracture irregular, cleavage one perfect; transparent to translucent.

stilpnomelane Hydrous iron magnesium aluminum silicate, $2(Fe,Mg)O\cdot$-$(Fe,Al)_2O_3\cdot5SiO_2\cdot3H_2O$; monoclinic, micaceous; luster brassy to submetallic; color black, yellowish, greenish bronze; H, 3–4; G, 2.77–2.96; becomes magnetic on heating. **Chalcodite** is a rare brown variety, occurring in minute scales, often with a bronze luster.

stolzite Native lead tungstate, $PbWO_4$; isomorphous with **wulfenite,** q.v., and probably with **scheelite** and **powellite**, q.v.

stream tin Cf. **cassiterite**.

strengite Hydrous iron phosphate, $FePO_4\cdot2H_2O$; orthorhombic, generally in spherical and botryoidal forms; luster vitreous, color pale red; H, 3–4; G, 2.87; cleavage one perfect. Cf. also **metastrengite**.

stromeyerite (copper silver glance) Silver copper sulfide $(Ag,Cu)_2S$;

orthorhombic, generally compact massive; luster metallic, color and streak dark steel-gray; H, 2–2.5; G, 6.15–6.3.

strontianite   Strontium carbonate, $SrCO_3$; orthorhombic–rhombic bipyramidal; luster glassy; colorless, green, pink, yellow to brownish, white; H, 3.5–4; G, 3.7; fracture uneven; cleavage one good, one poor; brittle; transparent to translucent.

succinite   Mineralogic name for **amber,** *q.v.*

sulfur   Element, S; orthrhombic–bipyramidal; luster resinous, color yellow to amber; H, 2; G, 2–2.1; fracture conchoidal, cleavage basal, brittle.

sunstone   An **aventurine feldspar,** *q.v.*, containing inclusions of **hematite** and **goethite,** *q.v.*

sylvanite (graphic tellurium)   Gold silver telluride $(Au,Ag)Te_2$; monoclinic, bladed crystals and massive; luster metallic, color silver-white to yellow, streak silver-gray; H, 1.5–2; G, 7.9–9.3; often present in gold districts where tellurium occurs. The tellurium can be driven off by heating, leaving a button of gold-silver alloy. Cf. **calaverite.**

sylvite   Potassium chloride, KCl; colorless cubes or crystalline masses like rock salt, taste sharper than table salt; H, 2; G, 1.98. Occurs naturally in large quantities; used extensively as a fertilizer.

szaibelyite   Hydrous magnesium borate, $2MgO \cdot B_2O_3 \cdot H_2O$; orthorhombic, fibrous; color white; H, less than 3; G, 2.6. This mineral combines **ascharite, camsellite,** and **beta-ascharite.**

talc   Hydrous magnesium silicate, $Mg_3Si_4O_{10}(OH)_2$; monoclinic–prismatic; luster greasy to pearly, greasy feel; color blackish, gray, greenish, white; H, 1; G, 2.7–2.8; cleavage micaceous; opaque to translucent.

tantalite   Iron manganese tantalate $(Fe,Mn)(Ta,Cb)_2O_6$; orthorhombic–rhombic–bipyramidal; luster submetallic to resinous, colorless to black or reddish brown; streak brown to black, white; H, 6; G, 5.2–8; fracture uneven, cleavage front and side pinacoid, brittle; opaque to transparent.

taranakite   Possibly $K_2Al_6(PO_4)_6(OH)_2 \cdot 18H_2O$, basic hydrous potassium-aluminum phosphate; massive, claylike; color white, gray, yellowish white; very soft; unctuous to touch; G, 2+. Taranakite is found as a deposit in caves or along sea coasts, produced by chemical alteration of bat or bird guano.

tektite   Small, round, vitreous objects resembling glass with internal swirl marks, or grooved and channeled on the outside; a Texas variety known as **bediasite** has H, 5–6; G, 2.3–2.4; color greenish to black and dark brown; fracture conchoidal, tough. Cf. also **meteorite.** Of unknown origin, tektites are thought by some astronomers to be fragments of the moon knocked off and into the earth's gravitational field by impacting asteroidal masses.

tellurium   Element, Te; hexagonal–trigonal trapezohedral; luster metallic, color tin-white; H, 2–2.5; G, 6.1–6.3; fracture uneven; cleavage prismatic good, poor basal; brittle.

tennantite   Cf. **tetrahedrite.**

tenorite (melaconite)   Cupric oxide, CuO; monoclinic; in minute scales, also as an earthy powder, massive; luster metallic to dull, color and streak black; H, 3–4; G, 5.82–6.5. Massive material is commonly termed **melaconite.**

tephroite   Manganese silicate, Mn_2SiO_4; orthorhombic, usually massive;

luster vitreous to greasy, color grayish red to smoky gray, streak pale gray; H, 5.5; G, 4.1; cleavage one distinct. Soluble in HCl with gelatinization.

terlinguaite   Mercuric oxychloride, Hg_2ClO; yellow monoclinic crystals; H, 2–3; G, 8.7.

tetradymite   Bismuth telluride, Bi_2Te_2S; hexagonal–rhombohedral, commonly in bladed forms foliated to granular massive; luster metallic, color steel-gray; H, 1.5–2; G, 7.2–7.6; cleavage perfect basal.

tetrahedrite   Copper iron antimony sulfide $(Cu,Fe)_{12}Sb_4S_{13}$; cubic–hextetrahedral; luster metallic, color gray to black; H, 3–4.5; G, 4.6–5.1; fracture subconchoidal to uneven, no cleavage, brittle. Common in many gold and copper mines, occurring in small amounts mixed with galena, sphalerite, chalcopyrite, and other sulfide ores. The mineral **freibergite (argentian tetrahedrite)** is the silver variety and most common form found in Calif. mines.

thaumasite   Variety of snow-white, chatoyant **prehnite**, *q.v.*, weakly chatoyant, soft masses occurring in cavities in pillow basalts.

thenardite   Sodium sulfate, Na_2SO_4; orthorhombic–rhombic bipyramidal; luster glassy, colorless to brown or yellow; H, 2.5–3; G, 2.7; fracture uneven, cleavage good basal; transparent to translucent, fluorescent greenish yellow.

thetis hairstone   Cf. **quartz.**

thinolite   Cf. **calcite.**

thomsonite   A **zeolite** mineral, *q.v.* Complex hydrous calcium sodium aluminum silicate $(Ca,Na_2)Al_2Si_2O_8 \cdot 2\frac{1}{2}H_2O$; orthorhombic; fibrous, extremely compact, nodular and composed of radiated masses of microscopic needles; color white with concentric markings in cream, black, and green; H, 5; G, 2.3–2.4. **Lintonite** is a compact, translucent variety of dull green color.

thorite (uranothorite)   Thorium silicate, $ThSiO_4$; tetragonal, usually in square prisms with crystals resembling **zircon,** also massive compact; luster vitreous to resinous; color black or orange, when altered (usually containing H_2O); H, 4.5–5; G, 4.4–5.4; cleavage distinct; transparent to nearly opaque. Altered **thorite** is termed **orangeite.** Characteristic of pegmatites and often occurring in gold placers.

thorogummite   Hydrous thorium silicate, $Th(SiO_4)_{1-x}(OH)_{4x}$; fine-grained aggregates, as a result of hydration of **thorite,** *q.v.,* with nearly identical cell size. The name takes precedence over **hydrothorite, nicolayite, maitlandite, mackintoshite,** or **hyblite,** which are minor chemical variants of a single phase.

thulite   Fluorescent pink **zoisite,** *q.v.*

thunderegg   Special type of nodule, concretion, or aggregation of chalcedony with external rind of silicified volcanic ash and star-shaped core of translucent, usually banded **chalcedony,** *q.v.,* rarely **carnelian;** externally covered by "warty" protuberances, while interior chalcedony is often beautifully patterned with fine plume, sagenitic or moss **agate;** occurs sometimes as singles (usually), doubles, and/or triples.

thuringite   A chlorite family mineral (basic aluminum iron silicate), occurring as an aggregation of tiny scales; olive green, luster pearly.

tiemannite   Mercuric selenide, $HgSe$; hextetrahedral; generally massive, compact; luster metallic, color steel-gray to dark lead-gray, streak black; H, 2.5; G, 8.19–8.47. Gives off a "rotten radish" odor of **selenium** when heated on charcoal.

tiger's-eye   Cf. **hawk's-eye.**

tin   Element, Sn; tetragonal; luster metallic, color tin-white; H, 2; G, 7.31; fracture hackly, ductile, malleable. Tin is a mineralogic rarity, usually occurring as irregular rounded grains.

tincalconite (mojavite, mohavite)   Hydrous sodium borate, $Na_2B_4O_7\cdot5H_2O$; hexagonal–rhombohedral, fine-grained crystalline powder; color dull white; soft, G, 1.88; forms rapidly whenever borax is exposed to air.

tinstone   Cf. **cassiterite.**

titanite   Alternative name for **sphene,** q.v.

topaz   Aluminum fluosilicate, $Al_2SiO_4(F,OH)_2$; orthorhombic–rhombic bipyramidal; luster glassy; colorless, bluish, browns, yellow brown, yellow, white, orange yellow, purple, red, pale green; H, 8; G, 3.5–3.6; fracture conchoidal, cleavage perfect basal; transparent to translucent. **Golden topaz** is pale yellow; **imperial topaz** is deep orange yellow; crystals sometimes very large.

topazolite   Variety of topaz-yellow **andradite garnet,** q.v.

torbernite   Hydrous copper uranium phosphate, $Cu(UO_2)(PO_4)_2\cdot8\text{-}12H_2O$; luster vitreous to pearly, color green; H, 2–2.5; G, 3.2–3.6; no fracture, cleavage perfect basal, brittle; transparent to translucent.

tourmaline   A series name for aluminum silicates that include **lime-dravite, lithia-tourmaline, rubellite** (red), **indicolite** (blue), **schorl** (black), **soda-dravite,** q.v.; luster glassy; other colors various shades of green, colorless (**achroite**), pink, white; H, 7–7.5; G, 3–3.3; hexagonal–ditrigonal pyramidal; fracture conchoidal to uneven, cleavage poor prismatic and rhombohedral; transparent to opaque; often two or more colors per crystal; characteristic bulging triangular cross section, usually occurs as long striated crystals with strong color change according to direction (blue and green through sides, pink and red through ends).

travertine   A water-deposited **calcite,** q.v., laid down by hot springs; soft, porous, variously colored by impurities.

tremolite   Calcium magnesium silicate, $Ca_2Mg_5Si_8O_{22}(OH)_2$; monoclinic–prismatic; a light-colored **actinolite,** q.v.

tridymite   Silicon dioxide, SiO_2; orthorhombic–rhombic bipyramidal; luster glassy, colorless to white; H, 7; G, 2.3; fracture conchoidal, cleavage prismatic; transparent to translucent. Cf. **quartz,** but distinguishable by tabular crystallization; a high-temperature silicate.

triphane   Colorless to yellow **spodumene,** q.v.

triphylite   Lithium iron phosphate, $LiFePO_4$; orthorhombic–rhombic bipyramidal; luster glassy, color blue-green-gray; H, 4.5–5; G, 3.4–3.6; fracture uneven; cleavage one fair, two imperfect; brittle; transparent to translucent; usually associated with **lithiophilite,** q.v.

troilite   Ferrous sulfide, FeS; hexagonal; massive, compact granular; luster metallic, color light grayish brown speedily tarnishing to bronze brown, streak black; H, 3.4–4.5; G, 4.67–4.82. This mineral is known principally from meteorites; its only known terrestrial occurrence is massive in a sheared zone of serpentine in Del Norte Co., Calif., northeast of Crescent City at a copper mine.

trona (urao)   Hydrous carbonate and bicarbonate of sodium, $Na_2CO_3\cdot HNaCO_3\cdot2H_2O$; monoclinic; in plates or slender crystals, often fibrous or columnar massive; luster vitreous, glistening; color gray or yellowish white; H, 2.5–3; G, 2.11–2.14; cleavage one perfect. Occurs in the deposits of saline lakes or produced by evaporation of their waters.

troostite   Brownish, opaque variety of **willemite**, *q.v.*

tschermigite (ammonia alum)   Hydrous aluminum ammonium sulfate $(NH_4)_2SO_4 \cdot Al_2(SO_4)_3 \cdot 24H_2O$; isometric; octahedral crystals (brilliant), fibrous crusts; luster vitreous, colorless or white; H, 2; G, 1.64; water-soluble, found in geyser regions.

tungstite   Tungsten oxide plus water, $WO_3 \cdot xH_2O$; orthorhombic; color yellow, streak yellow; H, 2.5; G, 5.5; powdery, cleavage two; closely associated with **huebnerite** and **wolframite**, *q.v.*

turquoise   Hydrous basic aluminum phosphate with copper, $CuAl_6(PO_4)$-$(OH)_8 \cdot 4H_2O$; luster porcelaneous, color greenish blue to sky blue; H, 5–6; G, 2.6–2.8; fracture smooth, brittle; translucent thinly to opaque; chalky appearance in rough.

tyuyamunite   Hydrous vanadate of copper and uranium, $Cu(UO_2)_2$-$(VO_4)_2 \cdot nH_2O$; an important uranium ore.

ulexite   Hydrous sodium calcium borate, $NaCaB_5O_9 \cdot 8H_2O$; triclinic–pinacoidal; luster silky, color white; H, 1; G, 1.6; soft and cottony; translucent. Compact fibrous variety is strongly chatoyant (H, 2–2.5); cuts pure-white cat's-eyes and spheres.

unakite   A light-green **epidote**, *q.v.*, in which is mixed an equal proportion of bright red to pink **feldspar;** named after Unaka Mts. between N.C. and Tenn.

uraconite   Hydrous uranium sulfate, SO_3,UO_3,H_2O; orthorhombic; minute laths, earthy, or scaly; color lemon yellow; soft, soluble in acids. This "yellow uranium ocher" occurs as an alteration product of **pitchblende**, *q.v.*, in coatings.

uraninite   Uranium dioxide, UO_2; cubic–hexoctahedral; luster dull, submetallic; color steel-gray to brownish black; streak gray, brownish black, green; H, 5–6; G, 6.4–9.7; fracture conchoidal, no cleavage, brittle; opaque, radioactive. Cf. **pitchblende.**

uranophane   Hydrous calcium uranium silicate, $CaU_2Si_2O_{11} \cdot 7H_2O$; orthorhombic–rhombic bipyramidal; luster glassy to pearly, color yellow to orange yellow; H, 2–3; G, 3.8–3.9; translucent, moderately fluorescent greenish yellow.

uranospinite   Hydrous calcium uranium arsenate, $Ca(UO_2)_2(AsO_4)_2 \cdot 8H_2O$; as green tubular crystals.

uranothorite   Cf. **thorite.**

urao   Cf. **trona.**

uvarovite garnet   Cf. **garnet;** calcium chromium silicate, $Ca_3Cr_2Si_3O_{12}$; color emerald-green; H, 6–7.5; G, 3.8.

valencianite   Cf. **orthoclase feldspar.**

valentinite   Antimony oxide, Sb_2O_3; orthorhombic; in prismatic crystals, generally columnar massive; luster adamantine; color snow white, ash gray, lemon yellow; streak white; H, 2.5; G, 5.76; cleavage one perfect. An oxidation product of antimony minerals, especially of **stibnite**, *q.v.*, and usually present in antimony ores.

vanadinite   Lead chlorovanadate, $Pb_5(VO_4)_3Cl$; hexagonal–hexagonal bipyramidal; luster resinous; color brown, yellow brown, red-orange-brown; H, 2.7–3; G, 6.7–7.1; fracture uneven, no cleavage, brittle; transparent to translucent.

vanadium mica　Cf. **roscoelite.**

variscite　Hydrous aluminum phosphate, $Al(PO_4)\cdot2H_2O$; orthorhombic–rhombic bipyramidal; luster porcelaneous, color green; H, 3.5–4.5; G, 2.2–2.8; fracture conchoidal to smooth, no cleavage, brittle; thinly translucent.

verde antique　Impure, translucent variety of **serpentine,** *q.v.,* used as a decorative building stone.

verdite　Massive, fine-grained, opaque **serpentine,** *q.v.;* H, 3; G, 2.82–2.96. A South African import.

vermiculite　A group name for micaceous minerals, all hydrated silicates, in part closely related to the **chlorites,** *q.v.*

vesuvianite　Cf. **idocrase.**

vivianite　Hydrous iron phosphate, $Fe_3(PO_4)_2\cdot8H_2O$; monoclinic–prismatic; luster glassy to pearly; colorless to greenish blue, indigo, violet; streak white; H, 1.5–2; G, 2.6–2.7; fracture subconchoidal (striated), cleavage micaceous, leaves flexible; transparent to translucent.

volborthite　Hydrous copper vanadate, $Cu_3(VO_4)_2\cdot3H_2O$; as small 6-sided tabular crystals or globular forms; green or yellow.

wad　Cf. **psilomelane.**

wardite　Hydrous sodium calcium aluminum phosphate, $Na_4CaAl_{12}(PO_4)_8(OH)_{18}\cdot6H_2O$; tetragonal–tetragonal pyramidal; luster glassy, color bluish green to white; H, 5; G, 2.8–2.9; fracture conchoidal, cleavage good basal, brittle; transparent to translucent.

wascoite　Silica-rich jaspery sediment from bottom of Lake Wasco, Wasco Co., Ore.; color brown; variety of patterns resembles petrified wood.

wavellite　Hydrous basic aluminum phosphate, $Al_3(OH)_3(PO_4)_2\cdot5H_2O$; orthorhombic; luster glassy to silky; color black, brown, green, gray, yellow, white; H, 3.5–4; G, 2.4; fracture subconchoidal to uneven, splintery, cleavage domal and side pinacoid, brittle; transparent to translucent.

wernerite　Cf. **scapolite.**

wheelerite　Fossil resin (**amber,** *q.v.*) found in Sandoval Co., N.M.

white arsenic　Cf. **arsenolite.**

willemite　Zinc silicate, Zn_2SiO_4; hexagonal–rhombohedral bipyramidal; luster glassy; color gray, yellowish, white, green, yellow green, reddish brown, orange; H, 5.5; G, 3.89–4.18; fracture conchoidal to uneven, cleavage basal; transparent to translucent.

witherite　Barium carbonate, $BaCO_3$; orthorhombic–rhombic bipyramidal; luster glassy; color gray, yellowish, white; H, 3–3.5; G, 4.3–4.7; fracture uneven; cleavage one good, two poor; brittle; translucent; fluorescent blue.

wolframite　Iron manganese tungstates $(Fe,Mn)WO_4$; includes **ferberite** $(FeWO_4)$, **huebnerite** $(MnWO_4)$; monoclinic–prismatic; luster submetallic, color reddish brown to black; H, 4–4.5; G, 7.1–7.5; fracture uneven, cleavage perfect side pinacoid, brittle; opaque.

wollastonite　Calcium silicate, $CaSiO_3$; triclinic–pedial; luster glassy to silky; colorless, gray, pink, white; H, 4.5–5; G, 2.8–2.9; fracture splintery, cleavage perfect pinacoidal; translucent; sometimes fluorescent orange or yellow.

wonderstone　Variety of colorfully banded **rhyolite,** *q.v.*

wulfenite Lead molybdate, $PbMoO_4$; tetragonal–tetragonal pyramidal; luster adamantine; color brown, gray, orange, yellow, off-white; H, 2.7–3; G, 6.8; fracture subconchoidal; cleavage pyramidal good, two poor; transparent to translucent.

wurtzite Zinc sulfide, ZnS; brownish black hexagonal hemimorphic crystals or fibrous; polymorphous with **sphalerite**, *q.v.*

xenotime Yttrium phosphate, YPO_4; usually as brown or yellow tetragonal crystals and rolled grains (containing thorium, erbium, cerium, etc.); H, 4–5; G, 4.45–4.56.

xonotlite Hydrous calcium silicate, $Ca_3Si_3O_8(OH)_2$; orthorhombic (?); compact fibrous; luster vitreous to silky; color snow white, pink; H, 6.5; G, 2.7; cleavage one perfect. Closely resembles **pectolite**, *q.v.*, in structure.

yttrocrasite Complex oxide of the yttrium metals; as pitchy black orthorhombic crystals; H, 5.5–6; G, 4.8.

yttrotantalite (yttrocolumbite) A mineral possibly related to **samarskite**, *q.v.*, consisting of oxides of iron, uranium, yttrium, calcium, columbium, tantalum, zirconium, tin, and other metals; $(Fe,Y,U,Ca,etc.)(Cb,Ta,Zr,Sn)O_4$.

zaratite Hydrous carbonate of nickel, $NiCO_3 \cdot 2Ni(OH)_2 \cdot 4H_2O$; amorphous; in mammillary incrustations, also massive compact; luster vitreous, color emerald-green, streak green; H, 3; G, 2.6; brittle. Always accompanied by **chromite**, *q.v.*, occurring as an incrustation on massive chromite; it should be distinguished from a similar incrustation of green **uvarovite garnet** crystals or green **chlorite**, *q.v.*

zeolite Family name for **analcite, chabazite, heulandite, natrolite, stilbite**, etc., *q.v.*, totaling some 30 members.

zincite Zinc oxide, ZnO; hexagonal–dihexagonal pyramidal; luster subadamantine, color orange yellow to red; streak orange yellow; H, 4; G, 5.4–5.7; fracture conchoidal, cleavage prismatic, brittle; transparent to translucent. Facet-grade transparent crystals are deep orange red, usually very small fragments from Franklin, N.J.

zinc blende Cf. **sphalerite.**

zinnwaldite An iron lithia mica near **biotite**, *q.v.*, in composition and appearance; color pale violet, yellow, brown, gray. Occurs in pegmatites and hydrothermal veins.

zippeite Hydrous basic sulfate of uranium $(UO_2)_2(SO_4)(OH)_2 \cdot 4H_2O$.

zircon Zirconium silicate, $ZrSiO_4$; tetragonal–ditetragonal pyramidal; luster subadamantine; color orange yellow to red (**hyacinth** or **jacinth**, reddish brown; **jargoon**, smoky yellow), pale yellow, golden yellow, green, greenish blue, blue, colorless, violet; H, 6.5–7.5; G, 4–4.7; fracture conchoidal, cleavage two poor; transparent to translucent; fluorescent yellow orange. Heat-treating brownish or reddish crystals converts them into blue or colorless varieties.

zoisite Hydrous calcium aluminum silicate, $Ca_2Al_3(SiO_4)_3(OH)$; orthorhombic–rhombic bipyramidal; luster glassy; color brown, gray, pink (**thulite**, *q.v.*); H, 6; G, 3.3–3.4; fracture subconchoidal to uneven, cleavage perfect side pinacoid; translucent; sometimes fluorescent yellow orange.

Glossary

The definitions in this glossary are drawn from *A Glossary of the Mining and Mineral Industry,* by Albert H. Fay, U.S. Bureau of Mines Bulletin 95, and from Webster's Third New International Dictionary.

accessory mineral   A rock-forming mineral occurring in such small amounts that it does not contribute to the classification of the species. Cf. **essential mineral.**

acicular   Needle-shaped, slender, resembling a needle or bristle, as some leaves or crystals.

acidic rocks   Igneous rocks that contain more than 65 percent silica (SiO_2), as contrasted with intermediate or basic rocks. The term salic may occasionally be used.

adamantine   Having a luster similar to that of a diamond.

aggregate   Rock composed of mineral crystals or of mineral or rock fragments cemented together.

alluvium   A sedimentary deposit of soil, sand, gravel, or similar detrital material laid down by running water, as in a delta, floodplain, or riverbed.

amorphous   Having no definite molecular structure.

amygdule   Small globular cavity in an eruptive rock, such as lava, caused by expanding steam or vapor at time rock cooled; generally lined with secondary minerals.

aphanitic   Descriptive of a dark rock of such close texture that the individual grains are invisible to the naked eye.

arenaceous   Sandy or largely of sand.

argentiferous   Producing or containing silver.

argillaceous   Producing or abounding in clay.

argillite   An argillaceous rock, differing from shale in being metamorphosed and from slate in having no slaty cleavage.

banding   Parallel layers of different minerals, colors, or textures.

basalt   Dark gray to black, dense to fine-grained igneous rock consisting of basic (containing the chemical radical $-OH$) plagioclase, auguite, and magnetite.

basic   Of rocks comparatively low in silica (45–52 percent silica is the upper limit); the term femic is occasionally used.

bladed Decidedly elongated and flattened, like a knife blade; used to describe certain mineral structures.

book A term describing muscovite or biotite mica crystals from which individual thin sheets can be stripped.

botryoidal Having the form of a cluster of grapes. A mineral has botryoidal form if the surface is a series of round bumps, each about the size of a small grape or large pea.

breccia A rock composed of angular fragments cemented together.

clastic rock Rock made up of broken fragments of preexisting rocks or minerals cemented together; contrast **breccia.**

colors Small particles of native gold left in a pan after washing.

concentrate Separation of useful minerals from gangue in a rock by washing or mechanical methods of concentration; to increase in percentage and value. Also used as a noun.

conchoidal Shell-shaped; having elevations or depressions like one-half of a bivalve shell. The more compact rocks, such as quartz, flint, argillite, feldspar, obsidian, etc., break with a conchoidal fracture, as glass breaks.

concretion A rounded mass of mineral matter compacted about a nucleus.

conglomerate A rock composed of rounded fragments, varying from small pebbles to large boulders, in a cement of hardened clay; (verb) to gather or form into a ball.

contact-metamorphic Occurring at or near the contacts of intrusive rocks with sedimentary beds which carry minerals characteristic of contact metamorphism, such as garnet, pyroxene, and epidote.

contact metamorphism General term applied to the change that takes place along an intrusive contact (of an intruded igneous rock of high temperature and the enclosing rocks, usually cold, into which it has been thrust), such as the recrystallization of limestone with the development of typical silicate minerals.

country rock The general mass of adjacent rock, as distinguished from that of a dike, vein, or lode.

cryptocrystalline Formed of crystals of microscopic fineness, but not glassy.

crystal A body formed by an element or mineral compound solidifying so that it is bounded by plane surfaces symmetrically arranged, which are the external expression of a definite internal molecular structure.

crystallography The science of crystallization, dealing with the form and structure of crystals. (Appendix I provides the crystal structure of minerals, as hexagonal–hexagonal scalenohedral; monoclinic–prismatic; hexagonal–trigonal trapezohedral, etc. Definitions for crystal forms must be referred to any good textbook of crystallography.)

decahedral Having ten faces, as of a crystal.

detritus Any loose material, such as rock fragments, resulting directly from disintegration; debris.

diastrophism The process or processes by which the earth's crust is deformed, producing continents, ocean basins, mountains, etc.; also the results of these processes.

dimorphism Crystallization in two independent forms of the same chemical compound, as quartz vs. tridymite.

disseminated Scattered or diffused through; a disseminated mineral is one which has grains scattered through the country rock or other mineral rock, rather than being concentrated in masses or veins.

disseminated deposit   A natural occurrence or accumulation of ore minerals scattered throughout the rock, as copper minerals occurring in grains throughout granite porphyry. The term impregnation is sometimes applied to deposits of this nature.

dodecahedral   Having 12 faces, as in a crystal like garnet.

drift   Rock material deposited in one place after having been moved from another, as glacial drift. Also a horizontal mine passageway driven on, or parallel to, the course of a vein or rock stratum.

drusy   Covered with tiny crystals, as drusy quartz.

dump   Pile of waste gangue materials taken from a mine.

effervescence   Bubbling, foaming, or hissing through application of an acid to any carbonate, such as limestone, dolomite, etc. The gas given off is carbon dioxide.

efflorescence   A blossoming forth, or flowering, of a mineral substance on the surface of mine walls or timbers by crystallization from a mineral-saturated atmosphere, also occurring around mineralized hot springs, geysers, etc.

effusive   Formed by solidification of magma at the surface; volcanic.

ejecta   Matter ejected, as from a volcano.

electrum   A natural pale yellow alloy of gold and silver.

element   A substance which cannot be separated into other substances different from itself by ordinary chemical means; one of a limited number of distinct varieties of natural matter.

eruptive   Descriptive of igneous rock, usually an extrusive type such as lava; eruptive rock is one which has broken out, as lava or ashes, from an active volcano.

essential mineral   A mineral which is necessary to the classification of a rock species, even when occurring in small amounts; contrasted with **accessory mineral.**

evaporite   A sedimentary rock, like gypsum or halite, that originates by evaporation of water in enclosed basins.

exposure   A bed of mineral matter exposed to view, as an outcrop.

extrusive   Descriptive of igneous rock forced out at the surface and solidified; cf. **effusive** or **volcanic.**

face   The surface of a crystal; the end or wall of a mine tunnel, drift, or excavation at which work is progressing.

ferri-   A combining prefix indicating ferric iron as an ingredient.

ferro-   A combining prefix indicating the presence of, or a connection with, iron.

ferruginous   Resembling iron rust in color.

float   Bits or pieces of mineral or fossils found on the ground surface at some distance from their places of origin as a result of erosion and water transportation.

fluorescence   Emission of light from within a substance while it is being exposed to direct radiation or, in certain cases, to an electrical discharge (as from an ultraviolet-ray lamp).

fluvial deposit   Mud, sand, gravel, or rock deposited by water action; also fluviatile.

foliated   Leaflike. The meaning is similar to that of laminated, but the latter generally indicates a finer division of layers.

friable   Easily pulverized.

gabbro   Any of a family of granular igneous rocks essentially of plagioclase with a ferromagnesian mineral and accessory iron.

gangue   The worthless rock or vein matter in which valuable ore minerals occur.

geode   A hollow nodule or concretion, the cavity of which is later lined with crystals or ultimately entirely filled with mineral matter, such as agate, chalcedony, carnelian, etc.

geosyncline   A great downward flexure of the earth's crust depressed by the weight of accumulating sediments.

glance   Any of several mineral sulfides with a metallic luster.

gneiss   A laminated or foliated rock of metamorphic origin, corresponding in composition to granite or some other feldspathic plutonic rock.

granite   Any very hard natural igneous rock formation of visibly crystalline texture, consisting essentially of quartz and orthoclase or microcline feldspar.

granitoid   The suffix "-oid" means like. Thus granitoid means resembling granite.

grano-   A combining prefix meaning granite, granitic, as in granodiorite, granogabbro, etc.

groundmass   The fine-grained base of a porphyry in which the larger distinct crystals are embedded; usually glassy or crystalline.

hardness   The cohesion of the particles on the surface of a body, as determined by its capacity to scratch another, or be itself scratched. The hardness of a mineral is expressed semilogarithmically in terms of the Mohs scale: 1, talc; 2, gypsum; 3, calcite; 4, fluorite; 5, apatite; 6, orthoclase feldspar; 7, quartz; 8, topaz; 9, corundum; 10, diamond.

helio-   A combining prefix meaning the sun, as in heliotrope (bloodstone).

hydraulicking   Washing down minerals in a placer ore deposit with water emerging from a giant nozzle, called a giant, under extreme pressure.

hydrous   Containing water chemically combined, as in hydrates.

igneous   Formed by crystallization from a molten state; said of rocks of one of the great classes, contrasted with metamorphic and sedimentary rocks.

inclusion   Foreign mineral, rock, water, or fossil enclosed in the mass of a mineral or rock.

incrustation   A coating or crust, usually of one mineral over another, as kämmererite incrusting chromite.

iridescence   The quality of prismatic (rainbow) colors in the interior or on the surface of a mineral, similar to an oil film on water exhibiting a display of colors.

joint   A fracture in rock, smaller than a fault and not accompanied by dislocation.

jointing   Hexagonal, more commonly irregular polygonal, separation in columnar slabs characteristic of basaltic lava flows, sills, and dikes and which results from the cooling of their materials.

juvenile water   Water given off by magmas and considered new water.

lava   Fluid rock such as that which issues from a volcano or a surface flow of molten rock issuing from a volcanic fissure. Lava may solidify into such rock forms as basalt or rhyolite.

lens   An ore body more or less elliptical in outline, thickest at the center and thinning out toward the edges; lenticular in shape.

lignite   A noncaking, usually brownish black variety of coal intermediate between peat and bituminous coal, often revealing the original wood texture.

lode   A mineral deposit that fills a fissure in the country rock; any ore deposit within definite boundaries, separating it from adjoining rocks. Contrasted with placer or disseminated deposits.

magma   Molten rock material within the earth from which an igneous rock results by cooling and crystallization.

magmatic segregation   The process by which different types of igneous rock are derived from a single parent magma or by which different parts of the mass become different in composition and texture as they solidify. Also termed magmatic differentiation.

malleable   Capable of being extended or shaped by beating with a hammer, as gold, silver, etc.

matrix   The rock or earthy material containing a mineral, crystal, or metallic ore. Also termed **groundmass.**

metamorphic rock   Rock that has been extensively altered from a previous igneous or sedimentary condition by the effects of heat, pressure, or chemical action.

metamorphism   Any change in the texture or composition of a rock after its induration or solidification, especially by deformation and rise in temperature.

micaceous   Composed of thin scales or leaves, like a mass of tiny mica flakes.

mine   A pit or excavation from which ores, precious stones, coal, etc., are taken by digging; loosely, an ore deposit.

mineral   A homogeneous chemical element or compound of inorganic origin, usually having a definite atomic structure and often a regular external crystal form.

mineralization   The process of change or metamorphism by which minerals are secondarily developed in a rock, especially the formation or introduction of ore minerals into previously existing rock masses.

Mohs scale   Cf. **hardness.**

native (element)   A metallic element (gold, silver, copper, platinum, bismuth, etc.) found in nature as a mineral.

nodule   A rounded mass of irregularly shaped mineral; a little lump.

nonmetallic   A mineral substance, usually clay, kaolin, phosphate rock, bentonite, etc., which does not contain a metal worth recovering.

nugget   A rounded or irregular lump or mass of native metal, as of gold, occurring in placer ground.

ocher   Earthy or powdery mineral; a mineral paint. Usually an impure ore of iron (red, hematite; yellow, limonite) used as a pigment.

ore   Any material containing valuable metallic constituents for the sake of which it is mined and worked; often loosely applied to nonmetallic materials, as sulfur, fluorite, kaolin, etc.

organic rock   Rock material produced by plant or animal life, such as coal, petroleum, limestone, diatomaceous earth, etc.

outcrop The emergence of a stratum of rock to the surface of the ground; that part of a stratum which appears at the surface.

overburden Soil or worthless rock which covers a mineral deposit.

oxidized zone That portion of an ore deposit which has been subjected to the action of surface waters carrying oxygen, carbon dioxide, etc.; that zone in which sulfides have been removed or altered to oxides and carbonates.

pegmatite Coarse variety of granite occurring in dikes or veins.

phenocryst One of the prominent embedded crystals in a finer-grained groundmass or porphyritic rock.

pisolitic Consisting of rounded grains, like peas or beans.

placer A place where gold or other heavy mineral (platinum, cassiterite, etc.) is obtained by washing; an alluvial or glacial deposit containing particles of gold or other valuable mineral. A dry placer lacks water, so separation of the desired mineral from the worthless sediment is done by a blast of air.

placer mineral A heavy mineral found in a placer deposit, usually gold, platinum, cassiterite (stream tin), magnetite, zircon, etc.

plutonic Formed by solidification of a molten magma deep within the earth and crystalline throughout.

pocket A cavity containing gold, other minerals, or water; also, a small body of ore.

porphyritic Characterized by distinct crystals (phenocrysts) as of feldspar, quartz, augite, etc., in a fine-grained base.

porphyry Any igneous rock of porphyritic texture.

primary mineral A mineral which has been crystallized from magma or deposited directly from solution, not transported or produced by the chemical effects of weathering.

primary ore Those minerals and ores which retain their original form and composition, as original sulfides.

pseudomorph A crystal, or apparent crystal, of some mineral having the outward appearance and form of another species which has been replaced by substitution or by chemical alteration.

pyroclastic Formed by fragmentation as a result of volcanic or igneous action.

quarry An open or surface excavation from which nonmetallic minerals, usually building stone, slate, traprock, or limestone, are obtained.

radioactivity The property, possessed by certain elements (chiefly radium, uranium, thorium, and their disintegration products), of spontaneously emitting alpha, beta, and gamma rays by the disintegration of the nuclei of atoms.

rare earths Any of a large series of similar oxides of metals, chiefly lanthanum, cerium, praseodymium, neodymium, illinium, samarium, europium, gadolinium, terbium, dysprosium, holmium, yttrium, erbium, thallium, ytterbium, and lutetium.

replacement The process by which one mineral or chemical substance takes the place of some earlier substance, often preserving its structure or crystalline form, as in a pseudomorph.

replacement deposit A mass of ore and gangue formed by the alteration of limestone, dolomite, and other rocks; usually irregular in form and in many places grading into the surrounding country rock.

rosette A mineral form or outward structure resembling a rose.

schist Any metamorphic crystalline rock which has a foliated structure and which can readily be split into slabs or sheets.

seam A thin stratum of ore, coal, etc., sandwiched between thicker layers of country rock.

secondary mineral A mineral which was formed later than, and often from, the substance of earlier mineral deposits (as by weathering or by ground-water action).

streak The color of the fine powder of a mineral, as revealed by scratching or by rubbing against a hard, white surface, usually a piece of tile or ceramic.

strike A sudden finding of rich ore in prospecting or mining; the angle which bedded rocks make with a north–south line.

superposition Principle that a stratum or bed of rock at the lowest level is the oldest one, the layer first laid down, and that other strata followed in orderly succession toward the top. Sometimes the normal superposition may be inverted, as by overthrust action.

system A division of rocks usually larger than a series and smaller than a group and deposited during a specific period; as the Silurian system.

tailings Refuse material separated as residue in the treating of ores; mill tailings seldom have collectable minerals.

talcose Pertaining to or containing talc.

talus Rock debris at the base of a cliff.

telluride A binary compound of tellurium with another element or a chemical radical; formerly termed telluret.

terrace A level and rather narrow plain, usually with a steep front, bordering a river, lake, or sea.

thrust A form of fault that is nearly horizontal.

till Unstratified glacial drift consisting of mingled clay, sand, gravel, and boulders.

tillite Consolidated or lithophied till; till materials cemented together.

trap Any of various dark-colored, fine-grained, igneous rocks, including especially basalt, amygdaloid, etc.

tufa A porous rock formed as a deposit from springs or streams.

tuff A rock composed of the finer kinds of volcanic detritus, usually stratified.

umber A brown earth valued as a pigment and used either in the raw (natural) state or calcined (burned), in which case it has a slightly reddish hue; its color is due to manganese and iron oxides.

unconformity Lack of continuity in deposition between strata in contact, corresponding to a gap in the stratigraphic record.

uplift An upheaval; a raising of a mass of rock through forces of diastrophism, counterbalancing a downwarping elsewhere owing to intensive sedimentation.

vein A single body of minerals occupying or following a fissure, both walls of which are generally well defined; a fissure in rock filled by mineral matter, usually by deposition from solution. Where several veins are so closely spaced that the ground between them becomes in places ore-bearing and in its whole width constitutes an ore body, the assemblage is termed a lode. The term vein is often used for both individual veins and lodes.

volcanic   Formed by solidification of molten magma erupted from the top or sides of a volcano.

volcano   A vent in the earth's crust from which molten rock, steam, or chemical vapors issue; a hill, or mountain, composed of the ejected materials.

vug   A small unfilled cavity in a lode or in rock, usually lined with crystalline incrustation; differs from an amygdule in that the latter was formed in a lava rock by expanding gases.

vulcanism   From Vulcan, the Roman god of fire; pertains to volcanic action.

wash   Loose surface deposit of sand, gravel, or boulders laid down by running water. To subject earth, gravel, or crushed ore to the action of running water to separate the valuable minerals from the worthless, as to wash gravel for gold.

water of crystallization   Water which is regarded as present (chemically combined) in many crystallized substances and which can be released by heat.

xenolith   A fragment of rock incorporated in congealed igneous rock, hence older than the igneous rock enclosing it.

zinciferous   Containing or yielding zinc.

zone   A belt, layer, or series of layers of rock characterized by some particular property, action, or content.

Reference Libraries and Mineral Museums

The following directory lists by states the major libraries which maintain geological and mining literature and gem and mineral museums open to the public. A geological library is indicated by (L); a museum (M); if the institution has both (L,M).

ALABAMA

Auburn: Alabama Polytechnic Institute (L,M). *Birmingham:* Birmingham Southern College (L), Howard College (L), Public Library (L). *Mobile* (Spring Hill): Spring Hill College (M), Thomas Byrne Memorial Library (L). *Montgomery:* Department of Archives and State History, State Capitol (L). *Talladega:* Talladega College (M). *Tuskegee Institute:* Hollis Burke Frissell Library (L). *University:* University of Alabama (L), Alabama Geological Survey (L), Alabama Museum of Natural History (M).

ALASKA

College: University of Alaska (L,M).

ARIZONA

Holbrook: Petrified Forest National Monument Museum (M). *Phoenix:* Department of Library & Archives (L), Department of Mineral Resources (L), Public Library (L), Arizona Museum (M). *Tempe:* Arizona State College, Matthews Library (L). *Tucson:* University of Arizona (L).

ARKANSAS

Clarksville: College of the Ozarks (L). *Conway:* Hendrix College (M). *Fayetteville:* University of Arkansas (L,M). *Jonesboro:* Arkansas State College (L). *Little Rock:* Arkansas Geological Survey (L). *Magnolia:* Southern State College (L). *Russellville:* Arkansas Polytechnic College (L).

CALIFORNIA

Arcata: Humboldt State College (L). *Bakersfield:* Kern County Free Library (L). *Berkeley:* University of California (L,M). *Claremont:* Pomona College (L,M). *Davis:* University of California (L). *Eureka:* Eureka Free Library (L). *Fresno:* Fresno County Free Library (L),

State College Library (L). *La Jolla:* Scripps Institution of Oceanography (L). *Long Beach:* Public Library (L). *Los Angeles:* California State Exposition Building (M), Department of Water & Power (L), Los Angeles County Museum of History, Science, and Art (L,M), Los Angeles Public Library (L), Los Angeles State College (L), Occidental College (L,M), University of California at Los Angeles, (L,M), University of Southern California (L). *Northridge:* San Fernando Valley State College (L). *Oakland:* Oakland Free Library (L), Oakland Public Museum (M). *Pacific Grove:* Pacific Grove Museum (M). *Palm Springs:* Palm Springs Desert Museum (M). *Palo Alto:* Stanford University, Branner Geological Library (L), Stanford University Natural History Museum (M). *Pasadena:* California Institute of Technology (L,M), Pasadena Junior College (M). *Redding:* Shasta County Free Library (L). *Redlands:* University of Redlands (L). *Riverside:* Public Library (L), Riverside Municipal Museum (M), University of California (L). *Sacramento:* California State Library (L), City Free Library (L), California Museum Association (M). *San Diego:* San Diego Society of Natural History (M), Natural History Museum (M), University of California, La Jolla (L). *San Francisco:* California Academy of Sciences (L), California State Division of Mines Museum (L,M), Mechanics Mercantile Library (L), Memorial Museum (M), Public Library (L), San Francisco State College (L), Sierra Club (L), State Mineralogist (L). *San Jose:* San Jose State College (L). *Santa Barbara:* Santa Barbara Public Library (L), Santa Barbara Museum of Natural History (M). *Santa Clara:* University of Santa Clara Museum (M). *Stockton:* College of the Pacific (M), Free Public Library (L), Stockton College (L). *Twenty-Nine Palms:* Desert Branch, Southwest Museum (M). *Yosemite:* Yosemite National Park Museum (M).

COLORADO

Boulder: University of Colorado (L,M). *Colorado Springs:* Colorado College (L,M); El Paso County Pioneer Association, Pioneer Museum (M). *Denver:* Colorado Geological Survey (L), Colorado State Library (L), The Mining Record (L), Museum of Natural History (L,M), Public Library (L), Regis College (L), State Bureau of Mines (L,M), University of Denver (L,M), U.S. Geological Survey Office at Denver Federal Center and at 468 New Custom House (L). *Fort Collins:* Colorado State College of Agriculture and Mechanic Arts (M), Colorado State University (L). *Golden:* Colorado State School of Mines (L,M). *Grand Junction:* Public Library (L). *Gunnison:* Western State College (L). *Idaho Springs:* Western College of Mining (L). *Sterling:* Logan County Historical and National History Society Museum (M).

CONNECTICUT

Bridgeport: Bridgeport Scientific and Historical Society (M), Public Library (L). *Greenwich:* Bruce Museum (M). *Hartford:* Connecticut State Library (L), Geological and Natural History Survey (L), Public Library (L), Trinity College (L,M). *Middletown:* Wesleyan University (L,M). *New Britain:* New Britain Institute Museum (M). *New Haven:* American Journal of Science (L), Yale University (L), Peabody Museum of Natural History (M). *New London:* Connecticut College

(L). *Stamford:* Stamford Museum (M). *Storrs:* Connecticut Agricultural College (L,M). *Wallingford:* Choate School (M).

DELAWARE

Newark: Delaware Geological Survey (L), University of Delaware (L,M). *Wilmington:* Society of Natural History of Delaware (M), Wilmington Free Insitute (L).

DISTRICT OF COLUMBIA

Washington: Catholic University of America (M), Georgetown University (M), George Washington University (L,M), Howard University (L), Library of Congress (L), Smithsonian Institution (L,M), United States Bureau of Mines (L), United States Geological Survey Library (L), United States National Museum (M).

FLORIDA

Coral Gables: University of Miami (L). *Deland:* John B. Stetson University (L,M), Monroe Heath Museum (M). *Gainesville:* Florida State Museum (L,M), University of Florida (L,M). *Jacksonville:* Public Library (L). *Lakeland:* Public Library (L). *Miami:* Miami Public Library (L). *St. Augustine:* Crichlow Museum of Natural History (M). *Tallahassee:* Florida Geological Survey (L), Florida State Library (L), Florida State University (L). *Tampa:* University of Tampa (L). *Winter Park:* Rollins College (L,M).

GEORGIA

Athens: University of Georgia (L,M). *Atlanta:* Atlanta University (M), Division of Mines, Mining and Geology Library (L), Georgia State Museum (M), Public Library (L), Emory University, Asa Griggs Candler Library (L). *Macon:* Mercer University (M). *Oxford:* Emory University Academy Museum (M).

HAWAII

Honolulu: Bishop Museum (L,M), College of Hawaii (L), Geological Survey, 225 Federal Bldg. (L), University of Hawaii (L).

IDAHO

Boise: Public Library (L). *Caldwell:* Strahorn Memorial Library (L). *Moscow:* Idaho Bureau of Mines and Geology (L), University of Idaho (L,M). *Pocatello:* Idaho State College (L). *Rexburg:* Rich College (L).

ILLINOIS

Abington: Hedding College (M). *Bloomington:* Illinois Wesleyan University Museum (M). *Carbondale:* Southern Illinois State Normal University (L). *Carlinville:* Blackburn College (M). *Carthage:* Carthage College (M). *Chicago:* Chicago Academy of Sciences (M), Chicago Museum of Science and History (L,M), Field Museum (L,M), John Crerar Library (L), University of Chicago (L,M), University of Illinois (L), Western Society of Engineers (L). *Decatur:* Millikin University (M). *Elgin:* Elgin Scientific Society (M). *Elsah:* The Principia Library (L). *Evanston:* Northwestern University (L,M). *Galesburg:* Knox College (M). *Joliet:* Public Library (L). *Lake Forest:* Lake Forest College Museum (M). *Lincoln:* Lincoln College, Millikin Museum (M). *Monmouth:* Illinois State Normal University (L). *Naperville:* Northwestern College (M). *Normal:* Illinois State Normal University (L). *Peoria:* Public Library (L). *Rock Island:* Augustana College (L,M),

Rock Island Public Library (L). *Rockford:* Public Library (L). *Spring-field:* Illinois State Museum (M), Illinois State Library (L). *Urbana:* Illinois Geological Survey (L), University of Illinois (L,M).

INDIANA

Bloomington: Indiana Department of Conservation (L), Indiana University (L,M). *Brookville:* Brookville Society of Natural History (M). *Crawfordsville:* Wabash College (L,M). *Evansville:* Public Library (L). *Fort Wayne:* Public Library (L). *Franklin:* Franklin College of Indiana (M). *Greencastle:* De Pauw University (L). *Hanover:* Hanover College (L,M). *Huntington:* City Free Library (L). *Indianapolis:* Butler College (M), Children's Museum (M), Department of Conservation (L), Indiana State Library (L), Indiana State Museum (M), Public Library (L). *Lafayette:* Agricultural Experiment Station (L), Purdue University (L,M). *Muncie:* Public Library (L). *Newcastle:* Henry County Historical Society Museum (M). *New Harmony:* Workingmen's Institute (M). *North Manchester:* Manchester College (L). *Notre Dame:* Notre Dame University (L,M). *Richmond:* Earlham College (M). *Terre Haute:* Indiana State Teachers College (L), Rose Polytechnic Institute (M). *Upland:* Taylor University (M). *Valparaiso:* Valparaiso University (L).

IOWA

Ames: Iowa State College (L). *Cedar Falls:* Iowa State Teachers College (L,M). *Cedar Rapids:* Coe College (M). *College Springs:* Amity College (M). *Council Bluffs:* Free Public Library (L). *Davenport:* Public Museum (L,M). *Des Moines:* Drake University (L), Iowa State Mines Inspector (L), Iowa State Traveling Library (L), Public Library (L). *Dubuque:* Carnegie Stout Free Public Library (L), Hermann Museum of Natural History (M). *Fayette:* Upper Iowa University (M). *Grinnell:* Grinnell College (L). *Independence:* Independence Public Library (L,M). *Indianola:* Simpson College (L). *Iowa City:* Iowa Geological Survey (L), State University of Iowa (L,M). *Lamoni:* Graceland College (L). *Mount Vernon:* Cornell College (L,M). *Muscatine:* Muscatine Academy of Science (M). *Sioux City:* Sioux City Academy of Science and Letters (M). *Toledo:* Western College (M). *Waterloo:* Young Men's Christian Association (M). *Waverly:* Wartburg Normal College (M).

KANSAS

Baldwin City: Baker University (L,M). *Emporia:* College of Emporia (M), Kansas State Teachers College (L,M), Kellogg Library (L). *Hays:* Fort Hays Kansas State College (L). *Lawrence:* Kansas State Geological Survey (L), University of Kansas (L,M). *Lindsborg:* Bethany College (M). *Manhattan:* Kansas State Agricultural College (L,M). *McPherson:* McPherson College (M). *Pittsburg:* Kansas State Teachers College (L). *Salina:* Kansas Wesleyan University (L,M). *Topeka:* Kansas State Library (L), Kansas State Historical Society (L), State Board of Agriculture (L), Washburn College Museum (M). *Wichita:* Porter Library (L), University of Wichita (L).

KENTUCKY

Ashland: Public Library (L). *Bowling Green:* Ogden College (M), Western Kentucky State Teachers College (L). *Danville:* Centre College

(M). *Frankfort:* Kentucky Geological Society (M). *Lexington:* Kentucky Geological Survey (L), University of Kentucky (L,M), Transylvania University (M). *Louisville:* Free Public Library (L), Louisville Public Library Museum (M), University of Louisville (L).

LOUISIANA

Baton Rouge: Louisiana Geological Survey (L), Louisiana State University (L,M). *Lafayette:* Southwestern Louisiana Institute (L). *Lake Charles:* McNeese State College (L). *Natchitoches:* Northwestern State College (L). *New Orleans:* Law Library of Louisiana (L), Louisiana State Museum (M), Public Library (L), Loyola University (L), Tulane University (L,M). *Ruston:* Louisiana Polytechnic Institute (L). *Shreveport:* Shreve Memorial Library (L), Centenary College (L).

MAINE

Augusta: Maine Public Library (L,M), Kennebec Historical Society (M), Maine State Museum (M). *Bangor:* Bangor Public Library (L). *Brinckley:* Bates Museum (M). *Brunswick:* Bowdoin College (L,M). *Lewiston:* Bates College (L,M). *Orono:* Maine Geological Survey (L), University of Maine (L,M). *Paris:* Hamlin Memorial Hall (M). *Portland:* Portland Society of Natural History (L,M). Public Library (L). *Thomaston:* Knox Academy of Arts and Science (M). *Waterville:* Colby College (L,M).

MARYLAND

Annapolis: Maryland State Library (L), State House (M), United States Naval Academy (M). *Baltimore:* Enoch Pratt Free Library (L), Goucher College (M), Johns Hopkins University (L,M), Maryland Academy of Sciences (M), Peabody Institute (L). *College Park:* University of Maryland (L). *Ellicott City:* Rock Hill College (M). *Westminster:* Western Maryland College (L,M).

MASSACHUSETTS

Amherst: Amherst College (L,M), Massachusetts State College (M), University of Massachusetts (L,M). *Boston:* Boston Museum of Science (L,M), Boston Society of Natural History (M), New England Museum of Natural History (M), Boston University (L,M), Public Library (L), State Library of Massachusetts (L). *Cambridge:* Harvard University (L,M), Harvard University Geological Museum (L,M), Massachusetts Institute of Technology (L,M). *Chestnut Hill:* Boston College Museum (M). *Dover:* Dover Historical and Natural History Society (M). *Fall River:* Fall River Public Library (M). *Fitchburg:* Wallace Public Library (M). *Framingham:* Framingham Historical and Natural History Society (M). *Gloucester:* Cape Ann Scientific, Literary, and Historical Association (M). *Jamaica Plain:* Children's Museum (M). *Leominster:* Leominster Public Library Museum (M). *Marion:* Marion Natural History Society (M). *Marlborough:* Marlborough Society of Natural History (M). *Medford:* Tufts College (L). *Northampton:* Smith College (L,M). *Pittsfield:* Museum of Natural History and Art (M). *Salem:* Peabody Historical Society Museum (M). *Somerville:* Tufts College Museum (M). *South Hadley:* Mount Holyoke College (M). *Springfield:* City Library (L), Museum of Natural History (M). *Taunton:* Bristol County Academy of Sciences (M). *Wellesley:* Wellesley College (L,M). *Williamstown:* Williams College (L,M). *Worcester:*

Clark University (L,M), Free Public Library (L), Holy Cross College (M), Worcester Natural History Society (M).

MICHIGAN

Adrian: Adrian College (M). *Alma:* Alma College Museum (M). *Ann Arbor:* University of Michigan (L,M). *Battle Creek:* Public Schools Museum of Natural History (M). *Bloomfield Hills:* Cranbrook Institute of Science (L,M). *Detroit:* Detroit Children's Museum (M), Public Library (L), University of Detroit (L), Wayne University (L). *East Lansing:* Michigan State College of Agriculture and Applied Science (L,M). *Grand Rapids:* Kent Scientific Museum (M), Public Library (L). *Houghton:* Hillsdale College (M), Michigan College of Mining and Technology (L,M). *Ishpeming:* Lake Superior Mining Institute (L). *Kalamazoo:* Kalamazoo Museum and Art Institute (M). *Lansing:* Michigan State Library (L). *Muskegon:* Hackley Public Library (L). *Port Huron:* Port Huron Public Library Museum (M). *Saginaw:* Hoyt Public Library (L). *Three Oaks:* Edward K. Warren Foundation, Chamberlin Memorial Museum (M).

MINNESOTA

Collegeville: St. Johns University (L,M). *Duluth:* Public Library (L). *Minneapolis:* E. J. Longyear Company (L), Minneapolis Museum Federation, Public Library Science Museum (M), Minnesota Geological Survey (L), Public Library (L), University of Minnesota (L,M). *Northfield:* Carlton College (L,M), St. Olaf College (L,M). *St. Paul:* Hamlin University Museum (M), James Jerome Hill Reference Library (L), Minnesota Historical Society (L), Minnesota State Library (L), Public Library (L), Science Museum (L,M). *St. Peter:* Gustavus Adolphus College (L,M). *Winona:* Winona State Teachers College (M).

MISSISSIPPI

Columbus: J. C. Fant Memorial Library (L). *Hattiesburg:* Mississippi Southern College (L). *Jackson:* Millsaps College (M), Mississippi State Library (L). *Oxford:* Mississippi Geological Survey (L), University of Mississippi (L,M). *State College:* Mississippi State College (L,M). *Vicksburg:* Mississippi River Commission (L).

MISSOURI

Canton: Culver-Stockton College (M). *Cape Girardeau:* Southeast Missouri State College (L). *Columbia:* University of Missouri (L,M). *Fayette:* Central College (M). *Fulton:* Westminster College (L,M). *Glasgow:* Pritchett College (M). *Jefferson City:* Lincoln University (L), Missouri Resources Museum (M). *Kansas City:* Linda Hall Library (L), Public Library (L,M), Missouri Bureau of Geology and Mines (M), Rockhurst College (L), University of Kansas City (L). *Rolla:* Missouri School of Mines and Metallurgy (L,M), State Geologist (L). *St. Joseph:* St. Joseph's Museum (M). *St. Louis:* St. Louis Public Schools Educational Museum (M).

MONTANA

Agate: Cook Museum of Natural History (M). *Bozeman:* Montana State College (L,M). *Butte:* Montana School of Mines (L,M). *Ekalaka:* Carter County Geological Society (M). *Helena:* Historical Society of Montana (L), Montana State Library Museum (M), Public Library (L). *Missoula:* University of Montana (L,M).

NEBRASKA
   Fremont: Midland College (L). *Hastings:* Hastings College (M). *Lincoln:* Nebraska Conservation and Survey Division (L), Nebraska State Library (L), University of Nebraska (L,M).
NEVADA
   Carson City: Nevada State Library (L). *Las Vegas:* Southern Regional Division Library (L), University of Nevada (L). *Reno:* Nevada Bureau of Mines (L), University of Nevada (L,M).
NEW HAMPSHIRE
   Concord: New Hampshire State Library (L). *Durham:* Hamilton Smith State Library (L), New Hampshire College of Agriculture and Mechanic Arts (M), New Hampshire Planning and Development Commission (L), University of New Hampshire (L,M). *Hanover:* Dartmouth College (L,M). *Keene:* Keene High School (M), Keene Natural History Society (M). *Manchester:* Manchester Institute of Arts and Sciences (M). *Wolfboro:* Libby Museum (M).
NEW JERSEY
   Atlantic City: Free Public Library (L). *Bayonne:* Free Public Library (L). *Camden:* Camden Free Public Library (L). *Convent Station:* College of St. Elizabeth (L). *Dover:* Dover High School (M). *Elizabeth:* Public Library (L). *Hoboken:* Stevens Institute of Technology (M). *Jersey City:* New Jersey Public Library (L,M). *Madison:* Drew University (L). *New Brunswick:* Free Public Library (L), Rutgers University (L). *Newark:* Newark Museum Association (M), Public Library (L). *Paterson:* Paterson Museum (M). *Princeton:* Princeton University (L,M). *Trenton:* Department of Conservation and Development (L), Free Public Library (L), New Jersey State Library (L), State Museum of New Jersey (M). *West Caldwell:* Potwin Memorial Library (M).
NEW MEXICO
   Albuquerque: University of New Mexico (L,M). *Mesilla Park:* New Mexico College of Agriculture and Mechanic Arts (M). *Santa Fe:* New Mexico Historical Society (M), State Library (L). *Socorro:* New Mexico School of Mines (L,M).
NEW YORK
   Albany: New York State Library (L), New York State Museum (L,M). *Alfred:* Alfred University (L). *Aurora:* Wells College (M). *Binghamton:* Binghamton Academy of Science (M). *Brooklyn:* Brooklyn College (L), Brooklyn Institute of Arts and Science (M), Brooklyn Institute of Arts and Science, Children's Museum (M), Long Island Historical Society (M), Polytechnic Institute of Brooklyn (M), Pratt Institute Free College (L), Public Library (L). *Buffalo:* Buffalo Museum of Science (L,M), Cassius College (M), Grosvenor Library (L), Public Library (L), State Normal School (M). *Canton:* St. Lawrence University (L,M). *Clinton:* Hamilton College (L,M). *Cortland:* Public Library (M). *Farmingdale:* State Institute of Applied Agriculture (L). *Flushing:* Queens College (L). *Genesee:* Genesee Valley Museum (M). *Glens Falls:* Crandall Free Library (L). *Hamilton:* Colgate University (L,M). *Ithaca:* Cornell University (L,M). *Jamaica:* St. Johns University (L). *New Rochelle:* Glen Island Museum of Natural History (M). *New*

York: Academy of Mount St. Vincent (M), American Geographical Society (L), American Museum of Natural History (L,M), The Chemists Club (L), College of the City of New York (L,M), Columbia University (L,M), Cooper Union (L,M), Engineering and Mining Journal (L), Engineering Societies (L), Fordham University (L), Hunter College (L), H. W. Wilson Company (L), Manhattan College (M), Metropolitan Museum of Art (M), New York Academy of Sciences (L), New York Botanical Garden (L), New York University (L,M), Public Library (Astor, Lenox, Queens branches) (L), Scientific American (L), Society of Ethical Culture (M), Staten Island Institute of Arts and Sciences (M), Torrey Botanical Club (L). *Niagara Falls:* Niagara University (M). *Potsdam:* Clarkson College of Technology (L). *Poughkeepsie:* Vassar College (L,M). *Rochester:* Rochester Academy of Science (L), Rochester Museum of Arts and Sciences (M), Public Library (L), Rochester University (L). *St. Bonaventure:* St. Bonaventure College (L). *Schenectady:* Union College (L,M). *Schoharie:* Schoharie County Historical Society (M). *Seaford:* Fox Museum of Natural History (M). *Skaneateles:* Library Association (M). *Staten Island:* Wagner College (L). *Syracuse:* Syracuse University (L,M). *Troy:* Public Library (L), Rensselaer Polytechnic Institute (L,M). *Utica:* Public Library (L). *West Point:* United States Military Academy (M). *Yonkers:* Yonkers Museum of Science and Arts (M).

NORTH CAROLINA

Chapel Hill: University of North Carolina (L,M). *Davidson:* Davidson College (L,M). *Durham:* Duke University (L,M). *Greensboro:* Agricultural and Technical College (L). *Greenville:* East Carolina College (L). *Raleigh:* Department of Conservation and Development, State Geologist, Division of Mineral Resources (L), D. H. Hill Library (L), North Carolina State College (L,M), North Carolina State Library (L), North Carolina State Museum (M). *Tryon:* Polk County Museum (M). *Wake Forest:* Wake Forest College (L). *Winston-Salem:* Public Library (L).

NORTH DAKOTA

Bismarck: State Historical Society (L). *Fargo:* North Dakota Agricultural College (L,M), North Dakota State University (L). *Grand Forks:* North Dakota Geological Survey (L), University of North Dakota (L,M). *Minot:* State Teachers College (L). *Wahpeton:* North Dakota State School of Science (M).

OHIO

Akron: Municipal University of Akron (L), Public Library (L). *Alliance:* Mount Union College (L,M). *Antioch (Yellow Springs):* Antioch College (L,M). *Athens:* Ohio University (M), State Normal College (M). *Berea:* Baldwin-Wallace College Museum (M). *Bowling Green:* State University (L,M). *Cincinnati:* Cincinnati Museum Association (M), Cincinnati Society of Natural History (L,M), Public Library (L), University of Cincinnati (L,M). *Cleveland:* Adelbert College (L,M), Case Institute of Technology (L,M), Cleveland Museum of Natural History (M), Public Library (L). *Columbus:* American Ceramic Society (L), Geological Survey of Ohio (L), Ohio State Library (L), Ohio State Museum (M), Ohio State University (L,M), Public

Library (L), State Board of Agriculture (L). *Dayton:* Dayton Public Library (L,M). *Delaware:* Ohio Wesleyan University (L,M). *Fremont:* Hayes Memorial Library Museum (M). *Granville:* Denison University (L). *Greenville:* Carnegie Library Museum (M). *Hiram:* Hiram College (L,M). *Marietta:* Marietta College (L,M). *Oberlin:* Oberlin College (L,M). *Oxford:* Miami University (L). *Sandusky:* Sandusky High School (M). *Tiffin:* Heidelberg University (M). *Toledo:* Public Library (L), Toledo Institute of Natural Science (M). *Urbana:* Urbana University (M). *Westerville:* Otterbein University (M). *Wooster:* Wooster College (M). *Youngstown:* Public Library (L).

OKLAHOMA

Ada: East Central State College (L). *Alva:* Northwestern State College (L). *Bacone:* Bacone College (M). *Durant:* Southeastern College (L). *Edmond:* Central State College (L). *Enid:* Carnegie Library (L). *Langston:* University Library (L). *Norman:* Oklahoma Geological Survey (L), University of Oklahoma (L,M). *Oklahoma City:* Oklahoma City Library (L), Oklahoma State Library (L). *Shawnee:* Oklahoma Baptist University (L). *Stillwater:* Oklahoma State University (L). *Tahlequah:* Northeastern State College (L). *Tulsa:* University of Tulsa (L).

OREGON

Ashland: Southern Oregon College (L). *Corvallis:* Oregon State College (L,M). *Eugene:* University of Oregon (L,M). *Forest Grove:* Pacific University (L). *Portland:* Library Association of Portland (L), Mazamas Library (L), Reed College (L), State Department of Geology and Mineral Industries (L), U.S. Geological Survey (L). *Salem:* Oregon State Library (L), Willamette University (M).

PENNSYLVANIA

Allentown: Muhlenberg College (L,M). *Annville:* Lebanon Valley College (M). *Beaver Falls:* Geneva College (M). *Bethlehem:* Lehigh University (L,M). *Bradford:* Carnegie Public Library (L). *Bryn Mawr:* Bryn Mawr College (L,M). *Carlisle:* Dickinson College (L,M). *Chester:* Pennsylvania Military College (M). *Easton:* Lafayette College (L,M), Northampton County Historical and Genealogical Society (M). *Erie:* Public Library (L). *Gettysburg:* Gettysburg College (M). *Harrisburg:* Pennsylvania State Library and Museum (L,M), Topographic and Geological Survey (L). *Haverford:* Haverford College (L,M). *Huntington:* Juniata College (L). *Lancaster:* Franklin and Marshall College (L,M). *Lewisburg:* Bucknell University (M). *Meadville:* Allegheny College (L,M). *Media:* Delaware County Institute of Science (L,M). *Myerstown:* Albright College (M). *New Brighton:* Merrick Art Gallery (M). *New Wilmington:* Westminster College (M). *Philadelphia:* American Philosophical Society (L), Franklin Institute (L), Free Library of Philadelphia (L), Philadelphia Academy of Natural Sciences (L,M), Philadelphia Commercial Museum (L,M), Temple University (L), University of Pennsylvania (L), Wagner Free Institute of Science (L). *Pittsburgh:* Carnegie Library (L), Carnegie Free Library of Allegheny (L), Carnegie Institute (M), Engineer's Society of Western Pennsylvania (L), University of Pittsburgh (L). *Reading:* Public Library (L). *Scranton:* Everhart Museum of Natural History, Science and Art (M), Public Library (L). *State College:* Pennsylvania State University (L).

Swarthmore: Swarthmore College (L). *University Park:* Mineral Industries Library (L), Pennsylvania State University (L). *Warren:* Warren Academy of Sciences (M), Warren Library Association (L). *Washington:* Washington and Jefferson College (L,M). *Westchester:* State Teachers College (M). *Westtown:* Westtown Friends School (M). *Wilkes-Barre:* Kings College (L), Wyoming Historical and Geological Society (L,M). *Williamsport:* James V. Brown Library (L).

RHODE ISLAND

Kingston: Rhode Island State College (L,M). *Providence:* Brown University (L,M), Park Museum (M), Public Library (L), Rhode Island State Library (L). *Westerly:* Public Library (L).

SOUTH CAROLINA

Charleston: Charleston Museum (M), College of Charleston (M), South Carolina Military Academy (M). *Clemson:* Clemson College (L,M). *Clinton:* Thornwell Museum (M). *Columbia:* South Carolina Geological Survey (L), University of South Carolina (L,M). *Greenville:* Furman College (M). *Newberry:* Newberry College (M). *Orangeburg:* Claflin University (M), State Agricultural and Mechanical College (L). *Rock Hill:* Winthrop College (L,M). *Spartanburg:* Wofford College (M).

SOUTH DAKOTA

Brookings: Lincoln Memorial Library (L). *Mitchell:* Dakota Wesleyan University (L). *Pierre:* South Dakota State College (L). *Rapid City:* South Dakota State School of Mines (L,M). *Sioux Falls:* Carnegie Free Public Library (L). *Spearfish:* Black Hills Teachers College (L). *Vermillion:* South Dakota Geological Survey (L), University of South Dakota (L,M). *Yankton:* Yankton College (L,M).

TENNESSEE

Chattanooga: Public Library (L). *Clarksville:* Southwestern Presbyterian University (M). *Harriman:* Public Museum (M). *Jackson:* Union University (M). *Jefferson City:* Carson and Newman College (M). *Johnson City:* East Tennessee State College (L). *Knoxville:* University of Tennessee (L,M). *Lebanon:* Cumberland University (M). *Maryville:* Maryville College (M). *Memphis:* Cossitt Library (L,M), Southwestern College (M). *Milligan:* Milligan College (M). *Nashville:* Fisk University (L,M), Joint University Libraries (L), Nashville Public Library (L), Sewanee University of the South (L), State Geological Survey (L), Tennessee Division of Geology (L,M), Tennessee State Library (L), Vanderbilt University (L,M), Walden University (M).

TEXAS

Abilene: Hardin-Simmons University (L). *Alpine:* Sul Ross State College (L), West Texas Historical and Scientific Society (M). *Austin:* State Bureau of Economic Geology (L), Texas State Library (L), University of Texas (L,M). *Brownwood:* Payne College (M), Walker Memorial Library (L). *Canyon:* West Texas State Teachers College (L). *College Station:* Agricultural and Mechanical College of Texas (L). *Commerce:* East Texas State Teachers College (L). *Dallas:* Dallas Museum of Natural History (M), Public Library (L), Southern Methodist University (L), Texas Institute of Natural Resources and Industrial Development (M). *Denton:* North Texas State College (L). *El Paso:* El Paso Museum (M), Public Library (L), Texas Western

College (L), University of Texas (M). *Fort Worth:* Public Library (L), Texas Christian University (L). *Galveston:* Rosenburg Library (L). *Houston:* Houston Museum and Scientific Society (M), Public Library (L), Rice Institute (L). *Huntsville:* Sam Houston State Teachers College (L). *Kingsville:* Texas College of Arts and Industries (L). *Lubbock:* Texas Technological College (L). *San Antonio:* San Antonio Scientific Society (M), Texas Natural Resources Foundation (L), Witte Memorial Museum (M). *Waco:* Baylor University (L,M).

UTAH

Bryce Canyon National Park (M). *Logan:* Utah State College (L). *Provo:* Brigham Young University (L,M). *Salt Lake City:* Free Public Library (L), U.S. Geological Survey, 504 Federal Building (L), University of Utah (L,M), Utah Academy of Sciences (L), Utah Geological and Mineralogical Survey (L), Westminster College (M). Zion National Park (M).

VERMONT

Burlington: State Geologist (L), University of Vermont (L,M). *Middlebury:* Middlebury College (L,M). *Montpelier:* State Building (L,M), Vermont State Library (L). *Northfield:* Norwich University (L). *St. Johnsbury:* Fairbanks Museum of Natural Science (M). *Westfield:* Hitchcock Memorial Museum (M).

VIRGINIA

Blacksburg: Virginia Polytechnic Institute (L,M). *Charlottesville:* University of Virginia (L,M), Virginia Geological Survey (L). *Emory:* Emory and Henry College (L,M). *Fort Belvoir:* U.S. Engineer School (L). *Lexington:* Virginia Military Institute (L,M), Washington and Lee University (L,M). *Richmond:* Virginia State Library (L). *Roanoke:* Virginia Museum of Natural History (M).

WASHINGTON

Burton: Vashon College (M). *Olympia:* Division of Mines and Geology (L). *Port Angeles:* Klahhane City Museum (M). *Pullman:* Washington State College (L,M). *Seattle:* Public Library (L), State Museum (M), University of Washington (L,M). *Spokane:* Public Library (L), Public Museum (M), U.S. Geological Survey (L). *Tacoma:* College of Puget Sound (L), Public Library (L), Washington State Historical Society (M). *Walla Walla:* Whitman College (L,M).

WEST VIRGINIA

Athens: Concord College Library (L). *Charleston:* Department of Archives and History, State Library (L). *Huntington:* Marshall College (L). *Morgantown:* State Geologist, Geological and Economic Survey (L); West Virginia University (L,M). *Salem:* Salem College (L).

WISCONSIN

Appleton: Lawrence College (L,M). *Beloit:* Beloit College (L,M). *Green Bay:* Neville Public Museum (M). *Madison:* State Geological and Natural History Survey (L), State Historical Society (L), University of Wisconsin (L,M), Wisconsin State Library (L). *Milton:* Milton College (M). *Milwaukee:* Milwaukee-Downer College Museum (M), Public Library (L), Public Museum (L,M). *New London:* New London Public Museum (M). *Oshkosh:* Oshkosh Public Museum (M). *Platteville:* Wisconsin Institute of Technology (L). *Racine:* Public Library (L), Racine Memorial Museum (M). *Ripon:* Ripon College (M). *Stevens Point:* Wisconsin State College (L). *Superior:* Public Library (L), Superior State Teachers College (L). *Watertown:* Northwestern College (M).

WYOMING

Casper: Natrona County Public Library (L). *Cheyenne:* Wyoming State Geological Department Museum (M), Wyoming State Library (L). *Laramie:* University of Wyoming (L,M). *Yellowstone National Park:* Yellowstone Museum (M).

Bibliography of Selected Readings

The books, magazines, and area field guides have been selected from an extensive gem and mineral literature and listed here as supplementary materials. While most of the gem and mineral collecting localities described in the field guides are included in Part II of this volume, many other localities with detailed directions were omitted for lack of space. The guides listed here by states also include regional geological information pertinent to the localities described.

GENERAL WORKS OF REFERENCE

Averill, C. V. *Placer Mining for Gold in California*. California Division of Mines and Geology, Bulletin 135, San Francisco, 1946.

Dake, H. C. *Popular Prospecting: A Field Guide for the Part-Time Prospector*. Mentone, Calif.: Gembooks, 1955.

Dana, Edward S., and Ford, W. E. *Dana's Textbook of Mineralogy*. 4th ed. New York: John Wiley and Sons, 1932.

Dana, James D., and Hurbut, C. S., Jr. *Manual of Mineralogy*. 17th ed. New York: John Wiley and Sons, 1959. (An intermediate textbook of crystals, properties of minerals and gemstones, descriptions, and identifications.)

————. *Minerals and How to Study Them*. 3rd ed. New York: John Wiley and Sons, Inc., 1949. (An elementary textbook describing mineral properties, descriptions, and how to grow crystals.)

Fay, Gordon S. *The Rockhound's Manual*. New York: Harper & Row, 1972. (A fine introduction to gem and mineral collection, well illustrated, covering many aspects of collecting, identification, storage, and rockhound photography.)

Fenton, Carroll L., and Fenton, Mildred A. *The Rock Book*. New York: Appleton-Century-Crofts, 1943. (An excellent elementary discussion of rocks and minerals, well illustrated.)

Fritzen, D. K. *The Rock-Hunter's Field Manual*. New York: Harper & Row, 1959. (Color-coded description and identification keys for rocks and minerals.)

Gardner, E. D. *Guide to Prospecting for Lode Gold.* U.S. Bureau of Mines, Information Circular 7535, Washington, D.C., 1950.

Gleason, S. *Ultraviolet Guide to Minerals.* New York: Van Nostrand Reinhold, 1960. (One of the most complete books on mineral fluorescence for the amateur.)

Kunz, G. F. *Gems and Precious Stones of North America.* New York: Dover, 1968. (An unabridged reissue of the first edition of 1892, and still authoritative on gemstones.)

Palache, C., Berman, H., and Frondel, C. *Dana's System of Mineralogy.* New York: John Wiley and Sons, Vol. 1, 1944; Vol. 2, 1951; Vol. 3, 1962. (Modern revision of Dana's original work.)

Parsons, C. J., and Soukup, E. J. *Gem Materials Data Book.* Mentone, Calif.: Gembooks, 1957. (Useful for the gemologist and the lapidary.)

Pearl, R. M. *Popular Gemology.* New York: John Wiley and Sons, 1948. (A layman's survey of gems and gemstones.)

—————. *Rocks and Minerals.* New York: Barnes & Noble, 1956. (An everyday handbook of the mineral kingdom.)

Pough, F. H. *A Field Guide to Rocks and Minerals.* Boston: Houghton Mifflin, 1953. (A well-illustrated handbook of mineral and gemstone identification.)

Quick, L., and Leiper, H. *The Book of Agates and Other Quartz Gems.* Philadelphia: Chilton, 1970. (Covers basic information on quartz family gemstones, illustrated; provides locality information by states.)

—————. *How to Cut and Polish Gemstones.* Philadelphia: Chilton, 1959. (An excellent guide to lapidary work.)

Ransom, J. E. *Fossils in America.* New York: Harper & Row, 1964. (Covers basic geology and paleontology, with comprehensive national listing of significant fossil localities, including gemstone fossils.)

—————. *Petrified Forest Trails.* Mentone, Calif.: Gembooks, 1955. (The only popular authoritative work on petrified wood written for the amateur collector.)

Ricketts, A. H. *American Mining Law.* California State Division of Mines Bulletin 123, San Francisco, 1943.

Sinkankas, J. *Gem Cutting, A Lapidary's Manual.* New York: Van Nostrand Reinhold, 1962. (One of the most complete works on cutting and polishing gems and gemstones.)

—————. *Gemstones of North America.* New Jersey: D. Van Nostrand, 1959. (Comprehensive discussion of gems and gemstones, with localities listed for each species.)

—————. *Mineralogy for Amateurs.* New York: Van Nostrand Reinhold, 1964.

—————. *Prospecting for Gemstones and Minerals.* New York: Van Nostrand Reinhold, 1970. (An excellent, detailed coverage of basic geology and mineralogy.)

—————. *Standard Catalog of Gems.* New York: Van Nostrand Reinhold, 1968.

Smith, G. F. H. *Gemstones.* 13th ed. revised by F. C. Phillips. London: Methuen, 1958. (Possibly the most complete and thorough treatment of gemology in the English language.)

Soukup, E. J. *Facet Cutters Handbook.* Mentone, Calif.: Gemac Corp., 1959. (Lapidary techniques illustrated with diagrams.)

Spock, L. E. *A Guide to the Study of Rocks.* New York: Harper & Row, 1953.

U.S. Department of the Army. *Map Reading, Field Manual FM21–26.* Washington, D.C.: Government Printing Office, 1956.

Von Bernewitz, M. W. *Handbook for Prospectors and Operators of Small Mines.* 4th ed. rev. New York: McGraw-Hill, 1943.

Webster, R. *The Gemologist's Compendium.* London: N.A.C. Press, Ltd. (An excellent master reference of gemstone data for collectors and lapidaries.)

STATE FIELD COLLECTING GUIDES

ALABAMA

Pallister, H. D. *Index to the Minerals and Rocks of Alabama.* Geological Survey of Alabama Bulletin 65, 1955.

ARIZONA

Bitner, F. H. *Arizona Rock Trails.* Scottsdale, Ariz.: Bitner's, 1957.

Duke, A. *Arizona Gem Fields,* 2nd ed. Yuma, Ariz.: Alton Duke, 1959.

Flagg, A. L. *Mineralogical Journeys in Arizona.* Scottsdale, Ariz.: F. H. Bitner, 1958.

Galbraith, F. W., and Brennan, D. J. *Minerals of Arizona.* 3rd ed. rev. Tucson: University of Arizona, 1959.

Ransom, J. E. *Arizona Gem Trails and the Colorado Desert of California.* Mentone, Calif.: Gembooks, 1955.

CALIFORNIA

Dake, H. C. *California Gem Trails.* Mentone, Calif.: Gembooks, 1952.

Henry, D. J. *Gem Trail Journal.* 2nd ed. Long Beach, Calif.: L. R. Gordon, 1952.

Murdock, J., and Webb, R. W. *Minerals of California.* California Division of Mines and Geology Bulletin 189, San Francisco, 1956. (See Pemberton for update supplement.)

Pemberton, H. E. *Supplement to Bulletin 189.* California Division of Mines and Geology, Minerals of California for 1965 through 1968. Montebello: Mineral Research Society of California Bulletin, Vol. 3, No. 2, 1969.

Ransom, J. E. *Arizona Gem Trails and the Colorado Desert of California.* Mentone, Calif.: Gembooks, 1955.

Strong, M. F. *Desert Gem Trails.* Mentone, Calif.: Gembooks, 1966. (Laps over into adjacent Nevada.)

Troxel, B. W., and Morton, P. K. *Mines and Mineral Resources of Kern County, California.* California Division of Mines and Geology, County Report 1, San Francisco, 1962.

Weber, F. H. *Geology and Mineral Resources of San Diego County, California.* California Division of Mines and Geology, County Report 3, San Francisco, 1963. (Covers gem mines.)

COLORADO

Eckel, E. B. *Minerals of Colorado: A 100-Year Record.* U.S. Geological Survey Bulletin 1114, Washington, D.C., 1961.

Del Rio, S. M. *Mineral Resources of Colorado, First Sequel.* Denver: Colorado Mineral Resources Board, 1960.

Pearl, R. M. *Colorado Gem Trails and Mineral Guides.* 2nd ed. Denver: Sage Books, 1965.

————. *Colorado Rocks, Minerals, Fossils.* Denver: Sage Books, 1964.

Vanderwilt, J. W., et al. *Mineral Resources of Colorado.* Denver: Colorado Mineral Resources Board, 1947.

CONNECTICUT

Januzzi, R. E. *The Mineralogy of Connecticut and Southeastern New York State.* Danbury, Conn.: Mineralogical Press, 1961.

Jones, R. W., Jr. *Luminescent Minerals of Connecticut: A Guide to Their Properties and Locations.* Branford, Conn.: Fluorescent House, 1960.

Sohon, J. A. *Connecticut Minerals.* Connecticut Geological and Natural History Survey Bulletin 77, Storrs, 1951.

IDAHO

Henry, D. J. *The Rock Collector's Nevada and Idaho.* Long Beach, Calif.: L. R. Gordon, 1953.

Shannon, E. V. *The Minerals of Idaho.* U.S. National Museum Bulletin 131, Washington, D.C., 1931. (Old but good.)

ILLINOIS

Ekblaw, G. E., and Carroll, D. L. *Typical Rocks and Minerals in Illinois.* Illinois Geological Survey, Educational Series 3, Urbana, 1931.

INDIANA

Greensburg, S. S. *Guide to Some Minerals and Rocks in Indiana.* Indiana Department of Conservation, Geological Survey Circular 4, Bloomington, 1958.

KANSAS

Tolsted, L. L., and Swineford, A. *Kansas Rocks and Minerals.* Kansas State Geological Survey, Lawrence, 1957.

KENTUCKY

Richardson, C. H. *The Mineralogy of Kentucky.* Kentucky Geological Survey, Geological Reports, Vol. 33, Frankfort, 1925.

MAINE

Leadbeater, J. E. M. *Maine Minerals and Gems.* 1963.

Maine Geological Survey. *Maine Mineral Collecting.* Department of Economic Development, Augusta, 1960. (Contains 11 maps detailing 15 localities.)

————. *Maine Pegmatite Mines and Prospects and Associated Minerals.* Department of Development of Industry and Commerce, Mineral Resources Index I, Augusta, 1957.

MARYLAND

Ostrander, C. W., and Price, W. E. *Minerals of Maryland.* Baltimore: Natural History Society of Maryland, 1940.

MICHIGAN

Poindexter, O. F., et al. *Rocks and Minerals of Michigan.* Michigan Geological Survey Bulletin 2, Lansing, 1965.

MINNESOTA

Emmons, W. H., and Grout, F. F. *Mineral Resources of Minnesota*. Minnesota Geological Survey Bulletin 30, Minneapolis, 1943.

MISSOURI

Keller, W. D. *The Common Rocks and Minerals of Missouri*.

NEVADA

Gianella, V. P. *Nevada's Common Minerals*. University of Nevada Bulletin, Vol. 35, No. 6 (1941), Geology and Mining Series 36.

Henry, D. J. *The Rock Collector's Nevada and Idaho*. Long Beach, Calif.: L. R. Gordon, 1953.

Strong, M. P. *Desert Gem Trails*. Mentone, Calif.: Gembooks, 1966. (Laps over into adjacent California.)

NEW HAMPSHIRE

Meyers, T. R., and Stewart, G. W. *The Geology of New Hampshire;* Part 3: *Minerals and Mines*. Concord: New Hampshire State Planning and Development Commission, 1956.

Morrill, P. *New Hampshire Mines and Mineral Localities*. Hanover: Dartmouth College Museum, 1960.

NEW JERSEY

Jones, R. W., Jr. *Nature's Hidden Rainbows*. San Gabriel, Calif.: Ultra-Violet Products, 1964. (Fluorescent minerals of Franklin, N.J.)

NEW MEXICO

Northrup, S. A. *Minerals of New Mexico*. rev. ed. Albuquerque: University of New Mexico Press, 1960.

Simpson, B. W. *New Mexico Gem Trails*. 2nd rev. ed. Mentone, Calif.: Gembooks, 1970.

NEW YORK

Januzzi, R. E. *The Mineralogy of Connecticut and Southeastern New York State*. Danbury, Conn.: Mineralogical Press, 1961.

Luedke, E. M., et al. *Mineral Occurrences of New York State with Selected References to Each Locality*. U.S. Geological Survey Bulletin 1072 (F), 1959.

Manchester, J. G. *Minerals of New York and Its Environs*. New York: New York Mineralogical Club, 1931. (Covers a 50-mile radius around New York City.)

Whitlock, H. P. *List of New York Mineral Localities*. New York State Museum Bulletin 70, Albany, 1903. (Much outdated, but of some current value.)

NORTH CAROLINA

Conley, J. F. *Mineral Localities of North Carolina*. North Carolina Division of Mineral Resources, Information Circular 16, Raleigh, 1958.

Stuckey, J. L. *Geology and Mineral Resources of North Carolina*. North Carolina State Division of Mineral Resources, Educational Series 3, Raleigh, 1953.

NORTH DAKOTA

Budge, C. E. *The Mineral Resources of North Dakota*. North Dakota Research Foundation Bulletin 8, Bismarck, 1954.

PENNSYLVANIA

Gordon, S. G. *Mineralogy of Pennsylvania*. Academy of Natural Sciences of Philadelphia, Special Publication 2, Philadelphia, 1922.

Lapham, D. M., and Geyer, A. R. *Mineral Collecting in Pennsylvania*. General Geology Report G-33, Pennsylvania Geological Survey, Harrisburg, 3rd ed., 1969.

Montgomery, A. *The Mineralogy of Pennsylvania.* Philadelphia: Academy of Natural Sciences of Philadelphia Publication 9, 1969. (An update and supplement to Gordon's 1922 paper.)

SOUTH DAKOTA

Roberts, W. L., and Rapp, G., Jr. *Mineralogy of the Black Hills.* South Dakota School of Mines and Technology, Bulletin No. 18, Rapid City, 1965.

TEXAS

Simpson, B. W. *Gem Trails of Texas.* Rev. ed. Granbury, Tex.: Gem Trails Publishing Company, 1962.

VIRGINIA

Dietrich, R. V. *Virginia Mineral Localities.* Blacksburg: Virginia Polytechnic Institute, 1960, with a succession of excellent update supplements.

————. *Virginia Minerals and Rocks.* 4th ed. Blacksburg: Virginia Polytechnic Institute, 1964.

Pegau, A. A. *Mineral Collecting in Virginia.* Virginia Geological Survey, Virginia Minerals, Vol. 3, No. 2 (1957).

WEST VIRGINIA

Martens, J. H. *Minerals of West Virginia.* West Virginia Geological and Economic Survey, Morgantown, 1964.

WYOMING

Birch, R. W. *Wyoming's Mineral Resources.* Laramie: Wyoming Natural Resources Board, 1955.

Osterwald, F. W. *Wyoming Mineral Resources.* Wyoming Geological Survey Bulletin 45, Laramie, 1952.

REGIONAL AND NATIONAL GUIDES

Dake, H. C. *Northwest Gem Trails.* Mentone, Calif.: Gembooks, 1950. (Covers the Pacific Northwest states.)

Oles, F., and H. *Eastern Gem Trails.* Mentone, Calif.: Gembooks, 1967. (Covers the Middle Atlantic states.)

Quick, L. *The Book of Agates and Other Quartz Gems.* Philadelphia: Chilton, 1970. (Systematically covers all 50 states for quartz family gemstone localities.)

Ransom, J. E. *Fossils in America.* New York: Harper & Row, 1964. (Comprehensive coverage of all 50 states for significant fossil localities and names of species to be found.)

————. *Petrified Forest Trails.* Mentone, Calif.: Gembooks, 1955. (Describes and locates sources of petrified wood in the United States.)

————. *A Range Guide to Mines and Minerals.* New York: Harper & Row, 1964. (Locates all significant mines and ore-mineral deposits in the 50 states and identifies the ore minerals.)

————. *The Rock-Hunter's Range Guide.* New York: Harper & Row, 1962. (Lists state-by-state localities for all significant gems and gemstones and identifies the species to be found.)

Sinkankas, J. *Gemstones of North America.* New York: Van Nostrand Reinhold, 1959. (Lists more than 2,000 gem and gemstone localities by species of stone described.)

William, L. D. *Gem and Mineral Localities of Southeastern United States.* Jacksonville, Ala.: Jacksonville State College. (Lists localities mainly in Alabama and Georgia.)

Zeitner, J. C. *Appalachian Mineral & Gem Trails.* Lapidary Journal, Inc., San Diego, California, 1968.

————. *Midwest Gem Trails.* 3rd rev. ed. Mentone, Calif.: Gembooks, 1964. (Covers all the states of the Midwest.)

PERIODICALS

American Mineralogist. Journal of the Mineralogical Society of America. Chevron Oil Field Research Co., Box 466 La Habra, Calif. 90631. (Strictly for professional mineralogists.)

Earth Science. Journal of the Midwest Federation of Mineralogical Societies. Earth Science Publishing Co., Inc., Mount Morris, Ill. 61054. (Popular coverage of all phases of rock, mineral, and fossil collecting.)

Gems and Minerals. Official publication of the California Federation of Mineralogical Societies. P.O. Box 687, Mentone, Calif. 92359. (Devoted to the rock collector's hobby, including lapidary work, field collecting, gemology, etc.)

Geotimes. Journal of the American Geological Institute, 1444 N. Street, N.W., Washington, D.C. 20005.

Lapidary Journal. Lapidary Journal, Inc., P. O. Box 2369, San Diego, Calif. 92112. (Devoted popularly to all phases of gem and mineral collecting, cutting and polishing, and gemology.)

Rockhound Buyer's Guide. An annual special publication, appearing each April, of the *Lapidary Journal, q.v.* (Devoted to lists of clubs and mineralogical organizations, rockhound and lapidary suppliers and products, field trips, dealers, and accommodations, etc.)

Rocks and Minerals. Official publication of the Eastern Federation of Mineralogical and Lapidary Societies. Rocks and Minerals, Box 29, Peekskill, N.Y. 10566. (Provides excellent coverage of all facets of gemology, mineralogy, collecting, and lapidary work.)

Index to Part I